PRAISE FOR *LEAN LOGIC*

"David Fleming was a walking encyclopedia of ecological knowledge and wisdom. His brilliance, good humour, and deep insight were legendary and unforgettable. His writing, too, was of the highest calibre—witty, entertaining, profound, informative, and transformative. These books of his give us the opportunity to savour the great treasure that was his mind. To read them is to gain a superb education in ecology from one of the greatest masters in the field."

—DR. STEPHAN HARDING, resident ecologist, Schumacher College; author of *Animate Earth*

"This is an extraordinary book, uncategorisable, driven by a great rolling intellectual curiosity. Fleming fathomed the depth of the mess in which we find ourselves and left us clues as to how we might find our way through that mess."

—DOUGALD HINE, cofounder, The Dark Mountain Project

"David Fleming predicts environmental catastrophe but also proposes a solution that stems from the real motives of people and not from some comprehensive political agenda. He writes lucidly and eloquently of the moral and spiritual qualities on which we might draw in our 'descent' to a Lean Economy. His highly poetic description of these qualities is neither gloomy nor self-deceived but tranquil and inspiring. All environmental activists should read him and learn to think in his cultivated and nuanced way."

—ROGER SCRUTON, writer and philosopher; author of over thirty books, including *Green Philosophy*

"David Fleming gives a remarkable overview of our present situation and of possible future scenarios. His writing is clear, witty, insightful, and wise. *Lean Logic* is a delight to dip into, and every time I do so I feel refreshed. It is a work of genius."

—RUPERT SHELDRAKE, PhD, author of *The Science Delusion*

"Our current public discourse on such problems as resource depletion, climate change, and the economy is often hopelessly muddled; this book brings light and transparency. David Fleming didn't tell us what to think but rather how to avoid cognitive fallacies that masquerade as reason. *Lean Logic* is an instant classic that was many years in the making, and it should be essential reading for environmentalists, economists, policy makers, and anyone who wants greater clarity in understanding the most important issues of our time."

—RICHARD HEINBERG, senior fellow, Post Carbon Institute

"For me originality, passion, commitment, and sincerity are the words which describe David Fleming. All these qualities are present in his writing. His lifelong championing of Tradable Energy Quotas, one of the very few instruments which promote sustainable consumption in a progressive rather than regressive way thereby combining environmental gain with a simultaneous transfer of resources from richer to poorer people, propels him to an honoured place in the pantheon of green campaigners."

—TIM YEO, former UK Minister for the Environment and Chair of the House of Commons Energy and Climate Change Select Committee

"A splendid smorgasbord, *Lean Logic* provides rare insight into some of the key issues of our time! Fleming's underlying vision of a future founded in a reclaimed richness of community, culture, and conversation is both heartening and timely."

—HELENA NORBERG-HODGE, author of *Ancient Futures*; director of *The Economics of Happiness*

"David Fleming was the soul of provocative, exciting, and creative thought, and it was always a thought-provoking and pleasure-promoting experience to meet him. Amongst many virtues, his approach to climate change and ecology embraced the commons. Seeing this as a solution, with collective decision-making leading to a better future, was at the heart of his work. I am sure that Elinor Ostrom, who won a Nobel Prize for her work on the commons, would have appreciated David's comment that putting government in charge of commons was like placing the fox in control of the chicken coop. It is so sad that David is no longer with us, but his words are; these books are full of insight and enjoyment. I hope his laughter and enlightenment spread far and wide through new readers as well as those of us familiar with his thoughts already."

—DEREK WALL, author of *Economics After Capitalism* and the forthcoming *Elinor Ostrom's Rules for Radicals*

"The only scientific question left to us: how can we ensure a future for humanity? That includes: how do we free ourselves from capitalism, the form of social organisation that is destroying us? And how do we create something else? This book is a thoughtful and imaginative contribution to the debate about humanity's future."

—JOHN HOLLOWAY, sociologist; author of *Change the World Without Taking Power* and *Crack Capitalism*

"David Fleming's eye was sharp, and his words had a way of getting right to the heart of the matter. This book is remarkable and scintillating; the product of a truly original mind."

—PAUL KINGSNORTH, cofounder, The Dark Mountain Project; author of *The Wake*

"David Fleming's lifework is nothing less than an encyclopedia of the timeless art of living, encompassing the art of building enlivening communities, the art of allowing the economy to serve life and creativity, and the art of unmasking invisible brainwashing. Fleming has written a guide to becoming an authentic individual and to recognizing toxic relationships on every level of material and personal exchange. This is a serious guide to health on every level of relationships and at the same time a deeply humorous read. Whether the breakdown of technical civilisation will come (as Fleming is convinced) or humanity will just carry on muddling through as always, this encyclopedia of manners, grace, and style will make the reader's life more wonderful and thus inevitably help to build a saner society."

—ANDREAS WEBER, PhD, author of *The Biology of Wonder*

"In my words it's half encyclopedia, half commonplace book, half a secular bible, half survival guide, half . . . yes, that's a lot of halves, but I hope you get the picture. I have never encountered a book that is so hard to characterise yet so hard, despite its weight, to put down. *Lean Logic* is neither a policy manifesto nor a dry technical guide. It's an incredibly nourishing cultural and scientific treasure trove."

—JOHN THACKARA, founder and director, Doors of Perception; author of *How to Thrive in the Next Economy*

"A monumental achievement, David Fleming's *Lean Logic* is an encyclopedic guide to the crisis of industrial civilization. I challenge anyone to read so much as a page of it without finding at least one insight worth serious reflection. Individuals, families, and communities will find it invaluable as a guide to navigating the troubled waters of the future."

—JOHN MICHAEL GREER, author of *The Long Descent* and *After Progress*

LEAN
LOGIC

LEAN
LOGIC

A DICTIONARY *for the* FUTURE

and HOW *to* SURVIVE IT

DAVID FLEMING

Edited by SHAUN CHAMBERLIN
Foreword by JONATHON PORRITT

Chelsea Green Publishing
White River Junction, Vermont

Publisher's note: In order to honor David Fleming's voice, we have
forgone our typical Chelsea Green house style, including using
British grammar and spelling instead of American.

Developmental Editor: Shaun Chamberlin
Project Manager: Angela Boyle
Project Editor: Brianne Goodspeed
Designer: Melissa Jacobson
Indexer: Shaun Chamberlin
Editorial/Research Assistant to David Fleming: Beth Stratford

Printed in the United States of America.
First printing July, 2016.
10 9 8 7 6 5 4 3   20 21 22 23

Our Commitment to Green Publishing

Chelsea Green sees publishing as a tool for cultural change and ecological stewardship. We strive to align our book manufacturing practices with our editorial mission and to reduce the impact of our business enterprise in the environment. We print our books and catalogs on chlorine-free recycled paper, using vegetable-based inks whenever possible. This book may cost slightly more because it was printed on paper that contains recycled fiber, and we hope you'll agree that it's worth it. *Lean Logic* was printed on paper supplied by Sheridan that contains at least 30 percent postconsumer recycled fiber.

Library of Congress Cataloging-in-Publication Data

Names: Fleming, David, 1940– author. | Chamberlin, Shaun, editor.
Title: Lean logic : a dictionary for the future and how to survive it / David Fleming ; edited by Shaun Chamberlin ; foreword by
     Jonathon Porritt.
Description: White River Junction, Vermont : Chelsea Green Publishing,2016.
Identifiers: LCCN 2016006994| ISBN 9781603586481 (hardback) | ISBN 9781603586498 (ebook)
Subjects: LCSH: Environmental economics—Dictionaries. | Environmental policy—Dictionaries. | Culture—Economic aspects—
     Dictionaries. | Civilization, Modern—21st century. | BISAC: SOCIAL SCIENCE / Future Studies. | BUSINESS & ECONOMICS /
     Environmental Economics. | POLITICAL SCIENCE / Economic Conditions. | HISTORY / Civilization. | PHILOSOPHY / Social.
     | POLITICAL SCIENCE / History & Theory. | REFERENCE / Dictionaries. | PHILOSOPHY / Reference.
Classification: LCC HC79.E5 .F56294 2016 | DDC 304.203—dc23
LC record available at https://lccn.loc.gov/2016006994

Chelsea Green Publishing
85 North Main Street, Suite 120
White River Junction, VT 05001
(802) 295-6300
www.chelseagreen.com

In loving memory of David Fleming, 1940 – 2010

CONTENTS

On David Fleming's behalf, I am sure he would wish
to thank those who supported his work (I am aware of
David Astor, the R H Southern Trust, the Polden-Puckham
Charitable Foundation and the Organic Research Centre)
and the many who read, commented on, and contributed
to drafts of his great work during his lifetime.

SHAUN CHAMBERLIN

FOREWORD

I've never had to write a foreword like this one. And that's largely because I've never come across a book quite like this one. What's more, I never knew anyone remotely like David Fleming.

I honestly can't remember which particular Ecology Party Annual Conference it was where we first met. 1977, perhaps? But what I can remember is the joy of falling in love with David's intellect. With his spirit. With his crazy imagination.

As 'David and Jonathon', we then set out to capture the essence of green politics at that time, and to articulate it in ways that we hoped would set the world alight. Especially in the General Election Manifestos of 1979 and 1984.

We failed, of course. But neither of us ever stopped trying—for me, to this day; for David, till his still painfully inexplicable death in 2010. He was, in short, a true soul-mate.

That said, he could be the most irritating man on Earth! The work that you're about to venture into was in the making for more than thirty years. Finished as many times as it was started, and still unfinished at the end. It grew, shrank, grew again. The irony of needing 404 different "essay-entries", spread over 500 pages, to convey the basic principles of 'lean thinking' was all too apparent to David himself. But a startling combination of whimsy, perfectionism and mulish obstinacy ensured that the final endpoint he longed for, with the computer set finally aside, never came.

When David died, I worked my mourning way through *Lean Logic* all over again, in a forlorn effort to be with him in his words. And I've just done the same again, joyfully this time, to work out whether or not it would be possible to write a suitable foreword.

I put it like that because I know that *Lean Logic* will not be to everyone's liking. I used to think that David was wilfully making it hard for people by eschewing a conventionally logical narrative, by disappearing with self-indulgent abandon down intellectual rabbit holes of every conceivable kind, teasing, meandering along, and sometimes deliberately obfuscating.

He wasn't. That was just the way his mind worked, forever playful and provocative. He loved to wind up rather more earnest members of the Ecology Party like no other person I knew, intent on overcoming what he saw as a deeply problematic 'humour deficit'. *Lean Logic* is the way it is because that's how David was, gloriously eclectic, effortlessly holistic.

It may not work, therefore, as a new reader starting on page 1 and looking forward to getting to page 500 with hardly a break in between. See it more as an idiosyncratic almanac, an apothecary's storeroom, to be roamed around with as much curiosity and irreverence as you can muster.

I think the best I can do is to offer one or two aids as readers set out on their journey—a couple of walking poles, a few reference points (not so much a map, as that would be entirely foolhardy), a torch for some of those darker moments.

For me, the starting point has to be the one thing that most bugged David: today's dynamic, endlessly inventive but ultimately suicidal *market economy*. David was always quick to recognise the strengths of that economy, but following in the footsteps of Karl Polanyi and a host of heretical economists writing in the 1960s and 70s, he also recognised, very early on, that its dependence on exponential economic growth had already sown the seeds of its inevitable demise:

> This inherent need for eternal *per capita* growth
> will not go away—and yet, of course, it is
> impossible to sustain it in a finite world. This is
> the central problem of the market economy. If
> it does not sustain its growth, it will collapse,
> because unemployment will rise without limit,
> and both private incomes and public finances
> will fail. And yet, if it does sustain its growth,
> it will collapse even more dramatically, owing
> to the depletion of fuel and materials, the
> breakdown of soils, environment and climate.

So far, so unexpected. Many share that same analysis, and many alternatives have been advanced to avoid that kind of collapse, all entailing some kind of reform of that market economy: a rapid adoption of zero-growth policies; 'progressive degrowth'; an ethically-based advocacy of voluntary simplicity; the rather more pragmatic 'circular economy'. David was sympathetic to all of these 'half-way houses', but saw them ultimately as forlorn efforts to avoid the central insight of his work: that collapse is now inevitable.

Even back in the 1970s, he became convinced that it simply wouldn't be possible to transition from today's crazy world to a genuinely sustainable world by dint of incremental reform. He saw collapse as both inevitable and *necessary*, in order to set ourselves on a better path. What really mattered to him was what was going to happen *after* that "coming climacteric".

As will soon become apparent, David subscribed enthusiastically to the 'peak oil hypothesis': that global supplies of oil either already had peaked, or soon would peak, precipitating price rises and economic chaos as disruptive as anything that happened back in the 1970s—including the collapse of a system of food production largely dependent on inputs derived from fossil fuels. This has been a great big juicy bone of contention for many in the green movement (with me on the other end of the bone to David!), but it was a critical part of his overall thinking:

It is not about wrestling with the controls of economics to force it in the direction of degrowth, but about getting ready for the moment when the coming climacteric does the heavy work of degrowth for us; when the goods, materials, food and services—whose life-preserving growth has caused so much guilt—turn out to be not there. The informal economy that must take over is still tragically weak. Its development is intensely urgent. Degrowth will come on us all too quickly.

Hence the idea of the "Lean Economy"—as the only way of maintaining stability in an economy that would no longer be growing. In that respect, *resilience* is seen as critical ("a key property of the Lean Economy, and a key property of resilience is diversity"), to which he returns on many occasions.

Working closely with the Transition Towns movement, he adopted the language of "managed descent"

as the best option we could hope for, with both individuals and communities needing to embrace the principles and practice of a lean economy. Without that kind of narrative, he felt that people would *never* focus on the real alternative: to get the local economy moving as a resilient, self-reliant system, based on a radically different way of doing things, making things and exchanging things, on "reciprocal exchange" and on "the celebration of culture".

And that's the point where David's work becomes completely distinctive—in its exuberant exploration of what he meant by *culture*, both individually and collectively. In effect, culture becomes a direct substitute for the market economy—"The reciprocal obligation of common purpose which will fill the space vacated by the market". Even religion becomes a critical part of "building and sustaining the relationships of social capital". For David, trust was the cornerstone of this kind of living culture, nurtured by those reciprocal relationships and obligations. Pretty much everything got dragooned into this overarching sense of culture, including religion, the arts, play, food, and what he called "manners". And he drew on his wide knowledge of history to provide some sort of parallel:

All societies other than the market economy acknowledged, at least to some degree, that they could not make sense of their practical needs unless they made sense, first of all, of the community—and the culture which defined it, and which they were not aware of as anything different from the way they lived every day. Community is culture's habitat.

It's impossible to exaggerate the importance of this dimension of David's work. All sorts of apparent excursions and tangents link back to his belief that "culture today is decorative, not structural", just as he saw contemporary multiculturalism as having become "an attenuated tactic" rather than a lived reality. Many of the interventions that he believed needed to be made are based on building trust and cultural diversity at the local level, reinforcing old skills whilst creating a new economic vitality to protect what people really value in their communities. And what is characterised today as 'unacceptable inefficiency' would be an important part of that.

All of which depends, of course, on people caring for other people as the only way of maintaining social cohesion, on triumphing over the kind of "individual speak-for-yourselfism" that is so ruthlessly promoted at every level of the market economy.

To be honest, I was never entirely convinced that David himself completely subscribed to this benign and sometimes idealistic view of human nature. But he told himself that he did, and remained a passionate defender of democracy despite all its manifest inadequacies in terms of expediting the transition to a more sustainable world. He was a caustic critic of all those who espoused different shades of "green authoritarianism", which he defined succinctly as a "guarantee of failure".

So, in summary, here's what I think is perhaps the most important of the different 'logic flows' in *Lean Logic*, which I hope will be of some assistance to readers as they navigate their way around this unusually structured *tour de force*:

Our contemporary model of progress has come to depend entirely on achieving year-on-year economic growth, indefinitely into the future. If societies cannot keep on growing, collapse is inevitable. If societies succeed in growing, collapse is also inevitable.

↓

We're already in critical danger. Indeed, it's no good thinking that collapse can be avoided, as all attempts to reform the growth paradigm are doomed to failure. The best we can do is "manage our descent", conscientiously cultivating those habits of mind and practical behaviours that will help fashion a good life post-collapse.

↓

Prospects for that post-collapse good life depend on putting culture at the heart of tomorrow's lean economy. Culture based on trust, reciprocity, civility and "good manners" will be the direct substitute for today's market economy; resilience and diversity are critical characteristics of that kind of economy.

↓

We must therefore do everything we can to nurture humankind's intelligence and creativity, and fight as hard as we need to to protect our democratic entitlements. Without that, autocracy and dictatorship loom.

If you just keep that kind of logic flow in mind, all else starts to resonate, especially in the extensive margins of *Lean Logic*.

It is of course tragic that David never had much of a chance to present the essence of his lifetime's work in ways that he would have wanted—with the book out there to be read by all he encountered. But it's also something of a relief! One of my last (and fondest) memories of David was watching him trying to present 'a potted version' of the Lean Economy, on a panel of five people, in just 20 minutes. It was not a communications success, as he spoke faster and faster to beat the clock! But rarely have so many beautiful, elegant ideas been uttered, within such a short period of time, with such power and passion.

JONATHON PORRITT

EDITOR'S PREFACE

David Fleming was one of my closest friends; a mentor, and an inspiration. His sudden death in late 2010 came as a complete shock. At the time we were in the midst of final preparations ahead of the publication of a jointly-authored parliamentary report on his influential TEQs scheme (see the entry in this Dictionary), so getting that launched as he would have wanted was the immediate priority. It received international headlines but, for me, in the wake of the flurry of interest came the emotion, and the realisation that this book—his great work, his legacy to the world—remained unpublished.

There is no question that part of my motivation for undertaking the work on this book has been my deep love and gratitude for David, but I am driven far more by the sense that this is a genuinely important work, with a significant audience out there who deserve to read it.

For me, and for many others, it has been a touch-stone. When engaging in activities not tied to the logic of the market economy, we are forever told that our efforts are quaint and obsolete. It can be wearing, but *Lean Logic* is the antidote—a reminder of the deeper culture that such work is grounded in; that older ways of relating are no mirage, but rather the very foundation that society is built on; that our efforts matter more than we know. Indeed, if not for the weight, I might be tempted to carry a copy to gift to such critics!

This is, without any shadow of a doubt, a unique book. Conversations with David rank among the most startling and refreshing experiences of my life, and this book is the truest testament imaginable to the character and ingenuity of the man. The very structure of the book reflects his genius for drawing unconventional and revealing connections where they were never suspected, and it is all too easy to spend hours exploring his web of entertaining dictionary entries. And then astonishing to discover how they build, almost without being noticed, into a comprehensive vision of a radically different future. But I shall not say too much else about *Lean Logic* itself here, and let you experience it for yourself.

Instead, I have been asked to write a little about the past five years, and the process from the final manuscript on David's home computer to the book you now hold in your hands.

Some of you will have come to this book after reading the paperback *Surviving the Future: Culture, Carnival and Capital in the Aftermath of the Market Economy*.[1] I produced that book from this one, so your journey has been the opposite to my own, but I have had you in mind throughout, and I trust that you will find it a natural process to discover how the material from that book fits within David Fleming's wider vision. You will encounter content that you recognise, but it will be interwoven with other material (perhaps four-fifths of this book) that will be new to you.

The rest of you are on a path more similar to mine. Although David and I worked closely in his small Hampstead flat, until only a few weeks before his death he would not let me look at *Lean Logic*. He said that we were too close, and the project too dear to his heart, so that we would likely fall out if I were critical! So when I found his final manuscript for this book in the weeks after his death, it was an invitation to one last glorious conversation.

Shortly afterwards, a group of David's closest friends and family decided to self-publish 500 copies of his manuscript, as soon as possible and just as he had left it, for those who knew him and his work. Then, in 2011, we started talking with publishers about a full publication; the feedback was that a more conventional version might be necessary, as a 'way in' to the full work, so with advice and support from many of David's friends—Roger Bentley and Biff Vernon especially—I tentatively started work on what would become *Surviving the Future*.

As that process was coming to an end, the Dark Mountain journal put out a call for submissions to their fourth book, on the theme of 'post-cautionary tales': "That is to say, tales which do not seek to avert crisis or radical change, but which acknowledge that we are already living through those things and that we are going to have to deal with the consequences". In shock at encountering a category of any kind that *Lean Logic* actually seemed to fit perfectly, I felt obliged to submit some extracts. Despite being overwhelmed with submissions, the Dark Mountain team were so enamoured of the curious dictionary entries that they asked for an additional set, for their fifth book.[2]

And that is where Michael Weaver of Chelsea Green Publishing happened across them, and so made contact to ask whether they could help in any way with publishing or distributing David's work. Having worked with Chelsea Green before on my own Transition book, I was enthusiastic at the possibility.[3] Initially, we discussed the publication of *Surviving the Future*, but quickly came to the realisation that it was most appropriate to bring the two books out concurrently, allowing readers to explore both or either, according to their taste. That brings our story up to Autumn 2014, with much of my time since spent pulling both books together into their final published form. Writing this preface is one of my final tasks; in many ways the book in your hands has been both the starting-point and the finish-line for me.

So, you can imagine how much pleasure it gives me to invite you to step into the world of *Lean Logic*. David bestowed the subtitle *A Dictionary for the Future and How to Survive It*, but, if only for want of competition, it can surely claim to be *The Dictionary for the Future and How to Survive It*.[4]

But where to start with such a book? Well, one genuine answer would be "anywhere you like"—the index contains a complete list of entries to pique your interest—but if you would like some suggestions:

- If this is your first exploration of David Fleming's work, jump forward a couple of pages to his Introduction, which sets the context and ends with some guidance on how to approach his most unconventional creation.
- Or for those who have already read *Surviving the Future*, continue to David's Guide to Lean Logic, which offers a variety of possible starting-points, some of which will feel familiar, and are waiting to introduce you to their community.

SHAUN CHAMBERLIN

A GUIDE TO LEAN LOGIC

Welcome to the Dictionary of Lean Logic. You might think that a good place to start reading it is at the beginning. Well, that isn't necessarily so. For one thing, the first word in the Dictionary is Abstraction, and knowing what that is all about probably isn't a burning priority for most people. A better idea would be to begin with one of the questions that occupy, or preoccupy, many of us, and then dive in from there.

Here are some questions to start with, and some of the principal entries which think about them:

1. **Is there a problem?** Climacteric, Energy Prospects, Climate Change, Food Prospects, Population; Gaia, Wheel of Life; Economics, Delocalisation, Demoralisation, Tactile Deprivation; Growth, Intensification Paradox, Intermediate Economy, Regrettable Necessities; Genetic Modification, Nanotechnology, Nuclear Energy; Rationalism, Reductionism; Wicked Problems; Success.

2. **What is "Lean"?** Lean Thinking; Intention, Lean Means, Flow, Pull, Feedback; Five Whys, *Kaikaku*, *Kaizen*; *Muda*, Empowerment, Incentives Fallacy; Scale, Travelling Light.

3. **What solutions does *Lean Logic* explore?** Lean Economy; Slack and Taut, Intentional Waste, Lean Education, Lean Law and Order, Lean Energy, TEQs (Tradable Energy Quotas), Transition, Lean Food, Lean Health, Lean Materials, Lean Transport.

4. **What is there about community building?** Community, Reciprocity and Cooperation; Carnival, Common Purpose, Commons, Courtesy, Democracy, Eroticism, Freedom, Groups and Group Sizes, Home, Humour, Informal Economy, Narrative Truth, Place, Play, Public Sphere and Private Sphere, Social Capital, Religion, Ritual, Tradition, Transition, Trust.

5. **Are there practical suggestions?** Lean Economy; Manual Skills, Appropriate Technology, Lean Household, Lean Building, Lean Energy, Lean Food, Lean Materials, Lean Health, Lean Transport, Social City, Sorting Problem, Water; Local Currency, Gifts, Larders, Sleep.

6. **How does *Lean Logic* fit in with other lines of argument?** Sustainability, Sustainable Development, Needs and Wants, Money Fallacy, Ecology: The Scholars; Economics, Growth, Population, Unlean; Genetic Modification, Nanotechnology; Paradigm, Wheel of Life; Utopia.

7. **How does the principle of "small is beautiful" stack up with *Lean Logic*?** Scale, Place, Needs and Wants, Community, Resilience; Appropriate Technology, Boundaries and Frontiers, Nation, Closed-Loop Systems, Complexity, Connectedness, Dollar-a-Day Fallacy, Economics, Growth, Intentional Waste, Manual Skills, Systems Thinking, Protection.

8. **Can I have some context, please, given the super-giant society we are living in now?** Market Economy, Regrettable Necessities; Scale, System Scale Rule, Land, Ingenuity Gap; Complexity, Competitiveness, Climacteric, Gaia, Leisure, Multiculturalism, Myth; Groups and Group Sizes, Small Group, Neighbourhood, Parish, County, Nation.

9. **Does the spirit get a mention?** Spirit; Ironic Space, Carnival, Religion; Culture, Eroticism, Imagination, Implicit Truth, Invisible Goods, Liturgy, Narrative Truth, Performative Truth, Ritual, Script, Second Nature, *Tao*, Truth.

10. **What guiding principles are there, in addition to lean thinking?** Local Wisdom, Conversation, Culture, Leisure, Reciprocity and Cooperation, Resilience, Social Capital, Truth; Abstraction, Anarchism, Closed-Loop Systems, Cohesion, Commons, Harmless Lunatic, Harmonic Order, Holism, Informal Logic, Localisation, Metamorphosis, Practice, Presence.

11. **What about manners and ethics?** Manners, Ethics; Blame, *Caritas*, Casuistry, Character, Compassion, Courtesy, Dialogue, Dirty Hands, Ecology: The Scholars, Encounter, Gifts, Good Faith, Humility, Innocence, Insult, Interest, Presence, Promiscuous Ethics, Public Sphere and Private Sphere, Reflection, Responsibility, Trust, Virtues, Violence.

12. **And guidance on logical thinking?** Informal Logic, Fallacies, Manners; *Ad hominem*, Begging the Question, Big Stick, Cant, Causes, Composition, Deceptions, Distraction, Expertise, F-Word Fallacy, False Analogy, False Consistency, False Inference, False Opposite, Grammar, Hyperbole, Hypocrisy, Identity, Ideology, Irrelevance, No Alternative, Self-Evident, Straw Man, Time Fallacies, Unfalsifiability, Wolf Fallacy. (See also "How to Cheat in an Argument" on page xxiii.)

13. **Doesn't all this call for a fresh perspective on economics?** Economism, Economics, Regrettable Necessities; Green Economics, Lean Economics, Planned Economy; Capital, Growth, Intentional Waste; Competitiveness, Protection, Slack and Taut, Informal Economy, Gifts, Usury, Lean Household, Reciprocity and Cooperation, Well-Being.

14. **And where is nature in all this?** Encounter; Ecology: Farmers and Hunters, Ecology: The Scholars, Gaia, Ecological System, Wheel of Life, Resilience; Lean Food; Home, Play, Relevance, Spirit, Hippopotamus.

———

Or for a full list of all the entries in the Dictionary, see the **bold** entries in the index.

Note on links between entries

Asterisks in the text indicate words which have their own entries, but not always in the same form of the word: e.g., *Elegant refers to the entry "Elegance". *Reciprocity and Cooperation ❭ Balance refers to the section on "Balance" within the entry "Reciprocity and Cooperation".

INTRODUCTION

I never volunteer for anything. It only gets me into trouble. So when we were asked to volunteer for parts in a game to illustrate the virtues of what is known as lean thinking, I stood at the back, and stared at the floor. This was especially necessary because the other people on the course were senior management in industries which I had read about from time to time, but who lived on a different planet from the one I mooch about in: aerospace, automotive, logistics, reinsurance. One of them made tanks. I concentrated on not catching anyone's eye.

What I didn't realise was that the last person to volunteer—or anyone foolhardy enough not to volunteer at all—was punished by being nominated for the job that nobody wanted.

"Okay, you're the CEO."

"?"

"Yes, you."

"?"

"Chief Executive Officer."

"?"

"The Boss."

"No, really, I'm not that ambitious."

"You're the Boss. Now, let's get a move on."

Well, they put a lot of thought and effort into designing the games they play in business schools. And here is what they had us doing. They wanted us to assemble little plastic coloured bricks together in a very particular way. If you got it roughly right, that wouldn't do. If you got it almost exactly right, that meant you had built an aeroplane that would stall on take-off. It had to be exact—and agreed to be exact by the incorruptible referee, the lady who was making this distressing event happen.

Most of the twenty-four people on the course had sensibly volunteered to be production workers. The remaining one third were management. The production workers were divided into four groups, sat down at four tables, and required to put the bricks together in subassemblies, each one an exact replica of the model which had been placed in front of them on their table. Each subassembly then had to be taken to the next table to have some more bits added to it. The object was completed by the fourth group and handed to the referee for inspection. The task of the managers was to make sure the workers got it right. My task was to make sure the managers got it right.

A lot of things happened at once. Putting those little bricks together was tricky. At each table, piles of duff subassemblies collected. Sometimes a completed object did make it to the end of the line, only to be rejected. Disputes broke out between the tables. There was a lot of shouting. My team of managers were worked off their feet. I realised it is hard work being a manager. The workers blamed the management. The management blamed me. I tried to remember how to look calm and confident. If anyone, having lost their way to the university's art department, had looked in on the scene, they would reasonably have been impressed by the sheer scale of activity. Everyone was furiously busy checking, carrying, informing, suggesting, inspecting, disagreeing. This, clearly, was a group of highly-motivated people. If people can work with this level of enthusiasm on the task of assembling little plastic bricks, what chance has the competition? The world is beaten.

The problem was that not one single assembly was put together correctly. The sound and fury signified nothing. It began to become clear, even to me, that there must surely be a better way of doing it.

After some trial and error, the tables were rearranged; they were pushed against each other in a row. The group at each table now worked to a rule: only one subassembly to be made at a time, then to be placed in reach of the group at the next table, waiting to be picked up. When the next group found that there was something wrong with it, the two groups would get together and work out the problem. There was good reason, now, to apply their minds. Neither table would even attempt to make another assembly until the problem with the first one had been cracked, and only one subassembly could now be in play at the same time. Problems were revealed quickly; people talked to each other. The shouting stopped.

And then the talking, too, got quieter. The production workers had worked out how to get it right, every time. Something new began to come from the tables: a sense of quiet satisfaction.

And the management? Quite suddenly, I remembered my pivotal role as CEO, and looked round to see what the other members of my management team were doing. It can be easily summarised: we were standing in a straight line, with our arms folded. We were observing the scene, and trying to make ourselves believe that we were in some way responsible for this smoothly-running model of diligence, accuracy and intelligence.

But then we realised: we were out of work. I would have been out of work anyway, so for me it was a lucky reprieve; I could leave with relief and honour. But for the others in my team it was a moment of truth: if you declutter things so that the problems become visible, and you set things up so that people talk to each other and start to believe they can work things out for themselves, you are calling on information-processing power which has a tendency to be overlooked. It is there in the space right above the nose. You need some reasonably well-defined intention in the first place, but within that frame of reference there is freedom to invent. It is called "lean thinking".[†]

The lean thinking described in this book should not be taken as a comprehensive guide to how to run a railway or to make tanks. Rather, it is about how to recruit the intelligence and purpose of the people in the extraordinary task of inventing a future. And here is why we need to do so.

The story

When long-established systems break down, they often do so in many different ways at the same time. Our economy and society depend on a lot of things working right, all the time: cheap and reliable flows of energy, a stable

climate, fertile soils, abundant fresh water, productive oceans, an intact, diverse ecology, high levels of employment and a cohesive culture. These are all in trouble.

How should we respond to this? Well, with care, application and references, no doubt, and we shall come to that, but for now: four kinds of response are possible—that is, four paths which lead off in their different directions, each of which counts as the most enticing and delightful one, depending on who is looking at them:

- *Growth.* Market economies, like bicycles, are only stable when they are moving forward—and that, for an economy, means growth. Growth keeps unemployment down and governments solvent. These are extremely good reasons to keep it going: how could any responsible government and business establishment contemplate anything else? The snag is that growth destroys the foundations on which it relies. This is the double-bind of growth: we are damned if we do, and damned if we don't.

- *Continuity.* Could we not reform the economy—to protect those foundations from further damage or, better still, repair them? For instance, why not work out how to achieve the double delight of growth *and* repair? The snag here is that there is no sign whatsoever of that being possible. Alternatively, we might try continuing while calling a halt to growth itself. But there are problems with that, too. It would do nothing to reduce the accumulated damage, which is already more than the Earth can bear. And the lack of growth would break the economy.

- *Descent.* This is a steep winding-down of the size of the industrial economy. It strips away its burdens and complications, nurses the human ecology back to health, builds local competence and discovers a sense of place. It thinks afresh about how to get out of the aforementioned double-bind. The descent itself is inevitable, as is the breakage that follows, and yet, this is managed descent, in contrast with descent that forces itself on an economy blindly straining for growth. The shock is as gentle and as survivable as foresight can make it.

- *Collapse.* This future sees events moving out of our grasp.

[†] For full discussion of the principal concepts in this Introduction, with references, see the relevant entries in the Dictionary. All Dictionary entries are listed in **bold** in the index.

Lean Logic is about Descent. It is the path that has both reality and hope.

The ways in which the descent could develop are so varied that there is a risk of being paralysed by the uncertainty, so *Lean Logic* focuses on a particular aspect of it—an aspect that matters intensely to all of us. As the industrial economy descends, unemployment will rise, and there will come a point when government revenues are so deeply reduced that funds are not there to support the unemployed or to pay for such fundamentals as education, health and law and order. Households and communities will find it hard, bordering on impossible, to pay their way. Such necessities as food and even water supplies could be hard to get. Communities will therefore have to provide these things for themselves, or do without. They will need to rediscover their locality and local skills, rebuild a culture, and apply the power of lean thinking; sharply focused, widely shared.

The shocks of descent converging (as outlined in the Dictionary) into our culture's "climacteric" will leave nothing in our lives unchanged. We cannot now avoid it, but it can be managed, mitigated, made survivable, recognised as our species' toughest, but greatest, opportunity. At such moments of discontinuity, with sharp changes of direction, societies—or at least the technologies they use—can slip back, not by years, but by ages: when the Romans arrived in Britain, they found a thriving, technically advanced Celtic Iron Age society; when they left, it retreated, not to the Iron Age, but another 2,000 years further, to the Bronze Age. But we know what we need to do. We need to build the sequel, to draw on inspiration which has lain dormant, like the seed beneath the snow.

––––––

Here are three guiding principles that may serve us well:

Manners

"Manners", in *Lean Logic*, are about treating ideas with the respect, attention and good humour needed to hear them. They open us up to encounter with nature, with each other and with our own thinking minds. Logic and manners are closely linked. The rules of thinking, informal logic, judgment and reasonable conversation are rules of good manners, and this guide to thinking about the future is also a Book of Manners.

The art of recognising the difference between honest argument and fraud has been in poor health of late. That's good enough for a political economy which is overflowing with the riches of oil and held together by the self-interest of the market, and where there is a range of choice, with plenty of ways to be right, and second chances if you're wrong. But in our new, urgent world, getting it right matters more. If we are to usefully think through systems-solutions—as lean thinking would have us do—the first system to be aware of is the system of language, insight and self-deception that guides, or confuses, the way we think.

For a taster of some of the hazards that can arise in conversation, see "How to Cheat in an Argument" at the end of this Introduction. The accepted name for these hazards is "fallacies", and they are so common that it is sometimes hard to think of any argument in which at least one of the participants has *not* built his or her case on one of these fault lines. The potential for mayhem and grief is large. They are best avoided or, at least, understood. It is partly a matter of taking the time to reflect, to listen so carefully to what nature and people are telling us, and to what we are telling ourselves, that we may discover, over time, practical and astonishing responses to a fiercely difficult future.

Scale and presence

It is widely supposed that large size confers advantages. It is claimed to be more efficient, since there are economies of scale: once you have got things set up for a particular task, you can get a lot more done for relatively little extra cost and effort (lower unit costs), and you can go on building on that principle—up to a point. And yet, large-scale systems have problems, many of which apply to large-scale *anything*—including animals. They need large quantities of stuff (water, fuel, materials, information), which must be gathered over long distances; they may require complicated infrastructures; they then have to get rid of the waste; and they need complex specialisms to do all this. And, in the case of a big-city state, there is disempowerment. It is like a wave: you can ride it, but not steer it.

In contrast, small scale has its own economies: shorter transport distances, less waste, less infrastructure (lower total costs), more attention to detail, more flexibility, and it opens the way to empowerment: *you can make a difference*. For instance, given a chance, communities on a small enough scale for individuals to feel real influence can be so effective that doing the apparently impossible is their daily bread. Anarchists in terms of their independence, orderly in terms of ownership and responsibility for their particular places, surprising in their inventiveness, they are, even now, beginning to wake up to a long transition from the global city, towards located habitats on a human scale.

This is *presence*. It is about rediscovering citizenship, taking part in the life and creativity of well-beloved places that would not, without it, have a hope of coping with their future. There was something of this in the mind of one of history's early defenders of what we might now call the Big Society, Pericles.[1] In his 431 BC funeral oration for those who had fallen in the most recent year of the Peloponnesian War, he spoke of the virtues and values for which Athens was fighting. At the heart of this culture he placed ordinary citizens: these "fair judges of public matters", he said, bring "daring and deliberation" to politics, and "regard him who takes no part in these duties not as unambitious but as useless".[2]

That is the spirit of our age: the Transition movement, *Lean Logic's* "presence", lean thinking, the principle of co-production, local people who care for local people . . . the idea is getting about. And there are those who haven't waited for local participation to be invented and given a name, for they have been doing it for generations anyway. But the rediscovery of something as obvious as presence (in this sense of participation) is not trivial: since the early days of the Industrial Revolution, and especially in the century since 1914, it has been draining away. Many of the would-be participants died in the trenches and their sequels; the command-and-control culture of war acquired the standing of a public virtue; the large-scale state, dazzled by its good intentions, saw itself as provider; iconic liberties engaged our attention while regulation closed in; economic competitiveness usurped other standards. While democracy has advanced, the part we ordinary citizens have played in the making and sustaining of the places and communities we live in has diminished. Never has so much been decided for so many by so few.

And yet, as that accursed century—*saeculum maledictum*—draws to an end, we may have learned enough to come together, to develop ideas with brilliance and authority, being present, participating, investing imagination, being inspired by, and bringing inspiration to, the places we live in.

Slack

It is a truth universally acknowledged that competitiveness is a good thing. It is a life-saver, in that it enables an economy to pay its way. It is a provider of equity, in that it enables people to achieve wealth and status on their own merits. And it is the only way in which a price-based market economy will work. But it comes at a cost.

A competitive market economy must, by definition, be "taut". The price charged by Fred for his goods will hold only so long as the price charged by Dan for the same goods, in the same place, is no lower. If it is, Fred will need to reduce his prices, or else to go out of business. Prices for goods therefore tend to converge to the same level. And that level requires all the producers in the market to be efficient—to work full-time, to use the methods that cost least, and to sell as much as they can. Producers all understand this necessity—there is little choice in the matter; what distinguishes them is how good they are at doing it. There is a requirement to innovate, because the competitive market is *taut*: everyone else is doing so, and anyone who does not is quickly priced out of business.

In the future, it will not be like that. Producers will not always want to provide their goods and services in the most efficient way. They may—for good local reasons— want to use a technology which is more expensive. For instance, it could make sense, from the point of view of the resilient community, to use less energy, water or material, at the cost of having to spend more on labour. Or local craftsmen may be able to keep up with local demand for long-lasting goods despite working for only three days a week. Or producers may simply decide not to produce the maximum quantity, and to take it easy and produce according to what they see as reasonable need, or what they have the time for, after spending time with family and neighbours.

All these choices would have the effect of raising the price of the goods supplied by that producer or—if other producers did the same—by the community as a whole. In a taut market, such decisions could not be made. If they were, they would not stick, because a producer that tried to do so would be quickly put out of business by others who went for the cheaper option, the efficient and competitive one. Any market that did manage to make such sensible, yet inefficient, decisions stick, would be *slack*—and it would be at constant risk of being stymied by competitive producers seizing the opportunity to make easy money by producing and selling at a lower price.

How can a community, despite all this, be mistress of its own fate in this sense? How can it sustain that condition of slack—that is, have the freedom to make enlightened decisions and make them stick? Well, here is the good news. The "normal" state of affairs, before the era of the great civic societies, and in the intervals between them, has consisted of political economies—perhaps better known in this case as villages—where the terms on which goods and services were exchanged were not based on price. Instead, they were built around a complex culture of arrangements—obligations, loyalties, collaborations—which express the nature and priorities of the community and the network of relationships and reciprocities between its members. No, don't scoff. This is what households still do—and friends, neighbours, cricket teams, magistrates, parent-teacher associations, allotment holders; this is the non-monetary 'informal economy', the central core that enables our society to exist. It is outrageous to the received values of now: it is not transparent; it is nonconformist; social mobility in it is limited; it is neither efficient nor competitive; it is full of anomalies. But it keeps things going.

So, back to the question: how does this political economy manage to keep such an apparently unstable regime going? Well, it turns on culture. Sheer naked loyalties and family values can only go so far. There needs to be something interesting, connecting, going on too—something to talk about, to cooperate in, to mull over, to aim for, to laugh at; there needs to be a story to tell, something to coordinate and to do together. A culture is like the upright strands that you begin with in basket-making, round which you wind the texture of the basket itself: no sticks, no basket; no culture, no community. It is the context, the story, that identifies a

community and gives it existence. It is both the parent and child of 'social capital'. And the social capital of a community is its social life—the links of cooperation and friendship between its members. It is the common culture and ceremony, the good faith and reciprocal obligations, the civility and citizenship, the play, humour and conversation which make a living community, the cooperation that builds its institutions. It is the social ecosystem in which a culture lives.

Ever since Adam Smith observed that people are willing to carry out almost any service for each other despite being motivated by nothing more than commercial self-interest, it has seemed to be unnecessary and ridiculous to suppose that there is any significant role for such higher motives as benevolence. Economists simply haven't needed such concepts. Well, they do now. The economics of the future will be benignly and inextricably entangled with social capital—with intense links of reciprocity—in comparison with which the reduction of economic and social relations to the piteous simplicities of prices is not up to standard any longer, and is due for retirement. It is now all right to speak of benevolence as an economic concept, for economics is at the early stages of being reintegrated into community, and community into the whole nature of the living things that belong there. It will not be from the impersonal price-calculations of the butcher, the brewer or the baker that we expect our dinner, but from the reciprocal obligations that join a community together, and the benevolence among its members.

Slack is the space in which judgment lies. The early shocks of descent may leave little room for choice: just one tolerable option could be a fine thing, and that may be as much as most of us can hope for, at least for the time being. In the mature settlements that could follow, however, the tyranny of decisions being made in lock-step with competitive pricing will be an ancient memory. There will be time for music.

———

So what does that leave *Lean Logic* to do? In fact, hang on, how does one deal with such a book? Is it a dictionary to be consulted for the occasional word? Is it a book to read right through? Or is it some mixture of the two? Well, the answer to that is that it is a lean book. It does not have the last word. You, the reader, are invited to explore ideas from more than one point of view, to follow the links, to build up your own familiarity with the key concepts, in your own way.

Lean Logic is a community of essay-entries about inventive, cooperative self-reliance. Each entry is complete in itself, but also joins up with others, and signposts to those connections are supplied in the entries. Inheriting and inventing families of enabling principles (such as the rules of chess, the instruments of music or the grammar of language), we can construct things with more confidence and ambition than we could if we had to invent everything from first principles. Whether *Lean Logic* has a place on the edge of these enabling principles it is too soon to say. But it may, perhaps, provide some of the little bricks that, with luck, judgment and conversation, turn out to fit together.

A useful place to start is at A Guide to Lean Logic on page xv, which lists principal entries under fourteen questions that might occur to you on coming to the book for the first time. Links between them are suggested—it may help to make sense of one idea when you know something about related ones, from which more links extend, without any guarantee that you will discover a place where the logical sequence starts. It is, perhaps, like arriving in a group or a community: you learn about its members and their relationships with each other by being in the middle of it: there is no beginning or end. The more you know the group, the more you yourself become part of it, and part of its story. It is a story about the shared experience of something discovered, something discussed, something done.

HOW TO CHEAT IN AN ARGUMENT:
A BEGINNER'S GUIDE

(or, even better, how to catch yourself doing it)

*Asterisks mark terms with full entries in the Dictionary

Absence. Stop listening.

***Abstraction.** Keep the discussion at the level of high-flown generality.

***Accent.** Use tone of voice to smuggle fraud past the listener without suspicion.

Access. Reduce a complex subject (which requires thought) to gossip (which everyone can take part in).

***Ad hominem.** Have a go at the other person, rather than their argument.

Air-castle. Declare a fine objective. Argue from the assumption that you have already achieved it.

Anecdote I. Accept a mere anecdote as crucial evidence.

Anecdote II. Dismiss crucial evidence as mere anecdote.

Anger. Present it as proof of how right you are.

***Assent.** Go with the flow of authority or opinion.

Assertion. Simply assert your case, without any argument at all.

***Begging the question.** Use your conclusion as an argument to prove your conclusion. A circular argument.

***Big stick.** Threaten.

***Blame.** Assume that the problem is solved when you have found someone to blame.

***Bullshit.** Talk at length about nothing.

***Calibration.** Keep to yourself an opinion which might cause trouble. Go with the flow.

***Cant.** Offer assurances of goodness and good intentions, showing that no nice person could possibly disagree with you.

***Causes.** Assume that an event which follows another event was therefore caused by it.

***Certainty.** Be unaware of the possibility that you may be wrong.

***Choice.** Assume that we do what we choose, and we choose what we want.

Cold argument. Present a case so cold and impersonal that the other side freezes.

Common nature. Assume everyone else is as good-natured—or not—as you.

***Composition.** Argue that since one person can do it (e.g., come first in the race) everyone can do it.

Correlation gambit. Assert that "they" are all the same.

Counterexample. Cite one instance which disproves the other side's entire belief system: "But I have a friend who . . ."

***Damper.** Refuse to recognise anything except moderation.

Decisiveness. Sweep aside all argument by the supercharged simplicity of your reaction.

***Definition.** Define a word to mean what you want it to mean today, and defend that definition at all costs.

***Devil's voice.** Make your point only half seriously; if it goes down badly, you can claim to be only joking.

***Dialectic.** Explain everything in terms the struggle between two powerful forces: workers and capitalists, heaven and hell, us and them.

***Disconnection.** Fire off slogans. Don't worry about whether they join up.

Discretion. Do not tell them the truth, because they, unlike you, are not intelligent or strong enough to cope with it.

***Empty sandwich.** Say something that sounds plausible and avoids being wrong by virtue of actually meaning nothing at all.

Evil motive. Explain away the other side's argument by the brilliance of your insight about their real intentions.

*Exception. Insist that a statement is entirely untrue because there is (or might be) one case where it does not hold.

*Exit. Walk out.

*Expectations. Assume that if the other side does not say what you expect, they need help.

*Expertise. Appeal to your own, or someone else's, expert knowledge. Now it's beneath your pay-grade to listen.

*F-word. Proof that you are getting to the heart of the matter, while everyone else is dithering.

*False analogy. Derail the argument with an irrelevant example.

*False consistency. Avoid having to choose between two incompatible alternatives, by going for both.

*False inference. Draw false conclusions from observations.

*False opposite. Define a word in terms of it *not* being its opposite. Example: regulation is good, because its opposite is chaos.

*False premise. Start with nonsense. Build on it with meticulous accuracy and brilliance.

*False sameness. Assume that every new event or argument is the same as a previous event or argument which you have already made up your mind about.

Familiarity bias. Believe things that sound familiar; disbelieve things that don't.

*Fine-distinction-intolerance. Refuse any critical judgment at the margin (e.g., where pass/fail hangs on one mark).

*Fluency. Be so fluent in your delivery that no one notices what you are saying.

Fragmentation. Disrupt with such persistence that the other person's argument is reduced to disjointed remarks, which can be picked off at leisure.

Give up. Assume that, if you cannot think of a solution, there isn't one.

*Grim reality. Assume that good qualities are either fantasy or nostalgia. Lends plausibility to claims of harsh necessity.

Half-truth. Speak the truth, but leave out the part that matters.

Hearing-trouble I. Don't listen.

Hearing-trouble II. Hear every challenging argument as belonging to an "-ism", or a "wing", and reject it in boredom and disgust.

Hearing-trouble III. Hear no challenging argument unless it belongs to an "-ism" or a "wing" which you can recognise.

*High ground. Capture the moral advantage by insisting that the fates of real people are at stake here, which the other side appears to overlook.

*Humility. Expose your humility as proof of your good judgment.

*Hyperbole. Use wild exaggeration—especially useful for making the other person's case look ridiculous.

*Hypocrisy scourge. Don't worry about whether the person is right. Just assert that he doesn't live up to the standards he argues for and accuse him of being a hypocrite.

*Icon. Reduce the argument to one ready-made idea: a silver bullet solution.

*Ideology. Live and die for a single seductive theory that explains everything.

*Ignorance. Exploit your ignorance of a subject as freedom to say anything you like about it.

*Implicature. Use a true statement to imply a false statement. Example: "Cassio has got Desdemona's handkerchief in his pocket."

Inattention. Don't trouble to read what has been written before disagreeing with it.

*Indignation. Dismiss the other side's case as too repugnant to contemplate.

*Innocence. Present yourself as the sweet innocent, who cuts through all the clever stuff and with refreshing childlike simplicity gets straight to the point.

*Intelligence. Rest secure—someone of your intelligence can't be wrong.

*Internal evidence. Select only evidence which confirms your case.

Interrupt. Destroy all possibility of a sensible conversation, by not allowing the other side to speak. If necessary, shout.

*Irrelevance. Assume that if you cannot immediately see the relevance of something, it is off the topic and merits no further thought.

Irrelevant past. Dismiss former times as of no significance: they weren't as clever then as we are now. (*Time fallacies)

Lunch bias. Agree with anyone who buys you lunch. (see also *Digestive Ethics)

***Many questions.** Mix the agreed with the debatable. Example: "Has your objectionable boyfriend got a corkscrew I could borrow?"

Memory as irrelevant. Assume that you don't need to remember anything because your opinion is enough, and anyway you can find it on the internet.

***Mindset.** Sustain your opinion inflexibly without regard to any argument at all.

***Money.** Assume that money is the only measure that matters, and the only motivation that works.

Nit-pick. Use an error of detail to rubbish the other side's whole case.

***No alternative.** Conclude that, since options A, B and C are impossible, *therefore* there is no alternative to option D. But D may be impossible, too. And what about option Q?

No evidence. Assume that anything you haven't taken the trouble to find out, doesn't exist.

Nothing new. Respond to all information—including the most astonishing—in the same way: "I know".

***Numbers.** Give your case plausibility by quoting your own precise statistics; fall for the statistics quoted by the other side.

Old hat. Dismiss an argument on the grounds that you have disregarded it before.

Permanent present. Assert that the future, or at least the direction of progress, will be much the same as now. (*Time fallacies)

Perpetual notion. Assume that today's scientific opinion will hold good in the future.

***Personal experience.** Use your personal experience (e.g., surviving a train crash) to claim expertise (e.g., how to run the railway).

***Pharisee.** Assume that a person as good as you can only have good opinions, exempting you from the need to think.

Plausibility. Bluff your way through. Get the grades.

Possession. Quarrel with any thought that is not your own.

***Reasons.** Dismiss an argument as wrong if the other side cannot give reasons for it. Cite their irrational intuition as proof of how rational you are being, as needed.

Recency. Allow recent events to crowd out all other considerations.

***Reductionism.** Dismiss the entire argument other than the simplified bit of it you want to talk about.

Repetition. Make the same argument over and over again, until the other side is screaming.

***Rhetorical capture.** Be carried away by the other side's rhetoric, or your own.

***Scepticism.** Dismiss anything that is surprising.

Scientism. Explain that you're a scientist, so that, if you don't understand it, it can't be true.

***Sedation.** Send the other side to sleep.

***Self-evident.** Assume that because something is self-evident you don't need to find out whether it is true or not.

***Shifting ground.** As each of your arguments is defeated, try another one. Reduce the other side to exhaustion.

Shock tactics. If someone disagrees with you, freak out.

Simplification. Simplify, to the point of lunacy. It makes you audible in politics.

***Sincerity.** Use your sincerity as a licence never to have to apply your mind again.

***Slippery slope.** Rubbish a proposal on the grounds that it would cause mayhem if taken to a ludicrous extreme.

Smiler (The). Dismiss the other side's case with amiable contempt.

***Spiking guns.** Admit that your argument has trivial flaws, so that you can dismiss the other side's objections as trivial.

Spillover. Use your expertise in one field as a licence to pronounce on all other topics with authority.

***Straw man.** Invent an argument which your opponent did not use, and then launch a horrified attack on it.

Strife. Think of every argument as a battle you have to win as proof of your identity.

***Sunk cost.** Value a project on the basis of what you have spent on it in the past, not the net benefits it will bring in the future.

*Survivor bias.** Defend a bad practice by pointing to the (few) examples or people which have survived it.

*Tautology.** Repeat your assertion in different words, hoping that the other side will think you have made a case for it.

Truism. Try to destroy the argument with a loaded statement of the meaningless: "Democracy is democracy."

Ultimatum. Threaten to walk out: "I don't want to live in a society like that."

Uncertainty. Dismiss the possibility that you may be right.

Undeniable words I. Insert "hooray" words (equality, democratic, competitive, vibrant) which no one could disagree with.

Undeniable words II. Insert "boo" words (old boy network, toff, elitist, like-the-Nazis, outdated, bigot, hypocrite) which everyone can agree to hate.

*Unfalsifiability.** Use a form of argument that can never be shown to be false; e.g., "If only we could all be peaceful, there would be no wars."

*Unknowable future.** Insist that, since we don't know what will happen tomorrow (e.g., to the weather), we cannot possibly know what will happen in 20 years.

*Unmentionable.** Live in hope that since you do not speak about something, it does not exist.

War on truth I. Say nothing that can be believed.

War on truth II. Believe nothing that is said.

*Wishful thinking.** Say what you have made yourself believe, because you wish so much it were true.

*Witch-hunt.** Find a victim.

*Wolf.** Insist that, because expectations of trouble were false in the past, they will prove false in the future.

DICTIONARY

of

LEAN LOGIC

A

ABSTRACTION. Displacement of the particular—people, place, purpose—by general principle.

Abstraction supplies principles to die for—socialism, nationalism, equality, humanity, progress. Large scale turns human society into a rich provider of abstraction; the space that was once occupied by practical observation and direct affections is filled with *ideology. The ideology is then enforced. As industry, population and rootlessness grew in the nineteenth century, abstraction got everywhere and smudged everything, like the smoke:

> To the question of daily bread, liberalism
> did not give much serious thought. It is too
> romantic to trouble itself with such gross
> requirements. It was easier for liberalism to
> invent the people than to study it.[1]

Alexander Herzen (1812–1870) made the case for the particular—for local detail, for pragmatic decision-making, for the near-at-hand, for *presence. As for the great altruistic ideologies and systems of thought which lift people's gaze from the local, from their own friends, values and talents, demanding big sacrifices, offering general solutions and explaining the meaning of life, these he recognised as monstrous delusions.[2]

For Herzen, the values to be trusted consisted of such things as earning enough to feed a family, enjoying one's work, living in peace. Such aims are manageable, and have a good chance of being met without horrible and *unintended consequences. Herzen believed that the individual is responsible for his own *choices; the big abstractions and projects with a long, never-to-be-achieved vision usurp that responsibility: the person is reduced to the currency of politics—and spent. Although citizens have cogent views of what is good, just, beautiful or *true, abstraction abstracts the possibility of bringing them about.

And here, Herzen is in the good company of other scourges of abstraction and pretension: Oliver Goldsmith, for example, with his plain insight that "there may be equal happiness in states that are differently governed from our own." Goldsmith's insight about the different personalities of different places was simple, but it needed to be said, for the Enlightenment's scientific and economic presumptions favoured the single vision supplied by reason. And Aristotle, of course, was aware of this, with his distinction between two ways of thinking, between the universal and the particular, between *general theory (*episteme*) and practical *wisdom (*phronesis*). Aristotle recognised that there is no reason why arguments should be consistent with each other if they apply to different moral problems; there can be different, but equally reasonable, interpretations of the same argument in different places; diverse ethical theories, he noted, are not mutually exclusive: they are complementary. They call for informed *prudence about the particulars of the case.[3]

Another telling critic of abstraction is the well-beloved mayor of Bordeaux, Michel Eyquem de Montaigne (1533–1592). He was a follower of the Stoic philosophy, so when he writes of giving attention to himself, it is not a selfish lack of concern for others that he means. On the contrary, it is a direct alertness to people, place and circumstance; there is no veil of cleverness and strategic abstraction between what you see and what you think. Montaigne gives us a fresh, direct vision, a quality of *encounter which is the starting point of moral judgment:

> As far as in me lies, I give all my attention to
> myself; and even here I would willingly curb
> my feelings and keep them from plunging
> too deeply into an object that I possess by the
> favour of others, and over which Fortune has
> more right than I.[4]

But, all too often, the allure of abstraction is irresistible. Vigorous policy and *reform programmes almost invariably consist of abstractions; the opposite approach—relying on particular local knowledge, on skills and inspiration—leaves politics with less obvious, less elevated things to do, such as preserving the peace and the *law, supporting the *institutions of *social capital and the active presence and participation of citizens, and giving the society in its care the benefit of reliable long-term foresight about, for instance, *energy, *climate, *population, *food, and the need for long-term solutions to the *growth problem in

A

economics. But politicians with such a role would be reduced to public servants . . .

One powerful enticement to abstraction, then, is that it provides grounds for almost any form of destructive intervention; abstractions and the *rationalism they express can easily be made *unfalsifiable: they cannot be disputed by pointing to the particular because their existence means that the particular has already been discounted. Abstraction is above such *dirty details; it is detached.

For a perceptive take on abstraction, and on the paralysis and disempowerment that come with it, it is not a bad idea to turn to novelists, whose medium is the particular. Joseph Conrad's Lord Jim is introduced to us as "a seaman in exile from the sea, [who] had Ability in the abstract, which is good for no other work but that of a water-clerk". His exile and abstraction were due to a devastating incident in his past, in which he, along with all the other officers, had escaped in the few lifeboats from the steamer *Patna*, which they believed about to sink, leaving 800 pilgrim passengers to what they supposed (wrongly) to be their deaths. Here was a man who had become undefined, unidentified, in the "extreme weariness of emotions, the vanity of effort, the yearning for rest". At the inquiry even "the sound of his own truthful statements confirmed his deliberate opinion that speech was of no use to him any longer". The novel is about Jim's recovery of a concrete *identity, through unstinting commitment to a distant and troubled locality and its people; it costs him his life, but as the trusted narrator, Marlow, concludes, tentatively, "There are days when the reality of his existence comes to me with an immense, with an overwhelming force"; and not so tentatively: "Not in the wildest days of his boyish visions could he have seen the alluring shape of such an extraordinary success!"[5]

Matthew Arnold summarises,

> The great safeguard is never to let oneself become abstract, always to retain an intimate and lively consciousness of the truth of what one is saying, and, the moment this fails us, to be sure that something is wrong.[6]

Whether *Lean Logic* lives up to that standard is an open question. But at least it is not a grand project. It starts with the working-day particulars of who we are, and what we are about.

ACCENT. Tone of voice, used to smuggle fraud past the listener without arousing suspicion.

For Aristotle, this could be a significant source of error because, in classical Greek, what a word means often depends on how it is accented. With some minor *exceptions, this does not apply in English, yet the accent problem does arise in another sense not intended by Aristotle: the effect that accented words and tone of voice can have on the meaning of a sentence.[7]

For example, an argument can be reinforced by a tone of weary *boredom, implying that the argument is already settled, and that one's opponents are simply as wrong now as they have ever been, or that the matter is too *self-evident to be worth spelling out and you would have to be mad to question it. Anger or bright cheerfulness can also make it seem absurd or offensive to disagree, and emphasis can change the meaning. "We will depend on *technology*" conveys that technology is going to solve our problems. "We *will* depend on technology" conveys that technology will of course have a part to play but this is by no means enough. "We will depend on technology" (with no accent at all) could be saying anything, including: "I am not going to abandon the usual line that technology will get us out of this problem, but I don't think we have a chance, whatever we do." "I was *tempted* to have another glass of wine" means you didn't have one; "I was tempted to have another glass of *wine*" means you did.[8]

More generally, the written report of a speech can be misleading unless it uses italics to show where the emphasis lies in an ambiguous sentence. Deadpan delivery is a warning that the official is not going to be thrown off course by ridicule or by a sense of proportion. Skilful use of accent can allow you to tell lies without speaking an untrue word.

*Implicature, Equivocation.

ACCESS. See Closed Access, Open Access.

AD HOMINEM. A *distraction which takes on the other person, rather than the argument itself. The Latin name for it, *[Argumentum] ad hominem (or ad personam if this is seen as less gender-specific) is used because there is no short equivalent in English: "personal attack" is often suitable but not always. Here we have a distraction in which the argument is unheard; the discussion slips into politics: who is talking? who is paying them? who influences them? how to deal with them? It is on the basis of arguments such as these that, for instance, the science of *climate change is dismissed by the accusation that the scientists are bribed to reach their dire conclusions by the promise of research grants.[9]

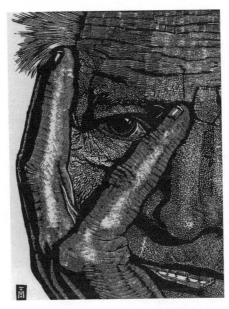

The distraction is effective: avoid the argument; concentrate on the person. Once he is on the defensive it can be hard to recover: nothing he says can be taken as true. Aristotle objected to this in 330 BC, and it was still giving trouble 2,000 years later when John Locke described it as one of three devious means of reducing your opponent to silence:

1. cite the eminence or *expertise of people who disagree with him;
2. insist that no mere argument is enough—he needs to provide proof; and
3. the straightforward *ad hominem* attack on the man and his principles, rather than his argument.[10]

The most usual application of *ad hominem* attack is the accusation of hypocrisy:

STOTHARD: (speaking of the BBC): [There is a] duty to correct a mistake you may have made.

TOYNBEE: I think the BBC should be a little cautious before it takes advice from the Murdoch Press on honesty and truth, light and beauty. . . . It really is quite astonishing the lessons the BBC is getting from an extremely disreputable British press.[11]

The charge of *hypocrisy is efficient, popular, and turns up everywhere. But it is flawed, for what matters

is not the arguer, but the argument. Though my lifestyle may be regrettable, that does not mean that my arguments are wrong; on the contrary, it could mean that I am acutely aware of values that are better than the ones I achieve myself. If I lived an impeccable life, I could be lost in admiration for myself as an ethical ideal; failings may keep me modest and raise my sights.

But *ad hominem* keeps things simple. It enables the crowd to speak with one voice, so that it can actually change things. Unfortunately, that change is quite likely to involve finding someone to *blame—a *witch-hunt which takes people's minds off the real problem. Here is the *mindset summarised with approval by Karl Marx: the job of philosophy, he shouts, is not to understand the world but to change it: "[History's] essential emotion is *indignation*; its essential task is *denunciation*."[12]

Accusation makes it clear what to do. It shrugs off the need to tangle with the difficulties of actual policy; instead, the victim can be gleefully demonised and swept away. He may have made the mistake of being associated with an *interest, class or party taken to be disreputable. Or he may have a private life that does not bear inspection.

Some private lives deserve this treatment, and yet awful private lives have coexisted with outstanding artistic and public judgment—and *vice versa*. Among history's famous men with immaculate private lives we have the members of Joseph Stalin's Politburo. Georgy Malenkov, just one of your ordinary killer-bureaucrats, was happily married and a wonderful, poetry-reading father to his children. Nikolai Yezhov was tender with his adopted daughter and played with her on his return from work. As the historian Amy Knight comments, "Let us hope that Yezhov, who liked to engage directly in the killing and torture of the NKVD victims, washed the blood off his hands first."[13]

A

And closely related to the charge of hypocrisy is the variant which discounts what a person says on the grounds that she has not experienced it *personally: you cannot know anything about *education unless you are a teacher; about poverty unless you have come from a poor background; you cannot know which horse won a horse-race unless you are another horse . . . On the other hand, if you *do* have the relevant experience, the inverse applies—"He would say that, wouldn't he?"

And yet, in spite of all this, there are some forms of *ad hominem* that are appropriate. For example, a person may be justified in being critical of the other person, and in allowing this to reduce the credibility of their argument. This can happen, for instance, in an oppressive regime. In Communist Eastern Europe in the 1970s and 1980s, intellectuals who had secured their own position by going along with what the regime wanted—e.g., by denouncing opposition movements such as Charter 77—inevitably contaminated their own case in all other arguments: if *he* (who has sold out) asserts an argument to be true, then there *must* be something wrong with it; it has to be a trap. The response may be to attack the person, however plausible his argument, or it may be to come to terms with the intolerable life- and family-threatening position of intellectuals under a tyranny. Either way, attention in this morally-impoverished context is forced away from considerations of the subject itself, and towards the person. Sometimes, there is little room left for anything but *ad hominem.*[14]
*Genetic Fallacy, Interest, Cognitive Dissonance, *Tu Quoque.*

ADVOCACY. See Special Pleading.

AGRICULTURE. See Food Prospects, Lean Food.

ANARCHISM. "Anarchism", from the Greek *an* and *arches*, means "no chief"—hence "no rule". But there is more than one way of interpreting this, and it has been anarchism's big problem that people tend to settle on the wrong one—the idea of anarchy as mere chaos. It was in this sense that John Milton used it—as the state of affairs . . .

Where eldest Night
And Chaos, Ancestors of Nature, hold

Eternal Anarchie, amidst the noise
Of endless warrs and by confusion stand.
For hot, cold, moist, and dry, four Champions fierce
Strive here for Maistrie

John Milton, Paradise Lost, 1667.[15]

Let us instead look to the main body of anarchist literature. We cannot really speak of "mainstream" anarchism because anarchist writers, as you might expect, have tended to disagree with each other. But there is a fundamental proposition in common: governments have a poor, even catastrophic, record, guided by almost any motive other than the interests of the people to whom they are in principle *responsible. If governments could somehow be persuaded or forced to back off, the people could make a far better job of things.[16]

There are some famous names in this literature, and they deserve a mention:

- William Godwin (1756–1836) argued that the guide to our actions should be *reason*, the logic of the Enlightenment. Once people have a rational understanding of their duties, there is no need for such sensibilities as honour, generosity, gratitude, promises, or even affections; nor for such limitations on individual judgment as marriage, orchestras or the theatre; nor, of course, for government. He did admit that this enlightened *deference to reason would not be easy to achieve; it would require ceaseless vigilance and self-examination, he supposed, but beyond that, there were no suggestions about how it was to be done, and Godwin's rule of logic lives on in the literature as perhaps the most heroic of all statements of the perfect society, a fantasy with remarkable staying power, for here we are considering it two centuries later.[17]
- Max Stirner (1806–1856) took individualism as far as it would go: no state, government, private property, religion, family, ethics, love or associations beyond what individuals happen to want, when they want it.[18]
- Leo Tolstoy (1828–1910) looked to the Gospels for the peace and love which is all that is needed, he claimed, to sustain society without governments, laws, police, armies and private property.[19]

- Pierre-Joseph Proudhon (1809–1865) was an early and strong supporter of localisation: the best safeguard of liberty and justice lies in food producers and craftsmen working together in cooperatives.[20]
- Mikhail Bakunin (1814–1876) looked to the violent overthrow of the state, and its replacement as a bottom-up federation of trade unions (anarcho-syndicalism).[21]
- Peter Kropotkin (1842–1921) developed his advocacy of communal living and the abolition of private property in an extended and valuable discussion of land, biodynamic farming, decentralised urban planning, technology and the history of effective local action.[22]

The common factor for most of these (but not Matthew Arnold, see "Culture and Good Sense" sidebar) is the desire to see the end of government, and the most explicit statement of this is Bakunin's anarcho-syndicalism, which sees trade unions as the spearhead of revolution, destroying both the government and the capitalism that sustains it. In this way, the strengths of traditional anarchism's positive visions and insights were impaired by the tendency to focus on one ideal solution—an *ideology in its own right—as the magic preliminary pain that had to be endured before anarchism itself could have a chance. A broader, more real vision was suggested by Alexander Herzen (1812–1870), who warned of the consequences of *abstraction, and insisted, instead, on the case for focusing on the local, the feasible, the practical, the tangible, the proven—on the freedom to make and care for the particular *place. It was this grounded vision which, a century later, was taken up by Colin Ward.[23]

For Ward (1924–2010), anarchy (or, perhaps less confrontationally, "anarchism") is the study of *organisation*—of rule of a particular kind: self-rule; the orderly habits and interactions that come into being with the formation and maintenance of human groups. Anarchism, as Ward explains,

> is about the ways in which people organise themselves,[24]

and . . .

> Anarchists are people who make a social and political philosophy out of the natural and

---

CULTURE AND GOOD SENSE
Matthew Arnold's orderly anarchism

For Matthew Arnold (1822–1888), the *cohesive principle is a common culture. By "culture" what he had in mind was the very highest standards, "a pursuit of our total perfection by means of getting to know, on all the matters which most concern us, the best which has been thought and said in the world".[25]

Later critics picked him up on this: culture is not limited to the best; it is, less ambitiously, the common *story and *tradition of a *community. But Arnold's point holds: the way in which a community can preserve itself from anarchy (in its chaotic, Miltonian sense), is to build a community which is interesting enough to recognise itself as a particular place with its own *identity, *loyalties and obligations. The previous sentence fills in the logic which Arnold does not spell out, but the outcome, as he put it, is that a community learns "to like what right reason ordains".[26]

---

spontaneous tendency of humans to associate together for their mutual benefit.[27]

As Ward points out, the reality underlying this is undeniable: the speed, efficiency and *imagination with which people bring order to a situation which has potential for chaos is revealed whenever a group of people are *aligned*, in the sense of having common interests and a *common purpose. Such alignment applies, for instance, at times of protest—at Climate Camp in the United Kingdom in 2008, for example, or in the uprisings in Budapest in 1956 and in Prague in 1968, when good order and altruism were as solid as the commitment to sustain the revolutions. During the Hungarian uprising, it was the custom in Budapest . . .

. . . to put big boxes on street corners, and just a script over them, "This is for the wounded and for the families of the dead." They were set out in the morning and by noon they were full of money.[28]

A

Happenings like these are exceptional, of course. Eventually the revolutions are either suppressed or successful, and things go back to normal; and yet they have something to tell us which could be useful. Among the students of revolution who have noticed the remarkably competent groupings and councils that come into being if given a chance, Hannah Arendt writes,

> Each time they appeared, they sprang up as the spontaneous organs of the people, not only outside of all revolutionary parties but entirely unexpected by them and their leaders. They were utterly neglected by statesmen, historians, political theorists and, most importantly, by the revolutionary tradition itself. [Even sympathetic historians] regarded them as nothing more than essentially temporary organs in the revolutionary struggle for liberation; that is to say, they failed to understand to what extent the council system confronted them with an entirely new form of government, with a new public space for freedom.[29]

The emphasis here is on what can be done in practice (a bottom-up way of thinking), rather than on ambitions that require a lot of demolition first.

On the other hand, the state's natural reflex is indeed to make things difficult, even without intending to do so. The essential freedoms and resources which enable local action are eroded by governments, and, in some cases, such as education, their elimination is comprehensive. And in terms of sheer practical possibility, too, the option of effective local community is becoming more remote: it is harder to make practical sense of things, for instance, in a locality which has lost its post office, hospital, school, surgery, shops, abattoir, railway station, local trades, church, magistrates court, probation services and local *presence in farmland, and where it is difficult to decide on a collective celebration, owing to (amongst other things) prohibitions on grounds of health and safety, the fees and lead-times needed for an entertainments licence, and the sense that there is no cultural expression which does not exclude or offend many or most of the people living there (*Multiculturalism).

And yet, anarchism, in the cool, practical, local sense intended by Colin Ward, recognises that we innate

community builders ought to concentrate on what we can positively do. We have a talent for order, and the inherited *culture and accomplishments of the modern world are mainly the product of this talent. The history of social inventions—the institutions and *social capital that give us existence as a recognisable and living society—is the history of anarchism in this sense. Medicine—both the science and the institutions—was the product of voluntary persistence, backed by charitable donations, as were the schools and universities. The whole of our inheritance of *education was invented and made to happen by citizens, investing their time and talent in schools and colleges, in teaching as a *creative skill in its own right, in sustaining *diversity, and in increasing access. Even such fundamentals as insurance against accident, sickness and loss of income—arranged through the friendly societies, owned by their members—were voluntary enterprises and, from their start in the eighteenth century to their displacement by a state system in 1911, they had expanded their reach to almost universal coverage of working people in the UK. The *organic movement began as a citizens' inspiration, developing its authority and its scientific standing via its *freedom to decide for itself.[30]

The weak point in that capacity for invention—in the spontaneous order that is the primary aim and accomplishment of anarchism—is that it is exposed to the distrust and jealousy of centralising governments. If it works, it tends to be taken over, and the spontaneous order tends to die.

Anarchism has had its moments. There are insights there that are relevant to a future of insolvent government, a deeply diminished *economy, and no alternative for communities other than to invent everything for themselves, including the meaning of community. *Lean Logic* will borrow from it, and will mix it with other lines of enquiry which most anarchists would have been horrified by. But, then, anarchists have always had trouble with their allies.[31]

*Lean Household, Commons, Assent, Constructivism, Democracy, Incentives Fallacy, Cheirarchy.

ANOMALY. Life-giving detail characteristic of a *resilient system, and hated by the *rationalist and the person with a mission—for whom, to describe something as an anomaly is enough to condemn it without the need for more reasons.

Anomaly may take the form of:

1. an instructive deviation from the expected;
2. the natural expression of an evolving *complex system; and/or
3. an affront to the tidy or controlling mind, warning that a *system has more complexity and independence than had been assumed, and that it will consequently be a source of pain and surprise until eliminated.

In other words, anomaly can be valuable and *creative. Here are two examples. The first comes from a study of police forces in the metropolitan areas of the United States. During the late 1960s and early 1970s, there were proposals to reduce the number of forces (departments) in eighty areas by amalgamating them. Underlying these proposals was the assumption that their diverse size should be standardised—and that they should in *general be substantially larger.[32]

Is it not *self-evident that the anomalous differences in the sizes of police forces would cause problems? This was the question that Elinor Ostrom set out to investigate, and she was able to show that small forces can in fact have substantial advantages in efficiency, giving better services at a lower cost than large police forces serving similar neighbourhoods. She showed that the areas with the largest number of small police forces can put more officers on patrol (relative to the total number of officers employed) than areas dominated by a few forces operating on a large scale. Overall, a higher standard of service is provided in metropolitan areas where there are many police forces, where no single large force dominates, and where there is a *diversity of size: the anomaly, far from being a handicap, is an advantage.[33]

There are good reasons for the effectiveness of what could be dismissed as a muddle of diverse *scales and distinctive approaches. Different urban conditions require different styles of policing; forces learn from each other, imitating the most successful initiatives and avoiding the least successful; it is easier for citizens to become properly informed about their police presence if there are other forces with which they can compare them, and small police forces may know their local

areas better. They may also have less rigid procedures, allowing local invention and diversity; for the larger forces, in turn, there is an *incentive to innovate and maintain high standards as they compete for *contracts to use their services.[34]

The proposition, which is indeed normally taken to be self-evident, is that large-scale organisation, organised to a standard design and on a standard scale, is better— that is, more efficient—than smaller structures which lack consistency and tidiness: common sense tells us so. However, the claim that something is self-evident should be viewed with suspicion—as a sign that a complex system is being observed and summarised at a glance, in preparation for radical deconstruction in the name of *reform.[35]

The second illustration of creative anomaly comes from medieval Europe. Beginning late in the tenth century, considerable thought was given to the matter of how to reduce the damage and the frequency of wars, and the church took the initiative in doing something about it.

The plan they adopted (in 1027) was to outlaw war at weekends: any war in progress must stop at midday on Saturday, and must not be resumed until Monday morning. This made it possible for everyone involved to go to church on Sunday, and to have an early night the evening before, and it was so successful that it was decided to extend the truce to the other holy days of the week. The ban was therefore extended to Saturday mornings (in memory of Christ's Entombment), Fridays (the day of the Crucifixion), and Thursday (the day of the Ascension and of the first Eucharist), the periods of Lent and Advent, and to the twelve most important saints' days.[36]

It was then extended to places: whatever day of the week it was, war was banned in churches and courtyards, and in fields at harvest time. And it included people: women, children, old people and farmers working in fields, were all to be left unmolested.

This was the *Treuga Dei*, The Truce of God, and the remarkable result was that, to some extent, the truce held. Circumstances were stacked against it, and there were many occasions when it was broken; it was common practice not to pay soldiers—it was part of the job to fend for themselves, and if, in the process, they wrecked the enemy's farms and communities, so much the better. Warfare was therefore more a matter of

A

constant raids (*chevauchées*) than of the pitched battles which history remembers.

In the "Great War" of the Middle Ages—the Hundred Years' War (1337–1453) in which France was under constant attack from England—the set-piece battles, such as Agincourt and Crécy, were interruptions to the normality of freelance pillage, and fair play had precious little to do with them. In the case of large-scale, far-from-home wars, especially if they involved hordes of savage English archers, the *Treuga Dei* did not work: no rules did, except the one about not running away. But, for smaller-scale affairs, closer to home, local secular authorities could enforce it to protect non-combatants. And the *Treuga Dei* was an important principle, precisely because it was an anomaly: it announced the idea that, even in something as ruthless and horrible as war, there could be some sense of fairness and legality. It indicated that justice has a life of its own, and endurance. If war and justice can coexist, justice must be more than it seems; it has depth; there is more to it than today's righteous *indignation.[37]

And yet, that coexistence of two contrasting ideas is an affront to the tidy mind of *empire, and the *Treuga Dei* was abolished (or at least trumped and superseded) in the reign (1493–1519) of the Holy Roman Emperor Maximilian I. He decided it was time to sweep away the anomaly, to introduce an overdue reform suited to the modern world, to demonstrate his *sincerity and his commitment to peace. So he announced the *Eternal Truce of God*. From now on, war would be prohibited on any day of the week, and for ever: total peace was established. What followed was total war, maturing to the Thirty Years' War and its sequels, unrestrained every day of the week—no one, and nowhere, exempt. Now, at last, they could have a proper, efficient, anomaly-free war, with consistency and transparency, and no *pity for anyone.

*Ideology resents exceptions. Deprived of anomalies and the theoretical chance to negotiate—"don't kill us today, it's Sunday"—which at least *started a conversation*, *communities and churches became irrelevant to the task of keeping the peace. The top-down decision had left them with nothing to say.

Anomaly in a system is a sign that it tolerates *intelligent life.

*Internal Evidence, Presence, Script, Good Shepherd Paradox, Personal Experience Fallacy.

APPROPRIATE TECHNOLOGY. Technology designed to fit the particular circumstances of the people who are to use it; if they need a solution which is cheap to build, small-scale, made from local materials, easy to operate, simple to maintain and energy-efficient, then appropriate technology can set about providing it. It is adapted to the small scale of local *skills and *materials, as distinct from the large scale of mass production.

Unfortunately, appropriate technology has an identity problem. E.F. Schumacher, who developed the concept, preferred "intermediate" technology, so for the moment we will stay with that: we will come back to the matter of the name for it in a minute.[38]

The principle of *intermediate* technology arose from Schumacher's observation of what happens when communities in developing countries are persuaded to install equipment which does not match their needs and resources. Large-scale systems, supplied without thought for the consequences, can push them into *debt and unemployment; their maintenance is beyond local capability, and if the equipment works as intended it produces on a scale beyond local needs, typically putting local producers out of business. All this can erode or destroy local autonomy, imposing the need for imported expertise and expanded *markets which are invitations to takeover by outside interests. And it can *demoralise communities, as the whole idea of local economic development turns sour.[39]

But if the technologies needed for success in the international market are *irrelevant and wrong in those situations, what is the alternative? Must the community stay with the very basic level of equipment that many of them have been using so far? Must they choose, as Schumacher put it, between "the hoe and the tractor, or the [sickle] and the combine harvester"?[40] He believes not, discussing an intermediate option . . .

> . . . vastly superior in productivity to their
> traditional technology (in its present state
> of decay), while at the same time being
> vastly cheaper and simpler than the highly
> sophisticated and enormously capital-intensive
> technology of the West.[41]

A

WAKE UP TO THE DETAIL
Extract from the article that first brought intermediate
technology to the attention of the public and politics

The first task of any society is surely to avoid the extremes of misery and frustration. If "the people" are left out of development planning; if economic growth merely intensifies, as it tends to do, the appalling features of the "dual economy"—a small sector of opulence surrounded by an ocean of misery—then the final outcome will be disastrous.

The primary task of developing countries now afflicted by mass unemployment and mass migration into a few metropolitan areas would therefore seem to be clear: go straight into battle with these evils. This means:

1. Workplaces have to be created in the areas in which people are living *now*, and not primarily in metropolitan areas into which they tend to migrate;
2. These workplaces must be, on average cheap enough so that they can be created in large numbers without this calling for an unattainable level of savings and imports;
3. The production methods employed must be relatively simple so that the demands for high skills are minimised, not only in the production process itself but also in matters of organisation, raw materials supply, financing, marketing and so forth;
4. Production should be largely from local materials for local use.

These needs can be met only if (a) there is a regional approach to development [i.e., each development project should apply to the particular needs of the district], and (b) there is a conscious effort to develop what might be called an "intermediate technology".

What stands in the way? . . . Is it lack of imagination on the part of planners in resplendent offices who find ratios and coefficients more significant than people?

E.F. Schumacher, "How to help them help themselves", *The Observer*, 29 August 1965

He suggested that intermediate technology has four defining properties:

1. *It is accessible*—that is, affordable: it does not burden the community with debt.[42]
2. *It is small*—that is, it does not require levels of energy, materials or a market on a scale greater than the community can supply.
3. *It has the simplicity* needed for local people to maintain and, ideally, build it themselves, using their own skills and resources.
4. *It is non-violent* in three senses: It does not make bigger demands (in terms of raw materials or *pollution) than the local environment can support. It does not come at the cost of people's mental and physical *health. And it does not start a sequence

of damage and repair, with clean-up commitments, repairs and costs extending into the future.[43]

Reading that, you could be forgiven for wondering what it is all about. Surely local communities don't want unaffordable, large-scale, energy-intensive equipment beyond the limits of what they can sell, maintain and renew? Well, surely not—unless, of course, they take advice from an *expert. Schumacher has something to say about this:

There are countless development 'experts' who cannot even conceive the possibility of any industrial production unless all the paraphernalia of the Western way of life are provided in advance. The 'basis of everything', they say, is of course electricity, steel, cement, near-perfect organisation, sophisticated accountancy. . . . In the blind pursuit of [a] highly questionable utopia, these 'experts' tend to neglect everything that is realistically possible. More than that, unfortunately, they denounce and ridicule every approach which relies on the employment and utilisation of humbler means.[44]

As he notes, many societies in the past have achieved a fair general level of wealth without that paraphernalia. Their technologies have been appropriate to their needs and resources.

And that brings us to the question of the name. In many ways, "intermediate technology" is the most comfortable name. It captures Schumacher's sense of belonging in the middle ground—the "disappearing middle", as he called it. It is the one he used in his famous article in *The Observer* (see "Wake Up to the Detail" sidebar on page 11). It is widely recognised—having been used for the Intermediate Technology Development Group (ITDG), the charity which he founded with George McRobie and Julia Porter in 1965. And it does not have the problem that it sounds *self-evident: surely all technology is appropriate to something?

The wide use of "appropriate" as the name for it today is due to insight about the need for considered choice on the technology to be used. It needn't always be intermediate; there are occasions on which the most advanced and largest-scale means available are the right ones to use, and the simplest ones have their uses, too. It can be a difficult choice: a technology which is not capable of competing internationally may be best for the way the community is now, but not for the way it wants to be, or would be if it were able to attract the needed capital. The choice of technology must take into account the community's vision, or expectation, of the future—yet there may be more than one vision.[45]

In practice, the convention is that "appropriate" usually refers to a technology which falls well short of the most advanced and labour-saving available (i.e., intermediate technology), and it is used in this sense in *Lean Logic*. It looks to its technology to be a form of *protection—of jobs, the environment and freedoms—and to be an accurate and realistic reflection of what the locality can commit itself to from its own resources.

And it is in these senses that the question of appropriate technology is central to the *Lean Economy. The hypersophisticated, miniaturised energy and information systems of today are almost ideally suited to the necessary task of *localisation. The "almost" is in there, however, because they depend on imports from centres of manufacturing which rely on a global industrial establishment. If local self-reliance is needed, that could be precisely because a global-scale manufacturing establishment no longer exists. And that would take us from *local lite*—where communities can buy in the equipment they need for localisation—to *deep local*, where they have to provide that, too, for themselves. Technologies may have to be chosen which are profoundly different from present *expectations about what self-reliance means.

Whether the Lean Economy is actually going to be able to make *choices* about this, as distinct from accepting whatever it can get, is another matter. *Reflection is needed on the level of self-reliance that we will have to cope with—and on the expectations, the *education, *food production and technology that, in the circumstances of the time, will turn out to be appropriate. But deep local is by no means an unrealistic prospect, and the technology appropriate to that should now be developed with the level of urgency currently directed towards visions of high-tech localisation.

*Borsodi's Law, Leisure, Productivity, Dollar-a-Day Fallacy.

ARGUMENTUM AD . . . "Argument on the grounds of".

This way of classifying arguments was invented by the philosopher and physician John Locke (1690).[46] Examples:

Ad Hominem, Big Stick, Cant, Expertise, Fear, Genetic Fallacy, Ignorance, Money, Pity, Wolf Fallacy.

ARMS RACE. The ratchet effect in which international rivals each feel compelled to advance the technology and scale of their armaments because the other side is doing so. Also a *metaphor for the race of *technical change, in which each advance creates new risks which can only be solved by further advance.

*GRIN (Genetics, Robotics, Information Technology and Nanotechnology), Reductionism, Regrettable Necessities.

ARTS. Explorations of meaning expressed in *narrative truth.
*Carnival, Culture, Ironic Space, Second Nature.

ASSENT, THE FALLACY OF. The *fallacy that an argument is correct because it is approved by the majority, or by the authorities.

The power of the majority has been recognised, from Aristotle onwards, as a potential form of tyranny. It is capable of "the most cruel oppression and injustice" (Edmund Burke); "The tyranny of the majority is among the evils against which society requires to be on its guard" (John Stuart Mill).[47] And, for Alexis de Tocqueville,

> No monarch is so absolute that he can gather
> all the forces of society into his own hands
> and overcome resistance as can a majority
> endowed with the right of enacting laws and
> executing them.[48]

And the risk is real, because *populist views, whether in the majority or not, are biased towards *reductionism and *memory fillers, such as fixation on recent symbolic events without context. Received opinion can quickly *calibrate to a new idea of what is normal, or the discovery of someone new to *blame.

This was demonstrated by intended and unintended experiments in the twentieth century. They are probably the most famous experiments ever done in sociology, so there is nothing new here, but they deserve *reflection. Solomon Asch showed the extent to which people will go along with a consensus view even if this means refusing to believe the clear—and, in other circumstances undeniable—evidence of their eyes. In the figure, which line—B, C or D—is the same length as line A? What about C? Not in the eyes of a person (with a few heroic exceptions) who finds himself in a minority of one in a group which (in collusion with the experimenter) insists otherwise. In another experiment, by Stanley Milgram, subjects were willing to torture others with powerful electric shocks "for research purposes" if instructed to do so by a person with apparent authority in a laboratory setting with the trappings of official endorsement.[49]

In the same tradition, Philip Zimbardo and his colleagues set out to discover what would happen if

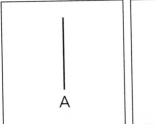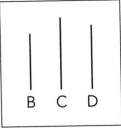

Subjects were shown two cards. One bore a standard line. The other bore three lines, one of which was the same length as the standard. The subjects were asked to identify this line.

college students were placed in positions of near-absolute power as prison warders over (fellow-student) prisoners. The rules were that there was to be no physical or sexual assault; otherwise, this was an "anything goes" regime. The experiment was flawed, with the experimenters getting close to encouraging the guards to make life hard for the prisoners; nonetheless, the "guards" played their part with enthusiasm, and the experiment was terminated prematurely on account of their cruelty: they had their cowed victims in a state of advanced depression, with crying, rage, helplessness and loss of *identity; they simply gave up and "stopped behaving". The guards' behaviour was conscientious and dutiful; it was their ethic; they worked diligently, putting in overtime without pay. The most hostile and tyrannical of the guards set the ethical standard for the rest, and there was "tyranny creep", as each new level of hostility became the baseline from which further hostility and harassment would begin.[50]

Yet not all the people involved in these experiments submitted to the pressure of group or official assent to the same extent. In the Asch and Milgram experiments, some refused to submit at all—having confidence in their own *judgment and being able to engage with a subject on its own terms rather than in terms of winning approval.

From the point of view of life after oil, perhaps the most significant aspect of these make-believe experiments is the law-abiding normality of the subjects in their real lives. The breakdowns of normality when oil outages begin will be seen by many as a licence to flip into a different *ethical code which, from where we stand, will be hard to recognise or believe. A well-behaved society is contained in a thin membrane which has been assumed to be a given. But it is not a given: it has to be slowly constructed, *intelligently maintained, understood and not undermined. Its significance and the consequences of breakage may escape attention until the early stages of the coming *energy-famine place them under pressure.

*Metamorphosis, Humility, Character, Anarchism, Constructivism, Democracy, Ideology.

AUTHORITY. See Freedom.

B

BAD FAITH. A breakdown of common *presence, *conversation and common *interest. It can take several forms:

1. No common presence: My approach to interaction is to appeal to *abstractions and rules which allow me to avoid noticing or recognising anything about you or your situation (*Hyperbole).
2. No conversation: Language is *disconnected from *truth in any of its forms. The other person (the victim) can have no idea whether the information he is getting from me is true or not. Every statement is a ploy, a tactic.
3. No common tolerance: I relish your misfortune; what is bad for you is good for me, and I may go to the lengths of damaging my own interests in order to cause you harm. Example: a regulatory system that, having lost touch with what it is there to do, switches from its duty to sustain best practice to the pleasure and profit of catching you out.

Bad faith is, in one sense, rational. It is what remains when the exacting task of dissolving and liberating *loyalties, implicit *contracts, *traditions and common *narratives has been accomplished. But there may be still a little way to go before then.

BALLETIC DEBATE. A debate whose participants are so *fluent that they can dance past each other in a performance of great beauty and skill. But to no purpose.

*Harebrain Fracture, Rhetorical Capture.

BARTER. Barter can make a contribution to *reciprocity in a *local economy whose income flow has broken down, but it is limited.[1] With barter, you can make a direct exchange of goods and services without having to get hold of the cash first, and this copes well with simple trading relationships between nations (e.g., arms for oil), or between allotments (carrots for cucumbers), but in a market it is impracticable. Each exchange pair (such as haircuts-for-bread) is one "trading post", but to make a barter market work, you need a lot more trading posts than you might think (in fact, $G(G-1)/2$ trading posts in a market in which G goods are traded), so that in a market of 100 goods you would need 4,950 trading posts (haircuts-for-bread, haircuts-for-apples, apples-for-bread . . .). Finding the trading post you need (if it exists at all) could take some time. Then there is the problem of quantity: for the haircut you supply, you would receive more bread than you really want; and then there is storage: the barber cannot store vegetables for his retirement.[2]

In fact, barter is quite a limited means of exchange. The strict tit-for-tat exchange to which the label "barter" has been applied is the kind which exists between people who do not know each other, and who have to get both sides of the deal done and finished there and then because they may never meet again. It is therefore different from other forms of exchange such as the varieties of *reciprocity in the local lean economies of the future. Barter deals can work out from time to time when two strangers need to exchange their respective surpluses of hogs and corn, or when two Boy Scouts want to swap sandwiches, but it is inflexible and inconvenient as a main form of exchange. It cannot be relied on to meet a large community's needs for an exchange system and for a store of value. That is why we have *money. But if the money has drained out of the locality, you need more appropriate means of exchange: reciprocity and *local currencies, both in the context of *lean economics.

*Dollar-a-Day Fallacy.

BEGGING THE QUESTION (*Petitio principii*). A circular argument, which uses its conclusion as part of the argument to prove its conclusion, sometimes in light disguise.[3] For instance:

QUESTION FOR DISCUSSION: Would the use of biotechnology help to feed the world?
ANSWER: Yes. Why? Because, if we don't use it, many will starve.

That discussion is evidently getting nowhere; the person who argues in this way may or may not be aware that the assumption which she implies is already agreed is what the argument is actually about. More examples: There is no need to worry about oil depletion. Why? Because the people who worry about oil supplies are being alarmist. Why do you say that? Because there is no need to worry about oil depletion. *Or*: We must take our place at the heart of Europe. Why? Because, if we don't we will be missing an opportunity. What opportunity? The opportunity to take our place at the heart of Europe. *Or*: Christopher Marlowe survived his attempted murder and lived to write Shakespeare's plays for him. How come? Well, he escaped out of the back door and went to live in Spain. How do you know? Well, if he hadn't, he wouldn't have been able to write Shakespeare's plays for him, would he?

It is possible to deliver a speech which consists almost entirely of sentences which beg the question, especially during the passages designed for *rhetorical arousal:

We now have an opportunity to truly transform our system into a world class system fit for the 21st century. . . . There is a real appetite out there to embrace change, to improve our system and to end the two-tier culture which brands so many of our young people as failures at the age of 11.

I relish the challenge of transforming our outdated and unequal education system into a modern and flexible one that places equality of opportunity for each and every child at its core.

I believe such a system will not only continue to deliver academic excellence for the few but can deliver it for all.

Caitríona Ruane, Education Secretary,
presenting the Northern Ireland Government's
decision to abolish grammar schools, 2007.[4]

Begging the Question is common, but there is so little awareness of it that the phrase is generally taken to mean no more than "this raises the question whether . . .", leaving the *fallacy without even a reliable name.

Its career as a destroyer of argument, however, is unchecked, and it can lurk in single words ("anachronism", "modern", "Luddite", "scientific", "accessible", "elitist", "reality", "stereotype"). Even the tone of voice, if weary enough, can suggest, deceptively, that the matter is too obvious to need explanation.

Here is an example from the debate about *globalisation:

The former head of the World Trade Organisation, Mike Moore, writes persuasively about the benefits of free trade. He shows that the lowering of trade barriers has stimulated growth, that the countries that have been the most *open to trade have enjoyed the most economic progress and the greatest rise in the incomes of the poor. And, as former prime minister of New Zealand, he has the experience of making that country a pioneer of free-market *agriculture, with benign effects across the economy. How, then, can there be doubts when he argues that the anti-globalisation movement, if successful, would bring catastrophic consequences, not just for the poor in developing economies,

but for all of us? Can Mr. Moore and the anti-globalisation protestors really be talking about the same thing?[5]

The opposing argument states that globalisation and free trade, in opening up *small-scale production in the non-industrialised countries to competition from multinationals, leads to unemployment and dispossession. It makes agriculture dependent on imported energy; it devastates soils, ecosystems and communities; it raises incomes in part by destroying local subsistence and forcing people into the cash economy; it is supported by the governments of the affected countries not least because of the *debts into which they have been lured. Food security, with higher overall yields and greater diversity, less damage to the soil and higher real local incomes, would be more fruitfully sought by helping farmers to make the best use of their own *skills, applied to local conditions.[6]

Both sides beg the question: they are each correct if their premises are accepted: if the priority is to expand world trade, to push ahead with the global market, Mr. Moore's conclusions naturally follow; if it is to build on the *resilience of communities, to protect them from the turbulence of the global market, and to improve their food security, his critics are correct. The begged question is the one thing they should actually be talking about.[7]
*Different Premises, Constructivism, Rationalism, Ideology, Internal Evidence, Tautology.

BETRAYAL. If *trust exists, the possibility of breaking it—betrayal—exists, too. In a culture which values trust, betrayal is viewed with horror. It opens up the possibility that the friendships, *loyalty and trust that hold society together and make it comprehensible are not what they seem. Dante's *Inferno* reserves for traitors the deepest pit of hell.[8] Betrayal destroys any "now" in which logic can operate: an enemy has at least the merit of existing in the present; the betrayer derives his value in his new life from what he was, and yet his old life has been repudiated; there is nothing there. The Psalms reflect on this with a summary of why it hurts:

For it is not an open enemy, that hath done me this dishonour: for then I could have borne it. Neither was it mine adversary, that did magnify himself against me: for peradventure I would have hid myself from him. But it was even thou, my companion: my guide, and mine own familiar friend. We took sweet counsel together: and walked in the house of God as friends.[9]

Betrayal is an uncomfortable idea. It is out of its time, like *character. We will become aware of it again.
*Bad Faith, Lean Economics, Promiscuous Ethics.

BIG STICK, THE (*Argumentum ad baculum*). The threat, or use, of force as a means of persuasion.[10]

The role of force in argument was discussed by Antoine Arnauld and Pierre Nicole in their *Logic, Or the Art of Thinking* (1662), and it was the strongest form of the *fallacy—physically attacking one's opponent until he gives in—that they had in mind. Naturally, they disapproved: "Any reasonable person will reject whatever is urged in so offensive a manner and not even the most stupid will listen."[11]

The threat can take many forms—blackmail, loss of job, execution—but its original meaning persisted in its name—*ad baculum*, "the big stick".

Arnauld's rejection of force as a means of argument was not a platitude. It was written not long before the Revocation of the Edict of Nantes (1685), the decision by Louis XIV to end years of tolerable coexistence with the Protestants and, instead, to apply persuasion in the form of the

dragonnards—soldiers billeted at Protestants' houses, with instructions to cause trouble—and to silence contrary arguments by breaking the Huguenot pastors at the wheel.[12]

This was also a time when the state was still working out, by trial and error, whether and how to come to terms with the way in which the individual's place in society was being shaped by the *market rather than by ancient structures of citizenship, *tradition and *religion. There is no doubt that leaving matters to the market, to the price mechanism and to individual *choices and *contracts saves a good deal of trouble. The market can appeal to something even more persuasive than the big stick—namely, simple self-interest—and when this began to be recognised in the seventeenth century it was all a great relief. "*Douce commerce*", sweet commerce, wrote Jacques Savary, an early management consultant, in a textbook for businessmen (also in 1685), "makes for all the gentleness of life". The authorities themselves agreed: commerce is the most "innocent and legitimate way of acquiring wealth", observed an edict of the French government in 1669; it is "the fertile source which brings abundance to the state and spreads it among its subjects".[13]

The market to a large extent replaced the network of duty, responsibility and social capital which had been the basis for social *cohesion and *reciprocity. This was the "Great Transformation", which has delegated to the market so much of the burden of decision-making: it is prices that now do the heavy work of signalling shortages and excesses, drawing the attention of business to the detail of demand, and supplying an *incentive to deliver. The government's main task in a mature market economy is to keep it free of obstacles that might stop it growing—like a bemused farmer would treat the enchanted goose: keep the foxes out so that it can go on magically laying its golden eggs.[14]

The shock is that this period is coming to an end. During the early decades of the century, the market will lose its magic as a stabiliser. The main burden of holding society and economy together will shift to *culture and reciprocal obligation, embedded in *social capital. Those assets will need to be remade. It will be difficult; we are starting in the wrong place. Our society and *economics, *food and *transport, culture and *politics, have evolved for a different world, and are riddled with cracks ready to break apart under pressure. But the alternative, should that fail, could be the big stick. You might think that the big stick is not the form of argument favoured by philosophers, even if it is the method used by the other side. But here is one who, from time to time, is driven to conceding that maybe there may be something to be said for it, after all:

What is a rational man to do, in the face of an appeal *ad baculum*? Knock-down arguments, alas, must be overcome not with a syllogism but

a stick. Liberty *and* order are the prerequisites of reason. . . . [In order to] protect and defend our rare and happy heritage of freedom and stability, let us have the courage, patience and wisdom to *enforce* restraint (without repression) upon our erring children. Then and only then, can the dialogue of reason continue.[15]

*Distraction, Fear, Humility, Decency Fallacy, Character.

BINARY. See Bivalence.

BIOFUELS. See Energy Prospects.

BIOMASS. See Energy Prospects.

BIOTECHNOLOGY. See GRIN (Genetics, Robotics, Information Technology and Nanotechnology).

BIVALENCE. Bivalence exists where an argument is about a matter of either/or, true or false, black or white, self-hate or self-love. There is no middle position—or this is thought to be so.
*Dialectic, Fuzzy Logic.

BLAME. The *fallacy that you have explained and in part solved a problem when its complexities have been focused, summarised and embodied in a person, a group, or other agent. A goat, perhaps.

Blame is therefore a quick way of making up your mind about a situation which you have not understood, or it at least provides a useful *distraction. It avoids the need to explain a person's behaviour or an event, still less to trace the sequence of cause-and-effect through to its origins. It is a way of making sure that trouble, once it comes, will settle in, its causes forever undiscovered.

If blame for an action is to have any meaning, it must be the case that the person was free to choose a different action. And yet, if the sequence of cause-and-effect is traced properly, there is no space left in which "free choice" makes any sense. Why not? Because the *choice the person made was shaped by circumstances which were themselves beyond his control—and without free choice, blame becomes meaningless. This does not in any sense eliminate the role of responsibility in making

B

B

a judgment; a choice is undoubtedly a person's responsibility and he or she must be held to account for it. *But the possession of a sense of responsibility is itself a matter which is largely or entirely a gift of inheritance or upbringing, or other circumstances not of the person's own making.*

What, then, can you make of an undesired action or circumstance? You can apply *judgment, or you can apply blame. If you apply *judgment*, you may simply, but reasonably, judge the action, or the person, or any of the circumstances surrounding it, to be bad (or good), against any standards you wish to use, such as the *laws and *expectations of the time, and you can then proceed to punish (or reward) accordingly. Equally reasonably, but at greater depth, you may wish to apply judgment by understanding how the event came about. The alternative is to apply *blame*. The problem is not just that, when you do this, you fail to understand how the action came about, but that, having failed to do so, you then proceed to plug the gap in your understanding with the pretence that the action *has* been understood: it fills the gap with blame, the thought-equivalent of fast food.

It matures easily into the witch-hunt. It is evidently comforting, when there is a crisis, to have someone to blame for it. Typically, the search for someone to blame crowds out all other deliberation. Blame seems to explain everything: any part of the analysis which is *not* blame is seen as evasion: to blame is to affirm and establish one's own moral standing beyond challenge—for if you challenge it, you are defending the guilty. And a common variant is the conspiracy version: no action or statement, not even the most benign ones, can be understood until the evil intent underlying them has been ruthlessly exposed. That ability to discover the true, rotten heart of everything is seen as proof of *intelligence and moral standing.

The number of people on whom anxiety and confusion will be dumped in the form of blame is likely to rise as, in the future, unexpected events crowd in. There is *witch-hunt potential. But *lean thinking does not blame. As far as it can, it explains.

*Choice, Causes, Devil's Tunes, Five Whys, Trust.

BOREDOM. (1) Distress caused by exposure to circumstances offering low levels of stimulus, an *unintended but life-threatening consequence of the banality, regulation and risk-aversion which corrodes our culture.
(2) Adaptation, or addiction, to a life with minimal stimulus, leading in due course to an inability to cope with an argument or an event that surprises.
(3) A moment of freedom from urgency, opening the way to the *reflection that makes you a person.
*Narcissism, Calibration, Exhilaration.

BORSODI'S LAW. "Distribution costs will tend to move in inverse proportion to production costs."

That is, although small-scale local production of food, goods and services tends to be more expensive (per unit produced) than large-scale centralised production, these costs are offset by lower distribution costs (i.e., less transport).

It does not follow that locally-produced goods will always be cheaper, because so many variable factors (such as wages and fuel costs) are involved, as well as the economies of *scale that are available to larger systems. However, it does follow that, as the cost of fuel for transport increases, the relative advantages of local production can be expected to increase.[16]
*Localisation, Energy Prospects, Lean Household, Regrettable Necessities.

BOUNDARIES AND FRONTIERS. Boundaries and limits are *necessary conditions for a system to have any meaning and *identity. They give a system its structure and stability; as E.F. Schumacher writes, boundaries . . .

> . . . produce 'structure'. . . . Now, a great deal
> of structure has collapsed, and a country is like
> a big cargo ship in which the load is in no way
> secured. It tilts, and all the load slips over, and
> the ship founders.[17]

Boundaries have three crucial functions. First, they control access to the system, to the commons and the community, empowering the people who live within them with the *expectation that what they decide on has a reasonable chance of happening. This assurance that their decision-making is not mocked by events and interests outside their control is a key condition for successful management of the *commons and for the evolution of *community.

Secondly, boundaries are central to the principle of a *closed-loop system. For a system whose boundaries give it the benefit of a *small-scale, *modular structure, it becomes realistic to conserve its materials and other assets—developing the *proximity principle, keeping *transport and *intermediate *needs to a minimum, conserving, *sorting, reusing and recycling, and trading materials across its *edges. This *complex, *holonic, bounded structure opens the way to a resilient *ecology that wastes none of its foundation *capital.

Thirdly, boundaries have a complementary effect for the people who live within them: they limit access to territories *beyond* the boundary. In this sense, "boundaries" are the opposite of "frontiers". "Frontiers" can carry the implication that, if things get difficult at home—if fertility is in decline, if the demand for goods and services is allowed to rise beyond what can be supplied in the locality, if there is overpopulation or *conflict or any other persistent problem—the natural thing to do is to cross the frontier and start again somewhere else. There are clear easy-option benefits here: you do not have to manage *land in a sustainable way, nor do you have to resolve disputes: you can just move on.

The *market economy has demolished its boundaries and turned them into frontiers. Its communities have lost control of their own decisions while at the same time pretending that there are always new frontiers beyond which new wealth can be plundered to solve troubles brought about by mismanagement at home. The principle of the *localised, resilient *Lean Economy, on the contrary, celebrates its limits and recognises that, when you can't either walk away from a problem or export it, you need instead to organise your brain. This is a world without a frontier—a "beyond". It has to solve its own problems, or at least try to.[18]
*Commons, Closed Access, Closed-Loop Systems, Resilience.

BUILDING. See Lean Building.

BULLSHIT. (1) The waffle produced by someone who is expected to know what he is talking about, but does not. (2) An accusation thrown at a person who is hoping to lift the discussion from the *reductionist torpor into which it has sunk.

(3) Brief description of a content-free argument.[19]
*Charisma, Icon, Intelligence, Empty Sandwich.

BUTTERFLY EFFECT, THE. The case where small causes lead to big consequences. This applies to a system with an energy source which enables events to ripple through it, improving, impairing, or simply changing its behaviour or its fitness for the environment it is in. It applies most obviously in the field of weather forecasting, and was discovered by the mathematical meteorologist Edward Lorenz in 1959.

While experimenting with a computer programme designed to supply forecasts for months ahead, Lorenz set out to verify a simulation that he had already run, and to extend it further into the future. For the new run, he fed back into the computer a set of numbers which he assumed to be identical to the set he was already using, since he copied them off a printout. Then off he went for a (now famous) coffee, leaving the computer to chunter away to itself with this re-entered data set. But when he got back, he found something surprising. The first couple of days of modelled weather were reasonably similar to the original, but then they departed from it and eventually became completely different. The reason was that whereas the computer was working with numbers to six decimal places, the printout just showed the first three decimal places. Although the difference between the numbers was extremely small, it radically altered the result. Evidently, in a chaotic system such as the weather, small differences can have big consequences. Lorenz had demonstrated sensitive dependence on initial conditions.[20]

He published his results at a scientific meeting in Tokyo in 1962, and then went on to develop the idea. Ten years later, at a meeting in Washington DC in 1972, he presented a paper, "Does the Flap of a Butterfly's Wings in Brazil Set off a Tornado in Texas?" and the image has stuck.[21]

The weather is a good way of demonstrating the butterfly effect because it is chaotic. It can produce almost any result within a certain range and still be weather. Complex systems—antelopes, for instance—do not have this quality. On the contrary, they sustain a high degree of *homeostasis: they must maintain a more-or-less unchanging temperature, metabolism and form under all circumstances short of catastrophe (being eaten by a lion). But even antelopes can fail to prevent chaos entering their systems. Grazing in the wrong place, near where some lions are hiding, or being pricked by a thorn which causes an

infection, will probably not prove fatal, owing to the antelope's powers of prevention and recovery—its *resilience—but it might.

Little events can ripple through an orderly complex system and change it completely. Chaos can break into even the most orderly system, giving the butterfly's wing its slim, but significant, chance.

Here is an example of a small event with big consequences. No complex system is without its weaknesses, but in the early years of the twentieth century, the complex system called Europe had achieved, to an extraordinary degree, qualities which might be seen as ideal in a civilisation, with a strong *culture and a strong—though still far from completed—trend of improvement in measures of social justice such as *education, *social security and *political participation.

The future Kaiser Wilhelm II, Emperor of Germany, was born on 27 January 1859. It was a breech (feet-first) birth. At the time, only some 2 percent of babies born in the breech position survived. The greatest risk in a breech birth is that the baby's head squeezes the umbilical cord running up alongside it, causing it to suffocate. To avoid offence to royal decency, Dr. Eduard Martin, who was in attendance, did not like to raise the Empress' long skirts, and had to do everything by feel.[22]

When the child was in the birth canal with its head still in the uterus, and with both arms raised above its head, Dr. Martin manoeuvred its left arm down out of the canal, using (as he explained in his report) "considerable force"—that is, enough to tear the brachial plexus in the complex of nerves in the baby's neck. He then, as was required, rotated the child's trunk in the birth canal. The only way to achieve this rotation without injury is to use both hands to grip the upper trunk

firmly before turning it. Dr. Martin did it by pulling on the now protruding left arm.[23]

The baby was thought to be dead for several minutes following the birth, and modern medical judgment estimates that he would have been hypoxic (lacking oxygen) for at least eight minutes, sufficient to produce "minimal brain damage", a condition whose symptoms are now well-recognised. It is not associated with loss of intelligence, but with psychopathic disturbances, hyperactivity, loss of attention span and inability to develop social sense or empathy, with the person having little or no understanding of the impact of his behaviour on others.[24]

The young prince's left arm was paralysed and six inches shorter than his right arm, and the effects of the injury were soon also revealed in his twisted neck. His mother, Vicky, Queen Victoria's eldest daughter, referring to his "deformity" and "disfigurement", never came to terms with his injury; she felt revulsion towards him, and lavished affection, instead, on her other children. Prince Wilhelm developed a hatred towards his mother and towards the English in general.[25]

As he grew up he showed symptoms typically associated with minimal brain damage, such as requiring his advisers and generals to participate in a court life that was to a significant extent based on practical jokes. The head of the German Military Cabinet, Dietrich von Hülsen-Haeseler, died of a heart attack while dancing for the Kaiser in a large feather hat and a tutu. He required his advisers to take part in morning gymnastics, which he spiced with pranks such as cutting General Scholl's braces with a penknife. The British foreign secretary Sir Edward Grey found the Kaiser "not quite sane, and very superficial". He reminded him, he wrote, of "a battleship with steam up and screws going, but with no rudder"; he could well "cause a catastrophe some day".[26]

His politics were largely shaped by an appetite for revenge, which his ministers were usually able to ignore. When the German envoy was killed by the Boxer rebels in China in 1900 he ordered that Peking should be razed to the ground. During a tram drivers' strike in Berlin in the same year, he ordered that troops should move in and gun down at least 500 people. In 1919 (after his abdication) he wrote that no German should rest until all Jews on German soil had been exterminated.[27]

His one consistent pleasure was the company of tall young men in the army. He explained that it was in his regiment that he found his family, his friends, his interests, everything which he had previously missed. In their daily company he was able to reduce each complex issue to a "purely military question".[28]

In retrospect we can always see the big-brained *reasons for big events: the rivalries between the *empires of that time, the excessive confidence that comes when small nations join up into an empire, the knowledge learned from industry about how to organise large numbers of men, the implications of German dominance of Europe's North Sea ports and trading routes, the trouble with the ailing rivals—the Austro-Hungarian and Russian empires—dangerously played-out in the Balkans. Realpolitik can explain everything backwards.

On the other hand, these were states which had achieved an astonishing degree of accomplishment, along with links of *family, friendship and passport-free travel in a diverse European culture described and celebrated by critics such as Stefan Zweig. There is no reason to believe that the First World War would have taken place without the lifelong and anachronistic commitment of the Kaiser to that end. And there is no reason to believe that this commitment would have occurred if it had not been a breech birth, or if the doctor has been sufficiently skilled to deliver the baby without injury, or insufficiently skilled to achieve a live birth. Or if he had felt it was all right to raise the Empress' skirts.[29]

The series of events set in train by that failure is arguably the most catastrophic in human history, decisively shaping the modern world, and giving its problems a rootedness; even a sense of being under a curse. The war of two halves that followed—and the revolutions and genocides that came with it—traumatised our civilisation. Some butterfly . . .

Evidently, a high degree of sensitivity to initial conditions is a quality that can shape history. But there are two points to note about it before finally abandoning all confidence in the idea that there is any point in planning ahead. The first is that a resilient system—a *complex system as distinct from a merely chaotic one—is usually capable of dealing with disturbances and maintaining its stability, its homeostasis, for a long time. That is what resilience means.

The second point is that even a resilient system can indeed be destroyed or transformed by an event which hits the spot—which happens to have the right *leverage. That maximum result from a minimum cause may be exactly what we want when working with a system: it is the ideal aim of effective *systems-thinking. But, if it hits the wrong spot, it can travel like a tsunami, and destroy comprehensively. Maybe if the system in question were perfectly resilient, that would not happen. But perfection is at risk from outside events which, on arrival, disrupt it. Behaviour which had previously been good—a *polite reluctance to lift a lady's skirt even in an emergency, for instance—can, if luck is bad enough, leave even resilience overwhelmed.

*Resilience is the stability which confers life and form in a living world which otherwise, as the victim of chaos, predation and bad luck, would never have got anywhere. Most little random disturbances—like most little random mutations—don't get anywhere. But sometimes they do, with good or bad consequences, however well the system may be defended against them. It is the weak point in resilience: it has a gambling addiction—the Butterfly Defect.

*Gaia, Connectedness, Emergence, Entropy, Unintended Consequences.

C

CALIBRATION. The scale against which an institution measures what is "good" and decides how to act. Example: if guided by a scale calibrated in terms of "Health and Safety", an institution may develop a busy and elaborate burden of regulation—and, given a chance, keep adding to it.

But the scale may be recalibrated quite suddenly and radically. "Health and Safety" could be sharply replaced by other calibrations, such as "Boredom Kills"—which might approve without question anything which reduces the burden of regulation, and helps people to sustain the *interest and joy in life whose absence increases the likelihood of resentment, depression and suicide. Or another calibration might accept, without inspection, any policy, however absurd and authoritarian, just so long as it could be presented as necessary for reasons of preventing climate change or terrorism.

The governing calibration is so powerful that *judgment itself is suspended, and it crowds out higher-level

thinking able to choose between the two. Calibration saves the trouble of having to think things through afresh every time—and this may be sensible and necessary—but once the scale of measurement has been settled, it is hard to judge by any other standard until, in an unexpected flip, it is exchanged for another one.

Groups with a purpose tend to calibrate their *mindsets and prejudices to extreme positions. This is borne out by experiments which bring together small groups of strangers to discuss a given subject, unsupervised, having previously suggested to each person a moderate view (which they were prepared to agree with). As the conversation progresses, views begin to shift towards the extremes. The behaviour psychologist André Martins summarises a trial:

> [Within the range of opinions held by a group] opinions become very extreme, with each agent basically sure that his choice is the best one. This can help explain cases where people are led, by social pressure, to believe blindly in whatever opinion is shared by its local group, despite divergent voices in the larger society they live in.[1]

In a population as a whole, the views of most people tend to be middle-of-the-road; they want, for instance, reasonably safe living conditions, but they would not go as far in this as the health and safety professionals. But this is at least understandable. If you are in a group of people paid by the state to consider matters of health and safety, you are unlikely simply to maintain a collective view which goes, "Oh, well, we ought to keep an eye on things, place the emphasis on personal responsibility, and chase up people who are really negligent, but let's keep this in proportion . . .". Groupthink and diligence will carry you along: all governments and pressure groups find themselves drawn to extreme positions, and this effect is intensified as individuals who would resist this are naturally-selected out.

Grand error makes truth look shabby. And yet the effect of extremism depends on what it is applied to. If the aim is to establish delegated bottom-up decision-making, built on the ethic of *lean thinking, principles about affirming community members' responsibility for their own institutions and lives

---

RECALIBRATION
. . . but not yet

Arthur Koestler writes in 1941 of the passive compliance with the occupation of France:

As long as they do not receive definite encouragement from hard facts, the French people will remain partial but passive observers. . . . The French people have been too deeply disillusioned to risk their lives once more without being fairly certain of victory. They have to learn to hope again, like a man after long bedriddenness has to learn to walk. When the scales of success turn in favour of England, the barricades will emerge from the pavements of towns in France, the snipers will appear behind the attic windows, and the people will fight as in the old glorious days—but not before.

ARTHUR KOESTLER, *Scum of the Earth*

could be passionately-upheld—that is, a fierce defence of *moderation.[2]

*Assent, Expectations, Green Authoritarianism, Cowardice, Cognitive Dissonance, Big Stick.

CALL AND RESPONSE. The principle by which localities can call on their local authorities for assistance to develop projects, without themselves losing the initiative: a variant of the principle of *pull.

A well-established example comes from Portland, Oregon, now widely recognised for its neighbourhood associations and the extent of their initiative-taking in decisions affecting the city: local government *responds* to citizens' requests for action, providing an *incentive for participation to deepen over several decades. It did not come easily: the discussions that led to it were often acrimonious, and maintaining the dialogue is recognised as the specific responsibility of the citizens, who have to "educate" new officials (with the help, if need be, of introducing them to committed residents in the shape of a room full of "100 people screaming mad"). But "call and response" is close to the centre of *lean thinking, as *Lean Logic* uses the concept: it has *flow, pull and *feedback; it has the focused *intention and *lean means of local people with the confidence to know what they want and to believe that there is a chance they may be able to accomplish it.[3]

So it is not that the government has no role here; rather, it rediscovers its role as public servant, working for people that have recovered their confidence. An initiative within this framework has been launched in the United Kingdom with the Sustainable Communities Act (2007). This has been organised at a higher level than the Portland scheme—it is about local authorities calling on assistance from central government rather than local communities calling on local authorities—but the principle is there, and it may well extend downwards. A less formal approach, which is likely to have a better chance of recovering local *presence, is the *Transition movement.[4]

*TEQs (Tradable Energy Quotas).

CANARD. An assertion which is simple, widely-accepted and wrong. The derivation is uncertain but it is thought to come from the French *vendre un canard à* *moitié*, to half-sell a duck (i.e., not to make the deal at all). Usually used to dismiss an unwelcome truth: "That old canard about *nuclear energy being dangerous . . .".

*Self-Evident, Fallacies.

CANT (*Argumentum ad cantum*). An argument based on assurances of goodness and good intentions.

Little Red Riding Hood and her grandmother were suckers. First, the grandmother opened her cottage door to the bass-voiced wolf claiming to be Little Red Riding Hood. Then Little Red Riding Hood got into bed with, and was eaten by, the wolf, who had disguised himself by wearing the grandmother's clothes. She had noticed some *anomalies: "What big ears you have", she said, doubtfully. "The better to hear you with", said the wolf. Oh, that's all right, then.

The story, though changed in many details over the centuries, maintained its role as a warning against cant: do not fall for affectations of goodness or for sanctimonious declarations of morality, even if smooth, reasonable and convincing. "Cant"—which comes from "chant", *liturgical song—was once applied to the ingratiating whine of mendicant friars, hence Dr. Johnson's 18th century definition: "a whining pretension to goodness". More recently, Valéry Giscard d'Estaing, president of the European Convention, provided an illustration of cant with a singsong description of the proposed European Constitution as only a "coordination of competences". "What big competences you have, M. Giscard d'Estaing". "The better to coordinate you with".[5]

C

In a way, there is nothing wrong with cant. Faking it is part of nature, part of the human comedy. But it is not cant that is the main problem; it is the addiction to falling for it, for cant should not be hard to detect, and a person who fails to do so is ready to be distracted by a seductive promise which should have been easy to rumble. So, why does it happen? Well, there are many reasons: loneliness, wanting to belong, to be wanted, to be comforted, seduced; a sense of emptiness, of being incomplete and unfulfilled, which could be healed if only the promise were true. Naïvety helps, perhaps due in part to a lack of childhood grounding in stories and folk tales in which the characters learn the hard way how to detect the fake: it isn't always a good idea to believe everything a frog tells you. Or the speaker may be seduced by his own goodness: with intentions as patently good as mine, I don't need to think this through; just look me in the eye.

The subject on M. Giscard d'Estaing's mind offers much to fall for:

> . . . sustainable development based on balanced economic growth and price stability, a highly competitive social market economy, aiming at full employment and social progress, and a high level of protection and improvement of the quality of the environment [and promotion of] scientific and technological advance.[6]

This is not from a competition to pack as many policy clichés as possible into a sentence. It is from Article 3 of the Constitution he was advocating. To be *sceptical about balanced economic *growth, price stability, the *competitive social *market economy, full employment, social progress, or improvements in the quality of the environment would be to propose violations of the

Constitution. Logic cannot rescue it—but it doesn't need to, for constitutions are law.

Cant has a short life. Soon, in his true identity, the wolf jumped out of bed. Then he did sit and eat.[7]
*Distraction, Diplomatic Lie, Pharisee.

CAPITAL. Capital (in *Lean Logic*) is a particular kind of arrangement of matter, energy and information. The default arrangement of these three elements is disorderly and diffuse—*entropic—but sometimes, in the right conditions, they clump together in unlikely and interesting ways; as life, for example.[8]

The key property for such 'unlikely arrangements' to qualify as capital is that of being of *instrumental value to something. Something, somewhere finds them useful. This means that arrangements of matter, energy and information may move in and out of being capital, depending on context.

Examples:

1. A local herd of antelopes is capital to a local family of lions. It produces a flow of value in the form of food for the lions, without that flow actually diminishing the size and productivity of the herd itself. For the lions, the herd is definitely capital. But for a shoal of pink maomao fish off the coast of New Zealand, the antelopes are not capital.

2. Cars are capital, just as long as drivers can buy the fuel they need. If fuel were to become completely and permanently unavailable, cars would be reduced to rather curious objects, whose shape, though sometimes intriguing, had no particular meaning; like clouds.

3. The body of scientific knowledge and written *culture in books and on the internet is capital, just as long as there is someone who can read it, understand it, and derive some use from it, even if that consists of no more than the pleasure of an interesting read. If the standards of *education were to fall so far that no one could understand it, it would cease to be capital.[9]

In each of these three examples, it is the existence of a user that determines whether the 'unlikely arrangement' qualifies as capital. But what about the user? Is he/she/it capital? Well, suppose the lions in the example were only useful to themselves—their bodies athletic sources of life: if the 'unlikely arrangement' is useful to itself then yes, it can be seen as capital: life lives for its own sake.[10]

Such a utilitarian view of creation could seem improper: what about a tree, deep in the jungle? Or a starlit night? Well, the tree is useful to the jungle and to itself; the starlit night, among its many depths and uses, makes your heart leap. Utilitarianism in this sense is not a view of the world through the eyes of a predator: it is about interactions. The nature of capital is revealed most clearly when it becomes absent: a cathedral or a cantata which no one could make sense of any more would be in trouble: the cathedral would fall down since maintenance would be seen as a misuse of scarce funds which could be better applied to building prisons; the cantata, unregarded age in corners thrown, would not be heard. Capital is capital if someone or something is hungry for it.[11]

Types of capital

First, a disclaimer, which applies to the remainder of this entry: there are *fuzzy boundaries here; the types of capital are clusters around defining principles, rather than clearly distinct groups.[12]

1. *Natural capital* is the living ecology which nature provides—and which it could provide more abundantly, if only we would allow it to do so. It includes soil fertility, water, fish stocks, material resources . . . The whole of the *ecosystem and its *climate; the essential conditions for a living Earth.[13]

2. *Human capital* is embodied in people as *inherited or learned capabilities and knowledge: *health, *intelligence, *education, *character, *skills, beauty . . . A critical property of human capital is its potential for growth, in the form of both its ability to reproduce itself, and its potential to work, using up or altering natural capital in the process. And that work in turn has the ability to multiply by making tools, equipment and technologies, which in turn can produce more tools, equipment and technologies in a positive (amplifying) feedback. Natural capital, too, has the notional capability of reproducing itself in this way, but it is held close to equilibrium by natural balances: with

C

rare exceptions, no single part of it can grow out of control, because the other parts will prevent it—and even the exceptions eventually get their comeuppance. The exception to this (but not to the endgame) is the case of species which, by migration or evolution, escape from the natural balances of the ecology.[14]

3. The *social capital* of a community is its social life—the links of *cooperation and friendship between its members. It is the *institutions, the common culture and *ceremony, the *good faith and *reciprocal obligations, the *civility and citizenship, the *play, *humour and *conversation which make a living community; it is the social ecosystem in which a culture lives. Some people might be startled by such an elaborate definition, which would be hard to summarise in an equation: the more typical textbook *definition is "the set of institutions and customs which organise economic activity".[15] The reason for the difference is that the textbook's authors are thinking of the *market economy, contained in well-behaved parameters, as the process by which society is sustained. For *Lean Logic*, by contrast, what matters is *community itself. Social capital, the living essence of community, is the organ grinder; the market economy is the monkey.[16]

4. *Scientific/cultural capital* is the information and *culture which is available to be grasped in our minds, and/or applied (we may apply it without fully understanding it). Its status as capital depends on the ability of human society to understand and/or use it. If that ability were to decline, so would the capital.[17]

5. *Material capital*: *buildings, roads, equipment, *materials, ships, computers and their *networks, etc. Material capital provides the clearest illustration of why materials, energy and information are all important to defining capital: if new information comes to light about (say) a deposit of copper, *and* the energy exists to exploit it, material capital is increased. If the energy needed should become unavailable, the deposit would cease to qualify as capital; indeed, with energy-famine, most of the other forms of material capital, including the oil-fuelled equipment we use, would also cease to

qualify as capital. Cars, as suggested above, would be just rather curious-shaped objects (and would only even maintain their curiosity value if they were reduced to rare examples).[18]

6. *Financial capital*. There is a case for omitting financial capital, because its value depends on, and is a representation of, the existence of the other five forms. It is included because to some extent its existence is independent: a financial crash can occur for reasons notionally unconnected with the other five. The connections, however, would be revealed as the crisis rippled through to the point of greatly reducing, or destroying, other forms of capital. So it is useful to have it in the list, despite the double-counting.[19]

Foundation capital and growth capital

A critical distinction within capital is that between foundation capital and *growth capital. Foundation capital is the ecological context on which the *community depends: chiefly soil, *water and *climate, and the information contained in various forms—*tradition, *identity and (literally) DNA. The loss of such information ripples out in the form of the permanent loss of species, *cultures and *ecosystems; failure to conserve it is tantamount to stealing from future generations. This is capital that needs to be protected at all costs.

Growth capital, on the other hand, *needs to be limited*, for its growth—rising numbers of people, cattle, technology, machines—produces more growth. This is the *intensification of the *intermediate economy, and unless its growth is constrained, it will become ever more expensive to maintain, while its swelling numbers and the demands it makes on the ecology will in due course erode and ultimately destroy the foundation capital. Resilient societies are as meticulous about limiting or destroying growth capital as they are about conserving foundation capital.

All the six forms of capital listed above have *some* part to play as both foundation capital and growth capital, but there are big differences of emphasis:

- *Natural capital* is the condition on which all other capital depends. It would be reasonable to argue that this is the only form of capital which can justifiably be called foundation capital. But *Lean Logic* takes a cautiously broader view, recognising that for a human ecology, some broader foundations are needed.

- *Human capital* is foundation capital in terms of its capabilities: the talent, creativity, insight, emotional qualities and so forth that make a society. Growth is *enabled* by human capital in this sense.

  Yet the multiplication of the number of people among whom such capabilities are duplicated is growth capital (the fuzzy boundaries, overlaps and dependencies between the two kinds are, of course, acknowledged). Growth is *driven* by human capital in this sense: large numbers of people applying their capabilities to do work, much of which involves drawing on, or actually reducing, natural capital.
- *Social capital*, similarly, is foundation capital that can become a driver of growth as a society's population increases and its reach extends.
- *Scientific/cultural capital* can also be seen as foundation capital: every society, no matter how small, needs its culture. Scientific knowledge can deepen quality without producing growth. Even technical knowledge can be innocent of any growth programme. There is no essential (as distinct from economic) reason why technical advance should produce growth either in GDP or in environmental impact. And technical knowledge *can* be merely decorative: the East Anglian Traction Engine Society has lots of it.[20]

  And yet, the reasonable presumption is that such technical *expertise is of a kind which is indeed part of the growth problem. Technical capital clearly implies growth. If we know how to do it, we will do it. This sequence from knowledge to action is regrettable, leading to technologies such as *genetic engineering, *nanotechnology and *nuclear energy which we would be well advised to forgo, but it is hard to stop.[21]
- *Material capital*. Any human society will have at least basic equipment and housing which could, on some interpretations, be recognised as foundation capital; it is consistent with maintaining the foundations of a social order rather than building on them without limit. But the extended range of manufacturing, plant and equipment consists of growth capital.
- *Financial capital*? Here we must remember the double-counting problem (money is only a representation of the other forms of capital). Money is not therefore included in this distinction between foundation capital and growth capital.

The entry on *Intentional Waste describes how stable societies avoid getting stuck on the spiral of compound growth by either preventing the formation of growth capital, destroying it, or keeping it occupied with the production of goods and services which they then proceed to squander. This prevention or culling of growth capital is central to *resilience in any of its forms. Reason does not need to define the difference between the forms of capital exactly, so long as, by instinct or accident, the society limits its growth.

The capital stock principle

If capital is of utilitarian value to something, somewhere, there must be a sense in which it produces a *flow* of value. There are two ways in which it can do this. One of them is the case where the *stock* of capital is destroyed in the process. For example, a domestic coal-heap is capital so long as it lasts. The other is the case where the stock produces a flow of value without being destroyed—as in the case of an apple tree, in that it (and its progeny) produces apples without being destroyed. Or the case of financial stock, which produces a flow of income and may maintain or increase its value at the same time—the principle of capitalism.

The idea of capital of the second kind—that which produces a flow of value without being destroyed in the process—is central to one interpretation of *sustainable development. This view argues that a defining aim should be (by the use of technology and structural change) to learn how to live on the flow derived from our capital stocks—notably the endowment of the natural environment—so ensuring that the stock remains unchanged for as long as possible, if not indefinitely. This is the core of the argument developed by, for instance, Kenneth Boulding in his famous essay "The Economics of the Coming Spaceship Earth", and by Jonathon Porritt in *Capitalism as if the World Matters*.[22]

C

There is nothing in principle wrong with this, other than a practical difficulty. A *large system, finding itself committed to *growth, is all too likely to continue to grow well beyond the point at which it can continue to live on the flow generated by its stock of capital, and it will press on to the point at which it finds itself feeding on the stock of the capital itself. The result, of course, is that the capital shrinks, while the system itself continues to grow, and then it will consume the capital even faster. Arguing that we should subsist on the flow derived from a deeply depleted capital has right on its side, but it is problematic. It is reasonable and sensible to argue that we should not kill the goose that lays the golden eggs, except when it is even more important to wake up to the fact that the goose is already dead.

Anyway, we would be better off trying to get along with ordinary geese that lay ordinary eggs—not all that many of them, but enough to keep body, soul and community together. Golden eggs are no use to a self-reliant economy. Real geese, unlike magic ones, produce edible eggs, and bring together the three elements of capital—matter, energy and information: goose-capital for a *small system.

CAPTURE AND CONCENTRATION (often shortened to "concentration"). The practice, characteristic of *civic societies, of concentrating *population and production in *large-scale centres (hubs), and maintaining an extended transport system to support them. As the civic society gets larger, it has to build even bigger infrastructures for *energy, *food, communication, *waste disposal, *law and order, administration and transport. This is the giant *intermediate economy which will fail when reliable flows of energy break down, and it is the key aim of the *Lean Economy to devise ways of living without it.

Efforts to address the concentration by making structures more efficient (high-speed trains, for instance) tend to have the perverse effect of increasing concentration in the hubs, leading to even greater dependence on *transport: a positive (or amplifying) *feedback.
*Intensification Paradox, Neotechnic, Complexity, New Domestication, Wheel of Life.

CARBON CAPTURE AND STORAGE (CCS). See Energy Prospects.

CARBON OFFSETTING. A system by which individuals and organisations arrange for part or all of their emissions of greenhouse gases (mainly carbon dioxide) to be offset—reduced to net zero—by paying someone else to reduce or absorb emissions by the same amount.

The value of carbon offsetting as a response to *climate change is debated. It is criticised on the grounds that it does not address the fundamental task, which is to reduce our fuel-dependency and carbon emissions *and* to work with others to the same end—that is, to achieve the *energy descent. On the contrary, carbon offsetting eases consciences and reduces the pressure to do anything about your own uses of fossil fuels. And the usefulness of the system is also impaired by poor practice in the way in which it is applied. For instance, tree-planting may qualify for payment under a carbon offsetting scheme, but the planting process itself releases carbon, and the trees will in due course release their stored carbon back into the atmosphere when they are felled and turned into paper or used as fuel, so it is impossible to make sensible estimates of the carbon absorbed. In any case, estimates are so varied and inaccurate that matching them to the known quantities of energy/emissions saved sits more comfortably in the world of the casino than of physics.[23]

And carbon offsetting is open to fraud. Companies may cite, as an "offset", efficiency improvements in their operations which they were already planning to implement, qualifying for credit for something that they would have done anyway. And when a large company proposes a scheme—such as a large new dam—the canny way forward is to commission a report proposing projects which plausibly justify and write off the environmental impact of its main project. Such projects may include undertakings not to destroy another natural asset (which they had no plans to destroy, yet). Skill is channelled into presentation and fudge, rather than into the thinking needed to make radical decisions.[24]

On the other hand, a search for a system without flaws could take some time. Meanwhile, carbon offsetting has the case in its favour that it does provide energy users at least with an incentive to think about their energy use; and that it can apply the funds generated to opportunities for carbon reduction that may be more cost-effective than anything available to the donor. For example, suppose the energy user (the donor) has the choice between spending the money herself (on a solar hot water panel, or a more efficient car, or on moving home to be nearer her place of work) *or* contributing the money for another, more cost-effective, purpose. That other purpose could be:

- to provide efficient cooking stoves in Gambia, which greatly reduce the amount of wood needed to make a meal; or
- to help to pay for political action to steer government decision-making away from actions such as draining the central Borneo swamp forest and turning it into a giant rice paddy, destroying the wilderness and the carbon sink, and so releasing in one year carbon equal to almost half that released from all uses of fossil fuels (and then discovering that it would not even work as a rice paddy). Just a five percent chance of forestalling such an event would make your money work hard in terms of expected results.[25]

Offsetting broadens the range of choice and projects available for tackling carbon emissions. It may provide an incentive for energy users to make careful and accurate assessments of the opportunities available to them for achieving reductions. And it provides an incentive to think about energy-using options in a constructive way.

And yet, it is no substitute for direct personal commitment by consumers, firms and government to actual reductions in their own dependency on fossil fuels. Carbon offsetting may *weaken* the *incentive to put one's own energy/carbon house in order, because it presents the option of buying-off a bad conscience. If we were serious about reducing carbon emissions, we would establish *TEQs (Tradable Energy Quotas), while maintaining maximum worldwide cooperation in the common task. Encouraging others to try harder is persuasive if you are doing all you can yourself.[26]

CARITAS. Caring *encounter: a principle associated particularly with medieval Christianity, by which a *community recognised the duty of care among its extended networks of family relationship and *reciprocal obligation. *Caritas* is close to *charity (meaning 2), except that (a) it is the expression of a humane and orderly *culture and community, whereas charity has more the sense of an individual act; and (b) it has no *implication that the other person is in trouble or worse-off than you: it is the mutual bond of care between equals that holds the *political economy together, giving it the stability it needs to cooperate with others, whether they are in trouble or not.

CARE IN THE COMMUNITY
From a Commentary on Psalm 23, by Myles Coverdale (1537)

. . . A sheep must live only by the help, defence, and diligence of his shepherd. As soon as it leaveth him, it is compassed about with all manner of peril, and must needs perish; for it cannot help itself. For why? It is a poor, weak, and innocent beast, that can neither feed nor guide itself, nor find the right way, nor keep itself against any unhappiness or misfortune; seeing this, that of nature it is fearful, flieth and goeth astray. And if it go but a little out of the way, and come from his shepherd, it is not possible for itself to find him again, but runneth ever farther and farther from him. And though it come to other shepherds and sheep, yet is it nothing helped therewith: for it knoweth not the voice of strange shepherds; therefore flieth it from them, and runneth so long astray, till the wolf ravish it, or till it perish in some other ways.

. . . This is the office of a good shepherd, that he doth not only provide for his sheep pasture, and other more things that belong thereto, but defendeth them also, that no harm chance unto them. Besides this, he taketh diligent heed that he lose none. If any go astray, he runneth after it, seeketh it, and fetcheth it again. As for such as be young, feeble, and sick, he dealeth gently with them, keepeth them, holdeth them up, and carrieth them, till they be old, strong, and whole.[27]

C

"Care in the Community" (see sidebar on page 29) has the intense concern and care intended in *caritas*. You might think, at first sight, that the sheep is in trouble—worse off than the shepherd—but that isn't necessarily so (it may be enjoying its day out). What is clear in the story and its meaning is the shepherd's intense care for the sheep or (by implication) for people around him, his neighbours. Care in the community—in the *neighbourhood and in the *parish—has deep roots, as we see, for instance, in the medieval kinship community (*Reciprocity and Cooperation ❭ Balance).
*Compassion, Gifts, Good Faith.

CARNIVAL. Celebrations of music, dance, torchlight, mime, games, feast and folly have been central to the life of *community for all times other than those when the pretensions of large-scale civilisation descended like a frost on public joy. Carnival is a big word: it spans the buffoonery of the Feasts of Fools, the *erotic Saturnalia of Rome, the holy holidays of the Church's calendar and the agricultural year, and local days of festival in which communities, for most of history, have put down their work and concentrated on enjoying themselves.

The making and sustaining of community requires deep *presence and *empowerment, with three key properties:

1. *Radical break*. This is the community's break from the normality of the working day. Conventions are broken; there is misrule, in the medieval sense of good order being turned upside down, and stepping briefly over the edge of chaos, before—slightly changed and refreshed—stepping back into regular life.
2. *Second nature* is the animal spirit at the heart of the tamed, domesticated citizen: the deep reality which, if recognised and cared for, connects us with the red-blooded truth about ourselves (see "Unrealistic Expectations" sidebar).
3. *Sacrifice-and-succession* affirms the ability of the community to survive—to be immortal—in spite of, or because of, the *death of other communities and (eventually) of its own living members. The death of individuals in the community is overcome by birth and renewal, and the failure of some communities may be essential for the survival of the system as a whole (*Resilience).

UNREALISTIC EXPECTATIONS
Second nature, if not cared for, can go feral

In 1425, Fra Bernardino persuaded the people of Perugia to ban their Battle of Stones; an understandable reform, since the fatalities were beginning to get excessive. However, at the same time, he also insisted on an end to gambling, elaborate clothes and cosmetics. At first, citizens agreed to go along with all this, starting with a huge bonfire of the vanities in the Piazza, but the pious mood passed, and in due course they were back to their old ways—without the Battle, but with a new and exaggerated tendency to homicide and mugging.

Likewise, the saintly Savonarola's death in 1498 released the people of Florence from similar inhibitions, and they reverted with enthusiasm to "the gambling-hells, the taverns, the brothels . . . and scenes of profanity such as Florence had never before witnessed".[28]

In a day of magic and colour, carnival enables, declares and celebrates these encounters with the nature of our situation, ourselves and our community. It is the central event of community building at the scale of the *parish, as we will now explore.

Carnival: uses and origins

Carnival is, first of all, a form of *ritual. There is in carnival a quality of exuberance which distinguishes it from the sedate proceedings which would usually go by that name, but it possesses, nonetheless, the seven properties of ritual:

1. *Membership*. Ritual is a regular meeting place, and taking part in it affirms that the participants are members of the community.[29]
2. *Emotional daring*. The emotion felt by any one individual on his or her own is deepened and intensified when it is shared. This is poignantly

illustrated in a reflection by the French historian, Jules Michelet, who, as a child, was kept away from the carnival:

> My childhood never blossomed in the open air, in the warm atmosphere of an amiable crowd, where the emotion of each individual is increased a hundredfold by the emotion felt by all.[30]

3. *Continuity.* The unchanging quality of ritual bears out beliefs and hopes about the permanence of the community.
4. *Consciousness of time and events.* The progression of the year, and events in the community (and in the lives of its members), are noticed and affirmed by ritual and rites of passage.
5. *Practice.* The practical skills required by carnival build *practice—craftsmanship, with its three properties of citizenship: *truthfulness, justice and *courage.
6. *Meaning.* Ritual does not supply answers; it suggests insights and raises contradictions to be explored, to grow into through a lifetime (*Ironic Space).
7. *Locality.* Ritual marks the community's residence in a place. It puts down emotional roots, and makes a *place you can love. And when it takes the form of carnival, local diversity goes to *imaginative extremes. York's signature carnival was the lavish display of Corpus Christi. Dunmow's famous Flitch of Bacon is awarded to the married couple who had lived together for a year without quarrel or regret. In Orkney, carnival was organised around a ploughing competition in which the "farmers" were young boys and the "horses" were young girls. Cider-growing areas took care to have carnivals near their apple trees, and to pour cider on their roots to make them feel appreciated.[31]

In the past, there were in addition two substantial assets that were brought to community by the ritual of carnival:

8. *Social rank on hold.* For the duration of the carnival, at least, social rank became less important, and hard to sustain with due seriousness. The carnival created its own temporary, unofficial, popular aristocracy; rank, privilege, received common sense and norms were suspended. Carnival was always, in a sense, the Feast of Fools, in which the powerful, the pompous, the monstrous, outrageous and some of the frightening aspects of society could be laughed at and made safe. A marketplace full of laughing people is hard to impress. Laughter upstages rank.[32]

And ecstasy upstages rank too. It need not be ecstasy of a kind to be wary of: it can be the spectacular dancing joy we encounter in, for instance, Bach's *Freue Dich* in his Cantata No. 30, music with its own precedence and authority. Unconstrained joy is an equaliser: as the historian of carnival, Barbara Ehrenreich, notes, "It's difficult, if not impossible, to retain one's regal dignity in the mad excitement of the dance."[33]

9. *Peace.* Carnival is a promoter of peace. The lack of discipline and hierarchy make carnival a poor foundation on which to build an army; other *incentives to fight, such as attack by neighbours, may brush aside carnival's preference for peace, but it is still a property of some value: carnival does not need the further excitement of war.[34]

Carnival persons

The sources of carnival belong to the later history of apes as much as to the early history of humans, but here are two persons ("people" doesn't seem to be quite the right word here) who hold a place of honour in its evolution. The first is Dionysus, the Greek god of wine and ecstasy. Dionysus had a difficult start in life. Zeus (a god) was married to Hera (a goddess), but made Semelē (a mortal) pregnant. When Hera found out about this, she arranged for Semelē to be consumed by Zeus' own lightning, but Zeus managed to rescue the foetus from the ashes and plant it in his thigh, from which in due time the young Dionysus was born. He was immediately torn to shreds on Hera's instructions, but (providentially) his grandmother, Harmonia, was on hand to put him together again. The infant Dionysus was then to be looked after by his aunt, but this came to grief when Hera condemned her to madness, whereupon she jumped into the sea and became a sea-goddess. Finally, Dionysus was brought up by the nymphs of Mount Nysa, where his divinity became manifest, and before long he was travelling and preaching the virtues

C

of wine, ecstasy and peace. He attracted disciples, men and women who spent their days possessed, intoxicated and dancing. But this, too, brought trouble, for the undisciplined band provided little protection against robbers, and Dionysus was kidnapped by pirates and tied to the mast. Fortunately, he was able to command the bonds to fall off him, and a vine to grow about the mast in their place. He himself turned briefly into a lion, and the alarmed sailors jumped overboard and turned into dolphins. We are not told how the ship got back to port, but evidently it did so, for Dionysus had a long and varied career ahead of him.[35]

Dionysus was remarkable even by the standards of a god. Whereas other gods merely existed, Dionysus could be brought into being by dance: here was a dance-god that demanded no sacrifices but existed for the joy of the dance itself, and these were qualities which made him popular with women who, at a signal, would put down their spinning and rush off into the mountains to dance in his honour, toss their hair, drink wine and (though this bit—omophagia—might have been a wicked rumour put about by men) eat wild animals raw.[36] One day the poet Edmund Spenser's Elfin Knight actually came across a group of women in the midst of their Dionysian dance, and he could hardly believe his eyes:

> An hundred naked maidens lily white,
> All raunged in a ring and dancing in delight.
>
> *Edmund Spenser, The Faerie Queene, 1596.*[37]

The second significant person in the story of carnival and dance is Jesus, and—as Barbara Ehrenreich shows—the two had much in common: both had a father-god and a mortal mother, enjoyed wine and meat, were healers, were popular with women but, it seems, had no *sexual partners, were lovers of peace, defended the poor, turned water into wine, were dismissive of the citizen-virtues of work and planning ahead, and were worshipped with ecstatic dance which could bring people to a state of the deepest communion and bliss.[38] Indeed, it is a matter of some doubt whether Dionysus and Jesus can really be regarded as *two* persons at all, rather than as two representatives among many—Pan, Sabazios, Osiris—of a deep and sustained consciousness of our second nature: ecstatic participation in the

natural world, the sacrificial *gift, spontaneity—all remembered dimly, despite being overlaid by *civic *responsibility, by the need to be sensible, to calculate, to plan strategy, to look about warily. Our second nature is comfortable with, and secretly delights in, levitation from the laws of physics and economics, with enchanted logic taking us into the world of anti-reality and dream. It is hard to get at. It is not a matter to be talked about. But it can be danced.

Outside to play

The natural form taken by ritual is dance, and of course the music that goes with it. In the earliest centuries of Christianity, it was a danced religion, and evidently the dance could get wild. It included, for instance, hair tossing which, according to accounts from various times and places, has been one of the recurring actions of wild dance: women's ecstatic tossing of their long hair could sometimes make it crack like a whip. St. Paul's famous injunction that women should either keep their head covered, or at least keep their hair short, may have been intended to discourage what he saw as these excesses: "the woman [ought] to have power on her head, because of the angels".[39]

And that anxious plea that the ecstatic worshippers should cool it set the theme for a stand-off between the church hierarchy (which advocated decorum) and the worshippers (who preferred ecstasy) which has shaped the development of both carnival and churches ever since. In broad terms, music and dance are forms of extravagance, and extravagance was a virtue defended by Jesus. He approved of wine and feasting; when the woman came to him with an alabaster box of precious ointment and anointed his feet with it, prompting *indignant protests from the disciples who said that it would have been better to sell it and give the money to the poor, Jesus' reply was withering. And it happened again in his reply to Martha's complaint about being "cumbered about with much serving" in the kitchen while her sister Mary sat in conversation with their guest:

> Martha, Martha, thou art careful and trouble about many things: But one thing is needful: and Mary has chosen that good part, which shall not be taken away from her.[40]

But churches increasingly began to see the bottom-up creativity of music and dance as the wrong kind of exuberance, and around the early thirteenth century, the long-held priestly assumption that the church ought to be above spontaneous joy began at last to take effect. So, carnival had to move outside—to the churchyard, the street, the village green. This was a major source of complaint, and François Rabelais' story of what happened to the sacristan who would not let a villager borrow some priestly robes for him to wear in a play in which he had been cast as God, tells us something about how deep this ran. The villagers, armed with saucepans and sticks, ambushed the sacristan on his horse, so that the horse bolted—the sacristan fell off but caught his foot in the stirrup. When eventually the horse was caught, there was nothing left of him but the stump of his foot. Villages were evidently short of patience with people of the priestly persuasion who wanted to throw them out of the best building in the place and spoil their fun.[41]

The expulsion of carnival from the churches had, however, its good, if *unintended, consequences: carnival became extraordinarily developed, with dance, decoration and invention happening throughout the year, especially those parts of the year when less work was needed in the fields. We hear a lot about the hardships of the Middle Ages, the famines, plagues and wars—all true. What we find harder to believe, since it violates our right to feel smug about the wonders of modernity, is that the Middle Ages were also a time of inventive joy, an age of art, participation and festivals—all of which, as the historian E.P. Thompson notes, "were, in an important sense, what men and women lived for".[42]

The long descent

But then, with the transition from a rural-centred culture to a city-centred one, carnival began its decline. In fact, that transition has been in various states of advance or retreat for thousands of years, and reports of its death, and that of carnival's impresario, Dionysus, have come and gone accordingly. One of them, told by Plutarch from the reign of Tiberius (14–37 AD) came in the haunting lament from the island of Palodes (where the preferred name for Dionysus was Pan). The story tells of a Greek merchant ship, whose crew, passing the island of Paxos, heard a loud cry instructing Thamus,

a sailor on the ship, to pass on a message: "The Great God Pan is dead". When they came to Palodes, Thamus duly shouted the message. In reply came a wailing and lamentation from many voices, unseen in the forest.[43]

And, more subtly, a story from much earlier. Homer (c.700 BC) tells us how the art of the ancient dream world lay in wait to seduce Odysseus and his crew as they were about to encounter the Sirens, whose bewitching song lures everyone who hears it to their death, their bodies added to the pile of mouldering skeletons in the meadow where the Sirens sat. On the advice of his mistress, Circe, the goddess who lives on the island of Aeaea, Odysseus stopped up the ears of his crew with wax so that, unable to hear the song, they were not distracted from the real work of rowing. He himself, being securely strapped to the mast, could now listen to the Sirens' voices "with enjoyment", as Circe puts it, and without being drawn irresistibly into their power. This has various interpretations, but one of them makes it a decisive detachment from art: the sound of ancient myth which once drew its hearers in, without means of escape, is rendered sensible and civilised, reduced to a concert, a sort of Hellenic musical evening with female chorus and a professor of Greek to tell us something about the local legend that lies behind it.[44]

On this view we see the breaking of the link between art (music, in this case) and politics: now you only need to buy your ticket, be a spectator of the arts for an hour or so, and then home for herb tea and bed (implications of this are discussed in *Narrative Truth). As Alasdair MacIntyre notes,

> The contrast, indeed the opposition, between art and life . . . provides a way of exempting art—including narrative—from its moral tasks. And the relegation of art by modernity to the status of an essentially minority activity and interest further helps to protect us from any narrative understanding of ourselves.[45]

In the seventeenth century, the decline of carnival in the West began in earnest. There were many reasons. The early stirrings of capitalism encouraged habits of soberness, and it has this fixation about people turning up for work on Monday morning. Some carnivals were getting out of control, becoming the starting point

C

for rebellion and riot: Robin Hood's career began as a carnival king; Ben Kett's rebellion in 1549 started in Wymondham at a festival for St. Thomas à Becket. And the invention of firearms had its effect: it meant, of course, that a reckless crowd could also be dangerous, but—more important than that—it introduced a need for discipline, especially in armies. The loading and firing of a musket is complicated; it requires a sequence of steps—forty-three of them, according to Prince Maurice of Orange's "drill"—each of which must be done exactly, at speed, and (on occasion) under fire. Discipline becomes critical: sober citizenship, which is good for armies, and good for trade, calls for self-awareness and self-control, and it gets lost in the spontaneous exuberance of carnival.[46]

At the same time, the loss of carnival is serious. It invites the bleak question: "What is the point?" The consequences are various, no doubt, but among them may be loneliness, *boredom, anxiety and depression; if society is less fun, its inequalities are more resented. There is no constant reminder of the teeming vitality beneath the surface of other people; there is a loss of *authority by the local community, which becomes less audible, less visible, less alive, less fertile as a source of laughter. Barbara Ehrenreich wonders whether the waning of carnival might have had something to do with the awareness of depression which, in the early seventeenth century, seems to have developed almost on the scale of a pandemic. Before then there was, of course, pain, and grief—all the dark emotions—but loneliness and anxiety . . . ? *Tactile deprivation (the sadness of not being touched) . . . ? The sense of the party being over . . . ?[47]

Here, for instance, we have a solitary lament from the touch-deprived John Clare, long after the passing of carnival:

I am: yet what I am none cares or knows,
  My friends forsake me like a memory lost;
I am the self-consumer of my woes,
  They rise and vanish in oblivious host,
Like shades in love and death's oblivion lost;
  And yet I am, and live with shadows tost

Into the nothingness of scorn and noise,
  Into the living sea of waking dreams,

Where there is neither sense of life nor joys,
  But the vast shipwreck of my life's esteems;
And e'en the dearest—that I loved the best—
  Are strange—nay, rather stranger than the rest.

John Clare, I Am!, 1848.[48]

On the other hand, we have Robert Burton's prescription, his cure for the black humour of melancholy. Your depression would have to be truly awful not to lift when that cheerful Dr. Carnival shows up:

Let them use hunting, sports, playes, jousts, merry company . . . which will not let the minde be molested, a cup of good drinke now and then, heare musicke, and have such companions with whom thy are especially delighted; merry tales or toyes, drinking, singing, dancing, and whatever else may procure mirth.

Robert Burton, The Anatomy of Melancholy, 1621.[49]

Carnival and community

At the start of this entry, there was a claim that carnival brings the three central properties of community building—the radical break, second nature and sacrifice-and-succession—to the making and sustaining of community. So, how have we done?

1. The *radical break* is there. The key insights come from Rabelais, whose subject was laughter, the language of *fearlessness.[50] In a strange way, laughter confers protection, and this may help to explain why Rabelais had a long and comparatively trouble-free life, at a time when much milder criticisms of the established order would lead to their serious-minded authors being burned at the stake. Carnival is about laughter, and laughter inspires insight and solidarity; it would be going too far to say that a radical break is impossible without laughter, but it certainly helps: like the screen behind which legendary mime Marcel Marceau momentarily disappeared when switching from being a fierce giant to a terrified pigmy (and back again), laughter gives you a brief phase of invisibility in which you can change your mind, and perhaps your life, without having to explain yourself. Change? What

change? In the presence of laughter, you don't have to answer impertinent questions like that.

2. *Second nature.* With its folly, its jokes and lack of dignity, its laughter at the intellectual, its wildness and its equality, second nature would be a distinct nuisance if it were allowed to get involved in matters of political graft and calculation. But it is a lifeline. It is the difference between belonging to the community because you feel you ought to, and belonging to it because its artistic expression engages your soul. There is a big difference between the citizen and the soul, and Rabelais makes this plain. Here is the citizen . . .

> Well, consider a man who watches over his private affairs and domestic business . . . who attends to his household . . . who keeps his nose to the grindstone . . . who understands thoroughly how to avoid the error of poverty. . . . That, according to the world, is a wise man. Yet, in the eyes of the celestial spirits, he may be the most unmitigated ass.

On the other hand . . .

> And whom do those spirits consider wise? Ha, That is a horse of another colour. For them a wise man, a man not only sage but able to presage future events by divine inspiration, is one who forgets himself, discards his own personality, rids his senses of all earthly desires, purges his spirit of all human care, neglects everything.[51]

3. *Sacrifice-and-succession.* One of the symbols of carnival is the act of giving birth. In his *Italian Journey*, the journal of his visit to the Roman Carnival of 1788, the poet Johann Wolfgang von Goethe describes a curious scene in the opening stages of the carnival. It is not really all that comic, nor original, nor exciting; it occupies, instead, a position in between these, a sort of mimed logo for the meaning of carnival. A group of (usually) men appears. They are dressed up in various ways: some as *peasants, some as women, and one of the "women" shows signs of heavy pregnancy. A quarrel breaks out, fake swords are drawn; there is duelling and fake death. The "pregnant woman"

is terrified, falls down in the street and goes into labour. The others gather round her, and in due course produce — well, a cat, perhaps, or a bag of potatoes, or a "formless object". It is the sheer wetness of this joke which gives it significance; it seems to come from far away, borne on the wind from a Greek island, a mime of the single phenomenon of death-birth, an assertion of collective immortality.[52]

And, in Goethe's journal, the same theme comes in a collective sketch as the carnival closes. It is night-time now, and in the final procession down the Corso in the Festival of Fire, everyone has a candle — *un moccolo* — to carry. Then comes the chant, "*Sia ammazzato chi non porta moccolo!*" — "Death to anyone who is not carrying a candle!", whereupon they try to blow out each other's candles, sort of condemning each other to death: "*Sia ammazzato il signor Padre!*" "Death to you, sir father!"[53]

It doesn't seem a friendly way to end a family day out. But that process of sacrifice-and-succession, *stirb und werde* (die and become) — death of the parts in the interests of the whole, birth and death belonging on the same cobblestones — is as intrinsic to resilience and to continuity as oxygen is to water, and in his poem, *Selige Sehnsucht*, Goethe reflects on this:

> *Und so lang du das nicht hast,*
> *Dieses stirb und werde,*
> *Bist du nur ein trüber Gast*
> *Auf der dunkeln Erde*
>
> And as long as you do not possess
> This: die and become,
> You are but a gloomy guest
> On the dark earth.[54]

———————

Order and misrule, *death and life, the sage and the ass: strange attractors, dependencies and *paradoxes have their day in carnival. The community building of the future will explore the intensely unfamiliar; the assumptions of the present will be laughable. Emerging communities, in contrast, will grow their own common sense, releasing the *creative potential of collective folly, while breeding new strains of good *judgment for a different world. Carnival is the act which gives the community its life — its conception. Start with a party.[55]

CASUISTRY. Case-by-case judgment. It is a meticulous approach, acknowledged in essence by Aristotle but developed in full as one of the accomplishments of the Middle Ages.[56]

Casuistry cultivated what it saw as good practice in thinking. It aimed at, and often achieved, a benign combination of:

1. closely-observed detail of the individual case,
2. a frame of reference (here, the Christian ethic) within which to think about it, and
3. well-defined *feedback, so that opinion could evolve *incrementally in the light of the individual cases.

Within the church, there was—along with the universal principles—a *reflective theological *tradition which could make diverse judgments, kindly and charitably, against whatever criteria seemed most suitable: virtues, sins, nature, experience, circumstance, precedent, reason . . .[57]

There is, in this approach, a humanity and *intelligence, as well as common sense, and the combination of local detail and broad principle in the medieval period was similar in some ways to those of the radical environmental movement today. Community was fundamental: man's place in nature being "to know the truth about God and to live in communities". Local self-sufficiency in food was urged as a virtue by St. Thomas Aquinas; there was a distrust of international trade and of economic *growth; excess profits were condemned as "filthy lucre" (*turpe lucrum*); local *credit unions provided cheap loans; *common *land-ownership was widely practised; fair terms of employment, responsibility for the poor and *defence of *peasant farmers against eviction by enclosures, were collective *virtues.[58]

It was partly for his defence of such as these that medieval virtue's last hero, Archbishop Laud, was to be executed in 1645. R. H. Tawney wrote in admiration of Laud and his civic principles:

> An intense conviction of the fundamental
> solidarity of all the manifold elements in a
> great community, a grand sense of the dignity
> of public duties, a passionate hatred for the
> self-seeking pettiness of personal cupidities
> and sectional interests—these qualities are not

among the weaknesses against which the human nature of ordinary men requires to be most upon its guard, and these qualities Laud possessed, not only in abundance, but to excess.[59]

The problem was that, by the early seventeenth century, *economic and social change was so fast that a constant (or slowly-evolving) frame of reference within which to deliberate could not keep pace. The first response to this was to dig in—to develop casuistry as far as it would go. Conscience was moved up into the front line of moral reflection, perhaps in a way not equalled before or since. *Judgment came under stress from an increasing tension between (on one hand), the principles and (on the other hand) the specific circumstances which profoundly affect the way in which they are interpreted, and which can sometimes seem to be in direct contradiction to them. An oath has to be honoured; but what happens when a new government comes in that requires you to take an oath of loyalty which is contrary to the previous one? You must tell the *truth; but no businessman who revealed all to his *competitors would survive very long. Special cases seemed to arise at every turn, and internal battles of conscience were sometimes taken so seriously that they required analysis by learned counsel.[60]

So casuistry started to retreat, and this turned to rout—giving casuistry its bad name—when it was rubbished as a hopeless mess of inconsistencies and fast-talking in Blaise Pascal's *Lettres Provinciales* (1656). The clear-out simplified matters a lot. As the historian John Selden observed scornfully over dinner one day in the 1680s,

> Some men make it a case of conscience, whether
> a man may have a pigeon-house, because his
> pigeons eate other folks Corne; but there is
> no such thing as conscience in yᵉ businesse; yᵉ
> matter is whether he be a man of such quality
> that yᵉ state allows him to have a Dovehouse: if
> soe, there's an end of yᵉ businesse; his pigeons
> have a right to eate where they list themselves.[61]

That is: Relax, my dear fellow, you're doing fine; don't worry about things so much. Let the law worry its head about all that stuff; you have now entered the world of civil society and tolerant fellowship. A satisfactory role model for "my dear fellow" in eighteenth century Britain was found in Jesus Christ himself: he gets an encouraging pat on the head as "the best and happiest man that ever was".[62]

But casuistry will outlive the *market. It matters because it is the opposite of *ideology. It looks at the detail. It applies judgment. It resists tyranny. It looks you in the eye. It consults the emotions. It does not envy *character, nor seek to destroy it. It affirms the freedom to think within a desired and agreed frame of reference. It is lean.

*Caritas, Green Authoritarianism, Humility, Lean Thinking.

CAUSES, THE FALLACY OF. The *fallacy that an event that follows another event was therefore caused by it. Among the crimes against the logic of causes, we have the cases of . . .

1. . . . *claimed credit*. Example: "The high quality of research at our top universities is a tribute to the success of this Government's education policy."
2. . . . *looking no further*. The immediate cause is taken to be a complete explanation. Example: "The train was late because the driver didn't turn up." Contrast with the *Five Whys, which dig through layers of explanation.
3. . . . *the invisible shadow*. The use of imaginary history—what *didn't* happen—to bear out your interpretation of what did happen. An argument based on the invisible shadow might claim, for instance, that:
   a. we would be in dire straits if it had not been for the National Health Service—no doubt we would be facing a distressing catalogue of high costs, long waiting times, bureaucracy, errors, sloppy cleaning and infections if it had not been there to eliminate these problems, and if the former system had had sixty more years to adapt and develop; or
   b. what peace and quiet we would now be enjoying in the Middle East if only Saddam Hussein and the Taliban had been left in power.
4. . . . *confusion between cause and effect*. Example: "We both have to have full-time jobs to pay for the large mortgage we need." But mortgages are large because so many households have two full-time earners. The interaction of cause and effect may make it impossible to identify a single cause. A normality emerges which reinforces itself.
5. . . . *correlation*. When two trends move in the same direction, one may be supposed to cause the other, but it may be the other way round, or both may be the effects of a common cause, or they may be substantially unrelated to each other.

But the chief form of this fallacy is *Post hoc propter hoc* ("after it, therefore because of it"). Along with its variant *Cum hoc propter hoc* ("along with it, therefore because of it"), its potential to mislead is well-established. The absence of war between the nations of Western Europe since 1945 has been credited to the European Union project—but there was no reason to expect a war between European nations during that period. Governments habitually claim credit for good economic performance, and blame the problems on factors outside their control. And misfortune is flattered with more meaning than it deserves: unwelcome events through the ages have become bearable and understandable when someone has been found to blame.

*Systems resist straightforward analysis in terms of cause and effect. This is because the effect is an outcome not just of the particular event which might seem to be the cause, but of the whole complex potential of the system to react in a certain way. The idea of cause-and-effect therefore gives way to a sequence of influence → response → influence, stretching back far into the non-obvious: the white billiard ball moved in that direction because I struck it with my red ball, because I had decided to play billiards that evening, because I wanted to be out of my house, because I had had a quarrel with my lover, because she didn't want to spend the weekend with me in Scunthorpe. Taiichi Ohno, president of Toyota and pioneer of lean thinking, instituted the *Five Whys, a discipline for understanding the root cause of errors. It is an approach which not only makes it hard to sustain the idea of *blame—that useful short cut through causes that you have not yet understood—but it disconcertingly manages to involve *you*: just five steps—five whys—away from the problem

Here is a test of having begun to understand and tolerate the *paradox and mild *complexities of an easily-understood system. If the conclusions you have drawn about it are obvious and *self-evident, you probably haven't.[63]
*Choice, Systems Thinking, Special Pleading.

CEREMONY. A form of *ritual, typically formal and on a relatively large scale. It affirms, or can affirm, an implicit *contract of membership between a *community and its members.
*Culture, Carnival, Religion.

CERTAINTY, FALLACIES OF. Certainty—confidence in a *material truth beyond reasonable doubt—is not itself a *fallacy. A fallacy does occur, however, when certainty takes the form of:

1. defence of a position, by all means, logical and otherwise; or
2. insistence that the other person's proposition has to be certain and proven beyond any conceivable challenge, before it can be accepted as *relevant. Example: "It was the excellent music teaching she had at home and at school that made it possible for her to become a professional pianist." "You see, you simply don't know that: she might have taught herself on the piano at the Youth Club."

*Precautionary Principle, Bad Faith, Self-Deception, Disingenuousness.

CHARACTER. Moral courage, depth, resourcefulness—being capable of originality and surprise, not being easily destroyed by criticism or failure. In the authoritarian state, character in this sense is a nuisance, unpredictable and hard to seduce with *cant; the state's task is therefore depersonalisation, making people mild, dependent, programmable with imposed and universal principles. In the *Lean Economy, by contrast, character will be built, by slow prudence, to make a mild people rugged.[64]
The idea of character is out of phase with a depersonalising culture that places its confidence in process, technologies, regulations, rights and the unchallenged guidance of *economics. But it is central. A clue to it comes from Ralph Waldo Emerson, in his essay

is often enough to establish you, if not as a cause, at least as an accomplice.

But there is a deeper meaning here. Even if real, more complex, meanings for cause and effect are acknowledged, the whole notion of cause becomes difficult to sustain. Shortages are both the cause and effect of hoarding. Loving is a cause and effect of being loved. The hunting of prey by its predator is not only a *necessary *cause* of the population of the prey being sustained, protecting its *ecosystem and its *food resource and selecting for the survival of the healthiest animals; it is also the *effect* of—enabled by—the maintenance of the prey's large and healthy population. For our own society, hunting has presented it with the task of having to think about *natural systems and about the value of *hunting to sustaining healthy fox and deer populations—along with their habitats, the wild animals and plants that depend on them, and the living rural *communities that depend on the hunt. But the thinking has degraded to *compassion. Compassion without understanding is cruel.

"Politics". He is arguing in favour of small (lean) government—and then comes this:

> Hence the less of government we have the better, the fewer laws, and the less confided power. The antidote to this abuse of [the powers of] formal Government is the influence of private character, the growth of the Individual; the appearance of the principal to supersede the proxy; the appearance of the wise man; of whom the existing government is, it must be owned, but a shabby imitation.

. . . followed by one of the most remarkable statements in the literature:

> The appearance of character makes the State unnecessary.[65]

The same word shows up in Tony Gibson's study of people joining together to take control of their own *neighbourhoods, using "sweat equity", renovating and caring for the *houses they want in the way they want them:

> What counts is the borrower's potential—the personal ability to make the most of a promising situation—and behind that, what can best be called *character*, the quality which sustains the enterprise in spite of setbacks. This staying-power means that the community will still be around whilst the neighbourhood takes shape and grows.[66]

And in different words, Max Gammon, the doctor who reviewed the impact of the National Health Service in 1976, and revisited the subject thirty years later, notes:

> By definition, nonbureaucratic systems are "voluntary" systems. Their working depends on a mixture of knowledge and wisdom, i.e., soundness of *personal* judgment.[67]

Although character is not the same thing as leadership, the two ideas have much in common, leading into, and reinforcing, each other. Qualities of character imply qualities of leadership. Here are seven of those qualities noted by John Elkington and Pamela Hartigan in their study of "unreasonable people", and the leadership they bring:[68]

1. *Enthusiasm*. There is an intense desire, a yearning, for a particular aim—not an *ideology, but engagement with a place, person, pragmatic idea. The enthusiast expresses inspiration, in a clean uncluttered way, without feeling it necessary to bring along a lot of other baggage at the same time.

   There is *intention—and this gives *relevance to events and circumstances which would otherwise have none. Someone comes along and asks if she can build a boat in your church hall: a *what*? But, come to think of it, this is exactly what you need at that moment. It would not have occurred to you, but when luck drops by, you recognise it. Your intention turns an *anomaly—a ripple of random noise—into a godsend.[69]

2. *Local knowledge*. When you see things from outside, you will miss the detail, so you have to stereotype. From inside, you can accurately observe. And when you are inside with enthusiasm, you can *feel* the detail.

3. *Mind*. The *intelligence available in the community is its central asset, and it is applied when it has something to focus on. The leadership's enthusiasm wakes the community's mind to options it had not been aware of.

4. *Visibility*. The leader-character as a person is visible (i.e., seen around) . . .

5. *Flexibility*. . . . and is able to be flexible, to respond quickly to opportunity; he or she is open to information and ideas which, if listened to and understood, may require a change of mind.

6. *Affection*. Character is not embarrassed by affection. It does not see why professional standards should insist on emotional paralysis. There is affection for the project, the *place and the people in it. The indifference—the impersonal procedures and hate that spread through a managed bureaucracy—does not happen. The *subjective and *emotional are not embarrassments: they are critical assets.

7. *Irrationality*. *Creative projects are irrational in that at the time of conception their implications are unknown, and those that are known may look absurd or impossible.

Here are some examples of these at work:

C

- Bunker Roy's Barefoot College in Rajasthan, founded in 1972, has taken generations of people without formal *education, living on less than $1 a day, and trained them as solar engineers, water engineers, IT specialists, teachers and architects. The College, preferring to train women students (men tend to use their certificates to get jobs in towns), has transformed the quality of life of rural communities in India and around the world. These are communities and people without the financial resources for the purchase of plant and *expertise—a market invisible to any assessment of the economic opportunity. By rational business standards—since it is advisable to make sure that you are working in a *market which has some money—this is not a promising idea, and for Roy himself, his decision as a young man to leave behind his glittering opportunities in the Indian diplomatic service was perverse. Only by the standards of his insight about the latent talent of the rural poor was this a rational thing to do.[70]
- The inspiration of Muhammad Yunus' Grameen Bank—which began as a research project in 1976—providing *small-scale credit to the urban poor, and applying the principle of "group credit" to bring peer pressure to the commitment to repay loans, along with very small-scale deposits. This, too, was irrational, or seemed to be, not least because it looks for a return on its investment expressed in terms other than *money: in benefits to people and the planet.[71]
- A third instance of the power of unreasonable people is Andrew Mawson's sustained commitment to Bromley by Bow, a district in east London with little evident potential. The Centre that has grown up there following his inspiration and character has brought more than jobs and a degree of wealth and confidence: it has *empowered the place.[72]

A project which is securely rational after the event may well be irrational before it: it *can't* be done until it *is* done. Leadership of this kind is a form of do-it-yourself (DIY)—like Mrs. Beeton's reputed recipe, "First, catch your rabbit", it starts at the very beginning: First, invent your logic.[73]

Is there a risk of excessive focus on the leader? Probably—but there is a greater risk in suppressing that talent. People with the ability and *imagination of Bunker Roy, Muhammad Yunus, Andrew Mawson, Rick Aubry (the Rubicon Programs of housing for the homeless), and Cristóbal Colón (the La Fageda company with its workforce of the mentally ill), are assets which no organisation can afford to lose. The good ones have no particular desire to be seen as heroes or for power and permanence; as John Elkington and Pamela Hartigan write,

> Any group of entrepreneurs, business or otherwise, will have its share of egomaniacs, but the social entrepreneurs we have met and worked with to date seem strongly skewed to the good-fun-to-be-around end of the spectrum. . . . Indeed, one of their most striking characteristics is their ready admission that the challenges they relish are way beyond any single entrepreneur or enterprise. . . . [They] have a great deal to offer and teach the rest of us.[74]

And then there is the flexibility that comes when character and motivation survive in an organisation with a lean freedom from heavy regulatory control. Mawson demonstrated this when he went along with the passionate enthusiasm of Billy, an unemployed builder, about his idea of landscaping the park round the centre. Billy proved himself to be one of the best garden designers in the country, transforming the Centre. And Margy set up the pottery business there on the strength of seeing an advertisement, KILN WANTED. These were not committee decisions. There is a risk of error in such an approach, and developing a community centre in an urban borough is not the same as building a whole *Transition community, but an informal organisation has the flexibility and individual engagement needed to bring on the potential and character of the people in the organisation or community. There is a sense here of "leader" and "servant" fusing into a single role—the ancient idea of the "servant leader" found in Lao Tzu's treatise on leadership (c.600 BC), in the Gospels, and in the literature of our own time.[75]

When in due course more formal organisation is needed, there is a range of options, and they include, of course, the elected committee with *defined areas of responsibility for some or all of its members. But the principle, as summarised by Mawson, remains: "*People before structures*." And the responsibility, insight and enthusiasm of individuals—which create the local leadership, build *cooperation and make things happen—are in direct opposition to a culture whose values are defined in terms of rights. Mawson recommends,

> Give more personal responsibility and hold individuals to account for what they do. This is difficult in a culture that has chosen to go down the legislative route of human rights. The litigiousness which results from it breaks down relationships and severs the bonds of trust that make any community possible. It will, I believe, bring with it a terrible price and fracture for some of Britain's poorest communities.[76]

In the long run, it is likely that natural leadership will emerge for aspects of *community life. In seventeenth century England, writes Peter Laslett,

> . . . the plain Richard Hodgsons, Robert Boswells, Humphrey Eltons and John Burtons of the English villages, the labourers and husbandmen, the tailors, millers, drovers, watermen, masons, could become constables, parish clerks, churchwardens, ale-conners, even overseers of the poor.[77]

Communities of the past hung on to their talent. The assumption that it should be captured and carried off to urban centres in the name of *social mobility—leaving the locality as the embodiment of serve-you-right failure—will not persist in a culture in which the action that matters is *local.
*Assent, Calibration, Constructivism, Cowardice, Frankness, Fortitude.

CHARISMA. (1) The gift of grace that enhances the moral *authority of a leader in the eyes of his or her followers.[78]
(2) The ability to express interesting and inspiring opinion; the quality of *leadership.
(3) A tactic for achieving promotion, recognition or status, despite being intellectually not up to it. Charismatic exhibitionists are entranced by their own mental ability; they try to control others, whom they tend to see as extensions of themselves, and they are intolerant of criticism. They tend not to believe that others have anything useful to tell them, they are liable to take more credit for success than is legitimate, they avoid acknowledging responsibility for failure, they make judgments with such confidence that others tend to believe them and, given the opportunity, they rush to fill positions of leadership. Motivated often by the best of intentions, they find it hard to believe that they could be wrong.[79]
(4) A tricky combination of (2) and (3): good ideas and leadership, but a lot of *bullshit too, and it can be hard to tell them apart.
*Intelligence, Fluency, Character.

CHARITY. (1) Assistance with money or time for a person or cause which lies outside the range of the giver's *reciprocal obligations; givers and receivers do not generally know each other's names; no reciprocal response is expected.
(2) Warm *manners. Manners on their own, for all their virtues, can sometimes suggest coldness and distance; charity cures this. It means, for instance, the manners to hold back from exploiting an advantage (e.g., in an argument); to suppose that the other person may have a case which works for her, though you do not agree; to care for a person, despite being, for the moment, angry, *bored, or exhausted; to be supportive to a person driven by an inspiration which may be more heroic than rational; to be alert to friends' needs, and to help them.

"Charity", the word, is needed because it does something love cannot do: you can decide to be charitable, but whether you can decide to love someone is open to question. Love is what you feel. Charity is what you do.
*Caritas, Compassion, Encounter, Gifts, Good Faith.

CHEIRARCHY (the first syllable rhymes with "sky"; Greek: *cheiros* hand + *archos* rule). The rule of hands—self-government by the people who are doing the work: making and sustaining their own local *institutions and *social capital, applying their own *judgment and *skills, participating in the *ecosystem, affirming the natural *authority of *presence.
*Lean Education.

41

CHOICE, THE FALLACY OF. The assumption that we do what we choose.

It sometimes happens that a well-intentioned friend or relation takes it as an assumption that the things you do in your life reflect choices that you have made. After all, if you hadn't chosen them, you wouldn't be doing them, would you? But it may not be as simple as that. You may find yourself committed, for instance, to your local *Transition initiative, or to any of the things you do as a citizen, because you believe that it has to be done, whether or not you have time for it and really enjoy doing that sort of thing more than, for instance, practising the flute. Or your energy may get "funnelled" (as the *Natural Step would put it) into Transition because you see no sensible alternative. In fact, the more you look at what "choice" means, the less clear it seems to be, and the less satisfying is the idea that choice actually determines what you do.

Is there a way of unpacking this clearly? Maybe not. But here is a start. The conditions that have to be met for a choice to exist are (a) that at least two options must be available, and (b) that they must be comparable—with a roughly agreed balance between what there is to gain (or lose). Okay so far.

But there is also the question of what choice actually means: given two comparable options, is a person free to make a choice between them at all—as distinct from observing the dictates of personality, experience and circumstance? There are two views about this: one of them is that nobody really makes any choices; they just respond to the various influences on them. The other view agrees that these influences can be important, but insists that people do actually make choices all the same, and that there is always an area of free will, or "sheer naked choice"; to deny this would take us into the nonsense of denying that people have responsibility for their actions.[80]

Now, to take this slowly. We need to distinguish between *before* the event and *after* the event. Before the event, there is a choice; there is free will: the person may not know how she will choose until she has chosen. The influences on her choice are a complex mixture: they include the actual circumstances of the case, and *also* a host of other things in which the person had no choice— like personality, *trust, experience, genetic endowment,

*intelligence and anxieties, hormones, health, and early training in personal responsibility. This mixture of circumstances may be too complex to allow a prediction of the outcome. The person feels free to choose: there is space to deliberate, something to think about.

After the event, matters become clearer: the choice was the product of all the circumstances over which, in the final analysis, the person had no control. But it *reveals* something about her: with hindsight, it is indeed explained: it could not have gone any other way. If any uncertainty remains, it tells us only that we still have not understood it properly.

And this in turn tells us something about *blame. If, after the event, a person's actions can be understood and explained, there is no "sheer naked choice", no free will to which blame can be attached—for, if everything can be explained (or could be explained if we knew the whole story), blame does not mean anything. *Judgment*, on the other hand, does have a meaning: although a person cannot be blamed for a wicked act, that does not mean we like what we see; *ethics and/or the *law can condemn it; she and the act can both be judged, and informed action can be taken. Judgment can be reached without being encumbered with agonising questions of blame.

So—now we know what choice means, we can go back to the two conditions that make it possible. Do we in our time have comparable options between which to choose? Well, the range of options is narrowing. There are few matters on which we can say, "Here we have a set of nice alternatives which are both available and comparable". Reasonable decision in the future will not be about choosing between responses that are available and comparable—but grasping at the single acceptable or least worst option. And if no such option exists, the remaining option will be to invent it.

*Causes, Freedom, Second Nature, Slack and Taut, Sustainability, Wicked Problems.

CIVIC SOCIETY. A developed *political economy; part of the sequence of civilisations which have risen and fallen during the last 10,000 years or so, whose traces are found in their architecture and artefacts.

Our own Western society—now reduced in *intelligence and *resilience, but much increased in *size and *complication in the form of the global *market economy—is the latest in that sequence. In fact, not all of them have fallen. China, for instance, has gone through many phases of creative destruction, or *kaikaku, none of them conclusive (*Unlean).

*Regrettable Necessities, Relative Intelligence, Touch-Down.

CIVILITY. The settled *manners which underwrite the existence of a republic. This is "republic" in the sense of a society whose members contributed to its *laws and decisions sufficiently to feel some sense of ownership, upholding the *freedom to build *communities with distinctive, individuated, *character and *common purpose.

CLIMACTERIC. A stage in the life of a system in which it is especially exposed to a profound change in health or fortune. One theory in early medical thinking was that climacterics occurred in the human life at intervals of seven years; a variant was that they occurred at odd multiples of seven years (7, 21, 35, 49, etc), and this survives in the use of "climacteric" as a name for mid-life hormonal changes. Climacterics for human society could be taken to include the end of the last ice age, and the beginnings of *agriculture and of industry.[81]

The climacteric considered in *Lean Logic* is the convergence of events which can be expected in the period 2010–2040. They include deep deficits in *energy, *water and *food, along with *climate change, a shrinking land area as the seas rise, and heat, drought and storm affecting the land that remains. There is also the prospect of acidic oceans which neither provide food nor remove carbon; ecologies degraded by introduced plants and animals; the failure of keystone species such as bees and plankton; and the depletion of minerals, including the phosphates on which we depend for a fertile soil.

This could be followed by economic and social fracture, taking *law and order with it, and the breakdown of *education systems able to pass on the essentials of culture and competence. And these events may be expected to lead to large movements of refugees and to steep reductions in *population comparable with those associated with the climacterics of previous civilisations. The large *infrastructures, such as those that transport energy, are likely to be out of commission. The constant supply of water, energy, money, security

and professional skills needed to prevent stores of high-level *nuclear waste from leaking and catching fire may not be available. Justice—which, in an affluent society, is seen as the only defensible criterion for judgment—will be open to new interpretations. This is deep, interconnected, planetary tragedy; grief reaches out to grief: one deep calleth another.[82]

As mentioned in the Introduction to this book, the breakdown of Roman society in Britain in the fifth century was followed by a retreat, not to the pre-Roman Celtic Iron Age, but to an earlier form without such simple artefacts as potters' wheels. To sustain even a technology as basic as pottery you need a supply chain to provide clay, wheels and kilns, some assurance of stability and peace, and customers who can pay—or who can at least be expected to be around long enough to keep their side of the *barter agreement or *reciprocal obligation. To crawl back towards this level of material comfort in post-Roman Britain took some four centuries. Small *communities made those conditions survivable.[83]

Lean Logic argues that community holds out at least a possibility of supporting *presence, social *cohesion, *economic realism, shared *cultural depth—and survival. In other words, the climacteric could be one of those rare historical turning points when society switches into a new mode of production—into a radically different way of using its resources; its labour, *capital and *land—changing its *expectations and values. The shift could be partly voluntary and partly an involuntary reaction to circumstances. Potentially, this could be an opportunity, for it is at such turning points that it is practical to make deep, *radical breakthroughs, before new conditions settle in which we can do little to change. We do not know, of course: the climacteric may be so severe that opportunity is the last thing on anyone's mind; this hinge of history may turn out to be just dust and grief, but if rational *judgment is to be salvaged from the depths where it has lain for so long, the coming climacteric could be the moment for it (*Systems Thinking ❭ Feedback ❭ Time).

It is unknown how fast the climacteric will develop. One view is that it will unfold as a slow deterioration—a long descent—with periods of respite allowing time for intelligent responses to be worked out and applied.[84] Another view is that, because our civilisation is so *connected, urbanised, and equipped with complex and fully-functioning energy and distribution systems — along with the property rights and financial systems that support them — the downturn will be more delayed than some expect: there is, as Adam Smith observed, a great deal of ruin in a nation.[85]

But when it comes, those tightly-connected dependencies will likely make it more abrupt. This is a typical pattern. The archaeologist Joseph Tainter summarises his review of the life and *death of civilisations,

> Collapse is a fundamentally sudden,
> pronounced loss of an established level of
> sociopolitical complexity.[86]

Core elements such as food provision depend on the whole sequence of cultivation and delivery working properly, all the time, from a benign climate and reliable supplies of oil, gas and electricity to *transport and distribution infrastructures, peace and social order, banking services and incomes. Yet when *complex systems break down, one failure can trigger more failures so fast that it seems almost instantaneous: shifts in the planet's *climate between icy and temperate have been abrupt; the financial crisis of 2008–2009 arrived in a flash, and the impact was crueller still because the rumblings we had been hearing for a few years had become so much part of life that we tended to discount them. The timing of the climacteric is uncertain.

In 2009, John Beddington, the chief scientific advisor to the UK government, forecast a "perfect storm" of food, energy and water shortages in 2030. Jonathon Porritt, chairman of the UK's Sustainable Development Commission, wrote that 2020 is more likely.[87] Richard Heinberg, the prolific commentator on energy and economics, proposed 2016 as his most optimistic (furthest postponed) date, but added,

> . . . the whole conversation makes sense only as a
> way of motivating coordinated action *prior to the
> crunch*. Once the unwinding has begun, no more
> preparation is possible. Our strategy must change
> from crisis prevention to crisis management.
> That's where we are right now, in my view.[88]

Previous *civic societies, having experienced their breakages, have typically — in the case, for instance, of the Roman civilisation of Western Europe — emerged in due course with a much reduced population to build decentralised, low-cost, local, lean *political economies; communities which have proved to be durable. The breakdown of the Chaco culture — which, until the early years of the twelfth century, lived in what is now the US state of New Mexico — followed many years of experiment with what we would now call *sustainable development: improvements in the *eco-efficiency of agriculture and economics in response to resource depletion (especially water and wood) and regional climate change. In this case, the shock took place quickly, shortly after the society's peak of wealth and artistic accomplishment. What followed was the Pueblo economy; the surviving remnant following the collapse. Jared Diamond writes:

> It took many centuries to discover that, among
> those economies, only the Pueblo economy was
> sustainable "in the long run", i.e., for at least a
> thousand years.[89]

In our own case, the crash, when it comes, is likely to be greater than those on previous occasions, with the joining up of all the elements extending beyond the regional shocks that have been experienced in the past. The regional climate changes that have affected our predecessors will, in our case, be global.[90]

There are no certainties here. It is not *certain that the climacteric as outlined here will happen. Some sustainable technologies are moving ahead rapidly; renewable energy is on course to transform the world's energy economies. The likelihood, however, is that the energy gap will open up as fossil fuels deplete, well before the renewables have had a chance to fill it, and that a solution to the *energy problem on its own will fall far short of holding off the other events whose combined weight can be expected — quite abruptly, and quite soon — to deintensify our political economy (*Intensification). Our social and economic order may be out of time.

And yet, the question about what the future holds does not really make any difference to what we decide now: there is just one way forward, and that is to build the sequel. The focus now should be on preparing with the aim of building a social order for the probably

ENDGAME
The scientist's view

Here, in summary, is another, earlier view of the climacteric, from a scientist's standpoint.

General Features of System Collapse

COLLAPSE

1. The central administrative organisation of the state collapses, with the disappearance of the hierarchy of government, almost complete disappearance of military organisation, abandonment of civic buildings such as palaces and temples, and effective loss of literacy.
2. There is disappearance of the traditional elite class, abandonment of their residences and of the manufacture of luxury goods.
3. The economy breaks down with near, or actual, cessation of large-scale distribution and market exchange, coinage, external trade, crafts, and agriculture apart from local subsistence.
4. There is "marked reduction in population density", with abandonment of many settlements in favour of a dispersed pattern of small settlements, often in defensible locations—the hills.

AFTERMATH

5. There is transition to a lower, or earlier, social order, with a "segmentary" society—that is, small settlements lacking any common political participation within a chiefdom or a state, although chiefdoms may form quite quickly. There may, however, be "possible peripheral survival of some highly organised communities still retaining several organisational features of the collapsed state". There may be remnants of religion in the form of folk cults and beliefs, and some crafts may survive as degraded imitations, especially in pottery. And it is to be expected that there will be "local movements of small population groups resulting from the breakdown in order at the collapse of the central administration (either with or without some language change), leading to destruction of many settlements".
6. There will be "Dark Age" myths as new power groups attempt to establish legitimacy by tracing connections with the former state.

COLIN RENFREW, "Systems Collapse as Social Transformation:
Catastrophe and Anastrophe in Early State Societies", 1979.[91]

diminished population of the future. That aim stands, whether it is realistic or not; and it stands, too, even if it is seen as an operation to *prevent* the shock, rather than to cope with its consequences.

The question to consider, therefore, is not whether the crash will happen, but how to develop the *skills, the will and the resources necessary to recapture the initiative and build the *resilient sequel to our present society. It will be the decentralised, low-impact human ecology which has always taken the human

story forward from the closing down of civilisations: *small-scale *community, *closed-loop systems, and a strong *culture.
*Lean Economy, Torments, Unintended Consequences, Wicked Problems.

CLIMATE CHANGE. The Earth's climate is part of an *ecological system which, despite spinning in cold space, manages to regulate its temperature and support life. Its ability to do so is shaped by three things:

C

1. Endowment: the physical properties of the Earth—its size and distance from the sun and moon; its continents and oceans; its life; the composition of gases; the laws of physics; the whole of its inheritance; the story so far.
2. Internal dynamics: the way in which the many parts of the *system interact, with *diversity and ingenuity.
3. Forcings: changes which are imposed from "outside". But what "outside" means is, of course, rather arbitrary, since it could reasonably be argued that most are part of *Gaia. So here it is simply affirmed that forcings consist of changes in the intensity of radiation from the sun; emissions of greenhouse gases arising from human activity; other human assaults on Gaia, such as the destruction of forests; and (a rare but spectacular forcing) meteorite strikes. Volcanic activity and discharges of methane are also taken to be forcings.[92]

The story of climate change in our time is one in which a massive intervention—a forcing—is in progress in the form of an imposed change to the composition of the atmosphere. The Earth's ability to get rid of excess heat is being damaged, with results that—if left unrepaired—will be as destructive to the planet's present *ecology as a breakdown in the removal of waste heat would be to any other living system.

The greenhouse gases which are responsible for this take their name from the key property of the glass in a greenhouse: it is transparent to short-wave radiation from the sun, but not to the long wave radiation (heat) that is generated when the sunlight comes into contact with material objects such as dust particles, water, vegetation or the ground. Greenhouse gases keep heat in. In small quantities, they do an essential job since, without them, Earth would be too cold to support life. But, like any other good thing, you can have too much of it. The greenhouse gases that are the *unintended consequence of industrial civilisation are present in excess.[93]

The six main greenhouse gases are these:[94]

- *Carbon dioxide* (CO_2), which is long-lived in the atmosphere, is the most important of the greenhouse gases. About half of the CO_2 emitted by man is quickly removed by fast processes such as photosynthesis. Other removal processes, such as absorption by the oceans, work on longer timescales, and the timescale for removal by weathering of rocks is longer still, so that some 20 percent remains in the atmosphere for thousands of years. Carbon dioxide is the product of combustion, respiration and decay; the default chemical that remains when the complex organic compounds from which life is made have broken down.[95]

Carbon itself is the defining element of organic chemistry—the chemistry of life—but (relative to the total quantity on the planet) the amount of carbon that actually participates in the living stages of the carbon cycle at any one time is minute. The great majority of it is safely stored out of the way in the rocks that, for the past four billion years, have by various means bonded it into their structures. Some of it is in more recent deposits of oil and gas. The quantity of carbon in the form of carbon dioxide that remains free in the atmosphere is tightly limited and regulated by the *ecosystem, whose most powerful instrument is photosynthesis by plants and algae in their various forms, on land and in the oceans. In excess, carbon dioxide would spell the death of the planet. The atmosphere of Venus, being thick with it (but also closer to the sun), scorches at a temperature of 450°C.[96]

- *Methane* (CH_4) is made when organic matter is decomposed by microorganisms in places which are both wet and low in oxygen, such as peat bogs, the guts of ruminants (e.g., cows) and decomposing forests on their way to becoming coal. There are very large quantities of methane frozen into the permafrost of the land and seabed of the high latitudes, buried in the peat bogs, or lying undisturbed in crystalline form in sea beds round the world. Generally, it stays put. The last time the Earth's methane was released in substantial quantities, some 251 million years ago, it raised the temperature so much, and turned the oceans so acid, that 95 percent of the species in existence on the planet at that time became extinct. This was the third Great Extinction—the Permian Extinction, the biggest of them all, coming statistically close to a complete elimination of life. If the permafrost of our own time were to thaw, in turn warming the sea by the few degrees needed to destabilise the crystals, methane would pour into our atmosphere, raising the temperature as it did so. That is not happening, as yet, on a scale which compares with the Third Extinction, but there is an amplifying *feedback here—methane emissions warm the atmosphere, causing more methane emissions—and the current rate of species decline is on a path which already has some scientists describing our own epoch as "The Sixth Extinction".[97]

Methane has only a short life in the atmosphere—half the methane emitted will be gone within twelve years, broken down to CO_2 and water—and much less methane (relative to carbon dioxide) is released into the atmosphere from human activities. And yet, a released tonne of methane has some 72 times the warming impact of a released tonne of carbon dioxide, over the first 20 years. Measured over 100 years, the climate impact is about 25 times that of the same mass of carbon dioxide. After taking all these factors into account, the Intergovernmental Panel on Climate Change (IPCC) estimates that the radiative forcing (total contribution to global warming) of anthropogenic methane emissions (i.e., those arising from human activity) is currently about 29 percent of that of carbon dioxide.[98]

- *Nitrous oxide* (N_2O)'s main anthropogenic source is from *agriculture, including the use of nitrogen fertiliser, biomass-burning and cattle-raising, and industrial processes such as the production of nylon.

  It has a lifetime of about 114 years in the atmosphere. Over 100 years the global warming potential of a tonne of nitrous oxide is about 298 times that of a tonne of carbon dioxide, but it is released in small quantities, and the IPCC estimates that its net impact is about 10 percent of that of carbon dioxide.[99]

- *Halogenated compounds* are synthetic chemicals in which one or more of the carbon atoms they contain is bonded with a halogen—chlorine, fluorine, bromine or iodine. Their stability makes them useful for pesticides (e.g., organochlorates), for the enrichment of *nuclear fuel (uranium hexafluoride), and for refrigerants such as CFCs.

Some halogenated compounds are now prohibited, notably CFCs and HFCs, because of the damage they do to the ozone layer, but they are long-lived, and those which were not listed in the 1988 rules on ozone depletion are still widely-used.

The global warming potential of these compounds is generally high—for example, HFC-23 has an expected life in the atmosphere of 270 years, and its global warming potential per kilogram, measured over 100 years, is about 14,800 times that of carbon dioxide—but they are released in low quantities, and the IPCC estimates a net impact of about 20 percent of that of carbon dioxide.[100]

- *Ozone* (O_3) in the lower atmosphere (tropospheric ozone) is a by-product of highly-energetic reactions such as photocopying and the combustion of fossil fuels, and of the action of sunlight on carbon dioxide, solvents and nitrous oxide. It has a life of only a few days, and its effects on the climate depend (for instance) on where it is, and its interactions with methane. The IPCC estimates that, overall, its impact is about 20 percent of that of carbon dioxide.[101]

- *Water vapour* (H_2O) is a significant greenhouse gas. The amount in the atmosphere depends mainly on the temperature, so that it has a gearing (amplifying/positive feedback) effect: the greater the warmth produced by atmospheric carbon dioxide, the greater the evaporation from the oceans, which tends to raise the temperature yet further. And the presence of water vapour in the atmosphere also affects the formation of clouds, whose impact on the climate is complex—both cooling (since clouds provide shade) and warming (since they keep the heat in).

In fact, both sides of the equation of forces which control atmospheric carbon dioxide levels (concentrations) are in trouble. Carbon is being emitted at the rate of about 8.7 billion tonnes per year (32 billion tonnes of carbon dioxide) by the burning of the fossil fuels (oil, gas and coal), with additions from the burning of forests and the draining of peat bogs; at the same time, the 'sinks' which take it out of the atmosphere (such as absorption by plants and oceans) are diminishing.[102]

Throughout the history of the Earth, the quantity of carbon dioxide in the atmosphere has varied widely and often, but there has been a pattern to it. Since the beginning of the more recent "ice ages" starting some 2.9 million years ago—actually a series of ice ages and interglacials, with each cycle lasting some 100,000 years—the quantity has been about 400 billion tonnes during the cold periods (the glaciations), and 600 billion tonnes during the warm periods (the interglacials). But that long-lived oscillation between deep cold and tolerable warmth may now have ended for a time. There are now more than 800 billion tonnes of carbon dioxide in the atmosphere, and rising.[103]

For the last twenty years, the implications of all this have been *monitored in detail by the Intergovernmental Panel on Climate Change. It was set up in 1988, and it has published major bodies of work—its Assessment Reports—in 1990, 1995, 2001 and 2007: landmark studies with wide (unpaid) participation. Now, time-lags are inevitable between the time of a scientific advance and the time when it is considered suitable for publication in a report. Often, the most important insights are those which it is hardest to be *certain about, and which may take many years to bring up to the level of verification which the IPCC ranks as "very likely", or justifying "high confidence". There is therefore a conservative bias in its work, but it nonetheless sets a standard and provides a common point of reference.[104]

In its 2007 report, the IPCC supplied estimates of the reduction in global emissions of carbon dioxide that would be required to maintain concentrations in the atmosphere within approximately the range in which we are now—350–400 parts per million (ppm). In order to achieve this, the IPCC finds that emissions of carbon dioxide would have to peak by 2015 and be reduced by between 50% and 85% (relative to 2000 levels) by 2050. The report adds that, even if this were achieved, the global mean temperature of the planet would continue to rise from the present 0.8°C above the pre-industrial equilibrium level, eventually settling at a new long-term equilibrium between 2°C and 2.4°C hotter.[105]

We have a comment on the implications of temperature rise from the climate scientist James Hansen. Hansen's projections of the consequences are not shared by the majority of climate scientists, but they do tell us something about the range of possibilities being debated at present:

> Global warming of 2–3°C above the present temperature [i.e., 2.8–3.8°C above pre-industrial levels] would produce a planet without Arctic sea-ice, a catastrophic sea level rise in the pipeline of around 25 metres, and a super drought in the American West, southern Europe, the Middle East and parts of Africa.[106]

Now, it is for the reader of the IPCC's work to make his or her own *judgment about its conclusions on the temperature rises in prospect. The starting point is to note that the IPCC's work is based on a combination of good data and good modelling. Its quality is explicitly discussed in the report, which gives three reasons to believe that the modelling is sound. First, it is based on established physical laws, such as the conservation of mass, energy and momentum, along with a wealth of observations. Secondly, it can predict events in the present climate in some detail, such as monsoon patterns and regional changes in temperature and pressure. Thirdly, the modelling performs well not only when it is asked to reproduce the essential features of the climate in the recent past, but also, in broad terms, older changes such as ocean temperatures during the last glaciation. The modelling is criticised by climate contrarians on the grounds that the science is biased by political pressure, by the system of grants that are more available to research which shows that there is a problem than to research that concludes that everything is just fine, and by the money to be made out of responses such as international *carbon credits. It would be surprising if climate science were an exception to the rule that everything that can be exploited will be exploited, but the field of climate and paleoclimate is one of the most brilliant and *necessary that has been opened up by science, and this is reflected in the modelling and in the current imperfect but impressive understanding of our planet as a dynamic living system.[107]

And yet, there is a problem here. The problem is not that the models may be exaggerating the changes in prospect, but that they may be underestimating them. Here are three things to consider:

C

1. *Feedbacks

There can be positive (amplifying) and negative (damping) feedbacks in any *system, where each effect knocks on to other effects which intensify, or reduce, the consequences. Negative feedbacks in the climate system include the stimulating effect of higher levels of CO_2 on the growth of plants, and the rise in the amount of dust in the atmosphere—produced by industrial activity, drought and loss of vegetation—reducing the amount of sunlight that penetrates. But such effects are recognised to be short-lived: the effect of CO_2 on plants peaks, easing off as concentrations rise, and the dust would clear after a week or two if industrial activity were to cease. The feedbacks that are most evident and likely to have the greatest impact are positive feedbacks.[108]

Positive feedbacks are difficult to model. First, there are a lot of them, and they include events which no one has thought of, and about which we know little. One example is the recent realisation that, as the ice sheets of Greenland melt, water pours down to the bed rock, creating a slippery surface which could enable very large sheets of ice to slide off into the sea, so that the melting of Greenland could unfold much faster than had been thought.

Secondly, there is the problem of "second-order" feedbacks, where one feedback triggers another which intensifies the first, or where it triggers several more, producing a range of feedbacks so complex that the difficulty of modelling rises exponentially. This is a familiar problem with drug testing: one drug can be tested in a straightforward way, but when it is tested for interaction with other drugs, things get complicated. If each drug had to be tested against all the other treatments or *foods to which a patient might be exposed, the permutations would increase exponentially, quickly exceeding the budget of any company (or the scope of any model). In the case of drugs the risk is more tolerable because the consequences of an unexpected interaction are individual, rather than global.

Here are some examples of feedbacks. No doubt all of them have been programmed into climate models somewhere, but the emergence of consensus about how severe they are, what the second-order feedbacks will be, and how they interact, could take some time:

- Ocean temperatures and mixing. At temperatures above 4°C, the specific gravity of water declines (the water becomes lighter). As a consequence, a layer of warmer water tends to rise and form at the surface of the ocean; this layer is then further warmed by sunlight and so becomes increasingly stable. This stability weakens the circulation of carbon-dioxide-rich water from the surface to the colder, deeper layers. But water that is already relatively saturated with CO_2 absorbs less CO_2 from the air. So the direct absorption of carbon dioxide from the atmosphere by the surface of the oceans is becoming less efficient as the temperature rises.[109]

- Ocean nutrients. A related effect of that warmer surface layer is that it prevents nutrient-rich water from the depths reaching the surface where it could support a population of plankton. Plankton are to oceans as grass is to meadows: when the surface water becomes sterile, plankton's vital role in absorbing carbon dioxide is not done.[110]

- Acidity. Even though the take-up of carbon dioxide by the ocean is impaired, higher concentrations in the atmosphere do lead to higher rates of absorption in direct chemical exchange, with the result that the oceans are becoming more acidic, turning into weak dilutions of carbonic acid. This is now building up towards levels which are lethal to marine organisms (including plankton) which are critical to the ocean's effectiveness in mopping up carbon dioxide. For instance, among the significant organisms from this point of view are the minute sea snails—pteropods—which use large quantities of carbon to form their calcium carbonate shells. They are essential to many marine ecosystems and, when they die, the carbonate falls to the seafloor. It has been shown that, in seawater at the level of acidity expected later this century, the integrity of their shells is destroyed.[111]

- *Decline in plants' ability to absorb carbon dioxide.* The effect of higher temperatures on plants has already been studied. At 2–3°C above pre-industrial levels, there are lengthening periods of the annual cycle during which vegetation becomes a source of carbon dioxide, adding to the carbon dioxide which is already in the atmosphere, rather than absorbing it as a sink.[112]

- *The impact of drought on forests.* There is an increasing loss of vegetation available to soak up the spare carbon. This is happening for several reasons. The tropical forests of South America are getting drier, and there are already signs of dieback. Stretches of the forest depend on each other, in the sense that much of the rain that falls on one area is promptly recycled, being taken by air currents to fall again and again on other areas of the forest further along. This means that if one area fails the rain will not be recycled, and the other areas will quickly dry out, releasing carbon dioxide in large quantities as they do so. And if the forest survives drought, it may not survive fires that follow. The fire releases most of the carbon the forest absorbed during its lifetime, together with the carbon stored in its soil.[113]

- *Albedo.* Snow and ice reflect back into space most of the solar energy that reaches them. As the ice retreats, the dark surfaces of the land and sea are revealed, so that most of the solar energy that reaches them is absorbed, increasing the rate of warming. This effect is well established in the models, but that has not banished surprise. For instance, the rate of melting of the Arctic sea ice is now acknowledged to be higher than the models have generally predicted. If, or when, the Arctic is ice-free, then there will be consequences for the Greenland ice sheet, as discussed in the following.[114]

- *The stratosphere.* The sequence is complex and it is not surprising that it has only recently been (tentatively) described:

> The troposphere—the lowest layer of the atmosphere (about the first 10 kilometres)—warms up as carbon dioxide concentrations rise.
> ↓
> So less heat escapes from it, and this in turn cools the next layer—the stratosphere (between 10 and 30 kilometres up).
> ↓
> The cooling changes the energy distribution in the stratosphere in a way which increases wind speed, particularly that of the 'stratospheric jet' which circles the Arctic, especially in the winter.
> ↓
> The stratospheric jet influences the speed of the warm westerlies in the troposphere, and they become faster, too.
> ↓
> The westerlies drive further into the Arctic, warming it, and contributing to a further cooling of the stratosphere . . .[115]

2. *Abrupt changes*

The typical graph we see, illustrating the rise in temperature and carbon dioxide concentrations over the years, is smooth. But *complex systems do not keep to such behaviour. They may mature smoothly and incrementally, but when they break down, they do so abruptly; breakdown tends to be untidy and messy and, as the stresses on the climate build, it becomes increasingly probable that the tension will snap. The IPCC recognises the likelihood of abrupt change affecting aspects of the system—and perhaps especially the ice sheets—and it adds, "If a large-scale abrupt climate change were to occur, its impact could be quite high."[116]

In fact, it is only since ice cores from Greenland have been studied—with their preserved record of temperatures and conditions back through the

C

whole of the last glaciation and into the temperate Eemian interglacial period that preceded it—that the truth about a fundamental property of the climate has dawned. The Holocene period in which we live, which started some 15,000 years ago, has been untypical in one fundamental way: it has been remarkably stable, by the standard of the climate's previous behaviour.[117] But turbulence is deep in the nature of *Gaia, and even the Holocene has had its ups and downs . . .

- From the end of the last glaciation to about 3500 BC, the area of Northern Africa which we now know as the Sahara Desert was a lush forested region of intense sunshine, reliable rain, massive rivers and *water-loving animals such as *hippos and crocodiles. The precession of the Earth (the slight wobble as it spins) had helpfully positioned the region for the fullest possible intensity of the sun during the summer, causing strong convection currents of rising warm air which drew in rain. Abruptly, it came to an end: when the precession shifted, the ecosystem changed into the rainless desert which we know today.[118]

- The Mayan civilisation in the Yucatan Peninsula (Mexico) was 2,500 years old and apparently flourishing when, between the eight and tenth century (about the start of the Medieval Warm Period) it was hit by a series of droughts, by which it was completely destroyed.[119]

- The four-century-long Medieval Warm Period which began in the tenth century had vineyards growing in Derbyshire, provided the agricultural wealth which paid for the cathedrals, and lured a Norse colony to settle in Greenland.

- The Little Ice Age that followed destroyed the Norse colony and provided the intense cold represented in the European snow scenes painted by Breugel and Hendrick Averkamp. Iceland, being surrounded by ice for many miles, could not be approached by shipping. Intensely cold weather in North America brought conditions which decisively ended the earliest colonists' attempt to live off the *land on Roanoke Island in Virginia. In Italy, wood grew

exceptionally slowly in the cold, providing the dense maple and spruce used by Antoni Stradivari for his violins.[120]

- The most dramatic climate shock, 13,800 years ago, was the Younger Dryas event, named after a *small, but hardy, white rose that thrived in cracks in exposed rocks between the ice, in an environment that practically no other plant could stomach. This was the 1,500 year encore at the end of the last glaciation, when meltwater from the giant Lake Agassiz covering much of the American Midwest burst through the ice dam which had contained it, and flooded into the North Atlantic—the place where the warm Gulf Stream reaches the end of its world tour, sinks deep beneath the surface, and heads back south. The driver of this circulation is the interaction between the salt water and the very cold temperatures: as salt water reaches freezing point, it separates out into fresh water and *very* salt water. The fresh water then freezes, while the very salt water sinks towards the seafloor, and this acts as a pump which pulls the Gulf Stream's surface water north, while pushing the cold, salt water down into the depths for the return journey. When the fresh water from Lake Agassiz flowed into the area it diluted the salt water so much that there was not enough of it to drive the pump, and the Gulf Stream stopped. Without its warming effect, Northern and Central Europe was back under ice and tundra.

With the exception of the Younger Dryas—which really belongs to the preceding glaciation more than to the Holocene—these events were comparatively minor and localised, relative to the violent changes which preceded the Holocene as far back as current *ingenuity allows us to see. This earlier record is one of Dansgaard-Oeschger events—short, (century-long) periods of respite from the deep cold of the ice age—and Heinrich events—longer periods of deep cold—and the dramatic lurches into the depth of the glaciations themselves. Climate history, apart from the special case of our own benign Holocene, has been a story of abrupt fluctuations. An apt analogy is the confused behaviour of a driveway light, activated by movement: when you approach it in the twilight it doesn't know whether it's night (when it is meant to switch itself on) or day (when it isn't), so it switches neurotically on and off. It has only two states: it is a *binary system; it doesn't do *moderation.[121]

Except that, in the case of the climate, the two states—icy vs. temperate—that have existed for the last three million years may not apply in the future, because the planet is being presented with a new situation. The quantity of carbon dioxide in the atmosphere is outside the range of the whole of that period; and the planet has *never* before experienced high levels of carbon dioxide while at the same time supporting ice caps at the poles. This is disequilibrium on a new scale. It won't stay put: disequilibria never do. In the past, the change from warmth to ice and back again has represented an oscillation "between two apparently quasi-stationary stages". When it moves, it tends to move fast—over a period of twenty years or less. As the disequilibrium of high carbon dioxide levels coexisting with icecaps has not been known before, there is no observational basis here for scientific confidence. And yet it is certainly outside the established range of periods of sustained warmth followed by sustained periods of cold. When equilibrium has been dislodged, giving way to disequilibria, we can expect chaotic, surprising and sometimes violent interactions, over a long period. From the planet's point of view, the new turbulence could be normal.[122]

3. *Politics and practicalities*

Concentrations of carbon dioxide, along with all the other gases in the atmosphere with an impact on global warming, are already in a state of "overshoot". If we are to have any chance of maintaining the climate system in the relative stability of the Holocene period, they would need to be brought down from the roughly 390 parts per million (ppm) in 2010 to 320 ppm or less. The timescale is *fuzzy, with scientific opinion ranging in emphasis: there is the view that the reduction has to be "as soon as possible" (ideally tomorrow morning)—that is, an almost immediate cessation of carbon emissions, together with extensive reforestation and an end to any further felling of forests or exploitation of peat

bogs anywhere in the world, might have a chance of making useful progress in the right direction. And there is the view that it is not so much the timing that matters, as the cumulative emissions— although, of course, the downturn must be soon and steep if those cumulative emissions are to be kept within the needed limits.[123]

The best that international debate can aim for at present is stabilisation at 450 ppm. Even this would require deep cuts in emissions, starting soon. In fact, after a peaking point no later than 2015, emissions of carbon dioxide and its equivalents from all energy and industrial processes would have to fall by 4 percent each year. At the same time, emissions from deforestation would have to cease (if they didn't, emissions from energy and industrial processes would need to fall by as much as 6.5 percent each year, as a kind of nominal compensation). Is that going to happen?[124]

If not, try something more realistic—a turning point of 2020, followed by a reduction of emissions by 3 percent each year. That would eventually lead to a notional stabilisation at 650 ppm. It is "notional" because it assumes that there are no feedbacks. At 650 ppm of CO_2 (or the equivalent, when all greenhouse gases are considered), the temperature would rise to around 4°C above pre-industrial levels. The effects of this would, in turn, carry the planet up to six degrees above pre-industrial levels, and to a level of trauma comparable to the Permian Extinction.[125]

Points of inflexion: where the curve changes direction

We do not know what is going to happen, but we do not need to be completely *innocent of any suspicion about what might happen. Here are three possible sequences:

1. *Methane*

The very large stores of methane on the planet are maintained mainly by low temperatures, with the methane on land and at sea in the Arctic kept stable under a lid of permafrost. However, there are signs that escapes of methane from these stores have already begun, and that this is beginning to take the form of a major feedback, with decisive potential.

C

In September 2008, researchers off the north coast of Siberia observed the sea foaming with gas bubbling up through "methane chimneys" from the seafloor; the conclusion they have drawn is that the permafrost seabed is melting. Orjan Gustafsson, one of the leaders of the expedition, comments,

> Yesterday, for the first time, we documented a field where the release was so intense that the methane did not have time to dissolve into the seawater but was rising as methane bubbles to the sea surface.[126]

The climate scientist Sarah Raper points out that the interpretation of observations such as these is difficult, owing to the lack of a baseline with which to compare it:

> The trouble is we don't know if this is 'normal' or not—i.e., we don't have a long historical record to look at.[127]

But we do know that, unless there are compensating feedbacks, methane releases set up classic positive feedback as the higher temperatures produced by more methane lead to the escape of yet more methane.

2. *The Gulf Stream*

It is possible that all the summer sea ice in the Arctic will have disappeared before the end of the decade 2011–2020. The substantially higher Arctic temperatures that will follow will speed up the melting of the Greenland ice cap, pouring vast quantities of cold fresh water into the North Atlantic. We do not how great the loss of salinity (saltiness) and change in sea temperature would have to be for the Gulf Stream to break down as it did in the Younger Dryas, nor how long it would take. But if that flow of water stopped, it could lower the temperatures of Northern Europe to the point at which its *agriculture becomes impossible, at the same time as drought develops in the lower latitudes.

Conditions would be similar to those of the Younger Dryas although, in our own day, things would be complicated by the high level of greenhouse gases in the atmosphere, which would tend to make the lower latitudes considerably warmer than

they were in the Younger Dryas. They might also moderate the cold in the northern latitudes, but the absence of a Gulf Stream—and less tropical forest to sustain the flows of water vapour and heat away from the lower latitudes—could create conditions for large temperature differences between the low latitudes and the poles. Storms could be expected.[128]

So, will the Gulf Stream stop? We don't know. But try that as your report to a general, whose whole information set consists of uncertainty. Reconnaissance does not present a collection of *disconnected uncertainties. It builds up a picture. And the picture is one of interlinked stabilising mechanisms across the planet being driven close to the edge.

3. *Reprieve*

There is, evidently, something about the Holocene era which has enabled it to maintain relative stability, in spite of a continued record of disturbances related to the sun—changes in the Earth's orbit, its tilt precession (wobble), and variations in the amount of radiation it receives. The stability has survived despite the invention of agriculture, which itself was a substantial source of carbon dioxide and methane, and shocks such as the drying-up of the Sahara region. We are, at the time of writing, still living under the benign regime of the Holocene.

At the same time, the world's stock of oil, gas and coal is declining (*Energy Prospects), and the option of reducing consumption at a rate much faster than energy resource depletion alone would impose would open up if *nation after nation were to take up the use of *TEQs (Tradable Energy Quotas), within an effective global reduction framework. Even the sun seems to be lending a helping hand; at present it is getting by on reduced power, and this will be in our favour for the early decades of the century. So we may have good luck and hope on our side; we may scrape through. Not without surprises, but with the possibility of being shocked and shaken into a better frame of mind, good order and improved *judgment.[129]

From the point of view of deciding what to do, it does not matter which (if any) of the above three sequences come to pass. There is only one way forward, and that is to reduce carbon emissions on a trajectory of decline much steeper than seems reasonable or comfortable, and to turn at last to the ingenuity and *good faith of people to achieve unreasonable results. The point is not that we know what will await us if we don't do these things, but that we know what resources of invention and *intelligence are available to us if we do. The information technology that we carry in our heads has been underestimated of late. If this were activated, it could, just possibly, be a match for the melting Greenland ice sheet and the bubbling methane.

In the end, this is a matter of good housekeeping; a *practical skill which has been devalued in a regime preoccupied with the magic of constant *growth. We are looking now for something more down-to-earth and less fantastic: the individual and collective *empowerment of *lean thinking.

*Climacteric, Self-Deception, Butterfly Effect, Unintended Consequences, Systems Thinking, Resilience.

CLOSED ACCESS. A *necessary condition for the management of a *commons. With limited numbers of people within its boundaries, the demands made on it, too, are limited, making them realistic and *sustainable.

The members of a managed commons must undertake to comply with the rules necessary for its maintenance; it follows that they must exclude others who do not comply with those rules, or whose demands would exceed the limits of what it can supply.

The principle underlying this is known as "subtractivity", or "rivalness"—the idea that what one person harvests from a resource subtracts from the ability of others to do the same. There is a simple recognition here of the objective reality of the resource: it has its limits, and no amount of technical trickery or *emotional pleading can make that fact go away. Recognising subtractivity is a case of growing up—as in realising that the powers of your parents to provide are not unlimited; moving on from the child-think of unqualified confidence that the *political economy you live in can provide.[130]

And a second principle follows from this. If the resource is limited, then there has to be some way of excluding people who, if their access were unlimited, would destroy it. That is, there has to be a way of defending it, which may be relatively straightforward in the case of, say, farmland, but is harder in the case of a fishery, or a forest, or a river, or a culture, or an atmosphere with a limited ability to absorb *waste; it is also harder when the damage caused by exceeding the limits will only become evident in the future, by which time it may be too late to repair.[131]

This is an especially difficult problem for a super-scale *civic society such as our own. Our *size, *growth and *technical powers insulate us for a time from having to think about the limits to the resources we depend on. There therefore seems to be no need to think about the cost of *protecting them. Maybe we can all be free riders, benefiting from assets which we have done nothing to produce or protect: we can affirm a liberal right to be a free rider. It is an attractive, inclusive philosophy. It would be immoral to disagree with it—until, that is, it comes face-to-face with the laws of physics.

For the human societies to which the laws of physics are more immediately evident, closed access is the determining and shaping property of their *culture. This does not by any means imply a Scrooge-like hoarding of an underused resource without regard for the needs of other people who could make use of it. Closed access, once established as the enabling condition for the sustainable management of the commons, can provide the foundations for an extensive and rich culture of sharing and generosity: it can be expected to allow access to others for particular purposes, such as harvesting medicinal plants, or hunting a prey across the territory; it is able up to a point to share the proceeds on a regular basis.[132] Sometimes a softening of strict closed access extends to "sleeping territoriality", in which, say, a Pacific island reserves the right to exclusive access of a fishing-ground, but applies it only at times of scarcity.[133] What we might see as uncaring exclusion is seen by the participants in a closed-access commons as responsibility, as belonging to the land:

> Expression of worldview through respect, patience and humility; and people being viewed as a part of nature are common in traditional communities. The Lax'skiik and Gitksan of British Columbia, in general, have a personal and spiritual identification with their territories and resources, which form the basis of their cultural and economic life.[134]

C

But, in order for qualities of sharing and altruism to happen, the responsibility of a particular group, and their ability to sustain the commons and determine access to it, must be unambiguously defined:

> . . . the management of common property
> is impossible unless the land is owned by a
> well-defined community.[135]

The alternative is the 'Tragedy of the *Commons', the destruction of a common resource as individuals make ever-greater demands on it, benefiting from what they can get individually, but not seeing as their problem the damage done by those ever-greater demands to the commons as a whole.

In a society used to cheap travel, and to the idea that destruction—when it comes to *boundaries and the *rhetoric about "tearing-down barriers"—is a good thing, the idea of closed access at first invites unease; there is a sense both of being locked-in, and of unfairly locking-out. But in fact it works the other way. Almost wherever you go in the *market economy, you find yourself in the same place—in the globalised market with its shared banality, its fullness; at the end of every lane is a busy road and a housing estate like the one at the beginning of it.

You cannot get *out* of a *globalised world, because there is no *out*. Closed access does not mean closed-in, it means the protection of distinctiveness: when you are out, you are somewhere else, in a different *in*.
*Boundaries and Frontiers, Open Access Fallacy, Closed-Loop Systems, Climate Change.

CLOSED-LOOP SYSTEMS. There is a fiercely rigorous definition. In a closed-loop (aka "closed") system, Kenneth Boulding explains,

> There are no inputs from outside and no out-puts to the outside; indeed, there is no outside at all. Closed systems, in fact, are very rare in human experience, in fact almost by definition unknowable, for if there are genuinely closed systems around us, we have no way of getting information into them or out of them; and hence if they are really closed, we would be quite unaware of their existence. We can only find

out about a closed system if we participate in it. Some isolated primitive societies may have approximated to this, but even these had to take inputs from the environment and give outputs to it. All living organisms, including man himself, are open systems.[136]

And there is a more relaxed understanding where the system is "closed" only with respect to *materials, while allowing energy and information in and out. But even that has problems. Living systems produce *waste which, unless released to another system, would become toxic and destroy them; or, to see it from another point of view, every activity involves some disordering and dissipation, along with losses of materials, and it is only outside systems—that is, systems working to different rules—that can do the necessary re-ordering and re-supply. So, unless we think of a material exchange system on a vast scale such as that of the planet, there is no such thing as a closed-loop system. Tim Jackson writes,

> The concept of a "no waste economy" is just an illusion. No such thing can exist.[137]

So we have to be content with a pragmatic view which looks to the benefits of a system being "roughly" closed—being substantially self-sufficient because it recycles most of what it uses.

And here a further source of vagueness comes in: it is impossible to be exact as to which closed-loop system we are talking about. For every large system, there are many *holons (smaller systems, subsystems or subassemblies) within it, and even smaller ones within these. Yes, a degree of self-sufficiency applies at every level in this hierarchy, but if the *hierarchy as a whole is to work this is largely due—especially at the lower levels—to the exchanges and interdependences. That is, exchange and self-sufficiency are complementary, with interdependence becoming weaker—systems becoming more realistically closed—at the higher levels.[138]

If that nuanced structure degrades—if it blows up to an enormous *size and loses its *harmonic order—the default position it will triumphantly but briefly enjoy will be a through-and-through open system, importing orderly materials (i.e., materials with low *entropy), and then dissipating them.

So the property that a *resilient system looks for is not the elimination of openness, but limits to it: it uses the exchange and recycling of surpluses and wastes at lower levels as enabling conditions by which higher levels can achieve greater degrees of self-reliance.

Closed-loop systems in *Lean Logic*, then, are systems or *communities that have worked out how, collectively, to reuse most of their materials. For a natural ecology, this is routine, a *necessary condition for its existence; in an *open system such as a *market economy, this condition is absent. For a community intent on a degree of eco-independence, the closed-loop system is a necessity; in a sense the definition of what it is aiming to do. To maintain a closed-loop system, it will need to establish and conserve the *small-scale, attuning to the *elegance of not needing a vast infrastructure of *regrettable necessities. It will conserve its foundation *capital in the form of fertile soils, a conserved genetic and *cultural endowment and a *protected *climate, and it will limit access and scale to levels which will not lead relentlessly to that foundation capital being destroyed.

Closed-loop systems are, at best, an approximation. The principle does, however, provide the central, elementary principle by which the burnout, dissipation, and *entropy of the human ecology could, perhaps for the long term, be delayed.

COGNITIVE DISSONANCE. A condition of anxiety or internal conflict which arises when new information, or pressure from other people, is in *conflict with an opinion which has already been settled, or an action which has already been taken.

Possible responses include a deliberate attempt to explain away the new information, or to block it out. If this fails, rationalisation may allow the person to come to terms with the decision by deciding that it was all right, after all—coping with the unbearable by learning to like it.

Ultimately, there remains the risk, or possibility, of switching—*calibrating—suddenly to a new position.[139]
*Wishful Thinking, Diplomatic Lie, Galley Skills, Special Pleading.

COHESION. Society's ability to hold itself together over a long period, despite stresses which would otherwise break it apart. The *market economy is an effective

system for sustaining social order: the distribution of goods, services and other assets is facilitated by buying and selling, supporting a *network of exchange to which everyone has *access. But if the flow of income fails, the powerfully-bonding combination of *money and self-interest will no longer be available on its present all-embracing scale, and perhaps not at all. It will then be necessary to rely instead on the cohesive properties of a robust common *culture, and the *loyalties and *reciprocities supported and sustained within it. Without this, there will be no basis for a cohesive society. And that, of course, is putting it mildly, because the time-interval between the demise of the market and the birth of a cohesive culture may be expected to be turbulent.

Reliance on the market economy has led to the asset of a common culture falling into neglect; sometimes we pick through the ruins like tourists marvelling at a lost settlement and guessing at what was once there. It would be helpful—though late in the day—to stop dismantling what remains of a culture in today's *political economy, and to start to re-grow cultural and *artistic links as an essential basis for cohesion in a future which, from where we sit, will be barely recognisable.[140]
*Casuistry, Civility, Humour, Trust, Play, Public Sphere and Private Sphere.

COMMON CAPABILITY. An aim which becomes available if and only if it is a collective aim—the transformation in possibility that takes place when others join your focus on achieving something. It is the opposite of the Fallacy of *Composition, which deals with the case where something which is possible for one person (e.g., the pleasures of a deserted beach) is not available for all. Common capability, by contrast, underpins the whole phenomenon of *civic societies in every age: it is possible to travel by train only because lots of other people want to do so; it is possible to build pyramids, viaducts or a Roman Forum because many others are after the same thing.

Common capability is critically significant for *sustainable *resilience because many of the things that have to be done to achieve it are only possible if many other people are involved. For example, the measures which a household can take to develop its *lean energy potential are significant, but it is common

C

capability, rather than individual best efforts, that will achieve the transformation in patterns of *land use and movement—the *localisation—that will become the foundation of a resilient future.[141]

*Common Purpose.

COMMON PURPOSE. Common purpose is a shared intention to achieve a shared goal, where collective aims are advanced by the individual purpose, and individual aims are advanced by the collective purpose. *Common Capability, Emergence, Presence, TEQs (Tradable Energy Quotas).

COMMONS, THE. A common-pool resource, such as *land, or a marine fishery, or a *community, whose benefits are shared amongst the people who use it or live in it.

Private property rights are, by comparison, straightforward: the owner has (or can reasonably be presumed to have) a sense of responsibility towards the property he or she owns, and a desire for its continuity. He or she will stand to gain from its improvement over the long term, or lose if it deteriorates. There are many *exceptions to this, but the record of care for land where an individual has autonomy—as in the case of a family farm—is good. In fact it does not have to be literal ownership which is the issue here; what matters is the freedom to manage it as the user thinks fit, the *expectation of being able to go on doing so for a long time to come, and the belief that there is some point to the exercise, since he knows for (almost) sure that, when the fruits of harvest come in, no one is going to show up with a wagon, claim possession of them and carry them off.

In contrast with that, there is common ownership. There is no limit to the amount of work a commoner in this sense can put into the shared asset; the difficulty is that there is no guarantee that he or she will stand to benefit from it. This is the "Tragedy of the Commons". Here is how it works (or, rather, doesn't work). Imagine a group of grazers on the local commons, which is already well-stocked with their sheep. It could support more but, with each additional sheep,

there is additional damage to the grass and a decline in the extra yield that the extra sheep will produce for its owner. There is a decreasing *marginal* return, but that might be thought tolerable so long as, with each additional sheep, the commons' total yield is greater. As more sheep are added, however, there comes a point at which, with the extra sheep, the total yield itself will shrink: there is decreasing *average* return. The commons has reached the point of maximum yield, and is poised to fall if any further demands are made on it.

And yet, one of the grazers (Gian) now adds one more sheep. The extra sheep reduces the total yield, but it is hard to do anything about it, because Gian gets the whole of the benefit of the extra sheep, yet the damage it causes is shared out among all the grazers. So, here we have a problem. The individual (Gian) is clearly better off, even though all the other grazers are worse off. But if it is rational for Gian as an individual to add his extra sheep, it will be rational for everybody else, so long as they see the matter just from their own individual point of view, and don't talk to each other enough. The result is that, with tragic inevitability, the commons will be overgrazed. If every grazer tries to compensate for his subsequent losses by adding more sheep of his own, it will be destroyed.

It was the ecologist Garrett Hardin who called this the Tragedy of the Commons, and the conclusion he drew is that common resources cannot be sustained in good health by the people who use them and benefit from them unless they are protected from exploitation by an overriding authority. If they are unprotected, every individual will be able to extract what he or she can from it until it is no use to anybody.[142]

The controlling authority whose job it would be to stop this happening is in effect the "Leviathan" proposed by Thomas Hobbes (1588–1679) who, following the troubles of the English Civil War, concluded that an essential condition for an orderly society is an authoritarian sovereign, with power limited only by a *contract to keep the peace and by his responsibility to God. It is a view which (with modifications) has remained influential. And so has

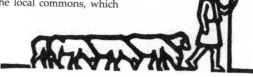

Hardin's approach to understanding the treatment of common assets, with its tragic *implications of an inevitable decline which only powerful authority can avert.[143]

What is wrong with it? Well, often there is nothing wrong with it. It certainly applies in the case of fisheries in our own time, a clear tragedy of the marine commons. And yet, it tells only part of the story—it applies just to *open access commons. This is the situation where there is free access, where anyone who feels like using the commons (fishers, grazers, etc) simply goes ahead and uses it. Commoners in this situation will indeed typically treat the commons in ways which work just for themselves, but which destroy it when everyone else does the same thing.

If the commons are closed and *bounded, however, things are different. There is now some point in *protecting it because the commoners can be confident that its wealth is not going to be stolen or destroyed by others who have no *interest in its preservation. The *closed access enables collective responsibility and awakens *common purpose. The boundedness keeps the scale small enough for the people in it to have eye contact with each other, to sustain *trust, and to have a sense of individual and collective confidence: I can make a difference; we can make it work.[144]

Now the commoners can prevent overgrazing: they can prevent both overuse by existing grazers and additional demands by new arrivals. The scope of *responsibility is clearly defined; there is an implicit or explicit contract which requires members to comply with the conditions of membership. As the naturalist Richard Mabey writes, Hardin "clearly knew nothing of the commons system in England, or for that matter in peasant societies throughout the world, where rootedness and neighbourliness made self-regulation second nature."[145]

Some twenty years after publishing his paper, Hardin acknowledged that the 'Tragedy of the Commons' is a problem that does not apply to self-managing closed-access commons and, seemingly without realising it, he stumbled on the fundamental requirement of a responsibly-managed commons: its *scale has to be limited (and the critical maximum size here is around 150—the largest *group size capable of establishing a network of *reciprocity and cooperation among people who know each other's names):

Perhaps we should say a community below 150 really is managed—managed by conscience. [But such] scale effect rules out the unmanaged commons as an important political possibility in the modern world.[146]

By building up "nested" *hierarchies of groups, each consisting of not more than 150, much larger commons can be sustained.

In summary, then: if the commons are closed in the sense of being able to limit the demands that are being made on them—and if they have dealt with the size problem in a way which enables that to happen—then they have the fundamental requirements for effective self-management. Indeed, once these two related conditions are recognised, it turns out that the problem is in a sense the *opposite* way round from Hardin's original analysis: without any network of *reciprocal obligations to restrain it, it is all too likely that a controlling authority—Leviathan—would plunder and destroy the commons which it was there to protect; a case of the fox set to guard the chickens.[147]

The *authority structure that works is the bottom-up one, where the community of users takes responsibility for the commons. In these circumstances, they can effectively limit the demands made on it to a level that will sustain it as an asset. From the perspective of history—though not in our time, with the present mismanagement of the ocean a tragic and exact illustration of the problem Hardin pointed out—closed access is the normal arrangement; open access is an *anomaly.

The Managed Commons: conditions for successful management

Here is the set of conditions needed for a self-regulating commons, developed by the scholar who has done most to advance our understanding of them, Elinor Ostrom. There are eighteen. Those two primary principles, above—closed access and a manageable size—are really places to start and they are implicit throughout, but to keep Ostrom's sequence intact, they are listed, respectively, as conditions 4 and 11.

The whole set is summarised here in terms a little less technical than Ostrom's—but for readers who would like to read each headline definition in exactly the language of the maestro herself, they are set out in the endnotes.[148]

C

This first group of four conditions tells us something about the commons itself (also termed the "resource", or "common-pool resource"), and about what the task of managing it and using it involves. Not every productive natural ecology has the potential to be a commons. Here are Ostrom's four conditions in this group:

1. *It is worth the attempt.* The task must be seen as realistic in that the common resource has not deteriorated so far that it can never be brought back; commoners recognise that, if restored and/or maintained, it will be a useful asset.[149]

   Like many of the conditions for a feasible commons, this seems no more than common sense. People won't set about building a collective asset if all around them there is such devastation that they see no point in trying, nor if the amount of work and the time it will take to get results are too great for them to see any benefit. Nor—at the other extreme—will they do so if, on the evidence of the present, they don't see a problem that needs fixing (but sometimes enlightened *leadership can change such perceptions).[150]

2. *Good information.* Management of the commons needs quick and easy access to information on its condition.[151]

   This is *feedback—but Ostrom prefers to write of "indicators", and there is a reason for this. Commons may be large and complex, and keeping track of their condition now, and of signs of problems to come, can be difficult (for a story of indicators on the health of fishing-grounds—and the informal information that may provide the best indicators—see *Harmless Lunatic).[152]

   Here are two relevant aspects of feedback. First, we have the idea of "adaptive management", which means learning-as-you-go. It sees the task of managing a commons as a series of experiments which will deal out success and failure in uncertain ways, but from which at least you can learn. And that is not a process that is ever really completed because, on the strength of what you have learned, you are likely to try something new, so you are back into uncertainty again. In other words, your approach evolves (*Kaizen).[153]

Secondly, Ostrom is emphatic about the connection between good understanding of a resource and—well, *conversation. A strongly-motivated group in stable conditions, with the opportunity for trial and error, and a lot of interactions between its members, "will tend to discover those strategies that an omniscient individual would have selected". Here is an information source not to be neglected: with the benefit of conversation and persistence there is a reasonable chance of being able to work out what to do, and how to do it—more or less perfectly.[154]

3. *Flow and predictability.* The commoners will need a roughly predictable flow of benefits (rather than the occasional windfall).[155]

   Flow (one of the five rules of *lean thinking), lies at the heart of there being any possibility of making sense of the commons. Here we have some benign regularity, where quite small variations show up clearly; the feedback coming from the system is intelligible. This is the "quiet life" condition at the heart of an effective commons, and its absence has tragic potential—turbulent conditions and constant change may actually stop you perceiving or taking the action needed to do anything about them: turbulence can be self-reinforcing.

   But, of course, the quiet life too has its dangers, for if change happens slowly you may not notice it until it has reached the stage when the turbulence returns. Ostrom cites the example of *population,

   > When the resource base itself grows very slowly, population growth may exceed the carrying capacity before participants have achieved a common understanding of the problem they face.[156]

4. *Manageable *scale.* The resource needs to be small enough for those *responsible for it to be aware of the local detail.[157]

   In *Lean Logic* (as in the introduction to this entry and in condition 18 below), scale is mainly about the numbers of people involved, but here it is about the physical size of the commons. If the actual area involved is very large, it is impossible to sustain closed access: you cannot *monitor the boundaries, nor can you really know what is going on within the area itself. There are two main responses to this problem: reduce the scale to a level that can be monitored, or subdivide it into smaller ("nested") areas within the authority of a larger group charged by those below it with responsibility for the whole.[158]

THE PEOPLE

The second set of conditions is about the commoners—or would-be commoners—themselves:

5. *Intention. The commoners need to believe that the success of the enterprise will bring results that they want. They must know what they want, and know that if they do not take the necessary action themselves, no one else is going to do it for them.[159]

6. Common understanding. There must be agreement in the community about the nature of the task and about the contribution that their actions can make towards it.[160]

    This is close to *Lean Means. Commoners agree on what needs to be done—on the priorities, and on what can be left out. As Ostrom emphasises, shared understanding is essential—it is hard to see how a commons could exist without it. If the members of a commons "do not share a common understanding of how complex resource systems operate, they will find it extremely difficult to agree on future joint strategies".[161]

7. The long view. Agreement is needed that it is worth taking action now to *protect the commons for the future, and that this is a lifetime commitment, not a short-term project.[162]

    The long view makes the difference between mining a common resource as an asset with little or no future value, and conserving it as *capital. This principle is central to Lean Logic, and it is the *ethic shared by ecologies of all kinds except those which, like the human ecology, have briefly broken out of their ecological limits.[163]

    The problem is that if natural ecological constraints (which, in effect, give space for no option other than taking the long view) are for some reason not in place, the ethic needed to stand in for them is fragile. If the commoners are entirely

preoccupied with present troubles, or if they feel awash with wealth and see plenty more natural assets to be exploited, or if current standards and norms of behaviour are too remote from any sense of foresight, or if they cannot prevent others from taking or destroying their commons at will, or if they simply spend too much time away from home—then the long-term view will fade. This is *demoralisation. The survival of the commons depends on les choses intérieures—matters of the soul and *spirit.[164]

8. *Trust and *reciprocity. Members of the community need to feel able to trust one another, and to sustain links of cooperation.[165]

    Commons are cooperative enterprises; they therefore depend on trust, on reciprocity, and on *social capital. The *market economy can get by, for a time, with a gravely-weakened culture and social capital, but the commons cannot. If you really want to save the planet and to give human society a decent chance of living on it, the first thing you should do is to join a choir. Or have dancing lessons, or both. That is not quite the *hyperbole it seems: in enduring communities, the thing which *defines and distinguishes them is their culture of *dance, music, *story and *tradition—so intertwined with trust that it is hard to tell cause from effect. As Leigh Anderson and colleagues, write,

> Social capital can be conceived of as an asset that *arises from and enables* the use of networks existing in a community in such a way that norms of trust and reciprocity are promoted.[166]

The making and sustaining of trust, reciprocity and social capital depends on relatively small-scale community—it may be nested, layer by layer, within a larger social order, but it is the small local scale that is critical, as Ostrom reminds us,

> . . . individuals repeatedly communicate and interact with one another in a localised physical setting. Thus it is possible that they can learn whom to trust, what effects their actions will have on each other and on the common-pool resource, and how to organise themselves to gain

C

benefits and avoid harm. When individuals have lived in such situations for a substantial time and have developed shared norms and patterns of reciprocity, they possess social capital with which they can build institutional arrangements.[167]

9. *Autonomy.* The community needs to be able to organise itself and decide as it thinks fit, making its own rules, with confidence that they won't be countermanded by external authorities.[168]

There is closed access here, as well as *pull, in the sense of responsiveness of circumstances and needs as they arise. The commoners can decide for themselves.[169]

10. *Competence.* At least some members of the community have organisation and *leadership skills.[170]

Ostrom emphasises the need for commoners to bring some experience to the task. She acknowledges the value of learning by doing, but recognises that if too many of the mistakes of inexperience are made at the beginning, the moment may pass at which a commons can be sustained or saved. Past experience, she insists, opens up the possibility of making real decisions, and reaching agreement on them.[171]

That is, commoners need to know what they are doing. The experience of some two centuries of market economy consumerism and the *education designed around it is no preparation for this. Deskilled and in many cases demoralised, the would-be commoners of the future have an urgent *incentive to build the needed experience rapidly, with limited time for trial-and-error. The initiatives—the blessed unrest—of our time, such as the *Transition movement, fall short as preparation for what is to come, but they are essential, and they are learning as they go.[172]

RULES FOR MAKING IT WORK (DESIGN PRINCIPLES)

This third and final set of principles is about the way the commons is managed, and how its rules are drawn up and maintained:

11. *Clearly-defined *boundaries.* Both the boundaries of the resource and the membership of the community responsible for it must be well-defined.[173]

Here is *closed access, that crucial condition of the self-regulating commons, strongly restated. As Ostrom writes, definition of boundaries,

> . . . ensures that appropriators can clearly identify individuals who do not have rights and take action against them.[174]

12. *Rules: local and specific.* Rules and decisions must be based on actual local circumstances rather than on theoretical principles and assumptions.[175]

Here again is the flexibility contained in *pull. Ostrom calls it "congruence", a close match between benefits and obligations. Costs and benefits are fairly balanced so that, for example, farms that receive large amounts of water from the irrigation system bear a corresponding share of the costs. The rules take into account local circumstances, such as soils, slope and the nature of the crops being grown.[176]

13. *Participation.* Members of the community must be able to develop their own initiatives and decide on their own rules.[177]

Here is *presence, with its characteristic link between the rules that a community makes for itself and its willingness to comply with them.[178]

14. *Monitoring.* Compliance with the rules should be monitored by people who are themselves members of the commons.[179]

15. *Sanctions.* Sanctions should be appropriate; though not severe at first, they may become so later.[180]

If there are rules for the management of the commons, it is essential that they should be monitored. If members of the commons break them, that must be noticed and sanctions should be applied. The sanctions themselves do not need to be severe—their task is to act as a reminder that the rules exist and that breaking them is unlikely to be a good idea in the long term. But that is consistent, too, with graduated sanctions: for repeated breaches of the rules, it is reasonable for penalties to be severe enough to make repeat offences an unattractive option.[181]

16. *Conflict resolution mechanisms.* There should be quick and effective access to the resolution of conflict between members of the community, and between communities.[182]

Communities can be destroyed by sustained *conflict, from within or without. The management of the commons is full of the risk of conflict, of misunderstanding, and accidental, half-accidental, or intentional failure to stand by reciprocal obligations. Even *character—a necessary condition for dealing with this—has its limits. Disputes are unavoidable, so some means of arbitrating between commoners will need to be integral to the design. As Ostrom writes, "It is difficult to imagine how any complex system of rules could be maintained over time without such mechanisms."[183]

17. *Rights to organise*. The rights of communities to devise their own institutions should be free of challenge from external government authorities.[184]

Ostrom is pointing here to a recurring problem, where authorities—such as the state government—do not recognise the rights of the commons to organise and self-regulate. This right needs to be established early on, before presenting the government with a done deal. Ostrom describes cases of long-term trouble when the needed recognition by the state government has not been in place.[185]

18. *Nested enterprises*. The commons should be organised from the bottom up, with local groups joining together to represent larger areas, and these areas joining upwards in a nested *hierarchy to represent the interests of a region.[186]

In large commons with many participants, nested representation allows commoners to take on problems at all levels, starting with the small-scale local detail. Large commons which have formed to manage irrigation systems—with 10,000 or more members covering very large areas—may be four layers deep, but, as Ostrom explains, the key to effective organisation at this level is to start with the smaller units, and to build on that foundation.[187] She illustrates this with water-management commons—formed with the aim of (amongst other things) ending the uncontrolled pumping of irreplaceable reserves of groundwater. From local beginnings, these evolved successfully into large-scale common enterprises, and she contrasts this with an attempt to organise a similar system in the Mojave Desert from the top down. The result of that was:

acrimonious political conflict, including several recall elections, front-page stories in the local papers that pushed aside stories on the Watergate scandal [and] no action . . . to limit groundwater pumping.[188]

But, once foundations in the form of *small-scale local institutions, their social capital and their self-recognition as a community have been laid, it becomes practical to build more complex institutional arrangements. The nesting of each level of organisation gives higher levels legitimacy in representing the smaller, local groups.[189]

And yet—this bottom-up principle depends, in turn, on top-down recognition and encouragement. Ton Schouten and Patrick Moriarty, whose book *Community Water, Community Management*, is an essential complement to Ostrom's work, explore the practice of the commons, as applied to local water management, and caution that:

> Community management builds from the bottom up, while decentralisation typically comes from the top down. Where they meet is somewhere in the middle, typically around the level of district or municipality government. Both community management and decentralisation will still take a long time to mature, but they cannot do without each other.[190]

The commons in context

The commons is an important idea, not least because many of its properties are intrinsic to community. At the same time, it is attractive, implying that here is a way of being sensible—a route to recovery from the limitations of the market. In fact, as Ostrom points out, commons are a generic solution to a particular kind of problem, and she helps us put them into context with the other means of working together.[191]

She draws our attention to two variables. The first, as we have seen, is *subtractability*. This is the property of a good which is depleted by consumption: if Fred consumes a subtractable good, or uses it, or owns it, that means that Dan cannot do likewise: Fred's consumption has (even if only slightly) reduced Dan's options. You might think this applies to all goods, but in fact it doesn't. Unless one reaches for some rather extreme assumptions, goods such as these are not subtractable: sunlight, joy, parks, pavements, bridges, *law and order, *carnivals, love, commas. Clearly, the buying-and-selling routines of the market economy apply more comfortably to goods that are subtractable than to goods that are not.

The second concept is the *difficulty of excluding beneficiaries*. In most cases, that is not difficult: if you don't have the money, you don't get the sweets. But if you are a farmer in an irrigation network, or a grazer who has inherited the right of access to the commons, or a traveller on the road, or a person who breathes air or enjoys sunshine, it is hard to exclude you from the enjoyment of such things. Plans to make money by making people pay for them may not work.

Having defined these two properties, Ostrom pairs them up, and suggests that, for each pairing, there is an appropriate form of exchange:

1. *Low subtractability* and *little difficulty in excluding beneficiaries*. The natural example of this combination is bridges: except at a trivial level, a bridge is not used up when a person crosses it; on the other hand it is not difficult to stop people crossing, so it is feasible to make them pay. These tend to be supplied as *toll goods*—a rather minor form of transaction.

2. *Low subtractability* and *much difficulty in excluding beneficiaries*. This group contains environmental assets such as sunlight, and the things (like roads) which we pay the government or local *authority to provide for us, which we then see as our deserts or rights as citizens: no one can take them away from us. These are *public goods* (joy and commas also belong to this pairing, though "public goods" doesn't seem to be quite the right label for them).

3. *High subtractability* and *little difficulty excluding beneficiaries*. This is the most common combination, the case of *private goods*, provided for payment—the simple exchange of goods and money.

4. *High subtractability* and *much difficulty of excluding beneficiaries*. The problem here is obvious. There is an asset which can be depleted; at the same time, it is hard to stop people helping themselves when they feel like it, as Garrett Hardin recognised.

These are suitable as *common-pool resources*, as discussed in this entry.

The commons, then, is a practical, and necessary, solution to a particular set of conditions. And it has crucial significance for the future. The *market economy has crowded out—privatised—the greater part of the goods and natural assets which, in an earlier age of community, belonged to pairing 4 above. In so doing, it has created the 'Tragedy of the Commons'.

The world of pre-industrial—and to an even greater extent, pre-state—community was indeed subtractable, and excluding beneficiaries required nothing short of the invention and maintenance of a *culture and society, a task sustained for a long period by the ethic of the commons. We don't know how far back along that road we will need to travel, but it will be some distance. *Script.

COMMUNITY. Community can mean many things. One of them refers to common interests—the Morris dancing community, the gay community, the Facebook community. These are reasonable understandings of community, but they fall outside the bounds of this entry, which explores community in the sense of living in the same place.

The character of such communities is varied, and many attempts have been made to devise a frame of reference for making sense of their differences. The best-known way of distinguishing between them was provided by Ferdinand Tönnies, who (in 1887) pointed to the difference between the internal bonding of *Gemeinschaft* (where *cooperation by members of a group is shaped by a commitment to its values), and the external bonding of *Gesellschaft*, (where it is shaped by their belief that this happens to be a good way of advancing their self-interest). Studies of community have used this as a starting point ever since. In fact the question of what makes a community and what part shared values have to play in it can get rather dry and arcane, but we need to visit it, if only briefly. Before that, though, let us visit some of the real-life communities of the past and present. The history of the world could be told in terms of the history of community, but this selective observation will start in eighteenth century Manchester.[192]

Community, some examples

UTOPIAN COMMUNITIES

Around that time, many communities came into being around the commitment to live in accordance with the teaching of the Bible (as they interpreted it). Generally they qualified as "communes", in the sense that they held most of their property in common, and a famous example was the United Society of Believers in Christ's Second Coming (the Shakers). They began with meetings in Mother Ann Lee's house in Manchester in 1772, where worship included ecstatic dancing, visions and trances, along with confession of sins, prophecy and a commitment to "perfectibility". Neighbours' and locals' reaction to this turned out to be less than encouraging, so she and her followers moved to America, but there too she had trouble, involving violent mobs, which contributed to her early death in 1784. However, the first of many Shaker communities in the Northeastern United States did become established three years later, and by 1840 there was a membership of 6,000, which then gradually declined to its 2010 remnant of just three members in the Shakers' last surviving community. Other religious communities of that time included three successful groups formed by German immigrants—The Harmony Society, Pennsylvania (1804–1904); Zoar in Ohio (1817–1898), and Amana in Iowa, (1843–1933). Then there was (among many others) Jerusalem in New York (1784–1821), the Seventh Day Adventists' Snowhill in Pennsylvania (1800–1890), and Oneida, an American Perfectionist community (1848–1881) in upstate New York.[193]

The religious communities were soon joined by others founded on a different philosophy—as models of socialism, trying out ways of living such as those of Charles Fourier (see "The Perfect Community" sidebar) and Robert Owen. Compared with the religious ones, these were short-lived. Yellow Springs lasted for six months in 1825; the Owenite New Harmony lasted from 1825–1827; Blue Spring, one year in 1826; the Order of Enoch from 1831–1834; and Utopia from 1847–1851. The North American Phalanx, founded on Fourierist principles in 1843, lasted for as much as thirteen years.[194]

In the twentieth century, the emphasis shifted again, this time towards psychosocial health and healing, with foundations such as Synanon in Santa Monica,

---

THE PERFECT COMMUNITY

. . . according to Charles Fourier

Charles Fourier (1772–1837) proposed communes, or *phalanstères*, consisting of 1,620 people, a number derived by a rather complex calculation from the "fact" that there are twelve common passions, key combinations of which should be represented by one member of either sex. The *phalanstères* were large buildings in which the whole commune lived, cooperating for efficiency of output, with the richest on the top floors and the poorest at the bottom, with gardens. Instead of trade there would be subsistence, with the produce being divided harmoniously according to the capital, labour and talent each member contributed.[195]

His vision, which was published in 1808, was influential. Ralph Waldo Emerson reminded his readers of it 65 years later in his essay, "English Traits" (1865):[196]

> Under an ash-coloured sky, the fields have been combed and rolled till they appear to have been finished with a pencil instead of a plough. The long habitation of a powerful and ingenious race has turned every rood of land to its best use . . . so that England is a huge phalanstery, where all that man wants is provided within the precinct.[197]

California (1958–1991), which specialised in drug rehabilitation, and "personal growth centers" such as the Lama Spiritual Home in New Mexico (1967–). Variants have followed, such as Bowden House in the UK (2004–), with the pragmatic and reasonable aim of "developing conscious and authentic community".[198]

Membership of a religious or socialist community was no easy ride, and one of the challenges was that prohibition on private property. In the Oneida community, for instance, all clothing was shared, as were *sexual relations. Love affairs, on the other hand, were not allowed, since they were seen as a form of ownership, and

C

members who fell in love were split up, with (at least) one of them being sent to another branch. Children, raised communally, were sent to live in the Children's House shortly after weaning. Excessive parental affection was not allowed. Even "self-possession" was considered a sin, so no detail of one's life or thoughts was considered too personal for public criticism.[199]

For the Shakers, sexual relations were not permitted at all (they recruited by adopting orphans), and perfectibility — an aim which suggests a degree of uniformity, and which was widely shared by both the religious and the political communities — was to be sought in the smallest details of life. As one ex-Shaker described it,

> Not a single action of life, whether spiritual or
> temporal — from the initiative of confession,
> to cleaning the habitation of Christ, to that of
> dressing the right side first, stepping first with
> the right foot as you ascend a flight of stairs,
> holding hands with the right-hand thumb
> and fingers above those of the left, kneeling
> and rising again with the right leg first, and
> harnessing first the right-hand beast — but has a
> rule for its perfect and strict performance.[200]

And uniformity was represented in clothes: Charles Nordhoff, a sympathetic contemporary observer of the nineteenth century communities, reported that women's clothes in the Amana community were made of dingy-coloured stuffs, including a black cap and a black shawl over the shoulders pinned across the breast: "This peculiar uniform adroitly conceals the marks of sex, and gives a singularly monotonous appearance."[201]

And yet . . . the members of a community of that period worked for not much more than three days a week, allowing for all the stoppages for Bible-reading and prayer. And could they even have been happy? Nordhoff, writing of the Amana community, gets close to deciding that they could:

> The people of the Amana appeared to me a
> remarkably quiet, industrious and contented
> population; honest, of good repute among their
> neighbours, very kindly, and with religion so
> thoroughly and largely made a part of their lives
> that they may be called a religious people.[202]

In view of what members of the religious communities had to endure, it is perhaps surprising that they lasted as long as they did. Maybe some of them were indeed happy: cooperation produces happiness; they had lots of music; they did not have the trouble of having to make decisions for themselves. And there are three other reasons why that may be particularly significant.

First, there was an intense focus on *ritual, which has a powerfully *cohesive effect: monastic communities, structured around ritual, and at least as austere as the Shakers and the Amana, sustained European culture through the Middle Ages.

Secondly, communities had a strong sense of *practice — as, for instance, in the *craftsmanship of the Shaker furniture, their elegant architecture, and their music. The Amana woollen mill supplied yarn and cloth, gloves, stockings and leather from the produce of some 26,000 acres. The Oneida community developed a thriving business (Oneida cutlery is still a recognised design). It had an intense emphasis on *education and sent many of its members to universities. There was competence and commitment — although in some cases the manufacturing overwhelmed the religion: in 1881, Oneida became a joint-stock company "with communal overtones".[203]

Thirdly, the successful communities called on an existing *grid*. This is a key idea (it is one of the bits of theory we are coming to), and we will have a hard look at it. But first, let's visit another kind of community.

ECOVILLAGES

> Ecovillages [writes Jonathan Dawson] can be
> likened to yoghurt culture: small, dense and
> rich concentrations of activity whose aim is to
> transform the nature of that which surrounds
> them. . . . The types of applied research,
> demonstration and training that ecovillages
> are engaged in are precisely those that will be
> needed to navigate the rough waters ahead.[204]

Ecovillages express an ideal of the spirit of the closing phase of the industrial era as clearly as the religious and socialist *utopias expressed an ideal of its early years. First of all, in a break with the principle that the government is there to make the big decisions, they take direct local responsibility for the way they live. Along with a hinterland of supporters, teachers, students and visitors, they explore in a practical way the principle described in *Lean Logic* as *presence. As Dawson puts it, they are "wresting back control over their own resources and ultimately their own destinies."[205]

They use that presence to develop ecological solutions. The principal aim is some variation on the theme of the *closed-loop system, with self-reliance in *energy, *water, *food, and *materials. And integral to that is a commitment to healing the Earth—or at least the favoured patches of it over which ecovillages manage to sustain some degree of control—where possible, cooperating with others in their *region. Auroville, in the state of Tamil Nadu in southern India, has restored the devastated land around it by careful water management and the planting of some two million trees. The Birse Community in Finzean in Aberdeenshire (though it wouldn't see itself as an ecovillage) is restoring the Highland forest around itself. The Centre for Alternative Technology in Machynlleth, North Wales cooperates on energy and conservation projects in its "bioregion", Ecodyfi. The Lammas community in Pembrokeshire has committed itself (as a condition of planning permission) to supplying 75 percent of its needs from *permaculture on its land, with each of its nine *households having the freedom to work out for themselves how to do that, with frequent meetings in their community centre to compare and consult.[206]

To do all this calls for a high degree of cooperation also *within* the community, but not the intense community building which we saw in the religious Utopias. For ecovillages, the community itself may be only a means to an end (providing useful numbers of people), or it may be central to its purpose, but it is the task that *defines the community: if the aim is to invent, demonstrate and teach environmental solutions, that will shape the way it works. And yet, when you're there, the sense of being in a community, even if only as a visitor, tends to be at the front of the mind. You see the practical results—you gaze in admiration at the technology, at the reed-beds which (you suspect) are actually more technically sophisticated than you would guess by looking at them; you feel the fine Welsh rain—but what really matters is the tenacity of the people who have been making it happen since the first day of eccentric inspiration. This is a community that is not be distracted by a quest for perfectibility. There is *practical work in hand; a lot of learning and unlearning to do.[207]

And practical reality bears on ecovillages in another sense, too. Most aspiring ecovillages and community groups fail: they do not happen or they crash after a short time. The survival rate is about 1 in 10. Money, written agreements, vision, privacy, psychology, recruitment and exclusion, expectations, consensus-building, conflict resolution . . . all these make the practice of community building intensely demanding, a professional *craft by any standards. Fortunately, we have guidance in the form of Diana Leafe Christian's book, *Creating a Life Together*. Don't even think of forming an ecovillage, or getting involved in one, without it.[208]

. . . or without being aware of the scale and competence of the ecovillage movement worldwide. As the Global Ecovillage Network explains, it is not short of ambition: its vision of the future comprises no less than "a planet of diverse cultures of all life united in creating communities in harmony with each other and the Earth, while meeting the needs of this and future generations". And it adds,

> We are creating a sustainable future by identifying, assisting and coordinating the efforts of communities to acquire social, spiritual, economic and ecological harmony. We encourage a culture of mutual acceptance and respect, solidarity and love, open communications, cross-cultural outreach, and education by example.[209]

This is now a large movement, with thousands of communities and millions of participants, forums for debate and information such as Wiser Earth, books inspired by the movement, such as Paul Hawken's *Blessed Unrest*, and a proven record of rapid learning.[210]

LOCAL LEAN ECONOMIES

Local *lean economies are slightly different from ecovillages in that they will often already exist as villages, or *parishes, or as communities in the sense of people living near each other. There will no doubt be a great deal of reorganisation, forming and reforming in the turbulent transition into life after *oil, and many people will find themselves living in new places with

C

new neighbours. But there will not be—as there is with the ecovillage or the utopian community—the simple possibility of leaving if you don't like it, or asking troublemakers to leave. We are not looking at intentional communities here, but at people and places that have community thrust upon them.

The implications of this are profound. At present, (while noting significant *exceptions in the case of, for example, some inner city estates), most of us face no particular challenges to our freedoms and well-being from our local community. But the increased significance of localities in the future has its darker side. These will be communities we depend on, which we cannot easily leave, which will need to coordinate their actions in many aspects of their *economic and social existence. Your community can be expected to experience scarcities; and as it becomes useful, rivalries and local *conflicts, not just within, but between, communities could mature into contest for the resources on which lives depend. So, now for the theory.

A framework for thinking about community

The anthropologist Mary Douglas gives us a helpful frame of reference with her distinction between *group* and *grid*—two kinds of influence on the way in which communities and societies hold themselves together, and on the interactions between the people who live in them. We shall look at this first, before turning to two related ways of thinking about it.[211]

GROUP AND GRID

Douglas argues that the social surroundings of an individual—her "social context"—consists of two dimensions. In communities with strong *group*, it is the group itself, rather than the wider setting of *culture and *expectations, that has the decisive influence on the individual's options and behaviour. The person's experience and social *identity is substantially defined by the group to which she belongs.

In contrast with this, the rules of the *grid* are taken to exist already—that is, they are not specific to the local community, but a given; a fundamental set of assumptions of how things should be. In the presence of strong grid, rules, roles and behaviours are well-defined, even pre-defined.[212]

GROUP AND GRID

		Group	
		WEAK	STRONG
Grid	**WEAK**	Fragmented individualism. There is *freedom in principle, but little *cooperation unless it just happens to be in someone else's interests too. There is little or no *social capital.	The group overwhelms the individual, who has no access to *lex*— guiding principles and *institutions, civility. There is more dissidence than *conversation.
	STRONG	Strong structures of social order, and a *culture and *ethic with substantial control on behaviour. A competent society with institutions able to cope, but too rigid for its own good.	Strong group commitment, along with civility, *manners and institutions, to solve problems. But personal freedom is scarce; there is rigidity which impairs *resilience.

These two dimensions are complementary, allowing combinations of each. This gives us four quadrants, as per the "Group and Grid" table:[213]

- In the presence of *weak group and weak grid*, we would expect to find little sense of status, distinct roles or specific obligations between individuals. This is consistent with the free, *competitive *market, but also with an interest in politicking and acquiring little groupings of allies, though they tend to be short-lived. If you fail in such a community, it is relatively unlikely that anyone is going to come to your aid.
- *Weak group and strong grid.* Here the individual's behaviour is largely ordained by key values, assumptions, classes, *traditions and/or laws of the social system. The individual is quite isolated, and there is no sense of a group that can intervene, nor in which she can participate to write the rules which shape her life.[214]
- *Strong group and weak grid.* Now the individual is anything but isolated. The group is everywhere; she belongs within it. On the other hand, it may be so powerful that freedom is close to zero and—in the absence of a grid of principles which exist independently of the group—there may be little or nothing to be done to challenge the group's authority. Conflicts remain unresolved, and are driven

underground, and for the individual that doesn't enjoy this there is little she can do other than take on the authorities, which could be dangerous. Or she could leave, which could also be difficult, not least because dissident tendencies are likely to be detected in advance, and that can lead to trouble.

- *Strong group and strong grid.* The group is powerful and controlling, but it is also competent, for it can use the rules of the grid to respond to trouble, to address and deal with *conflict, and to cooperate with other groups subject to the same rules. This range of options has at least the advantage of stability: strong group/strong grid has a longer life expectancy than the other combinations, but its rigidity limits its *resilience.

These are scarcely attractive choices, and yet, if they are seen as extreme positions on the axes of a graph, never meant to be taken to the limit, things look more promising. We might think that the best place to be from the point of view of a community would be somewhere near the centre: the group is defined, but it is not oppressive; distinctive roles and a confident culture are in place, but not so strongly that the system loses its flexibility. This seems close to the *grammar and *moderation of an enduring community.[215]

OTHER WAYS OF LOOKING AT GROUP AND GRID

The grid-group analysis is telling, and is reflected in two other ways of looking at community:

1. *Civility and enterprise*

 The political philosopher Michael Oakeshott pointed to the difference between two kinds of community: an "enterprise association", and (a drastically different animal), the "civil association" (or "civil state"). Both of these are consistent with freedom.[216]

 An *enterprise association* has a mission. Its rules and constraints are *instrumental, devised as a means of advancing its *common purpose. Some members of the community may not like those rules, but there is a safety-check in the sense that anyone who wants to leave can do so. It is this sense of community-membership being voluntary that gives validity to the specific purposes and rules of such a community.

Now, that's all right within a group or association—or "corporation", to use Émile Durkheim's word (*Profession)—but if a state embarks on enterprise-building of this kind, there is trouble. It imposes instrumental legislation to achieve its purposes but the individual who does not like it can neither prevent it nor leave. Moreover, the enterprise *state* is a jealous animal; it is not inclined to tolerate enterprise *communities*, and it will try to destroy them unless their aims precisely conform to those of the state:

> To the obedient will accrue a share in the profits of the enterprise. . . . The member of such a state enjoys the composure of the conscript assured of his dinner. His "freedom" is warm, compensated servility.[217]

Civil association, on the other hand, is quite different from all this. It has no particular mission other than to conserve the manners, or *civility—or "*lex*", to use Oakeshott's word—which enables a society to sustain and understand itself, to hold together, to maintain good order and protected freedoms. *Lex* is not about specific laws or processes; it is more the sense of being at home: Don knows what Sue is saying; he knows where she is coming from, he shares her *grammar. It is possible to have a conversation. The two of them may have nothing else in common—they may not even like each other—but citizens in this sense share unchanging obligations of allegiance, civility and promise-keeping.[218]

As a general principle, in every society held together by allegiance rather than by force, there needs to be (as John Stuart Mill writes):

> . . . something which is settled, something permanent, and not to be called in question; something which, by general agreement, has a right to be where it is, and to be secure against disturbance.[219]

This perspective on community is, of course, close to the distinction between group and grid. But here is the presumption (or aim, or hope) that *the society or state in which a community lives* is civil in Oakeshott's sense. *Civil* society provides the enabling conditions of tolerance, freedom and an orderly grid within which the local community can develop its own character.

2. *Civic virtue and civil society*

This is a vision of society which is best explored with the help of a story or two from history. It starts with an extreme view: a vision of society as a body—citizens are its "members", its arms and legs. The sixteenth century city of Geneva saw itself in this way, and its self-appointed physician was John Calvin, who wrote:

> No member . . . derives benefit save from those things which proceed from the common profit of the body as a whole.[220]

Members were minutely controlled. *Privacy was regarded as antisocial and suspicious; every household lived under observation. Geneva became known as the "City of Glass".[221] When a limb caused trouble, the solution was surgery, ranging from torture and scourging to execution. There was a dislike of children for their display of natural feelings, a disapproval of the notion that sex might be enjoyed. There was a high rate of clinical depression and suicide.[222]

In the light of such grief, it is a little puzzling that Calvinism was so successful, and yet it was willingly adopted in North America and the Netherlands, and it inspired the eighteenth century thinker Jean-Jacques Rousseau, who saw nothing wrong with this instrument for placing us, corrupted as we are by civilisation, "under the supreme direction of the general will".[223] Another person who saw merits in it was François Maximilien Joseph Isidore de Robespierre. He was noted for his immaculate, sleaze-free life, and for the trademark green coat for which Thomas Carlyle called him the "Sea-Green Incorruptible". The other thing for which he was famous was his tireless dedication as a social surgeon, amputating the limbs that gave trouble during the phase of the French Revolution known as The Terror.[224]

That, of course, was a crisis of *civic virtue*. For deep social solidarity in Western civilisation in a more enduring and normal form, perhaps medieval society will do. Closely integrated, it too saw itself as a body, but as part of the "Great Chain of Being" which stretched (as the poet James Thomson wrote at a later time) "from Infinite Perfection to the brink of dreary nothing". Here the significance of every individual, animals included, lay in his, her or its participation in the wider order. Society and *religion were so closely bonded that a modern historian has described the civil authority as "the police-department of the church".[225]

At the same time, there were cracks in this solidarity. The medieval period was also an age of heroes, of single combat in battle, of government on the basis of personal *loyalty and *courage, and a monastic system dedicated to (amongst other things) the cultivation of the individual's mind and *spirit. There was intense *interest in the affections, in individual dispositions, in the discovery of the "inner man"—the great scholar, Abelard, was in looks, genius, *charisma, ego, and (at least, until his castration) *sex appeal, as individual as it is possible to be. But in its religion, its celebrations, its understanding of politics (despite the stresses and discords), its cosmology and its economics, this was a society which saw itself as a *cohesive enterprise.[226]

For a fuller expression of civic virtue in Western civilisation, though, we may have to look back as far as Classical Greece. It was civic virtue that underpinned the ordered society of the Greek city states for most of their history, and it was not seriously challenged until the century of Aristotle. Christianity's interest in the destiny of individuals would have been incomprehensible to the earlier Classical Greeks. And yet, Greek mythology is not exactly free of personal ambition . . .[227]

So there seems always to be some ambiguity in Western civilisation's phases of social solidarity. In the great civilisations of the East, it appears to be different. Confucius' *Analects* gives such detailed, exact instructions about behaviour—how to eat, how many times to bow, what to say to a guest, how to get into a carriage, how to lie in bed—that the image comes to mind of a whole society acting as a giant *corps de ballet*.[228] The Bhagavad Gita, the sacred Hindu text, is a text of guidance, not to individuation and what we would see as *character, but to achieving the ultimate in solidarity:

> The man who, having abandoned all desires, lives free from longing, unpossessive and unegotistical, approaches peace. . . The man who depends upon nothing, who has given up attachment to the results of action, is perpetually satisfied, and even though engaged in action he does nothing whatsoever.[229]

Civil society lies at the other extreme from this. Here we find the optimistic view of the individual, the benevolent heart, the capacity for friendship, and an enlightened self-interest which knows the value of cooperation.[230] This laid-back position suggests confidence that there are a lot of sensible people around and that, as Immanuel Kant summarised it, "Hard as it may sound, the problem of establishing [the just social order] is soluble even to a nation of devils, provided they have sense."[231]

Here, the moral and social order is created and sustained by individuals, who can substantially be left to get on with it. The law's role leans towards the supportive—ensuring that the *contracts and arrangements that are made between these sensible people are honoured, and underwriting the key principles of property rights and the *trust between strangers on which the institutions of financial *capital depend. This is an attractive idea of autonomous individuals binding society together in a *network of promises, and it shows up in the contrast between the gradually-evolving English common law and the regulatory tradition in Europe, with its ultimate inheritance from Roman Law. One telling symptom of the English system's long-standing dislike of control and interference is its substantial past freedom from the use of torture.[232]

So money-making, too, has its rules. It needs that trust; it needs accuracy in keeping accounts, brilliance in engineering, a background of moral sentiments in a stable society, and good conduct by business towards all its stakeholders. Here was the philosophy of the hard-working Puritan (*Needs and Wants)—its intentions often fell far short in

practice, but it was the starting point for some clear thinking; not least a realisation of the link between individual freedom and individual responsibility. It produced, for example, the rules of good conduct in Richard Baxter's *Christian Directory* (1673), which anticipate the employee- and consumer-protection legislation of a later time.

In summary, civic virtue does not simply maintain social cohesion; it *is* social cohesion: it is no more necessary to keep a community intact if it is defined by civic virtue than it is necessary to keep water wet. Civil society is much looser; the society is not of one mind, but it is held together by the threads of *common purpose, *reciprocities, common *culture and enabling *institutions.

The communities of the future will need them both.

Lessons for local lean economies?

Now to the key question: where will communities get their values from? There are two answers to this. The first, dominant one, which receives strong emphasis throughout *Lean Logic*, is that they will decide for themselves. They will respond to local circumstances and will find themselves pulled along by events, inventing and adopting *diverse *practices which would astonish if seen from the point of view of the global market economy and its metropolitan values. That is close to the essence of *lean thinking: local people, *neighbourhoods and communities will be much better placed to apply their competence and good sense than any received, large-scale, standard and imposed practice.

But what guidelines are there as to how far this is taken? In a world of completely local ethics, it is hard for a local critic to claim that anything that happens there is good and bad, desirable or not; all that can be said is that stuff happens. The author of Psalm 12 seems to be in this place:

> Help me, oh Lord, for there is not one godly man left.

. . . and we see a modern version of this in Cormac McCarthy's book (and the film) *The Road*, which chronicles the journey of a father and his young son through a post-apocalypse world in which no one *encountered gives space for anything other than despair . . . until the very end, that is. We may be *sceptical about what would have happened *next*, and how realistic it is—but something good happens. The boy, who would otherwise have survived in such a situation for no more than a few hours, meets a decent man, and then his family. And their dog. In the film, we see a kind smile from a stranger for the first time. The boy asks,

"How do I know you're a good guy?"
"You don't. You have to take a shot."

What is missing in the destroyed world until that moment is values which transcend immediate circumstance—that is, a *grid*. What will the grid values of communities be? That is hard to say—but let's look, briefly, at the story so far:

- For the more successful communities we visited, a grid of some sort was in place. The religious communities, for all their excesses, and an intense groupishness extending to the most intimate aspects of their lives, had a grid which provided some framework in terms of which they could conduct their lives. Local group rules were intensely intrusive, and unendurable to many, but the context was that of an established *culture. There was music, *ritual, and an affirmation of shared values such as those of the Sermon on the Mount. The commune's rule book was not the only place in which they could get clarification as to what they were about.
- By contrast, that sense of duty—of the day being shaped by observance of shared *tradition, of collectively-agreed and non-negotiable obligation—did not apply so successfully in the case of the political utopias, for whom their latest thinking, as diverse as the people in them, was their only guideline, and none of which lasted for more than a few years.
- The ecovillages do have a well-defined aim, and an inheritance of science and *intention on which they can draw. It may not be enough in the long term, but a grid of some kind is in place.
- Michael Oakeshott's *lex* is a slender grid—a weak defence against *group* tyranny, for he is not referring to any law in particular—but although

lex (law) is not this or that law, its presence means that there *is* law in place: morality is not defined by your latest scheme or *ideology. In Geneva we visited an "enterprise state" more extreme than anything that Oakeshott had in mind, and in sharp contrast to the "civil association" that he urges, with its generally-acknowledged rules, widely seen as just. While these do not necessarily articulate any particular policy, their existence means that there is some representation of manners and a shared *grammar, as we saw in the civil society of the Enlightenment, shot through with a grid of protocols, rules and obligations.

Civility is not an *abstraction. It looks you in the eye. It is located; it is home. As the psychologist Mary Pipher writes,

> Communities are real places, chosen as objects of love, with particular landscapes, sounds, and smells and particular people who live there. Communities are about accountability, about what we can and should do for each other. People who live together have something that is fragile and easily destroyed by a lack of civility. Behaviour matters. Protocol is important. Relationships are not disposable. People are careful what they say in real communities because they will live with their words until they die of old age.
> Connections have a way of making us morally accountable.[233]

A healthy community, then, is a balance of group and grid. It has a strong *identity and confidence that it can decide for itself, but a recognition of the obligations which it can't change. It enjoys the enterprise of the group, and the *manners and *civility of the grid.

If the people of the future were able to live in a giant industrial economy, and to carry on living by trading in a healthy *market economy, community building would still be a desirable thing to do. You can do without community, but only for a time, like holding your breath under water.

However, that option of business-as-usual is not available. In a context of *energy and *material deprivation and, more generally, of the *climacteric, community—most especially in the sense of locally-competent *cooperative groups—will be the only way forward. Community will need to be reinvented as the defining form of human society.

*Lean Economy, Social Mobility, Groups and Group Sizes.

COMPASSION. There are two meanings. First, there is the important insight that it is possible to feel with—or to suffer with (Latin: *pati* to suffer + *cum* with)—one's enemies, or with people whom we don't know and whose interests are different from ours. The historian Karen Armstrong traces the way in which compassion in this sense began to develop consciously during the Axial Age (900–200 BC), which was the formative period of the great world traditions such as China's Confucianism and *Taoism, India's Hinduism and Buddhism, Israel's monotheism and philosophical rationalism in Greece. This was a time of maturing recognition that the *emotions matter: they reveal ourselves to ourselves; they enable us to feel what others are feeling. As Armstrong writes,

> Only by admitting our own pain can we learn to empathize with others.[234]

In this sense, compassion is crucial. We would be in deep trouble without it. It was compassion that matured when the Greeks felt empathy with the Persians who had recently devastated their city; in Aeschylus' trilogy, *The Oresteia*, the Erinyes (aka the Furies, the goddesses of vengeance) eventually acquit Orestes of his crimes, and are transformed into the Eumenides (the kindly ones); at the end of the *Iliad's* history of the Trojan War, the arch-enemies Achilles and Priam weep together.[235]

This is shared *presence; it is on-the-level *conversation and *encounter, not just with those who were formerly strangers and enemies, but with friends, colleagues and rivals; our fellow dwellers in the land. You do not have to be in trouble to qualify for it. It is all right to be competent; it is not a crime against the state. The *Lean Economy will encourage it.

A second sense of compassion is about care for those who are indeed in trouble. This is indispensable, too. All big religions press the case for it. There is no such thing as society without compassion in this sense. But the problem comes when it becomes the only acknowledged guideline for our relationships with each other. Between equals, none of whom are going through a particularly hard time relative to the other, compassion in this sense is not an appropriate response. If I were to tell my friend Tom that I feel compassionate towards him, he would have reason to be puzzled, *insulted and probably incensed.

The problem is that, while such a mistake is unlikely to be made between the friends, colleagues and acquaintances of our real lives, misplaced compassion has become established as a defining property of a plausible political philosophy. Catastrophic social engineering—Pol Pot's efforts, for instance—is routinely and blithely justified as compassion towards the poor.

And these two senses of compassion leave a gap—with no agreed and comprehensive name, and with little awareness that it merits consideration—in the matter of relationships among equals and friends. *Virtues that have no name can seem to be unimportant and disappear from the range of things that are recognised as worth getting right.

In a sense, it is easy to do the right thing for someone who is much worse-off than us and in need of a simple act of kindness (and we need to do so); but if we neglect the no-less-vital obligations of our more complex relationships, between people whose lives are chuntering on just fine at the moment—where acts of kindness, though they have their place, are really not what the relationship is about—we will be in trouble. And the poor will share that trouble—for, if they are to get the help they need, they need a society that knows what it is doing.[236]

Societies are held together by *networks of many kinds of relationships—between equals, between potential enemies, and between people who, in accomplishment, wealth, standing, health and/or happiness, are unequal. Where one person realises that another person is in trouble, they may, in *charity and *pity, be prepared to do something about it. But charity in that sense is only one part of it; a society whose core value is compassion is simply sorry for itself. There is more to life and relationships:

*Caritas, Encounter, Humour, Cupboard Love, Loyalty, Play, Trust, Truth.

COMPETITIVENESS. The production of goods and services at a price which is at least as low as that of other producers of similar things of similar quality. Competitiveness is a defining property of the market economy; it needs no justification—and just in case it did, it would be necessary only to point to the fact that producers who are not competitive have to raise their game or cease to exist.

And yet, economic competitiveness is not the fixed landmark it is thought to be. It is a special case. It exists only under the circumstances of a *taut market—that is, an efficient market, committed to employing the available resources to maximum effect and at minimum cost, so that those who fail to achieve this standard sink out of sight. The laws of competition apply to the pricing of goods and services supplied in a *market economy, but they are not universal: they are not intrinsic to the logic of *economics. This can be shown in two ways.

First, these laws apply only to production, and not to consumption. While producers are under pressure to be efficient (to maximise output from a given input), consumers are under corresponding pressure to be inefficient (to maximise input [consumption] for a given output [well-being]), so as to soak up the ever-*growing production which the economy needs as a condition of its stability. This is the divided self of the market state.

Secondly, the rules of the competitive market comprise the special case that arises when a *political economy leaves behind the texture of *reciprocity, *culture and *social capital in which it was once embedded. They replace that network of values with a single requirement: be efficient. You want to work a mere three-day week for a full living wage? Forget it. Competitors will soon put you out of business. You want to build with local stone, carving and shaping the masonry in the tradition of the last thousand years? There may be a niche for you, if you can find an *exceptionally wealthy client. You want to sustain a rich fertile soil and plenty of space for wildlife, because that is the way we ought to treat the *land? . . . weed your carrot crop by hand? Environmental *manners like that are a luxury item.

———

The market's answers sound authoritative and final, but what is really significant about them is how naïve they are. Most of human history has been bred, fed and watered by another sort of economy, where production for local use is supplied on the basis of *reciprocal obligation and there is freedom from the tyranny of price; indeed, *monetary payments may have no part to play at all. Dwellers in a land in which there is deep integration and *common purpose between the individual and *community, and a *culture to hold it together, do not live in a taut economy governed by competitive pricing, but in a society that lives by *craftsmanship. There is discretion: competition does not have the last word; the economy is *slack.[237]

A slack economy is a difficult form of social order to sustain. But it may not be impossible.

*Leisure, Big Stick, Intentional Waste, Social Mobility, Lean Thinking.

COMPLEXITY. The property of a system consisting of many complementary tasks carried out by highly specialised parts, which are joined up in *networks of information, control and distribution.[238]

Each part of a complex system depends on most, or all, of the other parts being in good working order at all times and providing them with the *reciprocal services they need. This means that a complex system is vulnerable to shock. If something goes wrong, it is in trouble. It has poor *recovery-elastic resilience, but it compensates for this by having well-developed *preventive resilience: it is good at keeping itself out of trouble. A complex system, in general, is gifted. It learns. It invents. It adapts. It can be extremely intelligent. One remarkable example of a complex system is Aristotle.

Complex systems and modular systems

The counterpart of a complex system is a *modular system—a system consisting of parts which are similar to each other and substantially self-reliant.

A modular system has poor preventive resilience, but it compensates for this by having well-developed recovery-elastic resilience: it is good at repairing the damage after failing to keep itself out of trouble (for a summary of the four types of system discussed below and throughout *Lean Logic*, see the summary table in *Systems Thinking on page 450).

An antelope is a complex system, consisting of highly diverse parts (organs, limbs) with widely different, complementary roles, linked with taut connections and strong interdependence. A herd of antelopes, on the other hand, is a modular system, consisting of rather similar parts with narrowly-similar roles. These parts may be *competitive or *cooperative, depending on circumstances, and are linked up with *slack connections and weak interdependence. Complex systems (such as antelopes and humans) need modular systems to live in, for they need the freedom to apply the ingenuity and competence which a tightly-connected complex system would not provide. The slack *connectedness of a modular system provides the elbow-room needed for their competence to be expressed.

Modularity does not lend itself to major collective projects. Modular systems do not have the capability—the power of thought, invention and collective achievement—which complex systems have (although there is a special-case exception to this, as noted in *Modularity). So, suppose that, starting with a modular system, such as a community of communities, the decision is made to go for a grand project. The objective is, say, to build a pyramid, a railway system or an *empire, or to have a war—or, more generally, to follow the long path of *intensification which leads to a *civic society. The modular structure is not going to achieve such aims. To carry forward these ambitions it will be necessary to join together to build a structure that *approximates* to complexity. The modular parts of the system take diverse *roles*, although they cannot take the strongly *diverse *forms* of a genuinely complex system.

In a human society that has achieved 'complexity' in this sense, the differentiation in function intrinsic to all complex systems takes the form of a differentiation in roles between people, represented in differences in wealth, class and privilege. These differences may well reach exaggerated, pathological levels, leading to a society which is grossly inefficient in all senses, including a profligate use of environmental resources.[239] High levels of intensification in a *large-scale society, with its large *intermediate economy, will inevitably lead to a relatively high level of demand on the ecology.[240]

Complicated systems

Lean Logic's name for this approximation of a complex system is a "complicated system". In place of local self-reliance and sufficiency there is specialisation and interdependence. In the case of a community of self-reliant communities, the advance towards complication reduces their connection with the *local. Where there was local provision, complication requires a network of *transport links; local music is upstaged by a national orchestra. Complication—'as-if complexity' in a system which would otherwise be occupied by *modularity—signals the intention to go for results more ambitious than the community of communities could aspire to.

Let us stay for a moment with this idea of a modular system transforming itself into an 'as-if complex' one, and think about the case of a decentralised agricultural society evolving into a centralised urban state. What happens is *paradoxical.

First, there is that transformation from the modular to the complicated—with the result that the system as a whole will now collectively be more effective and capable than it was before. It will build big *infrastructures for production, transport and *waste disposal. It will be able to make history. Every public figure will see that as a good thing. The increase in complexity is *self-evident.

But, secondly, the transformation is *also* a process of simplification. Communities that once produced everything they needed now find themselves—not entirely but substantially—concentrating on just one thing. They become specialist exporters of that one thing and importers of everything else. And there is simplification in the sense that when a community that was formerly self-reliant becomes the specialist provider of a few *large-scale services, it moves away from the multitasking it is accustomed to; its task becomes conceptually much simpler than providing the whole range of goods and services that are required by a robust, self-reliant and broadly-competent locality.

So, what we have here is a combination of greater complexity *and* greater simplicity. Complicated systems put up with this trade-off because of the great increase in capability they acquire by doing so. The agricultural scientist, Kenneth Dahlberg, gets close to this:

> Industrial societies are 'complicated' (like a clock which has many interlocking parts, but only a few 'species'—gears, springs, bearings etc) . . . [They] are not complex.[241]

As we have seen, such complication is 'as-if complexity'. And it has profound flaws. Its skill in sustaining

C

THE STORY OF NOSS AND SCARP
From complication, back to complexity

Imagine that there is a little society with, say, four participants—they might be thought of (though not too literally) as four small villages. In order to look after themselves, they have to provide four different goods and services: bread, clothes, electricity and teaching.

Now, there are two ways of dividing this work up. Each village could specialise in just one thing, sending off supplies (or transporting people) every day to all the others. Or each could do all four things for itself.

If the villages specialise (as they do in the society of Noss), there has to be a lot of swapping around, and there are lots of chances for things to go wrong. When there is a shock—e.g., to the bread producer—it tends to ripple through them all. There is standardisation; there is separation between producers and consumers. Transport has to bridge the gap between producers and consumers. It is harder to maintain a *closed-loop system because the large-scale production creates a lot of *waste, making it harder to *sort, and users of large quantities of unsorted waste are hard to find. This is a society of separation, distance and dependency, kept going by rivers of traffic.

The other little society (Scarp) doesn't like this complication. It prefers complexity. In place of separation, there is integration. Each village provides all four goods and services for itself. Each locality contains a full range of skills and facilities; there is integration between what they produce and what they consume; this is a hands-on—or hands-in—*culture, in touch with its own *food and its own *needs. It has free agency, and the interdependencies between the villages in Scarp take place across a rich range of subjects and interactions. Diverse cultures and solutions can be sustained; instead of just one standardised procedure for baker/tailor/energy-supplier/teacher, there are four variants of each. There is evolution, guided by trial and error since, if one village innovates successfully, the others can imitate it, whereas if the innovation is a failure, the others are not affected. It is robust: a shock tends to be localised: if one bit gets knocked out, others can cover for it, or simply get along without.

*preventive resilience comes at the cost of *intensification: the process of developing ever more elaborate structures which bring new problems of their own, in turn requiring yet more workarounds, regulation and elaboration. More complication becomes a short-term fix for the problems of complication. Once that journey has begun, it is hard to stop. As we see in the *Wheel of Life, the complicated system's interdependent connectedness inexorably leads it towards a "release" or "breakdown" phase, where the system crashes like an avalanche under its own weight.

That story of rigidity, elaboration, high costs and ultimate collapse under excess complexity is well-recognised by other writers on these matters, but *Lean Logic*'s use of "complication" is not standard in other studies of complex societies, and there is potential for confusion here (though no real dissonance of meaning). Joseph Tainter's *The Collapse of Complex Societies*, for instance, uses complexity as the key defining characteristic of civilisations, listing properties such as these:[242]

- A high degree of stratification and social differentiation.
- Economic and occupational specialisation of individuals, groups and territories.
- Centralised control; regulation and integration of diverse economic and social groups by elites.
- Behavioural control and regimentation.
- Investment in accomplishments that define the concept of civilisation, such as monumental architecture, artistic and literary achievements.
- Substantial flow of information between individuals, between political and economic groups, and between a centre and its periphery.
- Sharing, trading and redistribution of resources.

- Overall coordination and organisation of individuals and groups.
- A large territory integrated within a single political unit.[243]

Almost all of these are aspects of complication—Tainter calls it complexity, but when you centralise, standardise, and control, you simplify. The 'complexities' in Tainter's list are *simple*; even *dumbed-down* in comparison with the nuance, *diversity and detail of local complexity. There is an aspect of the big *civic societies which is grossly simplifying, and it is implied in Tainter's list: regulation, regimentation, coordination. And in this sense we can see *reduced* complexity in many of the characteristic structures of civilisation:

- The ecology of the landscape under intensive *agriculture is vastly simpler than that of the small-scale biological husbandry that it replaced.
- The economic and cultural life of a commuter town is simpler than that of the traditional town it replaced: there is comprehensive disappearance of the local industries on which it could once depend; there is less diversity of social and practical *skills.
- The successful, yet unplanned, diversity of public and voluntary *institutions is taken over and simplified by centralised administration. "Orderly" (in the sense of *Harmonic Order) becomes "ordered" (in the sense of regulated and standardised).[244]
- The complex range of food crop varieties suited to particular locations and purposes is standardised to a small number of approved strains.[245]

That is to say, the standardisation and specialisation of a complicated society comes with aspects of *diminished* complexity, relative to the decentralised self-reliant order prevailing pre- and post-civilisation. In some ways, civilisation explores the extremes of complexity; in some ways it is greatly simplified. Indeed, *intensification—a society's accomplishment of a massive expansion of work by the division of labour—comes at the cost of extreme simplification not just for places, but for people, as observed by the division of labour's leading advocate, Adam Smith:

> In the progress of the division of labour, the employment of the far greater part of those who live by labour, that is, of the great body of the people, comes to be confined to a few very simple operations; frequently to one or two. But the understandings of the greater part of men are necessarily formed by their ordinary employments. The man whose whole life is spent in performing a few simple operations, of which the effects too are, perhaps, always the same, or very nearly the same, has no occasion to exert his understanding, or to exercise his invention in finding out expedients for removing difficulties which never occur. He naturally loses, therefore, the habit of such exertion, and generally becomes as stupid and ignorant as it is possible for a human creature to become. The torpor of his mind renders him, not only incapable of relishing or bearing a part in any rational conversation, but of conceiving any generous, noble or tender sentiment, and consequently of forming any just judgment concerning many even of the ordinary duties of private life.[246]

What Kirkpatrick Sale advocates is in complete contrast to this:

> I wish to *complexify*, not simplify. It is our modern economy that is simple: whole nations given over to a single crop, cities to a single industry, farms to a single culture, factories to a single product, people to a single job, jobs to a single motion, motion to a single purpose. . . . Human organisations are healthy and they survive when they are diverse and differentiated, capable of many responses; they become brittle and inadaptable and prey to any changing conditions when they are uniform and specialised. It is when an individual is able to take on many jobs, learn many skills, live many roles, that growth and fullness of character inhabit the soul: it is when a society complexifies and mixes, when it develops the multiplicity of ways of caring for itself, that it becomes textured and enriched.[247]

The complication of a large-scale system leaves a trail of simplifications. A Bruckner symphony is certainly more complex than home-grown music, but the act of going *en*

C

masse to sit in orderly rows to listen to Bruckner, rather than making *danced, sung, inventive, ecstatic, self-sufficient music of our own, integrated into local life, makes an evening out in our complicated spectator-society look, by comparison, quite simple (*Carnival).

On the other hand, you may prefer Bruckner's symphonies to Anon's dances. Sometimes it is a good idea to stop straining at orderly explanations . . .
*Resilience ❯ Resilient Systems, Ecological System, Butterfly Effect.

COMPLICATION. See Complexity.

COMPOSITION, THE FALLACY OF. The *fallacy that, because an asset or accomplishment is available to one person, it must therefore be available to all. In fact, there is a class of goods—known as positional goods—that can never be available to all, however much incomes may rise, and whatever forms of social engineering may be attempted. Examples:[248]

1. *Strict scarcities* (i.e., goods whose supply cannot rise in response to demand). There is only a limited number of idyllic houses in the remote countryside, period houses in pleasant towns and Old Masters. Even if incomes rose so that everyone could pay more for them, that would make no difference to the number of people who managed to own one.
2. *Savings.* It is sensible for one person to save a high proportion of her income in order to have more to spend in the future; but if everyone else did so, this would reduce demand and national income to the point at which everyone (on average) would have *less* to spend in the future (the Paradox of Thrift).[249]
3. *Contest for rank and/or scarce jobs.* If everyone improved their CV-writing skills, that would have no (direct) effect in getting more people into work. Napoleon liked to claim that every soldier carried a marshal's baton in his pack. Not true.[250]
4. *Labour-intensive work.* While it is possible for some people to employ servants, it is impossible for everyone to do so because servants' incomes have to be less than those of their employers. And domestic service belongs to a class of goods and services which does not benefit from the technological advances

which reduce the costs of most others. Services of this kind, described by the economist William Baumol as "technologically non-progressive", may well use modern techniques (such as email, or clinical drugs), but remain essentially labour-intensive. Other examples include social work, nursing, teaching and military service. The cost of technologically non-progressive goods and services will therefore inevitably rise relative to the cost of the technologically progressive sectors (such as manufacturing and, to some extent, large retail). This happens because estimates of price inflation, and the wage negotiations that are based on them, are arrived at by measurements of the changing cost of a standard "basket" of goods, most of which become, in real terms, cheaper over time, thanks to technical advance.[251]

Contrary to what you might expect, therefore, as an economy becomes richer, services such as nursing and domestic service become *less* affordable when compared with average levels of income. As overall productivity advances, the sector's cost disadvantage will increase. And this disadvantage falls disproportionately on governments because so many of the labour-intensive services (e.g., social work and teaching) happen to be in the public sector. This helps to explain why governments' financial troubles seem always to be getting worse. While it may be possible for a local authority to pay for social services for the elderly at the time a service is set up, it is likely to have greater difficulty in doing so as time goes by.

There are many trade-offs and mitigations here, but the central problem stands. The reason labour-intensive work is so expensive is that technological advance in the technologically-progressive sector has progressively priced it out of the market. Should the technologically-progressive sector go into retreat for any reason (such as *peak oil), then the relative price of labour-intensive work will fall.

It may be that the possession of positional goods brings status too—and status is itself a positional good, but we do not need the idea of status here: the goods themselves are positional goods; they are widely-desired goods that cannot be replicated—or at least cannot be replicated very much. A *necessary condition for some people having them is that other people don't.[252]

The problem of positional goods will develop in an acute form when there is competition for resources. The price of one person's success in getting hold of the resources he or she needs will be another person's failure to do so. This is not a zero-sum game, which is simply about distribution (with the average outcome remaining unchanged); it is a negative-sum game, in which declining supply leaves the average consumer worse off. If the scarcities were deep enough, it could be a super-negative-sum game, in which every individual—even those most successful in maximising their own share—is worse off.

Positional goods are one member of the class of ideas dealing with composition status—the effect that other people's intentions and actions have on your own. To put these into context, their effect may be:

1. Negative (*Positional Goods)—other people's actions may stop you doing something you want to do: the available *land, *energy and *food goes to the minority that has the money, power, ingenuity and ruthlessness to make sure they get it.

2. Positive (*Common Capability)—other people's actions enable you to do something you want to do. Example: public services such as railways, which are possible only because many people use them.

3. Uncertain (the Prisoner's Dilemma: see *Leisure)—there is clearly a *best* thing to do, but it would involve trusting everyone else to do it, too. You can't trust them to do it, so it doesn't happen. Example: During a downturn in business, taxi drivers work longer hours to make up for it. But that does not increase the total available business; it just protects them from even greater losses, because they know all other taxi drivers are going to work longer hours too. If they all agreed not to work the longer hours, they would still get the same amount of business, at less cost in time and fuel. But such an agreement would be difficult to reach and impossible to guarantee. So they all work the longer hours.

It will be the economics of composition goods, rather than of a well-ordered regime in which supply responds to demand, which is characteristic of life after *oil.

*Needs and Wants, Economics 〉 #6, Lean Economics.

CONFLICT. See Big Stick, Play, Reciprocity and Cooperation, Fortitude, Lean Defence.

CONNECTEDNESS. The extent to which the parts of a system are joined up in links of *reciprocity, dependency and/or control.

In a *complex system there is a *tautly connected network of exchange of information, instructions, control and stimulus—of oxygen, water, sugars, adrenaline and endorphins, or of food, goods and services, or of weapons and reinforcements. These lines of communication are key to the competence of the complex system, but they also make it vulnerable because they are costly to maintain; they can be destroyed, are hard to repair, and a breakage in just one of them can be enough to destroy the whole organism or system.

In a *modular system, by contrast, these connections are *slack; they do not need to be in working order all the time; there may be time-lags; they have relatively little work to do, because the parts of a modular system have a high degree of self-reliance. This means that a modular system has the advantage of *recovery-elastic resilience, but lacks the preventive resilience of the complex system.

As a modular system *intensifies—transforming itself into a *complicated system—it increases its connectedness, which brings many advantages of capability and preventive resilience, but comes at the cost of the heavy *infrastructure of connections which the system must maintain and repair. As it grows, and as its infrastructure becomes more costly (through wear-and-tear, loss of *practical competence by the system's centres of *intelligence and decision-making, and/or attack by predators inside and outside the system), the task of maintaining the network of connectedness becomes increasingly burdensome. And, with every response to these problems, there is a tendency to add another layer of connectedness and control.

In due course, a level of elaboration and hyperconnectedness is reached which the living system can no longer support, and it is destroyed. That shock may be at the level of creative destruction, which opens the way to a new, uncluttered beginning on the same basic model; or it may set the system on a different path, leading to a radically different form (*Lean Logic's* name for both these

C

kinds of shock is *kaikaku). Or it may be a hypershock, closing off the possibility of a living system of any kind. *Resilience 〉 Resilient Systems 〉 Connectedness, Systems Thinking, Wheel of Life.

CONSTRUCTIVISM. The idea that enlightened *leaders can steer a society in desirable directions. As attempted, for instance, by Vladimir Lenin and by many autocratic leaders and *democratic *reformers before and since. This is not in all cases a *fallacy: leadership and foresight can in principle do some good.

The point made by critics such as Friedrich Hayek is that *culture and civilisation are not, in fact, consequences of deliberate human design, but the products of society's gradually evolving *institutions; civilisation depends on behaviour, not on goals. Hayek saw Keynesian *economics as a form of constructivism, because it appears to establish governments in effective control of the economy.

Constructivism teaches "-isms" (see "The Sea Cucumber" sidebar)—supplying answers, rather than the *grammar which enables a person to think things through and work out her own answers. You are told the destination, but not given the map. And the rightness of that destination is likely to be defended strongly, because no one knows how to navigate to another one.[253] *Anarchism, Assent, Calibration, Democracy, Ideology.

THE SEA CUCUMBER

The sea-cucumber is a sluggish beast,
Lumpy, contemplative, and very slow.
So stiff and dull is he, that one deceas'd
Is so like one alive, you'd never know.

Yet, with full complement of harps and choirs
A cloud is ready for his final phase.
With airs to while away the tranquil hours,
And sunny slopes to feed his languid gaze.

The reason is, he has not specialised
In 'ologies, and 'ists, and 'isms vast.
With good and bad and sloth precisely poised,
To God of good and bad he'll come at last.

DAVID FLEMING

CONTRACT. An arrangement made between two or more parties, committing them to certain obligations which they are required to fulfil even if, at a later time, they do not want to, or find it difficult to do so.

The contract may be implicit or explicit, but even an implicit contract is likely to be signalled by gesture or *ceremony which affirms the contract's existence. Contract is endorsed by *law and custom and recorded in documents and other instruments, and sanctions may be material, but the contract itself has no material expression. You cannot see it. You cannot say where it is. The paper may be touched, but the contract itself actually exists only in people's minds and in the *institutional mind of the law. It exists because it is held to exist.

If minds change profoundly enough, as they do with a changed regime, the contract may cease to exist. Although the contract may be both *necessary and desirable—it is a powerful concept—the reality of a contract is a social construct, not a material fact; it depends on consent, and can be destroyed if denied and not defended.

It is similar to the concept of God—also a powerful concept, also vulnerable and dependent on the consent of those who affirm it.

*Trust, Informal Economy, Performative Truth, Gifts.

CONTRARIAN FALLACY, THE. An argument which dismisses one proposition by emphasising another one. For example, the proposition, "Many London households in the age of Handel achieved a high level of culture and civility" may be disputed on the grounds that "eighteenth century London still had desperate poverty and open sewers."

The problem is not that the objection is false; it is that it can effectively see off the original statement, which disappears from the discussion, allowing the easy ride of catch-all cynicism to continue uninterrupted. The Contrarian Fallacy—the inverse of the three monkeys who hear no evil, see no evil and speak no evil—sees evil in every accomplishment, and claims that this dismal insight is what conscience requires.

*Irrelevance, Tu Quoque.

CONTROL OVERLOAD. The final breakdown that occurs when an attempt is made to control a *system comprehensively. Every control usurps *local

THE LIMITS TO CONTROL
The trouble with fast–breeder reactors

There is a systemic problem with the design of breeder nuclear reactors. Nuclear accident is potentially so destructive that the possibility has to be practically ruled out under all circumstances. This means that the defence-in-depth systems have to be extremely complex, which means that the installation must be large enough to derive economies of scale—otherwise it would be uneconomic. However, that in turn means that no confinement dome can be built on any acceptable design criterion on a scale and with the structural strength to withstand a major accident. Therefore, the defence-in-depth systems have to be even more complex, which in turn means that they become even more problem-prone than the device they were meant to protect.

A study for the nuclear industry in Japan concludes: "A successful commercial breeder reactor must have three attributes: it must breed, it must be economical, and it must be safe. Although any one or two of these attributes can be achieved in isolation by proper design, the laws of physics apparently make it impossible to achieve all three simultaneously, no matter how clever the design."[254]

A moment of *deference is due to the power of conversation: often it comes empty-handed but sometimes, crucially, it is the bearer of good judgment, raising the collective IQ by—who knows?—20 points? Do nothing that matters without consulting a conversation.

(2) The *how* of *encounter.

(3) The interaction that builds a *community; the process of *emergence. As the artist Santiago Bell demonstrated at the Bromley by Bow community where he was resident, *craftsmanship and community building are in some senses the same process, building timber by timber, relationship by relationship, conversation by conversation.[255]

(4) Verbal grooming—a way of sustaining close bonds more efficiently than the actual grooming which, as the anthropologist Robin Dunbar suggests, it replaced.[256] Conversation has the advantage that you can do it with more than one person at a time, and that it differentiates better: grooming feels about the same, whoever is doing it for you; conversations (on a good day) are unique to the people who are there. Conversation *can* descend to the *instrumental, lacking the intrinsic *emotional depth which is contained in touch; it can be cold and distant—less engaging than physical reward, more rejecting than physical rebuke; it can be cruel. And yet, a conversation has originality and specificness to the people who are having it; it has freshness; it stays in the memory; it *plays; it bonds.

Here are the latter stages of a grooming-conversation between two people at the end of a difficult day and, until a moment ago, not quite agreed on the way home. At the end, there is even a touch of grooming:

> Tietjens let the cart go on another fifty yards; then he said:
> "It *is* the right road. The Uddlemere turning *was* the right one. You wouldn't let the horse go another five steps if it wasn't. You're as soppy about horses as . . . as I am."
> "There's at least that bond of sympathy between us", she said drily. "Gran'fer's Wantways is six and three-quarters miles from Udimore; Udimore is exactly five from us; total, eleven and three-quarters; twelve and a quarter if you add half a mile for Udimore itself. The name

decision-making, and needs to be controlled itself, so that, with each added control, there is more to be controlled, until the system is crushed by the weight of it all.

It is hard to stop because in the latter stages, failures keep occurring, which prompt the installation of more controls.

Examples: financial regulation; anti-terror/enemy-of-the-state regimes; state-controlled *health services; *law and order when rivalries develop; fast-breeder *nuclear reactors (see "The Limits to Control" sidebar).

*Complexity, Connectedness, Responsibility.

CONVERSATION. (1) Cooperative problem-solving and deliberation (Latin: *de* thoroughly + *librare* weigh), including deliberation with oneself.

C

is Udimore, not Uddlemere. Local place-name enthusiasts derive this form "O'er the mere". Absurd! Legend as follows: Church builders desiring to put church with relic of St. Rumwold in wrong place, voice wailed: "O'er the mere." Obviously absurd! . . . Putrid! "O'er the" by Grimm's law impossible as "Udi"; "mere" not a Middle Low German word at all . . ."

"Why", Tietjens said, "are you giving me all this information?"

"Because," the girl said, "it's the way your mind works . . . It picks up useless facts as silver after you've polished it picks up sulphur vapour; and tarnishes! It arranges the useless fact in obsolescent patterns and makes Toryism out of them . . . I've never met a Cambridge Tory man before. I thought they were all in museums and you work them up again out of bones. That's what father used to say; he was an Oxford Disraelian Conservative Imperialist . . ."

"I know of course," Tietjens said.

"Of course you know," the girl said. "You know everything . . . And you've worked everything into absurd principles. You think father was unsound because he tried to apply tendencies to life. *You* want to be an English country gentleman and spin principles out of the newspapers and the gossip of horse-fairs. And let the country go to hell, you'll never stir a finger except to say I told you so."

She touched him suddenly on the arm:

"*Don't* mind me!" she said. "It's reaction. I'm so happy. I'm so happy."

Ford Madox Ford, Some Do Not . . . , 1924.[257]

Conversation is one of the *arts in its own right: it is the hot centre of *culture. We recognise Horace's Lalage and her vitality because we come upon her in conversation:[258]

> Dulce ridentem Lalagen amabo,
> Dulce loquentem.
>
> I will always love Lalage,
> sweetly laughing and talking.

Horace, Odes, 23 BC.[259]

*Dialogue, Courtesy, Disconnection, Fallacies.

COOPERATION. See Reciprocity and Cooperation.

COUNTY. Counties began their career as the defining administrative unit in England under King Alfred's land reforms, introduced following his defeat of the Viking army at the Battle of Edington, near Chippenham in 878. Their essential form and function remained in place until the Local Government Act, which came into force on 1 April 1974.[260]

Before Alfred's intervention, shires got a mention here and there, but the recognised territorial unit was that of the long-standing settlements of the peoples, or tribes, of England. Places took their names from the people that lived there. Many of those names survive: the Wreocensætan (the Wrekin), the Pecsætan (the Peak District), the Hicce (Hitchin), the Hwicce (Shipton-under-Wychwood), the Cilternætan (the Chilterns) — along with the larger groups and more established names such as the East Angles, the East Saxons, the South Saxons and the men of Kent.[261]

The Viking attack was sustained and ferocious; it decisively overwhelmed East Anglia, Northumbria and Mercia and, despite their defeat at Edington, it was clear that they would be back. Alfred prepared for this for the next fourteen years by building fortified centres across Wessex, insisting that they should be occupied at all times and more-or-less self-sufficient in food, and specifying their *defence in detail. For each length of wall, measured in poles (5½ yards), four men were required, and each man, with his family, required one hide of land for subsistence (the exact size of a hide varied according to its quality and local conditions). For example, Oxford, with 2060 yards of wall to be defended, required 1,500 men and hides. Along with this came systematic arrangements for land-ownership, taxation and military service, and the beginnings of the collectively-managed open fields of the English manor.[262]

All this, despite variations in definition and in the pace of change, was contained in the network of English counties, which were allocated powers and responsibilities both as defenders of local freedoms and as the local authorities that enabled the government to govern. The first — and in some senses, never surpassed — project at which these shires proved themselves was to provide a framework for a comprehensive survey of every cultivated hide and property in the *nation. It was commissioned by King William the Conqueror following "much thought and very deep discussion" with his court over Christmas in Gloucester, 1085. And—not bad for an official database—it is still selling well 1,000 years later in paperback as *The Domesday Book* (the title it acquired soon after completion).[263]

Counties, however, are now widely seen to be *irrelevant: too small to act as the administrative unit for a continent-wide structure such as the European Union; too large to be accepted as having relevance to the *local. But the problem is that each topic on the administrator's to-do list is on a different scale from all the others. If America were to be divided up according to the main characteristics of particular areas, there would, as Howard Odum pointed out, be . . .

> The geographers' 700 soil regions and 5145
> agricultural regions, the ecologists' 17 watersheds
> and 97 river valleys, the city planners' 183 metro-
> politan regions and 683 retail-shopping regions,
> the anthropologists' American Indian "culture
> areas", the historians' sections and provinces, the
> political scientists' pluralisms and federalisms,
> and the literary critics' cultures in the South,
> Southwest, New England, and the Great Plains.[264]

As long ago as the 1930s in the UK, it was argued that the county was simply the wrong size for most of the things it was intended to do:

> . . . in the matter of certain aspects of water
> supply, river pollution, land and drainage,
> electricity production and supply, transport
> and police, the county as an *area*, and, in some
> cases, as an authority, not only shows signs of
> supercession, but is already superceded.[265]

There is no neat fit between local areas and local responsibilities. The right size for one function is unlikely to be the right size for another function. There is no *generally right size—except when it is agreed that what matters above all is participation.

Building the *Lean Economy will involve, amongst other things, making the shift from a society of consumers and customers to a society of stewards of the *place they live in. Counties lasted for 1,000 years because they

were on a *scale which was large enough to represent central government and small enough to enable their inhabitants to participate. On the scale of the county, there is a good chance that you can get to the county town and be home in time for supper. Even on a horse. Or, failing that, you can reach your local town, which is local enough to sort out the problem and able to make its case at the level of the county. At this scale, local circumstances are visible from the centre.

*Regions are approximately ten times the size, with a population of some ten million, rather than the county's one million. They belong to the culture of technical *expertise. Counties have eye contact and knowledge of their particular landscape. The people know where they live.

*Groups and Group Sizes, Nation, Reciprocity and Cooperation ❭ Exchange.

COURAGE. See Fortitude, Practice, Virtues, *Tao*, Betrayal.

COURTESY. The art of listening and *reflection. It requires a taught or instinctive *logic literacy and *manners—foregoing *distractions, *deceptions, *fallacies and *abstractions. It requires *presence, and particular courtesies such as not interrupting—and (a variant), not interrupting, guessing wrongly what the other person was going to say, and then launching into an unstoppable flow of disagreement with what you assumed he would.

It means not finishing the other person's sentences, not quickly losing concentration while the other person is speaking, not hurrying the other person along with impatient listening-noises ("yes . . . yes . . . yes"), not abruptly changing the subject (*Shifting Ground), not flatly and thoughtlessly contradicting or disagreeing as a matter of routine, not deliberately misconstruing as an absurdity what the other person has said, not assuming the other person to be an idiot unless you have considered the evidence, not catching the other person out by taking issue with the loose expression that happens in everyday *conversation, not taking the other person's observations as personal criticism, and not interpreting the other person in a different "colour" from that which was intended—i.e., being able to recognise a joke as a joke, and urgency as demanding attention.[266]

C

Courtesy brings *virtues which Izaak Walton ascribed to fishing: "a rest to the mind, a cheerer of his spirits, a diverter of sadness, a calmer of unquiet thoughts, a moderator of passions, a procurer of contentedness; . . . habits of peace and patience".[267]
*Bad Faith.

COWARDICE. Lack of courage to defend, by argument or action, a value which a person believes to be right. The reason may be that the idea requires more careful thought than the alternative position; or that persistence would be lonely, or risky.
*Betrayal, Calibration, Character, Ideology, Reflection.

CRAFTS. Highly accomplished *manual skills.
*Practice, Profession.

CREATIVE BLOCK. (1) The stage of uncertainty, pessimism and loss of confidence through which a person must pass in order to achieve a creative and rooted insight.[268]
(2) Failure which prevents a person, *community or *culture from carrying out a bad idea, and thereby forces development of a better one.

*Boredom, Wishful Thinking, Fortitude, Casuistry, Ingenuity Gap, Interest, Paradigm, Success, Hippopotamus.

CREDIT UNION. A small-scale fund set up by people with a common bond of some kind, such as living in the same area, or working in a firm that can make a useful contribution to local needs and employment, but could not compete if it were fully exposed to the *market economy.

Members of the union have to purchase some minimum number of shares, which may be as little as £1's worth, up to a usual maximum of around £5,000, for which they receive *interest in the form of dividends. The union then lends money to *local people and small enterprises, and this money is therefore kept working within the area, instead of draining away into areas with stronger *economies, or into the world market.

Credit unions' aim is *cooperative microcredit, rather than *competitive pricing, so they can maintain a constant rate of interest, independently of how much mainstream rates may fluctuate. They can also provide banking facilities so that local people can pay in money, draw it out, and pay bills without having to travel into the town centre, which is necessary in poorer parts of town where the commercial banks have no branches.[269]
*Vernacular, Casuistry, Socially Solvent, Social Mobility, Closed Access, Usury.

CULTURE. The culture of a *community is its *art, music, dance, *skills, *traditions, *virtues, *humour, *carnival, conventions and *conversation. These give structure and shape to community—like the foundational vertical strands used in basket-making, round which you wind the texture of the basket itself. Culture keeps *social capital alive and upright. It is . . .

. . . all those habits and customs whereby we identify ourselves as a community instead of as a collection of atomic individuals. And what makes that possible is a sense of shared destiny, shared history, shared home, being together in one place and that place being ours. And out of that we build institutions, religions, literature, art, and music. And they all reinforce each other, and I think that's what gives a place a culture. But, of course, by that very argument there are things that take that culture away. Mass immigration of people who actually don't identify with the surrounding community would take it away, and of course that is a problem that we're all facing. What would also take it away is a complete degeneration of the media of communication, so that people are no longer in touch with literature and art which is theirs, and that is also happening.

Roger Scruton, Any Questions?, BBC Radio 4, 2006.[270]

And . . .

. . . a communal order of memory, insight, value, work, conviviality, reverence, aspiration. It reveals the human necessities and the human limits. It clarifies our inescapable bonds to the earth and to each other. It assures that the necessary restraints are observed, that the necessary work is done, and that it is done well. A healthy *farm* culture can be based only upon familiarity and can grow only among a people soundly established upon the land; it nourishes and safeguards a human intelligence of the earth that no amount of technology can satisfactorily replace. The growth of such a culture was once a strong possibility in the farm communities of this country. We now have only the sad remnants of those communities. If we allow another generation to pass without doing what is necessary to enhance and embolden the possibility now perishing with them, we will lose it altogether. And then we will not only invoke calamity—we will deserve it.

Wendell Berry, The Unsettling of America, 1977.[271]

Starting some three centuries ago, the *market economy has, with growing confidence, been the source and framework for a loose and easy-going but effective civil society and social order. When it fades, there will be no option other than to turn to a rich culture and social capital to take on this role. The culture of the future will have a challenging job to do, which seems to be unrealistic at a time when it is substantially reduced to an optional, spectator activity. And yet it is the brief era

of the market as the dominant source of social *cohesion—no more than the interval between acts in human history—that has been the *exception. That interlude aside, the frame on which the texture of social order has been woven has not been the 'sweet commerce' of the market, but culture.[272]

The fabric of the *Lean Economy will again consist of its social *institutions and their expressiveness—an organic integration of the past into the present. That culture is both the supportive frame of reference for *presence, and the condition for the *reciprocal obligations and *common purpose which will move into the space vacated by the market. Culture will be the *creative expression of a community, giving it, and its members, *identity. In part, it will be expressed in *religion. Lean culture will be the soul of a society which, despite *sceptical beginnings and the serial culture-destroying traumas of the modern era, will build and sustain a cohesive civility comprising a *public sphere, *judgment and participation.

At present, culture is decorative rather than structural; although it may lift the spirits . . .

. . . these wings are no longer wings to fly
But merely vans to beat the air . . .

T.S. Eliot, Ash Wednesday, 1930.[273]

The Lean Economy, in contrast, will depend on its culture for its existence.

Now, the existence of a cohesive society organised around a common culture will not require everyone to change their character and become altruistic. Benevolence is indeed integral to a culture that works, but that is not the *way in*; it is an outcome. The crucial task is to capture self-interest and use it in the interests of the community. David Hume (1711–1776), reflecting on this core principle, wrote that the central rule of good design in social arrangements is that "every man ought to be supposed a knave and to have no other end, in all his actions, than private interest".[274]

A strong culture provides a structure such that when people do act in their own interests, those actions are in others' interests too:

• You want to sustain a friendship? You take part in a whole range of interactions—*encounter, *gifts,

C

*play and *ritual—drawing on an endowment of humour, memory, inference and points of reference which are supplied by the culture you live in.

- You want to find agreement with someone so that you can move forward in a common aim? You have conversations or arguments which draw on a common culture, or a history of participation in cooperative projects.

- You want to be trusted by someone, and it would be helpful if you could trust them in return? That *trust draws on *grammar, built on clues which cannot be faked. You smile and laugh at the same things; enthusiasms, *loyalties, values and memory converge. These are things that draw on the mind and body beyond the level of consciousness, at *spiritual and *emotional depth, maturing over lifetimes in a common culture.

These muscles of *intuition, and the culture on which they rely, atrophy unless they are used, and can fall into near-disuse if a simpler alternative is supplied. Here is one such alternative, supplied by Adam Smith in 1776:

Man has almost constant occasion for the help of his brethren, and it is in vain for him to expect it from their benevolence only. He will be more likely to prevail if he can interest their self-love in his favour, and show them that it is for their own advantage to do for him what he requires of them. . . . It is not from the benevolence of the butcher, the brewer, or the baker that we expect our dinner, but from their regard to their own interest. . . . Nobody but a beggar chooses to depend chiefly upon the benevolence of his fellow-citizens.[275]

THE SOURCE OF TRULY HUMAN LIFE

Scene: Pyongyang, North Korea

I was in the enormous and almost deserted square in front of the Great People's Study House—all open spaces in Pyongyang remain deserted unless filled with squads of hundreds of thousands of human automata—when a young Korean slid surreptitiously up to me and asked, "Do you speak English?"

An electric moment: for in North Korea, unsupervised contact between a Korean and foreigner is utterly unthinkable, as unthinkable as shouting, "Down with Big Brother!"

"Yes," I replied.

"I am a student at the Foreign Languages Institute. Reading Dickens and Shakespeare is the greatest, the only pleasure of my life."

It was the most searing communication I have ever received in my life. We parted immediately afterward and of course will never meet again. For him, Dickens and Shakespeare (which the regime permitted him to read with quite other ends in view) guaranteed the possibility not just of freedom but of truly human life itself.

THEODORE DALRYMPLE, Our Culture, What's Left of It, 2005.[276]

Scene: Torquay, UK

A skills-based curriculum demands that you make connections between different subject domains. That requires thought. Quite seriously, you have got to move beyond, "Should we or should we not teach Shakespeare?" Is the world going to collapse if they don't know "to be, or not to be"? Our national curriculum should be far more focussed on the development of life skills and ways of working than whether or not we teach the Battle of Hastings.

MARY BOUSTED, general secretary of the Association of Teachers and Lecturers, Annual Conference, 20 March 2008.[277]

Well, that's fine, but what happens when the *market economy is no longer around to work that magic? The cultural texture that has been broken up will take years to rebuild. We see an example of the slowness of such recovery (in a different field) in the thick turf of inter-weaving grasses which is strong enough to support cattle through the winter. It takes a minimum of twenty years to re-establish (*Lean Food). That tells us some-thing. The foundation assets of our civilisation will take time to recover, but our need for them is immediate. We have a timing problem.

And perhaps the rebuilding of a culture is impossible, even if we had the time. In fact, is there a way back at all? The sociologist, Paul Gottfried, in his history of that defeat, says no:

> I do not perceive any possibility of moving
> backward historically. . . . One simply cannot
> recreate the cultural benefits of the past, as one
> might its architecture or cuisine, through public
> projects or ad-hoc committees.[278]

And yet, maybe Gottfried does not perceive any pos-sibility of *peak oil, either, or the *climacteric. If he did, he could acknowledge that mass production and mass consumption—the ultimate sources of the postmodern-ism which demolished the idea that meaning is to be found in particular *places, traditions and texts—are themselves fading into the past.

Only in a prosperous market economy is it rational to go confidently for self-fulfilment, doing it on your own without having to worry about the *ethics and *narrative of the group and society you belong to. Even Classical Rome stalled halfway along that road, because it lacked the mass market which is the foundation of the individual speak-for-yourselfism that underpins the *democratic order. All societies other than the market economy acknowledged, at least to some degree, that they could not make sense of their prac-tical needs unless they made sense, first of all, of the community—and the culture which defined it, which they were not aware of as anything different from the way they lived every day.

Community is culture's habitat. Culture is the centre of the community's life; its essence and DNA. If the great orchestras and theatre companies with a global reach committed themselves to localising their culture, building local competence and participation, they would reveal that, in terms of the planet's present drama, they had understood the plot.[279]

For the post-market economy, the difficult task will not be to move away from our market-based civil society: that will fall away so fast that we will find it hard to believe it was ever there. The task, on the con-trary, is to recognise that the seeds of a community ethic—and, indeed, of benevolence—still exist. We now need to move from a precious interest in culture as entertainment, often passive and solitary, to culture in its original, earthy senses of the story and celebration, the guardianship and dance that tell you where you are, and who is there with you . . .

*Carnival, Big Stick, Social Entropy, Invisible Goods, Script, Local Wisdom.

CUPBOARD LOVE. A practical motivation which helps to sustain loving relationships. To be too explicit about it is, of course, quickly destructive, but what you get from a relationship doesn't have to be material. It may be exchanges of social, *emotional or intellec-tual stimulation, an occasional laugh, cheerfulness, encouragement, company, *courtesy, *good faith, love . . . But material *reciprocity helps, and *gifts, especially of *food, are central to social bonding. In the future, fiercely powerful bonds of friendship and *loyalty will be unconditionally *necessary. They will be sustained and deepened for many reasons, includ-ing material ones.

CURRENCY. See Nation, Local Currency.

D

DAMPER, THE. The presumption that only the *ordinary, the unremarkable, the banal, can be *true. If what you are saying is surprising, you must be making it up.

More generally, the damper is the argument that the truth can be presumed to be somewhere in the middle between the extremes. This can be a manipulative tactic, since the "middle position" can creep towards an extreme as circumstances and *expectations change. The damper can be a successful way of ensuring that the opposition never really gets going because it does not think the middle position is worth getting excited about; not realising that it is constantly moving ahead and being redefined. Today's middle is yesterday's outlier.[1]

And the damper can take the form of "striking a balance". Find a mid-position between reason and mayhem: reason now seems unreasonable; the road to mayhem is already halfway-travelled.

*Moderation, Calibration, Fallacies, Lean Education.

DANCE. See Carnival, Middle Voice.

DEATH. The means by which an *ecosystem keeps itself alive, selects its fittest, controls its *scale, gives peace to the tormented, enables young life, and accumulates a *grammar of inherited meaning as generations change places.

A *natural system lies in tension between life and death: death is as important to it as life. *A lot* of death is a sign of a healthy large population. *Too much* death is a sign that it is in danger; it is not coping; its terms of coexistence with its habitat are breaking down. *Too little* death is a sign of the population exploding to levels which will destroy it and the ecology that supports it. *No death* means that the system is already dead.

The reduction of life to an *icon—the assertion that life (*viz*, human life) is sacred—disconnects the mind from the *ecosystem to which it belongs. It is a fertile error. Beneath the exaggerated regard for life lies an impatience with, a disdain for, the actual processes that sustain the ecology that sustains us. Expressing faith in the sanctity of human life is a licence—in a series of little, well-intentioned, *self-evident steps—to kill the ecology that supports it.

The large-scale system, relying on its size and technology, and making an enemy of death which should be its friend, joins a battle which it cannot win. In *systems thinking, death is sacred.[2]

*Sacrifice-and-Succession, Wheel of Life.

DEBT. Funds and assets whose owner makes them available for use by another person, usually for a price and for an agreed period.

It is often asserted that debt is the driver of economic growth and hence of our discontents, but it is not as simple as that. Societies discovered growth a long time before they discovered *money and banks. Money smoothes the path to debt, and debt helps to smooth the path of *growth, but neither are essential. A growing *civic society has to build big *infrastructures (such as the 1st century Roman Pont du Gard viaduct across the River Gardon in the south of France, 48 metres high and 360 metres long), which may be paid for with borrowed funds, so that *interest—and often power—accrues to lenders. But it is the need for the infrastructures that drives the process, and if the debt were unavailable, alternative means could be found, such as draw-downs from capital or taxation, or the slavery that built the Coliseum, or retained earnings, or just widely-shared participation.[3]

Debt can though be used as an instrument of direct exploitation. Companies saw in it a means of sustaining control over employees in the early years of the Industrial Revolution, when a company could own the only available shop, so that a worker might owe his soul to the company store—attempts to make this illegal finally became effective in the UK with the Truck Act of 1831. And it has been used by the Bretton Woods institutions—notably the World Bank—as part of a programme to encourage or require developing economies to become market economies exporting *food and raw *materials, and importing services and finished goods from OECD countries. Debt undermines settled, *resilient, subsistence societies, turning them into unstable societies with substantial fractions of their populations living in poverty.[4]

High levels of debt in the developed countries will mean that many people and institutions will become bankrupt after the oil *peak, and lenders could go the same way. We saw a rehearsal for this in 2008–2009. The consequences are hard to predict. *Market economies are robust, but a major breakdown of the financial system as a result of unpayable debts could ripple through to the breakdown of employment, incomes and essential distribution systems.[5]

*Economics, Usury, Resilience, Complexity, Credit Union.

DECENCY, THE FALLACY OF. The *fallacy that there are decent limits to the determination of opponents. This presumption of decency applies in long-standing *democracies in which there is a common, or at least widespread, quality of *good faith, but it is partly for this reason that democracies are so vulnerable: they are ripe for capture by people whose determination and ruthlessness is greater. *Civility is not defended by the niceties of political correctness, but by, for a start, staying awake.

*Moderation.

DECEPTIONS. Arguments whose errors confuse and mislead.

Deceptions are forms of the general error of *non sequitur—"it does not follow" (e.g., "the cat is chewing grass, so it must be Thursday"). They *can* lead to correct conclusions, despite their failure in logic (it might really be Thursday); and they may be intentional, with the arguer knowing exactly what she is doing; or unintentional, with the arguer herself being the first to be taken in. They are, however, different from *distractions in that they go through the motions of accepting the rules of argument. The villainy can be just as great, but it is more insidious because it comes in the form, not of sabotage, but of cheating: it deceives because it can seem *logical.

One defence against deception is *social capital, due to its basis in extended *conversation. *Intuitive detection of the fake comes only with *practice, including seriously-engaged argument—adversarial *cooperation—with friends. But with the decline in social capital, the balance of advantage is shifting, to the benefit of deception: the deceiver gets more skilled as he evades detection, and the deceived are more vulnerable to his *cant.

And here are other reasons why defences against deception may be weakening:

First, there is deception in the *mindset of the institution—the big, bureaucratic producer and regulator; the managerial state. Deception is a natural expression of institutional capture—the absorption of the whole person by the *institution and its objectives: he is out of his mind, away from *home (*Metamorphosis).

Secondly, there is deception in the mindset of the citizen-consumer: deception is embedded in mellifluous talk—sweet talk—the easy sense that it does not matter what you say, but thank you for sharing it anyway. Good communication is taken to be communication which does not make trouble—and there is no reason why it should if, as this sweet-talk *ethic requires, we only ever speak for ourselves. If you disagree with my *truth, no problem, because it only applies to me. We each inhabit our own truths. Here, for instance—quoted by the language scholar Deborah Cameron—is a therapy session for young single mothers dependent on welfare; Mirna is talking about wanting to have a baby, when the therapist intervenes:

MIRNA: You know how that is, when you just want to have a baby, just something that is yours and belongs to you . . .

THERAPIST: No, Mirna, we don't know how it is. Please tell us, but don't say "you". It is your experience, not ours, so you need to say "I" instead of "you": this is how *I* feel when *I* see a baby.

MIRNA: OK. I.

"We" can confidently declare that I can only speak for myself . . . And if I do so, there are no grounds for cooperation or for *conflict, nor is there any notion of truth and error, since whatever I speak is true for me. Sweet talk is not an expression of good *manners—it is a natural *grammar for a society of *disconnected individuals with weakened and broken links of *reciprocity. It is a consumer marketing tactic, too, where the "I"—and the death of "one"—says that there are no wider principles at stake, but only a personal deal between two individuals, one of whom exists to pleasure the other. This portable and personal "I" is required, for instance, in call centres, including *sex-lines. As Cameron notes, instruction manuals for sex-line workers could, with little editing, be applied to a commercialised culture that needs rules

D

D

for interactions between strangers: "Always be bubbly, sexy, interesting and interested in each individual caller. Remember, you are not your character on the phone."[6]

A third, and closely-related, stimulus to deception is the reduced part played by direct personal reflection as a source of opinion. *Iconic *personal experience remains all too significant—as in the "Train Crash Fallacy" whereby being in a train crash makes you an instant expert on the railways; or having a family member killed in war makes you an *expert on foreign policy. But first-hand experience as the raw material for one's own creative *reflection is rarer—and the detachment of opinion from that experience destroys confidence in one's own critical *judgment. You get out of practice. Instead, your judgment is applied to something you have heard, on criteria that you have heard, using evidence that you have heard, and—in search of approval of your own self—shaped by opinion that you have heard. The morals of modern debate are permissive about getting into bed *promiscuously with heard opinions. The insubstantial view bluffs its way through, attaching itself to any plausible utterance that comes to hand.

In contrast with all this, the sharp authenticity of something directly and personally observed and known can come in quite narrow, direct, focused insights. It stays in the mind. Here are two examples from the poet Thomas Hardy. At a time of the breaking of nations, such as 1915, the need for something very precise, beyond deception, is intense; he observed,

> Only a man harrowing clods
>   In a slow silent walk
> With an old horse that stumbles and nods
>   Half asleep as they stalk.
>
> Only thin smoke without flame
>   From the heaps of couch-grass;
> Yet this will go onward the same
>   Though Dynasties pass.[7]

It is a limited and exact vision of a place and moment, which is precisely its deception-resisting strength. Something like it had happened to Hardy long before: walking behind a chaise—to ease the pony's load— Hardy was climbing a hill at Castle Boterel with his future wife:

> It filled but a minute. But was there ever
> A time of such quality, since or before,
> In that hill's story?[8]

First-hand vision is not necessarily *right*. The horse-and-harrow culture did not last; nor did the quality of Hardy's love, about which he was writing after his wife's *death. But its first-hand quality and *presence give it the scent of the horse, the hardness of the ground; there is nothing second-hand, no sweet talk. It is a fixed point to hold in the mind when observing the constantly-moving deceptions that we try—and which others try on us—when we argue.

————

Fallacies never fit easily into a well-defined group, but here are some which (perhaps) fit more comfortably into a group labelled "deceptions" than into any other: *Begging the Question, Diplomatic Lie, Disingenuousness, False Analogy, False Consistency, Hyperbole, Quibble, Cant, Self-Deception, Wolf Fallacy.

DEFENCE. See Lean Defence.

DEFERENCE. (1) Sycophantic submission to received ideas and admired people.
(2) Recognition of the particular, even though it is uncomfortable or difficult, as a starting point for *caritas*, with its caring obligation and engagement, and for *encounter, the act of recognising something on its own terms. Deference, or *creative deference, accepts the qualities of the subject—a work of art, a *tradition, an *ecology, a person—despite its dissonance with easy current values.

The two meanings of deference are not complementary, but rather in direct opposition to each other, with the first being so dominant that it obscures the possibility of the second. Nonetheless, it is the second meaning which is defended in *Lean Logic*.[9]
*Humility, Calibration, Character, Ideology, Intuition, Manners.

DEFINITION. Definition is a useful way of making it clear what you are talking about. The problem starts, however, when it is supposed that the word or phrase in question has one intrinsically right meaning; the problem gets worse when it is argued that everyone should accept that meaning, and it reaches its nadir when it is combined with *bivalence—a refusal to recognise any grey areas. Example: the Fallacy of Definition occurs when a person asserts that an embryo, however soon after conception, is a human, and so qualifies for all the rights that might be claimed by a citizen. The response may be to argue, in contrast, that the embryo does not actually become human until it is two months gone, or six months gone, or until it is born, or even later. There is no way of resolving such a debate; all participants are a little bit right, including those who would go further still and say that a person is not "fully human" until he or she has passed various *ritual rites of passage and is an established, *socially solvent member of society. And that, furthermore, for some *traditional societies this does not occur until the age of 40.

The solution to this problem is to reverse the *direction* of the definition. Do not argue from left to right—saying, "'Human' means [quality ABC]"—a description which is certain to be as murderous to innocence and observation as Bitzer's definition of a horse in Dickens' *Hard Times*:

> Quadruped. Graminivorous. Forty teeth,
> namely twenty-four grinders, four eye-teeth,
> and twelve incisors. Sheds coat in the spring; in
> marshy countries, sheds hoofs, too. Hoofs hard,
> but requiring to be shod with iron. Age known
> by marks in mouth.[10]

Instead, argue from right to left, as in: "I am referring, in this particular conversation, to these particular qualities (ABC described at length, perhaps), and I am labelling them 'human'. There are certainly other qualities which could be labelled human, by other people in other contexts, but this is what the label means when I use it today."[11]

The Fallacy of Definition is one of the most insidious of all logical errors; it is the source for furious entrenched debate, for breakdowns in communication, for fanaticism, for war. It is possible to solve if and only if the change in the direction of definition—remaining within the reasonable world of right-to-left labelling, rather than left-to-right definition—is understood.

*Fallacies, Conversation, Wicked Problems, Good Faith, False Opposite.

DELOCALISATION. The process of eliminating essential services from local towns and villages, requiring increases in the need for travel and *transport, *energy and *time, along with a loss of *social capital, self-reliance, *presence and morale. Examples: the centralisation of hospitals, schools, police, magistrates courts and probation services; the closing down of post offices, shops, pubs and abattoirs; and prohibitions preventing *skilled craftsmen from recruiting apprentices by imposing health and safety regulations beyond the means of a small rural business.

These developments—persistent symptoms of *capture and concentration—reduce ever-further localities' preparedness for *localisation and the *Wheel of Life. They also destroy the sense of there being any *place to which local people belong, or for which they can make any decisions, or bear any *responsibility. The French philosopher Simone Weil called this "uproootedness", and wrote that it is "by far the most dangerous malady to which human societies are exposed. . . . To be rooted is perhaps the most important and least recognised need of the human soul".[12]

*Demoralisation, Social Entropy.

DEMOCRACY. Democracy gives people the power to vote out a government which they do not like, and to install an alternative. It is a vital defence of liberty, and it is at risk.[13]

Some previous civilisations, including the Ancient Greeks, have had long periods of democracy, in which citizens were qualified to vote. Theirs was a slave-owning democracy. Ours—in the industrially developed world—is an energy-owning democracy, with political standing underpinned by widely-available access to *energy, the equivalent of many slaves working for each citizen night and day.[14] Democracy depends on the assumption that electors have some power and standing in the state which cannot be spoken for by others. As citizens' access to energy unravels, loss of political power is likely to follow.

Democracy is necessary for our freedoms, but it is fragile and, among its flaws, here are five:

1. "The majority support it" is not a sufficient argument from which to conclude that a policy is

D

advisable or just. For instance, a decision to kill all people whose name is Stephen and to redistribute their assets among everyone else could be considered rational, in that it would make the majority wealthier. This is not a merely theoretical point. Totalitarian regimes—the Soviet Union, Communist China, Nazi Germany—have all depended on large-scale support for the vision they propose, although some minority groups are invariably singled out for punishment. This support becomes strained in later years, but it is there, and the regime does all it can to reinforce it. Its existence is seen as proof of the justice of what it is taking such pains to achieve, and John Stuart Mill's *On Liberty* is written as a warning of this *deception. Democracy, he shows, is not a sufficient defence of liberty; on the contrary, liberty depends on its own vigorous and perceptive defence, especially if there is a democracy in place complacently insisting that it is taking care of all that. Democracy is both a child and parent of liberty, but will let it down if given half a chance.[15]

2. Democracy does not recognise any right of franchise for future generations, even though their interests are affected by decisions taken in the present. Nor does it recognise any right of franchise for past generations, who had an *interest in their genetic and *cultural bequest to the present. In fact, there is a notional case for giving the vote to the unborn: an independent Responsible Legacy Panel (RLP), with a substantial block vote, could represent the interests of future generations; a Responsible Inheritance Panel (RIP) could represent past generations in the same way. As Edmund Burke reminds us,

> it is only those who listen to the dead who are the fit guardians of the unborn . . .[16]

. . . for what the dead gave us is the whole of our cultural language, enabling us to exist as a society. Perhaps a block vote might be taking matters too far, but the two panels could be required to publish meticulously-researched and serious manifestoes before each election, and to bring another voice, a deeper debate and a source of *judgment to the unchallenged platitudes that

precede elections in which just one generation gets the privilege of the vote.

Democracy has the potential to support good judgment, since it recruits talent and is accountable, but the combination of *reductionist thinking and an *ethic strongly biased towards the present impairs its ability to steer a complex civilisation along the desired path of *sustainability. At the time when the right to vote was being extended, this possibility was discussed at length by historians such as Oswald Spengler and Arnold Toynbee, and with more brevity, by Flinders Petrie:

> When democracy has attained full power, the majority without capital necessarily eat up the capital of the minority, and the civilisation steadily decays.[17]

3. Elected governments are free to take huge, society-transforming action, such as opening its borders or surrendering powers to other states, about which there has been no democratic discussion or vote. The reasons behind election wins have more to do with things like the need for a change of government, given the evident failures of the previous one, than they are about considered discussion and approval of what the new government will actually do. There is in fact a case for this freedom to decide without consultation—Edmund Burke argued that electors should elect representatives, not policies; but in practice, they elect neither. Even the representatives themselves have little say in the executive decisions, and the large *scale on which democratic government operates means that decisions are disconnected from the local *presence necessary for right judgment.[18]

In fact, democracy gives a strong mandate to governments to get involved in the life of the *political economy that elected them. It invites the government to reinvent itself as management and service provider, and voters to reinvent themselves as customers. And it inherits a long and hard-to-reverse history of *intensification, relying on overall principles and bureaucratic regulation—that is, usurping the direct participation and presence of citizens and building failure into the systems they control.

4. Democratic debate is drawn to *reductionist thinking; it addresses symptoms, one at a time. Non-democracies may be as bad, or worse, in this respect, but it is exactly the wrong way to treat a *complex system. Democracy's potential for careful *systems thinking is undeveloped. As a general rule, it feels more comfortable with—as Bernard Crick puts it—"idiot simplification".[19]

The process of selecting representatives is biased towards those with a clearly-pronounced *mindset—a bundle of views which sit comfortably within an electable party. Passionate reductionism, often fuelled by resentments, is typical, but is not representative of the population as a whole, by whom it is seen as a misfortune. The best hope for the sufferer is a lifetime of palliative care in *politics, where, with luck, it will not be noticed, for the men and women there are as mad as he.[20]

5. A political class may develop, to which most politicians belong, whichever party is in power, providing a guarantee that the political elite's interests will be well-represented, so that it does not matter too much to them whether they are in government or not. Voting the government out will have no effect: it will just produce a reshuffle of the people you would like to get rid of. Proportional representation may in some situations provide particularly good growing conditions for this.[21]

But these are wrinkles in the democracy we already have. The heart of the matter is the democracy we will have, or will want to have, in the *local *communities of the future. It can come as a shock to realise that the representative democracy that we know is a rather feeble compromise, imposed by the *scale and centralisation of the modern state. Democracy began with direct decision-making: not voting for decision-makers, but getting together to decide. *Commons, Groups and Group Sizes, Virtual Crowd, Reciprocity and Cooperation.

DEMORALISATION. Moral fatigue. Loss of belief in one's own way of life, its *myth, and its competence. The salient forms of demoralisation are:

1. The loss of self-belief by a traditional society. Contact with a society with a more advanced technology and (so it seems) more comforts for less work has destroyed the confidence of almost all traditional societies which have found themselves in this situation. Examples: the collapse of culture and skills in the traditional self-reliant societies of Ladakh and Ireland that followed exposure to the *market economy.[22]

2. The hopelessness following trauma and loss, whether the final result is described as a defeat or a victory. Examples include the demoralisation of Europe following the two World Wars and, more generally, the traumas of the last century. As Chip Ward writes,

> There is reason to believe we have been traumatised by our recent history of global war, genocide, environmental dislocation, and fear.[23]

3. Disempowerment: the bunker mentality—the sense that you cannot make significant decisions, perhaps because you see nothing you can do to improve your situation, or because you have lost your sense of legitimacy and belonging: "Who are we to act? We don't really belong round here anyway. Whatever we accomplish will be judged, not by what we have done, but by who is doing it".[24]

Or here is an extract from a conversation about local decision-making being demoralised by the constant prospect of being bailed out, or overridden, from the centre (in the case of local responsibility for police forces):

> If we want local government to be accountable to local people, having national governments step in is the worst thing that you can do. It actually ends up by infantilising communities and their local representatives. They will never step up and take responsibility if we always have government taking decisions as a back-stop. The people who take the decisions locally, who choose to get involved, must live or die by those decisions. So local government has to take the responsibility; it has to be held to account, but that only works if it is allowed to make the mistakes and then pay the price for them.
>
> *Sir Simon Milton, Chairman,*
> *The Local Government Association, UK, 2008.[25]*

D

Disempowerment in the form of displacement is discussed in more detail in *Presence.

4. Loss of motivation: the sense that there is no point in doing something because someone else is going to do it for you.

Example: In the period of housing shortage after the Second World War, some families illegally squatted in disused army camps, and stayed put, but were never given the right to do so. Soon after this, other families were officially allowed to join them, since space in the camps was abundant, though squalid. The local authorities undertook to renovate the apartments of the legal squatters, but not of the others. Result: the unofficial squatters set to work with a will, improvising partitions, running up curtains, distempering, painting and using initiative. The official squatters, on the other hand, sat about glumly bemoaning their fate, without lifting a hand to help themselves. Until the overworked corporation workmen got around to them they would not attempt to improve affairs themselves.[26]

5. The process of becoming good-for-nothing. The classic illustration of this is the fate of Hannibal's army after enjoying a luxurious winter stopover at Capua in 211 BC. The Roman general Marcus Claudius Marcellus tells us what happened, as reported by Livy. Some of Hannibal's forces have taken time out to plunder the countryside, while . . .

. . . those who are fighting are enervated by the luxury of Capua and have worn themselves out through a whole winter's indulgence in wine and women and every kind of debauchery. They have lost their force and vigour, they have dissipated that strength of mind and body in which they surmounted the Alpine peaks. The men who did that are mere wrecks now; they can hardly bear the weight of their armour on their limbs while they fight. Capua has proved to be Hannibal's Cannae. All soldierly courage; all military discipline, all glory won in the past, all hopes for the future have been extinguished there.[27]

6. Lack of stimulus: an *education system that fails to inspire.

———

Demoralisation can be addictive; it is comfortable and non-judgmental and does not need to risk embarrassment by defending anything in particular. For the good news, see *Empowerment.

DENIAL. The refusal to recognise information which, if accepted, would present unwelcome *truths. Denial may call on techniques (not always intentional) of drawing up arguments and selected scientific data which, together, represent a formidable case for avoiding the unwelcome knowledge.

Examination of this phenomenon has been called "agnatology"—the study of *ignorance—and has concerned itself with, for example, the efforts of the tobacco companies in their campaign of denial on the links between their products and cancer. The *torments of the *climacteric (*peak oil, *climate change, etc) are suffering similar efforts. The result is denial-lag: fifty years to solve a major problem is used up in forty-five years of debate, followed by five years of panic.[28]
*Wolf Fallacy, Cognitive Dissonance, Ideology, Character, Reverse Risk Assessment Rule, Pascal's Wager.

DEPLETION PROTOCOL (aka Oil Depletion Protocol; Rimini Protocol; Uppsala Protocol). A proposal, drawn up by the Association for the Study of *Peak Oil, designed to ensure that the decline in production of oil, which is now beginning, is maintained at a steady rate, rather than being subject to the fluctuations in price and availability which can otherwise be expected.

Under the Protocol, oil-producing countries would commit themselves to reducing their production at a rate which relates to the amount of oil they have left. This 'depletion rate' is calculated as the amount currently being extracted each year, divided by the amount yet-to-extract (i.e., the total quantity remaining, including best estimates of the oil yet to be found). For example, if a country currently produces 300 million barrels a year, and it has ten billion barrels remaining of its entire endowment, then its depletion rate is three percent. Signing up to the Protocol would accordingly commit this country to producing three percent of its *remaining* total endowment each year from now on. Since this remaining endowment is itself diminishing as it is extracted, the actual quantity produced declines in a regular and predictable way, year by year. Meanwhile, the consuming countries would commit themselves to reducing their consumption at a depletion rate calculated for the world as a whole (less any oil they can provide for themselves).[29]

The Protocol does not contain any provision for less-developed countries that currently consume less oil to increase their consumption, on the grounds that those countries actually have the *advantage*, which they should not endanger, of not depending for their well-being on a fuel which will in due course become almost unobtainable. Nor does it seek to alter the distribution of world energy demand in the name of equality or fairness; it just enables a rapid but orderly descent from where we are now.

It is not a comprehensive response. It does not include gas and coal; it could be extended to include them, but estimating their reserves is harder and less reliable than is the case for oil. And if it were extended, that could imply an *intention to use up all remaining reserves, which would be defensible if the only objective were to address fossil fuel depletion, but not in the context of climate change. And the strict formula would need to be interpreted with flexibility from time to time, to allow for events such as production problems due to hurricane damage or interruptions in supply caused by local wars.

But an effective instrument would be an advance on where we are now, even if it did deal only with oil. The Depletion Protocol is the application of *manners to the depletion of a scarce and essential resource. It defines a global framework which would be implemented at the national level by *TEQs (Tradable Energy Quotas). There is flexibility in its design: as Richard Heinberg writes, "under an Oil Depletion Protocol, nations would agree to reduce their oil production and oil imports according to a consistent, sensible formula."[30] "Sensible" means recognising that the *energy peak and *climate change are two parts of the same problem, and that there have to be ways of agreeing on a response, since the alternatives are unattractive.

*Wolf Fallacy.

DEVIL'S TUNES. Simple, attractive-sounding solutions; *reductionist responses to *complex systems. Devils' tunes are much easier to argue for than solutions

which are consistent with *systems thinking, which have the disadvantage (from the Devil's point of view) of taking longer to explain, being harder to understand, and often involving action which is contrary to intuition and *expectation; they may also begin by making matters worse before they get better.

There is a powerful bias in a *democracy towards seduction by devils' tunes; it should, however, be a primary objective of democratic politicians not to exploit this, nor to fall for them, and to try to help others not to fall for them either.

*Witch-Hunt, Good Shepherd Paradox, Reverse Risk Assessment Rule.

DEVIL'S VOICE. The tactic of maintaining an argument on the ambiguous borderline between serious and "only joking". This allows the commentator to back both horses in a two-horse race: If the argument is accepted as sound, she can take the credit for it; if it is thought to be completely ridiculous, that's all right, because she's only joking (but it does make the point). "To make the point" is a popular but insidious form of argument: it hovers between *material truth and untruth, allowing a detachment, an absence from grounded discussion, whose main expression is noise.

*Hyperbole, Quibble, *Reductio ad Absurdum*.

DIALECTIC FALLACY, THE. The *fallacy that all problems can be understood in terms of the struggle between two tendencies: good/evil, light/dark, right/wrong, working class/ruling class, my religion/your religion, my politics/your politics—a way of winding all life's variety onto just two spools. The fallacy is important because it allows everything to be explained. If things are going well, that is, of course, because workers are winning the struggle for now; if things are going badly, that is down to the capitalists and they need to be punished. Here is an *identity-defining cause to which anyone can belong, and it gives its members plenty to do, without fear of ever being proved wrong—for the dialectic is *unfalsifiable: whatever the outcome, it can be explained by the theory.

The difficulty with this fallacy is that "dialectics" is a word to which almost everyone seems to ascribe a different meaning. The dialectic (Gr: *dialektos*, discourse) referred originally to the investigation of *truth in discussion, and it was used in this sense in the Wyclif Bible:

> Job . . . determyneth alle the lawes of dialatik,
> in proposicoun, assumpcoun, etc.[31]

Kant, Hegel, Marx and Engels all used it in different ways.[32] *Lean Logic* offers no guarantee that the meaning defined above is already recognised by anyone, but suggests that it would be useful if it were.
*Bivalence, Internal Evidence.

DIALOGUE. There are five types of dialogue.

First, there is the Critical Discussion, intended to resolve a difference of view, to understand a situation and to arrive at the *material truth of the matter; it is advisable to avoid *fallacies in a discussion of this kind.[33]

Secondly, Advocacy. This is intended to make a convincing case. In court, where a sharp adversary will expose them if she can, the use of fallacies is to some extent excusable, though risky. Otherwise, it is a bad idea—you are simply adding to the babble or rubbish passing for public debate.

Thirdly, there is Negotiation—and here, too, both parties recognise that the job is to persuade, so they may reasonably expect each other to commit some fallacies, such as the *Straw Man and *Hyperbole: the skill is in part to expose the fallacy. At the same time, there is a case for recognising the costs of this: plain speaking, and no fallacies at all, may get better and more enduring results for both sides.

Fourthly, the Quarrel. The purpose of a quarrel (as the logician Douglas N. Walton describes it) is "[to enable] hidden grievances to be expressed explicitly, acknowledged and dealt with, in order to make possible the smooth continuance of a personal relationship". He adds, "The closing stage of the quarrel is the healing . . .". This reconciliation is likely to be harder, and the quarrel will have revealed less, if the parties have logically cheated to get their way. However, the quarrel is only one form of strife-dialogue (or "eristic" dialogue: Gr: *eris*, "strife"). In other types, all that matters is to win—content does not matter, so there may be no benefit in avoiding fallacies, except for the risk of being found out.

The fifth kind of dialogue is *Play, where all presumptions about behaviour are temporarily suspended by the rules of the game itself: here is a chance to employ *distractions and *deceptions as outrageously as you can. Their use in play is a reminder of their destructive effect in reducing critical discussion to combat.
*Conversation, Informal Logic.

DIFFERENT PREMISES. If the starting point—the premises or assumptions—of the two parties in an argument are different, shifting them can be difficult. Socrates' technique was to change the other person's mind by showing that their premise led inexorably to an absurd or undesired conclusion. This is an application of what is now known as the law of non-contradiction: a statement cannot be true if it, or an inference arising from it, contradicts another statement that is known to be true. The weakness is that, if the premise is held firmly enough, the method may not work: the person "knows" that the premise is true, so even if an argument leads from that to an absurd conclusion, it must be the argument that is wrong, not the premise (*Denial).[34]

Disagreements between premises tend to be stable. If you are in a meeting, and you disagree with the conclusions, you may still be able to make helpful contributions to the discussion. If you disagree with the premises, you have to go in with a complex and lengthy explanation which no one wants to hear: you threaten the ability of the meeting to achieve anything at all. The probability is that, next meeting, you won't be there. Recommended response: get some allies. If there is just one person at the meeting who agrees with you, things may begin to go better. And yet, *institutions are defined by their assumptions, the premises from which everything else follows. Revision remains unlikely. A shock might do it (*Kaikaku), but by then it may be too late.
*Calibration, Division Fallacy, False Premise, Internal Evidence, Shifting Ground.

DIGESTIVE ETHICS. The positive correlation between the fullness of a person's stomach and the extent of his *compassion.
*Empty Sandwich, Looter's Ethics.

DIPLOMATIC LIE. (1) An essential lie to protect a person against an enemy. Example: lying to the Gestapo about the presence of Jews in the attic.

(2) A way of maintaining *privacy against intrusive enquiry.

(3) An essential lie to protect a person from hurt. Example: "No, I did not see your wife going off with Fred at closing time."

(4) A temporary way out of trouble. Example: "No, I did not go off with your wife at closing time."

(5) The sort of lie which *you* tell (aka a white lie). Other people's lies are plain lies.

*Self-Deception, Truth.

DIRTY HANDS. The sign of being prepared to compromise high-flown principle in the interests of *encountering a complex system, engaging with the detail and being capable of acknowledging awkward conclusions. A person willing to get his hands dirty is sufficiently secure not to need to make an *icon of himself and his own high moral standing, or to join the intellectuals' desertion of local *culture and *narrative; he gets to grips with the story.

This requires you to make the nuanced *judgments of *fuzzy logic, to get down into the detail, and perhaps to take a famously inconvenient route: it goes through the Slough of Despond, the Valley of Humiliation and the Valley of the Shadow of Death, passing Doubting Castle, maybe even encountering the giant Despair and the foul fiend Apollyon along the way.[35] And at the end of all that you can find yourself in a hole—which can be a good place for making judgments on the basis of encounter with inconvenient detail, but it is not quite enough, for you need *also* to see the matter in perspective, to refer critically to wider principles, and to do something about it—in short, you need eventually to get out of the hole. And for that, it would be very helpful to have a ladder. Oh, but can you get hold of a ladder when you need one? W.B. Yeats couldn't. He found himself down there with:

A mound of refuse or the sweepings of a street,
Old kettles, old bottles, and a broken can,
Old iron, old bones, old rags, that raving slut
Who keeps the till. Now that my ladder's gone
I must lie down where all the ladders start
In the foul rag and bone shop of the heart.

W. B. Yeats, The Circus Animals' Desertion, 1939.[36]

But then, it was only a story: in the *imagination, you can take immense risks. Anyone with the *narrative skills to imagine himself down there at the heart of the matter and the judgment to make sense of it can imagine and judge his way back again—or else he would never have dared to begin. The real risk is not being left without a ladder, but being left without a narrative, without a frame of reference which makes judgment possible and gives it meaning. That is not to be thought of: try it and you will simply be left behind in the City of Destruction.[37] *Harmless Lunatic, Harmonic Order, Grope, Expertise, Place, Practice.

DISCONNECTION, THE FALLACY OF. The use of disconnected language to convey connected meaning.

*Social capital—with its *network of linkages, *loyalties and commonalities which make a society—depends on *conversation as its primary expression. There is an intense significance about the activity of simply talking to each other: as John Milton remarked, its absence—being "yoked to a mute and spiritless mate"—is the worst of violences to the yearning soul; deprive children of stories, writes the philosopher Alasdair MacIntyre, and you leave them anxious stutterers in their actions as in their words. The three defining conditions of a living community, he suggests, are:[38]

1. a *narrative of its own, lived and updated by the lives of the present;
2. intelligibility (its ability to understand itself sufficiently to accept its *institutions and *traditions, or at least to *encounter them); and
3. accountability (an acceptance of the obligation to justice, *truthfulness and *fortitude).

All these are learned, expressed and recognised in conversation.[39]

However, conversation as a connected and connecting interaction may be in trouble. There are many reasons for this, including the growth of television watching and the decline of family meals, but one possible influence, and/or symptom, is a change in grammatical form: there is a shortening of sentences and of continuous trains of thought: fewer relative pronouns ("which", "whose"), participles ("having seen . . . ", "despite wanting . . .") and conjunctions ("and", "but"); fewer commas and

D

it lends itself to the opposite. At the extreme, it gives us statements each of which has only the force of the sentence to which it belongs, and they can therefore contradict each other without necessarily appearing to be inconsistent. Where there are no connections, there can be no inconsistency. There is therefore no basis for *judgment.

*Liturgy, Conversation, Logic, Fallacies.

DISINGENUOUSNESS. A pretence at *innocence, and a form of *reductionism. The argument is: "I'm a simple man; you're getting carried away with anxiety and complication."

Disingenuousness is "sanguine"—hopeful, not recognising a problem. This disposition is more closely related to the four humours of medieval medicine—blood, phlegm, yellow bile and black bile—than to the matter being considered, and the derivations persist:

- Sanguine (Latin: *sanguineus* blood): disposed to hopefulness.
- Phlegmatic (Greek: *phlégma* inflammation; Latin *phlegma* clammy moisture of the body, phlegm, mucous secretions): self-possessed; able to face problems while remaining calm and composed.
- Choleric (Greek: *khlolê* bile, anger, yellow bile): angry.
- Melancholic (Greek: *melan-* inflammation + *khlolê* black bile): sad, depressed.

Disingenuousness can be personally attractive, and often uses a mild, jokey self-deprecation, implying that the other person should loosen up and not take life so seriously. Example:

> I'm quite old fashioned; I'm not a great
> clever-sight guy. I love the House of Commons,
> I love Parliamentary democracy. Every
> international treaty for 500 years has been taken
> through our parliament . . .
>
> *Dennis MacShane MP, The Today Programme, BBC
> Radio 4, 26 March 2004, arguing against a referendum
> about the defence of national democratic freedoms.*

*Spirit, Devil's Voice.

semi-colons; more full stops. The effect of chopped-up language (asyndeton) is evident in the recent church *liturgies, whose former generous thought-sequences have been broken down into the abruptness of remarks, even lists of instructions, and this is significant because disconnected *grammar lends itself to disconnected meaning. It does not deliver a connected narrative.[40]

Long sentences that make connections are with us still in (for instance) the sustained 153-word metaphor of *water, washing, storm, waves and landfall in the Baptism Service of *The Book of Common Prayer* . . .

> . . . who of thy great mercy didst save Noah
> and his family in the ark from perishing by
> water; and didst also safely lead the children of
> Israel thy people through the Red Sea, figuring
> thereby thy holy Baptism . . . : We beseech
> thee for thine infinite mercies, that thou wilt
> mercifully look upon *this Child*; wash *him* and
> sanctify *him* with the Holy Ghost; that *he* . . .
> may be received into the ark of Christ's Church;
> and being stedfast in faith, joyful through hope,
> and rooted in charity, may so pass the waves
> of this troublesome world, that finally *he* may
> come to the land of everlasting life . . .[41]

—but they are the exception. The grammar of asyndeton *can* be used to form a connected argument, but

DISTRACTION. Any *fallacy which diverts attention from the argument: an usurping proposition—or the question of whether it is relevant or not—takes over, or is intended to do so. A potent source of disorder.

If you were having an argument with a person who was armed with a gun, angry and determined to make you see things his way, you might be tempted to concede the point, for now at least. He would have won a battle of sorts—forcing a switch of attention to something else. Distraction breaks the thread of argument by loading it with objections, threats, claims or other interventions which, whether they are true or not, have nothing to do with the case. It distracts attention and, in effect, sabotages any attempt to discuss things sensibly.

In the case of the man with the gun, of course, the distraction is all too obvious: the argument itself remains undecided, and it is likely to resurface to give him trouble in the future. The most common distractions do better than that. They insinuate; they come in disguise; they confuse. They are the knotweed of logic. Reasonable argument survives only in the habitats which distraction has not yet destroyed.

Here is the villainy of distraction revealed by the simplest of all possible subjects for debate: the proposition that two and two makes four. Distraction might urge, for instance, that the idea is old-fashioned, that the time has come to move on from *traditional thinking on the matter, or that it is too *technical for the public to understand. It could take the form of an ingratiating assurance that the only thing that matters, naturally, is the well-being and happiness of everyone concerned. Distraction might urge that it is perfectly okay nowadays to think that two plus two makes five; or that even thinking about it means an unforgivable neglect of the far more important proposition that three plus four makes seven. You might be invited to take note that there is money to be made by taking a different view of the matter, or that we have to move on from the notion if we are to be *competitive, or that the proposition is a bit rich coming from someone with a *private life like yours. Or it could insist with some passion that, contrary to the view that two plus two makes four, we must take our place at the heart of Europe. Distraction might add, with hoped-for finality, that the argument has already been lost: two plus two is going to make five in the future, whatever we do.

Distraction, evidently, has the power and freedom to cause havoc wherever it likes. It is a spoiler, worse than the cheat: the cheat at least recognises the existence of the rules on which argument depends if it is to make any sense, even though he then proceeds to break them, hoping not to be found out. Distraction recognises nothing except conquest: the argument is too serious to have any connection with the orderly rules of honourable play; it will be settled by other means. Rules? What rules? It presumes the death of *logic.

A characteristic form of distraction is to make an assertion which is not true, but which is hard to disagree with. This happens, for instance, with the appeal to the inevitable: the distracter does not argue for or against a proposal; instead, he simply asserts that it is going to happen anyway, and he may do so in a slightly bored drawl that passes off the sell-out as if it were a routine comment on the weather. Don't stand for this: it is one of the ways in which our citizen's right to have a say in deciding for ourselves dwindles into a loss of belief that we can influence anything at all. It is designed to induce give-up-itis, an acceptance that technology and the sweep of history make the decisions. What we are then supposed to do is to surrender, to make sure we are not in the way.

To prevent distraction developing its potential, it is necessary to be acutely aware of it, of its sources, consequences and remedies, of people who exploit it, others who resist it with *courage, and those who give way in bewilderment. Fallacies of distraction are varieties of fraud in action and disreputable ways of carrying on; they are, however, arguments we encounter often. All of us, undoubtedly, will have committed some, at least, of these logical crimes ourselves, perhaps quite recently, perhaps even today.

And yet, errors can be like scaffolding—not the building you want, but a useful start. When they are identified, captured and named, you have got their measure: fallacies become insights. In *Lean Logic*, alchemy lives on: each wrong—after some conjunction and congelation, precipitation and putrefaction, separation and sublimation, fermentation, fixation and fire—finally filters out into a right.

*Ad Hominem, Big Stick, Cant, Demoralisation, Icon, Innocence, Irrelevance, Many Questions, Pharisee, Rationalism, Shifting Ground, Straw Man.

D

DIVERSITY. Variations between the parts of a system. We can think of diversity as coming in two important forms:

First, there is strong diversity (or 'structural diversity'). This is the diversity of the parts which carry out specialist roles within a *complex system, such as the radically different—but strongly-*connected—organs within the body of an animal.

Secondly, there is the weak diversity (or 'textural diversity') within a *modular system. Its parts are similar to each other and only loosely interdependent, but the small variations may still be necessary for it to function.

Examples of weak diversity in a modular system include:

- Variation between individual members of a herd of antelopes.
- The acutely-discriminating personalities of *politics in a primate group, supporting its complex role in sustaining *cohesion and conserving genetic inheritance.[42]
- The different ways in which *resilient *communities adapt to local conditions.
- The limited range of diversity in a communications system. Language is only intelligible because its *grammar and vocabulary keep it within *boundaries. For example, where clothes have something to say about people, the nuance and meaning they convey depends on an agreed convention: the clothing worn by the Roman negotiators at the city of Tarentum in the third century BC was grossly strange from the Greeks' point of view; it was too different to be intelligible. For the Greeks, those billowing togas had nothing to say—gesture without meaning—and had them falling about with laughter. The negotiators took a huff and went home. Then there was war (*Needs and Wants).[43]
- And maybe the most familiar example is the difference between varieties within a species—sheep, for instance. Some (Romney Marsh) are good at coping with wet conditions, some (North Ronaldsay) thrive on seaweed; some (Border Cheviots) are hardy in bitter winters or (Comisana) scorching summers; some (Black Welsh) are natural mountaineers; some (Spæl) grow long smooth wool,

some (Roquefort) produce milk for blue cheese. Diversity could be reduced, and a hybrid vigour could perhaps be achieved, if all these breeds were blended into one Standard Eurosheep. But that gives us the Sheep Without Qualities, its character smoothed away, its hopes of resilience over. We would have sheep that had adapted to nothing in particular. Perhaps Hyde Park would suit them.

Or it may take the form of diversity in timing:[44]

- Budworms that attack spruce fir forests only become a plague when the forest is mature (when foliage is so thick that the birds cannot get at them). The forest cannot prevent budworm attack but, left to themselves, local areas die off at different times and recover, and the forest as a whole carries on (*Sacrifice-and-Succession). If you try to stop the budworm by routine spraying, then local life-cycles become synchronised, the whole forest dies back at once, and recovery is harder.[45]
- Differences in timing are core to the ways in which hunter-gatherers share hunting grounds (*Script). These arrangements reduce their risk by forcing all parties to *hunt over a wider, more diverse, range than they would if they did not share territories.[46]
- Complementary diversity in timing is critical to the process of succession as a recovery-resilient system finds its way back from trauma. In the "From Sand to Forest" sidebar we see an ecology—ultimately a woodland—owing its existence to the pioneering work of lyme grass many years previously.
- And there is the impressive case of the brief, ecstatic quickening of the desert toad, whose whole life-cycle is squeezed into the rare occasions when it rains, and who—in order to minimise the time from conception to conception, and to put on weight in the short time available—eats its little brothers and sisters.[47]

———

The weak diversity within *modular systems, then, supplies a robust ecology with the prospects of stability, evolution and *resilience. Meanwhile, strong diversity provides sharply different, but complementary, forms (e.g. organs, limbs) which join up to undertake different roles in support of the *complex systems (e.g., sheep) of which they are part.

FROM SAND TO FOREST
Getting the timing right

It takes an exceptionally hardy plant to be among the first to colonise a sand dune: salt, flood, drought, almost no nutrients in the soil, and no surrounding plants to protect it or to cooperate. Lyme grass has made a speciality of surviving these conditions. It tolerates salt; its leaves have a waxy coating to conserve water; it binds the sand and traps it as it blows.

But in due course the sand smothers it, and marram grass takes over. It, too, gets buried by the sand, but it can grow through it, and its roots bind the sand at a deep level, providing stability for more plants such as sand sedge, sea holly, sea bindweed, sea spurge and Portland spurge. The spurges contain a white latex which makes them taste unpleasant to rabbits.

Then come plants seeded by the wind, such as dandelions, groundsels, thistles, hawkbits, hawkweeds, hawk-beards and ragworts which, along with grass, grazed by the rabbits, form a short, tight turf, fertilised by the rabbit droppings. Next come lichens and mosses, followed by wild thyme, then grasshoppers, caterpillars, bees, and spiders and their predators, including mice, voles, skylarks and kestrels.

Now there is enough soil for bushes, such as hawthorn, elder and brambles, followed by creeping willow and orchids. Eventually, trees will dominate, and (unless something happens to break the succession) the area will mature into woodland.[48]

And within a natural *ecosystem, reciprocal exchange between species—providing and receiving nutrients, or supporting predators that keep your pests in check—is only made possible by diversity. Difference is necessary for *reciprocity; without it, there is nothing to exchange.[49]

Reports of a decline in diversity are therefore not merely matters of sentimental regret: they tell us something about the *system's health and expectation of life. Here is a description of diversity in decline in the case of the human ecology—John Stuart Mill's lament for its passing in the United Kingdom of the 1850s—inviting *reflection on why that matters. Diversity, he writes, is . . .

. . . every day diminishing. Formerly, different ranks, different neighbourhoods, different trades and professions, lived in what might be called different worlds; at present to a great degree in the same. Comparatively speaking, they now read the same things, listen to the same things, see the same things, go to the same places, have their hopes and fears directed to the same objects, have the same rights and liberties, and the same means of asserting them. And the assimilation is still proceeding. The increase

of commerce and manufacture promotes it. A more powerful agency than even all these, in bringing about a general similarity among mankind, is the complete establishment, in this and other free societies, of the ascendancy of public opinion in the State [so that] there ceases to be any social support for nonconformity. The demand that all other people shall resemble ourselves grows by what it feeds on. If resistance waits till life is reduced *nearly* to one uniform type, all deviations from that type will come to be considered impious, immoral, even monstrous and contrary to nature.[50]

If the increase of commerce and manufacture promotes uniformity, their coming *decrease* will *demote* it. *Localities will develop approaches adapted to their particular circumstances and places, going their separate ways, some of which may (as Mill puts it) "be considered impious, immoral, even monstrous and contrary to nature". Kirkpatrick Sale agrees: local communities of the future will . . .

. . . create their own political systems according to their own environmental settings and their own ecological needs, and there is no reason to think they would necessarily be compatible—or even, from someone else's point of view, *good*.[51]

Given a chance, local economies work out their own solutions. The surge in creativity and *small-scale enterprise following the disaster of the collapse in grain prices in the last two decades of the nineteenth century is one example of small farmers and horticulturalists, under pressure, using their nous in diverse ways. The agricultural historian Joan Thirsk writes,

> Innovative activities under a regime of alternative agriculture were branching out in a multitude of different directions, but most were modest, local efforts, which only the assiduous seeker in out-of-the-way places was likely to uncover. The statisticians were the very last to become aware of them and give them regular attention.[52]

And she summarises,

> The economic strategies of small-holders were bewilderingly diverse: they might well exasperate politicians seeking truths that could be expressed in a few crisp generalities.[53]

There are hard times ahead for regulatory agencies and for *generalities. The *lean economies that succeed will do so because they have made use of local diversity, the distinctive challenges and troubles, the airs and graces, of particular *places and *times, working in very diverse ways towards the *common aim of life after *oil. *Resilience ⟩ Resilient Systems ⟩ Diversity, Capital, Lean Food.

DIVISION, THE FALLACY OF. The *fallacy that what is true of the whole must also be true of the parts (or at least some of them): the Welsh are good at rugby; Dai must, therefore, be good at rugby. This is the inverse of the Fallacy of *Composition.[54]

The fallacy comes in arguments like these: "Since we cannot save *all* the pictures from the fire; there is no point in saving any of them; since we cannot provide the best *education to everyone, we cannot justify providing the best education to anyone; since we cannot get rid of every tyrant, there we cannot justify getting rid of any of them." (See "Drained" sidebar)

DOLLAR-A-DAY FALLACY, THE. The fallacy that poverty can reliably be measured in terms of *money.

DRAINED
The Marshes of Iraq before 1991

The natural beauty of the place was hypnotic. Black and white pied kingfishers dived for their prey all around us, clusters of storks arced high above, snow-white flotillas of stately pelicans fished the lagoons; there was always at least one eagle in the sky. The reeds we passed through trembled or crashed with hidden wildlife: otters, herons, coot, warblers, gaudy purple gallinule, pygmy cormorants, huge and dangerous wild pigs. And often, out of some apparently deserted reed-jungle, a full-throated human voice soared into the silence—a young Marsh Arab singing a love-song as he harvested the rushes. The canoe-boys might stop paddling to listen and they grunted appreciatively if the voice was good. They were moist-eyed and soulful only when they themselves were singing. I found the sound of those unselfconscious singers invariably moving. The young voice throbbed and choked with sadness, real or feigned. In that great solitude, where the men of Ur once poled their canoes and where "in the beginning", according to Sumerian legend, Marduk, the great God, built a reed platform on the surface of the waters and thus created the world, the effect is one of unquenchable and universal yearning.

GAVIN YOUNG, Return to the Marshes, 1977.

For instance, more than one person in three, in the developed and less-developed countries, lives on a desperately low income—less than two dollars a day. At this level, we are down to a wage at or below subsistence, often combined with toxic and even lethal working conditions—that is, employment on terms no better, and on some comparisons worse, than slavery.[55]

And yet, it is also true that extremely low incomes do not always mean devastating poverty—income is not always the appropriate measure for statements about living standards. This is because stable pre-market societies, such as that of Ladakh before it was thrown off course by globalisation, do not measure their *living standards in terms of money; they are economies based on *reciprocal obligation, and despite their evident well-being, a conventional economic estimate of incomes would conclude with horror that they were living on nothing at all.

Another example is the economy of Burma, which had endured in its traditional form when E.F. Schumacher was there in 1955 as an economic adviser to the Government. Interpreted in the framework of *economics, the very low levels of *per capita* income indicated a desperate level of poverty; seen in terms of real life, it was not as simple as that. This persuaded Schumacher to argue that there is more than one kind of appropriate economic system, distinguishing between "economics" and "meta-economics"—the economics of people and nature—and we get a first look at this in a letter to his wife,

> There is an innocence here which I have never seen before . . . In their gay dances with their dignified and composed manners, they are lovable; and one really wants to help them, if one but knew how. Even some of the Americans here say, "How can we help them when they are much happier and much nicer than we are ourselves?"[56]

However, as their traditional *reciprocities break down, they move into the world of *market economics, in which their incomes are measured in money, and so their progress can be described as moving from "Nothing-a-Day" to "Ten Dollars-a-Day"—a great endorsement of the benefits of *globalisation. In fact, it would represent not just a decline, but a collapse from a *sustainable, non-monetary *local economy to deep poverty and dependence. Incomes should therefore not be used as a measure of global advance in *well-being without careful *definition of the terms; to do otherwise simply *begs the question, assuming that the market economy is the only option.[57]

The Indian economist, Vandana Shiva, summarises,

> I have witnessed again and again that as people's resources are commoditised and people's economies are commercialised, money flow does increase in society, but it is mainly *outflow* from nature and people to commercial interests and corporations. The money economy grows, but nature's economy and people's economy shrink.[58]

*Distraction.

DUAL ECONOMY. The principle by which transition to the *Lean Economy moves ahead while the *market economy alongside it is still capable of delivering social order, *energy and incomes. The further that transition can advance before the *climacteric, the better. There is no case for dismantling the market; that will be done for us, all too soon. The priority is to make sure that there are at least some elements of *resilience in place to take over. In summary: do not destroy anything; concentrate on building the sequel with the time and resources that we have.

"Dual economy" in this sense should be distinguished from the pathological sense indicated in E.F. Schumacher's case for intermediate technology (see *Appropriate Technology).

*Transition.

E

ECO-EFFICIENCY. The consumption of natural assets—*materials, *energy, *water, etc—per unit of output.

There is a five-step sequence:

1. the derivation of products (e.g., usable materials, oil, collected water) from the available *natural capital;
2. the production of goods from those products;
3. the services derived from the goods that have been produced;
4. the use made of those services; and
5. the consumer's behaviour and way of life which determines his or her need for the service.

Each of these stages provides an opportunity for improvements in *efficiency, which multiply up: for instance, a 40 percent improvement at each stage multiplies into a 92 percent improvement overall.

*Lean Materials, Lean Energy.

ECOLOGICAL SYSTEM. One of the four types of system discussed in *Lean Logic* (for context, see the summary table in *Systems Thinking on page 450).

The ecological system occupies the space between the *complex system and the *modular system, and incorporates both. Here we have both strong *and* weak *diversity, taut *and* slack *connectedness; a *panarchy of systems and subsystems (*holons) known to us as forests, meadows, deserts, oceans, the *ecology of lions and antelopes and, on a larger scale, *Gaia herself.

Ecological systems challenge the concept of *resilience because, whatever the shock, an *ecology of some kind will endure—if one ecology fails, another will take its place, probably with its own different normality. Actually, that should read *"almost whatever the shock . . ."* because a hypershock could comprehensively destroy the life needed to qualify as an ecology. Insufficient action by our generation could start the planet on the path to that conclusion.

The complex system, the modular system and the *complicated system are things that can be discussed at length, and perhaps usefully. The ecological system

does not allow that in quite the same way. It is not a thing. It is everything.

*Wheel of Life.

ECOLOGY: FARMERS AND HUNTERS (see also Ecology: The Scholars). Our human ecology, with its two signature properties of (1) being based on agriculture, and (2) supporting a large population, is shot through with dark dilemmas. Its awareness of this now is acute, but not, perhaps, all that much more so than it was around the time of its birth, some 8,000 years ago.

Being understandably prejudiced in favour of the way of life we know at first hand, we tend to dismiss the life of hunter-gatherers as laughably *irrelevant to anything that matters to us now. However, we do in fact have considerable knowledge about that precursor to the familiar urban civilisation that we see as normal. Our main source of knowledge comes from anthropologists' studies of the many groups all over the world who have been able—at least until very recently—to hold out against the transformation of their lives, societies and minds by the development of *agriculture, and the explosive growth in *population that follows. No romantic text along the lines of "Let's go back to being hunter-gatherers", or supposing that these societies were free of grief, is implied by recognising that they may have something to say to us which we need to know.

The first thing it is useful to know is that they knew what they were about. Stone Age *craftsmen, with their mastery of working with crystalline rocks and their slender stone "laurel leave" knives, worked to a standard in their medium which has never been matched. Until the *climate change at the end of the last ice age, when increased rainfall and expanding forests altered the equilibrium that had lasted 100,000 years, they maintained a balance with their environment and its food sources. They had reliable supplies of meat. They cooked it. They sustained conditions which supported natural selection for the brains we have now. They kept astronomical records. They would have had their Einsteins. They were artists. They lived *sustainably.[1]

And they had *freedom. We can guess, no doubt, that there were *exceptions to this, but what we know from studies of hunter-gatherers is that the *political *culture which was most suited to their lives, skills, numbers and environment was egalitarian individualism. The anthropologist Hugh Brody lived with and studied the Inuit in northern Canada. He writes of their respect for each other's minds and decisions; individuals recognise each other as experts, and they may be willing to take advice, but the *leader of the *hunt does not give instructions. Others will follow if the plan is good or if the leader's expertise is persuasive, but whether they do so or not is their decision.[2]

This is a *cooperative, capable society with shared ends and means. People (and other animals) with a high degree of *community interdependence can develop the powers of shared thinking, acquiring some of the attributes we might think of as a collective brain (*Modularity). One of the central concepts in Inuit culture is the sense and reason of deep belonging to the *group. The *education of Inuit children is based on imitation, inspiration, belonging, *play and *practice, with little explicit instruction: the children want to belong in the community, and they learn that participating in its culture is a good way of doing so. As Steven Pinker, Geoffrey Sampson and others argue—with unconcealed irritation at having to do so—there is indeed such a thing as human nature, despite the claims of the "blank slate" theory which has argued to the contrary: if the assumption around which we organise education is that our minds are passive and not much better than "potty putty" (as Sampson puts it), it is not surprising that we see education as an enormously difficult uphill task. The Inuit, in contrast, do not see it that way; they go with the flow of the developing insights for which their children's minds are prepared.[3]

So we do not need to have reservations about their competence when we read such delineations of hunter-gatherer societies as this:

In most band and village societies before the evolution of the state, the average human being enjoyed economic and political freedoms which only a privileged minority enjoy today. Men decided for themselves how long they would work on a particular day, what they would work at—or if they would work at all. Women, too, ... generally set up their own daily schedules and paced themselves on an individual

basis. ... A man might decide it was a good day to string his bow, pile on thatch, look for feathers, or lounge about the camp. A woman might decide to ... collect firewood, plait a basket, or visit her mother. If the cultures of modern band and village peoples can be relied upon to reveal the past, work got done in this way for tens of thousands of years. Moreover, wood for the bow, leaves for the thatch, birds for the feathers, ... fibre for the basket—all were there for everyone to take. Earth, water, plants and game were communally owned. Every man and woman held title to an equal share of nature.[4]

Why has it been necessary to pay this visit to Stone Age society when the matter at hand is the ecology of our time? Because we need to have some idea of a starting point and, in order to do that, we need to be aware of *the state* as a newcomer on the planet, and to note the differences between it and the very different form of human society and ecology which it replaced. There is, of course, debate about why so many human groups made the transition from the sustainable hunter-gatherer system to an expansionist agriculture in so many parts of the world at roughly the same time. One version of events is that, as the climate warmed and the ice retreated, as rainfall increased and the forests grew, conditions became less favourable for the large grassland-dependent animals (the megafauna) on which Stone Age society depended. This was a crisis which led to an *intensification—and an improvement in the technology—of hunting, with the result that the megafauna were depleted and approached extinction, leaving their human predators with no alternative other than to domesticate their own plants and animals, to raise them in one place, and to call it home. But let us leave that matter unsettled and turn from *why* it happened to *what* happened, and what the consequences were. And— from the point of view of concise storytelling, combined with fierce insight into what it was like to be there and to experience that revolution at that time—there is no better source than the Book of Genesis.[5]

We join the story in the second chapter. From the dust of the ground (adamah), God made Adam (Genesis 2:7). God planted the Garden of Eden but warned that

E

the fruit of the tree of knowledge was not to be eaten, on pain of death. He made Eve from Adam's rib. Then in chapter three, the serpent tempted Eve to eat the apple, despite the prohibition. It was so good that she persuaded Adam to have one too. God, who had been walking in the garden in the cool of the evening, realised what had happened, and came looking for them. He threw them out of the garden, placed angels with flaming swords at the entrance to make sure they stayed out, and issued seven interesting curses. All of them have something to tell us, but curses 4, 5 and 6 have intense *relevance to the transformation from hunting to agriculture—to mankind's new role as a farmer:

1. The serpent will crawl on its belly and be hated by human beings.
2. The woman will endure intense pain in childbirth.
3. The woman will yearn for her husband, but (he told Eve) "he shall rule over thee".
4. The soil will be unproductive, full of thorn and thistles.
5. Humankind must "eat the herb of the field".
6. In order to get enough to eat, the man will endure intense hardship: "in the sweat of thy face shalt thou eat bread".
7. In death, Adam will then return to the ground, "for out of it thou wast taken: for dust thou art, and to dust thou shalt return".[6]

With Adam's two sons, Cain and Abel (in chapter 4), we begin to see these curses at work. Cain is an agriculturalist. Abel has somehow escaped the curses, and is a herder—that halfway stage from the life of the hunter-gatherer. They both make sacrifices to God. Abel offers a succulent lamb; Cain comes up with what sounds like a veggie box of rather middling quality. God evidently prefers the lamb. That makes Cain jealous and—despite a short lecture from God about needing a sense of responsibility towards his brother—Cain murders him. This is followed by God's new curse—this time on Cain: he will find the ground where he has

murdered Abel to be unproductive; he is condemned to move on, to be a vagabond, to live in the land of Nod (the land of wandering). And now two things happen. One is that Cain turns out to be very successful as an agriculturalist—the founding father of a whole people, building the first city, Enoch, complete with musicians, craftsmen working copper and iron, and a population that will restlessly spread (wander) far afield. The other is that Adam has another son, whom he calls Seth, and his wife takes pains to explain what he represents: "For God, said she, hath appointed me another seed instead of Abel, whom Cain slew". Clearly, hostilities were to be permanent between the new order of agriculture and cities and the old order of pastoralists and hunter-gatherers. The new order would win every time, but the matter would never be settled, least of all in the mind.[7]

And that's the story. We know that actually the process of domesticating plants took place over millennia, and indeed that hunting for food (fish, game) and foraging (blackberries, mushrooms) is still practised, but the shift from hunter-gathering to agriculture must have seemed sudden, and to many it undoubtedly was: the original hunter-gatherer population of Europe was practically wiped out—except in the areas such as northern Scandinavia which were unsuitable for agriculture—in about the fifth millennium BC. The near liquidation of the indigenous Indians of North America took as little as two centuries. Wherever an agricultural people became established, their *population would grow to the *scale of the city, and they would expand outwards, destroying the hunter-gatherers as they went.[8]

And now this city-building, forest-felling, ground-breaking, pastoralist-murdering, serially-cursed, crazily-expansionist, *energy-addicted, *water-insatiable, ruthless family of Cain, having won every other battle by foul means, has piously invented environmental ethics and wants to know how it can win with regard to the ecology.

*Ethics and algorithms

One of the many things which that story leaves us to think about is the way in which matters turn out not as (we might think) they ought to. Abel, who is closer to nature and to God, is killed; Cain, who is cursed, prospers. His family is fruitful and multiplies; the knowledge derived from that forbidden tree is turning out to be rather useful. He and his descendants worked out how to domesticate plants and animals. Before long, God himself is seeing the sense of this, and takes to calling domesticated animals "clean" and wild animals "unclean". In modern language, Cain and his descendants get out of jail free. By using knowledge and applying thought, they (we) can open up a range of choice which defies *expectations, and seems to be free of the most elementary standards of right and wrong.[9]

Clearly it pays to bend the environment to our will. Cain's extended family, after being hit by an overwhelming curse which might have had anyone else spending the rest of time in sackcloth and ashes, walked away and worked out how to make wine. The tree of knowledge could equally well have been called the tree of opportunity. Its apples make you free.[10]

Freedom is a good thing. That is an absolute and unconditional value. But even absolute and unconditional values come at a cost. The cost in this case is related to *feedback. A rule for sustaining *resilience is "tight feedback loops"—rapid response to a stimulus or shock. But then, the *exception to this is the case of a large system in which there is a time-delay between events and consequences, and which uses that delay to apply its knowledge and intelligence; to dig itself in. It suffers grief and uncertainty because it knows much and sees many solutions, but knows it will not change: ecology's nudges are simply ignored. The death penalty prescribed for those who eat from the tree of knowledge is carried out first in the sense of the death of innocence—freedom's freedom to destroy itself and the world around it. Knowledge and *intelligence can be a curse.

And stupidity, as the philosopher Daniel Dennett explains, can be an advantage. He explains why in his outline of the key principle of *algorithms*. An algorithm is a certain sort of formal process that can be counted on, whenever it is run, to yield a certain sort of result—the game of tossing a coin will always produce a winner and a loser; long division will always reveal factors of a number. Dennett's interest in algorithms stems from his consideration of ecologies where species

consistently reproduce more rapidly than the ecology can support, and therefore find themselves in competition. Following Darwin, Dennett shows that repeated waves of competition and selection will lead to a natural selection of traits, resulting in the *emergence of a progressive advance in capability well beyond anything that could be consciously designed or predicted. It is not intelligence that has achieved this, but trial and error in response to the simplest of rules:

> Darwin's dangerous idea: the algorithmic level *is* the level that best accounts for the speed of the antelope, the wing of the eagle, the shape of the orchid, the diversity of species, and all the other occasions for wonder in the world of nature. It is hard to believe that something as mindless and mechanical as an algorithm could produce such wonderful things.[11]

Dennett's observation about the stupidity, the underlying mindlessness, of algorithms is emphatic:

> Although the overall design of the procedure may be brilliant, or yield brilliant results, each constituent step, as well as the transition between steps, is utterly simple. How simple? Simple enough for a dutiful idiot to perform—or for a straightforward mechanical device to perform.[12]

Cain's children did not reject algorithms. They could not have developed their technology and cities and taken over the world if they had. But they used their knowledge to override—or to react differently to—the feedbacks of detail supplied by their ecology. The thorns and thistles indeed showed up as forecast by the curse, but instead of taking this as a sign that the environment did not like what they were doing, they took it as a sign that they needed to work harder and know more. More research was needed. And more sweat.

The yearning for an orderly ecology

One of the long-standing assumptions of thinkers about ecology is that it is ordered. For St. Thomas Aquinas (1225–1274), for instance, animals are . . .

> . . . ordered to man's use in the natural course of things, according to divine providence.[13]

and he cites the authority of Psalm 8:

> Thou makest him [i.e., mankind] to have
> dominion of the work of thy hands: and thou
> hast put all things in subjection under his feet.[14]

"Ordered" implies care, *protection, continuity, an obligation not to destroy, because (Aquinas adds) what ultimately matters is "the perfection of the whole [which is] providentially cared for by God".[15] And Aldo Leopold emphasised this sense of order and continuity in his land ethic (see *Ecology: The Scholars):

> A thing is right when it tends to preserve the
> integrity, stability, and beauty of the biotic com-
> munity. It is wrong when it tends otherwise.[16]

and Leopold fuses this order with the idea of community:

> A land ethic changes the role of *Homo sapiens*
> from conqueror of the land-community to plain
> member and citizen of it. It implies respect for
> his fellow-members, and also respect for the
> community as such.[16]

In fact, *community is central to ecology. The sense of community, equilibrium, cooperation, order and *health was at the heart of ecology for much of the last century—a counterpoise in the mind, if not in practice, to the accelerating environmental destruction. The ecologist Paul Sears pressed the case for restoring bio-logical order as a key task of public policy. For Frederic Clements, one of the characteristics of that order is that an ecology should not be prevented from maturing nat-urally towards, and then conserving, its "climax". And the climax is a stable state in which its parts interact with each other almost to the point of forming a "super-organism", with many of the self-organising properties of a single plant or animal.[17]

Science both enriches ideas and amends them, and it did both to the idea of climax, adding the physics of energy flows, trophic levels (nutrition), mineral exchanges between living things and the physical envi-ronment to the central principle of *diversity, and so forming the robust and coherent principle of the "eco-system", brought together by Eugene Odum. Much of the observation and science—perhaps most of what is most important—is correct: forests do undoubtedly promote and protect the high rainfall they need; clear, shallow lakes do provide habitat for the plants and fish that keep them clear; a failed state, awash with disor-der and distrust does provide conditions for disorder and distrust to settle in and stay. That is the nature of *resilience. But if the inference is drawn from this that natural systems have a purpose—the principle of "tele-ology"—there is trouble. And Odum gets into trouble. What all systems have in common, he tells us, is . . .

> . . . a strategy of development . . . directed
> toward achieving as large and diverse an
> organic structure as is possible within the
> limits set by the available energy input and the
> prevailing conditions of existence.[18]

The principle of teleology is not only attractive and inspiring, but influential. It influenced, for instance, Edward Goldsmith, perhaps the most inspirational writer on ecology of all:

> Ecology has to be teleological, for purposive-
> ness is possibly the most essential feature
> of the behaviour of living things. Only a
> methodology that accents this can enable us
> to understand the roles that living things play
> within the Gaian hierarchy of which they are
> the differentiated parts.[19]

But there is a difficulty with this—it is inconsistent with the principle of natural selection, with its simple algorithms leading, by a process of competition and selection, towards increasing competence and diver-sity. It is possible, with care, to argue that animals have capabilities which are not at present recognised by most Darwinian scientists, but the basic principle of natural selection is now well out of the range of critics, and the idea of purposive progression towards climax and *homeostasis is now not recognised as science.[20]

Maybe forests do tend to mature to what looks like a complex condition, but some do not; and those that do are themselves in a constant state of change. Some ecologies' progress towards maturity is interrupted; some destroy themselves, like inland lakes which even-tually turn themselves into land; forests burn; some get so clogged and dark that they die back. None are exempt from the contest between *Gaia (order) and

Medea (disorder)—a satisfying story, but an uncomfortable one: while we naturally want to join together to progress towards an orderly future, we know that, in the long view of ecology, nature sees this as a rather naïve aim.

A question of scale

The *Wheel of Life entry traces the sequence from the pioneering stage of an ecology to its maturity and ultimate failure. This 'adaptive cycle' is widely acknowledged in the science of ecology at present, and it may well prove to be robust because it is a coherent view of how complex and *ecological systems in general can be expected to behave, given what we mean by complexity—a system containing lots of species interacting with each other and their environment in diverse ways. To refer to Barry Commoner's Fourth Law of Ecology (though filched from economics): "There's no such thing as a free lunch". It would be strange if complexity were indeed a perfect system untouched by old age and decay and vulnerable only to some unkind external force that comes along to spoil it.[21]

But a large complex ecology is made up of smaller, less complex ones—*holons—which build their own capabilities. The holons join up, adapt and change, forming a *hierarchy or *panarchy of subsystems which *cooperate in a positive and symbiotic way with the larger system. But even individually and on their small scale, they have the advantage of rapid *feedback and *recovery-elastic resilience which may enable them to endure in some form, even if the wider *system does not. It could go the other way—with the whole ecosystem failing and taking everything with it, *small-scale holons included. But at least those local holons are in with a chance.

Cain and his extended family of (now) some 7 billion people have received plenty of feedback cues about inadvisable courses of action, but their response has been to insist that their knowledge and their size gives them the freedom to do it anyway. We do not live in the domain of algorithms. We have a plan, and we have the freedom to carry it out. Would living in the domain of algorithms mean being unfree? No, it would mean being small.

*Ecology: The Scholars, Good Shepherd Paradox, Spirit.

ECOLOGY: THE SCHOLARS (see also Ecology: Farmers and Hunters). Ecology is the study of the interactions between living organisms and their environments, and the word refers equally to these *natural systems themselves (a woodland, a pond). The closely-related subject of ecological, or environmental, ethics extends moral *judgment beyond human affairs to the ways humans interact with nature. The two aspects of ecology combined—the science and the ethics—is a field as large as the planet's history. Here is a shortened version:[22]

The science of ecology[23]

1. *Evolution and adaptation* (or "autoecology") studies the ways in which species come into being and adapt to or change their habitat, what they eat and how they defend themselves, reproduce and extend their range.[24]

2. *Population ecology* is about *population numbers, their rise and fall, their predators and prey, the symbiosis and synergy with other populations, and the ways populations respond to the fundamental problem that, given a chance, they will increase (short term) beyond the (long term) ability of their environments to support them.[25]

3. *Communities and *ecosystems.* Here we have the study of *community in the sense of organisms (including people) that live together, how they are influenced by "bottom-up" influences such as changes in water quality, and "top-down" factors such as the arrival of an alien predator. This is the field of ecology that studies community-defining relationships such as competition, predation, facilitation (where one species' existence assists another), and mutual services (where species take positive action in each other's interests, as well as their own). It is here that we find rigorously scientific approaches to *resilience, *diversity and *complexity.[26]

4. *Landscapes and biospheres* explores real landscapes and regional biospheres, their productivities and their sensitivities to shock.[27]

5. *Conservation biology* addresses the practical problems and solutions related to the task of conserving species and their habitats, learning from previous extinctions, providing assistance when habitats get sick, and restoring them when they have been damaged.[28]

E

E

6. *Ecosystem services*. This is the aspect of ecology which sees things from the point of view of human society, valuing the environment for the massive and enduring service of making the planet habitable by us. Its influence still has a long way to go, because the immediate spoils from exploiting the environment and destroying *ecosystem services are obvious to the individual who does so, whereas the damage tends to be less obvious, delayed, and seen as no one's responsibility. The study of ecosystem services makes our dependency on them explicit.[29]

7. *Managing the biosphere*. Fisheries, wildlife, water, disease, the commons, the economy as it affects the ecology—nature itself—all need management in some form, given the competing claims on, and uses for, the world's ecosystems. Barry Commoner—along with Rachel Carson one of those who established public awareness of environmental matters in the 1960s and 1970s—defined "Four Laws of Ecology", of which the most famous is his Third Law: "Nature knows best." It needed saying, because at the time nature was being given a helping hand with DDT and organochlorates (*Food Prospects), and it is now being given wheelchair assistance with *genetic modification, but it has often been misinterpreted as the principle that we should not intervene in nature at all. It is widely agreed now that nature does need active and vigorous *protection if it is to have a future.[30]

The *ethics of ecology[31]

8. *Values: Nature in the service of Man*. For a long time, it has been taken as an article of faith that humans are (in a sense) at the centre of the universe. From this point of view, plants and animals have been seen—by thinkers such as Francis Bacon (1561–1626) and John Locke (1632–1704)—not as miracles in their own right, but as a resource for the benefit of Man, and far short of Man's accomplished brilliance. This is "anthropocentrism", and it gathered strength decisively in the period known as the "Axial Age" (800–200 BC), when there was a widely-shared shift in *mindset towards an awareness of the distinctiveness of humans, and of individual obligations and conscience. It was

an image of the human with nature only weakly represented in the background, and with a single God as an exemplar of what Man ought to be.[32]

Underlying this attitude to nature was the principle recognised by Thomas Aquinas (1225–1274) of *The Great Chain of Being*, which has humans at the peak of a *hierarchy with inanimate matter at the bottom, and then rising, stage-by-stage, through the simple microorganisms, plants, invertebrates and vertebrates to humans and then, finally to God and the company of Heaven. And related to that was the view that it is only humans that have a soul, and that nature—as René Descartes (1596–1650), and Isaac Newton (1643–1727) argued—can be thought of as a machine that exists for our convenience. Locke summarises,

> God, who hath given the world to men in common, hath also given them reason to make use of it to the best advantage of life, and convenience.[33]

Nature therefore has no moral standing in its own right, although some moral sense does find its way into the discussion with Immanuel Kant (1724–1804), for a person who is cruel to animals, he wrote, "becomes hard also in his dealings with men".[34]

The anthropocentric view was not all bad, for command over a God-given resource can also be taken to imply a responsibility towards it. And yet, it has provided other contributors to environmental ethics with a point of departure—it is a proposition with which most of them have been able to disagree.

9. *Values: Nature in its own right*. Here we have the opposite view. Nature matters. It has intrinsic value, which holds good whether there is a human around to benefit from it or not. Among the many writers making this case were Henry David Thoreau (1817–1862, author of *Walden*), John Muir (1838–1914, founder of the Sierra Club and critical to the establishment of the US National Parks), and the thinkers of our own day—John Passmore, Mary Midgley, and Chip Ward. Ward turns the tables on anthropocentrism with his observation that, if it is reliably intelligent life that we are looking for, the natural world has a better record than humans. In fact, nature's self-organising ability may be more

complex than any thinking that our own brains are capable of, so . . .[35]

> . . . we must wipe off that smirk and pay attention to the evidence of intelligence all around us. When we perceive and respect the self-organizing intelligence at work in the natural world, we try to dance with nature, not drive it.[36]

10. *Moral judgment: where does it apply?* This is the discussion about how to decide on a frame of reference for our obligations towards nature. The mere fact of living and eating means that we constantly override the interests of other organisms, however much we respect animal rights (vegans no less, since they capture land that would otherwise be used by animals, defend crops from animals, drive cars and heat their homes). The insistence that we should have "respect" for nature helps, although there are doubts about what that means, since our grossly inflated human numbers show little respect, however much we may protest about it.[37]

The most promising way of thinking about this is to be *holistic about it—to be aware at least of the existence of human civilisation, in its huge numbers, and to count it into our thinking and behaviour. A clear case of holistic thinking is James Lovelock's *Gaia, providing the foundation for the environmental thinker David Keller's observation that . . .

> . . . the entire biosphere, as one unitary system, should be the focus of environmental ethics.[38]

For Aldo Leopold, holism's most significant expression was community:

> When we see land as a community to which we belong, we may begin to use it with love and respect.[39]

. . . and, in his *Round River*, Leopold reflected that human beings, plants, animals, soils and waters are . . .

> . . . all interlocked in one humming community of cooperations and competitions, one biota.[40]

In summary, we get Leopold's famous maxim—the land *ethic:

> A thing is right when it tends to preserve the integrity, stability, and beauty of the biotic community. It is wrong when it tends otherwise.[41]

If we really do take a holistic view, how can we know whether a thing will preserve the integrity, stability and beauty of the biotic commonly or not? How do we know which (if there are two options) will do it better, or (if there is an unavoidable trade-off) which part of the biotic community to favour? Well, environmental ethics produces only rather general answers to this: we need to know what we are doing; and we need to feel for the nature that is on the receiving end of our actions. That is, we need *both* ecological literacy *and* bioempathy. And that needs to apply to everything—wilderness, the oceans, *agriculture, cities, homes, and the giant and troubled human ecology itself.[42]

11. *Frames of reference for thinking about environmental ethics:*[43]

- *A psychological awakening?* Urban life insulates us from having to think about nature. The Norwegian philosopher Arne Næss stripped away that insulation by living for many years high up in the Hallingskarvet mountains, in a cabin he built for himself and named Tvergastein—the place of crossed stones. Out of that came a psychological awakening, expressed in due course in the set of eight principles which proved to be the foundation statement for the "deep ecology" movement, drawn up jointly by Næss and the philosopher George Sessions (see "Principles in Summary" sidebar on page 112).
  Why is this seen as a psychological awakening rather than an ecological one? Well, underlying it is the idea of "biocentric equality" . . .

  > . . . all things in the biosphere have an equal right to live and blossom and to reach their own individual forms of unfolding and self-realisation within the larger Self-realisation.[44]

  That capital S is significant: Self = the whole Lifeworld. As for "equality"—that is more controversial, and the philosopher Warwick Fox, for one, disagrees with it: whereas we can

E

PRINCIPLES
IN SUMMARY
Deep Ecology

1. Nature has intrinsic value, apart from its practical value to humans.
2. A rich diversity of life forms is a value in itself.
3. Humans have no right to reduce that diversity.
4. Present human intervention in nature is excessive and should be reduced.
5. The present population is too large for a healthy natural environment.
6. Policies—*economics, technology and *ideology—must be changed radically
7. A new ideology is needed which values life quality rather than consumption quantity.
8. Anyone who agrees with these points is obliged to take action to do something about it.[45]

agree that all living things have their intrinsic value, he argues that the idea that this value is equal everywhere is without foundation.[46] And critics of deep ecology also argue that, while it usefully draws attention to our dependence on a conserved and cared-for planet, it pays little attention to the particular interests, needs and nature of society itself. The philosopher Freya Mathews, for instance, objects that . . .

> . . . many feminists, socialists, and Christians who respect the natural world for its own sake might nevertheless not want to count themselves members of a movement which was neither feminist, socialist, nor Christian in its essentials.[47]

And yet, Stephan Harding has no trouble with it. For him, the Lifeworld, that is, *Gaia, is close to home. In fact, it is inside him:

> To act well, we need to experience the Earth not as "nature" out there, nor as an "environment" that is distinct from us, but as a

mysterious extension of our very own sensing bodies that nourishes us with an astonishing variety of intellectual and aesthetic experiences—with the roar of the sea and with the wonderful sight of the night moon reflected in a calm lake. Right action requires us to *live into* the body of the Earth . . .[48]

- *Environmental virtue ethics.* This is about how we should live our lives. John Muir took his cleansing encounters with nature to the extreme—behind the Yosemite Falls, for instance:

> After enjoying the night-song of the waters and watching the formation of the coloured bow as the moon came round the domes and sent her beams into the wild uproar, I ventured out on the narrow bench that extends back of the fall, without taking sufficient thought about the consequences. [Then the wind changed and the full force of water and ice crashed down on him] Instinctively I fell on my knees, I gripped an angel or the rock, curled up like a young fern frond with my face against my breast; I moved a few feet along the bench to where a block of ice lay. I wedged myself between the ice and the wall and lay face downwards [Eventually making his escape back to his cabin, where, in the morning] I awoke sound and comfortable, better not worse for my hard midnight bath.[49]

and Henry David Thoreau . . .

> I went to the woods because I wished to live deliberately, to front only the essential facts of life, and see if I could not learn what it had to teach, and not, when I came to die, discover that I had not lived.[50]

Or we could grow our own vegetables. We have a wonderful literature and an emerging ecology of support groups to help us to take our own action in the pursuit of *green living. *Lean Logic*'s dark recognition of the limits to this should not discourage us from going as far along that road as we can.[51]

- *Continental environmental ethics*. This sees the matter through the eyes of an arcane branch of philosophy called "phenomenology" which investigates human experience as a phenomenon in its own right, without reference to whether what is experienced is real or not. It is associated with philosophers such as Edmund Husserl, G.W.F. Hegel, Maurice Merleau-Ponty, Martin Heidegger, Hans-Georg Gadamer, Jacques Derrida and Michel Foucault.[52]

- *Political environmental ethics*. *Politics erupts into environmental ethics in many ways. Here are two. The first is social ecology—the argument that we cannot make sense of the environment until we have made progress in sorting out society; ecological problems, it claims, are rooted in class hierarchy. It is represented by, for instance, Murray Bookchin—who takes issue with both Arne Næss and Thomas Malthus on the grounds that their analysis of environmental degradation seeks to lay the *blame on the overpopulating underclasses. He requires any programme for the future to "challenge the basic corporate property, bureaucratic, and profit-oriented social structure at its most fundamental level of ownership and control". The political critique is also represented by Derrick Jensen's analysis of the question, "Why civilisation is killing the world."[53]

- And the politics comes with *ecological feminism*, which links the "twin oppressions" of women and nature. Both are said to be based on the logic of domination, which has several outcomes, of which racism is another. Whereas nature (it is argued) is organic and associated with the feminine, the modern *conception* of nature uses mechanistic technology and science to further the masculine urge to dominate.[54]

- *Environmental pragmatism* argues for a practical and politically savvy approach to environmental protection: do not waste too much time thinking about the principles, concentrate on what can be done and on what works. Keller has examples: In Utah, "free-market ideology reigns supreme and environmentalism is generally seen as a form of socialism in danger of fettering the Invisible Hand", so an argument about the health effects of air pollution will not get anywhere. As an alternative, try "Utah Moms for Clean Air". This makes the same argument, and the moms are praised for their 'values'. Arguing that the "intrinsic value" of the Dwarf Bearclaw Poppy merits protection from all-terrain vehicles will (if anyone notices) provoke derision; pointing out that protecting it improves the recreational opportunities for retirees (and raises property values) can get results.[55]

- *Direct action*. Greenpeace, Earth First! and the Climate Camps (among others) have shown that direct action can achieve some results, as well as drawing the attention of the public and government to particular problems quickly and in ways which are not available to well-behaved debate and the environmental literature. It can complement the more orderly approaches, but it is not a substitute for them, and some critics find its relationship with terrorism too close for comfort. The debate on direct action between, for instance, Dave Foreman and Edward Abbey (for) and Eugene Hargrove (against) continues.[56]

- *Permaculture*. Here we have the case made by David Holmgren that the frame of reference which is needed is nothing short of deep, *reflective participation in the ecology: a combination of the key principles which *Lean Logic* calls *presence and the *vernacular. Guided by permaculture, we ourselves become part of the mosaic of ecosystem services we depend on—not as clever technologists, high on fossil fuels, but as integrated participants over the long-term, going with the flows of its energy and nutrients. Holmgren writes,

  > [Permaculture] draws together the diverse ideas, skills and ways of living which need to be rediscovered and developed in order to empower us to move from being dependent consumers to becoming responsible and productive citizens.[57]

E

E

12. *The environment of the mind.* This is about what we do to a concept when we think about it, how we change it around so that it fits our assumptions and expectations, and why the environment may be especially liable to this moulding and remaking.[58]

We think about nature, not just in the light of our own *expectations as individuals, but in a way that is shaped by the *culture we live in. The influence of that culture is likely to be strong when, for instance, we are thinking about such ideas as "nature" and "wilderness" which have no *objective *definition. "The state of nature" would, for Thomas Hobbes, be something we want to get out of as fast as possible; for Henry David Thoreau, it would be something to be in, and stay in. And "ecology", like "organic", can be used in matters remote from the soil as a catch-all phrase to persuade the other person that what you have in mind is good, and natural (*Hyperbole).

In this way we can live in a self-sustaining world of language which has been adapted to help us to feel good about things as they are and the *intentions we have adopted, and we can devise and use technology in ways that reinforce this make-believe. Our cultural assumptions shape the technologies we want and develop; the technologies shape and reinforce the assumptions. In this sense, our understanding of the environment creates a virtual landscape: some of it is real; some is what we want to see; some is what we fear; some is what we dare not look at.

13. *The science and the ethics.* Science describes and explains; it does not take a view as to whether the things it has described or explained are good or not. Should this same discipline apply to ecology? Most scholars of environmental ethics think not. For the ecologist Paul Sears (1891–1990), it must maintain a "continuing critique of man's operations within the ecosystem", and he compares ecologists with doctors: doctors don't simply describe tumours as interesting contributions to our understanding of medicine: they do something about them.[59]

In any case, as Mark Sagoff argues, if nature's design is good, corruptions of it must be bad. The extreme case of corruption must surely be the fact that the damage we are doing to the planet is on a *scale that threatens to destroy our civilisation and its whole planetary habitat. Jared Diamond, author of the bestselling *Collapse*, argues that we do know what to do about it, but whether we will join up the science and the ethics effectively and quickly enough is, of course, another matter.[60]

14. *Environment and public policy.* This range of subjects takes environmental ethics to questions discussed in depth in other entries in *Lean Logic*: *population, *agriculture, *economic policy, socioeconomic and environmental justice (*Climacteric, Growth, Presence, TEQs, Scale).[61]

———————

"To feed people or save nature?" That is the question asked in a celebrated paper by Holmes Rolston. And his answer is that—well, it depends . . . If the planet's ecology is under such stress—with so many choices having closed—that hunger is an inevitable symptom of the way things are, and treating this symptom directly will only increase the hunger, then, perhaps, effort should be concentrated on addressing the underlying problem. That task, he writes in conclusion to another paper "The Future of Environmental Ethics", is . . .

> . . . the most fundamental of our responsibilities. We are searching for an ethics adequate to respect life on this Earth, an Earth Ethic.[62]

Lean Logic wonders about that. With the gift of *intelligence comes the duty of *responsibility. On the other hand, maybe we are intelligent enough to learn from beetles. They don't have an Earth Ethic. They have an ecology of *place to fit into.
*Ecology: Farmers and Hunters, Ethics.

ECONOMICS (see also Green Economics, Lean Economics). To the question, "What is economics?", there are two answers. Economics in one sense is about policy. It is interested in the way that goods and services are produced and distributed, in markets and the conditions that help or hinder them, and in the *complex system of the national economy, its cycles of crisis and recovery, and its interactions with other national economies.

Economics in another sense, less widely recognised, is that which brings to problems an understanding of *choices and consequences. The starting point for this is the principle that, although people are aware of what they value, and alert to the opportunities and constraints which surround them, the consequences of what they do may be transformed by what others do, or intend to do, at the same time. Here we have patterns of interaction and outcome which, unless considered with close attention, are likely to be surprising and perverse, the opposite of what was expected. Economics makes no claim here to have the gift of foresight, but it does claim that, if the circumstances of choice and consequence are carefully read, actual outcomes can be reasonably forecast. Economics in this second sense is a main ingredient of Lean Logic.[63]

But it is economics in the first sense — as policy — which is the stuff of this entry. What we have here is a set of ideas, assumptions and interpretations which have been pieced together since the start of the industrial age. Foundations were laid by the Scottish Enlightenment, notably by Francis Hutcheson, followed by the classical economists (e.g., Adam Smith, David Ricardo, Thomas Malthus and John Stuart Mill), who mapped out an anatomy of *value, prices, *capital and markets. Then marginal analysis focused on the demand side of the market, specifically the utility which the buyer of a product or service would gain from consuming more of it, or which he or she would have to forgo if consuming less of it. And this opened the way to the mathematical modelling around which economics has since been substantially organised (e.g., Stanley Jevons, Léon Walras, Carl Menger, Alfred Marshall). Key sequels were the cool, non-judgmental evaluation of theory, behaviour and statistics known as positive economics (e.g., John Neville Keynes); neoclassical economics, which integrated supply and prices, demand and income into a single frame of reference (e.g., John Hicks); and then the work of John Maynard Keynes and E.F. Schumacher, which brought in the state and liquidity (the availability of money to spend) as having a decisive role in maintaining economic stability. Many variants and refinements followed, such as the principles of imperfect competition (Joan Robinson), savings, growth, employment and inflation (Edmund Phelps), the positive *feedback, or multiplier, in national economies (Richard Kahn), the part played by technical advance

in economic growth (Robert Solow), and general equilibrium theory (Kenneth Arrow and Gérard Debreu).[64]

To some extent, a working synthesis of three centuries of creative brilliance has been arrived at, but there remain variants, interpretations and specialisms more or less without limit — industrial economics, institutional, ecological, development and international economics and others have made their contributions, so statements about "economics" do not mean much without some more exact definition. The economics that is intended in what follows is the dominant *paradigm, which sees an essentially free *market economy as indispensable to the steady rate of *growth needed for full (or almost full) employment, and the reliable flow of tax revenues needed by governments.

Economics in that sense has a lot to be said for it. But there are difficulties, and critics have for many years been pointing them out. Some of the criticism has come from outside the profession, and one of the earlier collective critiques came in the form of The Other Economic Summit (TOES), first held in 1984; a radical shadow-conference which ran in parallel to the (then) G7 summit in London. TOES in turn led to the formation of the New Economics Foundation (nef), whose critiques of market economics and contributions to *green economics have been sustained.[65]

In 2009, the challenge came from inside the profession with the formation of the Institute for New Economic Thinking, whose aim is "to advance reform in economic thinking and policy worldwide". Among the difficulties which the Institute believes need attention are the idea that the "efficient market's" allocation of resources should be more-or-less beyond challenge, and that the swarming turbulence of real life economics can be adequately modelled by mathematics. It also notes the failure of economics to come to an agreed view on such fundamentals as the role of governments in stabilising markets — a severe case of professional indecision which for a generation has been known as the debate on "rational expectations".[66]

Lean Logic's critique extends further (and the case moves beyond criticism to reform in *Green Economics and *Lean Economics):

1. Economics builds its understanding of stability on the assumption of sustained growth

E

The assumption of sustained *growth is an intrinsically irrational and impossible basis for any enduring system. As their size advances, large systems must eventually fail under the weight of their own *complication; they destroy the natural environment on which they depend and reach *energy and *material limits, leading to *entropy and disorder. The market economy has to grow because technical advances—steadily learning how to make more efficient use of labour—free labour up for other work, and if that work is found, it adds to the economy's output, and that means growth. With each pulse of technical advance, further growth is needed to keep the labour force fully employed.

The problem is that growth-dependency puts the economy in a dynamic equilibrium which, like a bicycle, is stable only so long as it is moving forward. If it stops, it falls over.

If economic growth were zero or negative for an extended period, while technology continued to advance in response to *competition, the economy would crash; and "crash" would mean unemployment rising to rates so high that—at the level of *hyperunemployment—tax revenues would fall below the level the government needs to provide subsistence payments for the unemployed (even if supplemented by borrowing). What that means—no job at all means no money at all—merits *reflection.

So there is a flaw. *Market economics is a system which is damned if it grows, and damned if it doesn't.

And there is another flaw: growth is not just a problem with economics; it is what *populations do when they have easy access to abundant food and energy, few predators and no effective culture of population restraint. It is intrinsic to the process of *intensification. And in due course attention needs to be focused on the problem that the *sustainable carrying capacity of the *ecology is lower than the numbers that it is being required to carry. The temptation to attribute to economics—rather than to its fertile and fortunate beneficiaries—the responsibility for growth, leading to insupportably large *scale, should be resisted.[67]

2. *It gives insufficient recognition to turbulence*
Cyclical boom and bust is intrinsic to large complex systems and ecosystems (*Wheel of Life); the most graphic example perhaps being the fire forests, which burn and start again. Economies are no exception, and crash for many reasons. One is that, while banks' assets and liabilities can keep pace with each other at a time of growth, assets can fall much faster than liabilities at a time of decline—and rescuing banks when they hit this problem has been one of the key roles of the Bank of England since it was founded in 1694.

The system can be tipped into shock by events such as a sharp rise in oil prices (households' fuel costs soak up money needed to repay mortgages) or, more generally, by anxieties about being able to repay high levels of borrowing (the more households try to repay their loans, they less they spend, so demand and incomes fall, so they find it harder than ever to repay their loans . . .), or by a combination of these and other effects. The more *taut, *connected and efficient the system, the more often, and violently, will it crash.

Economics is comfortable with moderate cycles, and the practice of economics is in part about the stimulus and restraint that can be applied to smooth them out. Normality is its aim. What it finds harder to think about is the shocking turbulence that from time to time disrupts a complex system to the limit of survival, or beyond (*Systems Thinking 〉 Form 〉 The Power Law). And the implications of this are profound. In a famous article on *debt and deflation as drivers of the 1929–1933 depression, the economist Irving Fisher used the analogy of a boat which constantly rights itself in response to moderate turbulence—up to the point at which . . .

> [t]here is . . . no tendency of the boat to stop tipping until it has capsized. Ultimately, of course, but only after almost universal bankruptcy, the indebtedness must cease to grow greater and begin to grow less. Then comes recovery and a tendency for a new boom-depression sequence. This is the so-called "natural" way out of a depression, via needless and cruel bankruptcy, unemployment and starvation.[68]

The "of course . . . then comes recovery" does not apply if there is no oil to fuel it. But the analogy of the boat does apply. There need to be bulkheads to hold back the water, lifeboats . . . In marine engineering, damage limitation is routine, yet the existence of failure and the limits of *control are not recognised as intrinsic to the structure of the system to which economics belongs; they are recognised only as part of the debris that remains when that structure has failed.

3. *There is an uncritical presumption in favour of economies of *scale*

It can be shown that, in some situations, you get better results when you do things on a large scale (see *Sorting). In fact, microeconomics is aware that there are limits to this, after which the assumption that larger means more efficient no longer holds, and knows that it is advisable to prevent production at (say) a single factory from growing any further. Despite this, the presumption of economies of scale has become *self-evident, along with other things seen as too obvious to argue about, such as *competitiveness, free entry to—and *exit from—a market, and the other golden rules of perfect competition. This has led, more by association than by logic, to choices such as these:

- The 1999 repeal (in the interests of economies of scale) of the US Glass-Steagall Banking Act, which required a separation between high street banks and the much riskier business of the merchant banks. This was copied elsewhere, and it was part of the same thinking that produced the demutualisation of the building societies in the UK—allowing building societies to operate as banks.[69]
- The legislation (in the interests of *opening up the market) which required US banks from 1977 to make sub-prime mortgages available to applicants who would formerly have been considered too risky.[70]
- The breakdown of all barriers to competition and *access to markets worldwide, which gave us the global market, with its extreme vulnerability to a firestorm of shock.[71]

The problem is that economics has no non-trivial concept of scale. The vague presumption that, up to a point, efficiency (an idea which is itself accepted uncritically) comes with size, says nothing at all. It is as useful as "this situation is good apart from the ways in which it is bad", unless there is some sense of *why* the economies of scale break down at certain levels and in particular situations, and *what those levels and situations are*. Should any such arguments briefly surface, however, they are quickly eliminated with references to *competitiveness, to the need for a global reach, to being able to take on the big players, and (of course) the need for a level playing field.

There is a tragic quality in centuries of insight about the *political economy we live in failing to survive the transition to policy, and being displaced by half a dozen clichés, capable of easy use with confident and passionate conviction: the mountains laboured, and brought forth a mouse.[72] It is understandable that the little idea of being big should come to dominate, since the whole of the industrial process—at the level of both the factory and of the economy as a whole—was a spectacular demonstration of how large scale could transform productivity, and build a civilisation with a technical sophistication and *living standards for some that had never been imagined before. Crowd behaviour is understandable. But a coherent acknowledgement of *scale would have made economics a different discipline, less at risk to the simplifying parodies of mathematics, and turning instead to rich and specific application of what we know about motivation, *cooperation, information, *ecology, *systems, thermodynamics and spatial geometry. Having, however, gone for *abstractions in support of the large-scale, it is committed to the eventual dismantling of the structures which make a civilisation.

4. *It has no rational sense of *time*

Neoclassical economics lacks a coherent concept of time—or, at least, it has a mechanical technique for dealing with time which can be applied uncritically. Three aspects of this are especially significant.

First, there is the case of time-lags (*Systems Thinking 〉 Feedback 〉 Time). The *market cannot pick up a price signal until the prices in question actually

E

move and, by that time, it may be too late to act on the signal with any hope of success. For instance, it would take some fifty years to provide a comprehensive replacement for oil and gas, so waiting for high prices and (later) interruptions in supply to trigger a response is a way of ensuring that the response, when it eventually comes, is fifty years too late.

Secondly, there is the Fallacy of the Permanent Present (*Time Fallacies)—the presumption that conditions now are a good guide to what they will be in the future. Variants are that the path being followed now (*growth, *technical advance), will be straight, and that it is all right to fix short-term irritants in ways which will bring long-term disaster.

A third problem is that the key principle underlying the treatment of time in economics is *interest. Economics recognises that if a person needs to borrow money from another person with whom he or she is not in a close *reciprocal relationship (e.g., *family or friendly *neighbour), then the lender will reasonably expect to get something back for the money he provides (usually interest), in the same way as any other provider of goods and services (see *Usury). That introduces the principle of "discount"—money you won't have until a future time is worth less than it would be worth if you had it now. The problem arises when the discount principle is applied to other assets. For example, the value in a hundred years' time of a stock—such as a fishery—discounted at a rate of 3% per year, is just 5% of its present value, and if a valuation of this kind is taken literally, it can be used as a justification for fishing it to destruction now, because it is a depreciating asset. The fact that the interest rate calculation can be made does not necessarily mean that people will be foolish enough to make it, or to apply it uncritically, but, if they do, economics provides an apparent justification.

5. *It has trouble with values to which no price is attached*
Good and bad things to which no price is attached (bad things can have prices attached when people pay to avoid them or to prevent them, or have to bear the cost of the consequences) are "external" to the market, and known as "externalities".[73] It is

no longer true that externalities are overlooked by economics; since at least the 1960s, schemes have been devised for bringing them into the market: punitive tobacco taxes and carbon trading are two examples, so we know that responses can be developed. Finding solutions is another matter.

There are, then, two main kinds of externality:

a. *The external cost of bad things.*

These are the undesired by-products and consequences arising from the supply of a product or service. All forms of *pollution are externalities in this sense, and they can be "internalised" if a price is attached. Tax (e.g., on leaded petrol) can be a clear, simple instrument if there is a readily-available alternative (unleaded petrol). If the alternative would take a long time to develop, and/or if an additional tax burden is to be avoided, and/or if some flexibility is to be conserved, schemes which require producers of the bad things (e.g., carbon emissions) to buy and trade rights between each other may have advantages.

But the benefits of such means of internalising bad things—giving them a cost which the producer has to pay—are mixed. There is obvious common sense in making bad things more expensive than good things, and yet, this is a principle rich with *unintended consequences:[74]

- A scheme that is focused on the market may be seen more as a way of making money than as a means of getting rid of the problem: the "bad" thing then tends to turn out to be rather a "good" thing, because of all the money that can be made out of it, so there is an incentive to keep it going—and to keep the "bad" thing circulating in abundance—for a long time. That aim is assisted if the scheme is confined to a group of institutions which qualify on the basis of, for instance, their size: the sense of wider *dialogue and *common purpose is lost.
- The scheme will almost always be *reductionist, focusing just on the internalised cost and not on the context and *culture within which it is produced. Far from drawing focus to the fundamental underlying

challenges, it can tend to endorse everything else that an institution is doing on the strength of its stellar performance in, say, reducing carbon emissions.

- . . . and see also *Carbon Offsetting and *TEQs (Tradable Energy Quotas).

b. *The external cost of good things.*

There may be benefits supplied by a service which are not represented in its price. For example, the decision to close down a local post office, hospital or railway line is made in terms of whether the service is cost-effective to the owners (such as the government department acting on behalf of the public). The costs that have to be borne by a consumer when the service is closed are not registered, though they may be much greater than the savings achieved by the change. If a maternity ward is closed down, so that parents now have to drive a long distance to another hospital, arrange accommodation, take time off work and organise care for their children at home, it is likely to turn out that—had that money (plus the extra costs borne by the centralised hospital) actually been paid to the (now closed) maternity ward—this would have amply covered its costs. That is, if the cost of all the externalities—whoever finally picks the bill for them—were counted in public decisions, outcomes would be sharply different.

And there is the case of the entire unpaid *informal economy, including child-rearing and cooking, which has no price attached to it at all, and which is therefore devalued and overlooked. The neglect of the informal economy—the economy with *presence—has been encouraged by the presumption that it is in the world of work that a fulfilling life is to be found and aspirations fulfilled, and in which society's claims to justice and equality are tested. Money is the perfect measure: transparent, precise, universally desired, *objective, non-judgmental. The informal economy, in contrast, not only resists measurement, but lacks money. The problem is that we fall for a dominant idea with the awed *deference of worshippers observing their fetish—and *money fetishism induces blindness to the informal economy, devaluing the work of the men and women who devote their lives to it.

This matters intensely. It means that it is possible to do good economics, complete with rigorous mathematical modelling, and to overlook the whole set of informal *reciprocal arrangements and *loyalties—stable *community, *culture, *leisure, friendships, a sense of being at *home, citizenship, making people, being young, growing old, being beloved; things that are not measured and made visible by monetary exchange. Where economics has the last say, all these are ignored.

The problem is not that that the informal economy is not "internalised" and paid for—that would really destroy it, though indeed encroachments, setting prices for things that might be done better for love, have been relentless for three centuries—but that its absence from the accounts makes it inaudible. Money speaks a language that the market can hear. The informal economy doesn't.

The conclusion that has been drawn from economics' recognition of the externalities problem is that money is, by default, the instrument to use. It is presumed in a strange, *intuition-busting way that people will not do anything that needs to be done unless supplied with a financial incentive. But, as the entry on *incentives shows, financial rewards can actually be demotivating. They successfully get people in through the door; they can provide a reason to persist in simple repetitive tasks like picking strawberries; they do not, however, provide the frame of reference in which people are motivated and inspired to think through a shared problem, to invent new solutions, to achieve something difficult. They buy participation reduced to the simplest reflexes and geared to material rewards. As the anticulture of material incentives extends towards comprehensive coverage of our lives and of our response to environmental change, it reduces the possibility of recruiting the *intelligence, *imagination and passionate, self-motivated commitment which, together, represent our one chance of building a *resilient relationship with a damaged and angry *ecosystem.

E

And yet, it is not fair, either, to dump all the *blame onto economics. The *market, seeing value as money, took the colour out of society, burying *loyalties and cultural detail in a blizzard of prices. Economics described the whitened, smoothed-out landscape that it saw; and it was attractive to people who, on the basis of simple assumptions, could build mathematical models to describe parts of it with precision and sparkling brilliance. It is called being "parsimonious".[75] There is pride taken in reducing complex problems down to the essentials, preferably essentials which can be used as assumptions on which to build mathematics. It can be a good thing: mathematics is a way of exploring an idea and testing common sense; its models are often elegant and beautiful, and they can be used to produce unexpected results, some of which are *true. But its models are caricatures of reality, offering sharp observation sharpened by what they leave out, and what they exaggerate—not to be mistaken for the whole story. The difficulty is that the models do tend to be taken literally—a case of what Alfred North Whitehead called *misplaced concreteness—and they have a hard time accounting for value, unless there is a price attached. They become icons; and in common with most *icons, they can lead you astray.[76]

Neoclassical market economics engages with the things that fit neatly into the market, and which can generally look after themselves anyway. The things that are most needed and vulnerable—*culture, mental *health, *families, belonging, *character, happiness, *household skills, *reciprocity, *community, *empowerment—are either left out in the cold to die, or else become latchkey kids, gathered up by an authoritarian, overstretched government which takes over the responsibility because the rightful carers are away from home.

6. *It treats all goods as if they were produced*
Goods which are made—in factories, workshops and on farms, for instance—tend to obey the laws of supply and demand: if they get scarce, the price rises, so producers make more of them (and *vice versa*). Economics is comfortable with this, and models of great sophistication can be constructed

around it, exploring implications—taxes, inflation, technical change, competition. But not all goods are of this kind: some are not produced—or are produced too rarely and slowly for their production to rise in response to demand. Their supply is fixed and, if they get scarce, there is not much that can be done about it. Non-produced goods are of two main kinds:

First, there are the natural resources, such as agricultural *land, phosphates, *water and oil. The depletion of these essential assets is hollowing out the *material basis of our economy and civilisation. However, when economists have applied their discipline to the question of oil depletion in recent years, they have followed a simple logical sequence: as current reserves are used, prices rise, and it is argued that this will act as a stimulus for further exploration, for improved extraction rates, and for the development of unconventional supplies like oil shales, heavy oils and tar sands.[77]

This is no mere carelessness; it is based on an influential principle of resource economics. Harold Hotelling, professor of mathematics (Stamford, Columbia and North Carolina in the 1930s and 1940s), published a rule to follow when the aim is to optimise the present value of a non-renewable resource. It is expressed and proved in abstract terms of maths and *money and, in summary, it says that the resource should be depleted in such a way that the rate of growth of its price is equal to the rate of discount (i.e., the interest rate). This means that an abundant resource may rationally be extracted relatively quickly without the risk of the price of the remaining reserves rising too far (that is, faster than the discount rate); whereas a scarce resource should be depleted only slowly, in order to prevent the discount rate being overtaken by the rising price of the resource. One implication of this is that the optimal rate of extraction changes with the interest rate. Another, more reassuring one, is that, as a resource gets scarcer, its price rises, so extraction must fall if Hotelling's rule is to be obeyed, and there is therefore an incentive to provide an alternative.[78]

That is (as summarised by David Pearce and Kerry Turner) . . .

... as the price of the finite resource rises there will be some substitute for the resource. For example, oil from conventional sources is much less expensive than oil from tar sands or shale. As the price of oil rises it must eventually 'hit' the cost of extracting oil from these more expensive resources.[79]

A smooth hand-over to alternative resources, then? So the mathematics tells us. What it does not realistically take into account are the sheer practical problems of *technology, the *dirty detail of the quantity of *energy you have to put into tar sands to get any net energy back, the problems of logistics, fierce Canadian winters, the other resources that are required (such as water), the environmental and *climate impact, the long *time-lags and, at the end of all this, the small-scale output relative to the abundant flow of crude oil. The mathematics occupies a rigorous high ground: you can't argue with its combination of proof, precision and transparency—but it is a misplaced analysis which dismisses the practical pains and impossibilities and sees in the maths a concrete response to the energy shock.[80]

The problem is, of course, that reality on matters of depletion comes in bits and pieces of information which are hard to fit into a model of any kind. It is about the detail of production rates around the world, the decline of new discoveries, and the present scarcity of any alternative source of energy, renewable or otherwise, for *transport. Clearly, Hotelling was by no means making the gross error of supposing that oil was a produced good—made in factories like waistcoats—but his analysis derives from deep assumptions governing the supply, demand, price and quantity of produced goods— that is, the guidelines, or heuristics, which give economics its foundation. In the domain of this logic, a rise in price has to lead to a response in terms of increased supply. It is not the economist's business to get into how that increase is achieved—econo-mists do not need to know how to make waistcoats nor how to get oil out of tar sands—but it is the economist's task to understand and explain how the universal essentials of supply and demand work.

And that is the tragedy, for depletion is not to be understood in terms of *abstractions, but of *anomalies. This is data of a kind more suited for the detective or even the barroom gossip than the mathematician (*Expertise). In such a setting of anecdote, tip-offs, lies, bluff, politics and detail, broad economic principles have nothing to offer but error, just when the detection of anomalies, lurking there beneath the surface, is the one thing that could save the day.

The second class of non-produced good with an impact on economic thought consists of positional goods: *composition goods with the common char-acteristic that they can be enjoyed only by people whose income or other bargaining position is large *relative* to others. However high average incomes rise, access to positional goods remains unchanged. When desirable goods are available only in a fixed quantity which is significantly less than people want or need, their distribution is generally by some form of auction: the high bidders get the goods—but note that "auction" here may consist of many kinds of *competition, including money, connections or battle. Examples of positional goods include the house that you want to live in, but can only just afford, leadership positions, the alpha male role in a group of baboons, and *access to *land, *energy (*TEQs), *food and other assets at a time of scarcity.[81]

There are several ways in which positional goods may throw economic analysis off balance. For instance, there is the basic problem of wealth and welfare: if the incomes of everyone were to rise by equal amounts—or even if they were to rise faster for the worse-off than for the better-off—this would not necessarily reduce inequalities or improve *liv-ing standards, so long as those standards were due in part to being able to bid high for the inadequate supply of positional goods that happens to be available. Positional goods in this way represent an impassable limit to aspirations about the benefits of higher real incomes being shared by all. And a substantial proportion of households' spending on positional goods (such as houses, where purchasers on average bid up to the limit of what they can

E

afford) may actually become a form of saving (by the seller) along with *debt (by the buyer), both of which can have an effect on demand, providing a further source of volatility between boom and recession in the economy.

The presence of the rigidities imposed by non-produced goods in a market are substantial complications to a neat concept of economics which supposes that producers produce what buyers want to buy—and that if they run out of stock, they can always make some more.

7. *It is predatory*

On some matters, *market economics is far from neutral. It is normative: it has an opinion. It takes the view that the *competitive market is the only sound basis for a *political economy, and it advocates its case with evangelical conviction: if there is a society somewhere which is not based on the market, it needs to be saved. Here is an example, from E.F. Schumacher. Imagine the case of a small, unambitious, labour-intensive local economy that has existed happily for years in a remote region without being troubled by its backward condition—or saved from it by a more efficient producer with a mission to introduce it to the joys of life in the global market. One day, the efficient producer, along with its associated industries, does finally arrive. At first, the new arrivals, whose prices undercut those of our inefficient mini-economy, enjoy buoyant sales. However, this puts the mini-economy's own producers out of business: unemployment follows; so its households can no longer afford to buy the competitive firms' goods; the result is that both the inefficient traditional economy *and* the competitive one collapse.

Schumacher called this, variously, "mutual poisoning" or "maldevelopment" and he often watched the sequence at work when efficient companies arrive in third world communities, with the intention—naïve, patronising or just greedy—of "helping" them to achieve lift-off into the industrial age. They arrive in an inefficient but stable economy, in which there is a carefully protected environment, full employment, and no

requirement for economic *growth; they leave behind a destroyed economy with mass unemployment, none of its former *skills, a collapsed social structure, alcoholism, an exploding *population and a degraded environment.[82]

In response to the problems faced by undeveloped economies in the globalising world of the 1960s, Schumacher and George McRobie developed the principle of intermediate technology (aka *appropriate technology). It was in radical contrast with the assumptions of the time—which have proved persistent. Here they are summarised by Colin Ward:

> In those days, it was thought that access to high technology held the secret of success for all nations, great and small. [Schumacher and McRobie] grasped the fact that then, as now, the dilemma of the poor regions was their dependence for imports on the export of cash crops and raw materials. If they tried to diversify, they found that there was always some other country which could produce more cheaply. If they sought to build up their own modest production units to supply local needs, on the Gandhian pattern, they found that another country could mass-produce the same goods and deliver more cheaply too, while the industrial plant they would like to buy was geared to the advanced technology of the rich countries.[83]

This is a form of Gresham's well-known Law about the effect of a debased currency: bad money drives out good money.[84] The market state (in which price displaces *reciprocity and cooperation) drives out social ecology. This is the tragedy of economics.

Schumacher was, by any standards, one of the leading mainstream economists of his time—substantially the author of the "Keynes Plan" leading to the establishment of the International Monetary Fund; the main author of Sir William Beveridge's (1945) *Full Employment in a Free Society*; and Economic Advisor to the Economic Sub-Commission of the British Control Commission in Germany. He recognised, however, that economics dances to more than one tune: there is the Economics of Materialism, but . . .

. . . other systems of Economics are possible
and necessary and are even already available in
rudimentary form.[85]

The difficulty is that it is hard, even impossible,
for two head-to-head systems of *value to coexist.
Gresham's Law stands in the way: the cheap will
win. Unless very deliberate measures are taken to
protect the other economics (Buddhist Economics,
as Schumacher came to call it), the mainstream will
dominate—in the short term. In the longer term,
it will be necessary to find ways of *protecting
economies that have devised or inherited another
way of doing it (*Lean Economics, Local Currency).

———————

Unfortunately, the critics of economics have had a
tendency to discuss the whole structure as a tissue of
misconceptions. It is a critique that fails. The strength
of economics is its considerable, if far from complete,
understanding of the flows and comparative advantages
that underlie trade, jobs, capital and incomes, and the
logic of optimising behaviour, all backed by glittering
accomplishments in mathematics. That makes it a
powerful analytical instrument, so that just a few misconceptions—such as a failure to understand the informal
economy or resource depletion—can have leverage: like
a baby monkey at the controls of a Ferrari, they can turn
it into an instrument with extraordinarily destructive
potential. If it were a tissue of errors, it would not be dangerous: it is its 90 percent brilliance which makes it so.

Economics has therefore been seductive. It has
appealed to minds glad of a cognitive technology which
enabled them to make decisions according to mathematical models, and with little fear of contradiction. Its
professionals, with careers and families to think of, are
under some pressure to sustain a close and uncritical
embrace with the form of political economy in which
they happen to live, accepting the irrational proposition
of sustained growth, and being associated with (this
always helps, though other motives are stronger) a
discipline from whose practice they can make money.
But the reduction of a society and *culture to mathematical, *growth-dependent economic *abstraction has
infantilised a grown-up civilisation and is well on the
way to destroying it.

Civilisations self-destruct anyway, but it is reasonable
to ask whether they have done so before with such
enthusiasm, in obedience to such an acutely absurd
superstition, while claiming with such insistence that
they were beyond being seduced by the irrational
promises of *religion. Every civilisation has had its irrational but reassuring *myth. Previous civilisations have
used their culture to sing about it and tell stories about
it. Ours has used its mathematics to prove it.
*Economism, Galley Skills, Elegance, Green Econom-
ics, Lean Economics.

ECONOMISM. The presumption that matters of public
policy can be interpreted mainly or completely in terms
of *economics, particularly a technical and *constructivist
view of economics designed to sustain *growth. Economics builds *abstractions; economism takes them literally.

The scale of this category error is so large that it tends to
capture all our *judgment. Everything but the principle
of the *competitive *market is assumed-away, leaving
economics *disconnected from the texture and purposes
of society, *ecology and *culture which it exists to serve.[86]
*Rationalism, Misplaced Concreteness, Different Prem-
ises, Money Fallacy, Social Mobility, Looter's Ethics.

ECOSYSTEM. See Ecological System.

EDGE. The edge of a system is the *boundary where
it interacts with its neighbours and environment. This
is where it *protects, *cooperates, *competes; where it
exports waste and imports nutrients; it is where *systems meet. And there are three principles to note:

1. *Diversity and productivity.* At the join between two
   systems, there is mixing and interaction which can
   make the edge more complex and more productive
   than either of the systems on their own. This effect,
   as Patrick Whitefield explains, is used in *permaculture, with its intimate mixture of woods and fields,
   its layered crops of diverse varieties and heights,
   and the use of ponds, river margins and shallow
   water. River estuaries, where fresh water and sea
   mix, and which receive a supply of nutrients from
   the land and daily refreshment with oxygen from
   the tides, are exceptionally fertile: some estuaries
   are as productive as a tropical rainforest.[87]

E

2. *A high edge ratio.* Edge ratio is the ratio of a system's edge relative to its area (or, for a system considered in three dimensions, its surface area relative to its volume). As discussed in the entry on *scale, if we compare figures of the same shape but different sizes, the smaller a system's size, the greater its edge ratio. Small systems, having a relatively high edge ratio, can import nutrients and exchange wastes across short distances. Large systems that are well subdivided into smaller *holons with a substantial hinterland—space for their primary needs: *energy, *food, *water and *materials, for *reciprocal exchange with other systems, and for *waste disposal—may develop a high degree of efficiency and self-reliance.

3. *The Edge of Chaos.* The idea suggested by the computer scientist Christopher Langton in 1990 about the point of intersection between two states: solid and fluid. In the solid phase, there is no movement; in the liquid phase, there is no stillness; at the borderline between them, there is the possibility of structures developing and then holding their new shapes—or holding new information, like a semiconductor. The extent to which this should be taken as a *metaphor, and what kinds of system it should be applied to, is debated, but the principle applies in many situations, such as teaching (the case for moderate discipline) and *lean thinking, where the *common purpose defines a frame of reference for individual decision-making.[88]

The edge of a system is the place to observe closely for signs of change which is likely—for better or for worse—to affect the system as a whole. At the "active fringe", interesting things happen, as explained by the systems analyst Alex Trisoglio:

> Most organisations and entities have a core, where most of their activity is focused, so diversity must be expressed largely at the fringes. The fringes are the source of most truly innovatory ideas in cultures, economies and organisations.[89]

Totnes (the first *Transition Town) is inventive because it is on the fringe, neither a village nor a substantial town. Small companies are *diverse and inventive. Small

schools would be too, if they were allowed to be. If you are in the mainstream, it is harder: you are swept along.

Surprising happenings at the fringe may be a warning that the system will in due course need to transform itself if it is to survive. A radical vision will tend to be resisted, but the system's *resilience depends on whether it is able make sense of such visions, rather than dismissing them as *harmless lunacy.

EDUCATION. See Lean Education.

EFFICIENCY. See Systems Thinking 〉 Function 〉 Efficiency, Eco-Efficiency, Competitiveness, Economics, Lean Economics.

ELEGANCE. The property of a small-scale, or subdivided, system which does not, therefore, need the *complication of a large-scale infrastructure.

Self-reliant community, being substantially free of the complications of the large-scale, has economies of reduced scale. The *holonic form, consisting of many smaller parts interacting for a *common purpose, means that there are lots of *edges extending throughout the system. With this high edge-ratio, material needs can be exchanged, and the waste they produce can be recycled on the *proximity principle—work is done close to where its output is wanted; *waste is produced close to where it can be recycled.

An elegant *system does need an infrastructure—an *intermediate economy—but not on the giant scale (relative to its size) which *civic societies, especially our own, must sustain at great cost in *energy, *materials, organisation, labour and *capital. A high proportion of a small-scale community's work consists of action from which it derives a *direct* benefit, as distinct from having first to meet indirect, intermediate needs—the *regrettable necessities which it must endure simply to cope with the problems of large scale. It is not encumbered.

A *scale-literate *community makes modest, and realistic, demands on its *ecosystem. There is no insatiable ambition which will take its environment, both near at hand and far away, into shock. And it has only a small *sorting problem. It does not find itself with large accumulations of waste products, and of goods and people needing to be sorted. Detail comes to it naturally.

Elegance is therefore an idea with *leverage: it goes to the heart of the subject, changing the way it is understood, and getting large results from accurate responses. It relies, not on visionary, large-scale ambition, but on the gentle nudges of *feedback.[90]

EMERGENCE. The evolution of complex outcomes from simple circumstances or rules. For instance, chess is defined by fewer than two dozen rules, but new possibilities in the game are still being discovered without limit. Ants build complex structures without having an idea of it in their minds. Richard Dawkins' computer programme designed to simulate the evolution of species is able to produce virtual organisms of limitless variety from the expression of just nine genes. But note the corollary—if the number of rules or "genes" is reduced a little, the number of possible outcomes or types of outcome is reduced a lot. So a complex system could be drastically simplified or dumbed down if just one or two of the rules are lost or abandoned.[91]

This phenomenon of emergence is important for many reasons. Here are four:

1. The many properties of a *system may originally have been the product of chance—that is, of events and circumstances which just happened to come together to make it in a particular way. But the system that results cannot be described simply as the sum of these initial properties, for they will then interact in *complex ways. The system is more than just a mixture; it is the unique product of a particular *story so far—it has its own integrity and *identity.

    Its character will govern its behaviour, taking it along a path which gives it particular experiences and presents it with particular options. And the system's character is itself "path dependent"—its behaviour in the future will be profoundly influenced by the path it has followed thus far. This process of feedback and emergence will continue to shape it as it responds to the further experiences coming its way, and all this happens without any need for the idea of *intention.[92]

2. But intention may indeed be central. There are, for instance, rich possibilities for *creative expression at the borderline where intention meets random events and makes sense of them:

Intention has an aim, and recognises that some of the random events that come its way may help to achieve it.
↓
Trial and error shapes its initial responses to them, with mixed results.
↓
Intention recognises which of these responses promote its aim, and identifies them as rules.
↓
Rules allow for the replication of those helpful responses, whenever the opportunity arises to integrate them into behaviour.
↓
Intention revises its rules and behaviour in the light of experience.

Rules in this way become the *grammar of emergence: conditions for its existence and meaning.

3. *Lean thinking—and its expressions, such as *TEQs (Tradable Energy Quotas) and the *Lean Economy itself—can be understood in part as a set of rules, opening the way to a new space for creative expression and emergence, almost all of which is still waiting to be explored. Once the essential principles of the Lean Economy have been developed, its complex reality and variety can emerge.

4. Finally, there are the emergent properties of *groups. If the *incentives, the *freedom and the *scale of the task are right, groups and teams can develop a level of performance beyond what would have been predicted from the individual membership. There is *common capability.[93]

*Connectedness, Butterfly Effect, Ecology: Farmers and Hunters, Reductionism.

EMOTIONAL ARGUMENT, FALLACIES OF. (1) The fallacy that the strong presence of emotion in an argument validates it: the expression of real feeling is taken to show that the person is *sincere, so she has to be right. (2) The fallacy that the strong presence of emotion in an argument invalidates it: the expression of real feeling is taken to show that the person is not being rigorous, so she has to be wrong.

But neither of these are necessarily *fallacies. The logician's view of this is generally austere. Madsen Pirie writes,

> Emotion . . . motivates us to do things, but
> reason enables us to calculate what to do.[94]

Not in *Lean Logic*. For reasons why the emotions should be recognised as central to judgment, see *Spirit.[95] *Intuition, Eroticism, Icon, Distraction, Reflection, F-Word Fallacy.

EMOTIVISM. The doctrine that *judgments are no more than expressions of preference, attitude or feeling. It is most closely associated with the philosopher G.E. Moore (*Principia Ethica*, 1903), and may be taken as the inverse of the *practical, *place-based, roughly communitarian view developed by Alasdair MacIntyre.[96]

EMPIRE. A pathological condition consisting of the usurpation, or surrender, of decision-making and sovereignty from smaller communities, including *nation-states.

Empire is defined, not by physical *boundaries, but by conformity in terms of *ideology and compliance, which then has to be enforced. It generally presents itself as a force for peace, but the imposed conformity is a source of *conflict, both external and internal. A repressive regime is likely to follow, and to persist until the empire breaks up.

Empire is the inverse of the *modular and *diverse structure of *resilience. It can be resisted if it is recognised and tackled early: against the *rhetoric of *large scale—which consists of constantly-repeated violation of the *System Scale Rule and boundless ambition—the only effective responses are patient explanation, early mockery and zero tolerance.[97]
*Nation ❯ Empire, Butterfly Effect, Groups and Group Sizes, Character.

EMPOWERMENT. Empowerment, applied to the individual or the *community, means being confident, being assured; having the *authority to think things through and to act accordingly. In contrast, disempowerment speaks of apathy, futility, lack of hope and lack of influence over one's own destiny. The disempowered person, population or class is one that no one listens to—the electorate that is patronised and reduced to an *abstraction of consumers, not to be entrusted with doing anything for themselves unless they see a *private advantage. It is about accepting passively what comes

along, because there is *no alternative. Empowerment, in contrast, dances to a different logic: it is about investing *imagination and energy in the *place we live in, and in the people we live amongst. In fact, *Lean Logic* prefers the label *presence: it suggests permanence and natural competence, without the rather breathless sense of self-assertiveness and 'recovery as work-in-progress' that we get with empowerment. Indeed, as the management writer Daniel Pink points out, empowerment is an awkward word—almost an oxymoron—since it suggests that some kind authority is giving you lots of empowering flexibility—like a dog on a long lead—which is far from the *autonomy* of being able to choose your own route and apply your own mind:

> [Empowerment] presumes that the organization
> has the power and benevolently ladles some of
> it into the waiting bowls of grateful employees.
> But that's not autonomy. That's just a slightly
> more civilized form of control.[98]

But "empowerment" may communicate more clearly than "autonomy"—and the process of recovering, or wresting, or even being donated with, powers and freedoms that we didn't have before is in fact what is typically and urgently needed—so, with Pink's caveat in mind, we shall stay with it, for now.

The civilisation which we have *inherited is a product of empowerment, widely-shared. In the medieval period it built *institutions of great competence. The monasteries, for example, acted as schools, hospitals, centres of the arts, history, science and horticulture; they provided assistance for the poor, old peoples' homes, safehouses and prisons; and they were effective instruments for the control of *population. The manorial system of *land tenure and cultivation—though contained within a strong and at times harsh framework—was kept functioning by the people who belonged to it, sustaining *cooperative *commons as a central enabling institution for some four centuries. The *law, to an increasing degree, arose out of deliberation by the "republic"—the community of citizens with responsibility for the place they lived in, and it was sustained, not least, by local people as juries and magistrates.[99]

Through that period and beyond, local competence sustained *carnival, music, architecture, and the

E

*reciprocities of *social capital; it supported *households, delivering the routine miracle of making people, teaching language, building *emotional development, *humour, handiness, and the accomplishment of listening and friendship. And its achievements continued into the modern period through the Industrial Revolution. It built the institutions—the schools, hospitals, local government and (later) friendly societies which, though voluntarily taken up, provided widely-shared *protection against loss of income through sickness and unemployment. It developed to

keep pace as the social order broke beyond the limits that could be sustained by local self-reliance and needed to be invented and rebuilt on the scale of the city-everywhere.

In a sense, the roots of disempowerment that followed can be traced a long way back, to the invention of *money by the Greeks—the turning point at which the integration between skills and community began to fracture. Informal *reciprocal exchange began its long descent towards being a residual—merely the parts that monetary *economics hadn't yet reached. In our nearer history, early signs of what was to come began with the dissolution of the monasteries, the Enclosures—the loss of common land—and by the progressive retreat of domestic competence and local reciprocity, as money exchange—detached, impersonal, efficient, neat—tore through the *informal economy, which had no immunity. And now, *economism has brought the presumption that all values are economic values, and a demolition of confidence that there is any such thing as society, a thing which we can love (*Public Sphere and Private Sphere).

The power of economism has been formidable. The progressive removal of hands-on responsibility for the community has been carried through almost without challenge. And here are the losses: our sense of *place and the idea that it is in our power to care for it and to take responsibility for it; our regard for and accomplishment in *manual skills; our confidence that we have anything to teach, and can cope without massive institutions

behind us; that combination of originality and persistence known as *character; a *culture committed to the making and sustaining of emotional development; our land as a rich, living *ecology, protected (unconditionally) from *genetic modification and *nuclear contamination and (substantially) from concrete; our *manners and our sense of the wild (which, in deep ways, are the same things); our *spirit; our consciences and, perhaps, our future.

The balance sheet we have inherited is a wasteland. And yet, buried under economism and its anticulture, a seed growing secretly, is a human ecology. That is what—in the early stages of working out what empowerment means—we may with persistence, recover.

EMPTY SANDWICH, THE. A statement which sounds plausible but which is discovered to actually mean nothing at all. It does not even have the distinction of being wrong; it inhabits a dry and barren logic of its own:

> The more people see of one another and the more they do business with each other, the less likely they are to go to war. A more mobile world will also be a more stable world, both politically and socially.
>
> *Rod Eddington, outgoing chief executive of British Airways and the government's transport advisor, presenting the case for a national/EU-wide road pricing scheme, June 2005.[100]*

*Fallacies, Informal Logic.

E

ENCOUNTER. The act of recognising something—a person, a *practice, a *system—on its own terms; the particular character and wholeness of the other is acknowledged; *judgment and opinion about him/her/it are set in a *relevant context, rather than in the context of universal *general principle or immoveable *mindset.

To acknowledge the wholeness of a system—a woodland, a person, a planet, nature—means being aware that you are in the presence of something which has business and an agenda of its own, and which cannot be tamed by your understanding. To see nature as a whole, as its own self, you need to approach it with the *manners of the stranger—as noted by the great ecologist, Henry David Thoreau (1817–1862),

> To conceive of it with *a total apprehension* I
> must for the thousandth time approach it as
> something totally strange.[101]

When the animal ecologist, Stephan Harding, observed the little muntjac deer in Rushbeds Wood—little pools of life, chewing their cud, pausing for a moment of meditative tranquillity, and seeming to radiate light in the shadows—there was encounter. When the system you have been studying looks back at you, it is not understanding that hangs in the air, but a "hallo". There is a *conversation. You are not alone.[102]

Encounter is about the fundamental experience of not being alone. It is free of the curse of understanding, which opens up the path to *control. If, for instance, Harding had programmed the muntjac he was observing (perhaps with *genetic engineering, implanted chips and wireless technology), he would understand it better, but there would be no encounter, just an extension of his clever self, a lonely scientific experimenter in a wood. To control is to be alone: there is nothing there which calls for engagement and a response. There is no need, if alone, for logic.

The starting point for encounter, then, is the hallo reaction, the acknowledgement that there is something there which is *quick—which has the gift of life, self, soul and the ability to surprise. It is also the starting point for thought, the signal for *logic to stir into life. By filling its environment with things it can control, the industrial *market economy has lost its grip on logic at roughly the same speed and time as it has emptied its

environment of things it can say hallo to. Observing a little system chewing its cud among the shadows on a summer afternoon is good. Encountering a little muntjac is better. It can start you thinking.
*Deference, Expertise, Holism, Courtesy, Reflection, Spirit, Truth.

ENERGY. See Energy Prospects, Lean Energy, Energy Descent Action Plan.

ENERGY DESCENT ACTION PLAN. The "energy descent" is the phased decline in energy dependence needed in response both to *climate change and to the depletion of fuels (*Energy Prospects).[103]

The idea of descent in this context was suggested by Howard and Elizabeth Odum in *A Prosperous Way Down* (2001). Ted Trainer, in his *Renewable Energy Cannot Sustain a Consumer Society* (2007), pointed out that the decline in fossil fuel supply will leave a gap which cannot be filled in the foreseeable future, leaving no alternative to a steep reduction in our dependence on energy. And the permaculturist David Holmgren's work over many years has shown that this reduction in energy use will require change and invention in every aspect of the material consumption on which we now rely.[104]

The idea was taken forward to an Energy Descent Action Plan (EDAP) by the 2005 class of second year students at Kinsale Further Education College in County Cork, Ireland, and their course tutor, Rob Hopkins. As their local plan developed, it became clear that it provided the framework for constructive thinking on the ways in which a *community could work out how to live with a drastically reduced demand for energy

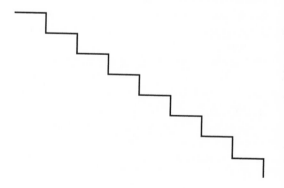

and *materials, and increased local competence in providing for the community's diverse needs from its own resources. So this tells us the first thing we need to know about Energy Descent Action Plans—they are *not* just about energy, but they *are* a reminder that energy is there at the heart of everything we do. And the idea can be seen as the starting point for *Transition—the movement in which local people commit themselves to working with their communities to find ways of living with less.[105]

The Kinsale EDAP's breadth of vision was impressive. It covered *food, youth and community, *education, *housing, *economy and livelihoods, *health, tourism, *transport, *waste and *energy. It was guided by the twelve principles of *permaculture. And lessons were learned about how to work with the talent that already exists in a community for the common benefit: include everyone—don't *blame people (the local council, for instance) for the lack of action so far; inspire visible and interesting events—projects, conferences, happenings, *carnivals; have a coherent and positive view of what the plan is aiming for; and be flexible in the light of experience about what that plan should be. Underpinning this is the technique of "open-space" meetings, which are a way of involving quite large numbers (100+) of people in thinking through the needs and opportunities of the community they live in. The principle is simple: the people present are asked to suggest subjects for discussion; they then (choosing the subjects that interest them most) come together in small groups to discuss them; their conclusions are collected together and worked up into objectives and plans for making things happen.[106]

And now we have a new generation of plans in other communities, building on what has been learned since 2005.[107] Several local authorities have written their first EDAPs, documents that can be expected to have increasingly ambitious sequels and, in part, to shape their future. The plan developed by the City of Bristol in the UK, *Building a Positive Future for Bristol after Peak Oil*, is explicit about the extent of the change that is in prospect:

> An oil crunch would fundamentally threaten the way our city operates. . . . Current alternatives aren't scalable—there is no alternative available that can replace the amount and type of energy that we receive from oil at a comparable cost.[108]

The plan then develops responses with respect to emergency planning, transport, food, health, public services, energy and the utilities. Clearly a future of radical thinking is unfolding here, and as further evidence for this, the 2009 EDAP from Oakland in California begins its transport planning for conditions of energy scarcity by making the case for "urban villages":

> Petroleum independence is proposed in a way that will build and strengthen local communities.[109]

This is *lean thinking in action. The plan provides the framework, inviting or requiring the community to think about how to make their visions for their future happen. And the practical detail of how this works is demonstrated by the Devon town of Totnes' experience of having done it—or, at least, having made a start. They suggest eight steps:

1. Develop a framework—the core organisers *define the area in question and do the research about its history, its present character and its needs.
2. Develop the communications tools—posters, leaflets and an initial vision of the future to form the starting point for discussion.
3. Involve the community in many different ways at once—public events, open-space meetings, talks, meetings with the *Parish Council and other local bodies.
4. Hold a celebratory public launch to communicate the developing collective vision of the future and invite speakers—community *leaders and others— to contribute to this.
5. Organise public workshops on specific themes such as *energy, *food and *education. These are the crucial ideas-harvesting events, in which people develop their visions, practical ideas and strategies for the transition.
6. Begin the "backcasting" process, in which participants work out the timing of the steps that need to be taken to accomplish what they have *imagined.[110]
7. Draft the EDAP and consult on it. This is the stage of intensely grounded detail, with the community working out the implications and detail of the plan. The key is to ensure the widest possible knowledge

E

129

about it and participation in it, so that there is a sense of ownership and *empowerment: here is the area's own plan, made by the hard work and imagination of its people.

8. Make it happen—put the plan into action.

PEAK OIL
Where did the idea come from?

In the 1950s, a dependable way of predicting the peak and decline of oil production from a large province was devised by the geologist M. King Hubbert. Look back, he advised, at the rate of discovery of new oil reserves; this invariably reaches a peak and, after an interval of some decades, the peak of production will follow. By studying the pattern of discovery and production, you can work out how long the interval between peak discovery and peak production is likely to be. His theory was borne out by his prediction, 15 years ahead of the event, that America would reach its production peak in 1970.

From 1966, the year after which discoveries of oil went into sharp decline worldwide, it became possible to make sensible forecasts of oil's global future. Detailed statistical foundations for estimating regional reserves began to be published by another geologist, Harry Wassall, through his company Petroconsultants (now IHS Energy). By the 1970s the evidence was available that, at current rates of growth in consumption, conventional oil would reach its peak around the turn of the century.

And in the 1990s, it was confirmed in detail when Colin Campbell and Jean Laherrère brought together Wassall's statistical detail and published the global picture. Their work was then taken up by Roger Bentley, Michael Smith and others, and forecasts for the turning point for the world's production of conventional oil converged with substantial consensus on the early years of the new century.[111]

Idealistic? Well, not necessarily. We should not rule out vision on the grounds that its convergence with reality is approximate. As Shaun Chamberlin shows in *The Transition Timeline*, the EDAP . . .

> . . . is, as much as anything, a new story for the community . . . a celebration of the creativity of the community, weaving together artwork, 'Transition Tales', local history, the practicalities of moving away from oil addiction, and much more. We often stress in Transition that we need to create visions of a post-carbon world so enticing, so compelling and attractive that people leap out of bed in the morning determined to dedicate their lives to its implementation.[112]

In fact, an example of such ideals has been worked out and accomplished in practice in the form of the Totnes EDAP, which was published in June 2010. The detail is there; the realistic view of what the landscape and local resources will actually allow; and the timelines, with step-by-step advance from 2010 to their target year of 2030. Can a community write a book? A brilliant one? Full of detailed local knowledge, tested and discussed? Well, yes. They had a little help from someone who did most of the actual writing (Jacqi Hodgson, with assistance from Rob Hopkins)—but the task couldn't go wrong, because it had assistance from 500 people who applied their minds and did the work. A lot of it, anyway. Enough to make it their plan. And Totnes' former inhabitants had a hand in it too—Mr. Heath, for instance. George Heath once supplied the local shop with year-round vegetables from his nursery in the centre of town—now a car park. On the timeline for 2016: turn it back into a vegetable garden.[113]
*Lean Energy, TEQs (Tradable Energy Quotas).

ENERGY PROSPECTS. Here is a summary of the prospects for each of the main energy sources on which we now rely:

THE FOSSIL FUELS

Oil

For the first 100 years of the oil industry's dazzling history, alarms about the imminent depletion of oil were commonplace (*Wolf Fallacy). These alarms were false,

LIFE STORY 1
Oil

Both oil and gas consist of molecules of hydrogen and carbon. The gas molecule is the simplest form of hydrocarbon—four atoms of hydrogen and one of carbon; and in the case of oil, these basic molecules are strung together in chains of varying lengths. The carbon is a signature of the fact that hydrocarbons were once part of living cells belonging to animals and plants.

The life of a barrel of oil starts between 60 and 500 million years ago with the detritus of dead algae which fell to the bottom of stagnant seas and deep lakes, mostly in the Jurassic and Cretaceous periods. A small amount of this dross made it to the bottom, where it was mixed in with fine-grained sediments from clays and muddy limestone, which eventually formed the oil's "source rock". The organic matter was then broken down by microorganisms, releasing carbon dioxide and methane, and producing an insoluble compound called kerogen, some of which then became buried beneath the surface at a depth of between 1,500 and 3,500 metres—known as the "kitchen" or "oil window"—where it simmered gently for 200 million years or more at a temperature of between 65°C and 150°C.

In these conditions, the chemical structure of the kerogen gradually matured (the name of the process is catagenesis) into oil. The oil is slightly less dense than the kerogen so that, as it forms, it expands, breaking out of its source rock and mostly escaping up to the atmosphere where it oxidises and fades out of the story. However, a tiny proportion became trapped before it reached the surface, in some cases under a layer of salt or hard (anhydrite) rocks, in other cases under a rather more leaky seal of shales or clay. It is these traps—anticlines, domes, faults, salt zones, pinchouts, pinnacle reefs, uncomformities and subtle traps in all their variety—which caught oil at the last stage in its epic escape back to the sunshine, and so give us exploitable oilfields.[114]

E

but the alarmists were right about one thing: there is a limited amount of accessible oil in the ground and, if it continues to be used, the rate at which it can be extracted will eventually go into decline, from which it will not recover. "Peak oil" is the view that "eventually" means about now—that is, the second decade of this century, and some of the people who first drew attention to the peak and its significance are introduced in the "Peak Oil" sidebar. The shock to the global market will be profound, because the decline in oil will proceed too fast for any other form of energy to take its place.

At the start of the oil age (in the mid-19th century), there were about 2,000 billion barrels of potentially-recoverable conventional oil in the ground, and around half of this now remains. Oil has been found and produced by over 100 nations, most of which have now passed their production peak; the turning point for the UK was in 1999. The world depends on a small number of giant fields for most of its oil. Of the 70,000 fields in use, just 120 account for half of the oil produced, and almost all

of them were discovered before 1965. Since then, there have been few major discoveries and, for every five barrels of oil now used, just one is discovered.[115]

For a closer look, we need to distinguish between conventional and unconventional oil. Conventional oil comes in these forms:[116]

REGULAR OIL

This is oil which is relatively easy to get at, and it is the largest source. The wells are on land or offshore on continental shelves of relatively shallow water. In 2010, regular oil contributed 73–74 million barrels a day (mbd)—or about 85 percent of the total flow of all liquid fuels.[117]

DEEPWATER OIL

Some conventional oil lies in sub-ocean reservoirs at depths of between 500 and 5,000 metres. They are a geological *anomaly, the product of algal deposits in sediments in the stagnant water of deep rifts, in the era when the Americas separated from the land mass of

Europe, Africa and Asia. These rifts then descended into the depths of the Atlantic, and over a period of 100 million years or so acquired a protective layer of silt brought down by rivers. Some of the silt was then washed by the Coriolis currents driven by the rotation of the Earth, leaving clean sand which formed an oil-tight seal.[118]

The task of producing oil from those deep sea deposits is heroic: the water is close to freezing, and the oil may need to be heated before it can be pumped to the surface; and the reservoirs are separated from each other, so that the intensely high pressure in a reservoir drops rapidly as the oil is pumped, leading to a heightened risk of fire and explosion. A blowout at a depth of 5,000 metres—and so accessible only to robots—is borderline impossible to contain using current technology. The main deposits of deep sea oil are in the Atlantic off the coast of Brazil, in the Gulf of Mexico and off the coasts of Angola and Nigeria.

It is expensive to maintain the installations so, once they are in place, the operators extract the oil quickly and, when a deepwater project has reached its peak, the decline is rapid. Deepwater oil contributes some 7 mbd a day, and is expected to peak at around 11 mbd in 2015.[119]

POLAR OIL

This is formed in the normal way but happens to be in the Arctic. The first problem is that it is hard to get at, being buried beneath polar ice, but it is becoming easier as sea ice retreats in the Arctic Ocean (*Climate Change). Secondly, there is a greater likelihood of gas than oil, because any oil reservoirs are likely to have been crushed under the weight of ice, pushing them below the oil window (see "Life Story 1" sidebar) and down to the level at which it cracks to gas.

Polar oil is expected to sustain a modest flow of up to 3 mbd for the first half of the century.[120]

NATURAL GAS LIQUIDS

Each of the three sources described above may also produce natural gas liquids (NGLs) along with the crude oil. NGLs come in various forms: some condense out from gas to liquid as soon as they reach the surface; others shift into a liquid phase under pressure. NGLs consist of relatively short-chain molecules such as ethane, propane and butane, and they should not be

TO THE LAST DROP
When is an oilfield exhausted?

The men at the oil-face do all they can to slow the decline. When a new regular oil field is started up, it gushes. Then the flow declines; then it has to be pumped; then it gets difficult. Some oil wells yield as much as 80 percent of their oil; with others, the limit is reached at around 10 percent; the overall average is around 40 percent. A constant research objective in the oil industry is to find ways of extracting a little bit more, and the methods vary. Detergents are sometimes pumped into the well to retrieve the oil as minute droplets (but the detergents tend to break down with the heat); fire is used to make the oil more liquid and to produce combustion gases to help it along (but this tends to produce sulphuric acid which eats the plumbing); liquefied gases such as butane and propane are used to dissolve the oil (but this requires a lot of expensive gas); and carbon dioxide is sometimes injected to dissolve into the oil to increase its bulk and drive it along. Sometimes, steam is used. If all else fails, it may be possible to use mining techniques, digging out galleries below the reservoir to catch any remaining oil. All of these can work, up to a point, and so it is sometimes suggested that "enhanced oil recovery" (EOR) can not only extend the life of an oil well after it has peaked, but postpone the global peak itself. But estimates for reserves of conventional oil already include the best that these improvisations can offer.[121]

confused with synthetic liquid fuels for which natural gas is the raw material (discussed later, in the "Liquid Energy" sidebar on page 141). NGLs are an important source of oil, with an expected flow of 12 mbd, remaining roughly constant until 2050.[122]

Until recently, it was these conventional oils that supplied all that was needed. But now we are having to turn to the "unconventional" sources:

HEAVY OILS

Heavy oils are deposits which, in the early part of their lives, went through the whole process of being formed into oil (see "Life Story 1" sidebar on page 131), but then came closer to the surface. This allowed the lighter molecules to evaporate, leaving behind a heavy tar, or an even heavier bitumen. The tar sands of Alberta in Canada can be processed into liquid crude oil, but the process is lengthy. The tar has to be mined and treated with steam, hot water and caustic soda; it is then diluted with naphtha, centrifuged to produce hot bitumen, and subjected to a coking process to produce a synthetic oil. This all requires large quantities of energy (usually natural gas, though building *nuclear power stations on the sites has been suggested) and *water: a single project to produce 235,000 barrels of oil a day in Alberta is estimated to use 3.5 million m³ water per day, and a river has been diverted to supply it.[123]

The heavy oils of Venezuela are slightly more fluid than the Canadian tars (not least because they are warmer); they consist of bitumen which must be extracted by injecting steam to drive it to a central well. The treatment then needed to produce oil is so punishing that a short cut has been invented: the bitumen is mixed with water and detergents to produce Orimulsion, a dirty fuel which can be burned only in power stations equipped to capture and dispose of the large quantities of sulphur it contains. Although the stock of oil sands and bitumen is very large, the flow of production is expected to be limited to between 3 and 5 mbd—some 4 percent of all production—for the foreseeable future.[124]

OIL SHALES

Shales are impermeable sedimentary rocks built up into tightly-compacted layers. They exist in large quantities (whole landscapes are made of them), with deposits in America, Australia, Russia and China; just one basin in Colorado contains shales theoretically capable of yielding 600 billion barrels of oil. These rocks contain kerogen which did not descend to the 'oil window' in which it would have been cooked at the correct temperature (see "Life Story 1"sidebar on page 131). There are ways of mimicking the conversion of kerogen into oil—speeding up the process from millions of years to a few hours—but the process has problems: the shale has to be mined, crushed

and heated to 350°C; all this requires very large amounts of energy and water, and it produces waste, much of it toxic, which bulks up into a quantity greater than that of the shale that was mined in the first place. And, when it is heaped up in tips, it is unstable. On a small scale, the use of shale as a source of oil has not yet been shown to be economic; on a large scale, the options are even more doubtful: as the operation grows it is increasingly at risk of being buried under its own waste. Shales will not be a significant source of oil on a useful timescale.[125]

LEAN REFLECTION ON OIL

In summary, several studies have pointed to the probability of the world's oil production reaching its peak in the near future, followed by a sustained decline. The authors of the UK Energy Research Centre's 2009 report, Global Oil Depletion, summarise,

Despite the apparent divergence between "peaking" and "non-peaking" forecasts, a degree of convergence is now becoming apparent . . . .

On balance, we suggest that there is a significant risk of a peak in conventional oil production before 2020. Given the potentially serious consequences of supply constraints and the lead times to develop alternatives, this risk should be given urgent consideration.[126]

And four of the authors of the UK Energy Research Centre's report repeat that warning in an independent journal article, adding . . .

At present, most OECD governments are failing to give serious consideration to this risk, despite its potentially far-reaching consequences.[127]

Chris Skrebowski, a contributor to The Oil Crunch, the 2010 report by the UK Industry Taskforce on Peak Oil and Energy Security, sees 2014–2015 as the time when the oil market will experience rapidly rising prices, with demand outrunning supply.[128]

And Dr. Robert Falkner, in the same report, writes that we are not just talking about energy shortages here; there are . . .

. . . important knock-on effects throughout the UK economy. . . . Any disruption to this complex distribution network would have far-reaching economic consequences, as the fuel protests of 2000 vividly illustrate. Back then, supermarkets ran out of essential food products as supplies dried up and consumers resorted to panic-driven hoarding.

The lesson from this experience is clear. Sudden supply-side shocks generated by oil supply restriction or hikes in oil prices would not be isolated events.[129]

The peak will not be a cut-off point for oil. It will be the start of a downward trend that will reduce supply year-by-year for the remainder of the century. But it is unlikely that the decline will be smooth, for the *market will have switched from being a buyers' market (with a large number of buyers, competing for low prices) to a sellers' market (with a small number of sellers, each of which can drastically raise the price of oil by restricting its supply). At the same time there are likely to be rivalries among sellers, and disruptions as the buyers face the stress of energy scarcity and compete for shares of the diminishing supply. The probable outcome will be a series of outages of increasing depth and duration. The benign economic conditions, including a reliable *transport system, in which there could have been an orderly transition to renewable energy, will have passed. The global network of *food supplies, *transportation and *economic interdependence will start to fracture.[130]

Unless, that is, another fuel comes to the rescue in time. What about gas?

Gas

In the case of gas, too, we need to distinguish between "conventional" and "unconventional". Here the standard approach is to describe gas as "conventional" if it is simply extracted from a gas well, needing little or no further heavy-duty encouragement to force it out. "Unconventional" is gas obtained in other ways.

CONVENTIONAL GAS

Conventional gas in its most familiar form (from the point of view of the UK) is the stuff that has for forty years or so come out of wells beneath the seabed of the North Sea. In fact, that source reached its peak in

---

LIFE STORY 2
Gas

The life story of gas is the same as that of oil, except that it is cooked at greater depths and higher temperatures. Most gas comes from leaves and other plant remains which fell or were washed into lakes and seas. There they formed the raw material for a different form of kerogen (vitrinite, as distinct from the sapropel which produces oil). Gas, like oil, can also begin as algae, but the result is the same because, when the source rock in which oil is being formed is forced down to greater and hotter depths—into the gas window—the complex molecules of oil crack into the much simpler molecules of methane which comprise natural gas.

Most deposits of oil and gas will live out their days undisturbed. There are tea-cup sized deposits beneath the surface, but they would require more energy to extract them than they could ever yield. Some, however, are in large deposits, the footprints of ancient, stagnant seas, now valued as the fuel which made it possible to sustain a confident high-technology civilisation.[131]

2000, and production is now falling rapidly. Instead of being an exporter, the UK is having to import gas from Norway and Russia. It is a convenient fuel, easy to recover, but its decline, when it comes, tends to be abrupt. Gas is hard to transport in quantity, except by pipeline; for shipping, it needs to be condensed at high pressure and low temperature, while the pipelines themselves are major projects requiring much money and time. That means that consumers' chances of getting the gas they need vary greatly around the world. One response—in the United States, for example—has been to construct giant terminals for offloading gas from liquefied gas carriers.[132]

So, prospects for gas have been looking highly uncertain, and have been discussed less in terms of a global peak than of supply agreements between consumers and producers around the world, the presence or absence of pipelines, and the ability to pay. Hanging over all this has been the fact that, when a gas province gets towards the end of its life, the fall-off in production tends to be abrupt. Until recently, it seemed that, following the oil shock, a gas shock would not be far behind. That could still be true, but with developments in unconventional gas things have started to look a lot more complicated.

SHALE GAS

Shales (the impermeable sedimentary rocks that we met above in the discussion of oil) contain gas when they are buried deep beneath the surface: the pressure and depth converts the oil they once contained into gas. The gas, however, is trapped so tightly in the rock that extracting it was thought to be impossible until the discovery of ways of fracturing ("fracking") the rock by injecting water into it with explosive force, producing a minor earthquake to open up the layers. What follows is an initial rush of gas from the fractures, followed by a much slower flow from the pore spaces and from the organic materials embedded in the rock.

Shale is the most common of the sedimentary rocks, and almost all of the shales found in deep strata contain at least some gas. In theory, therefore, the discovery of how to extract it opens up a large resource. The world consumes about 3 trillion cubic metres of natural gas each year, and the International Energy Agency estimates that some 180 trillion cubic metres of shale gas is recoverable. Taken together with the other sources of conventional and unconventional gas, this could keep the world supplied with gas at the present rate of consumption for approximately a century.[133]

And that is good news twice over—for, as well as being abundant, gas also burns cleanly with regard to *climate change, producing half the emissions of carbon per unit of energy, in comparison with coal. It is claimed that shale gas is the fuel that will displace oil and coal, that the United States is "swimming" in it, that the fall in gas prices and the mothballing of terminals for imported gas was due to its arrival, and that it will play a major role in saving the world.[134]

But there are snags. The first one is *pollution. The fracturing disturbs geological structures and opens up cracks over distances long enough to connect the shale

deposits with aquifers, or to reach the surface. The drinking *water in (amongst other places) Dimock, Pennsylvania, has become so rich in methane that a flame can be lit under the kitchen tap when it is opened. Domestic water wells have been exploding. In Cleveland, Ohio, an entire house has blown up. Residents have reported ill *health—dizziness, blacking out, rashes, swelling of the legs and elevated blood pressure. Pets and farm animals have been losing their hair. In Colorado, contamination of drinking water has been specifically traced to fractures opening up between gas layers deep underground and aquifers close to the surface.[135]

The water used for the fracturing process is spiked with chemicals whose identities have not yet been published, because the industry has been exempted from providing this information. The shale rock itself typically contains heavy metals such as cadmium, molybdenum and uranium which are dislodged by the water and migrate to wherever it happens to flow. Methane, having a small molecular structure, migrates quickly, and it is likely to be followed by the other, slower-moving, contaminants. This is a technology whose teething problems suggest a future—as yet unconfirmed—of large-scale chemical contamination of the soil and water, making water on the scale of whole watersheds unfit for drinking. Our understanding of all this will improve as the industry learns from experience and as research results come in, but the tension between the unconditional need for fuel and the unconditional need for water could become acute.[136]

The second snag is that the undoubted presence of gas does not necessarily mean that it can be extracted in the quantities needed to close the coming gap in the supply of fuel. It is a technology that lends itself to *false inference and false hopes, in that the gas races out immediately after the rock has been opened up, but this promising phase then falls away quickly. In the Barnett Shale in Texas, for instance, operators originally expected gas wells to have a life of about 30–40 years. In fact, early results suggest an average life of around 7.5 years, and most of the gas that a well will ever produce comes in the first year of its life.[137]

That does not necessarily make a well less useful: an extremely strong flow in the first few months can be seen as a bonus, rather than as a handicap. But rapid die-off could have something to tell us about the scale of the resource as a whole. The strong flow of gas from a well in its first year is an indication that it will turn out to be productive, but, when seeking funding for the enterprise, the *incentive to make optimistic estimates of future reserves in the light of current, if short-lived, results is strong.[138]

And this same incentive applies to a company's decision on whether or not to drill. The act of sinking a well can be taken as evidence that *money will be made from it, whether the company actually expects to do so or not. And big money-costs invariably mean big energy costs, more generally known as low energy return on energy invested (EROEI)—EROEI is the decisive measure which tells us whether a fuel resource is worth developing, regardless of the finances. This is a young industry, and neither advocates nor *sceptics can be sure of their case. But when the high monetary and energy costs of getting shale gas out of the ground are combined with the possibility of smaller-than-expected results and with the prospect of large liabilities arising from the contamination of *land, air and water, it is possible that the shale gas boom will yet turn out to be a bubble.[139]

Shale gas will make a contribution to gas supplies around the world. It is already starting to do so. As to how big that contribution will be, it is still uncertain. But it is not too early to work out some early perspective on the matter. This is done at the end of the present discussion on gas, and at the end of this entry on fossil fuels.

COALBED METHANE

This is the methane—the "firedamp"—that makes coal mining so dangerous, and was the bane of miners' lives from the earliest days. In principle, its extraction is simple: insert a pipe into the mine and allow the methane to flow up the pipe under its own pressure. In the first decade of exploiting this source there were *expectations that it would provide very large flows of gas, and its contribution of some 7.5 percent of annual gas production in the United States was useful, but its growth has now stalled.[140]

The main problem for the industry is what to do with the water it gets out of the mine along with the gas. The coalbed is typically permeated with water, and this has to be extracted and disposed of. It is saline and rich in sodium along with other contaminants such as chlorides, ethyl benzene and metals, so it cannot be used as irrigation water nor dumped into rivers. The problem remains unsolved. And there are other problems: removing the water from the coalbeds can lower the water table by between 200 and 800 feet; there can be spontaneous combustion leading to underground fires, smoke and pollution from the burning of *waste coal; and there are the spectacular and deafening explosions (and sometimes fireballs) produced by "cavitations", when the operator suddenly releases a gas build-up in a mine to create the underground cavity needed for the operation.[141]

All forms of mining for gas have their environmental hazards, but these problems for coalbed methane, combined with a relatively slow rate of release of the gas, have reduced *interest in the technology for now.

BIOGENIC GAS

All methane comes from organic materials, but in most cases the materials in question lived a long time (millions of years) ago. In the case of biogenic gas, the gas is of much more recent origin, ranging from hundreds of thousands of years to a few weeks.[142]

Theoretically, methane could be captured as it escapes from warming permafrost (see *Climate Change > Methane). This would involve covering hundreds of thousands of square miles of Canada and Siberia with plastic sheets. It has a disturbing logic about it—and if it were black plastic sheeting, it would absorb heat from the sun and accelerate the melting, so you would get even more methane.

A more realistic source is the methane released by rotting vegetation, sewage and slurry from cattle (milking parlours and indoor rearing). This can often provide the energy needed for the operation itself (the farm, the sewage works and some local domestic heating), with some left over. But its role as a solution to the coming energy scarcities will be minor.[143]

METHANE HYDRATES

Under conditions of high pressure and low temperature, methane and water combine to form stable crystalline structures which are found in large quantities in relatively shallow seas such as the Arctic Ocean, in outcrops in the deep oceans, at the surface of high-altitude inland plateaus, and in some deep sedimentary rocks. So far they have been left almost unexploited, and there are good arguments for leaving them that way. The global warming potential of methane in the atmosphere is many times that of carbon dioxide—25-fold over 100 years; 72-fold over the first 20 years. The process of mining these methane hydrates and capturing the gas would unavoidably release large quantities of methane into the atmosphere. And methane becomes a massive presence when we consider its potential as an amplifying *feedback, responding to every rise in temperature with further releases from the permafrost and the Arctic seabed. Methane hydrates are a sleeping giant which we would be well advised not to poke a stick at.[144]

And yet, concern about the prospects for oil and gas supplies has provided an *incentive for wild surmise about methane hydrates as a source of natural gas. One study by the US National Academy of Sciences has emphatically ruled out the idea that the risks of developing the potential of methane hydrates out-weigh the rewards:

> Research on methane hydrate to date has not revealed technical challenges that the committee believes are insurmountable in the goal to achieve commercial production of methane from methane hydrate in an economically and environmentally feasible manner.[145]

And energy analysts in China recognise the case for making use of its methane hydrates (aka "combustible ice"). Note the "clean":

> China's western Qinghai Province, containing major deposits of the country's "combustible ice", will see increased explorations for this emerging clean energy. . . . The plateau province plans to allow large energy companies along with researchers to tap this new source of energy while minimizing environmental threats.[146]

One widely cited estimate places the global methane hydrate resource (measured in terms of the carbon content) in the range of 500–2,500 billion tonnes—a wide range, but not so wide as to be useless, since it is unlikely that the industrial *political economy would

survive to explore beyond the smaller one. To put that estimate into perspective, there are currently around 800 billion tonnes of carbon in the atmosphere.[147]

LEAN REFLECTION ON GAS

One of the received principles guiding decision-making on natural gas is the observation that gas is a clean-er-burning fuel than either oil or coal in terms of the carbon dioxide released per unit of energy produced. Methane releases about 180 g/kWh, compared with coal's 351 g/kWh. This is why it is described as "clean" fuel, and why plans to develop the potential of gas to the limit—despite the extreme problems presented by shale gas and methane hydrates—can be presented as a way of reducing environmental impact, rather than as part of a process of diligently destroying the stability of the *climate.[148]

What this assessment of natural gas overlooks, however, is that its impact on the climate comes from two different sources. One of them—the obvious one—consists of the release of carbon dioxide when fuel is burned, and the claimed comparative advantage of gas in this context is justified. The other one, however, consists of the effect of (unburned) methane, whose warming potential over a century (as just noted) is 25 times that of the same mass of carbon dioxide. This means that methane that escapes at any point in the supply chain between drilling and final consumption will have an important direct impact on the climate, even if only released in small quantities.[149]

How small? A study by the independent analyst Chris Vernon points out that if just 3 percent of the methane escapes into the atmosphere at any point before combustion, then the global warming impact of natural gas (per unit of energy produced) will be the same as that of coal.[150]

We do not know how much methane leaks along the supply chain from wellhead to final consumption. Vernon suggests that it might be around 1.5 percent in the UK, and that it could be more than this when gas is transported over long distances and across national *boundaries, as in Eastern Europe. And if operations *before* the wellhead are included—that is, the whole cycle from rock face to consumption is considered—then it seems probable that leaks will be well in excess of 3 percent of the total volume of gas produced. We already know that shale gas mining can release enough methane to turn kitchen taps into flamethrowers. And when the oil was flowing from the blown-out Deepwater Horizon well in the Gulf of Mexico in 2010, methane escaped uncontrollably into the water at a rate some 500 times faster than that of the oil. It is probable that, if methane hydrates are disturbed by mining, then the release of methane into the atmosphere will be hard to prevent.[151]

Some readers may conclude that the argument in favour of natural gas as the ideal fuel is more nuanced than it is sometimes taken to be.

Coal

We shall come to the statistics, but let us first pause for a moment of awe at the story so far:

COAL'S PAST

Coal is the product of the ancient Carboniferous forests which covered much of the planet 300 million years ago. In long, leisurely periods—like deep sighs, each lasting tens of millions of years—the *land was submerged under seas and river deltas, recovering again and again to re-grow as forest, giving us layers of alternating coal and sedimentary rock, stretching from the surface to the unmineable depths, too hot to handle.[152]

It is hard to think about coal without hearing, if only in the imagination, the distant echoes of the outrageous and untamed jungle which it once was. It is relatively tame now, a well-trained industry in most places, but this good behaviour took a long time to come. Coal was used in the Bronze Age and in Roman Britain; in the medieval period it was a routine export from Tyneside to London; and from 1550–1700 it grew into an industry with an output of about 3 million tonnes a year, requiring systematic mining with underground working, and facing the endemic problems of geological faults, roof falls, flooding and fire.[153]

Coal mining meant daily trouble, detail and surprise; men, women, boys and girls worked by hand, with shovels, ponies, baskets, string, wood, candles and blind *courage. Later, steam engines helped with lifting the coal and pumping the water, but the mining itself did not really have an industrial revolution of its own. Hand-cutting, hand-hauling, pony power, wooden pit-props, fire, flooding, lung disease and labour-intensity remained; the detail of having to adapt, with *ingenuity, to weird faults and formations in the geology continued in the UK until well into the second half of the twentieth century, and in many coal mines around the world all these are with us still.[154]

It was dangerous. In the early years of the nineteenth century, the fatalities in the collieries of Tyne and Wear touched 300 a year. There were *deaths from flooding: even the Newcomen steam engine, which relied on atmospheric pressure to do the lifting, could do little for the deep mines, and it could do nothing in emergencies. At the Heaton colliery near Newcastle in 1815, over a century after the engine had been invented, it still took nine months to pump out the water that blocked the way to seventy-five men and boys who had been trapped by water coming from a neighbouring disused mine. By the time they were reached, they had eaten their horses, candles and the bark from the fir props, and the would-be rescuers noted that one man had not long been dead.[155]

And there were deaths from fire, caused mainly by methane, the infamous and explosive "firedamp" released by the exposed coal and sparked by the candles. Safer forms of illumination were tried, including phosphorous and putrescent fish, but the pale glimmers of light they provided were next to useless so—until the invention of the safety lamp in 1815—it had to be unprotected candles. When the miners became aware that firedamp was building up (which in some mines happened three times a day), they withdrew from the face and sent a fireman ahead to explode it. He would cover himself in damp rags and crawl forward, in distant imitation of the jungle-fauna of a previous era, holding a candle at the end of a very long stick, and hoping, when the moment came, to be able to lie flat enough to avoid being blown to bits. The alternative method was to dig a man-sized pit close to the place where the methane was concentrated; the fireman would climb into it, get his mates to cover the hole with a board and piles of wood, and then draw towards him a candle attached to a string . . .[156]

Technology eventually came to the rescue, reducing the fatalities—in the United Kingdom at least—to five per million tonnes of coal in 1900, and then down to the present rate of 0.5. But the phenomenal *complication

of the industry remains. Indeed, it is not one industry at all, it is many: its business consists of construction, surveying, tunnelling, ventilation, mechanical-, chemical- and electrical-engineering, *transport, *waste disposal, decommissioning, landscaping . . . And the *complexity continues with the users of coal, who must cope with the *pollution of *water, air and *land, disposing of slag and fly ash, and handling coal's bulk. Coal is greedy for men: in the UK in 1913, well over a million men worked in its service in coal mining itself, and over half a million more worked in the various power industries—producing gas, coke and electricity—and in the industries that serviced them: making the equipment, driving the coal trains, distributing the coal. The capture of energy from coal is not a technology; it is an establishment. It consists of layer on layer of *infrastructure, *capital, damage limitation and special skills; and it depends on a heroism and mastery of its own. In the United Kingdom, it took centuries to build, and just a few years to substantially demolish. Will it now be rebuilt?[157]

COAL'S FUTURE

If we were able to choose which fuels to use, ranked in order of the energy that can be extracted from them (by weight), coal would be low on the list. The best fuel from that point of view is natural gas, which contains around 50 megajoules of energy per kilogram (Mj/kg), with crude oil falling well short of that at 40. The highest grade of coal (anthracite) yields 30; bituminous coal 20–30, sub-bituminous 10–25. Wood comes in at around 10.[158]

Compared, therefore, with oil and gas (and even compared with wood, which also has the advantage that it absorbed its carbon content from the atmosphere rather more recently, and that the trick can be repeated), coal produces more carbon dioxide for each unit of energy delivered. And it has other disadvantages. Coal requires large mining and transport infrastructures. It leaves a lot of ash. Its boilers need constant management and frequent maintenance. Coal is large-scale trouble.

And yet, worldwide, the consumption of coal is growing fast. This is mainly because of a massive increase in the demand for electricity in the newly-developed countries, notably China and India, both of which have increased their consumption of coal fivefold since 1980. In the OECD countries, coal consumption has generally levelled off or declined as they have switched into alternatives—especially gas—but globally, from 1980–2010, total energy consumption has doubled, and coal's 25 percent contribution to that has held.[159]

Now, one of the points of agreement over the last twenty years of *climate and energy discussion has been that the planet still possesses very large stocks of mineable coal—that is, coal that can be physically extracted from the ground and used in its many applications on the surface. 200 years' supply of coal from proven reserves has been the more-or-less undisputed estimate.[160]

In 2004, that began to change, when the World Energy Council had a closer look at the estimates that they had made in 1980. The revisions were substantial. Botswana's 'proved recoverable reserves' were revised down by almost 99%, from 3.5 billion tons to 40 million (0.04 billion) tons; the United Kingdom's proved recoverable reserves shrank 95%, from 45 billion tons to 220 million tons; Germany's came down by more than 99%, from 23 billion tons to 183 million tons. Some other countries, such as India, did report increases over the same period, but in most cases, they were dramatically down.[161]

In 2007, these revisions were summarised and evaluated by a German think tank called the Energy Watch Group. Above all, they found great variation in the quality and accuracy of data but, based on the best we have, they reached some interesting conclusions.

In the United States—the world's second largest producer—production (mining) of anthracite peaked in 1950; production of bituminous coal peaked in 1990; and, importantly, the total *energy* from coal reached its peak in 1998. Coal of all kinds in the United States has become harder to obtain; since 2000, *productivity per miner has declined by about 10 percent (and this is measured in tons/miner, but the energy content of each ton is also dropping).[162]

Other countries are also well past 'peak coal'. Germany's hard coal (anthracite and bituminous) peaked in 1958; Canada has large reserves of subbituminous coal and lignite, but its total production nonetheless peaked in 1998.[163]

In the world's largest producer, China, the best estimate is that mineable coal production can be expected to peak around 2015, before falling away to around half by 2040. But even this needs to be revised to take into account the annual loss of reserves due to underground fires burning out of control, equivalent to 5–10 percent of production; it should also make allowance for likely downward revision in China's estimated reserves as more realistic evaluations are made of how much of the resource can actually be recovered.[164]

As the coal industry turns to ever poorer grades—down from anthracite (which is now almost entirely depleted) to bituminous, sub-bituminous and lignite—even maximising the production of mineable coal leads to a predicted worldwide peak in *energy* produced in around 2025.[165]

Other studies have reached similar conclusions. A report by the Uppsala Hydrocarbon Depletion Study Group concludes that the world's production of coal will increase by about 30 percent to a turning point in the mid-2020s, followed by some 25 years in which it holds constant, but at the cost of turning to lower grades. A report by the Institute for Energy, *The Future of Coal* concludes that mounting production costs will lift the price of coal relative to oil and gas, and that coal may no longer be "abundant, widely available, cheap, affordable and reliable". And an analysis by David Rutledge and Jean Laherrère, using a more mathematical and abstract approach than the close-range local detail of the EWG and Uppsala reports, comes in as an outlier with the coal peak postponed to the 2040s.[166]

The end of coal? Well, it may not be, because here is some news just in . . .

UNDERGROUND COAL GASIFICATION

It is beginning to dawn on the coal industry that, to generate electricity from coal, it may not be necessary to mine it—it can be done *in situ*, underground. In fact, this was first suggested by the engineer William Siemens in 1868, but there was plenty of easily mineable coal around then, so no one took any notice. It is based on the principles which have been used for almost two centuries to convert the solid and awkward bulk of coal into the much more convenient form of gas. Apply heat and (often) high pressure to a mixture of coal, steam and oxygen. The carbon will partially oxidise, producing carbon monoxide and hydrogen. Contaminants such as hydrogen sulphide, mercury and ammonia can then be removed (along with solid waste in the form of particulates, ash and slag). What you get is "town gas" or "illumination gas"—the mixture of nitrogen, carbon monoxide, hydrogen and carbon dioxide which lit the nineteenth century's streets and pubs, and—until the 1960s—fuelled the UK's domestic cookers, gas ovens, and boilers.[167]

Underground coal gasification (UCG) applies that principle underground. Oxygen is injected into the mine, a fire is started, and the carbon monoxide, hydrogen and (in some conditions) methane that is produced are piped to the surface. It is still early days, but the *incentive to develop UCG is now intense. The technology exists, gas has been produced in a pilot project in Queensland for a decade or so, and the signs are that it is ready to go.[168]

It could turn out to be a massive source of gas, and it would be *additional* to the development of shale gas discussed earlier in this entry. The subject is still rich with uncertainty but UCG could, in principle, make it possible to generate all the electricity we need, supplemented by liquid fuel for road *transport (see "Liquid Energy" sidebar). The toxicity of the carbon monoxide it contains would be a significant hazard, probably requiring further processing to deliver a flow of reasonably pure hydrogen. And the process of converting town gas to liquid petroleum uses up about half of the energy contained in the gas; but that may not be thought to matter if there is enough gas—and on the evidence now becoming available, UCG is potentially such an effective means of putting the planet's coal resources to use that there would indeed be enough.[169]

LIQUID ENERGY

Coal-to-liquids

The technology which derives liquid fuel from coal seems at first to be just what we need as we face a future of oil depletion. Its feasibility was demonstrated by wartime Germany, and South Africa's Sasol company started coal-to-liquids (CTL) under the Apartheid embargo and still produces 150,000 barrels of liquid fuels a day. A new plant has also been started up in China.[170]

There are two ways of doing it. The first converts the coal into gas and then employs the Fischer-Tropsch process: reacting it over a catalyst to extend the hydrocarbon molecules to the length needed for a liquid. Alternatively, the Bergius process subjects the coal to high temperature and pressure to produce liquid directly.[171]

Yet the energy analysts Mikael Höök and Kjell Aleklett see the large losses of energy in the conversion from coal to liquids—meaning the technology has a voracious demand for coal—as a severe limitation. In principle it makes more sense to generate electricity from the coal. Coal which is used to generate electricity will drive an electric car three times as far as the same quantity of coal used to produce fuel for a petrol-driven car.[172]

Gas-to-liquids

This process starts with gas, and so its use of the Fischer-Tropsch process is much more *efficient than coal-to-liquids. It is the fastest-growing development in the oil industry. A reminder: the "liquids" produced here are long-chain fuels such as gasoline, diesel, paraffin, kerosene, airline fuel and lubricants, not the short-chain 'natural gas liquids' (NGLs), which are much less versatile, bulkier and harder to transport and store.[173]

And the snags? First there is the problem of fire. The normal means of controlling the underground fire is the supply of oxygen: if it is shut off, the fire goes out. If that doesn't work, try *water: the presumption is that UCG would only be carried out at depths below the water table, so to extinguish the fire you would only need to let the water flow back in. But heat rises, and if the fire spread above the water table that fail-safe device would not work. Nor would it work if the flow was not fast enough to extinguish the fire: some deep geological deposits are dry. There are many underground fires burning in the world. Those in China have already reduced its mineable resource by almost a fifth; in the United States, the Centralia mine fire in Pennsylvania, started accidentally in 1962, is one of dozens still burning out of control in the state. And underground peat fires in Indonesia have been pouring carbon dioxide into the atmosphere at a variable rate ranging around a billion tonnes a year.[174]

It is unlikely that UCG could be developed on a large scale without starting a new generation of fires, with corresponding releases of carbon into the atmosphere.

Indeed, the very efficiency of UCG—relative to the avoided cost of mining and the construction of industrial-scale gasifiers—would encourage it. Labour *productivity may be some four times greater than in the case of mining; no long-distance coal *transport is needed; there are no slag heaps; and you don't need to build *complex, capital-intensive gas plants above ground (a *capital saving of some 60 percent has been estimated). The essential requirements are boreholes and pipes. Enterprises could develop UCG projects with modest backing and relaxed procedures. There could be a black market in coal gas whose sources and methods its buyers prefer not to know about.[175]

Secondly, there are the emissions of carbon dioxide both from the process of underground gasification itself, and from the eventual combustion of the gas in centralised facilities such as power stations. The natural response to this would be carbon capture and storage (CCS—see page 143), if it existed on a scale adequate for the task, but it doesn't, and it is unlikely to do so.

It's time for a look at the quantities we are dealing with here. For context, in 2010, approximately 6.5

billion tonnes of coal was mined from a global reserve of approximately 900 billion mineable tonnes. Estimates of the quantity of coal available using UCG vary widely: the World Energy Council stated in 2007 that around 600 billion tonnes of otherwise unusable coal may be suitable for underground gasification; a 2010 study by Dermot Roddy and Paul Younger suggested that the total potential resource could be as high as 4,000 billion tonnes.[176]

Let's stay with the latter estimate. If this resource were used, the carbon dioxide releases into the atmosphere might amount to some 12,000 billion tonnes. This would be enough (other things being equal) to raise carbon dioxide concentrations by 6,000 parts per million, which in turn would notionally raise the global temperature by 18 degrees.[177]

Lean reflection on fossil fuels

"It's obvious that the whole idea of peak oil—or peak fossil fuels—is blown completely out of the water." That observation, following a *conversation in a summertime wood in Buckinghamshire about shale gas, methane hydrates and underground coal gasification, seems at first hard to fault. If we want to get hold of fossil fuels in large quantities in the future, we will probably be able to do so.

But to what extent does this indeed destroy the peak oil argument? "Peak oil" is widely and understandably used as shorthand to refer not just to oil itself, but to the idea that energy scarcities of various kinds will in the near future damage the *market economy to the point of destruction, or at least to the point of change beyond recognition. Well, there are a few things to point out.

To start with, specific fuels are required for specific purposes. Oil (in its various liquid derivatives) is by far the best fuel for *transport; petrol and diesel have a higher energy-density (by volume, not weight) than compressed natural gas, which contains only around a quarter of the energy for the same volume of fuel. The proposed solution to this is to convert the natural gas to petroleum—a process which, though slightly more *efficient than the conversion of town gas, still comes at the cost of losing some 40 percent of the energy contained in the gas itself—and large installations for this purpose are coming on line in Qatar, Indonesia, Yemen and Peru. Meanwhile, a new floating LNG technology has the

potential to make use of the many gas reserves around the world which were formerly too small to develop.[178]

And yet, *general statements about the existence of fuel in quantities sufficient to meet the world's energy needs can be misleading. For what our civilisation needs to fuel the continuity of its present progress along the path of economic *growth is not just "energy" in general terms but:

1. Specific forms of fuel and energy in the right place: Fuels must be constantly available to satisfy *all* the market economy's needs, including transport, heating and power generation.
2. *Time: Any transformations in energy *infrastructure, such as for the conversion of gas to liquids, have to be available in time to make up for the shortfall in the supply of transport fuels due to peak oil.
3. A protected *ecology: (1) and (2) have to be delivered without destroying the planet's *ecosystems. It cannot be said that peak oil has gone away unless the additional threats presented by the candidates to replace oil are emphatically removed.

It appears unlikely, therefore, that peak oil will be avoided. Or, as the oil analyst Chris Skrebowski puts it, seemingly inviting his readers to read between the lines:

> Whether the development of unconventional gas supplies is fast enough to have an impact on the oil crunch remains to be seen. . . . It should be remembered, however, that fuel supply changeovers take time and investment.[179]

Regular oil—the light, sweet crude that keeps us all moving—has benign qualities, along with its problems. It is already a liquid with a high energy-density; it does not leak methane; it does not give rise to underground fires; it is easily transportable; it can be used for all purposes; its mishaps are not catastrophic. It is a hard act to follow. Yet the probability is that deepening oil scarcities will begin in the decade 2015–2024.

In fact, far from peak oil being blown out of the water by the new discoveries, its impact is intensified by another difficulty. At a time of energy deficit, there will be an incentive to develop those new sources of gas. There will also be a need to prevent the carbon emissions that this would produce.

Until now, *green critics' task of drawing attention to a turning point ahead has been comparatively easy and uncontroversial: peak oil was on its way; it was no one's fault, the product of no one's *choice or policy. The other message, "we must reduce carbon emissions to deal with climate change", though vigorously argued, could take second place in terms of imposing a profound and immediate transformation on our civilisation, not because it was less important, but because peak oil—the immediate problem, and probably the first to strike with radical consequences—would happen whatever anyone did.

But now it is necessary to base the argument on an *intentional commitment to prevent the explosive release of carbon dioxide and methane emissions from the new gas resources, in a market that is already in deep trouble owing to oil shortages. All this new energy potential can be seen as coming to the rescue of our civilisation in its hour of need. Anyone who wants to stop that happening risks being entangled in accusations of destroying the economy our civilisation depends on. What is blown out of the water is not peak oil, but the beautiful "not my fault, guv" simplicity of the story so far—the friendly warning that energy scarcity is not something we need to enforce, but something we need to prepare for and respond to.[180]

And these considerations are sharpened by the nature of the technology involved. We are in the era of *methods of last resort*, involving risks which would not be contemplated unless all other options had closed. It is not just that they present extreme difficulties—the development of deep-sea oil wells, for example, is at least as difficult as the exploration of space, and *nuclear energy generates radioactive *waste that must be actively managed for decades. The key problem is that when things go wrong with technologies built on this massive *scale, the consequences tend to be catastrophic. The Gulf of Mexico dies; whole watersheds become unusable; unquenchable underground fires burn; carbon and methane emissions erupt out of control. Regular technologies have their accidents, but, beyond the reach of the local trouble, life carries on. Once the boundary of last resort has been crossed, taking technologies from the regular to the extreme, some accidents will have global consequences. You don't need many of those.[181]

CARBON CAPTURE AND STORAGE

Carbon capture and storage (CCS) is the proposal that the carbon dioxide produced by the combustion of fossil fuels can be permanently stored away in places where it cannot harm the atmosphere. The intense *incentive to develop it as a solution is clear, since there is no other way of combining the use of fossil fuels with anything remotely corresponding to the emissions reduction needed to protect the climate.

It is suggested that the CO_2 could be stored in disused oil and gas fields; in unmineable or exhausted coal seams; in saline or basalt formations (porous rock saturated with brine); or in deep oceans, where liquid carbon dioxide would form a dense lake on the seafloor. CCS is widely cited as a mitigation or even a solution to the problem of carbon dioxide emissions from coal-fired power stations: it is what allows shale gas, underground coal gasification, and even methane hydrates to be presented as sensible options.[182]

Various ways of capturing carbon dioxide have been developed. One method is to extract as much carbon as possible from the exhaust flue after combustion of the fuel. In the case of coal, there is the option of partially-oxidising the coal to produce town gas (see "Underground Coal Gasification" on page 140), and transforming the carbon monoxide into carbon dioxide which can then be quite easily captured. A third alternative is to burn the coal in oxygen, mix the flue gas with water vapour, and then extract the water vapour to leave a stream of carbon dioxide.[183]

Demonstration and pilot plants for carbon capture have been constructed by Imperial College (London), by Total at Lacq (southwestern France), by Scottish Power in Longannet (Scotland), by Doosan Babcock in Renfrew (Scotland), and many other organisations. It is not yet settled whether CCS can deliver as promised, but there are problems associated with it:

1. *Scale*. At present about 30 billion tonnes of carbon dioxide are released from all industrial, *transport and domestic uses of fossil fuels each year.[184] If, by some means, this quantity of carbon dioxide could be condensed into a liquid (compressed and cooled to zero degrees) and injected into underground spaces, it would occupy approximately 10 cubic

143

E

BREAKTHROUGH
Dramatic advance in
Carbon Capture and Storage

MIKEL: I quite like the idea for digging up every
12 tons of coal, burning it, and putting the 44
tons of carbon dioxide back in the hole.

DAXR: I'm wondering how much cheaper it
would be instead to just bury coal itself?
If we used the holes and shafts that coal
mining leaves in the ground, we'd save lots
of costs there too.

GREENISH: I think you're on to something. In
theory, it would even work if we pushed
it one more step back. Just leave it in the
ground. We could call it "in situ non-gasifi-
cation" or something.

Exchange by commenters on *The Oil Drum*.[185]

kilometres. This is more than twice the total volume
of coal mined each year.[186] Nonetheless, the Intergovernmental Panel on Climate Change's (IPCC)
technical report on carbon capture and storage
estimates geological potential for at least 2,000 billion
tonnes of carbon dioxide storage worldwide.[187]

The idea that carbon dioxide could in fact be
contained at low temperature and high pressure in
underground spaces, either natural or man-made,
is, however, open to debate. It is disputed by, for
instance, Michael Economides, professor of chemical engineering at the University of Houston, but
the objection has been strongly rebuffed by other
specialists in the field and by the Carbon Capture
and Storage Association. Indeed, the matter is complicated because, in the right conditions, the carbon
dioxide doesn't just sit there as a gas, waiting to
leak; it combines with minerals in the rock to form
a stable carbonate.[188]

In summary, the balance of the argument appears
to support the view that large-scale storage is
feasible in principle, but the key question—"can
it work on a large enough scale to make a difference?"—is not settled, for implementation on a

*scale approaching the need is still at least twenty
years away. Even then, CCS is only relevant to flue
gas emissions, and can do nothing about emissions
from (for instance) domestic heating, petrol- and
diesel-driven transport and equipment, nor about
emissions of carbon dioxide and methane from
the mines, wells and transport systems of the fuel
providers themselves.

2. *Other practical consequences*. The reliability of the
various forms of storage being considered is uncertain. The concern that some underground storage
sites could leak is not laid to rest by the belief that
others probably wouldn't. There is also concern
that, if deposited on deep ocean floors, CO_2 would
contribute to the acidification of the oceans, which
already threatens to be a catastrophic consequence
of *climate change. On the other hand, the authors
of another IPCC report conclude that appropriately
selected geological reservoirs are likely to retain 99
percent of the carbon stored in them for 1,000 years,
and that the release of carbon from ocean storage
would be gradual over hundreds of years.[189]

Yet that does not settle the matter. The IPCC's
emphasis on the careful choice of sites is a reminder
of the possibility that this young technology too
requires *judgment and trade-offs, and would
experience its accidents. It may also be *relevant
that seabed storage would kill off marine life in the
area where it lies; we may wonder whether this is
any more acceptable than a policy which, in the
interests of saving the planet, destroyed all living
organisms in large areas of rainforest. Moreover,
there are uncertainties as to whether the spaces
vacated by the *new* sources of gas—shale gas and
underground coal gasification—will provide the
gas-tight underground structures suitable for storage. Methane hydrates in any case do not generally
vacate any underground space at all.

3. *The cost*. First, there is the energy-cost. The IPCC
estimates that a coal-fired power station whose
carbon dioxide emissions were sequestered would
need about twice as much coal to produce the same
amount of power. As for money costs, the IPCC's
estimates depend on the type of fuel being used.
For an efficient gas plant the cost increase could be

between 25% and 40%; for a coal plant it could be between 50% and 100%. The energy analyst Richard Heinberg settles for an increase of around 80%.[190]

CCS' biggest problem is that the *scale of the task counts against it. Two influential reports published in 2010 argued that it is not enough to demonstrate that it can work in principle; it needs to be shown that it can work on a large enough scale to capture most of the carbon produced by the combustion of coal and gas worldwide.[191] The evidence on this is decades away. Yet in the meantime, the option of carbon capture and storage is typically proposed as a solution to the dangers of the new generation of gas projects. As the science writer Fred Pearce points out:

> The trouble with CCS right now is that it is being sold as an imminent fix when it is very far from that.[192]

CCS is the technology that makes the case for unconventional gas as a realistic option. But CCS is itself a method of last resort, and arguably the largest-scale industrial project ever. It requires everything to be in working order: the prospecting of suitable repositories, the capture, the transport, the injection, the leak-proofing of the entire system and the *monitoring, the *law, the banks, international agreements and confidence that there is still some *point* in trying to save the *climate; that it is not already too late. All this will be required at a time when energy supplies are becoming ever tighter, and when the wealth and energy available for such large projects are already depleted. CCS is not a means of providing energy—that could be done at far lower short-term financial cost without it. It will, rather, be a dead weight on an already poor *political economy, keen to use every scrap of energy it can get, just to keep going. It may well be seen as a way of making a bad situation worse, at a time when people will be in no mood to make present sacrifices for an extremely uncertain future.

There is undoubtedly a case for CCS to be developed. And yet this is a moment for sympathetic *scepticism. An energy-poor, money-poor, climate-stressed global economy may not be able to *both* develop giant-scale, last resort fuel supplies *and* connect them up with an equally-large-scale system designed to prevent the damage which they cause. Here is the *debtor's downfall: he *knows* he can borrow now; he does so in the *hope* that he will be able to pay it back later; failing that, he can at least promise to do so, loud and often. CCS, the Climate-Credit Sting, allows us to carry on borrowing. For a time.

If CCS' chief significance is its role in removing doubts as to whether it is a good idea to open up a massive new flow of global warming gases, that is not an argument against developing it. Rather, it is an argument against developing shale gas, underground coal gasification and methane hydrates *on the assumption* that CCS will shortly be ready—with massive geological sites selected and surveyed, with legal titles arranged and the agreement of locals, with pipes linking them to the sources, with pumps and (in some cases) refrigeration all in place, with *technical challenges overcome and reliability assured—for final disposal of the carbon.

The large-scale renewables

And then there are the very large-scale projects and proposals based on renewable sources of energy. There is desert solar: the building—already started in several of the world's deserts—of arrays of solar concentrators, producing electricity to be transported by cable around the world. And there is the proposal for large-scale off-shore wind, which would supply much of Europe with energy generated from fixed and floating turbines in (for instance) the North Sea and North Atlantic.[193]

Whether such projects are developed in practice on the needed scale depends primarily on factors beyond the reach of the technologies themselves—notably money, *materials (especially copper) and time. If there were no prospect of an energy crunch in the near future, then the construction of such massive-scale proposals could be feasible. But they need to be based on an economy which is thriving and competent, able to sustain its *capital, its ability to plan, and a *transport system which reliably gets people into work. It also needs to have a power grid in full working order and large infrastructures for construction and maintenance.

The expectation that the energy crunch will come before such projects are able to make a serious and useful contribution is not really an argument against

E

making the attempt. But *large-scale visions—including *nuclear energy—cannot be seen as reasons to be diverted from a radically different energy strategy. We must *frankly recognise that the large energy sources on which our society depends face the same collective risk of failure as the other conditions for sustained global industrial *growth. Large-scale *connectedness is intrinsically and critically vulnerable.

No dismissal of desert solar is implied in the observation that the *climacteric—itself partly the product of the converging failure of the large energy establishments—will shortly be upon us, and will demand a profound rethink with regard to *resilient energy supply. The alternative to these large-scale technologies is to choose, instead—starting now—to make something quite different happen: deep planned reductions in the energy we use, along with brilliance about how to respond to the challenge of doing so. That is, to think lean.

The logic of community energy

"Into each life some rain must fall", as P.G. Wodehouse observed in connection with the troubles of Otis Pilkington. Well, this entry has pointed out some of the problems bearing down on the energy sources on which we rely at present, so it would seem that the next thing to do is to describe the rich *diversity of renewable energy sources available now, in a state of constant improvement, and suited to the small-scale, local, *Lean Economy.

However, this is the road not taken. Three reasons. First, it is a large subject and there is no space for it. Secondly, energy solutions are being developed and improved all the time, and the best sources are the latest books and internet sources. Thirdly, *lean thinking is a philosophy about working things out for ourselves.[194]

So, a last word: reclaim the streets; they are your streets. Don't believe the impossible—like the claim that large-scale, oil-dependent biofuels are an abundant net source of clean energy. Some logical possibilities (such as the use of algae as a third generation biofuel) can emerge usefully from things that seemed once to be technical dead ends, and they are especially useful if they can be done on an *informal and local scale. But how to use these options is your choice, based on your inventiveness and on applications of renewables which are only at the early stages of being thought of.[195]

The energy prospects for the global *market economy, then, are poor. We face an energy shock. The large-scale, last resort solutions will stall under the weight of *unintended consequences. *Local energy solutions will be as good as the resources and *intelligence of the people who are there. Some starting points are outlined in these entries:

*Entropy, Energy Descent Action Plan, Lean Energy, TEQs (Tradable Energy Quotas), Depletion Protocol.

ENTROPY. A measure of disorder and randomness in a system. Every living system consists of orderly and *complex structures, as in the intricate tissue of plants and animals. The Second Law of Thermodynamics tells us that, as events take place—as work is done—this order dissipates: the tissues decay. It can be repaired if there is a sufficient supply of the energy of the right kind and in the right concentration. In the case of our planet, that source of energy is almost entirely the sun—both the modern sun (sunlight) and the ancient sun (stored in oil, coal and gas)—supplemented on a minor scale from *nuclear energy, and by heat from deep inside the planet itself.[196]

A high level of entropy, or disorder—cold, dark, silent, meaningless—is the default condition (equilibrium) for physics, and it is everywhere, unless something both remarkable and energy-driven happens to prevent it, or to bring order into it. We do not need to be aware of the laws of thermodynamics to know that the consequences of the depletion of fossil fuels will take the form of disorder of many kinds, nor that a *political economy that relies on sustained *growth is impossible. But the laws of thermodynamics are a convenient summary of the problem, and the idea of entropy—the bleak baseline from which the making of order starts—is central: it stands at the opposite extreme from everything that matters to us.

If the *energy to sustain a large *political economy is not there, there is something to be said for planning for a *small one.[197]

*Social Entropy, Touch-Down, Wheel of Life.

EQUIVOCATION. The use of words in ways which are strictly true but which the other person is intended to interpret differently. Example: "Maybe there was something in the cake that didn't agree with him" (after gangsters leapt out of the cake and machine-gunned the hero in *Some Like It Hot*).

*Implicature.

EROTICISM. Our society fills much empty space with thoughts of sex, yet it is not comfortable with the erotic. Far from integrating it into its *culture, it buries it deep in the *private sphere—a personal matter, like remembering to take your medication. At the end of the road we are travelling on, desire will be not a hunger to be celebrated, but an issue to be sorted.

The erotic is an energy source. Its energy is desire—intense, beyond your own control and *intention, and unsafe, like a cliff path without a handrail. You lack detachment: you are there, right at the edge. This is not your territory: you are on the lip of someone else's. *Lean Logic* argues that this energy feeds into—gives intensity to—all our other emotions. The erotic is the dazzling power supply, the soular energy, on which we depend for the whole of our emotional lives.

At its heart is the possibility of a *gift. Things that you take are more-or-less under your control and, to that extent, lack excitement. Things that you are given have an independent life of their own: you can never be quite sure that they will come your way, nor that, if they do, they will be the real thing, nor that what you give back is as real as what you receive. But you live in hope on all these, aware that this garden will yield its *reciprocal gifts only if it is cultivated and watered and walked in:

> *Mane surgamus ad vineas, videamus si floruit vinea, si flores fructus parturiunt, si floruerunt mala punica: ibi dabo tibi ubera mea.*
>
> Let us rise up early and go to the vineyards; let us see if the vine flourish, whether the tender grape appear, and the pomegranate are ripening: there will I give thee my breasts.[198]

Eric Gill gives us an engraving of this, called "*Ibi Dabo Tibi*".

This sense of giving and surrender irrigates every other aspect of our culture. The extent to which we enter into a Corot landscape or a Vermeer household is the extent to which we surrender ourselves to them. The English poet

George Herbert was intent on surrender, seeming not to mind too much whether it was to a woman or to God. He needed the erotic. He knew . . .

> . . . the ways of pleasure; the sweet strains,
> The lullings and the relishes of it;
> The propositions of hot blood and brains;
> What mirth and music mean . . .
>
> George Herbert, The Pearl, 1633.[199]

. . . and here is Richard Crashaw being rather carried away, it seems:

> Lord, when the sense of thy sweet grace
> Sends up my soul to seek thy face.
> Thy blessed eyes breed such desire,
> I dy in love's delicious Fire.
>
> Richard Crashaw, A Song, 1652.[200]

We have this idea, too, in the mystic tradition of Islam—Sufism—intoxicated with love, living with ecstasy, for which . . .

> . . . the soul needs the wings of human love to
> fly toward divine love; [it is] the ladder leading
> to the love of the Merciful.[201]

And this is also the unlikely location of medieval monasticism, empowering with erotic energy a multinational *institution designed for spiritual observance, care of those in need, *education, publishing, archiving and *population control. Although the monks and nuns of that long-lived *tradition did in some ways "leave the world upon a shelf" as Chaucer observed in *The Canterbury Tales*, the principle was: do not repress energetic drives such as sex; use them as the energy source for talent, love and hard thinking, but set them in a different context.[202] There was, it is true, an evident risk of

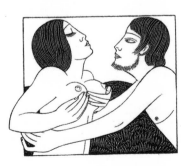

failure and compromise in redirecting these drives from the erotic love of people to loving God, but the monastic discipline was skilful and experienced: it knew how to handle large resources

E

of emotional energy—and how to contain it within the context of music and poetry, the graphic arts and prayer, architecture, *charity, philosophy, *community building, and that daily workout for the emotions provided by the Psalms (see "Feeling Better?" sidebar).[203]

The result could not be described as repressed: the aim, wrote the twelfth century scholar Hugh of St. Victor, was "to see what the untutored eye does not see, and to form desire", by subjecting oneself to *authority and learning how to recognise *virtue—in short, learning to master a *skill, to love your subject and get *emotional about it.[204] "Tears of desire for heaven" were positively encouraged; emotional energy was recognised as a reserve, waiting to be tapped.[205]

It was an emotional training which lasted into the seventeenth century, and one way of keeping in trim was to do the programme of Spiritual Exercises which had been devised by St. Ignatius Loyola: four weeks of contemplation of the Life, Passion and Resurrection of Christ could wake the soul from its torpor and make "the south wind blow over the garden of the soul", bringing the tears of intense affection.[206]

The Judaic-Christian is—perhaps this is its most astonishing quality—a culture of emotional depth. This is not mysticism; it is not ascetic; it is no exercise in willpower and self-control. On the contrary, it celebrates the passions. The Passion is a story of wringing emotion: pain, grief, love, derision, resolution. It consists almost

---

FEELING BETTER?
Emotions are laid bare by ritual in the Psalms

The emotional *capital of Western culture is, in part at least, a gift from its *religion—and the spectrum of emotion is clearly visible in the Psalms, composed for *ritual which contains and socialises the difficult emotions—violence, vengeance, *betrayal, yearning, lament. In the thin rituals of the *market, this full-blooded recognition of the "bad" emotions—along with the "good" ones—is censored and discarded. But if only the good emotions are permitted, the bad ones develop unsupervised: the possibility of recognising them and of learning how to handle them closes down. Better to celebrate them.

Delight: Then was our mouth filled with laughter: and our tongue with joy. 126:2

Vengeance: O daughter of Babylon, wasted with misery: yea happy shall he be that rewardeth thee, as thou hast served us. Blessed shall he be that taketh *thy* children and throweth *them* against the stones. 137:7–9

Sickness: I am poured out like water, and all my bones are out of joint: my heart also in the midst of my body is even like melting wax. My strength is dried up like a potsherd, and my tongue cleaveth to my gums: and thou shalt bring me into the dust of death. 22:14–15

Desire: Like as the hart desireth the water-brooks: so longeth my soul after thee O God. 42:1

Anger: Let their eyes be blinded that they see not: and ever bow thou down their backs. Let them be wiped out of the book of the living. . . . That thy foot may be dipped in the blood of thine enemies: and that the tongue of thy dogs may be red through the same. 69:24,29; 68:23

Displeasure: Let hot burning coals fall upon them: let them be cast into the fire and into the pit, that they never rise up again. 140:11

Love: Whither shall I go then from thy Spirit: or whither shall I go then from thy presence? If I climb up into heaven, thou art there: if I go down to hell thou art there also. If I take the wings of the morning: and remain in the uttermost parts of the sea; Even there also shall thy hand lead me: and thy right hand shall hold me. 139:6–9

Pleasure: That he may bring food out of the earth, and wine that maketh glad the heart of man: and oil to make him a cheerful countenance, and bread to strengthen man's heart. 104:15

Saving the day: He chose David also his servant: and took him away from the sheep-folds. 78:69

entirely of emotional events and expression, as Bach demonstrated when he set it to music. The *narrative (or poetic) truth is about a raising from the dead, but there is some direct *material truth in there too, for love—being the source of emotional life—can claim, rather more literally, to do the same thing. Richard Crashaw summarises this in a three-line request, confident of his answer:

> O let that love which thus makes Thee
> Mix with our low mortality,
> Lift our lean souls . . . .
>
> *Richard Crashaw, Lauda Sion Salvatorem, 1652.*[207]

A culture which contains such emotional energy makes it available for the relationships between the people who live there, for the *common purpose of making and sustaining community, and it celebrates this private good in the *public sphere. All animal behaviour is driven by the emotions, so it is a good idea to keep them fit and well, observant and in training for their life on the *edge between us and everything else. The erotic is but one emotion among many, but maybe it is the deepest and most ancient one, and, for *Lean Logic*, it is the critical energy source for all others. Emotions know the ways of pleasure, the lullings and the relishes of it, the proposition of hot blood and brains, what mirth and music mean. Erotic energy is their blood supply.[208]
*Encounter, Play, Invisible Goods, Spirit.

ETHICS (see also Ecology: The Scholars). There is a sense in which the core ethic is the one which guides (or would guide, if it were observed) our relationship with the natural environment. There is strict *feedback here: if it is not obeyed, it will in due course destroy.

The problem is the *time-lag: the payback may be deep in the future, or even unknown to those who are engaged in the choice. *Choices made now by you will have consequences after your *death, beyond your foresight, in places that you have never visited, for species of which you have no knowledge. And the links between cause and effect may be non-linear, with large and horrible effects coming from modest actions reflecting good intentions and concern for home and family (*Butterfly Effect).

Environmental ethics affect and intensify our understanding of ethics in all its senses. It takes us straight to the distinction between ethics and opportunism. It makes us face up to situations where there is no option available which seems to be fair. It requires careful tracing of long threads of complexity and *unintended consequences, where the primary task is not to weigh ethical choices, but to admit the *relevance and urgency of challenges which are almost invisible to the criteria and judgments of today's common sense. These long-chain interactions are the protein of ethics, giving strength, structure and character to our choices as ecocitizens. They make us recognise that the close-range evaluations of distributive justice—in situations where causes are visible and effects are predictable—belong with the comfortable assumptions which civilisations grasp to convince themselves that their state is permanent, and that their ethical common sense is definitive and final.[209]

Lean Logic therefore acknowledges the profound significance of environmental ethics, yet it does not treat it as a separate field. It is intrinsic to the principles of (for instance) *resilience, *scale, *community, *manners, *empowerment, *lean thinking and *character, which are among the defining characteristics of the Lean Economy (Greek: *ethos* character). Those principles will often take the form of first discovering what *can* be done, and then holding on to that insight as the foundation for what *ought* to be done. Like *permaculture, lean ethics will adapt to the lie of the land, guided by feel, opportunity and observation as much as by conscious decision.

And yet deliberate and conscious choices will also be part of it, and there may be some guidelines around which those choices can be sharpened and ordered. Here are two:

1. *What we get or what we do?*

   The distinction between what we get and what we do is made by the philosophers Alasdair MacIntyre and Roger Lundin in the context of the intense debate surrounding the nature and purpose of liberal *education. The debate starts with a criticism of the teaching of *tradition in the form of the canon of *art and literature on which cultures such as our own are founded. Critics argue against it on the grounds that it does not concern itself with the personal preferences and desires of people of our time: all that stuff from a previous age does nothing to help us to be happy now; the only guideline as to what we *ought* to think and do is what we *want* to think and do. As the influential book summarising the liberal position, *The Politics of Liberal Education* (1991), has it, what matters is that we should find ways of fulfilling our personal preferences. Ethics in this context, then, is about equality of getting.[210]

But there is another view of the matter. This sharply different concept of ethics argues that citizens have been disempowered, and that this ought not to have happened. It is around our *own* actions and motives guiding our conduct in our lives that the central ethical questions should turn. What it is fair for us to *get* is important, but it becomes relevant only as a sequel to what it is right for us to *do*. Distributive justice picks up the pieces after *empowerment has failed.

Building safety features into a design is always a good thing, but it presents its own risks: if the emphasis is on failure, failure is more likely to happen. A radical shift of emphasis from "what we get if we fail to do" to "what we do" is not only a defence of *freedom in its own right, but the only way forward in a future in which the established structures of security and equity have comprehensively broken down. We are looking here at a new frame of reference; a different equity landscape shaped less by shared benefits than by shared *virtues. Lundin fixes it in an imaginary conversation:

> "Have you noticed," asks the normally cynical Mr. Compson in William Faulkner's *Absalom, Absalom!* "when we try to reconstruct the causes which lead up to the actions of men and women, how with a sort of astonishment we find ourselves now and then reduced to the belief, the only possible belief, that they stemmed from some of the old virtues?"
>
> To which one can only imagine most of the contributors to *The Politics of Liberal Education* responding, "No, that hadn't occurred to me, nor does your mentioning it *cause* it to occur to me."
>
> Roger Lundin, The Culture of Interpretation, 1993.[211]

2. *For all times and places or just for our own?*
A key property of the Lean Economy is *resilience, and a key property of resilience is *diversity, with

all that it implies in terms of different solutions to the problems and opportunities faced by people and communities in different places.

The case for a universal ethic, appealing to universal values, has long been debated against the case for specific, circumstantial ethics designed for the particulars of *time, *place and *culture. *Lean Logic* argues for both these points of view. Principles such as *manners, the geometry of *scale, the enabling conditions of resilience, and the congruence embedded in *trust, have, in *Lean Logic*'s vocabulary, universal application. On the other hand, *practices, *traditions, *culture and concepts of justice and right and wrong vary enormously between different places and times, and it is hard to show that any particular place and time has the *authority to define an ethical code which is right for all. Local lean communities will need to develop their own normalities and ethics in response to their circumstances. *Empowerment is defined at least in part as being able to make a particular shared practice or *value last locally, even though other people in other places may disapprove.

This is sometimes called "moral relativism", but the neat label does no justice to a subject with such potential for self-delusion and insoluble ethics-defying clashes of culture and values.

As the brief story of moral relativism opposite suggests, settled outcomes, while they may be possible, can bring no promise of comfort.
*Ecology: The Scholars, Diversity, Spirit.

EXCEPTION, THE FALLACY OF (*Secumdum quid*). The argument that a principle is contradicted (not merely qualified) by exceptions. The possibility of understanding an issue can be blocked by an instance in which it does not apply. Example: "Too many exams make children depressed and demoralised." "Not at all—our Prudence *loves* her exams!"
*Generalisation Fallacies, Composition, Personal Experience.

EXHILARATION. The state of mind and body that occurs after accomplishing something difficult against

THE NECKLACE

This was the New World. Anne was one of the first white women to set foot in it. She brought with her a husband, and her father's blessing; in her belly the beginnings of a daughter, and round her neck, a necklace, which her mother had given her the night before they left. She had added her blessing too. That was only to be expected, for the family went about doing good, and the necklace was Puritan and plain. The coast of America had welcomed them from two hundred miles off, with air that was loaded with the scent of rich fruit and herbs. At the coast they received another welcome: gifts and food from people who were armed and dangerous and very kind. The whites came ill-equipped. The Indians gave them seed and animals and tools, and taught them how to live.

It was those acts of necessary friendship in those first years that, in her old age, Anne remembered and talked about. Her daughter, now the possessor of the necklace, and the authority in the household, put up with it, as was proper. But she did not shrink from speaking up for common sense either. She pointed out that Anne was unfeeling, insensitive and out of date. The Indians behaved as if the land was God's gift to them. They did nothing with it. They allowed the forests to run to waste. And when a new settlement from Plymouth tried to clear-fell the trees and fence off the grassland, they killed.

Her own chain of office hung heavy on her. Her duty was plain: to make the state safe for her daughter. Or else the necklace would have no inheritor.

But Anne of the third generation was born to it. For her, it was a matter of elementary good husbandry, pest-control. Indians were permitted beyond the enclosures, that is beyond the state, then beyond New England, then beyond Massachusetts, then beyond Virginia.

Well it was their own choice. If they did not want to be trapped, hunted, shot, concentrated in camps, eliminated, then they should not trespass onto the whites' lands.

Anne's great great great great great grand-daughter, necklace swinging gently in the dying sunlight, sang her little girl to sleep. The lace curtains rested still on the windowsill, and the child's face was scrubbed shining and clean and she asked for just one more story about the secret garden in the Old World, and the death of the wicked Indian in the New. And her mother sang a little night-time Puritan hymn in thanks for their safe world.

And then there were none. Except, of course, in the West. And where the West began was a matter for other people to consider. But as for Anne of the twelfth generation, she had her own family to attend to. It was her aim to be an example to the community, to breathe into her children the love of God, and the laughter and love of friends. She had standards to maintain. She descended, as everyone knew, from one of the oldest Puritan families in the Union. And she had a necklace to prove it. Beautiful, plain, priceless. No gewgaws, no make-believe. As true as the three-pronged pitchforks the men used on the estate at hay-making time.

So when the West came suddenly close to home, she knew what to do. It happened in 1848. The authorities in Washington invented the principle of Manifest Destiny. It claimed that the whole of the territory of North America, from coast to coast, was manifestly destined to be dominated, governed, and made their own, by the whites. The Indians, without legal existence, were to be removed from fertile lands and destroyed; some provision would be made to concentrate some few of them on reservations in areas which were too infertile to be used in any other way.

Anne was shocked. She petitioned. She turned public opinion in the states of New England, whose Indians had long gone, firmly against the principle. New England could claim to be on the side of justice, and against greed, on the side of workmanship, and against barbarism, for morality, against outrage. But New England was alone.

When they struck oil in southern California, Anne of the seventeenth generation and her husband felt it would only make good sense to buy a little estate over there, and when their grand-daughter got married, they gave her and Wayne a wonderful present: a little jet that would take them right across the States and down to their ranch in Malibu on Friday evenings. Here Anne, who is a fine harpsichordist, gives impromptu evening concerts to their friends among the Los Angeles intelligentsia.

Sometimes she plays the Baroque repertoire, Scarlatti and Corelli, and sometimes she accompanies singers in English Jacobean love songs by Thomas Weelkes and Thomas Arne. On summer evenings, they leave the French windows open wide, and the last of the sun, shining off the Pacific Ocean, catches her necklace as she moves with the music.

DAVID FLEMING

E

the odds, especially if it has involved *cooperation. It is the product in part of the release of the hormone serotonin, in the sequence: accomplishment → serotonin → exhilaration. The psychologist Oliver James discusses evidence of a fall in serotonin levels during the twentieth century, but they could rise again, with exhilarating consequences, in step with the *successful accomplishment of the *Wheel of Life.[212]

EXIT. The tactic of walking out of an argument which is not going your way, or of switching your business from a trader who does not supply what you want. This is the presumed and normal sanction in the *market economy. The alternative is "voice": to stay with the argument (or with the same trader), to communicate, and open the way to an improvement. Community building will need voice.[213]
*Loyalty.

EXPECTATIONS. The attitudes and assumptions which shape the way we make sense of events and plan our response. Unless our expectations are right, or at least expressed as a considered set of probabilities, we plan to fail. But, right or wrong, expectations are self-reinforcing, for we see what we expect to see. We may not realise how critical expectations are in guiding perception, but they are decisive. In the context of our perception of *art, the art historian E.H. Gombrich reminds us of . . .

> . . . the role which our own expectations play in the deciphering of the artists' cryptograms. We come to their works with our receivers already attuned. We expect to be presented with a certain notation, a certain sign situation, and make ready to cope with it.[214]

The experience of approaching the *climacteric will affect our expectations in three ways. First, options which were formerly dismissed will now be grasped with both hands, and we may wonder how we could have been so stupid as to turn them down when they were still available. Secondly, opinions and fundamental values, hitherto seen to be sacrosanct and *self-evident, will be challenged and may break down rapidly. Thirdly, there is likely to be expectations-creep,

as the (bad) new conditions are seen to be as acceptable as the (good) old ones used to be, without people being explicitly conscious of having changed their opinion. Events will change the frame of reference in which we make *judgments.

And there may be a *time-lag, leaving us always one step behind, fighting the last war, although *lean thinking, for which fast *feedback is a core principle, would help us keep this lag brief. Critical to this is a sense of history. History forms our expectations; it is our data. Without a sense of history, our expectations are the product of how we live now.
*Different Premises, Frankness, Social Mobility, Success, Damper.

EXPERTISE, THE FALLACY OF (*Argumentum ad verecundiam*). Argument based on an uncritical appeal to expert opinion, pointing to the shame that (in the expert's opinion) the other person ought to feel at challenging their expertise.[215]

Those who consider themselves experts defend their status in many ways, and here are six:

1. The *Train Crash Fallacy*: a claim to instant expertise derived from a single *personal experience.[216]
2. The *Genetic Fallacy*: judging an argument by its source rather than by its content.
3. The *Spillover Fallacy*: belief that expertise in one field of science confers the right to pronounce on other areas, whether the scientist has studied them or not.
4. *Perpetual Notion*: faith that expert scientific opinion which is held to be true at the present *time will always be so.
5. The *No Evidence Fallacy*: allowing the statement that "there is no evidence [that a proposition is true]" to be interpreted as "there is evidence [that the proposition is untrue]." But the lack of evidence may be due to a reluctance to look for it, or to believe it when it comes.
6. The *Anecdote Fallacy*: the related idea that occasional, or surprising, events and local particulars cannot be taken to be significant unless they are replicated in large-scale trials. But many of the most important clues on questions of the deepest significance come as individual straws in the

wind, gold-dust information which it is reckless to ignore: the sickness caused by pesticides, the effectiveness of particular alternative treatments to particular symptoms in a particular person, the case for *diverse *education free to encourage diverse talents in diverse ways: these are matters which do not call for expertise but for the *humility to encounter detail on its own terms. The expert's research model may dismiss what matters as *anomaly and noise (*Ignorance).

Among matters of detail which are dismissed as anecdote is the question of resource depletion, which may consist of *local gossip about depleting oil wells, or of fishermen's reports of the changing behaviour of North Atlantic cod—a calamitously dismissed warning sign of the coming collapse in the fishery. Science prefers calculation, but sometimes what we need is moments of life-saving insight. The expertise of the future will be about acute observation and inference, used to create, for example, strategies for *agriculture that work with the detail of the local *ecosystem.[217]

We have a long view of the power of observation and local invention, as distinct from the *generalities of established authority, in the crises of oversupply that have shaped the last 700 years of farming. In each case, the effective responses have been the most innovative ones—the ones most certain to outrage the experts. The crashes happened in 1351 (after the Black Death), in the 1650s (following improvements in agricultural production), in 1879 (with the start of large-scale imports of cereals from the United States), and in our own day (productivity, imports and subsidies). On each occasion, recovery has been invented and developed from below, coming from experiment and ingenuity, incrementally building a *diverse

agriculture—at first dairy, pigs, rape, flax, saffron and new vegetables and herbs, followed by selective breeding, pumpkins, beans and mustard, then hops and sugar beet and, most recently, the *organic movement. It has been the work of individuals, as the historian Joan Thirsk writes, "groping their way, after many trials and errors, [despite being] dismissed as harmless lunatics". As for official policy,

> The state may help indirectly, but it is unlikely to initiate, or select for support, the best strategies; and, out of ignorance or lack of imagination, it may positively hinder.[218]

Experts can drive the car, but they don't know the way. The future is safer in the *dirty hands of *harmless lunatics.[219]

Experts and citizens

Not all experts claim to be the only people qualified to participate in a conversation about the application of science, but the claim is nonetheless common. Once it has been made, experts can then generally be relied on to endorse established *institutions, to defend the *paradigm of the day and to advocate *large-scale technologies and standard procedures. When governments seek expert advice, these are the experts whose advice they will get. Expertise—fitness to be consulted on matters of public importance—becomes visible when it has floated to the top, where it will defend with vigour the work of institutions in endorsing and elaborating on current assumptions.

The debate on *genetic modification (GM) is an illustration. Attacks on those who argue for a completely different kind of understanding of the problems and responses surrounding food production may appear to be gentle—the gentleness of the parent comforting the child who is afraid of ghosts: for the scientist and philosopher, Baroness Warnock, critics of GM are "confused and vaguely frightened".[220] Or such attacks may be fierce: for Lord May, in his 2002 anniversary address as President of the Royal Society, opposition to GM is to be compared with the dogmas of Fundamentalism. Such breakdown in the

E

quality of thought, he warns us, was responsible for the teaching of Creationism, and the Taliban prohibition of education for women. There is an assumption here that the application of scientific advance leads obviously and without question to corresponding improvements in human lives and probably to benefits for the environment as well. In the light of that assumption, Lord May contrasts anti-science—i.e., cautious insistence on evaluating the value of *technical advance in its social, *economic and environmental aspects before applying it—with the open-hearted values of the Enlightenment, "rational, humane, questioning", which (he says) have been at the heart of the Royal Society since its foundation. Here we have a clear *binary choice: the alert *intelligence of the enlightened expert, or . . .

> . . . a kind of Fundamentalism that wistfully
> looks to a throw-back world in which nineteenth
> century agricultural practices can feed today's
> burgeoning population and unproven alterna-
> tive medicines can afford the same protection as
> the products of the pharmaceutical industry.[221]

But the argument about whether, and how, a scientific advance should be applied in practice needs an analysis as careful as—though belonging to a different discipline from—the science itself.

Citizens' ability and willingness to participate in, or to be responsible for, decisions affecting them has been devalued by technical expertise. The privilege and responsibility of citizens has been dismissed. One scholar who has studied this problem at depth is Frank Fischer, Professor of Political Science at Rutgers University. Although it is widely supposed that the citizen is out of his depth in making sensible contributions to decision-making in which science and technology are involved, he writes,

> . . . hard evidence demonstrates that the
> ordinary citizen is capable of a great deal more
> participation than generally recognised or
> acknowledged.[222]

But surely citizens are incompetent in these matters? Some of the answers received by a survey of scientists' attitudes to the debate on GM foods might tempt scientists to believe that they are:

> I had a lady from a magazine ring me up about
> genetic manipulation and said their readers
> were worried, and they were worried about
> this fact that they were eating DNA. And I said,
> "Well, look, you know, OK, but we're eating
> DNA all the time, you know." "Are we? Really?
> We're eating DNA?"[223]

Anecdotal evidence, as noted above, generally has a hard time in science, but in this conversation, one illustration of *ignorance adds its weight to a general assumption on the level of public ignorance about GM technology. Wearily, the presumption is confirmed that what is needed is not consultation, but instruction. As Professor Janet Bainbridge, Chair of the UK Government Advisory Committee on Novel Foods and Processes explains, "Sometimes, you have to tell people what's best for them."[224]

Some citizens are ill-informed about matters of science. It does not follow, however, that scientists have the information and mature *judgment needed for its application. As Fischer points out,

> While the scientific community complains of
> intervention in the pursuit of knowledge, the
> public increasingly comes to see that scientists
> are themselves laypersons in matters concern-
> ing political goals and social judgment.[225]

So it may not be the public's expertise in science that is lacking; it may be scientists' expertise in citizenship. Science-based expertise is often no more than today's *populism; urban myth dressed up as expert opinion. Likewise, the conflation of technical advance and social progress is naïve:

> . . . failing, for example, [writes Fischer] to sort
> out the differences between the kinds of welfare
> benefits resulting from computer-assisted
> medical diagnosis and the warfare potentials of
> computer-guided missile systems.[226]

In the *Lean Economy, expertise will be restored to where it belongs—the *community. Technical specialisms will undoubtedly exist in the minds of the scholarly, but the heart of the matter will be local intelligence. Those rich with expertise in the first of those

NOTHING TO SAY
Expertise and the paradox of exactness

Suppose you look out of your window and you see a field, bounded by a stone wall. That is a satisfactory image. You could elaborate it if you like; you might see some taller grasses, some nettles round the edge, some windswept hawthorn trees, a gate at the far end, a few wavy paths made by generations of sheep, a rusty horse-drawn hay-rake and a drinking-trough. That is a satisfactory image, too. But now suppose you wanted to be more scientific about it. You could see it as a field of photosynthesising plant cells, bounded by slabs of calcium carbonate. Well, you're a scientist, so you like to be more exact about things. But the problem here is that in reality the calcium carbonate is highly impure, containing iron and traces of quartz, and covered with lichen. The description of the surface as a simple spread of photosynthetic plant material is also far from accurate. In fact, the attempt to see the matter from the scientific point of view—to be more precise—has introduced such gross inaccuracies that it is scarcely justifiable in those terms to say anything about the field at all. The romantic, seeing the field from the window, though he may never have heard of calcium carbonate, would get closer to the truth. But then, no one, apart from his closest friends and his dog, really cares about what he thinks.[227]

senses will have a modest role, providing an occasional service when called upon, like the economists imagined in John Maynard Keynes' essay, "Economic Possibilities for Our Grandchildren":

> If economists could manage to get themselves thought of as humble, competent people, on a level with dentists, that would be splendid![228]

The application of expertise in the sense of local *intelligence is a defining quality at the heart of *Lean Logic*'s concept of *presence. Presence is the whole accomplishment of living in a local ecology, responding to it on its own terms, being part of it. The path to presence therefore deserves to be mapped, and Frank Fischer helps us to do so, making the case for three properties—deliberation, legitimacy and ordinary knowledge—each of which, in a sense, is both a condition and an outcome:

1. *Deliberation*

   Deliberation is the chance to talk about options before they have been settled, with the confidence that the *conversation matters—that its conclusions can have an effect on what happens. It confers ownership of the task on the people involved, and it takes responsibility for local initiatives, for their design, adaptation and endurance. During the era of cheap *energy and confident *growth, the participation of individuals in deliberation about how to serve the community, and in how to build the *institutions they wanted, was not seen to be particularly necessary: experts were there to decide and to apply *technical solutions; consumers were there to consume. But as we approach the energy transition, deliberation will be needed again.[229]

   In case there are any remaining doubts as to whether citizens have the knowledge needed to play a useful part in the complex decisions of our time, the sociologist Benjamin Barber offers a useful reminder that, when people feel there is something useful they can do with the knowledge, they will acquire it:

   > Give people some significant power and they will quickly appreciate the need for knowledge, but foist knowledge upon them without giving them responsibility and they will display only indifference.[230]

2. *Legitimacy*

   Legitimacy exists when there is a sense of ownership of an initiative by the people who are affected by it. There is an understanding of the task; there is intention to achieve consensus about it; there is a sense that they have the right to take action with respect to the community they belong to and the place that they know, and this right is confirmed by the fact of getting together to deliberate on it.[231]

The recovery of legitimacy in policy formation, especially at the *local level, is a matter of concern in both theory and practice. Robert Reich (Secretary of Labour in the Clinton Administration), has called it a process of "civic discovery". The practice is being vigorously advanced in some communities, and one example of this is the US city of Portland, Oregon. In 1974, the city created The Office of Neighbourhood Associations, which legitimised activism, built it into the official life of the city, and gave neighbourhood associations an official role in deliberation on (as the enabling legislation put it) "any matter affecting the livability of the neighbourhood". Central to this is the principle of *call and response: neighbourhood associations can make decisions and take initiatives of their own— that is, the government does not force itself onto them, but the community can call on government resources when needed and, when it does so, the government has an obligation to listen. It's the law. Outcomes have legitimacy.[232]

And it is in the early stages of being explored, though still tentatively, by *Transition and the Big Society.[233]

3. *Ordinary knowledge*

Thirdly, there has been a loss—which needs now to be repaired—of *ordinary knowledge*. Ordinary knowledge is . . .

> . . . knowledge that does not owe its origin, testing, degree of verification, truth, status, or currency to distinctive . . . professional techniques, but rather to common sense, casual empiricism, or thoughtful speculation and analysis.[234]

In the context of *agriculture (for example), ordinary knowledge is knowledge of the particular characteristics of fields and soils, *water and microclimates, varieties and breeds; it varies radically from place to place, and it is taught by word of mouth. In the context of *energy, it is detailed familiarity with the place, its assets and resources, and the whole range of behavioural changes available to it. Ordinary knowledge is the starting point for local invention directed to phasing-down dependence on fossil energy across the whole spectrum

of local detail—*food, *transport, *building, *water treatment, the management of *waste . . . .

From the expert, *rationalist point of view, ordinary knowledge is a disorderly set of *anomalies. In fact, it is knowledge of the locality as a living, unique resource, its physical assets, its skills and networks. It is the knowledge of the *harmless lunatic; the intense local observation and commitment in terms of which the *community thinks, deliberates, applies its mind.

———

There is nothing wrong with expertise as an accomplishment. The problem is that it has wandered into a lonely landscape of *abstractions, and has been reduced to falling in love with itself. *Lean Logic* brings it home, where there are real people and *places to engage with. *Deceptions, Practice, Galley Skills, Education, Household, Lean Food.

F

F-WORD FALLACY. The *fallacy that, by using the F-word, you make it plain that you are cutting through all elaboration and pretentious rubbish and getting to the heart of the matter with laser-like discipline (which the other side may lack). The F-word may reveal that you are so high on *certainty that you have forgotten to make any argument at all. And yet, in the presence of *bad faith, shock and absence, the F-word and its relatives may be well justified: it is a wake up call. The F-word is the *emotions' version of the discreet cough. *Indignation, Insult.

FALLACIES. Errors with staying power. To be a fallacy, someone must fall for it, as Lewis Carroll points out,

> Any argument which *deceives* us, by seeming to prove what it does not really prove, may be called a 'Fallacy' (derived from the Latin verb *fallo* "I deceive").[1]

Both *formal and *informal logic recognise the existence of fallacies. From the point of view of formal logic, a fallacy is an error which violates the laws of reasoning; it can be demonstrated as an error in many ways—with the use of (for instance) symbols, diagrams, words, maths, computer syntax. These, in the terms of formal logic, are "genuine fallacies".

Informal logic, on the other hand, recognises many other kinds of fallacies; a number do indeed violate the laws of reasoning (like *Begging the Question), but others are more about the equivocal use of language (*Devil's Voice), or *humour (*Play), or submission to a threat (*Big Stick), or *distraction (*Contrarian Fallacy), or a misconception about the way systems work (*Death), or long-held errors about matters of fact (*Ignorance). For a whistle-stop tour of such informal fallacies, see "How To Cheat in an Argument" (page xxiii).[2]

Informal fallacies can be used for good purposes or bad, but the risk of their causing trouble—especially for those unfamiliar with them—is significant. Studying them helps develop the art of coherent argument, as well as improving awareness of its importance, and assists the diagnosis when a *dialogue goes wrong. It may also suggest a cure.[3]

*Manners, Deceptions.

FALSE ANALOGY. The tactic of switching from the original question into an example or *metaphor which causes confusion.

The Duke of Clarence, the good guy who was drowned in a butt of Malmsey wine in *Richard III*, had a premonition in a dream about skulls on the seabed with jewels in their eyes. It was not a bad analogy, as it turned out. And, although it didn't help him much, it told him something about what was coming; wetness, *death and greed were neatly wrapped up. The trouble starts when the power of analogy is misused to take people's mind off the argument and leave them gazing into the eyes of an image that has nothing whatsoever to do with it. The former leader of the Liberal Democrat Party in Britain, Charles Kennedy, once asserted that if Britain continues to use the Pound Sterling (£) instead of the Euro (€), this would be like Manhattan deciding to withdraw from the dollar and set up its own currency. The *deception—the image of Wall Street switching its business from financial services into, perhaps, the cultivation of cucumbers, with the deranged support of the locals—was (one hopes) intended; it is true that Manhattan would be poorly-advised to take such a step, and if Britain's continued use of sterling were like it, then that, too, would be a mistake.[4]

Mr. Kennedy's tactic is successful, in that his opponent has no option but to point out that the analogy is not relevant to the question of Britain's membership of the Eurozone. All of a sudden, the argument has to make way for an elementary tourist guide explaining that the service supplied by the US banks and stock exchanges to their clients is not the same as the trading relationship between the UK economy and the rest of Europe; that a *national currency allows an economy to be responsibly supported by the economic policy and *interest rates that are relevant to it at the time; that the Eurozone's economic cycles are moderated by the presence of the United Kingdom as a trading partner on a different economic cycle; that flexible currencies have a stabilising effect, giving weaker economies the advantage of a soft currency operating at a low exchange rate, which makes it easier for them to sell their goods and services, acting as a *protective tariff, and enabling them to compete with stronger economies on more equal terms; and that the United States is not strictly a single currency area anyway: it is the world leader in the use of *local currencies, which have benign effects on jobs and *local economies, and which will be even more significant in the turbulent *economic conditions that can be expected to develop in the coming years.[5]

But, in the end, the absurd image of the false analogy persists, not least because the analogy is an easier subject to think about than the matter itself. If difficult questions are reduced to *conversation about (say) level playing fields, everyone can join in. Even a well-intended analogy can keep the argument indefinitely engaged in the question of whether the analogy applies or not—and that can often be harder to settle than the argument itself. Analogies are everywhere

in the English language, heard but not seen, like rats in a dark cellar, and a debate may be conducted almost entirely in terms of little analogies. They are fragments of the language of poets: comforting, a reminder of being at home. But they are also (as *The Tempest's* Ariel said of the victims of shipwreck) infected with the fever of the mad, and play tricks of desperation.[6]
*Straw Man, Distraction.

FALSE CONSISTENCY. The *fallacy that you can avoid having to choose between two alternatives by arguing for both.

This temptation can arise when you are faced with two or more options which, though desirable in themselves, are inconsistent, or cannot be adopted at the same time as key defining objectives. For example, in the field of *education, "access" and "excellence" are both things which any well-intentioned government might want, as are "tradition" and "change", not to mention "sustainability" and "development". The Utilitarian principle of "the greatest happiness for the greatest number" also has this flaw, which its chief advocate, Jeremy Bentham, recognised, later changing the formula to "the greatest happiness". *Sustainable development is sometimes taken, with unashamed faith in impossibility, to mean the maximum *growth with the minimum environmental impact.[7]

It seems a pity not to be able to go for two good things with equal determination—surely they are twice as good as one—but that's the way it often is, and communities will need to be able to make these difficult choices, particularly if trying to go for both means that they are likely to end up with neither.

A name for this problem is the "double maximand": the aim is to maximise two aims, despite there being an inevitable trade-off between them. A popular way of presenting this is to call it a "balance". Balance can, of course, be a good thing, but it can also be a plausible excuse for missing the point. For, example if someone told you to "run as far as possible as fast as possible", you would be left wondering whether to jog for 26 miles or sprint for 100 metres, or to compromise between the two. Actually, those instructions leave you with *freedom to do whatever you want, and if asked how you come to be lying in the grass listening to the skylarks, you could explain that you were striving to achieve a balance.[8]

Where there are two trade-off-related variables in an orderly system, one of them is the "control variable"; the other is the "residual". You cannot control them both. If there are several variables, you may be able to control some of them, but not all. The rule is that if there are n variables, the most you can control is $n-1$. That is, in any system, there is always at most one "degree of freedom" fewer than the number of variables. "Degrees of freedom" are a complex idea and the only secure definition is that they are "the rank of a quadratic form", but let's not disentangle that here.

Think, instead, of a system which has two variables. Example: a *nation with the *intention of reducing its carbon emissions. It can either cap the *quantity* of emissions in line with *climate science (e.g., through *TEQs) and let the *price* of carbon-intensive goods and services adjust accordingly, or it can set a *price* (e.g., through carbon taxation) and let the *quantity* of emissions adjust accordingly. Control of the quantity is enabled by flexibility in prices; control of the price is enabled by flexibility in emissions. It cannot control both.

False consistency lets the moment go by when it would have been helpful to face up to a problem. T.S. Eliot called it "obnubilation, [that is] reconciling, hushing up, patting down, glozing over, concocting pleasant sedatives . . .". And he added: "The sense of fact is something very slow to develop, and its complete development means perhaps the very pinnacle of civilisation."[9]

And yet . . . *Lean Logic* has to be cautious in making the case for consistency. Some of the complex matters included in its *conversation have not been sieved and *sorted down to the level at which no inconsistencies remain. Nor, perhaps, should they be. The last, ruthless rendering-down of an argument in the interests of consistency is rich with opportunities for mistakes which may wreck the whole enterprise. Anyway, inconsistency is fertile: it admits limitations; it invites the other person to apply his or her mind as required by *lean thinking. It suggests that maybe it's time for a walk in *ironic space.

*Good Shepherd Paradox.

FALSE INFERENCE. An argument that draws false conclusions from observations.

The observation may be true, but the inference drawn from it is false. In some forms of the *fallacy, the inference itself is never explicitly stated, but it turns out to be a necessary step to reach the conclusion. Example:

> [This year's] examination results published in your paper reveal that in A levels, girls outperform boys in 25 of 31 subjects at Grade A; in AS levels, girls outperform boys in 26 of 31 subjects at Grade A; and in GCSE girls outperform boys in 23 out of 27 subjects at Grade A*, and in 24 out of 27 subjects at Grade A (home economics and tied results excluded). Despite this incontrovertible proof of the intellectual superiority of girls at the highest levels . . .[10]

There are five inferences here:

1. That intellectual superiority is a quality which school exams measure accurately and
2. . . . at the highest levels.
3. That all other factors affecting performance in exams are equal or *irrelevant: these factors include the degree of application which boys and girls bring to school work, their respective aptitude for conformist behaviour, and the age at which they reach intellectual maturity.
4. That the results for one year can be taken as an indicator of how girls perform relative to boys in exams in all years.

5. A fifth inference—though this is one that the reader is encouraged to draw for himself—is that intellectual ability as measured by exam results comprises intellectual qualities of all kinds, including (say) creativity, persistence, personality, intellectual daring and a talent for conciliation.

It may, at a pinch, be reasonable to argue either for or against any of these; what is not reasonable is to try to make an argument hang on inferences which are taken to be *self-evident, but which can in fact be shown with some confidence to be fantasy. So, there are two problems here. The first is that such mistreatment of *logic threatens ultimately to mature to the point of destroying argument itself as a means of thinking and persuasion: it can simply insist that a certain inference is *true, and all sorts of execration and punishment can then be used to reduce the opposition to silence.

The second problem is that, since false inference is not rooted in any logic, it is unstable, and can flip, depending on current attitudes. The example above is a spirited advocacy of the abilities of women—clearly a good cause. However, the same form of false inference could be used to argue any other view—an opposite and outrageous one, for instance. *Disconnected opinions can quickly recalibrate to their opposite. And it is not just a matter of the person sneakily breaking the rules of logic and hoping that no one will notice, because the false inference is used most of all to fill the gaps and inconsistencies in the speaker's own opinion. The person who makes the false inference is the first to be persuaded by it.

Should her opinion shift, therefore, as the opinions of campaigners sometimes do, false inferences can be applied to their new task—from supporting the worthy to supporting the indefensible or the absurd: the economy is *growing, so we must all be getting happier; the Government doesn't believe in *peak oil, so it can't be a problem; the midges are biting me, so I must be delicious. The logical rootlessness that comes from the false inference is an incentive to grasp at anything that moves, and to drift downstream with it into the forgiving, logic-free, lethal comforts of the big idea.[11]

*False Premise, Ideology, Calibration.

FALSE OPPOSITE (aka False Antithesis/Dichotomy). A fallacy of *definition: a word is defined by *not* being its opposite. Example: "integration" must be a good thing because it is the opposite of "disintegration" (a bad thing). But integration could also be taken to be the opposite of concepts like independence or *freedom, which are good things, in which case such reasoning from opposites would make "integration" bad. The opposite of "consistency" is "inconsistency" (a bad thing); but it could also be "diversity".

This fallacy is trivial but it is popular, and it is often present as the *self-evident truth at the starting point of the *large-scale policy which imposes misjudgment in detail and at leisure.
*False Sameness.

FALSE PREMISE. A premise is a proposition (often *self-evident) from which another follows. An argument which starts with a false premise and draws consistent inferences from there is valid in logic, though its conclusions will almost always be wrong.[12]

An argument based on a false premise from which an *incorrect* inference is drawn has a greater chance of stumbling upon the right conclusion: I will find the way home by following the local ley lines, so we will get there safely.
*Different Premises, False Inference.

FALSE SAMENESS. The presumption that different things are in essence the same. This is what passes for acute insight—sweeping away the detail and getting to the heart of the matter. It is pub certainty which, in the morning, you unfortunately still believe: all uses of armed forces are forms of militarism; violent videos are no different from bedtime folk tales; the present *climate change is the same as previous wobbles in the climate; street crime now is the same as it was in the eighteenth century; a defence of the invasion of Iraq in 2003 means defending the idea of invading Iran in 2008. A fabric of argument may be woven by establishing agreement that one particular thing is bad, and then asserting that everything else that you are opposed to is nothing but another version of the same thing.[13]

The ancient story of *The Princess and the Pea* has been turned on its head. The princess' judgment (being that of a true princess) was so refined and discriminating that she was kept awake all night in discomfort, owing to the pea that had been placed beneath the twenty mattresses of her bed. That was then. The twenty-first century princess' judgment has been coarsened and dulled. She sleeps peacefully, whatever. To her, a bed of nails and a pile of soft mattresses are just the same.[14]
*False Opposite, Hyperbole, Slippery Slope.

FAMILY. See Small Group, Reciprocity and Cooperation, Home, Lean Household, Public Sphere and Private Sphere.

FEAR (*Argumentum ad metum*). An argument designed to force you to agree with a proposition by indicating the fearful consequences that could follow if you didn't. It is probably an empty threat. Stay cool and you will likely be able to make that plain.
*Big Stick, Violence.

FEEDBACK. See Systems Thinking > Feedback, Resilience > Feedback, Lean Thinking > Feedback.

FESTIVAL. Celebration of collective joy.
*Carnival, Invisible Goods, Intentional Waste, Play, Ritual.

FINE-DISTINCTION-INTOLERANCE. Refusal to make a substantial judgment which may turn—at the margin—on insubstantial differences. Example: selection for admission to a school or university.

But life is a network of fine distinctions; the ability to observe them is called *judgment.
*Fuzzy Logic, Disingenuousness, False Sameness, Slippery Slope.

FIVE WHYS. The practice of tracing a problem back through multiple layers of cause-and-effect to its ultimate cause—or at least back to the problem which, if repaired, would have a good chance of preventing it happening again. Observation finds that five layers of "Why?" are typically required. Although this is scarcely a new idea (in air accident investigation, for instance), the practice of meticulously tracing the source even of minor or routine errors was a major advance when it was established by Taiichi Ohno at the Toyota Motor

Company in Japan after the Second World War, as a standard response to the routine daily glitches of production. Without it, errors just out of sight—more than one step away—settle in and breed.[15]

A reasonable development of the Five Whys would be the Five Whats, which would consist of explicitly identifying five reasons for making an important decision where there is the potential for catastrophe if it is wrong. Decisions driven by one *iconic principle or argument have a tendency to be catastrophic; a rule which affirms that another four distinct reasons should be researched and thought through would be an application of *pull to decision-making.
*False Consistency, Reflection.

FLOW. One of the properties of a system designed according to the principles of *lean thinking (Rule 3). The aim is to achieve a regular flow of work on a scale small enough for participants to be aware of—and to respond to—local *diversity and detail. It avoids batches and blockbusting projects full of unexamined error. It enables incremental learning and improvement, and it invites participation from the people involved. When flow is in place, the conditions are right for *pull.[16]

But there is more to it than that. Flow is a key—perhaps *the* key—principle of a life that makes sense to the person who is living it. It is the experience of engagement in *practice in something difficult, where prompt feedback tells you how well you are doing it, how to respond to it, how to be part of the music.

How do we get there? Well, the psychologist Mihaly Csikszentmihalyi, who has explored the meaning of flow, asked people to think about the most positive experiences of their lives, and to tell him how they came about, and what they felt while they were happening. He concluded that there are seven conditions. Flow is most likely to come with a task we have a reasonable chance of completing. We must have time to concentrate. There are clear goals (for instance, you really do want to get up that rock face without falling off). And, of course, there is that critical condition for most things in *Lean Logic*—the rapid *feedback: the task answers back; we are drawn into *conversation; we are not alone. The last three items on Csikszentmihalyi's list are not so much enabling conditions as reinforcing consequences:

we forget (if only briefly) about our daily troubles; there is a suspension of our consciousness of time; and there is a sense of mastery, of knowing what we are doing.[17]

Flow means total engagement with your *intention. It means leaving out the *irrelevant, letting the task itself pull our responses along with honesty and accuracy, being alert to feedback and learning by repetition. Here we have gone beyond a self-conscious, cool acknowledgement of lean thinking. It is about what we do and who we are.
*Systems Thinking 〉 Feedback 〉 Feedback and Flow.

FLUENCY, THE FALLACY OF. A plausible facility with speech which upstages an actual understanding of the subject. It brings no surprises; it is sociable, and it has endurance: the argument goes to the last man or woman talking.
*Balletic Debate, Harebrain Fracture, Narrative Truth.

FOOD. See Food Prospects, Lean Food.

FOOD PROSPECTS. The world's ability to feed itself is not secure, and the headline concerns are well-recognised:[18]

- *Land*: Demand for land is increasing due to population growth, the need to produce food in bulk for cities and their supermarkets, and the spread of the "western diet" based on animal products and highly processed foods. This is forcing local farmers to leave the land or find ways of subsisting on minimal areas, allowing little or no space for crop rotation and local habitats. It has also led to the invasion of natural *ecosystems such as forests and peatlands, as well as of *nations.[19]
- *Water*: Intense demand for water from underground reservoirs has depleted the supply. Extraction and redirection has led to the frequent drying-out of rivers such as the Yellow River, the Colorado River in the southwestern United States, and even the Aral Sea (now the Aralkum Desert).[20]
- *Soil*: Many soils have been exhausted of their organic matter and nutrients.[21]
- *Energy*: Much of the world's agriculture has become dependent on fossil fuels for cultivation, the manufacture of fertilisers and pesticides,

F

storage, drying, transport and retail. Depending on the steepness of the decline in oil and gas supplies there is a prospect of deep, and maybe permanent, food shortages when energy outages begin.[22]

- *Food poverty*: The dependence on food markets—as distinct from subsistence—and global focus on food commodity trade has put people at risk of famine owing to lack of purchasing power, even if food is available.[23]

- **Climate*: Extreme events, such as drought and flood, are already beginning to destroy large areas of agricultural land at critical stages in the harvest year.[24]

- *Hybridisation*: Hybrid seeds have led to the use of identical varieties in large regions by a global agricultural industry. They provide a remarkable hybrid vigour, and rising yields and consistent quality for international trade and multiple retailers, but have led to a loss of agricultural biodiversity and increased the risk of large-scale damage by pests and diseases (*Genetic Modification).[25]

- *Industrialisation and specialisation*: The treatment of food production as an industrial process has made food producers dependent on ever-more-costly imports of seed, fertilisers, pesticides and equipment, forcing many local and small-scale farmers into crippling *debt. It also calls for the planting of large areas with a single crop (monocropping), which is invariably at a high risk of failure, requiring costly measures to prevent it (*Lean Food).[26]

- *Depleted oceans*: Overfishing is sharply reducing the value of oceans as a source of food.[27]

The world's food establishment is evidently in an uncomfortable situation. Conventional industrial agriculture is the short-lived product of cheap energy, enabling a small number of farmers, farm workers and industrial food processors to operate on a very large *scale. Science takes the credit, but it is oil and gas that did it. And the intense *competition to survive in this fuel-dependent *market has made it necessary for farmers to make use of every method available to them, including industrially-produced fertilisers and pesticides and the elimination of natural *ecosystems which stand in the way. Industrial agriculture brings the whole supply chain—from seed to mainstream supermarket checkout—under the commercial control of a few very large companies. It is without defences against the consequences of the coming *energy-famine, and it will retreat before it. Yet where *genetically modified crops have been used, the feasibility of converting from industrial agriculture to a less input-intensive regime will be reduced by depleted soil and super-persistent weeds; since genetic changes persist, it may even be impossible on any relevant timescale.[28]

CHRIS WHITE

But it is darker than this. Let us look more closely at one aspect. We tend to think of Rachel Carson's book *Silent Spring* as being a typical product of the 1960s, when the broad-spectrum ecological consequences of the organophosphate and organochlorate insecticides (DDT and the like) were not yet fully recognised, except by the people who lived close enough to nature to notice. Better now? No. It is just subtler now. There is no point in killing everything that moves when you need to kill only those species that are eating the crops. Modern pesticides aim to be highly specific in their targeting and systemic in their application: instead of being applied externally to the crops, where they will wash off in the rain or degrade in the sun, they are absorbed into the plant's tissues, where they are poisonous to the pests but not to other animals such as bees and humans.

At least, that is the theory. But the design of toxins which are as picky as that about whose nervous system to destroy and whose to leave alone is difficult. It is also difficult to test them; it takes a long time for any effects to become apparent, especially in the case of larger animals. And the effects are subtle, studies have to look for effects that are harder to detect than that helpful indicator that something is wrong: sudden death.

Bee-killing neonicotinoids, and why it's so hard to stop using them

The group of chemicals which has been most successful as a systemic pesticide is the neurotoxins (nerve poisons) known as the neonicotinoids. A survey from the industry's research establishment finds that they are "the most important chemical class for the insecticide market", thanks to their "target specificity [and the] relatively low risk for nontarget organisms".[29]

These features are important, since pollination by insects is essential to agricultural systems and other ecosystems alike. Yet bee-keepers in North America and Europe have observed that colony collapse—the disappearance of entire colonies of bees—is becoming common, raising the prospect of bees and their indispensable work of pollination going missing on a large scale.[30]

The type of neonicotinoid on which most research has been done is imidacloprid, but . . .

All neonicotinoids have a similar chemical structure, are mainly used as systemic pesticides, show a high toxicity to bees, and affect the nervous systems of invertebrates in the same way.[31]

Such findings have led many (very reasonably) to urge that the neonicotinoids should be banned.

And yet, the nature of large-scale monoculture, lacking any form of plant life other than the crop itself, means that the crop is intensely vulnerable to pests, since there is no local *ecosystem to support the life-cycles of their predators. And if neonicotinoids were not used, what should be used instead? No one would want a return to the organochlorates, yet banning the neonicotinoids which underpin this system (and equivalent pesticides), is at present beyond the reach of feasible policy.[32]

So agriculture has got itself into a technological trap. The agricultural establishment depends on these chemicals; as their advocates in the industry rightly protest, it cannot do without them. On the other hand, continuing to use them has its problems, too. A steep decline in pollinating insects—'peak bees'—would, like *peak oil, raise questions about whether our society on its present *scale can be fed.

And there are other unknowns here. It could be a cause for concern that we don't know whether the neurotoxins in food we have ourselves been eating for twenty years are as harmless as had been hoped, or whether they may now be well advanced in the work of confusing our own nervous systems. The causes of several neurological disorders in humans are still poorly understood. There are also unknowns as to the effect of neurotoxins on the nervous systems of the birds and other predators that feed on the pests—almost exactly the problem that was raised by Carson half a century ago. The bees may have something to tell us.

The trap: once a technology has started down a particular route, the logic leads it, step by step, in a direction which would not have been followed if there was choice in the matter—that is, if it had been designed in response to the question, "How do we want our food to be produced?" It was never intended to be like this. It is not, then, the neonicotinoids that should be banned. It is the system that depends on them. True, that system will break down rapidly when the energy shortages

F

start, but it would be a good idea before then to have made some progress towards a less toxic and inefficient system of food production—putting this dismal accumulation of *unintended consequences out of its misery before it crashes, taking us with it.

And yet that dependency on the fossil fuels and their products is now being ramped up even further, as if no one had the slightest inkling that any problems of *energy, *climate, fertility, toxicity or the control of disease could conceivably be in prospect: the new generation of hypergiant (2,000–cow) dairy farms, for instance. They are wholly dependent on oil and gas for nitrogen fertilisers and biocides for the feed, for *transport and *waste disposal, for every detail of their work. They are highly susceptible to disease, and rely on routine antibiotics, which will quickly and urgently be supplemented by *genetically engineered elaborations as a non-negotiable *necessity. And, by pricing milk from the remaining mixed farms out of the market, they are forcing them, too, into the same dependencies. Concentration into just a few giant food production centres removes all defences against the spread of trouble, which will ripple through into the wider industry, giving our security against famine the resilience of a house of cards.[33]

The key to all this is to recognise that the driving force behind industrial agriculture is not (as is usually claimed), the need to feed the world's *population of 7 billion or more. Indeed, as a way of providing food, industrial agriculture is inefficient: the use of giant-scale standardisation on single crops is not a way to get the maximum yield per acre of *land, but to get the maximum yield per worker; the machinery and chemicals are intended to depopulate the agricultural landscape. Those workers that do remain are a quaint rearguard in retreat from the robots.[34]

It is true that the food produced by a farming *culture that had not done everything it could think of to eliminate labour would be more expensive, but that would be reflected in higher minimum wages, which are based on the cost of subsistence. In equilibrium a higher cost of food would make no difference to *living standards other than providing uncontaminated food, rich with the complex nutrients provided by a *resilient ecosystem which is not on the point of collapse. And we would have a farming economy which did not have to get involved

in the fine-tuning of neurotoxins in order to provide you with a pizza, nor to treat animals reared for their meat with a depth of contempt which shames our age.

There is the option, but it is a *radical one (*Kaikaku), of turning agriculture in a different direction: breaking free from the model of supergiant, centralised production which is forced by *competition to stop at nothing in getting rid of human labour and other pests. Of moving on from a culture which traps even its most successful participants into a routine which they may profoundly loathe, but in which they have no options. The claim that industrial *agriculture is the only way of feeding a large population is about as scientific as a belief in Creationism—and far more damaging. The real task—to maintain a secure supply of quality, non-poisonous food and to sustain an environment capable of supporting it—has been buried by an industry weighed down with preoccupations other than those of food and soil.[35]

This is not a situation in which *technical advances will help—except to postpone the shock of the release stage in the *Wheel of Life, so that the break when it comes is as catastrophic as possible. *Lean Food suggests some of the forms that radical but non-catastrophic transformation could take.

*Genetic Modification, Climacteric.

FORMAL LOGIC. One of the two main kinds of logic. Formal logic deals with the form of an argument rather than its content, and it studies language, deduction and reasoning. It is closely related to mathematics.[36]

One of its core rules is *modus ponens* ("the affirming mode"): a technical term sometimes used by students as a brand name for the whole of formal logic, as in "*modus ponens* and all that". *Modus ponens* is an inference from two premises. The first premise is conditional, consisting of an "antecedent" and a "consequent"; the second premise simply confirms that the antecedent applies in this case. Example:

1. If you get some ducks [antecedent], your slug problem will be resolved [consequent].
2. You are getting some ducks [the antecedent is confirmed].
3. Therefore your slug problem will be resolved [conclusion].

The counterpart to this is *modus tollens* ("the denying mode"), in which a similar first premise is followed by a second premise that denies the *consequent*. Example:

1. If Mary is at home [antecedent], her car will be outside [consequent].
2. Her car is not outside [the consequent is denied].
3. Therefore she is not at home [conclusion].

It sounds banal, but the syllogisms of formal logic are the building blocks of reasoning which—in combination with a series of conditions, affirmed or denied in sequence and in parallel—can develop into a problem-solving capacity of great complexity, used as the logical structure on which artificial intelligence is based.[37]

Informal logic is, of course, the junior partner in all this, since it depends on the reasoning of formal logic, and its mixing up of *logic and content is exactly what you cannot do with formal logic. On the other hand, without content, logic has no purpose. Formal logic is the road; *informal logic is the journey.

*Fallacies.

FORTITUDE. Persistence in the face of trouble, danger, *conflict, mockery, fatigue, solitude, *demoralisation, guilt or *fear. It can be mere bloody-mindedness, of course; it is the connection with *judgment that matters. And yet, the judgment itself may be *intuitive. Bloody-mindedness can save the day.

*Humility, Moderation, Presence, Character, Promiscuous Ethics, Tradition, Virtues.

FRANKNESS. The exposure of ideas and opinions, formerly forbidden by the *ethics and values of society, which can be expected to erupt in the disorderly conditions that will follow the *climacteric. Under the surface in the well-behaved citizen, there is a *second nature, to whom outrageous thoughts and opinions occur, but which the person has no trouble in censoring and keeping in check. In deeply destabilised conditions, however, that second nature tends to break out; the *decency-censor is ignored; the person's second nature becomes, simply, her nature.

The shock of a new frankness has been experienced before—for example, at the time of the Renaissance,

when changing *expectations were forced into even more violent change by recurring outbreaks of the plague. Giovanni Boccaccio's *Decameron* explores this disorder with astonishment. The *conversations described in it (he explains) do not take place in church, nor in schools of philosophy, but in the whorehouse. In fact, the times are so out of joint that . . .

> . . . judges have deserted the judgment-seat, the laws are silent, and ample license to preserve his life as best he may is accorded to each and all. . . . If so one might save one's life, the most sedate might without disgrace walk abroad wearing his breeches on his head.[38]

*Carnival, Manners.

FREEDOM. Is *lean thinking consistent with freedom? There are clearly some senses in which it is not. The five rules of the *grammar of lean thinking—*intention, *lean means, *flow, *pull and *feedback—are designed to focus minds on a purpose, so there is a commitment there which may narrow individual options. The purpose may be the business of making cars or the *Lean Economy's aim of building and sustaining a *community, but it cannot be achieved in a *culture where—as Aristotle put it, warning us of the *fallacy—"freedom means doing what you like".[39]

Nor can we expect useful results from a collective activity organised around a second concept of freedom—the nineteenth century principle of Libertarianism, derived from the Enlightenment, and based on the belief, or hope, that when *intelligence is applied in the minds of different people, they will converge on the same thing. Here we have an even-handed account of Libertarianism by William Fleming:

> The doctrine of Libertarianism is that the Will is such a power as makes it possible to govern or control all the motive forces of our nature, including dispositions and passions, so as to determine personal conduct in accordance with the decisions of the understanding. It implies negatively that impulses or motive forces are not dominant in our life under its normal conditions; positively, that will is associated

F

with intelligence [with every intelligent decision] presupposing that motives have been subordinated to thought.

> *William Fleming,* Vocabulary of Philosophy, *1856.[40]*

To make sense of freedom, we need to look at it in greater depth. It comes in many shapes, and there is no definitive list of them, but a summary is suggested by the philosopher Richard De George:[41]

1. *Rational freedom.* This is the ability to act according to rules; it is also the ability to refuse to act according to them, or to act contrary to them. At first sight, it is a curious argument. How could we *not* have the ability to act according to rules? Well, for one thing, the rules need to exist, and in a chaotic society they don't. While they may be written down somewhere, like the blueprint of a car, you can't drive around in a blueprint: statements need to have at least a degree of acceptance before they can be recognised as rules. Also, if *freedom* to act in a certain way is to mean anything, there must be the possibility of not doing so. And freedom applies here not just to individuals, but to *groups: no choices can be made by the group if those choices are not accepted by its membership; without a means of reaching agreement, decisions made by any individual within that disorderly group may well come to nothing. The first essential for freedom in this sense, then, is an orderly environment in which sensible and realistic decisions are possible.

2. *Interpersonal freedom.* Here we have a much more straightforward aspect of freedom. You are not free if someone is stopping you from doing what you have decided to do. Actually, all of our freedoms are moderated in this way to some extent. Slaves, carers, employees, married people, children, teachers — anybody with responsibilities and obligations, whether freely entered into or not, has some loss of freedom, and it would be a lonely and a rather useless life without it. Good things are bad things at the extreme, and freedom (too much or too little) is no exception. Limits to freedom are the price of being part of something.

3. *Teleological freedom of action.* "Teleological" means purposeful (Greek: *télos* end, aim), and freedom in

this sense is the freedom to carry through what you have decided to do. It depends on two conditions: first, the extent to which you have the capability to do what you have decided upon and, secondly, the extent to which there are obstacles in your way. This kind of freedom, too, is likely to stand in some middle ground: you are more-or-less capable of doing what you intend, and the problems that stand in your way can be more-or-less overcome. In a totalitarian regime, of course, such *moderation may not apply.

4. *Negative freedom.* This is simply freedom from misfortune, such as sickness, poverty and want.[42]

These four kinds of freedom naturally overlap, and they are often interdependent, with expectations of positive *feedback: more freedom of one kind opens up the possibility of more freedom of another, so that a society that is on a benign trend towards freedom may well become able to progress towards further freedoms, while a vicious spiral will see each reduction in freedom opening the way to the next. But let us now stay with the idea of a society in which freedom of all four kinds is strongly supported, and consider how that might happen.[43]

There are several circumstances that may promote freedom. One helpful condition is mountains. A country like Switzerland which is surrounded by mountains and therefore easy to *defend, or hard to reach and seldom invaded, has the advantage of being able to work out its differences, its *institutions and its freedoms at leisure. Being an island may have the same effect. Another helpful, if less stable, condition is federalism, where small states or institutions are able to balance each other's power and learn from each other, although there is the risk of takeover by a *large, would-be *empire, as happened in nineteenth century Germany.

But the key condition for freedom in our context is authority. Authority is hard to define, and there are various understandings of its meaning, but *Lean Logic* takes the view that it is emphatically not the same thing as *control. For example, a man with a gun or a sadistic dictator could force you to do things you don't want to do and which would in the end be bad for both of you. Some critics would say that this is the exercise of an authority of sorts, and there is nothing wrong with that, except that *Lean Logic*'s intention is to reserve the use of "authority" for another purpose.

Just as there are several forms of freedom, so there are several kinds of authority, and one particularly revealing kind is "epistemic" authority (Greek: *episteme* knowledge)—i.e., authority relating to knowledge, *intelligence, insight. Teachers, books and maps are epistemic authorities. That is, they are sources of knowledge which is better than, or more than, that of the person who is receiving it. A child is an epistemic authority when she tells the doctor where she hurts; a tramp is an epistemic authority to a general when he shows him and his army the way through the forest. A strongly-developed *culture is an epistemic authority in its *traditions, assumptions, standards, language, literature, music, *humour, *skills, and in all aspects of its *social capital.⁴⁴

There are two reasons why the idea of epistemic authority is fundamental here. The first is that it is a reminder that authority does not by any means have to be embodied in a person, nor in an organisational structure such as a politburo: it may have a tangible embodiment, but that is a special case. It can reside in any source of reliable guidance, and the mark of a key source is one which is embedded in the atmosphere and the *spirit of the *place, in the culture, in a shared recognition of value and purpose—the personality of the hospital, ship, community, institution, society.

Secondly, epistemic authority introduces the principle of authenticity. A source of incorrect information is not an epistemic authority. Authenticity means that a person is entitled to the respect and admiration which she inspires. Authentic is good. And authority of all kinds, understood in these terms, is authentic. Authentic executive authority has a mandate to act on behalf of others, and/or to give them instructions. Its claim of authority is based on recognised knowledge or ability, and/or on fair appointment, and/or on natural *leadership or experience. And on the grounds of it authority it can exercise *judgment. Authority in this sense was used by the United Kingdom's then-shadow Chancellor of the Exchequer, speaking of the case for assigning more regulatory powers to the Bank of England:

> We have learned from this crisis the old truth that one cannot separate central banking from the supervision of the financial system and that sound regulation is not just about a checklist of rules but about the authority to exercise judgment and to see the bigger picture.⁴⁵

There are, of course, many other forms of authority justified in these same terms: political authority, parental authority, operative authority (invested in a person or group for a particular purpose)—and representative authority, arising from a person being able to speak for people who have invited him or her to do so. All of these forms of authority may be usurped, with savage consequences, but—in the terms of *Lean Logic*—the usurping force is not authority: it is power, tyranny, autocracy.⁴⁶

The reason why the interpretation of authority as something which is authentic and good has been made here with such emphasis is that it would be helpful to explore the idea that freedom is compatible with living and working in a *community or *institution, even one which has a well-defined purpose.

*Lean thinking is not, by any means, a system which says "Come along and do exactly as you want." It is not a holiday camp. It is a way of enabling a *group to accomplish difficult things in a focused way, to learn fast, and to keep an enterprise going. It is not an Enlightenment project—that is, it does not go back to first principles, discard all *emotions and prejudice, and rely on ideals of reason and *intelligence. Nor is it a form of genealogy—tracing the *genetic inheritance of its guiding ideas back to the point where it discovers that there is actually nothing there, apart (maybe) from the malice and power struggles that gave rise to them. On the contrary, lean thinking in *Lean Logic* gets its hands down into the particular, the earthy, the *local, into what is here.⁴⁷

The *loyalties of lean thinking are embedded in particular *places, for which they make no claim other than that they are the ones the people concerned know and care for most. *Lean thinking recognises the community's authority as being authentic—and *trusts it as central to its *identity and that of its members. Their aims are not simply permitted by the community, they are inspired and enabled by it. Call that *empowerment.

And the participants accept the premises around which their group or society has come into being. In fact, as Edmund Burke pointed out, any "controlling power upon will and appetite" has to be located somewhere, "and the less of it there is within, the more there must be without".[48] If authority comes from within—accepted, adopted, internalised—then . . .

> . . . interest, habit, and the tacit convention, that arise from a thousand nameless circumstances produce a *tact* that regulates without difficulty, what laws and magistrates cannot regulate at all.[49]

And the other freedoms hold, too. There is rational freedom, since the rules are sufficiently coherent, well-defined and supported for people to be able to act in accordance with them. There is interpersonal freedom—the weak interdependencies of *resilience. There is teleological freedom: you can get something done. And there is a reasonable chance of freedom in the negative sense of being spared the consequences of a failing system. In such a community, there is no need for autocracy, for force, for regulatory *control. Here *culture and authority join up, drenching the *community in shared purpose, sustaining the benign circle in which freedom makes freedom.

*Grammar, Choice, Subsidiarity.

FUZZY LOGIC. Logic which recognises that many qualities, such as baldness, tallness, happiness or *truth, are matters of degree, expressed in shades of grey, not black-and-white. Example: the fuzzy borderline between life and *death is celebrated by a lizard's tail for a long time after it has been shed (as a defence tactic by its owner). It glows and *dances in the sun, filling the space between life and death with the *sexy suppleness of the *kama sutra*.[50]

*Lumpy Logic.

G

GAIA. The idea of planet Earth as a *resilient *ecological system, able to maintain its environment in a state consistent with its needs.

In the early 1970s, the scientist James Lovelock suggested that the planet's living ecology regulates its

atmosphere and temperature to shape the conditions it lives in. It does not merely adapt to change; it influences change. It makes its planet inhabitable. At the suggestion of the novelist William Golding, Lovelock named this phenomenon after the Greek goddess of Earth, Gaia.[1]

Though ridiculed at first, Lovelock began to give it substance as a theoretical model with his Daisyworld, whose temperature is regulated by daisies. Imagine a planet on which only one kind of plant grows: daisies, which come in two kinds: white and black. The white ones cope best in warm conditions because they reflect sunlight back into space, and this keeps both themselves and the planet cool. The black ones cope best in cool conditions because they absorb heat, and this keeps both them and the planet warm. Now imagine that, at the start of the story, the sun (as has happened in fact) gives out substantially less heat than at present, so that the planet would be quite cold, were it not covered by black daisies which absorb much of the heat. However, the sun gradually warms up; conditions become hotter and less favourable for the black daisies and more favourable for the white ones, so white daisies increase, black ones diminish, and the temperature of the Earth remains benign for daisies. This continues until the surface is entirely covered with white daisies.

Then comes the turning point. As the sun now gets even hotter, there are no black daisies left to replace. Just a small further increase in heat from the sun is too much even for the white daisies, which die off—and there is nothing to stop the planet heating up beyond the range of the daisies to do anything about it. And that, for the simple computer model with its virtual daisies, is the end of the story. In a real ecology, with *complex relationships between millions of species, other kinds of interaction between the living members of the ecology and their material setting—its rocks, water and (mainly solar) power supply—will kick in, conserving the favourable conditions despite the external shock. But even with millions of species on the case, there comes a point where a shock—such as the heating up of the sun, or the relentless loading of carbon into the atmosphere by an industrial civilisation—reaches the limits of Gaia's resilience.[2]

That is what you might expect. What is much less obvious is that life itself, in the process of taking part in the web of interactions and *feedbacks which sustains and is sustained by Gaia, can take forms and present problems which are beyond Gaia's ability to cope. For example, some 2.3 billion years ago, microbes mastered the art of photosynthesis (the extraction of carbon from carbon dioxide, and the release of oxygen as a by-product). That was a brilliant breakthrough. However, those microbes then proceeded to suck up so much carbon dioxide that the Earth lost its ability to conserve heat, and the oceans froze solid for 100 million years. The same thing happened again (700 million years ago), when complex plants (i.e., plants with leaves and roots) evolved which not only absorbed carbon dioxide but speeded-up "weathering". Weathering is the process which wears away rock and releases phosphorus and other vital ingredients of a fertile soil—a good Gaia-like thing to do, you might think. But it takes a lot of carbon out of the atmosphere in the process. Result: another 50 million years of ice.[3]

Could it be, then, that Gaia has a self-destructive side to her character? Consider: Gaia produced *Homo sapiens* . . .

Gaia is, without doubt, the benign vitality which gives us resilience. But *success*, in the form of life itself, can lead on to shock. We can think of this either as the other side to Gaia's character, or as the work of a quite different character: Medea, perhaps. Medea was the enchantress— grand-daughter of the sun-god, Helios—who tricked the daughters of Pelias into boiling their father alive.[4] She

seems at first, with a cv like that, to stand for disorder to an extreme degree, but she is in fact quite law-abiding, by the standards of a goddess. Unfortunately, the law she abides by is the "Power Law", which says that the scale of shocks a system will suffer over time ranges in scale from the trivial (most shocks), and the moderate (some shocks), through to the rare but utterly breathtaking and cataclysmic. The Power Law tells us that failure is intrinsic to all complex systems, and to resilience (*Systems Thinking ⟩ Form ⟩ The Power Law).

This succession of *death and life is the time-signature of *Lean Logic*; it is present in *lean thinking, with its *radical break followed by slow *incremental development, and in the cycle of release and regeneration in the *Wheel of Life. A resilient ecology extends its collective lifetime by allowing *parts* to go through their Gaia-Medea cycles on a smaller, less destructive, scale (*Sacrifice-and-Succession). It can be a highly successful strategy, sustaining interlocking cycles of depth and renewal for long periods. It is with its breathing-out and breathing-in, its sigh and inspiration, that the system as a whole keeps going. Life doesn't give up easily, since it is almost infinitely adaptable, and capable of inventing and sustaining interactions favourable for life. For any particular form of life and ecological community, however, prospects are less assured.

And yet, consider dimethyl sulphide (DMS). Or, rather, consider, dimethylsulphoniopropionate (DMSP). DMSP, as its name suggests, is a long molecule, and it is found in the cells of marine organisms such as *Emiliania huxleyi*—abundant algae which are known for capturing carbon from the atmosphere and precipitating it to the ocean floor as chalk. The DMSP in the algae's cells keeps them from losing water by osmosis to the surrounding sea, but when the cells die DMSP degrades into DMS, which then floats up into the atmosphere (giving the sea its slightly tangy sulphuric smell) and degrades, leaving a residue of sulphate aerosol. This has the effect of 'seeding' clouds, meaning that, sooner or later, it will rain.[5]

So the algae's cells contain the DMSP, which releases the DMS, which seeds the clouds, which make it rain. But the algae itself depends on iron in the sea, which is scarce. Here peat bogs come to the rescue. When sphagnum moss there dies, it releases humic and fulvic acids which, in effect, pickle it, storing carbon and building

G

up a deep layer of soggy black peat. These acids also get to work dissolving the metals, including iron, out of the bedrock, and the iron-rich solution then drains into the rivers and thus into the sea, where it fertilises the algae which in turn make it rain.[6]

Meanwhile, down in the forest, bromeliads, small plants that live on trees, have leaves (technically, bracts) specially shaped to catch and hold pools of water, which are alive with bacteria and algae which maintain their own wetness with DMSP, which breaks down to DMS, which makes it rain. That rain turns the tropical forests into a heat pump, driving up warm, wet air into the atmosphere, where it is transported by (the Walker and Hadley) air circulations far into the Northern and Southern Hemispheres, cooling the forests enough to keep them near their optimum temperature, and distributing heat to parts of the planet which, without them, would freeze.[7]

All told, we do seem to get a lot of benefits from the decomposing *waste products of a chemical used by the cells in algae to keep themselves wet. And yet such connected and unlikely *elegance is everywhere. Every ecosystem, from the human body to slime mould to heathland, has connections and interactions in support of constancy. Any accident of nature whose outcome sustains these conditions is likely to happen again. Accidents of this kind reinforce themselves, steering the system they live in with constant adjustments of positive and negative *feedback, maintaining the subtle conditions for life of a particular kind.[8]

That particularity will not last indefinitely, but Gaia's stabilising feedbacks can keep a *system in an apparently unlikely condition for a long time. It will have started by accident, but its feedbacks make it seem intentional, giving it, it seems, a guiding hand, a stillness and integrity. What seems like purpose is in fact a more secure and reliable thing—a system stuck in a benign and brilliant rut. Gaia settles in. Medea bides her time. For now.
*Emergence, Climate Change, Wheel of Life, Good Shepherd Paradox, Spirit.

GALLEY SKILLS. Skills which, requiring a lot of talent, learning and practice, eventually trap the skilled person into moving in a direction about which he or she has no say. Examples:

1. There are only limited alternatives for an appropriately trained biochemist other than to work in the field of *biotechnology.
2. Molecular scientists are likewise drawn into *nanotechnology.
3. There is little *nuclear physicists can do other than design, build and operate nuclear power stations.
4. The most able *economists are able to build mathematical models of the economy which may be more brilliant than they are useful (*Reductio ad Absurdum).

At worst, galley skills can elaborate dominant models which threaten to destroy us. You have to be brilliant for your scientific contribution to the current predicament to be truly catastrophic.
*Cognitive Dissonance, Sunk Cost Fallacy, Metamorphosis.

GENERALISATION FALLACIES. (1) Too little: The insistence that it is not justifiable to make any statement at all unless you can give a complete story, covering every detail; the refusal to draw general conclusions, or meaning of any kind, from the particular.[9]
(2) Too much: A generalisation which misleads by:

a. asserting or assuming that what happened in one case, or a few cases, happens in most or all cases (*Memory Fillers); or
b. by leaving out essential details; or
c. by failing to recognise *exceptions.

In fact, it is dubious to think of either of these as a *fallacy. Lean Logic asserts the case both for intense awareness of the *local detail, and for using local detail to build principles as a frame of reference, allowing what is going on to be understood. The problem with generalisation arises because it may be done badly, not because it is attempted.
*Lumpy Logic.

GENETIC FALLACY. The *fallacy which judges the *truth of a statement mainly or exclusively by its source. In the case of *ad hominem, the source is a person; here the source is taken to be a theory, or a school of thought, or a political opinion—allowing the argument to be seen as typical and dismissed without further consideration.

One common expression of this is the dismissal of any statement about inherited characteristics of people (other than diseases), in reaction to the gross abuse and misrepresentation of genetic sciences by the Nazis.[10]

There is a good deal of overlap between the Genetic Fallacy and *ad hominem*. They are both guilty of what is probably the most common of all expressions of *bad faith, and of all ways of destroying sensible discussion—the Mandy Rice-Davies riposte: "He would say that, wouldn't he?" This is the long-standing guarantee that the two sides in an adversarial *democratic system don't have to listen to a word the other side is saying.[11]

In general, it is advisable to keep your arguments to the matter in hand—*ad rem*—rather than being diverted to the source. On the other hand, it is a good idea to be aware of the source. Statements should arouse suspicion if they come from fantasists, historians with an axe to grind, fanatics of all kinds, totalitarian regimes, bureaucrats, or those whose analytical powers have been taken over by resentments or by dramatics (*argumentum ad ludicrum*). W.H. Auden advises caution with respect to those who wash too much.[12]

*Identity, Judgment.

GENETIC MODIFICATION (aka Genetic Engineering).
A technique for modifying the genetic make-up of an organism by inserting into it a gene bearing a desired trait extracted from another organism.[13]

Several applications of gene technology are being developed—e.g., in medicine—but this entry discusses only the case of its use on plants and animals with a view to increasing *agricultural yields, improving pest resistance and generating other characteristics which are thought to be desirable.[14]

The promises

1. *Increased yields*

In fact, genetically modified organisms (GMOs) are not at present designed to increase yields directly—to produce, for instance, more beans or corn cobs per plant. Instead, they are designed to work indirectly—by, for instance, improving plants' resistance to herbicides so that stronger doses can be used to deal with persistent weeds. But the cost of this interference in the gene is high, and so the direct effect of GMOs

on yields can be to reduce them. GM yield is highly variable but, for example, studies indicate that the yield of GM rapeseed and soya is around 10 percent lower than that of conventional varieties—though other much greater declines in yield have also been reported—and that where an increase *has* occurred it has often been due to a conventionally-bred trait in the plant, rather than a GM one.[15]

Moreover, GM crops have been explicitly designed for industrial agriculture and are used (and trialled) in almost monocultural systems. With just one crop growing at a time, it is unable to take advantage of the substantially higher yields and improved weed- and pest-resistance that can be obtained from *diverse polycultures, such as the root vegetable *arracacha* along with onions (Brazil), or wheat along with faba beans (Ethiopia). And the focus on GMOs has tended to close down the use of rotations and intermediate (aka *appropriate, or agroecological) approaches, including green manures, cover crops and animal manures, and the substantial improvements in soil health and crop yields that they make available.[16]

That, in turn, locks agriculture into a simplistic understanding of the meaning of "yield", a rich man's throwaway *ethic which no *resilient community could ever afford. As the agronomist Vandana Shiva summarises it, the narrow *definition of yield required by industrial agriculture . . .

> . . . focuses on partial yields of single crops rather than total yields of multiple crops and integrated systems; focuses on yields of one or two globally traded commodities, not on the diverse crops that people eat; focuses on quantity per acre rather than on nutrition per acre; has very low productivity judged on the basis of resource use; and undermines food security by using up resources that could have been used for sustainable food production.[17]

GMO technology intensifies and deepens these properties of industrial agriculture.

2. *Improved resistance to pests*

The design of ways of defending crops from attack by pests such as lepidopterans (butterflies and moths) and their larvae is a main objective of agriculture. Industrial agriculture generally relies on chemicals for the *protection which its crops cannot provide for themselves. *Organic cultivation uses a *systems approach and a living ecology— soil fertility, rotations, a large repertoire of species and varieties, timing, companion planting and local habitats for predators—to build crops' resistance.

Genetic engineering uses the science of gene transfer. For instance, it inserts into the crop a gene for a toxin which is lethal to pests, but not to the animals and people that eat it. One toxin which is used for this originates in a bacterium called *Bacillus thuringiensis* (Bt). Bt was discovered in 1911 as a pathogen of flour moths in Thuringia in Germany, and its cells contain a powerful insecticidal crystal protein. It is claimed to be safe for humans and for all other higher animals, and the most widely-used strain (kurstaki) is claimed to be safe also for insects—and yet, Bt is lethal for the lepidoptera larvae (caterpillars). Newly-developed strains of Bt are effective also against the larvae of other pests, including mosquitoes, some flies and gnats, Colorado beetles and elm leaf beetles. But how come it is safe for animals but not for the pests it targets? The reason for this is clever: the protein containing the toxin itself (*delta endotoxin*) is insoluble in normal conditions; it is only in the highly reducing conditions (with a pH of 9.5 or more) which exist in the gut of lepidoptera larvae and other bugs that eat the crops that it becomes soluble—and when it dissolves, it releases the toxin.[18]

And yet, there have to be some concerns about combining this long-established insecticide with gene technology. Although Bt does not secrete its toxin when it is eaten by us, the health effects of eating food containing the bacillus have not been tested. In the past, Bt was sprayed onto crops, but there was little of it left by the time anyone ate it, since Bt quickly breaks down in sunlight.[19] But when it is genetically-engineered into a plant, the bacterium is of course present on a different scale—integrated into every part of the plant. The effect of substantial daily doses of a powerful bacillus unfamiliar to the bodies of humans and animals is unknown.

And then there is the immunity problem—for, if the *whole* crop has a *constant* content of the toxin, the bugs can build up their immunity at leisure. Bt is claimed by the agronomists to be a miracle, but for the pests with predatory designs on the crops, it is at first a tricky problem in chemistry—then, all too soon, it is lunch. The conventional pesticides (such as the organophosphates: *Food Prospects) established the pattern: as pests develop a resistance to the toxins that are designed to destroy them, the pesticides have to be made more powerful, so the pests adapt, and the technologies raise their game yet further . . .[20] GMOs, in the end, make little difference to this *arms race other than to speed it up. As the environmentalist Jonathon Porritt writes,

> It is astonishing that serious scientists can be so childishly enthusiastic at the prospect of swapping today's chemical treadmill for tomorrow's genetic treadmill, all in pursuit of the unattainable dream of pest-eradication.[21]

3. *Other characteristics*

Other intended benefits include the following:[22]

- Vitamin A-enriched GM crops have been promised for many years—but vitamin A is sustainably provided by improved crop diversity, and there are other ways of increasing the content of vitamin A in crops which do not involve genetic modification. Moreover, this GM promise (golden rice) is yet to be fulfilled.[23]
- Drought-resistant GM crops have been promised, but they, too, have failed to materialise. In fact, drought-resistance is *sustainably provided by varieties which have been bred for generations for that purpose and which have by some miracle survived the species-genocide committed by industrial agriculture.[24]
- Salt-tolerant GM crops have been promised, and they have been produced for some crops, but the performance of non-GM varieties has been shown to be better.[25]
- A new strain of soybean from Monsanto is promised that contains Omega-3 fatty acids. If soya oil from this strain were eaten regularly for

year after year (and assuming it is successfully cultivated on a commercial scale, and that the benefits were not outweighed by lower yields), it could increase the "omega-3 index" in the blood from 4 percent to 5 percent, and this, according to William Harris, professor of medicine at the University of South Dakota, would be associated with a drop of about 50 percent in the risk of heart attacks. But so would more exercise and less fatty food. Its real significance is the hope that it will break down consumers' resistance to GMOs, as Monsanto's vice-president for consumer traits explains:

> We've shown for years that GM crops can control pests. That's important to consumers, but not in a personal way. Hopefully this will be personal enough to make a difference.[26]

- Tomatoes genetically modified to contain more antioxidants are being tested. But the plainest and safest way of getting the antioxidants you need is to have a varied diet with plenty of fruit and vegetables—preferably organic.[27]

The problems

1. *Immunity*

The predators, the viruses and the weeds learn to cope, and the example of this which is most evident and current in the case of GMOs is the problem of weeds. These are becoming increasingly resistant to herbicides, to the point where the dose of pesticides needed to kill the weeds is enough to kill the crops too. The response offered by GMOs—to insert a gene into the crop which confers resistance—is applied to such widely established weedkillers as glyphosate, aka "Round-Up" (Monsanto), glufos-inate (Aventis), and imidazolinone (Cyanamid).[28]

Higher doses → greater immunity → higher doses . . . (see "Tough Weeds I" sidebar). The limit comes when the quantity of herbicide makes the crop unfit for consumption, or when the soil becomes so degraded that it is unable to support crops, or when herbicides contaminate the drinking water, or when farmers can no longer afford to buy the quantity of herbicide that is needed.[29]

TOUGH WEEDS I
Weeds that rise to the challenge of GMOs

Horseweed, a prolific weed in the soya crops of Mississippi, quickly developed an immunity which required a six- to thirteen-fold increase in the amount of glyphosate to achieve the same level of control as normal horseweed. Velvet leaf developed a tolerance for quantities of glufosinate larger than many farmers could afford; water hemp's response to glyphosate application was simply to delay germination until after it had been applied. In Iowa, after a few years of GM use, the 10 percent most heavi-ly-treated fields required at least 34 times more herbicide than fields in which GM varieties were not used.[30]

It seems at first to be a problem to which there is no *technical solution. But the technologists do not give up easily. Industrial agriculture is starting to turn to the development of completely new toxins: just moving genes around is no longer enough; it is necessary to start from scratch—and that means *nanotechnology. This opens the way to toxins that have never previously existed, which will stimulate the rapid evolution of organisms that can deal with them.

They in turn will present challenges which will require the convergence of four technologies: genetics, robotics, information technology and nanotechnology (GRIN). *GRIN has the potential to build prodigiously small robots, or "assemblers", which can in turn build materials and nanoscale instruments capable of tasks which would be impos-sible on a larger scale. And, as you might suspect by now, there are some problems here, too. There could be some resistance by consumers to a daily diet of foods which contain robots, even very small ones. And there is the problem of the technology not going according to plan. GRINs will escape into the wild *ecology. And, since GRINs are an information

G

technology, it will be possible to hack into and insert or develop a virus designed to cause trouble.

2. *Escapes*

Once genetically modified crops have been planted on a farm, it is certain that the modification will spread into the wider environment. The pollen will spread on the wind to fertilise related varieties; the seeds will fall from trucks and be dropped by birds. Why should that matter? Well, consider some of the modifications that are now possible. Here are four examples (although only the first is yet in commercial use):

- *Pesticide resistance*. Weeds with high resistance to herbicides—superweeds—are virtually indestructible unless removed by hand, or by the application of very powerful pesticides consisting, for instance, of some 70 percent of Agent Orange.
- *Terminator genes*. These are genes which sterilise the plant's reproductive system, making it necessary for the farmer to buy new supplies of seed for each season; he cannot use the seeds he has saved because they are sterile. For evident reasons, it would be advisable to be make sure that this terminator gene does not contaminate close cousins of the crop, and from there spread beyond them to other plants, and in due course to animals.
- *Cheater gene*. Varieties of seed containing an inserted gene which prevents them from producing seeds until they have been sprayed with a particular chemical, controlled by the supplier of the seed.
- *Zombie gene*. Although the plant with this gene is able to produce a seed, the seed will not germinate until it has been sprayed with the proprietary chemical.

Unfortunately, contamination is unavoidable. Tree pollen can travel 600 kilometres in a season, and pollen from all plants is industriously spread through the locality by birds, bees, insects, fungi, bacteria and rain. When this year's pollen has gone as far as it can, it fertilises the plant which will be the starting point for next year's journey. And, not far behind the

pollen come the seeds, spread by the wind, by birds, by the transport of grain, and by the contamination of grain elevators and combine harvesters.[31]

Then there is the matter of the wandering gene. When a gene is inserted into the DNA of an organism, it is bundled together in a "construct" with other genes needed for various functions such as the insertion itself and the activation and identification of the inserted gene. These constructs are designed to be mobile—and that mobility persists so that, when the gene has moved in, it is reasonable to suspect that it could all too easily move out again, in a process known as "horizontal transfer".[32] It is not yet known to what extent genes can continue to function after such a transfer, but among the accessible organisms into which the wandering gene could migrate are the gut bacteria of the animals (insects, bees, cattle and humans) that eat the GM food. There is also evidence that modified genes can migrate into the microorganisms and fungi that sustain the soil and the natural environment.[33]

And then there is competition between plants. GM plants do not necessarily have a competitive advantage in the natural world with non-GM plants—clearly plants with a terminator gene wouldn't—but in some cases their advantage could be decisive. GM trees containing insecticide-producing genes, for instance, may be able to invade wild ecosystems with ease, disrupting the system as they go.[34]

In large *natural systems, events that could occur generally do occur, as we see in nations which have established a large GMO industry. The cultivation of GM-free crops of maize, oilseed rape and soya is, for all practical purposes, no longer possible anywhere in Canada. There is no effective way of containing genetic *pollution.[35]

For the industry, it is matter of consumer *choice: just look at the label. As David Stark, Monsanto's vice-president for consumer traits, tells us,

> Consumers will have a choice: some may choose not to try it, but others will.[36]

There is no such thing as containment with respect to GM strains, so there is no such thing as coexistence between GM strains and non-GM strains. Once released, they will spread everywhere.

3. *Volunteers*

When a farmer plants a new crop, he has to be confident that the crop which grew in the previous year will not try to come back in force; or if it does, he may need to have the option of using herbicide to eradicate newly-germinated plants from that crop (farmers call them "volunteers"). However, if the volunteers happen to be genetically engineered to survive applications of the normal herbicides (glyphosate, etc), he has a problem: the remaining options are to turn to intensely toxic chemicals such as 2,4-D and paraquat, or to weed the fields by hand, or to abandon his model of varied cropping altogether (see "Tough Weeds II" sidebar).[37]

4. *Uniformity*

Hybrid seeds do not breed true, so growers have to buy in first-generation hybrid seeds every time. This produces uniformity, which helps in harvesting, in processing and in the identification of particular varieties and their breeders; it also, of course, helps the sales of seed.

The danger of this uniformity showed up in 1970: corn leaf blight swept through the southern states of America, encountering no genetic resistance for thousands of miles. By opening the way for greater intensification of cropping with a reduction in the *diversity of crop types, varieties and systems, GM technology reduces *resilience and increases vulnerability to virus and pest attacks.

5. *Surprises*

The principle on which GM technology is based is the expectation or hope that, when a gene is extracted from the DNA of its own species and implanted in another, it will simply carry on doing the same job as before. But the function of DNA is not as easy as that: it is not a self-service counter at which biotechnologists can pile up their plates with whatever combination of goodies they wish. What the science tells us is that the gene's activity depends on its interactions with the proteins and other constituents of the cell; when a gene finds itself in a new biological environment this

---

> # TOUGH WEEDS II
> ## When last year's crop comes back and back
>
> Tony Huether, who farms in northern Alberta, planted three different kinds of GM oilseed rape resistant to, respectively, Monsanto's glyphosate, Aventis' glufosinate, and Cyanamid's imidazolinones. The following year, he found his fields invaded by strains of oilseed rape which had acquired genes giving them resistance to all three herbicides: in order to clear his land, he had to use 2,4-D. In Manitoba, Monsanto has been reduced to sending out teams of students to weed out indestructible volunteer rape plants by hand.[38]

collaboration is disrupted. The biologist Barry Commoner explains,

> The living cell is a unique network of interacting components, dynamic yet sufficiently stable to survive. [It] is made fit to survive by evolution; the marvellously intricate behaviour of the nucleoprotein site of DNA synthesis is as much a product of natural selection as the bee and the buttercup.[39]

It is only to be expected, therefore, that the organisms into which genes have been implanted usually die, and that most of the survivors are damaged. Those with obvious damage are weeded out; the less obvious failures are those that survive but have a defect which becomes apparent later, in subtle ways. Some curious effects are being observed by farmers in the form of unexplained interactions between crops and the animals that eat them (or refuse to eat them). There are the pigs that do not farrow (conceive) when they are fed on GM grain, the cows, elk and rats that refuse to eat it, the soya plants whose stems split open before the harvest, or that fall victim to pests that the farmers have never seen before, or that refuse to germinate, or that prove to be highly unstable in successive generations.[40] The studies which could show for

G

G

INTERESTING POTATOES
. . . and the scientific community

"After a pointless experiment that involved feeding rats with potatoes modified to produce a poison," writes *The Economist*, "parts of Europe developed mass hysteria."[41]

This *hyperbole refers to a careful 1998 experiment by Dr. Árpád Pusztai, which compared the effects of feeding rats identical quantities of a protein (not toxic to mammals) either by (a) genetically modifying the potatoes to produce the protein, or (b) adding the protein itself to the potatoes. The rats fed GM potatoes showed significant changes, notably increases in the mucosal thickness of the stomach and the crypt length of the intestines, indicating that the GM process itself has consequences which we know nothing about. Dr. Pusztai noted, "It is therefore imperative that the effects on the gut structure and metabolism of all other GM crops developed using similar techniques and genetic vectors should be thoroughly investigated before their release into the food chain."[42]

Dr. Pusztai's conclusions were comprehensively rubbished: "Most of the adverse comments on this *Lancet* paper," he writes, "were personal, non-peer-reviewed opinions and, as such, of limited scientific value."[43]

certain whether such effects are due to GMOs or to some other cause, and which could explain why they occur, have not yet been done; all that can be said for the time being is that these effects are linked by experienced observers to the presence of GM crops, and that they are indications that the technology has unintended consequences (see "Interesting Potatoes" sidebar).

6. *Oil and gas dependency*

GMOs are a development of industrial agriculture. They depend entirely on cheap energy for cultivation, fertilisers, pesticides and transport, and on consumers able to pay for them. When farming turns—as it will—towards more *locally-based, low-energy, *closed-loop, *organic systems, it will find a major barrier in its way in the form of land which was previously used by industrial agriculture and its GMOs. Indeed, when your starting point is profoundly impoverished soil, super-persistent weeds, and seeds which are able to grow true only with the help of chemicals which are no longer available, conversion could prove difficult, even impossible. The *land in question could be unable to contribute fully to *food production for many years.

7. *The death of *trust*

The companies that provide GM seeds and chemicals press their case with vigour. GMOs, as we have seen, move around, so if one farm in a region uses GM products, they will quickly establish themselves on other farms. The seed and chemical companies—notably Monsanto—are then able to claim that the farmers on whose land the modified crops have turned up are using the patented seed without a licence from the company. Farmers are told that they have an obligation to report any neighbours whom they suspected of using the company's products without a licence. The company then sees to it that any farmer who is reported in this way is drawn into a legal process involving costs and grief on a scale which may destroy the business. In this way, the seeds of suspicion and mistrust rip through the farming community.[44]

A disaster is usually an accident of nature or inattention. A comprehensive catastrophe is more likely to be traceable to a big idea—a *self-evident *ideology, awash with good intentions. And in the case of GMOs, there is an added fusion of unctuous platitudes about feeding the world, breathless claims about the need to be scientific, and addiction to an intoxicating new technology. The technology is viewed with an awe which has something in common with the primitive forms of response developed by cargo cults, which worshipped the hats of white colonists in the hope that—with the help of the hats— they too might grow rich and powerful. Writing in the context of a related field, the medical scientist David Horrobin tells us something about how it happened:

From the 1930s to the 1960s, biomedical science bore some resemblance to an integrated whole. There were researchers working at every level of biological organisation—from subcellular biochemistry, to whole cells, to organs, to animals, to humans. This was a golden age.

... But starting in the 1960s, molecular biologists and genomics specialists took over biomedical science. Everything was to be understood completely at the molecular genomic level. Everything was to be reduced to the genome. ... Now we have an almost wholly reductionist biomedical community which repeatedly makes exaggerated claims about how it is going to revolutionise medical treatment—and which repeatedly fails to achieve anything. ... The idea that genomics is going to make a major contribution to human health in the near future is laughable. But the tragedy is that the whole-organism biologists and clinicians who might have helped to unravel the complexity have almost all gone, destroyed by the reductionists.[45]

New technologies present scientists with an invitation to develop them as far as they will go. With respect to the applications of gene technology in clinical science, there is at least a case to be made for accepting it. In the context of agriculture, there is not. Food production, shortly to be devastated by *energy shortages, is beginning to develop its remaining option—*localisation. The promotion of an energy-intensive food technology, wholly dependent on remotely-produced industrial inputs (including seeds), and having to be backed by intensive research and development to deal with the new organisms and threats presented by the technology, is ill-advised. Simply stated: we ought to be building solutions for life after *oil; GMOs are working in the opposite direction.

The cost of *expertise in science can be high, producing minds which have learned to be brilliant, but have never learned to think. And now, in a further application of that *mindset, we have the potential for extension of the technology in the form of *GRIN, to fix the problems it causes. This is not a science which we can say with confidence is under control, for GMOs

are lining up such unintended consequences that the long march of *technical fixes has to continue. And so will the *unintended consequences. The convergent technology that follows will be extremely powerful. And then, since this is a dynamic equilibrium, it will be necessary to take the step after that. Science cannot tell us what that step will be.[46]

*Galley Skills, Reductionism, Food Prospects, Lean Food.

GIFTS. Assets transferred voluntarily and without payment. At first sight, "giving" seems to be straightforward: the giver confers the gift freely. And yet, there is in return an unspoken expectation—it cannot be explicit—that he will in due course receive something back. The give-and-take of mutual obligation is so inseparable from the idea of the gift that there turns out to be no such thing as the "free" gift. The very notion of giving implies—or at least affirms an expectation of—receiving. All gifts have strings attached; indeed, the word itself is full of ambiguity: "gift", with its *implication of an object or a service that is pleasant, also bears the implication of its opposite: *Gift* is the German word for poison; the Greek and Latin *dosis* has a similar subtext—a "dose" of something with an ambivalent propensity to kill or cure. And there is ambiguity, too, in the notion of a "given"—imposing a hard-edged reality which you have to accept, whether you like it or not.[47]

In other words, gifts cannot be taken at face value. They are instruments of social *cohesion, creating networks of exchange and obligation which are not provided by *market exchange, as Lewis Hyde notes:

> It is the cardinal difference between gift and commodity exchange that a gift establishes a feeling-bond between two people, while the sale of a commodity leaves no necessary connection. I go into a hardware store, pay the man for a hacksaw blade and walk out. I may never see him again. ... I just want a hacksaw blade. But a gift makes a connection.[48]

A gift affirms the intention of *good faith. The giver affirms that she is aware of the other person's interests; she is willing to take the trouble and to give the thought needed to promote them, and to put herself in the mind of the other—to empathise with her. The power of gift exchange is witnessed by the plainly-stated formula for peaceful living in a traditional society for whom war with neighbouring groups came all too naturally—the anthropologist Marshall Sahlins quotes a Bushman's insistence on the need to give:[49]

> The worst thing is not giving presents. If people do not like each other but one gives a gift, the other must accept it, and this brings a peace between them. We give what we have. That is the way we live together.[50]

In a pre-market society the gift-obligation is so powerful that—as the anthropologist Marcel Mauss explains in his classic, *The Gift*—the whole society can be seen as a *network of transfers affirming and holding in place the obligations between its members, not only within generations but between them (*Script). It can be seen as the bone structure of society. Mary Douglas summarises,

> The cycling gift system is the society.[51]

In the *Lean Economy, gifts could be all the more telling for their scarcity, with the *arts, handcrafts and *festival becoming the currency of *reciprocal obligation: there is a deeper sense of self-bestowal in a gift you have made than in one you have bought. But whatever the gift itself, it is necessary for someone to take the initiative, without immediate returns, and without being instructed to do so—that is, to take a risk, to make a commitment to the social order. There is a sense of extravagance here, and just a short distance further along in that direction is—or was—giving on a grander scale: sacrificial giving. What is that all about? In *Intentional Waste, the question is answered in terms of the *necessary elimination of growth *capital. But there is a deeper context, closer to the core meaning of "gifts" as relationship-builders, and concerning the join between gift and sacrifice.

Ancient societies intervened in the natural world; they depended on it and, to a significant degree mastered it. And yet, they received unexpected shocks from it; clearly, it had a life of its own; they therefore needed to establish some relationship, some reciprocity, with it. Although a key to establishing a *reciprocal relationship is to make a gift of some kind, and living relationships

depend on the exchange of gifts, a gift to nature is not as simple as, say, a gift to your aunt. If you give something to nature, it has to be destroyed—otherwise it is a loan: you can just go into the forest next morning and take it back. Therefore gifts to nature take the form of sacrifice, which may involve inviting others to join in eating it—an opportunity to combine *ritual with redistribution (a high-protein meal) among the group.

Indeed, eating meat in traditional societies is so powerfully linked to sacrifice—turning a meal into a celebration—that we may wonder to what extent meat eating without sacrifice was practised at all. Grace before meals, which lingers on in places even in our own *culture—offering up the food to God before promptly eating it—seems to have something of this ancient quality.

There is an engaging custom here, but the problem with it, of course, is that it can become routine. To be effective—that is, to not be mistaken for a mere formality—sacrifices must sometimes be *charismatic, generous on a scale that hurts. A particularly telling sacrificial gift, given that he was credited with divine powers, would be the king himself, and the question as to whether that involved eating kings is much debated. But a reluctance to let a king die of natural causes is understandable: his robust health was a symbol of the community's own health, so *sacrifice-and-succession was arranged while he was still reasonably young and vigorous. In fact, so many early societies came independently to the conclusion that their king would be the ideal gift to nature that kings did not usually last very long. A refinement of this principle came—no doubt with the encouragement of kings—in the idea of substituting the king's son; he would die on the king's behalf and, through him, for the whole people.[52]

Giving lives in a domain ranging from deep symbolism to basic *housekeeping. It is the *currency of the *small-scale *resilient *community. It is sometimes magic, in that some kinds of gift can be given over and over again without loss—love, for example, and (in a different sense, since time cannot really be replenished) the gift of reciprocal service to each other. The "reciprocal" part happens, but not by arrangement. This is the opposite of transparency: you cast your gift upon the waters, and what comes back is *trust.

GLOBALISATION. A brief *anomaly arising from cheap *transport and communications: the *modular structure of self-reliant, diverse *political economies breaks down into a scale-free *network of production, consumption and exchange, working to common principles and standards. The outcome is an unstable social order, without the firewalls and *diversity needed to prevent problems (and recoveries) sluicing throughout it without containment or limit.

This smoothed-out, deconstructed pathology is seen as a *virtue, and as the defining goal of the *competitive, commercial ideal. It has freed itself from the *bounded *cultures of an earlier time which, though not wholly independent, had maintained their own distinctive political and *economic orders, adapted to particular *places and changing conditions.

This short-lived model of *connectedness and incoherence will not outlive the conditions of cheap and abundant *energy on which it depends.

*Localisation, Lean Economics, Population, Resilience.

GOOD FAITH. The existence of four qualities in relationships between people:

1. Common *presence, justifying the use of the word "we".
2. *Conversation: consensus on the rules of *logic and veracity, even if frequently breached.
3. Common tolerance: a presumption that, even if its conclusions are unkind, the conversation itself will ring *true—that, at this foundational level in people's relationship with the earth and each other,

   alle shalle be wele, and alle maner of thing shalle be wele.[53]

4. Common *courtesy, enabling participants in a conversation to be heard.

*Bad Faith, Social Capital, Decency Fallacy.

GOOD SHEPHERD PARADOX, THE. The paradox of the shepherd that cares for his sheep, even at the risk of his own life, only to surrender them for slaughter in the end. This *paradox is one of the keys to an understanding of *natural systems. All natural ecologies contain paired properties which seem to be inconsistent but are in fact enabling characteristics: making and unmaking, my lunch and your undoing, your lunch and my undoing, extravagance and *efficiency, life and *death.
*Hunt.

GRAMMAR. The way a language works: the received principles which enable it to communicate meaning, colour and joy.

That, at least, is the meaning of grammar as applied to language. But *Lean Logic* uses it in an extended sense as one of the key implications and elements of *lean thinking. Lean thinking affirms that it is those who are actually engaged in a task who are better placed to decide on responses to events and shocks, and to invent *local solutions, than is a centralised authority remote from the detail; there is local freedom to think. But this requires that there should be consensus on what the task is: without that, local *freedom turns into something else—simply a situation in which everyone decides what they feel like doing today: there is nothing wrong with that, but it is not a way of accomplishing very much.

Grammar in this sense, then, is the set of rules in terms of which collective action takes place. It exists, for instance, in the form of the rules of a game: it is because there is a requirement to obey the rules (a lack of freedom to disobey them) that the game is possible; it is the frame of reference, the set of genes, forming the structure which enables a *system or a *culture to *emerge. And the *paradox is clear: it is because of the existence of the rules (constraining freedom) that it becomes possible to build a complex system/game/culture whose expression can mean a formidable improvement in the range of available *choices and meanings: freedom is much increased because it becomes possible to do things which would not have been available to participants if the freedom-constraining grammar had not been in place.

So lean grammar is the endowment within which a system operates, providing the frame of reference for local *freedom of *judgment. It is the set of principles which enable *community to *create* meaning, colour and joy.
*Intention, Manners.

GREEN. The colour of hope, and of the desire, in response to the grey and brutal surfaces of the industrial city, to recover, *protect, affirm, or just be reminded of, the natural world. Political parties which made this their main purpose adopted the name in the 1980s, but the idea, latent since mankind began to live in cities, has been intense since the early days of steam power. Here it is, extravagantly but sharply stated by John Ruskin, *reflecting on the question, "What have we done?"

> Gentlemen of England, if ever you would have your country breathe the pure breath of heaven again, and receive again a soul into her body, instead of rotting into a carcase, blown up in the belly with carbonic acid, you must think, and feel, for your England, as well as fight for her: you must teach her that all the true greatness she ever had, or can have, she won while her fields were green and her faces ruddy; and that greatness is still possible for Englishmen, even though the ground be not hollow under their feet, nor the sky black over their heads.
>
> The Crown of Wild Olive, 1873.[54]

*Green Economics.

GREEN AUTHORITARIANISM.
Environmental hazards are just the kind of threat—the enemy—which authoritarian regimes need. A main purpose of *Lean Logic* is to argue that there is another option: *lean thinking, which does not tell people what to do, but sets up a clear frame of reference which stimulates—*pulls along—the ingenuity and intelligence of people to develop their own responses. Green authoritarianism starts *innocently with sensible-sounding regulation, and then grows without limit: it has the advantage that it never has to be argued through because it short-circuits straight to the *begged question: "You have to do [whatever the government happens to want you to do today] in order to tackle climate change—and if you make trouble, you are clearly an enemy of the planet."

Green authoritarianism fails to activate citizens' *intelligence and motivation; it refuses to recognise the decisive significance of local detail; it discards the potential of *trust and *imagination; it does not understand *incentives; it presents environmental action in terms of adversarial politics, instruction and surveillance; it is committed to the impossible task of

protecting the *status quo*, rather than going along with the *creative evolution of the *Wheel of Life; it guarantees failure; it lacks *presence and it is bad *manners.

GREEN ECONOMICS.
The original—and still the core—intention of green economics is to achieve consistency between the environment and *economics. But agendas of various kinds and the opportunity provided for a broadly-based critique of economics have complicated matters, so green economics now comes in many forms. Here are three:

First, there is *internalisation*. This consists of ways of bringing environmental variables (such as emissions of carbon dioxide) into the *market—into the world of measurable value and exchange—by attaching prices to them (see *Economics ❭ #5).[55]

Secondly, there is the *liberal agenda*. Green economics is seen as a new context in which to argue for ideas which are already established as liberal objectives, such as gender studies, peace studies, animal rights, and social and environmental justice. Some interpretations of green economics include "critical theory"—that is, depictions of economics as a struggle; the struggle of people to release themselves from what is seen as the oppression of commerce and class, and the complicit role of literature and culture in collaborating with that oppression.[56]

A third strand of argument which could be included under the heading of green economics is *reconnection*, the view that the proper field of study is a *systems one, linking society, *culture, the environment and economics within a single frame of reference. According to this argument, the disconnection of economics from society, allowing the exchange mechanism to be studied on its own, may be briefly helpful as a learning exercise and may achieve short-term aims, but as a practice applied to the human *ecosystem as a whole over the long term, it fractures the *logic—it can *only* produce ludicrous results, and its position as the guiding principle of public policy is acutely destructive. Green economics exists as a service to the human ecology, not the other way round. Nothing to argue with there.[57]

For all that, it is reasonable to wonder whether green economics has invented a line of enquiry which economics has not already thought about. The place to look for an

G

answer to this is the output of green economics—that is, the studies and recommendations on what to do about the present convergence of *torments affecting *energy, *food, *climate, society, mind and *money. *The Green New Deal* is one, and it clearly sees itself as making a break from economics as it is normally taught and understood. Under the heading "A new well-being", it notes,

> The conflation of a growing economy with rising well-being in wealthy countries such as Britain has become a "given" in conventional economic theory and the minds of policy makers. To question it remains an economic heresy, punishable by excommunication from the company of the professional commentariat.[58]

Well, it depends what you mean by "excommunicated". As long ago as 1920 the economist A.C. Pigou, in his famous book, *The Economics of Welfare*, was clear about the limitations of money as a measure of welfare. In 1972, the Yale economists William Nordhaus and James Tobin, with the encouragement of the great Paul Samuelson himself, demonstrated the parting of the ways between *growth (GNP) and well-being, and produced an alternative measurement, "Net Economic Welfare", which has been in the textbooks ever since. Principles on which well-being and incomes can be distinguished have been explored exhaustively since then by economists such as E.J. Mishan, Mark Lutz, Kenneth Lux, Richard Easterlin, Fred Hirsch, Ed Diener and Amartya Sen.[59]

The chief weakness of such alternative measures (discussed in *Well-Being) is not that they are heretical, but that they are hard to measure, and the use of GNP is a fundamental direction-finder without which it would be impossible to make sense of the behaviour of the *market economy at all. There is indeed a powerful correlation between well-being and GNP, as is cruelly shown when a falling GNP leads to rising unemployment and its consequences, including shortened life expectancy, marriage break-up and an increased likelihood of suicide. You have to be a wealthy society not to view a growing GNP (and the stable economy it produces) with the utmost gratitude—which does not preclude recognising its flaws: its less-than-ideal correlation with well-being, and its imminent passing.[60]

And yet, the actual achievement of the new, fresh thinking that has been coming into economics is better than its rhetoric would have us believe. *A Green New Deal* gives the *energy problem (i.e., oil/gas/coal/*nuclear + *climate) the focus and urgency which it needs. You do not have to agree with its advocacy of carbon tax and its top-down regulatory approach, nor with its proposed financial reconstructions, to recognise the value of a contribution which integrates *economics and *ecology as single subject. And the urgency and accuracy of its rethinking of the electricity grid—"every building a power station"—and of the "carbon army" of new *skills, immediately deployed, are beyond challenge.[61]

In the same tradition we have studies such as *The Oil Crunch*, an authoritative and devastating survey of the coming oil peak, its consequences, and responses to it. And we have a stream of studies from sources such as the New Economics Foundation, which has covered such matters as microfinance, time banking, social investment, *debt relief, post office banking, community-development finance, and a "public benefit" model for social services, instead of the present (and inefficient) efficiency targets. And now we have the first of what is likely to be a stream of studies on how to live without economic *growth.[62]

Mainstream *economics has not in fact comprehensively neglected key ideas—as green economists tend to accuse—but green economics' recognition of economics as the means to well-defined personal and *local ends is new and significant, and its early contributions to the matter of how to live without growth do indeed represent a break from the mainstream on the most fundamental topic of all.[63]

*Lean Economics, Usury.

GRIM REALITY, THE FALLACY OF. The assumption that good things, such as *communities where people talk to each other and help each other, are either fantasy (when proposed for the future), or nostalgia (when described as the past). Grimness lends plausibility: if the effects of a proposed new regulation are grim and joyless enough, that is proof that it is really *necessary.

*Time Fallacies.

GRIN. The convergent technology, now being developed, comprising *Genetic modification, Robotics, Information technology and *Nanotechnology.

GROPE. To feel your way, with the alertness that comes in the pitch dark, undeterred by not knowing whether you are going to get there, or how, and emboldened by your *ignorance from having to face up to how hard it is going to be.
*Success.

GROUPS AND GROUP SIZES. The table opposite summarises the basic structure of groups and their corresponding reciprocities. For the detail see the entries for each of the five groups, and the entry for *Reciprocity and Cooperation.

GROWTH. There are two meanings relevant to *Lean Logic*:

1. The natural development of an immature *system or organism to maturity.
2. A pathology in which a mature system or organism continues to grow.

This entry is about the pathology, an affliction of *economics. The necessity for growth will be discussed in two distinct contexts - the intrinsic need for growth in a market economy; and the intrinsic need for growth in *all* large-scale economies:

The intrinsic need to grow in a *market economy

Our present *political economy depends on economic growth measured in terms of gross domestic product (GDP: for definitions see *Well-Being). The main driver is a relentless rise in *productivity: improvements in technology and in the use of labour make it possible to produce more goods and services (on average) per person employed. As the economist Moses Abramovitz writes, it is the possibility of discovering ways of improving productivity that gives meaning to the idea of the *"competitive business":

> It offers new firms a chance to carve out lucrative markets to the peril of old firms. And it impels existing firms to make large investment

in new products and process research and its application in an effort to enlarge or, at least, to protect the markets they have. The threat posed by the obsolescence of existing products and methods leaves them little choice.[64]

The labour released by these efficiency improvements can be re-employed to produce more of the same; or it could turn to the production of something different. Either way, the outcome (in equilibrium) will be growth. In the absence of that equilibrium—that is, if the labour were *not* re-employed in some way—unemployment would rise towards *hyperunemployment, eventually reaching a level at which maintaining any unemployment benefits would be impossible, since so few workers would exist to pay for them in taxes. The state would go bust and "no job" would mean "no income", which in a market economy can be lethal.

In fact, the market economy is in a *dynamic* equilibrium, like an aircraft or a bicycle: it is only able to maintain its stability if it moves forward. For an economy, "moving forward" means growth in GDP, which it has to sustain just to reabsorb the labour released by those advances in productivity. The economy will stall or topple if the needed forward motion is not sustained, and the critical rate of about 2–2½ percent annual growth is little changed since the economist Wynne Godley wrote about it in 1993:

> It cannot be too strongly emphasised that no recovery can be said to have begun until national production starts to grow faster than the economy's productive potential, that is by at least 2 to 2.5 percent per annum. Growth at any slower rate will not even bring the rise in unemployment to a halt, let alone turn it round.[65]

And it is *per capita* (per person) growth in GDP that matters, to re-absorb those troublesome advances in *per capita* productivity. Aggregate growth (i.e., a rise in total GDP), is of no value to the market economy, except in so far as it attends *per capita* growth.[66]

Rises in output/total GDP that are due to a growing population (e.g., from immigration) rather than to improvements in *per capita* productivity will of course increase the government's revenues from tax, giving it more to spend on the *intermediate economy—i.e.,

Groups and the *Reciprocal Cooperation Within Them

Group Name Preferred/Alternative	Group Size	Name for Type of Reciprocal Cooperation Preferred/Alternative	Nature of Reciprocal Cooperation[a]
1. *Small Group (a) Primary Group Up to about 5–6. Family; household group; supper table. (b) Sympathy Group Up to about 12–15. Extended family; close friends; gang.	The typical group gathering is 2–5. Five (or six) feels complete, but is small enough to sustain a single *conversation. Its members are drawn, at least in part, from a wider group of 12–15.	Direct engagement Group solidarity. Generalised reciprocity.[b]	Members provide services for each other without expectation of reciprocal exchange. Individuals' own interests are essentially the same as those of the group.
2. *Neighbourhood Precinct; compartment; (army) company; large group.	Collaboration among 150 active participants, if this comprises one from each family, forms a neighbourhood of around 500.	Collaboration Working together. Neighbourliness. A mixture of generalised and balanced reciprocity.	Community membership requires cooperation and services, but contributions vary. Since deals are never completely closed, they leave a benign, bonding, network of mutual obligation.
3. *Community (or) Parish Intentional community; village, or group of villages; the local landscape; town.	The upper limit to the scale of a community with small-scale *elegance, *judgment and *presence is about 5,000.	Balance Balanced reciprocity.[c]	When goods and services are supplied, this sets up an obligation which must be repaid (balanced). But these need not necessarily be money deals, nor the "best" deals: *gifts, cooperation on projects and delayed completion sustain a network of obligation.
4. *County	A group of communities, small enough to reflect local knowledge and represent local needs.	Exchange Negative reciprocity.[d]	Buyers and sellers go for the best deal, and deals are closed, with no obligation remaining. At the same time, the county is vital for networking, sharing ideas, and mutual aid between communities, including representation at national level.
5. *Nation	So long as they comprise a *modular *panarchy of groups of the *scale suggested in this table, the size of nations may vary widely.	Latency Negative reciprocity.	Although negative exchange exists at this level, interaction is mainly *cultural and *political. The nation affirms *identity and keeps the peace. There is potential for *encounters at national level to mature into any of the smaller-scale reciprocities.

a. The column on the nature of reciprocal cooperation is influenced by readings of Marshall Sahlins, "On the Sociology of Primitive Exchange", in Michael Banton, ed. (1965), The Relevance of Models for Social Anthropology; Marshall Sahlins, (1972), Stone Age Economics; and Manning Nash (1966), Primitive and Peasant Economic Systems.

b. "Generalised reciprocity": Sahlins, "On the Sociology of Primitive Exchange"; Sahlins (1972), pp 193–4.

c. "Balanced reciprocity": Sahlins (1972), pp 194–5.

d. "Negative reciprocity": Sahlins (1972), pp 195–6.

on infrastructures such as *transport, *waste disposal, *law and order, emergency services and administration. However, the demands made on these services will also be higher, owing to the larger population, so no one is better off, except perhaps some ministers who now find themselves with larger budgets, and the government, which can claim credit for a higher rate of growth, hoping that no one will notice that it is referring to the *irrelevance of aggregate growth, rather than the *per capita* growth which (in this context) is the only sort of growth that actually does anyone any good (see "Growth at all Costs" sidebar on page 184).[67]

GROWTH AT ALL COSTS
The Plan

The assumption that aggregate growth is a good thing in its own right has been influential—arguably the dominant frame of reference for economic management since the Second World War. It was the motivation for ambitious National Plans in the United Kingdom. The 1965 Plan, which adopted the aim of a 25 percent increase in national output between 1964 and 1970, tells us that "Productivity alone is not enough to achieve the 25 percent growth. There is a *manpower gap*, for which provision will be made by enhanced rates of recruitment of high-quality trained personnel from overseas, especially from the Commonwealth."[68]

It is sustained *per capita* growth, then, that is a *necessary condition for stability. It does not *necessarily* benefit *households themselves, because the proceeds may be removed as tax—*per capita* growth is the main source of funds for the welfare state (or for totalitarian regimes buying power, patronage, bureaucracy and arms). And yet, its absence, if significant in time and scale, would lead to rising unemployment and, eventually, to a breakdown of income flows of any kind to the unemployed. This inherent need for *per capita* growth will not go away—and yet, of course, it is impossible to sustain it in a finite world (unless we assume a decline in the *population at least as fast as the advance in productivity). It is certain that there are no *simple* answers to this—none that could be proposed without proposing at the same time a transformation in the whole of the way we think, work and order our lives.[69]

And yet, once that path of growth has been trodden, if only for a short distance, it is difficult, or impossible, to stop. There is positive/amplifying *feedback: growth leads on to growth at a compound rate, and this evidence of success allows the *myth of "permanent growth" to become established, leading to the concept of "sustainable growth" (often misrepresented as *sustainable development). However, any system which

grows beyond its mature state without limit will in due course crash. It may not know it, but it is in danger. And the more successful it has been in sustaining its development in this sense, the greater will be the crash.

This is the central problem of the market economy. If it does not sustain its growth, it will collapse, because unemployment will rise without limit, and both private incomes and public finances will fail. And yet, if it does sustain its growth, it will collapse even more dramatically, owing to the depletion of fuel and *materials, the breakdown of the soils, environment and *climate, the costs and *complications of its *intermediate economy, and the decay of *social capital. As soon as a society pulls free of its roots in *reciprocal obligation and the *culture in which it is embedded and moves forward into the market economy, it is marching towards collapse. It is then bound to keep marching as the only way to postpone the reckoning, but the more successful it is in sustaining growth, the greater the ultimate crash will be. In the language of *resilience, the shock is the "release" stage in the adaptive cycle (the *Wheel of Life).

It is no individual's fault. It is not due to greed, to rising aspirations, or to lenders wanting their money to grow (*Usury), although those may all jump on the rolling wagon of growth. Once growth has become established, it makes itself essential.

The intrinsic need for
growth in all *large-scale societies

Now, that is only half the story because, as it has been told so far, it applies only to the *market economy. In fact, all previous societies have gone through the processes of growth, both *per capita* (advances in the *productivity of labour) and aggregate (massive increases in *population). But it is only the market economy that is under *competitive pressure *both* to maintain the advances in productivity *and* to keep practically its whole workforce employed. We now need to look more closely at the *other* story of productivity advance and sustained growth, which is not about competitive pressures, but about other commitments which have applied to civic societies throughout history. So, we will start again with that (now familiar) improvement in the productivity of labour.

At its most basic level, this takes the form of simple increases in output—as in the case of Adam Smith's example of labour specialisation leading to increases in the output of pins and nails per person (*Intermediate Economy). And improvements in productivity can also come in other ways, such as increases in working hours (members of a *traditional society that are recruited into the labour force of a *civic society might increase their working hours from some two hours a day towards full-time work), or the development of equipment (pulleys were an early breakthrough), or in the organisation of work. All these are unequivocal improvements in labour productivity—and routes to growth.[70]

But now comes the catch—the question of what all this extra output is needed for? In essence, it is about building and maintaining the *intermediate economy—the *regrettable necessities which are required to support a large-scale civic society. Those intermediate goods and infrastructures are enabled to grow by improvements in productivity. Or, to put it the other way round, the increased output arising from productivity advances substantially feeds through to the support systems needed for a large-scale economy to exist.

The process of building these infrastructures is the process of *intensification. It builds the support systems needed by a large-scale system. And, owing to the diseconomies of *large scale, the support systems and the tissue of *connectedness which they weave increase *relative* to the size of the society for which they are needed. So (other things being equal), the larger the system, the larger the proportion of its total energy and output needed to build, and then to maintain, its own complicated *infrastructures. In other words, in terms of that ratio between the size of the support system and the size of the society, intensification is a process of increasing inefficiency.[71]

In summary: as intensification advances, individual output becomes more efficient and so more output per worker is *produced*. At the same time, the economy as a whole becomes less efficient, so more output per worker is *required*. The match between the growth in productivity and the growth in *regrettable necessities will of course vary from place to place. But civic societies consist largely of structures, services and practices which, owing to their *large-scale and *complicated form, they could not forgo without extreme

difficulty, or at all. What we have here is a ratchet effect: increased population and *per capita* productivity produce infrastructures on which the economy quickly comes to rely. Going into reverse—doing without those infrastructures—takes us into the territory of the almost impossible. It is the "almost" on which we need now to concentrate, making use of and—as far and fast as possible—expanding what little elbow-room we have.

Can growth be stopped?

Considerable thought has been given to the idea of halting growth but, first, there are some points to note about this:

1. *Zero-growth won't do*
   Calling a halt to growth will not be enough. The world economy is already well into overshoot (*Systems Thinking > Feedback > Time) and, if it is to avoid shocks which would destroy it, will need to shrink, rapidly and soon. That is, it will have to go into "degrowth".

2. *The taut market is designed to destroy inefficiency*
   Many past *civic societies have in fact made efforts—with varying success—to block further growth by setting limits to working time, by requiring producers to maintain intentionally inefficient practices, or by preventing the expansion of growth *capital by means of *intentional waste.
   But the *market economy does not do that: it depends on *taut, *competitive pricing to maximise efficiency (minimise the labour needed per unit of output) and has no *tradition or instinct for intentionally wasting either goods or potential productivity. That does not mean that the option of introducing *slack is impossible, but getting from here to there would not be an adjustment; it would be a radical transformation.

3. *Population changes are not an available instrument*
   As it faces the problem of excessive *scale and recognises the need to reduce it, the *democratic market economy understandably rules out a reduction in population as part of the solution. Very long-term demographic change due to (for instance) falling fertility rates are too slow-acting to be relevant to the rapid corrections that are needed and in prospect for

G

economic growth; indeed, most current projections foresee a rise in the global *population rather than a fall. Former societies did not have this problem, since their populations adjusted promptly to changes in the ability of their economies to support them (*Unlean). That is no role model for us, but it provides some insight as to why we find the problem of growth so hard to solve.[72]

4. *The scope for reducing output without increasing hardship is limited*

Here we encounter the ratchet effect. So many of the products of economic growth—the goods, services and *intermediate infrastructures it produces—are things genuinely needed to support a tolerably humane life in our giant civic society that it would present *households with substantial problems if a significant proportion of that production were reduced or eliminated as required by "degrowth".

Average-income households are not big spenders; they have little scope for pulling back their consumption. Nor is the opportunity for cuts in output to be found in forcing the super-rich to fire their butlers or to eat out less expansively. A relevant reduction in output would involve a massive transformation—a reversal of *intensification—of the support systems needed for a large-scale society, which have been established not in response to greed, but for the good reason that they were necessary (*Needs and Wants). In the absence of a strengthened *informal economy, it would have implications not just for the quality of life, but for life and death.

The *abstract assertion that we are all consuming too much and that we would be better off if we consumed less—despite its popularity in *green circles—will not do. There is indeed scope for consuming less and improving the quality of our lives at the same time, though the opportunity for doing so varies, but consistent reductions on a scale which are deep enough to make the difference that is needed would bring deep distress and hardship to households across a broad spectrum of income levels. Critics in the developed countries have benefited from growth all their lives, and may not all be completely aware of what the consequences

of a deep reduction in economic output would be. The Renaissance scholar Desiderius Erasmus made this point about advocates of war: "*Dulce bellum inexpertis*" [War is sweet to those who know it not].[73]

5. *The rising costs of labour-intensive services present a non-negotiable need for growth*

A substantial share of the intermediate economy consists of work that fundamentally relies on human input (labour), such as the social services. In a large market economy, this includes much work which former civic societies would not have done on a large scale, such as special *educational needs, long-term care and prisons. For reasons detailed in *Composition, the relative costs of such services (where people are hard to replace with automation) *rise* with advances in technology and economic growth, and so constantly need more revenue, which can only be provided by more growth.

There is a vicious problem here. As *productivity increases in other sectors and the economy grows (and intensifies), these services are more in demand and thus provision requires more revenue. This can only be found through further growth . . .

So, providers of such labour-intensive services (such as the government) need the rising income *provided by* growth to cover the rising costs which are *caused by* growth in the first place.

Such labour-intensive services are only part of the intermediate economy. But their cost rises relentlessly, relative to:

a. the declining cost of the typical basket of all goods—which is substantially set by years of advance in technology and process; and

b. wage levels—which are set with reference to the cost of that basket.

And the rising cost of such services is seen as a *further* reason for the necessity of growth. To any public sector accountant charged right now with paying for nurses, teachers, officials and soldiers, degrowth is out of the question.

6. *Growth will shortly be needing no encouragement to stop. And then go into reverse*

As oil production begins to decline from its peak, with or without the support of the other aspects of the *climacteric, it is likely that growth will falter, and turn into decline. We will wonder how we ever came to be talking about halting growth; it will be happening, faster than we might wish.

The task we face, therefore, is not the generality of "degrowth", but the detail of "deintensification". OK, it's a longer word, but it takes us to what we are actually trying to do. What has got us into this situation is centuries of *intensification, with its voracious use of natural assets to build the complicated and concentrated economy in which we now live. The road back is deintensification, in the form of reconfiguring those infrastructures to support its sequel—a much smaller-scale, *localised community, distributed as a *modular system, enabling its parts (*small groups, *households, *neighbourhoods . . .) to achieve the critical property of *elegance.

We have the advantage that much present-day science and technology lends itself to a *small-scale, *neotechnic order, which was not available in the early and middle stages of industrialisation. We cannot be sure, however, that in the future these technologies will be available.

The case for deintensification—getting improvements in efficiency by moving towards that modular order of highly-developed local *resilience—is robust. What is in doubt is how far it can be achieved from the starting point of today. *Lean Logic* is *sceptical as to whether an *intentional transformation on the needed scale is possible, arguing instead that what lies ahead is a *climacteric with numerous consequences affecting every aspect of our lives, including *population. But that is not a debate that needs to be settled, for two reasons:

First, the same set of objectives presents itself, whatever the prospects for the future, or the *expectation of *success. Our global *political economy—as is typical of a *complicated system in trouble—is busy responding to the problem by adding to it, frantically building *infrastructures or shoring them up, even though they are too large, too centralised and concentrated, too degraded and too overstretched to have anything more than a short expectation of life. As such, every effort should be made now to achieve the transformation—to *localise, reskill and rebuild *culture and *community, and to develop the *informal economy which is the

means by which households can meet substantial needs elegantly and directly. It produces goods and services without financial reward, for direct consumption by the people involved, and without dependence on growth or the infrastructures of intensification.

Secondly, the only way of knowing the extent to which the process of deintensification is possible is by trying it. One framework for doing so, at the local scale, is the *Energy Descent Action Plan (EDAP). Another—complementing the EDAP at the national scale—is *TEQs (Tradable Energy Quotas).

Can we look to reduced working time as at least part of the solution?

The question of how to achieve managed degrowth has been studied by several recent critics, and one much-discussed means to that end has been the idea of reduced working hours. Significant contributions on this topic have been made by Gerhard Bosch, Peter Victor, Tim Jackson and a joint report by Anna Coote, Jane Franklin and Andrew Simms.

Bosch considers some of the conditions that would have to be in place to make a reduction in working time possible. He argues that the option of shorter working hours will not be taken up unless people can afford it, and that this in turn will call for high levels of productivity, with training to make it happen, and wages to match. He also emphasises the need for flexible hours.[74]

Victor's discussion of the case for shorter working time emphasises the need to ensure that those whose income already leaves them close to the poverty line do not find it reduced yet further. He notes that effective action would at the same time be needed to protect the environment, along with taxation and *incentives to reduce the flow of fuels and materials and to conserve capital assets. Efficiency improvements would be directed to the conservation of *energy and *materials, rather than to raising output. Action would need to be taken to limit international trade to the central task of meeting a *nation's needs, rather than making money from each nation's comparative advantage. Victor recognises that measures like this would present problems for nations (first movers) that implemented them while others did not, and that solutions would require them to live simply. He cites Henry David Thoreau's *Walden*, and E.F. Schumacher's

G

Small is Beautiful as inspirations for the prospect of "voluntary simplicity", which would open up the possibility of getting by on the reduced consumption.[75]

Jackson writes that reduced working time would need to be in the context of reduced inequality and strong *social capital, developed in *resilient communities, and he suggests that we can look to the *Transition movement for inspiration. Changes in working time would require profound changes in the present direction of travel, away from the culture of consumerism, and Jackson wonders whether, and in what senses, it would mean the end of capitalism. He settles on three key practical policies to reduce growth:

1. a greater emphasis on service-based activities, with less demand for—and more conservation of—*material goods;
2. increased investment in ecological assets which should be recognised as a form of *capital—yielding a flow of value, and
3. the reduced working time policy itself.

His answer to the question of whether this would still be capitalism is ambiguous: there would be more public and employee ownership, and there would be less focus on the return on financial assets, since it would be environmental assets that would be the focus of economics in this sharply different, zero-growth form. This would not be a society which saw its aims in terms of ever-increasing consumption, nor its worth in terms of financial capital.[76]

Coote *et al*'s analysis is tightly focused, in that it is based on a steep reduction to the 21-hour week; it is also comprehensive, in that it outlines many of the arguments both for and against a much shorter working week, the reactions to such a change, safeguards to deal with the problems it would raise, and steps towards achieving it. They argue that it would improve the quality of lives in the economy we have now by giving us more time at home with *family and *community, as well as reducing stress and improving relations between the genders. They suggest that (in the light of the experience that already exists of a three-day week), it could also improve the *productivity with which we use the time we spend at work. It would make it easier to contemplate a shift in the focus of our working lives from the formal economy

of paid work, to the *informal "core" economy of working directly for ourselves and families.[77]

These contributions are valuable and groundbreaking, but they do invite some observations, three especially:

First, an imposed shorter working week would be difficult to enforce in the context of the *taut *market economy, and would tend to quickly snap back to full-time work (*Leisure). It would also be hard to distinguish between formal work (e.g., working in the horticulture industry) and informal work (e.g., growing vegetables for family and friends).

Secondly, what sort of shorter working week are we talking about? There are two kinds:

One is where it goes with a rise in hourly rates, so that incomes remain unchanged. The other is where hourly rates remain unchanged, so that weekly wages—incomes—reduce in step with the fall in working time. Coote *et al* give us a hint of what is in their minds about this:

> If hours are to be reduced incrementally . . . over, say, 15 years, it may still be possible to increase hourly rates gradually during that time to offset, at least partially, the effect on total earnings.[78]

So pay rates rise to compensate, leaving take-home pay unchanged. Companies' labour costs remain constant, but their output goes down. Unless all other producers in the market do the same, or watertight tariff barriers are established, what happens next is that producers who shorten their working week are priced out of business; their workers become unemployed. You might try it with a large non-competitive organisation like a National Health Service, but then the cost has to be paid by tax, so this, too, leads—via reduced demand and high costs—to unemployment.[79]

Or what about the alternative version, where a shorter working week leads to a *pro rata* reduction in pay? This, too, would be unstable, with workers strongly motivated, for reasons of income, to get back from their reduced hours to a full working week (*Leisure).

Thirdly, there is the problem that we have come to depend on what the economy produces. A 40% reduction in working hours (from 35 to 21 per week) would, realistically, mean a 40% reduction in incomes, and that—even if mitigated by redistribution—would have consequences in terms of both *living standards and *politics which would make it unlikely to happen. As discussed above, it carries no weight to assert that in this consumerist society we consume too much anyway. Indeed, it is hard to make sense of this at all without a firm basis in that key concept of *intensification. We are all at present stuck with, and dependent on, the shared cost of maintaining a giant, intensely *complicated *civic society, and if that commitment is not met, we are in trouble. The case for voluntary simplicity, with the example of Henry David Thoreau, who lived by a pond, does not accurately reflect the detail of the lives of households on middle or lower income in twenty-first century cities.

In short, the use of the shorter working week as a *means* of achieving degrowth is back-to-front. This would be an *outcome* of success, and it is some way down the line: there is a lot of genius to be accomplished first.

What deintensification requires is a rebuilding of the *diverse *informal economy of communal self-reliance—growth of the "core economy", as Edgar Cahn and Coote *et al* call it.[80] The first steps to making that work are consistent with a full working week, or minimal reductions in it. A helpful start would be widely-established flexible working time—ready agreement that employees should be able to negotiate shorter working hours if they want to, so that the building of the informal economy can be accomplished *incrementally. But the motivation to gear-up the informal economy to delivering more must be in place from the outset—otherwise, extra hours of enforced *leisure will be experienced as authoritarian control, and as an incentive to bust the system.

And, remember, too (as introduced briefly above), that the shorter working week is only one of the many ways in which an economy can work towards a reduction in the scale of its output—towards developing the *slack economy. Other ways include the use of intentionally-inefficient technologies (such as handcraft for tasks that could be done by machine) and of processes that minimise environmental impact—or have a *positive* environmental impact. On the same principle, local *materials that require substantially more work could be used instead of imported materials. Or labour could be absorbed in projects involving *intentional waste, such as *carnival. Or there could be positive, deliberate teaching of the art of idleness, with the focus on the *arts, and life as a citizen rather than as a professional.[81]

It may well be that life in the Lean Economy will be very busy and stretched indeed—at this stage there is no reason really to have confidence that the prospects ahead will be a leisure-rich *utopia (who knows?). Either way, building local informal economies is the priority—but *if* we are thinking about ways of turning growth round from positive, to zero, to negative, and *if* the shorter working week is the method that is being considered, we should also be aware that quite a range of other growth-killing options is available.

The heart of the matter is this. If the motivation and opportunity exist, and if the objective of building the informal economy—deintensifying—is established first, the incrementally-shortening working week would naturally flow from this, as a sign that we were getting things right.

Conclusions on growth

The task then, is not properly specified in terms such as the degrowth of the *market economy. It is about growth of the *informal economy, its sequel. It is not about wrestling with the controls of economics to force it in the direction of degrowth, but about getting ready for the moment when the coming *climacteric does the heavy work of degrowth for us; when the goods, materials, food and services—whose life-preserving growth has caused so much guilt—turn out to not be there.[82] The informal economy that must take over is still tragically weak. Its development is intensely urgent. Degrowth will come on us all too quickly.

If deintensification were achieved on the needed scale, and in the available time, without a correspondingly steep descent in *population, this would, on the available evidence, be the first time in history, but it is the right aim, and there is no downside; if it is not achieved, we face the prospect of an unmitigated crash in the economy and the population alike.

We have inherited a system that depends on growth. That growth will end, by accident or design, and soon. Probably, growth will go into reverse, without the need for assistance, and more decisively than any zero- or negative-growth programme could accomplish. Whatever the cause, the system that develops without it will not be a revision of what we have now. It will be a complete rewrite.

*Lean Economy, Dual Economy, Debt, Entropy.

H

HAREBRAIN FRACTURE. A condition in which the victim has become *disconnected from reality but is able to persuade herself and others by the *fluency of her delivery.

*Irrelevance, Virtual Crowd.

HARMLESS LUNATIC. A person whose interpretation of a problem is radically different from the received view, and who therefore lives in a storm of ridicule and contempt before turning out to be right. Oh, all right— not all harmless lunatics do turn out to be right, not all lunatics turn out to be harmless, and not all harmless people are lunatics, but the record of dissidents in thinking afresh about problems, and developing solutions despite *expert scorn, is impressive. In the cooler language of the research monograph, summarising its results,

> Local-level institutions learn and develop
> the capability to respond to environmental
> feedbacks faster than do centralised agencies.[1]

Lean Logic was introduced to harmless lunatics by the historian Joan Thirsk, describing the *local wisdom and inventive contributions made by farmers at times of *agricultural change.[2] They exist at sea too. Among the different varieties of fishermen earning a living from catching cod in the North Atlantic were some who worked on a *small scale. Most of the cod were caught by large, refrigerated trawlers that spent weeks at sea, were able to fish through pack ice, used the most advanced equipment to locate the cod and to handle smaller-sized fish, and were owned by companies with boards of directors and pension schemes. The inshore fishermen, by contrast, used small boats with crews of self-employed labour, and they were out and back

in a couple of days or less. They couldn't afford the high-tech equipment, but they didn't need to because the skipper knew what he was about. He had probably learned it from his father.[3]

Starting in the 1970s, the inshore fishermen noticed that something odd was happening; the migration patterns and numbers of cod were changing, and both the ages of the fish caught and the size of inshore catches were falling. They reported on this to the Canadian authorities, but their concerns were dismissed as anecdotal. Eventually, they themselves commissioned a report which was published in 1986, showing that the estimates prepared by the official body (Canada's Department of Fisheries and Oceans) were overstating stocks by up to three times the reality. This led in due course to two official reports being commissioned, one of which, published in 1990, led to action. But by that time, the cod was poised for collapse. A moratorium—simply a recognition that the cod had gone—was imposed in 1993.

Why were the officials so reluctant to take any notice of the local knowledge of the inshore fishermen? The study that was commissioned after the event pointed to three errors in the science on which the officials relied:

- They treated the entire stock as a single unit, whereas it actually comprised distinct populations with different patterns of migration.
- They measured the survival of cod of different ages as an average of wide fluctuations, whereas it is the fluctuations themselves that supply the needed data—the averaging-out wipes the model clean of the useful information.
- They relied on measurements taken over a short period, which proved to be untypical.

But the politics were significant, too:

- Perhaps the scientists *did* know what was happening, but were not allowed to say anything because it would have meant problems for the management.
- The responsible authority was a bureaucracy, and bureaucracies are naturally defensive.
- The task of fisheries management calls for the skill of working alongside independent-minded people like inshore fishing communities, and there is no recognised discipline for doing this.

- Scientists' communications with policy-makers tend to be poor in any case, with the scientists feeling under pressure to moderate bad news in order to avoid being frozen out: the theory is that it is better (when a sharp warning is needed) to be heard merely sounding a note of caution than not be heard at all.[4]

But whatever the reason, the lifetime *wisdom of the informal, inshore fishermen was dismissed until too late. Life-saving information tends to come in local dialects.

The difficulties faced by dissident views in the face of established scientific orthodoxy were described by Thomas Kuhn in 1962. Science, he argued, is developed in consistent frameworks within which there is a high degree of consensus; the problem is that discussion within those frameworks is, at least in part, circular and mutually-reinforcing. Dissidence is rejected; in a sense it is inaudible. Sometimes something happens: new ideas break through and become established, causing a *paradigm shift, but until that breakthrough happens, the dissidents have to cope with ridicule, stalled careers, even death threats, especially if they are whistle-blowers whose work has implications for an established industry.[5]

But being in the minority doesn't make you wrong—as the Russian thinker Alexander Herzen (1812–1870) observes:

> Is a man less right merely because no one agrees with him? Does the mind stand in need of any other warrant than that of the mind? And how can universal insanity refute personal conviction?[6]

The small-scale local detail of an *ecosystem responding to a particular mix of species, soil, ocean currents, *climate and management is below the horizon of the scientific model. The implication is not that, one day, models will be made big enough to take account of all the *anomalies, but that local detailed observation is intrinsically different from the data supplied by a model. By the time a person has observed a particular (but apparently insignificant) pattern, lived in the *place long enough to think about it, and learned enough from local *traditions to make his own original contribution, he is getting close to an accurate and sufficient interpretation. It is extreme observation that matters. But,

from the point of view of the scientific model and the coordinated policy, all the local observer of detail has to offer is anecdote.

We are living at present under a paradigm of paradigms—the presumption that, should one paradigm be eventually defeated, another will take its place. In the future, that metaparadigm will make way for the appreciation of a different kind of understanding: when it has had its day, ordinary knowledge will take its place, in all modesty, in long observation of local detail and local experience. Here is the sustained *reflection of the harmless lunatic, walking in the garden in the cool of the evening, engaged, self-reliant, peculiar to the place, alert. *Sunk Cost Fallacy.

HARMONIC ORDER. The seeming untidiness of a *resilient system which has been allowed to develop *diverse and appropriate responses to local detail.

Small groups do not need orderly structures of organisation with a manager at the top. Larger groups do—unless they are subdivided into *small groups or *holons working to a *common purpose and building up their own competence.

One of the reasons why managing a large organisation is difficult is that it is hard to see what is going on. Managements therefore turn to the next best thing, which is summary data. Statistics make work visible. The result is that managements can seem to be remarkably well-informed. Unfortunately, it tends to be about the wrong things. The focus is on such measures as . . .

- Volume . . .
  This is the obvious statistic: the *number of boxes going out the door, the number of cabbages produced, patients treated, A-grades awarded:

  > When I arrive in a service center, I generally find managers know everything about volumes and activity, but little or nothing about the real nature of work. . . . I have yet to find a British government-inspired specification that is based on knowledge. They are all based on opinion. The implementation of these opinions makes performance worse, not better.
  >
  > *John Seddon (management consultant),* Freedom from Command and Control, *2003.*[7]

H

H

- Budgets . . .

These are well-defended by the *Slippery Slope, aggressively applied: "Are you telling me that you don't need a budget?"

> There was a shift in culture and priorities in the MoD [Ministry of Defence] towards "business" and financial targets, at the expense of functional values such as safety and airworthiness.
>
> *Charles Haddon-Cave, QC,*
> *presenting the conclusions of the inquiry into the*
> *Royal Air Force (RAF) Nimrod air crash, 2009.[8]*

> In the days of the RAF chief engineer in the 1990s, you had to be on top of airworthiness. By 2004 you had to be on top of your budget if you wanted to get ahead.
>
> *A former RAF officer,*
> *giving evidence to the same inquiry.[9]*

- Text . . .

Here *imagination and the critical practice of learning as you go are ruled out by the controlling presence of the written report:

> It is telling that, almost without exception, whenever we have applied for funding from statutory agencies, we have felt there to be no interest or desire to get really involved and connected; no thought of getting properly engaged and forging a relationship with us and our community. It has all been about the written word.
>
> *Andrew Mawson,* The Social Entrepreneur.[10]

- Standardisation . . .

The 1870 Education Act in Britain established the new Boards of Education, which in turn set up state-funded primary schools, ending the comprehensive and *diverse system of paid-for and charitably-funded schools that already existed. One of the inspectors of the new schools in Lambeth observed what happened . . .[11]

> A consequence of this reform which is clearly to be regretted is the disappearance of different and interesting types of school, adapted to the varied social requirements and religious convictions of different classes.[12]

- Control . . .

The 1943 Labour Party report which exposed the failures of health provision in the United Kingdom thought the existing health services looked disorderly. It found no problems of waiting lists, quality, hygiene, innovation, staffing or management, and it recognised the role of health insurance and of arrangements which assured access to treatment whether the patent could pay for it or not. What it did find, and deplored, however, was (to let the paper speak for itself):

- No one is in a position to make or direct a coherent plan of health services for the nation as a whole;
- It does not allow the Ministry of Health to exercise a control wide enough to ensure an energetic, comprehensive, National Service for Health;
- The general public lacks the knowledge for appraising the quality of [the general practitioner's] service and his efficiency is not in fact subject to an adequate public control. If he has a manner which ingratiates him with his clients, he can retain and even increase his practice, even though his technical competence may be very low;
- The agencies dealing with maternity in London are numerous and uncoordinated;
- The hospital system is an unplanned medley of public and voluntary institutions, without any unified control, in contrast with the army:
- Just as the Ministry of War directs the strategic placing of the Home Forces for defence against invasion, so this Central Authority should be able to plan the strategic disposition of the nation's defences against ill-health.[13]

Yes, it seems to have been something to do with control. Diversity—a *flow of hands-on originality, combined with universal access to a *resilient, self-regulating *system—was not to be tolerated, for top-down colonising government distrusts decentralised *incremental achievement. Diversity must be destroyed. Order must be imposed. Fortunately, we have Dr. Max Gammon on hand to explain to us why this is a mistake:

It is of the first importance not to confuse bureaucracy with orderly administration. The difference between *ordered* (in the sense of according to the compulsion of commands), and *orderly* (in the sense of according to harmonic order) is crucial here.[14]

What is lacking in all these perspectives is the essential asset of *presence—of engaging with actual circumstances and objectives, rather than imposing some other set of preoccupations. Presence does not require; it evolves; it moves by incremental advance in response to real events; it does not impose top-down order; it learns, it discovers and tests as it goes. Its accomplishment, Gammon continues, is harmonic order—where . . .

> . . . continuous *ad hoc* procedural adjustments are made on personal initiative rather than imposed by remote directive. If successful, these local adjustments are likely to be more generally adopted. If unsuccessful, they are usually eliminated without widespread damage. The efficient non-bureaucratic organisation has a Darwinian internal economy involving a process of natural selection and survival of the fittest procedures. . . . An essential component— the motor—of such systems is the dependence of their survival on their performance.[15]

From the top-down perspective, harmonic order is an incoherent, unplanned, uncontrolled, uncoordinated medley, lacking unified control. It dismays those unfamiliar with it. It is open to surprise. It makes space for the competent. It copes with detail. It is rooted in *trust. It is balanced by *humour. It is guided by *intention.

*Commons, Presence, Anarchism.

HEALTH. See Lean Health.

HIERARCHY. A model of systems design, in which the parts of a system are grouped together into *holons (aka subassemblies), and those holons are in turn grouped, and so on upwards in a hierarchy of increasing complexity. Each holon comprises a hierarchy of smaller holons; and each holon itself exists within a larger hierarchy.

The problem with that understanding of the intimate connections of parts and wholes within a *system is that—if taken too literally—it is too neat. *Ecosystems are irregular and *complex, with many hierarchies overlapping in space, time and function, so they are better known as "panarchies", implying a *harmonic order and the rule of many. For more detail on panarchies and the interactions within and between them, see *Systems Thinking ❭ Form ❭ Holons and Hierarchy.[16] *Scale.

HIGH GROUND, THE FALLACY OF THE. This is the simple tactic (a *distraction) of insisting that the argument is very much more serious, with much greater moral substance or urgency, than the other person appears to think, and that to continue with his line of argument would therefore not only be wrong but also irresponsible. It may, truly, be *necessary to point out the urgency of a problem, but that is only the context for the argument; it should not be allowed to usurp the argument itself. Example: "Get real, we're talking about total collapse of *energy → we have to develop *nuclear power" (*or* ". . . *food supplies → *biotechnology"). An emergency, real or manufactured, can be used as an excuse for claiming the high ground over practically everything. The 1933 Reichstag fire provides a demonstration of this *fallacy in action.[17] *Pharisee, Expertise, Indignation.

HIPPOPOTAMUS. A symbol of the limits to the ability of argument to make sense of things, in the presence of the big facts of nature. The hippopotamus in this sense comes from the Book of Job in which, after a lot of argument, God speaks from the whirlwind and draws the chattering intellectuals' attention to the facts of nature, heavy with energy and *charisma: the lion, the thunder, Orion's Belt, the whale who makes the sea boil, and the battle horse who, having swallowed the ground with fierceness and rage, "saith among the trumpets, Ha, ha; and he smelleth the battle afar off, the thunder of the captains, and the shouting." But even this show is stolen by God's invitation to "Behold the Behemoth". Scholars are undecided as to whether this is a hippopotamus or an elephant. Anyway, it is big, its bones are like iron, it can drink a river, and it cuts short overlong debate, living proof of David Hume's observation that "Nature will always maintain her rights, and prevail in the end over any abstract reasoning whatsoever."[18]

These are hard times for a civilisation that has long been, or felt, in control of the whole of itself and its environment, and which can choose what it means by justice. The possibility that transformations in our *ethical standards may be forced on us is shocking. But the whirlwind which is now approaching seems to be asking us something: "Who is this that darkeneth counsel by words without knowledge?" At this point, the best thing to do is to behold the hippopotamus.[19]

*Ironic Space, Reflection, Metamorphosis.

HOLISM. The art—in contrast with *reductionism—of seeing a *complex system as a whole. Holism knows the limits to its understanding; it acknowledges that the *system has its wildness, its privacy, its own reasons, its defences against invasive explanation. It does not approach systems with crafted *innocence and call it evidence-based science. It does not pretend to understand the whole school just on the evidence of dissecting the geography teacher. It is not embarrassed by the application of *judgment.[20]

But holism can lead the way into *fallacies. First, it can be misconstrued as a mandate for top-down control, without regard for detail and for the system's structure of parts and subassemblies. For example, it is sometimes argued that an appropriate model for a carbon *rationing system would be a global system in which people trade worldwide within a single carbon budget. On the contrary, such a system would require well-developed subsystems (e.g., at the level of the *nation and below) to manage their own rationing schemes adapted to *local circumstances, but within the wider global framework. As the *System Scale Rule has it: large-scale problems do not require large-scale solutions; they require small-scale solutions within a large-scale framework.

Secondly, holism is sometimes reduced to a brief and benign glance at the surface, rather than persistent

and deep engagement with a system, including some painstaking understanding of at least some of its parts. Without that, you are not being "holistic"; you are flattering your *intuition with powers of insight which you may not have fully earned.

Despite the risks, holism is a key ethic. It is both *lean thinking and *systems thinking, but it can make a claim to be more than either. To *encounter the connections between the particular matter before you today and all other matters is to get close to the quality of *Tao—the Way which connects us to the logic of our existence.[21] It is an *ethic which we cannot *define, but which we can explore, though it is uphill work.

> On a huge hill,
> Cragged and steep, Truth stands, and he that will
> Reach her, about must and about must go,
> And what th' hill's suddenness resists, win so.
>
> *John Donne, Satire III, c.1593.*[22]

*Division Fallacy, Systems Thinking.

HOLON. A part, or subsystem, or subassembly, of a system. Every system consists of holons.

Other names—orgs, integrons—have been suggested for them; holon is the name coined by Arthur Koestler. It comes from the Greek *holos* (whole), with the suffix -on (as in neutron), which suggests particle or part.[23]

Local *communities are holons within the wider system of society, for example, and the *modularity which underpins recovery-elastic *resilience comprises diverse, independent holons. Holons have the characteristic property of "facing both ways": they are complete in themselves and have substantial powers to maintain their own health and integrity; at the same time, they are part of a wider system, depending on it and participating in it.

Whole-systems-thinking is an undoubted *virtue, but if it does not at the same time recognise the distinctive properties and needs of the parts, then it is as bad as *reductionism. *Systems-thinking depends, as a first step, on recognising the robust, semi-independent, *small-scale competence that is distributed throughout a *complex system, and on having a name for it.[24]

These subsystems within larger systems build up in complex and untidy *hierarchies, from the smallest *scale up to the scale of the system as a whole. That system might be a person, *household, *neighbourhood or *community; or the complex *panarchy of a woodland *ecosystem; or the established *skills and *practices that were brought together by medieval builders to build a church.

The architect Christopher Alexander, a hero of *lean thinking (though he doesn't call it that), applies this distributed, holonic structure as a fundamental principle of design. He believes that people know more about what they want and need in the *place they live in than architects do, and that if they are given the basic principles of good design in the form of what he calls a "pattern language", then they can use it to design forms which work for them.[25] These principles—or subsystems, or holons—are the words and *grammar of the pattern language; as Alexander writes,

We may picture the process of form-making as the action of a series of subsystems, all interlinked, yet sufficiently free of one another to adjust independently.[26]

. . . and if after that we still need a concise definition of holon, we have, from Elinor Ostrom,

a nested, whole-part unit of analysis.[27]

If the subsystems are well-established and in equilibrium, they can fit together to create designed forms which (as Alexander writes) are "unselfconscious", in that the designer does not have to invent the details and building blocks; instead, she uses elements that are tried and proven. And yet, conservative though it sounds, holons themselves are a setting for *incremental evolution: if one of the holons changes—it might improve significantly or it might be damaged or become unavailable—then there is a process of adjustment whereby the other holons in the system adapt until, by trial and error, they settle down into a new equilibrium. Equally, if the design as a whole advances or changes in some substantial way, it may be necessary only for one of more of the holons to adjust to enable it to happen.[28]

This idea of the holons within a wider system changing in order to take the pressure off the system as a whole is intrinsic to resilience and *lean thinking. The system is resilient because the holons' responses to shocks conserve the larger equilibrium; it is lean because there is the possibility of flexible responses and inventiveness deep down in the *hierarchy of the system. In the entry on *Tradition we see how a *culture is sustained by incremental change to small parts of itself, and the adaptive cycle of the *Wheel of Life shows how this deep-level flexibility is the enabling condition for the survival of a complex system.

If it is to benefit from such *resilience, then, a system has to maintain—or restore—significant freedom for its holons, by whatever means. It is not a case of "power to the people", because the people may be so uprooted that they lack a holonic structure of their own. Rather it is "power to the nested whole-part structure of household-neighbourhood-community . . .". As a rallying cry, that might take some time to catch on, but then rebuilding the *harmonic order of proven holons in a *complex system is always a slow process.

HOME. Home is the *household where you feel you belong.

The household is by far the most productive part of our *political economy. It makes people. It teaches near-perfect grasp of a language. It creates and makes in us the essential skills of *conversation, listening, looking at the person who is talking to you; it transmits *humour, *loyalty, love, *manners, *reciprocity; it builds confidence and *identity; it enables its members to discover which sex they are; given a chance, it arranges its own *food, cooks it, serves it up and sustains a conversation while it is eaten; it is a library and reading room, a first aid centre, a support service for the new-born, and a source of comfort for the elderly and dying. For its friends, it is a provider of food and drink, comfort and conversation, bed and breakfast. It is the building block from which society is made. It is self-regulating and self-sustaining; it provides its services free, and renews membership indefinitely.

And it has a past. There was an ideal of the household supported by an accustomed, ceremonious sense of good humour and continuity, which would bear the hope of quiet days, fair issue, and long life. Ben Johnson paid tribute to the "high huswifery" and "the mysteries

of manners, armes and arts" at Penshurst Place; Andrew Marvell reflected on Appleton House—"that dear and happy isle"; and the idea of the gentleman, with "a full appetite of fame by just and generous actions [but] an equal contempt of it by any servile expedients" reflected the domestic values enjoyed by the early seventeenth century circle which gathered regularly at Great Tew to think about them. It is the locus of happiness, thy fortress and thy ease. As Lionel Trilling writes, "The hope that animates this is the almost shockingly elementary one [which] has to do with good harvests and full barns and qualities of affluent decorum."[29]

This was not just an upper class conceit; William Cobbett's recipe for happiness for the labouring classes of his day was focused on sound economic management of the household, and H.J. Massingham writes of an English village at the start of the twentieth century,

> For both yeoman and master-craftsman, the
> holding of property was the guarantee of
> economic freedom and a dutiful right. Home,
> as the centre alike of the family and of industry
> and the nucleus of neighbourliness, was the
> ruling concept for them both.[30]

For the *market economy, however, the household, and the home it becomes if you feel you belong there, is not all that important. Its virtues fade into insignificance in comparison with the personal fulfilment that lies ahead on the journey to work and equality targets outside the home. The unpaid, *informal work done at home contributes nothing measurable to Gross Domestic Product and makes it invisible to a society with eyes only for *money. Individualism and *ideology have abandoned the home as obsolete. The post-war story has been a long goodbye, leaving home to those whose *competitive aspirations have come to little.

Many households are still in good heart; some are less so (see "Not Coping" sidebar); overall, this sector of the economy is in a state of decay. Its declining—or, in some cases, extinguished—ability to provide any of the services noted above deprives the rest of the state of the enabling capability it needs, leaving it with the task of picking up the pieces as households break down. But that's now. When there is no longer an office to travel to, when the brief interlude of full

NOT COPING
The social worker's tale

Violence, drugs, chaos: that's what I deal with every day. I can't take children into care for that. There's not the space for them. There's so many families like that, I don't think the public has any idea.

I go into houses and they don't live like we'd live. There can be dog faeces all over the floor, and beer cans, and so much rubbish that there's only a narrow path from the front door to the kitchen. There might be a lot of swearing and aggression, and the children are missing school, and no one works. But it's not my job to make value judgments on how adults live their lives. We're not allowed to do that.

Our only concern is whether the children are at substantial risk of harm, and that's the criterion we use to ask them to change. And they're often a bit sullen, but next time you go there's a bit less muck on the floor, and the kids are in school half the week, and the health visitor's been, and you think things are getting better. You hope it is, because the pressure's on you to keep that family together. Then a couple of months later it's all gone back again, and the kid might be in a bit of trouble with the police—but it's hard to tell when that all crosses the line and when you should be thinking, "Hang on, this really isn't working and the children shouldn't be here".

A social worker talks about her clients in South Yorkshire, England.[31]

employment in a confident *growth-fed *civic society no longer—looking back—seems to be a good basis on which to build our understanding of what interpersonal *ethics and fulfilment is all about, some revisions to the evaluation of households and their *community habitat will be needed.

The social order of the future will be built up from its households. As its *small groups, they will be the *holons from which the *Lean Economy is made. They will transmit the core *cultural, social and *practical *skills which enable people to live with each other in love and *cooperation. *Household production will be the key enabling property for local self-reliance.

And yet, we cannot quite leave it there—for, surely, our home is nature itself? William Hazlitt sorts this out for us:

> Thus Nature is a kind of universal home, and every object it presents to us an old acquaintance with unaltered looks. . . . For there is that consent and mutual harmony among all her works, one undivided spirit pervading them throughout, that, if we have once knit ourselves in hearty fellowship to any of them, they will never afterwards appear as strangers to us, but, which ever way we turn, we shall find a secret power to have gone out before us, moulding them into such shapes as fancy loves, informing them with life and sympathy, bidding them put on their festive looks and gayest attire at our approach, and to pour all their sweets and choicest treasures at our feet. For him, then, who has well acquainted himself with Nature's works, she wears always one face, and speaks the same well-known language, striking on the heart, amidst unquiet thoughts and the tumult of the world, like the music of one's native tongue heard in some far-off country.
>
> *William Hazlitt, "On the Love of the Country", 1814.[32]*

HOMEOSTASIS. See Systems Thinking 〉 Feedback 〉 Homeostasis.

HOUSEHOLD GROUP. See Small Group, Groups and Group Sizes, Reciprocity and Cooperation, Lean Household, Home.

HOUSEHOLD PRODUCTION. See Lean Household.

HUMILITY, THE FALLACY OF. The *fallacy that humility is a natural qualification for good *judgment.

Humility is a virtue. Its absence closes the mind, leaving the victim defended from inconvenient *truth. Its presence suggests a willingness to consider a contrary view, to defer to the unexpected, to encounter distinctiveness

and difference. But humility as an *abstraction, as an aim, an achievement in its own right, can make trouble. All too easily, it is a form of *Pharisaism: since I am humble, my motives are above suspicion; if you disagree, that is a sad sign that you lack my plain and humble nature; being humble, I am free of the aggression and greed which I see and deplore in those who disagree with me. I will express my sorrow at their misguidedness, but I will forgive them. With any luck, it may provoke fury and *violence, and I will forgive them for that, too.

But more than that, humility can be greedy; it can crowd out, and make obsolete, that complementary characteristic, *fortitude. Fortitude is one of the cardinal *virtues, a necessary condition for the other three—justice, prudence and temperance. It is, however, the neglected one, usurped by indifference and guilt, hesitating at the prospect of having to justify action against all possible criticisms. It is less easy to justify and explain than *compassion, the impeccably authorised but dangerous virtue which gives comfort to the reliably less fortunate, but tells us nothing about obligations among equals. Fortitude smells of old leather, but there is work for it to do. It affirms *loyalty to the *places and *narratives that make *identity; it is identity's defence; and identity is the foundation for rationality—for sense.

The link between fortitude and sense is at risk because, in an age addicted to *abstractions, fortitude has little to sustain it. It depends on the particular—particular

narratives, loyalties, actions, *practices, *ceremonies, places. The philosopher David Miller illustrates this with an imagined *dialogue from The Wind in the Willows. Mole accepts that water rats have a preference for river banks, but he asks: "What's so special about this river bank? Why is it a better place than any other river bank beyond the Wood?" Rat could only have one reply: "This is my place; I like it here; I have no need to ask such questions." It does not sound as though he will be easily persuaded to change his mind. His identity and his place are joined-up. He can believe what he is (*Home).[33]

It is the arbitrariness of fortitude that is critical. Rat's insistence on his particular stretch of river bank seems to come from nowhere—that is, from no reason beyond the existence of the place itself, and his own *presence in it. Certainly, there are no moral distinctions here, no inference that his river bank is right and others are wrong, but still he prefers his. It is the map on which rattish reason is located. Humility can simply mean a refusal to accept the map, for if this arbitrary preference cannot be explained, how can it be justified? And if it cannot be justified, how can insisting on it express humility? Actually, the fortitude to affirm the place you live in as special does come from somewhere: it comes from the story of you and the people you know, set in the place you know, which asserts your robust presence among creatures who would find imported abstractions of any kind rather out of place. If there is no local *story, the space can be filled by humility's refusal to do anything or believe anything without reasons kitted-out and made impressive with abstractions. But that does not make it a virtue.[34]

And there is a still darker side to humility which—unlike low self-esteem—is often, and confidently, claimed to be a virtue. As the *market economy weakens, the *democracy which it supports will weaken. Whether the acute *energy shortages and a destabilised *climate and *population will provide conditions capable of supporting authoritarian regimes is as yet unclear. But one of the strengths of authoritarian regimes is their ability to recruit the humble. They need people who will accept decisions without causing difficulties, and then carry out missions without taking it upon themselves to be moved by reason, common sense, or *pity. They need supporters who will defer to the language.

For example, as Françoise Thom shows in her study of the wooden doubletalk—langue de bois—of tyranny . . .

> . . . [b]y stating: "It is necessary to show increased vigilance", the orator testifies simultaneously to his loyalty to the ideological fiction of the 'enemies within' and to his aggressive intentions towards his fellows. Langue de bois has therefore this unique quality, without precedent in human communication: it can exhibit at the same time both the humiliation of the individual, his inner abasement, and his willingness to pass on the same degradation to others.[35]

But, for all that, back to the good side: humility can mean the recognition that there are qualities in the other, in the person or practice or thing, which you have not yet understood, and which may be too complex, too deep or too unseen for you (at the moment at least) to understand. It is good *manners, *encounter, an encouragement to listen. It is that sanctuary of imperfect comprehension which gives the other person his otherness and independence: you may destroy him, but you can never comprehend him. With humility, you know your limits; you may *reflect on the medieval poet Giovanni Boccaccio's question (about himself and his fellow men): "O wormës meate, O froth, O vanity: why art thou so insolent?"[36]
*Spirit.

HUMOUR. Sensory delight in *paradox.

Humour clears away inhibitions about exploring taboo responses and solutions. It makes it all right to acknowledge a mistake; it supplies the detachment needed to judge one's own work and improve its quality. It is a *necessary condition for the toleration—as distinct from enforcement—of differences in role, assets and influence within the group. It sustains *conversation and underwrites the existence of a group whose members work together and listen to each other; it is a source of shared belonging and mutual recognition: it . . .

> . . . remains one of the ways in which human beings enjoy each other's company, become reconciled to their differences, and accept their common lot. Laughter helps us to overcome

our isolation and fortifies us against despair.
. . . When you and I laugh together, we reveal
to each other that we see the world in the same
light, that we understand its shortcomings and
find them bearable.[37]

Humour sees through the fraud, the person who
makes an *icon of himself and his own high moral
standing. It is a test of team membership, distinguishing a team from a lonely *instrumentalism whose
sufferers have lost all their mirth and must put up,
reluctantly, with having other people around the place.
It builds "congruence", the property of an effective and
*resilient team that can think aloud. And central to con-
gruence-building among *cooperative equals is a blend
of humour and *play, some of which takes the form of
*insult. It communicates the possibility that, maybe, the
person is to be *trusted. An important quality when
applying for a job as a mechanic in Donsco's repair
shop for high-performance cars . . .

> the invitation to the back is a judgment of the
> young man's character and a large measure
> of trust. He will get some light supervision
> that is likely to be disguised as a stream of
> sexual insults, delivered from ten feet away by
> someone he cannot see (only his shoes) as he
> lies under his car. Such insults are another index
> of trust. If he is able to return these outrageous
> comments with wit, the conversation will cas-
> cade towards real depravity; the trust is pushed
> further and made reciprocal. If the young man
> shows promise, that is, if he is judged to have
> some potential to plumb new depths of moral
> turpitude, he may get hired: here is someone
> around whom everyone can relax.
>
> *Matthew Crawford*, The Case for
> Working with Your Hands, 2010.[38]

HUNT, THE. A *system for accepting *responsibility
(now that human beings have usurped so much of the
ecology) for maintaining a healthy population of wild
animals in an *agricultural landscape, protecting their
habitats, stabilising their population, culling the older,
sick and injured animals and treating nature with the
*ceremony and respect which it deserves. The complex

*paradox of the hunt requires *reflection which lies
beyond the easy certainties of guilt and *reductionism.[39]
*Causes, Good Shepherd.

HYPERBOLE. An argument that deceives by *metaphor or exaggeration, and sometimes by changing the
meaning of words.[40]

There is a lot to be said for exaggeration — the wilder
the better. Here are some suggestions about how to be
excused from having to talk to a lady you are trying
to avoid:

> Will your grace command me any service to the
> world's end? I will go on the slightest errand
> now to the Antipodes that you can devise to
> send me on; I will fetch you a tooth-picker now
> from the furthest inch of Asia, bring you the
> length of Prester John's foot, fetch you a hair off
> the great Cham's beard, do you any embassage
> to the Pigmies, rather than hold three words'
> conference with this harpy. You have no
> employment for me?
>
> *Benedick, in Shakespeare's*
> Much Ado About Nothing, c.1599.[41]

There is no danger of missing the point there, but
hyperbole becomes *deception when changes to com-
monly-received meanings are sneaked in, in the hope
that the other person will either fall for it, or will not
notice. Here is some hyperbole: the writer is arguing
that industrial *agriculture and *genetic modification
(GM) technology are nothing new:

> A few thousand years ago hybrid grasses
> thrown up by nature were gathered from
> the wild and developed under unnatural
> (i.e., weeded) conditions in a wheatfield (i.e.,
> monoculture) and fertilised artificially (i.e., with
> gathered dung). The dung was collected from
> genetically modified (i.e., domesticated) beasts.[42]

If the meaning of "genetic modification" is extended to
include the long *tradition of patient observation and selection which bred the crops and animals which now feed us,
then we are left with no name for the technology which
directly intervenes in the structure and composition of
DNA. The wheatfields of the past were not monocultures;

they were rotations, which planted and rested the land in different ways year by year; and dung returns fertility in a manner which is in no way artificial. But when the words mean whatever the writer wants them to mean, entering a dark area between the joke and the serious, you can amusingly say nothing, when there is something that urgently needs to be said. This is the *Devil's voice; if it's right, it's right; if it's wrong, it's only a joke.

Hyperbole, like a spirited horse, needs to be treated with respect and firmness, or it will run away with you. Aristotle suggests guidelines—not for hyperbole, but for rhetoric, which is close—clarity; aptness ("neither too mundane nor too high-flown: it must be appropriate"); and invention (it should contain something new). Shakespeare thought this through, too: on the one hand . . .

> Swear me, Kate, like a lady as thou art,
> A good mouth-filling oath . . .[43]

but plain speaking comes as a relief, too. After Falstaff's claim to have fought off fifty-three bandits in the dark, the Prince explains quietly:

> We two saw you four set on four, and bound
> them and were masters of their wealth—mark
> now, how a plain tale shall put you down. Then
> did we two set on you four, and, with a word,
> out-faced you from your prize, and have it, yea,
> and can show it you here in the house.[44]

Unfortunately, the horse Hyperbole is indeed running out of control, all the time: "Meat is murder." "Alternative medical practitioners are witch doctors for the gullible." "If the organic movement had its way we'd all be going out digging up roots and shooting game with bows and arrows." "American foreign policy consists of bombing the shit out of anyone they disagree with."

In fact, these are not hard to handle, but then we get to something more insidious. Here are seven techniques— members of the family of Newspeak introduced to us by George Orwell in *Nineteen Eighty-Four*, and studied in more detail by the linguistic philosopher Françoise Thom in her analysis of the language of Soviet Communism.[45] She supplies many of the examples:

1. *Summary dismissal*. This is simply name-calling: "reactionary", "potential terrorist", "racist",

"bigot", "elitist", "xenophobe" are nouns you cannot argue with; they are thought-crimes, sitting there banning further progress.[46]

2. *Lack of shifters*. A shifter is a word which acquires a meaning from its context; it does not impose a pre-defined meaning on the argument. For example, "now" in normal speech means "the time at which I am speaking" (but that could be any time). In Newspeak it means "at this stage in history, from which we will be swept along towards the fulfilment of our purpose". "We", in Newspeak, means "those of us who are destined to take this movement forward". This is linguistic fast food: you don't have to apply your mind; the authoritarian language does it for you. Just open the packaging and there it is.[47]

3. *Comparatives*. Aims are described in terms of progress towards a goal, rather than reaching it. The benefits of maintaining the needed signs of progress are facilitated if the goal itself is meaningless or impossible. Phrases like "more developed", "ever closer", "more competitive", "fairer", "greener", "more climate-friendly", tell us that the authorities are dancing as fast as they can, and that we have to dance with them, for longer and longer. Examples:

   a. Socialist hopes for convergence between the highest values of *spirit and *politics:

   > Under the conditions of mature socialism,
   > the bond between economic progress
   > and socio-political and spiritual progress
   > becomes ever closer.[48]

   b. The European Union's permanent progress affirmed in the constitutional treaty:

   > The peoples of Europe, in creating an ever
   > closer union among them, are resolved . . .

   As Roger Scruton notes, the treaty *defines "a project of 'ever closer union', without pausing to consider how much union has so far been attained or how much union would be desirable". Nor to ask the peoples of Europe these questions.[49]

c. The terms of the *climate change discussion, which sees the task as being to reduce emissions and impacts (or move towards agreeing to do so), when in fact the need is to halt them, or even reverse them, quickly enough to avoid the looming tipping point. As the energy analyst David MacKay points out, the phrase "Every little helps" is misleading. If it is not enough to stop climate breakdown, then it hasn't helped. He suggests that a more truthful way of putting it would be, "If everyone does a little, we'll achieve only a little."[50]

4. *The imperative.* Example: "The important changes in Soviet society *must* receive profound scientific expression."[51]

5. *Manichaeism.* The presumption is of a world deeply divided into two hostile and irreconcilable camps, creating a *dialectic which is an inexhaustible source of hyperbole. Everything can be discussed in terms of success and failure in the struggle: to bring evidence and thought to the matter can be seen as a punishable failure to take part in it. In Nazi Germany *Kampf* and *kämpferisch* (struggle, struggle-related) were in constant use as expressions of commitment to the cause.[52]

6. *The "organic" metaphor* suggests naturalness, wholesomeness, predestined *growth, continuity. It claims for current projects a status beyond challenge as the natural unfolding of evolution: the new technologies and applied sciences have their own momentum and inevitability which we should not question.[53]

And that's a shame, because *organic does of course have a positive meaning. So does the implied idea of the "inevitable". It may, for instance, be a property of every word in a poem, each one (as W.H. Auden writes) seeming "inevitable, the only word which could accurately express the poet's meaning". The poem is not just the medium, nor the message; it gives an idea an independence and a personality. But "organic", and "inevitable", alike, can cause trouble.[54]

7. *Passionate muddle.*

The hopes of the capitalists danced furiously on the still open wounds of the murdered people . . .[55]

And four more from a different *ideology:

8. *Imposed criteria* apply criteria from a different sphere. They deliberately miss the point: the Boy Scouts' camp fire is not hygienic; the butter knife in your picnic basket could be used to stab someone; the opera's casting director blatantly discriminates on the basis of gender and musical ability (*False Sameness).

9. *Unctuous *paternalism*: your *home, comfort and safety are what really matter to us (Latin: *unguentum* ointment, grease).

10. *Parody* (the *Straw Man) summarises the other side's argument in the most absurd way possible.

11. *Summary *abstraction*. The use of the generic (animal, fruit, vehicle, alcohol, education) instead of the specific (cat, blackberries, wheelbarrow, pint, story). This assists top-down instruction, disabling the local particular.

Here is an illustration of summary abstraction. A European Union directive which excludes dogs from farmhouse kitchens came into force in 2008: it is now illegal for the owners of 'bed and breakfast' guesthouses to allow dogs into food preparation areas (i.e., kitchens), and owners who cannot for practical reasons exclude their dogs (e.g., by keeping them in an outhouse or the car) are having to decide whether to get rid of their dogs or to close down their 'B and Bs'. Fortunately, there is an environmental health officer at hand to explain to us what that dog sleeping by the Aga really means. His explanation contains *summary abstractions*, IMPOSED CRITERIA and **parody**. Think of the implications of summary abstraction for "animals in kitchens": if he means every type of animal—cobras, tarantulas, komodo dragons, polar bears, seagulls and cane toads—he is, of course, quite right . . .

> Most people would agree it is not HYGIENIC to have *animals in kitchens where food is being prepared*. A bed and breakfast may be somebody's home but once a room is used to prepare HIGH-RISK FOOD that is going to be *sold to members of the public*, it takes on a different meaning. If **there was a food poisoning outbreak that was traced back to those premises, it would not**

be much of a defence in court to say "It is OK because it is our home."[56]

When everything peculiar to a person or situation has been blanked out, there is nothing for a response with any warmth or humanity to attach itself to. What remains is official detachment, slipping easily into cold hatred. The *expert-training for this involves learning to force the detail—luminous, dancing detail—into summary abstractions, sequences of instruction designed to classify details and to deal with them in bulk. You can get a professional qualification in not seeing the trees for the wood.

And yet, at the other end of the spectrum of hyperbole, there are the ecstatic exaggerations of Benedick in *Much Ado About Nothing*. So hyperbole is not all bad. It gets Benedick off on his travels. And it may be a necessary device in argument. It may be needed, for instance, to get people to concentrate on a critical question, to obscure differences sufficiently to achieve concerted action, to stimulate the *emotion needed to get action of any kind, or to shock an opponent into switching on her brain: its *deceptions are generally used for the bad purpose of corrupt logic, but sometimes they are needed. The important thing is to avoid being taken in by the other person's hyperbole, or by your own.
*Fallacies, Special Pleading, Necessity, Conversation, Humility.

HYPERUNEMPLOYMENT.
Unemployment so high that the government cannot raise enough taxation revenue to fund unemployment benefits and pensions (and cannot borrow enough to fill the gap). How high this is depends primarily on (a) the proportion of the workforce out of work, and for how long, and (b) the rate of taxation. Tax could in principle rise to very high levels. The authorities in the declining years of Rome were willing to take tax rates to the limit. Farmers in the third century were reduced to selling their children into slavery as the only way of meeting the tax demands from Rome, or to abandoning their farms altogether. In some cases the tax rates equalled the whole of their harvest, leaving farmers themselves with no way of feeding their families other than going to the cities in search of food hand-outs.[57]

Rome could test such extremes because it was unencumbered by *democracy but, whatever the politics, there is a degree of disruption beyond which there is not, by any standards, enough revenue to redistribute. At this point, no job means no income, and no means of staying alive—with the exception, of course, of those cases where the lack of a job is compensated by participation in the *informal economy. With the arrival of hyperunemployment, the career of the *market economy as a provider is over.
*Leisure, Growth, Economics, Lean Economics, Profession, Slack and Taut.

HYPOCRISY (SCOURGE), THE FALLACY OF THE.
The *fallacy that, if what I do falls below the standards of what I say, my argument can be dismissed without further ado. This fallacy arises from the obvious discomforts of a contrast between good words and bad deeds, like those of *Measure for Measure's* Angelo: upright in public, outrageous in private.

And yet, if an argument is a good one, dissonant deeds do nothing to contradict it. In fact, the hypocrite may have something to be said for him. For instance, he may not be making any claims at all about how he lives, but only about his values in the context of the argument. There is no reason why he should not argue for standards better than he manages to achieve in his own life; in fact, it would be worrying if his ideals were *not* better than the way he lives. He is not dazzled by his high personal standards; he does not make an *icon of himself as the model of good moral conscience. He is not defended by his *sincerity from the possibility of self-criticism. His ideals are not limited to what he can achieve himself.

What matters is whether his argument is right or not. With accusations of hypocrisy in the air, difficult questions about real problems short-circuit into *ad hominem* quarrel.

Hypocrisy is a bad thing with good qualities. Sincerity is a good thing with bad qualities; it shines a light on the simple certainties of your feelings on the matter, rather than on the awkward realities of the case. Some of the most intensely savage people this planet has ever produced were noted for their sincerity and their incorruptible and austere lives. There was Maximilien Robespierre (1758–1794), largely responsible for the

H

203

reign of terror during the French Revolution, but, in his own life, the "Sea-Green Incorruptible".[58] And there was Conrad of Marburg (d. 1233), thin with fasting, who, in imitation of Jesus, rode on a donkey from place to place on his mission to discover and burn heretics and *witches. For groundbreaking catastrophes, we have to turn to the incorruptible. We are safer with those who are not preoccupied with admiration of their own moral standing, confident that they can think no wrong.

If required to choose between sincerity and hypocrisy (writes the theologian David Martin), "Give me a friendly hypocrite any day".[59]

*Ad Hominem, Humour.

I

ICON, THE. An argument summarised in one ready-made idea: a silver bullet, often of the kind which thinks the job is done when it has found someone to *blame. Icons are words or phrases which act as a substitute for—or which distract attention from—the argument, crowding out *reflection.

Once fixed on the iconic word, the argument is over: "reform", "diversity", "competition", "qualifications", "level playing field", "equality", "transparent", "fair", "democratic", "accessible", "vibrant", "modernising"; or "selfishness", "greed", "violence", "privilege", "elitist", "exclusive", "discriminatory", "fascist", "sexist". With the use of 'hooray words' and 'boo words', writes the philosopher Jamie Whyte . . .

> You can win at least the sentiment of agreement without having to say anything that might be held against you later. Or without even having to know what you mean yourself.[1]

Such icon-words are like the hubs in a centralised, scale-free *network: once they are established, an idea has to connect with them if it is to get anywhere. The icon packs a busy future into a word:

Declaration of Iconic Principle: Harmonisation/rationalisation/centralisation/regulation will make life better for millions of our people.

Blame for Failure: Regrettably, there is opposition/sabotage from a minority who remain stuck in the past, but this only strengthens our determination.

Uplifting Conclusion: Therefore, by its progress in the face of such difficulties, the Principle is proving its quality and the need to press ahead fearlessly.[2]

In its material sense, an icon is a painted or carved image, a picture or a figure to assist in *religious *reflection and *ceremony. To the Old Testament Hebrews, icons were images of the ancient deities of Canaan, and they were used in ecstatic *festivals in the name of Baal, aka Dionysus. This pagan rivalry with God was one of the long-running themes of early Jewish history, and the depths of horror with which multiple idolatry was regarded are suggested by the words used to describe it: "vanity", "iniquity", "wind and confusion", "the dead", "things of naught", "carcasses".

The temptation to stay *loyal to the *dance and icons of the old gods was difficult to resist. The alternative called for some hard thinking. Judaism is a religion of constant reflection, embedded in the emotions. God is not a model for good behaviour and, for the people of Israel, he was the God of both Love and Wrath, both of which were needed by the embattled Judaic state. There was clearly potential for confusion here, and the rabbis' task of explaining it called for advanced skills, not only in joined up thinking, but in joined-up emotions, ranging from delight, tenderness and yearning to bitterness, anxiety and *betrayal. What came out of all that was a stunning, emotionally-rich culture, making the connections between thought and feeling, between mind and body. Friedrich Nietzsche reminds us of the importance of this, presaging the psychologist Antonio Damasio in our own day (*Spirit):

> Behind your thoughts and feelings, my brother, there stands a mighty ruler, an unknown sage—whose name is self. In your body he dwells; he is your body. There is more reason in your body than in your best wisdom.

It seems the rabbis knew what they were doing. What they invented was a habit of *reflection and feeling, a *culture rich in self-awareness, comfortable with *emotion, steeped in *humour, designed to make you think. When that weakens, the icon fills the space.[3]
*Ideology.

IDENTITY. The root condition for rational judgment.

"Rational" here has a particular sense: a rational decision is consistent with the individual's *intention, or *conatus*—what he is striving to do; what he is about. The intention may be selfish or enlightened; it may be mistaken; it may be altruistic or self-sacrificing: if the person wishes to do something for others without counting the cost, rational behaviour will take steps to do so. What rational decision *cannot* do is choose a direction in the absence of context, if the decision-maker has no identity, no intention—no *conatus*. Reason can exist without a rational person being present—the laws of Euclid would exist in a lifeless universe—but rational judgment about whether something is a good idea or not only make sense if there is some definition of whom it might be a good idea *for* (*Resilience ❯ Feedback).[4]

Without identity, there is no more reason for a person to make rational decisions with respect to himself and his *community than there would for him to make rational decisions in the interests of any other person or thing, such as an enemy, a rival, or a predator. Antelopes suffering from a loss of identity might forget they are antelopes that run away from lions: instead, they might be on the lions' side and give themselves up; or they might think they were goats, migrate to the uplands and starve in the rocky wilderness. Identity is knowing who you are. *Judgment without identity is madness.

Arguments which comprise only *abstract principles lack those roots in identity: assertions of good or bad intentions unconnected to the particular of people and places are, in this sense, not rational. If there is no identity in terms of which a person, a community, a *nation, is able to make rational judgment, then there is no one there, no defining *interest. Impressive analysis may be abundant—tests, procedures, *numbers, targets—but it cannot correct (though it may disguise) the lack of orientation needed to make it rational.

Being in a community or having a *cultural context is not a sufficient condition for identity being defined,

205

but it is a *necessary one. It means that there are coordinates: the person can take a fix on his position in terms of the community, its *place, its culture, its *tradition, its *narrative (the stories which link up with its past, explain its present, and give it meaning). Community, so identified, can—given a chance—provide the *authority of a defined, rooted, rational context in which the individual can think for himself or herself, apply judgment, express *emotion, be a person. There is a frame of reference in which rational judgments can be made: reason means something.

If you have a secure identity, you have freedom to explore the unfamiliar, to *encounter the surprising. You have the freedom to think. If, however, you are in the insecure condition of having no reliable identity, you need to affirm it in some other way: your opinion is your identity, so that, when making a judgment, you use it as an opportunity to declare—to yourself and others—who you are. The protection of your identity takes priority over actually engaging with the question; it leads you to a quick answer which says nothing about the matter in hand, but a lot about the opinions which you cannot afford to change—because if you did, there would be nothing left of you. In this way, our *freedom to think atrophies. Identity, then, consists of being *intuitively sure of who you are, having no need to *define this by any particular set of values and therefore being able to approach a question by applying judgment on its merits, rather than on your merits.

The economist and philosopher Amartya Sen disagrees with this: identity, he argues, is a product of a person's many characteristics, experiences and opinions—the case, for instance, of a person whose identity comprises being . . .

> . . . a stockbroker, a nonvegetarian, an asthmatic, a linguist, a bodybuilder, a poet, an opponent of abortion, a bird-watcher, an astrologer, and one who believes that God created Darwin to test the gullible.[5]

But it is deeper than that. Identity is not the sum of characteristics. It consists of a deep, rooted sense of being; though you may stop being a stockbroker and start on a new career, you do not start a new identity. Your being does not have to be *promiscuously defined

in terms of something else; it is already, as the poet Thomas Traherne has it,

> A living Inhabitant
> Of the Great World.
> And the Centre of it![6]

The soil in which identity grows is a lifelong immersion in culture, tradition and *manners. It is set in a particular place, so that place, landscape and located roots are integral to it. We must not be too rigid about this, since being of no fixed address does not necessarily mean having no fixed identity: gypsies and ships' captains are not necessarily prevented from discovering their identity—but their place is the road, or the sea. Specificness—non-*abstraction—is set in a particular place, and the idea that *ethics are located goes deep into the language. Greek *tópos* (place), from which we get both "topic" and "topology", was used by Aristotle in *tópoi* (patterns of argument) in his treatise *Ta Tópica*—"Commonplaces". Judgment is, first of all, located in the specifics of the particular case:

> Patterns of argument are not so many rival intellectual theories; rather, they are complementary practical theories, each of which is relevant to some specific type of moral problem. Decisions about which practical theory will best allow us to resolve any particular problem can only be made in the context of, and with an eye to, the detailed circumstances of that particular problem.[7]

Here is the principle of practical wisdom, *prudence, Aristotle's *phronesis*. It focuses on the particular. Particulars are found in *places. Places nurture identity. Identity enables reason.[8]
*Dirty Hands, Loyalty, Narcissism, Metamorphosis, Nation.

IDEOLOGY. A single, widely-applicable strategy or idea, typically well-intended, whose *scale is too large—or which is being dealt with at too high a level—to permit observable reality and detail. Ideology in the state sector is expressed in:

1. large projects, which can be persisted with and given a measure of plausibility due to the massive resources that are invested in them; and

2. *general principles—the *abstract *ethic in terms of which the regime *defines and justifies itself, and on which it bases its claim to be ethical.

Pragmatic thinking, focused on grounded local observation, is seen as an offence to these projects and principles, and suppressed, often by authoritarian governments impressed by their own good intentions.

Here is some news of ideology from history. First of all, the story of a man who was motivated by a grand vision—to bring the world the benefits of universal peace. This fine aim called for fresh new thinking, a *radical shake-up and overdue *reform, dragging his *tradition-bound *nation into the fourteenth century.

On 18th May 1291, the city of Acre fell to the Muslims. It was the last Christian stronghold in the Holy Land. Some people might have thought that this was the moment to draw a line under the Crusades, which had by now had 196 years to prove their futility. However, the King of France, Philip the Fair (1268–1314) had a big, idealistic project. He allowed himself to be persuaded by a Spanish mystic called Ramon Lull that he was destined by God to recapture the Holy Land and, having done so, to send teams of missionaries to convert the Muslim world to Christianity. Philip himself was to lead this crusade. He was to become the new Roman Emperor, with the right to intervene in the election of the pope. Having reconquered the Holy Land, he would then set up his court in Jerusalem and establish a worldwide reign of universal peace.[9]

In order to fulfil his vision, he needed to find a great deal of money, and either to unite under a single command the two rich and powerful monastic-military organisations—the Hospitallers (the Order of the Hospital of St. John of Jerusalem) and their rivals the Templars (the Knights Templar)—or to strip at least one of them of their wealth. The Templars were a multinational organisation of remarkable development and sophistication. Although their numbers were quite small—there were around 4,000 Knights in France—they were formidable

warriors and defenders of the faith; and they ran a respected international banking system, and provided safe lodgings, safe escort and financial services all over Europe. Reform, with some limitation to their power and influence, was needed, but Philip decided to see the end of them: he wanted their money; and he wanted to dissolve their rather independent command structure and replace it with his own military command over a crusading army.[10]

He made his move on Friday 13th October 1307. That morning, the Templars were visited by officers of the crown, who arrested them and handed them over to the torturers. They were required to make public confessions to living lives of extreme pornography, including roasting infants in order to anoint *idols with their fat, making magic potions out of the ashes of deceased Templars, and indulging in initiation ceremonies which included summoning up a Satanic cat to hover over the proceedings, which they were then required to kiss beneath the tail, and swearing on oath that they would be available to sodomy for the rest of their lives. Remarkably, some survived the interrogations, though the tortures could include having their feet roasted until the bones fell from their sockets—one, at a later inquiry, displayed the bones. The Templars were quickly and completely destroyed, but some of the accusations stuck: the task of fabricating an entire body of accusations out of nothing, and then compelling the innocent victims to substantiate them, was so extraordinary and seemed so improbable that it inevitably left the suspicion that maybe there was something in it—that there is no smoke without fire. Recent historical research has conclusively cleared the Templars' name, but a fabrication which must have shocked its contemporaries into thinking that no one can be *trusted, ever—and whose lies lasted for five centuries—has to count as a success for the art of the visionary.[11]

Nonetheless, the crusade did not happen; the vision died. In other words, the project was, by the standard of such projects, utterly typical, with all four defining elements in place:

I

1. the vision;
2. the obstacle;
3. the ruthless campaign to overcome the obstacle, thereby validating the vision; and
4. the forging of a new reality with regard to pain and busyness.

It is not success that matters, it is the signs of advance, crowding out all considerations, detail, circumstance and *diversity—everything but the ideal and *unfalsifiable cause: "universal peace" will do nicely (*Hyperbole).

It was Philip's bad luck that he did not live at another time. He could have been an economist. He might have observed, one December day in 1931, the crowd of unemployed outside the Municipal Lodging House in New York City, lining up in the hope of a free meal.[12] Adopting John Maynard Keynes' *General Theory* as his Bible, he might have committed himself to a lifetime of labouring to build the new Jerusalem of universal employment. He could have destroyed *local economies and *resilient *food production with oil-dependent industrial agriculture in a global *market economy. This crusade would have been in the cause of *economism and its *global reach, and the bright-eyed, authoritative vision would have been supported by the sharpest and most optimistic young minds around— such as that of Michael Stewart, an advisor to the UK's Labour Government in the 1960s:

> Whatever the qualifications, the basic fact is that with the acceptance of the *General Theory*, the days of uncontrollable mass unemployment in advanced industrial countries are over. Other economic problems may threaten; this one, at least, has passed into history.
>
> *Michael Stewart*, Keynes and After, 1967.[13]

You can see the attraction of vision. If you are looking at a crowd of the hungry, *demoralised and unemployed on a winter day, shortly after a world war fought in trenches, it is reasonable to want to do something big, and from the top. By contrast, the *virtues of the local particular which inhabit *Lean Logic* are, very often, on a minute *scale. The visionary who attempts to kick the habit, to turn her gaze away from the epic of large accomplishment to the detail of *tradition and local knowledge, is in

for a shock. She could, with due application, find herself woven into the conscientiousness, care and *imagination of being *located*—being somewhere and building *community. She could in due course find herself sufficiently fluent in the *grammar of her *practice to achieve something. She could walk in the company of the lore, rhymes and ballads of local gossip. The reformed and fully-recovered visionary, *reflecting in a damp field in a *place of no particular importance, could find that the big life-shaping decisions have already been made by the weather and the geology, by the *culture and local traditions. Some of the tasks, *skills and pleasures that remain are about providing food and are likely to be delicious. Some could be shocking. In fact, hang on—over there, on this big landscape, there are two tiny figures, and something strange seems to be going on . . .

Johnny Sands

1. A man whose name was Johnny Sands
   Had married Betty Haigh,
   And though she brought him gold and lands,
   She proved a terrible plague.
   For, oh, she was a scolding wife,
   Full of caprice and whim;
   He said that he was tired of life,
   And she was tired of him
   And she was tired of him.

2. Says he, "Then I will drown myself,
   The river runs below."
   Says she, "Pray do, you silly elf,
   I wished it long ago."
   Says he, "Upon the brink I'll stand,
   Do you run down the hill
   And push me in with all your might."
   Says she, "My love, I will."
   Says she, "My love, I will."

3. "For fear that I should courage lack
   And try to save my life,
   Pray tie my hands behind my back."
   "I will," replied his wife.
   She tied them fast as you may think,
   And when securely done
   "Now stand," she says, "upon the brink,
   Now I'll prepare to run
   Now I'll prepare to run."

4. All down the hill his loving bride
   Now ran with all her force
   To push him in—he stepped aside
   And she fell in of course.
   Now splashing, dashing like a fish
   "Oh save me, Johnny Sands."
   "I can't, my dear, though much I wish
   For you have tied my hands
   For you have tied my hands."[14]

Henry IV, Philip the Fair's successor 275 years later, understood this: he knew the importance of small things; he affirmed the tradition, for every French family, of a chicken in the pot every Sunday, and his name is remembered and honoured in some very fine cheese.[15]
*Reductionism, Internal Evidence, Genetic Fallacy, False Sameness, Sedation, Casuistry, Utopia.

IGNORANCE, THE FALLACY OF (*Argumentum ad ignorantiam*). The case of not knowing anything about the subject, but not letting that put you off. Its main habitat consists of trying to break the rule that "you can't prove a negative"—concluding that, since you can't find something (such as a black swan) it follows that it doesn't exist. Variants are:

1. The Scientist's Fallacy that something that has not been proved and understood therefore does not exist (e.g., homeopathy, morphic resonance, ghosts). This tends to be stated in the assertion that "there is no evidence that . . .", often reflecting a determination not to find it.

2. The Non-Scientist's Fallacy that something that has not been proved not to exist therefore does exist. Variants of this are the non-scientist's version of the Scientist's Fallacy: the view that a phenomenon around which there is still uncertainty (e.g., *climate change) is therefore untrue; and the Hypochondriac's Fallacy: that a problem that has not been shown not to exist therefore does exist.[16]

Other varieties of the fallacy:

3. Where your *ideology and intense conviction about a subject make it unnecessary to know anything about it.

4. Where your sweet *innocence would be polluted by the facts.

5. Where your *expertise in one area is so impressive that it makes you feel confident in other areas of which you know nothing (the Spillover Fallacy).

6. Where you are so consumed with work (e.g., doing brilliant science on climate change) that you overlook other commitments (e.g., communicating your results to non-scientists).

7. Where you are so determined to see the matter from others' point of view that you never develop or research a point of view of your own.

8. Where you don't believe that others (unlike strong-minded intellectuals like you) are up to being told the *truth, so you leave them in ignorance.

9. Where ignorance opens up brilliant possibility—for, without a blanket of ignorance about how difficult the task was going to be, you would never have attempted it.

*Expertise.

IMAGINATION. Creative *intelligence in action; the ability to learn and understand something without having experience of it.[17]

If the mature *market economy is to have a sequel on the *Wheel of Life, it will be the work, substantially, of imagination. But imagination will not have an easy time of it, for it is widely seen as a dissident to be suppressed, removed or re-educated. "Higher level learning", the ability to understand and analyse a subject, was achieved by one in five teenagers in 1976; as the psychologist Michael Shayer has shown, this is now down to one in twenty. The target-led routines of the *education of our time appear to be reducing our ability to apply the lateral thinking needed for transition to a lean and *resilient future.[18]

Given a chance, imagination can build whole civilisations of the unexpected. Once, for example, it went Baroque . . .

"Baroque" was a culture that flourished in England and Europe between 1630 and 1730. It began with the order, harmony, *authority and cool, universal proportion of Renaissance art and architecture. It groaned and rebelled, wondering what had happened to *local detail, to *paradox and to the pairs of opposites which walk together in the real world: science and superstition, the *charitable and the *violent, splendour and squalor, order and chaos, civilisation and nature, the *erotic and the divine. And, in response, it produced an *art and architecture, gardens, music, theatre and literature of systematic disorder. The historian Judith Hook explains,

> Disorder and asymmetry were made part of a whole which when seen as a whole was ordered. This explains the baroque artist's interest in total forms—the palace surrounded by its baroque gardens, town planning, or the opera—which gave full rein to diversity within an integrated overall design.[19]

The Baroque is widely associated with the pointlessly elaborate, but more exactly it refers to the disorderliness and asymmetry of real life, to thought in the process of being formed, to the mind thinking.[20]

And it worries the orderly mind. For instance, it worried the orderly thinking of those—notably the group at Emmanuel College, Cambridge: the Cambridge Platonists—who held on to the universal, orderly thinking of the Enlightenment, and saw, in imagination, nothing but confusion. As one of them wrote, with *indignation, the trouble with imaginative powers is that they are always . . .

> . . . breathing gross dew upon the pure Glass of our Understandings [which they so] sully and besmear . . . that we cannot see the Image of Divinity sincerely in it.[21]

The irritating thing about Baroque thinking, from that point of view, is that it seems to be both untidy and inconclusive. It is not interested in equilibria, in orderly vertical and horizontal geometry; it is interested, instead, in movement. It is less taken by conclusions than by the imaginative process of getting there, and its preferred shape is the spiral—or the helix, like the pillars of the porch of St. Mary's Church in Oxford—moving upwards out of the picture, forever inconclusive. It does not mark out the path to pleasure, but joins Thomas Hobbes in his quest for something more transient—"felicity". Felicity lacks finality; its *encounters with perfection are brief, at best; more usually, it simply makes do with the possibility.[22]

It is better to travel hopefully than to arrive . . . . The travelling is done by the imagination; it takes place in the person, in the body, the habitat of life and passion. We need have no doubt on this point, because John Donne tells us so:

> . . . for we are so composed, that if abundance, or glory scorch and melt us, we have an earthly cave, our bodies, to go into by consideration, and cool ourselves: and if we be frozen, and contracted with lower and dark fortunes, we have within us a torch, a soul, lighter and warmer than any without: we are therefore our own umbrellas and our own suns.[23]

*Narrative Truth, Second Nature.

IMPLICATURE. The presence of a subtext—another meaning—which makes a statement not quite as simple, or as *innocent, as it looks. Examples:

- "What did you think of the singer?" "Well, I liked her dress."[24]
- "We are tackling the problem of global warming." There is nothing wrong with the statement itself, but it implies that we are on the way to solving the problem; it may also be taken to imply that we can do the job on our own. It sounds reassuring, but it may be telling you that the efforts to tackle global warming are not having much success.

The philosopher Paul Grice, who coined the word, pointed out that implicature is commonplace in *conversation, and that it comes in many forms (e.g., *Accent, *Quibble). Given its potential to mislead, he argued for a code of good conduct in communication, which he called the Cooperative Principle: be as informative as required (but no more), do not say things which you believe to be false or for which you have no evidence, be *relevant, avoid obscurity and ambiguity, be brief and orderly . . .

. . . except when you're not. *Lean Logic* advocates asides, long-windedness if it comes with a story, frank untruths if there is a reasonable chance that the other person can untangle the *irony, broken logic if it reflects the difficulty of explaining things which break your heart or are hard to understand.[25] It does not share the modest self-restraint which we find in Psalm 131:

I do not exercise myself in great matters :
which are too high for me.[26]

Lean Logic finds that, when dealing with great matters, it can, from time to time, be a good thing if there are cracks and faults in the argument, for the repair of which help is invited. It is a reminder that a conversation is a cooperative affair, not just a series of beautifully-manicured statements.

*Narrative Truth.

IMPLICIT TRUTH. The product of *reflection, particular to the person. Reflections and *loyalties about the same thing may produce different *truths—both, or all, true despite contrasts in emphasis and meaning. The differences may be consistent with each other, or they may mature into deep contradictions: "This is my territory"; "The ideal place for our honeymoon would be Scunthorpe"; "We've won". All these are true or untrue, depending on who is speaking.

*Material Truth, Truth, Good Shepherd Paradox.

INCENTIVES, THE FALLACY OF. The presumption that a person will not carry out a substantial task unless given an incentive over and above—separate from—the benefits derived from the task itself.

It is taken as a *self-evident truth that the way to persuade people to make the effort to achieve a significant aim is to give them an incentive—a reward if they do, or a penalty if they don't. The possibility that people may want to achieve an aim for its own sake is not taken to be a sufficient motivation. This carrot-and-stick theory is at the heart of the system of rewards and grades in *education and public policy, and it is poised to be applied on a draconian scale to the measures which governments decide we must take in response to the *climacteric. The reward is *extrinsic*, it is nothing to do with the *intrinsic* rewards of doing a good job or doing the right thing; it is about supplying the people with a substitute incentive because (it is assumed) they don't care whether they are doing it right or not.

Extrinsic incentive schemes do work for simple quantity production. If the task consists of picking strawberries, it makes sense for earnings to be linked to the quantity of strawberries that a worker picks: the task

is already specified; no *judgment is needed. If designed for very routine tasks, or if sufficiently draconian and painful, extrinsic incentives can make people change their behaviour, although they cannot make them *want* to change their behaviour; nor can they make people apply their minds to inventing *creative solutions to problems, and to sustaining their commitment to getting results over a long period. That is, where it is quality rather than quantity that matters—where the organisation needs its people to have the incentive to *think*—extrinsic rewards and punishments pre-empt judgment and trivialise the task. The person, the *character, is discounted. Rewards for hitting quality targets—given to surgeons, for instance, as an incentive to carry out successful operations as distinct from botched ones—don't work.[27]

The case is illustrated by a simple experiment by Edward Deci, involving college students. Give two groups (with no contact with each other) an interesting task; tell just one of the groups that they will be paid for doing it. Let them start work and get into the task. Now call a coffee break. It is the group that isn't paid that will carry on working through the break. The financial incentive here has in effect announced to the students that the task itself is *not* intrinsically interesting—that it is not in your interests to continue with it, unless you are paid to do so. The inference is that a programme which depends on people's enthusiasm cannot buy it with financial incentives, with tricksy promptings of the carrot and stick. Instead, it has to win people's *interest and engagement on its own merits.[28]

Alfie Kohn summarises an exhaustive review of research in the field:

> Rewards usually improve performance only at extremely simple—indeed, mindless—tasks, and even then they improve only quantitative performance.
>
> . . . Not a single controlled study has ever found that the use of rewards produces a long-term improvement in the quality of work. Extrinsic rewards reduce intrinsic motivation. . . . The central finding has been documented beyond any reasonable doubt.[29]

The consistent finding of the research, then, is that the quality of the work produced by both adults and children is actually reduced by performance-related incentives. Sometimes the initial results are good—the initial offer of a reward is taken up, the required action is taken on the first day—but that establishes the action as something that no sensible person would do unless rewarded and the incentive to give the task any sustained attention is destroyed. Kohn suggests reasons for this.[30]

First, the flip side of reward, of course, is punishment: if the hoped-for reward is not achieved, then the *expectation is disappointed. Circumstances outside the subject's control are likely to be *blamed; the scheme is seen as manipulative.

Secondly, reward schemes can damage relationships: there is jealousy and a reluctance to cooperate. Winners have no need to *cooperate with losers; losers have nothing to offer. And they damage relationships, too, with the authorities who have devised the scheme: their seniority and power is emphasised; the scheme is not seen as a cooperative partnership, but as a bribe.

A third reason is that incentive schemes reduce the willingness to take risks, to invent and explore: people go for the solutions and short cuts that have worked in the past. And once you have got the reward or grade, the job is done.[31]

The central failure of incentive schemes, however, lies with the fourth problem: people who are engaged in an activity because they have been given an extrinsic incentive to do so (e.g., *money) are less interested in what they are doing than people who are doing the same task under conditions which are identical except for the lack of an extrinsic incentive. If you have to be bribed to do something, you would not have done it without the bribe, so the task is a *bore, on which you certainly aren't about to waste much enthusiasm or creativity.

There are some subtleties here, and the shock of discovering that incentives are in fact disincentives requires a pause for thought. It does not follow, for instance, that being paid for a job means that people will be *bored by it—and Kohn and his colleagues make a sharp distinction between the salary, which gets people through the door, and the performance-related incentive. He summarises,

The problem with financial incentives is not that people are offered too much money; earning

a hefty salary is not incompatible with doing good work. Rather the problem is that money is made too salient. . . . Pay people generously and equitably. Do your best to make sure they don't feel exploited. Then *do everything in your power to help them put money out of their minds.*[32]

The implications of this are profound. It means—as the research reveals with disturbing candour—that much of the incentive structure around which modern life is organised is perverse, reducing success in achieving intended aims and making *judgment obsolete. In this way, *education is reduced to an exercise in playing the system—you go through the motions of doing what they want you to do. Who needs judgment when you can simply be given dog biscuits? A more miserable preparation for productive citizenship or for the *intelligence and *imagination we need would be hard to invent. It is, in fact, a reasonable suspicion that incentive schemes are used despite being *known* to demotivate. They are instruments of control. Our society's political institutions do not dare to engage intelligence, which would change them. On the contrary, they feel threatened by it.[33]

The writer Daniel Pink reflects on this. He suggests that, when motivation is properly understood, and *institutions—schools, companies, public policy, our *culture—get the *cooperation of the people that live and work in them, three vital conditions of creative energy are released:

- Autonomy (the confidence and *freedom to apply your mind);
- Mastery (the opportunity to be so engaged in the task that you begin to know what you are doing); and
- Purpose (the sense that what you are doing is worthwhile—the opposite of *demoralisation).[34]

Put all these together, moving on from primitive intervention with carrots and sticks, and we get that crucial outcome: *flow. A phased withdrawal from fossil fuels will not be accomplished without it.

*Presence, Common Purpose, Exhilaration, Lean Thinking, Energy Prospects.

INCREMENTALISM. Progress consisting of small steps: little-by-little (Latin: *paulatim*). It is generally—but not always—based on a clear *intention as to where these steps will eventually lead. It corrects for errors, being guided by slight feedbacks, or algorithms; like the steersman of a yacht. It *may* in due course be so prolific and elaborate that it becomes unsupportable and breaks in a shock of *kaikaku*. Of course, that may not happen. For one thing, feedbacks and corrections do not necessarily have to deliver incremental advance (*kaizen*); they may deliver stability, as in the case of species that had remained unchanged over long periods, despite dramatic changes of climate (*Ecology: Farmers and Hunters, Systems Thinking ❭ Feedback ❭ Homeostasis).

Incrementalism can be powerful, and we have an illustration of this in the case of *land use and planning—a task which, in the *Lean Economy, will call for brilliance in the application and evolution of the *proximity principle. Bit-by-bit progress discovers solutions which rapid, broad-brush change misses. Here is the architect and planner, Patrick Geddes, approaching things incrementally in the British Raj in India in 1914. His first encounter with the problem was when he became aware of the British engineers' plans for wholesale slum clearance: the orthodoxy was demolition followed by a gridiron pattern of streets and expensive hygiene arrangements. Geddes, in contrast, pointed out that "the existing roads and lanes are the past products of practical life, its movement and experience". What they needed was not massive and sudden change at the instruction of British officials, but steady improvement:

> By our small removals, straightenings, openings
> and replannings in detail, a network of clean
> and decent lanes, of small streets and open
> places, and even gardens, is thus formed,
> which is often pleasant, and I venture to say
> sometimes beautiful. . . . As dilapidated and
> depressed old quarters reopen to another, the
> old village life, with its admirable combination
> of private simplicity and sacred magnificence,
> [turns out to be] only awaiting renewal.[35]

Peter Hall has dug into the reports Geddes wrote at this time, and into the reactions of the engineers with their authoritarian and expensive hygiene agenda. For them, Geddes was, "a crank who don't know his subject". But Geddes' incrementalism brought immediate

returns in the form of reductions in sickness and death rates, at a small fraction of the cost and time required by the clearances and rebuilding of the official plan. And yet, working at the level of detail has its problems, too. It calls on reserves of *time and patience—and the trouble it takes to build that detail, to encourage it to grow out of *local circumstance, is illustrated by Geddes himself:

> It requires long and patient study. The work
> cannot be done in the office with ruler and
> parallels, for the plan must be sketched out
> on the spot, after wearying hours of perambu-
> lation—commonly among sights and odours
> which neither Brahmin nor Briton has generally
> schooled himself to endure. This type of work
> also requires maps of a higher degree of detail
> and accuracy than those hitherto required by
> law for municipal or government use. Even
> after a good deal of experience of the game,
> one constantly finds oneself tempted like the
> impatient chess-player, to sweep a fist through
> the pieces which stand in the way.[36]

Geddes had recognised for a long time how much can be achieved when the potential of what is already there is understood and managed in the right way. Earlier in his career (in 1886) he had moved into an Edinburgh tenement block, and what followed was an illustration of incrementalism at work. He rented several adjacent rooms, joined them together to make a flat, and moved outwards from there. He encouraged a collective effort of owners and occupiers to conserve the façades and shapes of the buildings while refurbishing; he knocked down parts of the tenements to let light and air into the courtyards, and converted deadbeat slums to hostels, flats and halls of residence for students at Edinburgh University.[37]

The consistent theme in Geddes' philosophy was this incrementalism—or, as Geddes preferred, "evolution"—by which the assets that we have inherited are given the chance to evolve their individual identities and capabilities and, in doing so, become individuated and distinctive. He developed this idea in building (the Outlook Tower museum in Edinburgh was inspired and developed by him), in his work in the biological evolution of the cell—and in his application of this principle in his study of love, *The Evolution of Sex*:

I

For we see that it is possible to interpret the ideals of ethical progress, through love and sociality, co-operation and sacrifice, not as mere utopias contradicted by experience, but as the highest expressions of the central evolutionary process of the natural world. The ideal of evolution is indeed an Eden; and although competition can never be wholly eliminated, and progress must thus approach without ever completely reaching its ideal, it is much for our pure natural history to recognise that creation's final law is not struggle but love.[38]

And Geddes illustrates this with a steel engraving of six baby opossums being taken out for a walk by their mother, hanging on by their tails.

Incremental, observant advance; the maturing individuation of a conserved inheritance: the principle was taken to maturity in his book, *Cities in Evolution*. You do not destroy; you might intervene; you do not manipulate. Essentially, you enable.

Geddes' consistent theme of bottom-up incrementalism in a cared-for *culture, building on what is already there, belongs in the conservative tradition with ancient roots in Aristotle and Aquinas and more modern ones in Edmund Burke and Michael Oakeshott, and in *Lean Logic*'s principles of *empowerment, *presence and *lean thinking. When the task that lies ahead is almost impossible, the strategy of using what is there, revising it, and enabling it to build on its strengths endows the project with inherited *capital which the visionary *ideologue, whose first instinct is demolition, forgoes.

What matters is not being right, but being perceptive about the errors which you will inevitably make, about what they are telling you, and about the direction in which evolution could take you, if allowed. As Geddes' contemporary, Ebenezer Howard, the man behind the Garden Cities movement, precursor to *Social Cities, remarked,

> One should never be excessively realistic in human plans. Our aspirations should always be as far-reaching as they can be, so as to make it possible to retract from some of them if necessary; for great gains are not to be thought of.[39]

The social historian Paul Barker puts it the other way round:

> One brilliant feature of Howard's plan is that it could be created incrementally, by scores of local initiatives.[40]

Does incrementalism contradict lean thinking? Not really. *Intention is muted, but it is usually alert to opportunity, so *pull is in place. *Kaizen is there, in a gentle form. And what of *kaikaku, that act of destroying and starting again in a new direction and on different principles? Caution is needed here, because *kaikaku* can belong in the destructive world of *rationalism. And even it if it doesn't, it may be only a remote *necessity. It may come without an invitation, in the form of a *climacteric; or it may be the last resort when faced by a system paralysed by autocratic top-down administration; or by *large-scale dependencies and lines of supply that can no longer be supported; or by the death-trap whereby incremental improvements can do no more than deepen the trouble that a system is already in. Or we may see *kaikaku* in the sequence of life and *death (*Sacrifice-and-Succession) which gives a community its longevity. At the small scale its value lies in its frequency; at the large scale, in its rarity. *Radical Break.

INDIGNATION, THE FALLACY OF. Indignation is an urban emotion: it looks for action to be taken by someone else, believing that the way forward is agitation. It *begs the question: if you are indignant about something, it has to be an outrage, and caused by someone other than you—otherwise, of course, you wouldn't be indignant, would you? And it is urban in the sense that, in the city, it is easy to get away, so you can absent yourself from a conversation, indignantly telling the other person you find his views repugnant. You won't be needing to borrow his horse.

Out of town, it is different. It is a waste of time being indignant in a field of buttercups. You have to see to it yourself. That may involve time in a circumstance not of your choosing, in a *conversation not on your terms. *Anger, Blame, Empowerment, Unmentionable.

INFORMAL ECONOMY. That part of an economy whose members provide for each other and *cooperate on terms which do not involve money.

The informal economy—aka the "core economy"—consists of all the things we do for each other in families: cooking, bringing up children, *playing, discussing citizenship, building *character and *emotional literacy. And it includes the things we do as citizens: serving as school governors, organising societies and sports clubs, voting—the things which, taken together, add up to our "social capital". It is large; if the value of the informal economy were costed in terms of the wages that would have to be paid for doing all these things, we would get enormous *numbers. And yet, it is but a remnant in comparison with the economy of *reciprocal obligation in the medieval period. Or even compared with the communitarian *social capital that survived into the twentieth century, before the long withdrawal from *home and local community—due in part to the developments in domestic equipment—in favour of paid work, which is visible to the calculations of economics.[41]

The informal economy makes the *community. While money will be used for imports and exports between communities, the *Lean Economy will be founded on reciprocal services. There will be a fusion of society and *economics, of friendship and service, *local self-reliance and *presence.

A start-up version of this principle was proposed as "the Big Society", first introduced by the Conservative Party's manifesto for the 2010 election, and developed since—"a society where people come together to solve problems and improve life for themselves and their communities . . . redistributing power from the state

to society; from the centre to local communities, giving people the opportunity to take more control over their lives . . .". There is a convergence of thinking on this from the various directions of *lean thinking, *presence, *TEQs, and *Transition.

It is there in the principle of "co-production", where public services such as schools and hospitals build partnership with citizens as volunteers. In its report, *Co-production: A Manifesto for Growing the Core Economy*, The New Economics Foundation supplies examples of this rediscovery of an old idea, such as the aftercare arrangements at Lehigh Hospital, Philadelphia, where visits to discharged patients in their homes are done substantially by other former patients. The term "co-production" was suggested by Elinor Ostrom in the 1970s, when she argued that police forces should develop more and better routine contact with the public, pointing out that "the police need the community as much as the community need the police".[42]

Rebuilding the informal economy means re-awakening citizenship—doing things because they weave community together, and because in practical terms they provide the necessities that keep them alive.
*Reciprocity and Cooperation, Dual Economy, Lean Economics, Lean Household, Compassion, Barter, Growth.

INFORMAL LOGIC. One of the two main kinds of logic (the other is *formal logic). Almost all the *fallacies discussed in *Lean Logic* are informal. Informal logic considers the context, content and delivery of an argument; it recognises the fallacies that can destroy *dialogue, and teaches how to avoid, or use, them. It is often thought of as the disreputable relation of formal logic, for it has no solid set of rules from which conclusions can be deduced. It tends to focus on mistakes, and its discussion of logic in the context of subjects such as *religion, *culture, *law and the environment—by books such as this one—seems to violate the principles of logical rigour, which ought not to be contaminated by reference to any particular practical applications.

One of the symptoms of all this is that there is no definitive list of fallacies: you can (within limits) invent them as you go along, and it is possible to turn fallacies to advantage—using them, for instance, to persuade

215

the other person of a conclusion for the wrong reasons (though a person who is fluent in informal logic should be able to expose such schemes). In fact, informal logic is altogether too informal for some tastes, and some logicians conclude with regret that it does not exist. Here, for example, is the logician Jaakko Hintikka, more in sorrow than in anger:

> The [logical] structures I am concerned with uncovering are intended to be of the same kind as the structures studied in mathematical logic and foundations of mathematics. I have a great deal of sympathy with the intentions of those philosophers who speak of "informal logic", but I don't think any clarity is gained by using the term "logic" for what they are doing.[43]

Alternatively:

> OLD GENT (to Logician): Beautiful thing, logic.
> LOGICIAN (to Old Gent): Provided it's not abused.
> Eugène Ionesco, *Rhinoceros, 1959.[44]

*Fallacies, Fuzzy Logic, Lumpy Logic, Manners.

INFRASTRUCTURES. See Intermediate Economy, Regrettable Necessities, Intensification Paradox.

INGENUITY GAP. The gap between our ability to invent solutions and the *scale of the problems for which solutions are needed. The *market state is so impressed by its own ingenuity—by its ability to find technical solutions to its problems—that it finds it hard to recognise that it is not technical solutions that are needed. Forward movement (*Kaizen) is not helpful if what is needed is a change of direction (*Kaikaku). Ingenuity in extending the life of the familiar is most useful if the time it buys is used to prepare for the time when it reaches its limits.[45]

*Intelligence, Wicked Problems, Denial, Lean Thinking.

INHERITANCE. The *capital assets conserved and/or created by previous generations, on which we completely depend.

*Relevance.

INNOCENCE, THE FALLACY OF. "Innocence" has two related meanings here. First, it means innocence of knowledge—i.e., *ignorance, a gift to an adversary in argument, inviting the whole range of *rhetorical scams.

The second meaning is not another name for ignorance, but an addition to it: it embellishes ignorance with the qualities of irreproachable naïveté and purity. Innocence (noun): Freedom from the sin of knowing anything.

The arguer presents herself as the sweet innocent, who cuts through all the clever stuff and with refreshing childlike simplicity gets straight to the point. You are as innocent as a March hare, the outsider whose mind is unspoiled by knowledge and who can look with a fresh, uncomprehending eye at extraordinary goings-on.[46]

Jonathan Swift's Gulliver takes delight in this, telling his horrified hosts—the innocent horses, the Houyhnhnms—about the professions back home: the lawyers who are paid to tell the most enormous lies, the soldiers who blow people sky-high so that the populace can watch their bodies crashing back to earth.[47]

Innocence in this sense of holy ignorance has had a good press—or, at least, a good *myth. Its most famous moment came with the Emperor Who Had No Clothes: sweet innocence, over whose eyes the scales of sophistication had not yet grown—or rather, in whom the ability to appreciate myth had not yet developed—came in the boy's cry of amazement about his naked emperor. But innocence has a darker side, and it is on display in the medieval morality play, Everyman, which is the story of desertion in the hour of death. Inevitably, Fellowship, Kindred and Goods must take their leave; they are followed by Beauty, Strength, Discretion, and the Five Wits, leaving just Knowledge and Good Deeds: then, even Knowledge goes, leaving Everyman alone except for the permanent company of Good Deeds. Everyman will not be needing Knowledge where he is going: he is "crowned" as a reward for being ignorant, innocent of any knowledge at all. He is not even allowed to keep his Pride.[48]

INSTITUTION. A generic name for groups, clubs, churches, schools, universities, societies; the subdivisions and *holons that make a *community. They include *professional networks and associations—Émile Durkheim's "corporations". "Institution" is in this sense similar to *social capital, and the groups, friendships and *connectedness that it seeds.[49]

There is, however, a form of institution—the institution-with-a-mission—which exists, not for the benefit of its members but to advance another aim which stands the best chance of being achieved if its members surrender their interests to it. The members of such an institution are useful to it insofar as they contribute to those ends; they therefore have to be at one with the institution in terms of opinion, partially or comprehensively sacrificing independent critical *judgment to it; the person loses his or her *identity and suffers *metamorphosis into a creature of the institution. Franz Kafka's suggestion of a suitable institutional character in this sense was that of a cockroach.[50]

And the institution's breadth of judgment narrows down accordingly. The effect is a regrettable condition. It affects companies with a mission to dominate a *market (using their size or a capturing technology such as *genetic modification). It also affects pressure groups and campaigning institutions of all kinds, governments included; they lose their minds, overstate their case, and see the world as a system which can be substantially—or sufficiently—understood, wrapped up and sorted in terms of their own aims.

It is important to understand what an institution-with-a-mission is, because there are good reasons to believe that we are all living in one, whether we are on a payroll or not.

*Community, Metamorphosis, Instrumentalism, Social Entropy.

INSTRUMENTALISM, THE FALLACY OF.
The perception of a thing or person as useful for your purposes, but otherwise expendable and of little or no account.

It is a form of *abstraction, because the victim, forfeiting his, her or its claim to defining properties and characteristics, is recognised only in terms of that usefulness. An image of this is the nude observed coldly, but with *interest, by a man in a suit, complete with clipboard, biro, well-filled wallet, mobile phone, calculator . . . The instrumental detachment has the quality

of the scavenger, the asset-stripper; the victim is likely to be destroyed in the process, but that does not matter if it serves the exploiter's purpose. The characteristic art of instrumentalism is kitsch.

One victim of this instrumental detachment is the *nation. The nation exists as an asset, a character, a *community, in its own right. It is part of the frame of reference which give a person an *identity. It has its *place, its *narrative history, its *culture, its language, its jokes, its *politics. The people and parties of national politics can legitimately speak for the same community, however much they may disagree. This is the principle of the *loyal opposition—acknowledgement that disagreement at least starts from the same premises: debate and dissent are legitimised as *diverse expressions of a common identity; the participants are defined by the place. Without that, identity depends, instead, on opinion and on the security of belonging to power networks and faction, so that *institutions break: social cohesion is surrendered and reduced to obedience. A nation, in contrast, is a being, in a sense a personality, a person. It lives.

However, like all living things, it is vulnerable. It can be reduced to a mere instrument for the overriding priority of economism, which renders collective identity down to the pursuit of economic growth. Economism bundles together the whole inherited diversity of *skills and investment, of material, financial, human and natural *capital, as a single passive entity, naked and awaiting the attention of the *experts. It is practised at peak aggregation; it takes the imperative of growth and competition as the only reality to be tolerated; it is The Argument: like surreal announcements from Alpha Centauri, it tolerates no reply. It is an addiction which falls for the childish error of failing to distinguish between *per capita* growth, which market economies have to sustain, and aggregate (national) growth, which is not a coherent objective at all. Since abstractions do not have a beginning and an end, the signs that *growth is about to *touch-down at the end of its 300–year flight are missed.

The market economy takes over most of the need to make decisions; *networks of *reciprocal obligation, emotional literacy and *social capital are displaced by *competitive prices and regulation. However, when it is no longer capable of delivering its skin-deep social *cohesion, a secure setting, where the *communities of a particular society can live and have their being, will be needed again. The place capable of providing that wider context is the *nation. Whether it will have survived its rape by *economism and be in any fit state to live again, to be itself, is another matter.[51]
*Encounter.

INSULT. (1) Refreshing evidence of good *humour and *good faith.

(2) An ambivalent act, midway between endearment and assault, which is intrinsic to the politics and *play of bonding into stable and cooperative-competitive groups of male primates (*Small Group).

(3) Personal *ad hominem* attack, closing down the possibility of reasonable *dialogue.

INTELLIGENCE. (1) A public good. The intelligence of at least some people is a vital public good which we cannot do without if there is to be a future for the rest of us. The view of intelligence as a *private perk is a measure of failure to recognise society as a *connected system, which relies on individual talent as a collective asset. In the *market economy, attitudes to intelligence are ambivalent, and mixed in with them is unease about it—as an embarrassment; proof of how far we still fall short of equality of opportunity to fuck up.

(2) A public bad. The presumption is: I am intelligent, therefore I am right. Reliance on intelligence as reassurance of being right is a critical source of error

and failed arguments. It is also a licence to work to a different *ethical standard from those of lesser intelligence. The psychologist Carol Dweck describes studies of students who have been explicitly congratulated on their intelligence, compared with students in the same circumstances who have been explicitly congratulated on their hard work: students who are told that their success is a reward for their intelligence show an increased tendency to rely on intelligence alone to get them by, without having to make any serious attempt to get to grips with the substance of an argument. They are less motivated to make an effort in subsequent tasks; if they are seriously challenged by a task, they become disheartened (disillusioned about their intelligence), being paralysed by doubts about it, rather than being stimulated to application, and less able to see tasks as enjoyable. They feel the need to convince others of their ability and, in order to do this, they may lie (for instance, about their exam grades).[52]

And, all too easily, intelligence can be switched off—by, for instance, an *instrumental view of intelligence as a way of bluffing one's way through to performance goals such as grades, targets and qualifications. Dweck describes a comparison in which two sets of students were asked to carry out the same task of learning scientific principles, but given different reasons for doing so. One of the groups was given a performance goal (their ability would be evaluated by how they performed); the other was given a learning goal (the task would offer them the opportunity to learn some valuable things). After both groups had learned the material equally well, they were given a new set of problems, related to what they had learned, but requiring some serious new thinking:

> What happened next was very interesting.
> Many of the students with performance goals showed a clear *helpless pattern* in response to difficulty. A number of them condemned their ability, and their problem-solving deteriorated.
>
> In sharp contrast, most of the students with learning goals showed a clear *mastery-oriented pattern*. In the face of failure, they did not worry about their intellect, they remained focused on the task, and they maintained their effective problem-solving strategies.[53]

Intelligence is an instrument, and it is therefore value-neutral: its value depends on what you use it for. A person suffering from paranoid delusions—or simply mistaken—can reinforce the error by the application of intelligence. A regrettable and ill-fated scheme for world domination can be made plausible and even temporarily successful by intelligence. If you are going in the wrong direction, intelligence, like technology and an effective bureaucracy, can enable you to go in that direction faster and more effectively. Intelligence is not sufficient to be a net asset, and if it is developed out of context, it is a regrettable handicap. What matters is the judgment on which it is based. And *judgment is the accomplishment of the whole person—mind, *spirit and all.

And intelligence may be a source of insecurity: am I really as intelligent as I was yesterday? It cannot be confirmed by looking in the mirror, but temporary reassurance can be derived from intense discussion whose aim is to participate in the game of being intelligent—of being more-intelligent-than-thou. Agreement is avoided, because the argument itself is your best chance of displaying your intelligence in its full glory. Intelligent debate, and the status and self-respect of being thought to be smart, fall greedily on what is left of our environmental *capital. When *Death comes to Earthlings, he will find them being intelligent.

*Narcissism, Charisma, Pharisee, Humility, Local Wisdom.

INTENSIFICATION PARADOX. The paradox by which a developing economy, whose *productivity is improving, actually requires *increasing* quantities of labour (and the other factors of production, *land and *capital) to keep each individual supplied with food and shelter. Represented simply as the cost—in terms of labour, land and capital—of supporting the life of one person, the process of development is a process of declining efficiency.[54]

At first this seems odd because—as Adam Smith described—in the developing *intermediate economy, we see a vast *increase* in output per person, perhaps through improved technology. Surely those productivity improvements represent an improvement in efficiency? The explanation is that the increased output goes primarily into creating and maintaining intermediate goods such as aqueducts, *transport and administration—that is, the new infrastructures and gismos which the individual never actually gets to consume, but which become necessary for keeping the developing (intensifying) economy in existence. The need for all that stuff is the nature of intensification, and the essence of its increasing inefficiency.[55]

Here we discover the crucial distinction between *labour-saving* productivity advances and *scale-enabling* productivity advances. Those early productivity advances—which actually arose mainly from a massive increase in working time—were mainly scale-enabling: ploughed straight into intensification and its attendant multiplication of intermediate infrastructures. And that process, with varying degrees of intensity, has continued in our economy ever since. In a *large economy, it takes more work, more stuff, to keep you, dear reader, alive.

So, here we have the Intensification Paradox, elegantly summarised by Marvin Harris: *intensification inevitably leads to declining efficiencies.*[56]

The paradox is central to several key entries (listed at the end of this entry). And it is quite an optimistic idea, because it means that as the economy of the future deintensifies, it will become more resource-efficient: it will need fewer resources as it shrinks, *and* it will use its resources more efficiently. There are economies of downsizing. The deintensified society will be more efficient; it will require less labour and energy *per capita*. Hunter-gatherer societies were supremely efficient in terms of labour and energy. There is no argument to be made for "returning" to a hunter-gatherer society; and yet, the argument is widely made—not just in *Lean Logic*—for *permaculture, which is in a sense a half-way house. Herding is half way between hunting and livestock farming; permaculture is half way between gathering and vegetable gardening or arable farming.

A *frank recognition that the process of intensification is the upside of the adaptive cycle (as discussed in the *Wheel of Life) leads unavoidably to an equal recognition that the cycle will have its deintensifying downside too. Yet the ambiguity won't go away: there is no doubt that a small economy can achieve such efficiency gains (with its material demand shrinking faster than its size), but the extent to which it is possible for a large economy

I

to achieve them is not clear. But hold on, if the giant infrastructures are *needed* for a large economy, how can we contemplate the idea of our large economy getting by without them? Well, we can't, but there may be some scope for a reduction in their *scale. This is because the principle, or presumption, of *economies of scale has been so dominant that the practice has been taken even further than *necessary. Patterns of behaviour, once established, turn into *ideologies, powerful and unquestioned; there is overshoot.

We could still support our large-scale *political economy even if we had local abattoirs, post offices, schools, magistrates' courts, railways, more local food production and empowered local *communities. And modern small-scale technologies, so long as they continue to be available, enable deconcentrated—*localised—industry on the *neotechnic pattern, with some progress towards the *proximity principle. So, in this sense, a considerable amount of rowing-back from the present extremes of intensification is possible. And yet, that still leaves intact the big structures—the long lines of supply in *food, *energy, *water, *materials, equipment and *money. Intensification can, therefore, be mitigated; it cannot be reversed. And this is where the ambiguity stops: that mitigation, deintensifying as fast and as far as the size of our present *population allows, is essential. Whatever future is in store for us, a deintensified, somewhat-more-local economy will be a lot better placed to survive it than one in which the whole concept of local competence has been wiped off the map.

*Intermediate Economy, Regrettable Necessities, Lean Economics, Capital, Intentional Waste, Competitiveness, Slack and Taut, Culture, Unlean.

INTENTION. One of the properties (Rule 1) of a system designed on the principles of *lean thinking. This first, critical, stage defines what you want to achieve: resist the temptation to add numerous other objectives, since this will only destroy the focus and rule out the possibility of discovering a *common purpose. But you don't need to resist the temptation to adopt an aim which is beyond what you think you can achieve—for among the resources available to you is *pull, and its speciality is discovering solutions.

LIMITED AIMS
The case for chopping
the Intention down to size

The business analyst Robert Schaffer suggests four criteria for intentions that succeed.

> Urgency: Break it down into urgent and compelling objectives, which everybody can recognise as vital and necessary *now*. Realism: Get results soon. People should be able to look forward to a first success in a matter of weeks.
> Clarity: The objectives must be defined in specific terms: quantities, dates, quality tolerances.
> Commitment: The people involved should have the commitment, *authority and resources to get there.

He calls this the "Breakthrough Strategy", and uses the example of the Bonaventure Express [freight] Terminal of the Canadian National Railway, which had a history of terrible quality, late deliveries and rising costs—and had suffered a stream of company doctors, each with their own doomed prescriptions.

Schaffer proposed that they should concentrate on getting just one train—the 242—to carry a higher proportion of the load it was actually scheduled to carry: a mere 60% would do for a start. Hitting that modest aim was the first experience of success after years of *demoralisation, and it was followed by the recovery of the company and its managers—"no longer the passive losers whom everyone was trying to improve".[57]

But of course it isn't as simple as that, for two reasons. First, overall aims consist of many specific means towards that end, the first of which do indeed need to be recognised as realistic and achievable—and within a reasonably short time.

Secondly, there is the question of who decides what the Intention is to be. Four alternative sources come to mind:

1. It comes with the job. The original application of lean thinking, in car production, does not leave it to the production team to decide on their own Intention. The workers are there not just to apply their minds, but to apply their minds to the building of cars. They might decide that the best thing to do on a sunny day like this is to go out and play cricket, but the management might have a different plan.

2. Here the Intention is bottom-up; it comes from the *community itself—perhaps to hold a *carnival, to start a local school, or to establish a long-term *commons project such as installing and maintaining an irrigation *system.

3. It is imposed by an authoritarian regime whose decisions, extending beyond the Intention itself, include every detail of what is to be done, and how (*Unlean).

4. This is 'gap-lean'—where, for instance, an authoritarian regime leaves some gaps in its control in which lean can flourish. The ingenuity of prisoners-of-war in circumstances which are as controlling as the authorities can make them is, perhaps, a case of gap-lean—with room for super-lean responses, given the chance, thanks to the efforts of the regime to rule out any possibility of lean at all. Such a regime may leave little choice to its victims other than to focus their minds on the task with all the life-saving *ingenuity they can find, during the long wait for their chance to rebel.

As the entry on the Commons shows, the only enduring way of making or sustaining a large-scale commons in our own time is the long route of bottom-up decision, building the motivation of *loyalty layer-by-layer from foundations of personal commitment. And yet—we should not be so seduced by our admiration of this obviously-right way of doing it that we fail to notice that other models have also had their impressive records. Autocratic companies have had their moments. The blood-strewn hydraulic tyrannies described in *Unlean were successful for thousands of years: hyperprojects such as building the Great Wall of China or the Pyramid of Cheops were awesome exercises in effective management. *Organic farming invented itself in the gaps unintentionally left in the state-supported, agri-industrial establishment.

So, intention of various kinds and from diverse sources can still work, in the sense of providing a focused frame of reference. Does it therefore really matter what the source is? Well, it does, for several reasons, no doubt, but just one will do: Intentions of type 1, 3 and 4 have the problem that they crash. Type 1 depends critically on senior management deciding on the Intention, and recent problems in celebrated lean companies have suggested that it is subject to cycles of decadence and revolution. Type 3 also leads to decadence, followed by revolution and maybe civil war, followed by recovery for a time of stability, followed by another revolution. The crash in the case of type 4 differs in that it may be the context that crashes, leaving the long-sustained intention and its slow-motion revolution the winner. But, in whatever form, the moment of *kaikaku arrives.[58]

As for Type 2—the truly bottom-up intention—is this cycle/revolution-free? Well, it may be, so long as the conditions for its stability are maintained—and they may well be self-stabilising (*Commons, Wheel of Life).

Intention—rule 1 of *lean thinking—needs all the other rules really, to be fully understood. Yet an intriguing aspect of lean is that, in a sense, each of the five rules—intention, *lean means, *flow, *pull and *feedback—contains the whole story. If you think hard enough about any one of them it takes you into an understanding of all the others. Intention certainly does that. Reach for a long attention span and *reflect on it. That's lean thinking.

*Humility, Harmonic Order.

INTENTIONAL WASTE. The deliberate destruction of goods, or the production of goods and events which use up a lot of labour but are of no practical value. It has been widely practised in *traditional societies and, in some form, in most societies, with the partial but significant *exception of our own.

Fertile ecologies have one big problem in common: they are too productive for their own good. Surplus is produced that—unless checked, managed, destroyed or removed—will eventually destroy the *system. Lakes can become so rich with life that they die; many forests rely on periodic fire to clear out their choking abundance; the spruce fir forests of North America, left undisturbed for long enough, become so richly and

I

closely entwined that the birds can't get to the spruce budworm which, left to breed in peace, will in due course destroy the forest.[59]

Human societies, too, have been extraordinarily productive. The more successful they are, the more capital they accumulate. Here we need to use the distinction made in *Capital between:

a. the *foundation capital* on which everything else depends—essentially genetic inheritance and the fertile, watered *ecology—which has to be preserved at all costs; and

b. *growth capital*, whose growth produces more growth which, if not held in check, will ultimately destroy foundation capital itself.

In order to limit or prevent that *growth, growth capital has to be controlled, in one or more of three ways:

- By preventing its growth.
- By destroying it, or discarding it, following growth.
- By ensuring that—whatever it produces—its output does not take the form of further growth capital. That is, let it produce only useless ornaments, or extravagant, labour-intensive carnivals—let it be *wasted*. For then its impact on foundation capital is zero or minimal, in comparison to its impact if it did something useful, such as building machine tools or motorways, training construction engineers, or making productive investments that produced more growth.

If growth capital is allowed to accumulate unchecked, it will produce more than can be contained in a *closed-loop system, and the system will in due course break down. However, if part of that capital is intentionally discarded (in sufficient quantity), or used up in *carnival and *play, folly and fun, this will reduce production to a level at which it can be kept within the limits of a closed-loop system, making it possible that the *ecosystem (or *community) will endure.

Waste-reduction has a key place with respect to foundation capital, for soil fertility and some scarce *materials have to be conserved—ideally what is 'waste' to one part of the system should be a valuable input for another. *But the central economic ethic is not about reducing waste in all its forms;* it is about sustaining or—if necessary—increasing

it in some of its forms, acknowledging growth capital as having lethal potential and thus wasting it, managing it, using it for decoration and delight, or destroying it.

In response to this—whether by understanding, instinct or accident—former societies have devised many ways of getting rid of excess. Weapons, jewels, artefacts, even ships, would be deposited in the grave of a chief. Traditional societies organised an endless series of little crashes: creative-destruction-moments, *kaikaku*-parties. A frequent event would be the "potlatch" (the word is from the Chinook language of the Pacific Northwest coast of America, but the practice is widely present). This was a *competitive *ceremony of mutually assured destruction in which each contestant would have to more-than-match his opponent's sacrifice of his own possessions, often by burning, to the point of material devastation for the property of both. In this same profligate tradition, the Egyptians built more pyramids than there were pharaohs to bury in them; and the Florentines and Venetians of the Renaissance spent in abundance on churches, paintings and carnivals.[60]

But it was not only about sacrifice: when *gifts are given, something comes back. As the anthropologist Marcel Mauss writes,

> Gifts to humans and to the gods also serve the purpose of buying peace between them both.[61]

This is *contract making: there is a gift, there is the obligation to *reciprocate, and the imbalance between what is given and what is received can be rather large: whereas God gives the gift of life and the whole world, all He gets back is a mere cathedral. Mauss summarises:

> those gods who give and return gifts are there to give a considerable thing in place of a small one.[62]

The medieval cathedrals and the astonishing churches—big works of *art in little villages—used up the excess wealth which is the curse of a stable society. Cultures have to a large extent been organised around the task of finding celebratory ways of destroying *la part maudite*—"the accursed share", as Georges Bataille describes it—the capital which would otherwise endow *resilient societies with the curse of *growth.[63]

It can be a process of the utmost decorum. A modern demonstration of an ancient version of this comes from people who are not famous for their profligate lifestyles. At the Royal Academy in London in 1995, there was an exhibition of Tibetan art. In one of the rooms of the exhibition, four monks in their saffron robes toiled for weeks at a large and complex work of art: a sand mandala, made in intricate geometric shapes of coloured sand, guided by written instructions which they were translating from words into pattern. There was a sense of gravity, intense concentration, even reverence, in the room, and the great pattern, still unfinished, had a meaning for those who could read it, and beauty for the rest. The climax of this quiet *festival was to throw the whole lot into the Thames.[64]

Yet for the *market economy, things are different. From the early years of the Industrial Revolution, society needed all its resources to invent and build its way through its difficult, touch-and-go transition: from a *small-scale society depending on *local economies and firewood to a giant industrial economy depending on a correspondingly massive infrastructure of engineering, transport, *complication and *regrettable necessities. As it walked this punishing route, it could not afford to discard surplus over and above the unintended waste that came with its technology—with the vast investments into which it was being forced, material want was all too evident and it needed to use or invest all the resources it could get. At the same time, it gradually lost the *reciprocities of bonding, of *culture, *loyalty and *place, and turned instead to the price mechanism: "I will deal with you if and only if you are competitive; otherwise I will deal with Fred, whose prices are lower."[65]

The new market state, therefore, has not recognised surplus as a problem and destroyed it accordingly. Instead, its surplus has been conserved and valued; in fact, it has been reinvested. The modern economy has turned the problem of surplus into more surplus, to be used, in turn, in the production of even more, at compound *interest. *Capital—including human capital (population)—breeds capital. But a system that breaks free of constraints on its *growth is the curse of ecological *ethics; this is the sin that won't be forgiven. The resulting exponential growth postpones the necessary process of destruction, ensuring that human society loses control of its inevitable unleashing. Modern society doesn't understand surplus; it carefully conserves it, invites it in like

the Trojan horse. It stores up this excess—this accursed share—ready and waiting for the crash. As Bataille comments, "It causes us to *undergo* what we could *bring about* in our own way, if only we understood."[66]

The Lean Economy

What will the *Lean Economy do about surplus? It will be built on a systems-literate foundation of *closed-loop systems for all its primary resources. Its small-scale labour-*saving* *elegance will *waste* potential labour by making full-time work obsolete. Rediscovering the community building blocks that make a society, free of the *taut high-tension grid of *competitive prices, it will integrate *economics into a culture which recovers and values the *gift of choice.

Instead of having to produce to common competitive standards, it will instead be able to choose labour-intensive, inefficient methods: it will cultivate land as it wishes, work with whatever loving *craftsmanship it knows, take time off, make music, think, *sleep, cherish philosophy, control its own *population, know its own *political economy and *ecology well enough to understand the deep ambiguous meaning of *waste, and recover the *intelligence of the early cultures that knew that they had to destroy, or waste, or spend on spectaculars, because their ecology and their lives depended on it.

The inhabitants of the Lean Economy of the future could, perhaps, build cathedrals and pyramids, but there are probably enough of those. It would be better if they concentrated on being interesting. If so, they will have moved beyond the primitive ethic of competitiveness. Relations between inhabitants of these enduring and *resilient lean political economies will not be reduced to their ability to compete, but enriched by their talent for surprise.

*Growth, Lean Economics, Slack and Taut, Script, Leisure, Sorting.

INTEREST. (1) Money earned by money (*Usury).

(2) Engagement with a subject on its own terms; *encounter with it beyond preoccupation with the self.

(3) Rational advantage—that is, recognition of what you want: it is in your interests to eat if you are hungry. The interest is still rational even if it is mistaken—you eat

the food even though you should have suspected it contained salmonella; it is not rational if you know it has salmonella, *and* you don't want to get food poisoning, *but* you eat it all the same. That is not as improbable as it may appear, because of divided intentions. You want to drink five pints; you also want to keep your driving licence. Your decision as to which of those intentions is to be overridden is not necessarily a rational one: it may be a direct, pre-rational expression of who you are, of what your body, its hormones, its addictions, reflexes and nervous system instruct (*Identity).

(4) The pathway by which a person formed her opinion on a subject in question: the prior agenda and *loyalties that made her think the way she does (*Emergence).

(5) The potential for material or other gain from a subject which—unless successfully inhibited by *cultural, constitutional or practical constraints—will lead the person to concentrate just on that gain and on the falsehoods and *bad faith needed to procure it (*Looter's Ethics).

*Subjective, *Ad Hominem*, Incentives, Credit Union, Capital.

INTERMEDIATE ECONOMY. That part of the economy which consists of forms of production and other activities which, though necessary, do not directly provide the goods and services which consumers *actually* want and *need. That is, the intermediate economy does tasks which have to be done just to keep things going, to enable the *civic society to exist on its very large *scale: goods transport, sewage, landfill sites, electricity grids, social workers, police and prisons, regulation and policy-making, inspectors, bureaucrats, parking wardens, and the large and growing task of *protecting and repairing the environment. And it includes the remedial economy—the *social services, special *education, geriatric care, things which are added to the economy's commitments as *expectations change, as the stresses and casualties of large-scale anonymous living call for attention, and as *families and *communities become less willing and able to provide that care.

As *intensification develops, the need for these infrastructures and commitments increases, but should the size of the economy begin to fall, the intermediate tasks remain as pressing as ever. Either for practical reasons (keeping sewage and waste disposal systems going)

or in response to expectations (care, for instance, for those whose lives entirely depend on it), the intermediate economy remains unchallenged and unchanged as resources decline. There is a ratchet effect: it grows smoothly in response to economic *growth, and as governments give it priority for the funds that growth makes available; but any decline is in the teeth of opposition, and may in the end be catastrophic.

The intermediate economy exists in various forms in every large civic society; it is the signature of large scale. The big intermediate economy of the industrial age is not a way of making life in giant cities better, it is a way of making it possible. It is a necessity—a *regrettable necessity; the goods and services of the intermediate economy deliver no joy in their own right: we need these things to enable us to get by.

The most obvious example of a regrettable necessity is the transport of goods: it is a necessity, given the large-scale *economy and *population, which require long, *complicated supply chains to deliver energy, nutrients and *materials, and to dispose of *waste. But there is nothing in the actual process of *transport which adds to the quality of the goods or to the flavour of the *food: our hearts do not leap with delight at the sight of an articulated truck; we just put up with it. Yet this is where the bulk of demand for *energy and resources comes from. The intermediate economy is the price of size; the large scale of the economy both requires the big infrastructures, and makes them possible. It is the product, and the enabler, of growth.

The civic societies of the past—such as the highly-evolved, elaborate Roman civilisation—relied on growth, too, and for most of the same reasons. They had to become more *productive, not just to keep pace with the needs of their increasing populations, but to build their intermediate economies. So they intensified, producing more output *per capita* (per person). But that output was used to develop the intrinsically-undesired intermediate economy so that, in terms of their ability to sustain *per capita well-being*, their economies became increasingly inefficient. This is the *Intensification Paradox: intensification inevitably leads to declining efficiency.

Meanwhile productivity improvements generate growth; and the growing economy requires extended infrastructures; and extended infrastructures must be

INTERMEDIATE GOODS
Or: things we don't want but have to have

"Intermediate" is used here in a different sense from that which is current in *economics, where intermediate goods are "partly finished goods which form inputs to another firm's production processes and are used up in that process".[67]

Lean Logic uses "intermediate economy" and "intermediate goods" in the sense given by E.J. Mishan in the 1970s, who pointed out that much of what we actually buy as consumers consists of things which we would just as soon do without, but which are really just part of the toil and trouble of being a citizen:[68]

> A large proportion of the goods that enter into estimates of national income . . . are not, in fact, finished goods, or goods 'wanted for their own sake', as they ought to be. Rather they are *intermediate* goods . . . There is, as always, some uncertainty about where the line should be drawn . . . .[69]

Mishan lists goods and services of many kinds which could be understood as "intermediate" more accurately than "final": *defence, *law and order, travel (both business and leisure), *education (most of which is preparation for jobs), media information, *healthcare (treating the effects of congestion and urban life), vacations (recovering from the work of running the industrial machine), institutional lubricants (banks, employment agencies).

Another example is "defensive expenditure": "the purchase or provision of goods and services, such as ambulances and burglar alarms, which are intended to offset harm rather than positively enhance well-being".[70]

I

paid for with further productivity improvements. Those improvements in turn produce further growth which requires further expansion in the infrastructures. . . . This cycle of *growth—leading to dependence on a voracious intermediate economy—has been integral to all *civic societies.[71]

One trick for achieving the spectacular productivity improvements that all this calls for is the specialisation (division) of labour, and for an illustration of how effective that can be in producing growth, here is Adam Smith (1723–1790) on the subject, with the manufacture of nails and pins as his example. Division of the labour of pin-making, splitting up the task into eighteen parts, each done by one worker, makes it possible for each worker to make . . .

> . . . four thousand eight hundred pins in a day. But if they had all wrought separately and independently and without any of them having been educated to this peculiar business, they could certainly not have made twenty, perhaps not one pin in a day.[72]

Pottery offers another example. Start with a society of subsistence farmers, some of whom feel they could do with a few more mugs for the family breakfast. They *could* make potters wheels, get hold of some clay, practise making a few pots, and try firing them in the bread oven. In fact, they realise that it would be better to get Aelfrith in the next village to make them, because he has a wheel and kiln already set up, and he knows what he is doing. The anthropologist and mathematician Colin Renfrew agrees:

> A craftsman (potter) could produce far more of his product and of a far better quality than could five farmers each devoting one-fifth of his time to making the same product.[73]

This makes for a more elaborate and *complex system, but . . .

> . . . it is very sound strategy for a society to maximise specialisation through the agency of a central redistributive organisation. In this way it is possible, through economies of scale,

225

A STORY OF POTS
*Complication builds from an innocent start.

1. more pots
2. → more transport
3. → transport infrastructures
4. → more tax to pay for the roads
5. → more bureaucracy to raise the tax
6. → more jobs available in towns
7. → larger towns
8. → dislocation of rural social structures
9. → relaxation of sexual rules
10. → higher population
11. → greater need for food and resources
12. → military power and conquest
13. → flow of wealth into a growing society
14. → more pots . . .[74]

to support a very much larger population than would be the case if each individual family or village had to be largely self-supporting, producing all the commodities which it used.[75]

It is hard to argue with that. But try following through the implications: you get all the pots you need, but you get a whole lot of other things which you hadn't bargained for too (see "A Story of Pots" sidebar). Before you know where you are, you have built up a big civilisation with ox-drawn wagons trundling along the road, or fleets of cargo ships crossing the Mediterranean, or rivers of articulated trucks bashing down motorways, or forests felled for timber, or an industrial civilisation created to serve and be served by coalmines—and all you really wanted was enough mugs to go round for the family breakfast. Progress comes encumbered with a storm of *regrettable necessities.[76]

So, we get the spiral of *growth—and the *Intensification Paradox—where individual productivity improves, but the total quantity of goods and services needed grows so much that more work is needed to keep one person alive—that is, more work *per capita* of population. And there is more to it than that—for now

a ratchet effect clicks in. If (to stay with the pots), by the time the society has got to stage 14, the structures of transport, administration and power were to fail, it could not simply go back to the safety of stage 1: it would soon find itself in a much worse position—perhaps with no pots at all, and not much else either.

And intrinsic to all this is a change in the pattern of *land use—the way in which a society uses its space and understands the meaning of *'place'. If all the pots (and other goods) are to be made full-time by a few people, instead of just occasionally by every *household, it obviously makes sense (as suggested in the pot sequence) for people to live fairly close together. And the greater the degree of specialisation, the more the population moves from small dispersed settlements to become concentrated in towns: there is agglomeration. As civic societies evolve, they develop both the ability and the need to concentrate production and population in *large-scale urban economies.[77]

Moreover, the larger the town, the larger the area of land on which it depends—and the more *charismatic and decisive must the government be to hold the whole system together; notably, to raise taxes to pay for all the infrastructures and to defend them against other states on a similar path of expansion. Then the ratchet effect clicks in again: since the population is concentrating in towns, it has to build up its specialisms, its transport, its bureaucracy and its dependence on imports: there is nowhere else for growth and intensification to go except upwards.

. . . or downwards, of course. And if we take a long view of the archaeological record, we see that, while the pattern is sometimes one of *civic societies being destroyed by some external force—environmental, *climatic or military—there is a deeper sequence at work as well. As settlements become ever more large, elaborate, materially voracious and tightly-connected, they have less of the flexibility needed to respond to events and change, less *resilience, and need their *complex support systems to be in full working order, all the time. The depletion of *capital and critical assets—especially *water, forests and fertile soil—and the measures taken in response, which themselves depend on ever-increasing quantities of those scarce assets, deepen the state's inefficiency to the point at which any action it takes makes matters worse.

By the time it becomes clear that the state itself is part of the problem, it is on the way to collapse.[78]

It tends to happen quickly. Although the additional stresses on any day may be not especially greater than those of the day before, the accumulation may reach the cusp at which suddenly the ground falls away. The mathematical models of this tipping-point for the late stage of a civic society are the calculus-equivalent of a football rolling idly towards the edge of a cliff: it may even be slowing or coming to rest at the moment at which suddenly it . . . shifts into a new *paradigm.[79]

After the failure of the *market, our intermediate economy will rapidly deconstruct and cease to be available to provide essential services. The collapse will mean, in effect, a breakdown in distribution systems for *food, *waste disposal and running *water, in police services and civic order. The *Lean Economy is a concept of recovery and *resilience, rebuilding an enduring political economy on a scale matched to the assets and options actually available to it. What many people want to achieve now by reducing consumption in the interests of rescuing the planet will be accomplished quickly, but unkindly.

With a reduced *population and smaller settlements, requiring no elaborate intermediate economy, the state is brought back into equilibrium with its—now much impoverished—environment. But, because of their smaller *scale, the communities of the future will be less *complicated, with a correspondingly reduced intermediate economy. They will have *elegance. Our *civic society, like its predecessors, will break up. *Travelling light, being able to get by without the vast intermediate economy, is the key to the *Wheel of Life. *Localisation is about making a virtue out of this necessity. *Transition is about starting the process now.

*Touch-Down.

INTERNAL EVIDENCE, THE FALLACY OF. The error of judging a proposition to be true on the strength of evidence selected, intentionally or unintentionally, to confirm it. This is related to *Cognitive Dissonance and *Begging the Question, and to forms of *Expertise (the No Evidence Fallacy).

In some *cultures it is safe to assume that statements which are intended to be believed are in fact *true, but this state of affairs is easily eroded and lost. In its absence, the other option—when arguing a case which you are sure is right—is to meddle with the evidence to suit your case. This can help to persuade your victim, and yourself, but with some strange results.

One of the reasons why strange beliefs are so addictive is that they cannot easily be faulted by *internal* evidence. If you allow yourself to forget everything else you know about a subject, and listen with rapt attention just to the *story itself, the question of whether it is true or not does not even seem to arise. Here, for instance is Oliver Goldsmith (1730–1774), doctor, playwright, essayist, naturalist, writing about a patient (not one of his own) from a farming family that lived in such close and loving association with their cows that they became like them:

> The man in question was a citizen of Bristol, of about 20 years of age, and what seemed more extraordinary still, of a ruminating family, for his father was frequently subject to the same infirmity. This young man usually began to chew his meat over again within about a quarter of an hour after eating. His ruminating after a full meal generally lasted about an hour and a half, nor could he sleep until this task was performed. The victuals, upon return, tasted even more pleasantly than at first; and returned as if they had been beaten up in a mortar. If he ate a variety of things, that which he ate first came up again first; and if this return was interrupted for any time, it produced sickness and disorder, and he was never well till it returned. Instances of this kind, however, are rare and accidental; and it is happy for mankind that they are so. Eating is a pleasure of so low a kind, that none but such as are nearly allied to the quadrupede, desire its prolongation.[80]

This is from the man who gave us:

> Sweet was the sound, when oft at evening's close
> Up yonder hill the village murmur rose.[81]

Admittedly, it is an extreme case, but it illustrates the possibility of sustaining a ridiculous proposition simply by referring to more and more circumstantial evidence: your life can be given meaning and passion

by persistent invention, and your friends are those who see it the same way. There is no argument so absurd that it is impossible to find abundant evidence in its support.

A reliable source of convenient truths is the existence of sharply distinct factions, each on the defensive. And once you are in a group united by a strong opinion—a faction—it is hard, bordering on impossible, to think independently. If you do, you are likely to be excommunicated, losing the meaning of your life, including your friendships; to help you to stay in line, there are little mantras ("global justice", "the liberation of humanity") around which, or against which ("imperialism", "profit", "greed"), you can unite.

Here is a large-scale farmer mixing up exaggeration, fiction and outrage at a tendency he evidently detests: the "Organic Taleban", he writes, want us to believe that organic fertilisers are "made by little old Cornish ladies boiling up seaweed on the beach". Well, he does not really believe that; it is chortling *hyperbole, but he does believe that organic cultivation is no less absurd. He is, however, well-defended by the faction of those who couldn't agree more.[82]

*Relevance, Expectations, Memory Fillers, Imagination, Generalisation Fallacies.

INTOXICATION. The condition that arises when an enthusiast encounters someone with whom he can share his passion.

INTUITION. The ability to understand, or respond accurately to, a complex issue without consciously thinking it through and knowing the *reasons. The mind gets to the point without knowing why. Many skills, such as playing the piano, drawing, or quickly judging the veracity of a stranger, can only be performed if they are embedded in parts of the brain which get things done without having to consult the conscious mind. But you need to do a lot of work to get there. Antonio Damasio explains,

> The quality of one's intuition depends on how well we have reasoned in the past; on how well we have classified the events of our past experience in relation to the emotions that preceded and followed them; and also how well we have reflected on the successes and failures of our past intuitions. Intuition is simply rapid cognition with the required knowledge partially swept under the carpet, all courtesy of emotion and much past practice.[83]

Intuition (if it is correct) gives you answers. And yet, sometimes you are better off without them. That, at least, is what John Keats suggests with his "negative capability" which, as he explains in a letter to his brothers, George and Thomas, in 1817,

> . . . is when a man is capable of being in uncertainties, Mysteries, doubts, without any irritable reaching after fact and reason . . . the sense of Beauty overcomes every other consideration, or rather obliterates all consideration.[84]

The conscious mind, as Keats notes in *Ode to a Nightingale*, is a clumsy, uninventive instrument: "the dull brain perplexes and retards". Negative capability opens the way to going along with something, accepting it and dealing with it with good *manners, without having to understand it. It is an *encounter with beauty.
*Local Wisdom, Humility, Spirit.

INVISIBLE GOODS. The *paradox of a materialist society. We consume a very large number of goods—not least *intermediate goods and services which really are needs rather than desires. But what about the goods which we might be expected actually to enjoy? Well, responses are mixed, but there is often some guilt in there; a tendency to explain them away as *needs which leave us with little reasonable alternative; a hesitation to celebrate them as material artefacts in their own right. In this sense the modern *market economy is *less* materialistic than those traditional societies for which goods and their conspicuous display were central to *festival and *culture, over and above providing for subsistence. Along with all other forms of communication, goods, in all their extravagance and unnecessariness, drew the lines of social relationships. As the anthropologists Mary Douglas and Baron Isherwood write,[85]

> Forget the idea of consumer irrationality. Forget that commodities are good for eating, clothing and shelter; forget their usefulness and try instead the idea that commodities are good for thinking; treat them as a nonverbal medium for the human creative faculty.[86]

For various reasons, goods in our materialistic culture have become, in a sense, invisible—because they are losing their *implicit* functions—the symbolism, the social function which ought to travel with them. Here are some examples: *food, in addition to its *overt* function of providing nutrition, also has, or had, an *implicit* function in *reciprocal giving and in the daily interaction round a table, without which the durability of the *household in any structured sense is improbable. The implicit function of clothes as signals of social belonging, *courtesy and standing has waned. Sport has lost much of its implicit but crucial function of *ceremony and *play, and is left with the overt but futile business of winning. Perhaps *sex has lost a bit of its implicit function in cementing relationships and is becoming a simpler, reduced proposition.

The effect of this disenchantment, this *denial of the spirit and deeper significance of the currency of goods, services and behaviour with which we live, is to make it harder to recall anything about them at all. The object was eaten, worn, contested or had, but the implicit function—which is the only bit that engages the mind, *emotions and *spirit—probably did not happen at all, and if it did, you must have blinked at the wrong moment. Goods are finally becoming *instrumentalised, invisible except for their instrumental purpose. Austerity, in a sense, is upon us ahead of schedule.
*Carnival, Needs and Wants, Ceremony, Composition, Intentional Waste, Ritual.

IRONIC SPACE. The gap between contradictions—such as the contradiction between what you think about something and the evidence about it, of which you may only recently have become aware. It is a *paradox which, if recognised, demands a resolution, but may never get one. It is the obscurity that comes in inherited *myth or sacred language, bringing the plain delight and enigma of incomprehension. Or it is a clash between ideas which are consistent within themselves, but not with each other. A momentary loss of bearings gives us the disorientation enjoyed in *humour, quickly resolved. But, if the contradiction cannot be resolved except with long reflection—if at all—this is ironic space, a main source for, and a necessary condition of, *culture and *judgment.[87]

Ironic space is the habitat of questions from which there are insights to be derived, but no definitive answers. There is an illustration of this in Titian's painting *Noli Me Tangere*, which has Jesus shrinking from Mary Magdalene as she reaches towards him in a tension between closeness and separateness which invites *reflection, never quite resolved. Reason is not enough:

the *certainty it achieves is at the cost of simply ignoring the difficulties. Deep reflection in ironic space may not discover a solution, but may make a person. "What is at stake" comments Charles Taylor, "is the definition of those inchoate evaluations [i.e., not yet mature, but establishing and testing the most basic assumptions] which are sensed as being essential to our identity."[88]

*Lean thinking demands thought. Ironic space consists of questions and meanings which demand thought to be sustained for a long time. It is created by a society's culture. The most fertile form of culture in this context is *religion.
*Identity, Implicit Truth.

IRRELEVANCE, THE FALLACY OF (*Ignoratio elenchi*). The classic illustration of this fallacy is the case of a man who, on his way home at night, drops his keys. Instead of searching the area where he dropped them, he searches under a street light elsewhere, on the basis that searching is easier when well-lit. *Ignoratio elenchi* literally translates as "ignorance of the connection"—an *elenchus* in Rome was a pendant worn as an ear-ring: it joins up.[89]

This is a core *fallacy, in that many of the other fallacies can be seen as examples of it. Most arguments arise because one or both sides have missed the point. If, when you hear an argument about a matter of public policy, frustration builds up, and you say to yourself, or anyone else in earshot, "But the whole *point* is . . .", that argument has probably been corrupted by the fallacy of *Ignoratio elenchi*.

We have a good example of this happening—and being detected—in John Maynard Keynes' *General Theory*. In chapter 19 he is writing about the received view of his time that the way to take an economy out of recession is to keep wages low. That seems reasonable doesn't it? Low wages feed through to low prices, and that means that consumers can afford to buy more, which in turn means that the sale of goods will go up and the economy will rise out of recession. Yes, yes, but the whole *point* is that if people are earning lower wages, their incomes will be lower too, so demand will fall, leading to a cycle in which low wages and low prices reinforce each other, so that the low wages will simply reduce prices, and an economy which is already stuck in recession will stay there.[90]

If by some magic you could reduce wages *without* reducing demand, that of course would work fine. But, as Keynes points out . . .

> . . . this assumption reduces the argument to an *Ignoratio elenchi*. [The classical theory on which it is based] has nothing to offer.[91]

Sadly, the tendency to miss the point of an argument increases in proportion to the passion with which the arguer is committed to her case. For example, take the argument that every *household should, by law, have in its possession one red widget. All sorts of reasons can be advanced for or against: this requirement is key to the government's policy of health and fitness of young people; it is especially relevant to its healthy hearts programme, to the prevention of verrucas, and to the maintenance of a balanced diet; it is essential to the nation's *competitiveness and standing in the world, to equal opportunity and the maintenance of a level playing field; indeed, there is a target to achieve 80% household ownership of red widgets by 2020—a major challenge, but an achievable one within the context of the Europe-wide red widget policy which will play a critical role in the Union's role as a world player, a counterweight to the United States and China; a global problem requires a global solution.[92]

It is the passionate *sincerity that keeps the hare of irrelevance running. If the discussion were merely technical—whether red widgets work best when they are square or round, for instance—the engineers, not caring much one way or the other, would get to the point and solve it—correctly—in a matter of minutes.

There is nothing more that needs to be said about irrelevance: time for a coffee break, but, oh, there seem to be quite a lot of people with their hands up. Please give your names and speak clearly:

- Aristotle, here, wants to point out that, if the case a person is arguing is absurd, then every argument advanced in its favour is irrelevant.[93]

- A Member of Parliament demonstrates the technique of tossing a blanket of irrelevant comments over a talkative general when it is time for bed:

  > General Dannatt has crossed an important line. He is playing a high-risk game. It is not appropriate to play party politics at this time. Dannatt should just get on with the job. After the conflict, if there are lessons to be learned, we should do so in a considered manner.[94]

- A gentleman who prefers not to give his name offers an example of blather: "Did I steal the horse? Let me tell you, I have lived with horses all my life, and I have three children, and I am a qualified car mechanic . . ."

- A sympathetic acquaintance demonstrates misplaced emphasis: "So, other than that, Mrs. Lincoln, how did you enjoy the play?"[95]

- Artemus Ward, entertainer (1834–1867), confides, "One of the principal features of my Entertainment is that it contains so many things that don't have anything to do with it."[96]

*Relevance, Distraction, Necessary and Sufficient, *Reductio ad Absurdum*, Shifting Ground, Straw Man, Time Fallacies.

J

JUDGMENT. See Reflection, Encounter, Flow, Presence, Casuistry, Intelligence, Practice, Spirit.

K

KAIKAKU. A *radical break. See Lean Thinking, Paradigm.

KAIZEN. *Incremental advance. See Lean Thinking, Paradigm.

L

LAND. The problem of access to land is fundamental and acute. The self-reliant localities of the future will need land; including in the less industrialised *nations, whose small farmers have lost their land to the large-scale *agriculture of the global *market. Land is in many ways the hardest problem of all. Depending of course on the size of the *population, the demand for land can be expected to exceed supply. Most wars, including civil wars, are about land. The land problem is a *wicked problem.[1]

One interesting person to chew these things over with is Ebenezer Howard, the man behind *Social Cities at the beginning of the last century. He relished the unlikely. He had to face up to the improbability of reorganising a landscape whose essential structure had already been laid down. With their drainage and sewerage systems unalterably settled, and their physical structure and railways already built, existing cities could not be adapted to the latticed pattern he proposed. He was no *incrementalist; his solution was simple and outrageous: the only thing to do is start again "on a bold plan on comparatively virgin soil . . . ; and when that simple fact is well grasped, the social revolution will speedily commence".[2]

That solution is not available to us now; Howard was lucky. The depression in agriculture was so deep that, in 1919, he was able to pick up the land on which Welwyn Garden City would be built for a mere £34 an acre (£800 at 2001 prices). The deposit was raised at speed over a cup of tea at King's Cross with the chairman of the Garden Cities and Town Planning Association, and the rest of the money—£50,000 (£11 million at 2001 prices)—was raised or promised in a hasty cab ride round the City of London.[3]

The population of England and Wales was smaller too—about 600 people per square mile compared with 900 today—living in larger *households, with minimal land devoted to roads and no land at all given over to airports and out-of-town shopping centres: this was a landscape with space. There were even patches of *common land which had escaped the Enclosures, which local people could use as a basis for subsistence. And the First World War brought the land of *families with no surviving heirs onto the market. In those days, H.G. Wells' Mr. Polly could walk and cycle for days in the empty roads of Kent, crossing misty meadows by moonlight, meeting almost nobody.[4]

But that all changed with the road building, the smaller households, the higher population and the industrialised agriculture which started tentatively in the second quarter of the century, and became established in the third. If Howard's book had been published closer to the present time, its hopes of taking advantage of cheap land for a massive programme of resettlement would have been thin. And much of the landscape in the market economy is so worn, contaminated, entombed in concrete and lacking in living *social capital that there is no happy future for it anyway, short of a completely fresh start.

And yet, despite several centuries in which open land in cities—such as the Marais of Paris and the canalside kitchen gardens of Amsterdam—have been buried under streets, some remains for lean production. There is a remnant of gardens, allotments and parklands; and almost any land can be used as the hard standing for intensive raised beds, glasshouses and renewable energy systems. Flat roofs have potential, as do the top floors of multi-storey car parks. Earth-filled tubs can make use of hard surfaces in gardens and on fire escapes. Demolished office buildings in the cities will yield unused space ready for partial reclamation; the deep rafts of poured reinforced concrete on which they stand will be hard to reclaim, but there are solutions even for this, such as building up the level with mixtures of prepared demolition waste and organic matter, after which it is possible to begin to restore the land with trees.[5]

So *ingenuity in the use of space has a contribution to make, but with current populations most urban settings will still fall well short of the food-growing land needed per person, even with significant reductions in *waste, and will remain reliant on food being trucked in every night. What we must hope for, then, is optimistic continuity: not a *climacteric, but a gentle nudge. And yet, ingenuity is never wasted, and we cannot afford to be *demoralised by the evident shortage of land. We do not know how much land there will be *per capita*, especially if we are thinking of it as a problem common to all *nations with large cities; we do not know how much the sea will claim; nor how much will be lost to drought; nor the size of the *population. It will be factors like these that decide whether land-famine and *conflict over land can be expected, and how intense it will be.[6]

Maybe we can take comfort from Leopold Kohr's claim that a shortage of space *can* have something to be said for it, in that it stimulates the evolution of *diversity and detail. If limits are well-defined, "the rest can be left to the forces released by *implosion*": social energy is concentrated by lack of space—as in a pressure cooker—and organic form evolves in response; in the end, everything is squeezed into the place where it belongs. That seems optimistic, too, but there may be *something* in it: the productivity of intensely labour-intensive attention to detail in the cultivation of *food can be spectacular.[7]

*Social City, Proximity Principle, Commons, Access.

LARDERS. Cool food-storage rooms. North-facing in the Northern Hemisphere. Thick stone shelf to keep some of the night coolness circulating during the day. Window with fine wire mesh to keep out the flies. Uses no energy (except, perhaps, a light bulb). Large enough to allow entry, followed by extended *reflection on *food, and some petty theft of a bit of moist, aromatic chicken if such is in residence.

Sadly displaced by the fridge, which uses a lot of *energy. And hums. And uses noxious gases. And costs. And needs to be made, *transported and then unmade.

The larder is temporarily obsolete. It will be back.

LARGE SCALE. See Scale.

LAW. See Lean Law and Order, Law and Change.

LAW AND CHANGE. The law is a key asset. But its conservation is neglected. When law has recently become established and brought peace, it is appreciated, conserved and cared for with an urgency that we have forgotten. Deriving its *authority from its constancy, the law was once compared with the sun: in ancient Near Eastern thought, "sun" and "justice" belonged together, and in the lyrical poetry of Psalm 19 we have a dazzling statement of this:

> In them [the heavens] he hath set a tabernacle for the sun: which cometh forth as a bridegroom out of his chamber, and rejoiceth as a giant to run his course . . .

And that, come to think of it, is just like that other defining feature of creation, the law:

> The law of the Lord is an undefiled law . . . The statutes of the Lord are right, and rejoice the heart: the commandment of the Lord is pure, and giveth light unto the eyes.[8]

And yet, the law in our day is not as undefiled as the psalmist thought it ought to be. For one thing, it lacks constancy:

> There is much too much law-making. Thousands and thousands of pages of primary and subordinate legislation are turned out every year, reaching the point where it is virtually impossible for those who administer the law to discover what it is. One will get a regulation made, and before it has come into force there will be an amendment, and the amendment will be amended before the amendment comes into force. And the databases are not always capable of keeping up with it.
>
> Tom Bingham, Start the Week, BBC Radio 4, 2010.[9]

It can also be an instrument of social engineering or vendetta. When this happens, those who are at the controls claim with sanctimonious *certainty that anyone who challenges it is a hooligan and law-breaker. This happened, for instance, in legislation in Germany in the 1930s, in the Former Soviet Union, and in Maoist China: to be a law-abiding citizen merged into being complicit with atrocity. The action needed to get rid of a tyrant is almost

L

always strictly illegal—as Patricia Meehan notes in her study of the foreign policy of the British Government in the 1930s: "It was the core of the British attitude to the German Opposition that disloyalty to the Nazi Government was high treason and those who took that stand were traitors, no matter how vile that government might be."[10] Deposing Saddam Hussein was illegal: having gassed the Kurdish villages and destroyed the Marsh Arabs along with their habitat, by law he should have been allowed to develop biological and nuclear weapons, and to continue to tyrannise his people and the region at leisure.[11]

But, as John Locke pointed out, respect for the law of a tyranny—the view that all but one should be under the restraint of laws—

> . . . is to think that men are so foolish that they take care to avoid what mischiefs may be done them by polecats or foxes, but are content, nay, think it safety, to be devoured by lions.[12]

Law in the *Lean Economy is limited. The moral sensibility from which it comes is, as Michael Oakeshott put it, "educated"—the law is there not to require *virtue but to underwrite *contracts. More generally, it is there to establish the rule-making and rule-observing republic—a society whose liberty is sustained by a texture of rules which, if not actually made by the people, are the accomplishment of a just *culture in which the people participate, and towards which they feel ownership. Like the rules of games, the laws are not necessarily moral statements, and they may seem arbitrary, but they form the *grammar by which citizens can make and sustain their *community and its laws, its *fortitude and its *flow, *conversation by conversation.[13]
*Lean Law and Order, Assent, Calibration, Constructivism, Rationalism.

LEADERSHIP. See Character.

LEAN BUILDING. The design, building or conversion of houses using local *skills and resources, and suited to self-reliant *community.

The stock of buildings inherited by the *Lean Economy is likely to be larger than it needs. It might not, therefore, build many new homes, but there will be drastic transformations. Here are three guidelines:

The first requirement of building, or retrofitting, in the local Lean Economy is that it should use a form of *appropriate technology, in the sense that it is within the reach of what the community can do for itself.[14] We cannot be sure what technologies will be available. We cannot even be certain that core technologies such as photovoltaics will be obtainable on any significant *scale. But we can be sure that people will want to use their houses for more than just living in. Participants—with *character—will want to work there, to make a *practical reality of their self-reliant lives, and to adapt their houses to meet those needs.[15] Houses will have the dynamic, flexible quality which was recommended by a report in the mid-twentieth century:

> With the greatly increased rate of social and economic change, the adaptable house is becoming a national necessity. . . . We see the investigation of the practical possibilities of doing it easily and at a reasonable cost as one of the most important lines of future research into the development of design and structure. The sooner it is started the better.
>
> *The Parker Morris Report,*
> *"Homes for Today and Tomorrow", 1961.*[16]

The second requirement is energy-efficiency. The recognised standard for this is the Passivhaus, which combines the highest energy efficiency with real comfort. It is based on an airtight, super-insulated fabric, with ventilation designed for heat recovery—heat exchangers gather heat from stale air on the way out and transfer it to fresh air as it comes in. Depending on the weather conditions, the Passivhaus can reduce *energy dependency by some 85 percent. Crucially, Passivhaus standards can be reached by retrofitting existing houses.[17]

Short of the extreme standards of the Passivhaus, there is still a lot that can be done to improve the energy-efficiency of houses. Simple draught-proofing can halve the energy needed for heating. Then there is the familiar range of options such as double glazing, cavity wall insulation—the standard solutions described in today's rich literature.[18]

Thirdly, houses should be recognised, not as mere artefacts—things for living in—but as living parts of a pattern extending into the neighbourhood and landscape. This is close to the recurring idea of *grammar in *Lean Logic*, and it was famously developed by the architect Christopher Alexander and his colleagues at the University of California, Berkeley, in the 1970s.[19]

We are speaking a 'pattern language', they suggest, when we build houses in clusters, in terraces, as work communities, in *neighbourhoods, with small *public squares, high places such as church spires, and common *land, with space for *play, for living out-of-doors, for animals. They advise: treat every site as individual and plan specifically for it; build houses which face the sun, which let in abundant light, which join up with others. Have big common areas at the heart of the *household, such as farmhouse kitchens; family members need rooms of their own as well as spaces for *common eating and for their work. Alexander and his colleagues like window-seats and windows overlooking local life. They like fireplaces. They like terraced slopes, places of shade under trees, and garden walls. They recommend vegetable gardens. They argue for places which have been designed with the living, rather than the engineering, in mind. And the idea of the pattern language has more recently been explored for application on the larger scale of *Transition.[20]

*Home, Holon, Social City.

LEAN DEFENCE. From some points of view, there will be a greatly reduced incentive for defence in the Lean Economy. States will have fewer distant interests to defend. But the evolution to the post-market settlement will bring tensions of its own. There will be competition for *land. Large urban populations could quickly find themselves in some desperation for *food. The fault lines of a *multicultural society could mature into deep divisions. The tensions considered in the entry on *population could mature under the pressures of scarcity. Urban populations will not stay put.

Among strategies that present themselves for consideration, here are four:

1. *Scepticism*. This is the argument that a breakdown of *law and order is unlikely, and that, in any case, it should not be discussed, since this could stimulate aggressiveness, turning out to be a *self-fulfilling forecast. On the other hand, it could be argued that there is already wide awareness of such events around the world, and that the acting out of resentments in the form of *violence is probably not significantly held back by any lack of awareness of violence as a possibility.[21]

2. *Appeasement*. A psychotherapist living near Totnes, Devon, argues that *local preparation for an urban break-out should take the form of cultivating more food than the people of Totnes need for their own consumption so that, in the event of the arrival of groups of hungry visitors from nearby towns and cities, there will be enough food to share with them.[22]

3. *Participation*. Here we have the darker view that local lean economies will not be able to assume that they have the benefit of peace in the landscape they live in. Disruption on a ferocious scale can be expected, and it may not settle down for many years. Defence will be a non-negotiable need. Participation in it will be shared, and some forms of this that have worked in the past are discussed in *Lean Law and Order.

One thing that cannot be predicted with any confidence is the nature of warfare in the future. It may be that some states will inherit very advanced munitions; along with that, they may have computer systems with war game capability which is so realistic and authoritative that they do not need actually to fight wars, once they can accept the verdict of war games. Or if they actually exchanged their nuclear weapons and other weapons of mass destruction, there might be little sequel to speculate about. But there is a reasonable probability, consistent with *Lean Logic*'s line of vision, that the wars that shape the future will be local.

Firearms and ammunition are complex to manufacture, requiring an *infrastructure of mining, steel-making precision-engineering, money and *transport. A substantial stock of arms will be inherited from the *market economy, but the demand will substantially outstrip the supply, and this will have several consequences.

First, it will confer decisive advantages to any group that has contrived to get hold of firearms. There will be little possibility of resistance to such groups, except in cases of *conflict between groups similarly armed.

L

Secondly, some groups will not have firearms, but they will still feel capable of taking on local settlements whose assets or land they want to acquire. Knives and staves are effective weapons against any group that has not substantially sacrificed normal life in the interests of defence.

Thirdly, some groups may acquire extreme weapons such as spent nuclear fuel or even plutonium extracted from it. The world's stock of these materials is widely distributed, and it is far from secure. Moreover, the specialist electronic defence equipment which is now in use—and being developed further— to protect those stocks is unlikely to be in working order. Here we have another reminder of the need to close down the *nuclear industry and to sequester its *waste in the limited time that remains. Similarly, other weapons, such as gas, biological weapons and, in due course, the potential of *nanotechnology, could be used. A priority for the present should be not simply to make these technologies safe under present conditions, but to make them unavailable for the future. Containment measures in full working order, and fully supplied with the necessary *energy, electronics and organisation, will become less available as the need for them increases.[23]

4. *Coalition.* As soon as there is awareness that the peaceable conditions needed by local lean economies are no longer available, communities will try to form defensive coalitions. This will not be easy. Coalitions will naturally be made up of settled communities who are already on their way to local self-reliance. They will have the *land, the *skills, the *community. The offensive groups, on the other hand, will tend to comprise people from towns and cities who lack such resources, and see no option other than to take them, by whatever means. The idea that there is enough to go round for everyone is an anachronism some 300 years behind the times. It is not only a matter of land, but the means to cultivate it in conditions where there is a lack of fuel, of traction such as horses, of secure ownership, and of the detailed complex of infrastructures and skills needed to harvest and store *food to last through the year. The dark arithmetic of land and *population will be recognised.

And yet, even after those consequences have been substantially played out, there will still be the need for coalitions. For a thousand years after the departure of the Romans, the politics of Britain was shaped by a series of oscillations between stable, nationwide government (with many variations on the meaning of "nation") and war: between invaders (Danes) and the indigenous population; between small *nations (Welsh, Scottish, Irish) and their powerful neighbour; or between armies whose causes and commitments were linked to *loyalties related to the families they belonged to and the estates they happened to live on.

The dates of final settlement are mixed in with dates that looked final at the time, but turned out not to be. Among the phantom closures in European history, there were days—in 216 BC, in 1461, 1644, 1813, and 1918, for instance—which seemed to be final, but settled nothing. There is a temptation to assume that we have put such matters behind us. Well, that's true in a way, for *democratic *market economies do not make war on each other. But that is not the political-economic order to which the future belongs.[24]

Yet the idea of coalitions and alliances is central here. Coming from a peaceable *green point of departure—*Transition Belsize Park's first public meeting included lengthy instructions in knitting—we find it hard to imagine the dark terror into which our ancestors—farmers and *family men—have walked, accompanied only by their *courage and allegiance. It doesn't have to be a modern war. Archers were the machine-gunners of their day, firing at the rate of twelve a minute to produce an arrow storm:

> The enemy either stood still, being unable to reply, or, charging blindly, were thrown into hopeless confusion. The arrows could stop a rush, not because they brought a man down, because they made him wild.[25]

If there is to be a solution, it will come in the form of a state that can keep the peace. It is to be hoped, intensely, that it is a highly decentralised state, a *modular system organised around *local self-reliance. But significant disorder may open the way to an authoritarian response justified by the claim that there is no other way of dealing with it. And the possibility of the survival of the modular form will remain open only so long as:

a. there is no threat from a state which, being more *complex and centralised, is more capable of coordinated and aggressive action, and is tempted to make trouble by the mere fact of knowing that it can; and

b. there is that common *cultural frame of reference to which *Lean Logic* refers continually.

It will not be the *market that holds it together, for that option will have closed. If there is a framework for peaceable settlement, it will be the *authority of a common *identity, defined explicitly in a shared culture and its expressions—in *rituals and affirmations which the market economy has not yet managed completely to destroy, in affections shared, insights lived for.

———

Lean defence, then, is here in the room—large and unavoidable, an unwelcome need and commitment. So, what to do? Well, first of all, don't rush. The first and proper response is—do nothing. Instead, enter the space of *reflection, love, reason, *encounter, friendship, *ignorance, *presence. Here is St Basil—someone who knew a thing or two about defence—doing just that, at a turbulent time in fourth century Caesarea in a letter to the monk, Urbicius. He entered that space, and called it "prayer":

> Do please visit us, either to console us, or to give advice, or to send us on our way, but in any case, by the very sight of you to make us easier at heart. And—most important of all—pray, and pray again, that our reason be not submerged by the flood of evil, but that in all things we may keep ourselves pleasing to God, in order that we may not be numbered among the wicked servants who thank Him when He grants blessings, but when He chastises through the opposite means do not submit. Nay, let us derive benefit even from our very difficulties, trusting in Him the more when we stand the more in need.[26]

There is the possibility of civilisation ahead of us. It will need to be defended with steady *humility.

LEAN ECONOMICS. The conventional ideal of the perfect competitive *market can be summarised in seven conditions. In order for it to exist, there must be . . .[27]

1. no local intervention (such as government regulation to set standards)—and no discrimination except on grounds of price against another producer;

2. standardised products—so that all products compete on price rather than on differences in specification;

3. a large number of sellers and buyers, and all of roughly the same size—so that none of them can influence prices;

4. free entry and exit—sellers and buyers can come and go as they wish;

5. profit maximisation—sellers do not have any agenda other than making money; buyers are irresistibly drawn to the best deal;

6. perfect mobility of the factors of production—so that labour, capital and land are distributed according to price: they are free from other entanglements and strings; and

7. perfect knowledge—so that buyers can perfectly evaluate the quality of all products on the market.

Under these conditions, prices are set and resources are used with smooth efficiency, unsullied by human error, by economic *boundaries or by principles and agreements of any kind other than those of comparative advantage and competition. This does the theoretically useful job of opening the way to the greatest possible efficiency. There is no *slack; there is "Pareto Efficiency": it would not be possible to make better use of the economy's resources and assets: any gain made in one place would be at the cost of loss in another.[28]

Economists do not claim that this ideal of perfect competition ever happens in real life, nor that the rigorously-defined equilibrium enabled by it can exist. As a leading authority in the matter, Frank Hahn, remarks, "The economy cannot be in this state."[29] Nor do they even believe that, in practice, the existence of perfect competition is really desirable. For a start, it would rule out the existence of large companies; differences between brands of the same product would have to be banned, as

L

would natural monopolies such as railway and electricity networks, however competitively they were structured.

Nonetheless, it is the ideal baseline against which distortions, disequilibria, rigidities and the market failures which are suspected of causing unemployment are identified and defined. "Perfection" in the market consists in being *competitive and *taut, with every available resource used as efficiently as it can be.[30]

The *Lean Economy, being the opposite of this, affirms a critical role for intentionally imperfect competition, for "organisational slack".[31] In fact, building slack into a system as an instrument of *protection and stabilisation is already an accepted, though not universal, practice in management.[32] Instead of insisting that price competition should pre-empt and trump every other criterion of decision, such slack allows space for choice and for committed long-term relationships with business partners and suppliers—for what Milton Friedman described disapprovingly as "cumbrous political channels", an untidy jostling of argument, policy, *judgment and long-term vision.[33]

This is not the contradiction of *lean thinking that it might seem, since lean organisation makes good use of strategic slack. It may, for example, be prepared to work painstakingly with suppliers when they get into trouble, rather than rigidly buying at the lowest price from someone else, and it may earn *loyalty in return. It may take time out to think. And yet, the settled lean order of the future will take slack a long way further than any current enterprise would contemplate.

A Seven Point Protocol for Lean Economics

The stabilised *local economy—the economics of the *Wheel of Life—will violate all seven of the conditions listed above. All economies do so to some extent, but in the Lean Economy the impediments to perfect competition will be greater than ever, and this will be intentional. The ideal conditions of the post-market economy—those of *intelligent imperfect competition—are summarised in this alternative seven point protocol:

1. LOCAL INTERVENTION: INTERVENTION TO
PROTECT THE LOCAL ECONOMY, AND TO BUILD TRUST

*Protection. All the seven points of this Protocol for Lean Economics are implicitly or explicitly about the task of protecting local economies.

In a *taut, *competitive, *growing *market, it is true that protectionism is not a good idea. It reinforces inefficiencies and reduces the *incentives for improvements in quality, economies of *scale and reductions in price. It discourages the development of *technical advances and specialist skills, and it freezes flows of trade and *capital, setting up conditions for national and global unemployment.

But there are other circumstances in which free, unprotected trade is not what an economy needs. One of them occurs where an undeveloped, thus-far uncompetitive economy needs time to get its industries established before exposing them to international competition. In the early years, a developing region with an industry which is still too new to have developed competitive levels of efficiency is unlikely to survive without some advantage, such as a weak currency or tariff protection.[34]

Another case where unprotected trade is not what is needed is the *Lean Economy, whose sharing out of work makes it inefficient by design, so that it would quickly be destroyed unless protected from the competitive rigours suited to profoundly different conditions. The Lean Economy will be inherently uncompetitive in two main ways. First, full-time work as standard practice will be obsolete, and much of the work that is done will take the form of participation in the *informal economy. Secondly, its range of technologies will include labour-intensive production methods which would be priced out of existence in a competitive market. These two characteristics are discussed further at the end of this entry.

Labour intensification for its own sake is not advocated. It would make more sense to get the job done quickly and to spend any spare time smelling the roses. But the benefits of labour-intensive methods apply widely, and they include reduced *energy-dependence, simple equipment, suitability for the small, local *scale, greater *eco-efficiency, better *food and improved soil, and a higher quality of *craftsmanship.

In summary, the Lean Economy will be *slack, producing less per working man and woman than it could produce it if were able, like the industrial economy had been, to keep the majority of the working population at work full-time and with competitive efficiency.

Sustainable slack will be an immense achievement, more significant in its way than the Industrial Revolution's invention of unsustainable work. But that brings us back to the key problem. Slack economies are vulnerable to taut economies—a version of Gresham's Law, which says that bad money drives out good money.[35] And slack economies, once destroyed, do not become taut economies. They become broken economies. They will need protection.

Trust. Money will have much reduced significance in a local Lean Economy. Prices don't work well in a slack economy because (if everything were priced) slack would mean high prices, and there is always the temptation to give in to buyers' pressure to reduce the price, especially if the buyer is outside the community.[36] In the local Lean Economy—a culture of cooperation and *reciprocity —*exchange involving money is not the rule, but the backup*. The significance of such a change is hard to overstate. The *market economy's money exchange is impersonal: until they get into the bigger, longer-term transactions, such as rents or employment, the two sides of a money transaction don't have to trust each other, and even then there are ways of dealing with the situation if things go wrong.

In contrast with this, the *informal economy of the *neighbourhood will consist substantially of reciprocities which do not involve *money, and would break down immediately in the absence of trust. The central collaborative task of the local Lean Economy and of the *politics beyond it will be to build that trust. And yet, trust cannot be made; it is a slowly-growing outcome of getting other things right first—like lichen, that grows on a wall if you leave it undisturbed for long enough. It requires permanence, with people being in the same *place for a long time. Deep trust, able to survive stresses, to support substantial cooperation, and to sustain intense deliberation, requires the foundation of a common *culture and *identity.

The task of supporting that culture is itself a form of sustained intervention in the way in which people interact with each other. In other words, the community will protect its culture as the foundation for trust, which in turn will be the key enabling property of its economy.

2. PRODUCT DIVERSITY: NO PRODUCT IS QUITE WHAT IT SEEMS

A local shop provides a subtle mix of services—gossip, help for old people, surveillance of the street, accessibility—along with the groceries. These extras have to be paid for in higher prices (see "Loyalty" sidebar on page 240). It is not only the disadvantage of being unable to buy in bulk that makes the corner shop supposedly inefficient and expensive; it is the labour-intensive presence of the shopkeeper and all the intangible services he supplies: they are a *public good from which you benefit whether you buy from him or not.

The problem is that customers, though aware of these things as *local facts of life, appreciate what they are getting only when they are no longer getting it, and the local retailer is able to sustain them only because he is a mini-monopolist in his area; his *freedom to charge a higher price to cover the cost of the extras would wane or cease if a super-cheap superstore opened up which could not provide them.[37] Those subtle enlargements—strings attached to the goods provided by the local shopkeeper—are seen through the spectacles of neoclassical economics as impediments to the ideal of perfect *competition; such "diffusion of goodwill and mutual consideration" (writes the sociologist Ronald Dore) is feared as "creeping malevolence, [an] abuse of monopoly power".[38] However, in the local Lean Economy, the attachment of such strings to products and services will be seen as desirable; that is to say, there is no standardisation: the product's identity acquires just the sort of blurred borderlines that perfect competition cannot abide.

Economics' word for the other things you get, whether you want them or not, along with the economic output that you pay for, is "externalities"—that is, goods and bads that are external to the price system. Carbon emissions are an *undesired* externality; the friendliness of the local deli who will keep your keys for your daughter when you are out is a *desired* one. Much of environmental economics is about finding ways of "internalising externalities"—giving prices to externalities—so that better prices, which represent the reality more accurately, lead to better decisions. But even if externalities are priced, it is still the market that makes the decisions, as buyers search for the low prices which suit them.[39]

Lean economics, in contrast with this, deals with externalities directly. There is full awareness that products and services come encumbered with strings, and they may be exactly what the *community wants—such as the advantage of richly-encumbered enterprise keeping

239

L

LOYALTY
Getting more than you bargain for

When the Thanatopsis Club hit its centennial in 1982 and Mrs. Hallberg wrote to the White House and asked for an essay from the President on small-town life, she got one, two paragraphs that extolled Lake Wobegon as a model of free enterprise and individualism, which was displayed in the library under glass, although the truth is that Lake Wobegon survives to the extent that it does on a form of voluntary socialism with elements of Deism, fatalism and nepotism. Free enterprise runs on self-interest. This is socialism, and it runs on loyalty. You need a toaster, you buy it at Co-op Hardware even though you can get a deluxe model with all the toaster attachments for less money at K-Mart in St. Cloud. You buy it at Co-op because you know Otto. Glasses you will find at Clifford's which also sells shoes and ties and some gloves. (It is trying to be the department store it used to be when it was The Mercantile, which it is still called by most people because the old sign is so clear on the brick facade, clearer than the "Clifford's" in the window.) Though you might rather shop for glasses in a strange place where they'll encourage your vanity, though Clifford's selection of frames is clearly based on Scripture ("Take no thought for what you shall wear . . .") and you might put a hideous piece of junk on your face and Clifford would say, "I think you'll like those" as if you're a person who looks like you don't care what you look like—nevertheless you should think twice before you get the Calvin Klein glasses from Vanity Vision in St. Cloud Mall. Calvin Klein isn't going to come with the Rescue Squad and he isn't going to teach your children about redemption by grace. You couldn't find Calvin Klein to save your life.

If people were to live by comparison shopping, the town would go bust. It cannot compete with other places item by item. Nothing in town is quite as good as it appears to be somewhere else. If you live there, you have to take it as a whole. That's loyalty.

GARRISON KEILLOR, *Lake Wobegon Days*, 1985.[40]

local traders and the local economy solvent. In local lean economies, consumers know that there is more to be said about the product than what it says on the tin.

3. A SMALL NUMBER OF SELLERS AND BUYERS:
WITH A LOT OF INFLUENCE OVER THE LOCAL MARKET

In its essence, the Lean Economy will take the form of a radical transformation away from the *market economy's division of purpose between producers and consumers (each of us is, after all, both). The divide between supply and demand loses its focus and to a large extent breaks down. Here we have a human ecology that does not consume: it lives; it behaves; it *quickens.

And yet, there will also be *craftsmanship and specialisation, and a market will be needed to link them up. But the local Lean Economy's markets will be small markets, with small numbers of sellers and buyers. Just a few of them could influence prices or some other aspect

of supply and demand. Many trading relationships will be specifically organised as *reciprocal arrangements between (say) a producer and a small group of households; terms will be agreed on a case-by-case basis with little reference to prices elsewhere. For instance, local people (in their role as producers) may take a position on reduced working time, or on carefully-maintained *closed-loop systems, while (in their role as consumers) accepting the costs of this, as well as the *necessity for it. All this is in contrast with the "price-taking" idealised in the model of perfect *competition, where nobody has any influence on prices.

In the large and impersonal market, the *only* economic behaviour that makes sense is an *abstract pursuit of wealth (*chrematistics* [Greek: *chremata* money], to use Aristotle's word for this). In the short-range, local economy, by contrast, the intention is to promote the interests of the *household and *community in practical ways (in line with the roots of our word "economy": *oikonomia* [Greek: *oîkos* house + *nómos* managing]). Any money you make out of it is at most secondary: money is not the point of the exercise, and much of what you do—everything you do for your family, for instance—is for no money at all. For *oikonomia*, price is often *irrelevant. Economics in this core sense is beyond the reach of the parsimonious summaries of mathematics; it depends on *judgment.[41]

4. Barriers to Entry and Exit:
A helping hand for loyalty

There are two types of relationship between customers and suppliers. First, there is "exit"—to get out at the first sign of bother. This is how the *market economy is meant to work. Secondly, there is "voice"—to argue for change, to influence matters by getting involved rather than by walking away, to stay loyal. Such *loyalty is a vital asset in the *Lean Economy.[42]

And it is given a powerful helping hand by barriers to *exit—where conditions exist which make it hard to get out. One barrier which has shown itself to be effective in many cases in the market economy is geographical remoteness.[43] The decline and fall of the small-island economy of Inishbofin, off the west coast of Ireland, illustrates this. With local economic self-sufficiency in virtually all their needs, the islanders maintained a millennium or two of *resilience until the coming of the market economy. Inishbofin's low-tech fishing boats were no match for the trawlers; its farmers, who needed to sell at least some of their output in mainland Ireland in order to buy the goods they needed, were no match for industrial agriculture. And as the islanders, as consumers, became aware of the market's products and prices, they had, as producers, less and less to offer. They resisted for a time, since the island's remoteness provided a big *incentive to rely on what it could produce for itself, but when the lower prices, the wider range of goods, and the convenience of the market in mainland Ireland was made more accessible by a massive EU-funded pier, that was the end.[44]

Not that it could have been avoided. The people of Inishbofin could not conceivably have access to modern consumer goods and services from their own resources except with the help of imports and subsistence payments—and without those, the islanders

could reasonably be expected simply to leave. Life on the island formerly was hard, beyond the *expectations of our own time. And yet, unemployment and dole-dependency is hard too. When the subsistence payments can no longer cover the costs of living, or when they stop altogether, life on the island will be harder still.

Decisions which have profound long-term consequences are often made on the strength of short-term opportunities which, with hindsight, people would not have chosen. And barriers to entry and exit—such as the inconvenience of living on an island without a modern pier, or of living in a remote area without a modern road—mean that the temptation to take the actions which will destroy the local economy does not arise. This matters, because when that chance of giving in to temptation comes along, it is grasped with both hands.

The momentum of small, seemingly harmless *choices is powerful and virtually unstoppable, and the final result has to be accepted without a murmur. Alfred Kahn called it "the tyranny of small decisions", where people make decisions on the basis of the easy options now, without making the connection with the consequences to which those *innocent choices will eventually lead. Massive, long-term consequences, such as the tearing-down of the trade barriers which have protected a local economy for centuries, come along as unforeseen implications of little decisions about how you and the dog want to spend the afternoon.[45]

"Barriers to entry and exit" (aka sustainable protectionism) are restrictive of freedom, but only in that they prevent people from walking into the trap of the small decisions by which they would destroy what they value. One good barrier to exit from the locality is that members should want to stay inside it (see "Italian Games" sidebar on page 242). The Lean Economy will have barriers to entry and exit thrust upon it: localities will be hard-pressed to provide for their people, especially in the early years, and would quickly fail if overwhelmed by numbers. If you are already in a functioning local lean economy, you are likely to need and want to stay there.

"Loyalty", writes the economist Albert Hirschman, "can be compared to such barriers as protective tariffs."[46] There you have it. Loyalty means having the good sense to hang on despite short-term disadvantage, not taking too much notice of price signals—a

241

L

ITALIAN GAMES
Enjoying Being an Insider

Barriers to entry and exit have the effect of creating "insiders"[47]—people who belong to a group and who have an incentive to stay there. *Enjoying* being an insider can improve matters even more. In the Tuscan city of Siena, membership of one of the seventeen *contrade* means being strongly *identified with the locality, and belonging to a *culture of intense *loyalty. Loyalty cultivates benevolence, and in Siena it is built into the local *communities—held in place with the help of the exuberant *ritual of the Sienese horse-race, the *palio,* and by the fantastically cumbrous political channels that surround it. The *palio* is unquestionably a barrier to entry and exit—for instance, you need to be born in a *contrada* to be able to claim to belong to it and you need to participate in *palio* politics for your belonging to mean anything; the rivalry between *contrade* is an expression of *play, part of an actual texture of loyalties both within *contrade* and between them.[48]

deliberate inverse of perfect *competition.[49] It implies an economy where price does not have the final say; "protection" recovers its proper sense of stewardship.

Local lean economies will depend on it.[50]

5. MULTIPLE AIMS: BEYOND PROFIT MAXIMISATION

There has for a long time been the presumption that, as representatives of the shareholders, managements have no right to pursue objectives other than that of maximising profit. And yet, that simplification is well out of date, since other obligations—to the "triple bottom line" (economics, environment and social justice), for instance—are already recognised. The idea that a producer in the Lean Economy should work in the interests of the locality and its complex needs is therefore an evolution of current management principles rather than a contradiction; many businesses are already providing local services, productively encumbered with complex local aims—*community supported *agriculture is one example.

In the *Lean Economy, the distinction between producer and consumer will be weak; as the *household and *neighbourhoods build their competence, the two functions will merge. Profit in this context has little meaning.

6. BARRIERS TO MOBILITY: OF THE FACTORS OF PRODUCTION

The three factors of production in economics are *labour,* *capital and *land. They will all be scarce:

There will be plenty of people around, but *labour* that brings the *skills and the *trust that local lean economies will need will be prized, and efforts will be made to keep it in the community. At the same time, communities will not be able to assimilate new arrivals which would raise their numbers beyond what they can sustain: the first principle of an enduring *commons is *closed access. That does not mean a closed-minded lack of hospitality and *encounter: relationships bridging between communities and forming a network of learning and mutual support will be fundamental to the evolution of the Lean Economy. What it does mean is that the community recognises that a feasible and effective commons requires control of *boundaries, restricting access and *scale to numbers that the resource can support, with participants that accept the obligations that this requires.

The six forms of *capital in lean economics are: natural, scientific/cultural, human, social, material and financial. One of these (scientific/cultural) has the property that it can travel to another place without leaving the place it started from (like love, you can give it and still have it; or commas, whose supply knows no limit), and it will be important to the network of local lean economies that they should, with ease, share ideas, information and *culture. Apart from that, capital in the Lean Economy is subtractable (if you give some away, you have less of it), and it will tend to be immobile.

The idea that capital should be mobile is not recent but it became routine, rather than the exception, following the influence of the economist David Ricardo (1772–1823), who made the case for "comparative advantage"—that is, for the production of each kind of good and service to be concentrated in the places where it can be done most efficiently and cheaply. According to this principle, the efficient *nation will make things for its own use only if there is nothing else (either for home consumption or export) that it could produce more efficiently.[51]

Such dislocated economics is a natural feature of *large-scale *civic societies. Located economics is a central principle of the Lean Economy. Capital, in its various forms, recovering from the breathless globe-trotting recommended by Ricardo, will come home and underpin *resilient *communities.

Land, in economics, stands for the whole set of miracles and services which comprise the planet. As John Stuart Mill summarised, labour can do no more than move things around: "the properties of matter, the laws of nature, do the rest". However, this vast, but vulnerable, endowment has been taken for granted, summarised as "land", and reduced to a residual which (in the models and equations) can be left to look after itself. And, as "land", of course, it can be owned and inserted into a business plan somewhere, so that, in this sense, land in economics is mobile.[52]

In the Lean Economy, land will stay in one place.

7. IMPERFECT KNOWLEDGE:
MAKING A VIRTUE OUT OF IGNORANCE

Perfect *competition requires perfect information about all the products on the *market and how they are sold; the local Lean Economy, by contrast, will be largely ignorant of the goods that other consumers can buy in other places. Passive consumer-awareness of out-of-season strawberries will be replaced by intense knowledge of the range of goods, *food and skills that the place they live in can supply. And at a time of substantial uncertainty, knowledge will be rare, relative to inference. Knowledge, in a sense, is the final product, packaged and ready for use, and local lean economies would be stuck without some of that. But economies and lives, alike, will depend (as the Duke of Wellington described it) on working out "what you don't know by what you do; . . . guessing what [is] at the other side of the hill". The first steps towards self-reliance will be to explore and infer at a time when certain knowledge is scarce, and when the idea that you can "perfectly evaluate the quality of all products in the market" is a relic from another age.[53]

And there is something to be said for not knowing how big an almost-impossibly-big project is going to be. If you knew, you probably wouldn't start.

Imagine that you are at home in your small town or parish in the years after the *energy peak. International trade has substantially failed, taking the financial institutions with it. There is very high unemployment. The government cannot sustain unemployment benefits and can fund virtually nothing. Tax revenues have crashed. This is a society with—by the standards of the affluent market—no *money. Local economies depend, not on what they can buy, but on what they can do.

If their response follows the seven point Protocol for Lean Economics described above, local economies will be working to principles which are, in a sense, the inverse of those of the market.

Now for a bit of *reductionism in the positive sense: forget, for a moment, all the other problems that would arise in such a situation, and concentrate on how to get the local economy moving as a system that can support life and *community. There are two structural supports: the first one is *reciprocal exchange. The second is the *cultural setting which gives the community an *identity, and around which reciprocities and cooperation can form. There may also, for the larger scale of the *parish, be a *local currency. These are described under their own entries. What we need to consider now is the economics underlying this.

The demise of the *market economy will affect the demand for labour. The effect will work in two directions. Factors which will tend to *reduce* the demand will include:

- the reduced supply of energy and materials. Labour is *complementary with* (i.e., depends on) *materials and resources. If the supply of these were reduced, there would be less for labour to do. The consequence could be a large-scale closedown of the industry and services on which the economy depends.
- the small *scale of the local *Lean Economy, and its minimal infrastructure (i.e., its *elegance). The drastically reduced scale of *intermediate economy is the key to the feasibility of life after oil, but it has the corollary that the bulk of work currently required to sustain the intermediate infrastructures of the market economy will not be needed.

On the other hand, there will be factors which tend to *increase* the demand for labour. They include:

L

L

- the reduced supply of energy and materials. Labour is also a *substitute for* materials and resources. If the supply of these were reduced, there would be *more* for labour to do: labour will do, by hand, work which was previously done by energy-driven equipment. The scale of this effect is not predictable. It is plausible to suppose that at least some of the electrical apparatus on which we rely—such as hand tools and saws—will have power supplies from local renewable resources, but no assumptions can be made about the availability of good equipment and spare parts. Other kinds of work, such as farming, lacking abundant flows of oil and gas as fuel and feedstocks (raw materials for fertilisers and biocides)—are also likely to be more labour-intensive than they are at present.
- the task of *energy-provision and -conservation itself. Much of this will consist of building the equipment and installations needed for the zero-carbon economy, which will call for a lot of labour, although this will tend to be less when the task becomes essentially one of maintenance.[54]

The net outcome of these effects in terms of labour demand can be debated, and it will undoubtedly vary, depending on timing and circumstances. Indeed the whole question of "reducing unemployment" in an economy by increasing the demand for labour takes on a different and ill-defined meaning where there is free movement of labour with other economies ten times, or even a hundred times, its size. *Lean Logic*'s position is that, in the settled form of the *Lean Economy, the factors which *reduce* the demand for labour will dominate, by a large margin.

It is the essence of development that, as technology and labour *productivity advance and infrastructure grows (i.e., as the economy *intensifies), the demand for labour increases. This effect is not merely a change in one of the parameters—it is an absolute transformation in the way labour and the other factors of production are used. A developing economy is voracious for labour, *capital and *land (*Regrettable Necessities). In the de-development (or "deintensification") that lies ahead, this effect will be reversed. The small-scale *elegance of the Lean Economy will lead to a collapse in

the amount of work needed/available *per capita*. There will be *hyperunemployment.

The Lean Economy will never be able to provide full-time work for the whole of its workforce. It will be a *slack economy, and it will have to adapt to this. One way to do so is by sharing out the work with restrictions on working time (as was required through the medieval period). Another is to absorb spare labour with standards of *practice—such as *organic production—which combine labour-intensive methods with other benefits such as high quality and low environmental impact (such methods may also be the natural outcome of scarcities of energy and equipment). A variant of this second response is to supply goods for the purpose of destroying them, or to produce goods of monumental extravagance (pyramids, cathedrals, *carnival). Means of supporting surplus labour, and preventing the accumulation of *capital, become in this way both dependent on the common culture and supportive of it (*Intentional Waste).

Lean economics is the means of maintaining the stability of an economy which does not *grow. Its *institutions are designed as essential means to manage and protect its small *scale. It will do that by sharing out the available work, absorbing spare labour/time in activities which do not contribute to growth, preventing the accumulation of growth capital (capital which, if employed, would lead to growth) and underpinning a *culture and social order which can maintain *reciprocity and *freedom in conditions of slack, and in the absence of well-defined *competitive pricing.

*Slack and Taut, Leisure, Economics, Economism, Elegance, Green Economics, Lean Defence, Success.

LEAN ECONOMY, THE. The fabric of the *Wheel of Life, supported by richly-developed *social capital and culture, organised not around the *market, but around the rediscovery of community. It is based on *cooperation in a *slack *economic and social order, building on a *panarchy of social groupings, from *small groups and *household production through the close *neighbourhood and *parish to the *nation. It sustains solutions—*lean energy, *lean food, *lean materials and *water, along with *lean economics, *lean education, *lean health, *lean law and order, *lean defence, *religion, *carnival and *play. Guiding principles include *informal logic, *lean thinking and *manners, underwriting the three key, linked properties of *community, *closed-loop systems and *culture.

All these lean responses are set in the context of a key assumption: local communities will not have access to government funding for any of their needs; they will not have an income that enables them to buy in the goods and services they need from outside the local economy. The implications of this are explored by the "Lean" entries—and, inevitably, there is uncertainty about the extent to which local lean economies will be forced to rely on their own resources—with the range between *deep local*, where they cannot get supplies even of tools and metals, and *local lite*, where most, or almost all, routine needs (e.g., food) are produced locally, but the equipment needed to do this can be bought in. *Lean Logic*'s position on this spectrum is towards the *deep local* extreme, though some opportunities that would arise under less extreme assumptions are noted.

Writing of Thomas Hobbes' famous system—the *political economy of *Leviathan*—Michael Oakeshott notes,

> If it requires great energy of mind to create a
> system, it requires even greater not to become
> the slave of the creation.[55]

. . . that is, it becomes necessary to think consistently through the logic while recognising that it might turn out quite differently. The Lean Economy is not a forecast; it is a scenario.

LEAN EDUCATION. *Culture, science, *crafts, *play, friendship and the *ecology provide the medium in terms of which an individual fulfils his or her potential as a person, and a group fulfils its potential as a *community. Education is that part of the life of a community that contributes to those ends.

Community practice

The starting point is early education in the fundamental skill of belonging to a community, and here is a teacher with something to say about this. The philosopher Alasdair MacIntyre makes a connection (introduced in *Practice) between complementary forms of learning—between (a) acquiring a demanding skill and (b) embracing the virtues of community. Imagine for a moment that you are becoming accomplished in a

practice—that is, a skill (especially a *manual skill, but some non-manual skills have this quality too)—which requires deep commitment and reflection, and intense and accurate *feedback to scotch the delusion that you are better than you are. Learning such a skill builds and reinforces three qualities which extend beyond those which are specific to the skill itself. First, *truthfulness: it will be necessary to sustain a truthful relationship with the people from whose example or teaching you are learning. Secondly, fairness: you will need to be fair in your *judgment of yourself and others in the performance of the skill. And thirdly, *courage: you will need to have the courage from time to time to attempt something beyond your present capacity, and to persist despite criticism.[56]

It follows from MacIntyre's argument that the task of teaching children how to be responsible members of a community is about teaching them to be interested in something—leading on to being good at it. The accomplishment soaks into their lives; they grow to value the community that teaches them. These skills are, in essence, the skills of citizenship; that is to say, a by-product of learning skills is learning citizenship. It is the rapid and unambiguous feedback from manual skills that makes them effective. Intellectual skills are not always so reliable in this way: you can use your intellect to conceal your errors. The teaching that comes from manual skills, on the other hand, is clear and hard to misread. And, as the philosopher-mechanic Matthew Crawford points out, it comes in a sequence of trial and error, mutual aid and occasional inspiration:

> You break things, and learn something new by
> taking them apart and talking it through. Here
> work and leisure both take their bearings from
> something basically human: rational activity,
> in association with others. . . . To place oneself
> at the service of this master is to enter into
> community and . . . to open oneself to being
> schooled by one's elders. This is solidarity.[57]

Practical education, then, will be recognised as a critical accomplishment, and teaching it will be a core responsibility of the community. "The boy is in a school here", writes William Cobbett, "and an excellent school too: the school of useful labour."[58] And

L

L

START YOUNG
Too old to learn to make a wheel?
Not for your brain, but for your body . . .

With the idea that I was going to learn everything from the beginning I put myself eagerly to boys' jobs, not at all dreaming that, at over twenty, the nerves and muscles are no longer able to put on the cell-growths, and so acquire the habits of perceiving and doing which should have begun at fifteen. Could not Intellect achieve it? In fact, Intellect made but a fumbling imitation of real knowledge, yet hardly deigned to recognise how clumsy in fact it was. Beginning so late in life, I know now that I could never have earned my keep as a skilled workman. But with the ambition to begin at the beginning, I set myself to act as boy to any of the men who might want a boy's help.

And now,—how dare I go on to describe that swinging drive of the wheelwright's action fixing the spokes into the stock? He picks up one in one hand, and, with sledgehammer in the other, lightly taps the spoke into its own mortice. Then he steps back, glancing behind him belike to see that the coast is clear; and, testing the distance with another light tap (a two-handed tap this time) suddenly, with a leap, he swings the sledge round full circle with both hands, and brings it down right on top of the spoke—bang. Another blow or so, and the spoke is far enough into the mortice to be gauged. Is it leaning forward a little too much, or not quite enough? It can be corrected, with batterings properly planted on front or back or top, and accordingly the wheelwright aims his sledge, swinging it round tremendously again and again, until the spoke is indeed "driven" into the stock. It is battered over on the top, but the oak stands firm in the mortice, to stay for years.

 For an hour or so, until all the spokes had been driven into a wheel, this sledge-hammer work went on, tremendous. A wheelwright driving spokes, though not necessarily a very strong man, was able, with knack, to strike more powerful blows, and many of them too, in succession. With one hand close under the head he gave the sledge a great fling, then slipped the same hand down the handle, to help the other hand, hold it in and guide it truly round its circle. By the time it reached the spoke the sledge had got an impetus. With the momentum of a stone from a sling, it was so to speak hurled down on its mark, terrific.

GEORGE STURT, *The Wheelwright's Shop*, 1923.[59]

learning-by-doing will start young. The workplace and its apprenticeships will be recognised as integral to the community as a learning establishment. The difference between getting-by at a manual skill and being good it turns, not least, on how old the person was when he or she started to learn it. This is illustrated by the lament of a dairy farmer, the late Dinah Williams (founder of Rachel's Dairy), who told the author how difficult it was to get people to do the milking morning and evening, day after day. The job is cold, wet, noisy and repetitive; it requires patience and acquaintance with each cow— enough to notice if a behavioural change signifies a

problem. "Only the members of our own family seem to be able to stick it", she said, "but they have been doing it since they were children. We get graduates from the agricultural college, and they can manage the job all right, *but they never learn to enjoy it*, and then they leave" (see "Start Young" sidebar).

In the Lean Economy, hand-skills will be at least as valued as brain-skills. There will be no presumption that manual work is a sign of failure to ascend the ladder of equal opportunity. The association between skills and community *virtues is critical, and Sybil Marshall, in her classic *An Experiment in Education*, showed how, in the case of young children, it can be achieved effectively and economically. At Kingston Primary School in Cambridgeshire, where she was head (and often the only) teacher (1942–1960), the acquisition of learning was almost immediately translated into early community *leadership. The essence of her method, and one of the reasons for its cost-effectiveness, is that, for much of the learning time, the child is either being mentored by another, slightly older, child, or is teaching himself or herself—working on a task which bears some relation to what he or she understands already, but which brings new experience and learning. *Pull (rule 4 of *lean thinking) is not a sufficient condition for learning—some things (learning poetry, a musical instrument or Latin, for instance) have to be based at least in part on learning by heart or the sheer hard slog of repetition—but it is a *necessary condition: inquiry, aka "problem-based learning" makes the mind *want* the information before getting it (*Rote). It is the difference between a man in your living room who is there because you have invited him to dinner, and one who is there uninvited, having just forced his way through the window, or come to sell dusters in which you have no particular *interest. The invited guest is likely to be around longer.[60]

The proof of the method at Kingston Primary came in the results, with well-developed reading and writing skills at the age of five and, by eleven, accomplishment in all the primary subjects, along with a confidence in such basics of community practice as *cooperation, persistence and *reflection.

To get such results, the teaching has to be inspiring and confident, and if it is, it can build on its success, since much of the education day consists of time in which the children are doing-it-themselves in a range of activities—as distinct from passivities—such as reading. If children are *trusted and motivated to the point of being capable of focused enquiry, their learning becomes part of their relationship with the *place—not only its schools but also its *households and churches. To be a child in a local *community is to learn from the community intensively. If that sounds an ideal, it only tells us how far the *social capital of the *market economy has declined and fragmented.

As it happens, Marshall's approach to education has an unfortunate history; parodied and renamed "progressive education", it led to some spectacular and damaging failures, with (as she writes with horror) "the teacher abdicating the professional position of someone whose function is *to teach*".[61] But schools can't do it on their own; it is a method which probably only works in classes consisting mainly of children already familiar with some sense of orderly behaviour, aware of the possibility of listening, used to the idea of active *play, feeling some sense of affinity with a teacher that can (and is allowed to) inspire, and having some knowledge of the local area on which they can draw for ideas and inspiration. Primary education under the leadership of Marshall invited its participants to apply their *imagination—to show that *home has its stories to tell, to give *stories a home. It established the questions, the focused *interest, the engagement, and enabled the children to explore and invent within that space. That is, it was *lean (see "Home Ground" sidebar on page 248).

Community learning

Richard Hoggart quotes a former Conservative Education Minister who enjoyed a standing ovation at a party conference:

> We've taken money from the people who
> write about ancient Egyptian scripts and the
> pre-nuptial habits of the Upper Volta valley.[62]

Hoggart spits: "That's as easy as tickling a dog's stomach." But why *does* a society—the *Lean Economy included—need scholarship?

Well, first of all, our society needs brilliance, and in the future of the Lean Economy, the need for it will be especially intense. Brilliance is a public good, and one of the awesome insanities of the market economy has been the treatment of highly-developed *intelligence as a *private perk, the target for envy, grounds for *indignation and proof of injustice. Interventions that dampen brilliance in the name of *ideology will lose their shine. At the heart of self-reliance will be the Lean Economy's ability to grow its own minds.

Secondly, scholarship keeps our culture alive; if it does not exist in the minds of successive generations, it does not exist at all. It may be stored in books, or on the internet, but without thriving higher education to sustain the desire to read them and the ability to understand

L

HOME GROUND
From *narrative truth to *local intelligence

. . . it was just as illuminating to watch the child struggling to keep up with the adult, trying desperately to follow the adult's instruction on some abstract theme, and falling back on a bit on his own concrete experience to fill the gaps when his understanding failed. I cannot resist one example. A friend of mine, a head teacher at a small village school, had been telling her children about the guardian angels and, on her own confession, had been laying it on a bit thick.

"Wherever you are," she had said, "you need never be afraid. In the dark, just as in the daylight, when mummy's there, or when she's not, your angel is always there, looking after you."

It so happened that down in front of her there sat a little boy who lived at a very outlying and lonely farm called Alicky Farm. When she stopped, he said, wonderingly, "Are we got angels down at Alicky, then?"

The teacher thought that here she saw a good chance of pushing home the point of her lesson.

"Yes," she said, "even down at Alicky, if you are all alone and even in the dark, you needn't be afraid, because you have an angel there, always looking after you."

The child waited patiently and politely till she had finished, and then dropped his innocent bombshell.

"Well," he said, "I reckon that ol' angel's a-wasting his time, 'cos we don't need him. You see, *we've got a good dog.*"

SYBIL MARSHALL, *An Experiment in Education*, 1963.

---

them, the knowledge will fade. Higher learning is the anatomy and *grammar of our condition. Without it, we are left reaching for the instructions, for the *self-evident, for the terminal *certainties of fundamentalism.

The historian, Keith Thomas, takes up the case:

> . . . [scholarship] makes an essential contribution to contemporary needs. No assessment of human limits and potentialities can be informed if it does not take account of previous experience. By studying books, manuscripts and works of art, digging up sites and writing commentaries and histories, scholars resist the annihilation of what has gone before. Without their work, the past would survive only in the most selective and mythical form. By reminding us that there are other ways of living and thinking the learned contribute a crucial element to our self-awareness.
>
> . . . the life of learning still has an exemplary morality to offer. Where else, save in other forms of academic inquiry, can we find the same scrupulous concern for truth, the same requirement that all propositions which are not self-evidently true should be documented, the same conviction that getting things right is more important than a quick fix, the same acceptance of the complexity of things. . . ?[63]

In summary:

> We need scholars to resist the annihilation of our intellectual inheritance.[64]

Scholarship sounds remote, but it is actually about the culture and the *arts that are core conditions and properties of living in a society, as distinct from living in a place that has the misfortune of being infested with people. In a pre-literate society, education was recognised as a matter of searing importance, since the minds of the people were the information storage system for the whole of its *inheritance of knowledge and collective *reflection. Their way of life was to a large degree centred around teaching, and the personal *loyalties that produced. To be an adult was to be a teacher. *Myth, such as the Greek Homeric *tradition, now studied by the exceptional, was learned, like a language, by total immersion—part of the texture of *stories told and lived, and integral to their lives. "Higher learning" is in this sense like learning a mother tongue.

Scholarship underpins and desentimentalises our awareness and love of the *culture we live in. It has good *humour; it is talkative and companionable; it brings shared insights. It lifts the spirits. It is the habitat of the stories and arts without which *imagination dies. And it can come free (or almost free). There are these qualities in the Workers' Educational Association in the United Kingdom. Albert Mansbridge, who founded the Association in 1903, wrote of education as

> . . . pure wonder and enjoyment, ultimately of the spirit [and] perceived by the spirit only, reaching out to higher things, music and song [and revealing] the secrets of life. To anyone who has seen groups of men and women reading in a college garden or has heard their songs across the quadrangle, it is obvious that the Association has found the deep harmonies in the national life.[65]

The failure of the market economy will be accompanied by a collapse of university funding. The extinction of higher learning will be prevented only if a degree of social and economic order remains in which centres of scholarship can be sustained by varied forms of *reciprocity, supplemented with whatever funding is available, if any. They will set standards and contribute to the science, philosophy and poetry of the post-industrial world.

Localities were once rich with their own scholarship. No, that's not romantic nostalgia. Some were not, of course. And those that were, weren't all world class. But they made it happen. In Horwich, a small engineering town in Lancashire—and by no means exceptional in this—a series of papers was presented to the Literary Society in the 1920s by Mr. David Gibson, director of the local locomotive works. It was the Mechanics' Institute's building during the day, but in the evening the riveters and boiler-makers of locomotive-building would wash and come out to discuss literature and to make music. Mr. Gibson gave song-recitals, and his papers surveyed the prose and poetry of major writers in English from Shakespeare to his own day, with special reference to his hero, Thomas Carlyle. Poetry, he suggested,

teaches us to see beauty all around us. We see it in Horwich. We see it in the windswept streets with the old smoke-blackened houses with their decent fronts, on a clear east-windy day. We see it when we look down on the Blackrod and Horwich valley, with its houses and factories, the gleams of water in the lodges. We may even find this beauty and the poetic interpretation of it in some of our big stately locomotives . . .[66]

These papers were among many given at the time by members of the society. The honorary "University of Horwich" needed no government funding.

Research in technology and the sciences will happen if there is the money for it. But there may not be. That could take the sciences towards an emphasis on teaching—conserving what we already know. And the only useful technologies to conserve will be those that can be supported on a local *scale, using local resources, supported by the community (*Appropriate Technology, Lean Energy).[67]

Will that make society less aware of science? Maybe not. It could make us more aware of technology, of practical action that we can take for ourselves. But for most of us, the sciences themselves are remote from our knowledge and competence. As Douglas Adams noted of his space-travelling hero, Arthur Dent, "Left to his own devices he couldn't build a toaster. He could just about make a sandwich and that was it."[68] That is to say, *we* are not scientists. The supergizmos required to keep our oversize civilisation alive are not evidence that we are clever. Aristotle, Shakespeare and Darwin were no less clever because they didn't know about semiconductors; they just lived in a civilisation that had not yet got itself into such a pickle that it could not get by without them.

Educating friendship

You have to wonder at the idea that the purpose of education is to enable a *nation to compete in international trade. *Economics is not the only value. If the *intention is to provide serried ranks of dutiful contestants on a short fuse, alone and bewildered, with a high degree of accomplishment in the art of bluffing their way through, modern education is making good progress. But it is time, now, for a change of course.

To claim that there is a need to educate people for the task of being *nice* will undoubtedly invite a derisive critique: you can't educate people for niceness; they either are, or they aren't; anyway what is "nice" in your opinion? Probably no more than a dreary tendency to agree with *you*. Well, none of that is true—those are *fallacies arising from lack of practice in having to think through what "nice" means. In the mobile *market state, you don't have to worry very much about whether people are nice or not because, if not, you can usually get away from them. But sometimes you can't. If you are living in a leasehold flat in London, with *neighbours that must cooperate to make it work, you find out what "nice" means. It means the natural inclination to cooperate rather than a suspicious and resentful determination to destroy the enterprise and distribute misery.

Local lean economies will depend, unconditionally, on that *cooperation, and it will be vulnerable to wrecking strategies. Some guidelines on what to do about this, and where to turn for advice, are suggested in *Community, but here the question is whether education has a contribution to make. Well, it has: personality is made by inheritance, *family, friends, play, *culture—and education. In fact, the desire to cooperate is not unteachable—and starred academic distinction is of little value if it is simply going to make you better at causing trouble. Just being *aware* of neighbourliness—okay, niceness—as being a critical, central value would, if thought through, change the orientation of society and what it educates *for*. This is more than the familiar aim of teaching a sense of responsibility and duty, though these undoubtedly help; it is the gift of *wanting* to make cooperation work, acknowledging collective accomplishment and the friendships that are sustained by it as the purpose and point of being a person.

Education can't do this on its own. But nothing else can, either, if education walks away from it. *How* education might teach us to want to look each other in the eye, to listen, to want to cooperate, takes us to the heart of *lean thinking: if this comfort—this fit between us and our community—is acknowledged as the core value that it is, teaching of all kinds, formal and informal, will discover ways to do it. This is lean thinking doing what it is designed to do—inventing solutions. And in fact, a recognition of how crucial it is may not be so far away. Here, for example, is the philosopher Martha Nussbaum making the case for education committed to the care and cultivation of . . .

> . . . the ability to think what it might be like to be in the shoes of a person different from oneself, to be an intelligent reader of that person's story, to understand the emotions and wishes and desires that someone so placed might have [and to] activate and refine the capacity to see the world through another person's eyes, a capacity that children develop through imaginative play.[69]

So *play is in there—and the Dictionary entry explores some of the ways in which that works. Dance, itself a form of play, is there, too: one thing that we can be sure about with respect to pre-nuptial habits in the Upper Volta valley is that they would have involved *dance. And the form of dance—its use or rejection of rules and formality, its basis in individual or collective expression—reflects with surefooted accuracy the nature of the society it lives in.

So music is there, too. Music is education. It deletes the distinction between education and higher education. It is a *practice; it teaches maths, reading, *reciprocity and cooperation, emotional intelligence, *imagination, languages, discernment, accuracy, *encounter, enthusiasm, friendship, *judgment, shared *grammar; it calls on *tradition and it trains the *memory; it provides interim answers to questions about the meaning of life and the use of *time; it is integrated into other crucial community-building practices such as *carnival, *religion, *ritual and *social capital—that is, directly or indirectly, into the whole corpus of *culture. It is an intense bond within one's own culture, and a bridge to others. It forms *networks. It educates friendship.

And educating friendship is what friends do—not least, at *home. In our own time, home education is one of the most successful, as well as the least-cost, forms of education. The Lean Economy will apply the principle of home education in its community setting. Minds will be (as Wendell Berry describes it) made "competent in all their concerns", shaped . . .

> . . . by a passion for excellence and order that is handed down to young people by older people whom they respect and love.[70]

L

Home education will be a point of reference, a centre of competence in local lean economies. That does not mean that every child will do his or her learning at home. It will mean that homes are recognised as their primary centres of learning—and it is homes that take the initiative in delegating teaching to primary and secondary schools, to apprenticeships, to work experience, to *freedom, to churches, universities, storytellers and bell-ringers, to the whole range of learning and cross-generation *conversation available to the *place.[71]

This *diversity is friendship's habitat. The peer-group of competitive 15-year-olds can be one of the loneliest places on Earth; a society that relies on it to transmit its culture and the skill of acute and benevolent attention to the unexpected is making a logical error. Lean education will not be without its awards and qualifications—they are rites of passage and useful when someone who claims to be good with animals is operating on your sheep—but, as an index of whether a person is bringing *connectedness or mayhem, they are unhelpful. Local lean communities will look for, and provide, other qualities which cannot be expressed in simple *reductionist grades.

At the heart of this is *pull. It does not say "this is the way to do it". It *empowers *households and *communities to work out what they want and how to do it. That "how" will be radically constrained by the minimal financial resources available to the *Lean Economy. Small-scale places of learning—some of them called secondary schools—will form and reform, for good reasons and bad, learning and teaching as they go, with intense focus on *intention—on what they are there to do, for now. There will be the variety and the disorder of a rich ecology—that is, the *harmonic order, the sheer joy of being there, of being part of the *common purpose.
*Rote, Ecology: Farmers and Hunters, Economism.

LEAN ENERGY. The application of *pull to meet *communities' energy needs in conditions of *energy-famine.

When thinking about making energy-sense of the future, it is helpful to see it as a sequence of three related tasks.[72]

1. *Energy conservation*
   This is about looking for ways of doing what we are already doing, or planning to do, but with

> ## ENERGY'S USES
> ### Overlaps and intersections
>
> 1. Space heating, space cooling and air conditioning.
> 2. Light: street lighting, interiors by day and by night.
> 3. Energy embodied in materials (mining, processing, transport) and feedstocks (plastics, paint).
> 4. Industrial processes: machine tools, carpentry, pumps, process heat and refrigeration.
> 5. Service processes: retail, medical, dental, catering, research, education administration, etc.
> 6. Information processing, storage and transmission.
> 7. Travel and transport.
> 8. Agricultural production, food processing and distribution.
> 9. Construction.
> 10. Domestic equipment and processes.
> 11. Waste treatment and disposal.

much reduced dependence on energy (for a checklist/reminder of energy's uses—double-counting included—see sidebar).

Industrial advance and economic *growth can be understood as a story of getting more *value from less—extracting more from each unit of input (land, labour, materials, financial capital, energy). In the case of the use of energy, this sequence of improvement has been dramatic and sustained. Compare the vast boilers of a Victorian factory with the generators and electric motors of today, or open coal fires with today's central heating. Some processes are *less* energy efficient, in the sense that energy is used where none was needed before—the use of electrical equipment to do what was formerly done by hand, for example, or the case of being driven to school instead of walking. But, once the use of energy for a particular task has been established, ways are generally found to do the same thing with less energy.

This first stage in the sequence of lean energy is to get better results (in terms of energy-efficiency) than those likely to be achieved through companies' general pursuit of *competitive advantage. Some guidelines and inspiration are provided by the energy analysts Paul Hawken, Amory Lovins and Hunter Lovins. Among the conclusions they draw from their collective experience, there are two with special relevance to lean energy.[73]

First, there is the iterative approach to solving complex problems. They point out that, if you make a substantial improvement in one part of a system, it is likely that it will open the way to another. That is, a sequence of possibility opens up. An illustration of this which will be familiar to anyone who visits a small local supermarket is the problem of getting rid of heat. The chillers produce a lot of heat. So the shop gets hot. So the chillers have to work harder. So the shop gets hotter. There is a positive *feedback of energy-inefficiency. But suppose that a way is now found of breaking that cycle, by ducting the hot air outside: the shop cools down, so the chillers have to work less hard, so they produce less heat, so the fresh vegetables sell better, sales rise, energy costs fall, profits rise, success breeds success, and the owner discovers that she can afford a proper temperature control system for the whole shop.

Hawken *et al*'s own iconic example of this principle is the Hypercar. We shouldn't take it too literally, because the result is an extremely lightweight car, which could be tricky to drive on a windy day, and would surely grind to a halt if going uphill fully loaded with family, luggage, and the dog (a system has to be powerful enough to cope with its peaks) but it has become a landmark in the literature. A smaller engine makes it possible to install a lighter suspension, so it can get by with a less robust chassis, so most of the components can be downsized, which opens the way to a smaller engine . . . Although you probably wouldn't want to drive the theoretical endpoint of that process, the principle is good. And they offer many other (more realistic, and now widely-recognised) examples—improved designs in pumping systems, building design and construction, appliances, and city planning: it is all about seeing the *system as a whole, rather than as a *reductionist set of individual problems.[74]

Hawken *et al*'s second (closely-related) piece of advice draws philosophical lessons from eating a lobster. There are some good meaty chunks to be found (in the claws and tail). But if you stop there, you have really missed the point, because half of what the lobster has to offer is hidden in the bits that are hard to find, and it takes persistence and a certain amount of know-how to extract them. In the case of energy conservation, that half really matters; it can take you to the point when (in Hawken *et al*'s phrase) you can start to "tunnel through the cost barrier"—the breakthrough when you are getting close to understanding, or at last taking into account, the *whole* system. Instead of tinkering with a system that is full of contradictions, you get consistency—a *common purpose. Now the big cost savings can come.[75]

With the application of these principles, significant improvements in energy efficiency can be expected. And yet, there are limits. Even lobsters are eventually finished. Energy solutions on the scale of the local supermarket are not enough. The supermarket itself is just one component in isolation. What we are looking for is energy efficiency transformations in a whole economy. And that takes us to structural change.

2. *Structural change*

Structural change does not stop at making energy services more efficient. It is focused on doing without them. It looks at ways of getting the results—the *food and joy—we want with minimum recourse to goods, services, *transport and processing in all their forms. It is not about making the *regrettable necessities of life more energy-efficient, but avoiding having to use them at all. It is the essence of *Lean Logic*'s case. It is about doing things in a completely different way, minimising the *scale of the *intermediate economy—or coping after its comprehensive collapse. At the heart of it, it is about the *proximity principle, which provides services in the *place where they are to be used and matures towards a *closed-loop system. That means *localisation.

Consider the sequences of elaboration described in the entry on the *intermediate economy—notably in the Story of Pots. In our imagination we could unravel that elaboration, starting at the end, and deintensifying, backwards, step-by-step. This would be very much harder than it sounds—borderline impossible, in fact—because there is a ratchet effect here: it is all too easy to go forward but (almost) impossible to go backwards. The elaborations and infrastructure of a large-scale *civic society are there for a reason: they are part of the *intensification needed by a large *population. On a very much smaller scale—when we are thinking about cooling down a corner shop rather than ratcheting back a civilisation—the principles of intelligent energy conservation are a life-saver. But, on the large scale of step-by-step unravelling of complexity, we have to face the fact that it is fairly conclusively a one-way process: you can intensify—you can build a more and more elaborate *political economy without even fully realising what you are doing—but deintensification is orders of magnitude harder.

The exception to that statement comes with the possibility of a profound, population-reducing shock, whose outcome would be a radically deintensified economy. That may happen, and *Lean Logic* thinks about the kind of political economy that could be built to last after such a shock. But recognising the possibility of that shock—and preparing for it—is not the same thing as advocating it, nor assuming it. What it is realistic to advocate is the case for understanding deintensification, and making some progress towards it, whatever the probability of the shock and its timing. A significant degree of localisation is not inconsistent with the *market economy, but it has to be *intentional, and it goes against the grain of the *competitive market which, as a default position—barely even consciously—will centralise and delocalise.

So, that's the agenda of structural change:

- intentional localisation, starting while the market economy is still capable of supporting an ambitious programme of reform . . .
- using the principle of iterative progress applied both to energy conservation and to structural change itself, and then . . .
- continuing with persistence down an *Energy Descent Action Plan towards a deep reduction in energy-dependency.

It does not come from any particular breakthrough or technology; it comes from that iterative advance, a step-by-step opening up of possibilities made available by the interactions both within and between conservation and structural change. It could be by real-life experiment, or on paper, or in conversation, or in the virtual reality of a computer programme. And if policy-makers can be recruited than a supportive *national framework like *TEQs could be a key catalyst to the necessary local innovation.

3. *Energy sources*

Once energy conservation and structural change, in their iterative, step-by-step way, have established the frame of reference, it then becomes possible to develop a sensible strategy for the *sources* of energy on which the community of the future will depend.

Once those first two steps have been developed to the point of reducing energy demand by (say) tenfold or more, down to a realistic and manageable scale, the possibility opens up that solar power, wind power, water power, and the other renewable sources could supply that energy. Renewable energy systems designed to supply *all* the energy needs of a small-scale local system are quite different from those that are intended simply as a *useful contribution* to a large system, and the task required of them now begins to become clear—where the energy is needed, how much is needed, for what purposes, when (time of day, time of year), and in what form it should be delivered. The modern grids are based on these calculations anyway, but in the case of lean energy, they will be more detailed, more local. And local systems of all kinds will not be designed on the assumption of abundant energy, but with intense focus on their actual purposes, with energy-flows into the system being factored in only as a last resort, when all other possible solutions have been explored and exhausted. Lean energy solutions are not about energy solutions; they are about solutions.

On the small scale, there is a specificness. People don't need energy. They don't need energy services. They don't need the things that the energy services do for them. They need the final outcomes: *health, stimulus, friendship, security, time in a natural environment. There are ways of enabling these outcomes other than through the supply of energy; energy will be part of it, but when the nature, the volume and the timing of energy supply is closely matched to specific *intentions, the system begins to get close to sustainable *elegance—a defining property of a *complex system with a future.

As with energy conservation, there are synergies here. A modest level of energy demand makes it possible to use small-scale installations; transport distances for the energy itself are short; and there is a reduced need for (easily) portable energy—that is, liquid fuels such as petrol, which are hard to get in the absence of oil, gas or coal to start the process. Much less *capital is needed; the installation is local, accessible and owned by its users: this is a system that can be fine-tuned.

And low energy demand also has the crucial advantage of reduced reliance on the backup of a national grid. It is not known whether there will be a functioning grid to which local *lean economies can link their *networks. The presumption in *Lean Logic* is that there will not. The grid requires a complete industrial and financial infrastructure, whose prospects of long-term survival are poor. There is little to lose—and there is assurance to be gained—by *assuming* the absence of a reliable grid. A large-scale grid is an undoubted advantage because it evens up the supply, which is especially useful when a substantial proportion of the supply comes from renewables—notably wind. But it may not be available.

Certainly, the grid is no guarantee of a continuous flow. Indeed, should it fail for any reason—such as an outage in the gas-generated electricity which it is designed to carry—it will not be able to accept the flow of energy coming from

the renewable energy sources attached to it: it will cut out just at the moment when their contribution is most needed, with the failure of the main system rippling through to a failure of the backup. We might think of an analogy here: a luxury cruise liner equipped with state-of-the-art lifeboats, each equipped with hot cocoa machines and fleece sleeping bags. The only snag being that they are welded to the ship.

In a lean energy system, the production and distribution of energy is decentralised. It is not a top-down structure with energy being produced by large-scale generators and distributed down the wire; instead, all the participants, including *households, are active in the grid in several ways. Households generate electricity as well as using it. The local network, or "minigrid", carries the electrical current in both directions, probably using the efficiency savings of direct current (DC). If the technology is available, a smart grid and smart meters, applying well-established principles and circuitry, will keep demand and supply in balance, smoothing out the peaks and reducing the maximum capacity for which the grid and its energy sources has to be designed. Energy of all kinds will be included in the local network.[76]

For all these reasons, a *generalised installation of renewables *before* the design of the local systems which they will be supplying is unfocused, and likely to be an impressive solution to the wrong problem. And that takes us to the intensely-difficult question that opens up with the consideration of local solutions: what is "local"?

What is "local"?

When we think of local renewable sources of energy, it is natural to think of things like: photovoltaic cells in the form of solar panels attached to roofs and walls or film attached to windows; solar thermal systems using solar heat concentrated and tracked with mirrors, wind turbines, local hydropower, run-of-the-river turbines, tidal power, wave power and ground-source heat pumps. And we should think, too, of the gadgets attached to them, such as light bulbs, electric motors and equipment, refrigeration, information processors and the internet.

These are sophisticated machines, and they are provided by the industrial establishment, organised on a global *scale. If any part of that *network becomes unavailable, its capability is likely to be reduced drastically.

Now, it is not known to what extent that global industrial establishment will survive the *climacteric. Nor is it known how far deconcentration into self-reliant local economies will extend—and, in any case, it is likely to vary over time and by location. So we have to approach the matter from the other direction—to be prepared, if only as a thought-experiment, to question the assumption that today's advanced energy technologies will be available. In fact, there are four characters in the story—four variables . . .

1. The technology available locally.
2. Local technical knowledge and skills.
3. Local natural resources (including energy sources).
4. The extent and reliability of connections with trading partners providing access to resources and equipment which localities cannot provide for themselves.

. . . and they are mutually dependent. If one of them were significantly impaired, the consequences would be substantial. Would a local community then have access to solar panels? wind turbines? diesel- or bio-fuelled generators? electricity from any source? light bulbs?

These are unknowns, of course. We must hope, intensely, for *local lite*—where (as variable 4 suggests) the locality has access to the small-scale, hyperefficient technologies that enable the potential of small-scale production to be fulfilled. But that, of course, raises a question. If communities can get hold of all the equipment they need to be locally self-reliant in energy, that sounds like a well-ordered society and *market: so, whatever happened to the climacteric? Was it cancelled? And if they can get hold of all that equipment, perhaps they can also simply buy the energy itself? In fact, why bother to deconcentrate in the first place? Why not just carry on with the *status quo* of large-scale *capture and concentration? Perhaps we are looking at a golden age of energy-efficiency, with solar energy cabled all over Europe from Desertec installations in the Sahara Desert? Or from wind arrays in the North Sea and extending far out into the North Atlantic? Even if so, that may do little to mitigate any of the other shocks—*climate,

*water, *food—that are in prospect; on the contrary, easily-available energy could have the effect of allowing the other shocks to worsen at their leisure.[77]

And any shock which disrupts economic life in the mainstream political economy sufficiently to prompt the development of local self-reliance would also be likely to disrupt connections between self-reliant communities. There may be a period during which self-reliance is developed in anticipation of problems to come, but when scarcities bite, local communities seeking increased self-reliance can be expected to find themselves forced into *deep* self-reliance. In this situation, communities will be able to obtain little from outside providers, and have little access even to tools, or to materials such as copper, other than what they inherit from previous inhabitants and their central heating systems.

The good news here is that there is one asset which could be reasonably resilient to the shock. If the climacteric were to take us back to local self-reliance on the scale of (say) medieval Europe, there would actually be a substantial difference—it could be medieval-plus. Though short of technical equipment, we would at least have technical knowledge. We could make better glass. We would have an understanding of infections and the need for sterile conditions for open wounds and surgery. There would probably be knowledge of how to use local plant species as a source of anaesthetics and maybe even antibiotics. We would not need to invent wood-burning stoves and wheeled luggage. Our standards of *organic *agriculture would be high. We would not drink out of lead cups. We would have cavity-wall insulation and maybe double-glazing, methane and other biofuels, and the plant-based resins and plastics described in *Lean Materials.

And if the equipment and materials for the requisite level of metalworking are available, the possibility opens up of using forms of mechanical power as recommended by the charity Practical Action for communities which do not have the resources to buy, install and maintain an electricity grid. With mechanical power driven by wind, water, animals or humans in place, pumps, mills, threshing, pressing (for vegetable oil), carpentry tools and ropeways for local transport can remain in life-saving working order, providing a resilience to shocks whose first sign of arrival is that the lights go out.[78]

L

———

In its essentials, then, lean energy is simple. It is about developing conservation and structural changes as far as they will go, and then working out how to supply the energy needed for the relatively modest level of demand that remains. But the way in which that works out is not at all simple. Electricity needs more than the occasional inefficient generator. It almost certainly needs a trading *network—for the generation, transmission, and equipment. And it needs a grid. If the maintenance of a national grid is not possible, then that implies conditions which could well place a local grid, too, beyond the competence of local economies. A local grid offers some security from trouble affecting the national grid, so it is worth providing that local resilience if at all possible, but events which would knock out the national grid while leaving the local grid intact and fully maintained cover a relatively narrow range of probability.

Amid all this uncertainty, there are two principles that we can rely on. The first is that the sequence {energy conservation → structural change → energy sources} remains intact, however the story of energy supply develops. Acknowledging uncertainty does not diminish the probability of deep energy scarcities, and the nucleus of any response must be to reduce energy-dependence deeply and urgently. The second principle is that, whatever the circumstances, the flexible, rapid response that will be needed plays to the strengths of lean thinking—this is exactly what it is for. In our present, pre-shock era, reasonable competence can usually get us through: we can refer to established systems and methods. Lean energy needs more than that. The local Lean Economy will need to be brilliant.

*Energy Prospects, Energy Descent Action Plan, TEQs (Tradable Energy Quotas).

LEAN FOOD. Local self-reliance in food, where the *community can buy in little or nothing of what it eats. We will consider this by walking through the sequence of *lean thinking: *intention, *lean means, *flow, *pull and *feedback.

1. INTENTION: THE PROXIMITY PRINCIPLE APPLIED TO FOOD

As with all the other "lean" entries, the intention is to provide a starting point for thinking about how *local

lean economies might provide for themselves from their own resources. The degree of their local self-reliance will vary with time and place. It could lie anywhere between *local lite*—where communities have access to outside equipment and material resources to support their localisation—and *deep local*, where they do not. The ideal, for an enduring settlement in line with the *proximity principle, is for routine needs to be met from local resources, with some enabling equipment and *materials bought in, but the emphasis in Lean Logic is on the dark end of the spectrum, where almost no food—and none of the agricultural materials that depend on oil, gas and coal, such as nitrogen fertilisers—are available from outside the locality. This is a scenario, not a forecast, but it is a critical one to consider.

Communities will be of varying sizes, with varying quantities of *land of varying quality, and the *skills they will be able to bring will vary. They will have varying luck and *judgment. There is less variation, however, in the means available to them—in the logic of local self-reliance in food.

2. LEAN MEANS: ORGANIC FOUNDATIONS

If nitrogen fertilisers and the various defensive chemicals (biocides) that accompany them become unavailable, the remaining option for food production will be to turn to methods which are at least some approximation of "organic".

Any model of food production with a future must conserve its fertility. In principle, that means it must sustain a *closed-loop system, with everything it produces eventually finding its way back to the soil. But the need to feed large and distant urban populations makes this cycle hard to maintain, so the discovery by Justus von Liebig in the 1840s of a way to capture nitrogen from the air, and to combine it with oxygen to turn it into a form that could be spread on the land, was a major breakthrough. It enabled farmers to sustain the supply of food to urban populations without getting back any of the organic matter needed to sustain a healthy soil.

However, this use of manufactured nitrogen fertiliser has its problems. The first problem is that the form in which it is added to the soil—simple nitrate salts—is quite different from the complex compounds of plant

and animal residues in which it comes in a natural *ecology. It is a bit like the difference between drinking (or maybe sharing) a bottle of wine on its own and on an empty stomach, or drinking it in the course of a meal: the same wine will have quite different effects. The wine drunk on its own acts more quickly, gives you a rush of alcohol and makes you feel worse afterwards (though an *expert analysis of the matter might conclude that any difference in the effect is all in your imagination, since the quantity and nature of the wine in each case is identical).

In the case of agriculture, farmers noticed that when their crops were fed on these "neat" nitrates, there were various *unintended consequences (and Liebig himself was aware of this risk). The crops became more vulnerable to pests and diseases, so that the nitrates eventually needed to be backed up by an assortment of agro-chemical biocides. And there were consequences for the soil too, in the form of a loss of humus (we will come to what that is in a moment). This was not only due to the direct impact of soluble nitrates on soil life, but also because "bag nitrogen" encouraged farmers to reduce or even ignore crop rotation and the routine return of livestock manure and other types of organic matter to the soil.

Some farmers and researchers therefore investigated other ways of restoring nitrogen to the soil, and protecting crops from disease without the use of the chemicals—and these experiments, which drew on knowledge that had been available to farmers for a long time, proved to be successful. For instance, nitrogen is restored to the soil by leguminous plants, such as clover, beans and alfalfa, so that if crops of wheat are "rotated" over a period of, say, five years, with an annually-changing series of crops such as clover, grass (feeding sheep or cattle), beans and root vegetables,

before coming back to wheat, then (in the case of best practice on a mixed farm with livestock) the soil remains well supplied with nitrogen, without the need for any industrial nitrates at all.[79]

The second problem with neat nitrates (also recognised by Liebig) is that nitrogen is only one of the nutrients that plants need. There are many others. Phosphorus is needed both by plants and animals; plants need it for their enzymes to work properly, and livestock needs it for the formation of their bones. Potassium is used by plants for photosynthesis (the production of plant tissue and oxygen from carbon dioxide and sunlight), and animals use it in large quantities for the formation of their body fluids, muscle control and nervous systems. Calcium is used by plants to build their tissue, by the soil (to keep earthworms happy), and animals need it to make bones. And many other elements are needed in "trace" quantities: manganese, zinc, boron (to prevent internal rot in potatoes), copper, molybdenum, cobalt, iron (used by nitrogen-fixing bacteria)—and there is a long list of elements needed in extremely small amounts, such as chromium, nickel and selenium.[80]

With each export of nutrient-rich food from the farm, the nutrients in the soil are reduced, and they are hard to replace. For instance, the soil's stores of phosphates can be routinely topped up, mainly by phosphates imported from quarries in North Africa, but the world's reserves are being used up quickly. Potassium is contained in almost every kind of rock, but not all soil types are rich in potassium, and it takes a long time to rebuild levels in the soil by the natural processes of weathering. It is easily extracted in industrial quantities from rocks and added to the soil as a form of salt (potash), but that gives plants a "rush" of potassium, rather than the constant moderate levels that they are adapted to, and the only available source for that is animal manure

L

and urine. Calcium, by contrast, can easily be replaced with ground-up limestone and chalk (where these are available). The trace elements, however, are hard to replace; soils vary in their needs, and could be damaged if they are supplied in the wrong quantities, and the cost of adding them is high. Even if they were routinely applied, it could turn out to be to some extent a wasted effort, since the nitrogen fertilisers have the effect of making the soils more acid, which makes it harder for plants to absorb them.[81]

For these reasons, the export of soil fertility to cities—from which the nutrients will never return—is a problem that is not solved by the application of nitrogen fertiliser. Rather, it is masked. Farmers can get high yields, but the fine detail—what the food actually contains, what biocides have had to be used for the protection that the crops cannot now provide for themselves, the condition of the soil, how long the supplies of phosphates will last, and the steady loss of trace elements—generally escapes attention. With the discovery of artificial fertilisers, we can patch up the obvious, crude deficits that develop in the soil when its fertility is exported, but that is not the same as maintaining a healthy soil with a future as a source of healthy—that is, complete—food.

This is this problem that engaged the attention of the pioneers of *organic agriculture in the 1920s and 1930s. Here is one of them, Walter James (Lord Northbourne), in his book *Look to the Land*, which, in this context, made the first use of the word "organic":

> . . . the farm must have a *biological completeness*; it must be a living entity, a unit which has within itself a balanced organic life. The penalty for failure to maintain this balance is, in the long run, a progressive impoverishment of the soil. Real fertility can only be built up gradually under a system appropriate to the conditions on each particular farm. Artificial manures contribute to the soil only some of the elements which are removed in crops. By the proper conservation and preparation of wastes of all kinds, absolutely everything ever taken from the soil can be returned to it.[82]

The fact that human society depends for its existence on a healthy soil is, you might think, obvious, but the organic movement (it has also gone by other names, but can be identified by the principles listed in the sidebar) has been pointing it out for a century or so, and there is still some way to go. The case, in summary, is this:

- The soil is a biologically-active, living system.
- Fertility and minerals taken out of the soil should be replaced, bringing it as close as possible to a *closed-loop system.
- Those replacements should usually be composted so that the materials returned to the soil are already in a biologically active form.
- Food from a fertile soil is a necessary condition for the health of the people who eat it.
- The health of plants and animals and of the people who eat them are mutually dependent.[83]

Those five points are the essence of Lady Eve Balfour's classic, *The Living Soil*, a compendium of the work of the pioneers in the 1920s and 1930s. Sir Albert Howard was among the major influences on this work, and his *An Agricultural Testament* was the first connected explanation of what is meant by a "fertile soil". He placed the emphasis decisively on humus—which, he explains, is . . .

258

. . . a complex residue of partly oxidised vegetable and animal matter together with the substances synthesised by the fungi and bacteria which break down the wastes. This humus also helps to provide the cement which enables the minute mineral soil particles to aggregate into larger compound particles and so maintain the pore space. If the soil is deficient in humus, the volume of the pore space is reduced; the aeration of the soil is impeded; there is insufficient organic matter for the soil population; the machinery of the soil runs down; the supply of oxygen, water and dissolved salts needed by the root hairs is reduced; the synthesis of carbohydrates and proteins in the green leaf proceeds at a lower tempo; growth is affected. Humus is therefore an essential material for the soil if the first phase of the life cycle is to function.[84]

And humus, in turn, is a condition for the presence of mycorrhiza, the *network of soil fungi which form a link between the nutrients (especially phosphorus) in the soil, and the roots of the plants that depend on them. There is a two-way flow, with organic nutrients flowing into the fungus, and inorganic nutrients being taken up by the plants. The quality and nutritional value of food relies on the efficiency of this interaction; it therefore relies on the presence of organic matter in the soil.[85]

Just to be sure, Howard reminds us:

[It is] on the efficiency of this mycorrhiza association that the health and well-being of mankind must depend.[86]

And yet, none of this really deals with the loss of phosphates, potassium and the micronutrients from the land. There is no doubt that organic methods mitigate the problem. The well-developed humus in organic soil conserves its nutrients and reduces or prevents erosion. The mycorrhiza it supports make the micronutrients more available to the plants in an organic system, and organic agriculture's crop rotations invite the use of deep-rooting plants (e.g., chicory, dock) which bring micronutrients to the surface. And the depletion of micronutrients is a slow-moving problem which it is tempting, and to some extent justifiable, to defer for a time, especially when the

---

PRINCIPLES IN SUMMARY
Organic agriculture

Principle of health: Organic agriculture should sustain and enhance the health of soil, plant, animal, human and planet as one and indivisible.

Principle of ecology: Organic agriculture should be based on living ecological systems and cycles, work with them, emulate them and help to sustain them.

Principle of fairness: Organic agriculture should build on relationships that ensure fairness with regard to the common environment and life opportunities.

Principle of care: Organic agriculture should be managed in a precautionary and responsible manner to protect the health and well-being of current and future generations and the environment.

International Federation of Organic Agriculture Movements, Headline Principles.[87]

---

most pressing issue is supplying the food needed to keep people alive today. But, on a longer view, the depletion of micronutrients—peak micronutrients—needs a solution. Organic cultivation is not it, but it does provide the foundations on which solutions to it can be devised. It recognises the production of food as part of the interconnected network between soil, plant, animal and man (or, as we now prefer, soil, plant, animal, human and planet). It makes the case that (as Balfour writes),

. . . the health of man, beast, plant and soil is one indivisible whole; the health of the soil depends on maintaining its biological balance and, starting with a truly fertile soil, the crops grown on it, the livestock fed on those crops and the humans fed on both have a standard of health and power of resisting disease and infection, from whatever cause, greatly in advance of anything ordinarily found . . . ; such health as we have almost forgotten should be our natural state, so used have we become to subnormal physical fitness.[88]

"Health" is not now quite the key property that public opinion looks for in food; its place has been taken by other mainstream aims such as *choice, cheapness and quantity. And yet, it remains a priority for critics of industrial agriculture, and organic agriculture has crucial advantages. It avoids contamination of food with biocides. It manages the land in a way that works with *natural systems. It conserves the soil with its rich ecology of humus. It makes use of the natural behaviour patterns of predators—insects and birds—to control pests. It conserves the predators' habitats. It uses strategies such as companion planting (plants that thrive together are placed close together), and it times the planting and harvesting of crops on the basis of an understanding of predators' life-cycles. The principle here is not that the pests should be wiped out (not least because that would wipe out their natural predators, too), but that they should be kept in check so effectively that they do not damage the crop. Balfour describes the example of an organic farm that was expected to be under attack:

> A large-scale organic commercial grower,
> growing vegetables, fruit and flowers was
> visited by a team of scientists from Cambridge
> University—they included plant pathologists
> and entomologists. They knew it was an
> unsprayed holding and they came looking
> for disease and pests. They found isolated
> examples of everything they expected to find,
> but, as they put it, they failed to find a single
> case of crop damage.[89]

And she adds,

> Whenever pests appear in unmanageable num-
> bers, it is probably safe to assume that nature's
> balance of species has in some way been upset
> [by] man's mismanagement.[90]

Here, then, we have the bare bones of the art of getting food from the earth. And that takes us to the third snag arising from the use of soluble nitrogen and other agro-chemical fertilisers: *lean economies won't be able to get hold of them anyway. They will have to develop other ways of sustaining a healthy soil. Organic cultivation is the *only* means by which a community can supply its own food. It does not import fertility by the bag; it does all it can to stop it going to *waste; it protects its soil; it uses no manufactured biocides. In terms of its direct requirements (that is, not counting the energy needed to manufacture and drive its equipment), it is self-reliant, and close to being self-sufficient.

In its present form, it is of course profoundly dependent on oil and gas for *transport, and for equipment and operations such as drying grain or hay, but these dependencies are not intrinsic to it. The process *itself* (as distinct from the equipment it uses) would still be a functioning, productive source of food even if those energy supplies were not available, and that would by no means be true of conventional agriculture, whose use of nitrates and biocides makes it intrinsically dependent on oil, gas and/or coal. It is a measure of how far our industrial economy has distanced itself from the land that we are able to think of the baseline of rational, local organic food production as being a special case, even as a luxury. In the local lean community, decentralisation and a focus on local capability will not be a lifestyle choice. There will be no alternative.

So we have convergence here. What is right for a healthy soil is *also* right—in fact, indispensable—for a self-reliant community. It is always a good sign when the solution to one problem turns out to be a solution to one or more others at the same time. That should be no surprise, of course, because we are talking about a *complex system, and the insides of such systems join up: *common purpose matures to *common capability.

And yet, that is not the whole story. The problem of the micronutrients remains unsolved. And this description of the *means* of growing local food does not really explain how it can be done—how, from that baseline, to discover ways of feeding a community. So this is the moment to continue our progress along the sequence of lean thinking: the next stage is *flow.*

3. FLOW: FLEXIBLE APPLICATIONS

What, then, is *flow in the context of providing food for a community? It means inspired flexibility. That could take many forms, all of them right in their own way, and having a contribution to make. The best will no doubt come in the form of inventions of the *time and *place, but here, for the time being, are some suggestions:

a *diverse range of food crops that ripen over an extended time rather than all at once; the use of all the horizontal, vertical and below-the-surface spaces for its food; little in the way of clear *boundaries between one use of the space and another, or between one ecology and another; broadly-based participation in the supply of food in community; local synergies—that is, ways of joining up the many parts of the food cycle through the whole sequence from harvest to harvest, including the use of all human and animal waste; a convergence of *skills—hands and heads, *ecology and *community.

That sounds like permaculture. There is nothing new about that way of thinking, though the name (a combination of permanent + agriculture + culture)—was first published by Bill Mollison and David Holmgren as recently as 1978. What is new is the realisation that it is intensely *relevant to our time. Organic agriculture and permaculture are both intended as imitations of nature, but permaculture follows that principle through, working with natural ecologies including permanent grasslands, wetlands, estuaries, forests of various ages and types, and *edge-ecologies between one form and another. Permaculture's case is that, with enlightened intervention, those natural ecologies can be guided towards forms and mixtures of species which, despite the lack of assistance from fossil fuels, are extremely productive.[91]

Permaculture's most distinctive form is the forest garden. Forest gardens are based on the principle of "layering": instead of using the sunlight at just one level, and for a limited period of the year, plants of different heights use it at many levels and on different timings. For the extreme illustration of this we can look to forest gardening in places where there is no winter to speak of. In southeastern Nigeria, local smallholdings are layered in up to nine storeys, with crops consisting of fruit (breadfruit, pear, mango, orange, lime, papaya, bananas and pepper), tree vegetables, timber, fertilisers, thatching, snake repellents, gums, dyes, spices, ground vegetables, maize, melons, yams and peanuts. This is a virtuoso performance, not just in the variety of food and *materials produced in a small space, but in their quality. And making it happen—as Robert Hart, the pioneer of temperate forest gardens points out—takes "skilled craftsmanship".[92] He explains,

PRINCIPLES IN SUMMARY
Permaculture

Permaculture is designed to produce a yield within a *closed-loop system, recycling as much as it can of its own *waste, relying on renewable sources of *energy and on ecosystem services such as a healthy soil and natural predators. It uses the *diversity of plants and animals, devising ways to integrate them into productive, *small-scale, local guilds and ecologies. It applies tested patterns to local situations and it values the opportunities supplied at the margins between distinct ecologies.

There is emphasis on close observation and personal interaction with the ecology, on the need to adjust our own *intentions in the light of what we observe, and on creative response to changes in it.

Permaculture has application both to food production and to whole human habitats. It aims to build complex mosaics of ecological exchange, producing a rich flow of food and *materials with the minimum need for intervention.

Derived from the Design Principles in David Holmgren, *Permaculture*, 2002[93]

A tropical rainforest is a supreme and infinitely varied work of art, but with a touch of human genius, it can be converted into a forest garden system, even more beautiful and vastly more productive. . . . A forest garden, replete with fruit and foliage, blooms, birds and insects, mammals and fungi, fascinating scents and sounds, can be a work of art comparable to any of humankind's highest cultural attainments . . . a profoundly practical answer to the technology developed since the Industrial Revolution.[94]

Can it be done in temperate regions? Well, yes, it can, but that does mean a considerable revision to what is meant by "forest"—and whether it can be called a

L

"forest garden" is a matter of taste.[95] At the very least, there are gaps in the forest, perhaps containing grassland crops—grass, wheat, oats and barley—and water plants. Raised beds with cabbages, leeks and courgettes may also be found in a forest garden, and could look just like what most people would call a vegetable patch. What distinguishes this from more conventional forms of cultivation is that flow of *diversity, on the edge of disorder: comfrey for compost, fruit trees, nut trees, a fish pond and crops growing at different heights and to different timings, a *harmonic order of species together in the same place. That can only be done if there is a wide variety of species to choose from, to suit local conditions, and permaculture deliberately explores the much underdeveloped potential here. As a report by the UN Food and Agriculture Organisation concludes,

> Of more than 50,000 edible plant species in the world, only a few hundred contribute significantly to food supplies. Just 15 crop plants provide 90 percent of the world's food energy intake, with three—rice, maize and wheat—making up two-thirds of this.[96]

Stephen Hopper, director of the Royal Botanical Gardens at Kew, adds, "It is baffling that we are so reliant on so few species." And now, with extended studies from Ken Fern, Martin Crawford and others, we have comprehensive guidance on the edible plants, their nature, cultivation and use.[97]

There may also be larger fields and larger animals for cereals and milk, playing their part in the cycle of crop rotations, so the diversity will almost certainly include meat: future society would have to be rich indeed if it were willing to forgo the use of uplands for sheep, wild forest for deer, livestock as an integral part of crop rotations, the many uses of pigs and chickens in a *waste-free closed-loop system, and rabbits, pigeons and fish as easily-available sources of protein.

A hyperdiverse ecology of this kind undoubtedly encourages an intense spirit of experimentation—established examples include using perennial crops wherever possible (no need for annual sowing); ingenuity in joining systems up in productive ways; or developing the potential of close reciprocal collaboration with chickens. If chickens forage in an orchard in the autumn and winter, and corn marigold, fleabane and ox-eye daisy grow there in the spring and summer, the apples are unlikely to be troubled by pests and diseases. From the bugs' point of view, chickens are ferocious. They spell trouble for codling moth, apple-, plum- and gooseberry-sawfly, winter moth, scab, pear mite, slugworm, raspberry beetle and cane midge. And they can also warm up your greenhouse, clear vegetable beds of slugs and seeds ready for cultivation, provide manure, save the trouble of digging, pick the lice off pigs, get rid of household scraps and clear willow coppice of the brassy beetle. Oh, and they lay eggs and provide succulent meat, and you can make soup from their bones.[98]

In the midst of all this, there is an *intelligent, thoughtful species, with a light tread, that knows what it is doing, and has designed the local *ecology with insight, making constant interventions like digging unnecessary. Permaculture finds the point of *leverage in the system, so that it wants to do what you want it to do; it takes to the fullest development its economies of scale—that is, *small scale—and the very high levels of productivity per square metre that are possible under the care of a gardener who knows what

INTENSIVE FOOD PRODUCTION
Examples, with and without digging

The horticulturalists Alan Chadwick and (later) John Jeavons used physically-demanding, deep-bed, double-dig methods. They followed through the logic of closed-loop systems to their limit, recycling all waste, including *post mortem* human remains, and they had the benefit of the California climate. Their results were prodigious: they showed that a complete diet for one adult can be achieved on 2,800 square feet (260m²).[99]

Michael and Julia Guerra do it without digging: "Why double-dig when you can let the earthworms take the strain? In our 75m² no-dig urban garden, with raised beds, multilayered plants and about a million hard-working worms, we can get around 150kg of food per year (excluding the 25% that is returned to compost as kitchen waste). That works out at about 26 tonnes per hectare. For food self-sufficiency we would need around 250m² of perfect soil, climate and aspect per person. We do have to import stable manure to offset the loss via the flush toilet, but we can get by with 30% less of that by adding fertility as a mulch on top of the living soil instead of digging it in. That keeps the worms happy and we let them get on with it."[100]

Charles Dowding, in partnership with his local ecology, has created an enchanting and productive source of vegetables for his part of Somerset. His key recommendation: "Please don't dig!"[101]

he or she is doing. It provides an intense insight into the potential for gardening the world: food production based on attention to detail.[102]

And if you are still wondering, after all this, why you can't put your finger on what permaculture is, and where the difference lies between it and organic gardening, don't be alarmed, for (as the permaculture teacher Rob Hopkins observes) it is famously difficult to explain in the pub. The reason is that permaculture is not a technique; it is an enlightened *freedom to think. Although guiding principles have been devised, it is its commitment to breaking through into fresh uses of *local chance and detail that makes it so powerful. You can't really explain that to the man in the pub. You can explain the specifics of what you have done, or plan to do, but *abstractions about how you have opened your mind to anything suggested by the site and inspiration sound vague.[103]

The sequence is:

- *Observe* the site in detail and at length: *land, *water, soil, sunlight, gradients, buildings, *boundaries and walking distances.
- *Design* and map the ecology to take root there; review it, *reflect on it, *imagine living in it.
- *Enable* it. This is the hard work phase—planting; building raised beds and paths; maybe digging a

pond or a well; using spaces which catch the sun now, but won't when the trees you are planting are grown.

- *Participate*. No longer playing The Maker of your productive ecology, you can now take a rest. Well, in part at least, although those raised beds will need frequent attention, not far short of what a gardener with a family to feed would recognise. You are now part of it, living off it, and nudging it, joining up in the *network of *connectedness which makes an interactive *natural system.

Patrick Whitefield summarises, "Permaculture can be described as careful thought followed by minimum action."[104]

Permaculture is, in this sense, a return to normal. Its advocates explain it with enthusiasm, but in the end, it sounds completely obvious: "Yes, but what's special about it?" Nothing—that's the whole point. What is *special* is a model of farming designed in imitation of industry and relying on stocks of unreplaceable fuels to maintain its fertility, to distribute its produce, to protect it from attack by predators, and to support the growth-dependent, fuel-addicted, *market economy as the foundation on which the whole structure is built. Permaculture is, in contrast, but brilliantly, *nothing special*.

The output of permaculture or forest gardens is diverse and abundant, but it will not provide bulk deliveries of the identical quality and standards required by a supermarket. As Whitefield explains, a forest garden . . .

> . . . will almost certainly yield less top fruit than a simple orchard, less berries than a pure stand of soft fruit bushes, and less vegetables than a simple vegetable garden, but it will produce more in total than any of the single layer plantings.[105]

It is therefore a culture for the small-scale, for short distances, for the *informal economy. It is for ecologies whose human participants live close by. As Whitefield reflects:

> A forest garden does not need a lot of work, but it does need attention. Though it can stand the odd spell of neglect, if it only gets attended to in occasional bursts of energy a few vigorous plants will take over the lower layers and much of the food will go unharvested. It needs someone to wander through it regularly to see how it is getting on, to cut back a rampant plant here, add a little mulch there, pick those tender little leaves or juicy berries before they go past their best. In short it needs someone to inhabit it.[106]

And that explains why, among its inhabitants, teachers and advocates, there is so strong an emphasis on permaculture as an *ethic. Ethics acknowledge a frame of reference beyond immediate opportunism and the ethic of permaculture comes from the whole experience of the *place we live in; from intense engagement with a living ecology that you are part of, and that has a mind of its own. Here we have a network of obligations and mutual care, of sacrifice and ingenuity for the *common purpose. Permaculture is ethics made edible.

4. Pull: participation

Pull is about the invention of solutions; the motivation to accomplish more than you thought you could. And it is happening now, at the beginning of a wonderful worldwide wave of *interest in growing our own food,

of taking control of what we eat. We have a sketch-map of some of this from Tamzin Pinkerton and Rob Hopkins:[107]

- *Home-grown food*, after a long decline, especially during the affluent half-century 1955-2005, is now on the turn towards recovery. Advice and local support for people who want to grow their own is beginning to reach people who have never done it before, with visits to experienced gardeners and their gardens as sources of inspiration, backed up by websites and local tuition, now strongly encouraged by local Transition groups.[108]
- Space within or on the *edge of cities has always been needed as a resource, especially for fresh food, and the United Kingdom's *allotments*—which fell into neglect, along with a loss of local skills, after reaching their peak during the Second World War—are getting attention again. Most allotments are rented and tended by individuals, but some are collectively managed, allowing people to specialise in the jobs they do best, pooling experience, ensuring continuity, providing encouragement and supplying a wide selection of produce. The demand for them is increasing and some local authorities are responding to this by making more land available, but the problem of *land, which will prove to be so critical in the future, is already beginning to be felt as allotment waiting lists lengthen.[109]
- Some gardens are larger than their owners can care for; some would-be gardeners have a garden that is too small for them, or no garden at all. There is a natural solution to this: *garden shares*. Garden owners invite people to grow vegetables in their gardens in return for a supply for their own use. These schemes have been encouraged by the *Transition movement, and by freelance initiatives such as Landshare—an exchange service which puts people with garden space in touch with people who could use it. Pinkerton and Hopkins provide guidelines on how to make this rational use of resources work.[110]

- *Community gardens* make use of whatever space in the locality seems to be suitable and available—at least for now: neglected orchards, back gardens and spaces on housing estates. Some of this opportunism spills over into guerrilla gardening, in which local authorities and absentee owners may—or may not—be pleasantly surprised by the improvements that have been covertly made to the use of their land. If the results are both decorative and edible, they can attract legitimate offers of less marginal land, such as the garden at the local railway station. Out-of-bounds vegetable growing in a West Yorkshire town in the UK has led to a vegetable-rich urban landscape known as Incredible Edible Todmorden.[111]

- Of all ways of supplying local food, *community orchards* have the clearest potential for celebration. The fruit harvest is a natural *festival, with fruit to eat, to cook, to make into juice and cider, to give away. And there are the skills of orchard-keeping to be taught: pruning, looking after the land between the trees (sheep and chickens, maybe), bee-keeping, and the selection of trees and varieties that will pollinate together. As Sue Clifford, co-director of Common Ground, writes, orchards and their carers weave *culture and nature together in "a philosophy of living well with the world".[112]

- Then there is *community supported agriculture* (CSA). This is the model of local food production in which the growing is in the hands of a professional, who earns his or her income from it, but the members of the scheme make regular payments into it and, in return, receive weekly supplies of the food produced. The grower gets a secure income; *transport is minimal; there are no intermediaries to claim their mark-up; the schemes' members get the kind of food they want, grown to the standard they want, and there is the *freedom to test *practical ideas and take them forward. Some schemes, for instance, are using the opportunity to explore deep reductions in their dependence on fossil fuels. CSAs are designed on the presumption that there is a robust market economy in the background but if, or when, that changes, they will be relatively well placed to adapt.[113]

- *Farmers' markets* allow growers to sell to their consumers direct, supplying both fresh and prepared food in much smaller quantities than the supermarkets would take. And by doing without the intermediaries, they can get a better return for what they produce, without having to raise the price. And the markets are convivial, sustaining networks of acquaintance and *conversation across the *community.[114]

- *Food cooperatives* buy from known local growers producing to whatever standards the community wants. Prices are kept down because much of the work is done by volunteers—the co-production which means that co-ops have (at least) one foot in the *informal economy. This model, too, with its established short-distance supply lines, will be comparatively well placed for a future *economy with very little money.[115]

Is there really no one right way of doing it? That's *pull* for you, especially when it gets into the diverse experimentalism of the Lean Economy. These community food solutions are still on a small scale, and even if they are to some extent independent of the *market economy, they rely on the stability it provides, and on income flows to provide most of a *household's other material needs. But in the future, with no such market, and maybe no such stability, the task of inventing solutions will be several steps closer to reality where some of these foundations of local self-reliance in food are already in place.

5. FEEDBACK: ORGANIC CAPITAL, ORGANIC CONVERSATION

The feedback that guides and stabilises all this comes in two ways. First, the fertility cycle. This closes the loop by which—as Walter James (Lord Northbourne) puts it above—absolutely everything taken from the soil is returned to it. It is easily said, but hard to achieve. There is no easy way of ensuring that all human wastes are composted and returned to the soil—and that applies especially to potassium, whose transport medium is urine, which quickly leaves the area in a water-based toilet *system. As a general rule, the smaller the population, the more feasible it becomes to design and sustain ways of closing the loop in its use of *waste. There are, for instance, highly-efficient means of capturing and composting human waste, as well as using urine. One of them involves compost toilets, which work best when urine and faeces are kept separate; but are difficult to design for use above ground-floor level, and some reluctance to use them has been observed. Other means include digesters, which obtain methane, and therefore energy, from decomposing waste. And there are several ways of holding waste and extracting nutrients from the water—by, for instance, growing reeds and aquatic plants in it, and then composting them.[116]

The literature on the subject is large and seemingly addictive. It appeals to minds with an outlook on life which will be extremely useful—indispensable, in fact—to local lean economies that appreciate their waste as the *capital on which their future depends. It is about loving shit as much as once we loved money. This is the new capitalism.

And feedback in the second sense? Eating the food, of course. But nothing in the organic cycle comes on its own, and eating is no exception: eating invites *conversation; organic conversation invites the *reflection that supports a human ecology; the ecology supports the whole sequence of *reciprocal exchange and *gifts— between lovers, amongst *families, *neighbours and *communities—and the gift that is ahead of all others is food. It is given at *rituals called "meals".[117]

Mealtime conversations can go anywhere. But they are especially critical to—and often the only way of sustaining—conversations which are not *instrumental—that have no *practical* value. Such conversation-for-its-own-sake can, as Catherine Blyth writes "come close to heaven". It is the gift of *humour, affection, being interesting. It is by far the most important means by which human *groups stay together. It is hard to sustain a tedious and infantile *ideology over a meal: someone is likely to disagree, and you can't use notes, or slides. And you need to stop talking sometimes in order to eat. Even if *manners are observed, *deferential silence is short-lived. You can discover you like someone at a mealtime conversation. Shared meals are the starting point for the *common purpose of a community that is working out how to feed itself.

*Food Prospects, Larders, Planned Economy, Ecology: Farmers and Hunters.

LEAN HEALTH. Seen from the point of view of the affluent *market economy, the task for Lean Health is impossible. It is to provide for the medical needs of local communities at a time when there is no money—neither taxation revenues nor private funding—available for *large-scale medical services.

It could be argued that it will not be necessary to rely entirely on local resources for medical services in the future, but the task of *Lean Logic* is to ask that "what if?" question: if communities did have to provide their own entirely *localised medical services, what would they look like?

To begin, we need to think about the effect that the *climacteric might be expected to have on the health of the population in a developed country. It is reasonable to expect that the shock will have several direct consequences for health:

First of all, there will be the impact of the *food famine that will follow the *energy-famine.

Secondly, the pharmaceutical industry may not survive the shock on a significant scale, and this would remove the central resource of modern medicine. The supply of vaccines and antibiotics could break down, along with the drugs for the treatment and stabilisation of chronic diseases and mental conditions.

The third threat to health comes from new epidemics such as bird flu, which could be transmitted by the migration of people and their animals.

These three considerations represent more than a threat to health. The implication is of a rise in the death rate (see also "The Unwanted Inheritance" sidebar). But how, in this context, might the stabilised *Lean Economy be able to care for its people, despite the lack of money?

Prevention

For the post-market society which, in whatever form and in whatever numbers, has survived the failure of the market, the priority of medicine will be prevention. Even in the affluent market, preventing disease has become the priority, not least because of the cost of failing to do so.[118] Only one person in six survives his sixties without one or more of the major degenerative diseases: diabetes, arthritis, cancer, osteoporosis or heart disease; one third of the total healthcare budget is spent on mental health. And the antibiotics themselves,

THE UNWANTED INHERITANCE
Industrial pollutants and the threat to health in the Lean Economy

The Lean Economy will inherit a threat to health in the form of industrial pollutants. The subject is in need of further research, but the evidence to date is as follows.

One key industrial pollutant is the endocrine disruptors. Notable among these chemicals are DDT (and its degradation products), lindane, polychlorinated biphenyls (PCBs), herbicides and many of the styrenes present in plastic.[119] These chemicals damage the endocrine system of humans and other animals by mimicking the effects of natural hormones: they interact with hormone receptors which do not recognise them as intruders, and interfere with processes such as those by which the foetus and the breastfeeding infant build the structures of body and mind. Research has associated this with depleted neurological, sexual and endocrine development, and the precipitous decline in the fertility of men, reproductive problems in women, and changes in cognition and behaviour have been linked all too consistently with the exposure of embryos, infants and children to endocrine disruptors.[120]

There is an overriding priority to stop further releases of these chemicals into the environment, and to research and reduce their impacts. As Theo Colborn and her colleagues write,

> At levels typically found in the environment, hormone-disrupting chemicals do not kill cells nor do they attack DNA. Their target is hormones, the chemical messengers that move about constantly within the body's communications network. Hormonally-active synthetic chemicals are thugs on the biological information highway that sabotage vital communication. They mug the messengers or impersonate them. They jam signals. They scramble messages. They sow disinformation. They wreak all manner of havoc. . . . Chemicals that disrupt hormone messages have the power to rob us of rich possibilities that have been the legacy of our species and, indeed, the essence of our humanity. There may be worse fates than extinction.[121]

Another key form of industrial pollutant may be the Lean Economy's inheritance of untreated, and leaking, *nuclear waste. Some of this will catch fire if the electricity supply that powers its cooling systems breaks down, and/or when the needed round-the-clock management structures are no longer available. The only way to mitigate this is to deal with nuclear wastes as an overriding priority now.[122]

the central treatment resources for half a century, are losing their infallibility, as the superbugs fight back.[123]

There are four main prevention strategies:

1. *Nutrition.* The contribution that good nutrition can make to preventing disease came into prominence in the modern era with the work of Dr. Robert McCarrison, writing in 1927,

> When physicians, medical officers of health and the lay public learn to apply the principles which the newer knowledge of nutrition has to impart, when they know what malnutrition means, when they look upon it as they now

look upon sepsis and learn to avoid the one as much as they now avoid the other, then will this knowledge do for medicine what asepsis has done for surgery. I know of no disease-producing agency which reaps so rich a harvest of ill health as [faulty nutrition].[124]

And the frustration among family doctors with the treadmill of treating degenerative diseases which good nutrition could have prevented was famously summarised in the "Medical Testament", a manifesto signed by sixty Cheshire doctors in March 1939:

We are called upon to cure sickness. We conceive it to be our duty in the present state of knowledge to point out that much, perhaps most, of this sickness is preventable and would be prevented by the right feeding of our people.[125]

Advice on "right feeding" and right cooking was duly provided during the 1939–45 war by Robert McCance, Elsie Widdowson and others, producing the healthiest national diet of modern times.[126] After 1945, the work of this generation of food scientists was overshadowed by antibiotics, which reinforced confidence in clinical treatment, while rising incomes made it harder to sustain a sense of responsibility for the diet of consumers who could now afford to eat almost anything they wanted. But progress in the science of healthy eating was sustained, for instance, by Ancel Keys, a biologist at the University of Minnesota, who demonstrated a link between cholesterol in the body and the fat composition of the diet. And T.L. Cleave, Denis Burkitt and John Yudkin's work on the damage due to the lack of fibre and excess of sugar led in due course to one of the century's most successful books on diet, Audrey Eyton's *The F-Plan*.[127] Since the 1980s, the World Health Organisation and governments have consistently argued the case for eating less fat and more fresh fruit and vegetables: the phrase, "five helpings a day" is widely recognised.[128]

In a settled Lean Economy, localities will grow their own food. It will be eaten fresh, with little or no addition of the chemicals used for colour, preservation, enhanced taste and enhanced appetite, or the fat, salt and sugar which develop food's potential as an addiction. In a sense, the unfolding energy-famine will narrow the options: high-fat, high-sugar junk food is made possible by the availability of cheap oil and gas to fertilise, cultivate, process and transport it. As sugar gets scarcer, mental

health, for instance, is likely to improve, especially for children. And following the collapse of the market economy's import-based food processing and distribution systems (*Food Prospects, *Climacteric) and the establishment of the central role of the *household as a provider, food will tend to be eaten at mealtimes round a table.

All this is widely recognised to be a recipe for healthy eating. Would it be even healthier if it were organic? For a discussion of that question, see *Lean Food. But in some senses, the question is disconnected from the reality of future food. Self-reliant local lean economies will not generally be able to get hold of pesticides and fertilisers even if they want to. Local *systems-literate, fertility-building, *closed-loop food production—*organic cultivation—will be their lifeline. The impact on diet, then, will range between the ideal of varied, organic food, produced in a low-energy system, requiring minimal transport—and the shock of no food at all. Either way, the obesity problem will be solved.

2. *Exercise*. Inactivity is as great a risk factor for heart disease as a 20-a-day cigarette habit; people with risk factors such as smoking, hypertension or high cholesterol can (according to some research findings) reduce their risk of early cardiac death by as much as five-fold if they take enough exercise.[129]

3. *Behaviour*. Smoking in the Lean Economy is likely to be limited by the cost and scarcity of imported tobacco; heavy addiction to alcohol may be inhibited by an awakened social and *cultural order, and reduced by the collapse of incomes, though if the poor want to get it, or make it, they often can. The imported drugs like heroin are likely to be scarce, but localities will be free to experiment with anything that can be locally grown. Working practices will be changed by the scarcity of industrial and agricultural chemicals and by the nature of lean production. Health-promoting

behaviour such as breastfeeding and childhood *play in immunity-building dirt will sit comfortably with the gross earthy mixture of life in the Lean Economy.

4. *Social capital*. Belonging to a living *community is as important to physical and mental health as taking exercise, avoiding smoking, obesity and high blood pressure. As Robert Putnam reports, the more integrated we are into our community, the less likely we are to experience colds, heart attacks, strokes, cancer, depression and premature death of all sorts.[130] The protective effects of social capital for mental and physical health have been confirmed for close *family ties, for friendship *networks, for participation in social events, and even for simple affiliation with *religious and other civic associations. Putnam summarises,

> People who are socially disconnected are between two and five times more likely to die from all causes, compared with matched individuals who have close ties with family, friends and the community.[131]

In fact, if the Lean Economy can support the rich social capital of community—and it will need to do so if it is to work at all—then (holding other factors constant) it could reduce life-threatening illness by some fifty percent. Putnam cites studies which link lower death rates to . . .

> . . . membership in voluntary groups and engagement in cultural activities, church attendance, phone calls and visits with friends and relatives, and general sociability such as holding parties at home, attending union meetings, visiting friends, participating in organised sports, or being members of highly cohesive military units.[132]

The conclusion can be left to a statistic from Putnam:

> The bottom line from this multitude of studies: As a rule of thumb, if you belong to no groups but decide to join one, you cut your risk of dying over the next year in *half*.[133]

Treatment

In the cash- and resource-depleted post-market economy, medical treatment will be organised mainly as a decentralised, informal, *reciprocal service. It will be based on the principle of *lean thinking, with decision-making pulled along by the detail in decluttered, *small-scale organisations. The effectiveness of health care will be transformed, leaving today's costly elaborations behind as a nightmare, straining belief. Herbal medicine, which has been under attack since the persecution of women herbalists as witches in the fifteenth and sixteenth century, will be accepted and respected. Health care in the Lean Economy, no longer trapped in the *fallacy that things for which we so far have no explanation cannot be true, will recognise the value of homeopathy.

Local hospitals will not be able to afford the grief—the *muda*—of a regulatory bureaucracy and of excluding citizens from voluntary participation in the making and sustaining of their own hospitals and health services. Small local hospitals are limited in the treatment they can provide in a *profession which consists almost entirely of specialisms, but much of the work of local hospital care can be done using *informal reciprocities.[134] In the Lean Economy, the needed local labour will be on hand, along with (as far as possible) a core of medical professionals. The availability of the resources of (for instance) dentistry and surgery will depend on the depth of the post-market collapse but, over the long term, intensely effective surgery, dentistry and even pharmaceuticals could make some recovery, notably for the production of vaccines and antibiotics. Nonetheless, some treatments, such as surgical procedures which stretch the resources even of the pre-climacteric economy, will be abandoned, and the long-term care of the profoundly and chronically dependent comes at a cost which no society other than one enjoying the exceptional wealth of the *market economy could sustain.

In summary, the collapse of the vast medical establishment is to be expected, but its lightweight replacement is in many ways attractive, as well as *resilient. The transition from treatment to prevention will require some understanding of diet, of ways of avoiding the grief and expense of being ill, of how to be happy without drugs. And local hospitals and care homes will make use of the local potential for lean thinking, for voluntary work—for the talent and care that is available to *institutions when they are recognised as part of the *community.

LEAN HOUSEHOLD. A small group that lives in one place—and "one place" is defined here by the presence of a single (main) kitchen. The *group size will vary between a single person and an extended household of as many as twelve, at least some of whom are likely to be related by blood or marriage. Households in the *Lean Economy are likely to be larger than at present because, in the absence of reliable supplies of *food, goods and services of all kinds, the task of keeping a household fed, clothed and warm will need to be shared among several people.

Household production

In *economics, "household production" refers to the things that consumers must do with the goods and services they buy in order to derive the "utility" they are after—that is, to fulfil their intentions. Having bought the book you want, you then have to go to the trouble of opening it, and applying your reading skills . . .

In *lean economics, household production is about a profound shift of emphasis in production from the factory and office, back to the household (the *New Domestication). It is easy to overlook, but there was formerly a deep, civilisation-building *tradition of the *home being the place of work. It did not survive the early days of the industrial *market economy, and remembrances of how wonderful it was were no doubt romantically coloured, but there was also substance in it, and real regret about its passing. Here, for instance, is the early nineteenth century historian, Andrew Ure's, view of it:

> Their dwellings and small gardens [were] clean and neat—all the family well clad—the men each with a watch in his pocket, and the women dressed to their own fancy—the church crowded to excess every Sunday—every house well furnished with a clock in elegant mahogany or fancy case—handsome tea services in Staffordshire ware. The workshop of the weaver was a rural cottage, from which when he was

tired of sedentary labour he could sally forth into his little garden, and with the spade or the hoe tend its culinary productions. The cotton wool which was to form his weft was picked clean by the fingers of his younger children and was carded and spun by the older girls assisted by his wife, and the yarn was woven by himself assisted by his sons.[135]

Life was harder than that, really, but homeworking was defended, with passion:

> We all know but too well from the incessant clamours of handloom weavers, that there are many industrious men who, during a series of years, have carried on a domestic manufacture in small rooms, crowded by looms and weaving apparatus, breathing air loaded with dust, their hours of labour extending into the night, payment for such weaving very moderate—preferring all these inconveniences to factory labour, because they cannot endure stated hours and the regular behaviour indispensable in every factory.[136]

In the *competition between the factory and the household, the factories easily won, and households were accordingly reshaped and relocated to conform to the needs of industry, forcing a rethink of what households were *for*. As industry *captured and concentrated more and more of what had formerly been household production, the household economy responded by simplifying itself, shedding skills and cutting back on *cooperative relationships between *neighbours and within the extended *family. While the workload for many individuals increased dramatically, the household itself became less of a working institution: household production declined. The role of the *private, biologically-related family was simplified: it was to consume. Most of the production could be done elsewhere, and households, finding less and less use for their own labour at home, had no option but to sell it, working for their living outside the home.[137]

Faced with this loss of significance—*vis-à-vis* the overwhelming dominance of industry—two responses were open for households: one was to accept the fact of large-scale industry, and to look for ways of improving it, humanising it, reforming it, taking a greater part in it, or even taking it over in some way. The other was to try to disassemble it, to decentralise it back as far as possible to the household. The first of those solutions was pursued with some success; the second, the decentralist tradition, has remained much the weaker of the two, but it may prove in the end to have more staying power. Its early advocates—during the roughly four decades from 1770 when it was making the news, reaching its climax in the Luddism of 1811–1813—were militant, hammer-wielding defenders of domestic production; of the integration of home and *craft. It had seemed a permanent feature of life, with its handlooms, its domestic workshops, its high-quality craftsmanship, its cottage gardens and *common land, and a tolerably effective negotiating position for independent traders. The troubles of this rock solid *institution were surely a temporary aberration . . . ?[138]

But the loss of independence came from many directions, and settled in: the key change was the machinery, driven by water and steam, with eye-watering *productivity advances which could be of the order of 20:1. And the one man remaining (where twenty were needed before) was required to move to town, to accept factory discipline and breathe the smoke, and to leave the other nineteen with no evident solutions at all. Added to that was the absolute penury of being thrown out of work during the combination of a collapse of trade due to twenty years of war with France, freak cold weather and failed harvests, the loss of *land due to enclosures and—as a casualty of this moral earthquake—the break-up of custom, neighbourliness, reciprocities, households and community.[139]

So they took to the hammer. The hammer was called the "Enoch" after the firm of blacksmiths that made it; the movement was called "Luddism" after Ned Ludd, a village simpleton living in Leicestershire, who one day lost his cool with some boys who were teasing him, chased them into a cottage where, unable to find them, he vented his anger on a couple of knitting frames. The method of protest—physically breaking machines—was crude, but it is hard to see what alternative was available to them, and the intention was understandable. It was not just, as the silk workers of Derby put

it, that they conceived themselves "entitled to a higher station in society" than was available to them in large, autocratically-managed workshops. Their needs were more fundamental than that: they needed to cope with the end of a millennium of *community, which had been self-reliant not just in *material and *cultural needs but in the confidence that, when trouble came, they could deal with it themselves. This was trouble, however, of a new order: it gutted them of whatever capability they had.[140]

The Luddites were defeated in 1812, but the ideas quietly lived on through the nineteenth and twentieth century with thinkers like Max Weber and Lewis Mumford, and especially in the political philosophy of *anarchism. Pierre-Joseph Proudhon (1809–1865), for instance, advocated *small-scale production and (despite his famous phrase, "property is theft") property-ownership for such producers. Then came Peter Kropotkin.

Kropotkin (1842–1921) had the advantage that by the end of the nineteenth century, the massive concentration of industry in giant workshops—by now seething with labour, as had been inevitable in the early days—was starting to scale down a little; and there began to be some freedom of choice in the matter of location, thanks to technical advance and the use of electricity. "The leviathan factories offer great inconveniences", he wrote; and it follows that "the scattering of industries over the country is surely the next step to be made". Why? His answer to that looked forward to a development that was not to become a serious option for over a century: it would be "imposed by the very necessity of *producing for the producers themselves*"[141]—that is, local production for local consumption. Patrick Geddes, a committed supporter of this principle, called it the *neotechnic model of industry. It is an idea which was on hold for as long as the *market economy was in robust health, but its time has come.[142]

The logic of the argument that households should try to get back some of the production faculties that they have lost leads naturally from the factory floor to the domestic kitchen. This historic step was made, famously, by Mrs. Borsodi, whose husband, Ralph, a professor of economics at the University of New York in the 1930s, came home one evening after a hard day in the lecture room to find the kitchen table covered with shining glass jars filled with tomatoes and tomato juice. In reply to his searching questions, Mrs. Borsodi assured him that home-bottled tomatoes were cheaper than bought ones; he checked her *intuition with his calculations, which indeed revealed that the produce of one's own garden has a cost-advantage, in that it does not have to be carried long distances by road and rail to one's own kitchen.[143]

Ralph was so taken with this result of his researches that he spent the rest of his life writing a series of scholarly books telling the world how much money it was wasting on distribution and *transport between factories, their customers and their suppliers. He developed his Law: "Distribution costs will tend to move in inverse proportion to production costs"[144]—i.e., the savings that can be made with mass production are offset by the costs of distributing the goods over long distances. And so the introduction of the electric motor backed by the electricity grid meant that local production at home became a realistic and cost-effective option. When these revisions in costs are taken into account, he concluded, it turns out to be cheaper to produce goods locally than in the centralised system that was standard for nineteenth century industry. His findings gave a central place to the household as a production centre:

> I discovered that more than two thirds of the things which the average family now buys could be produced more economically at home than they could be bought factory made—that the home itself was still capable of being made into a productive unit and creative institution and that an investment in a homestead equipped with efficient domestic machinery would yield larger returns per dollar than investments in insurances, in mortgages, in stocks and bonds.[145]

To some extent, it was already happening. The period 1850–1950 can be seen as the century of the homemaker, in which (mainly) married women—the "industrious consumer"—took the opportunity offered by cheap and abundant consumer goods (soap, for instance) to bring their homes up to a standard of cleanness and comfort which had never before been known on a large scale. But this, too, came to an end in the 1950s, when women were able to delegate at lot of that work to the new domestic equipment such as central heating, freezers and washing machines, and so joined the workplace. So much for Mrs. Borsodi's bottled tomatoes.[146]

Most households now fall silent on weekdays, and it will be a long haul back. Even the planning laws are against it—shaped by assumptions and objectives which are the inverse of the *new domestication: home and work are kept separate. Until the 1950s, there was a degree of flexibility about this. In 1943, the County of London Plan recognised that

> There is much that is popular and convenient about this mixture of work-places and houses, where indeed, in many cases the factories are actually in the houses themselves.[147]

At the same time, practical advice was given by the Ministry of Agriculture and Fisheries on the rearing and slaughtering of that intensely efficient means of domestic production, the pig, citing with approval the method recommended by Cato the Censor in 200 BC.[148]

That flexible self-reliance ended abruptly. But now we can again recognise the need for households to have the skills and resources necessary for their own maintenance. Those *skills are short, the *tradition is all but broken, and we do not know how much of the technology available to the Borsodis—a reliable electricity grid, for instance—will be available after the *climacteric. But the future lies with the household. It takes a great deal of *energy and heavy equipment to keep a centralised industry at work. Whether we find ourselves with an impressive, energy-efficient, small-scale, neotechnic, locality-literate technology far in advance of 1930s America, or with the deep trauma of energy and infrastructure breakdown, it will be households that are best placed to keep things going.

Household life

Apart from being a producer, the household has a deeper meaning as a life-giving *cooperative *institution that makes people, feeds them, teaches language, practical skills, *culture, *emotional intelligence and sociability. Some make their own beer (no doubt to protect their virtue: see sidebar). Some cultivate a sense of *humour and philosophy. They sustain *conversation, working out a route to good *judgment.

HOW BEER PROTECTS VIRTUE
The case for home-brewing

Writing in 1821, the rural philosopher William Cobbett raged against the decline in home brewing. He looks back to "forty years ago, [when] to have a house and not to brew was a rare thing indeed. . . . There was not a labourer in his parish that did not brew his own beer". As households stopped brewing their own beer, so the consumption of beer fell and, to Cobbett's dismay, they started drinking tea instead:

> It must be evident to every one, that the practice of tea drinking must render the frame feeble and unfit to encounter hard labour or severe weather, while . . . it deducts from the means of replenishing the belly and covering the back. Hence succeeds a softness, an effeminacy, a seeking for the fire-side, a lurking in the bed, and, in short, all the characteristics of idleness. . . . The tea drinking fills the public-house, makes the frequenting of it habitual, corrupts boys as soon as they are able to move from home, and does little less for the girls, to whom the gossip of the tea-table is no bad preparatory school for the brothel.

> WILLIAM COBBETT, *Cottage Economy*, 1821.[149]

Given a chance, households live naturally by the *proximity principle. Proximity, a central condition of lean consumption, means the art of organising things so that they start off in the right place—so that the people, jobs, products and recreations of everyday life are near at hand. Benefiting from the small scale, the lean household will be *elegant and uncluttered; it will solve its *sorting problem. Everything it uses will be reused or recycled and the waste reused in a *closed-loop system. That does not necessarily mean that it will consume less, but its *regrettable necessities will be reduced: a much higher proportion of its consumption will consist of goods and services which people actually want, rather than those which they are obliged to use (cars, packaging, accountants) as a consequence of the massive *scale of the *political economy they live in.

And households will have craftsmanship—giving them a power of repair and renewal that they share with other *ecosystems, and which is among the most encouraging and powerful ideas in *ecology. In fact, as Fritjof Capra explains, organisms are primarily engaged in renewal.

> Every living organism continually renews itself, tissues and organs are replacing their cells in continual cycles. Our pancreas replaces most of its cells every twenty-four hours, our stomach

lining every three days; ninety-eight percent of our brain is turned over in less than one month. Our skin replaces its cells at the rate of 100,000 cells per minute.[150]

Yet such renewal (of living systems) and repair (of household goods, clothes and equipment) takes time. This is recognised by H.J. Massingham, observer of the crafts and *manual literacy of English rural life. Speed, he writes,

> . . . is the deadly foe of thoroughness. . . . The judgment of the earth is plain. It will have craftsmanship or nothing.[151]

This is also recognised by the growing Slow Food movement. Its *Manifesto* declares that "a firm defence of quiet material pleasure is the only way to oppose the universal folly of *Fast Life*", and proposes instead, "many suitable doses of guaranteed sensual pleasure and slow, long-lasting enjoyment".[152] Here is lean thinking's *"flow", made edible.

And the capacity of the landscape for renewal, its permanence, and its affinity with slowness, were celebrated by John Stewart Collis, a chronicler of farming in the war years immediately before it speeded into the era of industrial farming:

Beyond that hedge the winter wheat was shining now, so far, so green against the dark leafless trees and the pale blue winter sky. . . . Here is the thing that remains constant. Here is the order that does not break.[153]

As we now know, the order broke almost as soon as he put down his pen. It was displaced by a *culture of production and consumption committed to saving time. But with the end of the *market, things will slow down again. Slow means quick if you waste less time making mistakes. The lean household's critical asset will be *elegant competence.

*Home, Presence, Reciprocity and Cooperation, Invisible Goods, Household Group, Small Group.

LEAN LAW AND ORDER. Maintaining law and order, using only the resources of the *informal economy, would be . . . well, "impossible" is the word that comes to mind, and justifiably so in the case of a giant *civic society whose social order and *common purpose has long-since been dissolved. But in the *Lean Economy, the presumption is that there will be no alternative. Communities that cannot buy in their law and order will have to make their own. They will keep their own peace.

The key to such community law and order is prevention. *Social capital, *practice and apprenticeship, the structures of belonging, the legitimised joy and rebellion of *play and *carnival, and the *small scale of lean *community will all reduce the *incentives for crime. And *families will recover the confidence to build *emotional intelligence and citizenship. And yet, even *cohesive communities are not crime-free. The problem is, of course, that in the *Lean Economy there will be little or no money to pay for a police force.

Fortunately, the idea of local community being responsible for keeping the peace is well established. English law's recognition of the principle of community policing reached its full expression in the Statute of Winchester of 1285. According to the statute, every man (other than clergy) between the ages of fifteen and sixty was required to possess arms appropriate to his rank, ranging from the helmet, hauberk (coat of mail) and sword of the knight down to the poor man's bow, arrows and knife; it also affirmed the *tradition that every man is a policeman: all must serve their turn as night watches and constables, join the hue and cry (by which anyone who spotted a crime could summon bystanders to assist in the pursuit of the criminal), cut back the roadside trees, and bear mutual responsibility for crimes committed within their area. If need be, they

274

were also required to form a *posse comitatus* to deal with persistent trouble such as, for instance, incursions by the Scots from across the border.[154]

Despite the obvious drawbacks in a system which required every man to carry arms and to be expert in their use, and which demanded that merchants and artisans should be ready to break off work to take their turn as constables or, at a moment's notice, to join the hue and cry, it did at least make for a community which was active in preventing, and responding to, crime. In fact, the community's main task is prevention—to be a community to which people want to belong—but, as for crime after the event, there are three things for the community to do: solving crimes once they have occurred; sustaining appropriate systems of punishment; and containing the whole process within the framework of the law.

Solving crime

Unskilled investigation is at best inefficient, at worst intolerable. For medieval towns and villages, the preferred and obvious method was to find witnesses, but they could be unreliable, or know little, or they might not exist at all. An alternative was to invite "compurgators", predecessors of the jury, with a knowledge of the circumstances, to swear to the innocence of the accused. But in the absence of witnesses and established methods of investigation, a twelfth century local community, shocked by a crime, could have recourse to methods which expressed its desperation but did little to reveal the facts. Although torture was not permitted by English common law, there were exceptions, and trial by ordeal lingered on as a last resort. The accused might be required to thrust his arm in a cauldron of boiling water to pick out a stone; or he could be made to walk over red-hot ploughshares, place his hand in a glove of red-hot iron, or pick up a red-hot iron bar and hold it in his bare hand while he walked three paces. The hands or feet were then bandaged for three days; if at the end of the third day there was evidence of scalding, or a blister the size of half a walnut, this was taken as proof of guilt. Even the examination of witnesses—in itself a more rational and accurate way of getting at the facts—could, if frustrated, break down into retribution, since eye-witnesses were almost the only reliable source of forensic information

that the local community had. One woman found guilty of perjury (a capital offence) in a murder trial was spared execution: "she has deserved death but by way of dispensation let her eyes be torn out".[155]

As in the case of *lean defence, there is a sense here of a barely soluble problem—a gap between what is needed and the resources of a cash-poor *political economy which has not yet developed systems of investigation which we take for granted. The proper response is to recognise how effective well-motivated amateurs—citizens—can be, given the training and *incentive. Citizenship lends itself better to the prevention of crime than to solving it but, when the funds to pay for full-time professional public services are not there, other methods must be explored.

Lean policing could consist of a core of experts—craftsmen of law and order, and paid if resources allow—whose main function is to train citizens with the skills of policing when the need arises. Even now, some hybrid vestiges of this persist in the case of part-time special constabulary, rural fire brigades, the Territorial Army, and private detectives. The Lean Economy could be seen as a society based on inspired amateurism. Lean citizenship places its *skills at the service of the community.

Punishing crime

Local communities have almost no facilities for effective and tolerable punishment—and a distinction must be made here between short-term detention (for which the sheriff's lock-up, familiar from Western movies, will do) and longer-term imprisonment. The difficulty of sustaining a system of punishment in a society in which cash and *capital are scarce is illustrated in the ancient *sharia* system of punishment in Arab countries: a nomadic people, whose lower ranks possess little or no private property or money, cannot impose fines, nor maintain prisons. Individuals' only substantial assets are their bodies. Although *sharia* amputations and the finality of capital punishment are scarcely to be condoned, alternative punishments available to a society whose wealth is far below the *exceptional levels of our own are clearly quite limited.

Prisons will have to be sustained outside the *parish, and administered at the level of the *county or *nation, but even this could stretch the resources available, and, in any case, the lean response to crime will be an intense focus on repair, on understanding what had gone wrong, on bringing people back into the community. The core lean principle of diagnosis—the *Five Whys, tracing problems back to a cause or causes that could realistically be corrected—applies critically to the treatment of crime.

It is not an unrealistic aim. Crime is valuable *feedback about what childhood in that society means, about its *education, *economics and *culture—about whether this is a society that works or not. Listening to that feedback and acting on it will be the signature of the Lean Economy's principles on Law and Order. And, since the Lean Economy will recognise *blame for the *fallacy it is, it will hold punishment in reserve as an option, rather than using it as routine. It will fail, often: psychopaths and sociopaths exist in the nicest society. But it will have its priorities and preferences for the punishment of miscreants: service to the community in various forms, perhaps including enforced participation in music, dance, sport, *carnival, *conversation, or contact with and care for animals, especially horses. Maybe communities will nominate, not jailors, nor professional social workers, but mentors offering practical help and proof of community as an ally. The Lean Economy will be a place of *empowerment, work and celebration. It will be a place that people want to belong to, to get back into.

Failure at the end of all this will no doubt lead to prison or tougher sanctions. But prisons are not all bad. As the historian Guy Geltner tells us, when prisons began to be regularly used for punishment in Europe at the end of the fourteenth century, they were not necessarily the infested, lethal nightmares that we might imagine, but recognised as opportunities for sustained contact and responsibility for prisoners, for correction and redemption. There were the exceptions, of course, but there was also evidence that it is not just hospitals and schools that can be seen as opportunities for local citizenship. Prisons can be, too.

But it will be the last resort, because the Lean Economy's ability to sustain large prisons will be not much better than that of nomadic tribes, whose punishment systems were brutal, but cheap.[156]

Containing the whole process within the law

There is a tension here: local diversity and practice vs. the law of the state. It is, however, a *necessary and creative tension; were it to fail, one of its two extremes would triumph: either (1) the tyranny of an exclusively local code of law, or (2) the tyranny of exclusively state law, extending beyond its proper limits, into the detail of local regulation. In the Lean Economy, there will be deeply-rooted *diversity in local law, subject to a framework of *national law and legal institutions.

In early medieval England, the state sometimes had to shout for its side of the argument to be heard: the local lord had the right to enforce an obligation, such as rent or services, by seizing a tenant's chattels; on the other hand, tenants' own rights were protected by common law, and King Edward I decided to make this protection really effective. Maurice Powicke explains how:

> Suppose that the lord or his bailiff had seized a tenant's beasts, required for ploughing and carrying, and had driven them into his castle and refused to release them. The first Statute of Westminster (1275) enacted that in the last resort, after due warning, the castle or fortified place should be battered down beyond repair.[157]

But who is to hold the tension between the two extremes? The ideal candidate is someone who recognises an obligation to sustain standards more robust and universal than those of the locality—but who, at the same time, has a fierce local *loyalty and sympathy, is drenched in *local knowledge and experience, and is driven by affection for the *place. In other words, the ideal is the magistrate. Magistrates have *presence. They began their history in a healthy atmosphere of mild suspicion on all sides. The professional lawyers were especially suspicious, for magistrates were amateurs. Their appointment as keepers of the peace began within a few decades of the Norman conquest, but it was only after two centuries of their powers being by turns increased and reduced that, in 1368, their judicial powers were placed firmly on a statutory basis.[158] Another two centuries later, they finally earned unqualified official approval—with the comment from the great common-law lawyer, Sir Edward Coke, that the magistrates were . . .

. . . such a form of subordinate government for the tranquillity and quiet of the realm, as no part of the Christian world hath the like.[159]

Magistrates—Justices of the Peace, the Bench—were (and many still are) unpaid; they had (but generally do not now have) status; their tenure was secure (though is now less so); there were magistrates courts, representing local justice, in every town (now largely closed down and concentrated in the large towns). Their durability as an uncorrupt *institution was remarkable, and the crucial element here was status. It was uncommon for magistrates to be removed—and there is a reason for this:

> The idea that the social status of the magistracy must be maintained prevented any king from purging the county. This idea was sound. Magistrates varied in character, but their position in local society was a guard against the worst kind of corruption, for it brought out their sense of paternal responsibility.[160]

One of the things that the Lean Economy may have to reinvent from little more than a remnant is the local network of unpaid, independent magistrates. They will bring ordinary knowledge (*Expertise) to the problems that will occur as the new social order is explored and tested. And they are key to *connectedness—as Powicke describes it, "the interdependence of social relations from top to bottom—that makes a society".[161] Magistrates, along with the related amateur institution of juries, sustain a layer of common sense between the frigid intensity of official intervention and the *creative appreciation of local detail. They cannot be coerced; they have to be persuaded. They are sufficiently free of corruption and of a prior institutional *mindset to listen. They make the link between social standing and civic responsibility. If the Lean Economy does achieve interdependence of social relations from top to bottom, that link will be part of it.

———

The *Lean Economy, then, may have a small core of well-qualified police paid for by some form of tax or local contribution; this will be similar to the core of medical expertise in *Lean Health. The scale of this service will,

however, be drastically less than that seen in the *market economy: communities themselves will do much of the peace-keeping, and the world in which people learn how to live will consist of local communities and not just local streets. The legal system itself will also be reduced, relative to the current scale, with a much reduced commercial litigation, the demise of central regulatory intervention in local *practice, and the *common purpose of a society that is trying to heal itself. And the legal system will place central emphasis on its local unpaid presence in the form of the ancient and tested institution of Justices of the Peace. Self-reliance in law and order may seem at first to be a landscape inspiring wild surmise—and there is some mapping to be done—but it is where we are about to live.

*Community, Law and Change, Assent, Calibration, Witch-Hunt.

LEAN MATERIALS. There are two kinds of solution to the problem of providing materials from limited local resources—making the best use of local resources, and conserving materials in a *closed-loop system.

Making the best use of local resources

In this regard, four options are available. First, there are natural materials—materials that can be grown or quarried locally and used in more-or-less their original form. Secondly, there is the chemicals harvest, using locally grown plants as the main source. Thirdly, biomimicry copies *natural systems to produce high-quality materials from locally-available ingredients. For a fourth option (not recommended) see *GRIN (Genetics, Robotics, Information Technology and Nanotechnology).

1. *Natural materials*

   In the Lean Economy, *place matters and, in the case of lean materials, it is decisive. Particular places, with *diverse advantages, will develop particular solutions. Once, before being ironed out by the market economy, local distinctiveness was founded on local rock, and on the *water and *ecology that came from it. The long sequence of connections from geology to craftsmanship that followed is described by the agricultural writer H.J. Massingham in a suitably long sentence:

If, after the geology lesson of walking up the village street, the craftsmanly minutiae be attended to—the chamfering of a waggon in the shed, the carving of a corner-post or of a piscina or a poppy-head bench-end in the church, the ogee curves to the "guide" of a shepherd's crook, the wrought-iron work of a weather-vane or a chest, the moulding of a dripstone over a cottage window, the geometrical pattern of the thatch below the ridge-board or (if the roof be stone) the "valleying" of the angles of intersection . . . , the shape and colour of a mug at the pub, a carved settle opposite it . . . , the proportions of a pigsty, the raftering of a barn, the brasses on a horse's martingale, the harr [gatepost] of a field-gate, the pewter inlay of a butterfly bobbin on a lace-pillow, the carved boss in the groining of the church-porch—if the multiplicity of these details be taken in; if, again, another village, ten, twenty, fifty or only a couple of miles off be remembered as totally different in its materials, its forms, its mannerisms, its styles, even the tools (which also will have different names), then it will appear that, if we were a nation of shopkeepers in 1800 and are a nation of card-indexers and committees today, we were a nation of artists in 1500, 1600 and 1700.[162]

Building the lean material economy will be a matter of making the inspired best of what is locally available. The most immediately-available material resources consist of the natural fibres that can be grown locally, and others which are part of its geological endowment. These are the familiar materials which shaped, sheltered and clothed the village: wool, leather, bone and horn; wood, withies, straw and reeds, flax and hemp; natural oils and fats; sand, clay, lime, slate, mud. No area is endowed with them all, but all areas have at least some of them, and they become more useful in proportion to the skills—mainly *manual skills—that are capable of using them. The need to rediscover and revalue these skills, made briefly obsolete by oil and gas, will be intense. There will be a reskilling of society.

SKILLS
The craft of practical citizenship

It was of the essence of the old system that those living under it subsisted in the main upon what their own industry could produce out of the soil and materials of their own countryside. A few things, certainly, they might get from other neighbourhoods, such as iron for making their tools, and salt for curing their bacon; and some small interchange of commodities there was, accordingly, say between the various districts that yielded cheese, and wool, and hops, and charcoal; but as a general thing the parish where the peasant people lived was the source of the materials they used, and their wellbeing depended on their knowledge of its resources. Amongst themselves they would number a few special craftsmen—a smith, a carpenter or wheelwright, a shoemaker, a pair of sawyers, and so on; yet the trades of these specialists were only ancillary to the general handiness of the people, who with their own hands raised and harvested their crops, made their clothes, did much of the building of their homes, attended to their cattle, thatched their ricks, cut their firing, made their bread and wine or cider, pruned their fruit-trees and wines, looked after their bees, all for themselves.

GEORGE BOURNE, Change in the Village, 1912.[163]

2. *The chemicals harvest: biomaterials*
The second option open to local lean economies whose ability to buy in materials has been drastically reduced is to use farm crops—mainly plants, but animal products are used in this way, too—as sources of the chemicals for which at present we rely mainly on oil and gas. "Biomaterials" are, roughly, of two kinds. First, there are the *material products*, such as the gums, resins and adhesives, which make useful properties of plants available in a concentrated form. Secondly, there are the *chemical feedstocks*, derived from breaking down

farm products into the organic building blocks from which it is possible to produce a virtually unlimited variety of materials, including plastics, fats and oils, soaps and detergents.[164]

Here are some examples. First, material products. The resin of pine trees can be transformed into inks, rubber, varnishes and rosin; seaweed is an ideal raw material for thickeners, flocculants (tufted fibres), lubricants, sizing agents and edible gum. Vegetable oils (especially soy, in warmer climates) can be used in the production of resins, paints, varnishes and plastics, and castor oil for cosmetics, plasticisers, lubricants, binders, inks, adhesive, caulks, sealants . . .[165]

Secondly, chemical feedstocks. Synthetic fibres, dyes and solvents can be made from benzene; benzene can be made from phenols; phenols are derived from lignin which, in turn, is extracted from wood. Starches are used, for instance, to produce lactic acid, useful as a sizing agent in the production of paper and cardboard (sizing is applied to paper to keep ink and other liquids on the surface instead of soaking in) and as a source of ethanol (alcohol) which can be processed into plastics and synthetic rubber. More generally, methane, the starting point for the polymers, the joined-up structures of organic chemistry, can be produced by the fermentation of practically anything grown on farms.

Once, all these technologies had a collective name: "chemurgy". Not many people have heard of it, and the reason is that the use of farm products as a raw material for industry has been decisively overtaken by oil and gas. Farm crops remain a significant source of industrial materials—35 percent of detergents still come from plant material, for example—but, in the case of chemical feedstocks, the advantages of gas and oil have been decisive: their quality is more consistent, and they are supremely easy to handle and store. So long as their supply is reliable and their price is low, farm products cannot compete.[166]

"Chemurgy" is derived from the Greek roots, *Chemi* (their name for Egypt, source of the "black arts" of chemistry) and *ergon* (work). It began as a

serious study in America after the First World War, when the United States seized many of the patents of the German chemical industry. It was driven along by fears of oil depletion (at a time when the global endowment of oil was still unknown), by doubts about international trade as a reliable source of raw materials, by the deep depression in *agriculture and an urgent search for other ways of keeping farmers in business. And, of course, chemurgy neatly provided a new and urgent job for chemistry to concern itself with, now that it had become a well-developed science keen for new things to do.

The man who did most to drive chemurgy along was William ("Billy") Hale, a brilliant and prolific chemist, chairman of the US National Research Council's Chemistry and Chemical Technology Committee—and, in due course, husband of Helen Dow, daughter of H.H. Dow, founder of the Dow Chemical Company. There is no doubt about it: he was in love with chemurgy, and in his book, *The Farm Chemurgic: Farmward the Star of Destiny Lights Our Way*, the chemist grows lyrical. Thanks to chemurgy, he wrote, agriculture is . . .

> . . . no longer a pursuit to supply man with food and raiment, but a pursuit that shall bring into existence a vast array of chemical compounds to fit a myriad of ends. It presents the most fascinating of pictures and the most awe-inspiring of nature's wonders. The tearing asunder of composite matter, heretofore known and used generally under such prehistoric names as "corn", "wheat", "potatoes", "straw" and "wood" and the like, the allocation of several homogenous components thereof under their proper and clearly defined chemical characteristics, opens up a new world to man. It is the alphabet of a new knowledge; a knowledge that nature is now to inculcate in man.[167]

His enthusiasm was catching. During the 1930s, some 1,300 institutions were involved in research into chemurgy and in 1935, 300 leaders of industry, science and farming met in Dearborn, Michigan to sign the *Declaration of Dependence Upon the Soil and the Right of Self-Maintenance*: "When in the course of the life of a Nation, its people become neglectful of the laws of nature, . . . necessity impels them to turn to the soil in order to recover the right of self-maintenance" — and that right was asserted to be an inalienable right and part of the Divine Order. Chemurgy was unquestionably showing itself to be useful: sawmill wastes were turned into wood products and plastics; solvents (butanol, acetone and butyl alcohol) were produced from sugar beets and Jerusalem artichokes. Paper was made from flax, hemp and rice. Cellulose for synthetic fibres was derived from sweet potatoes, peanuts and cotton. Wastes that remained after processing were used for road-building materials. At the height of the war in 1944, half a million tons of synthetic rubber was produced from alcohol derived from crops.[168]

But there were snags. The new crops, in many cases, had to be transplanted from abroad, bringing trouble with pests and acclimatisation; the supply of raw materials could be irregular. From the point of view of our time, the critical snag would consist of the competition for *land which could otherwise be used for the production of *food. The decisive problem in the past was the increasing competition from cheap, convenient and abundant oil and gas.

But the end of chemurgy, which came quite quickly after the war, is not really the end of the story. For one thing, many industrial materials are still made from farm products. And this is a technology which can make a decisive contribution to the task of converting *waste products of all kinds into the *materials — and *energy — that will be needed with intense urgency in the future.

There were two men who proved this with particularly dramatic effect. One of them was George Washington Carver (1864–1943), the legendary black scientist based in Tuskegee, Alabama. He manufactured silk from sweet potatoes; he made face cream, dyes, and plastics from peanuts. He insisted that nature produces no waste, and he demonstrated this by producing soap, not just from peanuts, but from the waste scraped off the floor of the plant where they were shelled. And late in life, he became a friend of Henry Ford.

Ford used soybeans as raw material for paints, lubricants and plastic car parts, including body-work which was so strong that it did not dent when he swung an axe at it. He found ways of reducing the wood wasted in the production of his cars "to negligible quantities" — and with those negligible quantities he proceeded to produce acetate of lime, methyl alcohol, charcoal, tar, heavy oils, light oils, creosote and methane. *The New York Times* of 1930 was impressed: "After the raw materials — and even the smoke — have served their purposes in the production of automobiles, they are made to yield vast quantities of still other raw materials which are either employed in the plants or sold in the market." The annual value of these by-products, it noted, was $19 million.[169]

In the future, biomaterials will be a major source for local industry, substantially replacing oil and gas. Sophisticated chemistry is needed, but local lean economies will not have to invent their way into it, nor to build large plants. The essentials — the knowledge and the *small-scale equipment — may be within the means of orderly localities, which are not in a position to buy in their daily material needs. Small, local-scale plants will affirm localities' "Right of Self-Maintenance". The technology is better than it was in the prime of chemurgy in the 1930's, while the alternative source of hydrocarbons as the primary raw material is no longer secure and will soon be spluttering towards deep decline. Biomaterials will provide part of the solution. They can never be available on a scale to replace the fading of oil, gas and coal, but they can open the way to localities growing their own materials.

3. *Biomimicry (aka biological processing or "green chemistry")*
The third option is ambitious, and in its early days. It may never happen on a large scale, but the technology is there, potentially. The *intention is to copy the ability of animals and plants to produce materials with properties very much better than the best that our own industrial processes can manage, and to do so with no energy apart from a little sunlight, no special raw materials apart from what is available in the local soil or seawater, and no *pollution.[170]

One well-studied example of this is spider silk. Compared weight-for-weight, it is five times stronger than steel; it is five times tougher than Kevlar (used in bulletproof vests); it is 40 percent more elastic than nylon; and it is energy-absorbing, in the sense that when a spider web is stretched, it recoils so gently that it does not trampoline the fly back out. And the manufacturing process is neater: you do not see spiders pouring derivatives of petroleum into pressurised vats of sulphuric acid, boiling and then extruding the product under high pressures—and producing, in the process, large quantities of toxic waste. Similarly, the high performance of nature's ceramics—the hardness of seashells and the self-repairing horn of the rhino's tusk—is better, more sophisticated, more fit-for-purpose, than anything we can make, as is the variety of proteins which are present wherever there is life.[171]

So, the question is, can technology imitate this? This is the field of "biomimetics", or "biomimicry". It can at first be confused with "biomaterials" but is in fact sharply different and far harder to achieve: biomaterials technologies make industrial use of materials that are already made available by nature; biomimetics learns from the principles of natural processing to produce new material supplies in new ways. If it could be done, there would be immense advantages. Local economies would be able to make practically any material they needed from their basic natural endowment of, for instance, soil, water, sunlight and air. They would be left with no industrial waste. And they would have materials ideally designed for their purpose with the qualities of being both durable and biodegradable.

In fact, the technology is not all as unattainable as it sounds. For instance, one of the processes of biomimetics is fermentation, which has been used for as long as people have made bread and wine. Fermentation depends on enzymes to guide and catalyse the chemical reactions, and it is these large protein molecules—already used in industrial processes to produce vitamins, antibiotics and single-cell proteins—that give biomimetic

processes their typical benign characteristics. They happen at room temperature and pressure, they are quite easy to control, and there is a good chance that the enzymes may survive the process to be used again. This is a technology that could in principle make local economies self-sufficient in (for instance) polymers, which could be made to grow slowly and cleanly into all the proteins and starches that the locality might need. As the materials scientist Kenneth Geiser writes, the biomimetics industrial plant would look radically different from today's factory:

> The vision of materials factories of the future that look like large greenhouses with long tanks of microbially infused carbohydrates in which tiny organisms manufacture well-tailored materials from recycled organic wastes is intriguing and attractive.[172]

Whether biomimetics will be available in time to be of substantial help to local lean economies in the first half of this century is another matter. It does not look likely. One problem is that the organisms that do the work do not, in general, like to be crowded; they prefer low concentrations, rich with a wide variety of other organisms and other compounds which have little to do with the process that you actually want. This means that, though you may well get the product you want, you may then have to try to separate it from all the other products that you do not want. The process must in principle be possible, because molluscs do it, but what the Lean Economy will inherit will not be a scintillating set of solutions to material self-reliance but a long research agenda. The *market economy does not have the time; the *Lean Economy just might.

The other problem is that serious advances in biomimicry will require work at the molecular level; it will be, in some aspects at least, a product of *nanotechnology. The trouble is that *nanotechnology is not a well-behaved science; it is hard to contain; it is very powerful: it could take biomimetics well beyond the innocent aim of imitating nature.

L

Thinking systems:
conserving materials in a closed-loop system

Whatever the source of lean materials, *systems fluency with regard to them requires the application of the Seven R's: reduce, reuse, repair, recycle, re-grow, re-skill, review.

1. *Reduce*. The big reduction in the scale of local lean economies will not be an achievement; it will be an unavoidable, unwelcome inheritance. The response is to make a virtue of necessity: small-scale *elegance will bring a greatly reduced need for the *intermediate goods and services that sustain the infrastructures of life and citizenship. There will be reduction to the point of virtual elimination in (for instance) travel and *transport, packaging and handling, the structures of bureaucracy and regulation. This reduction is the point of entry back into the real world of *resilience and consistency with the *ecology on which life in all its forms completely relies.

2. *Reuse*. The first essential condition for *closed-loop system materials management is small *scale, opening the way to effective *sorting. The smaller the scale, the more realistic it becomes to sort and reuse goods rather than dumping them into the recycling stream.

3. *Repair*. Repair, too, becomes a realistic option on the small scale. In the market economy, there is material affluence and time poverty, and little patience for the

slowness and deliberateness needed for repair: wasting materials saves time. In the local Lean Economy, there is time-affluence and material poverty.[173]

4. *Recycle*. Effective recycling, like reuse, depends on effective sorting—or, better still, on preventing materials from getting mixed up in the first place. This detailed orderliness has potential: not only does it mean that recycling meets the crucial requirement of working with uncontaminated materials, but it is also a materials-ethic in its own right—looking towards the guiding, if unattainable, ideal in which recycling itself is unnecessary, because goods remain intact and in use.[174]

5. *Re-grow*. Organic materials—food waste, human waste, wood and textiles—can be contained within a closed-loop system by being composted, returned to the soil and re-grown, either as the raw materials themselves, or as the chemical feedstocks needed to produce them. Local lean economies will aim for all the materials they use, other than ceramics and metals, to be biodegradable, supplying material for compost systems, including digesters, which leave long-chain molecules of nitrogen to recycle into the soil, and supply methane fuel as well.[175]

6. *Re-skill*. Manual skills have the potential to be very efficient in their use of materials, since their attention to detail enables them to keep waste to a minimum. At the other end of the technology spectrum, the most advanced digital technology also has this potential, because of the small size of much of its equipment, and its accuracy. Comparisons of the materials-efficiency (and *eco-efficiency) of different kinds of production have the difficulty of not comparing like with like, but there is persuasive evidence that *both* manual skills *and* the advanced technologies have at least the potential to be more materials-efficient then the industrial production which built, and still sustains, our *economy. In fact, local-scale economies will have little use for large-scale production; instead, they will naturally tend to turn to manual skills, supplemented, where it is available, by digital equipment. The extent to which digital equipment will be able to make a contribution is uncertain—at present the world of microchips is embedded in, and needs, a global

industrial establishment. But the manual crafts and the best of the digital tools make a natural pairing as the material foundation of the Lean Economy.[176]

Regrettably, the *market economy has had a disdain for the *manual skills, seeing them as signs of failure in the equal opportunity contest for prestigious roles. The consequent shortage of such skills will mature to a famine when the task of building the *resilient economy begins in earnest. The skills of even those craftsmen who remain tend to remain frozen and untaught. Yet the closed-loop materials system of the Lean Economy will value them intensely, as it works to forge a pragmatic alliance of science and hands, engaged at the level of Massingham's "craftsmanly minutiae":

> The craftsman's relation to nature was non-predatory from first to last, from raw material to finished product. He did not conquer nature but married her in husbandry.[177]

7. *Review*. This last stage—step five in the sequence of *lean thinking—examines the progress to date critically, and works out ways, *incremental or *radical, of doing better. Sometimes, the force is with you. Each step opens the way to the next one, so that we have the iterative improvement which can be applied, too, to a locality, moving step-by-step towards a *closed-loop system. Fewer goods are thrown away, so there is less to recycle, so recycling systems are reduced to a manageable scale requiring minimal *transport, so goods can be properly *sorted, so high quality materials can be produced, so the goods that are made from them are built to last, so fewer goods are thrown away, so the flow of materials declines while the materials stock endures, and the locality begins to recognise its materials, at every stage in their life-cycle, as being a permanent part of their wealth.

*Invisible Goods, New Domestication, Energy Prospects, Lean Education, Expertise, Abstraction, Lean Economics.

LEAN MEANS. One of the properties of a system designed according to the principles of *lean thinking (Rule 2). It carries out the *intention, and that may involve the shock of bringing to an end a lot of activities which, up to now, had seemed to be important. From now on, the enterprise is *travelling light.
*Value, *Muda*.

LEAN PRODUCTION. The original form of the lean revolution in production systems, developed in the 1940s at Toyota's factory in Japan, under the direction of Taiichi Ohno. It maintained low backup stocks of parts and finished goods, and that forced the whole productive process to develop rapid reactions and to achieve very low rates of error. This in turn meant that workers had responsibility for taking timely decisions in response to local circumstances, forestalling errors rather than waiting for them to happen.

Since then, lean production has evolved into the more broadly-based system of management called lean thinking, the guiding principle of *Lean Logic*. It is important, however, to note two qualifications to this.

First, *Lean Logic*'s application of lean thinking to the question of how to survive the closing down of the *market economy is a considerable stretch from the original vision, and sometimes the strain shows (as discussed in *Lean Thinking). The use of the concept in *Lean Logic* may stray from the lean thinking which industrial practitioners and teachers of lean thinking would recognise.[178]

Secondly, the application of lean production in industry varies from place to place, and some are far from being a model for our future society. For example, lean production's precision and synchronised timing has in some places been coupled with ruthless treatment of the participating workers. The value of lean production and the lean thinking that came out of it is to be found in its insights, and not always in its commercial practice.[179]

LEAN SOCIAL SECURITY. Means of enabling subsistence for the unemployed and retired, when the government is able to raise little or no taxation and therefore has no *money.

At the heart of it, there is prevention. Sustained counsel and care is a task for the *neighbourhood, which will respond to the detail of individual circumstances. It will encourage and enable work at home in trades and *crafts suited to age and skills. Mentoring and

L

personal contact, the model pioneered by reformers such as Thomas Chalmers (*Scale), would be close to the principles of the local Lean Economy.[180]

The English Reformation dismantled the *institutions of the church that had the commitment and capability needed to care for the poor and retired, and the local arrangements that took their place were patchy. The recurring question was, "Who is local? Is he really one of ours..?" But even a rich *market society can provide no guarantees and, whereas social security can ward off hunger, it cannot prevent *demoralisation.

The ability of a *community to prevent or relieve poverty will reflect the vitality of its support networks, and the existence and effectiveness of a local *informal economy. The *Lean Economy will have the advantage that its *material heart—its *organic *ecosystem and its *permaculture, for instance—does not depend on a long supply chain, distancing it from the people it serves. Established lean economies will know what their local *systems can supply—both their potential and their limits.

*Hyperunemployment, Empowerment, Public Sphere and Private Sphere, Religion, Boundaries and Frontiers, Slack and Taut.

LEAN THINKING. A frame of reference for enabling people to join together in a shared aim.

"Lean" in this sense was originally derived from industrial *lean production in the post-war period, and the concept is widely applied in industry, as alluded to in this book's Introduction. *Lean Logic* applies this frame of reference to the shared aim of rebuilding a *political economy in place of the failing *market.[181]

The essence is this. Two ways of making something happen can be compared. One of them—top-down management—is to tell people what to do: issue instructions, regulations, *incentives, penalties, targets; exert managerial control; do the thinking for them; give orders, make sure they are carrying them out, check that they have done them right and, if they haven't, tell them to do it again.

The other way is to set people up with the necessary resources, the *skills and equipment, a *common purpose, and the *freedom to apply their *judgment. This has advantages: it brings to life the *imagination

and tenacity of the people; it transforms the quality of decisions; it is flexible; it sets up conditions for alert *feedback: it makes the needs of the *system quickly apparent, responding to the *local and real, rather than to a distant caricature.

An example of what we are looking at here is the difference between, on the one hand, policy in which the government tells us what to do and is then obeyed with *sceptical resignation; and, on the other hand, an agreed direction, enabled by a *leadership which knows the difference between management and inspiration, and which makes it clear what the aims are and why they matter, switching on minds, ingenuity and motivation. Those aims are general—e.g., "to achieve this long-term reduction in collective energy use, as defined by the Energy Budget, in order to preserve a benign climate. And it is up to you how you do it, though you will get all the help you ask for"—as distinct from detailed instructions backed by rewards and penalties.

This is regime change—from disjointed regulation to freedom to think, from command-and-control to concentration on the matter in hand. And in lean thinking such a *radical break is called *kaikaku*; whereas *incremental improvement is *kaizen*. The switch into lean thinking itself is almost always a radical break, prompted by crisis and reluctantly done. Whether further radical breaks, or creative destruction, are needed after that switch has been made is a more complex matter (*Paradigm, The Wheel of Life).

And yet, in a sense, there is nothing new about lean thinking. It is as old as *politics and *community, but it was business that rediscovered it and made it explicit in our own time, so the business context of the principle is still present. This turns out to be quite helpful because business, especially lean production's home territory of vehicle manufacturing—though far removed from post-market communities—provides a real-life setting for the five rules of the *grammar of lean thinking. *Lean Logic* suggests its own labels for three of them; the original names are given in brackets:

1. *Intention* (Specify *value)
   The Intention defines what you want to achieve; it is the core around which every activity is organised and given shape. In industrial lean production, the Intention is to achieve "value", and value is . . .

[a] capability provided to a customer at the right time at an appropriate price, as defined in each case by the customer.[182]

So, it works like this. We have a complex intention, and here again there are two ways of thinking about it. One way is to adopt a single task within that wider aim. It might be:

Require all workers to account for and record their time in full.

Now, why is that relevant to the Intention? What value does it bring? You might be able to think of ways in which customers get better value if all workers account for their time in full than if they don't do so. But if, as we shall suppose for this example, it turns out that, after examination of the matter from all angles, it is just a case of bureaucratic form-filling, a tedious encumbrance which takes workers' minds off their jobs, then it should not be there. Lean thinking *travels light. It concentrates on what contributes to value—to the Intention—and does without things that don't.

It sounds obvious; in action, it isn't. Organisations sustain many practices that are irrelevant to what they are there to do. Sometimes they do so because *other* practices require it, such as a structure based on top-down command-and-control which requires exhaustive recordkeeping—if the recordkeeping were removed, the whole structure could collapse. That could be exactly the *kaikaku event that is needed, but to the people around at the time, it is anything but obvious.

Another possible subsidiary task:

Make sure the handbrakes work.

Here we have identified an aim which at least has some relevance to making cars, though given such prominence that other aims, which are also intrinsic to "value", risk being forgotten-about: you could end up with cars in which nothing worked but the handbrake. That is a caricature, of course, but it is not a remote one in the context of schools with state-of-the-art security cameras and collapsing discipline, farms with awesome labour-saving equipment and a deteriorating soil structure, urban districts whose smoothly-functioning *social security system underwrites their crime and futility, factories whose milling machines work to a speed and accuracy far ahead of the rest of the system's ability to keep up, or societies paralysed under the weight of regulation and *control.

It is, of course, the aim that is wrong. The aim (again, it sounds obvious but it often isn't to the harassed people in nominal command-and-control) should not be simply to produce handbrakes that work, but to produce cars that the customers want. Here, then, is *reductionism in its most characteristic form, where it seems to let us off the need to think about working with the system as a whole, offering instead the satisfaction of concentrating on a simplified, one-item, to-do list. This will only destroy the shared focus on the overall aim and rule out the possibility of discovering a *common purpose.

And that would in turn opens the way to Advanced Reductionism, where those *iconic single-focus aims multiply, infesting the system like an extended family of clothes-moths. The cost of administering that collection of reductionist targets is high; inconsistencies either paralyse the system or impose a culture of pretence; *creative invention is disallowed. The system becomes rigidly connected up; paralysed into incompetence. There is disempowerment—the task imposed on that busy ecology is to labour, but not to ask for any reward save the joy of catching each other out. The only participants who are happy with the situation are the managers, who think that more control is needed. Despite being rushed off their feet, they still can't keep control, so it appears at first breathless glance that they have a point.

In contrast with all this, the Intention identifies the system's deep, central, aims. That does not mean that the idea of "value" should be so focused that it itself becomes a reductionist aim, for the "capability provided to a customer" may in fact be quite complex and require *reflection. The customer does not, for instance, want the company to go out of business, so she will expect it to make a profit; nor does she want to buy products from a company

L

285

that pollutes the groundwater. So value—the Intention of an industrial enterprise—can be expressed in terms of responding to the claims of its numerous stakeholders, such as customers, shareholders, staff, the local community and the environment. The "triple bottom line" recognises companies' obligations in terms of quality and income, and of the environment and social justice too.[183]

What is non-negotiable is that the enterprise, having decided what it wants to do, must avoid being burdened either by a host of other kinds of urgent commitments which are nothing to do with that Intention, or by *iconic reductionist obsessions which crowd out *encounter with the system as a whole.

So, value is defined in terms of what the enterprise is ultimately for, and leaves out all the other things it may want to do, unless they are also relevant to that defining purpose. Since an enterprise is a *complex system, many unexpected things may well be *relevant, such as blue skies research and a generous pension scheme, but the connection between them and the Intention needs to be explicit. There may be seductive reasons for being distracted from what you are trying to do, but unless there is a plain reason in support of something being part of the enterprise's Intention, it should be left out.

2. *Lean Means (Identify the value stream)
The Intention is defined, so now is the moment to purge the irrelevant—the legacy of stuff that clogs up and weighs down the system. For instance, in the case of a manufacturing company—the original setting for lean thinking—you don't have to maintain and pay for large numbers of supervisors to regulate the front-line workers on the assumption that no one can be trusted to think for themselves; you don't need a large inspection and testing establishment if quality and *judgment are intrinsic to every stage in the process. You don't need arbitrary targets if there is a structure of motivation and *trust, and a widely shared agreement on the Intention. Controls and written reports may in some circumstances be needed, but they do not in themselves add value, so they should be used only

if they are essential to value being added. You don't need centralisation if localisation will do as well or (more likely) better.

So get rid of all the irrelevant activities, elaborations and hassle (collectively known as *muda) which tend to accumulate in organisations—that is, everything that isn't part of the "value stream". With the shock of *kaikaku comes the sacrifice of much that may have been thought of as important or indispensable, and its replacement by lean-intelligent design, which is in turn followed by *kaizen: incremental improvement, working out how to do what is *necessary, and how to avoid what is not.

But, at the same time as purging the irrelevant, it is necessary to recruit the *relevant—the set of means that is needed. There may be a lot of them, and not all of them will reveal themselves at first. For example, good ventilation is essential to good patient care, as Florence Nightingale discovered, too late for most of her patients at Scutari; soil structure depends on rotations and on the use of natural fertility and compost; a shared *commons requires well-established conditions to be met if its users are to sustain it with the necessary autonomy, understanding and competence. Sifting the lean means from the irrelevant and achieving the needed convergence of focus and *complexity may be difficult; it is an idea which, as is the way of *systems, resists summary. In the end, learning about it means living it: heartbeat and respiration respond faithfully to—are pulled along exactly and promptly by—what the body needs.

3. *Flow
Flow keeps the system moving at an even pace. The lean industrial system delivers parts and finished goods as they are needed; it avoids large batches, bottlenecks and storage. There is no waiting time between frantic bursts of work; the system is synchronised. It is also connected up, so that tasks are arranged close to each other and in sequence; the people who are doing them can sort out problems together; their conversation enables their cooperation. There is a convergence of the system's aptitudes, timings, circumstances and purpose (for wider meanings of flow, see the separate entry).

4. *Pull

Once the system is connected up, action in one part of it is the cue for fitting responses in adjacent parts. Action and information converge. Everyone involved can see—or recognises that they must work out for themselves—what needs to be done to achieve the Intention; actions are focused responses to the particular.

This is how the two leading exponents of lean thinking explain it ("downstream" refers to activities nearer the completion of the process; "upstream" refers to activities nearer the start of the process):

[Pull is] a system of cascading production and delivery instructions from downstream to upstream activities in which nothing is produced by the upstream supplier until the downstream customer signals a need.[184]

Each activity responds to the needs of the next one along: it is *pulled along* in sequence. No one has to stand there giving instructions about what to do; participants respond to the demands of the processes downstream from them, whose needs they have to supply. The people involved see what is needed, and engage their brains.[185]

5. *Feedback (Perfection)

Reflect on results; improve the system *incrementally. Check outcomes against Intention. Decide in the light of all this: is what you are trying to do realistic? Where are the gaps? Where is the room for improvement?

This is another of the features of lean thinking which seems obvious but which, on close inspection, turns out not to be. You can look at a system from the outside—and perhaps from a little bit above—and come to the conclusion that it is all working just fine, just as scale models of horrendous proposed city developments, with their tiny figures and tree-lined walkways, tend to look nice litter-free places to live. So, how is this error of misty-eyed complacency to be avoided?

Well, the first rule is: don't look down at it from the sky. It is the people who are inside it who know it, and it is usually the dissidents, complainers and troublemakers who are most perceptive about it. What they are quite likely to see is the ways in which the bits do not join up: they will see the trade-offs: *this* can only work properly at the cost of *this*. But complex systems, given *time and feedback, can usually do better than that: instead of trade-offs, with one part having to bear the cost of another, they develop 'trade-ons', where the service being provided by one part of the system for another is felt as a benefit by both the recipient and by the supplier. In contrast with the exchange relationships of *economics, participants in such complementary relationships benefit *directly* from the very act of providing the goods and services to other parts of the system. Intrinsic advantage rolls through the system.[186]

Lean thinking is a radical approach. It begins with the break of *kaikaku*, which may be hard to bear, as it is a profound change from previous assumptions and methods and so is usually resisted until a shock intervenes. The changed thinking that follows, approaching the system in a profoundly new way, moves ahead with incremental improvement and evolution, guided by experience and local detail.

It is a philosophy with wide application, shaped by the context. But there are significant differences between lean thinking as it is now widely applied in industry and the use that *Lean Logic* makes of it—apart from the obvious one that the industrial case is about extending the flying-time of the *market state and *Lean Logic* is about bringing it in to land.

One of the differences—in fact it is more apparent than real, as we shall see—lies in the attitude to standard practice. Industrial *lean production requires its procedures to be carried out to a standard, and in a standard way. Individuals are encouraged to invent and develop new ways, but they are not adopted without testing and widely shared agreement that this is to be the new way of doing it. The reason for this becomes obvious when you think about what it means to introduce, say, a new procedure in an aircraft cockpit. Each cockpit is used by many different pilots and co-pilots, who must be confident that all the cockpits they enter are virtually identical; they need to be able to use the

L

equipment with *certainty, not only as a routine, but in the dark, in an emergency and when tired. Innovations in equipment and practice are constantly introduced in response to pilots' suggestions—this is key to the debugging process which is needed for every new model—but only after an established routine of evaluation, followed by briefings to everyone involved, and then the change is made to all aircraft of that type at the

---

FLEXIBILITY AND INVENTION
Reflection and Learning

I once did a course with Australian permaculture teacher Dave Clark, who talked about his experiences implementing permaculture in refugee camps in Macedonia. He was dealing with large numbers of people moving to places with no infrastructure, all of which had to be created. He did amazing work, erecting straw-bale buildings, food gardens, putting in miles of swales and hundreds of thousands of trees.

He spoke of having to work with professional engineers who would design something such as a drainage system, which Dave could see wouldn't work, but which, because the person was a 'professional', could not be questioned. He saw much money wasted through this unchallengeable 'rule' that the professional is always right.

He talked about how in his work he always worked from the premise that he was wrong. This designed into the process the openness to reassessment at any stage. An Energy Descent Action Plan should be like this. It is a collection of ideas that should be reworked and revised regularly.

Some 'Plans' become carved in stone, immutable and fixed: "We are working our way through the plan", even though that Plan may be long since irrelevant. By designing flexibility into the process, we can make it infinitely more powerful, and give the community a far stronger sense of ownership and involvement.

ROB HOPKINS, *The Transition Handbook*, 2008.[187]

---

same time. A similar case for standard practice can be made for any system in which a number of people use the same equipment, where customers want to know in advance what service they can expect, and where "trial and error" has to be strictly contained, and cannot be allowed to escape into actual practice.[188]

For a *panarchy, or *ecology, of communities, matters are more relaxed. The people who work in them and who depend on them tend to stay in the same *place; it does not matter that they don't know much about how things are done elsewhere; trial and error is not only acceptable, it is at the heart of their working practice. Their "errors" rarely have fatal consequences, and experiments can be extended and refined over many years; surviving mistakes; allowing successes to be gradually copied and locally adapted. At the same time, there is a presumption in favour of local practice, allowing a *lack* of standardisation that would be impractical in an industrial organisation.

And yet, a group of independent *communities will still not be without its standard practice. For instance, the *principles* of *organic food production and *permaculture are widely agreed. It helps, of course, that those principles advocate a high degree of diversity in application, depending on soil, *climate and the needs and numbers of the people involved in it, but the insights of teachers like Eve Balfour, David Holmgren and Patrick Whitefield have universal application, once the local *intention has been settled. These enabling principles are, in a sense, a standard practice; they can be learned.

And the same applies to the whole cluster of *practical and *cultural skills discussed in *Lean Logic* and beyond—in surgery and computer programming, for instance. This is not a case, then, of inventing everything from scratch, but of having a foundation of skills and relevant *expertise opening up possibilities and degrees of *freedom which, without that foundation, would not be available. As any musician will tell you, you must know the rules before you can invent interesting ways to break them.

The key to the freedom and flexibility of the Lean Economy, then, consists of a range of *skills, needing hands, mind, memory, *judgment, *emotion and cooperation. It will be a case of lifetime learning, starting not long after the first breath, and continuing with experience and *conversation for as long as a person is able to take part in making community work.

With that platform of competence, it is possible to sustain flexibility and pragmatism in the bloodstream of the Lean Economy, and this affects such fundamentals as the "The Plan"—the *Energy Descent Action Plan, for instance. There is nothing wrong with long-term plans: to learn from them is instructive, and to deliberate about them engages the wits, but to believe them is a betrayal of the creative *imagination which is the heart of the matter (see "Flexibility and Invention" sidebar).

And a more profound difference between mainstream lean thinking and its application in *Lean Logic* lies in the idea of a *slack economy. The lean enterprise is designed to be so *taut that problems immediately show up, with dire consequences, and everyone involved has the maximum *incentive to make sure they don't happen. This is the "Just-In-Time" (*kanban*) principle which does not allow backup stocks, so that supplies are delivered at the last minute. It certainly concentrates the mind but, even in industry itself, it has its risks, leading to stock outages if, for instance, there is a problem in supply which the company can do nothing about. And yet, there is slack even in the industrial version of lean thinking, in the sense of its responses to such challenges: it is unencumbered; it can respond quickly and effectively; it *travels light. There is extended freedom for the people involved in it—not just a remote well-intentioned management—to engage their minds.

The lean approach is not about apple-pie-sensible practices. It is about listening acutely to what a *system needs and responding accurately. It is not an ecology in which the waste of materials, money, labour, health, or environmental quality is *cut*: some *waste may indeed still be present, but here it is not inadvertently designed into the system.

Lean thinking switches on the information technology that we keep in the space between the bridge of the nose and the top of the head. Regulatory management has not been made aware of its existence.

*Lean Food, Incentives Fallacy, Paradigm, Metamorphosis, Lean Education, Harmonic Order, Relevance Fallacy.

LEAN TRANSPORT. Transport is the symbol of modernity: pictures of the future show the land, sea and air full of fast-moving vehicles. But that is, of course, an image of the failure of modernity—the relentlessly deepening incompetence of *place: local capability has leaked away and collected in giant hubs in which skills and assets are captured and concentrated. In an age of cheap energy and massive *material *needs and flows, distance is trivial, opening the way to a comedy of errors, in which everything starts off in the wrong place. If *Lean Logic*'s expectations of future *energy scarcity are correct, there is no way in which that depth of transport-dependency can be sustained by being made lean. The *Lean Economy will have to start again, thinking about space and distance in a completely different way.

The transport network needed to support a drastically reduced volume of traffic will not include motorways. Whatever we may think about motorways, it comes as a shock to think of them as obsolete and empty. And yet, the history of transport is a collection of stories with abrupt endings: transport systems which have reached an accomplished maturity, supported by *skilled labour-forces, generally turn out to be on the point of obsolescence. The Romans' roads, at the end of their day, reverted to scrub, and later proved unsuited to the heavy loads and heavy horses needed by the cathedral-builders in the Middle Ages. The eighteenth century's invention of express coaching along 20,000 miles of turnpikes (a breakthrough: paid for by their users, rather than by a charge on local residents) reached its peak of efficiency and speed in 1837: just five years later, defeated by railways, it had gone; the fine roads—dual carriageways thirty yards wide in many areas—were deserted; grass and weeds started to creep in from the margins, leaving a space just wide enough for two vehicles to pass. There is now the prospect of the mass road transport of our own day, too, coming to an abrupt end—to be followed, as before, by a forgiving shroud of grass and weeds.[189]

The motorways' decaying surfaces, unsafe bridges and rotting concrete, their heavy maintenance needs and their massive *land use (around 50 square miles, or 14,000 hectares in the UK) will be a curse on the landscape.[190] Rehabilitating the land on which they lie would be desirable, but the scale of the task—including breaking up and removing deeply embedded reinforced concrete foundations and disposing of the spoil—would

L

be not far short of that of building them in the first place. The probability is that the motorway system will be neither maintained nor decommissioned, except by local initiative, which would have the *incentive to close off this dangerous 'no man's land' (hard to police, and an express route for crime) and start the long process of bringing it back into use, in the first instance as woodland. Just breaking up the surface would be a start. In practice, the removal of any more than a small fraction of the network may well turn out to be impossible.

Railways are likely to go the same way. With a steep decline in use, the cost per passenger mile would rise beyond the possibility of maintaining any substantial part of the system. Rail makes sense only where there is the potential for mass transit: it needs a lot of people and money to pay for it. This is not an enterprise which can be expected to work on the basis of *reciprocities. And its energy source is in doubt. If substantial electrical energy should become available from (say) solar arrays in the Sahara Desert, then electrically-powered railways would be the ideal transport medium. But, failing that, there is a question about how railways would be powered, and where the energy would come from to fuel their infrastructures—making rails and trains.

We may get lucky. It depends on the depth of the collapse following the *climacteric. And, so long as the possibility of being able to run a railway cannot be ruled out, the inherited rail network is a crucial asset. It would have been even more useful, the infrastructure of localisation, had it not been for the errors—pathetic misconceptions, according to the transport analyst David St John Thomas—which led to its substantial closure in the 1960s. The prospect of what remains being unavailable to the *Lean Economy comes as another shock. The aim of conserving it—or, better still, reinstating some of the lost network—would be a priority if circumstances allowed.[191]

The *exception to this is high-speed rail, a deeply obsolete technology based on the assumption that society in the future will be based on ever-growing city hubs, requiring mass transit not only between them but to them, within the centralised *regions they serve. The case for high-speed rail has turned on two factoids: (1) it isn't air travel; and (2) journey times are shorter—but that will only encourage people to make more journeys—and, anyway, time on a train is Grade 1 useful time for work, *sleep, *conversation and thinking. In fact, the convergence of special conditions—cheap energy, *large-scale engineering and transport *infrastructures, and robust demand backed by high incomes—will no longer exist, either for high-speed rail or for air travel itself. The present drive to build high-speed rail will draw scarce resources away from the undoubted asset of local rail, breeding a new generation of white elephants, like the *nuclear power stations. Phantom tracks will be named after their advocate, like the Maginot Line.

As Neil MacGregor reminds us during a brief visit to ancient Persia in his *A History of the World in 100 Objects*, "nothing tells you more about a state than its transport system."[192] In fact, the relevant transport system for a localised economy organised on the *proximity principle is local roads—backed by lightly-used trunk roads. There may be no alternative to local maintenance, although that is a collective task which, for societies that have valued their *freedoms, has never been without its problems and *politics, with the quality of the maintenance variable. Local transport may include biogas-fuelled cars, buses and trucks, but the biogas will be sufficiently costly and scarce to make the use of road vehicles the exception, rather than the routine. Some reliable forms of transport will remain: walking, bicycles, horses and sojourn: staying at your designation for a long time, rather than going backwards and forwards; in this way, slow becomes fast—you simply spend less time travelling, for you are already there.

The unanswerable question at the heart of transport is the one asked by the farm labourer standing bemused one day in the mid-eighteenth century at the side of the Liverpool-Manchester turnpike, crowded with urgently-speeding coaches: "Who would ever have thought that there were so many people in the wrong place?"[193] Ivan Illich expresses the matter as an ideal: it is never to be realised, and in the gap between ideal and actuality, the Lean Economy will need transport, but the ideal itself is, in his words,

> space that offers to each person the constantly
> renewed experience that the centre of the world
> is where he stands, walks and lives.[194]

LEISURE. Leisure, widely-shared, has been the unfulfilled promise of economic development, a reward for mankind's achievement in (as John Maynard Keynes put it) "solving its economic problem".[195] Some of the makers of the Industrial Revolution looked forward to the day when hard work would be over, and society could devote itself to leisure. "Men and women", it was confidently forecast by a writer in the *Democratic Review* in 1853, "will then have no harassing cares or laborious duties to fulfil. Machinery will perform all work— automata will direct them. The only task of the human race will be to make love, study and be happy."[196]

And yet, in a *competitive *market economy, a large amount of roughly-equally-shared leisure time—say, a three-day working week or less—is hard to sustain, because any individuals who decide to instead work a full week can produce for a lower price (by working longer hours than the competition they can produce a greater quantity of goods and services, and thus earn the same wage by selling each one more cheaply). These more competitive people would then be fully employed, and would put the more leisurely out of business completely. Consider, for example, this thought-experiment:

The case of the vanishing economy

Imagine that there is an economy of 100 people (all in their dual role as producers and consumers). Add three strong assumptions:

1. They are consuming the maximum they want to consume: if they had more money, they would not increase their consumption.

   This might be because, for instance, producers and consumers alike want to reduce their carbon footprint, or because consumers are feeling insecure and want to save any extra money, or because they use all their additional income competing for non-produced *positional goods (those goods that by definition cannot be exclusively owned by every individual, such as unique and irreplaceable artefacts, works of art or houses in particular locations), which is simply a more roundabout way of increasing the level of savings.

2. They never believe each other's promises.

3. There are no unemployment benefits, so that the out-of-work die.

Now imagine that this miniature economy abruptly experiences a shock: there is a technological advance that doubles *productivity, so that the 100 workers now produce twice as much as they did before, but consumers (by assumption) do not consume more, so overall consumption remains unchanged. What happens?

Well, the doubled productivity means that now only 50 people are needed to produce enough for 100, so half the workforce becomes unemployed. There are no unemployment benefits, so they die.

That leaves 50 producers/consumers. They are still working to the same (doubled) level of productivity, so they produce enough for 100. This is twice as much as is now needed, so half of them become unemployed and die. That leaves 25 producers/consumers. And so on . . .

Now, if they were sensible, they would all decide to work half-time. That would give them the same quantity of goods as they would get if half of them worked full-time, and it would share out the leisure. But they do not do that because they can't get an agreement to stick; they are conditioned by the market economy; they have to be competitive, and cannot forgo an immediate advantage from which they would individually benefit in favour of a future (and larger) advantage from which everyone would benefit.

Competition now becomes a curse, frustrating all efforts at accommodation, but people are programmed to think only in those reductive terms. And that has particularly regrettable consequences if they are in a system which, when it is stressed, can become unstable.

Thus, George realises that if he works half-time, Jack can steal a march on him and work full-time, earning twice the money, selling his product at half price, and putting George out of business. Everyone is scared of opportunists like Jack, and they *blame each other for "forcing" them to behave in this way; they dare not trust each other, so they cannot take the simple step needed to solve their problem and enjoy leisurely lives (this is a version of the "Prisoner's Dilemma", see sidebar on page 292).

———

This is why it is difficult to sustain a part-time, *slack economy. There are obvious practical reasons too: it would be

L

THE PRISONER'S DILEMMA

When you can't trust people to choose what is best for everyone

The Prisoner's Dilemma is an allegory (told in many different versions) of two suspects that are being separately questioned about a crime which, in reality, they committed together. If they both deny it, then (since there is no proof) they will be allowed to go free. However, denying it is quite risky for both of them because if (say) George denies it and Jack confesses, George will be shot (and Jack will only get a ten-year prison sentence, as a reward for pleading guilty). They cannot talk to each other, nor trust each other to deny the crime, so they both end up confessing it and going to prison. If only they could have trusted each other, they would both have been let off. The problem is that the ideal solution is ruled out as suicidal unless some special reassurance—a binding declaration of honour among thieves—had been made in advance. It would have had to be quite a performance—an oath of undying loyalty, not just a fix-up in the pub.[197]

hard for pianists, brain surgeons, tennis champions and others with *skilled jobs to maintain the standard they need if they only worked part-time; and challenging to monitor the working hours of the self-employed, such as writers, who work at home. Unannounced visits by time-wardens might be viewed with concern and would anyway be less than fair, since the working hours of the less-skilled jobs (e.g., waiters) could more easily be monitored than the more-skilled ones (e.g., philosophers).

But the deeper problem is that agreements on self-denying measures—such as shorter working time, or a deliberately inefficient technology, both of which require people to forgo immediate advantage—are hard to sustain. Everyone who stays within the limit, forgoing the opportunity to be more competitive, is a potential sucker. That is the core, enduring *ethic of the *market.

In the *Lean Economy, however, that problem need not apply in the case of working time, for three reasons:

First, the aim is not, in essence, to reduce working hours; it is to build the *informal and *local economy to the point that it meets the wants and *needs which the declining market is conspicuously unable to provide. Indeed, the whole discussion of work and leisure makes more sense when it starts with the aim of increasing working time in the informal economy, rather than of reducing working time in the formal economy, which is on course to decline whether we want it to or not.

Secondly, the Lean Economy will be fully aware that there are other ways of inhibiting economic *growth: the use of labour-intensive methods, the selection of technologies for their minimal environmental impact rather than for their *productivity, the discarding of surpluses (*Intentional Waste) and various other strategies within the range of options open to the *slack economy. It is unlikely that they will be needed to end the growth of the formal economy, but they will certainly be applied in the informal economy of the future.

Thirdly, the Lean Economy is built on a strong *culture and on *social capital, underwriting a shared sense of *common purpose and enabling it to make decisions that stick: it can sustain desirable aims such as more leisure time if it needs to do so. *If* the sophisticated information and energy technology of our time continues to be available, the way is open in principle for a benign and positive progress towards the steady state economy; technical advance can in this context open the way to reduced working time without the initiative collapsing in disarray. This is a society that can implement its decision to enjoy ever-increasing leisure with each advance in technology. Result: a culturally-rich, steady state, *systems-literate, *resilient *political economy . . .

———

. . . at least, in principle. But the instability never goes away. Still, it is a core aim of *lean economics to keep its *choices and arrangements from unravelling, to restore to human society the power of decision, instead of being subject to the turbulence of competition and the opportunism of price. With a strongly developed culture, built on a well-articulated *grammar of *scale, it is possible. A decision to work shorter hours, the use of labour-intensive methods that can be done lovingly and in a *closed-loop system—these *freedoms are waiting to be rediscovered.

There are snags, of course. Living in a slack economy, supported by the culture rather than by opportunism, is a skilled task. Many of the abilities needed for it are best learned in childhood. The potential for *play, *judgment, *imagination and *manners must be activated early in life if they are to develop properly, but the narrow targets-based *education of the market economy passes them by. This means that more leisure could short-circuit miserably into poverty and resentment. Or it could be sucked up by addiction to television and its related media, through which the time available to make a personal commitment to social capital or to a new political-economic order is diminished. Having to build a new social order from the foundations is a challenge. When the builders don't turn up, the challenge is greater.

The other major snag is that the advanced technologies may not be available (*Appropriate Technology, Climacteric).

And yet, the possibility of a culture-rich, technically-advanced, sustainable political economy, with the key accomplishment of *slack—with time to think—is there. *Trust, Slack and Taut, Growth, Informal Economy.

LEVERAGE. See Systems Thinking 〉 Function 〉 Leverage.

LITURGY. The form taken by religious observance.

Why should this matter? Well, *Lean Logic* argues that the *culture of a society and its *communities will be central to its existence; that if a culture is affirmed and expressed collectively and regularly, it will have, to some degree, the properties of *ritual; and that the cultural framework within which a ritual is performed can be understood as a form of *religion. This is clearly a nuanced understanding of religion: it claims that the nature and intensity of the ritual shapes the nature and intensity of the religion which it affirms, ranging, for instance, from "slightly" religious to "intensely" religious, and indeed the intensity can be expected to vary over time. *Binary definitions—this *is/is not* a religion—have value only at the extremes, at which the identification of the religious is trivial in any case.

This gives ritual itself a central function. There is a sense in which the ritual *is* the religion; if a ritual should change, then the religion changes. It may continue unchanged in some senses—its core text, *narrative and set of propositions may be unaltered—but a change in the ritual will affect the *implicit perceptions and significance of those core properties. It follows that what actually *happens* at a religious celebration matters; and the language and choreography which comprise a ritual are, in turn, its liturgy (Gr: *leiton* [people] + *ergos* [work]—"the work of the people").

What happens at the liturgies of the religions of the lean future is no business of *Lean Logic*. And yet, the design and *practice of liturgy is not a field into which the industrial *market has provided much useful insight, so a perspective on the matter, drawing conclusions from recent experience, may have some value, whether it is something to agree with or disagree with: a particular, local irritant can be a good starting point from which to draw your own conclusions. Moreover, it is not always the case that the most helpful form of discussion is an *objective form, and this may apply especially to ritual; a liturgy seen from the perspective of a person who is in love with it is different from, and *may* mean more than, a discussion from the perspective of someone who does not care one way or the other. The following brief remarks are from the far-from-objective starting point of being in love with the Anglican *Book of Common Prayer*.

Until recently, this was the central ritual of the Church of England. It was based on the medieval Latin liturgy, and was the work of Thomas Cranmer (1489–1556), published in 1549 (revised 1552, 1559 and 1604, finally settled in 1662). This book was the identifying asset of the Anglican church worldwide. It is a poetry of narrative and insight, of sublime *encounter: the words are constant, remembered; their meanings are there to be uncovered, explored and *reflected on over time. A liturgy which is intensely poetic, whose constant, unchanging *words* are the event, is a lean liturgy in the sense that it is for the people to interpret and uncover meanings and *metaphors contained in them at their *leisure, and to the limit of their *imagination. By contrast with this, in a liturgy where the *meaning* comes first, and where there are many different ways in which the meaning could be expressed, the entry ticket to participation is not to chew over the words but to swallow the meaning: you can take it or leave it: if you are a member, you have to take it. That is the nature of a belief system, and it is brittle. Most people simply leave it.

In the 1960s, the depth and *intelligence with which the Anglican liturgy—and many other liturgies in the Christian church—endowed *religious observance came to be seen as inconsistent with what was seen as the exciting, liberated and vibrant informality of the time, and a series of simplifications were introduced. Like that period's urban reconstruction, *education and *health programmes, they began with large-scale demolition. Poetic, narrative *truth was cleared away. What followed was concrete. Questions to be reflected on were replaced by answers which the liturgical planners felt quite sure the people would be happy with. Everyone was presumed to be a beginner. Guidance was supplied on what to feel. Children were targeted. Teenagers cringed. Grown-ups tended to feel rather silly. People stayed away.

Recovery has been incomplete. Following forty years of serial revision, no liturgy has *authority, and local churches tend to devise their own liturgies, retreating with their declining numbers into a *private sphere, seeing their little congregation as a "family", with a role for the minister as their father or mother. The language combines tabloid modernity with an elderly desire to please. These disjointed snippets of sentiment have no interest in what previous generations could tell us, and no expectation of having anything to say to the future. Such detachment from *time and space makes it absolutely necessary to have faith, with smiling *certainty, that you are saved.

There are places in the Christian church with a large and inspired attendance, perceptive evangelical preaching and conviviality—all of which are sources of *social capital, and the valued core of many people's lives. But those hubs of crowdedness are aspects of the disconnection between people and *places. They are fine events, but they are not part of the everywhere-texture which gives us a society; religion has been separated out into something that some people come together to *do*, like rally-driving. Religion, the Anglican Christian religion, at least—and here it can be taken as an approximate representation of the religion of Western

civilisation—has been personalised. It is a personal journey for you, because that is the sort of thing you like. Here is the psychologist Gail Sheehy waving as you set off:

> If I could give everyone a gift for the send-off on this journey, it would be a tent. A tent for tentativeness. The gift of portable roots.... For each of us there is the opportunity to emerge reborn, *authentically* unique, with an enlarged capacity to love ourselves and embrace others.... The delights of self-discovery are always available. Though loved ones move in and out of our lives, the capacity to love remains.[198]

But, as we see continually in *Lean Logic*, bottom-up local *empowerment requires a shared *intention—to protect the group's *freedom and to sustain an understanding of what it is about: local groups who have forgotten whether they exist for weekend cricket or for Pilates classes are not lean; they are chaotic. A framework is needed to sustain the *grammar which the *community can use for its own *creative expression. It is only through that grammar that anything of any depth and significance can be understood: without it, there are no coordinates for meaning to be defined in terms of. In the case of the Anglican church, its grammar was its liturgy.

We cannot tell what forms the religion of future communities will take. Small communities, with cultures shaped by a closeness to nature, which is held in respect and awe, could be close to pagan spiritualism—like the *lelira* of the Inuit and the shamanic religions whose rituals sustain the *scripts which in turn sustain their local *ecologies. On the other hand, cultures which are settled, more domestic than wild, and with a religion to match, may find themselves in the Christian tradition. If they do, they will inherit a proven, full-mouthed, full-blooded liturgy of great depth and brilliance, the existence of which—if they have formerly experienced only the winsome banalities from the time of the late market economy—they might not suspect. And they will also inherit the architectural expression of that liturgy—the churches—spectacular assertions that community is a mere prelude to the great fugue of overlapping mysteries, parables, affections and accomplishments that give us *Gaia.

L

A good liturgy is inclusive. It allows personal commitment but does not compel it. It allows, but does not require, a literal interpretation of its *myth. It does not patronise. It confirms an adult's self-image as an adult, and a child's self-image as growing up into an adult world. It is a collective, community response. It resists being captured and privatised as personal therapy. It invites *reflection; it explores *ironic space. It has continuity, affirming its rock solid and constant existence as a focal point for *social capital, and as the foundation for community.[199]

What is true of one *tradition may have some relevance for others. Confidence in one's own and delight at its liturgy can be the platform for constructive dialogue; there can be mutual understanding between strong traditions, which can inspire the people that affirm them. The starting point for the community building led by Andrew Mawson at Bromley by Bow was a tiny congregation using the liturgy of the United Reformed Church. Its essential sympathy with religious tradition made robust, self-confident links with other traditions possible. Unconditional advocacy of *The Book of Common Prayer* is not inconsistent with equally unconditional love and *loyalty by others for their own traditions. It is only inconsistent with the view that, since other traditions exist, it is necessary therefore to be tepid about one's own. Coexistence is not toleration; it is resonance; it is the nature of the human ecology.[200]
*Religion, Ritual, Rote, Multiculturalism.

LIVING STANDARDS. *Lean Logic* makes a distinction between "nominal" and "real" living standards. Nominal living standards tend to be measured in terms of monetary income and *productivity. Real living standards are not. For example, feeling safe in our homes counts as a positive aspect of real living standards, but security gates and electronic systems bought in order to feel safe do not. They are (at best) *regrettable necessities. The transport that has brought these tomatoes to my table is a regrettable necessity, but no one would claim that the transport itself improved the quality of the tomatoes.

Nonetheless, such *intermediate goods—the things a *household needs to buy, directly or indirectly, in order to enjoy the things it wants—do tend to get counted-in to measures of living standards, and they shouldn't. They are a positive contribution to Gross Domestic Product (GDP), but they are only repairs to, and compensations for, the *intensification needed by a super-large economy, all of which GDP faithfully measures.

In other words, real living standards cannot be measured in *money. When, or if, the *informal economy of the future is well-developed, real living standards will be high, though purchases of goods and services will be low. GDP will be history.[201]
*Well-Being, Dollar-a-Day Fallacy.

LOCAL. See Localisation, Local Wisdom.

LOCAL CURRENCY. A form of money other than the national currency, set up and managed locally. The reason for establishing a local currency at present is that it enables local producers, handicapped by high costs, to *compete more effectively with *efficient national and international producers. The *intention is to give them a better chance of making a living, providing a needed local service and staying in business.

In a thriving *market economy, such *protection is not generally considered a good idea. The discipline of having to be *competitive keeps businesses efficient. But there is more that businesses, especially small ones, can do for the local *community than simply sell goods at the lowest possible price. They can sell locally-produced goods, services and *food, for example; and they can help to supply jobs. They have the advantage of being in easy walking distance, and they can be centres of local conviviality. Many small, less-efficient businesses survive, in spite of the higher price of their goods, because benefits such as these inspire *loyalty from their customers, and local currencies have for a long time been discussed and tried out as a means of supporting this survival, in a wider economy which tends to discount such benefits.

Local currencies are also, potentially, a crucial asset for the settled *Lean Economy that could eventually become established after the *climacteric. But at this stage in the discussion we will focus on local currencies in the context of their present potential role in helping high-cost *local producers to cope in a *large-scale, delocalised, competitive market economy.

To explain how local currencies can play their part in this, maybe it's time to get personal. The example is extreme (a caricature) to make the point. The author of *Lean Logic* always makes his own bread. If, lacking any other means of subsistence, he had to earn his living entirely by making bread, then—given his small kitchen and oven, and the limits to the size of the mixing bowl that would fit on the counter and then into the sink for washing-up—he could realistically manage to make no more than five loaves a day. To earn a tolerable living from this he would have to price his loaves at £20 each. Clearly, that's not going to work.

But, come to think of it, there might be others in the same situation. Sarah, Fred and Biff could maybe provide some vegetables which are very expensive because they have been reared with individual care and attention. Deidre's hand-stitched clothes use local *materials, far removed from the sweatshops and long-distance *transport involved in the production of cheap jeans. Joseph could perhaps supply an occasional pricey leg of lamb, and there is that fellow who shows up from time to time with a side of venison, but only after dark for some reason. Here we have the *creative-inefficient sector*, which will be central and crucial to the human ecology of the future. And there are no doubt other potential suppliers and buyers around that we haven't met, whose names we don't know, so it can't be done on the basis of *reciprocity between friends—at least, not yet. Suppose, then, that all these high-cost producers—no-hopers in the competitive market—agreed to charge each other high prices for our various kinds of produce—in other words, suppose we formed a cartel? Our standard of living would be low, because one day's work does not produce very much, but at least our inefficient output would not be squeezed out by a competitive market and we would be able to sell what we produced. It's a promising idea. The alternative would be to go out of business. And starve.

But there is a snag. Next time Sarah goes into town she finds bread costing one tenth of what she pays me as a member of the cartel—just £2 a loaf, and, since it is a hot day and it is the obvious thing to do, she goes into the shop and buys one. And that opportunism is catching: very quickly, our cartel will break down, and its members will all be out of work and out of money again.

So, the question is, how to stop that happening? How to protect the cartel so that it doesn't break down? There are several possibilities. One is to threaten to shoot anyone who breaks it. Another is to set up a local currency. Call it the Log. Now its members trade with each other in Logs and, next time Sarah goes into town, she can't buy that cheap bread because she only has Logs in her wallet and the bakery only accepts pounds. Logs stay in the local economy because they can't go anywhere else; the local economy's high-cost producers stay in business. Problem solved. Currencies that are explicitly matched to the economies they serve are an extremely powerful instrument. They have the ability to sustain a business life which would otherwise sink into unemployment and exclusion.

But—more snags, and they arise mainly at the point where two currencies interact. They may do so in either of two ways:

First, consider our Logs, operating "in parallel" with pounds, but now all traders in the area—both inside and outside the cartel—decide to accept both currencies. Here, things get difficult. Potential purchasers of those very expensive, inefficiently-produced loaves would not see the need to pay more for them than the £2 that a loaf costs from other bakers. The same goes for everything else the cartel produces. So it goes out of business, taking the Log with it.

So the only thing protecting the cartel from oblivion is the unwillingness of other producers to accept Logs. That's not a very stable basis for continued existence, and that's a shame, because the Log was a "good" currency. A lot of hard work went into it: you would have to work for ten days to earn the Logs equivalent to just one day's earnings in pounds. But the market is flooded with pounds, which are so much easier to get hold of, so hardly anyone bothered with Logs. As Gresham's Law tells us, "Bad money drives out good money."[202]

The pounds in this story are not really bad money: they are just easier to get hold of because *productivity advances have enabled people to get their stuff onto the market easily—and to get pounds into their pockets when they sell them. To get Logs into their pocket by producing in the *creative and inefficient way that the Logs market specialises in is much harder work for no greater reward. Kiss goodbye to Logs.

It may not be quite as drastic as that. It *may* yet be possible for an inefficient parallel economy to use its own currency to sustain a degree of stability, but the expensive cartel economy will never be more than an impoverished subset of the wider economy it belongs to. If one of its producers does improve its efficiency—if I, for instance, decided to invest in a proper baker's oven and a large mixer—then my prices would tumble and I would drop out of the cartel. Other members would have one less customer for their goods. There would also now be some cheap bread around, and the rational response, even for cartel members (in their role as consumers), would be to buy everything they could at the lowest possible price— that is, to put themselves (in their role as producers) out of business. There might be some marginal purchases for which Logs would be used, but they would not rise above being a small "alternative" economy.

Now consider the *second* possible format. Imagine that there are two distinct currency areas: one is rich, endowed with efficient, low-cost technology; the other is poor, with an inefficient, high-cost technology. And imagine, too that the rich area has a thoroughly competitive (cartel-free) currency—the Pound—while the poor area has a currency of its own—the Log. In this case there is a clear definition of currencies, with each currency being legal tender in its own area and not in the other, without any overlap. Now put yourself in the position of a person living in the rich area who makes a trip to the poor area to buy a loaf of their famous handmade bread, and some other goodies at the same time. Since the rich area's currency (the Pound) is not accepted here, the tourist has to change his pounds into Logs.

At what exchange rate? Well, the normal guideline for exchange is "purchasing power parity"—that is, the tourist can buy roughly as much with the currency he purchases as he could have bought with his national currency if he had stayed at home. It is an equilibrium condition, and there are in practice enormous exceptions to it but, for present purposes, we can suppose that it holds good. Our tourist wants to spend a whole day in the poor area, so he decides to convert one day's salary from pounds into Logs. A day's wages would buy him as much as fifty loaves if he wanted, so he goes into the poor area with his wallet stuffed with Logs, and the traders in the poor area do well from his visit.[203]

But when a person from the poor area visits the rich area, it is another matter. Sarah spends the whole of one day's income on buying pounds—but what can she get for that? Just five loaves, since one day's income for a person living in the poor area buys much less than one day's income for a person living in the rich area. So, on her visit to the rich area, she can buy hardly anything. That's unfortunate from the point of view of a day out, but it is good for her local economy. It means it is strongly placed to export its goods, and can import hardly anything, so it is on course to get richer and to be able to invest enough to make its industry more efficient. *Or*, it can just hold things as they are: its people earn enough to live on, and are not importing much. That is, they are self-reliant and may be happy to stay that way, for they are much better off than they would be if—without the benefit of their separate currency—they remained unemployed. The local economy is using its local currency to underwrite an invaluable stability. Subject to the detail and to troubles which fall outside the range of this story, that poor locality really has solved its problem.[204]

So, to sustain a stable *slack economy it would be necessary to maintain a single local currency, protected by an exchange rate with the different currencies of neighbours. The alternative, or additional, way of doing it is to make the revolutionary shift in thinking required to move on from the whole culture of *competitive pricing.

This latter course would involve looking towards a small-scale economy that builds in inefficiencies, space and slack from the beginning, and underwrites them with a strongly-developed *social capital and *culture. And it doesn't think in terms of *money. It is about *community and *reciprocity. This is the essence of *lean economics. Local currencies may be part of it.

Local currencies alone, however, rarely succeed in providing the decisive *protection needed by *small-scale, inefficient producers. But they come in many forms, each with their value. Here are some of them:

1. *Transition banknotes*
   These are banknotes issued by local communities, such as *Transition communities. They are issued at parity with the national currency so that, for

example, the local "pounds" issued by Transition Totnes, Lewes and Brixton exchange 1:1 with sterling. The publicity value is excellent, but their declared aim of keeping money in the local economy is less robust. People who buy them have to spend them in local shops, which in turn have to spend them on local goods or wages, but the effect is marginal, because anyone who buys a local "pound" is likely already to have the intention of spending that money in local shops. If it does anything for the creative-inefficient sector in the locality, the benefits are indirect: people are made more aware of local producers, but it does not provide any genuine value-advantage in doing so. That is, it may nudge gently, but it has no "forcing function"—no material *incentive to support creative inefficiency, to enable it to survive.

And yet, the banknotes are beautiful, and there is a sense of local celebration about them.[205]

2. *Local Exchange Trading Schemes (LETS)*

LETS are local networks of people who supply services amongst each other in return for credits held in an account in a central computer managed by the scheme's volunteer accountant. In a sense, this is "multiple barter": buyers and sellers don't have to find someone to swap with—that is, if you want a haircut and all you have to offer is bread, you don't need to find someone looking for precisely that trade. Instead, members of a LETS scheme provide their goods and services and get a credit which they can then trade with any other member.

LETS have a genuine function in protecting the creative-inefficient. They really do succeed in making a little separate economy for some goods and services and, within that narrow range, there are no exchange rate problems to make things difficult. And they make constructive, if limited, use of credit: you can start with nothing. Their membership tends to be small. They are cumbersome, requiring a cheque and a telephone call or email to the accountant for every transaction, and they tend to focus on things which the solitary trader can provide—things like aromatherapy, child minding, bread, cakes and home-grown

vegetables in modest quantities. The Camden LETS scheme in north London summarises,

> We have over 50 members, doing gardening, giving massages, making bread, giving lifts to the shops, DIY, typing and more.[206]

LETS schemes are in essence relevant to the task, finding a market for goods and services which would otherwise have little chance of a sale. And they have the potential to mature—that is, to omit the stage of accounting for each transaction and, instead, turn the relationships they have formed into the direct *reciprocities and cooperation on which the local lean economies of the future will substantially depend. A sign that they could be at least moving in this direction is that LETS schemes tend to last.[207]

3. *Time banking*

This is a means of recording exchange without money, and it works on the same principle as LETS. The time you spend—which is measured in hours, whatever level of skill you bring to it—is logged by a time-broker, and earns you a credit, in the form of the right to receive a service in return. The time-broker in this case is the central link which (on the principle of a dating agency) joins up service providers with service-users. A variant is the exchange of credits between people and agencies, which works well because the agency is well-informed about local needs, and able to organise time bank members to work together as a group and to sustain a regular service. A farmer who wants a team to clear away undergrowth can arrange it through an agency more easily than having to identify individuals. The agency is also able to provide training and advice, and to sustain and improve standards of work (see "Paid to Learn" sidebar). Another variant is agency-to-agency time banking, allowing spare resources (meeting rooms, transport, some labour) to be shared.[208]

Time banks are an asset in places with a comparatively high rate of unemployment and only a modest inventory of skills, and which are not well enough connected to provide a natural source of information about their needs, *skills, and availabilities. This is the kind of local knowledge which was formerly supplied by the hubs of *social capital, such as church, chapel, pubs, working men's clubs, local shops, schools, *festivals and events. In a sense, the laborious brokerage of time banking which requires time to be recorded and credited can be seen as the scaffolding of a heroic attempt to rebuild community with information flows and a *culture of reciprocal obligation. It brings in people who would otherwise be socially excluded. Communities whose inheritance of social capital remains intact do not need that scaffolding; the informal links of awareness and obligation are already in place. But where that rare ideal is not present, time banks meet a need.[209]

4. *Hours*

Hours—often known as "Ithaca Hours" after the original and best-known scheme, started by Paul Glover in Ithaca, New York, in 1991—are a form of local currency that has overcome many of the limitations of the others. They are in the convenient form of notes, denominated in hours' work (2, 1, ½, ¼, ⅛ and ⅒), so there is no central computer register to update. Each Hour is considered to be worth about $10, but that would change if, for instance, inflation reduced the value of the dollar, for the Hour is firmly based on one hour's work, whatever the value of the dollar.

And they differ from Transition banknotes in another vital way. New arrivals in the scheme receive a gift of two Hours; and every eight months they receive another gift of two Hours. This is crucial, for the following reason. It makes the goods and services in the schemes just that little bit cheaper, since you get the first $20-worth free, and that means that those expensive—creative yet inefficient—goods and services discussed at the start of this entry have their moment of being distinctly more affordable. *Lean Logic*'s in-house baker actually succeeds in selling some of his outrageously expensive loaves! And since he is in the scheme, he can go off and, at a more reasonable cost, buy some of the other creative-inefficient goods that locals produce. And that in turn brings a lot of people into a network; the advantage of

---

PAID TO LEARN
When skills are not completely intuitive

The time bank in Louth in Lincolnshire is a case study in benign *unintended consequences. Jean Vernon explains: "He came to do a couple of hours' weeding. Well, I spent a couple of hours teaching him how to do it, with special emphasis on knowing how to recognise a weed. He got his credits but perhaps I should have claimed some for myself for all the teaching."[210]

The main benign consequence of time banking is that, once people have established a good working relationship, and know what they are doing, they forget about the credits. They just do it. But that's the point.

---

those free two hours wears off in due course, but by then people have been brought into the magic circle of goodwill. A person who is good at altering clothes to fit growing children, or making fruit cake, and who would not normally think of selling these goods and services, finds herself *already* in a circle of *informal local contact and solidarity. This means that, when she thinks that she might as well sell some in a small way, she is in touch with people who are ready and listening. She has access to a local directory in which other potential providers are listed, and which providers and buyers alike are motivated to consult.

This is a system that has been thought through. The brilliance is in the detail.[211]

5. *Argentina's barter currencies*

All of the above schemes have something to offer as possible ingredients in the currency of the future. And the network of local currencies that developed in Argentina in the mid-1990s may be the most significant of all, because it was formed and tested in conditions having something in common with those that lie ahead. In the previous five years, inflation had hit 5,000 percent, so the government pegged the peso to the dollar to stop it. Unemployment then started to rise towards 25 percent, and the dollar—the only trusted currency—became increasingly scarce, so it was hard to pay for anything, and the government was on its way to going bust, defaulting on its public *debt.

When money is short, clearly *barter has advantages, and Argentina's famous love affair with local currencies started in the barter arrangements at a garage sale in Buenos Aires organised by three ecologists, members of the Regional Self-Sufficiency Programme. They developed into a wide variety of currencies that were recognised at the time as the only non-toxic currency in Argentina.[212]

The possibility of a solution to the crisis began when in 2002 the Argentine government decided to de-link the peso from the dollar. The collapse in the value of the peso that followed was catastrophic, but it opened the way to recovery and relative stability. And in the meantime, the experience of local resourcefulness has changed the culture. Well-developed local markets and currencies remain in Argentina, along with a sense that the *judgment of individuals and *localities can be trusted, in contrast with the judgment of central government, which proved itself to be so flawed.[213]

This last example is where local currencies come into their own. When the national currency fails, the balance of advantage changes fundamentally. It is the local currencies that—if any—are to be *trusted. Under conditions of hyperinflation or hyperdeflation, local currencies shift up a gear to being a necessity. And if the wider economy is not functioning, there is no alternative to buying *local produce and services, even though they look expensive, relative to what you can earn in a day. When the *market economy fails, *living standards will fall hard and fast. If some inefficiently-produced, high-cost local goods are available, supported and protected by local currency, then, as in Argentina, it will be a life-saver.

Here is a local market that matters. Nationally-traded goods will be scarce, like nationally-traded currency. So locally-produced goods are likely to be bought, with locally-produced currency, because both will be within the range of local competence.

To make this point as plain as possible: the Logs discussed at the beginning of this entry failed when they interacted with pounds because there were plenty of pounds and plenty of the goods that pounds could buy. There was no real point to the local currency—or, if giving a chance to our inefficient minority of producers was a "point"—then there was certainly no serious weight behind it. People don't pay substantially higher prices for essentially similar goods for fun, or on principle—or not often, anyway. The Pound-economy was doing just fine and the Log-economy was marginal, and had to struggle to survive.

But in the future, when energy and other goods in the wider economy get scarce, pounds will get scarce too. There is a famous formula in economics which goes:

Money × Velocity = Price × Quantity
(often shortened to MV= PQ)

So, think about it: the coming shock will have the effect (for any number of reasons, but let's suppose for a moment that the reason is *energy-famine) of reducing the quantity of goods available to close to zero. What will that do? Well, quantity (Q) falls. Prices (P) may rise, but they may not, because in the depression that follows, purchasers will have minimal incomes if any. From that, as the equation shows, either (or both) money (M) and the velocity of its circulation (V) must fall, too. Bank lending will be called in; bank balances will fall, and that will force the banks to call in even more of their lending. Result: money is seriously scarce. Paralysis.

Solution: Logs. Now the local currency doesn't have to fight its corner: it is the currency of choice. In fact, it is the currency. Localities take into their hands not only the production of the goods they need, but the currency needed to buy them. When we use local currencies at present, we are *essentially* going to a lot of trouble to solve a problem we don't have. Yes, there may be some value in them in present conditions, as we have seen. But the reason it is hard to make local currencies work is that the conditions for which they are required don't yet exist. But then everything changes. The spare wheel that people carry around in their cars is a complete waste of space—and you could, if you came from Mars, spend a lot of time experimenting with ways to find a use for it. Then the car has a puncture. And the penny drops.

The time will come when the strengths of local currencies, and the reasons for their existence, will become all too clear.

*Nation 〉 Currency, False Analogy, Lean Economics, Localisation, New Domestication, Usury.

LOCAL ECONOMY, THE. See Lean Economy, Localisation.

LOCALISATION. The *political economies of the future will be essentially local. They will use locally-generated energy and local *land and materials, producing for local consumption and reusing their wastes. They will be managed—given life, competence and resilience—by the people who live there, participants, in daily touch with the local detail. Their *infrastructures will be minimal. They will have access to equipment and resources which are as advanced as possible, given the limits imposed by the local *scale and the technology of the time.[214]

The local *Lean Economy, shaped and held together by a rich, earthy mixture of *reciprocities and *culture, will be the resilient successor to the *market economy in the tasks of meeting material needs, sustaining social order and keeping the peace. If a *lean thinking, *systems-literate society is to replace the market, it will have to be in the form of *communities whose size is consistent with what can be produced without reliance on long lines of *transport, except for (where possible) specialist materials and equipment which cannot be supplied locally. There are large uncertainties here: much of the technology of self-reliance, such as solar panels, depends on equipment which may not be available on a local scale for a long time. So the meaning of "local" ranges between extremes. On the one hand there is "deep local", to the point of there being little access to sources of such industrially-produced equipment—or even materials such as steel, and tools such as drills. This would be an economy that had suffered severe damage, but it is not impossible. At the other extreme—"local lite"—the assumption is that localities will be able to obtain the supplies needed to make use of modern technology as the foundation of local self-reliance.

But, however intense the localisation, it will take time to develop. A large system (such as a centralised urban civilisation) without a *modular structure cannot simply be divided up and declared to be local. Subdivision will undoubtedly help, bringing with it with many of the key advantages of small *scale, with the *recovery-elastic resilience of modularity, but the need for hinterland remains. Small-scale ecologies only achieve the benefits of modularity if they have access to primary goods—*energy, *food, *water, *materials (and a hard-working environment that recycles their *waste).

As a shocking reminder of what "local" means, consider: At present, almost every city, town and village in the developed or part-developed world depends on daily oil-fuelled deliveries. Start with an already tightly-stretched oil market which depends on the Middle East for most of its transport fuel. Into this add the shock of an (accidental or terrorist) event that closes the Strait of Hormuz, through which the tankers laden with oil from the Middle East must pass. Those food deliveries stop . . .

What happens next depends, of course, on how deep the stoppage is, and on whether there is a *rationing system in place. But in a tightly-stretched system, the disruptive consequences of even small disturbances are intense. It is not just one disruption we are talking about here. And it's not just oil. And it's not temporary. Localisation sings against the storm. Difficult though it is, it is the remaining option capable of continuity when the supply lines needed to sustain the cities and villages of the *market economy have failed.

Localisation stands, at best, at the limits of practical possibility, but it has the decisive argument in its favour that there will be no alternative. Does that mean the end of travel? On the contrary, it means the end of mass dislocation—and the recovery of *place. Travel now finds its purpose, taking you to a place which is not in essentials identical to the one you have left, but to one that is interesting and finds you interesting, that wants to hear your song, that dances to a different tune.[215]

*Local Wisdom, Credit Union, Presence, New Domestication, Delocalisation.

LOCALISM. The principle that local *communities and local authorities should have greater control over decision-making on matters which can conveniently and effectively be implemented locally. The principle

is extended further—towards substantial local self-reliance—with *localisation.
*Subsidiarity.

LOCAL WISDOM. *Intelligence drenched in *culture. Instinctive *systems-thinking. A state of *creative tension between intellect, *emotion, *place, *encounter and *tradition.

As a general rule, governments' record of decision-making is poor. If you had a family relation whose judgment were of this quality, it would be a kindness to make arrangements for him or her to be taken into care. There are examples closer to home, but look (for instance) at Russia's governments, whose performance substantially took the form of a criminal record of horror and black farce—despite periods of remission—from Ivan the Terrible to Stalin. And this cannot quite be dismissed as an extreme case, for the combination of error and aggression by many of the governments in Europe—the "Dark Continent"—in the twentieth century and beyond belongs to the same genre.[216]

The really remarkable thing about this, however, is less the incompetence of government than the ability of the people themselves to survive it without being brutalised. Village life in Russia, as witnessed by contemporary observers such as Olga Semyonova Tian-Shanskaia (1863–1906), could undoubtedly be desperately hard for long periods, and it was not immune from the wicked, but that was not the whole of the story. It had, so far, survived the madness of Russian governments: in their villages, there was *play, *ritual and social order; there were well-tended fields; self-possessed people smile out of the photographs.[217] It is as if there were a protective membrane between the psychosis of government and the responsible maturity of the people.

The sense of peace in Tsarist Russia's local *communities as we read about them now is wonderful, despite the turbulence in the urban centres of government. That is not to say that the peace was everywhere in the country, nor uninterrupted, but there was local *empowerment, which got on with its own business. The word for the community itself was *mir*—"peace". There was a culture of joint responsibility—*krugovaya poruka*—based on consensus-building in the community's *democratic assembly. The good *judgment which can be sustained when it is located. And the word which summed up these values was *pravda*, meaning truth, but also much more; in fact, as Geoffrey Hosking explains, it meant . . .

> . . . everything the community regarded as "right": Justice, morality, God's law, behaving according to conscience. The criterion taken by the village assembly was that it must accord with pravda. Pravda was the collective wisdom of the community, accumulated over the generations. The whole of life was regarded as a struggle between *pravda* and *nepravda* or *krivda* (crookedness). Pravda was order and beauty, where the home was clean and tidy, family life was harmonious, the fields were well cultivated and the crops grew regularly. *Nepravda* was a world of disorder and ugliness, where families were riven by conflict, the home was dirty and untidy, the fields were neglected and famine reigned. The orderly world was created by God and was under the protection of the saints; the disorderly one was the province of the "unclean spirit" (*nechistaia sila*), the devil. Outside the community, officials were judged according to whether their behaviour exemplified *pravda* or not. The grand prince or tsar was assumed to embody it through his status as God's anointed: if he manifestly did not, then he must be a "false tsar" and the true one had to be found.[218]

The success of local communities in preserving their sanity despite their psychotic governments turns on their ability to insulate themselves. They sustain—or have in the past sustained—well-defended cultural *boundaries, not only between themselves and governments, but between themselves and other communities. Here are the *parishes which are the decisive *neighbourhood-containing community. In the case of the Russian *communities, a clear distinction was drawn between *my* (we) and *oni* (they); *u nas*—in our village, at our workplace, in our country—conferred the benefits of being on this side of the boundary; the judgment *on—ne nash* (he's not one of us) could close the door.[219] And yet, the bonding and distinctive identity of one community was the foundation of bridging relationships with others. Communities need each other, for *skills and *material resources they don't have, for the alliances and *conversations that keep the peace, for interesting rivalries, for potential mates—who are more interesting and less likely to be related to you if they don't live close by. For a burlesque illustration of this mixture of love of the place you live in and the play-potential with places which have the misfortune of being somewhere else—the fusion of *insult and endearment—we have Rupert Brooke's homage to his village of Grantchester:[220]

> . . . And folks in Shelford and those parts
> Have twisted lips and twisted hearts,
> And Barton men make Cockney rhymes,
> And Corton's full of nameless crimes,
> And things are done you'd not believe
> At Madingley, on Christmas Eve.
> Strong men have run for miles and miles,
> When one from Cherry Hinton smiles;
> Strong men have blanched, and shot their wives,
> Rather than send them to St. Ives;
> Strong men have cried like babes, bydam,
> To hear what happened at Babraham.
> But Grantchester! ah, Grantchester!
> There's peace and holy quiet there,
> Great clouds along pacific skies,
> And men and women with straight eyes,
> Lithe children lovelier than a dream,
> A bosky wood, a slumbrous stream,
> And little kindly winds that creep
> Round twilight corners, half asleep.
>
> Rupert Brooke, The Old Vicarage,
> Grantchester, 1912.[221]

The significance of local boundaries between the self-reliant communities of the past is not that villagers were mutually hostile, antisocial or tight with *food, but that boundaries are intrinsic to the definition of a *place. It is the *particular* place which provides the substance from which community builds its *identity as *home, along with its *ethic, its *loyalties and its way of making sense of its situation, sustaining the local wisdom which keeps it going.

LOGIC. The rules of inference and reasoning. The study of these rules is called *formal logic, to distinguish it

from other, less rigorous discussions of reasoning, such as the treatment of *informal logic in *Lean Logic*.
*Lean Thinking, Hippopotamus.

LOOTER'S ETHICS. The *ethical code of a person who is able to think about an asset only in terms of asserting rights of *access or possession.

Variant: looter's ethics by proxy, which claims that you are doing it for someone else's benefit.
*Instrumentalism, Money Fallacy.

LOYALTY. Obligation, recognised and acted upon to promote the interests of a person or a *group, even though there is no evident advantage in doing so. The important word here is "evident": loyalty may involve short-term trouble or regret, but you may be able to influence the situation and make an investment—of thought, *emotion, work or *money—with better long-term results than you could have got from an early *exit.
*Lean Economics, Trust, Humility.

LUMPY LOGIC. The use of an argument which recognises that *systems—such as social systems—tend to settle down into reasonably well-defined characteristics. For example, a *nation contains a wide variety of schools, farms, forms of local government, etc, ranging from the good to the bad; however, *generalisations about them are quite likely to be true: e.g., "Nation A's schools are generally better than Nation B's" sounds like a ridiculous generalisation but may well not be. This is because all the schools in that particular society may be subject to the same system and develop in response to it.

The idea of "lumpiness" has been suggested in, for instance, the phenomenon of the size of animals in an ecology. The ecologists C.S. Holling, Lance Gunderson and Garry Petersen suggest that the phenomenon of groups of animals in an ecology being approximately the same size contributes to the system's *resilience: if one of the species in a *size group suffers a setback of some kind, others can step in and fill the gap. This is "imbricated [overlapping] redundancy". Many *complex systems, such as languages, have—and depend on—this bounded *diversity.[222]
*Needs and Wants.

M

MANNERS. (1) The practice of *courtesy, of *encounter with the other's space and values, of tact and good *humour, of acute observation, of listening to what a person is saying and—if really necessary—even reading what he has written before disagreeing with it. Manners spill over benignly into adjacent fields, directed not only towards the other person, but to the natural environment and to oneself.

(2) The whole behaviour of people—their thought and action, the way they go about things, the defining qualities of a person's existence.

The word "manners" has an early history in the ancient Sanskrit word *manu*, meaning "thinker". In due course it came to mean "hand"—as for instance in the Latin (*manus*) and French (*main*)—because "thinking", when applied, means doing something with your hands (or getting someone else to do so).

But thinking-and-doing is what makes a person, so the same word surfaces again in "man", meaning "people", as in the Germanic (*manna*) and Alemannic (itself meaning "all [or at least a wide alliance of] tribes"). And the root of "human" is the Latin *homo* (man).

If we trace through the tangled threads of inference that make language, man and manners turn out to be the same thing: the craft of thinking.

*'Introduction' ❯ Manners, Politeness, Civility, Conversation, Encounter, Deference, Logic.

MANUAL SKILLS. The Lean Economy will depend on manual skills; not only in the form of well-developed crafts such as building, gardening and cooking but, more fundamentally, as manual dexterity—being comfortable with, and attaching a high value to, the use of hands.

Manual dexterity itself is at present at risk. Recent studies have shown that it is common for children to arrive at school not knowing whether they are right or left-handed, having no familiarity with concepts such as weight, volume and measurement, and with attention deficit problems. Failures of development such as these

are acknowledged to be to some degree indelible—as suggested, for instance, by the restaurateur who reports that she is unable to find British employees under 25 who have the dexterity to peel a potato.[1]

The reasons are well-recognised, including the inactive lives of children due to screen-addiction, which is described by the psychologist Aric Sigman as "the greatest unacknowledged public health issue of our time". Other reasons include the lack of outdoor *play, and the health and safety advice that, to reduce the fear of cot death, parents should not let infants lie on their front (from which position they learn to crawl), with the result that they do not learn left-right coordination between their arms and legs.[2]

In addition, there has been a devaluing of domestic manual skills such as cooking and sewing, which were removed from the *educational curriculum in order to prevent gender stereotyping and to make more time available for learning *competitive cutting-edge skills such as the design of takeaway pizza cartons. The possibility that cooking is also a commercial skill may have been overlooked, along with the possibility that *households in which someone can cook are more likely to stay together, saving the expense of picking up the pieces when they don't. At the same time, the cost of manual skills has risen, relative to that of other goods and services whose costs can be reduced by technical advance: the cost of (say) a dressmaker, a thatcher, or domestic service—measured against the standard basket of goods which is used as the guideline for incomes—has risen many times over in the last 100 years, so that these labour-intensive manual skills have been priced out of the market (for more on this, see *Composition).[3]

And attitudes have followed the money. As the agronomist and campaigner Vandana Shiva noted in a discussion of the need to increase the number of people working in *food production:

> We have to stop thinking of physical work as degrading.[4]

In fact, the disdain for manual skills is one of the more regrettable properties of modern society, especially in the light of its constantly-protested concern for equality. Non-manual skills (only a minority of which can be described as thinking skills) are associated with success; manual skills are associated with failure—with being only a carpenter, like Jesus. In 1853, John Ruskin observed the early divisions which led on to this:

> we want one man to be always thinking, and another to be always working, and we call one a gentleman, and the other an operative; whereas the workman ought often to be thinking, and the thinker often to be working, and both should be gentlemen, in the best sense.[5]

Lean Logic commends the sense of touch, the direct hands-on experience of sharpness, roughness, coldness, the peculiar *character of things, *Die Tücke des Objekts*. And events are catching up, for in the early years following the failure of the *market economy, the skills shortage will be fierce. This capability-lite, out-of-touch civilisation will find itself without the services of *energy and distant *expertise. It will need, in its own local habitat, some hope of the beginnings of material competence. Mastery could come later.[6]

*Cheirarchy, Practice, Tactile Deprivation, Culture, Presence, Intentional Waste.

MANY QUESTIONS, THE FALLACY OF. The tactic of wrapping up a controversial argument in an *innocent and uncontroversial one, or a question that is more innocent than the message it brings (aka a "loaded question"). It is a form of *begging the question.

Example:

> Do you, as a citizen, want a Medical Service that is planned and directed in accordance with the needs of the nation as a whole, or do you think that we had better muddle along with the present system, distorted as it is by the influence of private profit?[7]
>
> *1943 Labour Party pamphlet outlining the future Government's plans for the National Health Service*

*Disingenuousness.

MARKET ECONOMY. The economic order on which modern society depends.

The "Great Transformation" in *politics, *economics and society came when the market economy hit its stride in Britain in the late eighteenth century. Before it, *cohesion was sustained to a large extent through the *social capital of *reciprocal obligation, *loyalties, *authority structures, *culture and *traditions. The Great Transformation consisted of their replacement by market exchange, income and price, and by the impersonal principles of *economics.[8]

Around these, *cooperative arrangements can be sustained with little need for a common culture of shared values or for a practice of reciprocal obligation. The stability of the market economy can be maintained because it depends on individual self-interest, which is in abundant supply. It requires little intervention to support *networks of at least a degree of social cohesion, so it tends to protect and promote liberty. It provides suppliers with the *incentive to know their markets and respond to them; it uses *pull rather than relying on top-down regulation, and it learns from experience, so it is effective and efficient. It supports a more egalitarian society than any other large-scale state has been capable of.

But it has weaknesses. First of all, its *competitiveness, demanding ever-increasing technical innovation and productivity, sets it up as a dynamic equilibrium whose stability depends on perpetual *growth, which is an impossibility, and which will lead in due course to its destruction. Former *civic societies have also been enabled by growth: improvements in *productivity are necessary to release labour for the *intensification on which they depended—the building and maintenance of infrastructures, and the provision of *food and other primary goods over ever-greater distances and in the face of ever-diminishing returns. But only the market economy, with its *taut efficiency and pricing and its insistence on the right to life for everyone, including the unemployed (cf. *Unlean), has the unconditional commitment to convert advances in productivity into increases in output, relying on growth as a condition for its survival.

Other weaknesses, plain for many years, are now pressing. It derives its *energy from stocks of fuel which are becoming depleted. It destroys its *climate and *ecology. It depends on price signals for most of its information, but they are liable to be incomplete and too late, indicating that *radical action should have begun many years ago. It allows the growth of *population to reach levels which, in any *ecosystem, would predict a crash. It supplies goods—such as tobacco, junk food, etc—which many of its consumers want not to want. It works for insiders only; people who fall out of the system are in trouble. It can be captured: big organisations may dominate and destroy it. It develops technologies whose significance and power it cannot understand or control. It is itself such a powerful concept that it has developed a global reach: nowhere is protected from it. It sees value in terms of *money, so it thinks in *abstractions. And it tends to usurp all other values, including *social capital and the *culture which sustains it—those essentials for a *slack, non-market economy. These have now substantially atrophied, and the need for them will become pressing after the market itself fails.

And yet, when it is gone, we will miss the essential simplicity of the market, its price mechanism, its self-stabilising properties, its impersonal exchange, the comforts it delivers to many, and the freedoms it underwrites. Its failure will be destructive. It is the aim of *Lean Logic* to suggest some principles for the design of a replacement.[9]
*Big Stick, Economics, Lean Economics, Regrettable Necessities, Needs and Wants, Globalisation, Climacteric.

MATERIALS. See Lean Materials.

MATERIAL TRUTH. A representation of reality which is accurate, or at least intended literally. Material *truth is the information you need to have available to you when, for instance, crossing a road, installing a boiler, filling a tooth or building a bridge.

MEMORY FILLERS. More strictly known as "availability biases", these are gaps in what we remember, and what we know about, which we fill in confidently, but often absurdly. They are habitual failures of *logic which can distort the way in which we observe and interpret events. We may remember just those matters of public policy in which there was a clearly-established villain. Seeing a picture of a problem may make the difference between whether we think it is important or not. We may forget about, or give less significance to, big events that happened some time ago, while being deeply concerned with minor events that happened recently. We may know nothing at all about Dick except the colour of his eyes, and deduce from that that he is an engineer. On the strength of our lack of acquaintance with any judges, we may assume (on hearing that one has been caught in a drink-driving offence), that they are all at it. Not knowing what we are talking about can have the reassuring effect of making us completely *certain about it (*Innocence).[10]

The data we have available to think about—however carefully we may do the thinking—can consist of a scrapheap of things which are weird enough, or simply recent enough, for us actually to remember them.
*Cognitive Dissonance, Mindset, Personal Experience, Lumpy Logic, Rote, False Premise.

METAMORPHOSIS. A metaphor for the transformation that overcomes people when they surrender their *judgment to a group, to a managerial *institution, to a complex bureaucracy, or to a government, as the price of belonging to it. For example, the ten-year-plus period of intense learning required in order to be able to cope with the detail, *diplomacy and *boredom of negotiating trade agreements with the World Trade Organisation and the European Union makes it unlikely that anyone who has achieved *expertise in it will question the aims of the organisations involved, or the essential assumptions of sustained *growth and *globalisation.

There is uncritical commitment to the aims of the institution; the person ceases to think as a free agent; her approach to a problem is not directed to understanding it, but to dealing with it in ways which reflect the institution's values.

The pressure to do so is strong. It might be better for everyone else that some institutions—a government, for instance—should do nothing other than benignly watch the world go about its business, except that most institutions that did this would quickly fall apart, because they derive their *identity and their claim for funds from what they do. They need a mission. Gross absurdities of *ideology can be pursued, energetically, ruthlessly, coldly and with a straight face by the individual member, because, locked in institutional capture, her speech and action reflect the corporate will. She has become a different animal.

And the matter is more critical when the institution involved is the urban institution itself. Urban society, in its inheritance and its deep character, is a machine driven by the coordinated action of its inhabitants. In the very earliest days of urban history, when the majority of even elementary technologies, such as pulleys, were still to be invented, the work of the city would have had to be minutely organised, not only by a top-down *authority, but by a

thick, all-penetrating sense of coordination, almost like a flock of birds that moves and shifts direction with simultaneous single-mindedness (*Unclean). Institutional belonging in that sense has weakened, but it has never gone away.

For medieval European towns and villages it was as much as they could do—and often more than they could do—to invent and sustain ways of keeping large numbers of people fed, watered and sheltered in one place; they were in many ways still rooted in the land, deeply aware of practical considerations of harvest and season. The modern urban state, by contrast, has much greater *freedom: urban impulse is insulated from rural causes and consequences; the time-lag between decision and consequence is long. Bad *logic can flourish; there is little or no quick, sanity-saving, *feedback. The modern urban-everywhere-institution—it spread its roots and its immune responses deep into the countryside long ago—has been able to impose its will at leisure.

So you don't need an interview to belong to an institution. You are already in one. If you are very lucky, you may spend some of your life groping and inventing your own way forward, but your escape from the institution may happen only on days off. It is the institutionalisation that presents itself as real life, and it may employ so much of the personality that the real person closes down.

And this means that the bureaucratic *economy seems to bring with it a particular and most remarkable occupational hazard, metamorphosis: "Candidates should be advised that they may find themselves turning into a golden ass, a wolf of the steppes, a crustacean, a cockroach or a rhinoceros. The employers regret any inconvenience that may be caused, but cannot be held

responsible." Metamorphosis seems almost routine in Western literature: the gods of Greece and Rome regularly change their victims into animals of various kinds; princes become frogs in the fairy tales, and there are variations on the theme of change and mistaken identity in the *Old Testament*, the *New Testament*, in the *Pygmalion* legend, *The Odyssey, Midsummer Night's Dream, The Ring, Swan Lake*. . . . Many of these cases of metamorphosis, despite their alarming symptoms, are relatively mild: the person takes a bit of time to discover, or to reveal, who he or she really is, and when the revelation happens, there is resolution and rejoicing. The metamorphoses of our own time, however—notably Kafka's disturbing story of Gregory turning into a giant and anguished cockroach, and Ionesco's story of *everyone else* turning into a rhinoceros—are not so sunny. Here we have, not a revelatory transition into becoming the person you really are, but deep burial inside an animal not noted for its independent thinking. The part of you that consists of a free agent with independent critical judgment ceases to exist.[11]

So, how do you cope? The French philosopher-novelist André Gide gives us a guideline—the opposite to the one he intended. For him, going along with what he saw as institutions built on *hypocrisy—such as the family or the state—is a case of *self-deception, a *deception no better than counterfeiting money: "Don't worry about appearances", he wrote, "what is important is *being*"—which, he notes, requires sincerity. But that does not take us much further, for you can quite easily be sincere about the role you are already in. Indeed, you will need to be, because otherwise it would be hard to fulfil it, least of all in a senior position. That is institutional capture for you: like the builders of the Bridge over the River Kwai, you embrace the role that has been thrust on you: *sincerity is about learning to love the cell into which you have been locked. And, once established, it is powerful: if you believe something, and if you are sincere about it, then that is all you need to know; sincerity itself is its own quality control, the entire justification for practically *any* view on practically *anything*.[12]

M.

But here we also have a clue to recovery from the dream world in which ideologies, *fallacies and sincerity give uneasy symbolic reality to whatever *idol or graven image happens along. What we need is at least *something* that stays still. *Identity is this fixed point; that which says that you are *you*. But it cannot do this if you are captured by an institution, or if you have institutionalised yourself as an intellectual or *expert. What gives identity roots and holds it still as *you* is *encounter*, the act of recognising something—a person, a *practice, a thing, the *spirit of a *place—on its own terms. And to do that, in turn, requires the world of real people and real places, with their own *traditions and *narratives. These are precisely the conventions, *manners, *institutions and *families that Gide railed against: the particular circumstances of a particular stock of *social capital belonging to particular people in particular places . . .

Still life at last. From particularity—from living its own particular *story and encountering those of others—identity derives roots. If its identity is constant, there is a real, wide awake chance that a place and its people may learn to cope. So it is possible to avoid metamorphosis; to bravely avoid, that is, starting a new, secure and pensionable career as a rhinoceros.
*Second Nature, Character, Calibration, Humility, Reformer Fallacy, Hippopotamus.

METAPHOR, THE FALLACY OF. Metaphor is part of communication, and it can have a useful function in communicating all forms of *truth, but it is easily open to abuse. If you don't know what you're talking about, the simple solution is to slip into metaphor:

> The 'easy oil' will run out in about 15 years' time. Companies will then have to mine some trickier and costlier waters. [13]

The thinking is as mixed as the metaphor itself, and yet it still sounds reassuring. The fact that the writer does not have a clue what those trickier and costlier waters are can be overlooked when the mind's eye is taken up with image of wave-lashed oil workers faithfully carrying out their task. The reader is reassured by their dedication. It is usually harder to free an argument from entanglement in a bad metaphor or *false analogy than to argue the case itself.
*Implicature.

MIDDLE VOICE. Verbs in English take either the active voice (I love) or passive voice (I am loved). Many other languages, including Classical Greek, have a "middle voice" which is half way between the two, and has properties of both.

This is a useful idea in the context of the Lean Economy, because it has special relevance to key principles such as *presence and *practice. A securely-developed skill is neither entirely voluntary nor entirely involuntary; there is a middle ground, intrinsic to *skills—both responsive to the will of the craftsman and shaped by the practised technique, both active and passive. This middle voice applies, for instance, to *dance—in part active participation; in part passive, with the person being swept up in it. The dancer, *encountering a skill, both grasps it and is grasped by it—or, to use the philosopher Alfred North Whitehead's word for it, she "prehends" it.[14]

And the same applies to a person's dedication of her skill to the making and sustaining of *community. It is neither voluntary nor involuntary. There is interconnected *intention and practice. Like a brain.
*Modularity, Complexity.

MINDSET. The frame of reference which guides our perception. It shapes our minds and the *logic they recognise. It *calibrates our evaluation of good and bad; it is the *paradigm in terms of which we think we understand something, or assert it to be *self-evident.

Freedom from control by the mindset is rare. Perhaps it doesn't exist. But this is by no means always a bad thing, since it provides the frame of reference needed to form a *judgment. Here are two examples of mindset in action. One comes from the most rigorous and *objective of sciences. The other comes from a man who needed a smoke.

Superstring theory, if correct, would get close to providing physics with its "unified theory"—linking up our understanding of gravity, matter and quantum mechanics with an explanation of the existence of the universe. It was developed by John Schwarz and Michael Green in 1984, and initially it seemed that it might achieve this without having to live with *anomalies which, for a theory in physics, would appear to disprove it. It is a complex theory, requiring ten dimensions (the three dimensions of space, one of time, and six others), but it flashed through the scientific community at the speed of FedEx (there was no email at that time) and remained the dominant paradigm for twenty years. However, it remained at the level of conjecture; observations that pointed in another direction were—as the physicist, Lee Smolin, writes—"ignored because, if confirmed, they would be inconvenient for our theorising". Careers were sucked into this mindset; other points of view and careers had a hard time overcoming it. At the end of such a process, as Smolin observes, "You have little more than you started with: a beautiful picture on the jacket of a book you can never open."[15]

There is nothing wrong with a widely shared focus of *interest on a theory as interesting as Superstrings. The problem arises when "widely shared" matures to an orthodox mindset which is intolerant of any other interest which seriously challenges it, or which is moving in a radically different direction—especially if that intolerance means that tenure and research grants are unavailable to potential challengers. But there may be a deep instinct here: mindsets are home territory, to be defended at all costs. Heresy can be silenced by the denial of a job, research facilities or publication unless (like Charles Darwin, or Miriam Rothschild, the pioneering authority on flower meadows) you have private means, or (like the scientist Rupert Sheldrake) you can write bestsellers, or (like the *organic movement and critics of *biotechnology in *agriculture) you are prepared to plod on, insecure and borderline broke, for generations, or (like the *oil heretic Colin Campbell, and the *population heretic William Stanton) you are retired.

The smoker's story comes from Antoine de Saint-Exupéry. He was a journalist in the Spanish civil war, and had been arrested by anarchist militia for watching the loading of goods onto a truck at three o'clock in the morning. He was taken to a basement . . .

From *Letter to a Hostage*

My captors handed round my camera as evidence to convict me. Some of those who were yawning, lounging on their rickety chairs, stood up with a bored expression, and propped themselves against the wall.

For the dominant impression was that of boredom. Boredom and sleep. The power of concentration of these men seemed to be exhausted. I almost wished for a sign of hostility, as a human contact. But they did not grant me any sign of anger, not even of reprobation. Several times I attempted to protest in Spanish, but my protestations came to naught. They gazed at me without any reaction, as if they were looking at a Chinese fish in an aquarium.

They were waiting. What were they waiting for? The return of a companion? The dawn? I thought: "Perhaps they are waiting for hunger". I also thought: "They are going to do a silly thing. It is absolutely ridiculous . . ." My feeling then, more than anguish, was a disgust of absurdity. I thought: "If they wake up, if they want to act, they will shoot!"

Was I really in danger? Did they still ignore the fact that I was neither a saboteur nor a spy, but a journalist? That my identity papers were at the hotel? Had they made a decision, and if so, which one?

Then the miracle happened. Oh! a very discreet miracle. I had no cigarette. As one of my guards was smoking, I asked him, by gesture, showing the vestige of a smile, if he would give me one. The man first stretched himself, slowly passed his hand across his brow, raised his eyes, no longer to my tie, but to my face, and, to my great astonishment, he also attempted a smile. It was the dawning of the day.

This miracle did not conclude the tragedy; it removed it altogether, as light does shadow. There had been no tragedy. This miracle altered nothing visible. The feeble oil lamp, the table scattered with papers, the men propped against the wall, the colours, the smell, everything remained unchanged. Yet everything was transformed in its very substance. That smile saved me. [. . .]

Nothing yet had been said. Yet everything was resolved. To thank him, I laid my hand upon his shoulder, as he gave me the cigarette. And now that the ice was broken, the rest of the militia also became human, and I entered into their smiles, as into a new and free country.[16]

*Calibration, Different Premises, False Inference, Humility.

M

Misplaced Concreteness. The error of inter-preting an economic model, representing a simplified version of reality, as if it were real life. For example, neoclassical *economics has a tendency to reduce com-plex ideas down to a level at which they can be fitted into equations. There is nothing necessarily wrong with that, so long as the conclusions drawn from the equations are recognised as only cartoons, or sketches of parts of the whole picture, and as true only under particular assumptions. The Fallacy of Misplaced Con-creteness occurs when these models are taken literally, and interpreted as the whole reality.[17]

Reductio ad Absurdum, Galley Skills, Metaphor, Reductionism.

Moderation, The Appeal to. The presump-tion that moderate ends can always be obtained by moderate means. But, as the sixteenth century French thinker, François Rabelais, warns us—don't count on it. He valued, perhaps above all else, *médiocrité*—which means neither mediocrity nor moderation, but "reason-able tranquillity", and he warned that the achievement of tranquil ends may well require means which include *fortitude, along with action that is anything but moderate. One of Rabelais' characters gives advice on the defence of tranquil space against the fanatics and authoritarians that would invade it:

> Burn them, nip them with pincers, slash them, drown them, hang them, impale them, break them, dismember them, disembowel them, hack them, fry them, grill them, cut them up, crucify them, boil them, crush them, quarter them, wrench their joints, rack them and roast them alive . . .[18]

But surely such behaviour is to be avoided if at all possible? As the Czech thinker of our own day, Nadia Johanisova, writes,

> There is no doubt that violence may be necessary. We should have defended ourselves against Hitler in 1938. On the other hand, in this country we have sad experience of immoderate means (torture, execution, imprisonment, being expelled from the country, job, university, etc) being taken to defend laudable ends (equality

between classes, employment for all, free education, an idea of Communism which some believed) and I would be very careful to suggest any form of extremism.[19]

Johanisova is right of course; when thinking about this subject, it is impossible to avoid playing with fire. The brutality that she reminds us of was in no way a defence of reasonable tranquillity—that is, of *civility. It was an exact expression of what happens when those defences break down. Yet civility and *médiocrité* do not come free. Moderate *defence is no defence.

*Calibration, Frankness.

Modularity. A modular system is one whose essentially similar parts, subassemblies or *holons have substantial self-reliance and independence. Modular-ity is intrinsic to *resilience and is the counterpart of *complexity (for modular systems in context with the four types of system discussed in *Lean Logic*, see the summary table in *Systems Thinking on page 450).

Its three critical properties are:

1. dispersal (weak interdependence between its parts, which prevents a shock rippling through the whole system);
2. flexibility (the substantial *freedom of parts to act in *diverse ways in their own and/or the system's interests); and
3. small scale of its parts (conferring the benefits of *elegance, *judgment and *presence).

Modularity gives the parts of a system the critical qual-ity of *recovery-elastic resilience, but a modular system does have limitations. Its weak interdependence means that it lacks the *connected brilliance of a complex sys-tem—even if the independent *holons that it is made up of are themselves complex systems. For example, *com-munities, being less complex than their members, find it hard to match their members' intelligence; likewise, groups of communities, being more modular than the communities which are their members, are no match for the intelligence of the communities they represent.

It is a common experience for *intelligent people to be dismayed at the obtuseness of the community they live in, or for communities to be dismayed at the obtuseness of government. This is not always because the man and woman in the pub think they can run the country better, nor because collective policy has to be agreed with those with least perceptiveness as well as those with most. It is because the modular system is intrinsically incapable of complex strategy. Its lack of connectedness, left to itself, leaves it stupid. It is capable, like a herd of antelopes, of doing simple-minded things like running away. And it can, crucially, do the most vital thing of all—act as the stable, non-interventionist but supportive *setting* for diversity, brilliance, learning, *politics, freedom, elegance, elasticity and recovery. It gives the complex systems that comprise it (the creatures that live there), the freedom to develop their potential. But it cannot *itself* sustain a complex idea and make complex connections, nor can it carry out a complex policy . . .

. . . *unless*, that is, it evolves *incrementally into an 'as-if complex' system (what *Lean Logic* terms a "complicated system"). This is clearly a tricky idea, even by the standards of the clutch of ideas surrounding resilience, complexity and modularity. The argument, as fleshed out in the entry on *complexity, goes roughly like this:

> A modular system can be shoe-horned into
> a form of 'as-if complexity' by an ambitious
> process of *intensification, with specialisation,
> division of labour and increased *connected-
> ness. Parts which were formerly self-reliant
> become dedicated providers of one thing to
> the wider system (and importers of everything
> else); despite their weak *diversity of form,
> they take on a wide variety of functions. A
> drift into *complication can end the quiet life
> of a modular system, launching it on the path
> towards a spectacular future (though maybe
> also a short one).

Modular systems, then, given time, can sometimes develop an 'as-if complexity' of their own—brains are not the only things that are capable of *intelligence. As Steven Johnson writes, an ant colony has . . .

> . . . collective intelligence. . . . Ten thousand
> ants, each limited to a meagre vocabulary
> of pheromones and minimal cognitive
> skills—collectively engage in nuanced and

improvisational problem-solving. . . . There is decentralised intelligence.[20]

That is, it has some of the properties of a brain. The *common purpose establishes the connections; and the serial interactions among those connections produce a collective intelligence which is closely attuned to the purpose. If deeply engaged people can think in the same way, their group may begin to acquire some of the *connectedness and competence of a complex system. For examples, we can look to groups such as the dedicated Little Sisters of Mercy, whose shared lives are based on the common purpose of caring for their patients, or the circle of scientists, natural philosophers, engineers and entrepreneurs who met regularly for "philosophical feasts" in London and the Midlands of the UK in the late eighteenth century (known as the Lunar Society). The story is taken up by one of the "Lunarticks"—as they called themselves—the inventor Richard Edgeworth:

> Arguments were fierce and fools were jeered,
> but as the knowledge of each member of such a
> society becomes in time disseminated through
> the whole body, so the talents of numbers could
> forward the ideas of a single person.[21]

And the historian Lisa Jardine, speaking of the early years of The Royal Society, develops this . . .

> The really defining quality of a group like the
> Royal Society is that they can bounce ideas off
> each other. Very few people make enormous
> change; it's groups together that do that. The
> isolated great man may light the touch-paper
> but it's the group. And that's true even with
> Newton. The great man isolated in his ivory
> tower can do the mathematics. That's lighting
> the touch-paper. Expanding that into the
> Inverse Square Law and the laws of gravity—
> that takes a group.[22]

A system or *community whose interdependencies or shared *culture are too weak will not achieve that; and nor will top-down decision-making that does not recognise its *holons as being competent at all. But a degree of interconnectedness within even a

M

and towards the other, the strong modularity (and *recovery-elastic resilience) of a herd of antelopes.

Complexity provides good *judgment; modularity makes the space for it to act on that judgment. And the union of opposites—complex parts within a wider modular system—gives us more than resilience. It gives us the brilliance of the *ecological system, capable of containing and supporting such *taut, *elegant systems as the nightingale. Complexity is the fine delight that fathers thought; modularity leaves yet the mind a mother of immortal song.[24]

*Nation, TEQs (Tradable Energy Quotas), Butterfly Effect, Resilience ❭ Resilient Systems.

modular system can confer the ability to think—the development, in some senses, of a collective mind.[23]

Now for the twist: if the wider group or society becomes more *complicated, *connected and closely-coupled, the holons or parts of that system may find that their own complexity *declines*. The complexity of the whole is predatory on the complexity of its parts. It is jealous of their competence. For example, consider a network of complex, self-reliant villages. If the complexity of each village, consisting of diverse, interdependent parts, remains intact, then they are relatively unlikely to be compliant to the demands of a higher-level complex system to which they in turn belong (*Character). There is in these circumstances a trade-off: increased complexity of the whole comes at the cost of decreased complexity of the parts. The (ultimately fatal) weakness that destroys the resilience of a tightly-coupled, rigid, *large-scale system arises as much from the weakened complexity of its deskilled, fragmented parts as from the increased connectedness—the brittle inflexibility—of the system as a whole.

To take it to the extreme, chaos is perfect modularity, zero complexity—perfectly resilient in the sense of being indestructible, since there is no order there in the first place; nothing to destroy. At the other extreme—zero modularity, full complexity—a system is so tightly connected up that it is unable to function at all, and quickly destroys itself. Between the two we find, not the *edge of chaos—that thin line of complexity and meaning—but a spectrum. Towards one end of that spectrum we find the strong complexity (and *preventive resilience) of, for instance, the antelope,

MONEY, THE FALLACY OF (*Argumentum ad crumenam*). The *fallacy that money speaks the *truth, that it is the unchallengeable basis for *judgment, and that argument can be reduced to financial calculation.

Money in the form of coins was invented by the Greeks in the seventh century BC (see "Money" sidebar), and the implications of this innovation were profound. A society without money has to organise all its exchanges and *reciprocities in other ways. In fact, there are three ways of doing it, only the first of which is benign:

1. *Community*. Here we have a network of duty, *loyalty, belonging, love, *gifts and cooperation within the *family and the locality—relationships of *reciprocal obligation and mutual dependence which come together to build a texture of *common purpose. The distribution of goods and services is integrated into the tissue of social interdependence. Deals are not closed with the payment of an invoice, and the network of open-ended, unsettled obligation joins people together and sustains the social order.[25]

2. *Contest*. This means of distribution and reciprocity without money is what remains after the failure of a state. There is no money; there is no settled community; there is *violence, *fear, uncompromising power and control. Tightly-knit groups, rivalries and chance do not underpin anything that

MONEY
What do you mean by that?

Exchange was taking place long before the invention of money in the form of coins, with slaves, sheep, tools (spades, hoes, knives and fire-spits) and ingots—or at least lumps—of precious metal changing hands. The Chinese were using coins in the twelfth century BC, but they were made of base metal, which limited their use, in effect, to small change. Precious metals began to be used in China as late as 1890.[26]

The evolution to coins was gradual, but the decisive step came in about 610 BC. Both Lydia (part of modern Turkey) and Ionia (Greece) took part in this, and they were in touch by sea. It was probably Lydia that made the breakthrough, but Greece that—by using coinage as their main medium of exchange—changed the way civilisation works.[27]

The classical scholar Richard Seaford gives us some guidelines for clarity on what money is. An exchange medium is money if and only if the following conditions are met, (1) its value lies in its ability to meet social obligations rather than as something for which there is a practical use; (2) it is easily quantified (counted in convenient units); (3) it is a measure of value, so that it enables (for instance) the value of a purchased good to be accurately represented if payment is made at a later date; (4) it has general acceptability as a means of exchange, and (5) that general acceptability applies exclusively to money; (6) there is *fiduciarity*—that is, collective confidence in the money, beyond its physical value (e.g., as a quantity of silver); (7) the state may be involved in its supply.[28]

He concludes: "The pivotal position of the Greeks in world culture stems largely from the fact that the sixth century polis was the first society in history (with the conceivable exception of China) to be pervaded by money. Coinage was invented towards the end of the seventh century BC, and spread rapidly in the Greek city-states from the beginning of the sixth. Did not the Babylonians, for instance, use silver as money well before that? On any sensibly narrow definition of money, no they did not."[29]

M

is permanent or attractive, but they are the default position when all else has failed. It is possible, over time, that they can learn, recover and establish a legal or *cultural framework for the recognition of rights and *contracts, but here and now—for a long first phase—we have grief mitigated only by proof that, when things are life-and-death critical, it is possible to get by without money.

3. *Autocracy*. A society that is organised around absolute control over what its people do has no use for money as a means of giving material expression to individual *choice. As the historian Glyn Davies summarises:

> The greater the stratification of society and the more efficiently meticulous the planning system, the less necessary is it for people to use money.[30]

We meet some extremely autocratic regimes in *Unlean, and one of the uses to which the

authorities put their power in these regimes is the construction of supergiant projects such as the Grand Canal in China and the Pyramids in Egypt. There is no freely entered *contract, no agreement on wages, in *political economies such as these.

Our word for the labour contract in such autocracies would normally be "slavery", but not all unpaid work is slavery; the "informal economy", which includes working without pay in one's own *household, in voluntary organisations, in the community or as an intern for work experience, are not forms of slavery. On the other hand, working in an autocratic economy and receiving no income from any source because money has not yet been invented is slavery, but in a special sense for which we have no word. "Moneyless employment" sounds like a terrible euphemism, but maybe it will have to do. In a pre-monetary society, all obligations—wherever they fell between the extremes of voluntary/benign and enforced/cruel—belonged somewhere in this range between local-family loyalties and control by the absolute power of the state.

So, a moneyless economy may or may not mean a profound absence of *freedom, but as a means of maintaining *resilient freedom under changing conditions, the effectiveness of money in the setting of a *market economy has been proved. That does not diminish the central importance of the *informal economy of mutual aid that to some extent we still have—not least in our own homes, in our communities and among our friends—nor the case argued by *Lean Logic* for substantially informal, moneyless community as the model for human society with a long-term future. But it is a reminder to do nothing to dismantle the money-based market economy before, all too soon, it starts to disintegrate of its own accord.

Let us now go back to the first of the three forms of moneyless economy, that of benign reciprocity. Ancient Greece was in many ways an authoritarian society, and its work was done on the basis of moneyless employment. But Greece did also develop a strong concept of citizenship. Its *politics varied, and it went through some bad times but, basically, it was not an obedience-based, power-based autocracy. It recognised the shared rights and obligations of citizenship and *conversation. It devised its own *democracy on several occasions. It had a rich *mythology. It produced scientists and philosophers of enduring world standing. The *network of obligations that enabled it to exist as a *complex society was based on a mixture of duties and *loyalties, involuntary and voluntary, intended and unintended, oppressive and relaxed.

Then—rather suddenly, and as an event outside anyone's experience—came the new development: money. Exchange would now be impersonal. Transactions—the supply of goods and services—were concluded when the payment was made, with no remaining sense of obligation. This is a convenient system, but it can be lonely, and we see the early shock of discovery of this new loneliness in the Athenian theatre of the time. Rules about unconditional obligations towards kin, and between subjects and rulers, seemed suddenly to vanish, and Greek tragedy explored the implications: the

breakdown of relations; incest and murder within families. Money became *the* value, 'the bottom line'; it put the grim into reality. We see this being recognised in the first decades after money's establishment: the *Theognidea*, an anthology of elegiac poetry noted, with regret, that . . .

> For the mass of humankind, the only virtue is money, compared to which self-control, knowledge, rhetoric, speed of foot are of no account. [Here we have] the power of money to displace all other values.[31]

Greek myth drew a moral from all this: spontaneity and money do not mix. Money makes you plan ahead. Midas, for example, is pleased to discover that everything he touches turns to gold—until he realises that this includes his food. Erysichthon, as a punishment for cutting down a sacred grove to build a banqueting hall, has the curse of insatiability placed upon him; after eating everything in sight, he eats himself. And money disempowers by weakening and, in places, ripping up, the network of connections by which we recognise each other, and which keeps us sane. It gears up error: if you make a mistake *and* there is money involved, you will be in big trouble.[32]

In fact, there have been long periods since its invention when the significance of money has been relatively subdued. Greece learned to live with it, to a considerable extent; and in the English medieval period, though it was by no means a money-free economy, most of the transactions of daily living were based on kinship and loyalties, on payments in kind (e.g., contributions of labour, or a share of the harvest), on the obligations of *common ownership, or on the duress—which could be harsh—of many forms of land tenure. Later on, the change brought by the Industrial Revolution was a slow process of the erosion of all other values by the market's single convenient *abstraction—money. But it was not the lurking existence of money that was the root of the trouble; rather, it was the market's dominance which allowed money to become the core value—the unit in terms of which *ethics became substantially defined.

In the mature market, it is taken to be *self-evident, despite some hard-fought exceptions, that money and prices are an accurate, if incomplete, *calibration of ethics. Rising incomes are taken to be a reliable sign of rising *living standards and *well-being; the life of a *traditional people can sometimes, carelessly, be taken to be benighted because their incomes do not register on the scale of money; equality of income and wealth is a core political aspiration; carbon trading can be judged a success because of the wealth that comes from it; the case for *genetically modified food crops is borne out by the wealth of the industry.[33]

Money can bring numerous benefits, such as security, power, food, housing, music—and freedom, when combined with *institutions such as *democracy. These are tasks for which the record of other models of large-scale social order is poor. But when money emerges as the unchallenged value, there is vacancy. Money does not love, or remember, or tell *stories; it does not care, recognise you or lick your face. It confers power, for good or bad, but in itself it is empty of meaning, and values and philosophy that are based on it are empty, too.

If money is the only criterion for justice, the only justice is equality, but at a time when the convergence of *economic, environmental, *energy and social problems threatens to destroy us, there may be larger aims—such as mitigating the crash, or recognising the human *ecology as a *complex system, or the defence of *freedom, or maintaining human ecologies on the *small scale which makes them possible. Such aims might not only take priority over an egalitarian distribution of money; they could be impaired or even blocked by it.

In fact, as Richard Wilkinson and Kate Pickett show in *The Spirit Level*, equality can indeed help to procure the conditions for many of the properties which we would recognise as essential for a decent life: mental and physical *health, and low levels of crime, drug-dependence and obesity. But they do not show that it is equality itself that does it—the connection that matters is not that between equality and well-being, but a more nuanced and well-established link from *social capital and *community to well-being; and equality may take its place there as a property of community.[34]

To see this, we need to be clear what scale of community we are talking about, for it is possible for a community with equality to exist in a *nation in which there is inequality. For example, English villages for a millennium or so enjoyed, in varying degrees, cooperation, *reciprocity, social capital and *trust, making the best of their equality of disadvantage, relative to those on whose manorial estates they lived. Some were too paralysed by poverty to do any such thing but, in the case of those that did build social capital, it is not evident how much, if at all, this was impaired by the existence of inequality within the nation as a whole. And Wilkinson and Pickett cite the example of the Chicago heatwave in 1995, where two communities with different degrees of social capital and trust responded in very different ways: African-American communities, with low trust and high levels of crime, were too frightened to open their windows or doors, or to leave their homes to go to local cooling centres and—since *neighbours did not check on neighbours—hundreds died, whereas . . .

> . . . in equally poor Hispanic neighbourhoods, characterised by high levels of trust and active community life, the risk of death was much lower.[35]

In a modern nation, in which local *holonic community is weak, equality is, by default, measured on a large, nationwide *scale. There is almost no such thing as a self-contained community, significantly distinct from the rest, and able to use the benefits conferred by its local equality and social capital to the full, despite inequalities at the national level (*Local Wisdom). In this context, Wilkinson and Pickett's evaluation of equality at a national level makes sense: here, the loss of community has led to intensive *competition for relative advantage: now you have to look after yourself, for the community isn't going to do it for you. The failure of social capital and community exposes people formerly protected by community—with its common destinies and equalities—to the inequalities endemic in the nation. And that means that failing to achieve equality or relative advantage is a much tougher and more miserable state than it would be if strong community still existed. So the cause-and-effect is from the loss of *social capital and *community to the loss of well-being; inequality and its resentments are symptoms.

But the usefulness of this *nationwide perspective is, in a sense, a special case. It is only helpful when studying industrial societies where strong communities of equality-within-inequality have declined, along with the overall decline of social capital. Where the complex

M

layers and deep structures of other societies' local communities and local equalities are taken into account, it
turns out that inequality at the national level can coexist
with community, social capital and trust.

The poverty—in *food, *water, shelter, liberty, money
and opportunity—of some half the *population of the
world is extreme, indefensible, and dangerous for all of
us. Nonetheless, "equality" has acquired the standing
of an *abstract good, the commonplace *ethic of progressive first world politics for which it is equality as
a monetary value—rather than *empowerment, social
capital and a future—that dominates. In that context,
equality and *well-being do not converge. The idea
that they do, and that money has the solution, is a *self-
evident, often paralysing *ideology that leaves a trail of
tears. Writing as someone who has done more to enrich
lives than any mere philosopher, and who knows how
essential *imagination and focus (*lean means) are to
getting results, Andrew Mawson does not recognise
such presumptions as helpful. He writes that they . . .

> . . . bedevil real change in the public sector and
> threaten to destroy initiative and enterprise.
> My experience . . . suggests that admitting the
> world is fundamentally unfair and unequal—
> but full of glorious diversity—is ironically the
> first step to simulating greater participation, a
> widening of opportunity for all and an increase
> in wealth creation. . . .
>
> Anyone who wants to know what [the
> overriding objective of] equality means in
> practice has only to look around the poor-quality
> housing on our estates to know just how unjust
> this thinking is. Here everything is fair and
> equal—equally mediocre.[36]

It is when people are able to take their minds off the
equality problem and the resentments it builds that a
sense of *trust can be created, and *social capital developed. Then we can . . .

> . . . grow a strong and honest sense of belonging
> and community, focused around a shared
> practical task.[37]

Money's distant, impartial measurements take the
pressure off having to be *present, as the Greeks

discovered to their dismay. The age of *economics is in
awe of money, and deferential towards it, as are some
of the liberal critics who have grown up in it. Despite
priding itself on its truculent lack of *deference in any
of its forms, the *market economy defers to money
as the real value, the bottom line, that everyone can
believe in. Deference crowds in with every sweep of the
broom intended to get rid of it. This dominant, *expert,
sycophantic, infantile vision, seeing only monetary
value, and full of *certainty that it is *true, eats its way
through the human *ecology.

*Economism, Dollar-a-Day Fallacy, Empowerment,
Nation, Local Currency.

MONITORING. It is justifiable to treat claims of
"monitoring" with some *scepticism—in *politics they
are commonly used as a pretence that action will, if
necessary, be taken (to solve a problem on which it
has already been decided that nothing will be done, or
which is already out of control).

But in a managed *ecosystem—notably a *closed-
access *commons—monitoring in the sense of frequent
*presence and assessment is fundamental. A well-
managed fishery such as that of Iceland is monitored
constantly, and fishing decisions are made on the basis of
this. Joy Measures, an *organic Hereford beef farmer in
Shropshire, visits her animals and chats to them at least
twice a day. The reindeer herders in the far north of Fin-
land monitor their herds and the weather in fine detail,
reading the night sky for guidance on the decisions of
travelling and fishing. The *permaculturist Martin Crawford wanders through his forest garden, often.

Here is the sharp *feedback of *resilience. Monitoring
is an *ethic at the heart of *lean thinking: it is not about
calculating but about being there.

*Harmless Lunatic, Food Prospects, TEQs (Tradable
Energy Quotas).

MUDA. A Japanese term used in the context of *lean
production and *lean thinking, meaning any activity
that consumes resources but creates no *value. Type
1 *muda* consists of activities which create no value
but which are, at present and for practical purposes,
unavoidable, such as issuing invoices. Type 2 consists
of activities which do not have a useful function: they

just happen, and things would go better without them. It is on this kind of *muda* that the attention of lean thinking is focused, and it comes in many forms:[38]

1. Mistakes and defects in products: the time and cost of making them and repairing them.
2. Excess production: producing goods which end up unsold.
3. Inventory: producing goods and parts which then sit for a long time in a warehouse.
4. Unnecessary processing, or steps in the process.
5. Unnecessary actions to carry out a process.
6. Unnecessary movement and transport of goods and parts.
7. Waiting time: standing around waiting for parts to be delivered.
8. Specification: production of goods and services which are not what the customer wants.
9. Job description: a task being left undone because it is not in the person's job description.
10. Obtuseness: a job being left undone because the person is not paid to think.
11. Signal failure: a culture which provides no motivation for success, or in which the *incentive structure (contrary to *intention) is set to reward inaction and failure.
12. An enterprise built on a foundation of blather.

You can probably think of more, or at least variants, such as bad communication, *demoralisation, effort diverted into appeasing litigious customers or an interventionist government, and loss of local control over critical decisions. However they are *defined, it turns out that the greater part of the work of *institutions (such as *health, *education and policing services) consists of tasks other than what they are there to do. Their effort is sucked into sequences of *muda*—making errors, being drawn into an extended series of errors when trying to correct them, maintaining structures of *control and recordkeeping, decision-seeking, standardised procedures, waiting, inflexible job definitions—and a prohibition of discretion and *judgment. The scale of *muda* in an organisation is indicated by the scale of the savings that can be achieved when it is removed.

Its removal can . . .

. . . double labor productivity all the way through the system. . . . If you can't quickly take throughput times down by half in product development, 75 percent in order processing, and 90 percent in physical production you are doing something wrong.

James Womack and Daniel Jones, Lean Thinking.[39]

The existence of *waste of this magnitude suggests that, in the settled, resilient economy of the future, *travelling light—living within a dramatically reduced scale of *intermediate economy—is a realistic option. With lean thinking in place, and *muda* purged, the effectiveness of local economies in the future could exceed *expectations and form the basis of a *resilient, long-lived *political economy.[40]

*Five Whys, Relevance Fallacy.

MULTICULTURALISM. This is usually taken to mean the coexistence of diverse *cultures and their corresponding *religions within a single community. *Lean Logic* argues that, in the future, the central uniting property of a society will be its culture. There is no doubt that, in order to accomplish this, the culture will need to be well-developed and strong, attracting consensus in the *public sphere rather than being simply a matter of private preference. It would seem to follow that culture can only do this work of sustaining unity if the culture concerned is a single, common culture, for which there is general consent.

In fact, while it probably is true that a genuinely common culture is best suited to do this, such a consensus is rare. Even in the medieval period—famous for its Catholic consensus—dissidents, aka heretics, persisted in their own interpretations in response to local inspiration, and much of the history of the medieval church consists of the business of what to do about them. For example, in the fifth century, the only reason the existence of Britain was even noticed by recorded European history was that it was influenced by the Pelagian heresy—which emphasised personal responsibility (rather than grace) as the means of salvation—requiring two visits to Britain by the Bishop of Auxerre in unsuccessful attempts to sort the problem out. Pelagius' tiresome English preference for going his

M

own way—his name is Latin for "the sea"—was a precursor in Europe of some sixteen centuries of differing takes on the received religion and culture. They led to persecutions, inquisitions and wars, but they did not, until the twentieth century, destroy the overarching culture in which Europe's people coexisted.[41]

But there are three circumstances in which the presence of sharply different cultures can have catastrophic consequences for social *cohesion:

The first is where there is the fusion of religious differences and material rivalries. Hindus and Muslims, despite tensions and flare-ups over many years, coexisted reasonably successfully in India until events leading up the Partition in 1947 created real conflict in terms of land and politics, and had them fighting for their lives, leaving some 1 million dead.[42] Buddhism and Islam coexisted successfully in the northern Indian region of Ladakh until the arrival of the *market economy in the 1970s destroyed confidence in every aspect of their lives.[43] The quality of coexistence of Jews and Christians in Europe through the centuries has been inversely correlated with the presence of stress—not least that brought on by bad harvests. The problem is that stresses which a society might otherwise have been able to endure lead to rupture along what turn out to be the fault lines of ethnic and/or religious difference, especially in a *political economy with a dense *population. It becomes hard to find the middle ground: resentment matures into deadly extremes and, because it has been so strongly inhibited, the break from coexistence can come with little warning.[44]

In this situation, it may not be possible to make decisions on the basis of what "we" think it is best to do. To promote multiculturalism or do the opposite, or indeed to pursue any policy at all—may not be a matter on which *choices can still be made. The historian Walter Laqueur observes, with respect to immigration in France at the start of the 21st century, that it could not necessarily be supposed . . .

> . . . that the situation was under control. A culture of violence and destruction prevailed that manifested itself, for instance, in torching cars (45,000 in 2005), and in gang warfare in general. It was not just a case of rejecting France

and its values but of *hating* French society and its institutions, as spokesmen of the young generation repeatedly declared.[45]

But the situation in the *zones* around the cities of France does not need to be accepted as typical.

The second kind of stress is the one which occurs when cultures and their religions cannot express themselves because there is not enough cultural uniformity to do so. For example, festival, *tradition, *carnival, and even daily assured companionship need a quorum—that is, at least sufficient agreement on language, music, idiom, graphics, timing and sheer heartening numbers of people—without which nothing happens. Without a collective existence, culture is reduced to a personal, maybe dissident, statement, with no significance for the community, which accordingly foregoes access to the *public sphere and its cultural expression. And, without that, a population's *identity and its existence as a *community are at best shadowy, and may turn inwards, towards *small groups and gangs defined by mutual hostilities. That retreat to the private sphere—as the public sphere becomes unable to speak with one voice—is in place in the United Kingdom and other nations today.

The communitarian thinker Amitai Etzioni reflects on the difference between pluralism and faction:

> The forces that combined all the plurals into one mosaic—one society and one nation—have waned. The notion of a shared community or public interest, which balances but does not replace the plurality of particular interests, has been eroded. . . . an ideology has developed, supported by some social scientists and intellectuals, that claims there is no such thing as communitywide (or "public") interest, only the give and take of particular interests.[46]

The third form of stress is less visible. The individual, or the *household, feels isolated, with no set of common memories, pleasures, fears, jokes, sympathies, comforts—no cognitive world to share. A strong local agenda such as the Bromley by Bow enterprise (*Presence) can transcend difference, but easy familiarity is less close to the surface when there is nothing particular going on. But this does not register as a social problem; it is considered a private matter (see "Dinner Lady" sidebar).

DINNER LADY
Life and death in Southall

My father worked in a greengrocers' shop for 35 years; my mother was a housewife before she committed suicide in 1987. They were both life-long Labour voters. My mother hanged herself in the house she lived in all her life, in Southall, west London, a town that had changed beyond all recognition. It is today the least white place in the whole of Britain.

She wrote in her suicide note, "I hate Southall. I feel so alone." In case anyone dare accuse of her of any racism, she may have hated Southall, but my mother was incapable of hating people. She worked in the last years of her life as a dinner lady in an all-Asian school, and was much loved. But she was lost. Her world had disappeared.

TIM LOTT, "White, working class—
and threatened with extinction",
Independent on Sunday, 2008.[47]

It is not inevitable that difference between cultures should mature into *conflict between them, but the more stressful the conditions—as in the case of shortages for essential resources such as *food, *energy or *land, for instance—the more likely it is to happen, and that makes it harder for a community to get positive results. Drawing on their experience of community-based water projects around the world, Ton Schouten and Patrick Moriarty write:

> A community with serious conflict between classes, castes, ethnic or religious groups will have little chance of successfully managing anything. . . . The key assumption is that "community" is a valid description for a particular group of people. If they do not represent a community, then community management is unlikely to work, particularly because active participation by all sectors of the community is absolutely essential. Opting out by any

important group of users will inevitably lead to conflict and eventual failure.[48]

Among the many suggested responses, that of Rabbi Jonathan Sacks is significant, because it is at least constructive. He suggests that the community could start again, inventing its own synthesis of the traditions it has inherited—its own evolved tradition and narrative—helping its members to adapt the cultures they bring with them. And he proposes a "Social Covenant"—a declaration of, and commitment to, friendly cooperation. There is certainly a case for a meeting point in the *arts, which are accomplished at bridging cultural divides. And there is a case too for being as positive as possible about any constructive suggestion and giving it the extended benefit of any doubt: the thought, well-defined *intention and effort that such a project would provoke would themselves be constructive and helpful. But there do have to be doubts about whether a synthesis of such diverse *narratives is possible, and some suspicions that a Covenant is a form of *begging the question: if there were a real prospect of such a Covenant being signed and ensuring mutual tolerance into the future, however difficult conditions become, there would not be a problem.[49]

An alternative is to encourage the strengthening of communities with distinct cultures in distinct localities. A precedent, or parallel—far from exact, but which at least refers to a system with a long and proven record—can be found in the form of the "tenurial shell". The scholars Janis Alcorn and Victor Toledo apply the principle to the coexistence of two or more different systems of property rights, which would be in conflict with each other if not for the recognised *boundary between them (*Script).[50] The boundary legitimises difference, and reduces the threat of one system seeing the other as a challenge to its own integrity and seeking to dominate or destroy it. But shells need not, of course, be defined only in terms of differences between property rights; a similar legitimising boundary could exist between cultures nested within the wider framework of a *nation. In this circumstance, stress can strengthen them both, as Alcorn and Toledo write:

> In times of stress, the political units *inside* different local shells have forged organizational links

M

M

CANDLES FOR PEACE
Monday, 3rd November 2008

There is a heavy drizzle outside Tooting Broadway station this November evening. I am early, and I stand against the railings, sheltering under my green tweed cap, and wait for something to happen. First, the Vicar comes, carrying some plastic sheeting and a bundle of poles, and with some help from bystanders he fits them together into a blue and white awning. Hanging from the awning are signs inviting us to LIGHT A CANDLE FOR PEACE. Then some people come with a poster: BALHAM AND TOOTING COMMUNITY ASSOCIATION. Two ladies put up trestle tables and lay out boxes of night-lights and a big baking dish to put them in.

Now there are fifty people there, and the prayers begin. The Vicar prays for peace in our community and in our hearts: "We don't need your money; we just need your prayer". Then a leader of the Hindus prays for peace, and sings us a chant. The Muslim leader reminds us that "Shalom" in Hebrew is the same word as "Salam" in Arabic, and that they both mean peace. A Buddhist monk speaks to us, rings a tiny bell which can just be heard above the traffic, beats his drum and chants. A Jewish elder speaks movingly of peace and sings his wild, wailing chant. Then the Sikh, with more chant. Then the Mayor himself, followed by the Vicar again, who reads us the prayer of St. Francis. Then the local chief of police. Then Lucy, from Transition Town

Tooting, who makes connections between care for each other and care of the Earth.

We light our scented night-lights. Claudia and I confer about whether they smell of apricots or strawberries. King Edward VII stands above us on his plinth. He does not take part in the proceedings but he clutches his sceptre and looks resolutely into the future. The plinth is dated 1911 and decorated with vigorous bronzes of angels delivering virtues and giving instructions for use. One of the virtues is Charity. The other is Peace.

"*Tout le monde* of Tooting was there", says Lucy as we go off for a herbal tea in a café, just in time before it closes.

---

between themselves to resist the destruction of their shells and their property rights.[51]

Stretching the idea even further, it is also conceivable that a 'protective membrane' could form round different cultures without there being any implication of boundaries defined in terms of *place: that is, without concentration of any one culture in any one location. Some scope for this is undoubtedly possible: Baghdad, for instance, was for many centuries rich with *diverse religions, with a famously thriving Jewish community.

But there are limits, because all social order and collective action requires a framework of *institutions— local community; places of worship; schools; clubs; neighbourhood associations; the rules and assumptions

which guide decision-making. If those institutions themselves differ, then the *public sphere fails: collective action becomes hard, or impossible. If no particular collective action is in fact needed because the economy is so prosperous, there may be no problem for a time, but if that should change, then the lack of an agreed set of institutional assumptions—of a *grammar underpinning political *conversation—will cause trouble. And, even if that trouble is mitigated, that task itself may absorb so much energy that little remains for the positive collective task of making a future. Or, if the way forward is seen to be a common *secular* culture and *ritual with a banal *myth—intended to be taken literally and intolerant of different interpretations—that takes us into the dangerous territory of the kind of grandiose *ideologies which gave us the regimes of the recent history of Russia, Germany, Cambodia and North Korea.

And yet, the celebration of cultural differences and mutual respect has a natural rightness about it. There can be doubt as to how deeply it penetrates: brave affirmative dialogue between the imam and the rabbi does not necessarily extend among all their followers; nor among all the leaders. But it is a first step (see "Candles for Peace" sidebar).

———

Those, then, seem to be the choices. Either a heroic attempt to build a new common culture: a common narrative or Social Covenant; *or* strong, distinctive, local cultures, sharing mutual respect for their common experience of religious faith and legitimised by their distinctiveness—and, notably, by their arts, which can communicate across boundaries better than plain words. Failing these, the default position is the absence of any culture at all, since each is diluted out of sight. This last is only a realistic option in a rich economy where consumption keeps the peace—and, in fact, all the concerned and urgent suggestions about ways to modify multiculturalism and create a peaceful and collective *identity are made on the assumption that *energy, *food, taxes and jobs will continue in good order. When that no longer holds, difficult revision is likely.

The interim conclusion is: keep alive the cultures that we have. To go quiet about your own culture in an attempt not to insult another is an insult to all cultures and a clean slate on which fundamentalism can have its way. Dan as a Christian can absolutely affirm and support Tejal's culture and practice as a Hindu. This is more than 'the dignity of difference', because they both know what commitment to a culture means; it is the mutual love of loving their diverse *traditions in the same ways; two cultures can affirm each other in an *encounter from which the *sceptic is self-excluded. If you really want to insult the other side's *religion, rubbish the whole idea of cultural and religious affiliation. When the stresses of the *climacteric set in with real intensity, people will rediscover strong religious associations which they may have almost forgotten.[52]

Bridging is possible: but bridges need firm footings. Dialogue from the strength of living *cultures should start while it is still possible.

MYTH. Among the meanings:

1. Ancient legend; story which seems to be as permanent as the landscape with which it is linked, giving it significance and personality.
2. The narrative underlying a religion; the meeting point between *religion and *culture.
3. A story which (the speaker insists) is untrue, though widely held to be true.
4. Shared common sense, about behaviour and opinion; a society's idea of normality.[53]
5. A *nation's history.
6. A nation's popular history.
7. A nation's history, revised with malicious intent.

But these are fragmented. The condensed meaning of myth is the most telling one. The myth of a *place is the *narrative that gives it *identity. The story is a mixture of *truth and untruth; it is in quantum space: to observe it too closely is to destroy it. The identity that derives from it is real, but fragile.

N

NANOTECHNOLOGY. The technology of the very small-scale. Nanotechnology works on the scale of nanometres (one billionth of a metre). At this scale, matter behaves in peculiar ways: chemical and magnetic properties are different; colours change (gold particles can be orange, purple, red or green). Here, science is dealing with individual atoms and molecules; it can put them together to produce not only materials but molecular-scale artefacts which have not existed nor even been *imagined before. Nanotechnology gives the scientist a measure of power which could transform life more profoundly than the Industrial Revolution itself, and could do so irreversibly. This technology is powerful and dangerous. And it is not receiving the public attention it deserves.[1]

At first sight, nanotechnology appears to promise or threaten nothing with the potential to change the world, and its applications already include such banal triumphs as invisible sunscreens: nano-sized titanium dioxide reflects the ultraviolet light that causes sunburn,

M

N

but it is smaller than the wavelength of visible light, so is invisible when smeared on the skin. Nanoparticles can improve the quality of clays, and they can be used in coatings which make windows water-repellent (self-cleaning) and fabrics stain-proof. And new products are now coming along, including paints with extremely hard surfaces; nanoparticles which can react with persistent environmental pollutants such as polychlorinated hydrocarbons (PCBs) and make them harmless, or lock up metals such as mercury into insoluble compounds which cause no trouble; and membranes which can improve the efficiency of fuel cells and batteries, sharpen up images on computer screens and provide cheap water purification. Nanostructures have the potential to reduce or replace the use of platinum in catalytic converters and to improve fuel efficiency. In the near future, there is the prospect of improved lubricants, new magnetic materials, durable medical implants such as heart valves and hip replacements, ceramics that can be machined, targeted drug delivery to specific cells in the body, and battle suits which can limit injuries and provide first aid when they occur.[2]

Well, it all seems rather standard stuff—some of it very useful, but nothing really to set the pulse racing, given the familiar onward march of technology. It becomes more interesting, however, when we consider the *material needs of local *lean economies, for this is a technology which can, atom-by-atom, build molecular structures to order. Carbon, hydrogen, oxygen, aluminium and silicon can be expected to be abundant resources for any locality; and that endowment of common elements could be enough to produce materials with almost any property that might be needed. As the Center for Responsible Nanotechnology enthusiastically tells us, "When most structure and function can be built out of carbon and hydrogen, there will be far less use for minerals, and mining operations can be mostly shut down."[3]

And, if you are building new materials atom-by-atom, you might as well build new equipment at the same time—for instance, nanocircuitry for super-powerful information processing, or nanorobots ("nanobots") that can repair cells in the human body. At this scale, the distinction between materials and equipment breaks down. But, of course, the problem is that the process of building things on this scale takes a long time. How long? It depends absolutely on the structure and the nature of what is being made, of course, but in the case of a complex structure such as a DNA strand, the production of a few ounces of material built atom by atom would take approximately 20 million years. To give an idea of the scale of such a project, Mark and Daniel Ratner write,

> If one atom were the size of a teaspoonful of water, this many atoms would be the size of the Pacific Ocean.[4]

Too long to be useful, you might think. But no, nanoscience has a solution for that, too: just one little prototype added to a piece of an existing structure could indeed take some time to make, but then this could become the template round which other atoms organise themselves. Electrical and magnetic interactions between molecules are much weaker than the strong bonds that actually hold the molecules together, but they are strong enough to assemble structures on that scale, and once the pattern of magnetic forces has been set up on a small fragment, other atoms will form around it like crystals, organised in the intended pattern. The structure "self-assembles".[5]

Now, think about this for a moment. If a structure can assemble itself, that might suggest that it could be designed to assemble other structures identical to itself.

It was the nanoscientist Eric Drexler who developed the concept, coining the term "assemblers":

> . . . [E]nzyme-like second generation machines will be able to use as "tools" almost any of the reactive molecules used by chemists—but they will wield them with the precision of programmed machines. They will be able to bond atoms together in virtually any stable pattern, adding a few at a time to the surface of a workpiece until a complex structure is complete. Think of such nanomaterials as *assemblers*.
>
> Because assemblers will let us place atoms in almost any reasonable arrangement, they will let us build almost anything that the laws of nature allow to exist. In particular, they will let us build almost anything we can design— *including more assemblers*.[6]

The term for this is "self-replication". In 2004 the Royal Society published a report which, amongst other things, considered whether self-replication is possible. It concluded that it is not:

> The working group found no convincing evidence that self-replication, a characteristic of a living organism, is possible.[7]

And the point matters rather a lot, because if nanomaterials can reproduce themselves, they might do so faster than we would wish, or supply us with self-replicating constructs which we do not want. Reassuringly, the Royal Society tells us that Drexler has since retracted his position, and points us to the paper in which he does so.[8] Some retraction—here is Drexler's own version of it (the paper is co-authored with Chris Phoenix):

> Although runaway replication cannot happen by accident, no law of nature prevents its deliberate development. . . . A programmable mechanochemical fabricator . . . should be able to be directed to build a copy of itself.[9]

. . . and indeed the debate has now moved on from the question of whether it is possible, to the question of how the dangers intrinsic in self-replication can be mitigated. The most prolific of the scientists participating in the debate is Ray Kurzweil. He talks of "engineers' pessimism", arguing that this is standard in technology—scientists tend to make modest projections of the future on the basis of the progress of their own work, but there is a gap in their logic, for today's advances can make tomorrow's advances more effective, bigger, quicker. It is this effect that has produced the compound growth in the power of the microchip (doubling in power every eighteen months for thirty years and still going strong), and in the thought-to-be-impossible speed with which the human genome has been mapped. And this effect also brings increased investment, so that there is a *double* exponential growth, with advances building on each other and racing ahead at a speed which surprises almost everybody.[10]

Self-replication, then, cannot be dismissed. The prospect of self-replicating nanostructures is real, and so is that of small 'nanofactories' (of the size, say, of a desktop PC), within which nanoscale self-replication takes place, and which can then proceed to make objects on a large scale, including copies of themselves. It is a truly extraordinary prospect, but there it is, in the literature of this new science of nanotechnology.

Here is an example, from the Center for Responsible Nanotechnology:

> It seems like magic. A small appliance, about the size of a washing machine, that is able to manufacture almost anything. It is called a "nanofactory". Fed with simple chemical stocks, this amazing machine breaks down molecules, and then reassembles them into any product you ask for. Packed with nanotechnology and robotics, weighing 200 pounds and standing half as tall as a person, it can produce two tons per day of products. Control is simple: a touch screen selects the type and number of products to produce. It costs very little to operate, just the price of materials fed into it. In one hour, $20 of chemicals can be converted into 1,000 pairs of shoes, or 50 shovels, or 200 cell phones, or even a duplicate nanofactory![11]

For the foreseeable future, such a machine is improbable. It would need to be spectacularly clever to go straight from the raw materials of (for instance) pure acetylene and acetone, to nanoassemblies on the scale of molecules, then to self-replicating assemblies of billions of molecules, and then on to the components of large structures which can then proceed to produce more large structures of virtually any specification. From any remotely sensible present-day point of view, the notion is ridiculous, and yet it is important, for three reasons:

First, there is a version of nanotechnology-based manufacturing called "convergent assembly", using building blocks consisting of a few billion atoms— smaller than a bacterium but large enough to be useful. Starting from that higher level of aggregation, it would be possible, as the nanoscientists Chris Phoenix and Mike Treder write, to build "anything from cars to computers".[12] The power of convergent assembly shifts the whole frame of reference within which we can apply common sense. Suddenly we have to recognise we are in a new world of technology in which it becomes very hard to make *judgments which reflect our own view

N

of ourselves as reasonable people. The criteria against which we can edit our own judgment for reasonableness are no longer as reliable as we would wish as defences against the absurd.

Secondly, a machine that can make a car can undoubtedly be made to make another version of itself. Those little factories could then proceed to produce whatever they were programmed to produce, such as nanoscale weapons. If the weapons are produced by a minifactory that can self-replicate, then the weapons themselves could self-replicate.[13]

Thirdly, the above discussion is itself a little primitive because it considers just molecular-nano-technology—which could be otherwise known as robotics-information-nanotechnology (RIN). Add genetics to that—*GRIN—and replication becomes routine. Starting when? Bill Joy, the celebrated chief scientist at Sun Microsystems and the inventor of the Java programming language, reflects,

> The breakthrough to wild self-replication in robotics, genetic engineering, or nanotechnology could come suddenly, reprising the surprise we felt when we first learned of the cloning of a mammal.[14]

The power of the technology makes it hard to resist with any consistency and consensus. The scale on which GRIN technology works—the building blocks it uses and the nanomaterials which it can produce—enables it to interact directly with the cells of the human body and use the same electrical language as the brain. Some of the advances that are made possible by this, though astonishing, could conceivably be welcomed—and are undoubtedly presented—as a good thing. For instance, if some varieties of nanobot could find, invade and repair diseased or ageing cells within the human body, others could greatly increase intelligence: even the unreliable meanderings of human thought require 10^{26} calculations per second; nanobiological intelligence, in the form of nanobots, could vastly exceed this rate by the middle of the century. Memories, suggests Kurzweil, could be expanded a trillion-fold. He may be exaggerating, of course, but one wonders how much difference it would make if he had overestimated this by a million or so?[15]

The nanobots could be introduced into the brain by injection, or by swallowing, or via the lungs. They could then take up positions in close proximity to every interneuronal connection, from which they could both communicate with the brain and receive communications—or orders—from outside it. It may not be your own brain which is controlling your thinking. Already scientists at the Max Planck Institute have succeeded in controlling the movements of a living leech from a computer.[16]

And from there, anything is possible, including applications which could not conceivably be welcomed. Self-replicating pathologies, on the principle of, for instance, fast-acting cancers, could be released, either by accident or design. GRIN-based weapons of mass destruction could be targeted to genetically distinct races or particular areas. Or aggressive, super-intelligent robots programmed to reproduce, to lodge in the brain and to solve problems could succeed in controlling the thinking and movements of living people.[17]

In sum, this is a technology which is inherently difficult to control, even in principle. We can be reasonably confident of a bomb not going off unless someone causes it to do so—and it goes off only once. In contrast with this, nanotechnology—and, particularly, GRIN technology—will be designed to make up its own mind, to adapt, to solve problems, and then to self-assemble new generations which will inherit those adaptations and solutions. This ability to pass on characteristics acquired during a lifetime—a phenomenon which is by general agreement not recognised in biology—will be programmed into GRIN technology, opening the way to fast evolutionary advance. "Fast" here refers to evolutionary adaptations taking place on a scale of days, or even hours.

And this could happen soon. Kurzweil writes,

> The means and knowledge will soon exist in a routine college bioengineering lab (and already exists in more sophisticated labs) to create unfriendly pathogens more dangerous than nuclear weapons. As technology accelerates towards the full realisation of biotechnology, nanotechnology and "strong" AI (artificial intelligence at human levels and beyond), we will see the same intertwined potentials: a feast

of creativity resulting from human intelligence expanded many-fold combined with many grave new dangers.[18]

A technology with such dangers must surely have much greater potential as a source of catastrophe than of good—so there is a case for calling a moratorium on it now, before that potential is fulfilled. As Bill Joy argues,

> The only realistic alternative I see is relinquishment: to limit development of the technologies that are too dangerous, by limiting our pursuit of certain kinds of knowledge.[19]

And there would be a sort of long-term sanity in doing so; it would be evidence of a civilisation *intelligent enough to know what it ought not to do. Joy cites Carl Sagan's long view of planetary civilisations: some of them . . .

> . . . see their way through, place limits on what may and what must not be done, and safely pass through the time of perils. Others, not so lucky or so prudent, perish.[20]

But relinquishment may not be possible. Nanotechnology is advancing on many fronts, invading almost every field of advanced science. It is distributed in laboratories around the world. It may well be that the worst that the technology can do will be done. That worst is a pathogen built on the molecular scale and released into the environment. It could reproduce itself in host organisms such as animals and plants. Its medium could be air or water. Already present in the language is "grey goo"—molecular particles able to reproduce themselves and floating in the wind. What matters is not the form, but the implications—and, according to Kurzweil, the implications are that we must avoid at all costs being left without a defensive technology when it happens:

> When we have "grey goo" (unrestrained nanobot replication), we will also have "blue goo" ("police" nanobots that combat the "bad" nanobots). . . . The surest way to prevent the development of the defensive technologies would be to relinquish the pursuit of knowledge in broad areas.[21]

And the Center for Responsible Nanotechnology brightly agrees on the need for nanobot defences—a nanoscale Star Wars—as another reason for hurrying on with developing the technology:

> Widespread detection networks may be necessary to deal effectively with grey goo. A system that can sample large volumes of air or water for sub-micron particles, and respond with sufficient speed to clean up an infestation, could only be built by molecular nanotechnology.[22]

Man-made viruses that infect computer networks, if not exactly under control, are at least contained. All they can directly damage is computers. Man-made nanoscale robots, collectively endowed with super-intelligence, which infest air, water, plants, humans and other animals, and which act directly on, and colonise, control or destroy the bodies and brains of their hosts, are out of control. All this is disputed, as Joy notes, on the grounds that, for instance, "We've heard all this before . . . " (*Wolf Fallacy). He wonders aloud: "I don't know where these people hide their fear."[23]

Nanotechnology is one of the big problems facing our civilisation. The potential for trouble is at least as big as *energy resource depletion and *climate change. It is bigger than, though related to, the threat of terrorism. It has already started: its full development may be unavoidable. It can offer the gambler's mirage of the-future-as-jackpot—extraordinary new powers for the mind, diseased and ageing cells that cure themselves, goods that make themselves—not all that far from the *utopian vision of fish that catch themselves, bake themselves and serve themselves up at the table. In its developed and constructive form, it could indeed be cheap and feasible as a source of local materials—in fact, just what local lean economies will need. With promise like that, it has, and will have, advocates. It is a knowledge technology: once the knowledge exists, it is virtually unstoppable, and the next phase is likely to be *GRIN, the convergence of genetics, robotics, information technology and nanotechnology. It is not, however, a rational technology; it is a form of surrender. It invites human society to revert to a kind of childhood, to leave the decision-making to a higher authority, to surrender itself to a technology with its own momentum and inertia, its own criteria, its own *judgment—its own agenda (*Metamorphosis). The time will come when society is forced into horrified disagreement with those judgments; the time may come when it is not human rationality, but another one, that prevails.

The decentralised, localised society of the future may not be short of options. It may have local sources of materials and the *skills to use them. It may have sustainable methods of *food production. It may have moved beyond the *technical fix, sustaining itself in a *closed-loop system. If all these things are true of it, it will have grown up. The threat of the nanobot, however, may never go away. The technology is seductive: it could do much to make local lean economies robustly self-reliant in materials, but the knowledge carries a curse—it is a case of damned if we do, and damned if we don't. It could well be *necessary to develop the technology to build defences against the consequences of developing it.

And yet, in the energy-strapped, climate-changed, post-market future, freelance out-of-control destructive science may not flourish as it does at present. It may even be that the apex of the danger is now. After the turning point to the *Lean Economy, there will be other priorities: to focus instead on the tangible and visible, on the human *scale, on surviving and coping, on making a *place, on taking delight in May mornings, on making a living, on thinking lean.

NARCISSISM. Love of the self. The person is entranced by his own mental ability and moral standing, to the point of being unable to hear any contrary view. Self-love is noted for its fidelity:

> The sin of self-love possesseth all mine eye
> And all my soul and all my every part;
> And for this sin there is no remedy,
> It is so grounded inward in my Heart.
>
> *William Shakespeare*, Sonnets, *1609.*[24]

Narcissism is the inevitable product of a society which has become so banal that there is all too little, apart from the self, left to love. This is fatal to argument because the person who loves himself has to love his own opinion, and is even *defined by it; a change of opinion would suggest that there had been a change

in the person himself, so that the person the narcissist formerly loved no longer exists, leaving him or her with nothing to love at all. In these circumstances, the argument that the opinion is wrong, and that the matter is more complex than it seems, has no chance of being heard or of getting anywhere. In a banal society, thought is dead.[25]

*Carnival, Dirty Hands, Internal Evidence.

NARRATIVE TRUTH. Meaning which is contained in *myth, *art, music and all forms of *culture. It applies most directly, however, to storytelling. Narrative is story which may or may not be *materially true, but—as is the way with stories—it has a shadow-meaning, ranging from the trivial or obvious to a deep, rich source of a lifetime's reflection. Narrative, to be distinguished from allegory, works fine just as a story if you don't want to look for the meaning beneath it; allegory's purpose is its deeper meaning. You don't by any means *have* to explore the meaning to enjoy a good narrative, whereas if you stay on the surface of an allegory, you are missing the point. Allegory "speaks otherwise" (Greek: *allos* other + *agor* speak).

This dual character—true and untrue, using narrative truth to communicate material truth, being *both* story *and* having something else to say—is shared with any work of creative imagination. A Jane Austen novel, say, which is untrue, since it is fiction; but is true, in that it traces *character and *manners with meticulous accuracy. Elizabeth Bennett certainly existed, as a real and rounded description of a lady of that age, station and temperament, and she has our affection; yet she certainly did not exist—she is a child of Austen's *imagination. This narrative, poetic ambiguity is the hot centre of our culture. It is also the victim of widespread misunderstanding, owing to the error of not knowing the difference between testimony and story:

Testimony works on the single dimension of material truth: if it deviates from material truth, it is bad testimony, so it is crucially different from story. Story works at two levels: the medium of the story itself (true or untrue), and the shadow it casts in the form of insight into truth at a depth which will demand (and reward) thought and reflection. Or the medium may take the form of a painting, which is both untrue and true, or music, which cannot be seen in terms of truth or untruth at all. The medium, in whatever form, invites you to *reflect, to sing, to pray, to build *social capital, to face the same way as your *neighbours, to sustain a point of reference in your life which is secure from the suspicion of being *squalid. The idea that allegory—or *religion, whose *grammar is allegory—should be taken for the literal truth is an extraordinary failure of mature judgment. A work of art—especially the work of art called religion—makes the question of whether it is true or not absurd. It is a category error and should not be asked. You might as well ask whether Schubert's String Quintet in C major Deutsch No. 956 likes broccoli.

Narrative, then, may or may not report the material truth. But it can lead to the discovery of both material truth and *implicit truth, as an explorer in search of the Holy Grail may discover and map real mountains and rivers. Story *uses* experience, giving it permanence and meaning; distilling memory into works of art to be *encountered, reflected on and loved—the features by which you can recognise a *place and a *community. The community's stock of stories is intrinsic to its *identity, to its culture and character. Its narrative is something which it recognises as its own, gives a name to, and uses as an expressive statement; without making the mistake of supposing the story to be true, any more than—despite being inspired by it—it would think that the Milky Way is made of milk. Story has emotional depth; hearts reach out to it; it may even be *believed*. That doesn't mean it is held to be materially true. Belief—the word, and the bundle of meanings with which it is linked—comes to our literal-minded age from a story-rich antiquity. It can be traced to the ancient Germanic root, *galaubjan* [to hold dear]; the Latin for "to believe" is *credere*, which comes from *cor dare*, to give [one's] heart.[26]

*Fluency vs. insight

The difficulty that plain speaking faces in communicating ideas which are complex and have emotional depth has been noted many times: the message itself may be rejected, or it may be just too big to talk about, or the storyteller herself may be far from having worked out the material truth buried in it; or she may be at risk. The curse of Cassandra was to be right but ignored:

everyone just carried on dancing; it was Salome that got results—but then she was a dancer. The prophets with the biggest things to say were intensely aware of the limitations of plain speaking. "I am not eloquent," Moses admitted; "I am slow of speech and of a slow tongue." Isaiah's "unclean lips" had to be purged with a live coal. Ezekiel was mute for a time. Jonah ran away to sea—and to his adventures inside a whale—rather than argue with the notoriously hard regime of Nineveh. "I held my tongue and spake nothing, though it was pain and grief to me", says Psalm 39, on the ropes. Even the great Catholic *liturgy, as the theologian Catherine Pickstock argues, was afflicted with a stammer.[27]

A solution is to turn complex truth into a story. The story can be about anything but—if the cultural and artistic depth explored by narrative and allegory is dedicated to the service of its people—the work of telling it, being reminded of it, exploring it, celebrating it, dancing it, or living it has the effect of binding a community together intensely. And the invention, or performance, of a good story (like *dance) takes a person as close to fulfilment, and to having a deeply good time, as it is possible to get. The risk in this is that allegory may acquire a life of its own, becoming story for its own sake, with no shadow-meaning—no purpose other than entertainment—and losing all sense of dedication to the community. Not that there is a problem with the existence of such materially-true narratives, but there is a profound loss for the community if stories exist only in that single dimension, leaving it with a narrative tradition that misses the point. Story is like a washing line: it is what is hanging from it that matters. The literal mind, seeing only the washing line, and never realising what it is for, leaves society unclothed, in a state of narrative deprivation. Probably the most famous expression of regret about this reduction of story to *only* entertainment—and surely the most impressive exit in English literature—is from Tennyson (and Monty Python):

> . . . behold an arm,
> Clothed in white samite, mystic, wonderful,
> That caught him by the hilt, and banish'd him
> Three times, and drew him under in the mere.[28]

What is waving farewell to us here is a robust confidence in the idea that the narrative, *manners, traditions, beliefs and *ceremonies of the society in which a person belongs are fit subjects for celebration. The pre-industrial (and, even more so, the pre-Reformation) society of Europe acknowledged *traditions and principles, often far from intuitively obvious, which had evolved through trial and error over a long period; they were taught to young people who participated in rites of passage to mark stages towards full membership of society. But they were not beyond challenge, and this was reinforced by such fragmenting advances as firearms, the waning of *carnival, the slowly-evolving *market economy and the Enlightenment's passionate and breathless surrender to reason. Confident, located values have been slipping into the bosom of the lake for a long time now, picking up speed around the time when Tennyson wrote his "Morte d'Arthur" (1842), but spanning several centuries of deepening artistic doubt as to how to replace them.

Allegory itself, of course, has lived on, but it has retreated by degrees into the *private sphere. It tells stories about grief and love; it explores *ironic space; it may be serious or just fun. It will be a matter of life-giving expression for the *community, and for the *resilient future. But nowadays it tends not to be, and Alasdair MacIntyre reflects on the consequences:

> The contrast, indeed, the opposition between art and life provides a way of exempting art—including narrative—from its moral tasks. The relegation of art to the status of an essentially minority activity and interest further helps to protect us from any narrative understanding of ourselves.[29]

Lean Logic brings whatever values and insights it can to the task of holding community together. If a robust market economy is not around to do that job, it will have to be done by a robust *culture; if culture does this, you can call it anything you like, but *Lean Logic* calls it *religion (Latin: *ligare* to bind + *re* intensely). It is the binding-together of people with stories, music, *dance, *emotion, *spirit, *death, *ecology, *caritas*—all really about the celebratory making of community, but "speaking otherwise", and real enough to give your heart to.[30]

*Invisible Goods, Dirty Hands, Truth.

NATION. A state which is defined by its own territorial *boundaries, whose people recognise that definition, and which has sovereign power over its affairs. Smaller territorial identities within the larger territory are part of the *modular, *diverse composition of the nation as a *complex system; they are not inconsistent with it.[31]

On the scale of the nation, *reciprocity is generally assumed to be "negative"—you get only what you pay for—but the strangeness of other people is mitigated. They speak the same language, are subject to the same *laws, are aware of the same debates; they have some of the essentials of being of one mind—with shared jokes, allegiances, *traditions and history; they live in the same *political economy and participate in the same *politics, which they enjoy or suffer together. There is—if only in moderation and imperfectly—*good faith. There is latency—potential for closer cooperation. The nation is the setting for the fundamentals of *culture and social order, for the character of society. Nations have had a bad press since the World Wars, on the grounds that they were fought between nations. They were not: they were fought between *empires, which we will discuss presently.

The state in the mature *Lean Economy will have three primary responsibilities which are intrinsic to the integrity of its structure. The first is to sustain its own *identity* as a nation, and the identity of citizens as participants with a shared sense of commonality, a willingness to *cooperate in the common public interest. Secondly, the state provides a setting for *politics*. It will sustain a confidence that people can safely and usefully participate in the making of policy and in holding government to account. And thirdly, the state must maintain a *currency* capable of responding quickly and effectively to its changing needs. Although the market can be expected to atrophy to a profound extent—profound enough to justify the term "post-market economy"—some trade will persist, and a currency will need to be sustained.

*Identity

A nation has an identity which connects the people who live there to a particular place, and to each other. There is a landscape which many generations have shaped and defended, and there is an endowment of culture, language and *institutions which, though they can be *betrayed, cannot be denied. The nation is a located, bounded, particular homeland. If defeated, it often manages, eventually, to come back into being, with a sense of renewal and justice. It exists in the mind of its people.[32]

Identity in this collective sense means that there is an identifiable meaning to the idea of "we". Of course, "we" can mean almost anything, but in this context, the issue is one of commonality between people on a scale beyond the local. It is not a vague sense that I ought to recognise, or do recognise, a *responsibility towards others; on the contrary, it is part of my understanding of myself that I belong to a particular *population within particular boundaries. Far from being a conscious and circumstantial *agreement* with what a nation is doing, or a liking for its weather, or an appreciation of the business opportunities, it is a recognition of emotional attachment to a *place and people, and of that attachment as a legitimate and essential asset.[33] The task for the Lean Economy is to rebuild social structure, *emotional engagement and obligation after the devastation and *social entropy of the *market economy; to reconstruct a community of obligation. As the political philosopher David Miller writes,

> Because our forebears have toiled and spilt
> their blood to build and defend the nation, we
> who are born into it inherit an obligation to
> continue their work, which we discharge partly
> towards our contemporaries and partly towards
> our descendants. [It is] a community which,
> because it stretches back and forward across
> the generations, is not one that the present
> generation can renounce.[34]

Now, why should an identity in this sense matter? For two reasons. First, it has a direct consequence in terms of action. Nations are communities that do things together, take decisions, achieve results.[35] A state that has this constructive resource available to it has an asset of value: the asset of citizenship. But citizenship is not a generalised inclination to good behaviour; it is a convergence between the interests of the person and the well-being of the community. For that to work, the community must have an identity—if it does, there is no need for the paraphernalia of secret police and bureaucracy to enforce participation; the community-nation can depend on its citizens to participate as members, doing things which (unlike obeying the law and paying taxes) cannot be imposed and secured by regulation. It means being willing to take active steps in the interests of other citizens, and expressing commitment to the society by playing a part in its politics. Its people—notwithstanding a *diversity of beliefs and styles of life—live together under laws and institutions which they can accept as legitimate.

The second reason why identity matters is that it provides the necessary basis for rational decision. There is an agreement that the national interest is something to be desired and promoted rather than avoided and prevented. There is a shared *intention. The logic is in place. The nation joins up varied interests into a shared rationality.

Whether a population can sustain such a common identity or not depends partly on circumstances which are outside its control. It is much more likely to be feasible in the case of states which have well-defined *boundaries, which have a common language, and which have a history of getting along together. With each breach in these conditions, identity and rationality alike become increasingly elusive, and public decision becomes disconnected from the rational interest of the state. Good intentions may abound, but there will be no consistent story, nor any assurance that decisions will be related to the state's own interests. National identity is the precondition for national virtue. As Jean-Jacques Rousseau summarised, "Do we want people to be virtuous? If so, let us begin by making them love their homeland."[36]

That widely-extended *virtue brings peace, a necessity if local lean economies are to have a future. But the sense of homeland on which it depends is in retreat; many nations—notably those of Western civilisation—are engaged in scrapping the conditions of *culture and identity which sustain this concept of the nation. The presumption of wider peace as a setting for community building in the future is at risk. And yet peace, extending over the horizon from the community we live in, is at the heart of all our futures.

*Politics

A state without that benign circle of shared *identity, citizenship and a common rationality will, in the end, tend to collapse into constant local war and/or tyranny,

N

whose way of coping with disagreement, as Bernard Crick writes, is to clobber, coerce or overawe all opposition (*Big Stick). He adds,

The establishing of political order is not just any order at all; it marks the birth, or the recognition of freedom. For politics represents at least some tolerance of differing truths, some recognition that government is possible, indeed best conducted, amid the open canvassing of rival interests. Politics are the public actions of free men.[37]

And Mr. Toad helpfully rounds off the logic: "Free! The word and thought alone were worth fifty blankets."[38] The essential condition for *freedom—for the successful functioning of a democratic state under the rule of law—is that those who are on the losing side in an argument about the design of that law should be willing to accept the result with good grace, acknowledging that the shared citizenship overrides the policy differences.[39] Here we have the central principle of the law being, as Larry Siedentop writes, "our own parent and child": we make the law but, at the same time, the law makes us; it guides our intentions.[40] Since we do not all think in the same way, we may not agree about what the law should be, but we have a solution—politics, which relishes *intelligent disagreement, giving debate itself an integral place in the nation's understanding of how things are done within its territory.[41] Politics is enabled by territorial boundaries. There is no limit to the power governments need if there is no limit to their territories. Winners and losers in the political debate recognise both the claim of future generations who will want to inherit a political economy in working order, and that of past generations who might have hoped that their work would not be destroyed before it was understood.[42] This large-scale solidarity, as John Stuart Mill warned, is nothing less than a *necessary condition for a free society. Miller summarises,

Unless the several groups that compose a society have the mutual sympathy and trust that stems from a common nationality, it will be virtually impossible to have free institutions. There will, for instance, be no common interest

in stemming the excesses of government; politics becomes a zero-sum game in which each group can hope to gain by the exploitation of others.[43]

Politics in this territorial setting is the enabling condition for a liberal culture. As John Laughland writes, with an urgency shared by many scholars in this field, "Without territorial jurisdiction there is no possibility of a liberal state."[44]

Currency

An economy with its own currency, which is "flexible" in the sense that it can move in response to supply and demand, and that it can be influenced by the government's (or an independent national monetary policy committee's) decisions on *interest rates, enjoys a degree of protection.[45]

One essential function of such flexible currency systems, wherein each nation is responsible for its own currency, is that they make it possible for a particular economy to get the economic management it needs—in the form of interest rates, taxation and government spending tailored to its particular circumstances, effectively steering it through upturns and downturns with the least possible damage. By contrast, in a multi-national single-currency area, economies can get very little effective management. Interest rates cannot be adapted in response to a single nation's situation. Taxation and government spending can be altered, but these policies are relatively ineffective (or they can even make matters worse) without interest rate management to support them.[46]

But, more fundamentally, national currencies allow exchange rates to move in ways that very approximately compensate for differences between the efficiency of economies, thereby allowing them to trade with each other comfortably without destroying one another—that is, without the stronger one driving the weaker one out of business, and the weaker one then dropping out of the market for the stronger one's goods (and/or the workforce of the weaker one simply migrating to the stronger one, where there are jobs). As a means of adjustment between different economies with different relative strengths, changes in exchange rates are simpler, and unsurprisingly cause less damage to communities, than tidal flows of workforces and *populations. In summary, currency flexibility provides a measure of *protection which gives the less *efficient nation a chance to catch up—to make its industry more efficient rather than having to close it down.[47]

Consider, for instance, the case of an inefficient national economy that has trouble exporting its goods. If the value of its currency falls, this makes its goods cheaper to buyers in other nations. It also makes imports more expensive, so the home economy's industries get a boost twice over.

Actually, a good case can be made for currencies to be organised on a substantially more local basis than even that of nations. As Jane Jacobs points out, a national economy is actually a set of city economies, each with different industries at different stages of development, with problems and opportunities affecting their ability to compete. If those changes in fortune are reflected in the value of a local/civic currency, the chances of a city being able to cope with bad times are much greater. Otherwise, one day it might find that the currency of the nation in which it is based substantially rises in value, making its own products much more costly and less competitive and—as happened, for instance, with much of the UK pottery industry in Stoke on Trent—putting it out of business.

Jacobs illustrates the problem of different cities and industries all having to work in the same currency in a famous and graphic image:

> Imagine a group of people who are all properly equipped with diaphragms and lungs but who share only one single brain-stem breathing centre. In this goofy arrangement, the breathing centre would receive consolidated feedback on the carbon dioxide level of the whole group without discriminating among the individuals producing it. Everybody's diaphragm would thus be triggered to contract at the same time. But suppose some of those people were sleeping, while others were playing tennis. Suppose some were reading about feedback controls, while others were chopping wood. Some would have to halt what they were doing and subside into a lower common denominator of activity. Worse yet, suppose some were swimming and diving, and for some reason, such as the breaking of the surf, had no control over the timing of their submersions. Imagine what would happen to them. In such an arrangement, feedback control would be working perfectly on its own terms but the results would be devastating because of a flaw designed right into the system.[48]

Nonetheless, flexible city currencies of the kind that would give such city-by-city *feedback don't currently exist. There is ambiguity here: there is a theoretical possibility that cities could operate with their own *local currencies (as the only currency available for purchases in the city), and this could become a reality in the future, but, for the present, they don't, and we will take this as a fact of life for now. That is bad luck for cities like Detroit, whose prospects of a comeback in the teeth of *competition from cities with state-of-the-art development programmes, training and skills—and *capital to match—are poor.

But we do have national currencies, which supply at least some of the needed feedback and flexibility. It was not enough to save the UK's pottery industry, but it is better than no feedback at all, which is what you get from (as Jacobs calls it) an "imperial currency" such as that of the Euro (€). Under that system, a relatively inefficient, high-cost economy such as Greece has to compete in the same currency and exchange rate as a cost-efficient economy such as Germany. Far from this acting as a boot camp challenge which forces the less efficient economy to make the necessary investment to raise its competitiveness, it essentially wipes it out as a serious competitor. A more competitive exception to this may be preserved in sectors where it has an absolute monopoly of supply, such as holidays in the Greek islands or visits to the Parthenon. But even there, the impoverished economy can be forced to sell these assets simply in order to keep going.[49]

An early illustration of the level of interventionism needed to coordinate the breathing of *complex systems was the tough action taken in Europe in the late 1990s to force the would-be Euro currencies down to the single, very low, rate of interest set by Germany. In 1990, Italy's

N

short-term rates were around 18 percent, with France at 10 percent, Spain at 15 percent, Germany at 6 percent—and the UK at 10 percent. By 1999, government action had got the rates in the Euro countries down to a common 3.25 percent (the Euro Interbank Offered Rate). Naturally, foreign direct investment boomed, as did stock markets and the price of houses and oil, but that made it hard for (for instance) pension funds that needed to get a decent return for their savers, so "structured products" designed to capitalise directly on that almost-free-money growth (betting on bets) flourished—with consequences that we know to our cost. Maybe high oil prices did have something to do with it, or maybe—as in the case of the reckless housebuilding in Ireland—they were simply another effect of cheap money. At most, they were only the final symptom of an assault on nations' duty of care in the matter of maintaining sensible interest rates for their national currencies.[50]

This matter of currencies is crucial, not only to the future of nations, but, on the minute *scale, to local lean economies. Only with an understanding of the way in which flexible local/citywide/national currencies can keep their respective economies in business, can sense be made of the argument for or against national currencies, and of the case for *local currencies.[51]

In the mature Lean Economy, nations will sustain their national currencies. There will be local currencies operating as well as the national currency, but guardianship of the national currency at the national level will be a non-negotiable duty of government. Loss of control of national currency ripples through into loss of capability in *economics, the progressive *irrelevance of policy and the fading of national *identity to a remnant of tourist stereotypes.

––––––––––

The nation, then—one of the damaged, but surviving, political assets of the late *market economy—is a necessary framework for building the stability needed by the Lean Economy. Scrapping it would be unwise, for the space vacated by the loss of national competence could be filled, all too quickly, by other, more regrettable, forces.

*Empire: a state with a mission

Rather than deriving an identity from long association with a particular *place, as in the case of nations, empire exists to fulfil a mission: to impose a single social and cultural regime from the top down. There is "unity in design, and perseverance, and boldness in pursuit", as Burke wrote of revolutionary France.[52] The Lean Economy, in sharp contrast with this, will need to invent and build *diverse responses from the bottom up, while at the same time looking to the top to keep the peace. And here lies a test for the nation: the disorder that follows the *climacteric will present the state with this indispensable task to do—as indispensable as maintaining the irrigation systems in the despotic regimes decried in *Unlean. If nations, and their accountability, are too weakened and devalued to fulfil that role, the sequel could be empire.

In empire, the sustained politics (disagreement contained with a common identity) which is one of the defining and enduring characteristics of nations does not exist; the state is either defined by its imperial mission or not defined at all. The empire stands for a particular programme, which *has* to prevail. And persuasion is never quite enough: it has to be backed up. New empires, as a general rule—intoxicated by their newly-acquired strength—tend to be aggressive. The security task has to succeed, whatever it takes. The consequences of this are illustrated by Hans Buchheim's explanation of the situation facing the security chief of an imperial regime:

> He can never fall back on the excuse that he has done everything possible for security within the framework of law and ethics; he may not rest until he has taken into account the final *conceivable* possibility of protection. Even if he himself were completely free of ambition and power drive, he would have to go all out to gain the last key position and to eliminate the final suspicious character. And since he is bound to no standards, he will in the end not limit himself to safeguarding the existing order but will try to bring about an order that offers the utmost possible security: the police state.[53]

Underlying that compulsion, there is always some proposition which, at first hearing, is quite plausible and reasonable. No one can reasonably disagree with the claim that there is a need for international coordination to contain terrorism and to address international problems such as *climate change; it does not, however, follow that the formation of a large new empire is the right way to set about it.

As the *System Scale Rule tells us, large-scale problems do not require large-scale solutions; they require small-scale solutions within a large-scale framework. What a major collective task needs is nations with identities and a culture, and a political system organised on the principles of *pull that are characteristic of *lean thinking. And it especially needs to avoid the reduction of *logic and argument to idiot simplifications, or the seduction of nations by one *charismatic person, no matter how enlightened or *sincere.[54] As Edward Gibbon warns in his story of the landslide from the brilliance of Marcus Aurelius to the homicidal psychosis of his successor (his son, Commodus), the victims "must often have recollected the instability of a happiness which depended on the character in a single man".[55]

By contrast, the *Lean Economy and its political context cannot be understood at first glance. It is a landscape of *judgment, *stories, *tradition and *politics, *common capability and *common purpose. It will be feasible if, and only if, it is in the stable setting of a nation.

The tragedy of the regions

Regions in Europe are now pressing their case for increased autonomy. However, as they develop political and administrative structures and confidence, they will, in a sequence analysed by Larry Siedentop, drain power from nations, only to pour it back into the imperial framework which sees it as its mission to abolish nations. The "tragedy of the regions" is the tendency of regions, while seeking greater independence from the nation state, to fall into the more authoritarian embrace of empire.[56] They may think that they can protect their independence and make their interests heard within the wider setting of the empire, but the error is naïve. Siedentop, writing of Europe, notes that:

> The lure of Brussels for resurgent regionalisms is that it provides a centre which can be played off against the traditional "oppressors" — i.e., existing nation-states. . . . The danger is that in throwing off the "shackles" of the

nation-state — rejecting national subordinations which are perceived to be oppressive — there will also be thrown away civic cultures which incorporate democratic norms.[57]

And there is a reduced chance — in a centralised setting such as that being developed by the European Union — of rebuilding a stabilised society from the bottom-up. Its organisational model is a bureaucracy with the right to make its own *laws. Indeed, smaller-scale political organisation, including *counties and their European equivalents, is already in trouble. The French counties were abolished by the French Revolution and replaced with large *Départements* named after rivers. As one analyst writes,

> The size of the regions makes every intermediate body between them and the communes [local authorities] totally redundant. At best the provinces can be used as a geographical and administrative frame for implementing national and regional policies; but as an independent policy body, their role is over.[58]

And the loss of counties, in turn, means the loss, or weakening, of the level of government and administration with the knowledge, accessibility and patience for *local detail. The claim of *subsidiarity is made by European leaders when they have to deal with popular fears about the centralising power and weakened democratic accountability of the Union. In fact, it is the right of regions to do as they are told.

Counties represent the scale on which the local can develop collective expression. They are small enough to be directly in touch with, and aware of, particular local *practice; being numerous (England has 50 counties, compared with 12 regions), they do not naturally form power cliques with central government; their *authority comes up from below, not down from above.

During the five years of the Second World War, regional government showed what it could do. It acted quickly; it distributed; it used local knowledge; it mobilised local resources and goodwill; it improvised. It planned a massive, necessarily authoritarian programme. Without it, according to the historian A.J.P. Taylor, "war socialism would not have been possible".

But on this occasion, he was too easily impressed: when the system was dismantled after the war, he wrote, "the chance was lost to give England the blessings of regional government".[59] Certainly, if the state really wishes to prepare for a life of the top-down control needed in wartime, the establishment of a regional structure is a good first step.[60]

The power of one tier of government is in inverse relation to that of the tiers immediately above and below it. The case can, no doubt, be made for the sequence:

> small group → NEIGHBOURHOOD → parish →
> CITY → county → REGION → nation → EMPIRE
> → planet

In the urban *market economy, with its good *connections, it is not out of the question for people to drive long distances to the regional centre to discuss matters of strictly local concern; and the regional city itself is the centre of economic and political gravity. But in an *energy-limited, *transport-constrained context, where the principle of *cohesion in a shared *culture will matter again, the decisive advantage of being able to support local detail lies with the county, in turn supported by the nation:

> SMALL GROUP → neighbourhood → PARISH →
> city → COUNTY → region → NATION → empire
> → PLANET

The planet needs devolution down to local decision-making; that in turn needs detailed support at the county level, and the effective *protection that nations can offer. The local needs the nation.

*Groups and Group Sizes, Reciprocity and Cooperation > Latency.

NATURAL CAPITAL. See Capital > Types of Capital > Natural Capital.

NATURAL STEP, THE. A *systems-approach to business strategy, based on the scientific principles that have to be satisfied if a system is to be *sustainable.[61] The method uses the "funnel" as a *metaphor for the narrowing range of options available to business and government; and a sequence of four steps (ABCD) for analysis and action:

Awareness of the conditions of sustainability and the place of their business in that wider context;
Baseline mapping of the gap between the criteria of sustainability and the business as a system— including its whole supply chain and social and economic context;
Clear vision of how the business would have to change if it were to fulfil the principles of sustainability—a "backcasting" method is used to trace a path from those principles to their application; and
Down to Action in implementing that vision.

The action will involve collective learning, new ways of working together, systems thinking, stretch goals (aims that may at first seem to be over-ambitious), and a step-by-step approach, starting with the easiest change, moving ahead *incrementally, and grasping the opportunities when these incremental advances start to bring stretch goals within reach.

In fact, as *lean thinking recognises, incrementalism is only part of the story: as you get close-up to the barriers to further progress, you may realise that overcoming them is impossible, except via the total transformation of *kaikaku, a step which will feel anything but natural.[62]
*Choice.

NATURAL SYSTEM. See Ecological System.

NECESSARY AND SUFFICIENT. A crucial distinction between two kinds of condition required for your argument to hold true, or for an outcome or event to take place.

As the words make plain, a condition is *necessary* if the event could not have happened without it; it is *sufficient* if it is enough on its own to cause or trigger the event (although, in some cases, something else could just as well have caused it). Example: Before having the energy to play in tonight's concert I need . . .

a. some bangers and mash [a sufficient condition, but steak and kidney pie would do just as well];
b. some supper [a necessary and sufficient condition].

But note that both "necessary" and "sufficient" are particular to the context: the context here is hunger, but of course I need to be a musician, too.
*Formal Logic, Necessity.

NECESSITY. (1) "The plea for every infringement of human freedom." (William Pitt, 18 November 1783) (2) The considered product of *reflection.
*Distraction, Hyperbole.

NEEDS AND WANTS. A distinction between needs and wants has been made by many critics in the *green movement and its predecessors, who have argued that consumption in response to our needs is justifiable and sustainable, but consumption in response to our wants is not.

The American economist Thorstein Veblen (1857–1929) insisted that the desire to satisfy wants had but one over-riding explanation: "conspicuous consumption". Wants, Veblen tells us, are manifested in unnecessary things like decoration ("architectural distress" in the case of buildings), and in such pointless symbols of an idle and wasted life as flowers, cats and dogs, sports and higher learning. Such conspicuous consumption, he tells us, has no practical value for human life and *well-being; its purpose is simply to impress, to intimidate and to provide evidence that the consumer is lucky enough not to have to do a full day's work and so can exploit other people's toil. Once people have felt the buzz of material excess, it develops an addictive hold over them as powerful as that of alcohol.[63]

So, that leaves "needs"—and what are they? The *utopian Marxist Herbert Marcuse (1898–1979) explains,

> The only needs that have an unqualified claim
> for satisfaction are the vital ones—nourishment,
> clothing, lodging.[64]

The distinction between needs and wants became an issue of even greater concern when people started to realise that the high levels of consumption enjoyed in the *market economy are too great to be sustained by the environment. Evidently consumption must be cut back: envy must be slain; wants must go; needs can stay. "Needs", wrote Duane Elgin in 1981, "are those things that are essential to our survival and growth; wants are those things that are extra—that gratify our psychological desires"—and to indulge wants is a bad thing, reducing "the vastness of who we are" to a mask, an image, an "ill-fitting shell".[65]

Mahatma Gandhi—and E.F. Schumacher, quoting him—came close to a simple equation of need

and greed: "Earth provides enough to satisfy every man's need, but not for every man's greed."[66] Jeremy Seabrook's view of the commodities that reflect wants rather than needs has been consistently blistering: they are akin to heroin, addictive and alienated from human need, and people are goaded into thinking they want them "by the vast and abstract power of capital. . . . Need has been turned against life".[67]

And the responsibility for much of this was down to industry, as Kenneth Galbraith explained. Producers, he wrote, create wants along with the goods to satisfy them, like the town doctor deftly knocking over pedestrians with his car in order to keep the town hospital full. Since these wants are synthesised by advertising, catalysed by salesmanship, and shaped by the discreet manipulations of the persuaders (which itself shows that they cannot be very urgent), consumers find themselves on a mad squirrel wheel of ever increasing, ever-unsatisfied, desire.[68]

Now, one thing to be noted about this critique is that it does not care about the nature of psychological desires; all that really matters is the means which are used to satisfy them. None but the most extreme critic, such as Veblen, really has any objection to wants so long as they are of a kind which non-material—or not-too-obviously-material—means can satisfy: poetry, *conversation and *dancing, it seems, are all right, as are "thinking, singing, laughing, reading books from the public library, interactive electronic entertainment, hiking, painting and playing cards": in Factor Ten's ethic, these are approved occupations.[69] The behaviour that causes the problem is the use of material means for psychological ends—especially if those ends are suspected of being related to social status. If people had a true understanding of what makes them happy, and of what their real needs are, they would keep their *material requirements down to an uncluttered, physiological minimum. They might, with Henry David Thoreau, be content to "derive a real vigor from the scent of the gale wafted over the naked ground, as from strong meats, and realize again how man is the pensioner of nature".[70] From this point of view, the austere repudiation of wants is claimed to be the road to enlightenment.

And yet, this distaste for material goods will not do as a response to the market economy's material

N

NO TIME TO INDULGE YOUR WANTS
Working like a Puritan

"The sound of your hammer at five in the morning, or eight at night, heard by a creditor, makes him easy six months longer; but if he sees you at a billiard-table, or hears your voice at a tavern, when you should be at work, he sends for his money the next day." This is from Benjamin Franklin's *Puritan Credo,* whose first instruction is, "Remember, that *time* is money."[71]

All work and no unnecessary expenditure is a recipe for getting rich; at first sight, it might also seem to be in conflict with the Christian ideal of poverty but, as Max Weber explains, the Puritans were able to see money as "a sign of God's blessing . . . and at the same time the most evident proof of rebirth and genuine faith".[72]

Here is John Wesley struggling with this problem:

I fear, wherever riches have increased, the essence of religion has decreased in the same proportion. Therefore I do not see how it is possible, in the nature of things, for any revival of true religion to continue long. . . . Is there no way to prevent this—this continual decay of pure religion?

His answer is heroic:

We ought not to prevent people from being diligent and frugal; we must exhort all Christians to gain all they can, and to save all they can; that is, in effect, to grow rich.[73]

The formula was certainly effective: the Puritan states of New England raced ahead of the different *traditions in Rhode Island and the South in their early economic development,[74] but the legacy of this, as Tibor Scitovsky writes, is "Puritan money-mindedness . . . distrust of all artifice aimed merely to enhance enjoyment . . . [and] an acceptance of dull food and drab surroundings."

This "joyless economy" cultivates a disdain for the knowledge required to cope with culture; it presses "for the progressive crowding out of a liberal, humanistic education by the requirements of science and technology" and, faced with *boredom, prefers quick kicks to the *reflective skills required for *culture. Culture, "the learning of the leisure class", writes Scitovsky, becomes distrusted and disliked; to the Puritans, "skills and learning aimed solely at enhancing one's ability to obtain enjoyment looked like instruments of the devil".[75]

intemperance. In the "No Time to Indulge Your Wants" sidebar, we observe a confused, if competent, John Wesley. He thought there was nothing inconsistent about making goods for other people while, for himself, his family and his co-workers, there was little comfort, and little time to enjoy the money he made.

For pre-market societies, on the other hand, goods had a significance which extended well beyond their functions as instruments for a practical purpose. Agricultural implements, household goods and weapons, along with houses, churches, fields and wells, were decorated, blessed and given names. And the conceit that goods have a life of their own—that you should therefore not only care for them, but be kind to them, and that

they might even one day answer back—survives, if only in a muted way. D.H. Lawrence once reflected on the furnishings in his seedy lodgings in Florence like this:

We have to choose between the quick and the dead. . . . In this room where I write, there is a little table that is dead; . . . and there is a ridiculous little iron stove, which for some unknown reason is quick. And there is an iron wardrobe trunk, which for some still more mysterious reason is quick. And there are several books, whose mere corpus is dead, utterly dead and non-existent. And there is a sleeping cat, very quick. And a glass lamp, alas, is dead.[76]

The idea that such objects can be alive is (aside from the cat) absurd, but an *imaginative engagement with them is not. A healthy delight in goods—Mary Douglas and Baron Isherwood's "visible part of culture"—is a characteristic, alike, of jackdaws and of enduring *political economies. And a regard for goods, which assigns them a value beyond their *instrumental function and pretends they have a life of their own, is not wholly unconnected with a regard for people. Neither the careful concern for the chattels of the eighteenth century household described by the historian Margaret Vickery, nor the consuming *interest in accumulated household goods demonstrated by the Dodson women in George Eliot's The Mill on the Floss, were cases of gullible and greedy acquiescence to clever advertising; the pleasure they took from the company of the meticulously pressed linen and from the artefacts of their households is *frank and refreshing and, in some cases at least, there was no visible join between their concern for their *household's goods and their concern for its people.[77]

A person's possession of material goods tells you something about him or her. In most societies until the late market economy, they elaborately communicated (among other things) social status, particular *loyalties, obligations and belonging. Clothes, goods and demeanour are signals of personal availability, statements you make about being interested in interacting with other people: invitations, in a sense, to play. In the market economy, the signals given out by goods are much weaker, but this is not a concern because social roles are substantially replaced by money exchange: it does not matter who you are, so long as your *money is good. But, in the absence of an efficiently-functioning market, the identity of the person you are dealing with will be important again; each party has to be sure that the other one can be reliably identified, that he will deliver when the *debt is called in, that he is a willing participant in the society and its culture, and that he is happy to show it.

And for signals to work in this way, another need will become evident: constrained diversity. The ability of signals to inform depends on their being contained within a limited range, with an implied or explicit *grammar and vocabulary. If the *diversity is too great, it forgoes its grammar and ceases to communicate; it

is merely off the scale. In the Lean Economy, signs of *identity, of *good faith, of availability, will be needed.[78]

Clothes in the Lean Economy, for example, may need to work hard as signals of recognition and belonging. This was the business of clothes—not an entirely serious business, because *play was integrated into it—before the weariness, the fever and the fret of a dirty and dislocated industrial *market descended at the start of the nineteenth century. Dress promptly responded to that horror by turning to black, both because conformity and anonymity became commercial assets, and because it disguised the soot. The function of dress as a signal was sharply diminished, though never quite lost; but with the decline of soot, and with the post-market economy's need to reinvent direct *reciprocity between identified people, it will be plain good business to develop the semiotic (signalling) possibilities of dress, and to play around with them.[79] And not just with dress. For the same semiotic reasons, material goods, dwellings and *places will again have something to say.

And here is an intention: what they will say in the *Lean Economy is that every place is a sacred place; every *ecology has its enchantment, its quiet music, its *authority. At the very least, every town and village will need to be visible and communicative: places will have a meaning, giving signals of particular loyalties, of rooted obligations and belonging, of a *cultural landscape. *Public places and private *homes will live up to the standards of the urban designer Francis Tibbalds' Tenth Commandment: "Thou shalt, with all the means available, promote intricacy, joy and visual delight in the built environment."[80] This will do as an aim for the local Lean Economy, whose inhabitants will have the confidence to be robustly materialist, fond of *things*, public and private—including attributes such as decoration which, through having least practical value, are able to give the strongest signals. The Lean Economy will restore the symbolic values and implicit functions of goods; it will be comfortable with material possession in a way that the market economy would envy (*Invisible Goods).

The notion that needs are good and wants bad does not survive inspection. For the anthropologists Douglas and Isherwood, it is a "curious moral split [that] appears under the surface of most economists' thoughts on human needs". Indeed, *Lean Logic* argues that those economists may have it somewhat back-to-front.[81]

The heaviest burden of the modern economy, by far, is that imposed by its own elaborations—the massive infrastructures and material flows of the *intermediate economy—which are needed because of the special problems of sustaining a system of such a *size. Regardless of whether we want them, we now *need* the sewage systems, heavy-goods transport, police forces, hospitals. Given the substantial scale of the task of feeding, raising and schooling a suburban family, and the increasing challenge of such routine needs as finding a post office, many of us undoubtedly need cars. The collapse of local self-reliance was both the cause and the effect of the massive elaboration of *transport, and when that need is no longer met, its life-sustaining function will be bitterly recognised.

It is, then, the multiplication of needs by large-scale industrial life that causes the trouble. Our *wants* are squeezed out, much missed and—if freed of much of the intermediate economy on which at present they depend—light by comparison, not least because they often involve labour-intensive crafts and services: pianists, craftsmen, dressmakers, waitresses, gardeners with minimum environmental impact. Some wants are also needs, of course, and they cannot be cleanly separated, but if we focus our efforts on finding ways, under the stresses of the climacteric, of achieving a substantial and rapid liquidation of our needs, we will be getting somewhere.

*Intentional Waste, Regrettable Necessities, New Domestication, Usury, Scale.

NEIGHBOURHOOD. A large group of around 150 participating adults (for a summary table of key group sizes see *Groups and Group Sizes).

In the history of *cooperation, there has been much agreement on the effectiveness of groups on this *scale. The number is suggested, for instance, by the frequency of the 150-person group in industry. "Compartments" of this size, writes Gerald Fairtlough, have a quality of communication which is "open, intensive, subtle and varied, which could not happen on a larger scale":

> There is a clear boundary marking off
> compartment members from non-members
> and a strikingly different expectation about
> openness, trust, shared purposes and shared
> language inside the boundary, compared with
> expectations across it. [This size of group can]
> create great creative energy in achieving a
> common aim, in carrying out a common project,
> in solving a common problem. It can assemble a
> rich blend of skills and knowledge, giving it the
> potential to produce extraordinary results . . .
> On such a scale, and in the right conditions,
> the creative capability of human beings is
> unlocked—perhaps to an unimaginable extent.[82]

There are many examples of groups of this size. One comes from the Hutterites—the Christian community of agriculturalists (similar to the Amish) now living in the Dakotas and southern Canada. For more than four centuries, they have successfully sustained communes with an upper limit of about 150 members, plus their families. They do not allow *private property, so they pay no wages, but members qualify for the material benefits of membership whatever they do. As a consequence, the only *incentives their members have to pull their weight are their conscience and sense of solidarity. They accept that there will always be people who try to get out of doing the work—they have a saying, "All colonies have their drones"—but solutions are at hand so long as the group remains small: the elders have a quiet talk with them; their fellow colonists encourage them. In a small community, members are ready to recognise their obligations, and prepared to listen to other members who point them out, but if it is allowed to grow larger than around 150 people (about

30 families), the drones multiply, and the colony is forced to split up.[83]

This a matter in which there are *fuzzy boundaries. For instance, some groups of 150 (such as the army company) are single sex, but the historian Peter Laslett includes both adult men and women in his estimate that 150 was the median size for an English village in 1700.[84] Nearly three centuries later, Ronald Blythe claims that the village he studied, Akenfield, tended to organise itself into *informal groups of about that number.[85] The critical point is that 150 is the maximum number with whom you—as a member of the group—can actually engage, cooperate and *reciprocate: you know the internal politics; who belongs to which *small group; how the lines of influence and leadership run. For the larger *community as a whole, if each of the members of the 150-group represent one family, that will allow a community size (including children and the elderly) of some 500–600. But the core network of close interactions holds. 150 is the number of active characters you can cope with in the group before engaged interaction begins to fade into mere acquaintance.

And the crucial role of the 150-group is borne out by the work of the anthropologist Robin Dunbar. As in the case of the size of primary groups (your closest friends and family: see *Small Group), Dunbar was able to show that there is a correlation between primates' neocortex ratios (the ratio between the size of the neocortex and the size of the rest of the brain), and the size of the neighbourhood-scale coalitions which are the foundation of their social standing.

This correlation is trickier than it may seem. Since the neocortex is the part of the brain that can process the politics of multiple interactions, the large neocortex ratio is needed to understand and deal with the complex relationships in the small group. Clear enough so far, but Dunbar argues that the larger the small/primary group you belong to, the larger the secondary group you can make your way in, which is why the neocortex ratio is associated with both group sizes. If you have the benefit of belonging to a relatively large, closely-bonded *primary* group of friends and allies, this power base makes it possible for you to survive and prosper in a relatively large *secondary* group: if you are on your own in a troupe of gelada baboons or in a

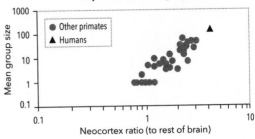

Neocortex ratio and size of secondary groups of primates, including humans

Mean group size / Neocortex ratio (to rest of brain)
● Other primates
▲ Humans

neighbourhood of human primates, it is hard for you to defend your interests. A primary group of close friends puts you in a tenable position in the secondary group/troupe/neighbourhood.

Dunbar demonstrates this by testing the scale of 150 against the neocortex ratios, and finding that primates with larger neocortex ratios do in fact live in larger groups. Those with the lowest ratios (1:1) are minimally socialised, living essentially solitary lives, but primates with a ratio of 3:1 live in groups of about 15. He then applies this correlation to the case of humans, with their neocortex ratio of 4:1, and shows that this corresponds to a mean (secondary) group size of 148 (see figure).[86] He summarises,

> Taken together, these results suggest that human societies contain buried within them a natural grouping of around 150 people. These groups do not have a specific function: . . . The figure of 150 seems to represent the maximum number of individuals with whom we can have a genuinely social relationship, the kind of relationship that goes with knowing who they are and how they relate to us. Putting it another way, it's the number of people you would not feel embarrassed about joining uninvited for a drink if you happened to bump into them in a bar.[87]

150—all lines of enquiry seem to lead to this number as the optimum size of the neighbourhood-community—plus families. And yet, just as twelve seems too many to be a realistic *small group in action, so 150 is too many for day-to-day business. It is, rather, an immediate local resource to be called on: it can bring substantial numbers—such as the 35-member groups which Dunbar describes as "overnight camps" — to a common project; or it can all come together for policy-making and changing locations; or for identity-building with parties and *ritual. The neighbourhood is the *household's setting, protection, labour-resource and store of *capital.[88]

This is what specialists in animal behaviour would call a "fission-fusion" social system, with flexibility, coming-and-going and kinship links both within and between communities.[89] The task determines the size of *groups within the neighbourhood, but *cooperation in the community grows out of the sense of living together, and the shared strengths, weaknesses, opportunities and threats that can be sustained between about 150 people and their families.

What the neighbourhood does

The neighbourhood has four functions. First, it has a material job to do. It is an active agent for lean production — for community-wide conservation and the provision of renewable *energy; for local *food, *water and *waste management and the conservation of fertility; and for the provision and management of *materials.

Secondly, it has a *political function. It defends the interests of its people in a fiercely political wider world. Small groups may well be able to speak for themselves at the *parish level, but it helps if they have a solid power base of support from their neighbourhood. Politics is about having allies.

The third function is social. The wider community is needed for the more elaborate *ceremonies and *religion, for *carnival, for people seeking discussion with specific matching *professions, talents, interests or *expectations, and for courtship, but in the neighbourhood there is conviviality, and it is the *place where the basic *skills of society and *culture are learned — a setting for fun, exuberance, *play and parties. Neighbourhoods — their internal politics and their relations with each other and with the wider community — are the starting point, the power base, from which to participate in the community and the *public sphere. They are ambivalently located with respect to the public and private spheres, but they have known you since you were little, and they care if you go away. They are where *home is.

The fourth function of the neighbourhood is as an enabler of events. In the future, it will be larger groups on the *scale of the wider community or parish — or the parishes in a town — which take the initiative, as we are seeing with *Transition Towns. But it is not really the parish that does the work; that comes from smaller groups, especially the neighbourhood. When sustained application is needed, the *community inspires it; the neighbourhood does it; the *household lives it. *Reciprocity and Cooperation > Collaboration.

NEOTECHNIC. A form of *political economy which takes advantage of the more *efficient, less labour-intensive new technology ("neotechnic") that began to develop in the early years of the twentieth century, replacing the former ("paleotechnic") technology with which the Industrial Revolution got started.

The word was coined by the biologist, sociologist, educationalist and town planner, Sir Patrick Geddes (1854–1932). Among neotechnic technology's critical features were that:

1. less labour was needed to supply the fundamentals, such as *energy;
2. industry could be decentralised, no longer needing to be so concentrated in huge industrial centres, heavily dependent on transport; and
3. local producers could, in principle, provide a higher proportion of their own needs, reducing their dependence on imports.

Geddes' leading example was the displacement of coal by oil:

> No one surely but can see that the practical disappearance of the legion of stokers, which coal fuel involves, is something, physiologically if not politically, comparable to the emancipation of the galley-slaves.
>
> *Patrick Geddes,* Cities in Evolution, *1915.*[90]

and Geddes followed through the logic of this is to the point of seeing the evolution of a *cooperative, *civic, beautiful *Utopia (good place), in sharp contrast to the Cacotopia (Greek: *kakós* bad + *tópos* place) which had preceded it:

> The escape from Paleotechnic to Neotechnic order is thus from Cacotopia to Utopia — the first turning on dissipating energies towards

individual money gains, the other on con-serving energies and organising environment towards the maintenance and evolution of life, social and individual, civic and eugenic.[91]

Although local production was a favourite idea of the time, Geddes differed from others who have seemed to be on the same case—such as Pierre-Joseph Proudhon, William Morris and Eric Gill—in that he saw the ben-efits coming, not from a form of technological retreat (handcrafts), but from advance towards high technol-ogy producing goods on a smaller, local scale, with less need for *capital, and less *pollution. The thinker with whom Geddes had most in common was Peter Kropotkin, whose *Fields, Factories and Workshops Tomor-row*, published in 1899—and taking a pragmatic view of what "local" means—looked forward to a society . . .

> . . . where every aggregation of individuals, large enough to dispose of a certain variety of natural resources—it may be a nation, or rather a region—produces and itself consumes most of its own agricultural and manufactured produce.[92]

Progress, in fact,

> . . . is in producing for home use.[93]

and its time is coming:

> To return to a state of affairs where corn is grown, and manufactured goods are fabricated *for the use of those very people who grow and produce them*—such will be, no doubt, the problem to be solved during the coming years of European history.[94]

What these two lean thinkers could not have been expected to foresee was the astonishing decline in the costs—and growth in the *scale—of *transport, and the consequent development of massive centres of concentrated production of (for instance) *food, manu-facturing and services. The potential of the Neotechnic principle recognised by Geddes and Kropotkin has not been developed. In our time, it is being retrieved.

But there is a snag. Just at the moment when small-scale local technologies are maturing to hyperefficiency, we are beginning to become aware that the prospects for a reliable grid, delivering cheap electricity, are less assured than they were, and that the global industrial establishment which produces the hyperefficient technology in the first place cannot be guaranteed (*Climacteric). Should those two requirements fail, the neotechnic will not develop as hoped.

Will we be back to the old version—paleotechnic? Our knowledge of science is better, as is our experience of *appropriate technologies specifically designed to lie within the competence of local resources and skills. And society may be smaller than the one those huge pieces of equipment, and the stokers that serviced them, was designed for. Coal-based industry is unlikely to make a comeback. But where we will stand on the technological spectrum—between giant, miniature and appropriate—is still uncertain.

*Lean Household, New Domestication, Localisation, Energy Prospects.

NETWORKS. See Systems Thinking ❭ Form ❭ Networks.

NEW DOMESTICATION. The building of house-holds' competence to the point at which they can provide most of what they want from their own, or local, resources. This entry will put on one side, for the moment, uncertainties as to how much of the indus-trial establishment needed to supply the equipment to produce local *energy will survive the *climacteric. Instead, let's project some trends . . .

Some 8,000 years ago, before *agriculture had been invented, people had to go off on hunting and gathering expeditions for their food. This worked well because it meant that they had no need for cultivation, nor for the *responsibility of rearing animals, caring for them and preventing them from straying or being stolen. Getting *food in this way did not take very long, so they had a lot of free time, and hunting also had the advantage of being a significant *ritual, making sense of the commu-nity's place in the natural environment and, in a settled hunter-gatherer *ecology, caring for it with *wisdom. The harvest was governed by the ecology, and by the human animals' understanding of it, not by the amount of work they did.[95]

But hunting and gathering did not provide food for many people, so that, with *productivity gains—cooking

N

(especially the discovery that grains could be made edible by cooking), selection of the most nutritious fruits, and improving *climate—the growing *populations of early societies gradually evolved a different way of doing it. Instead of relying on the wild to breed and provide their food, they did it themselves. It was harder work, but it was successful, bringing the cultivation of food and the rearing of animals within the perimeter fence, under their direct influence and care; and improving them, often out of recognition, in the process. That was the first domestication: a response to necessity and technology.[96]

The second domestication could be a similar response. It will mean bringing the provision of goods and services under the direct influence of the domestic economy. And it will need the right equipment:

The tale of the oven: a story of domestication

1. *Before the oven was domesticated, villagers had to go out and hunt for one.*

   Villagers in the Middle Ages did not usually have an oven in their possession, so they had to do their baking in the kitchens of the local manor or priory and, of course, there was a tendency among these oven-monopolists to exploit their position. If the loaves were burned or half-baked, for instance, there was not much the villagers could do about it. The other monopolist in the technology of food preparation was the miller. Even after small hand-mills had been developed, there were local bans on their use; villagers had to carry their corn to the mill, and when they got there they had to wait around, perhaps for days, for the job to be done, or for the millpond to fill, or for the wind to get up. Bakers and millers had villagers in their power, and used their advantage, with "all sorts of tricks and vexations", to wind them up.[97]

2. *Then, with domestication, ovens came to live in the kitchen.*

   Later, houses were built with "a big bread-baking oven in the wash-house. This was like a large cupboard with an iron door, lined with brick and going far back into the wall. Faggots of wood were lighted inside and the door was closed upon them until the oven was well heated. Then the ashes were swept out and baking tins with joints of pork, potatoes, batter puddings, pork pies, and sometimes a cake or two, were popped inside and left to bake without further attention."[98]

3. *Unfortunately, with the Enclosures, and the migration to towns, domestic ovens became rare luxuries . . .*

   "And at the same time there emerged from scores of by-streets, lanes and nameless turnings innumerable people, carrying their dinners to the bakers' shops. . . . In time the bells ceased, and the bakers were shut up [for a few hours], and yet there was a general shadowing forth of all these dinners and the progress of their cooking in the thawed blotch of wet above each baker's oven, where the pavement smoked as if its stones were cooking too." And then the bakers opened up again and the people picked up their cooked Christmas dinners and took them home.[99]

4. *. . . until twentieth century builders came up with a very tame version with a friendly suburban nature . . .*

   The specifications for a typical semi-detached house erected in North Ilford in 1934 and costing £745 included a gas cooker in the kitchen.[100]

5. *. . . which had the strange effect of starting to drive the family wild.*

   The traditional family meal is on its way out, according to a Mintel study. The revolution has been facilitated by the microwave. "Where is the witty conversation, the thoughtful table manners, the intergenerational communion that family meals are supposed to generate? Gone to a silence punctuated by grunts."[101]

6. *But maybe the technology that started the trouble was the fork:*

   "The invention of the cheap fork in the Industrial Revolution was the start of table manners, and the end of the communal practice of eating from a single dish and drinking from a single cup. It was a momentous innovation: from that time, the rites of the sacrament of holy communion and of family meals went their separate ways."[102]

The challenge presented by the failure of the *market economy will lead to a different way of meeting *material needs—that is, to the domestication of industry. Although the transition to this new domestication will never be complete, any more than that of the first domestication (for instance, fish and boar are still hunted and wild food is still gathered), industry will increasingly become part of the competence of *household production. This is the natural conclusion of industrialisation.

The domestic sector, ranging between the *scale of the *household and the *community, will supply itself. It will be enabled to do this by a deep reduction in its *needs, with a corresponding advance in the ability to meet needs and wants, alike, from its own *skills and resources and the *place it lives in.[103]

*Complexity, Localisation, Neotechnic, Ecology: Farmers and Hunters.

No Alternative, The Fallacy Of. (1) The *fallacy that there is no alternative (but you may not have looked hard enough).

(2) The fallacy that, because there is no alternative to the particular strategy under discussion, that strategy must be feasible. Example: It is argued that the other big *energy options are not going to provide solutions in the future, and that *therefore* therefore the solution is a vast expansion of *nuclear energy.

But this is a *non sequitur: the lack of feasibility of the other options tells us nothing about whether an expansion of nuclear power is feasible or not. *Lean Logic*'s response is to think about the problem in a different way, starting from *different premises.

Non Sequitur ("It does not follow"). An argument whose conclusion does not follow from the premise. e.g., "It is supported by the majority/It is a break with the past/I am an *expert/It is more accessible . . . *therefore* it is right."

Most fallacies can be interpreted as *non sequiturs* in some form. Anthony Weston, in his *Rulebook for Arguments*, further thought:

[*Non sequitur is a*] very general term for a bad argument. Try to figure out specifically what is supposed to be wrong with the argument.[104]

*Fallacies, False Inference, Irrelevance, Logic.

Nuclear Energy. The argument that is most widely made in support of nuclear energy is that there is *no alternative. In a sense, that is true. But there is a *fallacy here: if we are considering options A, B, C and D, the fact that options A, B and C do not exist cannot be interpreted as proof that D exists.

The big three energy providers are oil, gas and coal; nuclear, which supplies electricity to the grid equivalent to about 2½ percent of the world's final demand for energy, is very small in comparison. And those three, as detailed in *Energy Prospects, are in trouble, so the incentive to turn to nuclear energy as the only remaining alternative is strong. The catch is that nuclear energy is in trouble too.[105]

At first sight, the nuclear energy industry is a model of clean and orderly electricity-generation set in an idyllic environment. The favoured portrait shows a nuclear plant with its graceful cooling towers as a backdrop to a peaceful reed-lined lake, home to happy-looking ducks. But the industry has a rather unfair advantage in these matters. Most of the mess it makes is far away, both in space and *time; some of it is invisible; and nuclear fuel itself is a compact item, which most people have never seen. Relative to coal-fired power stations, with their heaps of coal and ash, nuclear reactors seem to be close to magic (*Energy Prospects ⟩ Coal).

But the reality of the nuclear cycle is rather different. It involves a sequence of many stages, almost all of which produce large quantities of radioactive *waste, and use large quantities of energy with carbon emissions to match. It starts—like coal—at the mine, and if you read on, and look at the table, you will find out what happens next. Roughly. It is something of a disgrace that the story cannot be made more robust, more immune from critics armed with contrary *numbers, than it is. The problem is that, with one exception, no one has ever carried out a comprehensive analysis of the whole nuclear energy chain, attaching fully-researched estimates of the energy used at each stage. That one exception is the nuclear engineer, Jan Willem Storm van Leeuwen, who (in partnership with the late Dr. Philip

N

LIFE CYCLE

Nuclear Energy

Carbon emissions associated with each stage in the life cycle				
FRONT END	TOTAL CARBON EMISSIONS gCO$_2$/kWh	BACK END		TOTAL CARBON EMISSIONS gCO$_2$/kWh
Mining (drilling and blasting, excavation, haulage, *sorting)		Management of overburden and waste from mines		
Milling (crushing and grinding, leaching, washing, clarification and filtering, solvent extraction, stripping, precipitation, drying and calcination. Product: uranium oxide (yellowcake))	2.95	Disposal of mill tailings and treatment waste. Reclamation of mining area		5.34
Refining and conversion (the yellowcake is converted to u-hexafluoride, UF$_6$)		Reconversion of depleted UF$_6$ back to uranium oxide, which must then be packed for final disposal in a geological repository		
Enrichment (the presence of the isotope U-235 is raised from 0.7% to 3.5%. Method: centrifuge and diffusion—world average)	5.83			6.44
Fuel fabrication (forming the ceramic-uranium pellets for use in the reactor)				
Reactor construction	23.20	Clean-up, dismantling and disposal of reactor in geological repository		34.80
Operation, maintenance and refurbishment of reactor	24.37	Management, packaging and geological disposal of spent fuel		4.85
TOTAL FRONT END	56.35		TOTAL BACK END	51.43
NUCLEAR LIFE-CYCLE TOTAL (ROUNDED): 108 gCO$_2$/kWh				

Source: Storm van Leeuwen (2008), "Nuclear Power: The Energy Balance", especially Part G, "Energy Analysis: Results". It is assumed that a relatively rich grade of soft ore (0.15 percent) is used. Reserves of this grade are in decline; hard ores (granite) yield less energy per kg of CO$_2$ released, because they require more energy in the milling.[106]

Smith, until his death in 2005) has produced a complete life-cycle assessment of nuclear energy.

It is criticised on all sides—both by the nuclear industry and by informed critics of nuclear energy—but, as one critic recognises,

Storm is the only person who has tried to put the whole nuclear chain together. His work is the best analysis we have at the moment.[107]

As for his critics among the uranium miners, who insist that there is still plenty of uranium available,

You have to remember that mining is optimism. It's a heroic and risky business. Optimism is what keeps them going; they just have to believe the stuff is there.[108]

The following paragraphs use Storm van Leeuwen's numbers. Don't take them too precisely, because by the time you read this, they will have been revised. But bear in mind that the overall story is clear and decisive—nuclear can only be a minor player for the rest of its short life and, before long, it will stop being a net supplier of energy; instead, it will be needing to *use* more energy than it can supply.[109]

So, back to the mine. A typical reactor needs 200 tonnes of natural uranium for a year's output. To keep a reactor in fuel for a year, therefore, it is necessary to mine around 140,000 tonnes of ore. How come? Well, uranium ore is contained in rocks at ore concentrations of between 0.2 percent and 0.01 percent (richer ores are rare and largely exhausted). Let's assume a generous average of 0.15 percent. At this ore grade, the milling process which extracts the uranium oxide from the surrounding rock is 95 percent efficient—and 200 × (100/0.15) (100/95) ≈ 140,000. At the proposed opencast Olympic Dam mine in Western Australia, the ore grade is 0.03 percent, and at this grade the milling process is 86 percent efficient, so some 800,000 tonnes of ore has to be mined for one year's supply of fuel for one reactor. Moreover, the ore bed itself is 350 metres down, so a large 'overburden' has to be removed before the mining itself can start.[110]

Extraction of the uranium oxide consists of crushing and grinding, leaching with sulphuric acid, washing and neutralising with salt, and then further treatment with (amongst other chemicals and solvents) ammonia, lime and nitric acid. The mill tailings must then be removed, and the ore has to be washed, clarified, filtered, further refined by precipitation, and then cleaned and dried to produce uranium oxide, or yellowcake.[111]

Next comes "enrichment". The isotope that starts the process off in the reactor is uranium-235, but there is only a trace of it—0.7 percent—in natural uranium, and this has to be brought up to 3.5 percent. The yellowcake is reacted with fluorine compounds to produce uranium hexafluoride gas, which is then placed in centrifuges. For every tonne of uranium hexafluoride enriched—and then fabricated into ceramic pallets for use in the reactor—some five tonnes are depleted. Depleted uranium hexafluoride is toxic, radioactive and explodes on contact with water; it abruptly turns from a solid to a gas if it warms up (to 56.5°C) and, as a gas, it belongs to a group of chemicals (the halogenated compounds) whose impact on the climate ranges up to some 20,000 times as much as the same mass of carbon dioxide. For final disposal, it must be converted into uranium oxide or into metallic uranium, before being placed in secure containers and buried deep underground in a geologically-stable repository.[112]

Nuclear fission itself does not produce carbon dioxide, but most of the processes surrounding that event are energy-consuming. The reactor itself has to be built, and then comprehensively refurbished at least once in its lifetime, before eventually being decommissioned, cleaned out, broken into pieces, packed in containers and buried. For each year of operation, 200 tonnes of fuel becomes 200 tonnes of high-level waste. That waste is very radioactive: stand close to it for a moment or two and you are dead. As they become more tightly-packed, the rods need to be separated by boron panels to stop active components of the waste—such as plutonium-239—forming a critical mass. It needs to be kept under water in cooling ponds for a minimum of 10-20 years before being placed in containers. At present, temporary containers are used. Permanent storage requires casks made of steel, lead and electrolytic (very high quality) copper, which are then buried in deep repositories lined with bentonite clay. And the cooling ponds in which fresh high-level waste is stored require a constant flow of *water; if they dry out, the spent fuel rods can be expected to catch fire. A power supply and stable *institutions are needed to keep the water circulating for the necessary decades.[113]

The processes listed in the table as "front end" are those involved in producing electricity for the grid; "back end" processes constitute the clearing up afterwards. At present, almost none of the waste produced by the nuclear industry has been treated and buried, but this must eventually be done. The total energy cost of the front end and the back end is indicated in the table by the carbon emissions which they produce. As it happens, the energy costs for the front end and the back end of the process are approximately the same, at around 55 grams of carbon dioxide per kilowatt hour of electricity delivered to the grid. At an ore grade of 0.15 percent, the energy needed by the front end is equal to about 25 percent of the gross output of energy to the grid. As is the energy needed by the back end. In other words, the net power available for consumption—after allowing for those front end and back end energy costs—is just 50 percent of the gross power produced.[114]

Now, all this depends crucially on the availability of high quality ore. The problem is that, as the industry matures, it has to turn to poorer grades, and there is a theoretical limit at which so much ore has to be mined and milled, and so much energy is needed for the task, that the energy balance turns negative: more energy has to be put in to the process than comes out of it. The theoretical limit for the grade of ore from which you can get a positive energy balance—assuming that everything goes according to plan—is (for hard rock) 0.02 percent, or (for soft rock) 0.01 percent.[115]

But that really is only a "theoretical" limit, because things do not generally go according to plan. Here we can draw on a crucially important measure of energy wealth: "energy return on energy invested" (EROEI). The EROEI of the entire economy of the United States in 2008 has been estimated at about 40:1—in other

N

words, about 2.5 percent of the economy's total output is devoted to gathering the energy it needs. If EROEI drops to 10:1, some 10 percent of the economy must be devoted solely to energy-gathering; at 1:1, it is 100 percent: energy limits, when they occur, are decisive. So it is important not to fudge the real value of EROEI, and to make a clear working distinction between the "theoretical return on energy invested" (TROEI) and the "practical return on energy invested" (PROEI). If (for instance) the ore deposit is very deep, or if there is constant flooding, or if there is no water (so that the process depends on desalinated seawater), or if diesel oil becomes scarce, then, in practice, the return on energy invested can be worse than 1:1. It can turn negative. For an energy project to be worthwhile, it needs to produce a PROEI of at least 20:1.[116]

So, how much high-grade uranium remains? Well, depletion estimates are never straightforward, but let us start with one that says there is some 60 years' supply of uranium rich enough to at least give us a positive *theoretical* energy return (TROEI). Suppose that, over this period, the number of nuclear reactors that now exist in the world could theoretically continue to produce a net flow of energy to the electricity grid:[117]

- Now deduct the energy that would be needed for the mining, milling and construction (front end) processes described above. That energy — approximately 25 percent of the gross output — is equivalent to 15 years' supply.[118]
- Now deduct the energy that would be needed for all the cooling, clearing up, container construction, dismantling, and burial (back end) processes needed. That also comes to about 25 percent of the gross energy output — another 15 years' supply.[119]
- Now remember that, while the industry is here assumed to have 60 years of life ahead of it, it also already has 60 years of life behind it, during which it has been steadily producing waste, none of which has been cleared. That will require energy equivalent to 25 percent of the gross output — yet another 15 years' supply.

If we add these together, it means that approximately 45 years of a 60-year total supply of uranium would be used up either in the (front end) production process

itself, or in the (back end) waste disposal. And that in turn means that our notional and optimistic estimate of 60 years remaining supply leaves us with just 15 years' worth of electricity delivered to the grid: from the turning point of 2025, the industry will effectively have to direct the whole of its output to the task of clearing up its own waste.

In fact, the idea that there is sixty years' supply of uranium at the present rate of demand looks optimistic. Already the production of uranium from mining falls well short of present demand of 65,000 tonnes a year; the shortfall (22,000 tonnes) is supplied by drawing down from stockpiles of uranium and dismantled missiles left over from the Cold War, which are expected to reach exhaustion around 2013.[120] So we have to ask: what if the available supply were significantly less than 60 years? If the supply of ore rich enough to satisfy the requirements of PROEI were half of that — 30 years — then the turning point after which the industry would need energy equivalent to the whole of its own gross energy output for the task of clearing up its own wastes is 2010. If there were only fifteen years' supply of ore at current rates of demand, then the turning point would have been 2000.[121]

If the clear-up is (or has already been) postponed beyond the turning point, then the industry will never be able to generate enough energy to clear up its own wastes, and will have to use other sources of energy which it will never be able to pay back. The alternative is to leave the waste dumps on the landscape indefinitely. But without attention and protection, and a constant supply of energy to circulate the cooling water, the unstable waste would in due course start to leak and catch fire. In many cases it would be flooded in the early years of rising sea levels.

But what if these depletion estimates on uranium supply are overly pessimistic? Suppose that rather than 60 years' uranium supply left, there were as much as 120 years' worth, enough to last at the present rate of extraction until 2130. Well, using the same estimates for the energy-cost of dealing with the waste, the turning point at which the industry would need to use the whole of its energy to clear up the waste would be 2055 — to be followed by 75 years of working to capacity on the task of waste clearance, with no energy sales to pay for it. It seems unlikely that, even if the industry did find vast and unexpected supplies of uranium, its past and future *waste dumps will ever be cleared up.

The impacts of an uncontrolled worldwide legacy of nuclear waste dumps, degrading and catching fire at their leisure, are not known for certain. Would there be a series of localised Chernobyls erupting around the planet indefinitely? If reactors and their spent fuel dumps are flooded as sea levels rise, what would be the implications for coastlines, the oceans and fishing? And how might all this affect our *health and well-being? This would be a dainty research project. What we do know is that, if the actual energy costs of preventing this outcome are factored into our understanding of the matter, the nuclear industry cannot any longer be regarded as an available source of energy.[122]

It is possible that more token reactors will be built. It will almost certainly have to be with government funds, since the industry itself is aware of the problems. And by the time the new reactors are ready to start paying back the energy that was used to construct them, the world's supply of uranium will be so depleted that it is likely that they will never be started up. Meanwhile they will have shifted the priority of energy policy away from solutions that actually work. If they are started up, and then shut down for lack of fuel, at the same time as the electricity grid is down owing to a lack of gas, then there will be no power supply to keep water circulating in the ponds. They will then dry out.

*Energy Prospects, Control Overload, Lean Energy.

NUMBERS, THE FALLACY OF. The *fallacy that if you cite precise numbers, particularly if they are large, you know what you are talking about. Example: a critic argues against taking action on *climate change: "Estimates indicate that the total cost of global warming will be about $5 trillion", whereas the cost of responding on the scale that "many suggest" would be $4 trillion, plus at least another $150 billion a year—so perhaps it isn't worth it, and we should spend the money on other priorities?[123]

It sounds authoritative until you wonder what basis there is for choosing the time horizon (5 years? 100 years?) that you need for a tidy costing, why there is no sign of taking into account the large saving derived

from improvements in energy efficiency, and why the estimate for the cost of climate change is so low; indeed, how can the prospect of runaway climate change be costed at all? It is necessary also to recognise that "other" uses of the *money, such as providing clean drinking *water, will become both impossible and pointless as global warming takes its expected course, unless a dramatic reduction in emissions is achieved in the near future. There is nothing there—no estimate, no investigation of the subject, no argument; and yet those hard-headed numbers have proved to be effective propaganda. One spoof number is worth 743 carefully-researched words.

*Pascal's Wager.

O

OBJECTIVITY. Evaluation of a subject, free from prior opinion or personal *interest. But what if your evaluation is governed by your determination to prove how objective you are? If you are going to be so dry about it, leaving nothing to uncertainty or to the *emotions, you may still be some distance from understanding it, being filled instead with a delicious sense of your impartiality. And if you don't bring some frame of reference or opinion—Burke calls it "prejudice"—to the matter, a sensible judgment on the matter will be elusive:

> We are afraid to put men to live and trade each
> on his own private stock of reason; because we
> suspect that this stock in each man is small, and
> that the individuals would be better to avail
> themselves of the general bank and capital
> of nations, and of ages. . . . Prejudice renders
> a man's virtue his habit; and not a series of
> unconnected acts. Through just prejudice, his
> duty becomes a part of his nature.[1]

*Casuistry, Encounter, Mindset, Scepticism, Big Stick.

OIL. See Energy Prospects.

OPEN ACCESS, THE FALLACY OF. The *fallacy that a common resource can be sustained despite the

members who have *responsibility for it being unable to control access to it.
*Commons, Closed Access.

OPPORTUNITY COST. The extent to which doing one thing means that you cannot at the same time do something else; the cost of having to forgo doing the next best thing—the thing which you would otherwise be doing with your time. For further definition, and discussion of its significance, see *Slack and Taut.

Note that the 'costs' of some actions are actually benefits. For example, when you weed the vegetable bed, this has costs, in that it requires you to do a couple of hours' work. However, if you enjoy it, if you benefit from the exercise which you would have to take anyway, and if you are not sacrificing some other important thing which you want or *need to do more, then the cost of weeding the bed is negative—i.e., not a net cost, but a benefit.

Another example: the cost of energy-efficiency in your *home as a measure to help to achieve the *energy descent and stabilise the *climate may not in fact be a cost at all. Unless it is expensive and inefficient, it will in due course *save* you money.

ORDINARY BIAS, THE. The presumption that because a proposition is ordinary, and presumes business-as-usual, it must be true.
*Damper.

ORGANIC. (1) A model of cultivation which focuses on maintaining a fertile soil as the enabling condition for producing food and raising animals with resistance to pests and disease, making it unnecessary to turn to industrial pesticides and fertilisers. See *Lean Food.
(2) A model for building a project, notably a *community, which is based on a *network of relationships built one step at a time: a form of *emergence, in which outcomes grow out of the project in ways which no individual, including the *leader or social entrepreneur, could have planned. This meaning of "organic" is in a sense the same as the first meaning above: it grows in the soil of a *system which is allowed to develop its potential.
(3) A word used as a rhetorical device to endorse the inevitability of a totalitarian *ideology. See *Hyperbole.

P

PAEDOMORPHISM (Child-form). (1) Failure by a system—an organism, person or society—to mature, leaving it childish, although some attributes (such as *size) may have achieved the adult state.
(2) The infantilising of society by a government which does not believe that people are capable of the thought or action needed for the collective benefit unless placed under constant supervision.
(3) The shedding of the elaborations accumulated by a mature system—hence, a form of *kaikaku*, enabling it to renew itself, achieving the flexibility and invention needed to cope with new conditions in new ways.[1]
*Paradigm, The Wheel of Life, Systems Thinking.

PANARCHY. See Hierarchy.

PARADIGM. A frame of reference which makes reasonably good sense of a complex subject, and enables us to think about it, to work with it and to get results which we can at least in part predict, and which we may be able to apply in useful ways. The word "paradigm" has been around some six centuries, in the sense of a story—an exemplar—retold many times to illustrate an argument or a group of ideas with something in common. It became a crucial idea in modern thought when, in 1962, the philosopher of science, Thomas Kuhn, published his book *The Structure of Scientific Revolutions*. in the context of the progress of scientific discoveries.[2]

The idea is important to *Lean Logic* for two reasons. It tells us something about how we as thinking people handle ideas which are too complex to work out from first principles. And it contains within it the idea of radical change: *kaikaku* is one of the key principles of *lean thinking, and is central to our future at a time when circumstances of *climate, *economics and society require revolutions in our thinking and in our assumptions.

Let's start with the first of those. When a complex subject is taught, there has to be an agreed frame of reference for it, and this forms the foundation of the *profession consisting of people who are competent in it. But, of course, there is a problem here. The frame of reference that is being taught is, in many ways, certain to be wrong. It will be better than nothing, but it will contain *anomalies and maybe even *paradoxes—signs that there are mistakes in there. In some cases, the people working in the field are aware of them but have not worked out how to correct them; in other cases they suppose things to be true that aren't: they don't know what they don't know. But they teach it as the *truth, all the same. As Kuhn summarises, this all adds up to "a strenuous and devoted attempt to force nature into the conceptual boxes supplied by professional education . . . into the preformed and relatively inflexible box that the paradigm supplies".[3]

So there is a sense here of making do with what we have, despite the imperfections, and the reward is a discipline—a story-so-far—which enables new entrants to learn quickly and to do useful work. And there is a stable basis from which specialists can then do the detailed research which Kuhn rather disparagingly calls "mopping up operations", but which enable them "to investigate some part of nature in a detail and depth that would otherwise be unimaginable".[4]

There follows a long-lasting phase of detailed study, or "normal science"—a period of steady progress—but this normality can be expected in due course to crack as it reveals more and more contradictions between the paradigm and actual observation. Scientists respond to these problems in a host of ways: they look again; they check their equipment; they develop what became known later as "auxiliary hypotheses" which solve—or explain away—the problem while leaving the paradigm itself intact. And yet, despite all these efforts to protect the paradigm, eventually the crisis is reached when there is no getting away from the horrible truth that it is significantly wrong, and the tension builds until something comes along to take its place. What follows is what Kuhn calls a "scientific revolution".[5]

Those are tough and exciting times for people working in the field. The most-established *experts who have been most successful in filling the gaps in the previous paradigm and polishing it up have most to lose, because much of their previous work now turns out to be *irrelevant (*Galley Skills). There is resistance; there are breakthroughs to be made, often by those who are relatively new to the field; there are difficulties in making the new, paradigm-busting work visible to those scientists who built their careers and *mindsets around the paradigm that is now under attack. At the end of this storm and stress, you get a new paradigm. The profession converges on a new way of thinking, and there is a whole new supply of uncertainties and interesting questions to keep those in the field busy for a long time to come.

But if it's wrong why put up with it?

Kuhn's story of the progress of science did not meet with complete approval. One critic was Karl Popper, the great champion of the open society, scourge of *ideology and defender of language from the unctuous, smiling emptiness which misshaped the twentieth century. As he constantly pointed out, evidence of being wrong is the only incontrovertible information we ever get about whether a universal hypothesis is right or not. It is like the "black swan" story: a theory that all swans are white is absolutely proved to be wrong by a single sighting of a black swan; but it is not proved to be right by a thousand sightings of white swans. That, for Popper, meant that when evidence that falsifies a theory comes along, it should be grasped with both hands, and the theory should be modified accordingly.[6]

An argument ensued. Popper's central insight about falsifiability was beyond challenge. But sometimes it is more complicated than that, and here are two complications:

1. *No evident alternative, yet*. There is no case for rubbishing a hypothesis, even if it is not true, if at the same time it is useful and you have no idea what to put in its place.
2. *More information needed*. If you reinforce one hypothesis which isn't fulfilling its promise (e.g., "Faith can move mountains") with another one (e.g., "Clearly you don't have enough faith"), there is of course the near-certainty of sinking out of sight into nonsense, and one of Popper's most strongly-expressed arguments was about the need to avoid adding auxiliary hypotheses to the point that the statement could not possibly be proved to be untrue. And yet, the addition of an auxiliary hypothesis may be *necessary: "Potatoes are perfectly safe to eat" is a dubious statement

P

DIGGING IN
Two other ways
of protecting a paradigm

1. *The destruction of immature science.* Fresh and creative hypotheses may have little research to support them. If they represent a significant challenge to the established paradigm, they are likely to feel the full force of its critique, and may indeed be effectively falsified by it, at least to the satisfaction of those who believe the present paradigm to be true. In this way, the dominant view may be securely defended from criticism while, in the process, developing a culture of macho refutation, constantly on duty for the task of bullying new arrivals into submission.

2. *Power and patronage.* Falsification can be further corrupted with the help of the political influence of the prevailing paradigm, its *institutions, its *experts and its *money, and the material advantages that tend to accrue to a mature paradigm in a self-reinforcing cycle where patronage buys influence (*Mindset). That in turn can blossom into utterly *sincere conviction in the minds of those who are too tired, busy or *ideology-led to think, and this in turn secures more patronage. The meticulous analysis of paradigms, falsifiability and intellectual honesty by thinkers of the standing of Kuhn and Popper is left far behind.

unless it comes with another statement, "You must cook them properly first". That is, developing the substance of a hypothesis with supplementary information which sets out the circumstances in which it appears not to be false is an entirely reasonable thing to do.

There are other ways of protecting a paradigm (see "Digging In" sidebar), but it was with these two complications surrounding falsifiability that the Kuhn-Popper debate was concerned. Their significance, under fair conditions of scientific debate, is real, and this was recognised by another member of the cast in this story: the Hungarian philosopher and mathematician, Imre Lakatos. In retrospect, his contribution seems to be obvious, and it is a modification, rather than a contradiction, of what Kuhn wrote in the first place: don't try to defend a *whole* paradigm, he argued; instead, decide, explicitly or implicitly, on its "hard core"—its central identifying principles. Around the periphery, there are invariably many things to be sorted out, and they may be substantial, but this can be done while leaving the hard core intact. As Lakatos pointed out, "All theories are *anomaly-laden"; so scientists should be prepared to add revisions and auxiliary hypotheses as research and experience suggest.[7]

Eventually the hard core itself may crash, but if it is sufficiently small, it may endure for a long time or even indefinitely, for the less it says, the less likely it is that part of it is untrue. And that hard core provides the foundation for ongoing science—its collapse and replacement by a radical new research programme remains a possibility, but scientists searching for the piercing new insights which could bring such fundamental change will not find them *unless* they plod on within the existing framework until they hit an obstacle. You only realise that a door is locked when you try to open it. So, although the resilience of the hard core is not guaranteed, at least its expectation of life is longer than that of a whole paradigm; and there is less to lose, with only a relatively small set of principles at the core, which even Popper might accept, for now, as beyond refutation.

And yet, however comprehensive or lite the paradigm might be, the pattern of advance is essentially the same. It is like a river flowing gently down a cascade of rocks. The water comes to quite still pools, each with a lot of river-life going on in it, and it may stay there for some time, before tipping over the edge through turbulence to the next pool, large or small. The waters in the higher pools will have no knowledge of the lower ones; those in lower pools will have an existential memory of the higher ones, but will know they can't be there any more: they are in a different *ethic, a different paradigm. Some of their hard core is likely to survive, but who knows? Some shocks are *extraordinary* (*Systems Thinking 〉 Form 〉 The Power Law).

The herringbone

Another way of visualising that pattern of rapid, turbulent change, followed by long periods of quiet, is Arthur Koestler's model of the herringbone. Each line and arrow represents reasonably steady advance within the framework of one paradigm (or hard core); each change in direction represents the shock of a "scientific revolution", followed by steady advance in the new direction/ paradigm. Although there is no knowing how long this will last, it will undoubtedly be for much longer than the period of shock. And each shock undoes at least some of the careful construction that has happened under the protection of the preceding paradigm (each new line does not start from the tip of the old one), so it will, for understandable reasons, be resisted or postponed for as long as possible. In some cases, it might be quite minor—a setback; in other cases, it could be so great that the whole of the achievement of the current arrow-paradigm is lost. An extreme shock could ripple through some or all of the arrows representing the shocks and recoveries of the past.[8]

Importantly, such a pattern of progress is characteristic of the *complex systems on which we depend, as we see with:

- *Kaizen and kaikaku. The incremental improvement of kaizen is interrupted and set off in a new direction by the shock of kaikaku. This principle is at the heart of *lean thinking.

- *Resilience. To protect the resilience of a system there is a case for severely limiting elaboration (i.e., preventing excessive advance along the arrow). This may be expected to postpone the shock, to reduce its scale and the damage it causes when eventually it comes, and to aid recovery.

- Punctuated equilibrium in evolution. There is evidence of very uneven rates of progress

in the evolution of new species and *diversity, ranging from massive and rapid change to long periods during which the *ecosystem and its resident species are fortunate enough to live in not particularly interesting times.[9]

- *Gaia and Medea. This is the principle that the ecology (Gaia), so long as it is not damaged by gross interventions, will maintain itself and its stability for a long period, but not indefinitely. When the shock (Medea) comes, it will cross the threshold into a different form; this is the crisis which Gaia cannot prevent, and it will be followed by a new stasis and equilibrium, maintained by a new Gaia whose standards and values are utterly different from those of its predecessor.

You might think, on the basis of the above, that whatever we do—as members of a large complex system which we cannot control—there is no way of avoiding the paradigm shift which will finally destroy everything we have made and depend on. You might be right. But you might not— at least, not for a long time—because, as the presence of "resilience" in the list above suggests, there are things we can do to contain and limit the shock. We can, for instance, make it happen ourselves and on a small scale, on the principle of the controlled explosion; it is not beyond our wit, though it may be beyond our inclination, to make sensible judgments (*Wheel of Life).

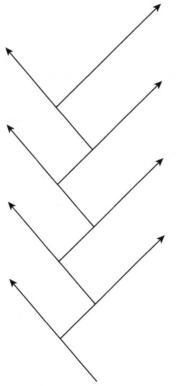

But the world which these *judgments inhabit may be profoundly different from the one that Kuhn, Popper and Lakatos were debating. Kuhn describes a sequence of deep breakthroughs—Copernicus' demonstration that the sun is at the centre of our solar system; Newton's laws of optics and motion; Priestley and Lavoisier's discovery of oxygen. But this paradigm-to-paradigm progression may have been of its time, characteristic of immature science, not (or not often) to be repeated. Maybe, in the case of a mature, large-scale science— whose many parts, once thought to be discrete, converge towards a single subject—the advances all take place around the edges. The larger the system, or the science, the longer its edge, and a long *edge means plenty of space for locally-revolutionary changes to take place which have a big effect in their immediate vicinity, leaving the bulk of the subject unchanged.

If that is the case, then two implications come to mind. First, we may have a convergence between Kuhn's large-scale paradigm—in the shape of modern science, its many strands persisting in essentially the same direction—and Lakatos' smaller-scale hard core, in which, at the edges, there is also continuous movement and revision of the ever-expanding scientific universe. Maybe, in a mature scientific *culture, we should not be looking for scientific revolutions, but for revisions of the detail. The big paradigm shifts, *kaikaku moments, may be characteristic of sciences and social movements in the middle years of their evolution. The *Transition movement, for instance, could perhaps reach that stage around 2015, when it has advanced far enough to learn the basics, but has hit a wall in terms of further developments. That is the point at which a breakthrough, a long time coming, and much resisted, could quite suddenly free the movement to move fast in a new direction.

And the second implication, in the strange way which is characteristic of this complex subject, seems both to confirm the first and to contradict it. While the scientific culture and establishment of our time is very sound, and while we should not be looking for revolutions except round the edges, it is also true that there is, even now, a profound stand-off between two scientific cultures. One looks for complex, big-science responses to our present condition—such as the convergence of *genetic engineering with robotics, information technology and *nanotechnology into a global *agricultural establishment, and super-projects such as giant dams and high-speed rail links. The other looks for simpler, small-science responses in the convergence of observation, local conditions and the experience in the minds of people, with perceptive husbandry, local *water management and functioning local rail systems, and

with disagreement between local paradigms being welcomed as *diversity; as an essential property of the planet's future, if it is to have one.

The stand-off between these two paradigms is as profound as anything that Copernicus, Newton, Priestley and Lavoisier were part of. If big science were to "surrender" to small science, it would need, not just to retreat back down one of the arrows of the herringbone, but to climb down much of its length. It isn't going to do that.

But supposing we change *it* to *they*? That means taking note of the *System Scale Rule and recognising the essential need for local, grounded, rooted responses in all their diversity, applying modern science where local conditions call for it, and applying scientific brilliance and observation in local conditions. "They" means scientists; it may also mean applied technologies such as microchips, materials science, and the application of informed biology to soil fertility, including such critical problems as the conservation of phosphates at a time when it is not being imported any more. "They" could bring us science's latest discovery: modesty—that is, science as a service to the people and to the *ecology.

This is listening science, with an ethic of *pull, a flexible *call-and-response science that provides assistance when it is asked for, brings great competence and observation to small places and does not, with today's *large-scale *certainties, kill off the local *imagination needed to make a future. It will no doubt require a *kaikaku* moment to get us into that new paradigm—but, maybe, once we're there, we will have stability: the requirement of shock after shock will no longer be built into the system.

Local resilience and scientific intelligence are going to need each other: there is nothing inconsistent there. The inconsistency lies between local resilience and *ideology. And large-scale science is degenerating into large-scale ideology. Small-scale science applies the best that science can provide without imposing a whole paradigm; it is flexible enough to work within whichever paradigm is right for a particular *place and *time.

The word for this process of being guided by, and learning from, the paradigm you are in is "heuristics". The possibility of being guided by a constructive heuristic means that we are not simply swept along the river like a cork; we can influence where we go, at least to some extent. Above all, we need to have a sureness of decision about which paradigm we want to be in. If, as Lakatos argued, we are in a "progressive" paradigm, we will have a positive heuristic, and may make some good decisions; if we are in a "degenerate" one, we won't. And to give ourselves a chance of being in a progressive paradigm, we need both to think and to observe—that is, as the philosopher Alan Musgrave puts it, to sustain "a subtle dialogue between the theoretician (armed with his heuristic) and the experimenter (armed with the 'facts')".[10]

The resilience of any large system requires the rise and fall of its smaller parts, on their different timescales—subcycles for subsystems. In terms of science and its paradigms, that means acknowledging the detailed local knowledge and small-scale research programmes which can succeed and fail, change and respond without *denial or delay; and without making waves big enough to destroy everything else.

Lean Logic's hard core consists of sustained and accurate alertness to the *ecosystem and to its demands for change. That is the heuristic which must be obeyed, for postponement serves to deepen crisis from a series of small new beginnings to a large-scale ending.
*Unfalsifiability, Genetic Fallacy, Humility, Harmless Lunatic, Ethics.

PARADOX. A statement which contradicts itself, or which seems to do so. Example:

> This sentence is false.

This is called the Liar Paradox; it can make you feel dizzy if you think about it too long, and it is said to have caused the premature death of Philetas of Cos, philosopher, romantic poet and tutor to the young Ptolemy II in the fourth century BC.[11] Paradoxes are extremely important because many of the most interesting truths contain seeming contradictions: as Francis Bacon remarked, "There is no excellent beauty that hath not some strangeness in the proportion."[12]

A person who is intolerant to paradox is likely to be excluded from an understanding of *systems, and to be confined instead to a fallacious world-view consisting of smoothly-consistent error and fraudulent simplification. But an excessive fondness for paradox can be dangerous too, allowing the person simply to accept contradictions without thinking about them or, in a Marxian way, revelling in paradox and refusing to accept that an analysis has been accomplished unless it ends in mind-numbing contradiction. Paradoxes are in a sense alive: greater understanding of them does not solve them but uncovers deeper layers of *interest. A paradox that is "solved" is not a paradox.[13]
*Logic, Self-Denying Truth, Ironic Space, Slippery Slope, Good Shepherd Paradox, Hunt, Sorites Paradox, Freedom.

PARISH. See Groups and Group Sizes, Reciprocity and Cooperation 〉 Balance, Community.

PASCAL'S WAGER. An argument set out by Blaise Pascal in his *Pensées* (1670). If God exists, and one commits oneself to a life of faith, the rewards in Heaven will be infinitely greater than any benefit one would get in life by *not* committing oneself to a life of faith (perhaps a bit of extra time for gardening on a Sunday morning?). Therefore, assuming that he does exist and committing oneself to a life of faith is a good bet. It would only be a bad bet if we knew for certain that God does not exist, which we don't.[14]

The Wager is a version of the *Precautionary Principle, but it is less vague, and it is a reasonable approach to risk in a constructive argument with (say) *sceptics on *climate change. If a breakdown of the present climate equilibrium—an event of infinitely high cost—were no more than a minor possibility, it would still be rational to take action, even expensive action, to try to prevent it. You do not at all have to be *certain that climate change is real to justify doing something about it.

PATERNALISM. The *fallacy that the government should have the role of father over the society for which it is responsible. Recently, it has been suggested that the government is taking on the role of a "nanny", making us a "nanny state". Actually, the role that it is developing towards is more that of the "father" (via the manager).

*Freedom-destroying governments from Caligula to Stalin—as well as modern-era leaderships in East Germany, Turkmenistan, North Korea, Libya and Haiti—have universally presented their top man as father of the state, which they see as a *household. The

father persuades himself, and others, of his benign concern, and everything he does as head of the daddy state is "for your own good". There is no appeal against a determined head of household. The state becomes Papa's private patch; it is his *private sphere.[15]
*Paedomorphism, Constructivism, Ideology.

PATHETIC FALLACY. The ascription to inanimate objects of feelings which correspond with the person's own feelings. Example: The lake I am looking at is sad/happy. It takes on whatever mood I happen to be in when I am looking at it.[16]

PEAK OIL. See Energy Prospects, Wolf Fallacy.

PEAK THINKING. Depletion of the *judgment needed to save our society and its planet; the gap between the supply of thinking and the need for it.
*Relative Intelligence.

PEASANT. A person practising *small-scale, mixed, energy-efficient, fertility-conserving farming designed chiefly for local subsistence. It is integrated into local *culture. It is the defining *practice of the *community. This model of agriculture, however, became briefly obsolete as the *market economy, with its abundant cheap *energy, enabled a different one to develop which did not need to supply its own energy and sustain its own fertility.

Peasant farming is a *skilled and *efficient way of sustaining *food production within the limits of the *ecology. It is an eco-ethic, sustaining the measured synergy with nature that we find in *Taoist philosophy. It has the five properties of *resilience.

But it has a flaw. It is highly productive, so it yields a surplus, and this is a tempting resource for the gradual evolution of an urban *civic society, with its unstoppable implications of *growth, hubris and trouble. Is there a way of learning from that dismal cycle, and sustaining, instead, a *localised, community-based, decentralised society, without the seeds of its own destruction. . . ?
*Lean Economy, Lean Food, Intentional Waste.

PERFORMATIVE TRUTH. Meaning that is created by a statement or a symbolic event, or even by a thought. For example, a contract or a commitment between two

or more people is brought into being by a deliberately-articulated statement—a performative utterance: "I challenge you", "I promise", "we celebrate", "I do", "I will". As the theologian Ian Robinson notes, a change in attitudes can change some things for real—marriage for instance:

> Mount Everest will remain the same whatever I make of it in my thoughts and emotions, and will not be changed if others make something quite different. Marriage is not similarly an unchanging object, and is affected by people's attitudes to it.[17]

A religious *liturgy brings into being a performative truth; not an as-if truth, but a truth which is as real as—and in many ways the same as—a *contract. Something happens.[18]
*Narrative Truth, Religion.

PERMACULTURE. See Lean Food.

PERSONAL EXPERIENCE, THE FALLACY OF. This is one of the most common and pernicious ways of destroying an argument. The *indignant private anecdote trumps all other collective experience, research, historical precedent or evaluation: I was made better/worse by the hospital ("I wouldn't be alive now if . . . "/"My brother would be alive now if . . . "), so I know how to run the health service. Time, now, for *wisdom to slink away in shame. You can't disagree with my personal experience because it happened to me. And if you do, I will take it as a personal attack (*Ad Hominem).

This may, at a pinch, be a justifiable position to take. If you have seen for yourself the fissures in Arctic ice, this may well add to the *authority with which you can speak about the reality of *climate change. But its chief contribution to argument is destructive. The point is, you can't argue against it, because you are pitting *logic against passionate *emotion, and it doesn't work. It can be useful to bear in mind, or even to point out, that personal experience can in fact be a substantial source of bias in a person's argument: she may be drawing *general conclusions from exceptional cases; she may be validating her career experience by reading more significance into it than it deserves. Personal experience erodes

355

objectivity, and can reduce knowledge of a subject by closing down any willingness to find out more about it. *Deceptions, High Ground.

PHARISEE, THE FALLACY OF THE. The assumption that you have higher moral standards than the other person. The form of the argument is: I have no problem in regarding anyone who disagrees with me as motivated by greed, cruelty, lust for power, lack of vision and a compulsion to deceive. Fortunately, I do not myself suffer from these handicaps, so my views on the matter can be trusted as pure, *objective and *compassionate. How could anyone as nice as me possibly be wrong? There are no limits to what I am justified in doing to promote my case, which is so clearly beyond reasonable challenge.

The remarkable thing about the Pharisee is the ease and comfort with which he believes that the other party is motivated by such horrible things, by the whole range of motivations whose vile nature is itself proof that they explain everything. It is a lonely life for the Pharisee; the world is so full of the wicked, and thinking through a problem consists of the thankless forensic task of identifying the particular kind of deplorable motive that shapes other people's opinions, and then fearlessly pointing it out. There is no risk of contradiction: if the accused defends herself, she just adds lying to her charge sheet. The Pharisee's work is never done.

Pharisaism is named after the strict priestly elite who did not compromise with paganism during the Babylonian captivity (597–538 BC)—unlike the Sadducees, who were left behind in Israel and made compromises in the interests of trade and a quiet life. At first, there was a robust *courage about the Pharisees' persistence, but it degenerated into self-regard and the famous mantras, "I thank God that I am not as other men are", and "Holier than Thou".

This is probably a moment to have some sympathy for the Pharisee. At least he hasn't given up. And yet, appearances of purity deceive. You may be able to get more surprising, more interesting *truths from unpromising places: blackened churches, shaken by city traffic (for instance), or noisy bars that smell of fish . . .[20]
*Narcissism, Dirty Hands, Humility, Cant, Hypocrisy, False Sameness.

PITY, APPEAL TO (*Argumentum ad misericordiam*). There is nothing necessarily wrong with appealing to someone's sense of pity. It can be exactly what is needed. But it can also throw an argument off course—a wrecking *distraction from what the discussion is actually about. It can apply either to you, the arguer ("please, take pity on a struggling *innocent in this subject"), or to them, the people you are talking about. For example, the historian Jules Michelet used this appeal to nudge his readers towards a sympathetic view of the French Revolution, encouraging them to see it as an uprising consisting mainly of starving widows and orphans.[21]

Stephen Toulmin *et al* wonder, "Can any sensible person ever fall for such tactics?"[22]
Ad Hominem, Compassion, Reductionism.

PLACE. Space whose local *narrative can still be heard, and could be heard again, given the chance. Place is the practical, located, tangible, *bounded setting which protects us from *abstractions, *generalities and *ideologies and opens the way to thinking as discovery. On this scale, there is *elegance, and some relief from the need to be right, for if you are wrong, the small *scale of place allows for revision and repair, supported by *conversation.

The philosopher David Hume considers the matter:

> There are in *England*, in particular, many honest gentlemen, who being always employ'd in their domestic affairs, or amusing themselves in common recreations, have carried their thoughts

---

O City city, I can sometimes hear
Beside a public bar in Lower Thames Street,
The pleasant whining of a mandoline
And a clatter and a chatter from within
Where fishmen lounge at noon: where the walls
Of Magnus Martyr hold
Inexplicable splendour of Ionian white and gold.

T.S. ELIOT, *The Waste Land*, 1922.[19]

very little beyond those objects which are every day expos'd to their senses. . . . They do well to keep themselves in their present situation; and instead of refining them into philosophers, I wish we cou'd communicate to our founders of systems a share of this gross earthy mixture, as an ingredient, which they commonly stand much in need of, and which wou'd serve to temper those fiery particles, of which they are compos'd.[23]

Place is the endangered habitat of our species.
*Neighbourhood, Social Mobility, Harmless Lunatic, Home, Localisation, Transition.

PLANNED ECONOMY. The meticulous, mapped plan of a *permaculture garden, allowing *ecological systems to develop within it.
*Lean Thinking.

PLAY. Think of it like this: there are forms of interaction with people which have a direct and serious *instrumental purpose: I am here to teach you Greek; I would like to order a goulash; please dig that ditch; what have you done with my socks? And there are all other forms of interaction: the reason we are talking about Barcelona is because we happen to be having sandwich lunch together and we are not strangers: if we were baboons we might do a spot of mutual grooming. If they could speak, they would call it "play".

Play resists definition, as one expert on the subject, Stuart Brown, protested on being asked for one . . .

> I adopted my usual academic stance. "I don't really use an absolute definition," I said. "Play is so varied, it's preverbal, preconscious."[24]

. . . but in *Lean Logic*, it consists of *all our interactions other than instrumental ones*. And even the instrumental ones are rarely quite free of it: at the checkout you still, quite often, get a hallo.

It comes in many varieties. There is no need to list them, but it may be useful to think about them as located approximately on two dimensions, ranged either between cooperation and competition (Table I), or between body and mind (Table II). All the combinations are interesting in their various ways, but especially important to the values of *Lean Logic* are the blends of *both* strong cooperation and competition, and strong presence of *both* body and mind.[25]

Those strong blends are close to the essence of play. The blend of strong competition and strong cooperation

Play Types I: Cooperation and Competition

Placings are typical but most could be anywhere on the table.		Cooperation	
		WEAK	STRONG
Competition	WEAK	Piano Reading Model building	Attunement with child or beloved Choir/dance
	STRONG	Chess/fencing Gambling Debating	Team games Rough-and-tumble Sparring

Note that "competition" includes soft competition such as (with infants and children) tickling and one-a-side football.

Play Types II: Body and Mind

A matter of emphasis: all forms of play use both body and mind.		Body	
		WEAK	STRONG
Mind	WEAK	Talking to the dog Window-shopping Staring out to sea	Sparring Rough-and-tumble Gym/jogging
	STRONG	Chess Story/make-believe Conversation/jokes	Object play Music Team games

is a medium in which the *identity of the individual in society is worked out and continually refreshed; and the strong presence of both body and mind is about becoming a person in the first place.

Now, to put these play-types into context, here are seven things which we may think of play doing for us, or helping us to do for ourselves:

1. *Becoming a person*

   Play has a critical role in the process by which the brain becomes active and competent, as distinct from simply a collection of neurons with potential. Together with *sleep, play practices, strengthens, differentiates and tests the circuitry by using it and linking it up with corresponding responses in the body and the emotions. In this sense it *makes* the person—developing *imagination and autonomy; a specific, unique, set of capabilities; the *freedom to respond, to feel, to invent and to interpret—the joined-up mind and body whose absence, and intense presence, is discussed in *Spirit.[26]

   In a deeper sense, becoming a person is about developing the powers of empathy. You can, in a sense, feel the other person's pain or joy. That sounds a little bit pious but, when it is missing, it becomes intensely real and, in a sense, the ultimate curse: it is the road to cruelty (since the person does not feel what the other person feels), to *ignorance (since the person who never speaks the *truth never believes what she is told), and to loneliness (since the person does not recognise that there is another person there, so the possibility of *emotional attachment does not arise). The significance of play as the maker of people is indispensable and beyond measure, and the consequences of its absence are devastating. The psychologist Bruce Perry writes,

   > The acts of holding, rocking, singing, feeding, gazing, kissing and other nurturing behaviours involved in caring for infants and young children are bonding experiences. Factors crucial to bonding include time together, face-to-face interactions, eye contact, physical proximity, touch and other primary sensory experiences such as smell, sound and taste. . . .
   > It should be no surprise that holding, gazing,

   smiling, kissing, singing and laughing all cause specific neurochemical activities in the brain. These neurochemical activities lead to normal organisation of brain systems that are responsible for attachment.
   > Children without touch, stimulation and nurturing can literally lose the capacity to form any meaningful relationships for the rest of their lives.[27]

   The *market economy's success in making people in this sense is mixed. Play with young children adds nothing to Gross Domestic Product (unless you get someone else to do it for you—but then the bonding can get complicated). But worry not, for the task of trying to repair the wreckage when the unplayed-with arrive at school shows up as an important contributor to GDP, and as an equal-opportunity job provider. A pity, then, that the *Lean Economy won't be able to afford it; it might be forced to prevent the problem arising in the first place.

2. *Play as teacher*

   Play teaches difficult *skills. One of the ways in which it does this is by easing the emotional pressure. There is a rule in the psychology of learning called the Yerkes-Dodson law, which says that, if we are trying to do something difficult, we will tend to do it less well if our arousal, or motivation, is too great: we do better if we are cool about it. So the context of play is helpful, reducing drive, anxiety and the potential for frustration.[28]

   The influence of play on learning is illustrated by many studies, including observation of the creative ingenuity of young children. In one example, children aged three to five were given the task of fishing a prize from a box that had been placed out of reach. To do that, they had to combine the length of two sticks by clamping them together. Beforehand, they were given one of four types of training: demonstration of the principle of clamping two sticks together, *or* practice in fastening clamps in single sticks, *or* an opportunity to watch the experimenter carry out the whole task, *or* simply being allowed to play around with the materials.

The children who had played with the materials did as well in solving the problem as the ones who had been given the full demonstration of clamping sticks together, and better than the other groups. Crucially, the opportunity to play had switched on their willingness to think about the problem when they were stuck:

> What was striking about the play group was their tenacity in sticking with the task so that even when they were poor in their initial approach, they ended by solving the problem. . . . They were playing.[29]

And play of that kind—object play—is fundamental to the process of switching on the current between the mind and the body. It teaches the child about weight, texture and balance, in the course of which the child discovers whether she is right-or left-handed.[30] As the child psychologist Otto Weininger writes,

> Play helps children to make use of their growing muscular skills and helps them co-ordinate the developing muscle systems, both gross motor movements and fine co-ordination. . . . Play increases the sensory input which, in turn, increases cognitive awareness of the environment. Children who are free to explore see, hear, feel, touch and sense more of the world around them become practised in noticing and being aware of their environment; they have more fuel for thought. . . . Play is the essence of learning for children.[31]

3. *Learning community membership*
And play is central, and in some cases indispensable, as a means of teaching and reinforcing the

P

conventions and skills of citizenship and of being part of a *community. Games of mothering, and mimicry of skills and roles, are almost universal. In some societies, the message communicated by the games could scarcely be more pointed. Children in the Tangu tribe in New Guinea, for instance, play a game called taketak where the object is to share out food fairly. There is no winner or loser; the aim is to tie.[32] In Switzerland the game of marbles' famous potential for flexibility in its rules is taken towards its extreme with the players deciding the rules by mutual discussion and consent, then codifying them, and then sticking to them—but still being able to amend them on one player's initiative if he or she can enlist general opinion on his or her side.[33]

And, of course, community membership is not only about *cooperating. It is about coping with non-cooperation and surviving offence. *Insult plus play equals friendship. Sometimes even love.

4. *Inclusiveness*

Play is inclusive. The young and old, and whole families with relatively little in common other than mutual goodwill, can play board games, do music, listen to *stories together. The social historian Richard Sennett writes,

> A child aged four is in ordinary social situations going to be excluded from much that a child aged six can and wants to do. In play, however, he gets the opportunity to interact with her as an equal, and so explore a kind of social situation he otherwise could not know.[34]

Indeed without some common forum for play, such as music, sport, or *conversation at meals, it is hard for a *family to find any frame of reference in which they can interact as a *group. And sport is well established as a defuser of potential tension, as in the Commonwealth (formerly Imperial) *tradition of cricket, or the now-traditional Whitby football match between Real Gothic FC—a scratch team selected from the pale, near-death Goths who gather for their biannual celebration in the town where Dracula reached England—and Athletico Gazette, a team of concerned locals drawn from the staff of the local newspaper.[35]

5. *Competition, cooperation and bonding*

Play opens up the possibility of that crucial combination of accomplishments in human and animal relationships: *competition and *cooperation. To see the significance of this, consider the case of a primate group such as gelada baboons, whose *politics is substantially organised around the existence of—and competition to replace—the alpha male. On approaching puberty, the young males are excluded from the privileged inner circle of the troupe, and in most cases live among the other males on the periphery. There they live their double lives consisting both of competition—expressed in a range of play routines, of which mock fights are a vital part, since some of those males will in due course be taking on the alpha male—and cooperation—no less important, because, being at the outside edge of the troupe, it is their task to warn of dangers and to deal with them, to come to each other's aid, to present a united front and to conserve the territory.[36]

Play is their medium. For the males in that characteristic and ambivalent situation—rivalry and alliance, battle and bonding—competition and cooperation are the *grammar of their coexistence.[37]

6. *A source of order*

Play is often disorderly, but it is bounded. When it is over, order is restored.

Medieval society was to a large extent kept intact by its busy diary of play and *carnival: the twelve days of celebratory misrule over Christmas, the boy bishops, Plough Monday, Candlemas, Valentine, Shrove, Passion, Palm, Easter, Hocktide, May Day, Whitsun, Rogation, St John, St Peter, Harvest, the season of fairs, hobby horses, Martinmas, All Saints . . . you do not cooperate in this amount of festival without getting on with each other rather well. That is capitalism for you, in another form—a wealth of *social capital, potential for cooperation in more serious matters. As Johan Huizinga writes:

> Play community generally tends to become permanent even after the game is over—and "permanent community" means "order". Play creates order, *is* order. Play demands order

P

absolute and supreme. The least deviation from it "spoils the game", robs it of its character, and makes it worthless. The profound affinity between play and order is perhaps the reason why play seems to lie to such a large extent in the field of aesthetics. Play has a tendency to be beautiful. It may be that this aesthetic factor is identical with the impulse to create orderly form, which animates play in all its aspects.[38]

7. *Play for its own sake—and for the sake of something else, which it is hard to be certain about*
Play is for fun, for exuberant self-expression; it is the content of carnival; it lifts the spirits; it prevents *boredom; it contains and neutralises aggression; it releases endorphins. It bridges the distance to another person; it *encounters. Love explores another country; play does so by invitation only. It may be formal (bound by explicit rules and within agreed *boundaries of *time and *place), or informal (where these restraints are implicit and flexible, or the rules may be invented for a moment of fantasy, benign insult or humour). The rules of play make it uninhibited: you can do and say things—aggressive or insulting things, for instance—which would be out of the question except in the shadow-world of play; aspects of personality which would never otherwise have been suspected, are discovered or displayed. Play manifests the person; it is intrinsic to the expressiveness of the *public sphere.[39]

So this is a moment to step back from it, not think about it too much, and acknowledge play as its own thing. We are familiar with the reasonings of science, the earnest explanations of behaviour in terms of natural selection and trophic (feeding) systems. But, as the naturalist Richard Mabey suggests, we may get closer to understanding play by not trying so hard. Animals do it because they enjoy it. And that, Mabey tells us, is how it eventually seemed to field biologist Professor Bernd Heinrich after five years of meticulous analysis of the behaviour of ravens while at lunch on a coyote-killed sheep. They yell out to others to join them, roll on their backs in the snow, flutter

in it, kick it and slide in it. After evaluating and rejecting all the hypotheses available to him from the sciences of behaviourism and natural selection, he settled for the obvious. They were doing what all young creatures do at feast times. They were . . .

. . . having fun.[40]

Perhaps even birdsong, along with all its territorial tasks, is at heart . . .

. . . a purely emotional outburst, an outpouring of sheer aliveness, and without referential meaning. In which case it is genuinely closer to music than language.[41]

And Mabey observes an egret (heron) playing with a large flock of a quite different species—lapwings—matching their wingbeats and swoons, their every move, in a wildly gratuitous celebration of life . . .

Was it seeking reassurance, or company, or just an outing in the sun? At times it seems as if the whole company of nature, ourselves included, is simply at play.[42]

And yet, play is fragile and is not in good shape at present. It does exist to a weakened extent in professional sport, but even there the aim of winning is increasingly taken as the literal purpose of the event, rather than the enabling *myth. Play relies on such critical *cultural assets as *trust, social capital and the *humour which blunts insult, and it is in trouble when these are in decline. Insult and rough-and-tumble are now largely forbidden; carnival is subdued; if an invitation to play is rejected or misconstrued, if a joke goes wrong, there is shame or worse.

The *market economy suffers from play-deprivation. But in the future we won't be able to get by without it. *Encounter, Invisible Goods, Lean Education, Shifting Ground, Tactile Deprivation.

POLITENESS. Politeness has never completely shaken off the meaning and importance it had in its eighteenth century prime. At that time, it signified a general agreeability and *courtesy, a disposition to please, skill in the practice and protocol of *conversation. The accent on politeness, as Roy Porter pointed out . . .

P

. . . was no footling obsession with petty punc-
tilio; it was a desperate remedy meant to heal
the chronic social conflict and personal traumas
stemming from civil and domestic tyranny and
topsy-turvy social values.[43]

But the age of industry changed the priorities. It
preferred conversation to be about something useful,
and politeness proved to be vulnerable to the rise
of the contrasting *virtue of authenticity: being the
real you, saying what you really think. This I'm-not-
messing-about ethic matured in some cases into a
take-me-as-you-find-me *ethic, expressed variously
in clothes, language, *sex and direct, straightforward
thinking, which reaches for the nearest *reductionist
conclusion and defends it with the claim that anyone
who disagrees needs to get real.

The virtuoso politeness of the eighteenth century has
not survived, but there is a polite-lite remnant which
still has a useful job to do. It means that you listen to the
opposing argument and understand it before attacking
it, you take measures to sustain and repair a relationship
after a disagreement, and you forbear to be authenti-
cally blunt about the other person's *politics, *fortitude,
hair, clothes and children without their consent. There
is *courtesy, so you may find yourself not speaking the
whole *truth, being drawn into the art of compromise
and tact. Politeness can therefore seem stuffy and dishonest; authenticity, by contrast, is refreshing, but it can
make things quite lonely, being more highly rated as a
virtue in oneself than in one's friends.[44]
*Frankness, Butterfly Effect.

POLITICAL ECONOMY. Society in the broad sense.
Despite many differences of emphasis, economics was
once understood in this way, as including the whole
range of society, politics and economy.

That understanding held in the period roughly
between the publication of a coherent theory of *value
(based on labour) by Francis Hutcheson (1694–1746), Professor of Moral Philosophy at Glasgow, and the launch
in 1891 of the narrower interpretation of "positive economics" by John Neville Keynes (1852–1949). Before that
period, economics had been discussed as a question of
moral philosophy; after it, economics became separated

into a much more technical question, opening up the
gap between the economy and society, and providing
the symbology and mathematics for *economism.[45]

As it is used in *Lean Logic*, "political economy" means
more than the more usual "society". It links it up with
*economics, *politics, the environment, the past and the
future—that is, the society and *ecology which economics exists to serve.

POLITICS. (1) Deliberation about collective decisions
by those affected by them.
(2) The grief that follows when (1) breaks down.
*Nation 〉 Politics, Abstraction, Anarchism, Blame,
Conversation, Democracy, Devil's Tunes, Green
Authoritarianism, Multiculturalism, Unlean.

POLLUTION. Material which impairs the living
system into which it is discarded. The disruption of
material flows may be due to the materials being alien
to the *ecology into which they are discharged, and/or
in excess of what the ecology can cope with. Pollution
is what happens when there is failure of the principle of
the *closed-loop system, whose parts exchange and use
their respective *wastes. The aim—and ultimately, the
requirement—of the *resilient *political economy of the
future will be to sustain closed-loop systems which waste
none of the foundation *capital on which they depend.[46]
*Sustainability, Lean Materials, Genetic Modification,
Nanotechnology.

POPULATION. The phrase *ceteris paribus*—other
things being equal—is absurd, because other things
are almost never equal. But it is useful. It is a way of
identifying the one thing that matters in the midst of a
lot of things that are beside the point.

In the case of population, the key point is this: the
growth in the population of organisms develops a
characteristic momentum. It is self-replicating. *Ceteris
paribus*, more produces more, in a process of exponential
growth, with each year's population rising by multiples
of the previous year's. The growth of non-self-replicating
things, on the other hand, is additive, and the additions
come from outside interventions, not from any internal
dynamic that gives them a life and growth momentum
of their own.[47]

Here is the story elegantly summarised by Thomas Malthus:

> Population, when unchecked, increases in a geometrical ratio. Subsistence increases only in an arithmetical ratio. A slight acquaintance with numbers will shew the immensity of the first power in comparison of the second.
>
> By that law of our nature which makes food necessary to the life of man, the effects of these two unequal powers must be kept equal.
>
> This implies a strong and constantly operating check on population from the difficulty of subsistence.
>
> This difficulty must fall somewhere and must necessarily be severely felt by a large proportion of mankind.[48]

Now, since other things are not equal, it doesn't work out like that. What we don't get is a "strong and constantly operating check on population". Instead, we get *time-lags, during which, from the growing population's point of view, things seem to be moving ahead just fine. But if the population takes advantage of this, and stops worrying about numbers, there will in due course be *overshoot*. The population will have to *fall* to get back into equilibrium with its environment. That fall may be abrupt and "severely felt". Time-lags switch off the automatic nudges and corrections which would keep us sensible. They make it necessary to think. In the case of something that matters as much as population — and where errors are so hard to correct — it is necessary to think a lot.[49]

The second thing to note is that, in the case of the human population (in common with virtually all other populations), there are things other than subsistence that can reduce or halt their growth; disease, for example. Human populations — before they invented civilisation — in fact had a long history of intentionally restricting their numbers rather than waiting for subsistence to do it for them. Other controls include changing social attitudes and priorities, prohibitions on marriage and coitus under certain conditions, advances in contraceptive medicine, wars and even infanticide. There are also many things which affect the match between the amount of food that the *land can produce

and the amount that people actually get. They include the presence or absence of cheap *energy, the weather, distribution in the sense of being able to buy and *transport food, crop diseases (such as potato blight), and shifts in *agricultural ownership from local subsistence farming to large-scale enterprises producing food for distant cities.[50]

It is during periods of sharp change and instability, especially when an economy *intensifies, that humans tend to lose control of their numbers. There are more jobs to be done, so there is an *incentive for having more people to do them. Insecurity encourages parents to have more children to increase the chances of some still being around to look after them in their own old age. At times of dislocation, the taboos and practices by which a settled population can limit its fertility (discussed later) are seen to be unacceptable, or forgotten. Migration, too, is associated with high fertility, as migrants do all they can to establish their presence. An illustration of this is supplied by a 2010 University of Leeds study, whose projections of the UK's population (2001–2051) suggest that, while the population of the White British group can be expected to grow by 4% between 2001 and 2031, the growth of the Asian, Black African, Chinese and Other Ethnic groups over the same time period are estimated at 95–153%, 179%, 202% and 350%, respectively.[51]

The arrival of new crops in a region can also lead to rapid population growth: for instance, the population of Ireland is estimated to have grown from 3 million in 1779 to over 8 million when the census was taken in 1841, and this is taken to be mainly due to the cultivation of potatoes which, along with milk or buttermilk, make a cheap and nutritious diet. All these factors, and feedbacks between them, contribute to pulses of population growth, but, thanks to those time-lags, it may be some time before it becomes clear what the consequences are, and how and when the environment will bite back.[52]

The 'demographic transition' to lower population growth

In nature, populations that grow out of equilibrium with their environments crash. In the case of the human population of the present, we are not, or not yet, seeing a crash, but we are seeing a reduction in the rate of growth. When urban society settles down, families realise that they are better off with a few children whom they can afford to feed and educate properly than with a large number of children that are beyond their means. And the range of choice changes: as domestic technology improves, and as service industries grow, opportunities for women outside family life, especially the ablest women, cause some to wonder whether they have better things to do with their time than to have children (in economists' terms, child-rearing acquires a higher *'opportunity cost' for those women). This leads to the inverse of Darwinian selection: a pattern in which the fittest produce the fewest children, the survival of the unfittest. And, in growing *market economies, labour-intensive forms of work that are least affected by technical advance—such as teaching and child-rearing—become increasingly expensive relative to other forms of work: child-rearing is priced out of the market (*Composition).[53]

All these effects, taken together, add up to the "demographic transition", a reduction in the growth of—or actual reductions in the size of—populations in a mature market economy. At least, the demographer John Weeks broadens out the meaning of the demographic transition to include all these factors. In its more familiar usage, it refers to a fall in the fertility rate—the number of children per woman—but Weeks insists that it is more complex than that. His transition includes changes in *health and mortality, fertility, age, migration, the growth of cities and changes in the *family and *household.[54] The net outcome of all these transitions, including the decline in fertility, is what we should have in mind when thinking about trends in future population, and the science writer Fred Pearce writes of this as a "peoplequake", unfolding in the present century:

> Once the trend has set in, it may prove very hard to break. As well as having ever fewer potential mothers, societies may get out of the habit of having babies. Children will be rare, exotic and unusual. We can see this already. Only a few years ago, going to a café in Italy would see you surrounded by noisy children. Now you will likely see only adults, including many young latte-sipping men and women who would once have been surrounded by kids.

And Pearce provides some startling estimates of populations in 2100, with Russia at some 20% of its present population and Italy as low as 14%. Undoubtedly, there has been a change in the trend, starting in the second half of the twentieth century.[55]

For example, China's one-child policy, introduced in 1979 at a time when the fertility rate was already on the way down, contributed to a reduction in fertility from 7.5 children per woman in 1963 to 2.5 children per woman in 1983. And yet this is also an illustration of how weak the link is between reductions in fertility and reductions in population—for, as a result of its former rapid growth rate, there are so many young women of reproductive age that China is still adding 7.7 million people each year, with an increasing proportion of old people to be looked after by the young. In due course, low birth rates will work through to declining populations, but it will take time. Over the whole period 1950–2000, China's population grew by 700 million; it is slowing, but in 2000 and 2050 it will still grow—by a further 150 million. In Japan, the fertility rate, at a mere 1.2 children per woman, is low enough to have relatively quick results: by 2050 its population is expected to have fallen from 127 million at the millennium to 100 million. Worldwide, the rate of growth is expected to slow from 76 million per year in 2010, to 34 million by 2050, but that will still take population up from a 2010 total of 6.8 billion to 9.1 billion in 2050.[56]

Weeks summarises,

> As the rate of population growth has slowed down over the past two decades, there has been talk of a population implosion, implying that "the world is in for some rapid downsizing". . . . The demographics of the world are shifting, to be sure, and there are pockets of potential implosion, especially in Japan and Eastern Europe, but there is no global implosion in sight.[57]

Difficulties severely felt

While acknowledging the uncertainties of forecasts about such *systems, then, there is nothing in the demographics to suggest prospects of any significant decline in the population . . .

. . . so long as our economies can keep it fed through the *climacteric, and supplied with its *energy needs in a liveable *climate, and in tolerable conditions of political and social order—aka peace—and . . .

The big driver of food production during the twentieth century was the abundant supply of oil, gas and coal. That abundance is over. This fact alone is on course to reduce the population on a scale that makes all demographic forecasts *irrelevant unless they take into account the possibility of catastrophic impacts, of which famine is one. Here are some of the critics that do so:

- John Weeks puts food and the prospect of famine in context with environmental change as a whole, including climate change:

    Can we increase the food supply enough to feed the nearly 80 million additional people on the planet every year while also improving everyone's diet in the process? We do not know. Do we have enough fresh water to support all those people? We do not know that either. . . . Still, we always have to come back to the fact that in the long run the only solution is to halt population growth; at some point, the finite limit to resources will close the gate on population growth.[58]

- Martin Rees considers the prospect of the end of civilisation, with a corresponding collapse in population, in the course of this century.[59]
- James Lovelock writes, ". . . the evidence coming in from the watchers around the world brings news of an imminent shift in our climate towards one that could easily be described as Hell: so hot, so deadly, that only a handful of the teeming billions now alive will survive."[60]
- A study by William Stanton, based on a worldwide historical analysis, concludes that, after an initial period when energy conservation and renewable energy sources are diligently developed, the link between oil and food will prove too strong: as oil production declines, so will population. There will be competition for survival, and some of the *conflict that will develop under the pressure of scarce resources will reflect ethnic divisions in *multicultural populations. Stanton argues that, even if all the correct decisions in response to oil depletion and climate change were to be made, the current population would still be far (some 7–14 times) in excess of the level sustainable under the conditions of the coming energy-famine. By 2050, he writes, the falling world population may stabilise at between 0.5 and 1 billion.[61]

- And it is now widely recognised that global transportation and identical hybrid crop strains provide conditions for both pandemics (such as bird flu) affecting the population and threats affecting crops; but there is no basis for an estimate of their effect on population numbers.[62]

The last time there was a population collapse in Europe was in 1348–9, when between a third and a half of the population died in the Black Death; it was, as Joan Thirsk describes it, "a Malthusian crisis that had long been waiting to happen".[63] One effect of this was to make much more *land available *per capita*—and this meant both a better, more varied diet and the freedom to experiment which opened the way for a revolution in agriculture. A new generation of crops and agricultural techniques was introduced, and there was substantial redistribution of wealth.[64]

The significance of this was recognised. Before the catastrophe, the need for bread had demanded desperate measures—felled forests, drained swamps, ploughed meadows; after it, as the historian George Huppert writes, the survivors became *prudent: they built "an artfully balanced social organisation" capable of controlling its own population. "Grim lessons had been learned. . . . They bowed to constraints, but they also achieved a degree of autonomy." It would be as wrong to deny the benefits that would be derived in our time from a reduced population as it would be to welcome them, but there is no need to do either. The *Lean Economy is designed not only to prevent or mitigate a reduction in population, but to provide the basis for a stabilised society far into the future, whether such a population collapse occurs at the start of the period or not.[65]

In fact, population has fallen out of the range of things which politicians think they can do anything about. On the presumption that population movements (shifting labour forces around according to demand) are good for the *economy, and in tune with the fact that "good for growth" trumps all other arguments, the European Union has abolished controls on migration across its national *boundaries—an engaging instance of the rule that the larger the consequences, the more infantile the decision. There is no substantial benefit to be derived from the economic growth produced by a growing population, whatever the source, and the belief that there is one arises from an elementary confusion between aggregate income (or growth) and *per capita* growth income (or growth). As the House of Lords economic affairs committee summarised in 2008:

> GDP—which measures the total output created by immigrants and pre-existing residents in the UK—is an irrelevant and misleading measure for the economic impacts of immigration on the resident population. The total size of an economy is not an indicator of prosperity or of residents' living standards.
>
> GDP *per capita* is a better measure than GDP because it takes account of the fact that immigration increases not only GDP but also population. . . . Rather than referring to total GDP when discussing the economic impacts of immigration, the Government should focus on the *per capita* income (as a measure of the standard of living) of the resident population.
>
> Although possible in theory, we found no systematic empirical evidence to suggest that net immigration creates significant dynamic effects for the resident population of the UK . . . , and it is possible that there are also negative dynamic and wider welfare effects.[66]

In fact, there are benefits, but they are minor and temporary. In addition to those discussed in the entry on *growth, topping up the workforce with immigration can absorb some of the inflation-potential in a chronically overheated economy; it allows the economy to import skills, briefly saving it the trouble of effectively *educating its workforce and developing *practice in the *manual skills; and it gives employers and middle-income householders access to labour which, for a short period, is prepared to work for little *money.[67]

On the other hand, such minor, short-term opportunism is no good reason for irreversible change. Immigration requires big increases in *infrastructure; it means less farmland and more people to feed in the event of food shortages; and it brings problems of increased *water demand and *waste disposal needs, a further reduction in the space available for local food and the natural environment, smaller *per capita* entitlements when energy *rationing begins, ethnic divisions as a factor in *law and order, and greater difficulty in sustaining the collective effort, the shared *culture and the latent *gift of *trust between strangers needed for the fluid conditions of the near future. Only the wealth temporarily conferred on the *market economy by oil, gas and coal removed population policy from the list of things we have needed to think about.

Intentional limits

How was population controlled in the past? There is debate about this. The conventional view is that *death rates in hunter-gatherer societies were very high (all those wild animals), so that humans were lucky to live long enough to have children and keep their numbers up. No doubt that was the case in some places. But a species that was developing tools and *intelligence, which had evolved a physiology capable of staying alive for up to a century and was engaged in taking over the world, is likely also to have been more successful than this. Humans during that long period, as the anthropologist Marvin Harris insists, were no bumbling amateurs.[68] For the stable clan and village societies that comprised (by far) the longest phase in human history, the need to maintain a steady population was non-negotiable. Their numbers were not kept down by predators, disease or starvation; rather, they had an accommodation with their environment, with food and materials in variety; they recognised that if they were to hold on to all that, they had to control their own population, and that in turn meant that, per woman, the number of children surviving long enough to have their own children could not be much more than two. Harris summarises,

> Each woman must have had on average less than 2.1 children who survived to reproductive age.[69]

Harris gives us a rough guide to how they did this, starting with the presumption that the fertile span for women would be from sixteen to forty-two, long enough in theory for twelve pregnancies. The principal way of reducing this was by prolonged lactations. It is not clear that this is still possible in our own day, when lactation does not appear to be so effective as a way of preventing menstruation, perhaps owing to high rates of exposure to oestrogen in the environment. But on the evidence of the past, a woman did not resume ovulation after giving birth until her body fat recovered to about 20–25 percent of her weight, which was difficult to achieve when she was nursing because the nursing infant needs 1,000 calories a day. Prolonged lactation (four years) would reduce the number of pregnancies from twelve to six.[70]

Reduced coitus in older women might bring that down to five; spontaneous abortions, accidents and predation might take it to four. But that is two more than a village with a stable population can support. Abortions during this period were rarely performed, not least because the techniques available were as likely to lead to the death of the mother as of the foetus. And that left infanticide.[71]

It was always a grief-drenched thing to do, and it was done with an array of *denials, delusions and taboos to fog the truth. A common means was neglect: the mother might not feed the infant enough, or she might abandon it in the wild, or accidentally drop it. Another mother could be asked to "look after" it for a day, while the real mother went foraging, to learn the sad news of her child's death when she returned. Feet-first (breech) births, or being born in the yard rather than in the house, were taken as signs that the child was not for this world. Even the foundling hospitals of the eighteenth and nineteenth centuries applied such principles of *deception. An infant left at a hospital would be placed in a revolving box in the wall of the hospital, allowing the mother surrendering her infant to hope that it would get a better life than she could provide for it. There was just a chance she was right: between 10 and 20 percent of them survived.[72]

For those groups and villages that kept the human race and its planet intact for so long, there was no alternative to maintaining stable numbers at a level at which food would be plentiful, or at an optimum where material affluence (in the terms of a traditional society) could be maximised. This stable society—as one eighteenth century missionary put it, this "rude image of the Golden Age"—would destroy itself if it destabilised its population.[73] The anthropologist Hugh Brody reports,

> [Inuit] families do not desire more than two small children at any one time, and to this end they do what they can to space births by about three years. Thus the apparent paradox noted by so many observers of hunter-gatherer societies: intense love for children, yet occasional readiness, at times of shortage, to use infanticide if a child just born is perceived as one too many.[74]

As for less drastic methods of birth control? Since pre-industrial contraception (e.g., beeswax, honey, pessaries, caps made of oiled paper and condoms made of animal intestines and herbal contraceptives) was unreliable and unpopular, the main alternative was abstinence, sustained by convents, monasteries, a celibate priesthood, and local rules such as those which did not permit a couple to get married until a house became available for them in the village. But those are methods suited to settled and comparatively rich states. For most of history, the urgent task of preventing death rates rising out of control demanded a sense of the gift of life being the intense, special outcome of getting a lot of things right at the same time.[75]

In the end, we do not need to make predictions about the scale of future population. The *Lean Economy has other business. Its aim is to explore how human society could sustain a *mannerly and decent civilisation despite the shocks, and we should not be distracted from this by uncertainty about the size of the population. What we do know is that, in an economy with richly-developed *reciprocities, *social capital and *culture, it is possible to support *institutions and *practices which limit the growth of populations. And one reason why the limits failed was that those structures of social order declined—slowly in the early medieval period, but gathering speed with the *growth of towns whose long commercial reach enabled them to break free of

P

the need to maintain a stable population. Then the larger population required an intensive, urban industry to meet the need not just for more goods, but for the increasing elaboration—the *intensification and *intermediate economy—that goes with *large scale. And that triggered a classic positive (i.e., amplifying) *feedback of further dislocation and further *growth.

Exploding populations in nature are never sustainable. The Lean Economy may, or may not, start with a much smaller population than that of now, but—however population numbers eventually settle down—it will support cultural standards controlling population with the effectiveness with which it delivers all its other solutions from energy to agriculture to music. This will be neither a voluntary *system nor an authoritarian one: it will be a *culture that has learned from experience.

POPULISM. See Calibration, Democracy, Demoralisation, Devil's Tunes, Emotivism, Harebrain Fracture, Virtue, Virtual Crowd, Wisdom.

POSITIONAL GOODS. See Composition Fallacy, Economics.

PRACTICE. A skill or craft, requiring a lifetime's learning, and whose tight *feedback loops reveal errors quickly.

This is in sharp contrast to activities which are in various ways protected against feedback (e.g., *politics, *economics). Without quick feedback, actions which will in due course lead to disaster can be assumed (on the *ignorance-is-bliss principle) to be successful, and firmly embedded and reinforced in irrational assumptions, appetites, reflexes and emotions which the person assumes to be right.[76]

The built-in feedback of practice does things. First, it nudges in the direction of the *incremental improvement, or evolution, of the skill. Secondly, as suggested by Alasdair MacIntyre, it requires a person *also to develop the skills of *truthfulness (because the craft will not allow you to bluff your way through), justice in dealing with associates (because there is usually little point in evaluating the work of other craftsmen—masters, learners, equals—unfairly), and *courage (in that to achieve excellence it will from time to time be necessary to make sacrifices and take risks).[77] By

building a distinctive skill, the person not only learns and practises the essentials of citizenship but commits himself to taking pains—with consequences described by John Keats:

> Do you not see how necessary a World of Pains and trouble is to school an Intelligence and make it a soul?[78]

Practice builds skills. Skills build citizenship. The significance of practice has been discussed by other philosophers such as Michael Oakeshott, and by Aristotle, whose concept of "practical wisdom" (*prudence), contains the same concrete grounding: you look at the situation, you respond to it, you observe what you have done, you evaluate it and revise it accordingly. The contrast between this practical wisdom (*phronesis*) and an appeal to universal and general theory (*episteme*) is the essence of the contrast between the diversity of *place and the *ideological principles of the managerial state, between Aristotle and Plato, between the fox (that knows many things) and the hedgehog (that knows one big thing), between a society that can respond under pressure, and one that breaks. Aristotle was a lean thinker.[79]
*Profession, Manual Skills, Middle Voice, Social Capital, Lean Education.

PRECAUTIONARY PRINCIPLE. If the unknown or uncertain consequences of a proposed action could be severe, the precautionary principle suggests that it is advisable to err on the safe side and to abandon the action, or at least to postpone it until more is known about it. However, the principle is widely redundant, or ignored, for reasons such as these:

1. The key decision (e.g., the introduction of a new technology) may have been taken a long time before the existence of potential dangers was widely recognised.
2. Technologies develop their own momentum and may *have* to be taken to the next stage, whether the precautionary principle argues against it or not (*biotechnology, *nanotechnology, economic *growth).
3. The *opportunity costs of *not* developing the technology—e.g., loss of *competitive advantage, and loss of opportunity for growth and

development—may be seen as being greater than the risks of the technology itself.

4. The undesired consequences may not be expected to develop for some time, allowing their costs to be heavily discounted (*Economics ❭ #4).

5. The duty of care may be distributed, by convention, in a way which bears no relation to the reality. For instance, if visitors to a site never have to take responsibility for an accident, no matter how reckless their behaviour, the owner may decide to avoid all risk assessments and simply close it down.

It is also important to appreciate that potential dangers come in four forms:

- Risk: you know what the undesired outcome is, and you know its probability. You accept or reject the odds.

- Uncertainty: you know what the undesired outcome is, but you don't know its probability, so you have to make a *subjective judgment. Given the nature of the undesired outcome, what odds of it happening would be low enough for you to decide to go ahead? If the undesired outcome is wholly unacceptable, no odds would be low enough for you to decide to do so.

- *Ignorance: you know neither the exact undesired outcome, nor its probability.

- Indeterminacy: your judgment of the risk is to some degree *self-fulfilling (or *self-denying). The probability you settle on for the undesired outcome will affect decisions which in turn affect the likelihood of that outcome. Your *intention changes the level of risk to which you are exposed, but overrides the risk assessment.[80]

Clear risks are straightforward subjects for *judgment, but uncertainty, ignorance and indeterminacy can permit an interested party simply to declare the risk to be whatever is appropriate to his or her case. Or they can prompt *scepticism, with the argument that an outcome (e.g., *climate change) is so uncertain that a costly response cannot be justified. And *reductionism encourages that we know little about how this will turn out, so let's do nothing (either to trigger the problem or to prevent it, depending on the agenda of the speaker) until we know more.

In fact, even when dealing with ignorance and indeterminacy, one can still *reflect on whether the risks in question are likely to be trivial (e.g., tripping on a paving stone), or catastrophic (e.g., making the planet uninhabitable). If the latter, a precautionary approach may well be sensible, but a *generalised precautionary principle is an *abstraction, providing no assurance of well-judged treatment of risk.[81]

*Wicked Problems, Pascal's Wager, Galley Skills, Certainty, Five Whys, Regrettable Necessities.

PRESENCE. Direct participation in *community and social enterprise. For *Lean Logic*, a social enterprise is any collective accomplishment, such as organising a *festival, maintaining a school, building a community, managing a *commons, helping the poor, or supporting *charities and local *institutions such as meals-on-wheels, churches, choirs, or the Scouts. Presence means being there, making a society, weaving a texture of belonging, motivations and affections. There is no such thing as society without it.

Throughout the modern era, however, presence has been in progressive decline. The loss of this crucial asset is widely suspected, but has not been speakable or audible in politics. But that may be changing—for, when the "Big Society" stepped onto the road towards wider participation in 2010, it joined a trend which was already quite crowded.[82] Among the more recent joiners are the *Transition movement, the principle of co-production and local initiatives such as those inspired by Participle, but *lean thinking, in some of its interpretations, has been moving in that direction for several decades, as has the *organic movement. In fact, the idea has never really gone away; it is embedded in the theory and *practice of *social capital and in those aspects of local *cooperation which have no name, but which have always maintained community in town and country, despite the best efforts of war-trained, dismally well-intentioned twentieth century social policy to destroy it.

Recognition is growing of the hidden wealth of *nations—the *intelligence, talent, time and goodwill of citizenship, its instinct as a *home-maker, and the incentive it has to maintain a low profile and simply be effective.[83] In general, there are four broad kinds of incentive. They can be thought of as magnetic

P

poles around which political values and assumptions are ordered. They are: (1) command-and-control, (2) financial rewards and penalties, (3) the managerial institution, and (4) presence:

Command-and-control separates decision from action: the actors—the people down there in the system—are not thought to have the information, motivation, ability or ethical standards to make sensible decisions for themselves. It is supposed that, if substantial participation were permitted, the system would fail, since, in individuals, there is no possibility of an incentive other than opportunism. So they are simply told what to do. The motivations for doing what this top-down *system requires are *extrinsic*: they are more about keeping out of trouble than about furthering the collective interest.

For those who see themselves as being in control of this arrangement, the motivations range from benign concern to *fear, *ideology and resentments. For the controlled, it is less a matter of motivation than of having no alternative. The focus is on enforcement.

As discussed in the entry on *incentives, the motivation provided by *financial rewards and penalties* is also extrinsic (and ineffective). Motivation is not directed towards the task, but towards the reward, preferably achieved by exploiting the system. The task itself is clearly of little worth—which is why they have to bribe you to do it. And yet this is the kind of motivation that government reaches for when it wants to motivate people to do something in the public interest. In the field of *climate science, for instance, it is taken to be

---

THE DISPLACEMENT LAW
Good intentions run into the sand . . .

In 1997, the Bromley by Bow Healthy Living Centre had been developing as a social enterprise for some fifteen years. It had provided a comprehensive service and setting for local people: doctors' surgeries, nurses, *arts, *education, a three-acre park, sheltered housing, support and care, along with shops selling fresh fruit and vegetables, a welfare and benefits advice shop, yoga, t'ai chi, aromatherapy, dance classes for children, circuit training and exercise classes and programmes for Bengali women and the elderly. It employed 150 people and paid its way. The Labour Government that would win that year's election decided to imitate it on a *large scale, making a manifesto commitment to open 257 more health centres at a cost of £300 million. The promise was fulfilled, but only in terms of the budget. The money was spent, and there are remnants here and there, but the programme was closed down soon afterwards, and the intention of bringing this valuable facility to a grateful public comprehensively failed.[84]

The mistake is to forget what a social enterprise is. Each one—the community, the school, the health centre or hospital—is invented afresh, the accomplishment of the people who live there, building on, and building, the *character and resources of the *place. The individual does not simply implement decisions; she has a personal attachment to the project, developing a sense of discovery about what can be done, and a sense that it would not be done as well, or at least not in the same way, without her own contribution. The effect of top-down *generalities is to control and kill off local inspiration, and to close down passionate commitment to making the social invention work: grown-up citizenship becomes seen as a disorder in need of treatment. The phenomenon is so universal and predictable that it seems justified to summarise it in The Displacement Law:

> If a social enterprise proves itself successful, bringing essential benefits elegantly and efficiently, it will be removed from the care of the citizens who have created it, brought under the bureaucratic control of the state, and turned into a problem.

Or, more succinctly (from Janet Daley):

> Government domination pushes out personal involvement.[85]

*self-evident that some form of financial incentive is needed to stimulate reduced emissions. Otherwise (it is argued) why would people bother? As a result, we have at present a policy-response shaped by a mixture of brilliant technology and pop behaviourism.[86]

The third form of incentive is *the managerial institution*. An impersonal regulatory culture takes over: procedures, permissions, prohibitions, protective rules, intense anxiety to be in the inner circle. There is *displacement* of *judgment, *intention and ownership; there is detachment and distance from the service it is there to provide (see "The Displacement Law" sidebar).

The fourth framework for collective action is *presence*, the property of a system which people take part in because their incentive to do so is *intrinsic*. This is the kind of incentive which made the Bromley by Bow social enterprise (see "The Displacement Law" sidebar), and it can take either of two forms (or it may lie somewhere on the spectrum between them):

First, there is *prehension* (*Middle Voice), where an action is prompted, less by conscious intention than by membership of a *group, by the momentum of participating in something that draws you in. This is easy to see in the case of, say, dance—especially traditional dance, in which each individual's movements are determined by a motivation midway between active decision and passive conformity: you are swept up in the *dance; you do it, but the dance decides for you.[87]

Secondly, there is *purpose*: the person wants to do a thing on its own terms. Here, too, the motivation is intrinsic. If it is integrated into the *community's own *intentions, there is the critical benefit of alignment, of *common purpose; the participants *want* to do what *needs* to be done. There is engagement with other people with the same objectives—an awareness of detail. It

is more than a bottom-up process: there is 'inside-out' decision-making, where collective achievements begin with one person's inspiration. People are present in the situation, and respond to it on its own terms.[88]

The power of presence

It is time for a glance at how normal presence used to be, as the way of making things happen, and at how intensely regretted and advocated it has been since its decline.

The products of social enterprise—*healthcare, *education, social insurance, *charitable work and *place-making in all its forms—happened because many individuals joined together to make them happen. The principle by which the institutions of our *culture came into being was direct voluntary participation—the path to both prehension and purpose. Every social invention which makes us recognisable as a society and a culture arose out of, and is sustained by, voluntary action—*cooperation, the dedication of time and lives—by citizens who are themselves present in schools, hospitals, the Bench, friendly societies, charitable giving, churches and libraries, the enabling *institutions which make us a people.

As we have seen, however, the recent pattern, once an institution has achieved a substantial degree of competence, is for the state to take it over. It is then forced to pay for services which had formerly been supplied voluntarily, to find funds which had formerly been donated, to motivate commitments which had formerly been vocational, and to apply central control in the space vacated by local intelligence, rapport and evolution. The state has difficulty in maintaining standards and will try to cope with these troubles by undersupplying, by overstaffing and regulation, by queue- or congestion-rationing, or by partly or wholly closing down the services it has commandeered.

SYSTEM	INCENTIVE
COMMAND-AND-CONTROL	Extrinsic: power/*fear/resentment/*ideology. Absence.
FINANCIAL REWARDS AND PENALTIES	Extrinsic: financial rewards and penalties. Rewards for fulfilling obligations which could be seen as already implicit are demotivating and build resentment. Absence.
MANAGERIAL INSTITUTION	Suppressed: no direction, *story or *common purpose. There may be compliance, but not creative *intelligence. Absence.
PRESENCE	Prehension: *middle-voiced; the person does not feel an explicit objective; he just does it.
	Purpose: the *incentive is intrinsic and explicit. The person participates in the decision-making that shapes her life.

Presence does better. This has long been recognised, with perhaps even greater clarity than elsewhere, in the United States. Henry David Thoreau (1817–1862), for instance, noted that . . .

> . . . government never of itself furthered any enterprise, but by the alacrity with which it got out of the way. *It* does not keep the country free. *It* does not settle the West. *It* does not educate. The character inherent in the American people has done all that has been accomplished; and it would have done somewhat more, if the government had not sometimes got in its way.[89]

Among many who pressed the case for leaving policy in the hands of citizens—directly participating in, and being responsible for, what happens in their locality—was Thomas Jefferson (1743–1826). He argued for local "wards", similar to the Swiss model of local participation, and small enough for citizens to take part in decision-making directly:

> Where every man is a sharer in the direction of his ward-republic, or of some of the higher ones, and feels that he is a participator in the govern-ment of affairs, not merely at an election one day in the year, but every day; when there shall not be a man in the State who will not be a member of some one of its councils, great or small, he will let the heart be torn out of his body sooner than his power be wrested from him . . .[90]

As for schools:

> If it is believed that . . . elementary schools will be better managed by the [state] governor and council, the commissioners of the literary fund or any other general authority of the govern-ment than by the parents within each ward, it is a belief against all experience.[91]

In fact, what we ought to be about is . . .

> . . . instilling the principles and exercise of self-government into every fibre of every member of our commonwealth.[92]

It went beyond the rhetoric. Doing-it-yourself means doing it on a manageable scale—which means making

it *local. It was in the name of local *empowerment that Ralph *Borsodi established his homesteaders and Arthur Morgan his communitarians, and Kirkpatrick Sale—in his extended and passionate review of this direct, hands-on, located form of self-government—lists groups such as the Greenbacks, the Grangers, the Okla-homa Socialists, the Knights of Labour, the Georgists and—achieving substantial political power for a time in North Carolina—the Populists.[93] More recently, the yearning for direct presence in politics was expressed in the Port Huron Statement ("The Hippy Charter", 1962):

> As a social system we seek the establishment of a democracy of individual participation, governed by two central aims: that the individual share in those social decisions determining the quality and direction of his life; [and] that society be organised to encourage independence in men and provide the media for their common participation.[94]

"True democracy"—the phrase comes from the "reformist *anarchism" school of thought—is about participation, with decisions and responsibility taken back into the hands of the public associations, schools, hospitals, *parishes, citizens. It seems idealistic, but this is only because it is so different from our present normal-ity. The mere idea of grown-up citizenship can bring on a panic attack in the context of the state's displacement of every enabling *institution of society-defining signif-icance. "The people", as the economist and philosopher Ludwig von Mises observes, "are reduced to the status of wards"—and recovery is still uncertain.[95]

Why, then, has government's encroachment and reg-ulatory capture been so comprehensive and relentless?

Among many reasons, one, of course, is the seduc-tive appeal of Marxist theory which encourages the state—on which power confers a monopoly of moral *judgment—to see itself as bringing order where liberty would mean class warfare. This is the state in its role as carer, peacekeeper, guide, disciplinarian and father of the people (*Paternalism).

A second reason is the logic of *democracy: govern-ments and parties, needing to attract votes, see voters as customers or patients—and this in turn can have a seductive appeal to voters who don't mind being wooed, if it comes their way.[96]

P

Thirdly, there is *expertise, that strange status-envy which dismisses ordinary knowledge—acute observation of the local particular—as a direct threat to expert credibility.[97]

Fourthly, *money. Money has no moral texture. It tells us nothing whatsoever about anything. We can study it and think all the time about it and still know nothing. A society that thinks money has equality of *innocence comes at problems naked as the day it was born, and thinks only of being lifted to safety.

Fifthly, there is the effect of war. The state interpreted the experience of (for instance) the Second World War as proving the competence of the government as an organiser, demonstrating its power to deliver results in bulk, legitimising the authoritarian control which had a chance to prove itself under testing circumstances. As shown in *Harmonic Order, this was key to the UK Labour Party's 1943 plans for the National Health Service, based on the need for the centralised control which was so enviably maintained by the army. War games, real and virtual, are addictive and, in fact, as Kirkpatrick Sale argues,

> We are still living in a war economy. Wars are centralising: that's why governments have them.[98]

A sixth reason is *economics itself. Keynesian economic management enables governments to enjoy the intoxicating delusion of being in command, and this is backed by appeals to economic criteria and *competitiveness as the basis for *judgment across the whole field of public policy. Government has found itself a job of overriding importance—a *necessary condition for all its other expensive controlling missions: to keep its citizens gratefully consuming.

Sale, who has done more than anybody to explore and map the subject, offers a reminder of how insidious the displacement of autonomous local institutions has been—and by authorities whose task it was to protect them. Writing of state services and regulatory agencies,

> There is not a one of them, not one, that has not in the past been the province of the community or some agency within the community (family, church, guild) and has been taken on by the state only because it first destroyed that province. There is not a one of them that could

not be reabsorbed by a community in control of its own destiny and able to see what its natural humanitarian obligations, its humanitarian *opportunities*, would be.[99]

The shredding of the *networks of *cooperative responsibility by which people once wove a social fabric has been so savage that the possibility of a world with an empowered and responsible citizenship has become hard to recognise as an option. Instead, not only is the *commons being destroyed by its protector, but the protector itself is sick—and busy making itself sicker. Here Dr. Max Gammon, introduced in *Harmonic Order, gives his diagnosis:

> In gigantic, centrally directed systems, unintended consequences provoke centrally prescribed adjustments that, in turn, will have their own unintended consequences. These will then require further adjustments, and so on until, to use an Information Theory metaphor—noise drowns out the signal. In a protected environment, shielded from competition, a bureaucracy will grow indefinitely and approach ever more closely the black hole state, in which externally supplied resources are entirely consumed by its furious internal activity . . .[100]

. . . and citizens who have lost any means of deciding for themselves will think that's normal.

Until now, that is, for a realisation that society is a living *system with powers of *judgment and the ability to act on them is beginning to stir into life, and to be spoken in public. The Big Society is not well-defined at this early stage, but there is an intention there which is interesting. It is to bring healing and presence to a deserted landscape, to join up the remnants of local *culture that survive, and to give them the chance to get their confidence back. Yes indeed, others will claim rights in that landscape, too, and whether we want that depends on who "we" are. So, at the same time as making the Big Society mean what we want it to mean, we need to discover our *identity. And our identities.

It was the *Transition movement that said it first. *Lean thinking, in some of its forms, has been thinking it for half a century. A case can be made for *permaculture, with its diverse participation of species—humans included—in a productive ecology, being an expression of the same principle. And the institutions of *social capital—the *neighbourhoods and *communities, centres of learning in their own right—have been doing it and teaching it since the invention of human *groups, and probably since the first sliver of life first became aware that maybe there was another one close by.

And not before time. Presence is beautiful; it is friendship; it is our being; it is what life is for. Absence makes things difficult. The task of rebuilding the competence of a *place, its *conversation and confidence, is hard by any standards, but especially so when there's no one at home. *'Introduction', Call and Response, Courtesy, TEQs (Tradable Energy Quotas).

PREVENTIVE RESILIENCE. See Resilience.

PRIVATE SPHERE. See Public Sphere and Private Sphere.

PRODUCTIVITY. (1) What you get back from a task for the work you put into it. That is: input × productivity = output.

Input usually refers to labour, but it could equally well be *capital, *land, or *energy. Or environmental impact (*eco-efficiency). For example, the *labour-productivity* of industrial *agriculture is high; its *land-productivity* is not so high; its *energy-productivity* is low.

(2) The extent to which a *system produces interesting, *diverse, life-enhancing results: friendships, *trust, inventiveness, the *arts, *social and *cultural capital.

Productivity can be seen and admired in a rock pool, with its variety of species, events and politics; or in a *creative civilisation; or in an *imaginative mind. Like the "potential" developed in the adaptive cycle (*Wheel of Life), productivity is enriched by *connections and *complexity, but only up to a point, beyond which the connections themselves produce rigidity and destroy it. *Appropriate Technology, Leisure.

PROFESSION. A skill or *craft which recognises obligations outside its own specialist field, taking shared responsibility for the wider *community, and dedicating time, care and *reflection to it in the common interest.

We have two points of departure for thinking about whether professions do actually have that quality. First, we have Alasdair MacIntyre's idea of *practice—the expectation that in learning a difficult craft, we are likely to learn the skills of citizenship at the same time: we will learn *truthfulness (for the craft will not allow you to get by without it), a sense of *judgment and justice (for the craft comes with its own robust criteria for judging the work of others) and *courage (for the craft will constantly take you to the limit of your skill, and you will need the bravery to go further).[101]

Secondly, we have Émile Durkheim's idea of the professions and professional organisations. Professions come together informally in *networks, or more formally in professional bodies or (to use Durkheim's word) "corporations", embodying the principles of morality and good conduct needed not only by the professionals themselves but also by the society in which they work. We should be careful about following Durkheim too literally—the sociologist David Martin dismisses him as "clapped-out old Durkheim", and his work does now read as antique when compared with MacIntyre, or with Robert Putnam's storming presentation of *social capital—but Durkheim's idea that the moral roots of our jobs reflect those of citizenship is an important one as we join together to make a society fit for the world after *oil.[102]

It is reasonable to expect that a craftsperson who has developed a significant degree of 'practice', with constant need to make judgments, will develop a sense of responsibility and motivation that will apply to wider interests beyond the limits of the daytime job. Doctors and carpenters are quite likely also to be magistrates, church wardens and football referees, as well as participants in the community in less formal ways. The nineteenth century friendly societies were explicitly managed by their investors, as James Bartholomew explains:

> A judge or a baron of commerce could easily be junior to a dockworker within a friendly society. A poor manual worker could become chairman of his local lodge. In the lodges of the Manchester Unity, the chairman would have two "supporters" who would sit on each side of him at a meeting. Traditionally the

chairman would choose a personal friend and someone who was experienced in the rules and practices of the society. The office of chairman was rotated so that, over time, almost everyone would hold the post.[103]

Here is an aspect of *cohesion, of commitment to the *community and to the *public sphere, which is indispensable.[104]

Those qualities of practice and social engagement—and indeed the word "profession"—are associated with the idea of "middle class". The causal relationship, however, is not from middle class to professional, but the other way round—it is from {practice and social responsibility} to {values described as middle class} to {supposed membership of the middle class}. There may then be reinforcement from that membership as to social responsibility—a stabilising interconnection, which disappears if *reductionism equates membership of the middle class with wealth. You do not have to be middle-income to possess the attributes of a profession and to be committed to the defence of collective *capital and *common purpose. However, the identification of "professional" with "middle class" has brought the key *ethic of profession, and people who giftedly defend their *culture, into the line of fire. Resentment, whose *mindset is *money, eats its way through society like the Ebola virus, whose mindset is flesh. And so the middle class is shot—almost.

The Italian communist Antonio Gramsci (1891–1937) also made the mistake of supposing that professional = middle class, but he did at least recognise the significance of that professional quality as a barrier to the overthrow of the state. He advocated its destruction as the necessary task of the revolutionary parties, but he concluded, with regret, that the idea of the profession gives liberal democracy its *resilience. Unfortunately, as he wrote in his *Prison Notebooks*, it holds *nations and communities together when disorder threatens—and that means that the first task of the revolutionary is to destroy the *institutions such as the church, the schools and the media, which sustain, and are sustained by, the professions. Imperial Russia, he added, had the enormous advantage (from the point of view of his revolutionary agenda) of lacking this public-spirited professional ethic: "the state was everything; civil

power was primordial and gelatinous" and, when revolution threatened, it had no resistance to offer.[105]

The *Lean Economy, by contrast, will intensely value its professions and the ethic of *practice which is cultivated by them. In the aftermath of the *climacteric, it will not be so flush with wealth and so impoverished in judgment that it feels it is okay to refuse the *gifts of citizenship and *presence when they are offered. Nor will it be diverted from the life-and-death need to think things through by a demonic *ad hominem* quarrel about who has a right to do the thinking.

*Leisure, Cheirarchy.

PROMISCUOUS ETHICS. The ethical code which consists of getting into bed with any point of view that confirms your opinion about what a beautifully ethical person you are.

As *culture declines, *ethics are reduced to the values which are easiest to defend, so that it becomes hard to support any values other than the value of there being no values: being real, spontaneous and true to your feelings is all you need. If the presumption that ethics consist of ideas that are *self-evident were to become a habit, it would be hard to distinguish an ethical *judgment from whatever impulsive responses happen to come along. They may not be ethical.

*Narcissism, Diplomatic Lie, Calibration, Identity.

P

PROTECTION. The act of caring for something which you value, or for which you are responsible. Protection is widely supposed to be a good thing, except in the case of economies, which are required to dance to the single tune of perpetual *competition.

Actually, the *market economy has little choice. Protectionism—in the sense of, for instance, trade tariffs against foreign imports—would allow domestic industry to settle into a comfortable inefficiency which will eventually ensure that it cannot sell its goods and services abroad; which it probably wouldn't be able to do anyway because trading partners would build their own tariff barriers in retaliation. So free trade is with good reason a fundamental principle of a rationally-managed market economy.

But, of course, there is a downside, and we are coming to a time when it can be discussed without inviting derision. *Competitive free trade comes with a commitment to *growth, i.e., to the rubbing out of *diversity and local self-reliance, to resource depletion, *pollution, the loss of *social capital and *resilience—and eventual collapse. It is too late to consider protection against these things; the damage has already been done. But protection of what is left of indigenous *food production and steps towards reduced dependence on fossil fuels would be rational. As E.F. Schumacher writes, protection of the intermediate technology (aka *appropriate technology) which could make progress towards such ends is not about "keeping alive activities which lack essential viability: it is concerned with creating a new viability".[106]

Protection is a deep behaviour which, in some senses, is shared by all living things. True, natural selection is a condition of all living things, too. But species with less *intelligence than ours use both. It is time we caught up. *Lean Economics, Local Currency, Nation > Currency.

PROXIMITY PRINCIPLE. The principle that the way to achieve a reduction in the need for *transport is to use space more intelligently, producing goods and services—especially *food—where they are needed, rather than having to transport them over long distances. The objective is to build competence across the whole range of *economics and *culture, and to enable personal lives to be organised so that extensive routine transport is no longer a *necessary condition for meeting material *needs, nor for *leisure, friendships or work. There is *localisation. Any progress made towards putting the principle into effect before enforced reductions in travel and transport are imposed by *oil depletion would be a life-saving benefit. The proximity principle is a central element of the *Lean Economy.[107]
*Boundaries and Frontiers, Elegance, Incrementalism, Lean Household, Neotechnic, TEQs (Tradable Energy Quotas).

PRUDENCE. This is Aristotle's "practical wisdom" (*phronesis*), the principle of engagement with the *small-scale and with local detail—and of freedom from universalised *ideology—that is at the heart of *Lean Logic*. *Dirty Hands, Judgment, Local Wisdom, Planned Economy, Vernacular, Virtues.

PUBLIC SPHERE AND PRIVATE SPHERE. The difference between the public sphere and the private sphere is one of the guiding principles of *community building. This entry will first discuss the difference between them. Secondly, a question: is the state private? Thirdly, despatches from an invasion: private invades public.

Towards a distinction between the public and the private spheres

The private sphere consists of everyday matters of love, *health, work, *money, food, trouble, gossip. Your family, and any others in your private sphere—your *small group—are likely to know quite a lot about such personal matters. They may even know about your verruca. There is a sense of being at home when someone you love is around, and yet, being at home sees you at your most blunt, at your worst as well as your best. There is a quality of behaviour in the private sphere which is unvarnished and untaught. You are accepted as you are; there is little *deference to rules, custom or *ceremony, unless invented, or specifically affirmed, at home. In the private sphere, actions correspond, sometimes all too closely, with thought. It is your occupation to be plain. You get to know each other, well. But if the community you live in consists only of the private sphere, you will feel the need to get away.[108]

The public sphere is different. Here a structure of rules and *civilities is accepted, not because it is immediately evident that they are sensible, but because they exist—they are part of the *culture, the rules of a game. They are expressive of the community as a whole, rather than of material and instrumental needs and relationships between individuals. The public sphere does not intrude; it does not tell you more about private lives than you want to know. Public life is guarded in what it reveals.

But the public sphere also *plays. It invites wide participation. There is immersion in the play, but the rules keep the distance between the players. In a healthy public sphere, there is a sense of reserve, even reticence—there is also excitement and enthusiasm, vitality and invention, but play is not a good setting for a player to open up his heart to the other players. It is best to wait until the game is over, and if the culture is organised around the principle of play, it is never over, except at focused moments of privacy—for instance, in the *family. And yet, despite the reticence, or perhaps because of it, there is also a sense that it is in the structured public context that your *identity is being shaped. Your imagination is stretched: you can develop your game persona and, towards your game partner, display aggression which you would not contemplate for real.

The public sphere, then, reaches beyond people's concerns with *instrumental needs. It can accomplish serious things, too: it can build a church or a hospital; and yet, its element is play; festival and *carnival are public in this sense, as is some theatre, music and architecture. There is decoration, *humour, deliberation, even a sense of collective enchantment—a sense of the *spirit of the *place, where the *anarchic power of people to organise themselves is unleashed. *Conversation between friends may border on the public sphere if it is not instrumental in the sense of discussion about, or seeking help on, personal problems. The public sphere is both impersonal and rich in *emotion, *imagination, *art—in things which transcend the self. There is a combination of creativity and a self-distance, in that you are expressing yourself but not necessarily revealing a lot about yourself.[109] The public sphere establishes a *presence behind which people can actually maintain their own privacy: a strong public sphere keeps privacy private, and indeed the two spheres depend on each other—the public sphere is built on private-sphere foundations.

All these things are expressed by, and comprise, a society's culture. And in the presence of a living culture, the public sphere comes alive; it rises above the daily grind; it has a *story to tell; it is awash with music. If there is to be an artistic culture, there has to be a public sphere—its habitat. If there is to be a public sphere, there has to be an artistic culture—its natural resident. There is a social ecology here, as interactive and self-stabilising as *Gaia—or, perhaps, there *was*, as Edmund Burke wrote:

> All the pleasing illusions, which made power
> gentle, and obedience liberal, which harmon-
> ised the different shades of life, and which, by
> a bland assimilation, incorporated into politics
> the sentiments which beatify and soften private

society, are to be dissolved by this new conquering empire of light and reason. All the decent drapery of life is to be rudely torn off. All the superadded ideas, furnished from the wardrobe of a moral imagination, which the heart owns and the understanding ratifies, as necessary to cover the defects of our naked shivering nature, and to raise it to dignity in our own estimation, are to be exploded as ridiculous, absurd, and antiquated fashion.[110]

Is the state public or private?

For most of the period of post-Roman history in the West, the distinction between private and public has been reasonably clear. There was some substantial crossing of the *boundary so that (as so often in *Lean Logic*) there were *fuzzy borderlines, but there were also central areas of sharp definition. The public sphere was large and strongly present.

And then, events began to stir into life which reduced the scale and significance of the public sphere. It was a long, slow process and it started a long time ago. It could perhaps be traced to the invention of *money in seventh century BC Greece. In our own culture, a decisive move came with the dissolution of the monasteries. Monasticism had been a powerful expression of the public sphere. It had its flaws; it had elements of politics and privacy and money-making in it, but at its best, and in *intention, it was a public institution. It was funded in part by charitable giving; its chief expression was in terms of *art and *culture, especially music, of the highest order; and it carried out a vital public function in that it provided hospitals, schools, colleges and systems of care and subsistence for the poor. Monasteries and convents provided care for the elderly (called corridans) and for people unable to work. Such schemes were not comprehensive, but they were important, and they set a standard.[111]

When they were dissolved (1536–1541), much of that work simply came to a stop. In particular, the task of care and maintenance for the poor was left undone and, since no other public *institution was available to take it over, the matter was left to the government. But the government had no instinct for the task: one of its first acts on taking over responsibility for the poor in 1547

P

was to pass a law requiring that idlers and wanderers should be branded. That law was repealed two years later, but the question of how the government ought best to carry out its responsibility towards the poor was never resolved. The friendly societies—set up by citizens as insurance against financial trouble, and one of the most significant accomplishments of the public sphere—took off in the nineteenth century, but this in turn was unpicked when, in 1911, the state established its own system of national insurance, making it the *responsibility of the state to administer pensions and welfare benefits, and to tinker with them as the *unintended consequences were revealed.[112]

Another sequence of events, linked in many ways with that, and starting at the same time, was the enclosure of common land which farmers had formerly maintained and relied on as a collective village asset. Enclosures—transfer of the *commons into private ownership—matured from being rare to being a transformation, spreading through the land at the cost of rebellion, resentment and disempowerment. Their consequences—the loss of jointly-managed responsibility for *local land, of accessible *land for grazing, and of shared rotations and very small-scale plots—are also still with us, complicating progress towards wider participation in *food production. The management of the commons had been an expression of the public sphere. The meetings of the Manor Court and its field jury in Laxton in Nottinghamshire—the last remaining area of land which is farmed in common—are a luminous remnant of the rural self-*monitoring public sphere in action.[113]

The deconstruction of the public sphere did not reach its climax in the United Kingdom until the twentieth century, after early warnings such as the decisive state intervention in primary schools in 1870.[114] In the second half of the twentieth century, encouraged by its experience as an organiser of war, the state's intervention in matters which had belonged in the public sphere advanced without restraint.

The question is not whether that was a good thing or not: *Lean Logic* would argue that, in terms of *efficiency and guaranteed access, the schools, hospitals and universities—and social security in the form of the friendly societies—would have been superior beyond

recognition as compared with the present state-run standards, if the public sphere—which had created them and brought them to their world-class standard—had been able to continue its work during the period of post-war economic recovery. But that isn't something we need to agree on, and it is not the point. The point is that this state takeover of services, and the other forms of takeover discussed above, were not additions to the public sphere, they were subtractions from it. They were forms of privatisation.

It makes no significant difference whether the services and responsibilities taken away from the public sphere finally end up in the hands of public companies or those of the state: their removal from the self-organising culture of presence and participation is a dismantling of the public sphere, and sucks meaning from citizenship. State ownership is a process of privatisation. Even though some of the money comes via taxation rather than direct exchange, the state, in its role as manager, paymaster and service provider, has the function of— has in essence become—a private-sphere institution.

The private invades the public

The distinction between private and public is no mere naming of parts: it matters. And it is not only about the loss of citizenship in a practical sense; it is about the whole ethic of interaction and relationship. For one thing, when the private sphere enters the space which would otherwise have been occupied by public *civility, its characteristic benign, uninhibited bluntness can become ugly. Just as public formality does not work in the private sphere, so private bluntness does not work in the public sphere, where it implies an intimate knowledge of the other person which is in fact intrusive, incipiently *violent: the other person's independence and distinctive identity are invaded—and so is the foundation for social order. Tribal groups that merge too quickly into large-scale societies may not have time to develop a culture of public *manners, which can be a route towards becoming *paternal tyrannies, with the tyrant claiming the title of "father", carrying forward the uninhibited culture of family privacy, and applying it to strangers.

The public sphere still exists in some instances (monarchy is one), but only in remnants. In the space where there was a public sphere, there is now (the remnants apart) only a big private sphere. Citizenship had meaning, responsibility, *common purpose and *presence, but the takeovers by state and commerce disempowered citizens, and told them to go back home to their private lives. At the same time, they plunged the state itself into the detail of an impossible top-down management structure, redefining the inherited institutions and services in terms of price and exchange as the previously self-motivated participants did as they were told. The public sphere was vacated.

And the consequences for the private sphere are profound. If there is no public context for private life, you tend to wonder if there is any point: is that all there is?[115]

And yet, the private sphere—the real thing—is itself non-negotiable. It nurses and cultivates; it produces the person who in due course will engage in the public sphere, if there is one; it is the place of love and *sleep, *home and close friends, childhood and lifelong *conversations. *Communities will need to protect their private sphere. They may begin with a strong sense of collective existence, but they will also need to be able to go home and shut the door.

The public sphere and the private sphere rely on each other, but if there is a survivor in the attrition between them, it is the private sphere. Bad *manners drive out good manners, and future building up of the public sphere will have to start from the basics. But it may be that it will have instinct on its side. One of the most dramatic rebellions against the assault on the local public sphere by enclosures was the one led by Ben Kett in Norfolk in 1549. When he rallied his pitchfork-armed troops under the oak tree in Wymondham—public address systems not having yet been invented—his message was amplified by the obviousness and resonance of what he was telling them. The case for being a responsible member of a self-regulating community, charged with the deeply informed and *skilled management of the local land, was not one that had to be heard in detail. Every man there already knew it. The distant music of his words was enough.[116]

PULL. One of the properties of a system designed according to the principles of *lean thinking (Rule 4). Pull recognises that the people best placed to deal with a complex task are those who are doing it—who are engaged with the practical detail. Once the *intention (or *common purpose) is defined, participants do not need forever to rely on instructions; they can respond to actual local circumstance, guided and pulled along by observation, rather than pushed through in response to rules or general principles, or a regulatory agency that claims a monopoly on decision-making.

In the context of the *energy descent, for instance, that means that the Government is freed from the task of having to micromanage the energy transition with detailed regulations; instead, it can call on the biggest intellectual energy source available to our society: the creative intelligence of the people (*TEQs). Pull means that people are allowed to switch on their brains—responding to a challenge on its own terms, and building on their *local wisdom as to the needs of a particular *time and *place. In a pull-system, the people involved apply their creative *intelligence to *pull* answers out of the situation; they *invent* solutions; they *discover* ways forward which management does not have to work out for itself.

In this context, aims can be defined without any reliable knowledge of how they are to be achieved, or even whether they are achievable, for pull can enable the *creative discovery of means which are at present unknown or out of sight and which, when they are invented or revealed, may surprise. The principle of pull is a political philosophy, and it is at the heart of the *Wheel of Life.

An inefficient, high-cost organisation will remain inefficient and high-cost so long as it is based on the principle of push. It is impossible to reform: like herding cats, it provides constant reasons for reform and correction, but it does not get anywhere. The *paradigm change from push to pull opens the way to improvement beyond recognition.[117]

*Call and Response.

Q

QUIBBLE. (1) Negotiation about the trivial.

(2) Noting the use of words which, while substantially true, mislead, evade or conceal the main issue. Example headline in *The Times*: "The Thirsty £1½m Car That Needs Only Water".[1] In fact, the car needs hydrogen, which is produced from water by the application of large quantities of power, which has to be supplied by oil, gas, hydropower or some other energy source: hydrogen does not actually reduce the quantity of fuel needed to drive cars—in fact, it increases it.[2] As the article eventually explains, the original energy source in this particular case is hydropower, so technically the headline is correct, but the super-confident hint—that, instead of filling up the cars of the future with petrol we will just add water (thanks to amazing new technologies)—is of course misleading. It reinforces the error that all we need in order to cope with the *energy peak is a few clever *technical fixes. The quibble can build giant structures of falsehood, without ever requiring the architect to tell a lie.

*Distraction, Special Pleading.

QUICK (adj). The dazzling condition of being alive.

R

RADICAL BREAK. This is a central idea in *lean thinking—known there as *kaikaku*. It means the shock—the large, and usually strongly-resisted break—that opens the way to an elaborate and dysfunctional *complex system being transformed into the flexible *elegance of lean thinking. This principle is the enabling condition for *Lean Logic*, but we should remember that it has its dangers: the radical break's value lies in its rarity: the serial *reforms of our time are, on the contrary, a pathology—the troubled responses of a *culture that has lost its *identity and wits, and is struggling with vicious pre-*climacteric problems to which there are no solutions.

Lean thinking has no patent on the idea of the radical break. It is present in the principle of "breakage" in *religion. And it is integral to the principle of "creative destruction", which was present in Marxist thinking, but developed and popularised by Joseph Schumpeter in his *Capitalism, Socialism and Democracy* (1942). In the years after the Second World War, intentional destruction did not seem to be a priority, but recently it has become more established as a principle of management. In particular, it has become part of the response to the downside of success which turns into large companies' biggest problem: successful (and therefore *large) companies are typically overtaken by small new companies which have the advantage of fresh thinking.[1]

Creative destruction is generally discussed as a continuous process—"Schumpeter's gale"—which, as he explains, is an . . .

> . . . industrial mutation that incessantly revolutionises the economic structure from within, incessantly destroying the old one, incessantly creating a new one. This process of Creative Destruction is the essential fact about capitalism. It is what capitalism consists in and what every capitalist concern has got to live in;
> . . . it cannot be understood on the hypothesis that there is a perennial lull.[2]

But for *Lean Logic*, the radical break is rarer, and darker, than that. And *Lean Logic* uses it also as an analogy, for times when there is a change of key—the opportunity to consider assumptions from a different point of view. The word that summarises this best is "ecstasy" (Greek: *ec* out + *histánai* place), and the community's most salient expression of it is *carnival: the opportunity to be ecstatic, to see things differently, to be enchanted; and then to recover its senses. A reminder that normal good behaviour is not a habit, but a matter of *choice—for now.

*Sunk Cost Fallacy, Incrementalism, Paradigm.

RATIONALISM. The presumption that there is one right—rational—way. The application of a universal *ideology to the local particular.

There is a divide in the personality of thought, shaped in part by the difference between the urban and the

rural. It is not inevitable, nor is it tidy—the thinking of towns spills over into the country—but it is powerful. Towns, with their *large scale, depend, at least to some degree, on standard principles and practice. Taxes, rules, the constitution, are in essence uniform. The Enlightenment that followed the early days of science, with its universal laws, followed that example, seeming at first to suggest that the *truths of science should apply to everything we do, and that dissidents should be enlightened and standardised for their own good, if necessary by force.

This is "rationalism", and the philosopher who has made the study of it most explicit is Michael Oakeshott. The essence of rationalism consists of seeing society as a tissue of problems and *anomalies calling for the application of reason. Such a task, of course, is beyond the powers of the ordinary people involved, whose access to reason (so the theory goes) is closed-off by their entanglements in local *interest and detail. Rationalism aims to help, confident that there is one way of doing things, and many able people—Rationalists—have dedicated their lives to telling others what that one enlightened way is.[3]

Unfortunately, the desire to put other people right has tended to crowd out *local wisdom and to discourage *creative invention and responsibility, so that the march of "reason" (in this rationalist sense) has caused a lot of misery and error, dismantling *tradition, inherited *skills and local *systems, and going so far as to establish horrific dystopias, accounting in part for our present discontents and the bewilderment as to what to do about them. All this is grounded in the principles of "positivism", which was developed notably by Auguste Comte (1798–1857) whose vision was of society understandable in terms of strict scientific principles, and evolving to a wonderful era when it would be governed by the universally-applicable laws of science.

The properties of rationalism, as described by Oakeshott, are familiar. It comes to questions with a mental clean slate—with no obligations and *loyalties, no point of reference other than reason. It is optimistic about the need for the standardised and correct solutions it is proposing, and it has a mission to promote them. It is not particularly interested in observing the evidence; nor in conserving and repairing what already exists; it insists that we must look beyond such trivialities, to the perfect results that will come when the mission is accomplished—which it surely must be, because reason has to win in the end. It often has to face disappointment, because the application of universal principles and *technical solutions to local *practice brings trouble—and yet the trouble itself is a rich source of opportunities to fix them. The rationalist can therefore expect a job for life.

It is a *distraction, of course. It is about looking away from the question in front of you and applying an

---

THE PEASANT'S DEFIANCE AGAINST THE ADVANCE OF RATIONALISM
David Fleming

Our place was made by long cooperation
With nature, rock, the rain, the ancient dead,
The living, by their day-by-day invention
A local ecosystem slowly bred—
All grievous error to the Enlightened head.
  But we'll outlive the onward march of reason;
  Our science rings true with system, time and season.

The Rationalist comes with plans for demolition;
He has no time for detail and repair,
Of loyalties and doubt he has no notion,
His certainties and sameness everywhere.
No meeting-up in conversation there.
  But we'll outlive the onward march of reason;
  Our science rings true with system, time and season.

To local detail, Gaia's rich endowment
He comes with high IQ and empty mind;
To trust, to inspiration, to enchantment,
He brings reforming regulation—blind
To local insight, life of every kind.
  But we'll outlive the onward march of reason;
  Our science rings true with system, time and season.

R

*ideology that comes from nowhere. It lies at the other extreme from *Lean Logic* and *lean thinking, which bring observation and nous to the local particular.[4]
*Second Nature, Ethics, Reformer Fallacy, Galley Skills, Objectivity, Indignation.

RATIONING (aka Entitlement). A system for ensuring fair shares of essentials such as *food or *energy at a time of scarcity.
*TEQs (Tradable Energy Quotas), Depletion Protocol.

REASONS, THE FALLACY OF. The *fallacy that, because a person can give no reasons, or only apparently poor reasons, her conclusion can be dismissed as wrong. But, on the contrary, it may be right: her thinking may have the distinction of being complex, *intelligent and *systems-literate, but she may not yet have worked out how to make it sufficiently clear and robust to objections to survive in an argument.
*Intuition, Reflection, Different Premises, Devil's Tunes.

RECIPROCAL OBLIGATION. A form of *reciprocity and cooperation, consisting of obligations, duties, *loyalties and the exchange of services not organised around *money.

RECIPROCITY AND COOPERATION. Reciprocity is about the ways in which people act in each other's interests. It may be conscious, or pleasurable, or permanent, or freely entered into, or none of these; it exists between *nations, between equals, between master and slave. In some forms of reciprocity, it can be hard to distinguish between giving and receiving—as in, for instance, the reciprocity between mother and infant: the baby gets what it needs to live, and in return the mother receives the satisfactions of giving, of love, of making a person. So it comes in many forms. But, within that wide range of meaning, there is one salient property: on the *definition of *Lean Logic*, reciprocity is usually *informal—that is, it refers primarily to means of distribution and exchange which work without *money.

Cooperation is about joining together for a shared purpose. No exchange is implied. In exchange, the parties involved are facing each other. In cooperation, they have joined together for a task that needs more than one

person on the case—sometimes many more—and they are facing the same way.

The terms on which reciprocity and cooperation are based depend on, amongst many other things, the size of the group within which they take place. The key group sizes (*small group, *neighbourhood, *parish, *county and *nation) are discussed in separate entries. Each of the five group sizes has its corresponding kind of reciprocity, but there is no general agreement on what to call them. The labels used by *Lean Logic* are, respectively: direct engagement, collaboration, balance, exchange and latency (for a summary table, see *Groups and Group Sizes).

1. *Direct Engagement*

This is the form of reciprocity in *small groups. Within the range of "small", there are two sizes of group which have particular significance and potential. First, there is the *primary group*, consisting of around 5 members, usually family, close friends or work partners. Secondly, there is the group consisting of around 12–15 members: a person's circle of close friends, about whom he or she cares very much—and "very much" means that he or she would be devastated on hearing of their death. This is termed the *sympathy group*. Primary groups consist at least in part of people recruited from, or into, the sympathy group, so a person has one sympathy group, but may belong to several primary groups. This is the scale of that fluid, definition-resistant but central group, the *household.[5]

In small groups, especially in the primary group, reciprocity and cooperation are equally important. Members work together. If one person minds the garden, that does not mean that she is "owed" anything by any other member of the group, it is simply part of her participation and engagement in it. Contributions may be out of balance, with (for instance) a high level of care being provided *for* one or two members (infants, old people, the sick) and/ or *by* one or two members. The level of engagement on this small-group scale may be extreme—members may be willing to devote their lives for the group. That commitment can be made in groups of all sizes, but there is a sense in which, in the case of the small group, it is close to the surface.

The critical significance of the small group lies in its powerful, almost unconditional, *cohesive bonding. There is cooperation, interdependence and affection. This may have something to tell us about why marriages and families in the late *market economy seem to find it harder to stay together. However evident the advantages of packaged convenience in food, heating, cleaning, entertainment and opinion may be, they reduce the need for real reciprocity and mutual dependency in the household. The opportunity and the need for routine, practical, *small-scale cooperation are less: affection has tougher conditions in which to grow, since it dwindles to the status of a voluntary activity, a bonus to be enjoyed while it lasts. It lacks the muscle conferred by interdependence—the unashamed, other-focused self-interest embodied in mutual *cupboard love. With each decline in the practical motivation for reciprocity, there is a little less certainty as to whether friends and family members have a *necessary role in one's life. The loss of material need for others opens up new opportunities for lonely comfort: a single-parent household becomes a more practical option when there are no fireplaces to be raked out every day.[6]

The small group is not free of *conflict, but reciprocity, with its frequent *gift-exchanges, is in itself a conflict-moderator: giving improves the chances of being forgiven. Conflict itself, in moderation, need not be a problem; and spirited disagreement is part of relationship-building. In fact, much of it happens between spouses, but, as Michael Argyle assures us, marriage remains far out in front on measures of the things that matter to us most: practical help, emotional support, shared interests and activities, low levels of stress, good mental and physical health, happiness.[7]

In all these ways, the small group is the locus of privacy. The *private setting allows informality—a friendly insolence—which would be startling if it were tried on anyone other than an intimate friend. One of the reasons experimental communities have such a poor record of success is the lack of privacy: anyone in the community can act as if he or she were your close friend. There is a limit, however, to

how much of this can be endured before you feel the need to get away. The coalition of intimates in small groups draws the line; and that can make the difference between being a member of the community and being taken over by it.

It is the personal warmth and reassurance of the small group that gives its reciprocal relationships their strength. You are not being pushed to love your neighbour. You already do love your circle of intimates; and can then participate in the neighbourhood with the option, but not the obligation, of *emotional engagement—building alliances of collaboration, *caritas and friendship. And, of course, the small group is the hot centre for practical results, in matters such as being born, learning to speak, eating, discovering and practising the emotions, providing, mourning, being loved, being happy. And having that friendly power base from which to participate in the neighbourhood and community.

Edmund Burke summarises:

> To be attached to the subdivision, to love the little platoon we belong to in society, is the first principle (the germ, as it were) of public affections. It is the first link in the series by which we proceed towards a love to our country, and to mankind.[8]

2. *Collaboration*

This is the reciprocity that can develop in a *neighbourhood of up to 150 households. The depth of engagement between neighbours is not as close as it is in the small group, but it is still intense enough for people to do things for each other and with each other, without expecting to be paid or rewarded specifically or by any particular time.

The most frequent form of relationship is likely to be cooperation—working together to achieve a *common purpose, but it is reciprocity that builds the *networks in the first place. The reciprocities are indirect—that is, if you provide a service for another member, she can "repay" that by providing a service for someone else, or for the group as a whole. The sequence of loose ends—services that haven't been directly reciprocated—create a

R

COMMUNAL SPIRIT
and radiant neighbours

There was a good deal of mutual help—a year's credit was usual and acceptable. We were all poor together, hence there was a magnificent communal spirit. When my father was so dreadfully ill in bed upstairs with rheumatic fever, the neighbours came and cheerfully cut a hole through the bedroom floor—larger than the bed, then lowered the bed with father in it to the room below, *y parlwr* where there was a fireplace, a wicker armchair and a bed—the so called guest-bed with a starched valance all around it to hide the chamber-pots. The guest-bed was dismantled, taken upstairs and the joists and boards replaced. It was a great comfort to know that one had such loyal helpful neighbours. We met this feeling again during the last war. . . . The coming of victory and of prosperity has vitiated this spirit—one could almost say "stained the white radiance of eternity".

JAMES WILLIAMS, *Give Me Yesterday*, 1971.

network of obligation which holds a community together. A person might make a particular contribution in growing food, or catching mackerel from his boat and giving them to neighbours; or it may be a collective and cooperative act, such as being part of the team that repairs a sea wall or provides a meal a day for the elderly, or which participates in collective responsibilities (see *Lean entries). These are the services of the *informal economy and are intrinsic to living there; earning and sustaining credit and affection by being part of the community and making it work. And the neighbourhood contributes to the *community in many ways:

First, it has those material tasks: lean production of *food, *energy, *water and *materials. There is no presumption that collective effort is an advantage in its own right; often, the best results come when people can get on with it on their own, but cooperation is often needed, too.

Secondly, the neighbourhood knows its people. It makes a *home for itself. It cares. Communal spirit (see sidebar) has deep roots, and it is real—a matter of what you *want* to do, as distinct from what you think you *ought* to want to do.

Thirdly, the neighbourhood has a *political function. It is the coalition which defends the interests of its people in a wider political world in which neither the individual nor the household, unaided, would have much chance. The neighbourhood is at the heart of politics in the *Lean Economy; it will act in the parish, representing its members' interests. And the need to do so will be intense: given the deep constraints on the supply of such fundamentals as energy, *land, food and social order, membership of a strong neighbourhood will be a life-saver.

The fourth function is social life. It is too small for much courtship, which needs a wider range—at least the range of the *parish—as do most public expressions of culture and *religion. But conviviality and common core values will still be indispensable, and the neighbourhood will be the place where the basic skills of society and culture are learned—the setting for fun, exuberance and rites of passage in which neighbours participate together in wider events, notably in *carnival on the scale of the parish. Neighbourhoods are therefore the base from which to participate in the wider world of the *public sphere, but they are not themselves the public sphere: they are home.

How does the neighbourhood hold together? There are seven principles. Because of their wide application, six of them are described in separate entries: *Boundaries, *Character, *Culture, *Play, *Gifts and *Common Purpose. But those will not always be enough to prevent conflict, so the seventh principle is about coping with it.

Conflict prevention and resolution has a large and deeply researched literature. Some suggestions about where to look are made in the endnotes, and a good place to start thinking about this in the setting of community is Diana Leafe Christian's *Creating a Life Together*. *Lean Logic*'s own take on it emphasises two points. The first is that conflict is a

R

symptom that reveals the strengths or weaknesses of the community—and these in turn are reflections of practically everything it does. So the whole of Lean Logic, from that point of view, is about *conflict resolution, or prevention.⁹

The second point is that, in the neighbourhood, as in the primary group, conflict is by no means always a sign that things are falling apart. When conflict does break out, repairs do not always follow quickly, but they can do so. Anger and indignation against people who try to take a free ride on other people's work has its uses in helping to bind groups together, as can the settlement that follows. The elaborate reconciliation, grooming and bonding that occurs after conflict in primate groups (e.g., baboons) provides the basis for strong alliances; coalitions are probably stronger and have greater *cohesion if their recent history has included some conflict, a reminder of the intense value of the cooperative solutions which the neighbourhood can provide. Indeed, *play itself explores an ambivalent boundary between adversaries, in which it does not always successfully distinguish the make-believe from the real.

There is an echo of this in the account of a retired fish-porter, Mr. Don Ruth, who had spent his working life at the old Billingsgate fish market in London. He spoke of the friendly joke-laden atmosphere that used to exist among porters and, as an illustration, he described the fights that took place—under strict rules, and always in the same place on the first floor, and attended by seconds and others to ensure fair play. Shortly after a fight was over, the contestants could be seen comparing their bruises and congratulating each other on their tactics—which is as close to baboon-like mutual grooming as human males usually get. Afterwards, the two were likely to remain firm friends, bonded by their ordeal and the reconciliation. "Then", said Mr. Ruth, "the fights were stopped, and the whole place became—oh, I don't know—impersonal."¹⁰

3. *Balance*
This is the reciprocity in the context of a wider locality or *parish which has developed its potential as an effective *Lean Economy. It is the scale

for substantial initiatives that take the community forward. *Politics, courtship, *carnival, *religion, *education, *healthcare, most *law and order, some *defence, *local currency and a secure context for *neighbourhoods and *households—all happen at the level of the parish, which is also at the heart of *lean economics. The reciprocity is not the close collaboration and cooperation of the household and neighbourhood—here there must be a balance between what you give and what you take—but transactions are not impersonal. There is an incentive to maintain the flow of services rendered and received, not least because the health of the parish as a whole depends on its own responsibility and *common purpose, and reciprocities are integral to its structure.

There are precedents. The obligations of membership of medieval communities were embedded in personal relationships, kinship and loyalties. Family relationships extended through the locality in a web of interconnectedness. Fraternities committed themselves, beyond the requirements of law, need and kin to "fraternal dilection"—concern, diligence, *charity and cooperation.¹¹ The meaning of "kinship" itself was extended: *compaternitas* was the principle which saw godparents as kin to the child's whole natural family. The community assisted its poor with food, goods, stock (animals) and hospitality.¹² It built and maintained churches and bridges and, within its central ethic of *caritas*, there was day-to-day care, duty, affection and reciprocal service.¹³

All this was celebrated in festival and carnival—in particular, in the celebrations of the church year. One example of this was *Corpus Christi*, the celebration of the body of Christ, a day of feasting and lavish expenditure on banners, garlands and lights hung from the houses—and another day off work, one of many *festa ferianda* in the church's year.¹⁴ It was a time of not only conspicuous consumption but conspicuous giving, substantial and regular enough for it to take the place of tax. As Catherine Pickstock writes, "the liturgical cycle of feasts and festivals freed charitable donation from the anxiety of private choice"; it also helped to sustain the

R

significance of a *gift—with its implication of a personal obligation and bond.[15]

But the strongest incentive of all to collective action is the knowledge—integral to *lean thinking—that if you don't come together to do it, no one else will. That was demonstrated by the famous case of the Orangi district in Karachi—a place characterised by official inertia and paralysis in planning and building regulations. There was a gross failure in the supply of food, water, shelter and sanitation—typhoid, malaria, diarrhoea, dysentery and scabies were endemic—and no systems of social order prevailed other than those imposed by warring local mafias and drug gangs. Then, in the 1990s, the community took action. Led by local people with technical knowledge, they installed latrines, drains and sewers, along with septic tanks between the latrines and the sewers to prevent them being clogged with solid waste; they established maintenance systems organised by local "lanes" (equivalent to neighbourhoods), and set up organised garbage collection. A 70% reduction in infant mortality followed, along with a ninefold increase in the use of family planning, a halving of disease, an 80% reduction in spending on doctors' fees, and higher rates of literacy.[16]

The Orangi example is, justifiably, seen as a model by people who recognise that the authorities cannot cope and that, if they want action, they will have to do it themselves. And now there are *Transition Towns, natural *lean thinkers, recognising that the most *creative initiatives are local. The parish is at the creative *edge between vision and local detail.

4. *Exchange*

Here we are moving from bonding to bridging. The scale on which this reciprocity is most comfortable is that neglected and supposedly obsolete social unit—the *county. On this scale, there is no particular obligation or expectation for *informal reciprocity. Instead, there is "negative reciprocity": the supply of goods and services prompts no reciprocal supply, leaving a gap which has to be filled by money. It is impersonal; both sides simply get what they bargain for.[17]

And yet, there is more to this exchange than calculation. This is the vital but often forgotten level of cooperation *between* communities within easy distance of each other—roughly the scale of the county. There is trade, and a market, with little fudging of the *intention to get a good deal. And yet, there is mutual endorsement and exchange in *education, experience and *skills. There is cooperation in *law and order, *conflict resolution and *lean defence. There is shared participation in the *arts. The county is explicitly in the *public sphere; the antidote to excess immersion in the parish. It is the bridge between the parish and the nation. It is the wider *ecosystem in which the parish is set, the place of unconformity and evolution. At the level of the county there is space for eccentricity and non-belonging. And at its heart is its landscape, which may be as diverse as chalk and cheese, beloved and basic to the county's *identity.

5. *Latency*

Now we reach the scale of the *nation. Here, too, the form of exchange is negative reciprocity but, again, there is more to it than is obvious at first sight. At the level of the nation there may be a shared predisposition—a latent mutual willingness—to cooperate if the occasion should arise. In brief encounters there is a flicker of recognition, in the sense that the *potential* for balanced reciprocities, for collaboration and even small group reciprocities is there. Latency, where it exists, is a shared sense of inhabiting a *place, of *good faith, confirmed by *civility, *humour and acknowledgement of the *common purpose and *culture, even between strangers.

If it is not there, you feel its absence. This is a place of strangers and unconcern, whose people can speak only for themselves, for all are separated by their individual rights, opaque interests and *privacies. This is the lonely, fractured state—and latency fractures easily: it breaks down if pushed too far (the *tradition of free overnight hospitality in the Scottish Highlands ended when it was overwhelmed by numbers), or when there is no sense of common destiny, or shared legitimacy in the claim to be there. When *food is short, it is tested to the limit (*Access).

The possibility of the non-existence of latency gives it meaning. In its absence, what fills the space is discussed by the French political philosopher Alexis de Tocqueville (1805–1859). He calls it "individualism", halfway house to *narcissism. Whereas such egoism (he writes) is an ardent and excessive love of oneself . . .

> . . . individualism is a calm and considered feeling which persuades each citizen to cut himself off from his fellows and to withdraw into the circle of his family and friends in such a way that he thus creates a small group of his own and willingly abandons society at large to its own devices. . . . At first, individualism attacks and dries up only the source of public virtue. In the longer term it attacks and destroys all the others and will finally merge into egoism.[18]

The shared sense of safely inhabiting a *place cannot be made to order. It comes of intense care, sustained over a long time. There is faith in permanence, the point of reference that reminds us who we are.

RECOVERY-ELASTIC RESILIENCE. See Resilience.

REDUCTIO AD ABSURDUM ("Reduction to the absurd"). A form of argument which exaggerates the other side's case to absurdity, and then argues against it. It is effective because, even though it is obviously absurd, it implies that your opponents' *actual* argument is no less absurd, and that she has not thought through the reality. It can very effectively remove any danger of the argument getting somewhere. This is similar to the *Straw Man, except that it takes particular delight in exploring the ludicrous extreme.

However, *reductio ad absurdum* can also be used as a means of constructive simplification to make a point. While many principles in *economics textbooks are grossly oversimplified with children's-storybook examples, it is also true that they can clarify some of the fundamental economic relationships: e.g., stories about Robinson Crusoe and Man Friday, or about a person whose shopping list contains just two items—apples and pears, or cummerbunds and kumquats. The

trouble is, some people who learn their economics in an engaging scale-model landscape find it hard to leave it. The models of great beauty and complexity which emerge can confirm the richly-misleading potential of absurd assumptions (*Economism). Example of a useful *reductio ad absurdum*: the discussion of "2+2=4" in *Distraction.

*Fallacies, Slippery Slope, Hyperbole.

REDUCTIONISM. The practice of considering a problem in isolation, as if it had no implications for the wider system to which it belongs, and as if interventions could be designed without taking account either of their wider consequences or of their effects over the longer term.

Serial reductionism can be understood as the idea that a complex *system can be understood by focusing acutely on parts of it, and then adding them together.[19]

Reductionism in its characteristic and familiar form consists of obvious and easy solutions, whatever the problem. Here are some examples: Too many weeds? → more herbicides. Expected rise in the demand for air travel? → more runways. Teenage pregnancy, drinking, drugs and violence? → more education on *sex, drinking, drugs and violence. Too few people going out to vote? → easy ways of enabling people to vote without having to go out. Youth crime epidemic? → set up a youth club in every neighbourhood. Young people vulnerable to abuse? → establish detailed vetting procedures which will dry up the supply of volunteers to work in youth clubs. Evidence that some herbal medicines may be ineffective? → ban them. To every problem, reductionism supplies a simple and direct solution, often in the form of regulation, prohibition or tax. These one-step responses save the sweat of understanding a system; they can give rise to decisive action; they are easily explained and defended. They do not require a long concentration span. It's sorted in time for lunch.[20]

This is the occupational curse of government and government ministers: they recognise a problem and set out to solve it; consideration of the ways in which their solution will affect other parts of the *system is not in the brief. And the only *time they are aware of is now. It is the nature of our *market-based political economy that it observes problems in terms of separate

R

components—immediately-adjacent causes and imme-diately-relevant action. And yet, as Paul Hawken, Amory Lovins and Hunter Lovins summarise,

> You can actually make a system less efficient while making each of its parts more efficient, simply by not properly linking up those com-ponents. If they're not designed to work with one another, they'll tend to work against one another. . . . *Optimising components in isolation tends to pessimise the whole system.*[21]

The immediate cause of a problem might itself be only one step in a sequence of causes and effects which has not been considered, but there is no space for this possi-bility in crowded minds that are focused and narrowed by the need to appear to be in control of the situation. *Relative intelligence declines. Simple fixes bring death by a thousand good intentions.

"Cathedral Camps" is a *charity which sends young people on week-long camps to help to maintain ancient church buildings while learning *traditional skills in cleaning stained glass windows and restoring ancient monuments. After 25 years without causing injury, it was threatened with closure in 2006 owing to health and safety fears, complex risk assessment regulations and the cost of insurance against potential compen-sation claims. The health and safety hazard that was overlooked was *boredom. It leads to things that, from the reductionist point of view, don't matter, such as depression, resentment, overeating, terminal disease, *violence, vandalism, destroyed relationships, and an indolent acceptance that there is no point in being alive. And thankfully, in this case the wider vision—that helping to keep cathedrals upright might be good for our *health—has so far prevailed.[22]

And yet, reductionism is not always a *fallacy. It can take the form of the replacement of ambitious but partial explanations with those that are more humble and more complete—a patient and necessary focus on detail. Our understanding of why algae produce dimethyl sulphide, for instance, helps us to understand *Gaia. And if there is one well-defined thing wrong with a system, there is nothing wrong with focusing on that. Scientific discovery depends on a reductionist focus as much as on systems-wide comprehension;

René Descartes' insistence that we have to study one thing at a time holds true, up to a point. *Crafts, lan-guage, music and *systems-thinking itself require an exhaustive grasp of the particular.[23]

So it is in its abuse and overstatement that reduction-ism has its malign influence on our lives. Descartes' just-one-thing-at-a-time method misleads because there is no limit to the just-one-things. If you add together all the things you have studied so carefully, you still don't get the whole system: you simply get high on trivia. The sage you took for Descartes turns out to be Mickey Mouse. Reductionists do not recognise the case for placing their work in a wider setting, but if complex questions are considered from just one point of view, then it is not a solution which is reached, but a pathology. Single-issue pressure groups wreak havoc with the complex tissue of forces in tension with each other; when politics addresses one issue at a time, it enters dark territory. Pornography is reductionism for the hell of it.

The philosopher Daniel Dennett writes that the problem lies not with reductionism but with greedy reductionism:

> in their eagerness for a bargain, in their zeal to explain too much too fast, scientists and philos-ophers often underestimate the complexities, trying to skip whole layers or levels of theory in their rush to fasten everything securely to the foundation.[24]

And yet reductionism accounts for one of the most important ideas of all time—natural selection:

> Darwin's dangerous idea is reductionism incarnate.[25]

*Ecology: Farmers and Hunters, Precautionary Princi-ple, Holism, Disingenuousness, *Reductio ad Absurdum.*

REFLECTION. Disengagement, in order to think. It may be brief and urgent: a matter of ducking out of sight for a moment, if there is no other way.

As Richard Chartres reminds us in his reflection on Ash Wednesday, that is what Jesus did, when pressed by an angry crowd—doodling reflectively in the dust before giving us the clincher argument against the *witch-hunt and its variants: "He who is without sin: let him cast the first stone." Chartres summarises: stoop, clarify, connect.[26]

In less crowded circumstances, reflection is thinking time; there is local self-reliance; a *flow of concentration. It is fractured by an oversupply of data that hasn't been looked for and *pulled in. It needs a long attention span: unhurried *conversation, a book, a remembered poem, a sense of being at *home, and sustained *intention. Given time and *practice, as Thomas Traherne discovered, it is conversation with the soul:

> And the soul is a miraculous abyss of
> infinite abysses, an undrainable ocean, an
> unexhausted fountain of endless oceans. . . .
> Infinity we know and feel by our souls: and feel
> it so naturally, as if it were the very essence and
> being of the soul.
>
> *Thomas Traherne, Centuries of Meditations, c.1670.*[27]

*Freedom, Ironic Space, Judgment, Humility, Sleep, Rote, Imagination, Success.

REFORMER FALLACY, THE. The *fallacy that the best reformers are driven by a burning desire to reform.

In fact, the person who sees himself as a fearless reformer is more likely to be driven by a desire to destroy, to simplify, and to ignore the pleas of the people who know the subject and are affected by the changes. The true reformer, in contrast, is a person who starts from a position of detachment and from no particular desire for change; instead, he is alert to the needs of circumstance, and may be able to push reform through with greater insight, precision and energy—and with more support—than he would be able to bring if he came to the task with the baggage of a prior commitment.

The big reformist movements of the modern era have been turned into acts of destruction by the Reformer Fallacy. The successful reforms—for instance, those of the great reforming Archbishops of Canterbury, Theodore of Tarsus (602-690) and Thomas Cranmer

(1489–1556), and of Florence Nightingale (1820–1910)—have started from a period in which the person is far from clear about the way forward, and is alert to fresh thinking about it. Fortunately, they did not have to take part in television debates in advance to set out precisely what they were going to do.

*Pharisee, Ideology, High Ground, Utopia, Reflection, Encounter.

REGION. See Nation ⟩ The Tragedy of the Regions, County.

REGRETTABLE NECESSITIES. Goods and services which are *needed for the subsistence of a large *civic society. The entries on the *Intermediate Economy and the *Intensification Paradox discuss the principles behind this need. Here is an example.

The story starts in seventeenth century Europe, whose growing population had a fuel problem. A lot of energy was needed for domestic heating (this was the "Little Ice Age", as discussed in *Climate Change), for cooking, and for industrial uses: forges, lime-burning, salt-boiling, dyeing, brewing, soap, candles, bricks, gunpowder and the metal industries. Although wood was the obvious fuel, that option was closing, as forests were cut down for firewood, ships and building, and cleared for *agriculture. The only alternative was to elaborate, to *intensify—and the sequence of elaborations that had to take place required a large amount of extra work from labour and land alike:[28]

Stage 1. Firewood—the starting point—has decisive advantages. It is widely distributed, easy to obtain by gathering or felling, easy to transport and clean; it has tolerable fumes and it is renewable. It is also easy to use in industrial processes such as smelting and soap-making.

Stage 2. Failing the ideal option of wood, the next best *choice is *coal from shallow mines.* This is accessible, and it had been in use for many centuries, but coal's disadvantages are severe. It lies in concentrated deposits, usually far from where it is needed; it has to be formally bought, rather than *informally gathered; it is heavy, and transport over roads in eighteenth century conditions was a nightmare of mud and ruts deep enough to drown in; its fumes are toxic and dirty; and its use for purposes such as smelting presents technical problems which were not to be solved for many years.

Stage 3. An even less attractive option, but—in due course—an unavoidable one, is *coal from deep mines*. Now the problems really start. Coal mines flood unless they are continually pumped, and this was for practical purposes impossible with the technology of the day: horse-whims (windlasses) could barely lift the long chains of buckets when they were full of water. The pressure to find a solution led on to the invention of steam power—which in turn required the invention of ways of making parts with an accuracy, durability and *complexity that had never been imagined—and then onwards through a sequence of trial and (spectacular) error to metal-bashing, new processes, industrial chemistry, the shock of very-large-scale engineering, and rapidly-growing industrial *populations (*Energy Prospects ❯ Coal).

Stage 4. Once deep mines became viable, it was necessary to establish a comprehensive system of *transport*. With a relentless step-by-step logic, the early Industrial Revolution, which had a non-negotiable need for coal, was drawn into building an immensely elaborate *transport structure—twice over, with the canals promptly being made obsolete by the even more ambitious network of railways.[29]

And the result of all this was an extraordinary increase in the average person's workload: so many *intermediate tasks (regrettable necessities) had to be accomplished that many of the final goods and services that were desperately wanted by so many people were never produced at all. Certainly, there was economic and social inequality, too, but the more fundamental problem was that of how to achieve an adequate supply of final goods on any terms. This was a society with its back to the wall; a *large and *complicated productive system had to be invented, built and run in order to produce the massive quantities of intermediate goods

and processes needed for the fuel, food, shelter and clothing that people actually wanted.

Far from being a matter of choice, all this was foisted onto society as a consequence of exhausting its preferred choice of energy. But there is a limit to an economy's ability to do more and more work simply in order to fulfil its needs—that is, to keep going, to carry out the increasing workload required just to provide for its own subsistence. During the English Industrial Revolution that limit was tested: for many people, it was overstepped—as Richard Wilkinson explains,

> The amount of work necessary to gain subsistence can—if all else fails—be allowed to increase until it begins to approach the maximum people are capable of doing. Beyond this the system is no longer viable. Undoubtedly this point was reached for a significant proportion of the English population during the Industrial Revolution: the workload rose to the limits of human endurance.[30]

From the standpoint of the people at the start of the process, this astonishing elaboration and total transformation of society in response to a simple shortage of firewood would have been unimaginable. But the logic led on relentlessly to. . .

. . . *Stage 5.* Even larger urban workforces, the break-up of small communities and face-to-face societies, the *capture and concentration of *populations and of specialist industries in particular places—and onwards to the mature transport-dependent *market economy, whose *energy problem has reached a climax which will turn out to be much more intense and dangerous than the firewood shortage which started the whole thing off in the first place.[31]

———

This story highlights the paradox at the heart of development—the *Intensification Paradox. Advancing technology and the specialisation of labour makes each worker more *productive: he can produce more nails per hour of work. But when that increased productivity is channelled into developing (intensifying) the economy, the *intermediate economy grows—there is a massive increase in the quantity of goods and services the economy needs in order to survive—and that requires a whole lot more nails. In that sense, development makes the economy *less* efficient—dramatically so—and its demand for energy and materials, for *capital and labour, rises accordingly.

Now, all of these problems inherent in large-scale development are not what we might expect, given that the principle of "economies of scale" has extended well beyond being a key presumption in *economics, and has become a household phrase. There is nothing wrong with economies of scale, of course: up to a point, they are completely obvious—this is the reason why we use shopping bags rather than carrying our apples back from the shop one-by-one. But it is equally well-recognised that those economies of scale become negative—becoming diseconomies, or inefficiencies—beyond a certain turning point: if you bought the whole crate of apples, you would have to get a taxi home, and install a chiller, or they would go off before you had time to eat them. Beyond that point, the needed infrastructures grow faster than the system they are there to support.[32] The principles that govern this are explained in *Scale.

In microeconomics, all that is fine: if the amount of stuff a factory is expected to produce increases beyond the turning point, then the obvious thing to do is to build another factory somewhere else, or to shift the turning point upwards by expanding the factory. But in the case of our industrial civilisation, we can't do that. It has to carry on even though the turning point into inefficiency and grossly inflated infrastructures has been left far behind. Further *growth increases those diseconomies yet further.

Yet the converse is also true, and that is the good news: if the size of the system should fall, those diseconomies can of course be expected to decline, producing an efficiency-dividend. This is the key to the feasibility of the *Lean Economy, which has the vital property of *elegance: it learns, *by scale-management*, to minimise the intermediate economy—the regrettable necessities.

This is a solution, but it is also a problem, for success in achieving the elegance required after the downsizing will mean a fall in the demand for labour. There is undoubted mid-term job-creating potential in the switch to a renewables-based economy, but the deep

*paradigm shift in prospect is towards the *slack, output-poor, Lean Economy. Here spare labour (aka spare time) is not a "problem of unemployment", but a property intrinsic to the life, *culture and *social capital of the *place. And *that* is both good news and bad news, because it is hard—when the *market economy is no longer functioning—to prevent no-job leading on to no-income and no-food. It can be done, but not by using only the instruments visible to *economics.[33]

*Culture, Leisure, Lean Economics, Hyperunemployment, Intentional Waste, Sorting, Unlean.

RELATIVE INTELLIGENCE. The match between mental capacity and the problems that have to be solved.

As society becomes more *complex, the relative intelligence of *Homo sapiens* declines, leaving us on a lower Relative Intelligence Quotient (RIQ) than a swan, or a beetle.

*Ingenuity Gap.

RELEVANCE, THE FALLACY OF. The *fallacy that the efficiency of a complex system can be sustained by purging the irrelevant.

Living systems, given a chance, are exuberant. The *excess* produced by a *natural system—the supply of seed and larvae, the material abundance—would threaten to choke it if it were not for the predators which prune it and control the surplus, stimulating an even greater variety. There is a wildness here, a sense of inexhaustible invention, of not knowing when to stop.

As the naturalist Gilbert White wrote to his friend Thomas Pennant in 1768,

> All nature is so full that that district has the greatest variety which is the most examined.[34]

If such a system is tamed and brought to order, the outcomes can be perverse. And this is certain to happen when the mistake is made of acting on an *abstract, *reductionist methodology, which listens to only one strictly delimited kind of *feedback. For a short period, there may be windfall results (on the *defined terms), but the loss of *complexity and *diversity will bring trouble, for characteristics which at first were taken to be irrelevant tend to turn out, after all, to have a purpose, or at least a value. For instance, the weeds and

R

wildness surviving in a cultivated landscape are more useful than they may seem to be: nettles are habitat for the species on which young ladybirds build up their strength before eating the aphids that attack crops; damp pond margins are habitat for the larvae of the gall midge that also feeds on the aphids; wildflowers feed the hoverfly that produce larvae—and they, too, do their bit in the control of aphids. Long grass is winter quarters for pest-eating beetles; insect-eating birds prosper in hedges; bats and chickens protect apple crops from coddling moths . . .[35]

An example of the Fallacy of Relevance—purging the irrelevant—in pursuit of efficiency is the closing down of traditional farming in Bali in the late 1960s and early 1970s. A *vernacular system had evolved over many centuries for managing *water, along with varieties of rice adapted to the local soil and *climate. This system was integrated into the culture and *religion of the society, and regulated by the priests, whose water temples were beautiful and prominent features of the landscape. When the national government of Indonesia decided that all this should end, that new hybrid strains of rice should be adopted, and that the water temples were irrelevant, the consequences followed a familiar pattern. After two or three years of blossoming yields, the pests and fungi came, the crops failed, and the Balinese religious institutions quickly became meaningless as they lost their relevance to the people's economy and daily lives. The exuberant beauty of Balinese *culture, dismissed as irrelevant, turned out in retrospect to have been indispensable.[36]

Seeming irrelevance gives texture, touch and warmth to life. Without it, our encounters with people are bleakly functional. They do the job—sell you the ticket, extract your kidney stone—as a functional, *instrumental service, thin and impersonal. The post-war liberal *market economy specialises in this hollow efficiency, taking it to be a borderline immoral act to recognise a service provider as a person: to be attribute-blind, person-blind, is now thought as much a virtue as observant, *humorous, warm *encounter once was. "There's a divinity that shapes our ends, rough-hew them how we will," said the surgeon as he was about to circumcise the infant author of Lean Logic on the kitchen table one stormy night some time ago. It was not irrelevant: you have to love that doctor.[37]

And yet, "lean means"—purging the irrelevant—is one of the five defining principles of *lean thinking. So what gives the relevant/irrelevant distinction its meaning? *Intention. A system designed to achieve a well-judged intention—e.g., *TEQs (Tradable Energy Quotas), designed to stimulate solutions for reducing fossil fuel dependency—would look very different if designed for a reductionist aim—e.g., to make *money for those involved. Equally, the *elegance of the system can be destroyed if a set of additional objectives is attached. Many ways of improving the TEQs model have been suggested: it could be focused on redistributing wealth, especially from the commercial sector to individuals, or it could work as an alternative *currency, or be applied as the basis for world government. This "Why doesn't it walk the dog?" fallacy turns up everywhere—e.g., tacking social engineering onto the core objective of *education—heaping up the camel with back-breaking baggage in the interests of *compassion.

The divide between the relevant and the irrelevant is not always obvious, but it is critical. It can, given thought, be identified. That is what thinking is for.
*Lean Thinking ❭ Feedback, Irrelevance, Rationalism, Harmless Lunatic, Reflection, Spirit.

RELIGION. Religions are *narrative truths affirmed by *ritual; they variously assert the existence of many gods, one God, a mystical union of three gods in one, or their *myth does not have a concept of God at all. The narrative truth and the ritual in which it is affirmed have essential functions for a *community, for the individuals within it, and for its *social capital. They embrace its *culture, giving it *identity and meaning.

Although narrative truth is central to it, religion also inhabits all five forms of truth:

- There is *material truth* in the historical account, and in at least some of religion's practical and ethical teaching.
- The *narrative truth* of religion is the allegory, the parable and myth which provide insights and deep sources for reflection.
- Religion's *implicit truth* is the insight derived from deliberation; it is the guidance, comfort, inspiration and prudence derived by a person's own participation in his or her religion.
- The *performative truth* of religion lies in its ritual, as in the performance of the Christian Eucharist and other practices of religion which affirm and bring into existence a reality, similar in kind to the reality brought into existence by a *contract.
- Religion also involves a *self-denying truth*, in that the commanding authority of a myth is impaired, or even destroyed, when it is described as a myth. The compiler of this Dictionary, as a critic, affirms

the truth of this description of religion—but, as an observant, he denies it and, instead, enters into the performative truth which gives religion real presence.

There are *paradoxes and shadow-meanings in all of these, especially in narrative truth and self-denying truth. Alfred North Whitehead, with the sureness of touch of a philosopher of science, captures it:

Religion is the vision of something which stands beyond, behind and within the passing flux of immediate things; something which is real, and yet waiting to be realised; something which is a remote possibility, and yet the greatest of present facts; something that gives meaning to all that passes, and yet eludes apprehension; something whose possession is the final good, and yet is beyond all reach; something which is the ultimate ideal, and the hopeless quest.[38]

Religion, like all other living things, dies if dissected; the dissector kills what he seeks to understand. It exists because it is performed, affirmed and loved. The view that dismisses religion on the grounds that it contains untrue statements is a solecism; a naïve failure to understand the significance of religion, the culture which it expresses, and the many natures of *truth. If a common practice celebrates the identifying narrative or *myth of the community, if it is expressed in one or more of the arts, especially music, if there is at least a degree of repetition and constancy in that expression, and if it requires some, or many, members of the community to participate, it is, for *Lean Logic*, an expression of religion.

In the process, religion provides meeting places in which people can come together, building and sustaining the friendships of social capital; it is the hub through which *needs are signalled and answered. That can be done in other ways, too, of course: by playing cards, or being a regular at the pub, or being on a committee. But religion can do it in ways which those other meeting places cannot. It enables a lot of people to participate in a collective activity, doing the same thing at the same time, to the same music. Its ritual is, in itself, of no direct practical value, and this makes it especially potent and effective as a statement by participants that they are

R

there as members of the community. In religious observance, friends, neighbours, beloveds and families face the same way; there is shared *presence.

Religion delivers *tradition to us, a present from the past. It brings core values represented in terms of exceptional beauty. The idea that every community, every village, no matter how small, should have, in the middle of it, a building of the greatest beauty they can manage, reaching up into the sky, a place of wonder and reflection, a seedbed of common purpose, made from *gifts of money and labour, coming to terms with the riddles of life and *death, and bringing *private lives and the setting up of *families into the embrace of the community—well, you might think it a ridiculous *utopia if it had not happened.

The critic will reach for the *Contrarian Fallacy, pointing out that religion can bring strife as well as concord; that there have been many abuses of power; that some expressions of religion misapprehend their own myths—by, for instance, naïvely supposing the Creation Story to be fact. Religion, like every other human enterprise, comes with no guarantee of being done well. It can be more drawn to guilt than to joy, to the personal than the collective, to righteous *narcissism than to *caritas. Religion can be intolerant, sanctimonious and cruel. But it is hard to think of any political or social order to which those regrettable properties do not

apply from time to time. The secular world, too, with chilling good intentions, and at whatever cost in lives and *capital in all its forms, sometimes tries to build a new and secular Jerusalem.

But look again at what religion *can* do. Religion is the community speaking. It is culture in the service of the community. It is a framework for integrating *caritas* into the community's life and culture; it takes charitable giving beyond the level of personal conscience and integrates it into the way the community sees itself and expresses itself.[39]

Religion uses allegory, opening up the *ironic space of questions unsettled, paradoxes unresolved, beauty undescribed. It occupies, with benign myth, the space in the mind which, if vacated, is wide open to takeover by *ideology. Akin to *carnival, it provides powerfully *cohesive rituals that give reality to membership of the community; that invite *emotional daring; and that alert the community to *time—to the natural cycles of day and season, as well as to its existence as inheritor from previous generations and benefactor of future generations. The ritual itself is a skilled *practice built on justice, truthfulness and *courage which affirms the identity of the community and builds social capital—it invites *reflection, recruiting the deep intellectual power which is available only to the subconscious mind, and locates the community as particular to—and steward of—the *place. It bears the gift of *encounter. In all these ways, religion underpins the *trust and permanence which make it possible to sustain *reciprocity—the network of interconnected talent and service which makes the local economy real.

Unfortunately, the religions of the world will not, in general, be in good shape for these creative responsibilities. There are four reasons for this:

The first is that religions have been shattered and depleted by the disintegration of social structure and the loss of social capital which have followed the advance of the *market economy. At the same time, the advance of science and the literal-minded, disenchanted thinking that is widely taken to be the only sort of thinking there is has made it harder to recognise and accept the poetic discourse of religion. Challenged by science, its leaders and ministers quickly surrendered to the idea that scientific, material truth is the only kind of truth there is. Argued on science's own terms, the religions that have been exposed to the debate in any serious way have been routed.

Secondly, and for similar reasons, a large part of (at least) the divided and confused Western Christian church, as it developed in the late twentieth century, has gone to great lengths to present the most plain-speaking of interpretations, abandoning the unchanging text needed if people are to have any chance of holding it in the memory. It has scrapped its *liturgies and strained, instead, at spontaneity, and at presenting the simple message of personal salvation in literal terms to be accepted as material truth or rejected as false. When it is presented in those terms, many reasonable people have no choice but to refuse to accept a proposition which they reject as simply nonsense. In this way, the church has thrown out the whole set of *implicit functions, narrative and allegorical truths which are integral to the *artistic and cultural meaning of the community, and which are the essence of religion. Christian religion in the market economy has found itself drawn into the idolatry of reducing complex meaning and the reflective Imitation of Christ to an *iconic Imitation of Marketing, falling for a technique which it can only do with breathless and piteous amateurism, in place of what it used to do with assured and numinous skill.

Thirdly, although at present there is a yearning for an expression of other, non-materialistic, non-scientific, *spiritual values, the established churches almost completely fail to benefit from this. They are not on that wavelength and, for much of the spiritual movement in the world of strongly-developed *green awareness, the affirmation of a Christian faith stands at the opposite extreme from what they need. It seems cold and absurd, full of confident reassurance about an afterlife which is not only grossly incredible but an offence to people whose concern is focused on how much longer there is going to be a planet for this life. Established religion, especially the Christian church, seems to be the embodiment of urban, and human-centred, alienation from nature, while green values look for ways to establish some real contact with—and come to the defence of—the rural. The childishness of happy-camper services is disempowering; in contrast, the green movement's central purpose

is *empowerment—to develop its *intelligence and resources, to empower its members to act, having observed for themselves the extent of the ecological *betrayal that has taken place at the command of centralised urban civilisation and its centralised religion since the invention of the plough.

It is not impossible that the Christian church, after the shock of realising that it is being sidelined in the biggest spiritual renaissance for centuries, could recover its intelligence and a sureness of emotional touch. In fact, many churches are contributing all they can to the greening of faith; for them, environmental awareness is a central *ethic. But turning the churches green is different from getting the Greens to see anything green about them at all, and a benign convergence of the two principles is some distance away. Lean religion, if it happens, will, like lean everything-else, start with the shock of *kaikaku. Maybe that shock, from the church's point of view, is happening now.[40]

The fourth handicap which religions have to bear—as they find themselves with their new society-building and life-saving responsibilities—is the mixing up of religions which has taken place over the same period. There is no doubt that they have something to learn from each other, gaining insights through their faiths which may not be accessible in any other way—the focus on the family, for instance, and the idea of God as a huge, complex, often difficult personality, are among the ideas which have been developed a long way by Judaism, and Christianity has inherited Judaism's gift for recruiting emotions into the whole of its religious expression. Islam has a text of rock solid beauty and, in Sufism, a philosophy of love. Confucianism's strength lies in the interweaving values of *Tao. Every religion has something to teach; they are each best in some way: the *Lean Economy, which will inherit pluralism, will have to derive advantages from them.

Nonetheless, pluralism is a *self-denying truth. It contradicts itself with multiple claims to *authority. If it is spoken too loud, the contradiction is fatal. It has introduced a sense of branding into the matter which, in itself, trivialises religious encounter: it effectively forces people to make an *instrumental choice with the conscious mind, rather than a bit-by-bit discovery of meaning and affection at the level of the subconscious,

R

CREATIVE BREAKAGE
and its benefits

"To break" is one of the curious words whose meaning, while clear enough, has a shadow which implies its opposite: the shadow-meaning of "to break" is "to make": the light breaks; to break-in a horse, to break a fast, to have a break, to give me a break, to break through, to break the ice, to break a glass as a symbol of marriage, to break bread: the latter is the symbol both of the Christian idea of *sacrifice as the condition for the sublime, and of domestic good *humour and hospitality, the making and sustaining of friendship.

In a constructive sense, there is a breaking of the will here, a *deference to more powerful circumstance as the starting point for making fresh sense of things. It is often the case that a word or an idea means its opposite, as if deep meaning were not a matter of cracking enough problems but cracking enough jokes. The joker who dreamed up Psalm 84, for example, hinted at a refreshing, thirst-quenching potential in tears—and his metaphor was real enough to drink:

Who going through the vale of misery use it for a well; and the pools are filled with water.[41]

It is with a related sense of double meaning—of successfully making a virtue out of vice—that breakage merges also with giving. In the Judaic *story, "a broken heart" is the ultimate gift: "Since thou delightest not in burnt offerings", dreams Psalm 51, I shall have to take the extreme step: "A broken and contrite heart O God shalt thou not despise."

It is John Donne that says it most directly and intensely:[42]

Batter my heart, three-person'd God, for you
As yet but knock, breathe, shine, and seek to mend;
That I may rise and stand, o'erthrow me and bend
Your force to break, blow, burn, and make me new.

Our *political economy will be broken. It may yet, on that account, rise and stand, but that depends on its *resilience.

R

starting in childhood when the foundations for this facility are laid. As Edmund Burke recognised (though writing in a different—political—context), the commitments *in which one finds* oneself have an ability to endure, and a sense of inevitability, which is not necessarily shared by commitments which are *chosen*:

Men without their choice derive benefits from that association [with the society in which they find themselves]; without their choice they are subjected to duties in consequence of these benefits; and without their choice they enter into a virtual obligation as binding as any that is actual. Much the strongest moral obligations are such as were never the results of our option.[43]

There can be no submission or creative breakage (see sidebar) in the context of a conscious *choice between the seductive appeals of competing retailers in the salvation market. Pluralism also means that society itself—and its institutions, such as schools—dare not favour one story over another, so collective expression of any one religion becomes an offence to the rest: many turns into none.

Maybe that leaves the option of inventing its own— the *common purpose expressed in the example of the Bromley by Bow Centre (*Presence) suggests the possibility of surmounting cultural difference—but any invented hybrid is likely to be raw and literal, lacking the settled subtleties and beauties of religion. Society is thus largely excluded from the benign shared vocabulary of *ceremony, celebration, solidarity, spirit and belief provided by religion; the *political economy, scrubbed clean of allegory, is filled with secular kitsch.

Of course, it is possible for *diverse religions to transcend this pluralism in shared recognition of each other's faith—"the dignity of difference", as Dr. Jonathan Sacks terms it—and this is something in which *art is particularly skilled. Such connection only works if the starting point is a robust loyalty to one's own *tradition—without that, there is nothing to connect—but when different traditions do develop their artistic differences to the fullest extent, they may derive an *intuitive sympathy and respect for each other from the experience of their own faith, and find common ground on which they can meet. In such circumstances, secularism—confronting religion—has nothing to say. You cannot argue with a song.[44]

But there are limits to how much of the dignity of difference can be borne. Local *identity depends on its culture: a divided culture makes a united community harder to achieve, and at a time of stress it may be impossible. Existing religious *loyalties are intense, and this can be expected to fracture some local *communities, with others defining their internal *cohesion in terms of opposition to the rest. Secular attempts to shift these loyalties tend to be savage, and new *ethics which fill the vacuum left by religion are often dangerous. Appropriate responses are discussed in *Multiculturalism, but this is the explosive mixture which many *nations have been diligently building since the mid twentieth century.

———————

None of this is rational from the point of view of the *market economy, whose instinct for worship is directed to its technology, but the idea that a society can be held together without *either* an *energy-rich market *or* a *culture-rich religion—that is seriously irrational. A coherent social order in the future will need a religion; a religion will need a rich cultural inheritance: it will give culture a real job to do, something to participate in, and not simply to be watched: something to give your heart to, to give you the moral strength you need to keep going because there is no big Something in the sky who is going to do it for you.

RESILIENCE. The ability of a *system to cope with shock.

That will do, perhaps, as a short definition. But this is a case where we need to know more, so here is a more considered way of looking at it. Resilience is . . .

> The capacity of a system to absorb disturbance and reorganise while undergoing change so as to still retain essentially the same function, structure, identity and feedbacks.[45]

There is nothing wrong with that except that it can still leave you wondering what resilience is really about, so here is another way of coming at it. Think of a shallow lake whose water is kept clear by the vegetation growing in it, which releases oxygen and maintains a healthy population of small water bugs which feed on nutrients in the water. Perhaps there are also some fish which feed on the bugs. This, we may assume, is a stable condition; sunlight gets into the water for the plants, and even though there are times when it gets an excess supply of nutrients from, say, falling leaves in the autumn, or from a local farm, it is able to cope with this by cleaning up the nutrients, and it remains clear.[46]

However, one day, it receives so many nutrients from various sources that it reaches a 'tipping point' at which, quite suddenly, it flips into a new state: turbid water, rich with algae which block out the light, killing the plants, and so reducing the oxygen level to the point at which much of the other aquatic life dies. Now it will remain in this new stable condition. Indeed, it will hold onto this condition even if the extra supply of nutrients then declines to a level which would have presented no problem for the pond in its former condition of plants and clear water. That is to say, there is a wide band of intermediate levels of nutrients at which the lake

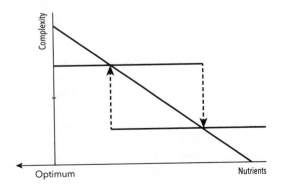

397

will remain turbid if it is already turbid, or clear, if is already clear.

So, what we have here is two states of resilience, both of which hang on to their current state with tenacity until they can do so no longer. But when the level of nutrients strays towards extremes, the whole pond ecology suddenly flips into a new state. The image often used to illustrate this consists of two adjacent basins, known as "valleys", or "basins of attraction". The system (like a ball kept in the basin by its high sides) is either in one condition or in the other, and "resilience" means that it tends to stay in the one that it is already in, unless an *exceptional disturbance comes along which jolts it into the adjacent one.[47]

C.S. Holling is the ecologist whose work on resilience in this sense is most widely recognised, and he defines resilience in this context as . . .

> . . . the size of the valley or basin of attraction around a state that corresponds to the maximum perturbation that can be taken without causing a shift to an alternative stable state.[48]

Lean Logic's definition is this:

> Resilience is a system's tendency to stay in the condition it is already in, despite shocks.

In fact, we could cautiously modify this by changing just one word: "Resilience is a system's *ability* to stay in the condition it is already in, despite shocks." That revision suggest that the system takes active steps to stay in the condition it is already in: it specifically compensates for, corrects and cures shocks, just as the white blood corpuscles in our bodies attack and destroy infections. The only problem with that one-word revision is that it suggests that nature is purposive—and the purposive, or teleological, view of nature implies the existence of a mind and of *intention which we cannot really claim in the case of a pond, or an *ecology, or a planet. This is the idea that has brought so much trouble to James Lovelock in his theory of *Gaia. So let us stay out of trouble and settle for "tendency" for now.

We can think of our definition as the Resilience Rule. *Ecological systems do not always succeed in staying in the condition they are already in: large events may overwhelm them, or small events (the *butterfly effect)

can start a sequence of events that overwhelms them. But the forces of continuity and stability (*homeostasis) are powerful—as demonstrated by the stable temperature and metabolism of our bodies. This holds true on scales ranging from small—e.g., a shallow lake—to large—e.g., Gaia—though it does not change the fact that ecologies' maintenance of conditions which favour their own continuation tend, ultimately, to fail (although . . . see *Wheel of Life).

That is resilience from the ecologist's point of view, but *Lean Logic*'s interpretation extends to *community. In the future, people may want to make conscious decisions about how to cope with disturbance. And unlike a shallow lake, they may give some thought to the matter. For instance, they may wonder whether there could be more than one kind of resilience, and whether there may be a *choice between them—and conscious strategies for getting to the preferred kind.

In order to think about this, a good place to start is with those basins, which are redrawn here. Let us suppose that the left-hand basin is the preferred state (an orderly, life-supporting community). The right-hand basin is undesired—some combination of chaos, crisis and failure which the community wants to avoid. Fortunately, there is a barrier between the two basins, so that the community can say that it is resilient in the sense of being reasonably confident of remaining in the left-hand basin, unless a shock comes along which is exceptional. On the other hand, that high barrier could turn out to be a problem because, if a shock does take you over the barrier into the right-hand basin, it could be hard to get out (like the turbid lake which remains turbid, even though conditions have improved). The new state will have a resilience of its own: undesired states can be resilient, too. You will be stuck in a place you don't want to be in. It might not be a place which can support the life of the community.[49]

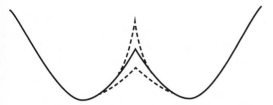

However, the community is also aware that exceptional shocks do happen. Quite often, in fact. So it decides to think about a strategy. The image of the basins suggests that there are two possible strategies. One is to raise the height of the barrier between them. This will reduce the probability that, when the shock comes, they will tip over into the right hand basin. The other strategy is to lower the height of the barrier between them. This will increase the probability that a shock might tip them over into the right hand basin, but it will mean that—if/when that happens—there is a much better chance of being able to get back. This suggests that there is a case for exploring two kinds of resilience:

1. preventive resilience; and
2. recovery-elastic resilience.

A visit to Tuscany

Think of two populations, each based in eight villages, living in practically identical locations, long ago—each in fertile Tuscan valleys beside small rivers.

Now imagine that, 200 years ago, their previously-similar histories diverged. One of them (call it L'Aquila) decided to join together as a town, surrounded by its fields. They argued that if they joined together, they could achieve things which were not practical as separate small villages. This *intensification would enable them to build larger buildings, including a larger church, maintain a library, attract visiting scholars, defend themselves better against troublesome neighbours, and even cause a spot of trouble themselves if they felt like it. The other population (call them the Passero villages) just carried on as they were, in loose contact with each other, falling out sometimes, but mostly getting along and learning from each other.

Then there are two disastrous events.

First a flood. One day, there is a massive rainstorm. The rivers rise rapidly. The valleys reveal their true nature as floodplains. The consequences for L'Aquila and the Passero villages are very different. Both L'Aquila and the villages had been aware of the danger of flooding and had followed the policy of enlightened inaction needed to keep it to a minimum. They had conserved the watershed, especially the forests that covered it. They left untouched the marshland that flourished in the higher reaches of the river, along with the meanderings that lengthened it and evened out the flow, enabling it to hold more water than it could have held if it had been straightened.

But then L'Aquila went further than that. They wanted water to irrigate their crops during dry summers, as well as reducing to the minimum the risk of flooding in the winter. To that end, they built a series of sacrificial lakes along the course of the river towards the valley. They allowed the lakes to fill up in the spring, and gradually emptied them (hence "sacrificial") in the summer, letting their water flow into the river for irrigation. They were then kept empty through the winter, except when a flood threatened, when they were allowed to fill up, holding back some of the excess water from the river, and preventing floods. During the summer, the flow of water from the lakes was used to provide power for a watermill, which ground all the flour needed by the town. Building the dams, the sluices, the canals and the mill for all this required a lot of labour. In fact, it required a whole class of manual workers, working intensely during the winter when there was less *agricultural work to do. It required a rather authoritarian profession of overseers and planners, and it needed to be managed by a class of priests, who lived in water temples and (since their role placed them in a strong position) demanded tribute and exercised power over everyone living downstream. But the arrangement made L'Aquila rich, and it was able to build fine roads for the transport of food to its growing population.

Now comes the rain. It is awesome, and yet a devastating flood is prevented. At the same time, L'Aquila has a reliable flour mill and in the summer it is protected from drought.

For the Passeri, such lakes were beyond their capability. The villages were well able to get together to deal with immediate problems, but they could not contemplate a large, long-term programme like that. Their *peasant

R

farmers would not agree to leave home for weeks on end in the winter to build dams and dig canals. They did not have the central organisation, nor the money to maintain a class of priests living in water temples. Instead, they adapted their farming to droughts, and made do with intermittent and rather inefficient water-mills which only worked in the winter (the one village on higher ground had an inefficient windmill). This was a largely egalitarian society, not without its *leaders and teachers, but seeing itself as a community of individuals rather than as hired or coerced labour. In any case, the villages did not always get on very well. One of them, in particular, was a troublemaker, and was suspected of a little bit of sheep-stealing (for immediate consumption) from its neighbours. It had not reached the level of a feud—priests from the other villages would go and tell them off, and there was intermarriage between all the villages—but they did not do large-scale cooperation. And another of the villages was quite beyond the pale, as we shall see. So serious coordinated action between all eight was out of the question.[50]

As such, when the rain comes to Passero, the valley is flooded, and the eight villages all respond in different ways. Here is what happens to them:

1. One of them loses almost half its livestock and some of its members; most of its stores of grain in the barns are swept away before the survivors manage to reach higher ground. And yet, they are philo-sophical about it. Some of the young leave home, but some come back with wives and husbands. Neighbours help them out with grain and livestock. Five years later, their barns are repaired, and they have as many people and livestock as before.

2. The second village also loses many sheep and some of its people, and their homes are wrecked. They are so devastated and *demoralised by these losses that they lose confidence in their *skill as farmers. They hold a council and decide to go into business making boats. They have learned the craft to some extent, building a few rudimentary fishing boats for their neighbours, but the flood has concentrated their minds. Some may go back to farming in the valley one day if the family expands, but for now they go into a new phase in the boat-building business.

3. The third village has a much more flexible response to the flood. They do not keep any livestock, so they have none to lose, and nobody has to risk their lives trying to rescue them. They have gardens, but they get their protein—and earn a living—from fishing. They lose most of their goods, and their houses are largely destroyed, leaving just the timber frames intact, but their fishing boats survive, tied securely to trees. The flood is flowing too fast to allow them to do anything with them, so they sit tight until the flood subsides. Then they begin the task of repairing the damage.

4. The fourth village is known locally for being the tough guys of the valley. They are wrestling cham-pions of their *region. No one for miles around would dare to steal any of their sheep, or try anything on with any of their women. They work on the principle of being prepared for anything: they do daily workouts and archery practice; their houses and their barns are built for endurance, on two floors. They have no use for carpets or soft furnishings. Even their sheepdogs are tough, trained to round up their flock in a moment and to drive them up into the barns. The flood when it hits them is just as deep as elsewhere, but they are not much affected by it. The flock is taken to safety in a well-rehearsed routine. Like the giant stones with which they built the foundations of their houses, and the solid wood frames which they placed on top of them, they are essentially undamaged and need time only to dry off. Repairs go ahead at speed and without complaint. No tears are shed. They have *Widerstandsfähigkeit*, resistance-capability.

5. The fifth village is the one with the bad reputation for causing trouble by stealing sheep. They are also caught by the flood, but they do not have far to go to reach higher ground. In fact, they get out so fast that they have time, before the worst of the flood, to go back with their horses to rescue as many of their neighbours in the second village as they can. And they make it clear that they expect to get some *land from them as a thank you when the second village announces that it is going into the boat-building business. After the flood they are rather better off than they were before it.

6. For the sixth village, the experience is quite different. In fact, it cannot really be called a village at all, for this group has still not moved on from its preference for the life of the hunter-gatherer. They have no livestock, gardens or settled territory. This offends the sensibilities of the agriculturalist villages, who often feel they ought to be exterminated, but they are related by marriage, and they sometimes do the villages a favour by culling the wolves that dine off their sheep. This *traditional society has the advantage of simplicity, or *elegance, in the language of *Lean Logic*. They live in tents made from skins. They have no infrastructures—no sheep, no houses, no gardens, no fishing boats. All their *needs are wants.

When the flood comes, they do not even need to saddle their horses—they ride bareback, and with the first sign of danger they pack up and vanish. A couple of hours later they are on one of their favourite upland camping grounds ten miles away, with the horses grazing as if nothing had happened.

7. The seventh village is completely swept away.
8. The eighth village is lucky. It lives a little bit up the hillside, where the land is less good, and is hard to cultivate because of the slope, but it keeps them out of danger when the water rises. They watch in horror as the other villages try, with mixed success, to save themselves. But it is a good thing that they survived, because they hold the original manuscript of the mass written for St. Maximus of Aveia, which is brought out and performed by all the villages in a *ritual show of solidarity and reconciliation on the Saint's Day (10 June).

Then the earthquake. Just twenty years after the flood, there is an earthquake. L'Aquila is by now a rich town, able to obtain the materials and labour it needs from the whole region. Over the years, it has used expensive limestone blocks to build impressive streets and a basilica with a dome. The Passero villages could only afford materials that were close at hand, especially wood, making for rather unimpressive timber-framed buildings rising to no more than two floors, with the spaces between the timber filled with various materials, including mud, reinforced as wattle-and-daub.

When the earthquake comes, the buildings of L'Aquila are devastated, and the loss of life is great. Much of the population has to evacuate, finding temporary accommodation all over Italy. The dams fail; the watermill is destroyed. The recovery of L'Aquila's economy and culture is in the balance, and people compare the disaster with the Lisbon earthquake of 1755.

For the Passeri, the effects are quite different. Their houses sway gently, and some of the mud fillings collapse, but they stay upright. People whose houses are most seriously damaged lodge with neighbours for the few weeks needed for repairs. Their watermills are damaged, but they have only ever worked for half the year, so many of the houses have handmills as a backup. Their economic life is almost unaffected, apart from the time needed for repairs, and the local farmers and other craftsmen, who are used to working with their hands and enjoy the luxury of a *slack economy with a short working week, patch up the houses. Soon, things are back to normal (for the sixth village, the earthquake is not a significant event at all: when the earth sways, they are amused by it).

So, let us now look at the forms of resilience displayed by L'Aquila and the Passeri.

Strategies of resilience

Here we have strategies of two fundamentally different kinds. L'Aquila's strategy is *preventive resilience*; the Passero villages' strategy is *recovery-elastic resilience*.

The common usage of "resilience" contains the sense of surviving adversity which would have destroyed a less resilient *community or person. In *Lean Logic*, the meaning of resilience includes all that, but it also extends closer to the source of the problem; applying highly-developed skills to prevent the shock happening in the first place.

PREVENTIVE RESILIENCE

Preventive resilience—like L'Aquila's sacrificial lakes— protects a system from being substantially damaged by a hostile environment. The system has the capability of changing its environment to suit its nature, or changing its nature to suit its environment, or both. The key to preventive resilience lies in the possession of a structure consisting of many differentiated parts and functions which join up: there is *connectedness—strong inter-dependence—forming a system, an organism, or a community with the defining characteristic of *complexity.

But it has a downside. The complex system's special-ised parts—and the long chains of interdependence between them—make it fragile. Damage to one part can disable the whole system. When a shock is not pre-vented, the consequences are likely to be devastating.

RECOVERY-ELASTIC RESILIENCE

Recovery-elastic resilience, by contrast, does not avoid shock: it responds to it. So far as it can, it goes with the flow; it uses its ingenuity and invents workarounds; it is elastic, flexible. Afterwards, it engages in repair and recovery; it has endurance. Corresponding to the stories of how the different Passero villages coped—or failed to cope—with the flood, the forms of recovery-elastic resilience they displayed are, respectively:

1. *Sacrifice-and-succession. Although parts of the system endure, other parts are destroyed. The system allows for this by producing more than it needs to replace itself (as we see in the high fertility of virtually all plants and animals in a natural *eco-system). It invests a large proportion of its assets in conserving the genetic code for the next generation and in educating the new generation in the *culture needed to keep the system alive. The sacrifice of parts gives the system as a whole immortality.

    In a sense, sacrifice-and-succession can be seen as a continuous process of repair. The repair doesn't always provide an exact replacement, but it fills the gap, either with more of the same, or with another part of the *ecology.

2. New phase. The system responds to the shock by shifting into a new phase, taking on a different character while the changed conditions last. One example of this is the forest which burns and then reverts to a grassland for a time, before becoming forest again. Ecologies and societies are trans-formed by *climate changes; the new state will last as long as the conditions which favour them.[51]

    An even more radical adaptation happens when part of the system changes permanently—or at least for the very long term. Hunting the giant herbivores of North America to extinction, urbanisation, *genetic change, climate change, desertification, the exhaustion of mineral and fossil fuel resources—these are all permanent changes, or associated with permanent change. If a living sys-tem changes out of recognition owing to a shock, but at least continues as a living system, that can be taken to be a form of resilience—but of course it is a reminder that we need to be specific about which "system" we are referring to. If it is, for instance, the giant herbivores of North America, they indeed proved not to be resilient to the climatic changes and other shocks following the end of the last ice age. But the *ecosystem they belonged to did: it adapted; life went on.[52]

3. Elasticity. This is flexibility in action. The system invents coping strategies; it bends with the storm; it behaves in a way which is not normal for it, survives the shock, then comes back to recover its former way of life as far as it can.

4. Resistance (but perhaps Widerstandsfähigkeit—resistance-capability—gets closer to the meaning). Here we have the hardness and imperviousness of a rock. It can endure large shocks without damage. It is the opposite of a house of cards: it hangs together. A person with this quality has a sense of *humour, being able to laugh off *insults; a community with it can cope with trouble without breaking down; it is thick-skinned, bombproof. It is not so much a case of recovering from shock, or being elastic in response to it, as being hard enough to be unaffected by it. If this is in place, then the shock would have to be on a very large scale indeed for the system to notice it.

5. Opportunism. Parts of the system use the damage as an opportunity. They fill the gaps. They use the reduction in—or absence of—competitors as a chance to flourish in ways which would have been impossible for them if the competitors were there. Plants that live in environments that no other plants could tolerate (such as lyme grass, discussed in *Diversity) demonstrate this form of recovery-elastic resilience.

6. *Elegance. The system has minimal infrastructure. It does not depend on long supply lines for food and

R

materials. It is not affected by damage to essential assets over which it has no control. It has little or no *intermediate economy, little or no stuff. All the Passero villages have elegance—this is one of the direct consequences of their *small scale—but the sixth 'village' has taken elegance to the limit. Or, rather, its inhabitants have kept their elegance intact, being hunter-gatherers and resisting the temptation to settle down and go into agriculture— which, from what they have seen of it, looks like hard work (*Ecology: Farmers and Hunters).

And the strategies of the seventh and eighth villages? The seventh village was swept away entirely, so it does not at first glance seem to provide an example of resilience. But in the context of all the other villages, this is a case of sacrifice-and-succession *on the scale of a whole village*, rather than only within one. It may allow the wider society to learn lessons. And the eighth village, which escaped the flood, reveals resistance in the collective sense, too, since recovery depends on the shock being survived by all the information it needs—by the culture and/or the DNA which it cannot rebuild. The eighth village was the system's continuity in this sense, for it was keeper of the Mass of St. Maximus. The Passeri could face the future with their key cultural icon intact.

All of these strategies of recovery-elastic resilience are possible where a system is subdivided into relatively small, weakly interconnected units, like the Passero villages. The system is *modular*.

Resilient systems

Since resilience is of two kinds—*preventive* and *recovery-elastic*—the properties of the systems capable of each are sharply different. Preventive resilience is the form of resilience mainly open to a complex system; recovery-elastic resilience is the form of resilience mainly open to a modular system.

Now, an important aside: the type of complexity that L'Aquila developed is in fact a special case. It is not the fully developed complexity of an organism, although it does achieve some of the qualities of such. No, what we have here is '*as-if complexity*'—which this Dictionary calls *complication*. In this present entry we consider cases of both true complexity and 'as-if complexity'

THE PROPERTIES OF RESILIENT SYSTEMS

	Preventive	Recovery-elastic
SYSTEM TYPE	Complex	Modular
DIVERSITY	Strong (Structural)	Weak (Textural)
CONNECTEDNESS	Strong (Taut)	Weak (Slack)

interchangeably, because the implications of the two types of complexity are similar—and highly relevant to our own future. Exactly what complication means and how it comes about is explained in the dedicated entry on *Complexity. But for now just bear in mind: complexity as applied to a developed human society is 'as-if complexity'.

And with that said, back to the lessons of Tuscany, where we shall use "complexity" freely, knowing that we get to grips with the small print elsewhere.

So, resilience is of two kinds, and it is possible to see a pattern here, as each kind has its cluster of complementary properties. As summarised in the table, "The Properties of Resilient Systems", we can think of resilient systems as ranging between the complex and the modular, with corresponding expressions of diversity and connectedness.

The characteristics of a system with regard to these three criteria define the nature and extent of the resilience it can achieve.

SYSTEM TYPE

Resilient systems, then, lie along the spectrum between complexity and modularity. In fact, they may occupy a range along the spectrum rather than a point, because many *ecological systems have attributes of both complexity and modularity. But let's first consider systems which have stabilised close to one extreme or the other—complex *or* modular: the antelope is complex; the herd of antelopes is modular (even though it is made up of complex antelopes).

1. *Complex

A system which is capable of preventive resilience is a complex system. Complexity can be interpreted in several different ways, but for *Lean Logic* it is the property of a system—such as an animal's body or a self-reliant community—whose parts have strong differences in function, carrying out different, complementary roles in the interests of the system as a whole. These interdependent parts and their functions are connected by extended links—such as the veins and nerves in the human body—and there is little redundancy or duplication.

In the case of an animal's body, the different functions are performed by organs with specialised structures. In the case of a human society, these different functions can take the form of specialised *professions, duties and abilities; and as we saw in the way L'Aquila set about the diverse and demanding tasks it set itself, one of the expressions of this differentiation will be varying degrees of inequality.

Either way, such differentiation of roles gives a system capability. A complex system with well-evolved specialisms can develop strategies of commanding brilliance, rising above the grim survival strategies which we associate with "resilience". Like L'Aquila, it may be able to foresee a threat and prevent it. It may use a range of connected and coordinated tasks to achieve high levels of ambition and beauty, such as the cathedrals and orchestras of a complex human society, or the athletic virtuosity of the falcon.[53]

However, the complex system has poor recovery-elastic resilience. It does not adapt easily in response to profound and sudden shock: all those connections inside a complex system make it quite inflexible and vulnerable to trauma. It cannot use the *sacrifice-and-succession strategy, for instance: if wounded, it is likely to die. A complex system would have been capable of some of the individual Passero responses—adaptation to a new phase and opportunism, for instance—but the mutually-dependent, tightly-connected functions of its parts would have made it hard, or impossible, to respond in more than one of those ways at the same time.

Complex systems do not *travel light. They can at times be inventive, but their complexity is likely to take the form of specialisation—e.g., swift running like an antelope; being capable of thriving in heat and drought like a cactus; or living in the deepest ocean depths like the eelpout. By these standards, humans have exceptional versatility—but outside their capabilities, complex systems find themselves in trouble. And they only have one shot at it, whereas modular systems can fail again and again and still survive. For a complex system, just one bullet, one fall from a horse, one snakebite, is likely to be the end of the matter. Complex systems *need* their ability to prevent shock, for their recovery-elastic resilience to a shock that they don't prevent is poor. The cost of their brilliance is their fragility.[54]

If the hero escapes to fight another day, that tells us something about his preventive resilience. With stop-at-nothing enemies like the ones he has made, recovery-elastic resilience wouldn't have been much help.

2. *Modular

Modularity is the property of being subdivided into parts (or subassemblies, *holons, modules . . .) which have a degree of independence. Every module carries out the essential functions required for its own self-reliance. There may be links of beneficial *reciprocity between parts, but they are not indispensable; if some modules are damaged or die, the effect does not ripple through to the rest—every antelope or Passero village is capable of feeding itself if needs be. The modules are *elegant in that they avoid long and vulnerable lines of supply, and this sets a limit on their size: all the six strategies of recovery-elastic resilience depend on the systems in question having the flexibility of *small scale. The other two key enabling properties of modular systems are weak diversity and weak connectedness, and we shall come to these in more detail in a moment.

Now for the key link between complexity and modularity. A modular system requires that each module within it must have a high degree of local competence and independence—and, in order to achieve that, the modules themselves must have complexity. If the modules are communities, they must be capable of aspects of self-reliance such as capturing and delivering the *energy they need, producing *food, dealing with *waste, maintaining *homeostasis—and that means that they will have internal structures that are far from modular. A modular (and therefore recovery-elastic) system consists of modules which are not recovery-elastic. So both kinds of resilience, both preventive and recovery-elastic resilience, can coexist within the same structure—but they inhabit different layers. Higher levels of complexity are characteristic of lower layers in the system: the complexity of the parts *supports* the modularity of the whole. There are qualifications to all this, but, as a general rule, preventive resilience is the individual accomplishment of a complex system; recovery-elastic resilience is the collective accomplishment of a modular system.

And a loose, modular structure has other positive features, too, beyond the defensive capabilities of resilience. It provides space and *freedom for its parts to develop and apply their complex *intelligence. It permits diverse solutions, trial and error, evolution and local flexibility. It confers responsibility on its members to take the initiative. It affirms, *protects and depends on *presence. The complex parts of such a system are weakly linked (loosely coupled) within its modular whole. Its resilience consists of *both* the local brilliance of its parts in keeping out of trouble *and* the collective ability of the whole in recovering when that fails.

These are critical, life-saving benefits. By contrast, modular communities that seek to build their intelligence and competence by joining up into an integrated system of tightly-coupled complexity (*complication) may have some success for a time, but the loss of modularity that this involves will in due course destroy them.

But note the *fuzzy borderlines and *anomalies here, which ensure that any statement has to come with disclaimers and *exceptions. There are modular properties in complex systems (cells are constantly replacing themselves in the body; the body's powers of recovery from non-lethal shock are considerable), and complex properties in modular systems (specialisms and exchanges of scarce materials between communities). And the crucial asset of *community itself sits between the two properties. So precision is off the menu. But the complementary relationship between modularity and complexity holds. Ask an antelope. The herd may lose one or many of its members and still be a herd. For a single antelope, one incision somewhere in the region of the throat is the end of it. That's complexity for you.

Diversity—the variety of forms, structures or species in a system—is a defining condition of resilience. And here, too, we find a spectrum, between:

1. *Strong (structural) diversity*
   In a complex system, the differences between parts—between the organs, the arteries and nerves of the body, for instance—are radical. There is little or no duplication of form, reflecting their very different tasks. And there is strong interdependence (connectedness), with each part owing its existence to successful coordination with the others. An animal is a network of transport links: if any of them get blocked, it will probably die. Individual freedom for the diverse parts in a complex system is minimal.

2. *Weak (textural) diversity*
   This is the diversity that exists between the parts of a modular system—the antelopes in a herd, the communities in a network like Passero, the varieties in a species. The diversity is intrinsically restrained: it is like variations on a musical theme. There is a lot of duplication of parts.

None of the six strategies of recovery-elastic resilience make sense unless the parts of the modular system are similar to one another. For instance, *sacrifice-and-succession* (as with the people and livestock in the first village, and the seventh village itself), only works if the parts are sufficiently like each other for the idea of replacement, or succession, to have some meaning. Adaptation to change in the form of parts collectively going into a *new phase* only makes sense if there is essential similarity between the parts in the first place. The *opportunist* strategy—rescuing neighbours in trouble and then claiming a reward—is not the action of an enemy or a predator, but part of *politics: unscrupulous behaviour being transcended (just) by shared interests.

That herd of antelopes is being cited in this discussion so often that they are in danger of becoming domestic pets. Nevertheless, they cannot be bettered as an example; here is a modular population of very similar parts, so recovery-resilient that it can survive for thousands of years in an environment full of animals that want to eat them, and consisting of individuals that have a high degree of uniformity—or, as Elinor Ostrom calls

R

it, homogeneity (*Commons). Indeed, if one part of a modular system is substantially different from the others, that is likely to bring trouble. The albino antelope has a short expectation of life.[55]

And such essential uniformity has practical benefits beyond its significance as a condition of recovery-elastic resilience. Basic similarity between the parts of a modular system provides a framework for their *cooperation, *reciprocity, *conversation and *trust within an agreed *culture and shared language; the ample presence of your own species means a range of *choice for breeding and the spreading of genes beyond the local population; it invites coming-together for *carnival, wide shared responsibility for the environment, rapid learning from each other's invention and experience and, if necessary, cooperation for *defence.

But there are, of course, limits to the benefits of homogeneity. In a modular system of communities like Passero there is diversity in the form of local variations, and local ecosystems too are adapted to the particular *place and circumstance; the specific local *character, particularity and enchantment is intact. Although some responses to local conditions won't work, others have at least a good chance of doing so, and the successful can then be imitated and reproduced, so evolution and *emergence are in place.

Such (weak) diversity is especially important if an ecosystem is under stress, and a classic study demonstrating this was published by David Tilman and John Downing in 1994. They cultivated hundreds of grassland plots on the flatlands of Minnesota, with varying degrees of diversity. The plots that performed best—notably in their ability to survive drought—were those with the most (bio)diversity.[56] Tilman puts such diversity into its context as only one of the conditions determining the resilience of an ecosystem, but emphasises that it is a *necessary one. He summarises,

> Diversity must be added to composition, disturbance, nutrient supply dynamics, and climate as a determinant of ecosystem structure and dynamics.[57]

The weak diversity within a modular system such as a grassland is still nowhere near the structural diversity inside a complex system—but some systems, such as

a woodland *ecosystem or an established *community, provide some sense of a middle ground. The woodland has modularity, with its recovery-elastic resilience; it *also* has a degree of complexity, with diverse roles and some interdependences. It has both preventive resilience and recovery-elastic resilience—up to a point. In a turbulent environment where there are no certainties this limited each-way bet provides the most secure *protection of all.[58]

*CONNECTEDNESS

Now we come to the third pairing: slack and taut.

So far, we have established that a modular system actually depends on having complex parts. So the independence (weak connectedness) within a modular system and the interdependence (strong connectedness) within a complex system depend on each other. The parts within a complex system are so strongly connected that they have almost no freedom—your heart and liver must carry out instructions coming from some combination of brain, nervous system and local chemistry. But this internal interdependence confers a high degree of freedom and capability on the complex system (in this case, you) acting as a whole.

It can apply this freedom of action within the space allowed by the modular system to which it belongs (in this case, your *community). In other words, a complex system like you can only make use of its powers of *intelligence and foresight—its ingenious response and avoidance—*if* it is part of a modular system which gives it the *freedom to do so.

So just as complexity and modularity are mutually dependent, so are strong connectedness (taut) and weak connectedness (slack). The taut brilliance of a complex system is only revealed and able to express itself because it lives in the context of a slack system. The complex system makes choices; the slack system enables choices to be made. And this allows the slack, modular system as a whole to benefit from the preventive resilience of its parts.

1. *Taut (strong connectedness)*

A taut, complex system makes few concessions to the freedom of its parts. The strength and astonishing capability of a complex system such as a peregrine falcon does not lie in its spare capacity and its ability to recover from trauma, but in its efficiency and in the exact, lean skill with which it earns a living. It has the *practised specialism of the hunter. Its assets consist of intense, taut athleticism, observation and precision, kept sharp by daily contest with animals who would prefer peregrines to starve. It is anything but slack:

Its shape is streamlined. The rounded head and wide chest taper smoothly back to the narrow wedge-shaped detail. The wings are long and pointed; the primaries long and slender for speed, the secondaries long and broad to give strength for the lifting and carrying of heavy prey. The hooked bill can pull flesh from bones. It has a tooth on the upper mandible, which fits into a notch in the lower one. This tooth can be inserted between the neck vertebrae of a bird so that, by pressuring and twisting, the peregrine is able to snap the spinal cord. The legs are thick and muscular, the toes long and powerful. The toes have bumpy pads on their undersides that help in the gripping of prey. The bird-killing hind toe is the longest of the four, and it can be used separately for striking prey to the ground. The huge pectoral muscles give power and endurance in flight. The dark feathering around the eyes absorbs light and reduces glare. The contrasting facial pattern of brown and white may also have the effect of startling prey into sudden flight. To some extent it also camouflages the large, light-reflecting eyes.

. . . The eyes of a peregrine weigh approximately one ounce each; they are larger and heavier than human eyes. If our eyes were in the same proportion to our bodies as the peregrine's are to his, a twelve stone man would have eyes three inches across, weighing four pounds. The whole retina of a hawk's eye records a resolution of distant objects that is twice as acute as that of the human retina. Where the lateral and binocular visions focus, there are deep-pitted foveal areas; their numerous cells record a resolution eight times as great as ours. This means that a hawk, endlessly

scanning the landscape with small abrupt turns of the head, will pick up any point of movement; by focusing upon it he can immediately make it flare up into larger, clearer, view.[59]

That is a taut system.

2. *Slack (weak connectedness)*

The slack comes at the level of the modular ecology of all peregrines in an area. They hatch many times more chicks than they would need to replace the population if they all survived. There is redundancy in the population of hawks; and also in the ecology of their habitat, whose existence depends on the succession of death and life of its members. The natural, *ecological system is designed to take losses. It can change—profoundly and quickly—in response to change in the *climate and setting. Internal to the hawk and its ecology alike, there are complex, taut structures with little or no freedom to change their highly-evolved forms in the light of present circumstances, but the modular ecologies that they live in have redundancy and room to adapt. They have slack; they therefore have recovery-elastic resilience.

The difference between taut and slack, then, is vital. Here is an illustration. It is about a disturbance occurring on two occasions—past and future—widely separated in time. The first time, the intensity of the disturbance was extreme and sudden, but the consequences for the slack systems of the time were moderate. The second time, the disturbance could be comparatively moderate, but the consequences will not, for the systems it affects have become taut and complex, and so much less able to cope with a shock they cannot prevent:

The next century of human-made global warming is predicted to be far less extreme than that which occurred at 9600 BC. At the end of the Younger Dryas, mean global temperature had risen by 7°C in fifty years, whereas the predicted rise for the next hundred years is less than 3°C; the end of the last ice age led to a 120-metre increase in sea level, whereas that predicted for the next fifty years is a paltry 32 centimetres at most, rising to 88 centimetres

R

by AD 2100. However, while future global warming may be less extreme than that of 9600 BC, the modern world is in a far more fragile state. . . . As a consequence, the threats to human communities and natural ecosystems are far more severe than those of prehistoric times.[60]

In a sense, a complex system is permanently on the threshold of collapse. It uses its taut complexity, and the capability it provides, to keep its nemesis at bay. When it can no longer do so, it reaches the tipping point which will take it back to a much less complex order. A slack, modular system lives much less close to the edge.

Feedback

Underlying all these properties of resilient systems is, of course, the matter of *feedback: "A resilient world", write Brian Walker and David Salt, "would possess tight feedbacks (but not too tight)."[61]

Systems—individuals and *groups—need to be aware of what is going on around them, but rapid awareness does not necessarily mean rapid response. The ideal timing is not always immediate; even procrastination can have its value if what you haven't yet got around to doing is nuts.

And yet, there is a danger of *begging some questions here. For we have got this far, almost to the end of this brain-busting entry on resilience, without being sure of how to tell *which* system we are talking about. Consider the case of the village that made its living in part by raiding its neighbours for their sheep, for example: was the resilience that mattered to them their own resilience as a village or the resilience of all the Passero villages? We are all, in a sense, parasites to our hosts and hosts to our parasites.

This is a moment to let a picture tell the story. Here we have our familiar pair of basins from the start of this entry, but now with another pair of basins inside one of

them. And of course we could extend that with a series of further basins without evident limit—both smaller ones inside the small pair and larger ones containing the large pair. There is likely to be interdependence between them: the small pair's resilience depends on the resilience of the basin in which it lives. And yet, there is also a need for judgment—for a choice of priorities, and for reflection on who you are—for defining the *identity which is a necessary condition for rational decision.[62]

If we were antelopes, we would not need to worry about such matters. If we made a wrong decision about who we were, and which basin it was that we wanted to stay in, then the mistake would quickly be corrected for us; we wouldn't survive to make it again. Humans, by contrast, with their powers of preventive resilience, can hold off such tight feedback loops. If only resilience were a formulaic guideline for how to cope in an intensely difficult time, that would make things so much easier. Thinking about it takes us into an exploration of complexity and modularity, the deep nature of systems and the strategies of life and *death in a turbulent environment. And it sets things up for the story of the *Wheel of Life, which sees complex systems like our own civilisation through their whole life-cycle.

Resilience does provide some guidelines. It can be an inspiring idea, and in critical ways it sets the agenda for *transition. But it does not do our thinking for us; it just tells us where to start.[63]

*Reflection, Gaia, Butterfly Effect, Climacteric.

RESPONSIBILITY, THE FALLACY OF. The *fallacy that intervention is necessary to make a *system work.

A *natural system does not, in general, require its participants to make any effort to sustain it. On the contrary, stability is maintained by the pursuit of self-interest. Lions eat antelopes; antelopes show every sign of being opposed to this arrangement; the system of lions, antelopes and the *ecology they support nevertheless thrives without their volition. The reason for that outcome is that the system is governed by rules—such as the laws of thermodynamics—which guide, or frustrate, intentions. And, in general, the rules governing systems do not only bring stability; just a few simple rules can lead to the *emergence of startling *complexity and *diversity.[64]

However, when this is applied to human society, there is an obvious snag. Whereas the rules which limit the ability of antelopes and lions to have their way are not made by the participants themselves, those which shape human society must to a large extent be made by the people who will then be constrained by them. What, then, are the constraints or rules that provide a foundation for stability and emergence in the case of human society?

The *self-evident answer is "laws". It is, however, the wrong answer. It is the function of laws to enable a society to do what it wants—to *grow, and to fulfil *expectations—with the least possible constraint and dissidence: if antelopes could legislate, the first law they would pass would be one that outlawed lions. *Laws do, of course, define rules and set up sanctions to enforce them, but the nature of the human society which *makes* the laws is derived from somewhere else.

It comes from the physical facts of *land and climate, from history, custom and *social capital; it comes from the moral deliberation and invention which can modify these inheritances for better or for worse. It comes from *tradition—the expressive and significant *narrative which identifies a community as particular and makes it intelligible; it comes from a perceptive engagement with the natural environment; it comes from the communitarian *ethic conferred by *practice; and it comes from *play, which learns, teaches, reinforces and gradually revises the traditions. If these grid-lines—providing a frame of reference beyond immediate opportunism—were removed, the broken-backed *community or state would indeed need someone to take over "responsibility".[65]

And it is when we start trying to take responsibility ourselves for the services which were once freely provided by a healthy system that we begin to realise how valuable that provision was. Here are some of the things that were once substantially supplied for free by the

*vernacular, products and *gifts of both social systems and natural systems: self-policing communities and secure social foundations for *law and order; public participation in *politics and an ability to sustain debate with comparatively little risk of it deteriorating into faction; the competence of *households in teaching children to speak, to know what *conversation means, to be socialised; a stabilised *climate; conserved fertility and micronutrients in the soil; abundant marine fisheries.

The point is not that these things were done perfectly but that, in spreading patches of systems breakage, they are now not being done at all. Filling the gaps becomes someone's responsibility at about the same time as it becomes impossible. Responsibility can be a sign of trouble.[66]
*Constructivism, Leverage, Encounter, Place.

REVERSE RISK ASSESSMENT RULE. The probability of a risk being recognised rises in proportion to belief in the existence of a solution.
*Choice, Fortitude.

RHETORICAL CAPTURE. An argument which is expressed with such rhetorical panache that the arguer convinces himself and everyone else that it is correct.

A variant is the case of the person whose rhetoric is so powerful that he or she is only able to make life *choices

R

which live up to it; the mundane and the merely sensible are ruled out, with *unintended consequences. *Hypocrisy, Balletic Debate, Emotional Argument, Harebrain Fracture, Metamorphosis, Icon.

RHINOCEROS. See Metamorphosis, Hippopotamus.

RITUAL. A *performative utterance which makes something happen, points to *spiritual depth and complexity, establishes or confirms the *identity of a *community or *institution, and gives recognition to the implicit functions and *reciprocal obligations which make up the fabric of social order.

The function of ritual is complex, but it centres on the fundamental matter of existence. Institutions—the communities and social inventions that make a society— have an identity problem. Does an institution actually exist, or is it just a collection of people doing something they happen to want to do today? Does a regiment exist? Does a *contract exist in any sense other than written good intentions? When you tear up the paper, do you tear up the contract? Although these things exist in *law, the same problem applies to the law itself: it is invisible; it can be described—but that is also true of UFOs. In any case, the description can be torn up. What gives such thought-institutions existence is ritual.

When the *market economy, with its networks of exchange, is no longer present to hold society together, the remaining alternative will be a powerfully-affirmed *culture in which people regularly participate, as distinct from being present only as spectators. And a regular, participative cultural event in which the essential framework and much of the content remains unchanged is a ritual. Ritual affirms people's sense of belonging to the community, and it does so in seven ways:

1. *Membership.* Taking part in ritual implies belonging. The ritual itself has no practically useful function, so the reasons for being there are to participate at a symbolic level—or simply because you want to. This sense of membership is often deepened by dance, once a central expression of the *religions, including Christianity. Dance is synchronised, interactive, and requires people to engage with, and sometimes even to touch, each other. It is

also *middle-voiced; that is, it is neither active nor passive but somewhere between the two; there is a sense of being willingly swept up in doing something dramatic and beautiful without having to make decisions about it. For the *resilient communities of the past, *dance was no mere entertainment: it was a key expression of membership.[67]

And ritual affirms membership also in the sense that it is a hub: it is a reason for regular meeting, for being mutually aware, being in touch, being around to help and cooperate. Unless there is such a regular meeting place, no amount of effort to "love your neighbours" is going to work: you won't know their names; you will scarcely meet them. Communities need to have some reason for getting together. If that reason is a *myth, nothing is lost. What matters is the getting together.

2. *Emotional daring.* When a group shares an emotion with you, it is likely that you will be able to feel it with more intensity and insight, or at least with more confidence, than you could alone. Personal joys and sorrows are placed within the context of collective joys and sorrows: you can feel emotionally uplifted by the exultant music of the *Messiah* or the great Harvest psalm; strong bonds can be built up in a community that is encountered at such depth.[68]

A community which not only feels the same emotion as you do, but enhances it, is a community you feel you can *trust. And there is an ecstatic quality about being happy among other happy people. It sometimes happens when playing in the snow.

3. *Continuity.* Ritual reassures by bringing constancy, with the same music, dance and choreography—*the way we do it here*—handed down between generations, and evolving slowly, if at all. It is a symbol of continuity, a stable code for the community.

This differentiates it from the daily schemes and politics of the moment. Its presence is real, dependable, reassuring; it is there on its own terms; it is something to which the individual can *defer. The shaman (priest) in the early religions who changed the ritual or *liturgy broke the spell, and would be in trouble, perhaps at risk of his life. The rules and practices confer timeless legitimacy on the community.[69]

4. *Consciousness of time and events*. Ritual is linked to *time and natural events, such as the closing down of the day's activity at dusk: the event is marked; it takes place in the mind as well as in the environment.[70]

It celebrates the *stories and events that made the community, acknowledging seasons and accomplished tasks, renewing members' awareness of their community's history, and of the stories and traditions which give it identity. Once, local saints and heroes were remembered; the *agricultural year was celebrated; rites of passage (baptism, adulthood, marriage, *death) were observed: a young man would be made explicitly conscious of becoming a full member of the community, and of the responsibilities and duties that conferred. Ritual was the performative utterance that turned events into the building blocks of a culture. James Roose-Evans comments on the barely-visible remnant of these rites of passage: "No wonder we undergo identity crises until we die."[71]

5. *Practice*. Ritual requires talent: music, speech, *building and decoration, often along with dance, acting and dressmaking, cooking, games, wrestling, organisation and stage-management. The effect of these carnival *practices extends beyond the material product to the cultivation of *truthfulness, justice and *courage, and these properties of citizenship are *virtues that can be placed at the service of the community.[72]

6. *Meaning*. Ritual's characteristic medium is *narrative truth—the poetic truth which raises questions that may demand long *reflection. In *Lean Logic*'s vocabulary, the space in which we think about almost-unanswerable questions is *ironic space, inviting a lifetime of exploration. It is artistic, so it cannot be completely understood; though introduced to it in childhood, participants will not grow out of it. Instead, they will grow into it, discovering its depth throughout their lives, and teaching as they learn, learning as they teach.

If you reflect for a lifetime on a not-immediately-understandable poem, or on the text of a ritual, you will have the freedom to live by your interpretation of it: nobody tells you what to think: you pull the meaning out of the words. Ritual is a form of *pull, and in this sense is a source of *freedom.

7. *Locality*. Ritual changes the nature of the place a little bit, making it special; because the ritual has happened there you will think about it in a different way for the rest of your life, like a tree under which you once made love, and which you still pass with musing nostalgia from time to time. Ritual events make places, bring them alive, haunt them or bless them, populate them with the *spirit of what happened, so that today's inhabitants are not alone. Ritual is not just *any* ritual: it is *yours*, because this is the ritual which you help to make, with the people you live amongst, in the *place where you live.[73]

The power of ritual as an effective means of sustaining societal structures was illustrated on a grand scale in the *imagination of Plato. In his *Republic*, goods are shared out amongst all members of the guardian class—an arrangement which would require highly developed altruism and commitment to the common good. But in his "City of the Magnesians", he went even further: here, goods would be shared amongst *all* citizens, and the problem was, of course, to find ways of making this exceptionally ambitious and unstable social *ethic hold up. His solution to the problem was to design the city's culture around the ceaseless performance of ritual; every day of the year had its own festival, binding the city together in a rhythmic pattern, integrating the gods into the enterprise. The citizens, as Catherine Pickstock writes, were "strung together on a thread of song and dance". The performance of ritual constantly renewed the commitment to the fragile ethic of common property. The City of the Magnesians is fiction—a *utopia—but Plato accepted, as a fact of life, that shared ritual is crucial for the delivery of social *cohesion.[74]

Ritual, though seemingly useless, asserts the legitimacy of the community (or institution, or *nation) and the *authority of its *traditions and *leadership. The presence of tradition sustains the idea that the community has an identity, permanence and depth. As the anthropologist Maurice Bloch notes, the ritual locates a particular social order in its setting as "a fact of the nature of the world". In a non-demoralised society, this sense of legitimacy provides a thread of continuity that extends through the social order as a whole. Ritual

R

411

and tradition can transform a community's chances of survival; giving it the courage of its conventions.[75]
*Carnival, Script, Rote, Truth, Tactile Deprivation.

ROTE. "Learning by rote" is a phrase used to dismiss the boon of learning by heart.

The difference between heart and rote was noted by Shakespeare: speaking by rote means speaking, not . . .

> . . . by the matter which your heart prompts you,
> But with such words that are but roted in
> Your tongue, though but bastards and syllables
> Of no allowance to your bosom's truth.
>
> *Coriolanus, c.1606.*[76]

The idea that teaching should not require learning by heart on the grounds that it is mere rote-learning is attributed to the philosopher of education John Dewey (1859–1952), but that's not what he meant, and he did not use the word "rote". What he was against was not the engagement of memory—by, for instance, learning poetry—but the practice of unloading large amounts of information onto children for no good reason. What he was for was education that connects with *culture, *community and *nature. He distinguished between going through the motions of learning and . . .

> . . . the readjustment of mental attitude, the enlarged and sympathetic vision, the sense of growing power, and the willing ability to identify both insight and capacity with the interests of the world and man. . . . [Culture is] the growth of the imagination in flexibility, in scope, and in sympathy, till the life which the individual lives is informed with the life of nature and society.[77]

That's *lean education.

S

SACRIFICE-AND-SUCCESSION. The succession of life-cycles of the subdivisions, *holons or parts of an *ecology, whose sequence of death and renewal sustains the longevity of the *ecological system as a whole and contributes to its *resilience. In this context, *death

is benign participation, the key enabling condition of resilient, living *community.
*Carnival, Wheel of Life, Resilience ❭ Recovery-Elastic Resilience ❭ Sacrifice-and-Succession.

SCALE. The size, or scale, of an object has a crucial influence on its nature.

The significance is as decisive as geometry itself. Consider: the two circles are identical except that one is larger than the other. Are there any differences between them other than that simple difference in size?

Yes. Their proportions differ in a fundamental way: relative to their respective areas, the circumference (*edge) of the large circle is less than that of the small one. The larger a circle, the smaller its edge relative to its area; the area rises with the square of the radius, whereas the circumference rises in simple proportion to the radius. And in the case of a three dimensional object, such as a sphere, the volume rises with the cube of the radius, where the surface area rises only with its square. Large shapes (and systems) have a low edge ratio, small ones have a high edge ratio.[1]

This rule of geometry can have some advantages for large organisms: for instance, having a small surface area (relative to its size) helps a large animal to conserve heat, enabling it to have the slower metabolic rate associated with long life. And there are other advantages such as improved powers to defend itself (but it may also be a more tempting target), the ability to forage over a large area (but it needs more food), a body capable of supporting a heavy brain, and (in the case of the human animal) being large enough to manage fire. And for human societies too there are advantages

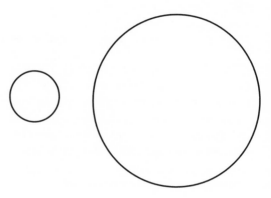

of scale—a bigger pool of talent and better orchestras, for instance—so scale is not a matter of small-is-always-best; it is a matter of being the right size. But there are good reasons for a strong presumption—a reliable default position—in favour of small.

The advantages that large scale does enjoy come at a high cost. The key to this is that a large system has a relatively short *boundary (border, edge, surface) across which it can obtain its *needs. Large animals and societies have to go to a lot of trouble to import sufficient nutrients and energy which then have to be distributed over larger distances in their bodies, with waste having to travel all the way back to the boundary. And in a large human *community, material waste comes up against the *sorting problem and tends to be lost from the system rather than recycled.

On the large scale (say, a modern city), decision-making is affected too—people lose the sense that matters affecting them are their responsibility or within their power. Meanwhile, top-down governance is so far removed from the local detail that the only option open to those responsible is to develop some form of *ideology.

The fundamental problem with large scale is that with each advance in size there is a *necessary increase in *complication. Large animals—whose ratio between volume and surface-area means that the absorption of food and oxygen is a problem—have to make up for this with *diverse and ingenious devices such as lungs, and the velvety textures which confer an enormous surface area on their guts. As the biologist J.B.S. Haldane writes in his classic essay, "On Being the Right Size",

> Comparative anatomy is largely the story of
> the struggle to increase surface in proportion to
> volume. . . . The higher animals are not larger
> than the lower because they are more compli-
> cated. They are more complicated because they
> are larger.[2]

Applying this to settlements and *economies, the inevitable complications of largeness lead to three things:

1. a loss of *elegance, as large infrastructures (the *intermediate economy) have to be maintained in order to enable the simple act of living;

2. a loss of *judgment, as inflexible, standardised, *rationalist solutions and ideologies destroy the local detail—that living part of the urban ecology on which the rest depends; and

3. a loss of *presence, as people surrender the power to build the *institutions they want, which would enable lives that make sense to them. The system as a whole sacrifices the *intelligence it needs: it loses its minds.

The relevant response to large scale is to transform the *system's structure: subdivide one big thing into many smaller ones; make it *modular. In the first diagram on page 414, the large system, at the cost of some loss of area, has increased its total edge many times over. In the second diagram, the same principle is applied again, taking the modular construction down to the local level, and building a nested hierarchy of *holons, or local communities—small enough to recognise themselves as communities, close enough to form clusters of *cooperation, while still having a generous edge across which to import their material needs and export their wastes in a small enough scale to allow for recycling.[3]

Here we have the rescaling of society. It is the essence of what the *Transition movement is trying to do. But then, of course, comes the snag: they need hinterland. Modularity does not provide solutions on its own; it needs a setting in the form of an *ecology which can supply *materials and *energy, and recycle its *waste. Without that ecological setting the small-scale holonic structure loses half of its point. Having access to a nearby edge across which to import materials and export waste is no advantage if, pressing up against that edge, there is another, virtually identical, holon, needing to do the same thing. But that does not make modularity any less critical: it is a *necessary condition. In any case, some communities do have access to the hinterland they need. And other communities will discover, and be surprised by, solutions which they would not have discovered if they had not developed a modular structure in the first place, against the odds.[4]

And here we have the testimony of a reformer who used small scale to good effect. Thomas Chalmers (1780–1847) was the vicar of the *parish of St. John in Glasgow, and invented the system of poor relief which established and maintained personal contact with poor families. It was based on fully-developed mentoring

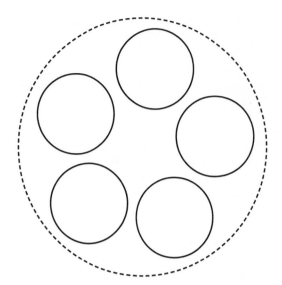

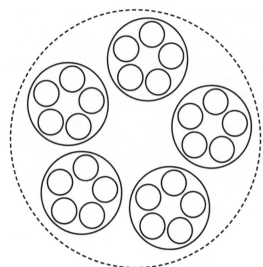

relationships between applicant and provider. Chalmers and his colleagues in the scheme talked through the options with each applicant; in the absence of alternatives, financial relief was provided, but personal contact was sustained. Its success in reducing poverty, in building morale, and in opening up the possibility of financial recovery, was recognised; the money saved was used to endow schools in the area, and the method was widely copied. The key to the scheme—intelligent personal engagement between the providers and the people in need—made it necessary to keep each area of administration small enough for that personal contact to be sustained.[5]

Such an approach works only on a small scale: a national scheme would need to be subdivided into local programmes. As Chalmers noted,

> There is a charm in locality most powerfully felt by every man who tries it . . . who has personally attached himself to a manageable portion of the civic territory. . . .
>
> The very visibility of the limit, by constantly leading him to perceive the length and breadth of his task, holds out an inducement to his energies, which, however difficult to explain, will be powerfully felt and proceeded on. There is a very great difference, in respect of its practical influence, between a task that is indefinite, and

a task that is clearly seen to be overtakeable. The one has the effect to paralyse; the other to quicken exertion.[6]

Small scale declutters. There is *elegance. The work it does produces the results it wants. It is not consumed and distracted with sustaining the large-scale infrastructures and *abstractions it is lumbered with. There is eye contact.

*'Introduction', Groups and Group Sizes, System Scale Rule, Social City.

SCEPTICISM. (1) *Precautionary defence against the untrue. Reasonable doubt.

(2) Unreasonable defence against the *true. William Fleming's *Vocabulary of Philosophy* summarises,

> Scepticism distrusts the very instruments of knowing, and discredits the claims of evidence to warrant certainty.[7]

*Certainty.

SCRIPT. A script (in *Lean Logic*) is a *practice of some difficulty, widely accepted and fulfilled by the members of a society or group, and reinforced and integrated into their values by their *culture and *rituals.[8]

It will be necessary, when inventing a survivable future, to develop routines and practices which are not *intuitively obvious. There will be many aspects of life—including the various means of limiting the *growth of *capital and *population and protecting the local culture and *ecology—which will not be guided by what seems to be common sense, and by what feels right. A script, which does not necessarily have to be written down, is a process or a procedure which a society believes it must carry through, but which is at the same time difficult, offering many temptations to cheat or forget about it. The script, therefore, is integrated into the culture, and made inseparable from what it means to be a member of that society.

Among the many examples of the principle in action in traditional societies, one that has been studied in detail is that of the *milpa* script, which has been sustained in varying forms for five centuries or more by the Huastec people, an indigenous community of some 120,000, in the Gulf Coastal slopes of the Sierra Madre Oriental region of Mexico. *Agriculture in this area of moist tropical forests has a basic problem. The forest is an essential part of the area's ecology, but *land is also needed for growing food. If forest land is maintained for agriculture for substantial periods of time, it degrades rapidly, there is erosion and flooding and it is colonised by weeds that compete with crops and inhibit the regeneration of the forest.[9]

Management of the land in such naturally forested tropical regions therefore has to be based on the "swidden" system, a principle of rotations which includes a long phase to allow new forest to mature before it is eventually felled again, followed by a relatively brief period for food crops.

However, this is quite a difficult kind of agriculture to sustain, for several reasons. For one thing, it requires periodic changes in the actual possession of land. That is to say, whereas the usual food crops lend themselves to smallholdings managed by a single farmer or *household (though extra help is sometimes needed), the forest is on a much larger scale, requiring collective responsibility, so some way has to be found of surrendering property rights over a patch of land, and then reclaiming them at a later time—say, twenty years later, or more. Secondly, there are stages in the process at which the action needed is possible only when the group works as a collective: for instance, when the

forest is felled or replanted. Thirdly, there are constant temptations to take short cuts by, for instance, felling the forest too soon, or encroaching onto neighbours' land, or not cultivating the main *milpa* crop (maize) to the standards which will enable the rotation cycle to be *sustainable for the indefinite future.

And the fourth reason why this form of management is demanding is that it requires continued vigilance that the land used for it will not be encroached on or mortgaged by conventional business interests. The stand-off between the *ejidos/comunidades* (the *commonly-owned landholdings managed collectively by a community), and the *mestizos* (the privately owned land which consists largely of pasture, much of it in poor condition) is intense and real. Indeed, this was the main motivation behind the Mexican revolution in 1910, which led to the execution by firing squad of the Emperor Maximilian (an event famously painted by Manet) and the firm establishment of the system of community-owned land in Mexican law.[10] The difference between the impacts of the two kinds of land use—one of them *protected by the legal "shell" that provides collective property rights—is clearly visible. Janis Alcorn and Victor Toledo explain,

> The tenurial shell that reinforces community and cultural values is physically visible at the border. Standing at the border where degraded pasture of large private holders meets the community's patchwork of *milpa* and forest, people tell stories of how their way of life and forests were threatened before the revolution, and how they were unable to reclaim parts of their territory (now outside the border). They say that the revolution was terrible, but they acknowledge that it saved their forests and their way of life.[11]

There is clearly a material incentive for the members of a *milpa* script community to sustain their standards of cultivation and their way of life. It keeps their *communities together; it provides them with *food and *water (since it maintains the watersheds); and it preserves a richly *diverse and productive ecosystem as a rich asset, with abundant edible species. The Huastecs, for instance, grow some 500 edible plants and, in the region as a whole, more than 1,000 species are cultivated.[12]

And yet, raw self-interest is not enough to sustain a collective enterprise. The temptation to cheat is always there: to ignore the strict protocols of *milpa* cultivation, to abandon the rotation system and to turn to weedkillers and herbicides instead, to encroach on a neighbour's land during a time when the borders are not defined, to fell a patch of forest ahead of time, or even to sell out to the *mestizos*, get rich and go. What holds it all together is the culture embedded in the *milpa* script. The aim is—it has to be—not just to produce the food and manage the ecosystem, but to maintain the local cultural *identity.

That identity is expressed in terms of the culture, and the culture is expressed in *rituals which belong within the Catholic *tradition, built in turn on traditions with roots in the pre-Hispanic Aztec period. The *milpa* ritual requires the care and dedication of a *craft; the process of making the *milpa* is regarded as sacred. This is a community in which enchantment has survived: obligations to the wild plants and animals are recognised; the land is regarded as part of the community; the *emotions are engaged. The rituals are especially intense shortly before the big seasonal events and turning points in the *milpa* cycle. There is, in this context, no visible join between culture and *practice, between work and *play, between song and memory, between the two parts of agri- and -culture. In summary, as Carl Folke and his colleagues write:

> Rituals help people remember the rules and interpret signals from the environment appropriately. Where traditions remain strong, people see no need to preserve esoteric knowledge; they simply practise their culture.[13]

Script, despite its name, takes us away from the written word. It recruits us into the *ecosystem, and makes us part of it. This is a time to move on from being lean, from being so *logical, from thinking so hard—and to grow into simply practising our *culture.
*Rote, Competitiveness, Slack and Taut.

SECOND NATURE. Our wild nature.

If you *act* as a pillar of the *community, you will be an invaluable part of the collective purpose of giving it stability and making it real. But if you *think*, in your heart of hearts, as a pillar of the community, you will be a bore: you will be limited to the *utterance*—*reductionist, joyless, banal. The mockery and critical faculty of your subconscious and its dreams will be banished until your retirement, or maybe your death.

Second nature calls your bluff: are you really an upstanding member of the community, or just on your best behaviour? It is the enabling folly which makes it okay to engage your subconscious mind, to listen to dreams, to recognise absurdity even if you are its source, to tolerate brilliance even if you are not its source, and to develop *judgment.

Our second nature takes us beyond being good citizens who know, privately, that we only have to pretend to be good, since no one will notice the fake. It takes us beyond being the brave and responsible soldier—that hero of Classical Greece and Rome, willing to defend his country, its fields and families. Instead, it belongs in the sacred world of chaos. This is an idea which, like lava, is buried somewhere deep inside all the major cultures, and sometimes erupts in Saturnalian excess (*Carnival). You can't tame it with your controlling and orderly good sense. But you have probably dreamed it, and it is inhabited during waking hours, too, by, for instance, musicians—such as Tchaikovsky when he wrote the symphonic poem *Francesca da Rimini*—and by poets such as Dante (who inspired the music), John Milton and William Blake. That poetic celebration of chaos and old night can leave us now bemused and puzzled, wondering not only at the allusions, but also at what on earth it is all about. We seem to have stumbled into a place where someone is feeling unusually strongly about something . . .

> "Crave not for the mortal & perishing
>   delights, but leave them
> To the weak, and pity the weak as your
>   infant care. . . .
> Wait till the Judgment is past, till the
>   Creation is consumed,
> And then rush forward with me into the
>   glorious spiritual
> Vegetation, the Supper of the Lamb & his
>   Bride; and the
> Awakening of Albion our friend and
>   ancient companion".

So Los spoke. But lightnings of discon-
tent broke on all sides round
And murmurs of thunder rolling heavy
long and loud over the mountains,
While Los call'd his Sons around him to
the Harvest & the Vintage.

> *William Blake, Milton, 1804–1808.* [14]

The *market economy is a fragile defence against such things. But they are going on under the smooth surface of the well-behaved, and there is a limit to how long it is possible to keep a straight face. Men need *wild*. Ay, and women, too, as C.P. Estés writes,

> No matter by which culture a woman is influenced, she understands the words *wild* and *woman*, intuitively. . . . The memory is of our absolute, undeniable, and irrevocable kinship with the wild feminine, a relationship which may have become ghosty from neglect, buried by overdomestication, outlawed by the surrounding culture, or no longer understood anymore. We may have forgotten her names, we may not answer when she calls ours, but in our bones we know her, we yearn toward her; we know she belongs to us and we to her.[15]

Lean community, by contrast, will depend, not just on our best behaviour, but on our whole nature.[16]

SEDATION. The art of making the *public compliant and sleepy:

> Officials and ministers followed an approach whose object was sedation.
>
> *The Phillips Report, the BSE inquiry, 2000.*[17]

*Distraction.

SELF-DECEPTION. The pretence that hard problems have been addressed.

Among the many ways of deceiving yourself, here are six:

1. *Sincerity: bury all contrary arguments under your irresistible and passionate conviction.
2. *Unfalsifiability: make a case which it is logically impossible to disprove or even deny.
3. *Blame: argue that your plan would have been successful if it had not been wrecked by others.
4. *False consistency: go for two incompatible aims; one of them is likely to do relatively well even (or especially) if the other one does not, and you can pretend that you were in favour of that one all along.
5. Rationalisation: think up reasons for believing that the events that happened were the best that could have happened.
6. *Distraction: Keep busy.

*Diplomatic Lie, Internal Evidence, Cognitive Dissonance.

SELF-DENYING TRUTH. A truth that contradicts itself—which undoes itself as soon as it is spoken. Examples: "The religious belief which unites us so securely is in fact a useful falsehood." "The reason we have such a loving relationship is that you remind me of my mother." "We have compulsory games at this school in bitter winter weather because it makes you boys philosophical." "The Lord Chancellor has announced that the office of Lord Chancellor has been abolished."

It is a matter of acknowledging the limits of what we can say without destroying the *truth in the process: you can kill an insight by analysing it, a god by naming him, love by telling it:

> Never seek to tell thy love
> Love that never told can be;
> For the gentle wind does move
> Silently, invisibly.
>
> I told my love, I told my love,
> I told her all my heart,
> Trembling, cold, in ghastly fears—
> Ah, she doth depart.
>
> Soon as she was gone from me
> A traveller came by
> Silently, invisibly—
> Oh, was no deny.
>
> *William Blake, Never Seek to Tell thy Love, 1793.*[18]

SELF-EVIDENT, THE FALLACY OF THE. The self-evident—a statement of the obvious which is likely to turn out to be untrue.

The social scientist Elinor Ostrom writes,

> I have learned to be sceptical whenever I hear the phrase, "it is self-evident" that some empirical regularity occurs in a sociological setting. Patterns of relationships among individuals and groups tend to be relatively complex and rarely lend themselves to simple explanations. Reforms based on overly simplified views of the world have led to counterintuitive and counterintentional results.[19]

In other words, avoid . . .

> a KISS (keep it simple, stupid) approach. If we keep it too simple, we lose our understanding of what's going on out there.[20]

And Ostrom offers an example of the limitations of the self-evident in her study of the organisation of police departments in the United States. It would no doubt be best if they were all roughly the same size and organised in the same way—until you look at it more closely, that is (*Anomaly).

Here are some examples of self-evident *truths that turn out to be untrue:

- Redundancy is inefficient.
- Local users of a resource cannot be trusted to take a long-term view.
- You can manage a whole region on a single set of principles.
- Order comes from centralised direction.
- The presence of agencies working to different principles is inefficient.
- Local decisions are always best.[21]

The ominous problem associated with the self-evident is that it tends to join up with good intentions to produce, not just *unintended consequences, but comprehensive deconstruction of the *institutions which it was intended to reform. There is scarcely an *ideology that does not come motivated by good intentions. That is, ideologies are not wicked cover stories for darker

purposes; they are migraine visions of the obvious and—especially if reinforced by resentments—they are hard to stop.

The problem is not only that the self-evident is typically wrong; it is that it departs from the central principle of *incremental discovery—the evolutionary, conserve-what-is-there *ethic which recognises truths, inconvenient or life-saving, which are not by any standards self-evident.

The philosopher Jamie Whyte suggests suitable candidates for self-evident truths: "I've just fallen in a puddle", or "This tea is hot."[22]

*Canard, Pharisee, Harmless Lunatic.

SELF-FULFILLING ARGUMENT. An argument which increases the likelihood—or even guarantees—that the case it is making will turn out to be right. Examples: "It is too late: we can do nothing." "You will fail." "Our relationship is in trouble." "We are going to be okay."

Self-fulfilling truth could be considered a sixth kind of *truth; an argument against (inconclusive) is that it is already there in *performative truth.

*Grim Reality, Self-Denying Truth.

SEX. See Eroticism.

SHIFTING GROUND. This is the attrition tactic: as each of your opponent's arguments is defeated, he tries another one, looking for weak points or simply reducing you to exhaustion:

> We were disagreeing about Muck, but to back up my case, I will have a go at you, in turn, about Staffa, Shuna, Eigg, Arran, Mousa, Canna, Lewis and Coll . . . and Yell . . .

At the level of the quarrel, this may be quite healthy, a release of accumulated resentments. Or, it may be more serious because—if what you have to argue against is not one point but a dozen—it can be hard to keep any one point in the frame for long enough to discuss it: my

S

nuanced observations about Eynhallow merely prompt a rant about Sgeotasaigh.

And if you do start getting somewhere with it, the opposition is likely to shift the ground again—and pretend he hasn't. People don't really think like that, they just argue like it, calling in at any proposition that catches their eye, like moths fluttering opportunistically around sources of light. There may be no end to this, short of a breakdown in all possibility of a *conversation, or—perhaps with help—some insight about what the conversation is *really about*, which may be nothing to do with islands at all, but an expression of deep resentments.

There are alternatives. One (recommended) is to stick to one subject at a time.

But another is to stop taking it so seriously. The idea that the outcome of an argument actually matters is a relatively new one, and in the history of *traditional societies, we find arguments being fired-off in sequence, not to change anyone's mind, but to keep the peace. An illustration of this from Old Germanic history describes what we may now think of as an extended dinner party of the time, held by Turisind, King of the Gepidae. His son has recently been slain in battle by the Langobards. So he invites the Langobards' chieftains round to dinner, where another of his sons addresses them. History conveniently summarises an extended argument:

Son: You are white-footed mares. You stink.

Langobards: Go to the field of Asfeld, there you
will surely learn how valiantly those "mares"
of yours can put about them, where your
brother's bones lie scattered like an old nag's
in the meadow.

After a lot of this, we are told, "they bring the banquet to a merry end". Altogether, a great evening. And, in the Old Norse and Old Germanic tradition, the hall in which such slanging matches were held was called "the great place of peace".[23]
*Distraction, Fallacies, Dialogue, Politeness.

SINCERITY. (1) Consistency between thought and speech.
(2) Engagement with a subject so close-up that you can neither see it nor think about it: your own conviction on the matter is taken as proof enough of how right you are.[24]

*Metamorphosis, Politeness, Hypocrisy, Reformer Fallacy.

SIZE. See Scale.

SKILLS. See Manual Skills.

SLACK AND TAUT. The two ends of the spectrum of *connectedness, and one of the three pairings of properties which define the extent of a system's *resilience.

Slack is central to the ability of a system to recover from shock. It enables it to cope with losses, and it makes space for *choice. It is also needed in well-defined ways for that special case of resilience—a post-industrial *Lean Economy.

By contrast, a price-based economy is taut. For goods to command a price they must be scarce, and a taut *market is one in which this scarcity is present. As summarised in one of the defining phrases of economics, attributed to Lionel Robbins: "Economics is the study of scarcity"—a shortened version of what he actually wrote in his *Essay on the Nature and Significance of Economics*,

> Economics is the science which studies human
> behaviour as a relationship between ends and
> scarce means which have alternative uses.[25]

A good or service is scarce if its production or consumption incurs an *"opportunity cost"—the loss of the benefits that could have been derived if the resources and time used for the chosen task had, instead, been used for something else (like leaving the money in a savings account to earn *interest, or buying something else with it). Opportunity cost is a central idea because it is intrinsic to the mechanism by which prices are set.

For example, a person does not have to accept a low wage if there is an alternative which would pay more. But consider the case when there are, say, more apples around than people can eat, or more available labour than job vacancies. There is no scarcity, no tautness—the economy is slack. In such circumstances, apples and labour have no opportunity cost: some (or many) remain unused and command no price.

In the case of labour, this is mitigated by state benefits paid to the unemployed. But when unemployment reaches the point at which the government's tax

S

revenues are so reduced that it is unable to pay unemployment benefits (the case of *hyperunemployment), the possibility of the opportunity cost of labour falling to zero—where jobs pay nothing because the alternative is no job at all—becomes more than theoretical.

Now, slack in economics occurs in two forms:

Unintentional slack

This is the case where the economy falls into depression which, at its extreme, matures to hyperunemployment. Reasons why that can be expected after the *energy peak are outlined at the end of *Lean Economics. At the heart of such a situation there is a *paradox, since there is both glut and famine at the same time. There may, for instance, be an abundance of apple orchards, abandoned because no one has the money to pay the farmer for the apples he could produce from them, thus leaving abundant food-growing potential untapped while people starve. Or there may be an abundance of labour, with plenty that needs doing—and yet that "plenty that needs doing" doesn't happen, owing to there being (for instance) no fuel to supply the *energy it needs, and/or no money to pay for it.

In a moderate form, and if the problem is the lack of money, this can be repaired, since governments can redistribute income to those who would otherwise have none; or spend heavily; or "print money". In an extreme form, there are so many without jobs that there is not enough tax revenue to redistribute or spend, and any government temptation to print money will immediately short-circuit into inflation. Recessions are dark reminders—or precursors—of the failure of urban economics when the large, city-based labour forces can no longer be sustained, since labour commands no price.

Intentional slack

This is the case where an economy learns to coexist with slack. It might, for instance, work a standard 2½-day week to reduce the demand for jobs, and/or use uncompetitive and labour-intensive (but *eco-efficient) methods of production to increase the supply.

In an obvious sense, this state of creative inefficiency is irrational: why should buyers in the market bear the high costs that this would bring? In a taut market, governed by price, there is no answer to that: such

inefficiencies would be wiped out in a moment and, on the large scale, this is a problem to which there is no solution. If some of the (part-time, creative and inefficient) workforce decided instead to work a full week and use the most efficient methods available, others would follow—some would be fully employed and some would not be employed at all; there would be excess labour, and wages would collapse to zero.

However, in an intentionally slack market there is a deliberate decision to build and sustain a *locally-based economy with a much lower level of output and consumption than it could produce if it were taut and *competitive (*Growth).[26] Its maintenance requires that work is shared out; that the inefficient technology is freely chosen; that nature is spared. This settlement, quite fragile—like our planet *Gaia herself—is the core principle of *lean economics.

On a small scale, intentional slack can be done easily enough (see "Slack and Evolution" sidebar). For example, the *informal economy of the domestic *household is prodigal with labour, and if it had to compete on price it wouldn't have a chance. It works because price is nothing to do with it, and it is this kind of essential-yet-slack economy which holds out to us the possibility of a future. But it is *protected by having opted-out from the competitive *market, and it is not easy to sustain such agreements at the *large scale.

Nonetheless, most human societies in the past, outside the taut, tense experience of urban civilisation, have been slack in this sense. Here, for example, is the historian Juliet Schor's view of the mixture of working life and days off in the Middle Ages:

> The medieval calendar was filled with holidays. Official—that is, church—holidays included not only long "vacations" at Christmas, Easter and midsummer but also numerous saints' and rest days. These were spent both in sober churchgoing and in feasting, drinking and merrymaking. In addition to official celebrations, there were often weeks' worth of ales—to mark important life events (bride ales or wake ales) as well as less momentous occasions (scot ale, lamb ale and hock ale). All told, holiday leisure time in medieval England took up probably about one third of the

SLACK AND EVOLUTION
Making space for trial and error

Freedom from the taut determinism of price competition opens up the space to develop flexible relationships. Instead of the written plans which effectively rule out *incremental experiment and advance, there can be evolution in the light of experience. Initiatives can be explored, with risks limited by their *small scale.[27]

In a slack system, there is the possibility of building elbow-room into *contracts. That is, contracts may have sufficient slack to allow for the unforeseen, as in the principle of "relational contracting", where there are informal agreements, unwritten codes of conduct, and relationships based on long-term loyalties which survive short-term trouble. Though practised since the dawn of *cooperation, this network of informal contracts only began to be recognised in *economics following the influential work by Oliver Williamson in the 1970s.[28]

The *reciprocal obligations sustained by local lean communities, based on *trust, will depend on flexible agreements if they are to last through periods of profound surprise and change.

year. And the English were apparently working harder than their neighbors. The *ancien régime* in France is reported to have guaranteed fifty-two Sundays, ninety rest days, and thirty-eight holidays. In Spain, travelers noted that holidays totaled five months per year.[29]

It was backed up by a well-established *ritual year, and when the rituals came abruptly to an end in the Reformation, the feast day slack was stopped too; in England by the Act of 1536, which allowed itself a rant at those who ought to be at work "being enticed by the licentious vacation and liberty of these holidays".[30] A strong *culture that can support slack has been in retreat ever since. But the inconvenient truth is that,

as the economy now begins to decompose, we have to rebuild a slack society to take its place.

The opening up of *choice—not least choice in the use of time—allows the economy to be interesting in a way which is impossible if it has to make *money with nearly everything it does. And yet, a market that is slack in terms of its relaxed use of labour, *capital and *land is unstable: it could at any time snap back to taut, full-time competitive employment for some (for a time), along with destitution for the rest.

Stopping that happening calls for things that are anathema to a *competitive economy: local *loyalties and *currencies, collusion and cartel, culture and confidence that it knows what it wants and where it is going—that it can choose how to live (*Leisure).[31]

*'Introduction' ❭ Slack, Resilience ❭ Resilient Systems ❭ Connectedness, Lean Economics.

SLEEP. Part of the progress towards *resilience. You take a rest from planning, arguing and campaigning, and keep out of trouble for a time. You gather your strength. You come to see things differently, as discovered by Odysseus, who spent much of his epic voyage in *negretos hypnos*—sleep deep enough to be the counterfeit of death—eventually waking so befuddled and different that he could not recognise his own homeland. This was sleep which was taking him somewhere—on a ship travelling faster than the falcon can fly—and he made it in the end.[32]

*Public Sphere and Private Sphere, Reflection.

SLIPPERY SLOPE. The evaluation of an argument or proposition by reference chiefly, or only, to its extreme form.

The Fallacy of the Slippery Slope is pernicious and hard to argue against, except perhaps with a weary "Oh, don't be ridiculous!" and a moment of mourning at the death of *good faith and *trust. The arguer insists that the thing he opposes, however innocent, would lead inevitably to its horrible extreme. A comforting hug leads to paedophilia; a dram of whisky to alcoholism; punishment to brutal assault; *authority becomes harassment; military action is genocide; concern about genetic inheritance leads to Auschwitz; expression of *erotic desire leads to rape; and, of course, without

S

intrusive health and safety regulation, we would be on the slippery slope to a litany of battle, murder and sudden death. No activity is immune to this particularly vicious fallacy. The moderate is overwhelmed by the extreme.

Yet the use of the *law to prohibit all activities with a horrible extreme would in due course prohibit everything. There is no activity—eating, *sex, discipline, work, alcohol, *religion, *humour—which does not have a monstrous and extreme expression. There are, of course, occasions when the feared extreme case does actually happen, so it is necessary to draw the line between what is a negligible risk and what is not. Life is a network of such *fine distinctions, and deciding how to respond to them is a matter of *judgment.

Unfortunately, the slippery slope belongs to a class of *fallacies which cannot tolerate *paradox. The most relevant here is the *Sorites Paradox, aka the "paradox of the heap" (Greek: *soros* heap). Imagine a heap of sand. Remove one grain. It is still a heap. Remove another, and another, until eventually it is only sort of a heap, or almost a heap, and finally it is evidently not a heap. There are transitions here, but no borderlines; our descriptions at each stage depend on judgments, and not on explicit rules: this is a "well, yes and no" world, open to debate.[33]

But if the *fuzziness of such transitions is not recognised, the argument snaps to the crude extremes: the moderate is only recognised in the terms of parody. Trust is derided as cringe and surrender, and all options for a post-industrial, post-market future are swept into a bin marked "going back to living in caves", or "taking us back to the Dark Ages". Reference to any *time before the present is lumbered with Thomas Hobbes' phrase "nasty, brutish and short", as the argument settles comfortably into a contempt for the past which makes the present and its predicaments incomprehensible.[34]

The slippery slope is a *denial of judgment, but it can be tricky to avoid, because the alternative lacks finality.

The critic William Empson knew this; the logic of considered *moderation, of ambiguity, fuzziness and paradox, he wrote, commits us to "maintaining oneself between contradictions that can't be solved by analysis". In fact, that tolerance of vague borderlines is essential if we are to think about the hard times ahead. It will be necessary to explore solutions which, taken to the extreme, would be difficult to defend. Every little local stratagem will cast a shadow—a hint of the extreme glowering over the *Lean Economy with hate and the threat of mayhem; but not paralysing it, for communities dominated by the slippery slope—lacking trust, moderation and judgment—will suffer natural deselection.[35]

*Institution, *Reductio ad Absurdum*, Systems Thinking, Damper, Hyperbole, Ironic Space.

SMALL GROUP. This is the nucleus, the little platoon identified by touch, *trust and *conversation which joins up with others to form the larger coalitions and associations which in turn make a society (for a summary table of key group sizes see *Groups and Group Sizes).

The size of the small group is much debated, with the case being made by different scholars for anything between two and twelve.[36] And yet, since 1988, significant progress in understanding small groups has come from the study of groups among non-human primates—especially chimpanzees and gelada baboons known as "bleeding heart" baboons, from the hourglass-shaped patch of bare skin on their chest.[37]

In a large group of observant, restless animals, any one individual on its own has problems: no status, no sustainable ability to defend itself—and probably not much *food either. It follows that every individual needs friends; in fact, he or she needs to belong to a small coalition which can stand up for itself, and whose members know for sure that if any one of them gets into trouble, the others will come to their help.

These coalitions of individuals within the wider group are an example of *holons. They exist for the *well-being and *protection of their own members; and they contribute as members of the larger group and enjoy the benefits it brings. There is a tension here that calls on the intelligent apes' social and political skills: they are more than simply aware of their own relationships with the other individuals in the group; they are also conscious of the relationships *between* other individuals, and they are able to use this knowledge to advantage. They sustain their small-group coalitions of close friends in many ways—and the most important of these is grooming, by which pairs of individuals interact for many hours each day—but they also play politics: they deceive, they rumble the *deceptions, they form alliances. They are explicitly aware of each other as individuals—their age, sex and kinship, their relative power, their past behaviour, their general disposition, their particular intentions, as judged by facial expressions, vocalisations, movement and posture.[38]

All of this calls for brain power which can carry out "parallel processing"—that is, it can imagine and compare alternatives. The anthropologists Andrew Whiten, Richard Byrne and Robin Dunbar have thought through the implications of this. The part of the brain which does all this is the neocortex, the layer of neural tissue which is wrapped and folded round the inner brain. As discussed also in *Neighbourhood, the most useful index of the power of the neocortex, correcting for differences which are due simply to different body sizes, is the "neocortex ratio"—the size of the neocortex relative to the rest of the brain. In most mammals, the neocortex comprises 30–40 percent of their total brain volume (i.e., a neocortex ratio of less than 1:1); in the case of primates, the ratio is between 1:1 and 3:1, rising, in the case of humans, to 4:1.[39]

The larger the small-group coalition, the harder it becomes to keep up with all the internal politics, and the greater the demands on the neocortex, so the neocortex effectively sets a limit to the size of the coalition in which an individual can sustain active membership.[40] And it turns out that neocortex ratios are indeed associated in practice with coalition size: the least gifted primates (with the 1:1 ratio) consistently maintain coalitions of as few as two members; with the greater social intelligence of apes such as the gelada baboons, coalitions rise to between three and five members; and it is consistent with this link between processing power and coalition size that humans can sustain collaboration in groups of as many as twelve.[41]

Twelve does sound rather a lot, and to make sense of this we have to move beyond the physiology, and think in a more pragmatic way about how human groups behave. We tend not to go around—nor indeed to collaborate closely and regularly—with twelve people at the same time. Nonetheless, in most people's lives, there are degrees of intimacy. Surveys of social contacts show that a person typically has around a dozen friends who are regarded as "close" in the sense that he or she would be devastated to hear of the death of any one of them.[42] This group is called the "sympathy" group, consisting of the main *dramatis personae* in the narrative of the individual's life. It includes—it may consist entirely of—close family and kinship bonds, which are generally very robust.[43] While friends often fade away following a change of job or leisure interest, or as a result of just growing up differently, kin often come to stay with each other, and they are more likely to maintain the relationship over a lifetime through difficulties such as illness and quarrels; more often than friends, kin are a source of major help (see "Kinship" sidebar on page 424).[44]

And yet, the sympathy group will almost always include unrelated friends, too. And it is relatively stable, changing only slowly as (for instance) members of the group die, and as younger people join. Here is a network of around twelve people (sometimes rising to fifteen) which, owing to its relatively large size—possesses a wide range of talents: its members participate in big events, such as *carnival and weddings, together; it is counsel in times of emergency—and it is a vital *social capital of intimates from which a *smaller* clique of around five or fewer can be drawn for most actual events, commitments, meals and conversations.[45]

It is, in fact, to such smaller groups that we turn when it is coordinated action, or even a sensible conversation, that is needed. A group of around five is generally enough, and it is in groups on this scale or smaller that people spend almost all their interaction time. Smaller groupings can take the form of strongly bonded permanent relationships, of which the most significant is the

KINSHIP
When trouble made a family

There is a dark but strong image of the power of kin in the story of the march of American pioneers who attempted in 1846–7 to cross the arid Great Basin of Utah on the way to Sacramento, California. They used an untested trail known as the Hastings Cutoff, got lost, were trapped by the snow, and began to starve slowly on a diet of their draft animals, their pets, then their own dead. The survivors, in almost every case, were those with the backing of kinship groups, who helped each other with material and emotional support, sustaining optimism and the will to live. But there was one group which showed something else which qualifies—or extends—the principle of kinship bonds: there was an alliance between two families; the Breens and the Reeds managed to bring their respective groups of nine and six individuals through the ordeal without loss of life, and in doing so showed that pure "kinship" is too simple a description for the bonds that can form to hold a household group together. The Breen-Reed household suggests that the household group can indeed consist of more than one family, under more than one roof; what matters is the commitment to hold the household group together—and kinship helps.[46]

Evidently, 'as-if' kinship can be created between families that have no blood relationship, given a firm enough commitment to do so; the potential for durable association is there. And it was used as a matter of course in large households such as that of the 17th century London baker whose 13 members included children who became workers for at least some part of the day when they reached the age of three. The only word used at that time to describe such a group of people was "family". The *Lean Economy will see forms of the family which are inventive, unexpected and substantially larger than those of the late *market economy. The Breen-Reed household and the baker's household needed to be highly effective and self-sufficient in some critical ways. Their coalition beyond the blood relationship—forming robust *household groups—gave them the practical and political weight they needed.[47]

*family, limited in size, sharing one house, one supper table, one hearth, and recognising a *reciprocal obligation which is "generalised" in the sense that—though not indestructible—it is unconditional.[48] Individual members affirm a commitment to promote the well-being of the other members, and of the group as a whole, and members may even see this collective interest as having priority over, and being more real than, their own *interests as individuals.

That "around five" indicates simply that variants occur: six is common (the army's "section"); in groups of seven there are likely to be some individuals who find they cannot participate enough ("can't get a word in edgeways") and they tend to self-correct themselves down to smaller numbers; groups of eight work notoriously badly: they tend to split into two equal factions, small enough for every individual to feel he or she is essential to it (and so has a power of veto), and large enough collectively to sustain a veto on the whole group. In groups of nine or more, minorities can form in small groups of three or four, which cannot dominate, but can talk things over in advance of the collective *choice. Larger groups of 12–20 have the benefit of bringing wide experience and are a good source of recruitment for smaller groups, but are themselves unwieldy and find it hard really to get down to the detail. Groups above 20 tend to be paralysed by their large size, since individuals (on average) can only speak for 90 seconds in every half hour. The next useful size up, with 35 members (sometimes called the "overnight camp"—*Neighbourhood), develops completely different kinds of discussion, with formal prepared debate rather than extended conversation.[49]

And now back to the primary group. The significance of the number five is that humans can quickly form intensely-interactive coalitions of up to this size, and easily sustain them. And therefore they *will* do so. It is easy for us because, unlike our primate cousins, we have speech, which enables us to collaborate with a group of five, while keeping alive an active and up-to-date relationship with a larger coalition of more than twice that number. For the (non-human) primates, five is beyond the upper limit that even the most gifted can realistically sustain for any length of time: not only is there a limit to the amount of domestic politics their neocortex can handle, but there are not enough hours in the day to sustain serial one-to-one grooming in support of relationships of five or more—and still have time to eat. By contrast, since humans do habitually sustain coalitions of this size, human coalitions of a smaller size are at a relative disadvantage, and there will be occasions on which this disadvantage tells.[50]

In the case of human groups, then, a distinction can be made between two types of primary group:

1. the small closely-collaborative group of five or fewer, which may be permanent (as in the family) or occasional (as in a group that often works together); and

2. the larger twelve-person coalition (i.e., twelve participating adults plus dependent children and old people) that provides the essential resource of close associates and friends.

In the *Lean Economy, members of the larger group might be expected often to live in nearby *households—as in the case of the informal groups of closely cooperative families whose reach extended round a "turning" (a street corner) in the East End of London.[51] This larger group is rarely a single household: as the social historian Peter Laslett notes, "the household has never been an autonomous and self-contained unit"—and in the Lean Economy the word "household" is used quite loosely, referring to family-centred groups, without specifying exactly whether it is a small group comprising an extended family, or one or two smaller groups.[52]

And this ambiguity about the small-scale unit—that "building block" of society—applies equally to the family, as the anthropologist Manning Nash insists, pointing us in a direction which we might not expect:

Developmental schemes, on the basis of evidence, can just as easily begin with the band, or the lineage, or some other kinship atom as they can with the family. The family is apparently a product of economic evolution, not the social substratum or elemental unit sometimes posited.[53]

In local lean economies, it will be as small groups of some kind that many—perhaps most—people take the first steps in investigating, forming or joining the community. The starting point for our existence and our affections is the family. The significance of the somewhat larger (sympathy) group is, in part, that it can call on the help of its members and may be able to use the politics of community to its advantage. The intelligent primates are able to sustain their *wider* communities of thirty individuals or more only by being able to rely on the *loyalty of their *close* friends—and by investing massive emotional effort and time in those coalitions by the proven and effective method of grooming. Lean politics will require the same degree of emotional investment in friendship. The disadvantage of having evolved beyond heavy dependence on grooming for this purpose is that no substitute has quite that direct power of physical contact; the advantages of speech go a long way towards compensating for this, but physical contact, about which the non-tactile *market economy is confused and embarrassed, has an important—and in some ways irreplaceable—part in forming and sustaining bonds between individuals. A "bond" implies both passive capture and active friendship, touch and speech, risk and security, service and *freedom: that is, it is a marriage of opposites: a *holon. It is the active principle of *community. The combination of *conversation and breaking bread together comes close, like grooming, to making and sustaining a *contract.

*Reciprocity and Cooperation 〉 Direct Engagement, Play, Public Sphere and Private Sphere, Tactile Deprivation.

SMALL SCALE. See Scale.

SOCIAL CAPITAL. The social capital of a *community is its social life—the links of *cooperation and friendship between its members. It is the *institutions, the common *culture and *ceremony, the *good faith and

S

*reciprocal obligations, the *civility and citizenship, the *play, *humour and *conversation which make a living community. Social capital is the *ecosystem in which a culture lives.

Imagine a society which shares an inheritance of *stories and poems which have grown out of its own story and experience; imagine that it consists of *neighbourhoods where the adults know each other, where they meet often, where members of *families have regular meals together, where people tend to live for a long time in the same *place, and where there are numerous interconnected *networks—music groups, churches, parent-teacher associations, *carnival . . . Almost every society contains this social capital to some extent, but, as Robert Putnam shows in his seminal book, *Bowling Alone*, a society in which it is strong can draw on the cooperation, energy and brilliance of its people; crime is less, education is better, *health is stronger, *democracy is more secure.[54]

A test of the power of social capital is *education. There are many things that can influence a community's schools; they include racial composition, affluence, economic inequality, adult educational levels, poverty rates, educational spending, teachers' salaries, class sizes, family structure, religious affiliation and the *competitive presence of schools in the *private sector. And yet, the single most important factor is social capital. In fact, efforts to improve the performance of schools in the conventional ways, unless backed by effective measures to defend or build social capital in the area are, to varying degrees, a waste of time and money. This is illustrated by a comparison of US Standard Attainment Test (SAT) scores in contrasting communities. In North Carolina, SAT scores are low; in Connecticut, they are high. The critical difference between the two states is not wealth, but social capital: social capital sets up the conditions in which successful education is possible. Putnam makes this point graphically: if North Carolina's residents wanted their efforts in education to be as productive as those in Connecticut, he writes, they could do any of the following:

increase their turnout in presidential elections by 50 percent; double their frequency of club meeting attendance; triple the number

of non-profit organisations per thousand inhabitants; or attend church two more times per month.[55]

And it is not just education which grows in the fertile soil of social capital: there is a direct impact on health and happiness, too. The more integrated we are into our community life by networks of friendship, with participation in social events and membership of religious and civic associations, the less likely we are to experience colds, heart attacks, strokes, cancer, depression and premature death. Indeed, the *positive* contributions to health made by social integration and social support rival in strength the *detrimental* contributions of well-established biomedical risk factors like cigarette smoking, obesity, elevated blood pressure and physical inactivity. Regular club attendance, volunteering, entertaining and church attendance are at least as powerful as conditions of happiness as getting a college degree, more than doubling your income, and maintaining a successful marriage.[56]

There is a sense here that everyone can be a pillar of the community, that citizenship is not just about obeying, and doing as one ought, but about loving one's society, being comfortable in it and even being stimulated by it—living means participating as a citizen; participating as a citizen means belonging to networks of reciprocal services; reciprocal service means a knowledge of, and regard for, local detail, and a tact and sociability that has the vital function of sustaining democracy. There is nothing intrinsic to democracy to prevent it from imposing tyranny and oppression over the minority, nor from collapsing into a bitter contest of aggressively-asserted and mutually-incompatible rights, nor from reducing all issues to facile *populism, nor from *betraying itself and giving its freedoms away. To endure, it needs the backing of shared common assumptions about fundamentals; it needs access to expertise—and roots in social capital. Social capital protects democracy, providing the essential foundation on which it is built, and it does this in at least four ways.

First, the presence of social capital means that people tend to meet each other a lot, providing the essential interactions from which it is possible to build mutual *trust; it sets up the conditions for friendship, for forging alliances, familiarity, tolerance and under-standing where otherwise there would be indifference or rivalry. Secondly, informal networks provide an opportunity for debate; talking about issues over meals, for instance, can enable crude, first-blush prejudice to mature to considered and moderated opinion. Thirdly, the clubs and local activities which are part of social capital can provide training in some of the skills of healthy *politics—the skills of organisation, listening and tact. And fourthly, social capital provides a local power base; a locality cannot be pushed around by gov-ernment with the same ease as individual citizens with no organised backing.

The way in which the local civilities of social capital form the building blocks of democracy has been studied in the case of the twenty *regional governments formed in Italy in the early 1970s. Some of them were dismal failures—inefficient, lethargic and corrupt; others were successful beyond *expectations. Why the differences? Putnam explains,

> The best predictor is one that Alexis de Tocque-ville might have expected. Strong traditions of civic engagement—voter turnout, newspaper readership, membership in choral societies and literary circles, Lions Clubs, and soccer clubs— were the hallmarks of a successful region.[57]

Another way of thinking of social capital is to see it (with the philosopher Michael Sandel) as society's "institutions": here we have the links, *loyalties, *coop-erations and meeting places that make a society: clubs, schools, universities, *families, villages, town councils, regiments, choirs, *traditions and churches, the struc-tures and detail which seed social capital and affirm *freedom. And pubs. Yes, like everything else, excess brings its problems but, by some standards, pubs are the most important hubs of all—places where people get together and talk to each other: that is what civili-sation is for. Governments that are really serious about reducing the costs of loneliness and mental health prob-lems could make no better investment than a reduction in the tax on beer.[58]

These institutions enable people to develop their potential and to align their aims in a *common pur-pose. Members retain their personalities, *identities,

friendships, *humour, inventiveness, and their ability to think—and they adopt the institutional culture with-out having to surrender their judgment to it. People make their institutions; the institutions make a society that gives the place and the community that lives there an *identity.[59]

Given that social capital is essential in all these ways, it is a matter of concern that it is going through a process of attrition which has much in common with the patterns of decline and depletion in *oil, *water, soil fertility and the biological systems which stabilise the *climate.

The decline of social capital

One reason for the decline is the high degree of individ-ual self-sufficiency made possible by the market and by its convenient consumer technologies; voluntary net-works of *reciprocity are not the indispensable lifeline they used to be before the days of convenience goods and the efficient *market.

Other reasons include:

1. A lack of time, particularly for women, who were the mainstays of social capital, but who are now too stretched between careers, their personal and family lives to have any time left over. And men's lives have not eased up to enable them to fill the gap. Equal opportunity is substantially *calibrated in terms of *money and incomes, and unpaid participation in the *informal economy of the community is not seen to have anything useful to contribute to that contest.

2. The lack of time in schools for education in the skills of social capital, such as music, literature, cooking, acting, debating and sports. The standard-isation of education makes people less interesting to each other;

3. Car dependency, which means that people rarely meet *neighbours in the street;

4. Inner city architecture, which often provides no space even for a table at which families can conveniently eat together;

5. The decline of *crafts and the interesting individu-ality they brought. The members of a community need to have at least *something* interesting to contribute if they are to build its social capital;

6. The industrialisation of *agriculture, and the waning of the rural economy, with its attachment to the *land, and to the people who provide the food.

7. The decadence and infantilism that has overtaken religious services, making them unbearable to grown-ups (*Liturgy);

8. Ethnic mixing, which (according to subsequent research by Putnam) tends to cause people of all ethnic backgrounds to "hunker down", keeping to themselves. In these conditions, *trust (even of one's own race) is lower, friends fewer, altruism and community-cooperation rarer, confidence in local *institutions weaker, and TV watching heavier.[60] A darker side of this is "communalism" — communities defining themselves by race, with variable obligations to citizens of other races, which may include the absence of any peaceable obligation within the wider community (*Multiculturalism).[61]

9. And Putnam's research suggests that very substantial damage to social capital has been caused by television

(see "Circuit Breaker" sidebar) and its close relations such as video games, which mean that many children never learn the principle of *playing with real people. There have to be some *caveats* here: the "circuit breaker" research referenced in the sidebar can clearly not be replicated, and there are those that deny that television has had much effect. Nonetheless, the evidence of the decline itself is telling.[62]

Putnam's research refers mainly to America, and no claim is made that it applies everywhere, but within the limits of his research, the results are striking. Participation is in decline across the range of political and civic life. Between the 1960s and the turn of the century, the following fell by around fifty percent (or more): the number of people who took a *leadership role in any local organisation, membership in a group with a political interest, newspaper readership, knowledge of politics among young people (e.g., a correct answer to the question, "Who controls the House of Representatives?"), and attendance at public meetings on town

CIRCUIT BREAKER
Television breaks up the networks that form the basis for social capital

"A major commitment to television viewing", writes Robert Putnam, "is incompatible with major commitment to community life".[63] People for whom television is their primary form of entertainment (compared with demographically matched people who differ only in saying that TV is *not*), volunteer and work on community projects less often, attend fewer club meetings, spend less time visiting friends, entertain at home less, picnic less, are less interested in politics, give blood less often, make fewer long-distance calls, send fewer greeting cards and less email, and express more road rage.[64]

A telling casualty of television has been the former practice of visiting neighbours in the evening for gossip, music, *stories, *dance, food. In the southwest of Ireland it was called "scoriarching";[65] in Wendell Berry's Kentucky, it was called "sitting till bedtime"[66] — and it ceased in place after place with the arrival of television. The Amish, with their celebrated willpower and foresight, kept television out of their communities on the grounds that it would destroy their visiting practices.[67]

A survey of research into long hours of television (more than four hours a day), starting in childhood, has been published by Dr. Aric Sigman. On this evidence, heavy exposure makes people ill-equipped for a positive contribution to social capital. It is associated with attention-deficit disorder, impaired development of the brain, speech and social skills, *sleep deprivation, minimal time spent in conversation, reading and *play, increased violence and bullying, overeating and lack of exercise — leading to obesity and related conditions: reduced libido, depression and poorly-developed social confidence and critical *judgment. The survey finds heavy television watching to be destructive across the range of practical, cognitive, social and emotional intelligences.[68]

or school affairs. At the same time, voting declined by a quarter, and the trend accelerated after 1985, with active involvement in community organisations falling by 45 percent.[69] And there is the same story of decline in religious participation. From the 1960s, attendance and involvement in religious activities fell by between 25 and 50 percent, and the remnants of religion have become personal consumer items: *religion's function as a collective act which defines a community, in the Christian church especially, has been buried.[70] Even picnics declined by half between 1975 and 1995. "Americans are spending a lot less time breaking bread with friends than we did twenty or thirty years ago", writes Putnam. "We engage less often . . ."[71] He concludes,

> In effect, the classic institutions of American civic life, both religious and secular, have been "hollowed out". Seen from without, the institutional edifice appears virtually intact—little decline in professions of faith, formal membership down just a bit, and so on. When examined more closely, however, it seems that decay has consumed the load-bearing beams of our civic infrastructure.[72]

Here is evidence from a different source that social capital, expressed in doing things together, is in trouble. An observer of British society, Bill Bryson, is writing of the Ashington Group of artists—the "Pitmen Painters", whose members were miners in the pit town of Ashington in Northumberland in the 1930s:

> It is quite astonishing, seeing it now, to realise just how rich life was, and how enthusiastically opportunities were seized, in Ashington in the years before the war. At one time the town boasted a philosophical society, with a busy year-round programme of lectures, concerts and evening classes; an operatic society; a dramatic society; a workers' educational association; a miners' welfare institute with workshops and yet more lecture rooms; and gardening clubs, cycling clubs, athletics clubs, and others in similar vein almost beyond counting. Even the workingmen's clubs, of which Ashington boasted twenty-two at its peak, offered libraries and reading rooms

for those who craved more than a pint or two of Federation Ale. The town had a thriving theatre, a ballroom, five cinemas, and a concert chamber called the Harmonic Hall. When, in the 1920s, the Bach Choir from Newcastle performed on a Sunday afternoon at the Harmonic Hall, it drew an audience of 2,000. Can you imagine anything remotely like that now?

And then, one by one, they faded away—the Thespians, the Operatic Society, the reading rooms and lecture halls. Even the five cinemas all quietly closed their doors. Today the liveliest diversion in Ashington is a Noble's amusement arcade.[73]

*Capital, Lean Economics, Presence, Public Sphere and Private Sphere, Dollar-a-Day Fallacy, Socially Solvent, Social Entropy.

SOCIAL CITY. A design for small cities which combines the advantages of dense housing with *neighbours and services in walking distance, and open space for food production and a rural setting.

Local economies, to quote William Cobbett, "must, of course, have some *land".[74] One way of providing it was explored and described in the first years of the twentieth century by Ebenezer Howard, with his vision of "Garden Cities". Howard believed that cities can be designed for fresh air, fresh *food, and the *freedom, sights, sounds and scents of the country. Although people need the jobs and *social life provided in towns, they do not have to be forced into choosing between one need and the other. The good city provides both:

> Town and country *must be married,* [to provide] better opportunities of social intercourse than are enjoyed in any crowded city, while yet the beauties of nature may encompass and enfold each dweller therein.[75]

The way to achieve this best-of-both-worlds, Howard argued, is to build cities with a dense population, but on a *small scale. Cities of 30,000 people living in houses with the narrow twenty-foot (6m) frontage and long 130-foot (40m) gardens which were typical of his day, could be built on a mere 150 acres (61 ha). At the

S

Detail of Garden City, as drawn by Ebenezer Howard, showing Grand Avenue, Crystal Palace, parks, gardens and access to open country.

same time, he allowed generous space for boulevards, a Grand Avenue, a large central park, gardens and a "Crystal Palace" complete with winter garden and a shopping centre (see "Detail of Garden City" diagram). When all this is included, the total area of the city is 1,000 acres (445 ha) — still small enough for every part to be easily accessible on foot. No inhabitant is further than 240 yards (220m) from either the Central Park or the start of the countryside outside the town.[76]

Although the scale is small, it is not small enough to sustain the *reciprocal cooperation of the *parish, whose upper limit is about 5,000. And in fact, Howard's model

suggested groupings of 5,000 in six "quarters" — a well-established subdivision in the medieval period, and approximately the anticipated population intended for the new town of Poundbury in Dorset, which is currently under construction. Howard's garden cities would be, in that sense, groups of six Poundburies, each with its own green space and food-growing areas, and the whole set of six collectively surrounded by open countryside. Howard then followed through the *holonic pattern suggested by this, imagining that each garden city could in turn be in a group of six, surrounding a seventh — somewhat larger (with a population of

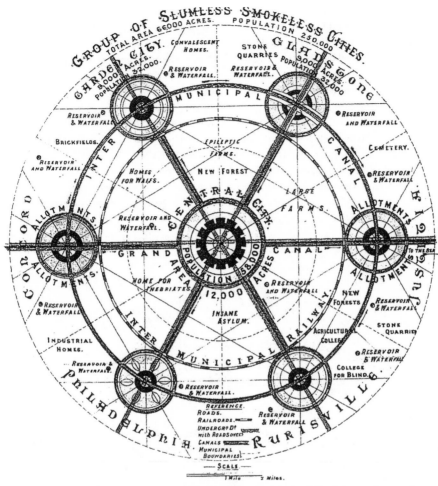

Ebenezer Howard's cluster of garden cities, with a large central city, *land for local *food, *water, *energy, *materials and recreation, and links between them. This image is the starting point for the modern concept of the social city.

58,000), a centre for administration and the more elaborate *arts. That pattern of cities could then be extended, with each group set in its own countryside; the cities of 30,000 would have a countryside of at least 5,000 acres (about 2,000 hectares), enough to provide much of their population's need for food, together with land for forest, water, wildlife and homes for some 2,000 people working in rural trades and *agriculture (see "Cluster of Garden Cities" diagram).[77]

The success of the towns inspired by Howard's principles, however, has been mixed. The first and greatest achievement was that some were actually built.

Letchworth and Welwyn Garden City were to a large extent based on Howard's design, and others, such as Hampstead Garden Suburb and New Earswick in the UK, Margaretenhöhe and Römerstadt in Germany, and Radburn in New Jersey were influenced by it. There is no doubt that these are in many ways good *places to live. They have space, trees, landscaping and the benefit of outstanding architects such as Barry Parker and Raymond Unwin.[78]

But what Howard had in mind was not just a model of town planning. It was revolution, designed to give people a say in their own affairs, to produce local food, to integrate industry within walking distance of where workers lived, to eliminate poverty, to transform the *health and nutrition of the population, and to fund their pensions from the incomes earned by the city from rents. The reality, however, has fallen far short of his complex ambition. None of the new towns built under Howard's influence have actually come close to the original specification. They have been built singly, not as part of a *network; the use of local countryside to provide food for the town has not been attempted; they have been built to the wrong scale (often too small, e.g., Römerstadt); or they have been dormitory suburbs with no industry (Hampstead Garden Suburb); and the financial arrangements proposed by Howard have not happened.

The balance between compact residential areas and open areas for gardens has never settled down into anything better than very approximate agreement about what a garden city is. There is nothing compact, for instance, about Hampstead Garden Suburb, which is a standing invitation to drive your Volvo a couple of miles every time you discover that there is no milk in the fridge. As for the Suburb's town centre, there is an indecisive space of rose-beds surrounded by public buildings without a shop or even a pub—all of which turned out to be a dry run for the architect Edwin Lutyens' enormous Viceroy's House and its setting in New Delhi.

In fact, the ambiguity is right there in the design. Even if you do live in a compact street in Howard's Garden City, you become a mere speck on the landscape as soon as you turn off it into the Grand Avenue. And the only message that people seemed really to agree on—at a time when cars were just beginning and there was an

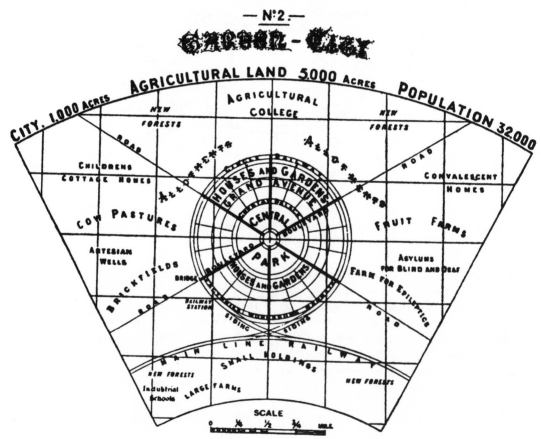

Garden City in its local setting, showing road and rail links

intense desire to get away from the smoke—was that it's all right to use lots of space.

The selective reading of Howard's all-embracing vision was inevitable, and it started almost immediately. The title of the first edition of the book, *To-Morrow: A Peaceful Path to Real Reform*, was thought to be too revolutionary, and the second and subsequent editions appeared as *Garden Cities of To-Morrow*. The beautiful diagram which showed the network of cities was omitted, leaving just a truncated version with a city sitting in the middle, with lots of space round it (see "Garden City in its Local Setting" diagram). Like *Small is Beautiful*, whose numerous non-readers claim to have got the general gist from the title, *Garden Cities of To-Morrow* inserted into the public mind the idea that it is about cities with lots of gardens at some undefined time in the future. This conceptoid was then grasped as an excuse for wholesale destruction of cityscapes and for their replacement by "projects" with their characteristic features of concrete, worn grass and communal space in the 'no man's land' between *private and public, whose possibilities for crime and local youth mafias have been exploited to much effect.[79]

It was against such authoritarian simplifications by the post-war planners—who appealed vaguely to the idea that "gardens", "cities", "space" and "community" could be stir-fried together—that Jane Jacobs launched her storming counterattack. She wrote from the point of view of a Jewish mum with a non-negotiable *need for a delicatessen within walking distance, along with streets that are well-used and safe, supporting the intricate *cultural life of a living city, with a good supply of friendly shops where you can meet *neighbours and with whom you could leave your house key if necessary. The use of space needs to be dense enough for people walking along the street to get to meet each other, and for shops and cafés to have potential customers in the vicinity, on foot. And, she added, "compact" does not rule out space for intensely-productive gardens. In place of these very obvious benefits, the massive projects minimised space where it would have been useful—in the flats, in small gardens, or on the threshold between households and street—and maximised space where it wasn't—in deserted areas whose only value was silence, interrupted at night by the occasional scream (see "Play Space" sidebar).[80]

PLAY SPACE
With *unintended consequences

A few days after the murder of two sixteen-year-old boys in a playground on the midtown of West Side Manhattan, I paid a morbid visit to the area. The near-by streets were evidently back to normal. Hundreds of children, directly under the eyes of innumerable adults using the sidewalks themselves and looking from windows, were engaged in a vast variety of sidewalk games and whooping pursuits. The sidewalks were dirty, they were too narrow for the demands put upon them, and they needed shade from the sun. But here was no scene of arson, mayhem, or the flourishing of dangerous weapons. In the playground where the night-time murder had occurred, things were apparently back to normal too. Three small boys were setting a fire under a wooden bench. Another was having his head beaten against the concrete. The custodian was absorbed in solemnly and slowly hauling down the American flag.

JANE JACOBS, *The Death and Life of Great American Cities*, 1961.[81]

Howard, then, was misunderstood. But he did rather ask for it. A system designed to be an urban, rural, democratic, food-producing, spacious, compact, poverty-eliminating pension fund is a poor example of the rule that systems work best when they are designed to do one thing well (*Relevance). "Compact" is a virtue, and if intense land use is subdivided too much by space, it becomes about as compact as confetti. Poundbury is compact: the town is proper town; the country around it (apart from its close neighbour, Dorchester) is proper country.[82]

The social city: attempts to live up to the ideal

It is now widely (but not universally) accepted that the living heart of the city—with shops, workplaces and railway stations—should be within walking, cycling or tram distance of where people live, producing a pattern with relatively small towns, linked to each other along a railway and lightly-used road—like beads on a string. That makes sense for so many reasons that we can be reasonably confident that the model would have been developed even without Howard's early approximation.[83]

Many versions of it have been produced in theory and practice. One "sustainable urban form" (developed by Susan Owens) consists of small settlements of 20,000–30,000 people living within walking distance of the main facilities they need; these small towns would often, but not always, be clustered in groups of around ten, to produce a social city of around 200,000. Another version (by Michael Breheny and Ralph Rookwood) has local centres with a mixture of activities to take pressure off the congested centre of cities, and to reduce the need for transport. Communities are arranged around dense, intensive developments at the centres, to which people can walk, and there is a use of local land for recreation, for storing water, and for growing food and firewood, fertilised with composted *waste from the town.[84]

The architect Peter Calthorpe's designs for suburban development in California are based on these principles, with clusters of intense activity within walking distance of where people live; high-density terrace housing keeps distances short, and his towns are separated by accessible food-growing areas in open country, a principle that is now embedded into the General Plan for Sacramento. The principle has also influenced the plans for Stockholm's "transit villages" and the "Thames Gateway" in the United Kingdom, which has towns on a relatively modest scale strung out along the metro route.[85]

We may wonder how relevant these models are to the settled *Lean Economy. They imply a large *population, *transport and *energy flows, high material *living standards and a thriving *market. There is a sense here of finding solutions to problems that are just on the way to going out of date. And yet, there does seem to be a common *grammar of village-planning here—urban villages and rural villages alike—akin to Christopher Alexander's "pattern language" (*Lean Building). The principle, for example, of compact living space, distinct from the wide landscape to which it belongs. This isn't really about a marriage of town and country; it is a chaste in-touch separateness—a *dance. *Lean food, *lean materials, *lean defence; all will call for the intense use of local space. For the Lean Economy, compact means compact.[86]

*Groups and Group Sizes, Modularity.

SOCIAL ENTROPY. The collapse of the complex social and *cultural structures of society. This is the social equivalent—welcomed at first as exciting *diversity—of the chaotic disordering of *natural systems and organisms when they are destroyed or burn. The process of destruction always has a positive side—burning wood gives out heat, for instance, and plants are broken down into energy when eaten—and social *entropy, too, has its attractions, since a society's orderly structures can be broken down in an *exhilarating time of licence, spontaneous self-fulfilment and economic *growth. The inhibitions are down: society consumes itself—burning up its inherited social structures to meet today's wants.

The critical question is whether some of the original order will remain—equivalent to the DNA of the organisms in an ecology—a point of reference, a guide to recovery. There is a lot of coding for social order in the human mind, but there may not be the benign external conditions required for recovery—as John Gray writes, "to put together the delicate spider's web of traditions that new technologies and unfettered markets have blown away".[87]

And yet, the powers of renewal, when the conditions do exist—in the case of the natural environment at least—are wonderful, as Walt Whitman's poem, *This Compost*, reminds us:

> Now I am terrified at the earth, it is that calm
>   and patient,
> It grows such sweet things out of such
>   corruptions,
> It turns harmless and stainless on its axis, with
>   such endless successions of disease'd corpses,
> It distils such exquisite winds out of such
>   infused fetor,
> It renews with such unwitting looks its
>   prodigal, annual, sumptuous crops,
> It gives such divine materials to men, and
>   accepts such leavings from them at last.[88]

*Kaikaku, Resilience, Capital, Needs and Wants, Gaia, Public Sphere and Private Sphere.

SOCIAL MOBILITY. When the values of a society switch from decentralised community building to centralised competition organised around making *money, then the ambitions of its people switch in the same way. The *cooperative ethic of *neighbourhood gives way to the *competitive ethic of relative advantage, with its corollary of relative disadvantage for those that have been less successful in the competition.

The social mobility of the late market economy has become a defining *ethic. It implies that *manual skills and the *places and *communities that are left behind by the socially mobile represent failure. Community is a place the talented want to leave. The *market economy mines society for its talent, confident that community won't be needing it.

This recognition that social mobility has its disadvantages as well as its merits lacks credibility in an economy which sees values in terms only of individual advantage, and to which the idea of community is invisible. But, in the *Lean Economy, community is central, and it will no longer be a standard assumption that the first thing talented people want to do is to get out of their inherited communities and concentrate in distant centres of talent, power and dislocation. Social mobility is one of the concepts about which we will need to start thinking afresh. When community is thought-through, it leads to conclusions which are unpalatable to the *expectations of the present.

*Freedom, Empowerment, Identity, Money Fallacy, Social Entropy.

SOCIAL SECURITY. See Lean Social Security.

SOCIALLY SOLVENT. The state of possessing the currency of *social capital: something—perhaps diverse *skills and *character—to bring to *reciprocal relationships.

SORITES PARADOX (the paradox of the heap). A pile of 10,000 grains of sand constitutes a heap; one grain does not. No problem so far, but it is impossible to put your finger on the *number of grains at which a non-heap turns into a heap.

The *paradox is an illustration of *fuzzy logic, which recognises that although two categories may be quite clear at the extremes—e.g., heap/non-heap, good/bad,

moral/immoral, tall/not tall; interrogation/torture, affection/abuse, punishment/abuse—there is no precise point at which one turns into the other; instead, there is a grey area, and dealing with these is one of the critical tests of *judgment.

It is often assumed that *truth is a black-and-white affair—something is either true or false, as in: children should be taught the difference between right and wrong. The Sorites paradox is an illustration of things being not so simple.

*Slippery Slope, Truth.

SORTING PROBLEM, THE. Work can be divided into two essential kinds: mixing and sorting (unmixing). There are *exceptions subject to circumstances, but as a rule it can be affirmed that mixing is most efficiently done on the large scale, while sorting is most efficiently done on the small scale. This latter is an example of a diseconomy (inefficiency) of scale.

Here we discover a way of making sense of mixed messages about economies of scale. *Lean Logic* tells a clear story about the importance of economies of scale and specialisation of labour in supporting civic societies (*Intermediate Economy). It also tells a story about the case for doing things on a small scale, locally (*Localisation). They are both right, but some *reflection is needed.

An example to start with: to mix (shuffle) a pack of cards, it is necessary to collect all the cards together—this is done quickly on the large scale, with little attention to detail. But to sort it into tricks and patterns you need step-by-step deliberation on the small scale.

For an example closer to practical matters, consider the case of bread. We start with the ingredients, ready and waiting in the village bakery: flour, water, yeast, salt; an oven, bread tins, wood; the *expertise of the baker. Now light the fire, mix the dough, bake, turn-out, sell. This is primarily a mixing operation; the stores of bulk ingredients are mixed and turned into a more complex product; and it has required a lot of energy, as proved by the ash, which is all that is left of the wood. It is clear that economies of scale apply. If the village baker—rather than each of the village's 150 households—makes the bread, the process requires only one fire, one mixing process, one delivery of ingredients, and one daily use of the equipment. The bread also benefits from the

S

baker's specialist *skills. If every household were to make its own bread, there would indeed be secondary benefits such as the satisfaction that comes from doing so, but from the point of view of economies of *energy, *materials and *time—that is, efficiency—the advantage of central provision by the village bakery are evident.

Economies of scale when mixing also apply in (for instance) making wine and beer, glasses, pots or nails, weaving cloth, baking bread, printing newsletters. The geometry of scale can work in favour of bigness: the larger the containers you use, the less glass or metal you need to store a given amount of liquid. In order to keep itself alive, our community has to do a great deal of mixing, and there is a case for doing some of it centrally, rather than on the scale of individual households.

But then there is the sorting out to do. From each of these processes, there is an end-product and there is also leftover waste such as: empty bottles, broken pots, bent nails, urine, faeces and unwanted paper. If a *closed-loop flow of materials is to be maintained, that lot has to be sorted. Now, the first principle of sorting is: try to stop it getting scrambled in the first place. In the case of *water management, for instance, an effective and manageable use of human sewage as a source of fertility requires (ideally) that urine and faeces should be separate, so that they can be used and treated in the different ways they need. Urine goes rancid quickly and, if it is to be used in the garden, it needs to be used quickly. Composted faeces should be handled on a small scale for many reasons: if it is in large bulk, it will be (unless constantly turned) deprived of oxygen, with the result that it will break down very slowly, anaerobically, producing a challenging smell, and losing nitrogen in the process. In short, waste in all its variety

A SMITH ON THE CASE

Another look at the distinction between (small-scale) sorting and (large-scale) mixing.

All mixing—all provision of goods and services—involves a certain amount of sorting, and some sorting involves mixing, so tolerance of *exceptions and that *fuzzy borderline is necessary here, along with, perhaps, a guideline borrowed from Adam Smith.

In his famous explanation of the improved *efficiencies that can be had from the division of labour, he suggests that there are three reasons for them: the dexterity that comes from repetition, the saving of time that comes from concentrating on one task rather than switching between tasks, and the convenient use of machines. Each of these are available to the task because it is being done in bulk—as, for instance, in the making of nails, where . . .

> . . . the division of labour, by reducing every man's business to some one simple operation, and by making this operation the sole employment of his life, necessarily increased very much the dexterity of the workman. A common smith, who, though accustomed to handle the hammer, has never been used to make nails, if upon some particular occasion he is obliged to attempt it, will scarcely, I am assured, be able to make above two or three hundred nails in a day, and those, too, very bad ones. . . . [By contrast,] I have seen several boys under twenty years of age who had never exercised any other trade but that of making nails, and who, when they exerted themselves, could make each of them upward of two thousand three hundred nails in a day.[89]

Perhaps if Smith were writing now, he would have used the case of bottle manufacture.

Every kind and shape of drinks bottle is routinely mixed by giant distribution networks and by households. Separating them all out and returning them to the drinks manufacturers to be reused would require a costly establishment of labour-intensive sorting, which is why it isn't done. If the drinks providers were on a small (village) scale, the sorting would happen easily: all bottles would be reused. At a *household level, jam makers reuse their bottles for many years.

has to be sorted—which in this context means, as far as possible and as a clear and feasible aim, kept separate. Sorting starts with the first moment of use. But all this depends on it being done on a small scale.

Generally speaking, the sorting of *waste on a small scale has these properties (relative to sorting at large scale):

1. The waste materials have more surface area (per unit of volume), making them more accessible both to the sorters and to the air.

2. The sorting is more accurate, allowing discrimination at a higher level of detail.

3. The sorting is a smaller task, which can be done easily as part of the day's work (rather than as a full-time job). This means that better *judgment, referring to context, needs and opportunities, can be made when considering the detail of how to bring this waste back into the local *ecology and economy.

4. There is the opportunity for effective *feedback and learning: the small-scale sorter is always looking for ways to reduce the task.

5. It avoids the disgusting and dangerous properties of industrial-scale waste.[90]

6. It is cheaper: small-scale sorting sits easily in the *informal economy. Large-scale sorting is a horrible job that has to be paid for.

7. It requires less energy: it can be done entirely by hand. Large-scale sorting requires heavy-material-handling equipment and the energy for magnetic-separation systems and the like.

8. It requires less transport, since waste materials do not have to be driven to a sorting centre and back.

The use of the small scale has benign implications. It limits the depth of disorder that is likely to build up if the sorting task is allowed to accumulate on the large scale.

It may, therefore, avoid the necessity for the comprehensive crash—or "release"—discussed in the *Wheel of Life. In fact, as discussed in that entry, within the bounds of the small scale, cycles of release and renewal can take place without being lethal to the system as a whole; they confer long life on a large—but subdivided (*modular)—natural or cultural community. Nature goes through these sub-cycles all the time. If they are allowed to happen, they can prevent the need for a large-scale crash, making the ecology as a whole *resilient.

Small-scale sorting, by preventing bulk chaos, can sustain a living ecology. The enabling condition is that the system should give it a chance. *Small scale is not a matter of preference: it is a requirement of *logic.

*Casuistry, Manual Skills, Vernacular.

SPECIAL PLEADING. An argument which, though strictly true, presents its case slanted by leaving out *relevant information or by giving undue emphasis to one part of the story. For some (estate agents, barristers), slanted arguments go with the job; and all arguments with persuasive content have special pleading within them somewhere, so we tend to be alert to the risk and to make allowances. In other cases, unless there is someone around to put the other side, the potential to mislead is powerful.[91]

Most arguments can be understood as statements arising from a particular context. Taking the fifth form on a hill walk would be a bad thing from the point of view of health and safety, insurance, cost, wear-and-tear on the mountain paths, and time away from studying; it would be a good thing from the point of view of cardiovascular fitness, fun, friendships, knowledge of geography, learning how to cook bacon and eggs in the rain, getting away from television, and having something to talk about. Emphasis on any of those arguments would be a case of special pleading.

So, what would we do without it? Would every enthusiasm get bogged down in impartial balance and indecisiveness? Perhaps a more tolerant name for this *fallacy is "advocacy". *Lean Logic* is an advocate for *lean thinking, *TEQs (Tradable Energy Quotas), *ritual, *carnival, *anarchism and many other things, claiming that these are support systems for *freedom of thought. But they are all expressions of particular contexts, and introduce bias. That does not make them wrong, but it makes them forms of special pleading.

Advocacy provides a service: it makes a case: it is the energy- and data-source for argument, an expression of the ethic of *incrementalism, guided in *conversation and in *practice by serial correction of error. Without advocacy, no errors would be corrected; no case would be made. There would be no impertinence. It would be night. There would be nothing to do, except . . .

S

... the sable Throne behold
Of Night primaeval, and of Chaos old!
Before her, Fancy's gilded clouds decay,
And all its varying rain-bows die away.

Alexander Pope, The Dunciad, 1742.[92]

SPIKING GUNS. Giving plausibility to an otherwise implausible argument by acknowledging that it is not perfect.

Format:

> "I admit the argument is not perfect, which means that any objections you may have are already fully discounted . . .".

Example:

> "Not even the most ardent Europhile would claim that the EU has achieved perfection . . . But sustainable development is a journey. Direction and rate of progress matter more than the precise point that has been reached at any time. By that measure, environmentalists and champions of the European project are on the same side."[93]

*Cant, Fallacies.

SPIRIT. St. Paul promised this:

> The peace of God which passeth all understanding shall keep your hearts and minds.[94]

There is a lot there. There is a radiant peace which we do not understand. It exists in the depth of our being. It is the gift of God.[95]

Properties like these seem to be beyond the competence of *Lean Logic's* *dirty-handed, located approach to matters, and beyond the reach of description. They can be *danced, perhaps. Made into music. But not described, because they live below the level of the conscious mind, in the dark territory explored by the German philosopher Johann Friedrich Herbart. His *Psychology as Science* (1824–1825) takes us *"unter der Schwelle des Bewusstseins"* — "below the threshold of consciousness". The phrase was shortened into Latin as *"sub lumen"* (below the threshold) and comes back into English as "sublime". *Lean Logic* once, briefly, maybe, encountered the sublime in the natural world, when the

surface of the River Stour in John Constable's meadows near Dedham burned bright with the setting sun.[96]

If the spirit is anywhere, it is in the natural *ecology. This entry therefore starts with one of the threads of recent history in which people's *encounter with nature was shaped by good intentions which crowded out the spirit. At first sight, this may seem to have nothing to do with the spirit—and this is in a sense true, for we shall now be visiting a place and time where the spirit becomes conspicuous by its absence. Then we get closer to it. Maybe. We can't be sure.

The Spirit of the Wild

Our illustration of the absence of the spirit comes to us from the story of the conservation of the American forests and the treatment of the wild animals that lived there. The mountain lions, wolves, wolverines, coyotes, bobcats, bears, beavers and birds were long-term residents, but (having no evident economic value, yet living on the forest's output) they were reduced to the status of vermin, aka "varmints". This seeming uselessness applies, in fact, to most of the native plants and animals in an ecology, and the conservation ecologist Aldo Leopold (1887–1948) commented on it in his essay "The Land Ethic":

> Of the 22,000 higher plants and animals native to Wisconsin, it is doubtful whether more than 5 percent can be sold, eaten, or otherwise put to economic use . . .[97]

. . . and from that point of view, there might seem to be little point in going to any trouble or expense to *protect them. But, as Leopold came to realise, there is a lot wrong with that conclusion. Closer study of "useless" species tends to reveal that they do have a useful function after all, one of which is to sustain an ecology that supports the useful ones. But, more to the point, life does not need to justify itself on the grounds of being useful. On the contrary,

> . . . these creatures are members of the biotic community, and if (as I believe) its stability depends on its integrity, they are entitled to continuance . . . [It is] a matter of biotic right, regardless of the presence or absence of economic advantage to us.[98]

That is, obvious utility is not the only frame of reference for recognising the value of things. HRH The Prince of Wales speaks in this context of the "sacred". Another common word for it is "spiritual". Nature's *ecological complexity, its *harmonic order, its grace and *elegance, its seemingly effortless competence, challenge humans to find a right response. The mind cannot fully understand it. The body cannot be fully part of it. The spirit, however, can affirm it; it can, given modesty and time, learn to love it.[99]

The conservation of American forests and the treatment of the varmints living there is the story of a long and bitter stand-off between the Progressive view of the need to eliminate the predators, and a supposedly Romantic view of the case for protecting them. Progressivism began as part of the Reconstruction programme following the American Civil War. Its aim was to smooth the way to an efficient transformation from an agrarian society to a modern industrial state, to clean up politics after the scandal-ridden presidency (1869–1877) of Ulysses Grant, and to purify the *nation's morals. It was also part of its purpose to *rationalise public management of natural resources, and one of the ways to achieve that was to eliminate predators once and for all.[100]

The officials put in charge of dealing with the animals in the American forest were conscientious. As the historian Donald Worster writes, they were . . .

> motivated by a strong, highly moralistic sense
> of mission to clean up the world around them,
> and that ambition encompassed the natural
> environment along with economic and political
> corruption. . . .[101]

Here are some examples. C. Hart Merriam, director of the Bureau of the Biological Survey in the Department of Agriculture in the 1880s/90s, assembled an impressive collection of 25,000 birds' stomachs. And no man was more unselfish or more devoted to the nation's moral and economic well-being than Gifford Pinchot, President Theodore Roosevelt's Chief Forester (1905–1910). Conservation, for him, meant "the development and use of the earth and all its resources for the enduring good of men" and the *efficiency and *productivity he imposed was manifest in his forests of orderly, well-trimmed trees.

Virtually everything you could see in a Pinchot landscape was a crop to be harvested and a source of profit. Animals that ate your profit before you could get it were a bad thing, and asking for trouble. Here was a conventional *ideology, widely accepted as *self-evidently true. The young (33-year-old) Aldo Leopold was committed to it. He promised not to relax his efforts until "the last wolf or lion in New Mexico" was dead.[102]

It is not just *economics and *economism that is speaking here. It is a conviction that order and control are *virtues in their own right, calling for decisive action on outlaws, animal or human. At a deeper level, it means reducing the *complexities of nature down to a system whose business can be summarised in terms of clean, rigorous, incorruptible maths—and this can be done by whittling the variables down to a single, measurable unit. *Energy will do nicely. An *ecosystem from this point of view is a natural system which collects energy, uses it, trades it and releases it in many different ways and with varying degrees of efficiency. Here we have the New Ecology, and a defining contribution to it was a 1942 paper by Raymond Lindeman, which brought to ecology—actually the ecology of Cedar Bog Lake in Minnesota—a kind of "unified field theory", in which measurable, testable gains and losses of energy could provide comprehensive explanations as free of mysticism and muddle as physics.[103]

And, even better than physics, a well-balanced ecology could have one foot in economics at the same time, making it not just the defender of good order, but the provider of funds. This—as H.G. Wells and Julian Huxley announced in their book, *The Science of Life*—was "Life Under Control".[104]

Except it wasn't, of course, and the more the *reductionists single-mindedly overlooked the unseen complexities and synergies—assuming that what they did not see or could not measure did not exist, ignoring or ruling out the spirit of complex ecologies—the more unstable these ecologies became (*Relevance Fallacy). An early warning was supplied in 1925, by the deer in the Kaibab forest of Arizona's Grand Canyon National Park. They seemed to be a model of good management, and, until that moment, things had been looking so good: the predators had been substantially eliminated and the deer population grew from 4,000 in 1906 to

100,000. Then, in the winters of 1924–1926, 60,000 deer starved. By 1939, on a devastated range, they were down to 10,000.[105]

That is plain bad management. You don't need spiritual insight to avoid such mistakes, and yet, the suspicion that there is more in a situation than you know or could know—the instinct for looking beyond the measurable, the useful, the understood—makes a difference. For Aldo Leopold, that began with an insight which matured quite slowly, starting when he and his companions were . . .

> . . . eating lunch on a high rimrock, at the foot of which a turbulent river elbowed its way. We saw what we thought was a doe fording the torrent, her breast awash in white water. When she climbed the bank towards us and shook out her tail, we realised our error: it was a wolf. A half-dozen others, evidently grown pups, sprang from the willows and all joined in a welcoming mêlée of wagging tails and playful maulings. What was literally a pile of wolves writhed and tumbled in the centre of an open flat at the foot of our rimrock.
>
> In those days we had never heard of passing up a chance to kill a wolf. In a second we were pumping lead into the pack, but with more excitement than accuracy: how to aim a steep downhill shot is always confusing. When our rifles were empty, the old wolf was down, and a pup was dragging a leg into impassable slide-rocks.
>
> We reached the old wolf in time to watch a fierce green fire dying in her eyes. I realised then and have known ever since, that there was something new to me in those eyes—something known only to her and to the mountain. I was young then, and full of trigger-itch; I thought that because fewer wolves meant more deer, that no wolves would mean hunters' paradise. But after seeing the green fire die, I sensed that neither the wolf nor the mountain agreed with such a view.[106]

Leopold called this insight "thinking like a mountain". It means deep engagement, being part of the ecology.

So, what does being "part of the ecology" mean? It means recognising that the ecology as a whole is connected and interdependent, that it is a web of life, to be understood only imperfectly, and only then after deep immersion in being there. In this sense, it is familiar to us through the idea of *Gaia, which requires us not just to acknowledge the existence of this web, but to sense it urgently, with our bodies and minds, if our response is to be in any way appropriate to what it is, and what is coming. As Stephan Harding writes,

> We are learning the painful way that we are embedded within a larger planetary entity that has personhood, agency and soul, a being that we must learn to respect if we are to have any sort of comfortable tenure within her.[107]

And *ignorance of what we are doing is no excuse, for, as the philosopher Alfred North Whitehead reflects, the ecology is an *ethic of interdependence. It is a densely woven *network of *connections. Any physical object which by its influence deteriorates its environment, commits suicide.[108]

That awareness of being joined together in a complex ecology started to become explicit with the growth of the Romantic movement in the eighteenth century, since when its influence has been more developed in the amateur tradition than in mainstream science, whose discoveries and understandings come at the price of narrowing vision down to principles that can be discovered and understood. For the scientist, as a rule, "spirit" is the fudge with which amateurs fill the gaps in their knowledge; for the dweller in an ecology, spiritual awareness recognises that, beyond a certain point, *explanation* misses the point: it has turned up at the wrong party. Mozart's music can be understood in impressive detail, but if you think that (given enough time to study the matter) you could wrap it up in complete explanation, you have not understood it. There is a boundary beyond which explanation has no relevance, where it is not knowledge that matters, but *encounter.[109]

And, if we ourselves are embedded in this community of nature—in the web of life—that brings moral obligations. As the ecologist and mystic Joseph Wood Krutch wrote, what is needed is more than just an awareness of the living ecology, of animals' joy and suffering. To

S

engage with the spirit of nature calls for reverence and love. If we don't extend our vision beyond matters of utility, we will be in deep trouble:

It is by no means yet certain that a society which believes in nothing except survival is actually capable of surviving.[110]

But what else is there? There is the spirit. As William Morton Wheeler concluded from a lifetime as a student of the ecology of ants, the spirit is intrinsic to the *story. The natural world, he declared, is "an inexhaustible source of spiritual and aesthetic delight". "Spirit" comes from Latin, spirare, to breathe. It is the essence of life.[111]

_____

Below the threshold

So, where does the spirit live? Is it in the *ecology, or in the observer? Or is it where they meet? These are matters in which, it seems, we may now be able to make some progress, thanks to the intense insights into the thinking faculties of the body and the brain by Antonio Damasio, and the work that he has inspired.[112]

Damasio's contribution is to show the extent to which our ability to cope and to make reasonable *judgments—either as individuals or as members of a community—resides in the emotions, and not in the conscious, accessible parts of the brain. It is true that *emotions can bias our judgment, and yet if they are missing, we are no longer able to make sense of events. We may be able to describe events and to analyse them *intelligently, but we have no frame of reference by which to see their significance, to be involved, or to care. For example (at one extreme), an event such as a lethal road accident, or (at the other) a welcome home scene, can be described without any particular meaning or significance being recognised. This is detachment.[113]

The leading symptom is that inability to feel the significance or meaning of events. The person does not see the difference in kind between a happy ending and a sad one; he is not in touch with the joy or grief; he misses the point. Another symptom is that the detached person is likely to lack the instincts of sociability. He or she has no feel for the kind of behaviour which might be expected to have positive consequences for him and

for his *community. It is typical for a person suffering detachment to be offensive and obscene; he is liable to rages, without any awareness of the implications. And the person is typically unable to make decisions. Instead, he lurches from impulse to impulse without any sense of realism or consistency. In summary, the detached person can be thought of as having no concept of "me". Intellect and emotion may be in full working order, but there is no *identity to give them meaning. Unless I am, I cannot think.[114]

Detachment is not a completely *binary, on-off, condition. Although the literature is still feeling its way about this, it is evident that some cases are more extreme than others. An extreme form would be the presence of intellectual analysis without the ability to supply any emotional context at all. A somewhat less extreme case could be where there is some coherent motivation, but it is detached and *instrumental. The person pursues a cold *ideological aim at the cost of grief and mayhem, but without a complete loss of personal involvement: the aim may at least advance his interests, or it may appeal to ancient survival motives, or to the contest for power and alpha status which is the signature property of the higher animals, and perhaps most conspicuously of the family of primates to which humans belong. Or, it may occur in a split-minded way, where the emotional life of the person is on hold until he gets home in the evening (*Ad Hominem).[115]

The extent and detail of the trauma of detachment depends on its cause, and the causes are of two kinds.

First, there may be physical damage. The missing abilities have their source in specific functions which reside in particular parts of the brain. It is the frontal lobe which is critical here, and normal decision-making takes place in the ventromedial prefrontal region. The clearest, most comprehensively-studied cause of emotional detachment is physical damage to that part of the brain, and this was illustrated in the dramatic case of Phineas Gage. He was the gifted and trusted foreman of a gang of railway builders, who, in 1848, were blasting their way through the rocks and escarpments of Vermont towards the town of Cavendish. A vital tool of this trade was the tamping iron—three feet seven inches long, one and a quarter inches in diameter, thirteen and a half pounds in weight—which was used

S

YOU REALLY CAN'T FAKE IT
The real smile

There are two sorts of smile. The fake smile just widens lips. The real smile both widens the mouth *and* wrinkles the eyes. The widened-lips part is easy: the muscle used is the zygomatic major, which is under a conscious motor-control part of the brain—the pyramidal tract. The wrinkled-eyes part is another matter. It uses the orbicularis oculi muscle, which is controlled by the anterior cingulate, an area of the brain over which we have no conscious control. To reward someone with a real smile, you really have to feel it.[116]

to tamp down charges of dynamite, deep into the holes that had been drilled for them in the rock. One day, in a moment of inattention, he tamped down a charge, not realising that the sand needed to stop it exploding prematurely was not yet in place. The explosion that followed shot the iron through his cheek, the base of his skull, his brain, and the top of his head. It landed a hundred feet away.[117]

He did not die. The wound was disinfected, and he was nursed back to health. His skills appeared to be unimpaired, and in due course he applied to get his job back. He did not get it, for his character had changed. The new Mr. Gage was foul-mouthed, subject to fits of rage, unable to plan ahead, given to decisions far removed from reality and mutually contradictory, and which he did not carry out anyway. His doctor gave him kind and firm advice about how to reform his behaviour, but it was a message he could not understand. The part of the brain needed to feel, to decide and act on decisions, had ended its days a short distance from the track of the Rutland and Burlington Railroad.[118]

Other head injuries with similarly decisive consequences include brain damage from childhood accidents where the skull itself remains intact, and whose effect may not become evident until later, and the effect of a tumour which is not removed in time to prevent damage to the brain.[119]

Secondly, there may have been a *lack of practice* in the use of the emotions. That is, the emotions may remain at the level of latent propensities, which have never developed because the child has rarely, or never, interacted with people who display emotions and bring them in as part of the daily *conversation of family and friends. If a child's emotional environment is seriously impoverished, he may be left to find his way with an emotional range reduced to a single response: malevolence, backed by *violence.[120]

If the family is not the locus of emotional famine, the state may do it. A dry, music-poor, *arts-free, emotion-lite *education can successfully ensure that emotional development never gets started, as can an authoritarian regime which deprives people of the *trust needed to sustain stable groups and the *cooperation that they bring. The informal contact between adults and children which once shared-out the privilege of inspiring and encouraging young people throughout a whole village is now substantially prohibited, excluding children from membership of groups of all ages from whom they can learn emotional literacy. In earlier times, Tsarist and Soviet Russia made it hard to sustain social *institutions in cities, even small informal groups of family and neighbourhoods; and Rome promoted the pathology of Coliseum entertainment in (as the historian Lewis Mumford describes it) the "collective torture chamber" of third- and fourth century Rome.[121]

What is at risk here is the possibility of a widespread collapse of the human capacity for applying feeling to the interpretation of events. Analysis and calculation may be flawless; detachment may even be seen as an ideal state, described—or even made mandatory—as *"objective", "transparent" or "non-judgmental". But if the emotions are disengaged, there is no point: the spirit is missing; our condition is reduced to the dead walking.

Waters of comfort

The treadmill was an instrument of punishment used in British prisons until the early twentieth century. It was a large, heavy squirrel wheel in which prisoners were required to walk endlessly uphill for up to ten hours a day. It was designed to break the will, to drain off the passions which could cause trouble—the emotional equivalent of the long-established medical technique of bleeding.

Elizabeth Fry (1780–1845) came as a reformer to prisons—notably Newgate—where the wheel was routine. The conditions she found were intended to persuade anyone who had endured them never again to risk a challenge to the *law: in addition to the wheel, there were long periods of solitary confinement and silence regimes, and if a person broke the silence, their already thin rations would be cut. But she was a revolutionary who believed that what prisoners needed was not *less* emotional development, but *more*.

She approached the inmates of Newgate as people valued in the artistic context of their and her *religion. She affirmed their personal *identity. Fry dug deep below the threshold, to the drivers of animal behaviour. She credited each prisoner with the possession of a soul. And since (as Damasio tells us) the soul breathes through the body, she gave them their bodies back, too. She offered responsibility and education, so that they had a chance of recovering the condition of being a person—not just a behaviour problem, a set of symptoms and a felon, but a person with emotional being. She restored their *conatus*. *Conatus* is the primal sense of striving, affirming the will to live and do. We can think of it as our "me", our soul, our morale, the key identity-affirming principle of—as the seventeenth century philosopher Baruch Spinoza has it—striving to persevere in our being.[122]

As a means to that end, she brought an emotionally-rich story about a God who cares, and who had this to offer: emotional life and depth, engagement, *ethical decisions to make, stories of *betrayal, forgiveness, fasting and feasting, obligations, gratitude, discretion, *judgment, resolution, striving, anxiety, encouragement, music, *dance, delight and love. She offered a resurrection of hope. These emotional competences had been intensely affirmed, as a matter of passionate urgency, by a revolutionary of a previous age, also living in a large *civic society in trouble. The Rome of Christ's day was a bureaucratic, militaristic, repressive society, increasingly *demoralised, weighed down by managerial institutions, interests, *complications and political correctness. It was a case of large-scale, long-lasting emotional drought, turning increasingly to savage extremes in the pursuit of the need to feel *something*. Christ brought emotion, like rain, to a parched land. Fry, drawing on that inheritance of emotional depth, and on the *narratives and parables that communicated it, also went into an emotional desert, bringing the waters of comfort, giving life and breath.[123]

In her evidence to a select committee of the House of Lords in 1835, Fry explained why her spiritual approach, and her Bible teaching, was integral to what she was doing:

> For though severe punishment may in a measure deter them and others from crime, it does not amend the character and change the heart, but if you have really altered the principles of the individuals, they are not only deterred from crime because of the fear of punishment, but they go out and set a bright example to others.[124]

The spirit, like a virus inside a cell, does not travel unattended. It comes in stories, in *myth, in music—in the music of wolves. It has *conatus*. It has *caritas*. It has insight. It brings hope. It has tenacity. It has attachment, connecting the body and soul, intellect and emotion, animal and *ecology. It is made speakable by *religion, which recognises and teaches more than reason, and gives us a language with which we can explain to ourselves what we are doing when we *encounter the dew sparkling in the grass and feel shamed by our preoccupations and grateful to our concerned and friendly God who enables us, if only briefly, to be simply present. It engages the whole of us in *conversation. It is our sigh and our inspiration.

*Humility, Second Nature, Cognitive Dissonance, Script, Lean Law and Order, Hippopotamus.

S

SQUALID (adj). The nature of the inherited problems to be considered in *public debate after years of incompetent decision-making.

STORY. See Narrative Truth.

STRAW MAN. The tactic of inventing an argument in order to demolish it.

This is *distraction at its most immediate, obvious and intentional. Summarise the other side's case. Make sure your version of it is as ridiculous as possible. Demolish the summary. Claim victory.

*ecosystems and animal welfare. It builds plants' and animals' ability to sustain their own health. It does not depend on pesticides and fertilisers produced from diminishing supplies of oil and gas. It conserves soils, *water and *energy; it protects habitats. It produces *food richer in nutrients than conventionally-grown food, and free of contamination by synthetic chemicals. And local food production, now a priority, will improve food security, relying less on the *transport which will be at risk when oil gets scarce, conserving local farming and *skills, and building local fertility on productive, *resilient principles known as "organic".

Have you quite finished? It makes no difference anyway, because the straw man stopped listening ages ago. Well, he really doesn't have to, for he has magic powers. He can make inconvenient *truths disappear at a stroke. And he can provide his minders with an intoxicating sense of being right. Actually, the straw man has a dark history (below), but in more recent times he has been a symbol of finality, an old fellow with a short life who had to die at the end of the harvest, and to hand over to the new generation. *Peasant societies used to unwind on the last day by making a straw man from the last sheaf, just to beat it to pieces with the flails they would soon be using to thresh the corn (perhaps to warn the rest of the corn what was coming). And there was a startling variant of this, where the man who cut the last bundle of corn was picked on for special treatment. His face would be blackened; he would be fêted and feasted, mocked and parodied. Fortunately, he had an understudy in the form of a straw goat, which he would carry about on his back. In the end, the goat would be placed on the ground and destroyed with the flails.[126]

You see, you have forgotten about organic agriculture already.[127]

A variant is simply to save yourself the trouble of understanding what the other side is talking about. Alternatively, launch into a free-wheeling parody—a song (Greek: *ōidê*) of mockery (Greek: *pará*). Your victim is forced onto the defensive, and possibly into fury. You're winning.

Here is an example. The target is the *organic movement; the tactic is to make it sound like a fundamentalist *religion.

1. Set up your straw man: "The high priests of the organic movement tell us that natural chemicals are good and synthetic chemicals bad."
2. Demolish it: "This is utter nonsense. . . . Arsenic, ricin, aflotoxin are all highly poisonous chemicals found in nature. Yet the supposed superiority of natural over synthetic is the rock on which the organic movement is built."[125]

Good. Now you can sit back and wait for the other side to go into a lumbering explanation (there will doubtless be something there which, if really necessary, will allow you to unleash another straw man). Here it comes:

Organic cultivation is not based on ridiculous claims about things being "natural", but on principles of fertile soils, crop rotations, local

In fact, the image is darker than it may at first seem. The Straw Man is a version of the *sacrifice ritual which marks conclusion and *death at the end of the summer, and takes us into the dark area of scapegoat and blame.[128] Julius Caesar describes straw man sacrifices in his *Gallic War*:

The whole Gallic race is addicted to religious ritual; consequently those suffering from serious maladies or subject to the perils of battle sacrifice human victims. . . . Some weave huge figures of wicker and fill their limbs with humans, who are then burned to death when the figures are set on fire. They suppose that the gods prefer this execution to be applied to thieves, robbers, and other malefactors taken in the act, but in default of such they resort to the execution of the innocent.[129]

By comparison with that, a mere *fallacy is small beer. But think of it like this. You make an argument. The other person does not understand it; it requires a degree of complex thought which is not in his powers. But instead of recognising that he does not understand it, he translates it into a different argument, and then attacks it. You try to correct the error, but fail. All sorts of anger and battle can follow.

This problem of misinterpreting an argument is explored by Lawrence Kohlberg, and summarised in his Moral Judgment Scale.[130] It consists of six stages of development (the seventh has been added by the present author):

Stage 1. Obedience and punishment orientation: egocentric surrender to superior power or prestige.

Stage 2. *Instrumental Relativism: egoism, and orientation to exchange and reciprocity. Right action is that which is instrumentally satisfying to the self.

Stage 3. Interpersonal Concordance: "good boy" orientation; eagerness to please; conformity to stereotypes of good behaviour.

Stage 4. Law and Order: orientation to "doing duty", to respect for *authority and the maintenance of social order.

Stage 5. Social *Contract: recognition that there is an arbitrary element in rules, but a willingness to conform for the sake of agreement. Avoidance of violating the will or rights of others.

Stage 6. Universal *Ethical Principles: orientation towards principles of choice having a universal value and consistency.

Stage 7. *Casuistry: rationally and *emotionally-integrated evaluation of the case in its context.

The trouble, as summarised by Kohlberg, is that people tend to be unable to comprehend moral *judgment more than one stage above the stage they themselves inhabit. What happens is that, instead of understanding that a different moral judgment could actually be better or more sophisticated than their own, they attribute motives of a kind that they themselves would recognise.

If they are low on the judgment scale—say, at Stage 2—they can be persuaded only of the other person's simple self-interest, or, at best, of his desire to be a "good boy", eager to please. Without the ability to handle either a complex idea, or a sharply unfamiliar one, they cannot believe that this capacity exists in anyone else. They may find it hard to see anyone else's point of view at all, and see disagreement in terms of apportioning *blame—a straw man needing to be punished. At the other end of the scale—evaluation of the case in its context (stage 7)—argument may find something close to the meaning of *encounter.

The Straw Man gets everywhere. When an argument misses the point—by accident or design—the Straw Man may well be at work.[131]
*Irrelevance.

SUBJECTIVE. The quality of an argument coloured by personal engagement. A subjective argument may bring prejudice to a case or distort it beyond the limits of *logic-literacy. Acknowledging this personal prejudice can bring clarity, as greater knowledge of what those interests are can help the listener to understand what is going on. Example:

Everyone is prejudiced; I am prejudiced myself; I am prejudiced by, for instance, my commitment as a practising Roman Catholic and my sense that we humans have the responsibility for stewardship of the Earth. It is in my view a legitimate and necessary part of evaluating an

445

argument to be aware of what prejudices and interests the people involved bring to it.

John Gummer MP, Centre for Policy Studies debate on *climate change, 23 February 2006.

*Ad Hominem, Emotional Argument, Expertise, Interest, Special Pleading, Survivor Bias.

SUBSIDIARITY. The principle, often advocated by the European Union, that decisions should be taken at the lowest practicable level. It sounds sensible, but it is in fact meaningless because the qualification ("practicable", or its equivalents) can mean anything.

It can, for instance, be used to justify a slow-motion process of removing the *authority of *nations: decide on a supra-national (imperial) policy; eliminate any interference at the national level; leave it to the *regions to implement the policy by doing as they are told. In this way, subsidiarity's claim to favour decision-making at the lowest possible level actually succeeds in capturing it for the highest possible level. Subsidiarity is a single word that contradicts itself, an oxymoron.

*Self-Denying Truth, Quibble, System Scale Rule, Localisation, Pull.

SUCCESS. Do you really think we will get through the *climacteric, and come in due course to a time of *resilience, *manners and *harmonic order?

Don't answer that question, for you may discover to your cost that your answer is either a *self-fulfilling or a *self-denying truth, and that both count against us. If we deny that there is a liveable future, then we will do little to secure one. If we affirm it, we come into other trouble, such as complacency, an optimistic view that what we are doing now is all that is needed, an *iconic focus on the simple solution, or the constant anxiety of life on the edge, between hope and doubt: positive thinking seems to be the right thing in the circumstances until you notice the wreckage.[132]

Instead, think of what happened to Orpheus and Eurydice. Eurydice, you may remember, died after having been bitten by a snake, and Orpheus went down into the Underworld to recover her. The goddess Persephone agreed to let her go on condition that Orpheus did not look back at her as she followed him.

Unfortunately, he forgot about this condition—he did look back, with the result that Eurydice vanished forever and Orpheus was torn to pieces by angry women who threw his head into the river Hebros, where it floated downstream, still singing.

That is, make the intense commitment. At walking pace. Plod on. Climb steeply uphill, out of the Underworld. Keep your eyes fixed ahead. You never know—you might get there; you might even find out where "there" is, and you might inspire others to come with you. Just don't look down . . .

We do not need to choose between hope and *expectation. What matters is to keep hope alive, which we won't succeed in doing if we are constantly checking up on it. It is not *certainty that sustains our focus, but the ambiguity that comes to us, for instance, in the prayer from another ancient moment of commitment against the odds: "Lord, I believe. Help thou mine unbelief."[133] *Grim Reality.

SUMMARY GAMBIT, THE. The use of summary to introduce distortion into an argument.

Example: The case for intervening in a country whose government is committing gross outrages on its population (Iraq in the 1990/2000s was the subject being discussed, but Germany in the 1930/40s is another instance) is summarised: "We can't simply say, 'Oh, we don't like your regime, we think you'll be happier without it, so let's invade you.'"[134]

The gambit is defended on the grounds that "the essentials" of the argument are there: it is evident, however, that they are not. The assumption that they are is a case of *begging the question—using the conclusion for which the person is arguing as the assumption on which her argument is based: *of course* we can't "simply say" that, but the whole point of the argument is about the actual reasons, not the parody which is passed off as summary.

The gambit is well defended because it can answer objections on its own terms: "So, you think we *can* simply decide to invade any regime that we don't happen to like?" It is possible for the opponent to escape from the trap that has been set for him, but the other person gets the advantage of first-use.

*Devil's Voice, Hyperbole, Special Pleading, Straw Man.

SUNK COST FALLACY, THE. The *fallacy that, when a *choice is being made between two or more alternatives, the costs that have already been incurred in bringing the alternatives to their present stage should be taken into account. In fact, only the costs and benefits expected in the future should be counted.

This can be hard: if millions have already been spent on developing alternative A, but alternative B is in fact better, simpler and (in terms of future costs) cheaper, then this is a matter of regret and embarrassment. It should prompt a *kaikaku moment, but the people who have built their careers in developing alternative A can be expected to argue against with passionate intensity: "We cannot just throw 20 years' work down the drain. . .".

In fact, decisions can only affect the future, so only future costs and benefits should be considered.
*Paradigm, Nuclear Energy, TEQs (Tradable Energy Quotas), Time Fallacies.

SURVIVOR BIAS. The advantage accruing to survivors in the evaluation of a risk. Examples:

1. Lifelong smokers who assert that smoking did them no harm, and therefore could not harm anyone else either. This biases the argument because those for whom smoking was lethal are not around to put their side of the case.
2. The credible material witnesses on the benefit of any current absurdity are those who have thrived on it; those who have not are not well placed to disagree.[135]

*Fallacies, Personal Experience, Expertise, False Sameness, Metamorphosis.

SUSTAINABILITY. Among the published formal statements of the conditions for *sustainability, two are notable for their clarity and urgency.

The first is from *The Natural Step*, which argues that the services provided by the natural world, and on which human society depends are:

1. The provision of the resources we need;
2. Absorption and recycling of *wastes, making them available for reuse; and
3. Maintenance of ecological services such as a benign *climate and pollination.

In order to sustain those conditions in good order, a further set of conditions must be met:

1. Minerals (including fuels) must not be extracted from the Earth's crust without effective provision to supply substitutes when they are depleted.
2. Waste must not be produced which nature cannot quickly break down into harmless forms, or in quantities which cannot be absorbed or broken down.
3. Natural *capital such as forests, soil and fisheries must not be degraded.
4. The assets of nature are used with fairness and efficiency, enabling the needs of all to be met.[136]

The second statement of sustainability is in the form of Richard Heinberg's "Five Axioms of Sustainability":

1. Tainter's Axiom: Any action that continues to use critical resources unsustainably will collapse.
2. Bartlett's Axiom: *Population growth and/or *growth in the rates of consumption of resources cannot be sustained.
3. To be sustainable, the use of renewable resources must proceed at a rate that is less than or equal to the rate of natural replenishment.
4. To be sustainable, the use of non-renewable resources must proceed at a rate that is declining and the rate of decline must be greater than or equal to the rate of depletion (see *Depletion Protocol).
5. Sustainability requires that substances introduced into the environment from human activities be minimised and rendered harmless to biosphere functions.[137]

Sustainability is not the same thing as *sustainable development. Sustainability consists of meeting a set of conditions; sustainable development is an aim.[138]
*Wheel of Life, Closed-Loop Systems, Natural Step.

SUSTAINABLE DEVELOPMENT. Herman Daly, perhaps the most authoritative voice on sustainable development, writes,

> Sustainable development is development without growth in the scale of the economy beyond some point that is within biospheric carrying capacity.[139]

It is possible to agree with that definition in principle while being aware of problems with it. As Daly himself recognised, there are reasons to believe we are already *beyond* the biosphere's carrying capacity—we are into "overshoot"—and if that is the case, sustainable development ought not to be about simply *reducing* the damage caused by *economic activity; it needs to be directed to environmental *repair*. Although (he writes) this is "very radical", anything less than that will take us to the limits of carrying capacity, or—if indeed overshoot is already upon us—even further beyond them.[140]

And the problem with *that*, of course, is that the *market economy has needs of its own in addition to those of the biosphere: it is a system which relies on *growth, and if growth were to stop for a long period or to go into reverse, the consequences could be as catastrophic for those who depend on it (i.e., all of us) as the collapse of the biosphere itself. So, if sustainable development as an idea is to have any acceptability to those whose lives depend *both* on the biosphere *and* on the economy, it will need to take the interests of both those spheres into account.

Here we have the United Nations World Commission on Environment and Development trying to do just that—with its definition of sustainable development, as:

> Development that meets the needs of the present without compromising the ability of future generations to meet their own needs.[141]

We need to take this apart a little. There are four characters (variables) in this story:

1. *Human *well-being*. Well-being is a complex idea, but for now, we can focus on the flow of goods and services needed to meet the needs of human society: this is not a sufficient condition for well-being, but it is a *necessary one.
2. *The environmental impact* of the task of providing those goods and services. This is the flow of damage suffered by the environment—the stock of *natural capital—on which the planet and its inhabitants depend.
3. *Technology*. This comes into the story in two ways: *Industrial technology* is the set of technologies used to produce the flow of goods and services;

technological improvement (from this point of view) would reduce the environmental impact per unit of output (*Eco-efficiency).

Domestic technology is the relationship between well-being and the flow of goods and services needed to sustain it. If, for instance, consumers could find ways of maintaining the same well-being with a smaller flow of goods and services, this would be an advance in 'domestic technology'.

4. *Population*. The environmental impact of economic activity depends (other things being equal) on the size of the population.

Now the question: is it possible to bring on improvements in *technology* to the point that human *well-being* is maintained while *environmental impact* is reduced to a level that conserves the stock of natural capital? This is known as the "decoupling" question. And the answer, broadly speaking, is No.[142]

As explained in *Growth, the market economy is a dynamic system which depends on growth as a condition of maintaining its stability. Decoupling would involve sustaining the needed growth in output while achieving the needed *fall* in impact. This is a long way from happening.

A less ambitious aim is "relative decoupling", where the environmental impact *per unit of output* falls, even though the total environmental impact rises with advances in growth. This is a recognition that more *efficient use of labour tends to go together with more efficient use of all the other forms of *capital and input that are needed. Each advance in growth still produces an increase in environmental impact, but the *relative* size of that impact does decline. That is only a *tendency* and there are many *exceptions (such as the use of systemic pesticides; see *Food Prospects) but, in general, relative decoupling has been successful. Compare modern manufacture with the smokestack industries of the past. Or think of Adnams' "carbon neutral beer". Variations on the theme of reducing environmental impact per unit of output—once the ecocatastrophic start-up phase of industrialisation had passed—have been central to the nature of *productivity improvements for most of the age of industry.[143]

As for the decoupling of domestic technology— the well-being derived by households per unit of consumption—there is no reason to believe that this has advanced at all. On the contrary—since the whole economy is in effect the collective household—economic growth depends on this becoming, year by year, *less* efficient (*Competitiveness).

So the problem is tough. What we need is not just slower growth in the flow of environmental impact (relative decoupling). We need actual *reductions* in the flow of environmental impact, despite sustained economic *growth (absolute decoupling). That has not happened. And even if it had, that would not in fact be enough, if we are already into overshoot. It is not enough to *reduce the rate at which we add* to the stock of damage to the environment that has already occurred; what the ecology needs is a *subtraction* from that damage: that is, economic activity which actually repairs the environment—or at least, gives it a breather so that it has a chance of repairing itself (strong absolute decoupling). At present, there is no prospect of this.[144]

So is 'sustainable development' dishonest? No. As Jonathon Porritt shows—with a wealth of evidence—businesses need to manage risk, to achieve deep efficiencies in the use of *energy and *materials, to build brand value and reputation, to attract and retain the best people, to motivate them, to innovate, to develop new markets and to sustain an accounting system which recognises the need to use performance measurements other than *money—and all of these imperatives call for an intense awareness of the whole *ecology in which a company is working.[145]

It is not the fault of its advocates or of the businesses that have practised it that sustainable development has been taken as a quick fix—the false promise that with the help of technology and being more *responsible, we can carry on pretty painlessly as we are, satisfy all our needs and still save the planet. But the phrase is open to that inference—"sustainable development" is there on the menu. If it had not been, we might have been left without any reassuring global statements about the environment at all.

But then, in due course, we would have had to own up to the fact that a shock is coming which we had not been able to bring ourselves to admit, or to prepare for. Perhaps the preceding silence would have made us alert to the urgent need to take notice; the itch that made us scratch. It could have been a moment of *humility and *truth.[146]

*Sustainability, Sedation, Script, Lean Economy.

SYSTEM SCALE RULE. The key rule governing systems-design: large-scale problems do not require large-scale solutions; they require small-scale solutions within a large-scale framework.

*Scale, Systems Thinking, Nation, TEQs (Tradable Energy Quotas), Wheel of Life.

SYSTEMS THINKING. Guidelines for thinking about networks of interaction.

Lean Logic makes a distinction between two kinds of system: the *complex system and the *modular system. It also recognises two more kinds of system which are special applications of these: the *complicated system and the *ecological system. The four are summarised in the table on page 450. This entry points to some typical properties of systems which it may be helpful to be aware of when thinking about them.

The first thing to note about systems is that, in general, they are not what they seem. Most of what matters is invisible. Here are some of the things you may not see:

- Their small-scale subsystems and components.
- The linkages and interactions between them.
- The large-scale context on which systems depend.
- The linkages between systems and that wider context.
- The rapid, but small, changes that take place inside them.
- The large, but slow, changes that will in due course transform them beyond recognition.

We cannot *control a system—practically everything we ever do has *unintended consequences—but we can look about us before rushing into the *indignant campaign or the *technical fix. This is called *manners.

Going beyond that—tracing through some, at least, of the often hard-to-understand causes and effects, and having some skill in thinking through the consequences—is called systems thinking. And even that can be inconclusive, in the sense that systems thinking, no matter how clear-sighted, may succeed in no more than improving a situation, falling far short of solving it. Or it may improve matters for some of the interests involved

COMPLEXITY, MODULARITY, COMPLICATION AND ECOLOGY
Defining properties

	*COMPLEX SYSTEM (Example: you)	*MODULAR SYSTEM (Example: a herd of antelopes)	*COMPLICATED SYSTEM (Example: globalised society)	*ECOLOGICAL SYSTEM (Example: a woodland)
FORM	A system whose diverse parts have little or no individual independence but take on specialised roles and interact for the collective purpose.	A system whose parts (*holons) have a high degree of similarity and independence. They all have essentially the same role, but may interact for collective purposes if the need arises.	A modular system which—by force or evolution—has acquired some properties of a complex system, although the transformation remains incomplete and is unstable.	A *panarchy; a mixture of complex and modular systems, and systems with both properties. This is typical for a natural *ecology.
***DIVERSITY**	**Strong diversity (structural diversity)** The system's parts are radically diverse in form, reflecting their specialist roles. The parts of a human body—and those of a complex, self-reliant community—are diverse in this sense.	**Weak diversity (textural diversity)** The differences between the system's parts are relatively minor; they are variations around a theme. But this weak diversity is sufficient to sustain *identity and meaning, and to enable evolution.	**Weak diversity (textural diversity)** The system requires its parts to take on profoundly diverse roles. But the essential modular form remains. As a consequence, parts have to adapt to functions to which they are not ideally suited.	**A mix of strong and weak diversity** This is diversity in depth, applying not only to individual organisms or parts but to whole systems or subsystems (holons).
***CONNECTEDNESS**	**Taut links: interdependence** Taut links and interdependence between the parts largely determine each part's actions. If any one of those taut links breaks, the system as a whole is in trouble.	**Slack links: independence** The parts may be mutually supportive, but they are not mutually dependent. There is substantial freedom for the system's (complex) parts to act as they choose without damage to the system itself.	**Taut links: interdependence** In addition to the usual vulnerabilities of a taut, complex system, inflexible, formulaic, top-down control may constrain the freedom of parts to play their roles as effectively as possible, producing ultimately damaging outcomes.	**A mix of taut links and slack links** The ecology has connections throughout its functions and energy flows, but there is extreme variety, including taut and slack links, occasional links, disconnections and opportunism.
***RESILIENCE**	**Preventive resilience** The system uses its well-developed competence to keep out of trouble, but if it fails to do so, it has poor chances of survival.	**Recovery-elastic resilience** The system has a well-developed ability to recover from shock—or to experience a shock while limiting the damage—but it is poorly-equipped to stay out of trouble in the first place.	**Intensification, leading to lower efficiency** The system responds to challenges through greater complication—making additional provisions which involve more work, and lead to greater elaboration and more challenges—right up to the point of collapse.	**A mix of preventive resilience and recovery-elastic resilience** There is an extreme variety of responses that evolves creatively. It does not stay still long enough to be described, but it has *harmonic order.

but leave things unaffected (or perhaps even worse) for others. This recognition of the limitations that are present as we move from thinking about systems to living with them is explained in some depth by "Soft Systems Methodology", and has its own literature.[147]

But that should not put us off thinking about the essence of systems—what they are and what they do. The following summary of systems' properties is set out in three groups, covering: the *form* taken by systems and their parts, the *feedback* they provide and respond to, and the usefulness of their *function*.

Form (see also *Resilience > Resilient Systems)

1. *Holons* and *hierarchy*

   Holons are the parts, or subassemblies, that make up *complex and *modular structures. An antelope is a holon, in that it is both complete in itself—looking after its own interests—and also part of a herd, with its place in the wider ecology, whose balance and *diversity it helps to sustain. Organs and cells in the antelope's body are holons in this same sense.

Holons join together in subassemblies and larger assemblies—for example, liver cells cooperate to make a functioning liver; the body's organs cooperate to make an antelope. And in these cases the sense of hierarchy is clear—the holons are, in a sense, pointing in the same direction.

Other systems contain holons and hierarchies which also belong to different systems with different missions, pointing in different directions—here there are often many hierarchies and it is hard to say which is at the "top". For example, a woodland consists of a host of interacting holons: the *cooperative, hostile, parasitic, complementary, benign, essential or *irrelevant coexist in the same system and the same space. Lumping all this lot together into one overarching super-hierarchy called the ecosystem is not convincing, so the collective name for the complex and seemingly disorderly muddle of many hierarchies that make an *ecosystem is "panarchy".[148]

And these holons, hierarchies and panarchies change over time. Systems change in response to events—they are dynamic—and this means that observations we make about the present form of a system may be true only temporarily. In particular, systems change as they move through the adaptive cycle discussed in the *Wheel of Life. Many of the

most profound changes will be slow-acting, but in some cases the pressure, having built slowly and over a long period, may break suddenly and violently (*Kaikaku, Climacteric, Resilience). The more effectively the change is held back, the more sudden will the breakage be, when it comes.[149]

2. *Networks*

Think of a network of connections between centres of activity—almost anything will do: towns, airports, film stars, academic researchers, websites. These centres are called "nodes" in the literature, and there are links between them. Depending on the kind of system, the links may take the form of (for instance) roads, air routes, friendship networks, co-casting (actors appearing in the same film), citations of academic papers, or links between websites. Those links come about almost by accident as a result of the nodes needing to be in touch with each other; they tend not to be planned in advance. And two kinds of pattern develop:

First, there is the "random" network. Imagine a scatter of nodes. Now gradually join them up with random links. At the early stages, you still have a lot of disconnected nodes, with just a few joined up: it is not a network. But then, as further links are added, it rather abruptly becomes a connected network: each new link joins nodes that are already joined, so the whole thing then becomes a system (see first diagram). Now you can reach any part

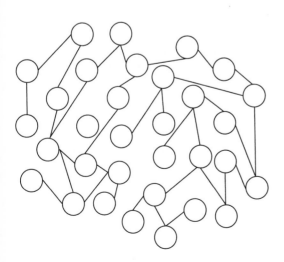

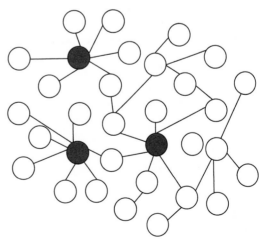

of it via the links between the nodes; each node has roughly the same number of links, and in that sense all the nodes are on the same *scale. Neighbouring towns and villages linked up by roads are a network of this kind.[150]

The second kind of network is the "scale-free" network. Imagine the same scatter of nodes, but this time a small number of them begin to be better known and more visited than the others (marked in black on the second diagram). Once that happens, people choose them for preference. For instance, some airports achieve a superstar—hub—status, as do some towns, and a few academics are hubs in that it would be foolish not to cite their papers if you are working in their field. Film stars are hubs in the sense that other actors want to be seen with them. These networks are scale-free in the sense that there no limit to the number of links that those few dominant nodes can have. For example, on the internet, while there is a long tail of sites with few links and visitors or none at all, others have millions of links: there is no sense of shared scale. Links are distributed between hubs according to the "Power Law" (discussed below), with a few hubs having many links, and many hubs having few.[151]

Now, why does this matter? Well, each type of network has its significance in specific situations. The scale-free network is the form that naturally occurs when it is the connections themselves that are the function of the system—as, for instance, in the case of air routes. If you want to fly from one small city to another distant city, it makes most sense to fly from hub to hub rather than travel via a random network, because then you may only have to change planes once. Direct links between every small city would require vast numbers of flights in small planes. For example, direct links between each of 1,000 towns would require half a million two-way flights; if all were routed via the hub, links between them all would require a mere 1,000 two-way flights.[152]

Random networks, on the other hand, work better when it is the nodes themselves, rather than the connections between them, that are the focus of

attention: the connections may still be important, but here the nodes have a degree of self-sufficiency which makes it less critical—not a matter of life and *death—that they should maintain efficient links with all other nodes at all times. Here there are no hubs; just nodes joined together locally. As such, a random network cannot compete with a scale-free network in terms of long-distance travel because to get from A to (a distant) B in a random network, you have to go through a lot of hubs (e.g., local towns, and stopping off at a lot of inns on the way, which is what horse-drawn transport was about).

But the random network, with its local links, has advantages. For one thing, it is *modular, and therefore has *recovery-elastic resilience—its built-in redundancy enables the system to survive even if some or many of its parts don't, making it much less vulnerable to catastrophic breakdown after a shock. If one of the hubs of a scale-free network is knocked out, the effects are traumatic: even if other less important hubs are brought into service, they risk being quickly overloaded and are likely to break down too. By contrast, the locally-linked network will have much slower connections, but its modular structure will survive all but extreme trauma, with links easily repaired or replaced with others. That rather homespun quality—the slower connections and responses throughout the system, the remoteness of distant parts of the system—is the cost of recovery-elastic resilience.[153]

There are implications here for the internet. We cannot be sure whether the internet will survive the *climacteric. And yet, it is hard to see how it can. It is a scale-free system, dependent on a relatively small number of giant hubs. If even a small number of hubs failed, then the whole system would be at risk of failure. It also depends on an uninterrupted flow of *energy (with carbon emissions to match), and it requires a large *infrastructure of minerals-mining, manufacture, distribution and maintenance. The *Lean Economy may have to get by without it. In fact, duplicate databanks and fail-safe sources for renewable energy are being built for the internet on an awesome scale, so its carbon emissions may be kept in some kind of check. But in an energy-scarce, *localised world, the force will be with the technologies which do not depend on a continuously functioning grid and a hyperconvergence of *material supplies, technologies, energy and financial flows. When resilience really matters, the advantage will lie decisively with technologies such as the book.[154]

3. *The Power Law*

Any system that has survived so far has resilience to at least some degree, though it may be trivial, giving the system no *protection—no ability to sustain its form—when the first significant shock comes along. So the question arises, how much shock ought a system be designed, or intended, to withstand? It is hard to answer this, for, in due course, a shock is likely on a scale beyond experience, *imagination, or the ability to cope. As explained by the mathematician Benoit Mandelbrot, the behaviour of *complex systems, natural or man-made, does not stay within the limits of a well-behaved distribution around an average, in the way that the differences between people's heights do. Instead, the scale of shocks (as in, for example, earthquakes, the turbulence of ocean currents, the flooding cycles of the River Nile, or the behaviour of economies and stock prices) behaves according to the "Power Law".[155]

We met the Power Law briefly in the discussion of networks, but let's take a closer look at it. This law exists where one variable changes in response to the *power* of another variable—e.g., the square or the cube of the other one. For instance, the scale of the maximum shock on record as having been endured by a system may be a power function of the number of years over which the record is taken. If you are measuring the height of the Nile over a period of time and you go back far enough, you will find catastrophic extremes. If people's heights were distributed according to the Power Law, most of us would be very short, but some would be 100 feet tall, and in a population of 6 billion someone, somewhere would be 8,000 feet tall. That is to say that, in systems of this kind, what seems to be normality will from time to time deviate into extremes—and occasionally

into spectacular extremes. In complex systems, extraordinary shocks are to be expected. An extended period of stability, such as the "Great Moderation" of the post-war period of *economics, is a special case.[156]

4. *Exactness*

A system's design is only as good as its detail. The Impressionist painters would not have been good system designers. It is the detail, leaving nothing to the imagination, that matters. An illustration of this comes from the early years of aircraft design. Reasonably affordable commercial passenger flights were not possible until, in 1935, the McDonnell Douglas DC-3 brought together five specific features: the variable-pitch propeller, retractable landing gear, a lightweight "monocoque" body, radial air-cooled engines and wing flaps. Four were not enough. All five had to be in place.[157]

Rough indications along the lines of "Oh, this is how it works" tell us nothing about a system except that here we have a set of good intentions which won't fly. They sound as though they ought to; they are fair; they are cheap; they are just what we need. But they won't. Systems are pedantic like that. They have an anorak personality. They need care and kindness, faithful observation, *deference to the detail, time to understand, a tolerance to surprise.

Feedback (see also *Resilience > Feedback)

Feedback is a property of all functioning systems, and is rule 5 of *lean thinking. The classic and *elegant example of feedback is the mechanism called the "governor", which keeps a steam engine running at constant speed. It consists of a spindle which spins at the speed of the engine, and it has two arms which, responding to centrifugal force, fly out as the speed rises. As they do so, they close the throttle, which slows the engine down.[158]

But a related meaning of feedback, less elegant but no less important, is the information which we receive as participants in a system (such as a bed of carrots, a garden, a *community, a *nation or a planet). If that feedback is accurate and quick, and if we do not close our minds to it, there is a possibility of influencing the system in ways consistent with resilience and reason. If it is inaccurate or slow, allowing mistakes to be merrily persisted in for a good long time before revealing themselves as mistakes, or if we are so important and powerful that we do not need to notice the feedback when it happens, then we will be on course to destroy the system and ourselves.

It does sound rather mechanical. That steam-governor is so beautiful that it invites a desire to stay at this sweet level of technical detail for the whole of one's life. But in reality, feedback is a big idea: as big as "rational", "reason" and "resilience". *Lean Logic* is all about feedback. Here we shall chew over some of what it means.[159]

1. *Feedback and forecast*

There is a sad-looking plant on your desk. You want it to cheer up. You water it. It becomes green and healthy: useful (positive) feedback. So you water it a lot. It goes brown: useful (negative)

feedback. So you water it in moderation, and it gets healthy again. Clearly the feedback is working. Then the plant goes brown again. Feedback tells you that something is wrong, but it does not tell you what: you won't know that it is zinc deficiency without more information. Moreover, even the feedback you have found so useful so far could have been misleading. Maybe it wasn't your watering that cheered it up, but the green-fingered cleaner who took *pity on it and fed it with liquid fertiliser. So the importance of feedback is not that it has all the answers you need, since it can be misleading, but that it is all the information you have. It is observation. You can be good or bad at reading it, and indeed there are ways of improving the quality of your observation and of the conclusions you draw (see "Causal Loops" sidebar).

CAUSAL LOOPS
Reductionism can have its uses

This is a case where *reductionist methods *can* be part of building up a coherent understanding. Start with a particular system which you would like to understand better. Now, every intervention can be associated with more or less of particular outcomes.

For instance, for a particular class in a particular school, a smaller class size could lead to (amongst other things) *less* noise, *more* individual attention, *more* motivated teachers and better education—but lower school income, cost-cutting, fewer teachers, and larger class sizes, an *increased* workload on teachers, who therefore demand higher salaries . . .

In other words, there is a series of consequences—"causal loops" between what you do and what happens. The sum of all the consequences can be positive (a signal to reduce the size of the class) or negative (to keep it large, or make it larger), or neither.

In principle these complementary effects will settle at an equilibrium, where the class size is at its optimum and, in principle, if you trace through all the causal loops—on paper, on a computer, and/or by experiment— you will get close to the class size that works best from all points of view.

The reason this approach is useful is that it provides a *protocol* for exploring—and to a significant degree forecasting—the implications of a proposal. You may be tempted to say, "larger class sizes save money", and have done with it. The protocol says, "Calm down; let's think this through", and the way is open to trace the links one at a time. For each causal loop, there are sequels and feedbacks: e.g., more individual attention → more discovery of individual talent → more resistance to the standard curriculum → more demand on individual teachers → more absenteeism → larger class sizes . . .

Your list, or diagram, of causal links can never be finished, but there is encouragement here for tracing the sequence of cause-and-effect—an advance on the passionate incomprehension which has shaped our world (*Five Whys).[160]

The important thing is to be alert to the information and consequences which you don't expect. For instance, if you come at a situation as an *expert in a narrow specialism of the subject, you may exclude yourself from noticing the information that comes from another part of it, or from making the connections between the bits of information you do get. Instead of seeing a system, *reductionism sees bits of it. Observing things is easy; joining them up is hard: it needs a long attention span, and the brain may need training.

2. *Feedback and flow*

A system tends to maintain its form and character, changing only slowly if at all, or maintaining a cyclical constancy despite shocks which would change it beyond recognition, if it were a cloud or a sand dune. And yet, this sustained integrity as a system is not achieved due to any of its members showing any particular self-restraint (*Responsibility Fallacy). Most populations—plant, animal or human—would quickly dominate their ecosystem with their numbers, given half a chance. The reason why such *amplifiers*, such as the propensity to breed without limit, do not continually destroy systems is that there are compensating *dampers* which stop them doing so.[161]

Amplifiers (positive feedback) tend to increase the effect that caused them; dampers (negative feedback) tend to reduce it. Practically all successful outcomes everywhere have aspects of positive feedback in them. Success goes from strength to strength. And it sometimes happens that, at first, there is no damper (negative feedback) on hand to suppress it. Confidence in stock markets and mortgage markets boils over. Plants *genetically modified to resist predators can be expected to multiply out of control. *Climate change, beyond a certain threshold (or 'tipping point'), triggers more climate change. Unless a damper can kick in at a reasonably early stage, allowing a flow of corrections, then the reaction may mature from feedback to shock or collapse. The problem lies, not with the positive feedback, but with the absence of early and effective dampers. And, to be effective, the dampers need, as a general rule, to have two qualities:

First, they need to be present in some variety. As James Lovelock shows, a modelled ecology that contains just two relevant animal species—rabbits and foxes—is unstable: if there are too many foxes, their population crashes, and that is followed by there being too many rabbits, whereupon the population of foxes grows. But as Lovelock points out, when we see . . .

> . . . a bank where the wild thyme blows,
> Where oxlips and the nodding violet grows,
> Quite over-canopied with luscious woodbine,
> With sweet musk-roses and with eglantine . . .[162]

. . . there is a good chance that, with that variety of species on hand to stabilise it, this is an iterative network of positive and negative feedback which conserves its form and nature for some time. It is the interaction of the *diverse species living there that gives the species stability.[163] Eugene Odum summarises,

> The ecosystem is the basic functional unit in ecology, since it includes both organisms and abiotic environment, each influencing the properties of the other and both necessary for maintenance of life as we have it on the Earth.[164]

Secondly, the damping process needs to be a continuous (or, at least, high frequency) one. Some ecosystems—such as forests that have adapted to periodic wildfires—do depend on infrequent limiters, but the immediate results are rather drastic. "Stability" is more comfortably associated, as Lovelock puts it, with "close coupling" between action and response—that is, with constant, *small-scale nudges and limitations (*Kaizen).

And Lovelock adds an aside:

> Perhaps it is a metaphor for our own experience that the family and society do better when firm, but justly applied, rules exist than they do with unrestricted freedom.[165]

In other words, systems are able to benefit from their parts' uninhibited potential for positive feedback because at the same time they maintain a steady flow of dampers. And yet, it is the positive

S

feedback that in a sense moves the whole process along, and the idea of positive feedback in an ecology is so often used in a disturbing context— such as runaway climate change, overfishing, overgrazing and deforestation—that we should acknowledge, too, its significance in a positive sense; the sense of reinforcement, the realisation of what we have the potential to become: pianist, doctor, friend, woman, man.

Birmingham, at the centre of Britain's largest industrial conurbation, is not often cited as an ecological example to follow. But it is in fact a story of reinforcement, of positive feedback in the constructive sense of its increasing, self-reinforcing confidence. It invented its own standards of engineering, technical ingenuity, teaching and apprenticeship, its radical politics—and Birmingham was a vital habitat for the Pre-Raphaelite movement. This city developed a brilliant critical mass of *creative talent, a storming contribution to the Industrial Revolution, and a culture of responding to acute observation—aka both negative and positive feedback. It had *flow.

We now need the magic of that energy and alertness, committed to a profoundly different aim.

3. *Fast feedback*

Guidance by feedback is everywhere we look, but we need to be aware of the occasions when it evolves to a level which is so fast-acting and sophisticated that it is not at first easy to recognise its existence. For example, a man on a tightrope is kept aloft by feedback loops. He responds to a slight tilt with a compensating action—a wobble. Tilts and wobbles present the man with a highly complex problem, in which he must take into account their speed, their direction in three dimensions and the resulting kinetic energy (depending on his weight, the length and weight of his balancing bar, and the movement of the rope). Each of these is strictly a causal loop, requiring evaluation in terms of positive and negative feedback. If he paused to work all this out on his calculator, he would fall off, so it is done at a subconscious level, using the principle of resonance (discussed below), which judges each changing state continuously.

The brilliance of our subconscious minds—and those of (for instance) flocking birds, or hawks standing on the wind or diving onto their prey—is awesome. The subconscious of a dog chasing a stick carries out millions of interactions with balance, electro-chemical muscle coordination, enzyme messaging, finely-tuned cardiovascular responses and parallax: the best the conscious mind can manage is 'dog fetch stick'.

The aim of skilled systems thinking—as in riding a bicycle, sustaining a *permaculture system, or making a *community—is to set things up in the first place so that the system runs itself. You then only have to think about it from time to time—interacting with, rather than intervening in, a healthy system, which responds faster than you can think.

4. *Synergy and *emergence*

Synergy is the interaction between parts of a system, producing results greater than would have been available to them acting on their own. Emergence is synergy which leads to the evolution of a *complex system.

Synergy and emergence are significant in the case of the collective action of a community. A community can achieve results—in, say, the transformation to energy-self-reliance—which are not simply the *sum* of what its individual members can do (added together), but the *product* of their interactions (multiplied together). Here is the power of *lean thinking and *common purpose. The big accomplishment may not be thought possible, so it may not be attempted, but—*if* the group possesses the relevant talent, *if* it persists, *if* it has the *freedom to decide for itself and the time to implement what it has decided, *if* the accomplishment is seen as a set of small tasks in which there is local *presence—if all these ifs and more are met, there will be emergence. The *exhilaration that comes with it can be spectacular.[166]

But synergy may turn negative, too, and this can be critically significant in the context of systems that have become stressed. For example, an economy that is in trouble owing to *energy depletion, changing *climate, declining soil fertility, a growing *population and declining *cultural confidence, may become sensitive to minor stresses. Just one thing could be the final straw that breaks the back of a system so weakened. A human society at that stage has reached the end of its ability to deal with additional trouble. Even a minor additional problem can nudge it across the threshold into an entirely different state, working to different rules (*Intermediate Economy).[167]

5. *Time

The impact of time on feedback is decisive. In the case of our own species' current large-scale systems, there is a long series of feedback lags between events and responses (see "The Lag Sequence" sidebar).

We can't wait that long. A systems-feasible future depends on tight coupling between event, observation and response, fulfilling the lean thinking requirement of *flow, with moderate early responses to small stimuli rather than late blockbuster responses to incipient catastrophe. *Lean Logic* is substantially defined by key principles which affirm and enable a flow of this kind, including *practice (the hands-on culture which observes events quickly and accurately), appropriate *scale (with its implications of *elegance, *judgment and *presence), and the principles of *resilience and *lean thinking.

But there is menace lurking in the concept of time. Here are three of its darker aspects:

The decision-window. In most situations, and for most of the time, big strategic decisions are unnecessary; you can simply let things ride. However, within a long period of time, there are occasions— sometimes short-lived and not much more than 'last moments'—at which crucial decisions can be made which will have radical consequences. And they *need* to be made, since the default position of making no decision will also have radical consequences. It is not always clear until later that the moment has passed.[168]

The anthropologist Marvin Harris offers an example of this. As described in the entry for *Unlean, the regimes of the Oriental civilisations of the past were organised around autocratic, giant-scale systems of *water management. The problem

---

THE LAG SEQUENCE
10 steps to being timed-out

1. Observation lag: from the time the problem begins to unfold, to its existence first being noticed by pioneers.
2. Comprehension lag: . . . to its significance being understood.
3. Communication lag: . . . to that understanding being first published.
4. Diffusion lag: . . . to wide awareness.
5. Denial lag: . . . to acceptance. But *denial may persist.
6. Action lag: . . . to action.
7. Project lag: . . . to completion of a relevant project.
8. System lag: . . . to termination of the practice which is causing the damage.
9. Pipeline lag: . . . to termination of the added trauma suffered by the system.
10. Overshoot: between the time of termination and the *earlier* time it would have had to be terminated.

---

is that, once such regimes are established, it is virtually impossible to reform them. Harris writes,

> . . . despotic forms of government may arise which can neutralise human will and intelligence for thousands of years. This implies . . . that the effective moment for conscious choice may exist only during the transition from one mode of production to another. After society has made its commitment to a particular technological and ecological strategy for solving the problem of declining efficiency, it may not be possible to do anything about the consequences of an unintelligent choice for a long time to come.[169]

Slow change. Slow changes are usually the big changes which transform systems, for better or worse. Examples:

a. the build-up of phosphorus from farmland surrounding the Everglades, with the result that

the native sawgrass ecosystem and the species
that depend on it are being replaced by an
emerging monoculture of cattail bulrushes;

b. gradual decline in the functional effectiveness of
the *family or the community's *culture;

c. the decline in male fertility.

Slow changes tend to be missed, or dismissed
on the grounds that there is nothing new there, or
that there is nothing to be done about it, or that the
evidence is weak, or that more immediate problems
claim priority.[170]

Overshoot is where action taken has already
caused damage, or it is too late to prevent it. It
belongs to a set of problems which can be illustrated by lags (see "The Lag Sequence" sidebar on
page 457) and inventories. Inventories take many
forms, with the most obvious being the stock of
finished goods in a company's warehouse, ready
and waiting for a sale. In good times, there is
nothing wrong with this. As soon as a sales order
comes in, it can be supplied out of what the firm has
in stock and, just in case an order comes in one day
which is exceptionally large, it is handy to have an
inventory, so that the customer is not kept waiting.

No problem so far. But suppose there is a
downturn in the economy, or the company begins
to feel less confident about the future, or is short
of cash. The obvious first thing to do is to let the
inventory run down: this leaves sales unaffected,
but it can reduce the costs of production: workers
can be laid off and orders for parts can be
cancelled, without this affecting the company's
prospects in any obvious way. And that means
that the existence of the inventory allows a *small*
problem for the company to turn into a *big* problem
for its suppliers: multiplied across the economy,
reduced confidence can quickly multiply into
recession. And even when demand starts to pick
up again, inventory-rich companies may still be
able to supply it from their inventories, so that the
economy as a whole remains in trouble . . .

. . . until the warehouse is empty, whereupon
firms must pile back into production quickly in
order to keep up with demand, despite having got

rid of their inventories. That is, inventories can lead
to large lags and shocks in a system. These do not
simply reduce the accuracy of feedback, but make
it profoundly misleading.

An engaging but hair-raising illustration of this
was devised at the Sloan School of Management
in the 1960s. It's called the Beer Game: a pop band
mentions a brand of beer (Lover's Beer) in a song;
demand for the beer doubles; the lags in the supply
chain, along with alarmed and understandable
overreactions by everyone involved, rapidly join
up. Retailers, wholesalers and the brewery run
out of stock. Then everyone does the obvious: the
retailers and wholesalers massively increase their
orders; the brewery goes into double time. The
result is that the whole supply chain suddenly
finds itself chock-full of over-ordered beer. Finally,
the point is reached where the brewery has to shut
down for a year to allow the inventories in the
system to clear.

In a sense, of course, it was an accident waiting
to happen. Communications were poor—this was
before the days of email—and the system was able
only to offer *quantity* responses to *time* problems.
And yet flaws of just this kind are present in other
time-related problems, such as *climate change. No
one actually does anything wrong. Lags are in the
system, killing *flow, and taking the system as a
whole forward to overshoot. Then everyone looks
for someone to *blame.[171]

6. *Closed-loop system*

A closed-loop system, using all (or most of) its
own material waste, is well placed to observe
and respond to feedback. It is close to events,
and the recognition that it cannot import what it
cannot provide focuses the mind. In a closed-loop
system, *hyperbole convinces nobody—unless (as
everybody knows, but doesn't like to admit), it is
too late.[172]

7. *Path dependence*

The character of a system, along with the features
of its local environment, is substantially determined by the path it embarked upon a long time
ago ("the story so far"). The way a system responds

to feedback is deeply shaped by this accumulated experience, leading to where it is now. Our lives congeal behind us, but watch us—like Tutankhamen's army—governing our *choices, uneasy witnesses to our flawed decisions (*Emergence).[173]

8. *Homeostasis*

Homeostasis is the ability of species and *natural systems to persist unchanged over very long periods in spite of profound changes in the environment and climate. The flow of *small-scale, rational adjustments to events, despite its mixed and largely failed record in human history, has a wonderful record in the case of natural systems. The attention of biology has been focused on its evolution rather than its stability, but its fundamental significance was recognised by Charles Darwin, who wrote in a letter to Charles Lyell, "If I had to commence *de novo*, I would have used 'natural preservation'."[174]

Function

This third and final group of principles is about getting the results you want from a system, avoiding the results you don't want, and (the ideal and leanest option) letting the system take its course to your mutual benefit.

1. *Composition gains*

These are benefits arising from the links between parts of the system, and/or from the extent of others' participation in the system. A well-tempered system yields three such gains:

 a. *common purpose*: shared intention to reach a shared goal. An alignment of individual and collective purposes, so that actions and aims which individuals recognise as in their own interests are also in the interests of the system as a whole, and *vice versa*.
 b. *common capability*, an aim which becomes available if and only if it is a collective aim, developing the system's potential for synergy; and
 c. *common resource*, a resource which is intrinsic to everyone's activities, so that events affecting its usefulness affect—and could ultimately transform—the system (e.g., the *political economy) as a whole.

2. *Leverage*

Leverage is accurate, small-scale, systems-literate action which makes a system want to do what you want it to do. It utilises resonance—that is, the tendency of a system to oscillate at maximum amplitude at certain frequencies.

Systems are drenched in resonance: events amplify each other with startling effect—like a child's rhythmically kicking legs on a swing—or they damp each other down, or change each other; there is rhythm and synergy, magnifying the effects of seemingly minor promptings and causes (small kicks while on the swing will sustain an oscillation containing a lot of energy). This is summarised by the science writer John Gribbin as a way of getting a large return for a relatively small effort, by making the effort at the right time and pushing the system in the way it wants to go.[175]

Leverage can sound at first like a case of scheming manipulation: find the weak point in the system and apply pressure to force it to do what you want. Well, perhaps sometimes it is just that, but more usefully, it is about working with the system. The example that Buckminster Fuller gives is the rudder on a ship:

> Something hit me very hard once, thinking about what one little man could do. Think of the Queen Mary [ocean liner]. The whole ship goes by and then comes the rudder. And there's a tiny thing at the edge of the rudder called a trim tab. It's a miniature rudder. Just moving the little trim tab builds a low pressure that pulls the rudder around. Takes almost no effort at all. So I said that the little individual can be a trim tab. Society thinks it's going right by you, that it's left you altogether. But if you're doing dynamic things mentally, the fact is that you can just put your foot out like that and the whole big ship of state is going to go. So I said, call me Trim Tab.[176]

And leverage works the opposite way round from the way you expect: to make the rudder turn right, you turn the trim tab left.

Well-designed, healthy systems do not need heavyweight management to produce intended

S

459

consequences. It may take no more than the "nudge" advocated by Richard Thaler and Cass Sunstein:

> Exceedingly small features of social interactions can have massive effects on people's behaviour.[177]

The alternative—to throw massive resources into trying to force the system to do what it doesn't want to do—does, however, have the advantages of keeping you very busy and setting you up with a job for life, so it tends to be preferred over looking for the point of leverage.

Nonetheless, the heroic, frantic effort is usually a sign that things have been left too late, that the opportunity of applying leverage has passed and that the outcome will be regrettable. Both the "flow" of lean thinking and the "nudge" of informal systems thinking are interventions with the time, knowledge and *manners needed to be effective.[178]

3. *Efficiency

This is the ratio between the outcomes desired from a system (e.g., the food, warmth and music delivered to residents of a large-scale *civic society) and the *regrettable necessities which it must maintain in order to produce them (e.g., the *intermediate economy of that society). A low ratio is *elegant.

But note that this (like many other concepts in Lean Logic) has *fuzzy edges. A snail, sliding modestly up the trunk of an apple tree, does not depend on any intermediate economy at all—no transport, no waste disposal contractors, no tax, no environmental consultants. And yet, it depends on the whole complex of global tectonic movements and ocean currents, the exchanges of gas and rock, the algae, the dimethyl sulphide which seeds clouds and makes it rain, and all the other interactions that comprise *Gaia. On one analysis, that's a terribly inefficient snail. On another, it might be best not to think of systems in such a *reductionist, snail-centred way.

Systems thinking is the art of holding a subject in the mind for long enough at least to recognise the existence of connections which are intrinsic to it—and, better still, of having a tentative idea of what some of those connections might be. It is enabled by a sustained concentration span. It is at the heart of Lean Logic, and its security as a defining property of our species and *culture is in trouble. This breaking up of vision is an almost unavoidable outcome of science—for it is easier to observe a thing than to trace through its connections with all other things—but there is a cost to this. As the pioneer of *organic thinking, Eve Balfour, writes,

> Whatever we study, our tendency is to break it up into little bits, thereby destroying the whole, and then to study the effect or behaviour of the separate pieces as though they were independent, instead of—as in fact they are—interdependent.[179]

And now, connected thinking has to contend with the forces of the electronic media, *distracting us from the attention span needed for *reflection, inductive problem-solving, critical thinking and *imagination. Systems are hard to think about by any standards. For the scattered and fragmented minds reflected on in Nicholas Carr's The Shallows, it may be becoming even harder. Systems thinking is not about understanding. It is deeper than that. It is about *encounter.[180]

*Resilience, Emergence, Gaia, Reductionism, Dirty Hands, Hippopotamus.

T

TACTILE DEPRIVATION. The loneliness, coldness and lack of communication in a society which, owing to anxieties about its abuse, has lost the language of touch. Touch has a large vocabulary of meaning, between bliss and pain, none of which can be abandoned without loss. Tactile deprivation leaves a misery of depression, isolation and *emotional withdrawal, followed by trouble when touch is the central skill needed for complex endeavours such as marriage and child-raising.[1]

At the same time, we are losing the touch of language, for language began as a replacement for grooming and, with careful, gentle articulation, it too has mildly *erotic qualities. It works best when you take your time, travelling hopefully rather than being distracted by arrival. *Community will be held together by both touch and

sound: soporific, inspissated, stretch, smooth, evocative, dappled, spinster, Limpopo. Slow and attentive is best.[2]
*Conversation, Reciprocity and Cooperation, Lean Education.

Tao. "The Way". A concept of Confucian thought which has something in common with the principles of *Lean Logic*. *Tao* refers to the ideal way of life, whose key features include the following:

Te is the *virtue—generosity, ritual, *humility—which enables a person (originally, the ruler) to tread The Way.

Jen—kindness—is a concern and engagement with all living things (related to *caritas and *encounter).

Li refers to *rituals, behaviour and *tradition as integral to a person's participation in the *community.

Yi is the sense of rightness, *truthfulness and *courage which underpins *judgment.

Confucian thinkers have disagreed about why the ideal should have any moral standing, with much debate centring on the significance of *hsing* (the intrinsic nature of something or someone), which came to mean the way a thing will develop its potential if unobstructed. One interpretation is that there is an intrinsic *ethical quality to what it means to be human in the natural world: human nature and Nature converge. The other is that *hsing* is a self-regarding cultivation of one's own potential.[3]

These debates do not do justice to the concept of *Tao* or—more generally—The Way, which appears to have been almost universal among traditional societies. It brings together in one principle the idea that there is an enchantment and rightness in common to the cosmos and to human affairs alike, whose absence is the leading symptom of a society or a community in trouble. *Tao* represents all that is right in the universe, including the human sphere itself and the spirit world which underpins it, which is the source of its order and of the possibility of happiness.[4]

In *Local Wisdom we see just this principle in the villages of Tsarist Russia. And in the *Lean Economy, the only way human society can survive at all is by developing an *ethic in the *spirit of *Tao*.

Taut. See Slack and Taut.

Tautology. An argument which uses the premise from which it starts as proof that the premise is true. This is a form of *begging the question, but it is more insidious because it does not even acknowledge that the question exists. It comes in the form:

> We have to be competitive, and therefore we have to be competitive [and now we have established that reason is on our side we can say anything we like].

This is effective because of its escape from reason: in defence of a blazing *certainty you can go straight into the heights of *hyperbole and *indignation:

> We reject all morality which has not a human, class perspective. We affirm that it is a fraud, a deceit and a form of brainwashing imposed on workers and peasants in the interest of plutocrats and capitalists. We declare that our morality is entirely subordinate to the interests of the working class in its struggle. Our morality is dedicated to the benefit of the class war . . .
> *And this is why we say so*: for us, morality detached from human society has no existence: it is a fraud. For us, morality is subordinate to the proletariat's class struggle.
>
> Vladimir Lenin, 1920.[5]

As Françoise Thom notes, the language of the tautology simulates *logical progression but remains completely motionless and reduced to an echo of itself.[6]

Technical Fix. The strategy of ignoring what a system in trouble is trying to tell you, and forcing it along in the same dismal direction even faster.
*Ingenuity Gap, Arms Race, Unintended Consequences, Galley Skills.

TEQs (Tradable Energy Quotas). A framework designed to achieve deep reductions in dependence on fossil fuels at the *national scale. It ensures

T

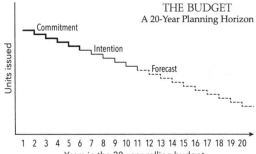

THE BUDGET
A 20-Year Planning Horizon

Units issued

Commitment

Intention

Forecast

1 2 3 4 5 6 7 8 9 10 11 12 13 14 15 16 17 18 19 20
Years in the 20-year rolling budget
set by the Committee on Climate Change

fair access to *energy as scarcities develop, guarantees emissions reductions in line with *climate science and supports the active participation and *cooperation of all energy users in the shared task.[7]

The TEQs system is, in essence, a system of legally-tradable electronic rations. It applies *lean thinking to stimulate the *local discovery of particular energy solutions that make deep transformations in fossil fuel use possible, as part of a *modular solution to almost-impossible global problems.

How TEQs works

At the heart of TEQs is the national Carbon Budget—set by an independent carbon policy committee informed by the latest climate science (in the UK this now exists, in the form of the Committee on Climate Change). The Budget (see diagram) states the quantity of carbon emissions that will be permitted each year, and so sets all energy-users in the nation a clear long-term time horizon in which to explore and implement ways of reducing their *need for the critical resource of fossil fuels.[8]

The TEQs system then shares out the rights to these emissions, by the *Issue* of TEQs units (see "The TEQs System" diagram). The Issue takes place in two ways.

First, an unconditional and equal weekly *Entitlement* to all adults, issued directly by electronic transfer into their TEQs accounts (around 40% of the available units would be issued in this way, reflecting the fact that roughly 40% of UK emissions currently come from individuals and *households).

At the same time, the remainder are sold by *Tender*, as part of the weekly auction that already takes place for

the sale of Treasury Bills and Government *debt. Banks and brokers obtain a supply of units on instructions from their clients, and distribute them to all non-household energy-users in the economy—to industry and services of all kinds, and to the Government itself. Being an auction, the Tender provides revenue, which the Government uses to facilitate, in every way it can, the process of reducing dependence on fossil fuels (more on this later).

On the first day of the scheme, one year's supply of TEQs units is issued into the national economy; it is then topped up each week, so that there is always a rolling year's supply of units in participants' accounts. Units are issued, and accounts maintained, by the Registrar.

When fuel or electrical energy is purchased anywhere in the national economy, the buyers pay for it as usual using money, but must also surrender a number of TEQs units corresponding to the carbon content of their purchase. Individuals who use less than their Entitlement of units can sell the surplus; those who need more can buy them. All such transactions take place at the prevailing national price—like topping up a mobile phone or travel smartcard, there is no haggling required.

The number of occasions on which individuals actually purchase energy is quite limited—perhaps eight times a year for utilities, although it could rise to some thirty times a year for individuals with cars—and most

THE TEQS SYSTEM

ISSUE ← | REGISTRAR QuotaCo | ← SURRENDER

| Entitlement 40% | Tender 60% | | Carbon Budget | Primary Energy Providers and Importers |

THE MARKET
trading between
Primary dealers
People   All other energy users.
Firms, Government, etc.

COMMITTEE ON CLIMATE CHANGE

Producers
↑
Wholesalers
↑
Retailers

£ Government revenue from Tender

UNITS FLOW THROUGH
THE ENERGY CYCLE
Government leads, assists,
and enables the Energy Descent

TEQs transactions are done by card and direct debit. Moreover, on each of these occasions, the surrender of TEQs units takes place along with the money payment, as part of the same transaction. If you have run out of units (or never had any—perhaps you are a foreign tourist) the energy retailer will simply add the cost of buying the units on your behalf to your bill. This is a system with low levels of hassle; it is 'hands-free', with no need for separate "carbon cards". Energy-users do not have to spend time thinking about the mechanics of the scheme and calculating carbon emissions. The whole of their attention is focused on the principal task of *creatively reducing their individual and collective use of fossil fuels—in line with the ambitious, transparent, long-term requirements of the Carbon Budget.

BACKGROUND PROCESSES

Meanwhile, the *Rating System* evaluates fuels and electricity in terms of the carbon they contain and release. One TEQs unit is defined as one "carbon unit"—corresponding to the quantity of fuel or electrical energy that produces one kilogram of carbon dioxide over its life-cycle (not only from its final combustion, but also from the combustion of the other fuels used in bringing that fuel to market). The system ensures that all electricity and fuel carries a carbon rating, e.g., 0.2 units per kWh, or 2.3 units per litre. Low-carbon energy sources thus cost consumers less, providing them with a competitive advantage.

The TEQs units flow through the economy just as energy does (though in the opposite direction), as illustrated in the diagram, "The TEQs System". Every time that energy changes hands, so do TEQs units, in exchange. So the units that an energy retailer receives from its customers when selling fuel or electricity are then surrendered to the wholesaler when the retailer buys its own fuel/electricity supplies. The wholesaler, in turn, surrenders them to the primary energy producer/importer. Finally, the primary provider surrenders the units back to the Registrar in exchange for the right to produce or import the fuel. Since the Registrar issued the units in the first place, this creates a *closed-loop system.

The flow of units round the loop can be accounted for in companies' existing stock-control systems, so TEQs is self-*monitoring, requiring no routine public sector intervention. Any retailer who failed to collect TEQs units at the point of sale would need to buy replacement units when purchasing their own supplies (just as with cash). And the fact that the carbon content is known when energy or fuel is sold avoids the need for direct measurement of emissions from exhaust pipes, factories or homes. It also makes unnecessary the impractical task of accurate, consistent carbon labelling for individual products and services within the economy. Instead, since carbon-intensive manufacturers will have to recoup the cost of the additional TEQs units necessary to run their businesses, consumers will simply find that lower-carbon options tend to cost less cash (and this also offers a competitive advantage to retailers of any product or service with a lower-carbon supply chain).

Key Benefits of TEQs

Any framework for collective action for deep reductions in dependence on fossil fuels must fulfil twelve criteria:

1. *Guaranteed emissions reductions.* TEQs is a guarantee that the trajectory of reductions set by the Budget will actually be achieved. The quantity of fuel is determined by the Budget; the price adjusts around it. Price in the TEQs model is the free variable, the expansion joint which adjusts to circumstances; it is the degree of freedom which enables the scheme to keep the Budget's promises. It is in everyone's interests that the price of TEQs units should be low—as low as possible.

   What is more, the price takes the temperature of the energy transition: the lower it is, the more successfully are energy-users and the *nation as a whole adjusting to the tough demands of the energy descent by discovering and inventing ways to reduce collective energy demand. The features detailed below are designed to facilitate this, and thereby mitigate the price pressures imposed on us by *energy depletion and the need to mitigate *climate change.

2. *Equity.* Although the *per capita* entitlement is equal, that does not necessarily make it adequate for the individual's needs. Instead, it brings into each individual's own life a direct encounter with the reality of diminishing access to energy. Where there are

T

households and individuals whose energy needs are very high (because, for instance, their house is poorly insulated or because they have to drive a long way to work), the equal entitlement draws focus to the problem and provides a powerful *incentive to deal with it. The TEQs entitlement engages with the inherently unjust consequences of climate change and fuel depletion, prompting urgent action where it is most intensely needed, in advance of the undiscriminating reductions in energy rations which—all too soon—will be imposed by nature.

3. *Time to plan ahead*. The guaranteed TEQs Budget gives a clear long-term warning of the scale of reduction in energy use which has to be achieved over a rolling 20-year time horizon: the trajectory of energy descent set by the Budget is held constant, with that constancy made possible because the price can adjust around it (see *False Consistency). The long-term perspective is essential. Decisions will have to be made now, and action taken now, which will take twenty years or more to come to fruition. The long-term view must be present as a defining property of any scheme designed to reduce—and, eventually, to end—our dependency on fossil fuels (*Time Fallacies).

4. *Leaves the money with the consumer*. The cost of achieving the energy descent will be high, requiring profound changes in lives and *expectations, in the use of land and technology, and in the pattern of industry and transport. Moreover, the economy may be in deep depression due to the effects of the *climacteric. Individuals and households will therefore need as much money as they can get in order to pay for the transformation. The free distribution of TEQs units to individuals ensures that the money stays where it is most needed. The revenue received by the Government from the Tender will also be used to create a fund to support the communication and training, expert guidance and *capital costs required by a decisive and steep energy descent.

Consumers' budgeting is also assisted by the price-balancing effect of TEQs. TEQs will tend to stabilise the price of energy in two ways.

First, it prevents scarce fuel (e.g., oil) being, in effect, 'rationed by price'—with access being limited to the highest bidders (or the fastest movers).

Secondly, the price of energy and the price of TEQs units will tend to move in opposite directions—if, or when, world oil prices reach very high levels, this will reduce the demand for oil, thereby reducing the demand for TEQs units and thus their price. So the net price paid by consumers (oil+units) is more stable than the price of either oil or units alone.

5. *Government there to help*. The Government, in a TEQs scheme, is in the same boat as everyone else (since it too is bound by the scheme). Its role is to do everything in its power to enable the economy to achieve the reduction set by the Carbon Budget with the least possible disruption. It will do so on the basis of *call-and-response, providing services such as training, infrastructures, loans, and changes or relaxations in regulation which open the way to comprehensive transformation in the energy and material structures of the economy. It is not spending its time issuing instructions and regulations; it is working out how to cope *intelligently with the transformation that is facing us all. The money to do so is generated by the Tender.

6. *Specified in terms of energy*. The problem is an energy problem, and it will call for *imaginative and highly-motivated energy solutions. If the energy descent were seen by consumers as, in essence, a *money problem, it would be just one more charge on the household budget. Although the most successful energy-savers in a TEQs system will be able to sell their excess units, financial *incentives are peripheral to the scheme. Instead of relying on an (ultimately demotivating) system of extrinsic rewards and punishment, TEQs is built on making our shared intrinsic motivation explicit: no-one need pay us (or punish us) to make us want to avoid catastrophic climate change and retain access to essential energy services.

7. *Ownership*. The scheme belongs to the people who use it—that is, to all energy-users. Everyone is involved, and the design of the policy means that there is no possibility of free-riders. The rise or

fall of the national price of units is *feedback on *our* progress in reducing reliance on fossil fuels in pursuit of *our* goals. The purpose of TEQs is to maximise *freedom of choice and *empower households and businesses, within the constraint of not jeopardising those goals.

8. *An assured entitlement.* At times of scarcity, consumers will need to be sure that they can obtain their entitlement of fuel and energy. Without such an entitlement—or ration—those who are unsuccessful in bidding for the energy they need, or who are not quick enough to get hold of whatever fuel is available, will be left with none. This absolute requirement for a ration/entitlement applies whether the aim is to reduce carbon emissions, or to cope with fuel shortages, or both.

TEQs guarantees individuals the right to buy fuel in at least the quantity specified by the entitlement. That is not quite the same as a straight rationing scheme—which also stops people buying more than a given amount—since, in the case of TEQs, you can buy more units (as long as others are willing to sell theirs). TEQs rationing does not set an upper limit for individual energy-users, but it does meet the essential, life-or-death requirement of fair access to energy.

9. *Both for fuel scarcity and the climate.* Even in the unlikely event that the scheme were being used exclusively to reduce carbon emissions—without there being any question of fuel shortages—there would still be a scarcity problem which would make an entitlement scheme essential. As the Carbon Budget declines, high-carbon fuel will necessarily become less widely available, and if the distribution were left entirely to the *market, it would exclude all but the highest bidders. That is, an imposed scarcity of carbon and an actual scarcity of fossil fuels would have the same effect, requiring the same guarantees. Since both climate change and fuel scarcity are upon us, any fuel-related scheme must be equipped to deal with either or both. TEQs is designed to do this.

10. *International advantage.* The first-mover nation will develop the advantage of reduced energy-costs and ahead-of-the-field technology. A nation with a TEQs scheme will be able to commit itself with confidence to deep reductions, breaking the inertia in international negotiations by showing the way for other nations to do the same.

11. *Pull.* TEQs is based on pull, which sets up a clear commitment to—and framework for—the energy descent, by whatever means energy-users can devise. Rather than dictating changes from the top down, TEQs is a framework for change to be pulled along by energy-users themselves. *Households, *neighbourhoods, *communities, local authorities and industry will have a common frame of reference in which to *cooperate in the ambitious reductions which are beyond the reach of individual consumers. The significance of pull is central: TEQs bring a sharp, intense focus to the aspects of energy use where action can be most effective; they provide the incentive to call on Government and other sources for assistance; they motivate action; they encourage people to work out what action to take if it is not immediately clear. They stimulate creative *intelligence.

12. *Common purpose.* If the *energy descent becomes a shared goal, then action taken by the individual in his or her own interest is the same as the action needed in the collective interest. The TEQs framework helps to achieve this common purpose. Confronting all participants will be major tasks such as developing the *proximity principle (shorter travel and transport distances; goods and services being produced in proximity to the people who will be using them) and building local competence to meet local needs. The only way in which an individual can achieve major changes such as these is by cooperating with others at the level of households, streets, towns, the nation; TEQs clearly specifies the task as one of cooperating to achieve an energy revolution.

In summary, the TEQs model is constructed on the foundations of the key concepts described in *Lean Logic*, including *lean thinking, *common purpose, *presence, intrinsic *incentives and *resilience. It makes a decisive break with the presumption that citizens will do nothing to transform their dependence on fossil fuels unless they are goaded into doing so by *green authoritarianism and its carrots and sticks. By contrast, TEQs is based on the recognition that the only way we will have a prayer of a chance of achieving that transformation will be by recruiting the whole-hearted commitment and whole-brained *intelligence of citizens to that task. TEQs provides a framework for that collective motivation and local inventiveness, and the grid below sketches out some of the forms of *cooperation it could support.

WHY A CARBON TAX WOULD BE LESS EFFECTIVE THAN TEQS

None of these desirable characteristics apply to a carbon tax. The unsuitability of taxation for the task of reducing carbon emissions needs to be recognised:

1. If taxation were high enough to influence the behaviour of the better-off, it would price the poor out of the energy market.

2. The focus of the scheme must be on the long-term energy descent, sustained over many years. There needs to be a framework to guide it, but this is not a job which taxation can do. It is impossible for

tax to give a steady long-term signal: if it remains constant, it will be inappropriate at certain periods of the economic cycle; if it fluctuates, it does not provide the steady signal.

3. Taxation would take money from people just at the time they need it most: to achieve the needed reductions, they will need to spend on a whole range of structural changes and technologies, and—especially in the likely event of deep recession during some periods of the scheme's life—it is essential that they should have as much discretionary income as possible to enable them to do this.

4. Taxation is based on the assumptions that the authorities know what people need to do, and that they won't do it unless pushed—in effect fined for not getting on with it. The energy descent, by contrast, requires a clearly-defined framework whose difficulties can only be solved by the application of local ingenuity. Tax may, at best, establish an *extrinsic* incentive to achieve compliance with a stated goal; effective motivation can establish a far stronger *intrinsic* incentive to achieve well beyond

	Households	Communities	Companies	Loc/Nat Gov
Households	Households cooperate in conservation, renewable energy systems, repairs and local *food.			
Communities	Communities and households cooperate in skills, cultivation, schools, services, materials recovery and jobs.	There is cooperation between communities in developing the potential for local self-reliance and resilience.		
Companies	Households and companies cooperate in *closed-loop systems and *household production.	Communities and companies cooperate in local sourcing, and the supply of specialist skills in the building of local energy systems.	Companies cooperate to sustain a flow of goods and services and promote best standards, even if at the cost of *competitive advantage.	
Loc/Nat Gov	Government assists households with training, funds and regulatory support for the energy descent.	Government provides assistance of all kinds on a *call-and-response basis. Communities develop self-regulation.	Companies cooperate with Government in technical innovation, building local infrastructures and reducing transport needs.	Local Governments sustain joint training courses on energy descent solutions and share information.

such a goal, and to cooperate with others to do the same (*Incentives Fallacy).

5. Taxation has no role whatsoever in the distribution of fair entitlements to energy at a time of scarcity. If oil prices have gone through the roof and most people can't, for love or money, track down petrol for their cars, it would scarcely help to increase the rate of fuel tax. If a tax regime did exist to phase down carbon emissions, it would still be necessary to have in place an additional rationing scheme specified in terms of entitlements to energy.

There is an argument for aligning tax with recognised values—being set at higher rates for bad things (such as tobacco) than for good things. But even here its effectiveness as a motivator and a deterrent is limited. It should concentrate on what it is good at—raising money. Where the task is the application of creative *imagination on a scale unequalled in modern times to transform the energy foundations of our society, deeper reasons are needed.

TEQs as response to outright fuel/energy shortage

The above discussion has focused on a TEQs scheme implemented primarily in response to the urgent challenges of dramatic reductions in emissions. However, the depletion of oil and gas—and the scarcities and outages that will follow—will make it necessary for governments around the world to install rationing systems, to provide every energy-user with fair access to energy, and to pre-empt the intense *competition for energy that would otherwise develop. Such systems need to be installed and tested well in advance of the start of energy shortages. If substantial shortages were to develop before a rationing system were in place, a breakdown in the orderly distribution of energy would follow.

TEQs could be implemented in response to either imperative, and is designed to be capable of switching between carbon entitlements and energy entitlements at short notice. All accounts and systems will already be in place, and the changeover from reducing carbon emissions to sustaining fair access to the scarce fuel—while continuing the reduction in carbon emissions from fuels unaffected by the scarcity—will require only the activation of the following prepared settings in the system's programming:

At a time of fuel scarcity—and assuming that a TEQs system is in place—the first step will be to estimate the available quantity of the fuel in question. That quantity is measured in units. If the scarce fuel is oil, petrol could be taken as the standard unit, with 1 unit equal to 1 litre. Other fuels derived from crude oil require differing amounts of energy to produce as compared with petrol, and their unit ratings would be adjusted to allow for this—so that highly-refined kerosene might have a rating of (say) 1.1 units, while other fuels might have a rating of less than 1. This allows the energy market the flexibility it needs to keep its production of fuels in balance with demand.

When an energy-user purchases petrol, he or she (or it—it may be a company) surrenders units corresponding to the amount purchased, so that, for a purchase of 10 units of petrol, he or she surrenders 10 units, alongside the usual money payment. Those units (in the same way as the ordinary money payment for the fuel) are then pulled along the chain of supply, back to the refiner, the primary producer/importer, and the Registrar. Each stage in the production and distribution uses energy, and those energy purchases, too, are covered by the surrender of units, which also find their way back to the primary producers and the Registrar.

This mechanism is identical to that used for controlling carbon emissions, with the single exception that fuels are rated in terms of the actual quantity of fuel they represent, rather than in terms of their carbon content. No procedures would have to change. When the system switches from a Carbon Budget to a Budget (or Budgets) covering specific fuel(s), a new Issue of units will be made, with a new Entitlement and Tender and a switchover to different settings in the software.

In the case where a second fuel, such as gas, is in short supply, rations (e.g., Tradable Gas Units—one unit per kWh) could be issued in addition to the Tradable Oil Units and the carbon units already in circulation.

The distribution of tradable oil units—or tradable gas units—to individuals will be the same in terms of design and implementation as the distribution of tradable carbon units. They will be issued by weekly top-ups into individuals' accounts. A likely scenario is that one fuel (say, oil) is in short supply, while the consumption of other fuels (say, gas and coal) has to be reduced as part of the continuing descent in carbon emissions. That is to say, concurrent budgets will be needed for, respectively, fuel and carbon emissions. The TEQs model is explicitly designed to sustain two (or more) budgets in this way.

It is possible that—in the case of shortages that are expected to be volatile or short-lived—the rolling period of issue will be shorter than the one-year's supply appropriate to the case of carbon units. It could, for instance, be as short as two months, backed by good information on the circumstances of the shortage and its expected duration.

THE TENDER

When TEQs is used for rationing carbon, the distribution of units to organisations is based on the auction of units at the Tender, where organisations receive their units at the settlement price—the price at which supply and demand are in balance.

However, at a time of actual—and perhaps sudden and profound—fuel shortage, the terms of the Tender may need to be revised. In this situation, the settlement price may prove to be so high that some participants do not succeed in obtaining any units—or not enough to enable them to continue services which are essential to the economy—so that some intervention may be needed to guarantee users' minimum access to energy. For example, *food producers could make a case for such a guarantee.

In these circumstances, the terms of the Tender will be modified to deliver units guaranteeing a minimum entitlement for *non-household* participants with a valid claim, while the remainder would be auctioned as usual. This hybrid Tender would have the benefits of meeting unconditional needs—insofar as the total quantity of available energy allows—and sustaining the market for units. However, the existence of the market element is essential. Some rationed assets (e.g., food) may have less need of a market in entitlements, because differences between individual needs are relatively minor, or at least predictable. But in the case of the distribution of energy entitlements, the wide diversity

of energy needs makes the flexibility of the market a central asset, as the means of sustaining an efficient allocation. The strict fixed cap on *national* emissions is the essential constraint on the market which defines the *intention of the scheme, but a strict fixed cap on *personal* emissions would simply destroy those *professions which inherently require more energy (and thus destroy the national economy).

The use of the hybrid Tender may also be required in the context of a market designed purely for carbon emissions, especially if action is delayed (*Denial). If an extremely steeply-declining Carbon Budget is necessary, this could potentially make carbon units unavailable to some service providers in the quantity needed to function, in the same way as a sudden decline in fuel availability. The use of guaranteed minimum allocations should be avoided wherever possible, however, because it impairs the efficient distribution of units—which is contrary to the interests of all participants in the economy. Nonetheless, it is an option for fine-tuning the market—requiring no modification to the scheme beyond adjustments to programme settings in the light of current circumstances—and it may be necessary as a means of sustaining supplies of the energy needed by essential services.

Such adjustments to the functioning of TEQs fall easily within the flexibility of the system. The key condition for them to be feasible is preparation time, but once a TEQs system is in place, the adaptations needed to respond to energy scarcities could be made promptly.

If energy scarcity were to develop before tried and tested rationing systems were in place, profound hardship would follow—that is, actual energy-famine for the losers in the *competition for fuel. All too clearly, this would be unjust. Indeed, the distribution of scarce fuel would involve some form of auction or contest which, in the case of severe scarcity, could be *violent. TEQs is designed to sustain orderly access to energy in these conditions. And the instrument is designed, too, to prevent an even greater injustice, in that it represents an effective and realistic response to *climate change, which has the potential to expose populations to impacts whose consequences would be unjust by any standards.

It is reasonable to conclude that we are running into danger. Energy shortages will occur. We do not know when, but the event is undoubted and it is not far distant (*Energy Prospects). There is a real possibility that this will happen before a rationing system is in place. The combination of energy scarcity and the absence of rationing provision has lethal potential and it needs to be corrected without delay.

A whole-economy, nationwide scheme

TEQs is designed to include all energy-users in a *national economy. Since the model was first published in 1996, several variants have been devised and debated under the *general heading of "personal carbon trading" (PCT). In some of these variants the scope of the scheme is limited to individual consumers, leaving out other energy-users such as business and the public sector which would be covered by some other scheme, such as the European Union Emissions Trading Scheme (EU ETS). In support of this format, it is argued that the EU ETS already exists and is immoveable, so that an economy-wide scheme is out of the question:

> The core economic instruments for managing
> emissions for the foreseeable future are the
> EU Emissions Trading Scheme (EU ETS) [and
> the domestic supplier obligations]. Analysis
> of any PCT system that does not operate in
> tandem with these instruments will be purely
> academic: this suggests that TEQs and similar
> designs of personal carbon trading schemes
> that assume organisations and individuals
> operating together in an economy-wide scheme
> are non-starters.[9]

But there are two ways of seeing the scale and format of a carbon/energy rationing scheme:

First, there is the Layered Format, in which different participants in the same national economy belong to different schemes, so that businesses would belong to one scheme, operating in its own market and governed by its own Carbon Budget, and individuals would belong in a different scheme, working to a different Carbon Budget, in a different market, and at different prices. The presumption is that the Layered Format would cross national *boundaries, as does the EU ETS, which includes some thirty nations; and that other national groupings, such as the North American Free Trade Area (NAFTA), or a global scheme, would use the same format.

Secondly, there is the Integrated Format. It is *integrated* in that all participants in the national energy market — companies, public sector bodies and individuals — operate in the same scheme. The *scale of this market is critical — it is sufficiently small and self-contained to enable a strongly developed sense of *common purpose and shared ownership. There is acceptance of the Budget as a just representation of national circumstances, and of the *authorities responsible for it as qualified to represent the collective interest. Each nation designs and manages the scheme in response to consultation, and to the particular circumstances and energy usage that exist within its *boundaries.

Under the Integrated Format, TEQs would be the means by which nations implement the energy/emissions targets they have agreed at the international level.[10] Wider multinational (e.g., EU) targets would become realistic as each nation committed itself to a single Carbon Budget corresponding to its own situation and endorsed by consultation with its energy-using public. In the case of small nations, there would be the option of joining forces in a "national" group on a scale equivalent to the larger nations.

It is useful to compare the merits of these two models against three criteria:

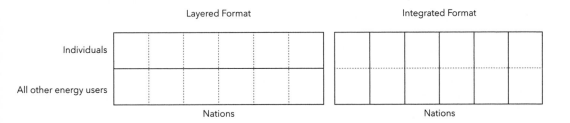

Layered Format

Integrated Format

Individuals

All other energy users

Nations

Nations

1. The Carbon Budget
2. Fuel Pricing
3. Rationing

THE CARBON BUDGET

The Carbon Budget—which defines the quantity of permitted emissions and their rate of decline—sets the *intention of the system. If the Budget were too steep, then the geographical area to which it belonged would find itself plunged directly into an energy problem: with too many buyers of units and too few sellers, the price would rise sharply, so that some participants would be plainly unable to afford to meet their needs for energy. Conversely, if the Budget was too unambitious, there would be no incentive to reduce energy demand, the price of units would decline towards zero, and the scheme would in effect cease to operate.

Even within a nation, of course, there are wide divergences of energy use, so that some users will find it harder than others to stay within the Budget or to buy the additional units they need—but it is for such adjustments that the flexibility of the market exists. Within a *multinational* TEQs scheme, the problem arises where *a whole nation* has energy needs substantially above or below the average for the other nations (as might be expected). This would lead to large-scale transfers of units from the nation with the lower demand to the nation with the higher demand, together with a large-scale transfer of funds the other way, which could reduce the scheme to simple international *money-politics—an unproductive mix of opportunism and resentments. The system would offer the nation receiving the windfall revenue little incentive to reduce its energy demand yet further, and the nation that bore the cost would pay less attention to driving down its energy demand than to challenging the scheme. If the imbalance were severe, the scheme would be short-lived.

A central condition of success, therefore, is that the Budget should be pitched at a *scale which is seen to be just and realistic, at which participants in the system can reasonably *cooperate, and on which they can feel a sense of shared ownership and *identity. The implication is that the scheme should be based on relatively small areas—roughly on the scale of the *nation—as specified in the Integrated Format.

FUEL PRICING

In the case of the Integrated Format (the TEQs model) a central principle is that the unit in which emissions are measured and traded is expressed in terms of energy (that which people actually want to buy), not in terms of emissions themselves. As explained at the start of this entry, carbon emissions are translated into energy units—that is, the amount of any given fuel needed to produce a kilogram of carbon dioxide. In other words, all fuels and electricity supplies are "carbon rated". This use of easily-measured units is a *necessary condition of a feasible carbon-rationing scheme involving individuals. There is no need to measure the carbon emissions of your car or house: they are already accounted for in the fuel you buy. The significance of this is not merely that it keeps things simple; it is the only realistic design for a scheme: people buy fuel exactly as they did before, except that they automatically surrender units at the time of purchase in accordance with its published carbon rating.

But it follows that any TEQs scheme must include all energy users. If it included only some, then fuel would carry two (or more) different prices, depending on who the buyer was: if you were to turn up at a garage in your car to buy petrol, you would be paying a different price for it than someone who showed up in a commercial vehicle (whose energy consumption would be covered by another scheme). Different prices for the same fuel would immediately lead to black market brokerage, and the scheme would break down.

It would be possible, no doubt, to remain aloof from such detail and to devise a very highly-regulated scheme in which people were required at the time of purchase to show the seller evidence of whether they were purchasing fuel for business or private use; people who used their cars (or homes) for both private and work-related purposes could perhaps pay two different prices for their energy (filling their tanks with, say, 13 litres at one price and 21 litres at another). The scheme would also have to do without *pull, where units are brought within the standard accounting systems of companies and then *flow through to the primary suppliers and the Registrar. But without this *elegance, the enforcement and anti-fraud costs would be prohibitively high: routine *closed-loop carbon accounting from oil well to petrol pump would not work if some of the final product (the petrol) were exempt from the system. The theoretical possibility that a misspecified scheme (the Layered Format) can be made to work if enough money and regulation is thrown at it invariably disappoints when it is put into practice.[11]

By contrast, the TEQs scheme is self-*monitoring — requiring no enforcement costs apart from the routine auditing needed for any significant initiative — but this property depends on it being a coherent, economy-wide model.

RATIONING

The use of the Layered Format as a means of rationing fuel, then, is highly problematic: the existence of separate schemes for businesses and households violates fundamental principles of the design of a rationing scheme.

A rationing scheme has to be a fair distribution of a scarce resource including *all* the users of that resource; it must distribute the limited quantity according to a single set of criteria which is transparent and widely understood; and the Government must be fully accountable for it. To deal with the distribution of fuel rations to households and businesses on different criteria — yielding two availabilities and two sets of prices, covering differently-defined and overlapping geographical areas, and over which the national Government has no control — would forfeit any confidence in the scheme. And it would sharply reduce any prospects for the *trust and alignment of interests that are required for joint, *cooperative effort to flourish.[12]

Furthermore, in the real world of rationing under conditions of scarcity, it cannot be predicted how nations will obtain their supplies of the scarce oil and/or gas. It seems probable that nations that are well placed — those which, for instance, own large reserves — will feel justified in taking full advantage of this, rather than sharing out fuel stocks equally to other nations which lack that advantage. And governments will undoubtedly negotiate for supplies of fuel in order to get the best deal they can for their populations. In these circumstances, an EU-wide trading scheme which provided an EU-wide budget without regard to the differences in energy stocks and sources available to the participating nations would be hard to reconcile with a feasible system of rationing.

There is at present intense concern to develop a system with *a global reach*, capable of — and committed to — *an ambitious phase-down of carbon emissions*, and able to *guarantee fair access to energy* for all energy-users. These three requirements can be provided by economy-wide *national systems within an overarching coordinating framework. That framework derives its effectiveness from the commitments made by governments acting on behalf of their national economies. The actual delivery of those commitments is achieved by national systems on the model of TEQs.

International and national schemes are complementary if, and only if, there is a well-defined and explicit distinction between their respective areas of activity. Solutions to the *energy problem will not be delivered by 'upstream systems', nor by 'downstream systems'. They will be delivered by full-stream integration of all participants in a system explicitly designed for *cooperative, complementary programmes. If suppliers, consumers and public bodies have reason to *trust each other and to talk to each other — if they are all in the same scheme and they realise they will not solve the problem without each other's help — then there will be a chance of achieving a fast, fair and effective energy transition.

Once the principle of electronic entitlements has been understood, a range of options opens up, allowing it to be designed and adapted to the priorities and prospects of the *place and *time. It could be designed for carbon emissions, or for oil and/or gas and/or electricity. It could be adapted to short term or long term scarcity; the Tender could be issued by auction or by allocation, or by a combination of the two. This is a generic instrument, permitting a high degree of flexibility. But there is clarity, too: the *intention is set, and there is no doubt that a form of rationing — using the established electronic technology of the day — is needed.

TEQs could be the game-changer, both allowing national *leaders to promise substantial reductions in fossil fuel dependency with confidence that they will actually happen, and emboldening them to throw down the powerful challenge to other nations: "We are acting, so must you."

It is now intensely urgent that nations should have an instrument, available and proven, which is capable of both dramatically reducing carbon emissions and rationing scarce fuel. The system capable of delivering that is TEQs.[13]

*Climate Change, Energy Prospects, Incentives Fallacy, Modularity, Subsidiarity, Common Purpose, Commons, Exhilaration.

TIME FALLACIES. Examples include:

The Permanent Present

The *fallacy which gives undue emphasis to the present when considering an option with long-term consequences. Examples include arguments that our present ability to import food justifies permanent burial of *agricultural land under new housing; that joining the Eurozone is justified by today's low interest rates there; that the state of the jobs market at the moment calls for migrant labour; that the current price of oil opens the way to a long-term expansion of air travel. This presumption of a constant present is a leading symptom of the dementia that afflicts the *judgment of governments—*dementia absens*: the patient is so elevated, so far removed from ordinary life, so taken up with a global vision, so protected by *experts, so busy, so short of *sleep, and so absent, that he or she has no sense of time or *place (*Abstraction, Presence).

And there is a risk that the values of the present may crowd out all other values. The question, "What is right?", short-circuits to the answer, "Whatever is now."[14]

The *Irrelevant Past

An argument that affirms that *now* is a special case, in that the present has achieved standards of reason and *ethics which have not been available before. The fallacy typically cites the fact that this is the twenty-first century as proof that the argument is correct:

> By the end of the 20th century, the independent sector had emerged pre-eminent in the British education system, but the only vision the independent sector has today remains entrenched in the 20th century. . . . We need new vision for the independent sector in the 21st century. . . . It is no longer tenable in 2008 to retain 20th century apartheid thinking.[15]

The Irrelevant Past argument *begs the question: if the proposal would change things around from how they were in the past, it is *self-evidently a good thing.

Here is the scientist-philosopher Mary Warnock being sympathetic with the unfortunates who are so stuck in the past that they are opposed to *genetically modified crops:

> [For] many confused and vaguely frightened people, the new biotechnology seems to have opened up possibilities of changing the genes of plants and animals in a way which nature, or God as the Creator, never intended. . . . [And now] the argument has moved on [to] the myth of an unnatural creature being formed in the laboratory whose growth and behaviour could not be controlled. It was upon such fears that Mary Shelley played, as long ago as 1818, in her story of Frankenstein.[16]

Oh dear. Perhaps we should learn from the future?

Availability

It's tough to get right. "The harder I work, the luckier I get." It was Thomas Jefferson who started the stream of variations on that theme. He should have added, "The harder I work on one thing, the unluckier I get on all the other commitments I haven't had time for."[17]

*Unknowable Future Fallacy, Tradition, Systems Thinking ❯ Feedback ❯ Time.

TORMENTS. The problems of our time (the *climacteric) that need to be understood and—in a sense—made use of, if we are to cope. As suggested by John Milton:

> Our torments also may in length of time
> Become our elements.
>
> Paradise Lost, 1667.[18]

TOUCH-DOWN. The stage in the history of a *civic society when it ceases being dependent on the *intermediate economy. A successful touch-down is one in which life goes on—in which parts, at least, of the civic society survive in a different form, having learned enough to avoid making the same mistakes all over again.

The study of *economic lift-off is well developed; touchdown has not been considered. There is an asymmetry here which would invite comment if applied to aviation.[19] *Lean Economy, Growth, Peasant.

TRADABLE ENERGY QUOTAS. See TEQs.

TRADITION. The standing of tradition at present is low. It is patronised as a theme for tourists; it is the nostalgia of old age, a repudiated symbol of the past, of privilege, of pre-scientific *ignorance, inconsistent with the serious business of a *competitive economy; an affront to common sense. Not so: tradition is indispensable for a functioning society; it is serious business. It does three vital things:

First, it is the substance of *culture. Culture does not necessarily advance in the sense of getting *better*; it changes slowly as each *creative contribution becomes part of it. As T.S. Eliot wrote,

> the most interesting parts of [the poet's]
> work may be those in which the dead poets,
> his ancestors, assert their immortality most
> rigorously. . . . The conscious present is an
> awareness of the past.[20]

Our culture has a voice because it has been endowed with one by tradition; if we have radical innovations to offer, the things we are being innovative *about*—the story so far, the language in which it is told, the point from which creativity starts, the culture and the coordinates by which we can work out who we are—are supplied by tradition. The more developed and interesting the tradition, the greater the expressive possibilities. Cultural tradition is the collective product of the people that have worked inside it and each added their bit. All expression is in terms of a tradition: no self, no expression, no distinctive "me", can exist without the inherited frame of reference provided by, for instance, tradition-derived language, *narrative, music, cooking, *humour, allusions, tact, *manners. Tradition is the voice of the self, the terms on which it is possible to find expression and define an *identity.[21]

Secondly, tradition makes available to us, for free, rules which have been learned the hard way. It may be difficult to work out, off the cuff, *why* a *festival is

a good idea in midwinter, *why* *sex at first meeting may be a bad idea, *why* *family meals are advisable, *why* celebrations are important, *why* archaic clothes for *ceremony and in *law courts may help to protect *freedoms, *why* *play is essential to a child's development, or *why* a musical and literary *education teaches the art of thinking—but there is no need to work it out, for tradition affirms it. It supplies (as Edmund Burke wrote) a way of "knowing exactly and habitually, without the labour of particular and occasional thinking". A society without tradition is a society without grown-ups.[22]

Thirdly, tradition protects the society of the future, and it does this in the *paradoxical way of speaking up for the past. It affirms that present concerns are not the only issues at stake: since virtually all the assets of the present have been inherited from the past, it follows that this *inheritance in its various forms is the most

THE RAIN

I hear leaves drinking rain;
   I hear rich leaves on top
Giving the poor beneath
   Drop after drop;
'Tis a sweet noise to hear
These green leaves drinking near.

And when the Sun comes out,
   After this Rain shall stop,
A wondrous Light will fill
   Each dark, round drop;
I hope the Sun shines bright;
'Twill be a lovely sight.

        W.H. DAVIES, 1908.[23]

T

important source of value that society has. It also follows that the ability of the current generation to guarantee the inheritance of the future is the defining condition for any claim to moral standing by the present.

————

Tradition, then, has three critical functions—as a source of the self, as the transmitter of *prudential rules, and as the medium by which a society is able to locate itself in *time. An excessively heavy responsibility, perhaps, to be entrusted to song? Yet this is characteristic of systems; they often seem to be not quite serious: what you observe is not the busy chemistry beneath the surface, but the finished result: it could be a poem about the rain . . . But traditions are the rules on which the *complex system of society depends.

TRANSITION. The evolution from dependence to *localised self-reliance.

The Transition movement was founded in Totnes, Devon, in 2006, and over three hundred communities around the world have joined to date.[24] The movement is part of a convergence of thinking towards the principle that, if areas and communities are to be prepared for the shocks of *energy, *climate, *economics and society, it will not be government and regulatory agencies that do it. It will be something they do for themselves. Transition, *lean thinking, the Big Society and others are, from their different starting points, pointing towards the same critical principle of *presence.[25] Here are some of its properties:

1. *The shared *ethic.* There is no presumption that the people's ethical standards and *judgment are lower than the government's, or that only the government has the competence to implement them.

2. *The shared *incentive.* The incentive drawn on to bring about *creative and sustained commitment to a difficult task is not the usual manipulation with carrots and sticks—payments and penalties—but a sense of *common purpose: individual and collective interests are aligned; individual contributions and insights make a difference; the exceptional becomes feasible.

3. *Place.* Solutions will be at the level of the detailed circumstances of particular places. They will

depend on the *efficiencies and *reciprocities made available on the small *scale.

4. *Local resources.* The *money available from the state will be severely limited and may be close to zero, so the only solutions available to communities will be those that they can put into effect and sustain for themselves.

5. *Community.* The enabling agency for the transformation.

6. *Trust.* A key enabling condition for the transformation.

Transition's pioneers are starting on the long, and maybe impossible, road towards what the catastrophe experts know and recommend as "deconcentration"— building local competence and self-reliance, implicitly recognising (as the analyst Charles Perrow describes it) "the inevitable failure of organisations, public and private, to protect us from disasters and [the need for] minimising the scale of our vulnerable targets".[26]

And their members are getting to know each other. The importance of this—so obvious that it has been overlooked—is beginning to be recognised, and it is central to the idea of the *checklist*. The checklist is a *professional routine which has been long established in aviation, and has been advancing in the field of medicine on approximately the same timescale as the Transition movement itself. The first item on the list—one of its key innovations—is: *get to know each other before trying to work together.* That is, aircrews and operating theatre teams get to know each other's names and roles, and any special concerns that anyone has about the task ahead, switching on—"activating"—their *presence as members of the team. Studies of what this means have been done at Johns Hopkins University in Maryland. The summary of their findings is dry:

> People who don't know one another's names don't work together nearly as well as those who do . . . When nurses were given a chance to say their names and mention concerns at the beginning of a case, they were more likely to note problems and offer solutions. The researchers called it an "activation phenomenon". Giving people a chance to say something at the start seemed to activate their sense of participation and responsibility.[27]

Transition is a more profound idea than it is sometimes taken to be. Several local groups that consider themselves to be part of the Transition movement have chosen to forego the usual "Transition Town x" moniker and instead call themselves "Sustainable x". But it is not, in its essence, about the familiar protocols of environmental *protection and *sustainability. On the contrary, the change of direction represented by the Transition movement is as profound as any intentional change experienced by a civilisation:

Starting point: the government promises to care for the people, relying on the money raised by taxation in the formal economy, but becomes less and less able to fulfil its promise as its *infrastructures and control systems become more elaborate, and the income flows provided by the economy fall.

Transition point: the people make no promises, but *incrementally work out how to care for themselves and each other, relying on *informal *reciprocities and on the efficiency dividend that becomes available at the *small scale—from a retreating infrastructure and advancing *elegance.

Now, the Transition movement is what its members worldwide think it is; *Lean Logic*'s slant on the matter interprets it as more-or-less indistinguishable from a pathway to the *Lean Economy, and if Transitioners disagree with this and argue that the movement is (for instance) about building *resilient local responses to *peak oil and *climate change, and setting an example of how to cut the carbon, there is no reason to disagree with that. There is the reality of distributed ownership here: Transition/Sustainable towns that are doing dazzling things in a practical way have an *authority which *Lean Logic*—which only writes and talks about them—cannot claim.

And yet, there is a convergence. The brewing industry is well advanced in its wonderful transition—from a locked-in structure of giant authoritarian brewers with marketing budgets, to space for independent local brewers with talent and passion. *Organic growers and farmers' markets are decentralising *food production and building on local experiment, widely shared. Some governments are beginning to get it, although they have the same disadvantage as company managements that suddenly announce that from now on workers are going to be allowed to think for themselves: not everyone believes them or knows what they are talking about, and they may not, themselves, have quite understood what they are saying.

But the tide is flowing. The direction is mapped, very simply, in the little hexagons of the *Wheel of Life. We do not need to agree on which particular straw it will be that breaks the camel's back, but there is little to disagree with in the observation that the *complicated, centralised, *energy-intensive, *materials-intensive, *money-intensive, *taut, *infrastructure-heavy, *feedback-blind model of society and economy on which we rely is in trouble from many directions. Transition, a wide awake, *modular *network of *small-scale responses, is one of the hexagons of *recovery-elastic resilience towards which talent and passion are being drawn.[28]

TRANSPORT. See Lean Transport.

TRAVELLING LIGHT. Adaptation to the failure of the *intermediate economy of big infrastructures and services which will follow the breakdown of the *market. The scale and consequences of the loss of these essentials will be shocking. The long-term task will be to build lean, *small-scale, *elegant, sustainable-resilient replacements. The Lean Economy will travel light. And there will be a major gain, since local enterprise such as hospitals and farms, can—relative to their giant equivalents—afford a greater flexibility and attention to detail; they can expect better morale, *closed-loop *waste management, a sense of *community, of being somewhere. The loss of the intermediate economy, though catastrophic at first, will release *local enterprise from a commitment it can no longer afford, and open the way to the land-, labour- and materials-efficiency of *lean thinking.

Travelling light, then, is about coping without the burden of giant infrastructures, which will fail, however much we might regret their passing. The heavily-burdened present will be separated from the travelling-light future by *kaikaku—by voluntary and/or involuntary shock. The *Lean Economy that emerges from it will have the advantage that, unlike its obese and tottering predecessor, it could have a future.
*Touch-Down.

T

TRUST. Trust is confidence that an obligation, explicit or implied, will be honoured. The motivation for keeping faith in this way is varied. It may be love, or a promise, or commitment to a *professional standard, or a matter of going along with the purpose of the *institution to which you belong. In *Lean Logic*, trust is a condition for the web of *reciprocal obligation which builds *community, and for the relationship between a *nation and its people.

And it is a critical *capital asset, distinct from the other forms of capital; it is both producer and product of *social capital. It is a necessary condition for the existence of a human *ecology in which decisions have meaning. But the existence of trust in this sense cannot be assumed. Evidence that it exists can be inferred from signals, such as a person's participation in a *cooperative project, long association, kinship, language, clothes, shared *culture, *ceremony, *humour or *ritual.

The significance of trust was borne out by the economist Francis Fukuyama who, in the 1990s, studied it as a condition for poor countries' economic development. His conclusion was that the nations which have not yet succeeded in climbing onto the ladder of development will not do so until they have established the trust in their commercial relationships without which enterprise will almost certainly fail. The problem, he writes, is that this essential framework of trust takes a long time to build: "communities depend on mutual trust".[29]

In the Lean Economy, *judgment will be shaped by the overriding priority to do nothing which could weaken the trust on which integrity depends—and "integrity" in this context means social *cohesion and authenticity, citizenship that brings with it little incentive to tell lies. It is a fragile asset. The dismantling of social capital which has occurred during the period of the *market economy has fractured that trust. The fractures could open up as the *climacteric unfolds.

At the same time, trust contains *anomalies and complexities which are sometimes overlooked:

1. It is not always a good thing; indeed, it may be immoral, as in the case, for instance, of a person who is trusted by Jack the Ripper; or where there is mutual trust between a logging company and its public relations advisers. And yet trust between close associates—honour among thieves—feels (to the thieves) like a *good* thing, part of the essential morality of being.

2. Criticism of a person on the grounds that "he has forfeited my trust" is dubious: it may be that you have forfeited his; it may, in fact, be no more than a pretentious way of saying that you no longer agree, and that you are claiming your right to the *high ground.

3. Having a strong motivation to trust someone is substantially *irrelevant to whether you can do so.

4. The absence of trust is *self-fulfilling—that is, people who are not trusted have no incentive to be trustworthy. Regulatory institutions can deconstruct trust and, with evolutionary logic, make themselves necessary.[30]

Transparency

As the Reith lecturer Onora O'Neill highlights, there are widespread calls for greater transparency—and accountability, and respect for human rights—as conditions for the existence of trust.[31]

In principle, the idea that the decisions taken by *public institutions such as hospitals and local government should be capable of explanation in terms of established, standard and transparent procedures is, of course, reasonable. It provides protection from allegations of unfairness; it saves time on detail. But there are problems. Full transparency means that someone who took no part in the decision-making can know (or find out) pretty well everything *relevant about the decision and how it was arrived at. There is a lot to be said for that, but when everything about a decision is clear there is no need—no space—to take anything on trust.

In fact, there are many circumstances in which transparency does not and cannot exist. The central point of the question of trust is whether you can trust the person to make a good decision—rational, with positive consequences for the people involved—even though you *don't* know the full circumstances of the case, and may never know. You may not know the person or people involved; you may not even know that the decision is made.

It is in those circumstances—in which neither transparency, nor indeed accountability and human rights, apply—that the question of trust is not only crucial, but arises also as a universal and daily event. We may not know, nor have any particular expectations about, what others are going to do, even in cases where their actions will significantly affect us, and especially in new situations where no established principles exist. You *do*, of course, have reasonable expectations about what your airline pilot will do, and what the driver coming in the opposite direction will do, and you can call that "trust" if you like, but if you think that is the extent of it, you are missing the point, and "expectation" might be better. *Trust* is about the conditions in which, despite the lack of transparency, accountability and a significant contribution from human rights, you are confident that the other person will get it right.[32]

A second problem with transparency is that it can affect the quality of decisions. There is a raft of decisions that can be based on routine procedures (think of medicine, for instance). But there are also *judgments requiring the application of *imagination and thought, which will on that account involve the acceptance of some degree of risk, for which the person who has applied the thought will bear some responsibility. Routine decisions are transparent; the imaginative ones are not. Given a commitment to risk-reduction and the rules of transparency, the only option is to stick to the routine. When something unexpected happens, it will fall outside the scope of the routine decision, so transparency will get it wrong. The needed risk is not taken.

"Well-placed trust", O'Neill states, "grows out of active inquiry rather than blind acceptance". For *Lean Logic*, that's well-placed expectation. What we will need in the future is reasonable confidence that, when people whom we scarcely know do unfamiliar things in circumstances which we cannot guess at, and which may not be what we would have done, there is a good chance that what they do is right.[33]

And now for a third difficulty with transparency. On closer inspection, it turns out that there is no such thing. Decisions in a transparent system depend on premises and presumptions which are quite arbitrary. Principles which seem to be too obvious to need any defence: "I think children should be allowed to follow their natural inclinations"—the platitudes of good intention, the avoidances of judgment, the presumed meanings of fairness and of moral authority—are in fact

propositions which, if they were reached by argument, would depend on a complex, closely-analysed case. The reason that kind of argument is so dominant is not that it has been constructed, but that it has been adopted as *self-evident. But the self-evident is a shedload of marginal assumptions, previous judgments and prejudice.

Transparency, then, trivialises trust down to the level of *expectation; diminishes decisions to the level of the safe, the routine, the easily-defended; and reinforces faith in the self-evident, which is subject to no examination at all. As suggested in the entry on *tradition, there is a role for unargued assumptions in the enduring structure and *practice which makes a society, but in the evaluation of individual cases in medicine, in education, in our relationships—in the case-by-case world of *casuistry—there is a choice to be made between deliberation and *ideology. Far more helpful than transparency is . . .

Congruence

Congruence is the gift of being able to talk to people revealingly and without reserve. This is critical: it is the quality, or "realness", which the psychologist Carl Rogers explores, describing it especially in the context of teaching. The effective teacher feels able—permitted—to teach as a real person; she enters into a relationship with the learner without presenting a front or a façade, or being *defined by her official role. Her feelings are available to her; she comes into direct *encounter with the learner, meeting him on a person-to-person basis. She is herself. That doesn't make her right, but it does mean that she believes what she is saying. And, in return, the learner will not feel he has to be strategic: he, too, can simply say what he believes: there is congruence.[34]

Suppose two people want to be in contact, to communicate with each other, and to continue this contact for a period of time. Rogers summarises,

> The greater the congruence of experience, awareness and communication on the part of one individual, the more the ensuing relationship will involve: a tendency toward reciprocal communication with a quality of increasing congruence; a tendency toward more mutually accurate understanding of the communications; improved psychological adjustment and

T

functioning in both parties; mutual satisfaction in the relationship.[35]

The medium of this is personal. It is hand-made:

> The person-centred approach is built on a basic trust in the person. This is perhaps its sharpest point of difference from most of the institutions in our culture. Almost all of education, government, business, much of religion, much of family life, much of psychotherapy, is based on a distrust of the person. . . . Teachers, parents, supervisors must develop procedures to make sure the individual is progressing towards the goal—examinations, inspections, interrogations. The individual is seen as innately sinful, destructive, lazy, or all three—as someone who must be constantly watched over.
>
> The person-centred approach, in contrast, depends on the actualizing tendency present in every living organism—the tendency to grow, to develop, to realize its full potential. This way of being trusts the constructive directional flow of the human being toward a more complex and complete development. It is this directional flow that we aim to release.[36]

If that is happening, trust has a chance of coming into being—and it both needs, and issues, signals that say, "This is a situation in which it is safe to trust." That does not come free; it has to be earned, and it takes us straight into the colourful, irregular world of *humour and *play, of shared experience, history, friends, complaints, *institutions—the *grammar by which people become intelligible to each other, and which gives people and events their meaning.

Under signal-free, person-free, *instrumental conditions, congruence is not only not there, it is actually seen to be unethical; it is ruled out. It cannot be imposed and, for a concerned government, whose limitations it reveals, the whole concept is unacceptable. But the absence of congruence means the absence of trust. A system constructed like that has brittleness built into it: it can bear no weight. It will break often, and then catastrophically. Fukuyama's "essential framework of trust", once burning, burns fast.

Building congruence back into our culture is so counter to our present presumptions that it may never happen. Eye contact, common *interest and humour, *character, *good faith and a *tactile, gentle *culture are society-enabling assets. If trust and the congruence on which it depends do recover, it will be because these are assets which—perhaps aided by new morsels of spring drifting in with the Big Society—the Lean Economy begins to reconstruct, with intense and determined creativity, and with its people gradually recovering their confidence.[37] *Betrayal, Reciprocity and Cooperation.

TRUTH. A family of connections between statements and meanings.

Truth can take many forms, and here are five of them.

1. *Material truth* is direct, plain, literal description of situations and events: no greater depth of meaning is intended. It is an account of a reality which is "bounded"—that is, there is no interest for the moment in exploring the deeper implications, insights and echo-meanings. This is the truth which tells you about the route taken by the hot water pipe from the boiler to the bathroom, how to make flatbread, how to photograph otters, what Darwinism is, why a herd of cows' milk yield is higher if the cows are named as well as numbered, what a well-tempered scale is, what a Higgs boson probably is, why pregnant women don't topple over, whether you went to the pub last night. Accuracy is not essential: it does not *have* to be true to belong in the domain of material truth, but it *does* have to be the speaker's intention that the other person should understand it to be true. It can use metaphor or simile that helps to get an unfamiliar idea across. The intention is to provide a truthful and uncluttered description. Here facts matter.[38]

2. *Narrative truth* (or poetic truth) is the truth present not just in storytelling but in *myth, art and the whole of our *culture. This is the truth of *Pride and Prejudice*. It is not materially true, in that it is fiction; on the other hand, it is true-to-life: it is as accurate an insight into human character as we have. Elizabeth Bennett's story can neither be dismissed as untrue nor accepted as true; it is in the middle

ground. The narrative says something that cannot be said in any other way. It extends beyond *metaphor.

Narrative truth may be a parable with a clear message, or a story for the story's sake, or the meaning may be forever unknown: a question to be reflected on, perhaps in a lifetime's exploration of *ironic space. It is the domain of poetry, music, laughter; if you ask whether it is true, you are at the wrong party.[39]

3. *Implicit truth* is the product of *reflection about a person, a thing, or an event. Two (or more) people may reach sharply different insights which may, however, all be true. They are different in that they are features in the landscape of the observers' different cognitive homelands. One student may think about the cypress tree growing in the quadrangle in a quite different way from another student. Two interpretations of the same observations may be different, even contradictory, but both represent implicit truths.

The crew of Coleridge's *Ancient Mariner* had good reason to think of home in a way which is resonant with this—as "their native country, and their own natural homes, which they enter unannounced, as lords that are certainly expected and yet there is a silent joy at their arrival". Native country naturalises common experience in different ways.[40]

4. *Performative truth* is the truth that is created by statements that do something: I challenge, I thee wed, I bet, I curse, thank you. The speaking makes the truth; a promise is brought into existence by being spoken: loyal cantons of contemned love make love come alive (for a variant—it does not quite qualify as a performative truth, but it is a good try—see "Making It Come True . . ." sidebar).[41]

5. *Self-denying truth* is *paradox which contradicts itself: it is (materially) true until it is spoken: the speaking of a self-denying truth kills it. Example: "I refuse to admit my addiction." Self-denying truth is the opposite of performative truth. It is a statement which makes itself untrue. By unpacking a useful mystery you are making it no longer a mystery, and maybe no longer useful.[42]

MAKING IT COME TRUE . . .
by saying it often enough

So if it's not focus that breeds success how do you get a project as vast and ambitious as Eden off the ground? Simple: you just announce you're going to do it. I discovered a technique that revolutionised my life. It's called lying—or rather, the telling of future truths. It's about putting yourself in the most public jeopardy possible and saying "I am going to do this", so the shame of not doing it would be so great it energises every part of your being.

TIM SMIT, Executive Director and Co-Founder of the Eden Project, Cornwall, 2009.[43]

Logic literacy depends on all of these forms of truth, with varying degrees of emphasis. All five are there, exuberantly, in *religion, which, if confined in the narrow space inhabited by material truth, decays into fundamentalism. And they are needed for the *common purpose of making a future, which needs brain and soul.

TU QUOQUE, THE FALLACY OF ("You, too"; "same to you"). A class of argument which dismisses the other person's position on the grounds that his behaviour contradicts it, or is no better than that of the person whose behaviour he is criticising. This *fallacy leads into sterile altercation, a grim and noisy dead end, from which it can be hard to escape. It is slightly broader than the Fallacy of *Hypocrisy because it does not need to show that the critic's own failures have any relevance to the argument, and it is summarised in responses such as "same to you", "you're no better", "how can you talk?", "it's a bit rich", and "well, what about your. . . ?". Don't go there.[44]

*Distraction, *Ad Hominem*.

U

UNFALSIFIABILITY. An argument presented in a form such that it can never be shown to be false.

An unfalsifiable argument can be qualified and amended at will. For instance, the statement "faith can move mountains" is unfalsifiable: if you cannot move mountains, that only shows that you haven't enough faith. Empty *abstractions about destiny, vision and optimism cannot be refuted; they can only be dismissed as meaningless. The philosopher Karl Popper summarises:

> It is the possibility of overthrowing [a theory], or its falsifiability, that constitutes the possibility of testing it, and therefore the scientific character of a theory.[1]

Despite Popper's advice, unfalsifiable statements are popular. Examples: The developing countries would all become thriving *market economies if only the West would give them enough aid. *Or*, The reason our *reforms haven't yet produced the promised results is that they haven't gone far enough. *Or*, Economic *growth will eventually make us all happier. *Or*, If we would only get round a table and talk to them, and build hospitals and schools, the violence would stop. *Or*, All we need is for everyone to be as softly-spoken and peace-loving as me—then there would be no *violence in the world. *Or*, There is a *rhinoceros in this room, but of a kind that you cannot see, touch, smell, taste or hear. *Or*, The reason we haven't achieved heaven on earth yet is because we haven't eliminated enough dissidents. *Or* (the Freudian version), "The woman you were dreaming about was your mother." "No, it wasn't!" "Now you're getting angry: that proves it was your mother." "Oh, all right, then." "You see...?"[2]

A famous instance of the constantly-revised argument is the model of planetary motion developed by the astronomer Ptolemy (Claudius Ptolemaeus, c.100–178). Having placed the Earth at the centre of the solar system, all he needed to do to reconcile this with the evidence was to design a complex set of cycles and epicycles: with every new observation, new elaborations could be added.[3] And we have a happy example from Jonathan Swift: on his visit to the Grand Academy of Lagado, Gulliver was introduced to a scientist working on technologies for renewable energy,

> He had been eight years upon a project for extracting sun-beams out of cucumbers ... He told me, he did not doubt, in eight years more, he should be able to supply the Governor's gardens with sunshine at a reasonable rate; but he complained that his stock [funding] was low, and entreated me to give him some as an encouragement to ingenuity.[4]

The idea that one more heave is all that is now needed is hard to disprove, even by experiment: if it is successful, that shows you were right; if it is unsuccessful, that shows that all that is needed is one more heave. Given that the required heave is the one that is *now*, the argument is unfalsifiable. If you impose a big idea but can constantly reform and fix it if it goes wrong, you never have to face up to the possibility that there could be something wrong with the idea.

And here are some more cases that invite its use:

1. Very large projects—such as super-giant water projects, or revolutionary change in schools, health services or constitutions—change the mental map: any argument that follows has to accept the premises imposed on it by the accomplished fact. There is no way back.

2. Elusive certainty: if you insist that no criticism of your argument can be admitted unless it comes

wrapped in *certainty proved beyond scientific dispute, it is secure against critics.

3. In a crisis, your empty proposition can be claimed to be the only hope, placing it beyond criticism.

4. It may be the only *ethical solution, obscuring the fact that it is impossible.

5. The argument, or assumption, may be integral to the person's belief in herself and in her own existence, so that a change of mind is impossible.

6. The idea may be so desirable—sunbeams to order— that to give up on it would break your heart.[5]

*Sunk Cost Fallacy, Self-Evident, *Kaikaku.*

UNINTENDED CONSEQUENCES. See Systems Thinking, Relevance Fallacy, Butterfly Effect, Self-Evident, Emergence, Humour, Climacteric, Precautionary Principle, Wheel of Life.

UNKNOWABLE FUTURE, THE FALLACY OF THE. The argument that, since we do not know what is going to happen in the short term, we are even less likely to know what is going to happen in the long term. This is true only sometimes. In other cases, the long term may be more predictable than the short term. For instance, if you are sitting in a room with a thermometer and a cup of hot coffee (and you don't drink it), you can forecast accurately the temperature it will be in five hours' time (the temperature of the room), but not the temperature it will be in ten minutes' time. You can forecast a long-term trend in the oil market (prices will rise) but have no idea what they will do in the next few days.

*Systems Thinking ❭ Feedback ❭ Time, Precautionary Principle, Butterfly Effect, Time Fallacies, Denial.

UNLEAN. The case for Lean is strong. It is clear about its *intention. It declutters tasks from *irrelevant preoccupations and commitments. It sustains a regular *flow. It invites original and exact responses. It learns from *feedback. It works. It has been proven. It is specifically suited to the *modular communities of the future, when the *market state will be too weakened to sustain the supply of goods, incomes and order on which we depend. Resilient local communities will, by accident or design, find themselves drawn into a political and economic order which, in essence, is lean.

And yet, Lean is not the only social and economic order with potential for a time when the market is no longer with us, and there is a case for looking at another one with a formidable record not only in terms of size, but also longevity. We are about to pay a brief visit to a form of society with *resilience. Although recently, and maybe temporarily, in retreat, it endured for thousands of years—far longer than any other system of statehood in history. It is the *political economy which started to form at various intensities and at various dates ranging up to 6,000 years ago in (among other states) China, northern India, Mesopotamia, Persia, Egypt, Peru and Mexico.

They had a problem: *water. Some of them received an annual monsoon, with a vast amount of rainfall over a few weeks, which often filled the rivers and caused flooding, while the rest of the year was dry and often very hot. Even if it rained, much of it evaporated before it could do anything useful, and evaporation kicked in hard as soon as forests were cleared for cultivation. Others had little reliable rainfall, and depended on the flow of giant rivers, such as the Yellow River—which receives meltwater from the Himalayas—or the Nile— which carries water from tropical Africa.[6]

Or, to look at it another way, their problem was people. They could get by in a landscape with long periods of low rainfall—and water being naturally conserved by forest—if the population was low, and the demands made on the *land were minimal. A society that left it to nature to supply its meat, fruit and vegetables saved itself a lot of trouble, and its people needed to work for only some two hours a day. But as populations rose, the only way of expanding the supply of *food to keep pace was by irrigation and related infrastructures—*intensifying their agriculture to build an ecology capable of supporting a lot of people.[7]

That—to open it up a bit—meant:

- *Infrastructures:* They needed to build and maintain irrigation systems to supply the water which became both more necessary and less available as they advanced into agriculture and felled the forests. And along with the work went the demands of harvest, storage, *transport and distribution, and the various stratagems needed to make the best of

U

less fertile soils, all supported by *institutions of administration and government.

- *Productivity advance*: In conditions of abundant unpaid labour and no *competition, the technical advances would have been of the *scale-enabling* kind (water management, domestications, eventually pulleys), rather than the *labour-saving* kind. The chief means of productivity advance was a massive increase in working hours (*Intensification Paradox).

There followed a relentless *growth sequence typical of intensification: more land *and* more labour is needed *per capita* (per person). At the same time, the *population itself grows. When exponential growth becomes established, you quickly reach large numbers, but once these societies had reached the limit of what their land and water could support, they remained at that level for century after century, hovering above and below the threshold of subsistence.[8]

To support this population, water had to be diverted on—eventually—a stupendous scale, to supply irrigation systems stretching over, for example, the low-lying, arid plains of China. But, being low-lying, these regions were also exposed to floods, so it became equally essential to establish means of flood control. And floods, when they happened, could be apocalyptic, not least because (as is characteristic of such a *'preventive resilience' approach) the containment measures, when they failed, multiplied the problem. In 132 BC, the Yellow River burst over its banks and the dikes that had been built to prevent such an occurrence, sending a branch of the river across the plain and inundating whole regions; 150 years later, the whole river changed its course, finding a new path to the sea. Presented with repair operations like these, nothing could happen until the emperor himself got involved, with a supporting cast of thousands. And with such workforces at their command, it was only natural to knock off a few more dainty projects, such as the Grand Canal (a thousand miles long) and the Great Wall (five thousand five hundred miles). And the Pyramids.[9]

It would be possible to discuss whether such super-giant systems of irrigation, flood control and water-transport could be organised on the bottom-up, lean basis advocated in *Lean Logic* (in, for instance, the entry on the *Commons). However, from what we know about the commons, about the scale of the hydraulic operations needed in these ancient empires, about the lack of earth-moving equipment other than men with spades, and about the death rates, it seems unlikely. Many of the criteria for a functioning commons—such as the need for local autonomy, for a shared sense that it is worth the attempt, for the task to be on a manageable *scale, and for a good match between the amount of work that would have to be put in and the benefits that could be expected by the people who did it—are conspicuously absent in the case of the giant hydraulic schemes. Paybacks postponed for generations and probable death in ant-like armies of workers; these are likely not opportunities for which we should expect a rush of public-spirited commoners to sign up.[10]

In any case, bottom-up programmes on that scale didn't happen. All the large irrigation systems were top-down projects involving extreme autocracy. These were regimes based on intimidation, reinforced by punishment. The Hindu Law book of Manu sets out rules for the conduct of the ideal king. It commends . . .

> Punishment, the protector of all creatures, (an incarnation of) the law, formed of Brahman's glory . . .
> Punishment is (in reality) the king (and) the male. Punishment alone governs all created beings, punishment alone protects them, punishment watches over them while they sleep; the wise declare punishment to be identical with the law. If the king did not, without tiring, inflict punishment on those worthy to be punished, the stronger would roast the weaker, like fish on a spit. The whole world is kept in order by punishment, for a guiltless man is hard to find. Even the gods give the enjoyments due from them only if they are tormented by the fear of punishment. Where punishment with a black hue and red eyes stalks about, destroying sinners, there the subjects are not disturbed, provided that he who inflicts it discerns well.[11]

It is not a bad king, or a bad system, that we have here, but a set of rules for how things should be. The *Arthashāstra*, the Indian treatise on statecraft, recommends eighteen kinds of torture with the added recommendation that for particularly serious cases, they should all be administered on the same day. The central place of punishment was acknowledged by Confucianism, and the Chinese Law Code describes the instruments to be used to extract evidence. The Egyptian *peasant who failed to deliver his quota of grain was beaten, bound, and thrown into the dike.[12]

The Great Cylinders of the Emperor Gudea of Mesopotamia (who reigned c.2150–2125 BC) describe how he restored the temple of Enninu, after its neglect had afflicted the land with a drought. So extreme was the crisis and the action needed in response that normal life had to be put on hold—in fact it was turned upside down, a vision of the impossible (like the lion lying down with the lamb in Isaiah) . . .

> He freed the prisoners. He remitted the taxes.
> A maid was in equality with her mistress. Her
> mistress did not strike her at all in the face. A
> servant walked in equality beside his lord. If
> a servant did wrong, his lord took no further
> thought thereof. The rod and the thorny switch
> he caused to be laid on one side, and the cudgel
> to be put away. [Even] the language of the whip
> was prohibited.[13]

The language of the whip. Not the ultimate sanction, then, but normal communication.

And, along with punishment, of course, comes obedience. Among the Greek *virtues, there is no mention of obedience; in medieval Europe, the knight was committed to loyalty to his lord, but not to total submission. But in the big civilisations of the East, obedience was central. In Mesopotamia, the "good life" was the obedient life; in Confucius' good society, the good subject was the obedient subject. And as for the masses—the "small people"—Confucius' code of honour did not apply at all: their role was, like grass, to bend low in the wind, directed by the threat of corporal punishment and by the principle of mutualism, which punished the whole family for the disobedience of just one of its members.[14]

And your obedience had to be confirmed at all times. If you approached a superior, you had to kowtow (touch the ground with the forehead, and maybe kiss it too); a meeting with a representative of the Pharaoh involved lying prone on your belly. And it got lonely,

because if you were in trouble, no one would dare to come to your assistance. The Chinese historian, Sima Qian, who differed with his Emperor's opinion on the abilities of a defeated general, was sentenced to be castrated in a darkened room. He wrote, "My friends did not come to my assistance. Those who were near and intimate with me did not say a single word in my favour."[15] Into the room.

Despite all this, the hydraulic civilisations were, and have remained, remarkably free of criticism. There were periodic revolutions in a sequence of *sacrifice-and-succession as dynasties became corrupt and decadent, the dikes silted up and the retaining walls decayed, but these *kaikaku moments were not challenges to the system itself. On the contrary, they renewed and strengthened it; they were integral to its *resilience. As the historian Karl Wittfogel explains, criticism was directed, not at the system, but at individual officials:

> Apart from mystics who teach total withdrawal
> from the world, these critics aim ultimately at
> regenerating a system of total power, whose
> fundamental desirability they do not doubt.[16]

And the reason was that those societies actually needed their giant construction projects, which in turn needed virtuoso administration:

> To say that the masters of hydraulic society are
> great builders is only another way of saying
> they are great organisers.[17]

Was there an alternative? Well, yes, if you had the weather for it. You needed regular rainfall. Rainfall farming, being locally self-sufficient in water, has no role for a central authority to provide it. The authorities can provide other things, such as *currency, a legal framework and *defence of the borders, but they are not indispensable in the way the governments of hydraulic civilisations are. If a state with rain-fed agriculture fails to carry out its duties, life will go on. If a hydraulic regime fails, then in due course there will be water shortages and/or catastrophic floods. Life will not go on. The people who endure that will want an effective government back, on almost any terms. Unlean works.

Areas with a rain-fed agriculture are the exception rather than the rule. If it had not been for them, with their freedoms to develop the *market and their incentives to apply technology, there is no reason to suppose that the hydraulic states would have moved on from the autocratic but highly effective and resilient economic structure they had been developing and sustaining for the last six thousand years. European freedoms, from this point of view, are the *exception. As the anthropologist Marvin Harris writes,

> In anthropological perspective, the emergence of bourgeois parliamentary democracies in seventeenth and eighteenth century Europe was a rare reversal of that descent from freedom to slavery which had been the main characteristic of the evolution of the state for 6,000 years. . . . No one who detests the practice of kowtowing and grovelling, who values the pursuit of scientific knowledge of culture and society, who values the right to study, discuss, debate and criticise, or who believes that society is greater than the state, can afford to mistake the rise of European and American democracies as the normal product of a march toward freedom.[18]

As for the Marxian view of history as the history of class struggle, Wittfogel comments,

> Class struggle . . . is the luxury of multi-centred and open societies.[19]

This leaves us with some *reflections, unresolved.

First of all, it is a reminder of how critical *and* vulnerable water supplies are around the world. In Western Europe our ability to produce *food is as good as the west wind—along with the higher latitudes—which can, generally, be relied on not to leave our crops unwatered for more than some two months at a time. The fragment of the song of a homesick troubadour appreciates this:[20]

Westron winde, when will thou blow,
The smalle raine downe can raine?
Christ if my love were in my armes,
And I in my bed againe.

Secondly, the lean, *local, *community-building, self-reliant response suggested for the multiple problems ahead seems to be a natural process of going back to our roots. It is where we came from. But the big hydraulic states of most of the world did not come from there. Well, originally they did, six thousand years ago, but even then it would have been at the level of the small settlements of the Iron Age, or the earlier Bronze Age or even, in some places, the Stone Age. Farming without irrigation in those areas had to be on a very modest scale. They do not have rain-fed villages like Wymondham, Stanton and Laxton as models and inspiration.

Thirdly, the government of a hydraulic regime would have no trouble in keeping economic output within the limits of zero-growth. There was no pressure to keep surplus labour employed—they could simply be directed into a mega-project with a low survival rate. Or the containing walls of some dikes protecting a floodplain could be breached. Or there was the well-established do-nothing option of allowing the surplus *population to starve. Once it had been established, China's population and output fluctuated through a sequence of shocks and recoveries, but remained on average at about the same level for millennia. That's a steady state economy.[21]

And, of course (fourthly), this story reminds us to be conscious of some insecurity with regard to our *freedoms. The hydraulic civilisations' model of despotic government travels with conquest and politics. Wittfogel suggests that the Mongol invasion brought it from China to Russia in the thirteenth century, and that it was faithfully followed by another seven centuries of Russian rulers, including Lenin and Stalin.[22] Its origins are all about water, but once it is established, a political *mindset develops a momentum, whatever the weather. The coming *climacteric, with its *energy-famine, could supply *green authoritarianism with a regrettable opportunity to become reinforced in those parts of the world where armies of workers will again be needed to keep water flowing, and to then extend to those parts which still have hope of building a future on freedom and self-reliance.

We may wonder if we know what we are doing. Our brave and truculent insistence on local lean autonomy is, in some serious senses, taking on by far the biggest and most autocratic form of *resilience that the world has ever known.

*Fortitude, Water.

UNMENTIONABLE, THE FALLACY OF. The *fallacy that, because a subject is taboo and cannot be mentioned, it does not exist; the curse that dare not speak its name.
*Death.

USURY. Lending money at *interest. This was a contentious matter long before *green critics began to see money-lending as the cause of economic *growth. For the last two thousand years or so, usury has caused trouble because it exposes the sensitive dividing line between the *public and *private spheres. Usury is incompatible with the relationship between close friends—in the private sphere—since it is a breach of the direct collaboration and unconditional *reciprocity which is the private sphere's main characteristic, and it is inconsistent with the *informal (non-monetary) relationships of the *neighbourhood. It can, however, be quite legitimately applied to the exchange relationships that apply at larger *scales. Defining and defending that *fuzzy borderline, however, has caused trouble.

Clear, simple rules on the matter are spelled out in the Book of Deuteronomy: "Unto a stranger thou mayest lend upon usury; but unto thy brother thou shalt not lend upon usury."[23] It is obviously important not to demand interest on loans within the private sphere, but Deuteronomy does not advise on what to do in the middle ground with a person who is neither a brother nor a stranger, but a neighbour. Such local *cooperation tends to be about matters on which the neighbouring farmer who seeks your help has no choice: if his working horse has died or he needs help with the harvest or with roof repairs, he has no room to negotiate, so that you—as neighbour-turned-usurer—could force him into a very bad deal, a lifetime of distress, if minded to do so. That is a matter for the neighbours concerned; the social scientists have no word for it with good reason: it is at the join between general and balanced *reciprocity, and the neighbours themselves are better placed to know the score than we are.

On the other hand, if it is a stranger, someone not part of the local economy, who is providing the loan, the farmer will expect to pay interest. Why else should the stranger bother? Between the two clear extremes, the turbulence and uncertainty have been substantial.

Psalm 15 compares usury with accepting bribes to convict the innocent. Folk tales in the Middle Ages told of the damnation awaiting usurers; one usurer was struck dead by a piece of falling masonry as he went into the church to get married. Usurers were not admitted to Christian burial, they were not allowed to rent houses, their wills were invalid; they were to be treated as heretics. Cities imported Jews to conduct a business that was forbidden to Christians.[24] Usury in Shakespeare reveals a brother as an enemy; and a thread of opposition to the idea of lending money at interest persists, for instance, in the radical environmental movement today.[25]

And yet, it seemed that everyone was at it. Calvinism—which sanctified economic enterprise—forbade usury, but quoted the going rate as "10 per cent or more".[26] The medieval cathedral chapters did it; priests did it; the building of Notre Dame was partly financed by it.[27] Kings borrowed at it; it was hard, even impossible, to get by without it. The imprecations against usury come with small print about when it is all right, after all. Jesus himself recommended it in the parable of the man who buried his talent instead of putting it out to usury.[28]

It was all about the borderline between public and private. If usury invades the private sphere, it brings a loss of innocence; it says "You are not my brother. You are not part of my local communion, but belong in another, external, sphere for which I have no name." And if the private sphere invades the public, there is trouble of a different kind. The private family-ethic, with a father at its head, is fine at the *household—and perhaps *community—level but not fine at all on the level of the city state or the *nation. On that scale it collapses into petulance and tyranny, into non-accountable invasive *paternalism such that, as Niccolò Machiavelli put it, "The way we live is so far removed from the way we ought to live, that anyone who tries to do as he ought to do takes the road to ruin."[29] In this overextended private world, there is one simple rule: be successful. If the logic of that calls for perfidy, cruelty, murder, then Machiavelli advised not to waste time being sentimental: you are unlikely to get "beneficent" results if you do.[30] There is a yearning, tragic confusion in it, expressed by Machiavelli himself in a tyrant's lament:

U

I hope—and hoping feeds my pain.
I weep—and weeping feeds my failing heart.
I laugh—but the laughter does not pass within.
I burn—but the burning makes no mark outside.[31]

Failure to have complementary public and private spheres ready when they are needed is a recipe for trouble. You can recognise them easily: the *public sphere does usury; the *private sphere doesn't.

UTOPIA. A place of ideal government, good *judgment and a perfectly cared-for *ecology. It is an important idea because it is a way of thinking afresh not only about what society ought to be, but what it will need to be, for it is argued that the world has become too dangerous for anything less than Utopia—as the futurist William Koetke puts it: "Creating a utopian paradise, a new Garden of Eden, is our only hope."[32]

Utopias do not have to be realistic to be interesting. They lift the spirits. Here, William Morris is being driven gently—in a carriage with the graceful and pleasant lines of a simple Wessex wagon, and pulled by a strong grey horse—through an area of rural forest called Kensington:

It was exceedingly pleasant in the dappled shadow, for the day was growing as hot as need be, and the coolness and shade soothed my excited mind into a condition of dreamy pleasure, so that I felt as if I should like to go on for ever through that balmy freshness. My companion seemed to share in my feelings, and let the horse go slower and slower as he sat inhaling the green forest scents, chief amongst which was the smell of the trodden bracken near the wayside.[33]

In the Utopia of Morris' *News from Nowhere,* industry, slums and suburbs had all been swept away, leaving an idyll of villages, meadow and woodland. The much-reduced population consisted of friendly, laughing people, given to *festivals and handcrafts, and needing no *laws: anyone who did wrong would be quickly overcome with remorse. Even the weather was better. Oh, and the women were lightly clad and affectionate, enjoying nothing better than waiting on and cooking for the men.[34]

Shaped by personal fantasies, Utopia belongs to an ancient tradition. It was often lyrical, especially with the ancient Greeks: once upon a time, wrote Hesiod, people lived free from sorrow, work and the pain of old age; the harvest yielded abundantly of its own accord. Yes, and it was eternal spring, added Ovid, and yet luscious autumnal harvests presented themselves to be gathered; golden honey dripped from the trees—and Edmund Spenser, too, made sure that in his Garden of Adonis,

There is continuall spring, and harvest there
Continuall, both meeting at one time.

Edmund Spenser, The Faerie Queene, 1596.[35]

The people in this land of perfection, according to Pindar, delight themselves with horses, wrestling, music and games of draughts, while all around them blooms the fair flower of perfect bliss. And from there, of course, there was plenty of scope for going seriously downhill. In the long, varied and outrageous *tradition of Cockaigne Utopias, fish come to the house, bake themselves, and serve themselves on the tables; parties of young monks come across groups of willing young nuns bathing in the river . . . This, we are assured, is better than Paradise.[36]

More recently, Utopias have tended to be rather more practical than this, and focused on the writer's favourite subject. There have been proposals for *population control: for reproduction being taken over entirely by state baby-factories; for a virtual prohibition of heterosexual *sex; and a lyrical description of a depopulated landscape reverting to the wildwood after an apocalyptic population collapse. Other Utopias propose the abolition of *money, psychological conditioning, total surrender to the passions, the replacement of commerce by a state-controlled industrial army, a single global language, a literary *education, the greening of Europe, subsistence farming and the simple life, a return to *manual skills, and a happy *innocent land inhabited by the noble savage.[37]

And after all that, it is reassuring to come across a prediction which actually came true, though a little short on excitement. In *The Diothas* (1883), John MacNie predicted the general use of the horseless carriage—capable of reaching twenty miles an hour—and the hero of this life in the fast lane deserves credit for accuracy:

"You see the white line running along the centre of the road," resumed Utis, "The rule of the road requires that line to be kept on the left, except when passing a vehicle in front. Then the line may be crossed, provided the way on that side is clear."[38]

But take heart, for the pace picks up again with J.D. Bernal and Freeman Dyson's technology of immortality, with its self-replicating machines capable of infinite work, and the colonisation of space by the forestation of giant asteroids with trees growing hundreds of miles tall, amongst which the human species would find once again the wilderness and *freedom that it lost on Earth.[39]

But then there are the darker Utopias. The states which see themselves as delivering a wonderful future and are prepared to put up with pain and tyranny as the price of getting there. Tyranny's diet, a mixture of good intentions, fantasy and terror, was there in the Soviet Union, the Third Reich, the People's Republic of China, Orwell's Oceania and Huxley's Brave New World. It was there, too, in Tzarist Russia, and we get an eye- and ear-witness account of it from the observant French tourist of the 1840s, Astolphe de Custine. Its most impressive accomplishment, he tells us, was the silence—it was quite a peaceful place, in fact:

> Russia is a nation of mutes; some magician has changed sixty million men into automatons who await the wand of another magician to be reborn and to live. Nothing is lacking in Russia . . . except liberty, that is to say life.[40]

It is a mistake to try to build a heaven on earth. This is the Millenarian Fallacy, and you can recognise it from its lack of rational aims, the support it gets from a dislocated and rootless population, and its catastrophic reality (see "The Millennium" sidebar on page 488). The turbulent decline of the *market economy could stir these ingredients into action.

Utopia's Golden Age

Once, there was a time when Utopia-invention could be taken seriously. In the summer of 1509, the scholar and lawyer Sir Thomas More (1478–1535) invited his friend Desiderius Erasmus (1467–1536) to stay with him at his house in Chelsea, while he recovered from a visit to Italy. They talked at length about what he had seen on his travels. The Pope at that time was the multitasking Julius II, who combined the careers of pope and general. As Erasmus explained, he rode off to battle followed by a retinue representing a range of skills and support services which maybe you didn't know were needed on military campaigns: whores, lawyers, cardinals, bankers and spin doctors who could prove that plunging a sword into your brother's vitals was an act of supreme *charity in accordance with Christian teaching.[41]

For Erasmus, the only thing to do about this was to laugh at it, and his *Praise of Folly* (1511) is a carnival of *irony and sarcasm, the portrait of a society of *erotic aggression, held together by little more than a web of mutual flattery—the habit, common in all the courts of Europe, of never daring to tell the *truth. The book was a bestseller. The Pope himself is said to have enjoyed it, but for More it was a shock and a reason to think about a better way of doing things.[42]

By comparison with the lunatic brilliance of Rome, More's *Utopia* (1516) comes as a relief. Here was the ideal state, calm and sensible, a haven of sanity and groundedness. The first thing to do, he tells us, is to make Utopia an island, decisively separate from continental Europe, and with the guarantee of freedom to decide for itself. If God hadn't already provided for this island status, then the omission should be corrected as soon as possible by a massive feat of collective digging. Now there would be a chance of a society that made sense, and More's Utopia duly defends *religious toleration and promotes lifelong *education; small towns are surrounded by the *land from which they derive food and fuel, in a model quite similar to that of Ebenezer Howard's *Social City; the houses have gardens, loved and cared for as sources of *food and delight; there is a supply of clean *water and proper drainage and sewage systems.

And yet, there is another side to this Utopia. It includes a bundle of ideas which suggests to us that even in this most benign paper-Utopia-creator, there is a controller who likes things done in his way: no private property; all houses reallocated by lot every ten years and built to a uniform design which would extend to town planning, dress and permitted games. The inhabitants even get up

U

THE MILLENNIUM
Fantasies of wealth, equality and happiness

The historian Norman Cohn tells us three things we should know about millenarian movements, those waves of *populist belief about the complete transformation in society, often involving the second coming:

No rational aims. It is characteristic of this kind of movement that its aims and premises are boundless. A social struggle is seen not as a struggle for specific, limited objectives, but an event of unique importance, different in kind from all other struggles known to history, a cataclysm from which the world is to emerge totally transformed and redeemed.

Springing from dislocation and rootlessness. Revolutionary millenarianism drew its strength from a population living on the margin of society — peasants without land or with too little land even for subsistence; journeymen and unskilled workers living under the continuous threat of unemployment; beggars and vagabonds — in fact from the amorphous mass of people who were not simply poor but who could find no assured and recognised place in society at all. These people lacked the material and emotional support afforded by traditional social groups; their kinship-groups had disintegrated and they were not effectively organised in village communities or in guilds; for them there existed no regular, institutionalised methods of voicing their grievances or pressing their claims. Instead, they waited for a *propheta* to bind them together in a group of their own.

Prompted by disaster. Because these people found themselves in such an exposed and defenceless position they were liable to react very sharply to any disruption of the normal, familiar, pattern of life. . . . The greatest wave of millenarian excitement, one which swept through the whole of society, was precipitated by the most universal natural disaster of the Middle Ages, the Black Death; and here again it was in the lower social strata that the excitement lasted longest and that it expressed itself in violence and massacre.

The old religious idiom has been replaced by a secular one, and this tends to obscure what otherwise would be obvious. For it is the simple truth that, stripped of their original supernatural sanction, revolutionary millenarianism and mystical anarchism are with us still.

NORMAN COHN, *The Pursuit of the Millennium*, 1957.[43]

and go to bed at the same time, they eat in *public halls, and discussion of *politics is punishable with death.[44]

It's disappointing, really. Why the retreat to teenage-authoritarian fantasy? Well, you can see More and Erasmus' problem. An earnest prescription of how life might really be lived, if measured, advisory and credible, would actually have been incredible. The storm of destruction in the Reformation to come — which included the sack of Rome by the Holy Roman Emperor's own army in 1527 — was to be a shock as yet unmatched, perhaps until the greater storm to be expected at the end of the age of fossil fuels. The mockery and exaggeration in their books signalled that this was not the time for policy prescriptions. Better to tease and goad: we, the readers, must work out our Utopias

for ourselves; the responsibility lies with us to do the thinking. Sanity does not run towards us in the form of spectacular ideas; we have to go looking for it. It matures in the minds of citizens. This Utopia is lean.

More was right: *Utopia* really did get people thinking, not least by giving a name to the literary form, and the century of turbulence in Europe that followed produced a library of utopian writing. Anton Doni's *The Wise and Mad World* (1552) outlined the role and *responsibilities of the state; Francesco Patrizi's *The Happy City* (1553) included an early exploration of the arguments in favour of eugenic breeding. By the early seventeenth century, utopian writers were getting the hang of this, with practical suggestions about sanitary arrangements, which at the time consisted of, well, almost no arrangements at all: sewage, garbage and waste from abattoirs and fishmongers were piled in the streets, scavenged by the "tossers", assisted by pigs, geese and rats. When the Catholic councillors were thrown out of the window of the chancery tower in Prague by an angry crowd of Protestant deputies on 23 May 1618, their lives were saved by the piles of *waste of various kinds heaped up against the walls of the building sixty feet below.[45]

The consequences of these conditions for *water supply and *health were regrettable, and the solutions proposed by the utopians were exactly what was needed: fresh water conduits, reservoirs, a regular programme of flushing away sewage, garbage collection, gardens, orchards, fresh air. In *The City of the Sun* (1602), Tommaso Campanella described a system of pumps, cisterns and rainwater collection; Ludovico Zuccolo (*The Republic of Evandria*, 1625) among many others, insisted on water stewards and inspectors of public health. Robert Burton (*The Anatomy of Melancholy*, 1621) recommended that the most *polluting and smelliest trades such as dyers, tanners and abattoirs along with the fire-using trades such as smiths, brewers, bakers and metalworkers should be out of town, and that every city should have its fire brigade.[46]

There were recommendations for personal hygiene and exercise (Johann Andreae, *Christianopolis*, 1619); proposals for a healthy diet, for midwives, prenatal and neonatal care, care for old people, euthanasia for the terminally ill if suffering extreme pain, and arrangements for burial and cremation. The anonymous I.D.M. (*The Kingdom of Antangil*, 1616) argued for the reform of medical training, ending the (then) unhelpful distinction between surgeons, apothecaries and physicians. Other matters of vital concern for these down-to-earth utopians included *education—especially in science (Francis Bacon, *New Atlantis*, 1624)—and vocational training, to be included as part of the school curriculum (Campanella). They deliberated on the legal structures of society, on property, the family, crime and punishment, including the option of community service as an alternative to prison; they recommended improvement in *agricultural methods, *economic policy, *monetary policy and social justice.[47]

It was all too much for Shakespeare's Gonzalo: he decided to design a Utopia of his own:

GONZALO: I' th' commonwealth I would, by contraries,
  Execute all things; for no kind of traffic
  Would I admit; no name of magistrate;
  Letters should not be known; riches, poverty,
  And use of service, none; contract, succession,
  Bourn, bound of land, tilth, vineyard, none;
  No use of metal, corn, or wine, or oil;
  No occupation, all men idle, all;
  And women too, but innocent and pure;
  No sovereignty—
SEBASTIAN: Yet he would be king on't.
ANTONIO: The latter end of his commonwealth
  forgets the beginning.
GONZALO: All things in common nature should produce
  Without sweat or endeavour: treason, felony,
  Sword, pike, knife, gun, or need of any engine,
  Would I not have; but nature should bring forth,
  Of it own kind, all foison, all abundance,
  To feed my innocent people.
SEBASTIAN: No marrying 'mong his subjects?
ANTONIO: None, man; all idle; whores and knaves.
GONZALO: I would with such perfection govern, sir,
  T' excel the golden age.

William Shakespeare, The Tempest, c.1611.[48]

———

The Lean Economy is set at a time when the potential for the extremes of disorder and tyranny is increasing. The default position—the failed state, extending to terror on a scale too large for a coherent response—is in prospect even in *nations which at present are orderly. Whether it is with a view to preventing such an outcome, or designing a liveable sequel to it, we need to think now about what kind of *political economy might have the best chances of life after *oil—that is, of the *Wheel of Life.

Does that make the Lean Economy a Utopia? Not quite: it is more interested in the feasible than in the ideal; it is about advocating *diversity, not promoting the best; its aim is *reflection, rather than persuasion. Local lean economies are unique expressions of particular *places, and lean thinking says that the people who live there are best able to work out what to do, if given the chance. Utopia has a universalist, one-size-fits-all tendency; it also means, ambiguously, "no-place" and "good-place". But the philosopher, Northrop Frye, suggests a way to interpret this:

> The question, "Where is Utopia?" is the same as the question "Where is nowhere?" and the only answer to that question is "here."[49]

And "Uchronia" — "no-time"? When is that? The only answer to that question is "now".

*Community > Utopian Communities, Rationalism.

V

VALUE. The word is used in two senses in *lean thinking:
(1) In the context of industrial *lean production, *value* consists of the potential benefits the customer gets when she buys from a company (they are only "potential" because what she actually does with what she has bought is another matter). So value is . . .

> A capability provided to a customer at the right time at an appropriate price, as defined in each case by the customer.[1]

In the application of lean thinking to the local *Lean Economy, value is what makes most sense for the people who live there; what they have decided, for now, to achieve.
(2) *The Value Stream*: When the "value" has been decided in lean production, the "value stream" is the series of things that need to be done to achieve it. It does *not* include the things that *don't* need to be done, and that is not a redundant statement, because most actual organisations waste most of their effort on activities that are not actually needed — on unnecessary paperwork, for instance.

The definition in the literature is:

> The specific activities required to design, order, and provide a specific product, from concept to launch, order to delivery, and raw materials into the hands of the customer.[2]

Rule 2 in lean thinking is to identify the elements which comprise this value — the "value stream". In *Lean Logic*, it is called *lean means.

VERNACULAR. (1) The local, applied to language, architecture and practice, especially where the local *practice belongs to an older *tradition than that of the wider society in which the vernacular survives.
(2) "Vernacular" is also used by Edward Goldsmith for the features of a society and ecology that are self-organising, self-governing and self-sustaining, and which therefore do not have to be supplied by the state and its institutions, or by commercial organisations. These life-giving, free services are essential to the work and functioning of both society and *natural systems. Examples: *communities that sustain their own *law and order; *ecosystems that protect themselves from predators; *families that naturally teach their children speech and *emotional literacy; self-regulating *systems that do not require constant intervention.

When the vernacular has faded, these assets have to be supplied by conscious decision, usually requiring payment; and often facing the impossibility of providing them adequately — or at all — where the *ecology that formerly did so as an intrinsic property of its existence is no longer functioning. One example of the failure of the vernacular is found in intensive farming systems which have so comprehensively destroyed habitats for pollinating insects that the pollination has to be done by hand.[3]

The *Lean Economy will aim to rebuild and protect the vernacular in both these senses.
*Local Wisdom, Social Entropy, Public Sphere and Private Sphere.

VIOLENCE. A form taken by argument when *logic and *politics fail. A response by members of a *closed-loop system, when the *closed-access condition on which it is based is challenged. Ultimate defence of the *freedom to say no.
*Big Stick, Lean Defence, Unmentionable.

VIRTUAL CROWD. A large number of people motivated by the simplified instincts of the crowd, but connected by the media and internet rather than by physical *presence.

VIRTUES. (1) *Christian*: faith, hope and *charity.[4]

(2) *Greek*: fortitude, godliness, prudence.[5]

(3) *Cardinal*: fortitude, justice, temperance, prudence.[6]

(4) *Lean*: *fortitude, *encounter, *prudence.

A recognised aim of education, in the recent past, has been to teach and cultivate collective virtue, embodied in the individual. For John Henry Newman, for instance, the aim of education was that . . .

> . . . people should be taught a wisdom, safe from the excesses and vagaries of individuals, embodied in the institutions which have stood the trial and received the sanction of ages.

The person thus educated . . .

> . . . is mainly occupied in merely removing the obstacles which hinder the free and unembarrassed action of those about him.

Here we have the lean and communitarian virtues of *courtesy and *encounter. The educated man has . . .

> . . . candour, consideration, indulgence: he throws himself into the minds of his opponents.

Newman has a word for the person thus educated: *education's great object, he writes, is . . .

> . . . to make its students "gentlemen".[7]

*Culture.

W

WASTE. (1) Material available for use by another part of the *system, or by a different system in a *closed-loop arrangement.

(2) Material discarded by a system as a means of preventing surplus which could produce unwanted *growth (*Intentional Waste).

(3) Material abandoned and made unavailable to the system (and to its neighbours and wider *ecological setting), which will in due course destroy it. The product of an open-loop arrangement formed by excessive *scale.

*Needs and Wants, Lean Materials, Pollution, Sorting Problem.

WATER. Options for water management are shaped by circumstances: the size of the future *population, the *size of the settlement, the nature of the local soil and the weather, the *inheritance of water infrastructures for collection and treatment, the presence or absence of groundwater and deep reservoirs, local rivers, crops and *politics . . .

It is true that all our options are shaped by such things but, given the *diversity of circumstances and the detail and ingenuity of water management, this, to be sure, is a moment to apply *lean thinking's principle of *pull—looking to the local particular for solutions rather than just accruing information because it is there.

There are crucial differences in the kinds of provision needed for water, ranging from the massive irrigation systems described in *Unlean to the chalk streams and water-rich villages of England's Hampshire. And there are thousands of organisations whose speciality is the conservation, treatment or use of water.

So here, in brief, are some of the questions, and some of the sources where answers may be sought:

1. Is local water abundant? Is coordinated work on the level of the *locality, the watershed or the *region needed to maintain a reliable supply?
2. How critical is water conservation in the area? Where do the opportunities for conservation lie: in the *household? in *food-growing? in manufacture? in power generation? in the wider—forested, grassland, or agricultural—environment?
3. What provision is needed to capture and conserve nutrients which would otherwise be carried off in waste water—that is, phosphates, nitrogen and the micronutrients—and at the same time, to conserve the quality of the water returning into the natural environment?
4. Is the local *community sufficiently developed to enable effective local water management? If not, how could it be improved?
5. What opportunities are there for developing aquaculture systems, linking up their potential as an exceptionally *productive source of nutrition with other needs such as *waste treatment and conserving local fertility?

A preliminary guide to sources on water is at this endnote.[1]

V

W

From the point of view of the long-term, decentralised *Lean Economy, then, there is a range of options and means, most of them well-researched and accessible. But there is another aspect of water to note. Short of a radical failure of the *climate, it is rather unlikely that today's developed economies in the temperate areas of the world will experience a breakdown in the *availability* of water, even after the *climacteric.

However, it is by no means unlikely that there could be breakdowns in *supply*. The total amount of water on the planet does not change, but its location and quality does. If there are enduring outages in energy supplies, and/or in the essential conditions which *transport water workers to work and pay their wages, then the water supply grids would be disrupted to the point that nothing will happen when we turn on the tap. At the same time, waste disposal systems will fail, dumping raw sewage into rivers on which we rely for clean water. We need also to recognise the risk of industrial *pollution from (for instance) shale gas mining or a *nuclear accident, making entire watersheds unusable. That is, breakdowns in the distribution of *energy and *food are likely to be followed by corresponding breakdowns in the distribution of water.

This belongs to the class of problems to which there is no solution after the event. And prevention itself is in trouble, owing to the many demands on the use of *land—notably the invasion of watersheds by housing and roads to accommodate a growing *population. The industrial economy's undefended and overlooked exposure to water shock ought to be factored into planning decisions even at this late stage.

It is not just that water is precious. It is magic. You can watch a spring with its constant gift of clear cold water and briefly think that all is right with the world.
*Casuistry, Commons, Encounter, Planned Economy, Script.

WELL-BEING. Accomplishment, laughter and the love of friends, in an *ecology able to sustain *community, peace and *freedom. No problem so far, but do we need to measure it? And, if so, can the national accounts help us to do so?[2]

Well, the items in that short list of uplifting things that comprise well-being are hard to quantify, and one measure that clearly does not do so is that which is usually taken as a guide to the performance of the economy—Gross Domestic Product (GDP). Indeed, GDP and its related economic indicators were never designed to tell us about the well-being of a *nation and the people living in it.

Shortly after the design of reliable measures of national income in the early 1930s, for which the economist Simon Kuznets was mainly responsible, he wrote a celebrated report about what "national income" really means. While it is true, he explains, that "economic welfare cannot be adequately measured unless the personal distribution of income is known", yet . . .

> . . . no income measurement undertakes to estimate the reverse side of income, that is, the intensity and unpleasantness of effort going into the earning of income. The welfare of a nation can, therefore, scarcely be inferred from a measurement of national income.[3]

The shortcomings of GDP as a measure of well-being are many and profound. Here are some of them:

1. *The vital contribution of the *informal economy is not measured in national income*
   The informal economy includes all the things we do for each other as *families or for the local community. They are unpaid, so are not registered in the national accounts. As the informal economy shrinks, with more of its work shifting into the formal economy and being paid for, GDP (other things being equal) rises, but this by no means suggests that there has been an improvement in well-being.[4]

2. *Externalities are not measured*
   Externalities are the things that we get for free: good things, such as work friendships and the services beyond value that we need from a healthy ecology, and bad things such as *pollution, *climate change and congestion. They affect well-being for good or ill, without any direct representation in the national accounts (see *Economics ❭ #5).[5]

3. *Defensive expenditure protects well-being, up to a point, but it does not improve it*
   Defensive expenditure is the cost of the things we have to do as a consequence of living in a

society that has grown to a very large *scale. The economist E.J. Mishan included the following in his radical analysis of defensive expenditure: internal and external *defence (the costs of *law and order as well as armies); travel and *transport (the transport of goods and people needed in order to cope with the centralised structure and remote supply that comes with large scale); *education (the training in technology and other skills needed for the specialist roles required by a large-scale economy); media information (we need to know what is going on); *healthcare (the cost of treating the impact of urban and industrial pollution and congestion on our mental and physical health); vacations (the cost of getting away from it all); and institutional lubricants (the whole establishment of administration and services—tax collectors, public relations companies, trade associations—which we have to pay for either directly or through taxes).[6]

Another way of looking at this is to note the paradoxical effect of trouble: an accident on the motorway—calling for emergency repairs to cars and people—will add to GDP. Delinquency—requiring police time, psychologists and long stays in prison—shows up as a boost to GDP.

And yet, hold your scorn: if we didn't have the ambulances and prisons on hand when we needed them, we would object. And they provide work. More generally, if you are out of a job, what you want to hear is news of GDP's growth, for it brings you a better chance of finding one. From the point of view of employment, it is output that matters—what sort of output doesn't really matter. Here the *abstractions of *economics and the abstractions of someone looking for a job join up (*Leisure, Needs and Wants).

Lean Logic usually refers to defensive expenditure as the cost of the *intermediate economy.

4. *Positional goods*

In a congested *market economy, it is high *relative* incomes rather than average national incomes which tend to be correlated with well-being because relative advantage can confer *absolute* benefits in the contest for positional goods, such as being able to live in the most sought-after part of town. In the case of key assets and advantages which are allocated by auction—such as housing—it is the relative size of bids, not their absolute size, that settles it. A general rise in incomes or wealth would make no difference to the outcome of this auction.[7]

5. *The decline in *social capital and stimulus*

As the industrial psychologist Frederick Herzberg outlined in a celebrated study, our wants can be divided into two different kinds:[8]

1. We want to prevent things we don't like—such as poor working conditions, poor management and inadequate equipment. He called these "hygiene factors", and their key characteristic is that, once we have sorted them out, we do not look for any further improvement: that's enough for now; we hit a ceiling.

2. We also want things we do like—such as achievement, recognition, the friendships, projects and *play of social capital, and interesting work. These he called "motivators", and there is no particular ceiling: we always want more.

This distinction is key to understanding the value we place on things in an affluent market economy. The things we spend money on—food, electric kettles, clothes, cars—are relevant to both hygiene factors and motivators, but the distribution between the two is uneven: electric kettles, for instance, tend to be more relevant as hygiene factors than as motivators.

The things we unequivocally recognise as motivators are things we tend not to buy: rewarding friendships, shared achievements, making music, being uplifted by the sight of the stars. A larger GDP does not increase the supply of such things. On the contrary, in an increasingly boring, excitement-lite, congested and regulated society, the attempt to compensate for the decline in motivators by spending money on stuff—trying to squeeze excitement from things intended to do no more than just keep us ticking over—is not only unstimulating, it is depressing. The psychologist Oliver James sees the clinical consequences of this in the form of a fall in the levels of serotonin—the hormone which makes us feel good after having accomplished something—and he sets out exhaustive evidence for the proposition . . .

> . . . that we are unhappier, that people who are unhappy tend to have low levels of serotonin and that levels thereof are largely caused by our social psychological environment. . . . If angst in general and depression in particular have increased since the Second World War, then it is highly probable that more of us suffer from low levels of serotonin . . . For once, it is no exaggeration to use the word "epidemic" in describing a social trend.[9]

Nonetheless, GDP is undoubtedly a valuable measure. By giving us the value of output *per capita* (per person), and comparing that with other *nations and with other years, it can tell us something about the wealth of the economy and its rate of *growth; about its character and the well-being of the people in it: if GDP is falling, for instance, the level of unemployment will probably be rising, and that has a big effect on well-being. Since our lives depend on the economy, it is a good idea to have some data on its size and growth, even though we also know it isn't going to last.

Adjustments and alternatives to the measurement of GDP have value, but criticism of it on the grounds that it does not measure well-being (taken sometimes to the point of proposing its abolition) is a *straw man argument. GDP can no more be criticised as a poor measure of well-being than an apple can be criticised for not being a potato. GDP is simply a *necessary but not a sufficient condition for understanding the state of the economy.

And if, having got the quantitative information we need about the economy, we want to know something about the impact of its growth and *scale, GDP can be elaborated in ways that will provide it.

Many other measures have been devised which attempt to give a better idea of well-being, such as the Genuine Progress Indicator (GPI), which corrects the raw *numbers provided by GDP, showing its costs in terms of resource depletion and environmental impact (see "Vital Statistics" sidebar). And, on a smaller scale, if the projected revenue from projects is corrected to

---

VITAL STATISTICS
Some economic indicators and supporting cast
(annual measurements implied)

Gross Domestic Product (GDP): the monetary value of all goods and services produced in the domestic economy.

Gross National Product (GNP): GDP plus net property income from abroad.[11]

National Income: GNP less depreciation.

Externalities: The good and bad things arising from production and consumption decisions, but not represented in prices.

Net Economic Welfare (NEW): GNP adjusted for externalities, plus the value of *leisure.[12]

Genuine Progress Indicator (GPI): NEW adjusted for resource depletion and environmental damage.[13]

Happy Planet Index (HPI): A measure of Happy Life Years, adjusted for their ecological footprint (i.e., environmental damage).[14]

Nominal values: values measured at current prices.

Real values: values adjusted by inflation.

Per capita. Per person: the expression of national accounts per person, rather than as an aggregate for the whole economy.[15]

---

take account of (for instance) the forests that have to be felled to make way for them, that can help to force the application of *intelligence to their evaluation.[10]

And yet, it is bigger than that. We are in trouble. What is in prospect is a *climacteric. Observation of subtle changes in average well-being do not, even remotely, capture the nature of the problem. We can probably come closer to it by taking a walk.

*Public Sphere and Private Sphere, Planned Economy, Generalisation Fallacies, Reflection, Local Wisdom.

WHEEL OF LIFE, THE. A way of thinking about the life-cycle of *complex systems (woodlands, companies, civilisations, *Gaia . . .).

These can be understood as inhabiting the space defined by two variables or dimensions:

Potential: a measure of the richness of the system, in the sense of being able to make interesting things happen—the quantity and *diversity of plant and animal life in an *ecosystem; the friendships, *trust and *social capital sustained in a society; the *skills and accomplishments of a *political economy . . .

Connectedness: the extent and strength of the linkages between different parts of the system, which influence or govern how they respond to events.

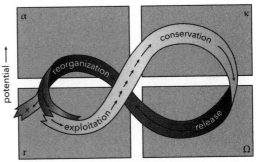

As you can imagine, these two properties relate positively to each other: the more connected the system is, the greater its potential, and greater potential opens the way to more fully-developed connections.

But there are limits to this progress. As a system's potential grows, so does the cost of keeping the whole thing going: for instance, it needs more inputs, it produces more *waste, and it becomes a more tempting prey for enemies. And as connectedness grows, the system eventually starts to become less flexible, slower to respond, less locally inventive, more "tightly coupled". There is now the risk that, when trouble occurs, it will ripple through the whole system.

The pioneers of *resilience thinking, C.S. Holling, Lance Gunderson and colleagues, put all this together for us in a story about four phases in the life, or 'adaptive cycle', of a system. This story can be summarised by an illustration in the shape of skewed infinity—redrawn here as a Möbius strip—and its explanation:[16]

The fore loop (the larger one in the diagram, moving up and to the right)

1. *Exploitation*: early entrants make use of the wealth of opportunity in their environment to multiply. Most fail, not least because they are poorly-connected individuals facing a dangerous world on their own, but some may eventually build a system with potential and connectedness. This is known as the r phase: r has for many years been used as a label for the rate of growth of the population of an ecology (example of phase: young trees).[17]

2. *Conservation*: the system persists in its mature form, with the benefit of a complex structure of connections, strong enough now to resist challenges for a long time, but with the weakness that the connections themselves introduce an element of rigidity, slowing down its reactions and reducing its inventiveness. This is the K phase, where the ecology reaches its carrying capacity (example: mature trees).[18] In due course, however, the tight connections themselves become a decisive problem, which can only be resolved by . . .

The back loop (moving from bottom-right to top-left in the diagram)

3. . . . *release*: at this point, the cost and *complication of maintaining the *large scale—providing the resources the system needs, and disposing of its waste—becomes too great. The space and flexibility for local responsiveness had become scarce, the system itself so tightly connected that it locked: a target for predators without and within, against which it found it harder and harder to defend itself. But now the stresses join up, and the system collapses (example: dying trees). This is the omega (Ω) phase, as suggested by Holling and Gunderson, and it is placed by them in its ecological context:

> The tightly bound accumulation of biomass and nutrients becomes increasingly fragile (overconnected, in systems terms) until it is suddenly released by agents such as forest fires, droughts, insect pests, or intense pulses of grazing.[19]

4. *Reorganisation*: the remains of a system after collapse are unpromising material on which to start afresh, and yet they are an opportunity for a

495

W

different kind of system to enjoy a brief flowering—decomposing the wood of a former forest, recycling the carbon after a fire, restoring the land with forgiving grass, clearing away the assumptions and grandeur of the previous regime. Reorganisation becomes a busy system in its own right (example: rotting trees). This is the alpha (α) phase.[20]

In this phase, there is a persistent process of disconnecting, with the former subsidiary parts of the system (*holons) being broken up. But our diagram is drawn on a graph of potential (increasing from bottom to top) and connectedness (increasing from left to right), which allows us to note a curious aspect of this back loop: the defining relationship of the fore loop—where *more* potential is correlated with *more* connectedness—is reversed. In the back loop (even) *less* connectedness goes with *more* potential. How can this be?

Well, potential can be the product of sharply-developed, well-connected structures: in the confident prime of life of Rome, with its army, its institutions, its transport networks and its wealth, who could tell what astonishing things they might produce? (That is, high connectedness goes with high potential).

However, potential is *also* the product of a system which is starting all over again. Where a forest has just burned, not much can grow there, but soon the charred tree trunks rot down: the land is weak on charisma, strong on potential. Grass and flowers flourish; it is now ready for anything. (That is, low connectedness goes with high potential).

And this is how Holling and Gunderson explain it from the point of view of *natural systems: during the conservation phase, the system's connectedness increases, until . . .

> [t]he resources sequestered in vegetation and soil are . . . suddenly released and the tight organisation is lost . . . so that the potential for other uses re-emerges.[21]

These four sequential stages take us through the life-cycle of a system, and show us two periods during which the system is particularly *resilient to shocks. One of these is in the later stages of exploitation, when the system's potential and connectedness are both well developed, but before the rigidities have set in. The other is in the reorganisation phase, when the remains of complex structures are broken down into a form that can be used in the next phase—since there is not much structure and connectedness here in the first place, little damage can be done even by large shocks. Also note the "x" indicated in the bottom left of the diagram; this is "the stage where the potential can leak away and where a flip into a less productive and organized system is most likely".[22]

What has this got to do with us?

It is the first of these two resilient stages—where a functioning complex system has a lot to lose, and needs all the resilience it can get—which is the stage that matters urgently to our society, now. The point on the diagram where we now stand is the one near the later stages of conservation, the K phase in which a mature tree lives. What is in prospect is the next stage in the cycle—release—where our tree falls to the ground, with the further prospect of break-up and reorganisation into a different system; into an utterly different world.

It is not unreasonable for us to want to postpone this development. Nor is it unreasonable to consider whether there is a way of going with the flow—that is, doing the right things in a systems-literate way to somehow extend the life of the cycle that really matters to us—the one we happen to be on. Can this be done?

Well, to answer this, let us first unpack the cycle a bit. It is helpful in fact to identify *six* stages in the cycle—to make this explicit, here is a simplified version of the adaptive cycle, just to clarify the point. It is drawn here as a hexagon (we lose the logic of the reorganisation but it makes this part of the sequence more intuitive and easier to follow):[23]

1. *Exploitation* (or *Renewal*). Here we have the phase of pioneers, working by trial-and-error, evolving as organisms and raising their *productivity, but in most cases failing to get very far, because they lack *connectedness: they are not embedded in rich ecosystems which protect them, join them up in alliances and *reciprocities and extend the length of their natural life-cycle from days to years.

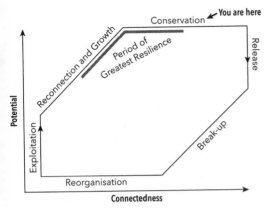

Nevertheless, some do survive and begin to join up with others into a system.

2. *Reconnection and growth.* This is the system's glad confident morning. It forges connections and grows in size and complexity; complex organisms inhabit it. There is a chain of stimulus and inspiration between one success and the next, and it becomes resilient, able to duck-and-weave, to recover in response to stresses.

3. *Conservation* (or *consolidation*). The system now extends, elaborates and reinforces its connections. In the case of a *civic society, there is *intensification as the *intermediate economy and its infrastructures develop: the burden of *transport, *law and order, *waste management and the rest—huge commitments which nobody wants for their own sake, but which are a necessary support structure for the large-scale. There is also growing regulation, imposed in support of the institutions which emerge as civic society becomes less diverse, requiring more coordination from the centre. There is consolidation: nothing (or nothing significant) can move without a lot of other things having to move at the same time. Problems spread at speed. There is top-down control, a loss of flexibility and *imagination, a loss of resilience.

And, perversely, the conventional responses to this phase seem to be devoted to the cause of making the system, in its hour of need, even less resilient. As the systems scientists Brian Walker and David Salt note, solutions are sought in standardisation and efficiency improvements, in increasingly centralised command-and-control and in tighter insistence on process, rules and procedures—that is, in stamping out any new vision, experiment and self-reliance, and in further elaborating expensive procedures standing in the way of getting things done.

The problem is the large scale, rigidity and *complication; the solution is seen as even larger scale, greater rigidity and further complication—a classic case of the amplifying *feedback typical of a *complicated system in trouble.[24] Fortunately, these mainstream solutions do not attract a consensus. There are some *harmless lunatics who think differently.

And this is where we are now—some way along the horizontal line labelled as the Conservation stage. We may wonder what lies ahead, and consider radical responses. Some people call this attitude *"green".[25]

4. *Release.* The more rigid the system becomes in trying to postpone the shock, and the longer it is postponed, the more catastrophic it will eventually be. The system's potential falls away; inflexible and complicated, it cannot defend itself. The big intermediate structures, still intact but not functioning, are a burden on the system, hastening its collapse.

5. *Break-up.* Now the connected system degenerates; its productivity falls to zero.

6. *Reorganisation.* This is the compost stage. The remains of the system's connected structure finally rot down, perhaps becoming rich with potential to eventually regenerate into a new system.

Is the sequence inevitable? To answer this we need to think about time, and about the networks of parts (or *holons), that make up any system. If these parts, each complete and functional in their own right—systems-within-systems—are to be useful to the larger system, they will vary in size, they will do different things in different ways; they will have the freedom to experiment, to repair and recover, to adapt and evolve. In a healthy system, each holon is able to operate at its own pace, according to its own clock. It is protected from above by the larger, slower-moving system to

497

which it belongs; it is stimulated by, and responds to, the smaller, faster, shorter cycles of innovation and response of the holons lower down.[26]

Here is an example of the faster reaction times of a subsystem relative to the large, slow-moving system to which it belongs: tropical forests have evolved such a thick canopy of leaves that it is hard for seedlings on the ground to get enough light to survive. The seed-holon has, therefore, comparatively recently, evolved a response in the form of very large seeds. These contain enough nutrients for the seed to grow despite being deprived of light and nibbled at by curious animals like tapirs, which eat the surrounding fruit and, in the process, spread the seeds around. The earlier seeding systems which depended on abundant light died, and gave way to systems that could cope with the deep gloom of the forest floor. This life-and-death flexibility—the rapid regeneration-response—of the subsystem enables the large system, the forest, to go on and on.[27]

Another example of a subsystem—a village—can be flexible in its own life, economy and society. In place of the sophisticated preoccupations of the city, it may be able to hang on to the realities of life and nature even if urban civic society cannot. Subsystems (the smaller hexagons in this second diagram) can come and go, adapt quickly, or die and reinvent themselves—they can go with the flow of trial-and-error, life-and-death. These are the strategies of *recovery-elastic resilience*, the ability to bounce back (see sidebar).[28]

The subsystem has greater flexibility to quickly explore these strategies because, in addition to the large relative surface area enjoyed by *small-scale systems, it is operating on a shorter life-cycle than the overall system. And when repeated many times by many parts of the system, this series of small-scale new beginnings can provide a community or civilisation with constantly-renewing resilience. *The more flexible its subsystems, the longer the expected life of the system as a whole.*

Such recovery-elastic resilience depends on the system's *holons/subsystems/*communities having four key properties:

They must have substantial independence (weak interdependence), so that the system as a whole is *modular.*

They must develop characteristics and behaviour in response to local conditions. Some of those responses will be unsuccessful—and *death will follow—but the variety makes it likely that other responses by other holons (e.g., villages) will do better. This gives the system as a whole textural-*diversity.*

It follows, in turn, that there must be some *slack in the holons, capable of being brought into play when needed, and allowing damage to be sustained at the periphery without destroying the core.

Exploitation / Reconnection and Growth / Conservation / Release / Break-up / Reorganisation

---

*RECOVERY-ELASTIC RESILIENCE
The strategies

1. *Sacrifice-and-succession: although some parts of the system fail, others take their place.
2. New phase: the system takes a different form for a time.
3. Elasticity: the system goes with the flow of change without suffering profound harm.
4. Resistance: it is robust—able to endure substantial shocks without suffering harm.
5. Opportunism: it uses the shock as an opportunity—to scavenge or to take advantage of weaknesses elsewhere in the system.
6. *Elegance: the system has minimum baggage, and little to lose; it reacts quickly.

And there will need to be alert *feedback—that is, the parts must be able to observe and respond quickly to events, not waiting for reassurance and permission from the centre.

A system which has this resilience, enabling its local subsystems to go into shock and live out their life-cycles on timescales shorter than that of the larger system, has a chance of enduring—of attaching an achievable meaning to "the Wheel of Life".[29]

In other words, what we have here, in principle, is a way of extending the life of a large-scale system indefinitely by enabling the ravages of time (the whole life-cycle from birth to death to birth) to take place with respect to the system's parts, or holons; the system as a whole is thereby constantly renewed. As the *System Scale Rule reminds us, large-scale problems do not require large-scale solutions; they require small-scale solutions within this kind of large-scale framework.[30]

And that is precisely what happens in every living creature; all its parts are in a constant state of *recovery-elastic resilience, extending the life of their host system, if not indefinitely, at least for much longer than their own lives.

The problem with the *large-scale *civic society is that the cost of *connecting itself up is a rigidity which stops a critical part of this process—the delegation of life-and-death—in its tracks, condemning the society as a whole to lumber into the death-stage, big time.

Independent local *lean economies are a means of restoring the system's immortality, or at least its longevity. But whether they actually succeed in doing this depends on how independent they are, how local, how alert, how quick, how diverse and how flexible. It may be too late to achieve a rapid transition into the modular structure of self-reliant, independent groups which is the foundation for resilience. It is not too late to try.

*Ecology: Farmers and Hunters, Resilience, Systems Thinking, Gaia.

WICKED PROBLEMS. Highly complex problems which cannot be solved in a straightforward way, and may not be soluble at all. We need to be aware of their existence because the problems we are now facing are wicked. If we cannot see a solution, that does not

necessarily mean that we have not understood the problem; it may mean that there isn't one.

The main features of a wicked problem are:

Vagueness: they lack clear *definition because they spill over into many different issues and *systems.

Hard to grasp: they can be recognised from one or two perspectives, but are too complex to understand in the round.

Populated: they affect many people: solutions are likely to be social rather than *technical.

No right answer: the best that can be done is to pick the least bad response.

Changeable: the problem, and attitudes both to it and to solutions, are constantly changing.

No definition: the problem may be hard even to identify in a form that allows it to be shared.

No solution?: there is no *objective clear definition of the problem, so no definitive solution.

No clean ending: the problem-solving ends when *money and *time run out.[31]

But do not believe that a problem is wicked because someone tells you so. Look again.

*Fortitude, Exhilaration, Climate Change, Growth, Squalid, Systems Thinking, Success.

WISDOM. See Local Wisdom.

WISHFUL THINKING. (1) A form of *denial, avoiding the need to do any thinking at all.

(2) Useful *self-deception as a means of maintaining morale when things are looking bad, or when the task ahead, though necessary, would not be attempted if you admitted how hard it would be.

*Reverse Risk Assessment Rule, Grope.

WITCH-HUNT. Extreme *reductionism: the easy explanation—or *blame—that has the bonus of seeming to raise or confirm one's own moral standing. Torpid *public debate stirs into life when there is the chance of a witch-hunt.

*Ad Hominem, Populism, High Ground.

WOLF, THE FALLACY OF THE (*Argumentum ad lupum*). The *fallacy that, since previous warnings of a

W

problem's arrival have been wrong, or premature, or misunderstood, the problem can safely be ignored.

One of Aesop's Fables is the story of the boy whose job was to look after the sheep but, having a nervous disposition, he was forever crying "wolf" when no wolf was there. One day the wolf really did come, and he cried "wolf" again, but nobody believed him, and the wolf was able to dine off the sheep, and the boy, at leisure.

There are two morals to the story. The first is: avoid giving false alarms. The second is: in the end, the wolf came, so do not be misled by previous false alarms into thinking that the latest alarm is false, too. Of these two, the second one is more significant—it highlights a key logical *fallacy. Believing false alarms wastes time, but it can lead to some helpful advice for apprentice shepherds; disbelieving all alarms can lead to a local lad being eaten, for starters.

We have an example of the Fallacy of the Wolf in the case of supplies of oil. A century or so ago, there were some false alarms about how little oil remained; the art of forecasting oil supplies earned a bad reputation. However, estimates of the quantity remaining in the world—and of the turning point (the "peak") at which oil production would start to decline—steadily improved and, in the 1970s, estimates of the easily-accessible liquid oil which had been in place at the start of the industrial era settled at, or around, 2,000 billion barrels, and that estimate has held.

The expected peak was estimated to be around the year 2000—later extended into the new century thanks to the slower growth in demand following the oil shocks of 1973–1979. The "2000:2000" warning, starting with a report by Esso in 1967, was independently confirmed by official sources, such as the UK's Department of Energy (1976), the *Global 2000* Report to the President (1980), the World Bank (1981), and by numerous independent studies such as Hubbert (1977), Petroconsultants (1995), Ivanhoe (1996), Campbell (1997), Bentley (2002), and so on through the first decade of the new century. Analysts have also pointed to the regrettable consequences of a breakdown in oil supplies on a global market which has neglected to make any serious preparation. Here is a wolf that gave more than forty years' notice of its arrival, and has been thoughtfully issuing reminders ever since (for detail, and more recent studies, see *Energy Prospects).[32]

It is, however, the *sceptics that tend to carry the day. "There is always a series of geologists who are concerned about imminent depletion of world supplies", an energy economist reassured a House of Lords Select Committee on Energy Supply in 2001. "They have been wrong for 100 years and I would be confident they will be wrong in the future."

So that's all right then: the anguished warnings are nothing more than that new kid trying to draw attention to himself. Aesop might be tempted to revise his fable slightly. Here we have the apprentice shepherd growing mature and experienced in the job. He has been giving precise fixes of the wolf's approach for as long as anyone can remember. He is specific and credible about the action that must be taken to save the village. And still he is disbelieved.[33]

*Unknowable Future Fallacy, Sedation, Spiking Guns, Transition.

Y

YONDER. A word used to direct attention to something with the properties of distance, hope, difficulty, competence, cooperation, uncertainty, space and anticipation. Obsolete.[1]

NOTES

The first mention of each book gives the author, date and title; subsequent mentions in the same note or those closely following give surname and date only. Full details of subtitles/publishers are given in the Bibliography. The dates given are the dates of the original authorship/publication, as per the Bibliography, but the page numbers refer to the edition utilised, which (if different) can be found at the end of each Bibliography entry. Articles are cited in full, but are not listed in the Bibliography, although in the case of articles which appear in collections of essays, the name of the collection is listed. Second-hand references (cited by authors cited in *Lean Logic*) are not cited in the Bibliography; instead, full publication details are given in these notes, or the reader is referred to the primary reference for details.

    Editor's note: A number of the endnotes in Fleming's final manuscript were incomplete and contained brief notes of further work required. Extensive efforts have been made to reconstruct these and present the endnotes as intended, but it has not been possible in all cases.

Editor's Preface

1. David Fleming (2016), *Surviving the Future: Culture, Carnival and Capital in the Aftermath of the Market Economy*, Chelsea Green Publishing. For more information see www.chelseagreen.com/surviving-the-future .
2. More information on the Dark Mountain books can be found at: http://dark-mountain.net/stories/books .
3. Shaun Chamberlin (2009), *The Transition Timeline*.
4. *Editor's note*: David had not quite completed his work on *Lean Logic* at the time of his sudden death in November 2010. As such, some parts of his final manuscript may not have been completed to his satisfaction. Nonetheless, the content proved to require no updating, and remains as Fleming left it—its clear relevance to our present circumstances only illustrates his great foresight.

Introduction

1. *Editor's note*: "The Big Society" was a flagship policy of the UK Conservative Party in their manifesto for the 2010 general election, aiming "to create a climate that empowers local people and communities, building a big society that will take power away from politicians and give it to people . . . encouraging people to take an active role in their communities." After the election, Conservative Prime Minister David Cameron stated that he wanted his vision of such a 'Big Society' to be one of the great legacies of his Government. See, e.g., www.gov.uk/government /news/government-launches-big-society-programme--2 .
2. Pericles' funeral oration quoted in Thucydides (431 BC), *The History of the Peloponnesian War* (translated by Richard Crawley, 1873), available at, e.g., www.gutenberg .org/files/7142/7142-h/7142-h.htm .

A

1. Alexander Herzen (1847–1851), *From the Other Shore*, p 93.
2. See Isaiah Berlin's introduction to Herzen (1847–1851), and Herzen's own account of the 1848 revolution in Paris, pp 45–52.
3. Oliver Goldsmith, dedication to "The Traveller", 1764, in (1756–1774), *The Complete Poetical Works of Oliver Goldsmith*, p 4.

    For Aristotle and the particular, see Albert Jonsen and Stephen Toulmin (1988), *The Abuse of Casuistry*, prologue, especially p 19, and chapter 2. In book VI, chapter 5 of his *Nicomachean Ethics*, Aristotle explicitly distinguishes between variable principles (e.g., geometry) and the circumstances of a particular case; it is only the latter which are subjects with which prudence concerns itself: "Nobody deliberates about things that are invariable."

4. Michel Eyquem de Montaigne (1580–1591), *Essays*, book 3, chapter 10, p 472.

5. Joseph Conrad (1900), *Lord Jim*.

6. Matthew Arnold, "The Function of Criticism at the Present Time", in (1865), *Essays in Criticism*, p 38.

7. Aristotle discusses accent in (c.350 BC), *On Sophistical Refutations*, 166 b. Exceptions to the rule that the meaning of individual English words is unaffected by emphasis include "*incense*" vs. "*incense*" (pointed out by Charles Leonard Hamblin (1970), *Fallacies*, p 24). Written English also fails to distinguish between "I read quickly" (past tense) and "I read quickly" (present tense), but that is a quirk of spelling. Hamblin (p 25), and Christopher Tindale (2007), *Fallacies and Argument Appraisal*, conclude that accent does not merit serious consideration as a fallacy, since not only did Aristotle not consider it in a sense that applies to English, but those modern writers who do include it "have difficulty in finding plausible examples" (Tindale, pp 57–58).

8. Writers on fallacies who do think that accent merits consideration include William Fleming (1856), *Vocabulary of Philosophy*, pp 156–157; David Hackett Fischer (1970), *Historians' Fallacies*, pp 271–274; and Madsen Pirie (2006), *How to Win Every Argument*, pp 3–5. Stephen Toulmin, Richard D. Rieke and Allan Janik's storming account of the fallacy in (1979), *An Introduction to Reasoning*, pp 170–171, leaves us in no doubt on the matter.

9. See Frans H. van Eemeren and Rob Grootendorst (1992), *Argumentation, Communication and Fallacies*, pp 137–140 and 212; Douglas N. Walton (1995), *A Pragmatic Theory of Fallacy*, pp 36–40 and 212–217, and Charles Leonard Hamblin (1970), *Fallacies*, pp 41–42 and 160–164.

10. John Locke (1690), *An Essay Concerning Human Understanding*, book IV, chapter 17, sections 19–21. Locke adds another argument which can silence the opposition—*Argumentum ad ludicrum*—where the arguer's case is built on recognised knowledge and proofs, but quite reasonably doesn't see anything wrong with this.

11. Polly Toynbee in joint interview with Sir Peter Stothard, *The Today Programme*, BBC Radio 4, 18 September 2003.

12. Karl Marx, introduction to "Zur Kritik der Hegelschen Rechts Philosophie", in *Der Historischer Materialismus, die Früschriften*, cited by John Laughland in "A Clockwork Orange? Or: What Makes Victor Yushchenko Tick?", *Chicken Kiev*, December 2004.

13. Amy Knight, "Everyone's Favourite Uncle", *The Times Literary Supplement*, 25 July 2003; a review of Simon Sebag Montefiore (2003), *Stalin: The Court of the Red Tsar*, Weidenfeld & Nicolson.

14. Example of Charter 77 suggested by Nadia Johanisova, personal communication.

15. John Milton (1667), *Paradise Lost*, book II, lines 894–899.

16. A helpful first reference on anarchy and its main thinkers is Ted Honderich, ed. (1995), *The Oxford Companion to Philosophy*, Oxford University Press (though it omits Colin Ward).

17. William Godwin (1793), *An Enquiry Concerning Political Justice and its Influence on Morals and Happiness*; William Godwin (1794), *Things as They Are; or The Adventures of Caleb Williams*. For an accessible summary of Godwin's anarchist thought, see Roy Porter (2000), *Enlightenment*, pp 455–459.

18. Peter Marshall (1992), *Demanding the Impossible: A History of Anarchism*, pp 220–234.

19. *Ibid*, pp 362–384.

20. *Ibid*, pp 234–263.

21. *Ibid*, pp 263–309.

22. See Peter Kropotkin (1899), *Fields, Factories and Workshops Tomorrow*, especially the 1974 edition by Colin Ward. See also Kropotkin's other works (1890–1896), *Mutual Aid* and (1892), *The Conquest of Bread*.

23. For more detail on Alexander Herzen, see *Abstraction.

24. Matthew Arnold (1869), *Culture And Anarchy*, p 6.

25. *Ibid*, p 82.

26. Colin Ward (1973), *Anarchy in Action*, p 4.

27. *Ibid*, p 15.

28. BBC sound archive, cited in Ward (1973), p 34.

29. Hannah Arendt (1963), *On Revolution*, p 249. See also Rebecca Solnit (2009), *A Paradise Built in Hell*, Viking.

30. A major influence on Ward's thinking was Percival Goodman and Paul Goodman (1947), *Communitas: Means of Livelihood and Ways of Life*, and it remains a core text of the anarchist literature, especially in the context of land use and planning. For brief histories of the evolution of medicine, education and social security in the United Kingdom, see James Bartholomew (2004), *The Welfare State We're In*.

31. See also José Peréz Adán (1992), *Reformist Anarchism 1800–1936*.

32. Elinor Ostrom, "The Danger of Self-Evident Truths", *PS: Political Science and Politics*, vol 33, 1, March 2000, pp 33–44.

33. *Ibid*, pp 5–7.

34. *Ibid*, p 4.

35. *Ibid*, p 14. Ostrom cites Michael McGinnis (1999), *Polycentric Governance and Development: Reading from the Workshop in Political Theory and Policy Analysis*, Ann Arbour: University of Michigan Press; and Vincent Ostrom (1997), *The Meaning of Democracy and the Vulnerabilities of Democracies*.

36. There is a discussion of the *Treuga Dei* from the point of view of scale in Leopold Kohr (1957), *The Breakdown of Nations*, chapter 2, and in Kirkpatrick Sale (1980), *Human Scale*, part 2, chapter 5. For a summary of the significance of the truce, see Richard Landes, "Peace of God: Pax Dei", 2007, available at www.mille.org/people/rlpages /paxdei.html ; and William Chester Jordan (2002), *Europe in the High Middle Ages*.

37. For an astonishing account of the implications of war for non-combatants—despite the *Treuga Dei*—see Christopher Allmand, "War and the Non-Combatant in the Middle Ages", in Maurice Keen, ed. (1999), *Medieval Warfare*, pp 253–272. The inference should not be drawn that the pitched battles were in fact confined to Mondays, Tuesdays and Wednesdays, though it would be interesting to know if they were.

38. Kelvin W. Willoughby (1990), *Technology Choice: A Critique of the Appropriate Technology Movement*, pp 5–9.

39. E.F. Schumacher, "How to help them help themselves", *The Observer*, 29 August 1965.

40. E.F. Schumacher, "Intermediate Technology: Its Meaning and Purpose", 1973, Intermediate Technology Development Group, p 1. Cited in Willoughby (1990), p 109; "sickle" is substituted for "pange" in the original because *Lean Logic* doesn't know what a pange is.

41. E.F. Schumacher, "Industrialisation through Intermediate Technology", 1964 paper presented to the Conference on Rural Development, Cambridge, in Ronald Robinson, ed. (1971), *Developing the Third World: The Experience of the 1960s*, Cambridge University Press, cited in Willoughby (1990), p 109.

42. Willoughby (1990), pp 109–115.

43. *Ibid*, pp 115–118.

44. E.F. Schumacher, "Industrialisation through Intermediate Technology", *Resurgence*, 1, 2 July/August 1964, in Schumacher (1997), *This I Believe, and Other Essays*.

45. Willoughby (1990), pp 7–8.

46. John Locke (1690), *An Essay Concerning Human Understanding*, books III and IV. Cited in Charles Leonard Hamblin (1970), *Fallacies*.

47. Edmund Burke, speech to the Bristol voters, 9 September 1780, in Burke (1774–1780), *The Writings and Speeches of Edmund Burke*, p 659; John Stuart Mill (quotation abridged), cited in Anthony Arblaster (1987), *Democracy*, p 46.

48. Alexis de Tocqueville (1835), *Democracy in America*, part 2, chapter 7, p 297. Modern scholars include Hans Daudt and Douglas Roe, "Social Contract and the Limits of Majority Rule", in Pierre Birnbaum, Jack Lively and Geraint Parry, eds. (1978), *Democracy, Consensus and Social Contract*, p 335.

49. See Elliott Aronson (1973), *Readings About the Social Animal*. Figure derived from Solomon Asch, "Opinions and Social Pressure", *Scientific American*, vol 193, No. 5, 1955, reprinted in Aronson (1973); discussed in Charles Hampden-Turner (1969), *Radical Man*. Image created by author.

50. Aronson (1973). See also Philip Zimbardo (2007), *The Lucifer Effect*.

B

1. As noted by Robert Clower, "The Keynesian Counter-revolution", in Frank H. Hahn and Frank P.R. Brechling, eds. (1965), *The Theory of Interest Rates*, chapter 5.

2. Nor can you store bread, except perhaps in the freezer, but not very much of it, and the energy you used would make it a bad investment. You could also invent a form of credit—you promise to provide a monthly haircut for the baker's family in exchange for daily bread for yours, but the values must be matched and there has to be a lot of negotiation and trust. It quickly becomes complicated.

3. *Petitio principii*: "Ask [your opponent] to concede the question-at-issue, so that you can use it to prove your point."

4. Caitríona Ruane, Member of the Legislative Assembly, 4 December 2007, "Outlining a Vision for Our Education System", Northern Ireland Assembly, Stormont, Belfast, available at http://cain.ulst.ac.uk/issues/education /selection/ruane041207.pdf .

5. Mike Moore (2003), *A World Without Walls*; Rosemary Righter, "Free for All", *Times Literary Supplement*, 26 September 2003, pp 6–8, a review of Moore (2003).

6. Jules Pretty (2002), *Agri-Culture*, chapter 4.

7. For the fallacy of Begging The Question, see Hamblin (1970), *Fallacies*, pp 32–35; Frans H. van Eemeren and Rob Grootendorst (1992), *Argumentation, Communication and Fallacies*, pp 153, 214; Christopher Tindale (2007), *Fallacies and Argument Appraisal*, pp 72–77; Douglas N. Walton (1989), *Informal Logic*; Douglas N. Walton (1995), *A Pragmatic Theory of Fallacy*, pp 49–54.

8. Dante (1320), *The Divine Comedy*, part 1, "Inferno", canto 11, 64–66.

9. Psalm 55:12–15.

10. van Eemeren and Grootendorst (1992), pp 109–115 and 212.

11. For Antoine Arnauld and Pierre Nicole, see Charles Leonard Hamblin (1970), *Fallacies*, pp 156–157.

12. Being "broken at the wheel" entailed being tied to a wheel and having your bones broken through its gaps. "The Revocation of the Edict of Nantes" is discussed in Barbara Tuchman (1984), *The March of Folly*, chapter 1, p 21; Heather Rae, "State Identities and

the Homogenisation of Peoples", *Cambridge Studies in International Relations*, vol 84, 2002, pp 114–116.

13. For *douce commerce*, see Albert O. Hirschman (1977), *The Passions and the Interests.*

14. Karl Polanyi (1944), *The Great Transformation.* For the increased recognition in economics of the significance of social capital, see James Alt, Margaret Levi and Elinor Ostrom, eds. (1999), *Competition and Cooperation: Conversations with Nobelists about Economics and Political Sciences.*

15. David Hackett Fischer (1970), *Historians' Fallacies*, p 295 (quotation abridged).

16. Ralph Borsodi (1933), *Flight from the City.*

17. E.F. Schumacher (1973), *Small is Beautiful*, pp 56, 58. Schumacher uses "frontiers" rather than "boundaries". The edit is to maintain consistency with the use of *boundaries and frontiers in *Lean Logic.*

18. For a discussion of frontiers, see Kenneth E. Boulding, "The Economics of the Coming Spaceship Earth", 1966, in Herman E. Daly and Kenneth Neal Townsend, eds. (1993), *Valuing the Earth*, pp 297–310.

19. Harry G. Frankfurt (2005), *On Bullshit*, p 67.

20. This summary of Edward Lorenz's work is based on John Gribbin (2004), *Deep Simplicity*, pp 54–58.

21. *Ibid.*

22. For survival rate from breech births, see John C.G. Röhl (1987), *The Kaiser and His Court*, p 25. For "raising the Empress' skirts", see Röhl (1987), p 26.

23. John C.G. Röhl (1993), *Young Wilhelm: The Kaiser's Early Life 1859–1888*, pp 15–16.

24. *Ibid*, pp 17–18.

25. Röhl (1987), pp 25–26; Röhl (1993), pp 32, 52 and 69.

26. Röhl (1987), pp 16 and 21; Röhl (1993), pp 18.

27. Röhl (1987), pp 13–14.

28. *Ibid*, pp 19–20.

29. For origins of the First World War, see Niall Ferguson (2005), *1914: Why the World Went to War*; Stefan Zweig (1942), *The World of Yesterday.*

C

1. André C.R. Martins, "Continuous Opinions and Discrete Actions in Opinion Dynamics Problems", 2007, available at www.arxiv.org/abs/0711.1199 . The paper is summarised and discussed in "Extremist Views Explained by Aligning Atoms", *New Scientist*, 24 November 2007.

2. Cf. "He had all the advantages of his passionate error against my shabby truth", Arthur Koestler (1941), *Scum of the Earth*, p 120.

3. For a discussion of the relative weight of citizen vs. government initiative, see Robert D. Putnam, Lewis

M. Feldstein and Donald Cohen (2003), *Better Together*, conclusion, especially pp 271–275. The Portland case study is in chapter 12.

4. Department of Communities and Local Government (2007), *Sustainable Communities Act 2007: A Guide*, available at http://tinyurl.com/ovhwsaj . See also Transition Culture at http://transitionculture.org/ .

5. Valéry Giscard d'Estaing, interviewed on *The Today Programme*, BBC Radio 4, 29 April 2004.

6. From the Treaty establishing a Constitution for Europe (TCE), article I–3: "The Union's objectives". Full text of TCE available at http://tinyurl.com/k5yotml . The treaty was adopted by consensus by the European Convention in 2003 and signed by representatives of the then twenty-five member states of the European Union in 2004, but eventually rejected by French and Dutch voters in 2005. After a "period of reflection" it was then replaced by the Treaty of Lisbon, which entered into force in 2009.

7. For the story of Little Red Riding Hood, see, e.g., A.H. Wratislaw (1890), *Sixty Folk Tales from Exclusively Slavic Sources*, p 86.

8. The economist and systems scientist, Kenneth E. Boulding, writes that "Systems may be open or closed in respect to a number of classes of inputs and outputs. Three important classes are matter, energy and information.", Kenneth E. Boulding, "The Economics of the Coming Spaceship Earth", 1966, in Daly and Townsend, eds. (1993), p 299.

9. Unless, of course, the books were useful in some other way, such as for decoration or lighting fires.

10. But, of course, it is never true that part of the ecology is useful only to itself. Lions, notably, are essential to their local ecology.

11. "Unregarded age in corners thrown", William Shakespeare (1599), *As You Like It*, act II, scene 3.

12. Michael Common and Sigrid Stagl's (2005), *Ecological Economics: An Introduction*, has five forms of capital (pp 91–92): durable (i.e., material) capital, human capital, social capital, natural capital and intellectual capital. Forum for the Future, as per Jonathon Porritt (2005), *Capitalism as if the World Matters*, chapter 6, has manufactured (i.e., material) capital, human capital, social capital, natural capital and financial capital.

13. See, e.g., Jonathon Porritt (2005), *Capitalism as if the World Matters*, chapter 7.

14. *Ibid*, chapter 8.

15. Common and Stagl (2005), p 92.

16. See Robert D. Putnam (2000), *Bowling Alone*. See also references under *Social Capital.

17. For discussion of scientific capital, see, e.g., William P. Fisher, Jr., "Bringing Human, Social, and Natural Capital to Life: Practical Consequences and Opportunities", 2008, accepted for publication in Nathaniel J. S. Brown, Brent Duckor, Karen Draney, and Mark Wilson, eds., *Advances in Rasch Measurement*, vol II, Journal of Applied Measurement.

18. Jonathon Porritt (2005), *Capitalism as if the World Matters*, chapter 10.

19. *Ibid*, chapter 11.

20. GDP (Gross Domestic Product) is defined and discussed in *Well-Being.

21. High Beam Research, "Baker Process: Deep Cone Paste Thickeners", 2000, available at http://tinyurl.com/oa2p4ma .

22. Kenneth E. Boulding, "The Economics of the Coming Spaceship Earth", 1966, in Daly and Townsend, eds. (1993), pp 297–310.

23. The case for carbon offsetting is made on the websites of the Carbon Neutral Company at www.carbonneutral.com , and Climate Care at www.climatecare.org . A case against it is made by Larry Lohmann, ed. (2006), *Carbon Trading: A Critical Conversation on Climate Change, Privatisation and Power*, chapter 3, section "The Special Problems of Carbon Projects".

24. *Ibid*, especially pp 147–152.

25. See Fred Pearce (2006), *The Last Generation*, chapter 12. See also *Climate Change.

26. For a blistering spoof of carbon offsetting as a form of conscience-money, see the film "Cheat Neutral", at www.cheatneutral.com .

27. This is Myles Coverdale, Bishop of Exeter's para-phrase-translation of Luther's commentary on Psalm 23, "Exposition upon the Twenty-Second Psalm" (Septuagint numbering), in (1537), *Remains of Myles Coverdale*. The Latin original was subsequently (1600) published in Luther's Latin works. However much, or little, of the original was actually written by Luther, the tradition is centrally medieval.

28. William Heywood (1904), *Palio and Ponte*, pp 155–157.

29. See references in *Ritual.

30. Jules Michelet (1869), *Le Banquet*, Paris: Calmann-Evy, cited in Mona Ozouf (1976), *Festivals and the French Revolution*, p 15. Ozouf is cited also in Barbara Ehrenreich (2007), *Dancing in the Streets*, p 147. Ehrenreich's work is the decisive guideline for this entry.

31. For York, see, e.g., Clifford Davidson, "York Corpus Christi Plays", available at https://tinyurl.com/p6ul5m4 . The Dunmow custom is still well-established; see also William Harrison Ainsworth's novel (1854), *The Flitch of Bacon*. For Orkney and cider-growing areas see Martin Green (1993), *Curious Customs and Festivals*, pp 18 and 131.

32. See Mikhail Bakhtin (1930), *Rabelais and His World*, e.g., pp 1–12 and 474.

33. Ehrenreich (2007), p 44.

34. For a discussion of the property of carnival as a promoter of peace, see Ehrenreich (2007), chapter 2.

35. For a life story of Dionysus, see Andrew Dalby (2005), *The Story of Bacchus*; or Mark P.O. Morford and Robert J. Lenardon (1971), *Classical Mythology*; or (summarised) Margaret C. Howatson and Ian Chilvers, eds. (1993), *The Concise Oxford Companion to Classical Literature*. For a discussion of the significance of Dionysus see Richard Seaford (2006), *Dionysos*.

36. See Ehrenreich (2007), chapter 1. Omophagia is discussed in Richard Seaford (1994), *Reciprocity and Ritual*, chapter 8.

37. Edmund Spenser (1596), *The Faerie Queene*, book VI, canto X.

38. See Ehrenreich (2007), chapter 3.

39. 1 Corinthians, 11, 4–15. See Ehrenreich (2007), pp 66–67.

40. Luke 7, 36–50, and Luke 10, 38–42.

41. François Rabelais (c.1532–1564), *Gargantua and Pantagruel*, book 4, chapter 13.

42. Edward Palmer Thompson (1991), *Customs in Common*, p 51. For the story of the expulsion of dance from the churches to the streets, see Ehrenreich (2007), chapter 4.

43. Plutarch, "On the Obsolescence of Oracles", in (c.100 AD), *Moralia*, vol 5, pp 401–403.

44. Homer (c. 700 BC), *The Odyssey*, book 12, p 180. The significance of this passage in symbolising the separation between art and labour is pointed out by Catherine Pickstock (1997), *After Writing*, p 163.

45. Alasdair MacIntyre (1981), *After Virtue*, p 227.

46. Philip S. Gorski (2003), *The Disciplinary Revolution*, p 72. On Maurice of Orange's drill, see Ehrenreich (2007), pp 122–123; she writes that there are 32 steps, citing Geoffrey Parker (1988), *The Military Revolution: Military Innovation and the Rise of the West 1500–1800*, Cambridge University Press.

47. On depression as the consequence of the decline of carnival, see Ehrenreich (2007), chapter 7. On tactile deprivation, see, e.g., Tiffany Field (2001), *Touch*.

48. John Clare was known as the 'Green Man', or the 'Northamptonshire Peasant Poet', and penned this poem while a patient at the Northampton General Lunatic Asylum, where he remained until his death in 1864. "I Am!" is widely available online, in a few slightly differing versions. This extract consists of two of the three stanzas.

49. Robert Burton (1621), *The Anatomy of Melancholy*, part 2, pp 117–118, subsection 4.

50. Mikhail Bakhtin (1930), *Rabelais and His World*, p 269.

51. Rabelais (c.1532–1564), *Gargantua and Pantagruel*, book 3, chapter 37.

52. Goethe cited in Bakhtin (1930), p 247.

53. *Ibid*, p 248.

54. Goethe, "Selige Sehnsucht", 1814, quoted in Bakhtin (1930), p 249. The translation is reprinted courtesy of The MIT Press.

55. For up-to-the-minute inspiration about the party see, for instance, the website of Transition Tooting at www.transitiontowntooting.org .

56. Aristotle (c.350 BC), *On Sophistical Refutations*.

57. Albert Jonsen and Stephen Toulmin (1988), *The Abuse of Casuistry*, p 296.

58. Richard Henry Tawney (1926), *Religion and the Rise of Capitalism*, pp 33, 43–47, 65, 142–154 and 175–178. "Filthy lucre" (p 47) is a quotation from 1 Timothy 3:3: [A bishop must be] "not greedy of filthy lucre; but patient, not a brawler, not covetous".

59. Tawney (1926), pp 174–175.

60. Keith Thomas, "Cases of Conscience in Seventeenth Century England", in John Morrill, Paul Slack and Daniel Woolf, eds. (1993), *Public Duty and Private Conscience in Seventeenth Century England*, pp 36–48.

61. John Selden (1689), *Table Talk*, ed. Sir Frederick Pollock, pp 35–36.

62. Marvin B. Becker (1994), *The Emergence of Civil Society in the Eighteenth Century*, p 5.

63. Joseph O'Connor and Ian McDermott (1997), *The Art of Systems Thinking*; Roger Scruton (1998b), *On Hunting*.

64. Cf. Alfred Tennyson, "Ulysses", 1842, in (1829–1864), *The Works of Alfred Lord Tennyson*.

65. Ralph Waldo Emerson, "Politics", 1844, in (1946), *The Portable Emerson*, p 200.

66. Tony Gibson (1984), *Counterweight: The Neighbourhood Option*, p 97. For an essay in praise of character, see Clive Aslet, "The National Character", in David Fleming, ed. (1997), *The Countryside in 2097*, pp 151–156.

67. Max Gammon (1976), *Health and Security: Report on Public Provision for Medical Care in Great Britain*, pp 26 and 28. See also Max Gammon, "Gammon's Law of Bureaucratic Displacement", Australian Doctors Fund, January 2005, available at www.adf.com.au/archive.php?doc_id=113 .

68. This discussion of the seven qualities and, more generally, of "the power of unreasonable people", is written with two inspirational sources in mind: John Elkington and Pamela Hartigan's (2008), *The Power of Unreasonable People*, pp 6–25, and Andrew Mawson's (2008), *The Social Entrepreneur*, passim.

69. For "boat in a church hall" example, see Mawson (2008), pp 24–25.

70. Bunker Roy at the Arkleton Trust seminar, "Community Preparedness for—and Resilience in Coping With - Impacts of Climate Change and Natural Disasters", Douneside, Aberdeenshire, 4–8 November, 2007; and Elkington and Hartigan (2008), pp 34–37.

71. See Elkington and Hartigan (2008), pp 17–18 and www .grameen-info.org .

72. See Mawson (2008). "The Power of Unreasonable People" is the subject and the title of Elkington and Hartigan (2008). The Bromley by Bow Centre is also discussed in *Presence.

73. With regard to Mrs. Beeton, this is one of those quotations which are only notionally true: it does not appear in her recipe for rabbit pie, but her thorough-going back-to-basics approach would have made it look comfortable there. See Isabella Mary Beeton (1861), *Household Management*.

74. Elkington and Hartigan (2008), p 33. Bunker Roy, Rick Aubry, Cristóbal Colón and Muhammad Yunus are discussed by Elkington and Hartigan (2008); Mawson (2008).

75. Mawson (2008), pp 63–65 and 114–115. Robert K. Greenleaf's (1977), *Servant Leadership* was a more recent book pioneering the titular concept, but it is now only one among a large literature. Lao Tzu's *Tao Te Ching* is available in several modern editions. For the Gospels reference, see Mark, 10:41–45 ("minister" in the Authorised Version means "servant").

76. Mawson (2008), p 169.

77. Peter Laslett (1965), *The World We Have Lost*, p 28.

78. Max Weber (1921), *Economy and Society*, chapter 14.

79. See Robert Hogan, Robert Raskin and Dan Fazzini, "The Dark Side of Charisma", in Kenneth E. Clark and Miriam B. Clark, eds. (1990), *Measures of Leadership*, pp 343–354.

80. "Sheer naked choice", from Rt. Rev. Richard Harries, Bishop of Oxford, "Thought for the Day", *The Today Programme*, BBC Radio 4, 19 December 2003.

81. *Oxford English Dictionary* definition of climacteric: "A critical stage in human life; a point at which the person was supposed to be specially liable to change in health or fortune."

82. The literature on collapse includes Joseph A. Tainter (1988), *The Collapse of Complex Societies*; Jared Diamond (2005), *Collapse*; Richard Heinberg (2003), *The Party's Over*; and Ronald Wright (2004), *A Short History of Progress*. For the very long-term view, see Peter Ward and Donald Brownlee (2002), *The Life and Death of Planet Earth*. The difficulties—"the multi-front

predicament"—of achieving a managed downsizing of a complex connected system which depends on all its mutually dependent parts being in full working order are discussed by David Korowicz (2010), *Tipping Point*. For "one deep calleth another", cf. Psalm 42:7.

83. Bryan Ward-Perkins (2005), *The Fall of Rome and the End of Civilization*, pp 116–119 and 183.

84. John Michael Greer (2008), *The Long Descent*.

85. Adam Smith in a personal communication to Sir John Sinclair, c.1782, reported in John Sinclair (1831), *The Correspondence of the Right Honourable Sir John Sinclair* , pp 390–391.

86. Tainter (1988), p 193.

87. John Beddington "Global crisis 'to strike by 2030'", available at http://news.bbc.co.uk/1/hi/uk/7951838.stm ; Jonathon Porritt, "Avoiding the Ultimate Recession", available at http://greenbiz.com/blog/2009/03/23 /avoiding-ultimate-recession .

   Editor's note: Both John Beddington and Jonathon Porritt are no longer in these roles at the time I am writing, in 2015. Nonetheless, to preserve the authenticity of Fleming's writing, I have refrained from terming them the *then* chief scientific advisor and *then* chairman.

88. Richard Heinberg, "MuseLetter 204: Timing and the Post Carbon Manifesto", April 2009, at http://richardheinberg .com/204-timing-and-the-post-carbon-manifesto .

89. Diamond (2005), p 155.

90. On climate change as a factor in destroying previous civic societies, see Diamond (2005), pp 12–13, and many of his case studies of the collapse of civilisations, notably the Anasazi (chapter 4), the Maya (chapter 5), and Greenland (chapters 7 and 8).

91. Colin Renfrew, "Systems Collapse as Social Transformation: Catastrophe and Anastrophe in Early State Societies", 1979, in Colin Renfrew and Kenneth L Cooke, eds. (1979), *Transformations: Mathematical Approaches to Culture Change*, pp 481–506 (quotation from pp 482–485).

92. IPCC (2007), *Climate Change 2007: The Physical Science Basis. Contribution of Working Group I to the Fourth Assessment Report of the Intergovernmental Panel on Climate Change*, Frequently Asked Question 1.1, "What Factors Determine Earth's Climate?", pp 96–98, available at www.ipcc.ch/pdf/assessment-report/ar4/wg1/ar4_wg1 _full_report.pdf . The IPCC distinguishes between internal dynamics and external forcings; it does not explicitly refer to inheritance in this context.

93. The essentials of global temperature control are explained in, for instance, *ibid*, and Fred Pearce (2006), *The Last Generation*, chapter 1.

94. See IPCC (2007), Frequently Asked Question 2.1, "How Do Human Activities Contribute To Climate Change And How Do They Compare With Natural Influences?", pp 135-137.

95. See David Walker (1979), *Energy, Plants and Man*, p 17.

96. Stephan Harding (2006), *Animate Earth*; Yiqi Luo and Harold A. Mooney, eds. (1999), *Carbon Dioxide and Environmental Stress*.

97. See Richard Leakey and Roger Lewin (1995), *The Sixth Extinction*. The previous major extinction events, in chronological order, were:

   1. the Ordovician-Silurian, 440–440 million years ago, thought to be caused by global cooling and a drop in the sea level, which saw off more than half of the quite primitive marine invertebrates of the time;

   2. the Late Devonian, 360–375 million years ago, the vaguest of them—probably also caused by cooling and a steep drop in sea level, and consisting of a series of smaller extinctions;

   3. the Permian, described in the text;

   4. the Triassic, 200 million years ago—perhaps due to volcanic activity, which saw off about half the species of that time, including the large amphibians;

   5. the Cretaceous, 65 million years ago, probably caused by a meteorite strike, which brought an abrupt end to the dinosaurs.

98. For radiative forcing of methane, see IPCC (2007), chapter 2, p 212, table 2.14. See also p 33, table TS.2. And a 2009 study further suggests that estimates for the GWP of methane should be raised by one third to take into account the effect of methane in breaking down the airborne sulphate particles, which help to cool atmosphere as they reflect heat. See Mark Henderson, "Methane's Impact on Global Warming Far Higher than Previously Thought", *The Times*, 30 October 2009.

   Editor's note: When measuring mass, Fleming uses the British English term "tonne". This is equivalent to the American English term "metric ton", and means a mass of 1,000 kg or approximately 2204.6 pounds. Note that this is different from *both* the American English "ton" (aka "short ton") of 2,000 pounds, *and* the British English "ton" (aka "long ton" or "imperial ton") of 2,240 pounds. To approximately convert a mass given in tonnes to the same mass given in American English tons, multiply the figure by 1.1023. To approximately convert a mass given in tonnes to the same mass given in British English tons, multiply the figure by 0.9842.

99. See IPCC (2007), pp 33, 115–116, 513 and 544–546.

100. See IPCC (2007), pp 33, 512 and 544–546; Arjun Makhijani and Kevin Gurney (1995), *Mending the Ozone Hole*.

101. See IPCC (2007), pp 33, 115–116, 513 and 544–546.

102. Carbon emissions figure (for 2009) from Global Carbon Emissions at http://co2now.org/Current-CO2/CO2 -Now/global-carbon-emissions.html . See also IPCC (2007), pp 115–116.

103. IPCC (2007), pp 533–538. For quantities in the atmosphere during and between glaciations see Pearce (2006), pp 298–299.

104. The IPCC explains its strict definitions of terms such as "unlikely", "very likely" and "virtually certain" at www. ipcc.ch/publications_and_data/ar4/wg1/en/ch1s1-6.html (see box 1.1). "Very likely" means a likelihood of more than 90%. For more on the strengths and limitations of the IPCC reports, see Shaun Chamberlin (2009), *The Transition Timeline*, chapter 18: "Climate Change—The IPCC".

105. IPCC Fourth Assessment Report, synthesis report, table 5.1, p 67, available at http://tinyurl.com/72p9wwd . See also Myles R. Allen, David J. Frame, Chris Huntingford, et al., "Warming Caused by Cumulative Carbon Emissions Towards the Trillionth Tonne", *Nature*, 458, 30 April 2009, pp 1163–1166, in which the authors conclude that: "Total anthropogenic emissions of one trillion tonnes of carbon (3.67 trillion tonnes of CO₂), about half of which has already been emitted since industrialisation began, results in a most likely peak carbon-dioxide-induced warming of 2°C above pre-industrial temperatures, with a 5–95% confidence interval of 1.3–3.9°C". But, as argued in *Energy Prospects, anthropogenic emissions in the future could more than double.

For further clarification of the terminology of climate science—radiative forcing, CO₂ equivalent, global warming potential, parts per million, etc.—see Shaun Chamberlin (2009), *The Transition Timeline*, chapter 17: "Climate Change Explained". Also available as "The Climate Science Translation Guide" at www.darkoptimism .org/2008/09/03/the-climate-science-translation-guide/ .

106. James Hansen, "The Threat to the Planet: How Can We Avoid Dangerous Human-Made Climate Change?", remarks on acceptance of WWF Duke of Edinburgh Conservation Medal at St James Palace, 21 November 2006, available at www.columbia.edu/~jeh1/ . Quoted in David Spratt and Philip Sutton (2008), *Climate Code Red*, p 22.

107. For criticism see, for instance, Christopher Booker and Richard North (2007), *Scared to Death*, chapter 14.

108. For a summary of climate feedback dynamics see David Wasdell, "The Westminster Briefing: An Introduction to Climate Dynamics", 2007, available at http://tinyurl.com /5te8ds . In the words of the IPCC, "The response of the climate system to anthropogenic forcing [heating caused by human activity] is expected to be more complex than simple cause and effect relationships would suggest; rather, it could exhibit chaotic behavior with cascades of effects across the different scales and with the potential for abrupt and perhaps irreversible transitions." Available at www.ipcc.ch/pdf/assessment-report/ar4 /wg1/ar4-wg1-chapter7.pdf , p 566.

109. See IPCC (2007), sections 7.3.4 and 7.3.5, pp 528–538.

110. Michael J. Behrenfeld et al., "Climate-Driven Trends in Contemporary Ocean Productivity", *Nature*, 444, 2006, pp 752–755; Daniel G. Boyce, Marlon R. Lewis and Boris Worm, "Global Phytoplankton Decline Over the Past Century", *Nature*, 466, 7036, 2010, pp 591–596, available at https://tinyurl.com/no2agu8 .

111. See Pearce (2006), pp 118–121.

112. Morello, Lauren, "Higher Temperatures Lessen Plants' Ability to Store CO₂", *Scientific American*, 20 August 2010.

113. Peter M. Cox et al., "Amazonian Forest Dieback under Climate-Carbon Cycle Projections for the 21st Century", *Theoretical and Applied Climatology*, 78, 1–3, 2004, pp 137–156.

114. Spratt and Sutton (2008), pp 3–10.

115. Drew Shindell's research on the role of the stratosphere in climate change is summarised by Pearce (2006), pp 287–291.

116. IPCC Fourth Assessment Report, synthesis report, p 53, available at http://tinyurl.com/72p9wwd .

117. The starting date of the Holocene depends on whether you start counting from the end of the Younger Dryas or (to get 15,000 years) from the start of the warm period that preceded it.

118. Claudio Vita-Finzi (2008), *The Sun: A User's Manual*, pp 68–70.

119. For the story of the collapse of the Mayan civilisation, see Diamond (2005), chapter 5.

120. See Diamond (2005), chapters 7 and 8. For Stradivarius violins, see David Whitehouse, "Stradivarius' sound due to the sun", BBC News, available at http://news.bbc.co .uk/1/low/sci/tech/3323259.stm , 17 December 2003.

121. R.B. Alley et al., "Abrupt Increase in Greenland Snow Accumulation at the End of the Younger Dryas Event", *Nature*, 362, April 1993, pp 527–529. It is discussed in John D. Cox (2005), *Climate Crash*, pp 119–200.

122. For the uniqueness of high carbon dioxide concentrations in the atmosphere coexisting with icecaps at the poles, see Raymond T. Pierrehumbert, "Climate Change and the Tropical Pacific: The Sleeping Dragon Wakes", in *Proceedings of the National Academy of Sciences*, 2000, cited in Cox (2005), pp 188–189. The research on abrupt changes is discussed in some depth in Cox (2005), chapters 7 and 8.

123. Spratt and Sutton (2008), pp vi and 27. For cumulative emissions (rather than timing), see Myles R. Allen, David J. Frame, Chris Huntingford, et al., "Warming Caused by Cumulative Carbon Emissions Towards the Trillionth Tonne", *Nature*, 458, 30 April 2009, pp 1163–1166.

   Editor's note: For the latest data on atmospheric CO_2 concentrations, plainly presented, see "Trends in Atmospheric Carbon Dioxide", Earth System Research Laboratory Global Monitoring Division, available at www.esrl.noaa.gov/gmd/ccgg/trends/. In 2015, the concentration is at around 400 ppm.

124. Kevin Anderson and Alice Bows, "Reframing the Climate Change Challenge in the Light of Post-2000 Emissions Trends", *Philosophical Transactions of The Royal Society*, 2008, available at www.tyndall.ac.uk/publications /journal_papers/fulltext.pdf. It is important to be aware how controversial this is. The analysis by Allen et al. is distinctly different from that by Anderson and Bows.

125. For "around 4°C" see IPCC Fourth Assessment Report, synthesis report, table 5.1, p 67, available at http://tinyurl .com/72p9wwd. For 4°C leading on to 6°C see, for example, Mark Lynas (2007), *Six Degrees*, chapter 6.

126. Quoted in a news report in *The Independent*, 23 September 2008.

127. Dr. Sarah Raper, personal communication.

128. For a summary of the flows of energy from the tropics to the polar regions and the critical role of the rainforests in this, see Peter Bunyard (1999), *The Breakdown of Climate*, chapter 4.

129. See Vita-Finzi (2008), p 118 on solar activity.

130. Nives Dolšak and Elinor Ostrom, "The Challenges of the Commons", in Nives Dolšak and Elinor Ostrom, eds. (2003), *The Commons in the New Millennium*. The definition of subtractivity in the first sentence is a quotation from this source. It is not quite the same as a zero-sum game, where the total reward is constant; subtractivity is about changing shares of a total reward which may increase (or decline).

131. *Ibid*.

132. Carl Folke, Fikret Berkes and Johan Colding, "Ecological Practices and Social Mechanisms", in Berkes and Folke, eds., (1998), *Linking Social and Ecological Systems*, p 426.

133. From Folke, Berkes and Colding's personal communication with Edvard Hviding, 1998, in *ibid*, p 426.

134. *Ibid*, p 428.

135. Maryam Niamir-Fuller, "The Resilience of Pastoral Herding in Sahelian Africa", 1998, in *ibid*, p 270.

136. Quotation from Kenneth E. Boulding, "The Economics of the Coming Spaceship Earth", 1966, in Daly and Townsend, eds. (1993), p 298.

137. Tim Jackson (1996), *Material Concerns*, p 55. See also Michael Common and Sigrid Stagl (2005), *Ecological Economics*, pp 29–30.

138. For weak interdependence, see Yaneer Bar-Yam (2004), *Making Things Work*, pp 28–29.

139. The main source is Leon Festinger (1957), *A Theory of Cognitive Dissonance*.

140. See Karl Polanyi (1944), *The Great Transformation*. For a magisterial analysis of what social cohesion means, see Jon Elster (1989), *The Cement of Society*, and Elster's later books, including (2007), *Explaining Social Behaviour*.

141. For a discussion of capabilities see Amartya Sen, "Personal Utilities and Public Judgements: Or What's Wrong with Welfare Economics?" *Economic Journal*, 89, 1979, pp 537–558.

142. Garrett Hardin, "The Tragedy of the Commons", *Science*, 162, 1968, pp 1243–1248; Hardin (1993), *Living Within Limits*, chapter 21.

143. For a discussion of how influential it has been, see Elinor Ostrom (1990), *Governing the Commons*, chapter 1.

144. For critique of Hardin's theory, see *ibid*; Susan Jane Buck Cox, "No Tragedy on the Commons", *Environmental Ethics*, 7, 1985, pp 49-61; and Ian Angus, "The Myth of the Tragedy of the Commons", *Monthly Review*, 2008, available at http://mrzine.monthlyreview.org/angus250808 .html. See also Raymond K. DeYoung, "Tragedy of the Commons", in David E. Alexander and Rhodes W. Fairbridge, eds. (1999), *Encyclopaedia of Environmental Science*; and Edward Goldsmith, Nicholas Hildyard, Peter Bunyard, et al., "Whose Common Future?", *The Ecologist*, 22, 4, July/August 1992.

145. Richard Mabey (2005), *Nature Cure*, p 127.

146. Garrett Hardin, "Tragedy of the Unmanaged Commons", 1994, in Dustin J. Penn and Iver Mysterud, eds. (2007), *Evolutionary Perspectives on Environmental Problems*, p 106; John A. Baden and Douglas S. Noonan, eds. (1998), *Managing the Commons*, pp 3–16.

147. For conditions for effective management, see for example Elinor Ostrom (1990); Elinor Ostrom, "The Danger of Self-Evident Truths", *PS: Political Science and Politics*, March 2000; or Joanna Burger, Elinor Ostrom, Richard Norgaard, David Policansky and Bernard Goldstein, eds. (2001), *Protecting the Commons*.

148. The three main sources for the following are Elinor Ostrom (1990), *Governing the Commons*; Elinor Ostrom, "Reformulating the Commons", chapter 1 in Joanna Burger, Elinor Ostrom, Richard B. Norgaard, David Policansky and Bernard D. Goldstein, eds. (2001), *Protecting the Commons*, pp 17–41; and Joanna Burger,

Christopher Field, Richard B. Norgaard, Elinor Ostrom, and David Policansky, "Common-Pool Resources and Commons Institutions: An Overview of the Applicability of the Concept and Approach to Current Environmental Problems", introduction to Burger et al. (2001), pp 1–15.

149. *(1) It is worth the attempt.* Original (spelling standardised): "R1. Feasible improvement: Resource conditions are not at a point of deterioration such that it is useless to organize or so underutilised that little advantage results from organising." Ostrom, "Reformulating the Commons", p 22.

150. The latter is the principle of "If it ain't broke, don't fix it". Discussed in two of the chapters of Burger et al., eds. (2001), *Protecting the Commons*: Ostrom, "Reformulating the Commons", p 25, and Joanna Burger, "Multiuse Coastal Commons: Personal Watercraft, Conflicts, and Resolutions", p 211. For the former, the demoralisation aspect, see Roger Scruton (2000), *England: An Elegy*, p249.

151. *(2) Feedback.* Original: "R2 Indicators: Reliable and valid indicators of the condition of the resource system are frequently available at relatively low cost." Ostrom, "Reformulating the Commons", pp 22, 25 and 27.

152. Ostrom (1990), chapter 6, "A framework for analysis of self-organising and self-governing CPRs", provides some context for this.

153. Fikret Berkes and Carl Folke, chapter 1, p 10, in Fikret Berkes and Carl Folke, eds. (1998), *Linking Social and Ecological Systems*. For more detail, see C.S. Holling, Fikret Berkes and Carl Folke, chapter 13, "Science, Sustainability and Resource Management", in Berkes and Folke, eds. (1998).

154. Ostrom (2005), *Understanding Institutional Diversity*, p 106.

155. *(3) Flow.* Original: "R3. Predictability: The flow of resources is relatively predictable." Ostrom "Reformulating the Commons", pp 22, 25 and 27.

156. Ostrom "Reformulating the Commons", pp 25–26.

157. *(4) Manageable scale.* Original: "R4. Spatial extent: The resource is sufficiently small, given the transportation and communicating technology in use, that appropriators can develop accurate knowledge of external boundaries and internal microenvironments." Ostrom "Reformulating the Commons", pp 22 and 25.

158. Ostrom "Reformulating the Commons", p 25. See also condition 18: "Nested Enterprises".

159. *(5) Intrinsic Incentive.* Original: "A1. Salience: Appropriators are dependent on the resource system for a major portion of their livelihoods or other important activity." Burger et al. (2001), Ostrom "Reformulating the Commons", pp 22, 25, 27, 33 and 34.

160. *(6) Consensus.* Original: "A2. Common understanding. Appropriators have a shared image of how the resource system operates (attributes R1, 2, 3 and 4 above) and how their actions affect each other and the resource system." Ostrom "Reformulating the Commons", pp 22, 25 and 34.

161. Ostrom "Reformulating the Commons", p 25.

162. *(7) The long view.* Original: "A3. Low discount rate: Appropriators use a sufficiently low discount rate in relation to future benefits to be achieved from the resource." Ostrom "Reformulating the Commons", pp 22, 25, 27, 33 and 34.

163. This is the case of—as Ostrom describes it —"appropriators who . . . discount the importance of future income from a particular resource [and] may prefer to "mine" one resource without spending resources to regulate it." Ostrom "Reformulating the Commons", p 26.

164. Ostrom (1990), p 35 (uncertainty about the future); Ostrom "Reformulating the Commons", p 26 (wealthy); Ostrom (1990), p 88 (current norms); Ostrom (1990), p 206 (away from home).

165. *(8) Trust and reciprocity.* Original: "A4. Trust and reciprocity: Appropriators trust one another to keep promises and relate to one another with reciprocity." Ostrom "Reformulating the Commons", pp 22, 26 and 34. For a full development of this theme, see Elinor Ostrom and James A. Walker, eds. (2002), *Trust and Reciprocity: Interdisciplinary Lessons for Experimental Research*.

166. C. Leigh Anderson, Laura A. Locket and Rachel A. Nugent, "A framework for analysing the physical-, social- and human-capital effects of microcredit on common-pool resources," in Dolšak and Ostrom (2003), p 276 (italics added).

167. Ostrom (1990), pp 183–184.

168. *(9) Autonomy.* Original: "A5. Autonomy: Appropriators are able to determine access and harvesting rules without external authorities countermanding them." Burger et al. (2001), p 22.

169. It could also be seen as *flow. Between these two rules of lean thinking there is fertile overlap.

170. *(10) Competence.* Original: "A6. Prior organizational experience and local leadership: Appropriators have learned at least minimal skills of organization and leadership through participation in other local associations or learning about ways that neighbouring groups have organised." Burger et al. (2001), pp 22 and 26.

171. Ostrom "Reformulating the Commons", p 26.

172. That is, blessed unrest as understood by Paul Hawken (2007), *Blessed Unrest*.

173. *(11) Clearly-defined boundaries.* Original: "1. Clearly Defined Boundaries. Individuals or households with rights to

withdraw resource units from the common-pool resource, and the boundaries of the common-pool resource itself, are clearly defined." Ostrom (1990), pp 90–92, and Ostrom "Reformulating the Commons", pp 28–30.

174. Ostrom "Reformulating the Commons", p 30.

175. *(12) Rules: local and specific.* Ostrom (1990), pp 90 and 92. The rule has been slightly revised in Ostrom "Reformulating the Commons", pp 29–30: "2. Congruence. (A) The distribution of benefits from appropriation rules is roughly proportionate to the costs imposed by provision rules. (B) Appropriation rules restricting time, place, technology and quantity of resource units are related to local conditions."

176. Ostrom "Reformulating the Commons", p 30.

177. *(13) Participation.* Original: "3. Collective-choice arrangements. Most individuals affected by operational rules can participate in modifying operational rules." Ostrom (1990), p 90, and Ostrom "Reformulating the Commons", p 29.

178. Ostrom (1990), pp 93–94 and Ostrom "Reformulating the Commons", p 30.

179. *(14) Monitoring.* Original: "4. Monitoring. Monitors, who actively audit common-pool resource conditions and appropriator behaviour, are accountable to the appropriators or are the appropriators themselves." Ostrom (1990), p 90, and Ostrom "Reformulating the Commons", p 29.

180. *(15) Sanctions.* Original: "5. Graduated sanctions: Appropriators who violate operational rules are likely to receive graduated sanctions (depending on the seriousness and context of the offence) from other appropriators, from officials accountable to these appropriators, or from both." Ostrom (1990), pp 90 and 94–100, and Ostrom "Reformulating the Commons", pp 29–31.

181. Ostrom (1990), pp 94–100, and Ostrom "Reformulating the Commons", pp 29–31.

182. *(16) Conflict resolution mechanisms.* Original: "6. Conflict resolution mechanisms. Appropriators and their officials have rapid access to low-cost, local arenas to resolve conflict among appropriators or between appropriators and officials." Ostrom (1990), p 90, and Ostrom "Reformulating the Commons", pp 29–31.

183. Ostrom (1990), pp 100–101.

The problem of conflict resolution within a community resists useful summary. Recommended reading, however, includes Oliver Ramsbotham, Tom Woodhouse, and Hugh Miall (1999), *Contemporary Conflict Resolution*; Diana Leafe Christian (2003), *Creating a Life Together*, especially chapters 5 and 17; and Dudley Weeks (1994), *The Eight Essential Steps to Conflict Resolution.*

184. *(17) Rights to organise.* Original: "7. Minimal recognition of rights to organise: The rights of appropriators to devise their own institutions are not challenged by external governmental authorities." Ostrom (1990), pp 90 and 101, and Ostrom "Reformulating the Commons", pp 29–31.

185. Ostrom (1990), p 101, and chapter 5. For an application of this principle to local communities' relationships with local authorities, see Alexis Rowell (2010), *Communities, Councils and a Low Carbon Future*, Green Books.

186. *(18) Nested enterprises.* Original: "8. Nested enterprises: Appropriation, provision monitoring, enforcement, conflict resolution, and governance activities are organised in multiple layers of nested enterprises." Ostrom (1990), pp 90, 101 and 189–190, and Ostrom "Reformulating the Commons", pp 29–31 and 181–182.

187. Ostrom (1990), pp 189–190.

188. Ostrom (1990), pp 145–149.

189. Ostrom "Reformulating the Commons", p 31.

190. Ton Schouten and Patrick Moriarty (2003), *Community Water, Community Management*, p 133.

191. Ostrom (2005), p 22–26.

192. Ferdinand Tönnies (1887), *Gemeinschaft und Gesellschaft.* A convenient explanation of Tönnies' distinction (which cannot be fairly explained in a summary as short as this) can be found in Jan Falk's essay "Ferdinand Tönnies", chapter 4, in Heine Andersen and Lars Bo Kaspersen, eds. (1996), *Classical and Modern Social Theory.* "Internal" and "external" come from Falk's essay.

193. The main source for this is Rosabeth Moss Kanter (1972), *Commitment and Community*, which describes, and puts into perspective, two centuries of community history up to 1970; Kanter outlines the first three phases on pp 1–31 (especially p 8), and sets out a summary timeline on pp 246–248. Regarding the terminal date for the Shakers, in 2010 there remained three elderly members in the last community at Sabbathday Lake in Maine, but the community—which does not permit sexual relations—was condemned to extinction by the United States legislation of 1960 which forbade adoption of children by religious groups.

194. Kanter (1972), pp 6, 32–35, 61–63 and 246–248.

195. Jonathan Beecher (1986), *Charles Fourier*, pp 241–258.

196. Ralph Waldo Emerson, "English Traits", 1865, in (1946), *The Portable Emerson*, p 353.

197. "Precinct" is already well established in the vocabulary of urban living in the United States, and of architecture, e.g., "The creation of the locality with its precinctual character is a major task of architecture, but it has been completely forgotten in the speculative building and in the housing estates of the past half-century." From

Henry Morris, "Architecture, Humanism and the Local Community", lecture to the Royal Institute of British Architects, 15 May 1956, reprinted in Colin Fletcher and Neil Thompson (1980), *Issues in Community Education*.

198. For Synanon foundation, see Kanter (1972), pp 194–212. It closed in controversial circumstances nineteen years after Kanter's book was published (see, e.g., Online Archive of California, at http://tinyurl.com/punnf76). For Lama, see Kanter (1972), pp 193–194. For Bowden House, see www.bowdenhouse.co.uk .

199. Kanter (1972), pp 9–16. For a more general view of practice in communities, see Kanter (1972), pp 32–57.

200. Kanter (1972), pp 33–39 (perfectibility), pp 39–30 (control).

201. Charles Nordhoff (1875), *American Utopias*, pp 34–35.

202. Nordhoff (1875), pp 40 and 43.

203. Kanter (1972), pp 148–152.

204. Jonathan Dawson (2006), *Ecovillages*, pp 66 and 77.

205. Dawson (2006), p 35.

206. For Auroville, see www.auroville.org . For Birse community, see www.birsecommunitytrust.org.uk and visit by the author. For Ecodyfi, see Dawson (2006), pp 78–79; www.ecodyfi.org.uk/ ; news reports at the Centre for Alternative Technology website www.cat.org.uk and visits by the author. For Lammas community, see http://lammas.org.uk/ .

207. As Dawson (2006) writes, to get such results, you need "a critical mass of people", pp 99–100.

208. Diana Leafe Christian (2003), *Creating a Life Together*.

209. Global Ecovillage Network, at http://gen.ecovillage.org/ .

210. Wiser Earth, at www.wiserearth.org ; Hawken (2007).

211. Mary Douglas (1970), *Natural Symbols*. Grid-group is developed in detail in Mary Douglas, "Cultural Bias", *Royal Anthropological Institute*, Occasional Paper, 34, 1978, in Mary Douglas (1982), *In the Active Voice*, pp 183–254 (this article is the main source for the present discussion). See also Mary Douglas and Baron Isherwood (1979), *The World of Goods*, chapter 2; and Michael Thompson, Richard Ellis and Aaron Wildavsky (1990), *Cultural Theory*, chapter 1. NB. "Group and grid" is more generally known (in the textbooks) as grid-group.

212. Douglas, "Cultural Bias".

213. For Douglas' quadrant-by-quadrant analysis, or "cosmology", see Douglas, "Cultural Bias", pp 205–208.

214. Thompson et al. (1990), see strong grid/weak group in their fatalistic and powerless case of the ununionised weaver. As Douglas ("Cultural Bias", p 202) recognises, there is some room for interpretation within this matrix. For *Lean Logic*, the "social classification" which Douglas indicates here may take the form of the legally-powerless weaver, but

also that of strong legal/cultural reinforcement. Grid can therefore be a source of strength as well as of weakness.

215. *Lean Logic* parts company on this with Mary Douglas, who reserves the central area of the grid for "the hermit", see Douglas, "Cultural Bias", pp 231–248.

216. The main source for this summary is Robert Grant (1990), *Oakeshott*, chapter 6, "Agency, Association and the State". Oakeshott developed the argument in (1975), *On Human Conduct*.

217. Grant (1990), pp 79–80 and 91–92.

218. *Ibid*, pp 81–83.

219. John Stuart Mill, essay on Coleridge, 1840, quoted in Grant (1990), p 87.

220. Richard Henry Tawney (1926), *Religion and the Rise of Capitalism*, p 126.

221. Tawney (1926), p 125.

222. Colin Campbell (1987), *The Romantic Ethic and the Spirit of Modern Consumerism*, pp 166 and 263.

223. Adam B. Seligman (1997), *The Problem of Trust*, p 109. In fact, the solidarity embodied in Calvinism was not as solid as is implied in this summary: it can also be seen as a case of well-to-do burghers organising their church and state as a club to which they chose to surrender much of their liberty. See Louis Dumont, "A Modified View of our Origins: The Christian Beginnings of Modern Individualism", 1985, in Michael Carrithers, Steven Collins and Steven Lukes, eds. (1985), *The Category of the Person*.

224. Lionel Trilling (1971), *Sincerity and Authenticity*, p 69.

225. For the metaphor of the body, see St. Paul, Ephesians, 4:29. For the Great Chain of Being, see James Thomson, "The Seasons", c.1895 quoted in Arthur O. Lovejoy (1936), *The Great Chain of Being*, p 61. Lovejoy's summary description of the Great Chain of Being is on p 59. For "police-department of the church", see John Figgis (1960), *Political Thought from Gerson to Grotius 1414–1625*, Harper Torchbooks, quoted in William T. Cavanaugh, "'A Fire Strong Enough to Consume the House': The Wars of Religion and the Rise of the State", *Modern Theology*, 11, 4, October 1995, pp 397–420.

226. Colin Morris (1972), *The Discovery of the Individual 1050–1200*, chapter 4; Michael T. Clanchy (1997), *Abelard: A Medieval Life*.

227. See, for instance, George H. Sabine (1937), *A History of Political Theory*, p 129; and Emmanuel Mounier (1950), *Personalism*, pp xix–xxii.

228. Confucius, *Analects*, book 10.

229. *Bhagavad Gita*, translated by W.J. Johnson (1994), 1:71, 4:20.

230. Adam Ferguson (1782), *An Essay on the History of Civil Society*, quoted in Seligman (1997), p 110 (a benevolent

heart). David Hume (1739), *A Treatise of Human Nature*, pp 392 and 521 (a capacity for friendship). Marvin B. Becker (1994), *The Emergence of Civil Society in the Eighteenth Century*, p 16 (cooperation).

231. Kant quotation from Marvin B. Becker (1994), p 59. Alison Van Rooy provides a valuable review of interpretations of civil society in "Civil Society as an Idea: An Analytical Hatstand?", in Alison Van Rooy, ed. (1998), *Civil Society and the Aid Industry*. After warning that a definition of civil society "must address major objections before being useful", she writes, "We define civil society as both an observable reality (civil society as a collective of conflicting, interdependent, inter-influential organisations), and a good thing (that having a civil society, warts and all, is better than not).", pp 29–30. For the central meaning of civil society, see Adam Seligman (1997), *The Problem of Trust*, chapter 4.

232. Seligman (1997), pp 87 and 99–100. His discussion of common law and contract in the English tradition is based on P.S. Atiyah (1979), *The Rise and Fall of Freedom of Contract*. For torture, see Thomas Babington Macaulay (1849), *The History of England*, vol 2, p 600. For the refusal of the judicial system in England to apply torture to extraction from the Templars in 1309–1310, see Karen Ralls (2003), *The Templars and the Grail*, p 108.

233. Mary Pipher, "In Praise of Hometowns", in Juliet B. Schor and Betsy Taylor, eds. (2002), *Sustainable Planet*, pp 135–136.

234. Karen Armstrong (2006), *The Great Transformation*, pp xii and 396.

235. Examples from Armstrong (2006), p 397.

236. See Stephen Toulmin, Richard D. Rieke and Allan Janik (1984), *An Introduction to Reasoning*, pp 147–148.

237. In this context, Herman E. Daly and John B. Cobb (1989), *For the Common Good*, chapter 7, cite Aristotle's distinction between *oikonomia* (the art of good management of the place you live in), and *chrematistics* (the art of making *money from the place you live in). See Aristotle (c.350 BC), *Politics*, book 1, chapter 10, pp 45–47.

238. This discussion of complexity should not be taken as representative of its treatment in the textbooks. Complexity in *Lean Logic* is taken to be one defining end of the spectrum along which a system can be placed; the other end of the spectrum is "modularity". For a more general approach to complexity, (contrasting complexity with simplicity rather than with modularity), readers may refer to sources such as Neil Johnson (2007), *Simply Complexity*; Melanie Mitchell (2009), *Complexity: A Guided Tour*; Mitchell M. Waldrop (1992), *Complexity*; and to teaching and research sources such as the London School of Economics Complexity Research Programme and the Economic and Social Research Council (ESRC) Complexity Research Seminar Series.

John Holland's description of complexity in Waldrop (1992), pp 145–147 can be summarised as follows: Complex systems are (amongst other things) systems that respond to events actively—revealing purpose, as distinct from inertia. The many properties of complex systems include four which are especially significant: (1) they consist of many levels of organisation, with parts joining up to create subassemblies or *holons at progressively higher orders of complexity; (2) control is widely dispersed throughout all the parts of the system; (3) they act on what they have learned, and this enables them not just to evolve and innovate with the development of new "species", but also to self-regulate and maintain their stability; (4) they discover, or create, niches in their environment, and they innovate, developing specialised attributes and functions to fill them. "Species" is used here literally (for ecologies) and figuratively (for distinctive cultures, craft and *character).

John Miller and Scott Page's understanding of complexity is consistent with the present discussion, but they place complication relative to complexity in a way which is almost opposite to the one suggested in *Lean Logic*: "In a complicated world, the various elements that make up the system maintain a degree of independence from one another. . . . Complexity arises when the dependencies among the elements become important." John H. Miller and Scott E. Page (2007), *Complex Adaptive Systems*, p 9.

239. Richard G. Wilkinson and Kate Pickett (2009), *The Spirit Level* gives many examples of the inefficiencies arising from pathological levels of inequality.

240. Ecologies themselves are a special kind of complex system, or might perhaps be better said to occupy the space between the complex system and the modular system, as discussed in *Ecological Systems.

241. Kenneth Dahlberg, "A Transition from Agriculture to Regenerative Food Systems", *Futures*, 26, 1994, pp 170–179.

242. See also Mancur Olson (1982), *The Rise and Decline of Nations: Economic Growth, Stagflation and Social Rigidities*, Yale University Press, pp 69–73; Charles Perrow (1984), *Normal Accidents: Living with High-Risk Technologies*, Princeton University Press. Both quoted by Tainter (1988), p 116.

243. Joseph A. Tainter (1988), *The Collapse of Complex Societies*, p 4 (slight paraphrase).

244. For a summary of the creation of the UK National Health Service as a means of eliminating the diversity of the

former arrangements, see James Bartholomew (2004), *The Welfare State We're In*, chapter 3; and Max Gammon (1976), *Health and Security: Report on Public Provision for Medical Care in Great Britain*.

245. For seed regulations and biodiversity, see the website of GRAIN (Genetic Resources Action International) at www.grain.org ; Alvaro Toledo, "Saving the Seed: Europe's Challenge", *Seedling*, April 2002, available at https://tinyurl.com/nvjo5fk ; Renée Vellvé (1992), *Saving the Seed: Genetic Diversity and European Agriculture*; Sue Stickland (1998), *Heritage Vegetables: The Gardener's Guide to Cultivating Diversity*; and Richard Douthwaite (1996), *Short Circuit*, chapter 6.

246. Adam Smith (1776), *The Wealth of Nations*, book 5, chapter 1, article 2d, p 429.

247. Kirkpatrick Sale (1980), *Human Scale*, p 403 (quotation slightly abridged).

248. Examples of positional goods are given in Fred Hirsch (1976), *Social Limits to Growth*, and David Fleming (1988), *After Affluence: A Study of the Market for Positional Goods*.

249. An increase in the desire to save can ultimately lead to a decrease in the realised level of savings: William H. Branson (1979), *Macroeconomic Theory and Policy*, p 40. The Paradox of Thrift is discussed at length in Paul A. Samuelson (1964), *Economics*, and in David Begg, Stanley Fischer and Rüdiger Dornbusch (1984), *Economics*. It was also stated in John Maynard Keynes (1936), *The General Theory of Employment, Interest and Money*, chapter 7, p 84 and by Bernard Mandeville (1714), *The Fable of the Bees*. The insight is not new. It appears, for instance, in Proverbs, 11:24–25.

250. Napoleon is widely quoted as saying this, though it may be an urban myth. Napoleon was pointing to the possibility of rapid promotion in his army, so we can see why he might have used that phrase, but that does not make it true.

251. William J. Baumol, "The Macroeconomics of Unbalanced Growth: The Anatomy of Urban Crisis", *American Economic Review*, 57, 1967, pp 415–426.

252. This Fallacy of *Composition is defined in Samuelson (1964), chapter 1. And see also van Eemeren and Grootendorst (1992), pp 213. Samuelson cites the Paradox of Thrift as an illustration of the Fallacy (chapter 12).

253. See Friedrich A. Hayek (1952), *The Sensory Order*.

254. Lawrence M. Lidsky and Marvin M. Miller, "Nuclear power and Energy Security: A Revised Strategy for Japan", *Science and Global Security*, 10, 2, 2002, pp 127–150.

255. Andrew Mawson (2008), *The Social Entrepreneur*, pp 52 and 104.

256. Robin Dunbar (1996), *Grooming, Gossip and the Evolution of Language*, pp 77–79.

257. Ford Madox Ford (1924), *Some Do Not . . .* , T. Seltzer, available at http://gutenberg.net.au/ebooks07/0700171h.html .

258. For further reading, see Stephen Miller (2006), *Conversation*. Also Michael Oakeshott, "The Voice of Poetry in the Conversation of Mankind", 1959, in Michael Oakeshott (1962), *Rationalism in Politics and Other Essays*.

259. Horace (23 BC), *Odes*, I, xxii.

260. Michael Wood (1986), *The Domesday Quest*, pp 82–83.

261. See Frank Stenton (1943), *Anglo-Saxon England*, pp 295–297.

262. Wood (1986), pp 83–85 and 92–93.

263. Geoffrey H. Martin, introduction to (2003), *Domesday Book*. The quotation "Much thought . . ." can be found in the *Anglo-Saxon Chronicle*, cited in Wood (1986), p 18.

264. This quotation is from Kirkpatrick Sale (1985), *Dwellers in the Land*, p 145. It is unclear whether he is paraphrasing Odum and Katherine Jacker (1945), *In Search of the Regional Balance of America*, Odum and Harry Estill Moore (1966), *American Regionalism*, or Odum (1936), *Southern Regions of the United States*.

265. Herman Finer (1933), *English Local Government*, p 56.

266. For Jay Heinrichs' closely-related treatment of "decorum" (but as a persuasive technique—get your audience to like you), see his (2007), *Thank You for Arguing*, chapter 5.

267. Izaak Walton (1653), *The Compleat Angler*.

268. See Peter M. Senge et al. (2004), *Presence*.

269. See Nadia Johanisova (2005), *Living in the Cracks*, which is recommended reading, as are Muhammad Yunus and Alan Jolis (1998), *Banker to the Poor: The Story of the Grameen Bank*; and Richard Douthwaite (1996), *Short Circuit*.

270. Roger Scruton, *Any Questions?*, BBC Radio 4, 4 August 2006.

271. Wendell Berry (1977), *The Unsettling of America*, pp 43–44.

272. There is ambiguity as to whether it is only the market economy that has the power to override community in this way. Perhaps a large and highly authoritarian society can do so. Paul Gottfried argues that Classical Rome progressed some way in this direction but stalled before it became a modern political movement because it lacked mass production, mass consumption and the mass market which is the foundation for individual autonomy and separateness: the sense that individuals can, and should, speak only for themselves. Paul Edward Gottfried (1999), *After Liberalism: Mass Democracy in the Managerial State*, pp 32–35. For brevity, *Lean Logic* discusses only the market economy in this context, but the question is not trivial, for some other models, such as a very powerful totalitarian society (see *Unlean), might be able to go some way, for a time, in maintaining society without community.

273. T.S. Eliot, "Ash Wednesday", 1930, in (1932), *Selected Essays*. See Roger Scruton, "Eliot and Conservatism", 2000, in Roger Scruton (2006a), *A Political Philosophy*.

274. David Hume, "Of the Independency of Parliament", 1741 in (1740–1776), *Essays, Moral, Political and Literary*, pp 42–46; quotation from p 42.

275. Adam Smith (1776), *The Wealth of Nations*, chapter 2, p 22.

276. Theodore Dalrymple (2005), *Our Culture, What's Left of It*, pp 114–115.

277. Mary Bousted, quoted in Alexandra Frean, "Tests twice a year put mental health of pupils at risk, teachers warn", *The Times*, 21 March 2008.

278. Paul Edward Gottfried (1999), *After Liberalism*, p 136 (cites Panajotis Kondylis).

279. Gottfried (1999), pp 32–35. The value of a conversation with Lucy Neal on this topic (13 October 2010) is acknowledged with thanks.

D

1. See Anthony Flew (1998), *How to Think Straight*.

2. See Lewis Mumford (1961), *The City in History*, especially pp 600 and 636.

3. For a discussion of debt as a driver of growth, see, for instance, Richard Douthwaite (1992), *The Growth Illusion*, pp 18–21; Richard Douthwaite (1999), *The Ecology of Money*, p 31.

4. For a discussion of debt as an instrument of dependence, see David C. Korten (1995), *When Corporations Rule the World*, chapter 9; Michael Rowbotham (1998), *The Grip of Death*.

5. For an extended discussion of debt, see Rowbotham (1998).

6. For a discussion of mellifluous talk, use of personal pronouns, expert information and call centres, see Deborah Cameron (2000), *Good to Talk*, chapters 1, 4 and 5. In the quotation "Always be bubbly . . .", Cameron is referring to the call-centre industry as a whole.

7. Thomas Hardy, *In Time of 'The Breaking of Nations'*, August 1915 (extract), in (1868–1928), *The Collected Poems of Thomas Hardy*.

8. Thomas Hardy, *At Castle Boterel*, March 1913 (extract), in (1868–1928), *The Collected Poems of Thomas Hardy*.

9. Michael Oakeshott uses "submission" in this sense: "[For the *Rationalist] there is, of course, no question either of retaining or improving [a *tradition of ideas], for both these involve an attitude of submission. It must be destroyed." From "Rationalism in Politics", 1947, in (1962), *Rationalism in Politics and Other Essays*, p 8.

10. Charles Dickens (1854), *Hard Times*, chapter 2.

11. Right to left definitions are explained in Karl Popper (1945), *The Open Society and Its Enemies*, pp 9–21.

12. For further reading, see Simone Weil (1943), *The Need for Roots*.

13. *Editor's note*: Fleming's notes indicate that the *Democracy entry is one that he had not finished revising at the time of his death.

14. As Richard Heinberg states, "If we were to add together the power of all the fuel-fed machines that we rely on to light and heat our homes, transport us, and otherwise keep us in the style to which we have become accustomed, and to compare that total with the amount of power that can be generated by the human body, we would find that each of us Americans has the equivalent of over 50 'energy slaves' working for us 24 hours each day." (2003), *The Party's Over*, pp 30–31.

15. For a discussion on mass support for totalitarian regimes, see Bernard Crick (1962), *In Defence of Politics*, p 25, where he also quotes Hannah Arendt making this point in her *Origins of Totalitarianism*.

16. Roger Scruton writing about Edmund Burke in Scruton (2006a), *A Political Philosophy*, p 207.

17. W.M. Flinders Petrie (1911), *The Revolutions of Civilisation*, p 124.

18. Burke's letters to the Sheriffs of Bristol, 3 April 1777, in Burke (1774–1780), *The Writings and Speeches of Edmund Burke*, pp 228–330.

19. Crick (1962), p 282.

20. See Roger Scruton (2006a), pp 150–160.

21. See Peter Oborne (2007), *The Triumph of the Political Class*.

22. Helena Norberg-Hodge (1991), *Ancient Futures* (Ladakh); Hugh Brody (1973), *Inishkillane* (the west coast of Ireland).

23. Chip Ward, "Is the Crown of Creation a Dunce Cap?", 2008, in David R. Keller, ed. (2010), *Environmental Ethics*, pp 143–146 (quotation from p 144). See also Roger Scruton (2000), *England: An Elegy*, pp 249.

24. For a discussion of the welfare state as a factor in this, see Theodore Dalrymple (2005), *Our Culture, What's Left of It*, chapter 1, "The Frivolity of Evil". For a challenge to the idea that the welfare state has a demoralising effect, see Nicolai Gentchev, "The Myth of Welfare Dependency", 1995, available at http://tinyurl.com/qj9k7a6 .

25. Sir Simon Milton, *The Today Programme*, BBC Radio 4, 28 March 2008.

26. *News Chronicle* report, cited in Colin Ward (1973), *Anarchy in Action*, p 72.

27. Livy (c.32 BC), *History of Rome*, vol 6, book 23:44.

28. On agnatology, see Robert Proctor (1996), *Cancer Wars*. See also Naomi Oreskes and Erik M. Conway (2010), *Merchants of Doubt: How a Handful of Scientists Obscured*

the Truth on Issues from Tobacco Smoke to Global Warming, Bloomsbury Press.

29. Heinberg (2006), *The Oil Depletion Protocol*, p 76.

30. *Ibid*, p 33.

31. Wyclif Bible, 1382, Pref. Ep. Jerome 68 (cited in the *Oxford English Dictionary* entry on "dialectic").

32. For a short and painless summary of these meanings see the entry "Dialectic" in Ted Honderich, ed. (1995), *The Oxford Companion to Philosophy*, Oxford University Press.

33. These forms of dialogue are discussed by Douglas N. Walton (1995), *A Pragmatic Theory of Fallacy*, chapter 4.

34. For an account of Socrates at work, see Alain de Botton (2000), *The Consolations of Philosophy*, pp 14–42.

35. John Bunyan (1678–84), *The Pilgrim's Progress*.

36. This extract is the ending of Yeats' forty line poem, in W.B. Yeats (1939), *Last Poems and Two Plays*.

   Reprinted with the permission of Scribner, a Division of Simon & Schuster, Inc., from *The Collected Works of W.B. Yeats, Volume I: The Poems, Revised* by W. B. Yeats, edited by Richard J. Finneran. Copyright © 1940 by Georgie Yeats, renewed 1968 by Bertha Georgie Yeats, Michael Butler Yeats, and Anne Yeats. All rights reserved.

37. John Bunyan (1678–84), *The Pilgrim's Progress*.

38. Milton quoted in Jessica Martin, "Marrying and Burying—The Book of Common Prayer and Translation", *Faith and Worship*, 53, Michaelmas 2003, pp 4–16.

39. Alasdair MacIntyre (1981), *After Virtue*, chapter 15.

40. Catherine Pickstock, "The Confession", *Theology*, 99.793, 1997, pp 25–35; Pickstock, "An Inquiry into Liturgical Syntax", *Faith and Worship*, 43, 1997, pp 14–21.

41. This prayer is from the service for the Publick Baptism of Infants, *The Book of Common Prayer* (italicised text to be adapted for sex and age of child).

42. For a narrative of the differing personalities in a primate group see Frans de Waal (1982), *Chimpanzee Politics*.

43. This story comes from the historian Dio Cassius, and is summarised in Mary Beard, "Ha ha", *Times Literary Supplement*, 20 February 2009.

44. Differences in timing and function within a resilient community are discussed by Yaneer Bar-Yam (2004), *Making Things Work*, p 108. See also Edward Goldsmith (1992), *The Way*, chapter 53, p 333.

45. Lance H. Gunderson and C.S. Holling, eds. (2002), *Panarchy: Understanding Transformations in Human and Natural Systems*, pp 30 and 206. Summarised in Brian Walker and David Salt (2006), *Resilience Thinking*, pp 79–80.

46. See Hugh Brody (2000), The Other Side of Eden, p 119; also Fikret Berkes, "Indigenous Knowledge and Resource Management Systems in the Canadian Subarctic", in

Fikret Berkes and Carl Folke, eds. (1998), *Linking Social and Ecological Systems*, pp 98–128 (pp 109–111).

47. See David Attenborough's programme on the desert toad, *Life In Cold Blood / Land Invaders / Desert Amphibians*, repeat broadcast 27 August 2008, BBC Four.

48. Offwell Woodland and Wildlife Trust, "Coastal Sand Dunes: An Example of Primary Succession", available at www.offwell.free-online.co.uk/successn/primary2.htm . See also the Trust's "Hydrosere—A Wetland Example of Succession in Action", at www.countrysideinfo.co.uk /successn/hydro.htm.

49. For a discussion of complementary diversity in an ecosystem, see Stephan Harding (2006), *Animate Earth*, pp 211–216.

50. John Stuart Mill (1859), *On Liberty*, chapter 3, pp 130–131 (quotation abridged).

51. Mill (1859), chapter 3. Kirkpatrick Sale (1985), *Dwellers in the Land*, pp 107–108 (quotation abridged). The localities to which Sale is referring in this passage are "bioregions".

52. Joan Thirsk (1997), *Alternative Agriculture*, p 218.

53. *Ibid*, p 213.

54. David Hackett Fischer (1970), *Historians' Fallacies*, pp 221–222; Madsen Pirie (2006), *How to Win Every Argument*, pp 53–55.

55. For an example of such wages and working conditions see Andrew Wasley and Jim Wickens, "Fishy Business", *The Ecologist*, December/January 2009, pp 24–29.

56. Letter to Schumacher's wife and discussion in Kelvin W. Willoughby (1990), *Technology Choice*, p 62. For meta-economics, see Willoughby (1990), p 93.

57. For a grounded discussion of this, see Norberg-Hodge (1991), pp 143–145.

58. Vandana Shiva, "How Wealth Creates Poverty", *Resurgence*, 240, Jan/Feb 2007.

E

1. For a discussion of cooking practices, see Richard Wrangham (2009), *Catching Fire* (but note Steve Jones' 17 October 2009 review in *The Guardian*, which warns that Wrangham does not adequately place cooking in context with the other conditions that led to the evolution of *Homo sapiens*).

   Alexander Marshack (1972), *The Roots of Civilisation*; Marshack, "Lunar Notations on Upper Paleolithic Remains", *Science*, 817, 1964, pp 28–46 (astronomy). Marshack is also the source for Marvin Harris (1977), *Cannibals and Kings*, p 16; and Paul Feyerabend: "the astronomy became part of a philosophical world view of considerable sophistication", *Knowledge Science and*

Relativism: Philosophical Papers Volume 3, 1999, p 206; Clive L.N. Ruggles (2005), *Ancient Astronomy*. For cave paintings as art, see Richard Mabey (2005), *Nature Cure*, pp 87–90. Note that this evaluation of Stone Age people is not free of controversy. Peter Ward, for instance, does not agree, in his (2009), *The Medea Hypothesis*.

2. Hugh Brody (2000), *The Other Side of Eden*, p 118.

3. Geoffrey Sampson (2005), *The 'Language Instinct' Debate*, pp 16–17 and passim. Steven Pinker (2002), *The Blank Slate: The Modern Denial of Human Nature*.

4. Harris (1977), p 101.

5. For the decline of megafauna after the end of the last ice age, and what followed, see Harris (1977), chapter 3. The following account, with its interpretations of Genesis, is based on Hugh Brody's groundbreaking work in Brody (2000), chapter 2. For an account of the domestication of plants and animals and the evolution of agriculture, see Jared Diamond (1991), *The Rise and Fall of the Third Chimpanzee*, chapter 10.

6. Genesis 3:14–19 (curses).

7. Genesis 4:17 (Enoch); Genesis 4:25 (Seth).

8. Hugh Brody (2000), *The Other Side of Eden*.

9. For "clean" and "unclean" animals, see Genesis 7:2 and 8.

10. Genesis 9:20–21 (Cain working out how to make wine).

11. Daniel C. Dennett (1995), *Darwin's Dangerous Idea*, pp 48–60 (quotation from p 59).

12. *Ibid*, p 51.

13. Thomas Aquinas (1264), *On the Truth of the Catholic Faith*, book 3, part 2, chapter 112, paragraph 12; Original: "Ex divina enim providentia naturali ordine in usum hominis ordinantur".

14. Psalm 8:6 (*Book of Common Prayer* version), cited in Aquinas (1264), book 3, part 2, chapter 112, paragraph 11.

15. Aquinas (1264), book 3, part 2, chapter 112, paragraph 5.

16. Aldo Leopold (1949), *A Sand County Almanac*, pp 224–225 and 204.

17. Donald Worster (1993), *The Wealth of Nature*, pp 158–159.

18. Eugene P. Odum, "The Strategy of Ecosystem Development", *Science*, 164, 1969, p 166, cited in Worster (1993), p 160. For Odum's own statement of ecosystem in this sense, see Eugene P. Odum and Howard T. Odum (1953), *Fundamentals of Ecology*, chapter 2.

19. Edward Goldsmith (1992), *The Way*, p 33.

20. See, for example, the case on morphic resonance, in Rupert Sheldrake (1988), *The Presence of the Past*.

21. Barry Commoner (1971), *The Closing Circle*, p 45. The adaptive cycle arguably has the quality that Dennett calls "substrate neutrality", which also speaks in favour of its likely robustness.

22. The two definitions are based, respectively, on Michel Loreau, "Communities and Ecosystems", in Simon A. Levin, ed. (2009), *The Princeton Guide to Ecology*, pp 253–355 (p 253); and on David R. Keller, "Introduction", in Keller, ed. (2010), *Environmental Ethics: The Big Questions*, p 1.

23. The main source for this summary is Levin, ed. (2009).

24. *(1) Evolution and adaptation*. See Jonathan B. Losos, "Autoecology", introduction to part 1 of Simon A. Levin, ed. (2009), The Princeton Guide to Ecology, pp 1–2, and the papers in this part.

25. *(2) Population ecology*. See H. Charles J. Godfray, "Population Ecology", introduction to part 2 of Levin, ed. (2009), pp 153–154, and the papers in this part.

26. *(3) Communities and ecosystems*. See Michel Loreau, "Communities and Ecosystems", introduction to part 3 of Levin, ed. (2009), pp 253–255, and the papers in this part.

27. *(4) Landscapes and the biosphere*. See Brian Walker, "Landscape and the Biosphere", introduction to part 4 of Levin, ed. (2009), pp 423–424, and the papers in this part.

28. *(5) Conservation biology*. See David S. Wilcove, "Conservation Biology", introduction to part 5 of Levin, ed. (2009), pp 511–513, and the papers in this part.

29. *(6) Ecosystem services*. See Ann P. Kinzig, "Ecosystem Services", introduction to part 6 of Levin, ed. (2009), pp 573–578, and the papers in this part.

30. *(7) Managing the biosphere*. See Stephen R. Carpenter, "Managing the Biosphere", introduction to part 2 of Levin, ed. (2009), pp 153–154, and the papers in this part.

31. The main source for this summary is Keller, ed. (2010).

32. *(8) Values: Nature in the service of Man*. See David R. Keller, "What is Anthropocentrism?", introduction to part 2 of Keller, ed. (2010), pp 59–62, and readings 1–8.
"Axial (pivotal) Age" term coined by the philosopher Karl Jaspers (1883–1969).

33. John Locke (1689), *Two Treatises of Government*, chapter 5, "On Property", reprinted in Keller, ed. (2010) as reading 6, "Nature as an Economic Resource", pp 77–81 (quotation from p 77).

34. Keller, introduction to part 2 of Keller, ed. (2010), p 59. Immanuel Kant, "Duties Towards Animals and Spirits", c.1784, reprinted in Keller, ed. (2010), as reading 7. Probable date based on Georg Ludwig Collins' notes on the lectures which he attended at the University of Königsberg in that year (in Immanuel Kant, *Lectures on Ethics*, Peter Lauchlan Heath and Jerome B. Schneewind, eds. (2001), Cambridge University Press).

35. *(9) Values: Nature in its own right*. See Keller, "What is Nonanthropocentrism?", introduction to part 3 of Keller, ed. (2010), pp 91–92, and readings 9–17.

36. Chip Ward, "Is the Crown of Creation a Dunce Cap?", 2008, in Keller, ed. (2010), pp 143–146 (quotation from p 146).

37. *(10) Moral judgment: where does it apply?*. See Keller, "What Is the Scope of Considerability?", introduction to part 4 of Keller, ed. (2010), pp 149–153, and readings 18–26.

38. Keller, ed. (2010), introduction to part 3, p 152.

39. Aldo Leopold, foreword to (1949), *A Sand County Almanac*, p viii.

40. See the discussion of this in J. Baird Callicott (1989), *In Defense of the Land Ethic*, reprinted in Keller, ed. (2010), pp 201–211. For the "humming community" quotation, see Aldo Leopold (1953), *Round River*, p 148, quoted on p 205 of Keller's book.

41. Aldo Leopold, "The Land Ethic", in (1949), *A Sand County Almanac*, pp 224–225.

42. Keller refers here to reading 26, Warwick Fox, "Developing a General Ethics", in Keller, ed. (2010), introduction to part 4, pp 213–220.

43. *(11) Frames of reference for thinking about environmental ethics*. See David R. Keller, "What Are the Prominent Alternatives to Grounding Environmental Ethics in Axiology?", introduction to part 5, in David Keller, ed. (2010), pp 223–229, and readings 27–84.

44. Devall and Sessions (1985), p 67.

45. The full text of *Deep Ecology's Basic Principles* by Arne Næss and George Sessions is in Bill Devall and George Sessions (1985), *Deep Ecology*, p 70. The principles are discussed in Arne Næss, "The Deep Ecology Movement: Some Philosophical Aspects", *Philosophical Enquiry*, 8, 1986, revised and reprinted in Andrew Light and Holmes Rolston III, eds. (2002), *Environmental Ethics*, pp 262–274; in Keller, ed. (2010), pp 240–245; and in Arne Næss (2008), *The Shallow and the Deep Ecology Movement*, reprinted in Keller, ed. (2010), pp 230–234. See also Arne Næss (1989), *Ecology, Community and Lifestyle*. For Næss' self-imposed exile on the mountain and the idea of "withdrawal and return", the classic text is Arnold Toynbee (1933), *A Study of History*, pp 217–240.

46. Keller, introduction to part 5 of Keller, ed. (2010), p 223; and Warwick Fox, "Transpersonal Ecology", reading 30, reprinted in Keller, ed. (2010), pp 213–220.

47. Freya Mathews, "Deep Ecology", in Dale Jamieson, ed. (2001), *A Companion to Environmental Philosophy*, pp 218–232. See also Warwick Fox, "Deep Ecology: A New Philosophy of our Time", *The Ecologist*, 14, 1984, reproduced in Light and Rolston, eds. (2002), pp 252–261; and Clare Palmer, "An Overview of Environmental Ethics", in Light and Rolston, eds. (2002), pp 29–31. For a review, see "Deep Ecology", part 2, in Michael Zimmerman et al.,

eds. (2001), *Environmental Philosophy: From Animal Rights to Radical Ecology*. Valuable context on the difference between the basic principle of Deep Ecology and the influential deep-green theory that has developed from it is supplied by Richard Sylvan and David Bennett (1994), *The Greening Ethics*.

48. Stephan Harding (2006), *Animate Earth*, p 244. See chapter 10 for a sympathetic discussion of deep ecology.

49. John Muir, "The Yosemite", 1912, in (1838–1914), *Journeys in the Wilderness: A John Muir Reader*, pp 450–451 (quotation abridged).

50. Henry David Thoreau (1854a), *Walden*, p 83.

51. See, for example, Howard-Yana Shapiro and John Harrisson (2000), *Gardening for the Future of the Earth*; Charles Dowding (2007), *Organic Gardening: The Natural No-Dig Way*; Carol Klein (2007), *Grow Your Own Veg*; Duncan Clark (2009), *The Rough Guide to Green Living*. See also Gilbert Harman, "Love Isn't All You Need" (a review of *On Virtue Ethics* by Rosalind Hursthouse), *Times Literary Supplement*, 26 January 2001, p 26.

52. David R. Keller, introduction to part 5 of Keller, ed. (2010); and Steven Vogel, "On Environmental Philosophy and Continental Thought", 1998, reprinted in Keller, ed. (2010), pp 257–267.

53. For Bookchin's argument, see Keller, introduction to part 5 of Keller, ed. (2010); and Murray Bookchin, "What is Social Ecology?", 1993, in Keller, ed. (2010), reading 33; and Murray Bookchin (1980), *Toward an Ecological Society*. Derrick Jensen (2006), *Endgame*, vol 1, pp 216–218; Vogel, "On Environmental Philosophy and Continental Thought", 1998, reprinted in Keller, ed. (2010), pp 257–267.

54. Keller, introduction to part 5 of Keller, ed. (2010). Papers developing this theme by Murray Bookchin, Carol Merchant and others are reprinted as readings 33–37. See also Clare Palmer, "An Overview of Environmental Ethics", in Light and Rolston, eds. (2002), pp 29–31, and readings 21 and 22 therein.

55. Keller, introduction to part 5 of Keller, ed. (2010). Papers developing this theme by Anthony Weston and Andrew Light are reprinted as readings 38–39.

56. Keller, introduction to part 5 of Keller, ed. (2010) and readings; the debate between Foreman/Abbey and their critics is reprinted in readings 40–44.

57. David Holmgren (2002), *Permaculture: Principles and Pathways Beyond Sustainability*, p xix.

58. *(12) The environment in the mind*. See David R. Keller, "What are the Connections between Realism, Relativism, Technology and Environmental Ethics?", introduction to part 6, in Keller, ed. (2010), pp 339–341, and readings 45–49.

59. *(13) The science and the ethics*. See Keller, "What Are the Connections between Ecological Science and Environmental Ethics?", introduction to part 7 of Keller, ed. (2010), pp 379–380, and readings 50–54.

   Keller, ed. (2010), p 379. Paul Sears, "Ecology—A Subversive Subject", *Bioscience*, vol 14, 17, 1964, pp 11–13, reprinted as reading 50 in Keller, ed. (2010). Donald Worster (1993), *The Wealth of Nature*, p 158.

60. Mark Sagoff, "Environmental Ethics and Ecological Science", in Keller, ed. (2010), pp 392–400. Jared Diamond, "The Ends of the World as We Know Them", *New York Times*, 1 January 2005, p 13, reprinted as reading 54 in Keller, ed. (2010).

61. *(14) The environment and public policy*. See David R. Keller, "What Are some of the Ethical Dimensions of Environmental Public Policy?", introduction to part 8 of Keller, ed. (2010), pp 415–421, and readings 55–71.

62. Holmes Rolston III, "Feeding People versus Saving Nature?", in William Aiken and Hugh LaFollette, eds. (1996), *World Hunger and Morality*, Prentice Hall, reproduced in Light and Rolston, eds. (2002), pp 451–462. See the other articles in part 7 of this anthology for a range of interpretations of this question and related dilemmas.

63. For a discussion of these two aspects of economics, see Thomas C. Schelling (1984), *Choice and Consequence*, especially pp vii–xi. Among economics texts on choices and consequences, and their outcomes in social behaviour see, for instance, Gary S. Becker (1976), *The Economic Approach to Human Behaviour* and sequels by the same author; Steven D. Levitt and Stephen J. Dunbar (2005), *Freakonomics*; Stephen E. Landsburg (1993), *The Armchair Economist*; John Kay (2004), *Everlasting Light Bulbs*; and Tim Harford's two books which show the starting point that behaviour can be understood in terms of radical choices: (2007), *The Undercover Economist* and (2008), *The Logic of Life*.

64. For a guide through the history of economic ideas, see Roger Backhouse (2002), *The Penguin History of Economics*.

65. For the critique developed by TOES in 1984 and its sequel in 1985, see Paul Ekins, ed. (1986), *The Living Economy*. The New Economics Foundation was founded in 1986. Recommended sources for constructive criticism of neoclassical economics include Herman E. Daly and John B. Cobb (1989), *For the Common Good*; Mark Lutz and Kenneth Lux (1988), *Humanistic Economics*; and—less a critique of economics than an analysis of what society really is—Jon Elster (1989), *The Cement of Society*. Elster's many books are a vital source on this.

   Editor's note: Fleming humbly fails to mention that he played a key role in the creation of the influential "The Other Economic Summit".

66. For the case for the Institute for New Economic Thinking and its task, see Anatole Kaletsky, "Three Cheers for the Death of Old Economics", *The Times*, 28 October 2009. The summary of the Institute for New Economic Thinking's purpose is on its website at www.ineteconomics.org/.

67. *Lean Logic*'s aim is to work out how to achieve stability without growth. Kenneth E. Boulding probably didn't say (as reputed), "Anyone who thinks that growth can go on forever in a finite world is either a madman or an economist", but he did write, in 1970, " . . . the growth of any particular growing structure must come to an end. The economic growth which has been characteristic of the last two hundred years is no exception to this rule." Boulding, "Economics and The Future of Man", 1970, in *Economics as Science*, chapter 7, p 143.

68. Irving Fischer, "The Debt-Deflation Theory of Great Depressions", *Econometrica*, 1, 4, October 1933, pp 337–357; quotation from p 346.

69. For Glass-Steagall see, for instance, www.investopedia.com/articles/03/071603.asp .

70. For a summary of the requirement under presidents Carter and Clinton that the banks should take on subprime mortgages, see, for instance, William Rees-Mogg, "Good Intentions Took Us on the Road to Hell", *The Times*, 17 November 2008. For supplementary discussion focused on the 1977 Community Reinvestment Act, see http://tinyurl.com/d9fezaa .

71. See, for instance, David C. Korten (1995), *When Corporations Rule the World*.

72. Cf. Horace: *Parturient montes, nascetur ridiculus mus*: The mountains will labour, and will bring forth a laughable mouse. Horace, *Ars Poetica*, 139.

73. Michael Common and Sigrid Stagl (2005), *Ecological Economics*, pp 325–332.

74. For a review of the impact of trading schemes, see Larry Lohmann, ed. (2006), *Carbon Trading*.

75. Albert O. Hirschman, "Against Parsimony: Three Easy Ways of Complicating Some Categories of Economic Discourse", *Economics and Philosophy*, vol 1, 1, 1985, pp 7–22.

76. For an extended discussion of Whitehead's concept of misplaced concreteness, applied to economics and a sustainable future, see Herman E. Daly and John B. Cobb (1989), *For the Common Good*, part 1.

77. See, e.g., "Special Report: More of Everything", *The Economist*, 14 September 2006 or Lynette Khoo, "Oil

crosses US$90 mark; may hit growth next year", *The Business Times*, 20 October 2007.

78. Harold Hotelling, "The Economics of Exhaustible Resources", *Journal of Political Economy*, vol 39, 1931, pp 137–175.

79. David W. Pearce and R. Kerry Turner (1989), *Economics of Natural Resources and the Environment*, p 275.

80. The maths does not take into account, for example, impacts of major significance to local people which take a long time to verify, and even longer to act on. Local evidence of people made sick by eating deformed fish in the polluted Athabasca River, which receives waste from tar sands mining, sits more comfortably in the space of *encounter and lived experience than of discount rates. See Liezel Hill, "Canada Names Panel to Study Oil Sands Water Concerns", *Mining Weekly*, 30 September 2010.

81. Fred Hirsch (1976), *Social Limits to Growth*; Fleming (1988), *After Affluence: A Study of the Market for Positional Goods*; Michael Schneider, "The Nature, History and Significance of the Concept of Positional Goods", *History of Economics Review*, 45, 2007, pp 60–81; Peter Saunders (2010), *Social Mobility Myths*.

82. E. F. Schumacher (1973), *Small is Beautiful*, p 139; Schumacher, "Paths to Economic Growth", pp 26–28, paper presented to the International Seminar "Paths to Economic Growth", 21–28 January 1961, Poona, India, published in Schumacher (1962), *Roots of Economic Growth*, Gandhian Institute of Studies, and quoted in Kelvin W. Willoughby (1990), *Technology Choice*, pp 84–87; and Helena Norberg-Hodge (1991), *Ancient Futures*. Schumacher also called it "unhealthy development" in his brilliant essay, "Healthy Development" in (1997), *This I Believe, and Other Essays*.

83. Colin Ward (1997), *Reflected in Water*, p 73.

84. Gresham's Law: bad money (e.g., coins containing cheaper metal than the precious metals that they are specified to contain) drives out good money (which is stockpiled or otherwise removed from circulation). See, for instance, www.britannica.com/topic/Greshams-law .

85. E.F. Schumacher, "Economics in a Buddhist Country", 1955 paper written for the Government of the Union of Burma, Rangoon, published in Schumacher (1962), *Roots of Economic Growth*, Gandhian Institute of Studies, p 3, cited in Kelvin W. Willoughby (1990), *Technology Choice*, pp 63–64.

86. For a full discussion of economism, see Larry Siedentop (2000), *Democracy in Europe*. Also John Laughland (1997), *The Tainted Source*, pp 163–167.

87. Patrick Whitefield (2004), *The Earth Care Manual*, pp 24–26. See also David Holmgren (2002), *Permaculture: Principles and Pathways Beyond Sustainability*, pp 226–228.

88. Mitchell M. Waldrop (1992), *Complexity*, pp 292–294; Steven Strogatz (2003), *Sync: The Emerging Science of Spontaneous Order*.

89. Alex Trisoglio, "Managing Complexity", paper presented at the LSE Strategy Seminar, 25 January 1997, p 31.

90. A nudge can be defined as "Any aspect of the choke architecture that alters people's behaviour in a predictable way without forbidding any options or significantly changing their economic incentives". Richard H. Thaler and Cass R. Sunstein (2008), *Nudge*.

91. Richard Dawkins (1986), *The Blind Watchmaker*, chapter 3.

92. Thomas Homer-Dixon (2006), *The Upside of Down*, pp 26–27.

93. See Dennis Sherwood (2002), *Seeing the Forest for the Trees*, pp 14–16. For further reading see Dawkins (1986); John Holland (1998), *Emergence*.

94. Pirie (2006), p 55.

95. For an extended discussion of the crucial importance of emotions in thought and behaviour, see Daniel Goleman (1994), *Emotional Intelligence: Why It Can Matter More Than IQ*.

96. Alasdair MacIntyre (1981), *After Virtue*, especially pp 14–16.

97. Roger Scruton, "Conserving Nations", in (2006a), *A Political Philosophy*. Chapter 1 makes the case for nations, and only by implication the case against empires.

98. Daniel Pink (2009), *Drive*, pp 89–90.

99. "Republic" is used in this sense by Roger Scruton (2006b), *England and the Need for Nations*. He writes: "Where citizens are appointed to administer the state, the result is 'republican' government", and adds (in a footnote): "I adopt this definition in order to identify an ideal that has been defended in various forms by Aristotle, Machiavelli, Montesquieu, Kant and the American Founding Fathers. Republic government is not to be contrasted with monarchy (our own government is both) but with absolute rule, dictatorship, one-party rule and a host of other possibilities that fall short of participatory administration.", p 6.

100. Rod Eddington cited in Ben Webster, "New Rail Lines, Roads and Runways Urged to Beat Gridlock", *The Times*, 6 June 2005. Owing to the extensive infrastructure required, any such scheme would be unlikely to come into operation until well after the *climacteric has made congestion a nostalgic memory.

101. Henry David Thoreau, journal entry for 4 October 1859, quoted in Donald Worster (1977), *Nature's Economy*, pp 91–92. See also Thoreau (1837–1861), *Journals*.

102. See Stephan Harding (2006), *Animate Earth*, chapter 1.

103. Energy descent 'steps' image created by author.

104. Rob Hopkins (2008), *The Transition Handbook*, especially pp 52–53, and 122–130; Howard and Elizabeth Odum (2001),

A Prosperous Way Down; Ted Trainer (2007), *Renewable Energy Cannot Sustain a Consumer Society*. For the David Holmgren source cited in Hopkins (2008), chapter 2, note 23, see David Holmgren, "What is Sustainability?", 9 September 2003, available at http://tinyurl.com/ndyesms .

105. For a description of the Kinsale EDAP and how it came about, see Hopkins (2008), pp 122–130. The Kinsale EDAP itself—*Kinsale 2021: An Energy Descent Action Plan*—is available at http://transitionculture.org/wp-content /uploads/KinsaleEnergyDescentActionPlan.pdf .

106. For a discussion of open-space, see Hopkins (2008), pp 123, 162 and 168–9.

107. The Totnes EDAP lives at http://totnes.transitionnetwork .org/edap/ .

108. "Building a Positive Future for Bristol After Peak Oil", Bristol City Council, pp 3–4, available at http://tinyurl .com/qg6epzo .

109. City of Oakland, "Oil Independent Oakland Action Plan", available at http://tinyurl.com/p5xgg9q , p 18.

110. For backcasting, see Shaun Chamberlin (2009), *The Transition Timeline*, p 100. This forms part of chapter 14, "Timelines and Energy Descent Action Plans", which offers an extensive practical guide to EDAPs.

111. Hubbert Linearisation plots the total "cumulative" production of a resource against the declining output year-by-year, producing an approximately straight line which, when projected into the future, gives an indication of when the resource will be exhausted, and how much it will by then have produced. See Kenneth S. Deffeyes (2006), *Beyond Oil: The View from Hubbert's Peak*. Note that linearisation was not Hubbert's first method: for a summary of Hubbert's contribution see David Strahan (2007), *The Last Oil Shock*. Or to witness Hubbert's prescience first-hand, watch the remarkable 1976 video clip, "Health Facilities and the Energy Crisis: A Conversation with M. King Hubbert", available at https://vimeo.com/19340602 .

Campbell's first book to signal the oil peak was Colin J. Campbell (1991), *The Golden Century of Oil*. His most influential article was Colin J. Campbell and Jean Laherrère, "The End of Cheap Oil", *Scientific American*, March 1998, and his most influential book was Colin J. Campbell (1997), *The Coming Oil Crisis*, which contains a bibliography of the most important publications before that date.

See also L.F. Ivanhoe, "Updated Hubbert curves analyze world oil supply", *World Oil*, November 1996, pp 91–94; David Fleming, "The next oil shock?", *Prospect*, April 1999 and "After Oil", *Prospect*, November 2000; Kenneth S. Deffeyes (2001), *Hubbert's Peak: The Impending World Oil Shortage*; Jean Laherrère, "Estimates of Oil Reserves", IXIAS-International Energy Workshop, Ladenburg, 19 June 2001, available at http://tinyurl.com/2zhjdt ; Roger W. Bentley, "Global gas and oil depletion: an overview", *Energy Policy*, 30, 2002, pp 189–205; David Fleming, "The wages of denial", *The Ecologist*, April 2003; and Steve Sorrell, Jamie Speirs, Adam Brandt, Richard Miller and Roger W. Bentley, "Global Oil Depletion: An Assessment of the Evidence for a Near-Term Peak in Global Oil Production", UK Energy Research Centre, 2009, available at www.ukerc.ac.uk/asset/865EFEEF %2D4727%2D4146%2D87D03A239D0A1DC4/ .

For a summary of reputable estimates of the oil peak from the 1970s, see Steve Sorrell, Richard Miller, Roger W. Bentley and Jamie Speirs, "Oil Futures: A Comparison of Global Supply Forecasts", *Energy Policy*, 38, 9, 2010, pp 4990–5003.

112. Shaun Chamberlin (2009), *The Transition Timeline*, pp 93–94.

113. Transition Town Totnes' Energy Descent Action Plan, scripted and edited by Jacqi Hodgson and Rob Hopkins (2010), *Transition in Action: Totnes and District 2030*. For reference to the car park, see p 183.

And for a summary of the practical manifestations that have already emerged from this young process, see "So What Does Transition Town Totnes Actually Do?", *Transition Culture*, 2010, available at https://tinyurl.com/2vjta35 .

114. Colin J. Campbell (1991), *The Golden Century of Oil 1950–2050*; F.K. North (1985), *Petroleum Geology*; Norman J. Hyne (1995), *Nontechnical Guide to Petroleum Geology, Exploration, Drilling and Production*; Fredrick Robelius, "Giant Oilfields: The Highway to Oil", 2007, PhD thesis, available at http://tinyurl.com/oe8t2u6 .

115. For concise summaries of the world outlook see, for instance, UK Industry Taskforce on Peak Oil and Energy Security, "The Oil Crunch: A Wake-Up Call for the UK Economy", February 2010; David Strahan (2007), *The Last Oil Shock*, and updates in Rembrandt Koppelaar's "Oilwatch Monthly" at *The Oil Drum: Europe*: http:// europe.theoildrum.com/ .

Editor's note: David Fleming's former colleague Roger W. Bentley offers the following clarification: The reference to "discovering one barrel of oil for every five consumed" refers to the discovery in new fields of "regular conventional oil", as defined by Colin J. Campbell. This definition excludes the discovery of deepwater oil, Arctic oil or very heavy oils. However, with regard to the first two categories, the quantity of oil available for discovery is relatively small (see, e.g., International Energy Agency, "Resources to Reserves 2013", 2013, available at

www.iea.org/publications/freepublications/publication
/Resources2013.pdf). And the location of most very heavy
oils, and of the non-conventional oils, is already known.

116. The distinction between conventional and unconventional oil set out here is consistent with that in Steve
Sorrell et al., "Global Oil Depletion: An Assessment
of the Evidence for a Near-Term Peak in Global Oil
Production", UK Energy Research Centre, 2009, p vi.

117. Rembrandt Koppelaar, "Oilwatch Monthly" at *The Oil
Drum: Europe*: http://europe.theoildrum.com/ .

118. Colin J. Campbell (1991), *The Golden Century of Oil
1950–2050*; F.K. North (1985), *Petroleum Geology*; Norman
J. Hyne (1995), *Nontechnical Guide to Petroleum Geology,
Exploration, Drilling and Production*; Fredrick Robelius,
"Giant Oilfields: The Highway to Oil", 2007, PhD thesis,
available at http://tinyurl.com/oe8t2u6 .

119. *Ibid.*

120. *Ibid.* See also Dave Cohen, "An Oil & Gas Shangri-La in the
Arctic?", ASPO USA, 10 October 2007, available at www
.resilience.org/stories/2007-10-10/oil-gas-shangri-la-arctic .

121. Colin J. Campbell and Jean Laherrère, "The End of
Cheap Oil", *Scientific American*, March 1998; Deffeyes
(2001), pp 106–108; Norman J. Hyne (1995), *Nontechnical
Guide to Petroleum Geology, Exploration, Drilling and Production*, pp 444–449. For a detailed survey of enhanced oil
recovery see Don W. Green and G. Paul Willhite (1998),
Enhanced Oil Recovery.

122. See, e.g., International Energy Agency, "Natural Gas
Liquids Supply Outlook", April 2010, available at www
.iea.org/publications/freepublications/publication
/ngl2010_free.pdf .

123. For the use of nuclear power to provide energy to extract
heavy oils, see Jeff Rubin, Chief Economist, CBC World
Markets, "Market Outlook", 2007, ASPO 6 Conference,
Cork, DVD available at www.aspo-ireland.org/index
.cfm/page/home . For a summary of unconventional
oil prospects in the context of the overall decline in oil
production, see Ray Leonard, "World Oil Reserves and
Future Production", 2008, summarised by Steve Andrews
in *Energy Bulletin*, available at www.energybulletin
.net/node/45679 .

124. For Orimulsion, see, e.g., "Orimulsion and Power Stations",
POSTnote 84, Parliamentary Office of Science and
Technology, October 1996, available at http://tinyurl.com
/ogqal3d . For a summary of unconventional oil prospects
in the context of the overall decline in oil production, see
Ray Leonard, "World Oil Reserves and Future Produc-
tion", 2008, summarised by Steve Andrews in *Energy
Bulletin*, available at www.energybulletin.net/node/45679 .

125. For an introduction to shale oil, see Walter Youngquist,
"Shale Oil—The Elusive Energy", Colorado School of
Mines, 1998. For comments on the potential scale of
production, see, e.g., Chris Nelder, "Peak Oil Media
Guide", *The Oil Drum*, 13 July 2008; or Rich Turcotte,
"Still Dealing with Peak Oil Denying Nonsense", *Peak Oil
Matters*, 22 November 2010. See also Randy Udall at the
Aspen Environment Forum, March 2008, video available at
http://tinyurl.com/6d2d3s . From the 6 minute mark Udall
comments—with tongue firmly in cheek—that: "Shell
has spent $200m to produce 1,700 barrels of shale oil in
the last decade. At that rate of production the shale oil that
we have here in Colorado will last six million years. This
is something that gives me great optimism for the future."
(cited in Shaun Chamberlin (2009), *The Transition Timeline*).

Editor's note: David Fleming's former colleague Roger
W. Bentley offers the following comment: Fleming was
writing before the rapid expansion in the United States
of production of 'light-tight' oil, which is relatively
light flowable oil, but trapped in very low permeability
shale or similar rock, from which it cannot be extracted
unless the rock is fractured. The latter is usually done
hydraulically ('fracking'), and using proppants to keep
the fractures open against the pressure of the overburden.
Production of this 'light-tight' oil has indeed been a
'game-changer' in the United States. But as the International Energy Agency's "Resources to Reserves 2013"
(available at www.iea.org /publications/freepublications
/publication/Resources2013 .pdf) shows, compared to
the perhaps originally 2,000 to 3,000 billion barrels of
global recoverable conventional oil, and the about 1,000
billion barrels of potentially recoverable shale oil (i.e., oil
from kerogen in rock), the global endowment of recoverable 'light-tight' oil is perhaps 250 billion barrels (i.e.,
only about 8 years' worth of global oil consumption),
and there have been significant difficulties in extracting
much of this oil outside the United States, in part due to
the geology of this oil in non-US regions.

126. Steve Sorrell et al., "Global Oil Depletion: An Assessment of the Evidence for a Near-Term Peak in Global Oil
Production", UK Energy Research Centre, 2009, pp 162.

127. Steve Sorrell, Richard Miller, Roger W. Bentley and
Jamie Speirs, "Oil Futures: A Comparison of Global Supply Forecasts", *Energy Policy*, 38, 9, 2010, pp 4990–5003.

128. Chris Skrebowski, "Opinion A", in UK Industry Taskforce on Peak Oil and Energy Security, "The Oil Crunch:
A Wake-Up Call for the UK Economy", February 2010,
chapter 3, pp 22–23.

129. Robert Falkner, "Opinion B", chapter 4 in *ibid*, pp 27–28.

130. The exposure of food distribution to shocks in the form of (amongst other things) fuel shortages is examined in Helen Peck, "Resilience in the Food Chain: A Study of Business Continuity Management in the Food and Drink Industry", report to the UK Department for Environment, Food and Rural Affairs July 2006, which concludes, "The fundamental problem is that it is the very efficiency of the nation's food and drink supply chains, under normal circumstances, that make (*sic*) them so vulnerable under abnormal ones", p xvii, available at http://tinyurl.com /37a8w39 . Lessons from the fuel transport drivers' strike in the UK in 2000 are drawn in Glenn Lyons and Kiron Chatterjee, eds. (2001), *Transport Lessons from the Fuel Tax Protests of 2000*; see also Lyons and Chatterjee, "Coping with a Crisis", Association for European Transport, 2001, available at www.abstracts.aetransport.org/paper /download/id/1299 ; and Public Safety and Emergency Preparedness Canada, Incident Analysis: *Impact of September 2000 Fuel Price Protests on UK Critical Infrastructure*, 25 January 2005, available at http://tinyurl.com/35hwy77 .

131. Colin J. Campbell and Jean Laherrère, "The End of Cheap Oil", *Scientific American*, March 1998. See also Campbell (1991), North (1985), Hyne (1995).

132. For a summary of gas prospects for the UK, see Shaun Chamberlin (2009), *The Transition Timeline*, pp 160–161.

133. Estimates from Helen Knight, "Wonderfuel: Welcome to the Age of Unconventional Gas", *New Scientist*, 12 June 2010, pp 45–47.

134. United States "swimming in natural gas", from "US Gas Fields Go from Bust to Boom", *Wall Street Journal*, 30 April 2009, quoted in Dave Cohen, "Natural Gas Boom Gets Put on Hold", *Energy Bulletin*, April 2010, available at http://dev .energybulletin.net/node/52499 . For a discussion of natural gas as clean and plentiful, see Helen Knight, "Wonderfuel: Welcome to the Age of Unconventional Gas", *New Scientist*, 12 June 2010, pp 45–47. For claims of gas displacing coal, see, e.g., Mike Graham of EnCana, quoted in ASPO-USA Commentary, 21 September 2009, available at www.energy bulletin.net/print/50174 . For positive views of the future of shale gas see, for instance, Danny Fortson, "The Scramble for Shale Gas", *The Sunday Times*, 6 June 2010; and Gideon Rachman, "Shale Gas will Change the World", *Financial Times*, 24 May 2010. For shale gas as possibly 'saving the world', see former Colorado Senator Tim Wirth, quoted in ASPO-USA Commentary, 21 September 2009.

135. For Dimock, Pennsylvania, see Josh Fox, *Gasland* (video), 2010, available at www.pbs.org/now/shows/613/index .html . For the exploding house in Ohio, see Ohio Department of Natural Resources, Division of Mineral Resources Management, "Report on the Investigation of the Natural Gas Invasion of Aquifers in Bainbridge Township of Geauga County, Ohio", 2008, available at http://tinyurl .com/pojv4j7 . For drinking water in Colorado, see Geoffrey Thyne, "Review of Phase II Hydrogeologic Study", 2008, prepared for Garfield County, available at http://tinyurl.com/pfuxr3t . For a review of the problem as a whole, see Abrahm Lustgarten, "Officials in Three States Pin Water Woes on Gas Drilling", April 26 2009, available at www.propublica.org/article/officials-in -three-states-pin-water-woes-on-gas-drilling-426 .

136. In 2010 the United States Environmental Protection Agency (EPA) announced a study of the environmental impact of fracking and a review of the exemption from identifying the chemicals involved: Tom Doggett (2010), "EPA Begins Study on Shale Gas Drilling", 2010, available at http://tinyurl.com/p5ou9nd . For the suggestion that methane could be the precursor of more chemical contamination to come, see Judith Jordan (representing Garfield County, Colorado), cited in Lustgarten, "Officials in Three States Pin Water Woes on Gas Drilling", April 26 2009. Concern has also been expressed about the implications of fracturing the geological foundations of large areas, especially those already unstable or prone to earthquakes, but no firm conclusions have yet been drawn. See, e.g., Courtney Spradlin, "Geologists deny fracking's influence in area earthquakes", 12 November 2010, available at http://tinyurl.com/ovyos4y .

137. See Dave Cohen, "A Miracle in the Marcellus Shale?", 19 April 2010, available at www.declineoftheempire.com /2010/04/a-miracle-in-the-marcellus-shale.html . The mothballing of terminals, Cohen writes, is due at least as much to the decline in the demand for gas as to the new supply from shale gas. Dave Cohen, "Shale Gas Shenanigans", 29 March 2010, available at http://dev .energybulletin.net/node/52235 .

138. For first year production as a poor indicator of long-term resource, see Cohen, "Shale Gas Shenanigans", where he also discusses the incentive when talking to the bank.

139. For a sceptical view, see Cohen, "Shale Gas Shenanigans"; and Cohen, "A Miracle in the Marcellus Shale?". For an advocate's view see Gwen Robinson , "Forget Oil, Shale Gas just Gets Sexier", *Financial Times*, June 16 2010, available at http://tinyurl.com/pwms9tg .

140. US Geological Survey, "Coal-Bed Methane: Potential and Concerns", Fact Sheet FS-123-00, October 2000, available at http://tinyurl.com/a6st2e4 .

141. Public Lands Foundation, "Coalbed Methane: A Major New Energy Source and an Environmental Concern",

Position Statement 21–02, 2002, available at
http://tinyurl.com/oz3em79 . US Environmental Protection Agency, "Evaluation of Impacts to Underground
Sources of Drinking Water by Hydraulic Fracturing of
Coalbed Methane Reservoirs", June 2004, see chapter 6,
"Water Quality Incidents", available at http://tinyurl.com
/phhsyds . For a helpful summary, see "Coal-Bed
Methane", from the Energy Justice Network, available at
www.energyjustice.net/naturalgas/cbm .

142. Or almost all. Note that methane from non-organic
sources ('abiogenic methane') is discussed, though this
is not a significant energy source. See, e.g., Juske Horita
and Michael E. Berndt, "Abiogenic Methane Formation
and Isotopic Fractionation Under Hydrothermal
Conditions", *Science*, 285, 5430, 1999, pp 1055–1057.

143. See, e.g., Fabien Monnet, "An Introduction to Anaerobic
Digestion of Organic Wastes", Remade Scotland,
November 2003.

144. For analysis of methane's role in abrupt global warming,
see US Climate Change Science Programme, "Abrupt Climate Change: Will It Happen This Century?", Geological
Survey, 16 December 2008, available at http://tinyurl
.com/op3hlsb .

145. National Academy of Sciences, "Realizing the Potential
of Methane Hydrate for the United States", 2010, p 6.

146. Press release from Xinhua News Agency, "China to
develop new energy source—combustible ice", 14 March
2010, available at www.energybulletin.net/51947 .

147. Alexei V. Milkov, "Global Estimates of Hydrate-Bound
Gas in Marine Sediments: How Much is Really Out
There?", *Earth-Science Reviews*, 66, 3–4, 2004 pp 183–197.
    Editor's note: When measuring mass, Fleming uses the Brit-
ish English term "tonne". This is equivalent to the American
English term "metric ton", and means a mass of 1,000 kg or
approximately 2204.6 pounds. Note that this is different from
both the American English "ton" (aka "short ton") of 2,000
pounds, *and* the British English "ton" (aka "long ton" or
"imperial ton") of 2,240 pounds. To approximately convert
a mass given in tonnes to the same mass given in American
English tons, multiply the figure by 1.1023. To approximately
convert a mass given in tonnes to the same mass given in
British English tons, multiply the figure by 0.9842.

148. The estimate that energy from gas is half as CO_2 intensive
as coal comes from the Energy Information Agency, "Voluntary Reporting of Greenhouse Gases Program", available
at www.eia.doe.gov/oiaf/1605/coefficients.html . Converted
into g/kWh by Chris Vernon, "Natural Gas, The Green
Choice?", 2010, available at http://europe.theoildrum.com
/node/6638#more . The coal in this case is anthracite.

149. Over 20 years, the global warming potential of methane
is 72 times that of carbon dioxide, as given in IPCC (2007),
chapter 2, p 212, table 2.14, available at http://tinyurl.com
/2n27cn . And a 2009 study further suggests that estimates
for the GWP of methane should be raised by one third
to take into account the effect of methane in breaking
down the airborne sulphate particles, which help to cool
atmosphere as they reflect heat. See Mark Henderson,
"Methane's Impact on Global Warming Far Higher than
Previously Thought", *The Times*, 30 October 2009.

150. Vernon, "Natural Gas, the Green Choice?".

151. This calculation is based on a BP executive's report stat-
ing that before the explosion gas was being removed at a
rate of 3,000 cubic feet of gas for every barrel of oil. There
are 5.64 cubic feet of gas per barrel at normal temperature and pressure. The equivalent barrel/barrel rate is
therefore approximately 532 barrels of gas per barrel of
oil. That methane would not escape into the atmosphere,
but as methane breaks down in water it removes the
dissolved oxygen, and it has substantially removed the
oxygen in the Gulf of Mexico. See, 'innereye', "Gas Leak
3,000 Times Worse than Oil", *Daily Kos*, 16 May 2010,
available at http://tinyurl.com/q4ct2f9 .

152. Peter James (1982), *The Future of Coal*, chapter 1; William
Ashworth (1986), *The History of the British Coal Industry,
vol 5, 1946–1982: The Nationalized Industry*, pp 64–73.

153. John Hatcher (1993), *The History of British Coal: Vol 1,
Before 1700: Towards the Age of Coal*, chapters 1–3.

154. Thomas S. Ashton and Joseph Sykes (1929), *The Coal Industry
of the Eighteenth Century*, especially chapter 3 and p 174.

155. For an account of the Heaton disaster, and links to
further information, see Durham Mining Museum at
www.dmm.org.uk/names/n1815-03.htm .

156. Ashton and Sykes (1929), chapter 3.

157. For accident rates, see World Coal Institute, *Sustainable
Entrepreneurship: The Way Forward for the Coal Industry*,
2001, p 22. For the number of coal-related industries, see
Ashworth (1986), chapter 3.

158. These are rounded estimates. With regard to coal
(including lignite), see Energy Watch Group, *Coal:
Resources and Future Production*, 2007, p 10, available at
http://tinyurl.com/q7eavva . For other fuels, see Jean-Paul
Rodrigue, "The Geography of Transport Systems",
available at http://tinyurl.com/q3gbpks .

159. US Energy Information Administration, *International
Energy Outlook 2009*, chapter 1.

160. See, for instance, John T. McMullan, "The Role of Coal in
Achieving Sustainability", 2002, in Richard Douthwaite,
ed. (2003), *Before the Wells Run Dry*.

161. Energy Watch Group, *Coal: Resources and Future Production*, 2007, pp 23–24, available at http://tinyurl.com/q7eavva .

162. *Ibid*, pp 13–20 and 30–39.

163. *Ibid*, pp 13–20 and 40–45.

164. *Ibid*, pp 13–20 and 27–29.

165. *Ibid*, pp 7–8.

166. Uppsala report: "A supply-driven forecast for future global coal production", 2008, available at http://tinyurl.com/p2w5v2g ; Institute for Energy report: "The Future of Coal", 2007, quotation from p 5, available at http://tinyurl.com/o4hjboe . Richard Heinberg's "MuseLetter 196: Coal and Climate", August 2008, notes a fifth report, by the German Federal Institute for Geosciences and Natural Resources (BGR), which sees no resource problem for coal until 2100. He points out, however, that the report assumes a decline in the demand for coal, and (in contrast with all other studies) a very sharp rise in the conversion of the "resource" (the estimated quantity of coal in the ground) into "reserves" (the quantity that can reasonably be expected to be mined). The basis on which these optimistic assumptions are made is not explained. Available at http://richardheinberg.com/196-coal-and-climate . See also Richard Heinberg, "MuseLetter 195: Coal in China", June 2008, available at http://old.globalpublicmedia.com/museletter_coal_in_china . Another study consistent with the Energy Watch Group's findings is S.H. Mohr and G. H. Evans, "Forecasting Coal Production until 2100", 2009, available at www.theoildrum.com/node/5256 .

167. William Siemens' (later Sir William Siemens) 1868 description of UCG was published in the *Transactions of the Chemical Society*, 21, 279. The final composition of town gas is 56% nitrogen, 25% carbon monoxide, 12% hydrogen and 7% carbon dioxide. See The Oil Drum website at www.theoildrum.com . See also Richard Heinberg (2007), *Peak Everything: Waking Up to the Century of Declines*, pp 129–132.

168. For the Queensland, Australia project, see www.lincenergy.com .

169. For conversion energy efficiency, see, e.g., "Coal-To-Liquids: An Alternative Oil Supply?", IEA Coal Industry Advisory Board, 2006, available at https://tinyurl.com/oymt8zb .

170. Mikael Höök and Kjell Aleklett, "A review on coal to liquid fuels and its coal consumption", International Journal of Energy Research, 34, 10, August 2010, pp 848–864. See also Richard Heinberg (2009), Blackout, pp 132–135.

171. Höök and Aleklett, "A review on coal to liquid fuels and its coal consumption", pp 3–6.

172. *Ibid*, p 19. For the car-efficiency comparison, see Heinberg (2009), p 134.

173. Paul Roberts (2005), *The End of Oil*, p 180.

174. For Centralia fires, see Joan Quigley (2007), *The Day the Earth Caved In*. For peat fires, see Fred Pearce (2006), The Last Generation, chapter 12.

175. The estimates of capital savings and productivity improvements are rough guidelines only. They are derived from 'Heading Out', "Tech Talk: Burning Coal in Place, or Underground Coal Gasification", 31 January 2010, available at www.theoildrum.com/node/6164 .

176. The estimates of global coal production/reserves are derived from the Energy Information Administration, "International Energy Outlook 2009", chapter 4, table 9. Those figures are for 2006, so the production estimate has been adjusted upwards in line with the global output rise indicated in chapter 1, figure 14. Short tons have been converted to tonnes. Cf. Energy Watch Group, *Coal: Resources and Future Production*, 2007, pp 21–26, available at http://tinyurl.com/q7eavva .

World Energy Council estimate: "Early studies suggest that the use of UCG could potentially increase world reserves of coal by as much as 600 billion tonnes", from World Energy Council, "Survey of Energy Resources", 2007, p 7. Dermot J. Roddy and Paul L. Younger, "Underground Coal Gasification with CCS: A Pathway to Decarbonising Industry", *Energy and Environmental Science*, 3, 2010, pp 400–407. See also International Energy Agency, "World Energy Outlook 2010".

177. The "18 degrees" estimate is based on the conversion factor proposed by H. Damon Matthews and cited in Hatice Cullingford, "'Matthews Measure' Proposed New Yardstick for Climate Change", *Science 2.0*, 10 September 2009: "In summary, independent of the timing of emissions or the atmospheric concentration of carbon dioxide, each tonne in carbon emissions means—as a best estimate—0.0000000000015 degrees of global temperature increase." For a survey of the caveats that should be taken into account, see H. Damon Matthews, Nathan P. Gillett, Peter A. Stott and Kirsten Zickfeld, "The Proportionality of Global Warming to Cumulative Carbon Emissions", letter in Nature, 459, 11 June 2009, pp 829–832.

178. For fuel energy density, see, e.g., Heinberg (2009); and "Fuel Energy Density", IOR Energy, available at https://tinyurl.com/ob8tn2g . For conversion energy efficiency of around 60%, see, e.g., Carmine L. Iandoli and Signe Kjelstrup, "Exergy Analysis of a GTL Process Based on Low-Temperature Slurry F-T Reactor Technology with a Cobalt Catalyst", Norwegian University of Science and

Technology, 2007, available at https://tinyurl.com/q4x7lxn . See also Tom Standing, "Natural Gas Vehicles—How Much Can They Reduce Oil Imports?", 2009, available at www.chrismartenson.com/print/14308 .

179. Chris Skrebowski (2010), "Opinion A", chapter 3, in UK Industry Taskforce on Peak Oil and Energy Security, "The Oil Crunch: A Wake-Up Call for the UK Economy", February 2010, pp 24–25.

180. This is a matter of emphasis, rather than being all that needs to be said on climate change and peak oil. The peak oil argument has never claimed that the natural reduction in the supply of oil and gas will be sufficient to reduce carbon emissions at the rate required by the climate. Still less has it argued that limits to coal reserves will do so. It has, however, been able to make a reasonable case about the need to be prepared for the decline in oil supplies starting in 2015–2024 and continuing downwards thereafter.

181. See, for instance, Viren Doshi, Hege Nordahl, and Adrian del Maestro, "Big Oil's Big Shift", *Strategy + Business*, 2010, available at www.strategy-business.com /article/00042?gko=62983 .

182. For a detailed but accessible account of Carbon Capture and Storage, see Open University Course Team (2007), *Energy for a Sustainable Future*.

183. For a valuable summary of forms of capture, linked to more detailed descriptions, see "Carbon Capture", Imperial College London, available at www3.imperial .ac.uk/carboncaptureandstorage/carboncapture .

184. Estimate published by the PBL Netherlands Environmental Assessment Agency, "No growth in total global CO_2 emissions in 2009", 2010, available at www.pbl.nl /en/publications/2010/No-growth-in-total-global-CO2 -emissions-in-2009 .

185. Comments following post by Rembrandt Koppelaar , "Carbon Capture and Storage: Energy Costs Revisited", *The Oil Drum*, 23 April 2010 (slightly edited).

186. See Heinberg (2009), *Blackout*, pp 141–142; Vaclav Smil (2010), *Energy Myths and Realities*.

187. IPCC report: Bert Metz, Ogunlade Davidson, Heleen de Coninck, Manuela Loos and Leo Meyer, eds., "Special Report on Carbon Dioxide Capture and Storage", 2005, prepared by working group 3 of the Intergovernmental Panel on Climate Change, available at http://tinyurl.com /oohr85o , p 12 and section 5.3.7: "Geographical distribution and storage capacity estimates", pp 220–224.

188. Bert Metz et al., eds., "Special Report on Carbon Dioxide Capture and Storage", 2005, p 6, paragraph 9.

For an introduction to the Economides critique, see Terry Macalister, "U.S. Research Paper Questions

Viability of Carbon Capture and Storage", *The Guardian*, 25 April 2010, and Robert Hokin, "Not Feasible at Any Price? Study Questions Carbon Storage", 27 April 2010, available at www.greenbang.com/not-feasible-at-any -price-study-questions-carbon-storage_14264.html . For the Economides argument in detail, see Michael J. Economides and Christine A. Ehlig-Economides, "Sequestering Carbon Dioxide in a Closed Underground Volume", *Journal of Petroleum Science and Engineering*, 70, 2009, pp 123–130. For a rebuttal, see A. J. Cavanagh, R. S. Haszeldine and M. J. Blunt, "Open or Closed: A Discussion of the Mistaken Assumptions in the Economides Analysis of Carbon Sequestration", Journal of Petroleum Science and Engineering, 74, 1–2, 2010, pp 107–110.

189. Bert Metz et al., eds., "Special Report on Carbon Dioxide Capture and Storage", 2005, p 14, paragraph 25 (geological storage); p 14, paragraph 26 (ocean storage).

190. Bert Metz et al., eds., "Special Report on Carbon Dioxide Capture and Storage", 2005, p 10. Heinberg's estimate of 78% is based on the United States Government Accountability Office, *Key Challenges Remain for Developing and Deploying Advanced Energy Technologies to Meet Future Needs*, Department of Energy report to Congressional requesters, 2006, available at www.gao.gov/new.items/d07106.pdf .

191. Massachusetts Institute of Technology, "The Future of Coal: Options for a Carbon-Constrained World", summary report, 2007, available at http://web.mit.edu/coal/The _Future_of_Coal_Summary_Report.pdf ; and International Energy Agency, "CO_2 Capture and Storage: A Key Carbon Abatement Option", 2008, available at www.iea.org /publications/freepublications/publication/CCS_2008.pdf .

192. Fred Pearce, "Greenwash: Why 'Clean Coal' is the Ultimate Climate Change Oxymoron", *The Guardian*, 26 February 2009.

193. For large-scale offshore wind, see The Offshore Valuation Project, at http://publicinterest.org.uk/offshore/ . For desert solar, see www.desertec.org .

194. Some suggested reading: Godfrey Boyle, ed. (2004), *Renewable Energy: Power for a Sustainable Future*; David J.C. MacKay (2008), *Sustainable Energy—Without the Hot Air*.

195. For a critique of biofuels on the grounds of their poor rate of Energy Return On Energy Invested (EROEI) see, for instance, David Pimentel and Tad W. Patzek, "Ethanol Production Using Corn, Switchgrass, and Wood: Biodiesel Production Using Soybean and Sunflower", *Natural Resources Research*, 14, 1, March 2005, pp 65–76; and David Pimentel, Tad Patzek and Gerald Cecil, "Ethanol Production: Energy, Economic and Environmental Losses", *Review of Environmental Contamination and Toxicology*, 189,

2007 pp 25–41. For a reply to the critique, see National Biodiesel Board, "Response to David Pimentel Biodiesel Life Cycle Analysis", July 2005 available at http://tinyurl.com/or624r7 . For an overview of the debate, see Frank Rosillo-Calle and Francis X. Johnson (2010), *Food versus Fuel, An Informed Introduction to Biofuels*.

196. For an explanation of entropy and its implications for economics, see also Common and Stagl (2005), pp 31–32.

197. See also Tim Jackson (1996), *Material Concerns*; Herman E. Daly (1992), *Steady-State Economics*; Nicholas Georgescu-Roegen (1971), *The Entropy Law and the Economic Process*; and Sven E. Jorgensen and Yuri M. Svirezhev, eds. (2004), *Towards a Thermodynamic Theory for Ecological Systems*.

198. Song of Solomon, 7:12. The Latin is from the Vulgate; the translation is the author's, deviating slightly from (but more literal than) the Authorised Version.

199. From George Herbert (1633), *The Temple: Sacred Poems and Private Ejaculations*, T. Buck and R. Daniel. "The Pearl" widely available online, e.g., at www.poetryfoundation.org/poem/173634 .

200. From Richard Crashaw (1652), *Carmen Deo Nostro*, Peter Targa. This book published posthumously after Crashaw's death in 1649. "A Song" widely available online, e.g., at www.poemhunter.com/poem/a-song-12/ .

201. See Satish Kumar (2002), *You Are, Therefore I Am*, pp 125–127. The quotation is cited in Nancy M. Martin and Joseph Runzo (2008), "Love", in John Corrigan, ed. (2008), *The Oxford Handbook of Religion and Emotion*, p 321.

202. Geoffrey Chaucer (c.1400), *The Canterbury Tales*, p 8.

203. Talal Asad (1993), *Genealogies of Religion*.

204. *Ibid*, pp 256–257.

205. *Ibid*, p 64.

206. John Carey (1980), *John Donne: Life, Mind and Art*, pp 49–50. The exact quotation—the English Jesuit, John Gerard, is describing the progress of one of his pupils in the programme of Spiritual Exercises which he ran—is, "then suddenly the south wind (so to speak) blew over the garden of his soul" and he wept for three days without stopping.

207. From Richard Crashaw (1652), *Carmen Deo Nostro*, Peter Targa. This book published posthumously after Crashaw's death in 1649. "Lauda Sion Salvatorem" widely available online, e.g., at https://tinyurl.com/q4f8uge .

208. "All animal behaviour is driven by the emotions." This statement is in Daniel J. Schneck and Dorita S. Berger (2006), *The Music Effect*, p 98. The significance of the emotions in this respect, and the treatment of them in Antonio Damasio's (1994), *Descartes' Error*, is discussed in the entry on *Spirit. Schneck and Berger also cite the following: Dorita S. Berger (2002), *Music Therapy, Sensory Integration and the Autistic Child*, London: Jessica Kingsley; Dorita S. Berger and Daniel J. Schneck, "The Use of Music Therapy as a Clinical Intervention for Physiologic Functional Adaptation", *Journal of Scientific Exploration*, 17, 4, 2003, pp 687–703; Antonio R. Damasio (1999), *The Feeling of What Happens*; Antonio R. Damasio, "Emotion and the Brain", in A.R. Damasio, R. Harrington, J. Kagan, B.S. McEwen, H. Moss and R. Shaikh, eds. (2001), *Unity of Knowledge: The Convergence of Natural and Human Sciences*, Annals of the N.Y. Academy of Sciences; Antonio R. Damasio (2003), *Looking for Spinoza*; Antonio R. Damasio and Henry Moss , "Emotion, Cognition and the Human Brain", in A.R. Damasio et al., eds. (2001); Joseph LeDoux (1998), *The Emotional Brain: The Mysterious Underpinnings of Emotional Life*, Simon & Schuster; and Joseph LeDoux (2002), *Synaptic Self: How Our Brains Become Who We Are*, Viking Penguin.

209. For a valuable review of topics in environmental ethics, and of the literature, see "Stanford Encyclopaedia of Philosophy: Environmental Ethics", 2002, at http://plato.stanford.edu/entries/ethics-environmental/ .

210. Roger Lundin (1993), *The Culture of Interpretation*, pp 11–17.

211. *Ibid*, pp 16–17.

212. See Oliver James (1997), *Britain on the Couch*; James Griffin (1986), *Well-Being*.

213. See Albert O. Hirschman (1970), *Exit, Voice and Loyalty*.

214. Ernst H. Gombrich (1960), *Art and Illusion*, p 53.

215. See Frans H. van Eemeren and Rob Grootendorst (1992), *Argumentation, Communication and Fallacies*, pp 135–139.

216. The "Train Crash Fallacy"—the fallacy that having experienced a train crash gives you special insight into how the railways should be run—is discussed in *Deceptions.

217. For discussion of North Atlantic cod, see Charles Clover (2006), *The End of the Line*, pp 91–95.

218. Joan Thirsk (1997), *Alternative Agriculture*, p 256.

219. Frans H. van Eemeren and Rob Grootendorst (1992), *Argumentation, Communication and Fallacies*, pp 135–139 and 213. David Hackett Fischer (1970), in his *Historians' Fallacies*, lists five ways in which historians use pedantry as a means of asserting their expertise: their use of particular language, references, detail and mathematical symbols, and the practice of writing at great length. See also Douglas N. Walton (1995), *A Pragmatic Theory of Fallacy*, especially pp 43–46.

220. Mary Warnock, "We Need Have No Fear of Interference with Nature", *The Guardian*, 15 May 2001.

221. Lord May's speech is analysed in Guy Cook (2004), *Genetically Modified Language*, chapter 2. The quotations

are from the extract from the speech on p 32. See also Jonathan Matthews, "The Great GM Miracle?", *The Ecologist*, 23 January 2008.

222. Frank Fischer (2000), *Citizens, Experts and the Environment*, p xi.

223. Extract from an interview with a scientist by Guy Cook in (2004), pp 38–39.

224. Professor Janet Bainbridge is cited in Cook (2004), p 40.

225. Fischer (2000), p 4.

226. Fischer (2000), pp 12–13.

227. I owe the image of the field, and the two kinds of description, to Roger Scruton, who uses them in a somewhat different context in his discussion of perception, in (1994), *Modern Philosophy*, chapter 24. The elaboration of the field and the use that is here made of the image are mine.

228. John Maynard Keynes, "Economic Possibilities for our Grandchildren", 1930, in (1931), *Essays in Persuasion*, pp 321–332 (quotation from p 332).

229. Fischer (2000) writes: "Few contemporary technocrats openly denounce politics. . . . [But] the technocratic argument more subtly manifests itself in a call for improving policy deliberation through improved technical inputs. Although there is nothing wrong with improved technical inputs per se, the effect of the argument—at least as it stands—is to emphasise and elevate technical over political discourse. As political discourse comes to be seen as inferior, typically defined as less rigorous, it is gradually but steadily denigrated.", pp 42–43.

230. Benjamin Barber (1984), *Strong Democracy*, quoted by Fischer (2000), p 29.

231. Fischer (2000), chapter 10.

232. Robert D. Putnam (2000); Robert D. Putnam, Lewis M. Feldstein and Donald Cohen (2003), *Better Together*, pp 241–268. The UK Sustainable Communities Act, 2007, has some of these properties. It enables communities and councils to apply to the Local Government Association, acting for the government, for support requiring grants and amendments to the law.

233. *Editor's note*: "The Big Society" was a flagship policy of the UK Conservative Party in their manifesto for the 2010 general election, aiming "to create a climate that empowers local people and communities, building a big society that will take power away from politicians and give it to people . . . encouraging people to take an active role in their communities." After the election, Conservative Prime Minister David Cameron stated that he wanted his vision of such a 'Big Society' to be one of the great legacies of his Government. See, e.g., www.gov.uk/government /news/government-launches-big-society-programme--2 .

234. Fischer (2000), p 194, quoting C. Lindblom and D. Cohen (1979), *Usable Knowledge: Social Science and Social Problem Solving*, Yale University Press, p 12.

F

1. Lewis Carroll (1896), *Symbolic Logic*.

2. For a comparison between the two kinds of fallacy, see Deborah J. Bennett (2004), *Logic Made Easy*, chapter 11.

3. There is a large literature on fallacies. For an introduction see, for instance, Jay Heinrichs (2007), *Thank You for Arguing*, chapter 14; Madsen Pirie (2006), *How to Win Every Argument*; Robert H. Thouless (1930), *Straight and Crooked Thinking*; Anthony Weston (1987), *A Rulebook for Arguments*; and Jamie Whyte (2003), *Bad Thoughts*. For more detailed treatment, see Douglas N. Walton (1995), *A Pragmatic Theory of Fallacy*, and Frans H. van Eemeren and Rob Grootendorst (1992), *Argumentation, Communication and Fallacies*. Maybe the best of all is David Hackett Fischer (1970), *Historians' Fallacies*.

4. Charles Kennedy said, "Trying to run the pound sterling alongside a single European currency while we were still part of a single market would have as much validity as an attempt by Manhattan to run a separate dollar from the rest of the United States. That is not the real world." House of Commons debate, *Hansard*, 7 December 1995, Column 544. For Duke of Clarence see William Shakespeare (c.1592), *Richard III*, act I, scene 4.

5. For a general introduction to currencies, see Jane Jacobs (1984), *Cities and the Wealth of Nations*, especially chapter 11; Noriko Hama (1996), *Disintegrating Europe*. For local currencies in the United States, see David Boyle (1999), *Funny Money*.

6. The fairness of an analogy "depends on whether the protagonist and the antagonist can agree on the conditions for its use" write Frans H. van Eemeren and Rob Grootendorst (1992), in *Argumentation Communication and Fallacies*, pp 161, 214. See also Weston (1987), *A Rulebook for Arguments*, pp 23–27; David Hackett Fischer (1970), *Historians' Fallacies*, pp 290–293; Charles Leonard Hamblin (1970), *Fallacies*, p 142.

7. For excellence and access in relation to re-education, see Estelle Morris, *The Today Programme*, BBC Radio 4, 16 October 2003. For tradition and change, see Tony Blair, speech to the National Federation of Women's Institutes, 7 June 2000, as reported in Giles Coren, "You can't expect people to like being patronised for making jam", *The Times*, 8 June 2000 and John Carvel, "Heckled, jeered, booed - Blair bombs at the WI", *The Guardian*, 8 June 2000. For sustainable development, see

Herman E. Daly (1996), *Beyond Growth: The Economics of Sustainable Development*, p 167. Here Daly corrects this fallacy, writing "Sustainable development, development without growth, is an economics of better, not bigger." For false consistency (aka the double maximand) and utilitarianism, see Geoffrey Scarre (1996), *Utilitarianism*, pp 24–25. As Jamie Whyte (2003) points out, there is nothing inconsistent about pragmatic choices, one or both of which are inconsistent with a principle which you accept: you choose that way because you want to do so. The inconsistency arises when you defend your choice in terms of the principle.

8. For a detailed explanation and critique of the double maximand, see James Griffin (1986), *Well-Being*, pp 151–155.

9. T.S. Eliot, "The Function of Criticism", in (1932), *Selected Essays*, 1917–1932. Obnubilation: Latin *ob-* "in the opposite direction from", and *nubere* "to marry".

10. Miriam Shaw, Letter to *The Times*, 26 August 2003.

11. *Ibid*.

12. In logic, a "valid" argument is one in which the conclusions logically follow from the premises. But validity says nothing about the truth of the premises. To be sure of the truth of the conclusion, you are looking for a "sound" argument—one which is both valid *and* has true premises.

13. This is one form of the error known as "relying on an inappropriate argumentation scheme", and it is discussed in the literature mainly as *false analogy. See Frans H. van Eemeren and Rob Grootendorst (1992), *Argumentation, Communication and Fallacies*, pp 96 and 160; and Robert H. Thouless (1930), *Straight and Crooked Thinking*, chapter 8.

14. *The Princess and the Pea* is a Hans Christian Andersen story, published in Copenhagen in 1835, but has ancient origins as a folk tale, probably Swedish. It has been adapted as a musical starring Carol Burnett, in a production called *Once Upon a Mattress*.

15. See James P. Womack, Daniel T. Jones and Daniel Roos (1990), *The Machine that Changed the World*, p 79; and James P. Womack and Daniel T. Jones (1996), *Lean Thinking*, p 348.

16. Womack and Jones (1996), pp 21–24 and 50–56.

17. Mihaly Csikszentmihalyi (2002), Flow, chapter 3, especially p 49. See also Mihaly Csikszentmihalyi (1975), *Beyond Boredom and Anxiety*; Mihaly Csikszentmihalyi (1996), *Creativity*; and the summary in Daniel Pink (2009), *Drive: The Surprising Truth About What Motivates Us*, chapter 5.

18. The increasing insecurity in the supply of food, and the prospect of famine extending to the industrialised countries, is explored in detail by Paul Roberts (2008), *The End of Food*. See also Charles Clover (2006), *The End of the Line*; Vandana Shiva (2008), *Soil Not Oil*; Tim Lang, David Barling and Martin Caraher (2009), *Food Policy*.

19. See, e.g., Kathryn Tulip and Lucy Michaels (2004), *A Rough Guide to the UK Farming Crisis*; Tim Lang, "Food Security or Food Democracy?", Rachel Carson Memorial Lecture, December 2007.

20. Fred Pearce (2005), *When the Rivers Run Dry*, chapters 7, 8, 24 and 25, and *passim*.

21. Davinder Sharma, "The Green Revolution Turns Sour", *New Scientist*, 8 July 2000.

22. See, e.g., Richard Heinberg (2003), *The Party's Over*.

23. Tim Lang, "Food Security or Food Democracy?", Rachel Carson Memorial Lecture, December 2007.

24. International Committee of the Red Cross, News Release, "Pakistan Flood- Stricken Farmers in Race Against Time to Plant Before Winter", 23 November 2010.

25. See GRAIN's 'Hybrid Rice Files (2002–2010)'—e.g., "Fiasco in the Field: an update on hybrid rice in Asia", 28 January 2005, or "New troubles with hybrid and GM rice", 27 July 2010, available at http://tinyurl.com/peax52p .

26. For small farmer indebtedness, see, e.g., Vandana Shiva and Kunwar Jalees, "Farmers' Suicides in India", Research Foundation for Science, Technology and Ecology, 2004. For the challenges facing monocropping, see, e.g., Sarina Macfadyen and David A. Bohan, "Crop domestication and the disruption of species interactions", *Basic and Applied Ecology* 11, 2, 2010, pp 116–125.

27. Clover (2006).

28. Many evaluations of industrial agriculture have been published. Brian Halweil (2004), *Eat Here* is especially recommended.

29. Peter Jeschke, Ralf Nauen, Michael Schindler and Alfred Elbert, "Overview of the Status and Global Strategy for Neonicotinoids", *Journal of Agricultural Food Chemistry*, 59, 7, 2010, pp 2897–2908.

30. The causes of 'colony collapse disorder' are as yet unknown. Suspected contributory factors include exposure to neonicotinoids, parasites, modern beekeeping practices, diseases carried by verroa mites, loss of appropriate habitat, climate change and fungal infection. See, e.g., CCD Steering Committee, "Colony Collapse Disorder Progress Report", US Department of Agriculture, June 2009, available at www.extension.org /mediawiki/files/c/c7/CCDReport2009.pdf .

31. Vicky Kindemba, "The Impact of Neonicotinoids Insecticides on Bumblebees, Honey bees and Other Non-Target Invertebrates", Invertebrate Conservation Trust, 2009, available at http://tinyurl.com/qbm57bf . The refereed papers on

which these claims are made are cited in the publication, pp 18–19 and 29. See also the report by the Institute of Science in Society, "Requiem for the Honeybee", 2007, available at www.i-sis.org.uk/requiemForTheHoneybee.php .

32. *Editor's note*: Fleming wrote this content before his death in 2010. In 2013 the European Union, pending the outcome of further research into the impacts on pollinators, voted for a two-year EU-wide moratorium on the use of three of the five neonicotinoids, including imidacloprid, on flowering crops attractive to bees. See, e.g., Charlotte McDonald-Gibson, "'Victory for bees' as European Union bans neonicotinoid pesticides blamed for destroying bee population", *The Independent*, 29 April 2013.

In July 2015 120-day emergency derogations from the ban were issued to specific areas in England due to oilseed rape crops threatened by the flea beetle. See, e.g., "Ban lifted on controversial 'neonic' pesticide", BBC News, 23 July 2015, available at www.bbc.co.uk/news/science-environment-33641646 .

33. For the challenges facing concentrated, large-scale monoculture, see, e.g., Sarina Macfadyen and David A. Bohan, "Crop domestication and the disruption of species interactions", *Basic and Applied Ecology* 11, 2, 2010, pp 116–125.

34. The higher food production per acre of small-scale, labour-intensive farms is long-established. See, for instance, Peter Rossett, "The Multiple Functions and Benefits of Small-Scale Agriculture", The Institute for Food and Development Policy, 1999; Gershon Feder, "The Relationship between Farm Size and Farm Productivity", *Journal of Development Economics*, 18, 1985, pp 297–313. Or indeed 2008's UN-backed International Assessment of International Science and Technology for Development (IAASTD) report—the result of four year's work by over 400 scientists and the biggest study of its kind ever undertaken.

35. The argument that the task of agriculture is to produce food, and how curious it is that this obvious fact has almost been lost from view, is developed by Colin Tudge (2003), *So Shall We Reap*. For a comprehensive critique of industrial agriculture, see Karl Weber (2009), *Food Inc*; and Eric Schlosser (2001), *Fast Food Nation*.

36. See Deborah J. Bennett (2004), *Logic Made Easy*.

37. For a summary of the value of formal logic, see Deborah J. Bennett (2004), *Logic Made Easy*, introduction.

38. Giovanni Boccaccio (1349–1351), *The Decameron*, vol 2, Author's Epilogue.

39. Aristotle (c.350 BC), *Politics*. This is discussed in Hannah Arendt, "What is Freedom?", in (1961), *Between Past and Future: Eight Exercises in Political Thought*, p 147.

40. William Fleming (1856), *Vocabulary of Philosophy*, p 237.

41. Richard T. De George (1985), *The Nature and Limits of Authority*, pp 117–119.

42. The distinction between "positive freedom" and "negative freedom" is discussed in depth in Isaiah Berlin, "Two Concepts of Liberty", 1966, in Isaiah Berlin (1969), *Four Essays on Liberty*.

43. Interactions are discussed by De George (1985), p 119.

44. De George (1985), chapter 3. The example of the child and the doctor is also De George's.

45. George Osborne, "Reforming Financial Markets", *Hansard*, 8 July 2009, Column 974.

46. Of course, we need to be tolerant to a lot of ambiguity here: the ground between usurpation and authority may be bitterly contested as, for instance, in the case of King Henry IV, whose usurpation of the crown from Richard II introduced a period of authoritative greatness in English *education and architecture, intertwined with instabilities, civil and foreign wars and resentments which lasted for a century.

47. The distinction between Enlightenment projects and genealogical projects is made in Alasdair MacIntyre (1990), *Three Rival Versions of Moral Enquiry, passim*, and summarised in Roger Lundin (1993), *The Culture of Interpretation*, chapter 1. "Genealogy" comes from Friedrich Nietzsche (1887), *On the Genealogy of Morality*, in which Nietzsche sets out to trace the sources and history of what he took to be the flawed, deformed morality and culture of the late nineteenth century, whose values he saw as little more than a disguise for power struggles, malice, hate and resentment. MacIntyre argues that the Enlightenment's displacement of all values other than reason itself produced a culture without defensible premises, exposing it to the attack which in due course matured from Nietzsche's critique to the extreme assault mounted by Martin Heidegger, who saw Western culture as nothing: the world is haunted by absence, by Nothingness, the thing that noths.

See also Roger Scruton (1998a), *An Intelligent Person's Guide to Modern Culture*: for further discussion of the Enlightenment, see chapter 3; and for the above-mentioned critique, see chapter 11, especially pp 125–126. For a general survey, see Roy Porter (2000), *Enlightenment*; and Marvin B. Becker (1994), *The Emergence of Civil Society in the Eighteenth Century*.

48. Edmund Burke, letter to a Member of the National Assembly, in (1790), *Reflections on the Revolution in France*, p 289.

49. Edmund Burke, "Thoughts and Details on Scarcity",
1795, in Burke (1794–1797), *The Writings and Speeches of
Edmund Burke*, p 128.
50. See Bart Kosko (1993), *Fuzzy Thinking*.

G

1. James Lovelock (1979), *Gaia*; James Lovelock (1988), *The
Ages of Gaia*; James Lovelock (2006), *The Revenge of Gaia*;
Stephan Harding (2006), *Animate Earth*, chapter 2.
2. For Daisyworld, see Lovelock (1988); Harding (2006),
pp 76–85. For the breakdown that follows when a
system is stressed beyond the limits of what it can cope
with (overshoot), see Donella H. Meadows, Dennis L.
Meadows and Jørgen Randers (1992), *Beyond the Limits*;
William Catton (1980), *Overshoot*; Ervin László (2006),
The Chaos Point.
3. For ice ages and weathering, see Peter Ward (2009), *The
Medea Hypothesis*, pp 51–64 and 113. Ice ages are discussed
in more general terms in Peter Ward and Donald Brownlee (2002), *The Life and Death of Planet Earth*, pp 70–76.
4. Medea also cut her young brother into pieces so that her
father would be delayed (by gathering up the body) in
his pursuit of the Argonauts. For better acquaintance
with this young lady, see Margaret C. Howatson and
Ian Chilvers, eds. (1993), *The Concise Oxford Companion to
Classical Literature*. The idea of Medea as the counterpart
of Gaia is Peter Ward's.
5. Stephan Harding (2006), *Animate Earth*, pp 130–136. For
details on DMS as a cloud-seeder, see K.L. Van Alstyne,
"Ecological and Physiological Roles of Dimethylsulfo-
niopropionate and Its Products in Marine Macroalgae",
which is chapter 8 of Charles D. Amsler, ed. (2008), *Algal
Chemical Ecology*, pp 173–194, especially p 187.
6. Harding (2006), pp 143–145. The scientific literature
includes Sjaak Slanina, ed. (1997), *Biosphere-Atmosphere
Exchange of Pollutants and Trace Substances*; and Robert W.
Howarth, J.W.B. Stewart and Mikhail V. Ivanov (1992),
*Sulphur Cycling on the Continents: Wetlands, Terrestrial
Ecosystems and Associated Water Bodies*.
7. Peter Bunyard (1999), *The Breakdown of Climate*, pp 78–80.
8. Such behaviour which tends to maintains the critical
order of the system can be termed "homeotely" (Greek:
homeo same + *telos* end). See Edward Goldsmith (1992),
The Way, especially pp 336–407.
9. See Frans H. van Eemeren and Rob Grootendorst (1992),
Argumentation, Communication and Fallacies, pp 156–167
and 214.
10. Note that such statements *are* allowed with regard
to horses.

11. Mandy Rice-Davies at the trial of Stephen Ward, 1963.
When the prosecuting counsel pointed out that Lord
Astor denied having an affair with her or having even
met her, she replied, "Well, he would, wouldn't he?"
12. See W.H. Auden, "Under Which Lyre", 1946. For a
discussion of the Genetic Fallacy, see Charles Leonard
Hamblin (1970), *Fallacies*, pp 41–42.
13. *Editor's note*: David Fleming's former colleague Lawrence
Woodward offers the following comment: "Genetic
modification" and "genetic engineering" are sometimes
used interchangeably, but there has been controversy
over the terms. "Modification" implies a relationship
with traditional plant breeding, which is often claimed by
protagonists, whilst "engineering" indicates a novel and
new technological approach, which critics argue is problematic and requires robust evaluation and regulation.

The European Union definition is in article 2(2) of
Directive 2001/18/EC: "genetically modified organism
(GMO) means an organism, with the exception of human
beings, in which the genetic material has been altered
in a way that does not occur naturally by mating and/or
natural recombination".
14. *Editor's note*: David Fleming's former colleague Lawrence
Woodward offers the following comment: Since David's
death in 2010 there has been a rapid development of
gene technology with approaches often termed "gene
editing", including site-directed nuclease techniques, oli-
gonucleotide-directed mutagenesis techniques and RNA
interference. There is much debate as to whether these
fall within the current regulatory definitions of GMOs,
and if not whether those definitions should be expanded
or whether these approaches should be regulated at all.

See, e.g., Michael Eckerstorfer, Marianne Miklau and
Helmut Gaugitsch "New Plant Breeding Techniques and
Risks Associated with their Application", Environment
Agency Austria, 2014; Sarah Z. Agapito-Tenfen and
Odd-Gunnar Wikmark, "Current status of emerging
technologies for plant breeding: Biosafety and
knowledge gaps of site directed nucleases and oligonu-
cleotide-directed mutagenesis", GenØk, January 2015;
"GMO lobby pushes new gene-silencing GMOs in spite
of safety risks", GM Watch, 18 August 2015.
15. Doug Gurian-Sherman, "Failure to Yield: Evaluating the
Performance of Genetically Engineered Crops", Union
of Concerned Scientists, April 2009. Another illustration
of this comes from a study of results in North America,
which found that, after the switch to genetically modified
varieties, the yield of soya fell by between 1 percent and
19 percent, with a typical reduction of about 10 percent

(the yield from some maize, engineered for pest resistance, rose very slightly, but in the case of oilseed rape, the study found a 7.5 percent reduction): Hugh Warwick and Gundula Meziani, "Seeds of Doubt: North American Farmers' Experience of GM Crops", The Soil Association, 2003, chapter 4, available at http://tinyurl.com/nk9ns3n . See also Ricarda A Steinbrecher and Antje Lorch, "Feed the World?", *The Ecologist*, November 2008, pp 18–20.

16. Ricarda A Steinbrecher and Antje Lorch, "Feed the World?", *The Ecologist*, November 2008, p 18.

17. Vandana Shiva (2000), *Tomorrow's Biodiversity*, p 66.

18. See, for instance, W.S. Cranshaw, "Bacillus thuringiensis", Colorado State Univeristy Factsheet, available at http://extension.colostate.edu/docs/pubs/insect/05556.pdf .

19. Most formulations last for up to a week; some of the newer formulations decay within 24 hours.

20. *Editor's note*: Research since Fleming's death has confirmed that pests are indeed evolving *Bt* resistance. See, e.g., Bruce E. Tabashnik, Thierry Brévault and Yves Carrière, "Insect Resistance to Bt Crops: Lessons From the First Billion Acres", *Nature Biotechnology*, 31, 6, 2013, pp 510–521.

21. Jonathon Porritt (2000), *Playing Safe: Science and the Environment*, p 85.

22. *Editor's note*: David Fleming's former colleague Lawrence Woodward offers the following comment: Only four crops—corn (maize), oil seed rape (canola), soy bean and cotton engineered for herbicide and *Bt* tolerance—make up over 90% of the global GM acreage. Since David's death a number of other crops have been developed which have not been commercially developed or widely grown despite great claims and widespread promotion. For a comprehensive review of GMO cropping, see John Fagan, Michael Antoniou and Claire Robinson, "GMO Myths and Truths" (second edition), Earth Open Source, 2014. See also www.gmeducation.org .

23. For instance, Bathua (Fat Hen or Good King Henry) is a rich source of vitamin A, but is destroyed in industrial cropping systems. See Vandana Shiva (1991), *The Violence of the Green Revolution*, p 206.

24. Rahul Nellithanam, Jacob Nellithanam and Sarvodaya Shikshan Samiti, "Return of the Native Seeds", *The Ecologist*, vol 28, 1, Jan/Feb 1998, pp 29–33. Jack Heinemann (2008), "Desert Grain", *The Ecologist*, November, pp 23–24.

25. Mark Anslow, "The Ongoing Quest for Salt-Water Wheat", *The Ecologist*, November 2008, p 25.

26. Mark Henderson, "GM Bean Could Help Prevent Heart Attacks", *The Times*, 3 November 2008.

27. For details on the GM tomatoes being produced at the John Innes Centre in Norwich, see Jonathan Leake, "GM Tomatoes May Ward Off Cancer—Shame They're Purple", *The Times*, 26 October 2008. For the nutritional properties of organic food, see Charles Benbrook et al., "New Evidence Confirms the Nutritional Superiority of Plant-Based Organic Foods", State of Science Review, March 2008.

28. "In 2002 . . . the dominant traits continued to be herbicide tolerance (75%), insect resistance (17%) and both traits (8%)", from "Genetic Technologies: A Review of Developments in 2002", Genewatch UK, 2003.

29. See Warwick and Meziani, "Seeds of Doubt: North American Farmers' Experience of GM Crops" , The Soil Association, 2003, chapter 4.

30. *Ibid.*

Editor's note: David Fleming's former colleague Lawrence Woodward offers the following comment: Since David's death in 2010 the problem of herbicide-tolerant "superweeds" has increased dramatically in GM crops. In the United States at least 14 new glyphosate-resistant weed species have emerged since 1995 and over half of US farms are plagued with herbicide-resistant weeds as a result of GM cropping. See, e.g., Doug Gurian-Sherman and Margaret Mellon, "The Rise of Superweeds—and What to Do About It", Union of Concerned Scientists, December 2013.

31. See Viola Sampson and Larry Lohmann, "Genetic Dialectic: The Biological Politics of Genetically Modified Trees", The Corner House Briefing, 2000, available at www.thecornerhouse.org.uk/resource/genetic-dialectic . Warwick and Meziani, "Seeds of Doubt: North American Farmers' Experience of GM Crops" , The Soil Association, 2003, chapter 7.

32. Mae-Wan Ho, "Recent Evidence Confirms Risks of Horizontal Gene Transfer", Institute of Science in Society, 2003, available at www.greens.org/s-r/30/30-14.html .

33. For a readable background to this, see Nathan B. Batalion, "Biotechnology Is A Vital Issue That Impacts All Of Us", available at https://tinyurl.com/og2cdqc .

34. See Sampson and Lohmann, "Genetic Dialectic: The Biological Politics of Genetically Modified Trees".

35. *Ibid*. Also Warwick and Meziani, "Seeds of Doubt: North American Farmers' Experience of GM Crops" , The Soil Association, 2003, chapter 7.

36. Mark Henderson, "GM Bean Could Help Prevent Heart Attacks", *The Times*, 3 November 2008.

37. Sampson and Lohmann, "Genetic Dialectic: The Biological Politics of Genetically Modified Trees".

38. Warwick and Meziani, "Seeds of Doubt: North American Farmers' Experience of GM Crops", The Soil Association, 2003, p 23.

39. Barry Commoner, "How Well Can Science Predict GM Impacts?", paper presented at the Gene Futures Conference, 11 February 2003 (quotation abridged).

40. Warwick and Meziani, "Seeds of Doubt: North American Farmers' Experience of GM Crops", The Soil Association, 2003, chapter 8.

41. The Economist, "Planting a Seed", 27 March 2003, available at www.economist.com/node/1647599 .

42. Árpád Pusztai, "Genetically Modified Foods: Are they a Risk to Human/Animal Health?", American Institute of Biological Sciences, June 2001, available at www.iatp.org /files/Genetically_Modified_Foods_Are_They_a_Risk _to_.htm .

43. Ibid. In 2005, the Federation of German Scientists honoured Dr. Pusztai with a whistleblower award.

44. Percy Schmeiser, "What Would GM Crops Mean for British Farmers?", lecture at Burgh House, Hampstead, 29 October 2008.

45. David Horrobin, "Not in the Genes", The Guardian, 12 February 2003.

46. Editor's note: For an extended briefing on biotechnology (adapted from an earlier draft of this book), see David Fleming, "Biotechnology: A Technology We Do Not Need", The Lean Economy Connection, October 2003, available at https://tinyurl.com/oebfvbv .

47. These ambiguities are described by John Milbank, "Can A Gift Be Given? Prolegomena to a Future Trinitarian Metaphysic", Modern Theology, 11, 1, 1995, pp 119–160.

48. Lewis Hyde (1983), The Gift, p 58.

49. Mary Douglas, "No Free Gifts", 1990, foreword to translation of Marcel Mauss (1950), The Gift: The Form and Reason for Exchange in Archaic Societies, pp viii. It was Mauss who made the breakthrough in the understanding of the role of gifts in underpinning social cohesion.

50. Marshall Sahlins' (1972), Stone Age Economics does not tell us anything about the Bushman who said this, but he was illustrating his general claim that "All . . . exchanges . . . must bear in their material design some political burden of reconciliation", p 182.

51. Mary Douglas, "No Free Gifts", 1990, pp ix.

52. This summary draws especially on Bataille (1967), The Accursed Share, vol 1, pp 19–77, and on James G. Frazer (1922), The Golden Bough, chapters 24–26. This is a controversial field, and Frazer's work is now dated, though not refuted. Peter Metcalf and Richard Huntington (1981) write, "It was Frazer's simplistic view that every

representation suggesting regicide inevitably meant the former existence of the practice. Evans-Pritchard's view reverses the practice, stressing the power of the idea itself, and stressing that the belief may be even more effective in strengthening the polity when the deed is not actually done." Celebrations of Death: The Anthropology of Mortuary Ritual, p 180. Of course, the substitution of a son opened the way for someone else to stand in for the son. As Bataille (1967) writes, "There is no possibility of a mistake here: This was a sacrifice of substitution" (p 55).

53. Julian of Norwich (1373), A Book of Showings to the Anchoress Julian of Norwich, chapter 8, p 245, line 72.

54. John Ruskin (1866), The Crown of Wild Olive, p 159.

55. See, for instance, Ahmed M. Hussen (2000), Principles of Environmental Economics, pp 103–106 and 246–253 (internalisation options); pp 228–232 (taxes); pp 253–264 (regulation and tradable permits); and Common and Stagl (2005), Ecological Economics, chapter 11.

56. For a sophisticated and modern representative of the liberal agenda, see Derrick Jensen (2006), Endgame. For general introductions to critical theory, see Craig Calhoun (1995), Critical Social Theory: Culture History and the Challenge of Difference; and Stephen Eric Bronner and Douglas MacKay Kellner, eds. (1989), Critical Theory and Society: A Reader.

57. See, for instance, David Boyle and Andrew Simms (2009), The New Economics; Zac Goldsmith (2009), The Constant Economy; Bill McKibben (2007), Deep Economy; Molly Scott Cato (2009), Green Economics; and Andrew Simms and Joe Smith, eds. (2008), Do Good Lives Have to Cost the Earth? For a discussion of the economics of zero-growth / negative-growth / degrowth, see Tim Jackson (2009), Prosperity Without Growth.

58. The Green New Deal Group (2008), The Green New Deal, p 32.

59. William D. Nordhaus and James Tobin, "Is Growth Obsolete?" National Bureau of Economic Research, Fiftieth Anniversary Colloquium, 1973, available at www.nber.org/chapters/c3621.pdf ; E.J. Mishan (1977), The Economic Growth Debate; Mark Lutz and Kenneth Lux (1988), Humanistic Economics; Richard Easterlin, "Does Economic Growth Improve the Human Lot?", in Paul A. David and Melvin Warren Reder, eds. (1974), Nations and Households in Economic Growth, pp 89–125; Fred Hirsch (1976), Social Limits to Growth; Ed Diener, ed. (2009), The Science of Well-Being; Amartya Sen, "Personal Utilities and Public Judgments: Or What's Wrong with Welfare Economics?", Economic Journal, 89, 1979 pp 537–558.

60. For effects of unemployment on well-being see, for instance, David Lester and Bijou Lang (1997), The Economy

and *Suicide: Social Perspectives on Suicide*; and Duncan Gallie, Catherine Marsh and Carolyn M. Vogler, eds. (1994), *Social Change and the Experience of Unemployment*.

61. Green New Deal Group (2008), p 3.

62. UK Industry Taskforce on Peak Oil and Energy Security, "The Oil Crunch: A Wake-Up Call for the UK Economy", February 2010; for New Economics Foundation see www.neweconomics.org ; Tim Jackson (2009), *Prosperity Without Growth*, chapter 4.

63. See also Herman E. Daly and John B. Cobb (1989), *For the Common Good*; Herman E. Daly (1992), *Steady-State Economics*; Herman E. Daly (1996), *Beyond Growth*; Michael Common and Sigrid Stagl (2005), *Ecological Economics*.

64. Moses Abramovitz, "Thinking About Growth", in Abramovitz (1989), *Thinking About Growth and Other Essays on Economic Growth and Welfare*, p 38.

65. Wynne Godley, "Lamont Gripped by a Double Bind", *The Observer*, 14 March 1993.

66. This point is discussed further in *Population.

67. It is arguable that a specially-recruited workforce, such as the Irish "navigators" imported to build the canal network in the eighteenth century, can raise *per capita* income by dealing with a bottleneck problem which is beyond the resources of the existing workforce. But the economic data (GDP, etc.) provides no insight into what is going on here, and the effect is short-lived since quite different circumstances apply after the bottleneck has been cleared.

68. Department of Economic Affairs (1965), *The National Plan*, Cmnd 2764, Her Majesty's Stationery Office, pp 1, 3, 7–8.

69. In fact, a profoundly totalitarian regime (*Unlean) may have an advantage here, since it is probable that it is presiding over a command economy rather than a market. That allows intervention in prices in a protected economy with closed borders—the wrong sort of *slack, but slack, and feasible, nonetheless.

70. Adam Smith (1776), *The Wealth of Nations*, book 1, chapter 1, pp 12–13. For the suggestion that it would have taken hunter-gatherers an average of two hours a day to provide their food, see Marshall Sahlins (1972), *Stone Age Economics*, p 27. This would today be considered rather a short working day.

71. This is in essence the argument of Marvin Harris' groundbreaking book (1977), *Cannibals and Kings*.

72. The Population Reference Bureau's "World Population Data Sheet", 2010, forecasts continued world population growth for decades. Key findings available at www.prb.org .

73. The original of this phrase comes from the Greek poet Pindar. Erasmus quoted it in Latin as the title for his 1525 pamphlet on war.

74. Gerhardt Bosch, "Working Time Reductions, Employment Consequences and Lessons from Europe", in Lonnie Golden and Deborah M. Figart, eds. (2002), *Working Time: International Trends, Theory and Policy Perspectives*. Routledge. For a summary, see pp 192–193.

75. Peter A. Victor (2008), *Managing Without Growth*, chapter 11.

76. Tim Jackson (2009), *Prosperity Without Growth*, chapters 11 and 12.

77. Anna Coote, Jane Franklin and Andrew Simms (2010), *21 Hours: Why a Shorter Working Week Can Help Us All to Flourish in the 21st Century*.

78. *Ibid*, p 28. They add that the minimum would have to be increased, too.

79. We will leave aside for now the suggestion, discussed in Coote et al. (2010), that the shorter working week could lead to improved labour productivity per hour. If there are such improvements to be made, they should happen anyway, especially with the application of *lean thinking.

80. Edgar S. Cahn (2000), *No More Throw-Away People*, pp 203–204; Coote et al. (2010), p 28.

81. See Tom Hodgkinson (2005), *How to Be Idle*.

82. For guilt over goods and services, see *Invisible Goods.

H

1. Carl Folke, Fikret Berkes and Johan Colding, "Ecological Practices and Social Mechanisms", in Berkes and Folke, eds. (1998), *Linking Social and Ecological Systems*, pp 431–432.

2. Joan Thirsk (1997), *Alternative Agriculture*.

3. Alan Christopher Finlayson and Bonnie J. McCay, "Crossing the Threshold of Ecosystem Resilience: The Commercial Extinction of Northern Cod", in Berkes and Folke, eds. (1998), chapter 12, especially pp 322–332.

4. *Ibid*. For an extended review of the story of scientific warnings being ignored, see Malcom MacGarvin, "Fisheries: Taking Stock", in Poul Harremoës, David Gee, Malcolm MacGarvin, et al., eds. (2002), *The Precautionary Principle in the 20th Century*, chapter 2, pp 10–25.

5. See Thomas S. Kuhn (1962), *The Structure of Scientific Revolutions*; or Alexander Bird (2000), *Thomas Kuhn*.

6. Alexander Herzen, "Omnia Mea Mecum Porto", 1850, in Alexander Herzen (1847–51), *From the Other Shore*, p 131.

7. John Seddon (2003), *Freedom from Command and Control*, pp 29 and 221.

8. Statement made in an oral presentation of the findings of the Nimrod crash inquiry, 28 October 2009.

9. Quotation from the report, in Michael Evans, "Damning Report Blames Defence Chiefs for Jet Crash that Killed 14", *The Times*, 29 October 2009, pp 6–7.

10. Andrew Mawson (2008), *The Social Entrepreneur*, p 164. See also the discussion of Mawson's work at the Bromley by Bow Centre in *Presence.

11. James Bartholomew (2004), *The Welfare State We're In*, pp 160–161.

12. Quoted in Bartholomew (2004) and Edwin George West (1965), *Education and the State*, pp 191–192 (no reference for the original is provided in West).

13. The Labour Party, "National Service for Health", 1943, pp 5, 6, 9, 10 and 12.

14. Max Gammon (1976), *Health and Security: Report on Public Provision for Medical Care in Great Britain*, p 28.

15. Max Gammon, "Gammon's Law of Bureaucratic Displacement", Australian Doctors Fund, January 2005, available at www.adf.com.au/archive.php?doc_id=113 .

16. For references on hierarchy and panarchy, see the entry on *Systems Thinking.

17. The Reichstag fire on 27 February 1933 was attributed to a Communist conspiracy, and Hitler used this to purge the German parliament of all its Communist members and consolidate his power in a one-party State.

18. Job 39: 25 (trumpets); Job 40:15 (behemoth); King James version—"Behold now behemoth". David Hume (1748), *An Enquiry Concerning Human Understanding*, chapter 5.

19. Job 38: 2 (darkeneth counsel).

20. The general principle of holism was concisely summarized by Aristotle in the *Metaphysics*, 1045a 10: "The whole is different from the sum of its parts".

21. For further reading, see Howard Jones (2008), *The Tao of Holism*.

22. John Donne, "Satire III", c.1593, available at, e.g., www .bartleby.com/357/177.html .

23. "Orgs" suggested by R.W. Gerard; "integrons" by F. Jacob. For details and references see Peter B. Checkland (1981), *Systems Thinking, Systems Practice*, p 82. Arthur Koestler's extended and groundbreaking discussion of holons is in (1967), *The Ghost in the Machine*, pp 45–70.

24. For further reading, see Arthur Koestler (1967); Lance H. Gunderson and C.S. Holling, eds. (2002), *Panarchy*; and Peter B. Checkland (1981).

25. Christopher Alexander, Sara Ishikawa, Murray Silverstein et al. (1977), *A Pattern Language*.

26. Christopher Alexander (1967), *Notes on the Synthesis of Form*, p 43.

27. Elinor Ostrom (2005), *Understanding Institutional Diversity*, pp 11–13.

28. Alexander et al. (1977), especially chapter 4.

29. For "accustomed, ceremonious", see W.B. Yeats, "A Prayer for My Daughter", June 1919, in (1921), *Michael Robartes and the Dancer*; Ferdinand, in William Shakespeare (c.1611), *The Tempest*. Ben Johnson, "Penshurst Place"; Andrew Marvell, "Appleton House"; The Earl of Clarendon's tribute to Falkland, in *The History of the Rebellion, III*, is quoted in Keith Thomas, "The Social Origins of Hobbes' Political Thought", in Keith C. Brown, ed. (1965), *Hobbes Studies*, p 207. Lionel Trilling (1971), *Sincerity and Authenticity*, p 39.

30. William Cobbett (1821), *Cottage Economy*. H.J. Massingham, introduction to Flora Thompson (1945), *Lark Rise to Candleford*, p 11.

31. Jenni Russell, "This Social Work by Computer System is Protecting No One", *Sunday Times*, 24 January 2010.

32. William Hazlitt, "On the Love of the Country" *The Examiner*, November 27 1814, in Hazlitt (1778–1830), *Selected Essays of William Hazlitt*, p 7. See also Patrick Curry, "Defending Middle Earth", 1997, in Laurence Coupe, ed. (2000), *The Green Studies Reader*, pp 282–287.

33. David Miller (2000), *Citizenship and National Identity*, p 25 (dialogue slightly edited).

34. Alasdair MacIntyre (1981), *After Virtue*; MacIntyre develops at length the idea of narrative, especially relating to locality and community, as a means whereby the community, and the identity of the person within it, become intelligible. See also Anthony Giddens (1991), *Modernity and Self-Identity*. Giddens writes, "The existential question of self-identity is bound up with the fragile nature of the biography which the individual 'supplies' about herself. A person's identity is not to be found in behaviour, not—important though this is—in the reactions of others, but in the capacity *to keep a particular narrative going*" (p 54).

35. Françoise Thom (1987), *Newspeak: The Language of Soviet Communism*, pp 115–116.

36. The source of this is unclear. It is quoted in Willard Farnham (1936), *The Medieval Heritage of Elizabethan Tragedy* (front cover), without attribution. It was used as a printer's device in a 1954 treatise on duelling by Vincentio Saviolo. Maybe it was the inspiration of a dueller on the point of fighting to the death?

37. Roger Scruton (2007), *Culture Counts*, pp 7 and 48.

38. Matthew Crawford (2010), *The Case for Working with Your Hands, or Why Office Work is Bad for Us and Fixing Things Feels Good*, p 183.

39. For a study of an ancient hunting culture in modern times, see Hugh Brody (2000), *The Other Side of Eden*. The case for the modern cultural ritual of hunting is made in Roger Scruton (1998b), *On Hunting*.

40. Hyperbole (Greek: *hypér* over + *bállein* throw).

41. William Shakespeare (c.1599), *Much Ado About Nothing*, act II, scene 1, lines 221–228.

42. Matthew Parris, "The Green Visionary Who Has Banished Famine From the World", *The Times*, 21 February 2004, p 28.

43. William Shakespeare (c.1597), *Henry IV*, Part 1, act III, scene 1, lines 247–248.

44. *Ibid*, act II, scene 4, lines 249–251.

45. Newspeak is the official language of Ingsoc, one of the three totalitarian superstates in George Orwell (1949), *Nineteen Eighty-Four*. It was designed to restrict language so that people could no longer think for themselves, nor respond appropriately to their predicament. It is standard in totalitarian regimes and gratefully adopted in regimes that are going that way. An understanding of *logic is an antidote.

46. Françoise Thom (1987), *Newspeak*, pp 21–22. This example is not Thom's. For thought crimes and George Orwell's description of them, see Roger Scruton (2006a), *A Political Philosophy*, pp 166–169.

47. Thom (1987), pp 22–23. The example of "now" is cited by Thom.

48. *Ibid*, p 24. The quotation is from Thom, citing Georges Marchais (1972), preface to *Programme Commun de Gouvernement*, Paris: Editions Socials, p 13.

49. Roger Scruton (2006a), *A Political Philosophy*, p 169. See also *Cant.

50. David J.C. MacKay (2008), *Sustainable Energy—Without the Hot Air*, p 3.

51. Thom (1987), pp 25–26. The example is from Marchais (1972), pp 37–38.

52. *Ibid*, pp 28–31.

53. *Ibid*.

54. W.H. Auden, introduction, in (1965), *The Sonnets*.

55. For the hopes of capitalists, see Henri Barbusse (1935), *Staline*, p 160, cited in Thom (1987), p 52; George Orwell supplies another, now famous, example: "The fascist octopus has sung its swan song", in "Politics and the English Language", 1946, in Orwell (1945–1950), *The Collected Essays, Journalism and Letters of George Orwell*, vol 4, p 134.

56. Simon de Bruxelles, "Brussels Orders Dogs Out of B&B Kitchens", *The Times*, 12 June 2008, p 6.

57. Joseph A. Tainter (1988), *The Collapse of Complex Societies*, pp 145–6. On pp 139 and 147 Tainter quotes Harold Mattingly (1960), *Roman Coins*, Quadrangle, p 186; and Robert Adams (1983), *Decadent Societies*, North Point Press, p 47.

58. The nickname "Sea-Green Incorruptible" is in Thomas Carlyle (1837), *The French Revolution: A History*, vol 2, book 4, p 198.

59. David Martin, "Shelves of Sincerity", *Times Literary Supplement*, 30 June 2006, p 28.

I

1. Jamie Whyte (2003), *Bad Thoughts*, p 62. Whyte develops his concept of 'hooray words' and 'boo words' on pp 61–63.

2. For a description of this form of argument, see Françoise Thom (1987), *Newspeak*, pp 54–55.

3. Antonio Damasio (1994), *Descartes' Error: Emotion, Reason and the Human Brain*; see also the review by Daniel C. Dennett, in *Times Literary Supplement*, 25 August 1995, pp 3–4; the quotation from Nietzsche is from (1883–1885), *Thus Spake Zarathustra*, "On the Despisers of the Body", quoted in Daniel C. Dennett (1995), *Darwin's Dangerous Idea*. Damasio's view on the emotions and the body being intrinsic to judgment is not unchallenged; see, for instance, Andrew L. Gluck (2007), *Damasio's Error and Descartes' Truth: An Inquiry into Consciousness, Metaphysics and Epistemology*.

4. The meaning of "rational" here is distinct from Michael Oakeshott's concept of "rationalism". *Conatus*: Latin, *conatus*, (past participle of verb *conari*, to try). For a discussion of the meaning of *conatus*, see the entry on *Spirit and Antonio Damasio (2003), *Looking for Spinoza*, especially pp 36 and 170–175.

5. Amartya Sen (2006), *Identity and Violence: The Illusion of Destiny*, p 28.

6. From Thomas Traherne (1636–1674), "Thanksgivings for the Body", in Christopher L. Webber, ed. (2004), *Give Us Grace: An Anthology of Anglican Prayers*, pp 110–115.

7. Aristotle, *Nicomachean Ethics*, in Albert Jonsen and Stephen Toulmin (1988), *The Abuse of Casuistry*, pp 298–299 (quotation abridged).

8. The idea of place is critical to identity as a "communitarian" position. See Michael J. Sandel (1982), *Liberalism and the Limits of Justice*; Alasdair MacIntyre (1981), *After Virtue*; and Michael Walzer (1983), *Spheres of Justice*. See also Jeff Malpas (1999), *Place and Experience*; Gaston Bachelard (1969), *The Poetics of Space*; Yi-Fu Tuan (1972), *Topophilia*; Irwin Altman and Setha Low (1992), *Place Attachment*; Anne Buttimer and David Seamon, eds. (1980), *The Human Experience of Space and Place*, notably Michael A. Godkin's essay, "Identity and Place: Clinical Applications Based on Notions of Rootedness and Uprootedness"; Simone Weil (1943), *The Need for Roots*.

9. Norman Cohn (1975), *Europe's Inner Demons*, pp 81–82.

10. *Ibid*, pp 77–83.

11. *Ibid*, pp 85–90. See p 86 for Cohn's categorical declaration of the Templars' innocence. The first to cast doubt on the accusations was F.J.M Raynouard in 1813.

12. This image of unemployment is from the photograph reproduced on the front cover of Amity Shlaes (2007), *The Forgotten Man: A New History of the Great Depression*.

13. Michael Stewart (1967), *Keynes and After*, p 254.

14. *Johnny Sands* is quoted in Frederick Woods, ed. (1983), *The Oxford Book of English Traditional Verse*.

15. A recipe for the chicken (*poule au pot*), attributed to Henry IV (or his cooks) is in *Delia's Complete Cookery Course* (2004), BBC Books, pp 188–189.

16. Madsen Pirie (2006), *How to Win Every Argument*, pp 92–94. Stephen Toulmin, Richard D. Rieke and Allan Janik (1984), *An Introduction to Reasoning*, pp 146–147; Frans H. van Eemeren and Rob Grootendorst (1992), *Argumentation, Communication and Fallacies*, pp 188–194 and 212–213.

17. On the topic of learning and understanding without having experience, see J.K. Rowling, Harvard Commencement Address, June 2008, available at http://harvardmagazine.com/commencement/the-fringe-benefits-failure-the-importance-imagination .

18. M. Shayer and D. Ginsburg, "Thirty Years On—A Larger Anti-Flynn effect? (II): 13- and 14-year-olds. Piagetian tests of formal operations norms 1976–2006/7", *British Journal of Educational Psychology*, vol 79, part 3, 2009, pp 409–418. The research was referring to the formal operational stage of cognitive development, when children start to learn how to think abstractly, and to use logic in drawing conclusions—that is, how to process reality and develop judgment. Shayer's research shows that children's performance at the lower—"creative operational" stage is actually improved. This stage carries out tasks such as sorting objects, and understanding properties such as size and shape. This classification of cognitive development is based on the work of Jean Piaget, which is surveyed in, for instance, Jean Piaget (1923–1979), *The Essential Piaget*, edited by Howard E. Gruber and J. Jacques Vonèche. For a press account of Shayer's findings, see Jessica Shepherd, "Teenagers of yesteryear 'were brighter'", *The Guardian*, 27 October 2008, available at www.theguardian.com/education/2008/oct/27/teenagers-less-bright .

19. Judith Hook (1976), *The Baroque Age in England*, p 11.

20. *Ibid*, chapter 1.

21. John Smith, "The Excellency and Nobleness of True Religion", 1660, cited in Hook (1976), p 117, whose source is C.A. Patrides, ed. (1980), *The Cambridge Platonists*, Cambridge University Press, p 144.

22. See Hook (1976), chapter 1. For Thomas Hobbes on felicity, see Michael Oakeshott (1946), introduction to Thomas Hobbes' (1651), *Leviathan*.

23. John Donne, letter to Sir Henry Goodyer, c.1609, reproduced in Edmund Gosse (1899), *The Life and Letters of John Donne*, I, 219.

24. "Implicature" is a term introduced by Paul Grice (1989), *Studies in the Way of Words*, chapter 2. The example of the singer comes from *The Penguin Dictionary of Philosophy*.

25. Grice (1989) acknowledges that irony, carefully used, can truthfully communicate the opposite of what the words say, pp 34 and 53–55.

26. Psalm 131, verse 2.

27. For discussion of the different effects of incentives on quality vs. quantity see, for instance, Simon Burgess, Carol Propper, Marissa Ratto and Emma Tominey, "Incentives in the Public Sector: Some Preliminary Evidence from a UK Government Agency", Discussion Paper 4010, Centre for Economic Policy Research, 2003.

28. This is a highly condensed summary of the research reported at length by Alfie Kohn (1993), *Punished by Rewards*, especially chapters 4 and 5. The original coffee break study, later much elaborated and replicated, was by Edward L. Deci, "Effects of Externally Mediated Rewards on Intrinsic Motivation", *Journal of Personality and Social Psychology*, 18, 1971, pp 105–115, cited in Kohn (1993), p 70.

29. Kohn (1993), *Punished by Rewards*, pp 46, 265 and 71.

30. See Kohn (1993), chapters 4 and 5. See this source for a fully-referenced survey of the literature, and Daniel Pink (2009), *Drive*, for the more recent work on incentives.

31. Simon Burgess, Carol Propper, Marissa Ratto and Emma Tominey, in their "Incentives in the Public Sector: Some Preliminary Evidence from a UK Government Agency", suggest that this is because there is no incentive to make further effort after achieving the target at which the reward is earned.

32. Kohn (1993), p 182, italics in original.

33. Pink (2009), pp 121–122; Carol S. Dweck (2000), *Self-Theories*, p 17. For "dog-biscuit", see Benjamin Barber (1984), *Strong Democracy*, p 13.

34. Pink (2009), chapters 4, 5 and 6.

35. Patrick Geddes, "Town Planning Towards City Development: A Report to the Durbar of Indore", Holkore State Printing Press, 1918; Patrick Geddes, "Town Planning in Balrampur: A Report to the Hon'ble the Maharaja Bahadur", Murray's Printing Press, 1917. Both quoted in Peter Hall (1988), *Cities of Tomorrow*, pp 246 and 245.

36. Jacqueline Tyrwhitt, ed. (1947), *Patrick Geddes in India*, Lund Humphries. Quoted in Hall (1988), p 246 (quotation abridged).

37. Hellen Meller (1990), *Patrick Geddes*, pp 75–76. Hall (1988), pp 242–244.

38. Patrick Geddes and John Arthur Thomson (1889), *The Evolution of Sex*, p 312.

39. Dennis Hardy (1991), *From Garden Cities to New Towns*, p 217 (quotation abridged).

40. Paul Barker (1984), *Founders of the Welfare State*, p 49.

41. For a vigorous presentation of the core economy, see Josh Ryan-Collins, Lucie Stephens and Anna Coote, "The New Wealth of Time: How Timebanking Helps People Build Better Public Services", New Economics Foundation, 2008. Their preferred name for it—"core economy" (rather than informal economy)—follows Edgar S. Cahn (2000), *No More Throw-Away People*, pp 203–204. In fact, "core economy" and "informal economy" are not quite equivalent. Core economy refers mainly to household activities, the core interactions that bring us into existence as people and on which everything else depends. Informal economy starts with this, but extends beyond—to all provision of goods and services without expectant of monetary payment.

42. For Lehigh Hospital, see Lucie Stephens, Josh Ryan-Collins and David Boyle, "Co-Production: A Manifesto for the Core Economy", New Economics Foundation, 2008, p 18; for "co-production", see Elinor Ostrom (1971), *Community Organization and the Provision of Police Services*, p 11. *Conservative Party* (2010), *Conservative Manifesto 2010: An Invitation to Join the Government of Britain*, p 37.

43. Jaakko Hintikka, "True and False Logics of Scientific Discovery", in Jaakko Hintikka and Fernand Vandamme, eds. (1985), *Logic of Discovery and Logic of Discourse*, p 3.

44. From the play "Rhinoceros", 1959, in Eugène Ionesco (1960), *Rhinoceros and Other Plays*, Grove Press.

45. See Thomas Homer-Dixon (2000), *The Ingenuity Gap*.

46. Frans H. van Eemeren and Rob Grootendorst (1992), *Argumentation, Communication and Fallacies*, pp 135–139 and 213. Douglas N. Walton (1995), *A Pragmatic Theory of Fallacy*, especially pp 43–46.

47. Jonathan Swift (1726), *Gulliver's Travels*, pp 470–473.

48. For *Everyman*, see Greg Walker (2000), *Medieval Drama: An Anthology*, pp 281–298, or Arthur C. Cawley, ed. (1961), *Everyman and Medieval Miracle Plays*. The English version (c.1509–19) is probably a derivation of the earlier Dutch *Elckerlije*.

49. Émile Durkheim (1893), *The Division of Labour in Society*. Discussed in *Profession.

50. Franz Kafka (1922), *The Castle*. Cf. the prayer of St. Ignatius of Loyola (1491–1556), "Teach us, good Lord, to serve thee as thou deservest . . .", available at www.spck.org.uk/classic-prayers/st-ignatius-/ .

51. David Miller (2000), *Citizenship and National Identity*, especially chapter 2. Bernard Crick (1962), *In Defence of Politics*, especially chapter 1. John Stuart Mill (1861), *Considerations on Representative Government*, especially chapter 16, "Of Nationality, as Connected with Representative Government". Larry Siedentop (2000), *Democracy in Europe*. John Laughland (1997), *The Tainted Source*.

52. Carol S. Dweck (2000), *Self-Theories*, pp 116–126.

53. Dweck (2000), pp 116–117 (italics added). There is a summary of this experiment in Daniel Pink (2009), *Drive*, pp 121–123.

54. Marshall Sahlins (1972), *Stone Age Economics*, p 27 suggests that it would have taken hunter-gatherers an average of two hours a day to provide their food. This would today be considered rather a short working day.

55. Adam Smith (1776), *The Wealth of Nations*, book 1, chapter 1, pp 12–13.

56. Marvin Harris (1977), *Cannibals and Kings*, p 266. The Intensification Paradox is discussed (though not called that) by Richard G. Wilkinson (1973), *Poverty and Progress*, chapters 6, 10 and *passim*; and Ester Boserup, "Environment, Population and Technology in Primitive Societies", in Donald Worster, ed. (1988), *The Ends of the Earth*, pp 23–38.

57. Robert H. Schaffer (1988), *The Breakthrough Strategy*. Schaffer assembles protocols under various headings, such as "The Zest Factors", "Breakthrough Project Design", "The Keys of the Kingdom", "Breakthrough Multiplication Routes", and "Top Management's New Job". These slogans may make it harder for his analysis to receive the attention it deserves. Schaffer's incremental approach contrasts with the more ambitious strategy proposed as ideal by Jeremy Carew-Reid, Robert Prescott-Allen, Stephen Bass and Barry Dalal-Clayton (1994), *Strategies for National Sustainable Development*. They write that "Objectives should be few enough to be achievable; broad enough to ensure the support of participants and encompass all aspects of the issue; and narrow enough and clearly defined enough to be measurable."

58. The cycle of tyranny and revolution in hydraulic civilisations is described in *Unlean.

59. Gunderson and Holling, eds. (2002), *Panarchy*, pp 29–30.

60. For potlatch, see Johan Huizinga (1949), *Homo Ludens*, pp 78–82. Marcel Mauss (1950), *The Gift*, pp 7 and 7–18. Lewis Hyde (1983), *The Gift*, chapter 2.

61. Mauss (1950), p 18.

62. *Ibid*.

63. Georges Bataille (1967), *The Accursed Share*, pp 37–38 and 67. John Milbank writes, "the chief or king who receives a surplus . . . must repay his debt to the community by expending the surplus in a festive, sacrificial manner, not by reinvesting it in production". John Milbank, "Can

a Gift be Given? Prolegomena to a Future Trinitarian Metaphysic", *Modern Theology*, 11, 1, 1995, pp 119–160. For further reading, see Huizinga (1949).

64. Marilyn M. Rhie and Robert A.F. Thurman (1991), *Wisdom and Compassion: The Sacred Art of Tibet*.

65. For the intense enforced investment in infrastructure in the Industrial Revolution, see Richard G. Wilkinson (1973), *Poverty and Progress*, chapter 6.

66. Georges Bataille (1967), *The Accursed Share*, pp 37–38 and 67. See also *Wheel of Life.

67. David Begg, Stanley Fischer and Rüdiger Dornbusch (1984), *Economics*, p 424.

68. The first to use "intermediate" in this sense were Nancy and Richard Ruggles: "a considerable portion of the expenditures of households could be considered to be intermediate . . . regrettable necessities", Nancy D. Ruggles and Richard Ruggles (1970), *The Design of Economic Accounts*, National Bureau of Economic Research. See also Wilfred Beckerman (1968), *An Introduction to National Income Analysis*, which references Ruggles and Ruggles' earlier work.

69. E.J. Mishan (1977), *The Economic Growth Debate*, pp 38–48.

70. Michael Common and Sigrid Stagl (2005), *Ecological Economics*, p 148.

71. And in our own political economy, productivity has an additional relentless driver in the form of *competition, which pushes ahead with technical advance (leaving companies that don't keep up to fold), and so reinforces the positive/amplifying *feedback of growth.

72. Adam Smith (1776), *The Wealth of Nations*, book 1, chapter 1, pp 12–13.

73. Colin Renfrew (1979), "Systems Collapse and Social Transformation: Catastrophe and Anastrophe in Early State Societies", in Colin Renfrew and Kenneth L. Cooke, eds. (1979), Transformations: *Mathematical Approaches to Cultural Change*, pp 481–506 (quotation from p 487).

74. The sequence illustrates the kind of elaboration and specialisation—and the increase in population—arising notionally from specialisation in pottery.

75. Colin Renfrew (1979), pp 487–488.

76. For the story of the creation of the coalmining industry—and the industrial and urban hinterland that grew up round it—in response to the energy shortages which developed in eighteenth century Britain, see Richard G. Wilkinson (1973), *Poverty and Progress*. Essentially the same analysis has been developed with respect to food production in Ester Boserup (1965), *The Conditions of Agricultural Growth*; and Ester Boserup, "Environment, Population and Technology in Primitive Societies",

in Donald Worster, ed. (1988), *The Ends of the Earth*, pp 23–38. But Wilkinson's thesis is criticised in Michael. S. Common, "Poverty and Progress Revisited", chapter 3 in David Collard, David W. Pearce, and David Ulph, eds. (1988), *Economics, Growth and Sustainable Environments*.

77. This is discussed in the context of a mathematical model by Colin Renfrew and Tim Poston, "Discontinuities in the Endogenous Change of Settlement Patterns", in Colin Renfrew and Kenneth L. Cooke, eds. (1979), *Transformations: Mathematical Approaches to Culture Change*, pp 442–447 (specifically p 444).

78. Regarding forests, see, for example, Clive Ponting (1991), *A Green History of the World*, pp 76–77 and 258. For collapse, see Renfrew and Cooke, eds. (1979), especially pp 487–488; Joseph A. Tainter (1988), *The Collapse of Complex Societies*; and Jared Diamond (2005), *Collapse*.

79. See, for example, Renfrew and Cooke, eds. (1979), pp 492–493.

80. Oliver Goldsmith (1774), *A History of the Earth, and Animated Nature*, volume 3, p 6.

81. Oliver Goldsmith, "The Deserted Village", 1770, in (1756–1774), *The Complete Poetical Works of Oliver Goldsmith*.

82. For a discussion of small-group factions, see Brian Davey, "Fundamentalism in Communities of Belief: Closed-Mindedness and the Human Condition", 2001, available at www.bgmi.us/web/bdavey/Fundamentalism.htm . For little old ladies, see Oliver Walston, "Do You Believe in Miracles? Yes. Then You Must Be a Worshipper of Organic Food", *The Times*, 9 April 2004.

83. Antonio Damasio (1994), *Descartes' Error*, p xix.

84. Letter from John Keats to George and Thomas Keats, 1817, in (1795–1821), *Selected Letters of John Keats*, pp 60–61.

85. Mary Douglas and Baron Isherwood (1979), *The World of Goods*, chapter 3, especially p 60.

86. *Ibid*, p 62.

87. For the delight and enigma of incomprehension, see Hugh Brody (2000), *The Other Side of Eden*, p 13.

88. In Charles Taylor, "Responsibility for Self", 1976, in Gary Watson, ed. (1982), *Free Will*, pp 111–126.

89. See Douglas N. Walton (1995), *A Pragmatic Theory of Fallacy*, pp 65–67; Charles Leonard Hamblin (1970), *Fallacies*, pp 31–32; and Frans H. van Eemeren and Rob Grootendorst (1992), *Argumentation, Communication and Fallacies*, pp 103, 133, 205 and 214. These authorities all agree with Irving Copi's argument in (1953), *Introduction to Logic*, that just about any fallacy can be seen as Ignoratio elenchi in some sense. An "elenchus" is also used as the name for a form of Socratic refutation which shows the interlocutor that what he thinks he knows is inconsistent

with his other opinions—it doesn't join up. This is used as a means to spur him on to think again—as distinct from a "sophistic" argument, which aims to refute the opponent by any means. See also David Hackett Fischer (1970), *Historians' Fallacies*, p 284.

90. John Maynard Keynes (1936), *The General Theory of Employment, Interest and Money*, pp 259–260.

91. *Ibid*. For *Ignoratio elenchi*, see *Irrelevance.

92. No offence is intended to widgets, which are fictional objects.

93. Hamblin (1970), *Fallacies*, pp 31–32.

94. David Crausby MP, member of the House of Commons Defence Select Committee, in reply to General Sir Richard Dannatt's suggestion that more troops and helicopters were needed in Afghanistan. In Jonathan Oliver and Michael Smith, "Labour Clashes with Army as Afghan Death Toll Mounts", *The Sunday Times*, 12 July 2009, p 1.

95. Abraham Lincoln, President of the United States, was assassinated at the theatre on 14 April 1865, during a performance of Tom Taylor's play, *Our American Cousin*. There is no evidence that Mrs. Lincoln was ever asked that question.

96. Artemus Ward, "Lecture on the Mormons", 1863, in Edward Peron Hingston (1865), *Artemus Ward: His Travels*, J.C. Hotten.

L

1. Some critics advocate the model of "land-value taxation"—proposed in Henry George (1879), *Progress and Poverty*—which imposes prohibitive taxes on the ownership of underused, but potentially productive, land. But tax regimes of any kind are unreliable from the perspective of the Lean Economy: tax collection is likely to be among the first casualties of the *climacteric and of *informal reciprocities, with their minimal reliance on money.

2. Ebenezer Howard (1898), *To-Morrow: A Peaceful Path to Real Reform*, pp 108–109.

3. Peter Hall and Colin Ward (1998), *Sociable Cities: The Legacy of Ebenezer Howard*, p 45.

4. Population figures based on population of England and Wales in Census 1911 and Census 2001. For Mr. Polly, see H.G. Wells (1910), *The History of Mr. Polly*.

5. For suggested reading on land reclamation, see Calvin Herbert Ward, John A. Cherry, Marion R. Scalf, eds. (1997), *Subsurface Restoration*; Robert L. France (2007), *Handbook of Regenerative Landscape Design*.

6. For example, Tara Garnett supplies a tentative estimate that, if all the available land in London were turned to the production of fruit and vegetables, that could supply about one fifth of Londoners' needs, in (1999) *City Harvest*, chapter 9: "How Much Could London Produce?".

Editor's note: Fleming's notes—and my discussions with his former colleagues—evidence that he was working on figures for the land area needed per person in different contexts. However, he evidently did not complete this work to his own satisfaction.

7. Leopold Kohr (1989), *The Inner City: From Mud to Marble*, p 110.

8. Psalm 19: 5, 8. For sun and justice, see A.A. Anderson (1972), *The New Century Bible Commentary*, Eerdmans Publishing Company, commentary on Psalm 19, introduction, p 167.

9. Lord Bingham (at various times Master of the Rolls, Lord Chief Justice of England and Wales, and President of the Supreme Court) on *Start the Week*, BBC Radio 4, 26 April 2010, talking about his book (2010), *The Rule of Law*, Allen Lane.

10. Patricia Meehan (1992), *The Unnecessary War, Whitehall and the German Resistance to Hitler*, p 210.

11. See William Shawcross (2003), *The Allies: The US, Britain, Europe and the War in Iraq*. Bingham (2010) also draws emphatic attention to this misuse of the law.

12. John Locke (1690), *Two Treatises of Government*, book 2, chapter 7, p 163. Locke has Hobbes' *Leviathan* in mind in this criticism (see *Commons).

13. A "republic", as Oakeshott used it, may equally well be a monarchy or not. What matters is that its citizens have participated in the formation of its rules, which have no particular factional agenda. The texture of rules is Oakeshott's *lex*. For a summary of Oakeshott's republic and *lex*, see Robert Grant (1990), *Oakeshott*, pp 80–83.

14. For appropriate technology in building, see Simon Fairlie (1996), *Low Impact Development*; and Roland Stulz and Kiran Mukerji (1981), *Appropriate Building Materials*, Swiss Centre for Appropriate Technology (SKAT). See also the Building and Construction Catalogue at Practical Action's bookshop, at http://developmentbookshop.com .

15. Tony Gibson (1984), *Counterweight: The Neighbourhood Option*.

16. The Parker Morris report, "Homes for Today and Tomorrow", Her Majesty's Stationery Office, 1961, quoted in Jon Broome and Brian Richardson (1995), *The Self-Build Book*, p 238.

17. For details, see, e.g., The Passive House Institute at http://passiv.de/en/ .

18. See, e.g., David Thorpe (2010), *Sustainable Home Refurbishment*; or Cindy Harris and Pat Borer (2001), *The Whole House Book*.

19. Christopher Alexander, Sara Ishikawa, Murray Silverstein, et al. (1977), *A Pattern Language*.

20. *Editor's note*: After Fleming's death, Rob Hopkins, founder of the Transition movement, published his 2011 book *The Transition Companion*, modelled on the structure of books like *A Pattern Language* and *Lean Logic*, both of which he cites as key influences. David Fleming was aware of the developing project.

21. Cf. the Positive Peace movement. The view that the priority is to avoid the causes of conflict wherever possible is beyond challenge, but the emphasis on positive thinking—peace thinking—as a route away from the delusion of violence, though highly influential, could increase the likelihood of violence, if it assumes it away as a prospect and so discourages foresight. See, for example, John Wilmerding, "The Theory of Active Peace", 2009, available at www.internationalpeaceand conflict.org/forum/topics/the-theory-of-active-peace .

22. Hilary Prentice, personal communication, July 2007.

23. "Barbed wire and armed guards won't be enough . . . Smarter detection technology will be needed", Benn Tannenbaum of the American Association for the Advancement of Science, quoted in Deborah MacK-enzie, "Can We Keep Tabs on Stockpiles of Nuclear Fuel?", *New Scientist*, 21 April 2010. Nuclear waste and nanotechnology are just two of the technologies whose safety depends on fully functioning containment systems which cannot be expected to survive the *climacteric.

24. 216 BC: the Battle of Cannae; 1461: the Battle of Towton; 1644: the Battle of Marston Moor; 1813: the Battle of Leipzig; 1918: WWI Armistice.

25. Quotation from John E. Morris (1901), *The Welsh Wars of Edward I*, p 102. For details on "the arrow storm", see Andrew Ayton, "Arms, Armour and Horses", in Maurice Keen, ed. (1999), *Medieval Warfare*, pp 203–204.

26. The letters of Saint Basil (330–379), Loeb Classical Library. The quotation is from letter 123, in volume 2, pp 254–257. There were deep divisions in the church caused by the Arian heresy, and natural disasters including drought and famine (in response to which Bishop Basil set up a soup kitchen). The "Caesarea" referred to was not the one in Israel, but Kayseri in modern Turkey. Its turbulence included exposure to attack by the Persians (who had destroyed the city 100 years before) and it remained vulnerable until the Emperor Justinian I fortified it with a wall 100 years later. The first two words of the translation "Do please" have been inserted by the author in place of "Pray do", in order to avoid confusion with the second meaning of "pray" later in the passage.

27. A distinction is usually made between perfect competition (which is satisfied by criteria 1, 2, 3 and 7), and pure competition (which needs all seven). An economy "with no distortions or market failure" (Begg et al. (1984), p 407) is, in effect, pure competition. In practice, there is some flexibility in the labels. For instance, Anna Koutsoyiannis (1975), *Modern Microeconomics*, pp 154–155, requires perfect information only as a criterion for the stronger assumption of pure competition, whereas Begg et al. (1984), p 162, make it a requirement for perfect competition. The present discussion uses all seven criteria as the benchmark against which the deliberate distortions of the local Lean Economy are defined, and labels that benchmark "perfect competition".

28. See, e.g., Anna Koutsoyiannis (1975), p 497; Begg et al. (1984), pp 314–318.

29. Frank H. Hahn (1984), *Equilibrium and Macroeconomics*, p 52. The "rigorously-defined equilibrium" is the Arrow-Debreu equilibrium.

30. Actually, there is some doubt as to whether the perfectly-competitive market is workable even in theory. G.B. Richardson argues that, if everyone was equally well-informed and equally efficient, there would be excess supply and general losses. The market depends on some producers being ahead of the game: "A profit opportunity which is known by and available to everybody is available to nobody in particular." G.B. Richardson, "Equilibrium, Expectations and Information", *Economic Journal*, 69, 1959, pp 223–237. This is another encounter with the Fallacy of *Composition, and there seems to be some leeway as to how seriously to take it in this case. If all identically-equipped producers move ahead in an identical fashion, the random sweep of the grim reaper could see to it that only some of them survived, and this would not violate the requirements of perfect competition. However, D.M. Lamberton (1971), *Economics of Information and Knowledge*, Penguin, argues that, in a world in which there was certainty, competition would rapidly degenerate into monopoly. Quoted in Peter E. Earl (1983), *The Economic Imagination*, p 111.

31. The case for, and the existence of, "organisational slack" in companies was argued by Richard M. Cyert and James G. March (1963), *A Behavioural Theory of the Firm*. Organisational slack (the difference between maximum performance and acceptable performance) is not quite the same as Harvey Leibenstein's X-inefficiency (the difference between maximum performance and actual performance) but it is not necessary to distinguish between them in this discussion. See Harvey Leibenstein

(1976), *Beyond Economic Man: A New Foundation for Microeconomics*. The third essential label used in this field is "relational contracting", which allows space in the contract for tolerance and for continuing the relationship, although either or both of the parties may be going through bad times, and may therefore be unable to deliver at a competitive price. The significance of these durable relationships is discussed by Ronald Dore, "Goodwill and the Spirit of Market Capitalism", *British Journal of Sociology*, Hobhouse Memorial Lecture, 34, 1983, pp 459–482. For a technical survey, see Donald Andrew Hay and Derek J. Morris (1979), *Industrial Economics*.

32. The evidence that slack is used in companies—and of its strong theoretical presence in industrial economics—does not mean that it is universally applied. Indeed, downsizing has shifted many companies strongly in the opposite direction. But downsizing has in many cases been to companies' cost, and is being reversed. Even downsized companies recognise commitments to long-term relationships, not least because they do not have the management resources to do otherwise. Organisational slack is not (necessarily) positively correlated with the number of people (for a firm of a given size) in management.

33. Milton Friedman, "The Role of Government in Education", in Robert A. Solo, ed. (1955), *Economics and the Public Interest*. He was arguing the case for school voucher schemes which, by allowing parents to easily take their children out of a school in which there is a problem, make it unnecessary for them to face up to the problem and help the school to correct it. Quoted in Albert O. Hirschman (1970), *Exit, Voice and Loyalty*, p 16. And judgment is hard work. Hirschman quotes the economist John Hicks: "The best of all monopoly profits is a quiet life", but adds "On certain assumptions about the existence and intensity of voice, competition can afford an even quieter life than does monopoly" (p 55).

34. For a brilliant discussion of this, and especially of the role and limitations of flexible currencies in providing protection, see Jane Jacobs (1984), *Cities and the Wealth of Nations*, chapter 11.

35. Gresham's Law discusses the effect of a debased currency: bad money (e.g., coins containing cheaper metal than the precious metals that they are specified to contain) drives out good money (which is stockpiled or otherwise removed from circulation). This parallel situation, in which the market state drives out the cooperation and reciprocity of a slack economy—the tragedy of economics—is further discussed in *Economics. For more on Gresham's Law, see, for instance, www.britannica.com/topic/Greshams-law .

36. This is a core reason for *local currencies, in which prices are set on the basis of a local agreement to operate in a slack regime, despite that prices *could* be substantially lower, if all producers worked full-time and used the most efficient methods.

37. Strictly, the local retailer is a case of "monopolistic competition". Begg et al. (1984), pp 191–196.

38. Ronald Dore, "Goodwill and the Spirit of Market Capitalism", 1983, p 478.

39. Michael Common and Sigrid Stagl (2005), *Ecological Economics*, pp 325–332.

40. From Garrison Keillor (1985), *Lake Wobegon Days*, Viking Penguin, pp 141–142.

41. Aristotle's distinction between *oikonomia* (the art of good management of the place you live in), and *chrematistics* (the art of making money from the place you live in) is cited in this context in Herman E. Daly and John B. Cobb (1989), *For the Common Good*, chapter 7. See Aristotle (c.350 BC), *Politics*, book 1, chapter 10, pp 45–47.

42. The distinction between "exit" and "voice" is made in Albert O. Hirschman (1970), *Exit, Voice and Loyalty*.

43. E.F. Schumacher pointed out the ambiguous effects of roads on local economies, as summarised by Kelvin W. Willoughby (1990): "Economic planners correctly surmise that the kind of development which has brought wealth to the Western industrialised nations cannot proceed without some kind of infrastructure, such as a fast, efficient transport system. The introduction of such infrastructure in the hinterland of the South, however, tends to destroy the natural protection originally afforded the relatively 'inefficient' rural industry by the existing slow, traditional transport.", pp 85–86. The effect of transport links in weakening local economies is also pointed out in Richard Douthwaite (1996), *Short Circuit*, and in David Fleming, "Towards the Low-Output Economy: The Future that the Delors White Paper Tries Not to Face", *European Environment*, 4, 2, April 1994, pp 11–16.

44. The case of Inishbofin is described by Richard Douthwaite (1996), *Short Circuit*, pp 4–9.

45. Alfred Kahn, "The Tyranny of Small Decisions: Market Failures, Imperfections and the Limits of Economics", *Kyklos*, 1966, pp 23–46. Quoted in Fred Hirsch (1976), *Social Limits to Growth*, p 40.

46. Hirschman (1970), p 79.

47. The advantage insiders have in the case of firms is described in Assar Lindbeck and Dennis Snower (1988), *The Insider-Outsider Theory of Employment and Unemployment*—an explanation of imperfect competition expressed in wage-rigidities leading to unemployment.

48. Alan Dundes and Alessandro Falassi (1975), *La Terra in Piazza: An Interpretation of the Palio of Siena*. For a valuable discussion of loyalty, see Ronald Dore, "Goodwill and the Spirit of Market Capitalism", 1983, p 480.

49. This sense of loyalty is implied also by Émile Durkheim (1893), in *The Division of Labour in Society*, who argued that social structure consists of a network of implied contracts—i.e., something more permanent than the fleeting agreement of today's price-based transactions. This derived from the fact that the division of labour "suggests two beings mutually dependent because they are each incomplete. . . . [It is] a condition of societies' existence. Through it, or at least partially through it, their cohesion would be assured; it would determine the essential traits of their constitution. . . . [Hence] there exists a social solidarity [for which] the visible symbol is law." Quoted in Kenneth Thompson and Jeremy Tunstall, eds. (1971), *Sociological Perspectives*, pp 99 and 101.

50. For further reading, see Herman E. Daly and John B. Cobb (1989), *For the Common Good*.

51. David Ricardo (1817), *On the Principles of Political Economy and Taxation*. The earliest statement of comparative advantage was probably that of Robert Torrens' (1815), *An Essay on the External Corn Trade*, Hatchard. The essence of comparative advantage can be shown by the (notional) case of a nation that can produce everything more efficiently than can any competitor: does such a nation have any incentive to trade? Yes. It is rational for it to purchase the items which it can produce least efficiently and buy them from an overseas supplier, if this allows it to produce more of the items it produces more efficiently. The overall efficiency of the importing nation is thereby increased. This makes perfect sense in a robustly growing world economy stretched to the limit to find ways of producing more with the resources at its disposal. That economy is the inverse of the Lean Economy.

52. John Stuart Mill (1848), *Principles of Political Economy*, chapter 1. For an explanation of the treatment of land in economics, see Herman E. Daly and John B. Cobb (1989), *For the Common Good*, chapters 5 and 13.

53. Duke of Wellington quotation taken from a conversation with John Croker and his wife, 4 September 1852, recorded in (1884), *The Croker Papers: The Correspondence and Diaries of the Late Right Honourable John Wilson Croker, LL.Dm F.R.S, Secretary of the Admiralty from 1809 to 1830*, Louis J. Jennings ed., John Murray, vol 3, p 276.

The idea that perfect information is required can easily be taken by *reductio ad absurdum*: there could be no bicycles, for instance, since a cyclist rarely knows, and

never uses, the equations that enable him to stay upright. This example of the bicycle was used by Michael Polanyi and is discussed in David Bohm (1985), *Unfolding Meaning*, p 18.

See also Amitai Etzioni, "Old Chestnuts and New Spurs", in Amitai Etzioni, ed. (1995), *New Communitarian Thinking*, p 27; and David Fleming, "The Economics of Taking Care, An Evaluation of the Precautionary Principle", in David Freestone and Ellen Hey, eds. (1995), *The Precautionary Principle and International Law*.

54. The case for green growth—and especially for the labour that will be required by renewable energy—is made in The Green New Deal Group (2008), *The Green New Deal*. One of the authors, Caroline Lucas, drew connections with the Transition movement during her visit to Transition Town Wolverton, available at http://tinyurl .com/lyxcg8 . See also Geoffrey Lean, "These Green Shoots Mean Business", *The Daily Telegraph*, 13 June 2009; and *Green Economics.

55. Michael Oakeshott (1946), introduction to Thomas Hobbes' (1651), *Leviathan*, p xv.

56. Alastair MacIntyre (1981), *After Virtue*, pp 188–196.

57. Matthew Crawford (2010), *The Case for Working with Your Hands*, pp 185–186.

58. William Cobbett (1821), *Cottage Economy*, p 79.

59. George Sturt (1923), *The Wheelwright's Shop*, pp 102–104 (quotation abridged).

60. Sybil Marshall (1963), *An Experiment in Education*; John Barell (2007), *Problem-Based Learning*.

61. Marshall (1963), pp xi–xii.

62. Richard Hoggart (1995), *The Way We Live Now*, pp 22–23.

63. Keith Thomas, "The Life of Learning: Why Scholarship Still Matters—or Ought to", *Times Literary Supplement*, 7 December 2001, pp 12–13, edited version of the fifth British Academy Lecture, in *Proceedings of the British Academy*, vol 117 (quotation abridged).

64. Keith Thomas, "What Are Universities For?", *Times Literary Supplement*, 7 May 2010, pp 13–15.

65. Albert Mansbridge (1920), *An Adventure in Working-Class Education*, pp xv–xvii, pp 59 and 66 (quotation abridged, with edited punctuation).

66. David Gibson, "Poetry and the Poetic Principle", 1922, private archive.

67. See Practical Action website at http://practicalaction.org/ .

68. Douglas Adams, *Mostly Harmless*, p 98.

69. Martha Nussbaum, "Skills For Life: Why Cuts in Humanities Teaching Pose A Threat to Democracy Itself", *Times Literary Supplement*, 30 April 2010, pp 13–15 (edited extract –from Nussbaum's forthcoming book *Not for Profit*).

Editor's note: Martha Nussbaum's book since published as: *Not for Profit: Why Democracy Needs the Humanities*, Princeton University Press, 2012.

70. Wendell Berry (1977), *The Unsettling of America*, pp 43–44.

71. Home education, at www.home-education.org.uk .

72. Two notes: (1) Energy is used for everything we do—in fact, for everything that happens, so that talking about reducing or "eliminating" energy use is, from a pedantic point of view, absurd. "Energy" here refers to fuel and power in the form of oil, gas, coal, wood or electricity— not to the energy we get from food. (2) "Energy services" are the things that energy does for us: heating the house, cooking food, driving industrial processes, etc.

73. Paul Hawken, Amory B. Lovins and L. Hunter Lovins (1999), *Natural Capitalism*, chapter 6 and *passim*.

74. Hawken et al. (1999), pp 116–118 (pumping systems); pp 82–90 and 102–104 (building design and construction); pp 104–106 (appliances); pp 288–308 (city planning).

75. *Ibid*, pp 118–119.

76. See, for instance, "The Advantages of DC Transmission over AC Transmission Systems", available at www .jcmiras.net/jcm/item/86/ .

77. For the Desertec concept of electricity generated in the great deserts and transmitted to consumption centres by High Voltage DC (HVDC) cabling, see www.desertec. org/. Regarding offshore wind, the Offshore Valuation Group's study concludes that installed capacity of 406 GW is feasible. "The Offshore Valuation: A Valuation of the UK's Offshore Renewable Energy Resources", Public Interest Research Centre, 2010, available at http:// publicinterest.org.uk/offshore/ .

78. See Liz Bates, Steven Hunt, Smail Khennas and Nararya Sastrawinata, "Expanding Energy Access in Developing Countries: The Role of Mechanical Power", Practical Action Publishing, 2009. This valuable but brief survey gives many examples of mechanical power in practice, setting it in the context of conditions where electricity is wholly or substantially beyond the community's reach.

An intermediate energy technology, in the sense of being midway between a functioning electricity grid and mechanical power, would take the form of local minigrids. Recommended reading: Yacob Mulugetta, Alison Doig, Simon Dunnett, Tim Jackson, Smail Khennas and Kavita Rai, eds. (2005), *Energy For Rural Livelihoods: A Framework for Sustainable Decision Making*, Practical Action; Joy Clancy and Lucy Redeby (2000), *Electricity in Households and Micro-Enterprises*, Intermediate Technology Publications; and Teodoro Sanchez (2006),

Electricity Services in Remote Rural Communities: The Small Enterprise Model, Practical Action Publishing.

79. Nicolas Lampkin (1990), *Organic Farming*, chapters 3 and 5. Some organic holdings without livestock also succeed in maintaining their soil quality. The best-known example of this is Iain and Lin Tolhurst's organic gardens at Whitchurch in Berkshire, UK.

80. Lampkin (1990), chapter 3. Alina Kabata-Pendias and Henryk Pendias (1984), *Trace Elements in Soils and Plants*.

81. David Rimmer, "Ultimate Interface", *New Scientist*, 14 November 1998.

82. Walter James, more commonly referred to as Lord Northbourne (1940), *Look to the Land*, pp 58–60 (quotation abridged, italics added).

83. These five points are based on the summary by Lawrence Woodward in his introduction to Lady Eve Balfour (1943), *The Living Soil*, p xvi.

84. Albert Howard (1940), *An Agricultural Testament*, p 24.

85. Lampkin (1990), chapter 2; Robert E. White (1979), *Principles and Practice of Soil Science: The Soil as a Natural Resource*, chapter 10; Jean-Michel Gobat, Michel Aragno and Willy Matthey (2004), *The Living Soil: Fundamentals of Soil Science and Soil Biology*, chapter 16.

Editor's note: David Fleming's former colleague Judith Thornton offers the following comment: Increasing numbers of bacteria as well as fungi are now recognised to be important for soil and plant health, forming symbiotic relationships with the plants they colonise. These organisms are known as endophytes.

86. Howard (1940), p 25. For more detail on mycorrhiza, see Arlene J. Tugel, Ann M. Lewandowski and Deb Happe-vonArb, eds. (2000), *Soil Biology Primer*, Soil and Water Conservation Society.

87. International Federation of Organic Agriculture Movements, www.ifoam.org/ .

88. Lady Eve Balfour (1943), *The Living Soil*, p 21.

89. Lady Eve Balfour, "Towards a Sustainable Agriculture: The Living Soil", paper given at a conference of the International Federation of Organic Agricultural Movements (IFOAM), 1977, p 7, reprinted in Andrew Dobson, ed. (1991), *The Green Reader: Essays Toward a Sustainable Society*. Also available at https://tinyurl.com/nnc9dyo (quotation slightly abridged).

90. Balfour (1943), pp 112.

91. Key texts on permaculture include: Bill Mollison and David Holmgren (1978), *Permaculture One: A Perennial Agriculture for Human Settlements*; Bill Mollison (1988), *Permaculture: A Designers' Manual*; David Holmgren (2002), *Permaculture: Principles and Pathways Beyond Sustainability*;

Patrick Whitefield (1996), *How to Make a Forest Garden*; Patrick Whitefield (2004), *The Earth Care Manual*.

92. Robert A. de J. Hart (1991), *Forest Gardening*, pp 120–121.

93. The full set of principles can be found in almost any basic text on permaculture, and were originally set out in David Holmgren (2002), *Permaculture: Principles and Pathways Beyond Sustainability*.

94. Hart (1991), pp 129–130.

95. We need, really, to go back to the Latin meaning of the word: *fores* outside—i.e., beyond the limits of cities and well-behaved agriculture, to outlandish places inhabited by wild beasts, experimental permaculturists, etc.

96. See UN Food and Agriculture Organisation, at http://tinyurl.com/ohjld8r .

97. Hopper is cited in Richard Gray, "Rare Crops Needed to Tackle World Hunger", *Telegraph*, 28 February 2009.

   Editor's note: David Fleming's former colleague Judith Thornton highly recommends John Warren (2015), *The Nature of Crops: How We Came To Eat The Plants We Do*, CABI Publishing, as a valuable supplementary resource on this topic, published after Fleming's death.

98. Patrick Whitefield (2004), *The Earth Care Manual*, pp 246–253.

99. John Jeavons (1995), *How to Grow More Vegetables Than You Ever Thought Possible on Less Land Than You Could Possibly Imagine*.

100. Personal communication.

   Editor's note: When measuring mass, Fleming uses the British English term "tonne". This is equivalent to the American English term "metric ton", and means a mass of 1,000 kg or approximately 2204.6 pounds. Note that this is different from *both* the American English "ton" (aka "short ton") of 2,000 pounds, *and* the British English "ton" (aka "long ton" or "imperial ton") of 2,240 pounds. To approximately convert a mass given in tonnes to the same mass given in American English tons, multiply the figure by 1.1023. To approximately convert a mass given in tonnes to the same mass given in British English tons, multiply the figure by 0.9842.

101. Charles Dowding (2007), *Organic Gardening*, p 15.

102. The higher food production per acre of small-scale, labour-intensive growing is long-established. See, for instance, Peter Rossett, "The Multiple Functions and Benefits of Small-Scale Agriculture", The Institute for Food and Development Policy, 1999; Gershon Feder, "The Relationship between Farm Size and Farm Productivity", *Journal of Development Economics*, 18, 1985, pp 297–313. Or indeed 2008's UN-backed International Assessment of International Science and Technology for Development (IAASTD) report—the result of four year's work by over 400 scientists and the biggest study of its kind ever undertaken.

103. Rob Hopkins (2008), *The Transition Handbook*, pp 135 and 141.

104. Patrick Whitefield (2004), p 4.

105. Patrick Whitefield (1996), *How to Make a Forest Garden*, p 5.

106. *Ibid*, p 12.

107. Tamzin Pinkerton and Rob Hopkins (2009), *Local Food: How to Make it Happen in Your Community*.

108. *Ibid*, chapter 3.

109. *Ibid*, chapter 4.

110. *Ibid*, chapter 5. For landshare, see www.landshare.net .

111. Pinkerton and Hopkins (2009), chapter 6. For Incredible Edible Todmorden, see www.incredible-edible-todmorden.co.uk/ .

112. Pinkerton and Hopkins (2009), chapter 7.

113. *Ibid*, chapter 8.

114. *Ibid*, chapter 9.

115. *Ibid*, chapter 10.

116. For ideas about the treatment of human waste in a closed-loop system see, for instance, Nick Grant, Mark Moodie and Chris Weedon (1996), *Sewage Solutions: Answering the Call of Nature*; Peter Harper and Louise Halestrap (1999), *Lifting the Lid: An Ecological Approach to Toilet Systems*; Patrick Whitefield (2004), *The Earth Care Manual*, chapter 5; and Lyla Mehta and Synne Movik (2010), *Shit Matters*, Practical Action Publishing.

117. For the anthropology of mealtimes, see Martin Jones (2007), *Feast: Why Humans Share Food*; for conversations close to heaven, see Catherine Blyth (2009), *The Art of Conversation*, p 4 and *passim*.

118. Most of the cost of medicine is due to having failed to maintain health in the first place. The growth in National Health Service funding will take spending to a minimum 10.6 percent of GDP by 2022, according to the Wanless report. Derek Wanless (2002), *Securing Our Future Health: Taking a Long-Term View*, Her Majesty's Treasury.

119. Theo Colborn, Dianne Dumanoski and John Peterson Myers (1996), *Our Stolen Future*. A list of the main chemicals involved is contained in the Wingspread Consensus Statement, reprinted in the Appendix on page 253. Substantial quantities of PCBs, insecurely contained, are lost in the oceans whenever a PCB-cooled transformer is lost there. For example, those on board the Piper Alpha oil platform which sank in the North Sea in 1988.

120. Colborn et al. (1996), *passim*, especially chapters 10–13.

121. Colborn et al. (1996), pp 203, 238.

122. See John Busby, "Rip van Winkel Wakes", 14 September 2006, available at www.after-oil.co.uk/winkel.htm .

123. Paul Clayton (2001), *Health Defence*, pp 21 and 26–27.

124. Robert McCarrison, "Diseases of Faulty Nutrition", 1927, reprinted in Robert McCarrison and Hugh M. Sinclair (1953), *Nutrition and Health*, pp 96–106.

125. Cheshire Panel Committee, "Medical Testament: Nutrition, Soil Fertility and the National Health", *British Medical Journal*, Supplement, 22 March 1939, p 157, available at http://journeytoforever.org/farm_library/medtest/medtest.html .

126. Margaret Ashwell, ed. (1993), *McCance and Widdowson: A Scientific Partnership of 60 Years*. Other writers in this early tradition include Weston A.V. Price (1939), *Nutrition and Physical Degeneration*, and Guy Theodore Wrench (1938), *The Wheel of Health*.

127. For link between cholesterol in the body and the fat composition of the diet, see, for example, Ancel Keys et al., "Epidemiological Studies Relating to Coronary Heart Disease: Characteristics of Men aged 40–59 in Seven Countries", *Acta Medica Scandinavica*, Supplement 460, 1996; Ancel Keys and Margaret Keys (1959), *Eat Well and Stay Well*. There are reservations about the quality of Keys' research results, but the central argument is borne out by more recent findings.

   For lack of fibre and excess sugar, see H.C. Trowell, Denis P. Burkitt and K.W. Heaton, eds. (1985), *Dietary Fibre, Fibre-Depleted Foods and Disease*; Andrew Stanway (1976), *Fibre in The Diet: Taking the Rough with the Smooth*; T.L. Cleave (1974), *The Saccharine Disease*; John Yudkin (1972), *Pure, White and Deadly*; Audrey Eyton (1982), The *F-Plan Diet*.

128. The recommendation that people should cut down on their consumption of fat and that they should eat at least 400 grams of fruit and vegetables per day (of which at least 30 grams should be in the form of pulses, nuts and seeds) was made by the World Health Organisation in, for instance, "Diet, Nutrition and the Prevention of Chronic Diseases", Technical Report Series 797, 1990.

129. Royal College of General Practitioners (1993), *Better Living, Better Life*. Royal College of Physicians of London, "Medical Aspects of Exercise, Benefits and Risks", Report, 1991.

130. Robert D. Putnam (2000), *Bowling Alone*, pp 327 and 329.

131. *Ibid*, p 327.

132. *Ibid*, p 327.

133. *Ibid*, p 331.

134. And informal funds. Local fundraising for local hospitals, crucial to hospital capital and income until the mid-twentieth century, has almost entirely dried up.

135. This description of Lancashire, around 1780, can be found in Andrew Ure (1836), *The Cotton Manufacture of Great Britain*, Charles Knight, vol 1, pp 191–192 (quotation abridged). See also Kirkpatrick Sale, "The Achievements of General Ludd", *The Ecologist*, vol 29, 5, August/September 1999, pp 310–313.

136. Ure (1836), p xv.

137. See Rosemary O'Day (1994), *The Family and Family Relationships 1500–1900*, pp 221–222.

138. For a history of Luddism, its context and significance, see Kirkpatrick Sale (1995), *Rebels Against the Future*.

139. *Ibid*, chapter 2. For "moral earthquake", see Charlotte Brontë (1849), *Shirley*, pp 29–30.

140. For Ned Ludd and silk workers, see Christopher Hibbert (1987), *The English: A Social History, 1066–1945*, pp 477–487.

141. Peter Kropotkin (1899), *Fields, Factories and Workshops Tomorrow*, pp 154–158, and Colin Ward's commentary, p 41 (quotation abridged, italics in original).

142. Patrick Geddes (1915), *Cities in Evolution*, chapter 4, "The Paleotechnic and the Neotechnic", and chapter 6, "Ways to the Neotechnic City". See also Colin Ward (1991), *Influences: Voices of Creative Dissent*, pp 103–110.

143. Ralph Borsodi (1933), *Flight from the City*, pp 10–15.

144. *Ibid*, p 15.

145. *Ibid*, p 15. Borsodi's calculations of costs, including labour costs, are set out in chapter 2.

146. Jan de Vries (2008), *The Industrious Revolution: Consumer Behaviour and the Household Economy, 1650 to the Present*.

147. Colin Ward (1993), *New Town, Home Town: The Lessons of Experience*, p 129.

148. Ministry of Agriculture and Fisheries (1943), *Home Curing of Bacon and Hams*, Her Majesty's Stationery Office, citing Cato the Censor, *De Agri Cultura*, 162, quoted in James Williams (1971), *Give Me Yesterday*, pp 55–56.

149. William Cobbett (1821), *Cottage Economy*, pp 12, 20 (quotation abridged).

150. Fritjof Capra (1996), *The Web of Life*, p 213. See also Fritjof Capra (1982), *The Turning Point*, p 293.

151. H.J. Massingham, "Norfolk", 1950, and "Remembrance", 1941, in (1882–1952), *A Mirror of England: An Anthology of the Writings of H.J. Massingham*, pp 137 and 191.

152. Slow Food Manifesto, available at www.slowfood.com (quotation abridged).

153. John Stewart Collis (1973), *The Worm Forgives the Plough*, pp 209–210.

154. See, for instance, May McKisack (1959), *The Oxford History of England, Volume V: The Fourteenth Century, 1307–1399*, pp 201–203; Christopher Hibbert (1987), *The English: A Social History, 1066–1945*, p 147.

155. Hibbert (1987), pp 141–143.

156. Guy Geltner (2008), *The Medieval Prison*.

157. Maurice Powicke (1953), *The Thirteenth Century 1216–1307*, p 368. The quotation is from chapter 17 of the First Statute of Westminster (abridged and slightly edited).

158. McKisack (1959), pp 201–202.

159. McKisack (1959), p 202, citing Sir Edward Coke's (1628–1644), *Institutes of the Lawes of England*, Societie of Stationers.

160. John Steven Watson (1960), *The Reign of George III 1760–1815*, p 47.

161. Powicke (1953), p 367.

162. H.J. Massingham, "The English Countryman", 1942, in (1882–1952), *A Mirror of England: An Anthology of the Writings of H.J. Massingham*, pp 65–66 (quotation abridged).

163. George Bourne (1912), *Change in the Village*, pp 77–78. Note that George Bourne is a pseudonym used by George Sturt, who later wrote (1923), *The Wheelwright's Shop*. An extract from that book appears in *Lean Education.

164. Kenneth Geiser (2001), *Materials Matter*, chapter 12. Mark R. Finlay, "Old Efforts at New Uses: A Brief History of Chemurgy and the American Search for Biobased Materials", *Journal of Industrial Ecology*, 7, 3–4, 2003, pp 33–46.

165. Geiser (2001), p 263.

166. Geiser (2001), pp 260–262; Mark R. Finlay, "Old Efforts at New Uses: A Brief History of Chemurgy and the American Search for Biobased Materials".

167. William J. Hale (1934), *The Farm Chemurgic: Farmward the Star of Destiny Lights our Way*, p 142.

168. Mark R. Finlay, "Old Efforts at New Uses: A Brief History of Chemurgy and the American Search for Biobased Materials", pp 34–39.

169. John S. Ferrell, "George Washington Carver and Henry Ford: Pioneers of Zero Waste", 2002, available at www.zerowaste.org/publications/PIONEERS.PDF .

170. Geiser (2001), chapter 11; Paul Hawken, Amory B. Lovins and L. Hunter Lovins (1999), *Natural Capitalism*, chapter 4.

171. See Janine Benyus (1997), *Biomimicry*, especially chapter 4.

172. Geiser (2001), p 304.

173. For a discussion of amateur, garden-shed skills taking a critical role at a time of national emergency, see Francis Spufford (2003), *The Backroom Boys*. For time-affluence in the Lean Economy, see *Leisure.

174. Geiser (2001), pp 224–22; Paul Hawken, Amory B. Lovins and L. Hunter Lovins (1999), *Natural Capitalism*, p 77.

175. See, for instance, Patrick Whitefield (2004), *The Earth-Care Manual*, pp 42–46.

176. For a discussion of the eco-efficiency of manual skills and advanced technology, relative to that of conventional industrial-scale systems, see Oliviero Bernardini and Riccardo Galli, "Dematerialization: Long Term Trends in the Intensity of Use of Materials and Energy", *Futures*, vol 25, 4, 1993, pp 431–448. Their work is based on Wilfred Malenbaum (1978), *World Demand for Raw Materials in 1985 and 2000*.

177. H.J. Massingham, "The English Countryman", 1942, in (1882–1952), *A Mirror of England: An Anthology of the Writings of H.J. Massingham*, p 66.

178. The key source on lean production is James P. Womack, Daniel T. Jones and Daniel Roos (1990), *The Machine that Changed the World*.

179. See, for instance, Joseph J. Fucini and Suzy Fucini (1990), *Working for the Japanese: Inside Mazda's American Auto Plant*.

180. For a summary history of social security in the United Kingdom, see James Bartholomew (2004), *The Welfare State We're In*, chapter 2.

181. The main source on lean thinking is James P. Womack and Daniel T. Jones (1996), *Lean Thinking*. See also John Seddon (2003), *Freedom from Command and Control*, and James P. Womack and Daniel T. Jones (2005), *Lean Solutions*.

182. Womack and Jones (1996), pp 16–19; quotation from p 353.

183. See John Elkington (1997), *Cannibals with Forks*. Simplicity seems to be yet further distanced by Elkington's development of that principle to seven "dimensions" of sustainable business management—requiring companies to change the way they think about their whole standing in the community now and in the future, before they can make serious progress with the triple bottom line itself.

184. Womack and Jones (1996), p 351.

185. For a summary of the principle of pull, see Womack and Jones (1996), pp 24–25.

186. For more on "intrinsic advantage", see *Incentives.

187. Rob Hopkins (2008), *The Transition Handbook*, pp 127–128 (extract slightly edited). See also Rob Hopkins, "The Lessons from Kinsale: Lesson 4—Designing in Flexibility", 2005, http://transitionculture.org/2005/12/16/the-lessons-from-kinsale-part-four/ ; and the principles of 'Action Learning'.

188. The example of standard practice in the airline industry was suggested by Jennifer O'Brien, personal communication.

189. H.C.B. Rogers (1961), *Turnpike to Iron Road*; and Albert C. Leighton (1972), *Transport and Communication in Early Medieval Europe AD 500–1100*.

190. The Road Users' Alliance estimates the UK motorway network at 2,361 miles (Road File 2008/9). Lane width is about 3.65m. Assuming an average of eight lanes per motorway, plus a margin equivalent to two lanes either side, the surface area covered by motorways in the UK is approximately 53 square miles.

191. For "pathetic misconceptions", see David St John Thomas (1963), *The Rural Transport Problem*, pp 166–168. For an analysis of the perverse economics of rail closures, see David Wiggins and Mayer Hillman, "Railways, Settlement and Access", in Anthony Barnett and Roger Scruton, eds. (1998), *Town and Country*.

192. *A History of the World in 100 Objects*, episode 26 (Oxus Chariot Model), BBC Radio 4, broadcast 22 February 2010, available at http://tinyurl.com/2u7cd6u .

193. The author read this quotation in approximately 1960, and has lost the source. If any reader could supply it, this would be appreciated.

    Editor's note: I share David's curiosity about the source!

194. Ivan Illich (1974), *Energy and Equity*, p 88.

195. John Maynard Keynes, "Economic Possibilities for our Grandchildren", 1930, in (1931), *Essays in Persuasion*, pp 321–332.

196. Quoted in Richard Easterlin, "Does Economic Growth Improve the Human Lot?", in Paul A. David and Melvin Warren Reder, eds. (1974), *Nations and Households in Economic Growth*, pp 89–125.

197. For the Prisoner's Dilemma see for example David Begg, Stanley Fischer and Rüdiger Dornbusch (1984), *Economics*, p 201; Anna Koutsoyiannis, (1975), *Modern Microeconomics*, pp 412–413.

198. Gail Sheehy (1976), *Passages: Predictable Crises of Adult Life*, Bantam Books, quoted in Charles Taylor (1991), *The Ethics of Authenticity*, p 44.

199. See *The Book of Common Prayer*. Among commentaries, see Peter Mullen, ed. (2000), *The Real Common Worship*; Charles Hefling and Cynthia Shattuck (2006), *The Oxford Guide to The Book of Common Prayer*.

200. Andrew Mawson (2008), *The Social Entrepreneur*, p 17. The Bromley by Bow Centre is discussed in *Presence.

201. The classical and clearest account of living standards is in Wilfred Beckerman (1968), *An Introduction to National Income Analysis*.

202. Gresham's Law: bad money (e.g., coins containing cheaper metal than the precious metals that they are specified to contain) drives out good money (which is stockpiled or otherwise removed from circulation). For more on Gresham's Law, see, for instance, www .britannica.com/topic/Greshams-law .

    Imagine that the 'good money' of Logs coins or notes could be cut up into ten parts, each of which retained the same purchasing power of a full Log. These parts might be called 'pounds'. Soon enough, there would be no Logs in circulation.

203. Purchasing power parity is discussed in standard macroeconomic textbooks, such as Robert J. Barro (1984), *Macroeconomics*, MIT Press.

204. For a crystal-clear explanation of how this works, see Jane Jacobs (1984), *Cities and the Wealth of Nations*, chapter 11; see also summary in *Nation ⟩ Currency.

205. For an extended description of Transition currencies and how to make them happen, see Noel Longhurst, "The first Transition currency: the Totnes Pound", chapter 11 of Peter North (2010), *Local Money: How to Make it Happen in Your Community*, pp 147–160.

206. See Camden Letslink, at http://letslink.org/camden /introduction.htm .

207. See Letslink, at www.letslinkuk.net .

208. Josh Ryan-Collins, Lucie Stephens and Anna Coote, "The New Wealth of Time: How Timebanking Helps People Build Better Public Services", New Economics Foundation, 2008. See also Edgar S. Cahn (2000), *No More Throw-Away People*; and Edgar S. Cahn (2006), *Priceless Money: Banking Time for Changing Times*, TimeBanks USA, available at http://coreeconomy.com/ .

209. For an inspiring introduction to time banking, see the website of the Holy Cross Centre Trust in London at www.hcct.org.uk . See also North (2010), pp 88–102.

210. Personal communication.

211. For a concise summary of Ithaca Hours and how they work, see Paul Glover, "Grassroots Economics", 1995, available at www.context.org/ICLIB/IC41/Glover.htm . See also North (2010), pp 103–110.

212. For alternative currencies, see Stephen DeMeulenaere, "Alternative Currencies in Argentina", 2001, available at http://archive.sustecweb.co.uk/past/sustec93/93-14.html . For a concise and clear introduction to the Argentine economic crisis (1998–2002), see http://tinyurl.com/kc78dhy .

213. This entry is not a comprehensive review of local currency schemes. One significant omission is the model of German regional currencies. For a detailed briefing, with special emphasis on practical advice on how to set them up, see North (2010). See also Richard Douthwaite (1996), *Short Circuit*. For a *tour-de-force* in the form of a comprehensive review of alternative currencies in all their variety, see David Boyle (1999), *Funny Money*.

214. See Colin Hines (2000), *Localization: A Global Manifesto*; Rob Hopkins (2008), *The Transition Handbook*; Shaun Chamberlin (2009), *The Transition Timeline*.

215. For the "relocalisation" movement, see the Post Carbon Institute website at www.postcarbon.org/relocalize/ .

216. Cf. Mark Mazower (1998), *Dark Continent: Europe's Twentieth Century*.

217. Olga Semyonova Tian-Shanskaia (1993), *Village Life in Late Tsarist Russia*.

218. Geoffrey Hosking (2001), *Russia and the Russians*, pp 16–18.

219. *Ibid*, p 17.

220. For an account of insult-matches as a play form in traditional societies, see Johan Huizinga (1949), *Homo Ludens*, pp 86–91. Prince Hal and Falstaff are at it in Shakespeare's (c.1597), *Henry IV, Part 1*: "'Sblood, you staveling, you eel-skin, you dried neat's tongue, you bull's pizzle, you stock-fish . . . you vile standing tuck!", act II, scene 4.

221. Rupert Brooke's poem, "The Old Vicarage, Grantchester", 1912 is widely available online, e.g., at http://poetrysociety .org.uk/poems/the-old-vicarage-grantchester/ .

222. C.S. Holling, Lance H. Gunderson and Garry D. Peterson, "Sustainability and Panarchies", in Lance H. Gunderson and C.S. Holling, eds. (2002), *Panarchy*, chapter 3.

M

1. Jack Grimston and Dipesh Gadher, "Youngsters Losing Hand Co-ordination: Children Are Struggling at School Because They Don't Know if They Are Left- or Right-handed", *The Sunday Times*, 9 November 2008; based on Madeleine Portwood (2000), *Understanding Developmental Dyspraxia*.

2. As the title of his book suggests, Aric Sigman is here referring mainly to television in (2005), *Remotely Controlled: How Television is Damaging Our Lives*. For coordination, see Madeleine Portwood (2000), *Understanding Developmental Dyspraxia*; a summary can be found in Jack Grimston and Dipesh Gadher, "Youngsters Losing Hand Co-ordination: Children Are Struggling at School Because They Don't Know if They Are Left- or Right-handed", 2008.

3. William J. Baumol, "The Macroeconomics of Unbalanced Growth: The Anatomy of Urban Crisis", *American Economic Review*, 57, 1967, pp 415–426.

4. Vandana Shiva, closing address, Soil Association Conference, Bristol, 25–27 January 2007.

5. John Ruskin (1853), *The Stones of Venice*, vol 2, cited in Fiona MacCarthy (1994), *William Morris*, p 71. MacCarthy also points out Eric Gill's and Raymond Williams' support for this point.

6. For details on *die Tücke des Objekts*, see Friedrich Theodor Vischer (1878), *Auch Einer, Eine Reise Bekanntschaft* (1923 Deutsche Kurzschrift Verlag edition). For modern appreciations of working with your hands, see Matthew Crawford (2010), *The Case for Working with Your Hands*, and John-Paul Flintoff (2010), *Sew Your Own*.

7. The Labour Party, "National Service for Health", pamphlet, 1943, p 14.

8. The concept of the Great Transformation in this sense was suggested by Karl Polanyi (1944), *The Great Transformation*.

9. Suggested reading: E.F. Schumacher (1973), *Small is Beautiful*; E.F. Schumacher (1969), "Healthy Development", in (1997), *This I Believe and Other Essays*; and Jonathon Porritt (2005), *Capitalism as if the World Matters*.

10. The key source for availability biases is Daniel Kahneman, Paul Slovic and Amos Tversky, eds. (1982), *Judgment Under Uncertainty: Heuristics and Biases*, especially the introduction by Amos Tversky and Daniel Kahneman, pp 3–22. They are discussed in a more accessible way in Stuart Sutherland (1992), *Irrationality*, pp 153, 176 and 189, and are related in some way to most other fallacies (see the Beginner's Guide to How to Cheat in an Argument on page xxiii of this book, and the entry on *Fallacies). For interpreting statistics, see, for example, Timothy C. Urdan (2001), *Statistics in Plain English*.

11. For metamorphosis, see Judith K. Krabbe (1989), *The Metamorphosis of Apuleius*; Franz Kafka (1915), *Metamorphosis*; and Eugène Ionesco's 1959 play *Rhinoceros*. In translations of Kafka's *Metamorphosis*, "Ungeziefer" is given variously as dung-beetle or cockroach. Cockroaches would seem to be more suited to urban bureaucracy.

12. André Gide's resentment of social convention (in common with Balzac, Flaubert, Sartre and Nathalie Sarraute) is discussed by J.C. Davies (1995), in his introduction to the translation of Gide's *Les Faux-Monnayeurs*, p 27. For a critique of sincerity, see Lionel Trilling (1971), *Sincerity and Authenticity*.

13. Leading article, "Crude Thoughts: Oil Price Fears Are Exaggerated", *The Times*, 13 May 2004.

14. See Catherine Pickstock, "Liturgy, Art and Politics", *Modern Theology*, vol 16, 2, 2000, pp 159–190; and William Norman Pittenger (1969), *Alfred North Whitehead*, p 16.

15. Lee Smolin (2006), *The Trouble with Physics*, pp 204 and 148.

16. Antoine de Saint-Exupéry (1943), *Lettre à un Otage*, part 4, pp 39–45, (quotation abridged, with omissions after paragraphs 4, 6 and 7). Thank you to Viv Scott for drawing my attention to this.

17. For Alfred North Whitehead's discussion of misplaced concreteness and the application of the concept in economics, see Herman E. Daly and John B. Cobb (1989), *For the Common Good*, part 1.

18. François Rabelais (c.1532–1564), *Gargantua and Pantagruel*, book 4, p 562.

19. Personal communication.

20. Steven Johnson (2001), *Emergence*, pp 74 and 224.

21. Edgeworth's description is summarised in Jenny Uglow (2002), *The Lunar Men: The Friends Who Made the Future*.

22. Lisa Jardine, *In Our Time—the Royal Society and British Science*, Episode 1, BBC Radio 4, broadcast 4 January 2010.

23. For non-centralised intelligence, see Chip Ward, "Is the Crown of Creation a Dunce Cap?", 2008, in David R. Keller, ed. (2010), *Environmental Ethics*, pp 143–146 (especially p 144).

24. Cf. Gerard Manley Hopkins' poem, "To RB", 1918. Widely available online, e.g., at www.bartleby.com /122/51.html .

25. For a detailed discussion of the isolation—and the consequences for reciprocity and social bonding—brought about by money, see Seaford (2004), chapter 14.

26. Glyn Davies (1994), *History of Money*, p 56.

27. Davies (1994), pp 60–51; Henry S. Kim, "Archaic coinage as evidence for the use of money", in Andrew Meadows and Kirsty Shipton, eds. (2001), *Money and its Uses in the Ancient Greek World*, p 10.

28. Richard Seaford (2004), *Money and the Early Greek Mind*, pp 16–20.

29. Richard Seaford, "Money makes the (Greek) world go round", *The Times Literary Supplement*, 17 June 2009.

30. Davies (1994), p 47.

31. Here Seaford (2004), pp 161 and 89–90, summarises lines from the elegiac verse (*Theognidea*), collected under the name of Theognis.

32. Midas is cited in this context by Seaford (2004), p 296.

33. For GMOs, see Carl Mortished, "Frankenstein Foods Are Not Monsters", *The Times*, 9 January 2008.

34. Richard G. Wilkinson and Kate Pickett (2009), *The Spirit Level*.

35. Wilkinson and Pickett (2009), p 57.

36. Andrew Mawson (2008), *The Social Entrepreneur*, p 139. Mawson's work at the Bromley by Bow Centre is discussed in *Presence.

37. *Ibid*, pp 144–145.

38. The first eight forms of *muda* are listed in James P. Womack and Daniel T. Jones (1996), *Lean Thinking*, p 355. The first seven were first listed by Taiichi Ohno (1978), *Toyota Production System: Beyond Large-Scale Production*. The eighth was added by Womack and Jones. The remainder are added by the author.

39. Womack and Jones (1996), p 24.

40. For an extended discussion of muda, see Paul Hawken, Amory B. Lovins and L. Hunter Lovins (1999), *Natural Capitalism*, chapter 7.

41. See, for example, Peter Hunter Blair (1970), *The World of Bede*, p 25.

42. Estimates for the number of deaths in the Partition vary. "One million" comes from Stanley Wolpert (1977), *A New History of India*.

43. Helena Norberg-Hodge (1991), *Ancient Futures*, pp 128–130.

44. For an extended discussion of this, see William Stanton (2003), *The Rapid Growth of Human Populations 1750–2000*, pp 48–53, 76–90, and passim.

45. Walter Laqueur (2007), *The Last Days of Europe*, pp 50–51.

46. Amitai Etzioni (1993), *The Spirit of Community*, pp 14 and 218.

47. Tim Lott, "White, working class—and threatened with extinction", *Independent on Sunday*, 9 March 2008, and *You and Yours*, BBC Radio 4, 11th March 2008.

48. Ton Schouten and Patrick Moriarty (2003), *Community Water, Community Management*, p 148.

49. Jonathan Sacks (2007), *The Home We Build Together: Recreating Society*. See also David Miller's comments in a review of Sacks' book in, "A Cake or a Covenant?", *The Times Literary Supplement*, 11 January 2008, pp 26–27.

50. Janis B. Alcorn and Victor M. Toledo, "Resilient Resource Management in Mexico's Forest Systems", in Fikret Berkes and Carl Folke, eds. (1998), *Linking Social and Ecological Systems*, p 218. This research is derived from extensive studies of tenurial systems in Mexico and is not applied to—nor implied by the authors as being relevant to—the subject of multiculturalism in developed countries. The notion that such a connection might usefully be made is the responsibility of the present writer.

51. *Ibid*, p 219, italics added.

52. Cf. Jonathan Sacks (2002), *The Dignity of Difference*.

53. For a discussion of "common sense", see Alain de Botton (2000), *The Consolations of Philosophy*. W.H. McNeil uses myth in this sense, too: it is "humankind's substitute for instinct" in, "The Care and Repair of Public Myth", *Foreign Affairs*, 6, 1, 1982, quoted in Donald N. Michael, "Learning in Turbulent Human Ecology", in Lance H. Gunderson, C.S. Holling and Stephen S. Light, eds. (1995), *Barriers and Bridges to the Renewal of Ecosystems and Institutions*, pp 461–485.

N

1. For an introduction to nanotechnology, see Richard Booker and Earl Boysen (2005), *Nanotechnology for Dummies*; Mark Ratner and Daniel Ratner (2002), *Nanotechnology: A Gentle Introduction to the Next Big Idea*; and The Royal Society, "Nanoscience and Nanotechnologies: Opportunities and Uncertainties", 2004, available at www.nanotec.org.uk/finalReport.htm .

2. The Royal Society, "Nanoscience and Nanotechnologies: Opportunities and Uncertainties", 2004, chapter 3.

3. Center for Responsible Nanotechnology, "Benefits of Molecular Manufacturing", available at www.crnano .org/benefits.htm .

4. Estimate by Richard Smalley is cited in Ratner and Ratner (2002), pp 54–55.

5. Ratner and Ratner (2002), pp 49–55.

6. K. Eric Drexler (1986), *Engines of Creation*, p 14. Italics in second paragraph added.

7. The Royal Society, "Nanoscience and Nanotechnologies: Opportunities and Uncertainties", 2004, chapter 4, p 28.

8. *Ibid*.

9. Chris Phoenix and Eric Drexler, "Safe Exponential Manufacturing", *Nanotechnology*, 15, 2004, pp 869–872. A self-confessed hacker adds a comment in the discussion at the end of Phoenix and Drexler's paper: "To say that 'runaway' replicating nano-machines isn't very likely is stupid, in my opinion. Why? Because there are people out there, like me, who desire such a scenario to happen. And we will make it happen eventually." Available at www.foresight.org/nanodot/?p=1556 .

10. Ray Kurzweil, "Testimony of Ray Kurzweil on the Societal Implications of Nanotechnology", 2003, available at www.kurzweilai.net/testimony-of-ray-kurzweil-on-the -societal-implications-of-nanotechnology .

11. Center for Responsible Nanotechnology, "Managing Magic", available at www.crnano.org/magic.htm .

12. Chris Phoenix and Mike Treder, "Safe Utilisation of Advanced Nanotechnology", 2003, available at www .crnano.org/safe.htm .

13. Chris Phoenix and Mike Treder, "Safe Utilisation of Advanced Nanotechnology", 2003.

14. Bill Joy, "Why the Future Doesn't Need Us", Wired, April 2000, available at www.primitivism.com/future.htm .

15. Ray Kurzweil, "Testimony of Ray Kurzweil on the Societal Implications of Nanotechnology", 2003.
    Editor's note: In 2014, Kurzweil was appointed as Google's Director of Engineering.

16. *Ibid*.

17. See, for instance, *ibid*.

18. *Ibid*.

19. Bill Joy, "Why the Future Doesn't Need Us", Wired, April 2000.

20. Carl Sagan (1994), *Pale Blue Dot*, Random House, cited in Joy (2000), pp 16–17.

21. Ray Kurzweil, "Testimony of Ray Kurzweil on the Societal Implications of Nanotechnology", 2003.

22. Center for Responsible Nanotechnology: "The Need for Early Development", available at www.crnano.org /early.htm .

23. Bill Joy, "Why the Future Doesn't Need Us", *Wired*, April 2000.

24. From sonnet 62, in William Shakespeare (1609), *Sonnets*.

25. See Christopher Lasch (1979), *The Culture of Narcissism*.

26. This derivation of Creed is discussed in Karen Armstrong (1993), *A History of God*.

27. Cassandra warned the Trojans that taking the Trojan Horse into the city would turn out badly, but was not believed. She was loved by Apollo and given the gift of prophecy, but when she refused his love he condemned her to the fate of always being right but never being believed. Salome danced before King Herod who promised to give her whatever she wished; she asked for the head of John the Baptist, and got it on a plate (Mark, 6:21–29). For Moses, see Exodus 4:10; Isaiah 6:5–6; Ezekiel 3:26; Jonah: Jeremiah 1. Psalms 39:10 ("I held my tongue"). For Catholic liturgy, see Catherine Pickstock, "An Inquiry into Liturgical Syntax", *Faith and Worship*, 43, 1997, pp 14–21; and *Pickstock* (1997), *After Writing*, chapter 4.

28. Alfred Tennyson, "Morte d'Arthur", 1842 (based on Thomas Malory's 15th century work), in (1829–1864), *The Works of Alfred Lord Tennyson*.

29. Alasdair MacIntyre (1981), *After Virtue*, p 227.

30. For further reading, see Alasdair MacIntyre (1981), *After Virtue*.

31. This view of the territorial definition of a nation is developed, for example, by Roger Scruton (2006b), *England and the Need for Nations*; and John Laughland (1997), *The Tainted Source*. Smaller nations within a large nation are discussed in Scruton (2006b), chapter 5.

32. David Miller (2000), *Citizenship and National Identity*, chapter 2.

33. Anthony D. Smith (2000), *The Nation in History: Historiographical Debates about Ethnicity and Nationalism*, p 62.

34. Miller (2000), pp 28–29.

35. Miller (2000), p 29. The argument in this paragraph is indebted to Miller, notably chapters 2 and 5 of his book.

36. Jean-Jacques Rousseau, "A Discourse on Political Economy", 1755, in (1772), *Rousseau, Political Writings*, p 70, quoted in Miller (2000), p 87.

37. Bernard Crick (1962), *In Defence of Politics*, pp 17–19. Crick cites Aristotle's discussion of tyranny in (c.350 BC), *Politics*, especially book 4, chapter 10, and book 5, chapters 9–10.

38. Kenneth Grahame (1908), *The Wind in the Willows*, chapter 10.

39. See Dan Atkinson, "The Eradication of Dissent", *The European Journal*, December 2001, pp 7–8.

40. Larry Siedentop (2000), *Democracy in Europe*, pp 26 and 23.
41. John Laughland (1997), *The Tainted Source*, pp 203–204.
42. See Anthony D. Smith (2000), *The Nation in History*, p 66.
43. Miller (2000), p 34, is here summarising John Stuart Mill (1861), *Considerations on Representative Government*, chapter 16, "Of Nationality, as Connected with Representative Government".
44. Laughland (1997), p 199.
45. The mechanism is explained in David Begg et al. (1984), *Economics*, chapter 28.
46. The importance that multiple currencies played in Europe's economic stability is explained forcefully by Noriko Hama (1996), *Disintegrating Europe*.
47. The main alternative to a weak currency as a means of helping weak economies is a system of transfer payments and subsidies. Donald MacDougall showed that the cost of intra-union subsidies (between nations, or between regions) necessary to offset the removal of the exchange rate and interest rate flexibility would require a federal expenditure of at least 7.5–10 percent of GDP, equal to 14 times the level of intra-union transfers in 2001 (calculated on the midpoint of 8.75 percent). Donald MacDougall, "Study Group on the Role of Public Finance in European Integration", 1977, cited in Ian Milne, "Euro: MacDougall's Advice Ignored", *Eurofacts*, 13 July 2001, p 1.
48. Jane Jacobs (1984), *Cities and the Wealth of Nations*, pp 161–162.
49. For the detail of the argument summarised here, see Jacobs (1984), chapter 11.
50. This sequence of events is set out in, for instance, Mona O'Connor, "The Euro Meltdown", *The European Journal*, 16, 8, December 2009, p 3.
51. The advantage of parallel currencies within a single economy does not persist into a case for the presence of, say, three currencies. This would triple the number of exchange options (from the single exchange available in the case of two currencies) and would also introduce an economic "layering" of society, which would be quite different from the localisation we need. Parallel currencies are discussed with guarded approval by James Robertson (1998), *Transforming Economic Life*, pp 56–7.
52. Edmund Burke (1790), "On the Genius and Character of the French Revolution as It Regards Other Nations", in Burke (1748–1797), *Burke's Politics: Selected Writings and Speeches of Edmund Burke on Reform, Revolution and War*, p 472. See also Jim McCue (1997), *Edmund Burke and Our Present Discontents*; and Hans Buchheim (1968), *Totalitarian Rule*, pp 18–21.
53. Buchheim (1968), pp 30–31.
54. Crick, epilogue to (1962), *In Defence of Politics*, pp 281–282.
55. Edward Gibbon (1788), *The Decline and Fall of the Roman Empire*, p 107.
56. Larry Siedentop (2000), *Democracy in Europe*, pp 174–176.
57. *Ibid*, pp 174 and 176 (quotation abridged).
58. Frank Delmartino, "Belgium: In Search of the Meso Level", in L.J. Sharpe, ed. (1993), *The Rise of the Meso Government in Europe*, Sage, pp 40–60, quoted in Liesbet Hooghe and Gary Marks, "Types of Multi-Level Governance", University of North Carolina Working Paper, 2001 p 10.
59. Alan J.P. Taylor (1965), *English History 1914–1945*, p 569.
60. Provisions for nuclear war include the immediate division of the United Kingdom into regions under autocratic rule. Peter Hennessy (2002), *The Secret State*.
61. For an exact statement of the conditions as applied by Forum for the Future, see www.forumforthefuture.org /project/natural-step-tns/overview .
62. Sarah James and Torbjörn Lahti (2004), *The Natural Step for Communities*.
63. Thorstein Veblen (1899), *The Theory of the Leisure Class*. In his introduction to the Unwin edition, Charles Wright Mills describes Veblen as "the only comic writer among modern social scientists".
64. Herbert Marcuse (1964), *One Dimensional Man*, p 19.
65. Duane Elgin (1981), *Voluntary Simplicity*, pp 165–167 (quotation abridged).
66. E.F. Schumacher (1973), *Small is Beautiful*, p 26.
67. Jeremy Seabrook, "Needs and Commodities", in Paul Ekins, ed. (1986), *The Living Economy*, p 61.
68. John Kenneth Galbraith (1958), *The Affluent Society*, chapter 11, "The Dependence Effect". See also William Leiss (1976), *The Limits to Satisfaction*, p 27; and Oliver James (2007), Affluenza.
69. Factor 10 Club, "Carnoules Declaration", 1994, available at http://tinyurl.com/4nxeuq . Factor 10 is an evolution of "Factor Four"—the theory that, with improvements in *eco-efficiency and patterns of living, we could halve our consumption of resources and double our wealth: a quadrupling of resource productivity. The name "Factor Four" has become generic, even though more ambitious efficiency improvements (e.g., Factor Ten, Factor Fifty . . .) are being studied. It is especially significant in its insight about the scope for improvements in energy-efficiency. See Ernst Weizsäcker, Amory B. Lovins and L. Hunter Lovins (1997), *Factor Four: Doubling Wealth, Halving Resource Use*, p xv and *passim*. For further reading, see Paul Hawken, Amory B. Lovins and L. Hunter Lovins

(1999), *Natural Capitalism*; or Amory B. Lovins, E. Kyle Datta, Odd-Even Bustnes, et al. (2005), *Winning the Oil Endgame: Innovation for Profits, Jobs and Security*.

70. Henry David Thoreau, journal entry for 8 January 1842, in his (1837–1861), *Journals*, p 361. See also the discussion by Donald Worster (1977), *Nature's Economy*, p 109.

71. Max Weber (1904), *The Protestant Ethic and the Spirit of Capitalism*, pp 48–49.

72. *Ibid*, p 172.

73. Quoted in Weber (1904), p 175.

74. *Ibid*, p 278.

75. Tibor Scitovsky (1976), *The Joyless Economy*, pp 202, 209, 211, and 228–229.

76. D.H. Lawrence (1925), "The Novel", in (1913–1930), *Selected Critical Writings*, p 183.

77. Mary Douglas and Baron Isherwood (1979), *The World of Goods*, p 66. Margaret Vickery (1998), *The Gentleman's Daughter*.

78. Mary Douglas and Baron Isherwood (1979), *The World of Goods*, pp 110–113.

79. The transformation in the clothes culture in Europe that took place around 1800 is discussed in chapters 11 and 12 of Johan Huizinga (1949), *Homo Ludens*, especially p 219.

80. Francis Tibbalds, "Ten Commandments", 1995; Tibbalds wrote this when he was President of the Urban Design Group, quoted in Hugh Barton et al. (1995), *Sustainable Settlements*, p 42.

81. Douglas and Isherwood (1979), pp 16–19.

82. Gerard Fairtlough (1994), *Creative Compartments*, pp 51, 55 and 88–89.

83. Garrett Hardin (1993), *Living within Limits*, pp 266–267. Malcolm Gladwell (2000), *The Tipping Point: How Little Things Make a Big Difference*, pp 177–181 and 185–186. See also www.hutterites.org/day-to-day/structure /daughter-colony/ .

84. Peter Laslett (1965), *The World We Have Lost*, p 57.

85. Akenfield in Suffolk had a population of 300 in 1961, but these were roughly divided into two groups—the native and the new villager; Ronald Blythe remarks that "the nearer [they] come together, the more obvious their difference". Ronald Blythe (1969), *Akenfield*. However, any conclusions drawn from the evidence of towns and villages in the present day and recent past are dubious. For one thing, the focus of community life and gossip has been shifted away from the community and towards a general semi-fictional public gossip. Sybil Marshall writes on the decline of gossip, "Maybe it was because for a lot of people the fictional communities of *Coronation Street* and *The Archers* had replaced interest in what was going on around them in their own community", Sybil Marshall (1993), *A Nest of Magpies*, Penguin edition, p 450.

86. The source for the graph is Robin Dunbar, "Neocortex Size as a Constraint on Group Size in Primates", *Journal of Human Evolution*, 20, 1992, pp 469–493. The correlation between the mean group size and the neocortex ratio illustrated in the graph is calculated from data on 37 species of primate, and produces the equation:

$$\mathrm{Log10}(N) = 0.093 + 3.389 \; \mathrm{log10(CR)}$$
$$(r2 = 0.764, t34 = 10.35, p < 0.001)$$

where N is the mean group size and CR is the neocortex ratio (the ratio of neocortical volume to the volume of the rest of the brain). The value of 147.9 indicated by the regression for humans is an extrapolation from the results for the other primates. The use of both major axis and least-squares regression, as well as alternative indices of relative neocortical size, all yield equations that are of about this magnitude. With a neocortical volume of 1006.5 cc and a total brain volume of 1251.8 cc, the neocortex ratio for humans is 4:1. If the same correlation between the neocortex ratio and mean group size holds for humans as for the other primates, the mean group size for humans is 147.9. This correlation, not drawn by Dunbar, has been added in the graph.

87. Robin Dunbar (1996), *Grooming, Gossip and the Evolution of Language*, p 77.

88. *Ibid*, p 70. Robin Dunbar, "The Social Brain Hypothesis", *Evolutionary Anthropology*, 6, 1998, p 187.

89. Dunbar (1996), p 120.

90. Patrick Geddes (1915), *Cities in Evolution*, p 32. For more on Geddes' career, see *Incrementalism.

91. *Ibid*, p 38. For the civic consciousness that arises from this, see chapter 12. For a valuable study of Geddes, see Helen Meller (1990), *Patrick Geddes*. Geddes' original spelling is "Kakotopia".

92 Peter Kropotkin (1899), *Fields, Factories and Workshops Tomorrow*, p 26.

93. *Ibid*, p 39.

94. *Ibid*, p 40, italics in original.

95. For a discussion of hunter-gatherers' ethic of long-term care of their ecology, see Hugh Brody (2000), *The Other Side of Eden*.

96. Richard Wrangham (2009), *Catching Fire: How Cooking Made Us Human*. For a model of evolution from hunter-gatherer to agriculturalist, see Ester Boserup, "Environment, Population and Technology in Primitive Societies", in Donald Worster, ed. (1988), *The Ends of the Earth*, pp 23–38; for an absorbing extended narrative of this, see Jared Diamond (1997), *Guns, Germs and Steel*, chapters 4–10.

97. George Gordon Coulton (1925), *Medieval Village, Manor and Monastery*.

98. Flora Thompson (1945), *Lark Rise to Candleford*.

99. Charles Dickens (1843), *A Christmas Carol*.

100. Christopher Hibbert (1987), *The English: A Social History, 1066–1945*.

101. Press Association report of a Mintel study, 9 October 1996. Mary Kenny, "Remedy for Families of Convenience", *The Sunday Telegraph*, 7 April 1991.

102. John Bossy (1985), *Christianity in the West: 1400–1700*, p 121.

103. Alvin Toffler coined the word "prosumer" to describe this "reintegration of the consumer into production", with consumers using advances in technology (*Neotechnic) to play a much bigger part in providing for their own needs. See Alvin Toffler (1980), *The Third Wave*, chapter 20.

104. Anthony Weston (1987), *A Rulebook for Arguments*, p 77.

105. For extended references on nuclear energy, see David Fleming (2007), *The Lean Guide to Nuclear Energy*.

106. Storm van Leeuwen, "Nuclear Power: The Energy Balance", updated report, February 2008, available at www.stormsmith.nl .

107. Dr. Gavin Mudd (mining engineer), personal communication.

108. *Ibid*.

109. As is standard for the work of whistle-blowers, Storm van Leeuwen's study of the energy balance of nuclear power is subject to criticism, especially from the industry body, the World Nuclear Association. While it would be surprising if it were accurate in all its details, van Leeuwen's study should be recognised as robust, for three reasons:

 1. It is a consistent exercise in evaluating the energy inputs and outputs at every stage of the nuclear cycle, down to the detail. Critics who dismiss his work find themselves at the same time dismissing comprehensively the literature on which our understanding of nuclear energy is based.

 2. Its consistent programme of evaluating the energy balances ties the research down to the detail, and van Leeuwen strongly encourages comment and criticism at that level, so that its accuracy is being constantly assessed and improved.

 3. The collapse in the quantity of net energy available as the ore grade approaches 0.02 percent is so dramatic that, even if there were substantial inaccuracy in his work, it would make little difference to his essential findings on the limited expectation of life for the nuclear industry. Even if no energy at all were needed to clear up the waste, nuclear power would still be closed as an option at that grade of ore.

 If it were really shown that van Leeuwen had made an error on a scale large enough to cast significant doubt on his findings, this would place his work in the kind of fantasy habitat in which you would be likely to bump into Calvin and Hobbes—that's not Hobbes the philosopher, but Hobbes the stuffed tiger.

110. van Leeuwen, "Nuclear Power: The Energy Balance", part D. Olympic Dam: part D8. Energy balance: part E, especially E2.4a, and G6.

111. *Ibid*, part E, especially E2.4b, and part G, especially G6.

112. *Ibid*, part E, especially E2.1, E2.2 and E3.3, and part G, especially G6.

113. *Ibid*, part E, especially E7 and E8. See also World Nuclear Association, "How It Works: Used Fuel Management", 2007, and (for the UK), Committee on Radioactive Waste Management, "Managing our Radioactive Waste Safely", July 2006, especially chapters 14–15. For an overview, see Rolf Haugaard Nielsen, "Final Resting Place", *New Scientist*, no. 2541, 4 March 2006, pp 38–41. See also John Busby, "Rip van Winkel Wakes", 14 September 2006, available at www.after-oil.co.uk/winkel.htm .

114. van Leeuwen, "Nuclear Power: The Energy Balance", part G, especially G6.

115. *Ibid*, part D (D3 and D4). See also World Nuclear Association, "How It Works: Getting Uranium from the Ground", 2007.

116. See Kurt Cobb, "The Net Energy Cliff", 14 September 2008, available at http://tinyurl.com/p3ra9z5 . The distinction between TROEI and PROEI is suggested in Fleming (2007), pp 11–13.

117. The 60 years estimate comes from van Leeuwen, "Nuclear Power: The Energy Balance", part H, especially H1 and H2. It is also accessibly summarised in Storm van Leeuwen, "Energy Security and Uranium Reserves", Factsheet 4, Oxford Research Group, 2006, available at www.oxfordresearchgroup.org.uk/sites/default/files /energyfactsheet4.pdf .

118. van Leeuwen, "Nuclear Power: The Energy Balance", part D (D3 and D4). See also World Nuclear Association, "How It Works: Getting Uranium from the Ground", 2007.

119. *Ibid*.

120. For data on world production from mines, see World Nuclear Association, "Uranium Production Figures", 2007, available at www.world-nuclear.org/info/uprod. html . Additional sources are Moukhtar Dzhakishev, "Uranium Production in Kazakhstan as a Potential Source for Covering the World Uranium Shortage", World Nuclear Association, 2004, available at www.world

-nuclear.org/sym/2004/dzakishev.htm ; Marcel Coderch Collell, "The Nuclear Mirage and the World Energy Situation", Real Instituto Elcano, 2006, available at www.realinstitutoelcano.org/analisis/925/925_Coderch _NuclearMirage.pdf ; Matthew Bunn, "Reducing Excess Stockpiles", 2003, Nuclear Threat Initiative (NTI), available at www.nti.org/gsn/article/increased-efforts -needed-to-secure-nuclear-stockpiles-researcher-says/ ; Jean-Paul Nicolet and Douglas Underhill, "Balancing Needs: Global Trends in Uranium Production and Demand", IAEA Division of Nuclear Fuel Cycle and Waste Technology, 1998, available at http://tinyurl.com/pd76gjb ; International Atomic Energy Agency, "Analysis of Uranium Supply to 2050", 2001, available at http://tinyurl .com/2t832q ; Werner Zittel and Jörg Schindler, "Ura- nium Resources and Nuclear Energy", Energy Watch Group, 2006, available at http://tinyurl.com/nc6o82m ; John Busby, "Rip van Winkel Wakes", 14 September 2006, available at www.after-oil.co.uk/winkel.htm .

121. For a table setting out these calculations, see Fleming (2007), p 34.

122. *Editor's note*: David Fleming's former collaborator John Busby offers the following comment on relevant developments since Fleming's death in 2010: Demand for uranium dropped when Japan—a major consumer— closed all of its reactors in response to the 2011 Fukushima disaster. The price has remained low since, and many low-grade ore mines have closed, since their operating costs were higher than the sale price. It is an open question as to whether investment will be available to bring these back into production if demand increases again. In addition, distributed energy such as small-scale solar PV is reducing the need for new centralised power stations. See John Busby, "Anaerobic Digestion and Distributed Energy", 20 December 2014, available at www.after-oil.co.uk/distribute.htm .

123. Bjørn Lomborg, "Time for the Climate Doomsters to Face Reality", *The Times*, 12 May 2004.

O

1. Edmund Burke (1790), *Reflections on the Revolution in France*, p 87.

P

1. The idea of paedomorphism is developed in Arthur Koestler (1967), *The Ghost in the Machine*, chapter 12.

2. For early use of "paradigm", see *Oxford English Dictionary*. Thomas S. Kuhn (1962), *The Structure of Scientific Revolutions*.

3. *Ibid*, pp 5 and 24.

4. *Ibid*, p 24.

5. For auxiliary hypotheses, see Imre Lakatos, "Falsification and the Methodology of Scientific Research Programmes", in Imre Lakatos and Alan Musgrave, eds. (1970), *Criticism and the Growth of Knowledge*; and Kuhn (1962), p 6.

6. Karl Popper (1945), *The Open Society and Its Enemies*. Karl Popper's most succinct statement of falsifiability was in his first publication, a two page letter in the periodical *Erkenntis* in 1933: "Scientific theories, if they are to deserve the name 'scientific', should be at least semi-decidable, one-sidedly decideable." That is, they might not be proved, but they might be disproved. Cited in Imre Lakatos (1973), *Lectures on Scientific Method*, lecture seven, "Falsification and Intellectual Honesty", p 89. For a valuable summary of falsifiability, see Brian Magee (1973), *Popper*, chapter 3.

7. Lakatos (1973), p 90.

8. The herringbone pattern is described in Arthur Koestler (1967), *The Ghost in the Machine*, chapter 12.

9. For more on punctuated equilibrium, see, for example, www.pbs.org/wgbh/evolution/library/03/5/l_035_01.html . See also Kim Sterelny (2001), *Dawkins vs. Gould: Survival of the Fittest*; and Stephen Jay Gould (2002), *The Structure of Evolutionary Theory*.

10. Brendan Larvor (1998), *Lakatos: An Introduction*, pp 54–55; Alan Musgrave, "Method or Madness?" and William Berkson, "Lakatos One and Lakatos Two: An Apprecia- tion", both in Robert S. Cohen, Paul K. Feyerabend and Marx W. Wartofsky, eds. (1976), *Essays in Memory of Imre Lakatos*. See especially pp 473 and 53.

11. Cited in R.M. Sainsbury (1987), *Paradoxes*, p 1.

12. Francis Bacon, "Of Beauty", in (1625), *Essayes or Counsels, Civill and Morall*.

13. For further reading, see R.M. Sainsbury (1987), *Paradoxes*; Glenn W. Erickson and John A. Fossa (1988), *Dictionary of Paradox*; Roy Sorensen (2003), *A Brief History of the Paradox*.

14. See Blaise Pascal (1670), *Pensées*, section 2. The wager is discussed in Nicholas Hammond, ed. (2003), *The Cambridge Companion to Pascal*, pp 53–74.

15. *Editor's note*: Fleming's final manuscript gives an endnote here which simply reads "see Laughland reference in Paternalism". The intended meaning is unclear, but the two John Laughland references mentioned elsewhere in *Lean Logic* are: (1997), *The Tainted Source*; and "A Clockwork Orange? Or: What Makes Victor Yushchenko Tick?", *Chicken Kiev*, December 2004.

16. The Pathetic Fallacy was coined in John Ruskin, "Mod- ern Painters: Of the Pathetic Fallacy", 1856, in (1843–1889), *John Ruskin: Selected Writings*.

17. Ian Robinson, "The Idea of a Christian Society in The Book of Common Prayer", *Faith and Worship*, 65–66, Easter 2010, pp 65–78.

18. The principle and significance of performative truth was first published by John L. Austin (1962), *How to Do Things with Words*.

19. Extract from T.S. Eliot, "The Fire Sermon"; part III of "The Waste Land", 1922, available at e.g., www.poetry foundation.org/poem/176735 .

20. For Pharisaism and Pharisees, see Isaiah 65:5; Luke 18:11. Thomas Aquinas, *Summa Theologica*, vol 1 and 2, pp 47 and 49, is cited in this context in Albert R. Jonsen and Stephen Toulmin (1988), *The Abuse of Casuistry*, pp 130–131.

21. The two uses of the Appeal to Pity are pointed out by Frans H. van Eemeren and Rob Grootendorst (1992), *Argumentation, Communication and Fallacies*, pp 213 and 215. Michelet's bias is cited as an illustration of the fallacy by David Hackett Fischer (1970), *Historians' Fallacies*, p 304.

22. Stephen Toulmin, Richard D. Rieke and Allan Janik (1984), *An Introduction to Reasoning*, pp 147–148. Toulmin et al. (1984) are writing here about *compassion, but it is "pity" (*Argumentum ad misericordiam*) that is generally discussed in the logic literature. See, for example, Charles Leonard Hamblin (1970), *Fallacies*, p 43.

23. David Hume (1739), *A Treatise of Human Nature*, p 272.

24. Stuart L. Brown (2009), *Play: How it Shapes the Brain, Opens the Imagination, and Invigorates the Soul*, p 15.

25. Useful suggestions about kinds of play and how to group them are made by Roger Caillois (1958), *Man, Play and Games*, pp 14–17; and by Brown (2009), *passim*, especially pp 66–70.

26. Brown (2009), pp 40–42.

27. Bruce D. Perry, "Bonding and Attachment in Maltreated Children: Consequences of Emotional Neglect in Childhood", available at http://teacher.scholastic.com /professional/bruceperry/bonding.htm . Adapted in part from Bruce D. Perry (1996), *Maltreated Children: Experience, Brain Development and the Next Generation*, W.W. Norton & Co. See also Tiffany Field (2001), *Touch*.

28. R.M. Yerkes and J.D. Dodson, "The Relation of Strength of Stimulus to Rapidity of Habit-Formation", *Journal of Comparative Neurology and Psychology*, vol 18, 1908, pp 459–482, available at http://psychclassics.yorku.ca/Yerkes /Law/. See also summary in Jerome S. Bruner, Alison Jolly and Kathy Sylva, eds. (1976), *Play: Its Role in Development and Evolution*, p 15; and Martyn Long (2000), *The Psychology of Education*.

29. Bruner et al., eds. (1976), p 16.

30. Jack Grimston and Dipesh Gadher, "Youngsters Losing Hand Co-ordination: Children Are Struggling at School Because They Don't Know if They Are Left- or Right-handed", *The Sunday Times*, 9 November 2008; based on Madeleine Portwood (2000), *Understanding Developmental Dyspraxia*.

31. Otto Weininger, "Play and Early Childhood", in Paul F. Wilkinson, ed. (1980), *In Celebration of Play*, pp 43–62 (quotation from pp 51, 53 and 61, abridged). For a review of object play among young primates, see Jacklyn K. Ramsey and William C. McGrew, "Object Play in Great Apes", in Anthony D. Pellegrini and Peter K. Smith, eds. (2005), *The Nature of Play*, pp 89–135.

32. Jerome S. Bruner , "Nature and Uses of Immaturity", in Bruner et al., eds. (1976), pp 28–65, p 49; first published in *American Psychologist*, vol 27, 8, August, 1972.

33. Jean Piaget, "The Rules of the Game of Marbles", in Bruner et al., eds. (1976), pp 412–441; first published in Piaget's (1965), *The Moral Judgment of the Child*, Free Press.

34. Richard Sennett (1974), *The Fall of Public Man*, p 320.

35. Pictures of the match available at http://tinyurl.com /y8ghnk6. See also www.realgothicfc.co.uk .

36. Play-fighting is recognised (though not necessarily in all cases) to be practice for real fighting, should that be needed. Peter K. Smith (2009), *Children and Play*, p 120.

37. Louise Barrett, Robin Dunbar and Patsy Dunbar, "Environmental Influences on Play Behaviour in Immature Gelada Baboons", *Animal Behaviour*, 44, 1, 1992, pp 111–115.

38. Johan Huizinga (1949), *Homo Ludens*, pp 31 and 29 (quotation abridged).

39. Joseph Michelli (1998), *Humor, Play and Laughter*.

40. Richard Mabey (2005), *Nature Cure*, pp 66–68.

41. *Ibid*, p 196.

42. *Ibid*, p 199.

43. Roy Porter (2000), *Enlightenment*, p 22.

44. For further reading, see Stephen Miller (2006), *Conversation*.

45. For Francis Hutcheson, see Peter C. Dooley (2005), *The Labour Theory of Value*, chapter 6. For John Neville Keynes, see Phyllis Deane (2001), *The Life and Times of J. Neville Keynes*; and his own book, John Neville Keynes (1891), *The Scope and Method of Political Economy*, Kitchener.

46. For a fuller discussion of pollution, see G. Tyler Miller (1975), *Living in the Environment*; or G. Tyler Miller, Scott E. Spoolman, John Soares (2010), *Environmental Science: What Can You Do?*, Cengage Learning.

47. Actually, there is plenty of food for thought about where exactly to draw the line between things that are self-replicating and things that aren't. Financial capital is to some extent, except that it depends on material

assets and markets that aren't. Food (you could argue, but not very convincingly) is—at second-hand—because the more people there are, the more labour becomes available to produce food. But let's keep it simple. There is more than enough complication to come.

48. Thomas Malthus (1798–1826), *An Essay on the Principle of Population*, p 71.

49. For a summary discussion of chaotic effects in population feedbacks, see Alan Hastings, "Biological Chaos and Complex Dynamics", in Simon A. Levin, ed. (2009), *The Princeton Guide to Ecology*, pp 172–176.

50. Harris (1977), pp 11–25 and 275–276; Hugh Brody (2000), *The Other Side of Eden*, pp 118–119; and Richard G. Wilkinson (1973), Poverty and Progress, pp 33–39 and 73.

51. John R. Weeks (1978), *Population: An Introduction to Concepts and Issues* (chapters 6 and 7) discusses factors favouring growth in the world's population, and the "transitions", factors that then tend to reduce the growth rate and which could in due course begin to reduce population itself. Leeds study on UK population: Pia Wohland, Phil Rees, Paul Norman, Peter Boden and Martyna Jasinska, "Ethnic Population Projections for the UK and Local Areas, 2001–2051", Working Paper 10/02, School of Geography, University of Leeds, 2010.

52. For details on the potato diet, see Cecil Woodham-Smith (1962), *The Great Hunger*, pp 30–31. The 1779 population figure is taken from *Arthur Young's Tour In Ireland (1776–1779)*: "The common idea is, that there are something under three millions in Ireland", available at http://tinyurl.com/pyfdhfr . This is a less reliable estimate than the census figure, but nonetheless plausible.

53. Weeks (1978); Fred Pearce (2010), *Peoplequake*, p 294.

54. See Weeks (1978), chapter 6, esp. p 41, and his detailed argument on global population trends in chapter 2. See also Pearce (2010), *passim*; and essays in Wolfgang Lutz, Warren C. Sanderson and Sergei Scherbov, eds. (2004), *The End of World Population Growth in the 21st Century*.

55. Pearce (2010), chapter 14.

56. A summary of worldwide population numbers can be found in Weeks (1978), pp 33–34.

57. *Ibid*, p 41.

58. *Ibid*, pp 453 and 463.

59. Martin Rees (2003), *Our Final Century*.

60. James Lovelock (2006), *The Revenge of Gaia*, p 147.

61. William Stanton (2003), *The Rapid Growth of Human Populations 1750–2000*, pp 185–213.

62. For avian (bird) flu, see, e.g., World Health Organisation, "Avian influenza", available at www.who.int/topics /avian_influenza/en/ . For crop strains, see, e.g., Sarina

Macfadyen and David A. Bohan, "Crop domestication and the disruption of species interactions", *Basic and Applied Ecology* 11, 2, 2010, pp 116–125.

63. Joan Thirsk (1997), *Alternative Agriculture*, p 254.

64. *Ibid*, chapter 1. Crops which either ceased to be exclusive to wealthy landowners, or which became established for the first time, included rabbit, pigeon, fish, flax, hemp, saffron, rape, buckwheat, apples, pears, scallions, chervil, chives, rosemary, carrots, parsnips and skirrets (water parsnips).

65. George Huppert (1986), *After the Black Death: A Social History of Early Modern Europe*, pp ix and 12–13. The benefits that can accrue to the survivors of pandemics and famine, based on a detailed case study of the famine among the Dinka of Sudan in the period 1983–1989, are discussed at length in David Keen (1994), *The Benefits of Famine*.

66. UK House of Lords Select Committee on Economic Affairs, "The Economic Impact of Immigration", First Report of Session 2007–8, published 1 April 2008, Her Majesty's Stationery Office, volume 1, chapter 1, paragraphs 49–51 and 69.

67. For a comment on the deskilling of the UK workforce see, for instance, Harriet Sergeant, "Schools Are Churning out the Unemployable", *The Sunday Times*, 21 February 2010.

68. Marvin Harris (1977), *Cannibals and Kings*, p 11, but note that there is controversy about this. For example, Peter Ward writes, "We were essentially cat food until the invention of Clovis technology about 10,000 years ago", (2009), *The Medea Hypothesis*, p 22.

69. With regard to the need for population control, see Harris (1977), pp 11–16 and 18.

70. *Ibid*, pp 23–25 and 21–22. On the evidence for a change in menstrual cycles, Rachel Bayer writes, "While the reasons behind why women menstruate remain unclear, research shows that the number of menstrual cycles modern women experience differs greatly from the number experienced by pre-agricultural women. It is impossible to know with certainty the reproductive patterns that prevailed 10,000 years ago. However, it is likely that the reproductive patterns of Stone Age women are more closely related to those of current hunter-gatherer societies than to those of Western women." (From "The Impact of Increased Menstruation Rates on Women's Health and Reproductive Cancers", 19 December 2001).

71. Harris (1977), pp 23–25.

72. Richard G. Wilkinson (1973), *Poverty and Progress*, pp 33–39 and 73; and Harris (1977), pp 22–23 and 275–276.

73. Wilkinson (1973), p 33.

74. Hugh Brody (2000), *The Other Side of Eden*, pp 118–119.

75. See, e.g., Planned Parenthood, "A History of Birth Control Methods", November 2006, and the references therein, available at http://tinyurl.com/pk4cz2x .

76. For tight feedback loops, see Brian Walker and David Salt (2006), *Resilience Thinking*, p 121.

77. Alasdair MacIntyre (1981), *After Virtue*.

78. John Keats, letter to George and Georgiana Keats, 14 February and 3 May 1819, in Hyder Edward Rollins, ed. (1958), *The Letters of John Keats 1814–1821*, Harvard University Press, cited in (1795–1821), *Selected Letters of John Keats*, p 291.

79. See Alasdair MacIntyre (1981), *After Virtue*, especially chapter 14; a definition of "practice" is on p 187. "The hedgehog and the fox" refers to a fragment of poetry surviving from Archilocus (680–645 BC); the idea is discussed at length in Isaiah Berlin (1953), *The Hedgehog and the Fox: An Essay on Tolstoy's View of History*.

80. The risk/uncertainty/ignorance/indeterminacy distinction is summarised in Larry Lohmann, ed. (2006), *Carbon Trading*, pp 160–161.

81. See David Fleming, "The Economics of Taking Care", in David Freestone and Ellen Hey, eds. (1995), *The Precautionary Principle and International Law*. For a critical evaluation of case studies on the precautionary principle, see Poul Harremoës, David Gee, Malcolm MacGarvin, et al., eds. (2002), *The Precautionary Principle in the 20th Century*.

82. *Editor's note*: "The Big Society" was a flagship policy of the UK Conservative Party in their manifesto for the 2010 general election, aiming "to create a climate that empowers local people and communities, building a big society that will take power away from politicians and give it to people . . . encouraging people to take an active role in their communities." After the election, Conservative Prime Minister David Cameron stated that he wanted his vision of such a 'Big Society' to be one of the great legacies of his Government. See, e.g., www.gov.uk/government /news/government-launches-big-society-programme--2 .

83. See David Halpern (2009), *The Hidden Wealth of Nations*.

84. For a description of the healthy living centre at Bromley by Bow, see Andrew Mawson (2008), *The Social Entrepreneur*, pp 110–111; for the Labour Government plan, see pp 116–118.

85. Janet Daley, "Does Optimism Have a Place in British Politics?", *The Sunday Telegraph*, 18 April 2010, p 22.

86. See the notion of "pop behaviourism", developed by Alfie Kohn in (1993), *Punished by Rewards*. For an alternative climate policy framework built around presence and intrinsic incentives, see *TEQs.

87. "Prehension" is used by Alfred North Whitehead in his discussion of the "middle voice"—that is, neither active nor passive. See for instance, William Norman Pittenger (1969), *Alfred North Whitehead*, p 16.

88. "Inside-out" in this context was coined by Germaine Greer, in conversation with Andrew Mawson about the principle of giving the responsibility for development of an idea to the person who had the idea in the first place. Mawson (2008), pp 123–124.

89. Henry David Thoreau (1849), "On the Duty of Civil Disobedience", in Thoreau (1854b), *Walden and Civil Disobedience*, p 386.

90. Thomas Jefferson writing to Joseph C. Cabell, 2 February 1816, available at http://press-pubs.uchicago.edu/founders/documents/v1ch4s34.html . For the printed version, see also Jean M. Yarbrough, ed. (2006), *The Essential Jefferson*, Hackett, p 544.

91. *Ibid*, p 543.

92. Thomas Jefferson writing to Joseph C. Cabell, 17 January 1814, available at http://founders.archives.gov/documents /Jefferson/03-07-02-0073 .

93. Kirkpatrick Sale (1980), *Human Scale*, pp 443–454.

94. "Port Huron Statement", 1962, available at www.hippy. com/article-129.html . For the printed version, see also James Miller (1987), *Democracy is in the Streets: From Port Huron to the Siege of Chicago*, p 333.

95. Ludwig von Mises (1949), *Human Action: A Treatise on Economics*, p 855. For details on reformist anarchism, see José Pérez Adán (1992), *Reformist Anarchism 1800–1936: A Study of the Feasibility of Anarchism*, especially section 2, chapter 5. For influential UK government advocacy of citizens' participation in local planning, see Arthur Skeffington MP and the Ministry of Housing and Local Government, "People and Planning" (aka 'The Skeffington Report'), report of the Committee on Public Participation in Planning, Her Majesty's Stationery Office, 1969.

96. See Bernard Crick (1962), *In Defence of Politics*, p 281.

97. See Frank Fischer (2000), *Citizens, Experts and the Environment*, pp xi and 194–201.

98. The Labour Party, "National Service for Health", pamphlet, 1943, p 12. Sale (1980), p 451. See also Colin Ward (1973), *Anarchy in Action*, pp 10 and 80.

99. Sale (1980), pp 476–477. Italics in original.

100. Max Gammon, "Gammon's Law of Bureaucratic Displacement", Australian Doctors Fund, January 2005, available at www.adf.com.au/archive.php?doc_id=113 (quotation abridged).

101. Alasdair MacIntyre (1981), *After Virtue*, especially chapter 14; a definition of "practice" is on p 187.

102. Émile Durkheim (1893), *The Division of Labour in Society*. He is most explicit about the role of professionals and their corporations in the preface to the second edition (pp xxxi–lix). David Martin, book review of Roger Scruton (2007), *Culture Counts*, in *Times Literary Supplement*, 11 January 2008; Robert D. Putnam (2000), *Bowling Alone*.

103. James Bartholomew (2004), *The Welfare State We're In*, p 48.

104. Labourers, husbandmen and drovers have worked as leaders of the community, as parish clerks and churchwardens since at least the seventeenth century (*Character).

105. Antonio Gramsci (1935), *Selections from the Prison Notebooks of Antonio Gramsci*, quoted in Geoff Eley, "Nations, Publics and Political Cultures: Placing Habermas in the Nineteenth Century", 1990, in Craig Calhoun, ed. (1992), *Habermas and the Public Sphere*.

106. E.F. Schumacher, "Industrialisation through Intermediate Technology", *Resurgence*, 1, 2 July/August 1964, in Schumacher (1997), *This I Believe, and Other Essays*. See also Tim Lang and Colin Hines (1993), *The New Protectionism*; and Jane Jacobs (1984), *Cities and the Wealth of Nations*.

107. For a discussion of the well-established idea of the proximity principle, see Rebecca Willis, "The Proximity Principle: Why We Are Living Too Far Apart", Campaign to Protect Rural England, May 2008, available at www.cpre.org.uk/resources/housing-and-planning /housing/item/download/449 .

108. This distinction between public and private is based on a reading of Richard Sennett (1974), *The Fall of Public Man*. Chapter 5 is especially helpful.

109. "Self-distance" is a phrase developed by Sennett (1974), pp 267 and 317.

110. Edmund Burke (1790), *Reflections on the Revolution in France*, p 77.

111. For a concise summary of the work of monasteries in providing services for the poor, and of the history of the friendly societies, see James Bartholomew (2004), *The Welfare State We're In*, chapter 2.

112. *Ibid*, chapter 2, especially pp 46–48.

113. J.V. Beckett (1989), *A History of Laxton*, pp 26–35.

114. William Edward Forster's *Elementary Education Act*.

115. To hear the song (by Peggy Lee), go to: https://tinyurl .com/cpl4leg .

116. See Mats G. Hansson (2008), *The Private Sphere*; and Meredith Minkler (1997), *Community Organizing and Community Building for Health*. For more depth on the public sphere, see Jürgen Habermas (1962), *The Structural Transformation of the Public Sphere*, and Alan McKee (2004), *The Public Sphere: An Introduction*.

117. For a summary of the principle of pull, see James P. Womack and Daniel T. Jones (1996), *Lean Thinking*, pp 24–25.

Q

1. Leo Lewis, "The Thirsty £1½m Car That Needs Only Water", *The Times*, 4 May 2004.

2. The fuel cells which power such cars are mini power plants in which hydrogen and oxygen react to produce energy and water. Like batteries, they are not an original source of energy—energy is needed to produce the hydrogen in the first place. See Rebecca L. Busby (2005), *Hydrogen and Fuel Cells*.

R

1. See Richard Foster, Pierre Ven Beneden and Sarah Kaplan (2001), *Creative Destruction: Turning Built-to-Last into Built-to-Perform*. See also Joseph Schumpeter (1942), *Capitalism, Socialism and Democracy*; Thomas K. McCraw (2007), *Prophet of Innovation: Joseph Schumpeter and Creative Destruction*, Richard L. Nolan and David C. Croson (1995), *Creative Destruction: A Six-Stage Process for Transforming the Organization*.

2. Schumpeter (1942), pp 83–84.

3. Michael Oakeshott, "Rationalism in Politics", 1947, in (1962), *Rationalism in Politics and Other Essays*.

4. On rationalism, see also Robert Grant (1990), *Oakeshott*; and the essays in Jesse Norman, ed. (1993), *The Achievement of Michael Oakeshott*. For a fuller treatment of rationalism and its technological foundation, see Daniel Bell, "Technocracy and Politics", *Survey*, 16,10, 1971; for a brief description, citing Bell, see Frank Fischer (2000), *Citizens, Experts and the Environment*, p 16.

5. Dunbar and Spoors, "Social Networks, Support Cliques, and Kinship", *Human Nature*, 6, 1995, pp 273–290.

6. Michael Argyle (1991), *Cooperation*, pp 16–17; David W. Johnson and Frank P. Johnson (1975), *Joining Together: Group Theory and Group Skills*. Both Argyle and the Johnson brothers cite Morton Deutsch's classic 1940s experiments, which compared cooperative groups with competitive ones (i.e., groups whose task was designed for cooperation versus groups where success depended on individual performance either relative to, or independently of, other members in the group). See George C. Homans (1951), *The Human Group*, p 111.

7. Johnson and Johnson (1975), p 305. Argyle (1991), p 111; Michael Argyle (1987), *The Psychology of Happiness*, pp 16–18.

8. Burke (1790), pp 46–47.

9. Diana Leafe Christian (2003), *Creating a Life Together*, especially chapters 5 and 17. See also Johnson and Johnson

(1975), pp 352–391. The problem of conflict resolution within a community resists useful summary. Additional recommended reading, however, includes Oliver Ramsbotham, Tom Woodhouse, and Hugh Miall (1999), *Contemporary Conflict Resolution*; and Dudley Weeks (1994), *The Eight Essential Steps to Conflict Resolution*.

10. Ernst Fehr and Simon Gächter, "Altruistic Punishment in Humans", *Nature*, vol 415, 2002, pp 137–140; summarised by Anil Ananthaswamy, "Moral Outrage", *New Scientist*, 12 January 2002. The discussion on fights is inspired by personal communication with Don Ruth.

11. John Bossy (1985), *Christianity in the West: 1400–1700*, pp 57–63.

12. For kinship, see Catherine Pickstock (1997), *After Writing*, p 140. For *caritas*, see Bossy (1985), p 61.

13. Pickstock (1997), p 143.

14. Eamon Duffy (1992), *The Stripping of the Altars: Traditional Religion in England 1400–1580*, pp 42–44.

15. Pickstock (1997), p 143 (quotation abridged).

16. For a summary and sources on the Orangi Project, see Paul Ekins (1992), *A New World Order*, pp 188–191; also Fred Pearce, "Squatters Take Control: What Started with a Scheme for Building Sewers Has Grown into an All-embracing Philosophy", *New Scientist*, 1 June 1996. The comparisons are with another Karachi community which had not taken charge in its own locality.

17. See, for instance, Marshall Sahlins (1972), *Stone Age Economics*. See also references under *Reciprocity and Cooperation.

18. Alexis de Tocqueville (1835), *Democracy in America*, vol 2, part 2, chapter 2, pp 587–589.

19. René Descartes was the first to describe such serial reductionism, in his *Discourses*, part V, 1637. In (1618–1650) *The Philosophical Writings of Descartes*, volume 3.

20. For a similar take on this kind of thinking, see Paul Hawken, Amory B. Lovins and L. Hunter Lovins (1999), *Natural Capitalism*, chapter 13.

21. For hypercar, see Hawken et al. (1999), chapter 2; for optimising, see *ibid*, chapter 6, especially p 117.

22. "Cathedral Camps" has now been rescued in a deal by which Community Service Volunteers agreed to include it in their insurance policy (Ruth Coates, Cathedral Camps: personal communication).

23. See René Descartes, *Discourses*, part V, 1637. In (1618–1650) *The Philosophical Writings of Descartes*, volume 3.

24. Daniel C. Dennett (1995), *Darwin's Dangerous Idea*, p 82.

25. *Ibid*.

26. Richard Chartres (2004), *Tree of Knowledge, Tree of Life*, chapter 3, "Ash Wednesday (2)", p 17.

27. Thomas Traherne (c.1670), *Centuries of Meditations*, The Second Century, numbers 83 and 81.

28. This interpretation of industrial development is based on Richard G. Wilkinson (1973), *Poverty and Progress*.

29. *Ibid*, pp 126 and 135.

30. *Ibid*, p 135.

31. *Ibid*, p 108.

32. All microeconomics textbooks explain this point.

33. On the job creating potential of rebuilding the economy based on renewable energy see, for instance, The Green New Deal Group (2008), *The Green New Deal*, pp 3 and 37–39 and *passim*; and Geoffrey Lean, "These Green Shoots Mean Business", *The Daily Telegraph*, 13 June 2009.

34. Gilbert White (1788), *The Natural History and Antiquities of Selborne*, letter XX, 8 October 1768, p 55.

35. These examples of the web of connections in a natural system come from personal communication with Richard Young.

36. The discussion on Balinese culture can be found in Albert Jonsen and Stephen Toulmin (1988), *The Abuse of Casuistry*, pp 60–62.

37. The quotation on divinity is from William Shakespeare (1603), *Hamlet*, act V, scene 2.

38. Alfred North Whitehead (1925), *Science and the Modern World*, pp 191–192.

39. In ancient pagan rituals, the "sacrifice" of meat ended up by providing food for everyone in the community. See Richard Seaford (2004), *Money and the Early Greek Mind*, pp 48–53 and 292.

40. The convergence of environmental awareness and Christianity is discussed in, for instance, Matthew Fox (1988), *The Coming of the Cosmic Christ: The Healing of Mother Earth and the Birth of a Global Renaissance*; and Tim Cooper (1990), *Green Christianity*.

41. Psalm 84:6.

42. John Donne, "Batter my heart", c.1609, in (1609–1620), *The Divine Poems of John Donne*.

43. Edmund Burke (1791), *An Appeal from the New to the Old Whigs*, quoted in Jim McCue (1997), *Edmund Burke and Our Present Discontents*, p 72.

44. Jonathan Sacks (2002), *The Dignity of Difference*. "You cannot argue with a song" is from Maurice Bloch (1989), *Ritual, History and Power*, p 37.

45. From the Resilience Alliance glossary—a useful source of definitions on systems-related topics—at www .resalliance.org/index.php/glossary . This widely-agreed definition is the same in essence as that given by systems analyst Paul A. Weiss: "A complex unit in space and in time, whose sub-units cooperate to preserve its integrity,

its structure and its behaviour and tend to restore them after a non-destructive disturbance", (1971), *Hierarchically Organized Systems in Theory and Practice*, p 99.

46. This example of the shallow lake comes from Marten Scheffer, "Alternative States and Regime Shifts in Ecosystems", in Simon A. Levin, ed. (2009), *The Princeton Guide to Ecology*, pp 395–406 (specifically, p 399).

47. Illustration created by author.

48. Marten Scheffer, "Alternative States and Regime Shifts in Ecosystems", p 398. Holling and colleagues' verbatim definition of resilience is "the capacity of a system to experience disturbance and still maintain its ongoing functions and controls. A measure of resilience is the magnitude of disturbance that can be experienced without the system flipping into another state or stability domain." This is taken from C.S. Holling, Stephen R. Carpenter, William A. Brock and Lance H. Gunderson, "Discoveries for Sustainable Futures", in Lance H. Gunderson and C.S. Holling, eds. (2002), *Panarchy*. The key influence of this work in the following discussion of resilience is acknowledged, but it bears no responsibility for the suggested distinction between recovery-elastic resilience and preventive resilience.

49. Illustration created by author.

50. For egalitarian individualism in a small-scale society, see Hugh Brody (2000), *The Other Side of Eden*, pp 196–199. Brody's account refers in particular to hunter-gatherer groups of northern Canada.

51. Coping strategies are discussed in Carl Folke, Fikret Berkes and Johan Colding, "Ecological Practices and Social Mechanisms for Building Resilience and Sustainability", in Berkes and Folke, eds. (1998), *Linking Social and Ecological Systems*, pp 425–426. For examples of the alternative stable state (the new phase) see, for instance, Gunderson and Holling, eds. (2002), chapter 2, especially pp 36–38.

52. For examples of the alternative stable state (transformation) see, for instance, Gunderson and Holling, eds. (2002), chapter 2, especially pp 38–40.

53. For the meaning of "capability", see Amartya Sen, "Personal Utilities and Public Judgements: Or What's Wrong with Welfare Economics?", *Economic Journal*, 89, 1979, pp 537–558.

54. And the cost of that fragility is that it will eventually destroy the complex system. For the story about local failure as the enabling condition for endurance of the larger system, see the *Wheel of Life.

The real L'Aquila, now capital of the Abruzzo region in Italy, came into existence by the merger of 99 local villages in the thirteenth century. The town has suffered destruction by earthquakes through its history. The earthquake of 1786 killed over 5,000 people, and in 2009, nearly 300 died. The present metaphor of L'Aquila (Eagle) and the Passero (Sparrow) villages makes no claims to be a historical account. In fact, a merger of 99 villages would be a more plausible fictional account than that of just eight villages, to produce a town of the sophistication of L'Aquila, but eight keeps it simple.

55. Elinor Ostrom cites an example of what happens when one or more members of a modular system have a significant advantage over others: the preventive resilience achieved by the cities on the banks of the Mississippi which built themselves massive flood defences. This ensured that, when Hurricane Katrina came, storm water was directed away from them and straight into New Orleans. See Elinor Ostrom's podcast at *Communicating Climate Change: Podcast Conversations with Social Scientists*, Episode 9, 13 February 2009, available at http://tinyurl.com/yzjqc2e .

56. David Tilman and John A. Downing, "Biodiversity and Stability in Grasslands", *Nature*, 367, 27 January 1994, pp 363–365.

57. David Tilman, "The Ecological Consequences of Changes in Biodiversity: A Search for General Principles", *Ecology*, 80, 5, July 1999, pp 1455–1474.

58. For discussion of diversity as a source of stability, see Stephan Harding (2006), *Animate Earth*, pp 212–216; or Edward Goldsmith (1992), *The Way*, pp 330–335.

59. John Alec Baker (1967), *The Peregrine*, pp 20 and 35.

60. Steven Mithen (2003), *After the Ice*, pp 507–508. Estimates of global warming and sea-level rise are higher now than they were when Mithen published this in 2003.

61. For tight feedback loops, see Brian Walker and David Salt (2006), *Resilience Thinking*, pp 122–123 and 146–147.

62. Illustration created by author.

63. Other proposals for the defining conditions of resilience: First, Brian Walker and David Salt (2006), *Resilience Thinking*, p 121, based on Simon A. Levin (1999), *Fragile Dominion: Complexity and the Commons*, Perseus Books, suggest three: modularity, diversity and feedback. Later, they settle on nine conditions: diversity, ecological variability, modularity, acknowledging slow variables, tight feedbacks, social capital, innovation, overlap in governance and ecosystem services.

Alternatively, Hartmut Bossel ((2007), *Systems and Models*, pp 184–185) argues for six "orientors", which represent the fundamental interests of self-organising systems, and which all have to be fulfilled if the system is to achieve its goals of survival, viability and success.

These orientors develop as a result of the system's co-evolution with its environment. They are:

1. Existence—causing organisms to avoid environments with which they are not compatible;
2. Effectiveness—causing organisms to develop effective and efficient means of using scarce resources;
3. Freedom of Action—allowing actors to respond appropriately to environmental challenges;
4. Security—causing search for shelter and food storage;
5. Adaptability—allowing actors to respond appropriately to environmental change; and
6. Coexistence with other systems in the same environment—enabling actors to interact appropriately with kin, competitors, etc.

64. John Holland (1998), *Emergence*, chapter 1.
65. For a helpful essay on laws and other forms of constraint, see Herbert L.A. Hart (1961), *The Concept of Law*, especially chapter 8.
66. For a discussion of the growth in the scale of the task of managing the ecosystem, see Edward Goldsmith, "The Last Word", in Edward Goldsmith and Gerry Mander, eds. (1996), *The Case Against the Global Economy*. Also Thomas Homer-Dixon (2000), *The Ingenuity Gap*. For vernacular, see Goldsmith (1992), *The Way*.
67. For dance, see Roderyk Lange (1970), *The Nature of Dance: An Anthropological Perspective*, p 91; and Paul Spencer, ed. (1985), *Society and the Dance: The Social Anthropology of Process and Performance*. For the 'middle voice', see Catherine Pickstock, "Liturgy, Art and Politics", *Modern Theology*, vol 16, 2, 2000, pp 159-190. See also Norman Pittenger (1969), *Alfred North Whitehead*, p 16.
68. For emotional daring, see Catherine Pickstock (1997), *After Writing*, especially pp 161–167; for harvest psalm, see Psalm 65; see also the quotation from Jules Michelet in the discussion of ritual/emotional daring in *Carnival: "My childhood never blossomed in the open air, in the warm atmosphere of an amiable crowd, where the emotion of each individual is increased a hundredfold by the emotion felt by all".
69. The extent to which dance in traditional societies changes with time and territory is discussed in Lange (1970), pp 104–105.
70. Pickstock (1997), pp 166–167.
71. James Roose-Evans (1994), *Passages of the Soul*, pp 7–8.
72. MacIntyre (1981), *After Virtue*, chapter 14.
73. See William T. Cavanaugh, "The World in a Wafer: A Geography of the Eucharist as Resistance to Globalization", *Modern Theology*, vol 15, 2, 1999, pp 181–196.

74. Catherine Pickstock, "Liturgy, Art and Politics", *Modern Theology*, vol 16, 2, 2000, p 160. The comparison between the *kallipolis* (good city) of the earlier *Republic* and the City of the Magnesians in his later *The Laws* is hers.
75. The phrase "the courage of its conventions" is owed to Jim McCue (1997), *Edmund Burke and our Present Discontents*, p 162. For ritual as establisher of fact, see Maurice Bloch (1989), *Ritual, History and Power*, pp 29 and 45. For a discussion of rituals as mechanisms for cultural internalisation, see Carl Folke, Fikret Berkes and Johan Colding, "Ecological Practices and Social Mechanisms for Building Resilience and Sustainability", in Berkes and Folke, eds. (1998), *Linking Social and Ecological Systems*, pp 414–436.
76. William Shakespeare (c.1606), *Coriolanus*, act III, scene 2.
77. John Dewey, "The School and Society", 1900, in (1899–1924), *The Middle Works of John Dewey*, p 38.

S

1. The circumference of a circle is $2\pi r$, where r is the radius. The area of a circle is πr^2. In the case of a sphere, the surface rises with the square of the radius: $4\pi r^2$, but volume rises with the cube of the radius: $(4/3)\,\pi r^3$.
2. J.B.S. Haldane, "On Being the Right Size", in (1927), *On Being the Right Size and Other Essays*.
3. Diagrams created by author.
4. For a wider view on scale, see Kirkpatrick Sale (1980), *Human Scale*; Leopold Kohr (1957), *The Breakdown of Nations*; Lewis Mumford (1961), *The City in History*.
5. See Bartholemew (2004), *The Welfare State We're In*, pp 42–45; and Karl de Schweinitz (1943), *England's Road to Social Security*, pp 100–113.
6. Thomas Chalmers (1821–26), *The Christian and Civic Economy of Large Towns*, Glasgow, vol I, pp 55–57, quoted in de Schweinitz (1943), pp 105.
7. William Fleming (1856), *Vocabulary of Philosophy*, p 354.
8. The main source for this discussion of scripts is Janis B. Alcorn and Victor M. Toledo, "Resilient Resource Management in Mexico's Forest Ecosystems: The Contribution of Property Rights", in Berkes and Folke, eds. (1998), *Linking Social and Ecological Systems*, chapter 9. Their definition of script is "an internalised plan used by people carrying out and interpreting routine activities", cited from R. Shank and R. Abelson (1977), *Scripts, Plans, Goals and Understanding*, Wiley.
9. See Janis B. Alcorn and Victor M. Toledo, "Resilient Resource Management in Mexico's Forest Ecosystems: The Contribution of Property Rights", in Berkes and Folke, eds. (1998), *Linking Social and Ecological Systems*, chapter 9.

10. Édouard Manet (1868–9), "The Execution of Emperor Maximilian", oil on canvas, Kunsthalle, Mannheim.

11. Janis B. Alcorn and Victor M. Toledo, "Resilient Resource Management in Mexico's Forest Ecosystems: The Contribution of Property Rights", in Berkes and Folke, eds. (1998), *Linking Social and Ecological Systems*, p 231. For another (tentative) application of the concept of the "shell", see *Multiculturalism.

12. *Ibid.*

13. Folke, Berkes and Colding, "Ecological Practices and Social Mechanisms for Building Resilience and Sustainability", in Berkes and Folke, eds. (1998), *Linking Social and Ecological Systems*, p 426.

14. William Blake (1804–1808), *Milton*, book I, part 28.

15. Clarissa Pinkola Estés (1992), *Women Who Run with the Wolves*, p 4.

16. James Roose-Evans (1994), *Passages of the Soul*, chapter 1. Neil Forsyth (1987), *The Old Enemy: Satan and the Combat Myth* and, for a short discussion, Robert Bly (1990), Iron John, chapter 6. For discussion of the wild man and "pretence", see Steve Biddulph (1994), *Manhood*, pp 256–260. For the wild woman, see Estés (1992).

17. The 'Phillips report' on the Government's handling of the BSE (Bovine Spongiform Encephalopathy, aka 'mad cow disease') crisis, published on 26 October 2000, volume 1, p 233, available at http://tinyurl.com/nqqdte3 .

18. "Never Seek to Tell thy Love" was first published in 1863 in Alexander Gilchrist's *Life of William Blake*, MacMillan and Co. As it was reproduced from Blake's hand-written notebook, featuring corrections, a few variants are extant. The poem is widely available online, e.g., at www .poetryfoundation.org/poem/172935 .

19. Elinor Ostrom, "The Danger of Self-Evident Truths", *PS: Political Science and Politics*, 33, 1, 2000, pp 33–44 (quotation from p 42).

20. Elinor Ostrom, "A General Framework for Analyzing Sustainability of Social-Ecological Systems", *Science*, 325, 5939, 2009, pp 419–22. See also summary in IU News Room, "Social Scientist Suggests New Research Framework to Study Complex Systems", 23 July 2009, available at http://newsinfo.iu.edu/news/page/normal/11424.html .

21. These self-evidently-true untruths are discussed as "challenged policy assumptions" in Bobbi Low, Elinor Ostrom, Carl Simon and James Wilson, "Redundancy and Diversity: Do They Influence Optimal Management?", in Fikret Berkes, Johan Colding and Carl Folke, eds. (2003), *Navigating Social-Ecological Systems*, pp 83–114.

22. Jamie Whyte (2003), *Bad Thoughts*, p 38.

23. The Shifting Ground tactic is a form of *irrelevance (*Ignoratio elenchi*); see Frans H. van Eemeren and Rob Grootendorst (1992), *Argumentation, Communication and Fallacies*, pp 133 and 214. For a discussion of the Old Germanic banquet, see Johan Huizinga (1949), *Homo Ludens*, pp 87–88.

24. For further reading, see Lionel Trilling (1971), *Sincerity and Authenticity*.

25. Lionel Robbins (1932), *An Essay on the Nature and Significance of Economic Science*, p 15.

26. The principle of degrowth is explored in Tim Jackson (2009), *Prosperity Without Growth*.

27. Andrew Mawson (2008), *The Social Entrepreneur*, pp 123–124.

28. See Oliver E. Williamson, "Transaction-cost economics: the governance of contractual relations", *Journal of Law and Economics*, 22, 2, 1979, pp 233–261; Oliver E. Williamson (1985), *The Economic Institutions of Capitalism*; especially pp 73–80; Robert M. Solow, "On Theories of Unemployment", *American Economic Review*, 70, 1, 1980, pp 1–11. For a summary see Ronald Dore, "Goodwill and the Spirit of Market Capitalism", 1983, pp 459–482, and more recent textbooks on labour economics.

29. Juliet B. Schor (1992), *The Overworked American: The Unexpected Decline of Leisure*, pp 46–47. For other views of medieval working time, see Eamon Duffy (1992), *The Stripping of the Altars* (40–50 days), pp 42–43; Keith Grint (1991), *The Sociology of Work* (one-third of the year including Sundays—i.e., 70 days), p 329.

30. For the 1536 Act, see Duffy (1992), p 394.

31. For a discussion of Peter Victor's work on the use of increased leisure to limit growth, see Tim Jackson (2009), *Prosperity Without Growth*, pp 134–136.

32. Homer (c. 700 BC), *The Odyssey*, book XIII.

33. For an elementary introduction to paradoxes, see Justin Leiber (1993), *Paradoxes*; the sorites paradox and others are discussed in R.M. Sainsbury (1987), *Paradoxes*; and Nicholas Rescher (2001), *Paradoxes: Their Roots, Range and Resolution*; Michael Clark (2002), *Paradoxes from A to Z*.

34. Thomas Hobbes (1651), *Leviathan*, chapter 13.

35. Frans H. van Eemeren and Rob Grootendorst (1992), *Argumentation, Communication and Fallacies*, pp 162 and 215; Christopher Tindale (2007), *Fallacies and Argument Appraisal*, pp 185–189. For vague logic / fuzzy logic, see Bart Kosko (1993), *Fuzzy Thinking*; Roy Sorensen (2001), *Vagueness and Contradiction*. William Empson, footnote to "Bacchus", in (1955), *Collected Poems*.

36. For a review of small-group sizes, see Richard L. Moreland, John M. Levine and Melissa L. Wingert, "Creating the Ideal Group: Composition Effects at

Work", 1996, in Erich H. Witte and James H. Davis, eds. (1996), *Understanding Group Behaviour*, vol 2, pp 11–36.

37. Andrew Whiten and Richard W. Byrne, "Tactical Deception in Primates", *Behavioural and Brain Sciences*, 12, 1988, pp 233–273; Richard W. Byrne and Andrew Whiten, eds. (1988), *Machiavellian Intelligence*.

38. Robert Barton and Robin Dunbar (1997), "Evolution of the Social Brain", in Andrew Whiten and Richard W. Byrne, eds. (1997), *Machiavellian Intelligence II*, p 255. The ability to keep up with relations between other members in your group is what is termed Machiavellian intelligence. The classic description of primate politics in action is Frans de Waal (1982), *Chimpanzee Politics*.

39. See references in previous two endnotes.

40. Robin Dunbar, "Coevolution of Neocortical Size, Group Size and Language in Humans", *Behavioural and Brain Science*, 16, 1993, pp 681–735. See also Robin Dunbar, "The Social Brain Hypothesis", *Evolutionary Anthropology*, 6, 1998, pp 178–190; and Robin Dunbar (1996), *Grooming, Gossip and the Evolution of Language*.

41. H. Kudo and Robin Dunbar, "Neocortex Size and Social Network Size in Primates", *Animal Behaviour*, 62, 2001, pp 711–722; and Dunbar, "Neocortex Size as a Constraint on Group Size and Behaviour", *Journal of Human Evolution*, 20, 1992, pp 469–493.

42. C.J. Buys and K.L. Larsen, "Human Sympathy Groups", *Psychology Reports*, 45, 1979, pp 547–53; also in Dunbar (1996), p 76.

43. Measured by frequency of contact (excluding the relationship between parents and young children), the strongest bond is between parent and adult children; this is followed by relationships between siblings, especially sisters; more remote kin, like cousins, nephews and grandparents, are seen much less often. Argyle (1991), *Cooperation*, pp 143–144.

44. *Ibid*, p 145.

45. Further discussion of group sizes can be found in R.A. Hill and Robin Dunbar, "Social Network Size in Humans", Human Nature, 14, 1, 2002, pp 53–72.

46. Pat Shipman, "Life and Death on the Wagon Trail", *New Scientist*, 27 July 1991, reporting Donald Grayson's historical research on the Dinner Party.

47. Peter Laslett (1965), *The World We Have Lost*, pp 2–3.

48. Jack Goody, "East is East?", *The Times Literary Supplement*, 15 February 2002, p 12.

49. For a discussion of the problems experienced by groups of 8 and groups of more than 20, see Mark Buchanan, "Explaining the Curse of Work", *New Scientist*, 14 January 2009. The article is a commentary on C.

Northcote Parkinson (1957), *Parkinson's Law, or the Pursuit of Progress*, John Murray.

50. Grooming can work for a larger group if its participants sit in a circle, as in circles of women doing each other's hair, but there is direct contact only with immediate neighbours.

51. W.J.H. Sprott (1958), *Human Groups*, p 91.

52. Peter Laslett, "The History of the Family", in Peter Laslett and Richard Wall, ed. (1972), *Household and Family in Past Time*, Cambridge University Press, quoted in Robert McCorkle Netting, Richard R. Wilk and Eric J. Arnould, eds. (1984), *Households: Comparative and Historical Studies of the Domestic Group*, p xxiv. The household and the family are not the same thing, and the consequences of assuming that they are were illustrated, for instance, by the clearing of the slums of Lagos with their maze of compounds and replacing them with single family apartments in suburban blocks, destroying the advantages of multiple family households for the urban poor. This is described by Peter Marris (1961), *Family and Social Change in an African City: A Study of Rehousing in Lagos*, Routledge & Kegan Paul, quoted in Netting et al., eds. (1984), p 18. Cf. *Incrementalism.

53. Manning Nash (1966), *Primitive and Peasant Economic Systems*, pp 43–44.

54. Robert D. Putnam (2000), *Bowling Alone*.

55. *Ibid*, pp 299–300.

56. See *ibid*, pp 326–333.

57. *Ibid*, p 345. For the Italian study, see Robert D. Putnam, Robert Leonardi, and Raffaella Y. Nanetti (1993), *Making Democracy Work: Civic Tradition in Modern Italy*, Princeton University Press. The discussion of democracy in the text is based on Putnam (2000), chapter 21.

58. For institutions as social detail, see Michael J. Sandel (1982), *Liberalism and the Limits of Justice*.

59. For the invisible body of rules, see Janis B. Alcorn and Victor M. Toledo, "Resilient Resource Management in Mexico's Forest Ecosystems", in Berkes and Folke, eds. (1998), *Linking Social and Ecological Systems*, p 219.

60. Robert D. Putnam, "E Pluribus Unum: Diversity and Community in the Twenty-First Century", *Scandinavian Political Studies*, 30, 2, 2007, pp 137–174, summarised at www.hks.harvard.edu/news-events/news/press-releases/putnam-social-cohesion .

61. See Walter Laqueur (2007), *The Last Days of Europe*, pp 69–76 and *passim*.

62. Sceptics on the role of television in reducing social capital include John Field (2003), *Social Capital*, and (quoted by Field) Peter Hall, "Social Capital in Britain",

British Journal of Political Science, 29, 3, 1999, pp 368–385. Putnam's findings on social capital itself are borne out by studies in other OECD countries; the central conclusions as to the deep and long-term decline in social capital are dismayingly consistent. References to findings in such other countries can be found in Stefano Bartolini, Ennio Bilancini and Maurizio Pugno, "Did the Decline in Social Capital Depress Americans' Happiness?", *Notebooks of the Department of Economic Politics, University of Siena*, 2008, available at www.econ-pol.unisi.it/quaderni/540.pdf .

63. Putnam (2000), p 229 (quotation abridged).

64. Putnam (2000), p 231.

65. For "scoriarching", see Patrick McCarthy and Richard Hawkes (1999), *Northside of the Mizen: Tales, Customs and History from the South-West of County Cork in Ireland*.

66. For "sitting till bedtime", see Wendell Berry, "The Work of Local Culture", Iowa Humanities Lecture, Schumacher Center for a New Economics, 1988, available at http://tinyurl.com/oehobl2 .

67. For the Amish, see Putnam (2000), p 235.

68. Aric Sigman (2005), *Remotely Controlled; How Television is Damaging Our Lives*. See also Guy Lyon Playfair (1990), *The Evil Eye: The Unacceptable Face of Television*, pp 145–147.

69. Putnam (2000), chapters 2 and 3.

70. *Ibid*, chapter 4.

71. *Ibid*, pp 100, 140, 110 and 115.

72. Putnam (2000), pp 72.

73. Bill Bryson (1996), *Notes from a Small Island*.

74. The context of this quotation is: "My work is intended chiefly for the benefit of cottagers, who must, of course, have some land; for, I propose to show, that a large part of the food of even a large family may be raised, without any diminution of the labourer's earnings abroad, from forty rod, or a quarter of an acre, of ground". William Cobbett (1821), *Cottage Economy*, pp 22–23.

75. Ebenezer Howard (1898), *To-Morrow: A Peaceful Path to Real Reform*, pp 11–12. Italics in original.

76. *Ibid*, chapter 1.

77. *Ibid*, pp 13–14, 19–20 and 23–24. Note that there is inconsistency between differing estimates of the amount of land needed for food and all other purposes. Some would deem Howard's suggestion of 2,000 hectares of surrounding land for all purposes to be on the low side, even if substantial quantities of food were grown in the gardens in the city itself. It seems right, however, to report on the numbers that have been provided by forbears rather than try to adjudicate between them. The resources for firmer calculations in the light of local circumstances are widely available.

78. Peter Hall and Colin Ward (1998), *Sociable Cities: The Legacy of Ebenezer Howard*, p 67. Peter Hall (1988), *Cities of Tomorrow*, p 100.

79. Howard (1898), *To-Morrow: A Peaceful Path to Real Reform*, Diagrams 2 and 3, p 14.

80. Jane Jacobs (1961), *The Death and Life of Great American Cities*, p 40.

81. Jacobs (1961), p 88.

82. See Dennis Hardy (2006), *Poundbury*.

83. Hall and Ward (1998), chapters 8 and 9.

84. Susan Owens' work, e.g., (1986), *Energy, Planning and Urban Form*, is summarised in Hall and Ward (1998), p 145. Michael Breheny and Ralph Rookwood , "Planning the Sustainable City Region", in Andrew Blowers, ed. (1992), *Planning for a Sustainable Environment*. See also summary in Hall and Ward (1998), pp 145–146.

85. Peter Calthorpe (1993), *The Next American Metropolis*, Princeton Architectural Press, summarised in Hall and Ward (1998), pp 146–149. For Stockholm and UK, see Michael Bernick and Robert Cervero (1997), *Transit Villages in the 21st Century*.

86. It is the idea of a set of principles in Alexander et al.'s (1977), *A Pattern Language* that is relevant here, rather than the principles they propose with respect to urban planning. Their principle of "fingers" of country alternating with town is anything but compact. Christopher Alexander, Sara Ishikawa, Murray Silverstein, et al. (1977), *A Pattern Language*, pp 21–25. See also Mike Jenks, Elizabeth Burton and Katie Williams, eds. (1999), *The Compact City: A Sustainable Urban Form?*

See also "Continuous Productive Urban Landscapes" (CPULs), another suggested system for remodelling cities to open up land for horticulture and agriculture, enabling them to become substantially self-sufficient in food, and healthier places to live. André Viljoen, ed., (2005), *CPULs: Continuous Productive Urban Landscapes*. For a summary, see www.energybulletin.net/17603.html .

87. John Gray (1998), False Dawn, p 37. In his powerful account of the dismantling of cultural traditions by the free market logic of the New Right, Gray argues that it is the unregulated free market experiment of the late nineteenth century and the 1980s—an Anglo-Saxon phenomenon, he claims—that has done the damage. It is argued in *Lean Logic*, however, that the market essentially replaces the more direct, social forms of reciprocal obligation; the free market expressed in globalisation is a logical development of that process, yet the real unpicking of direct reciprocity starts when the market moves centre-stage as it did in the eighteenth century.

The additional damage done by the free market—albeit avoidable and ill-advised—is an expression of the natural tendency of any social formula to mature towards its limit case.

88. Whitman (1855), *Leaves of Grass*, 159 (extract).

89. Adam Smith (1776), *The Wealth of Nations*, chapter 1, p 15.

90. For example, large-scale compost—with its smell, rats, flies, ground-water pollution and bacteria-rich air pollution—is a suspected health risk. See Richard Gray, "Giant Compost Heaps 'Are a Risk to Health'", *The Sunday Telegraph*, 28 June 2009.

91. For discussion of special pleading, see Robert H. Thouless (1930), *Straight and Crooked Thinking*, pp 199–203; and Douglas N. Walton (1999), *One-Sided Arguments, passim*, especially pp 87 and 107–110. For a cheerful introduction, see Madsen Pirie (2006), *How to Win Every Argument*, pp 155–157.

92. Alexander Pope (1742), *The Dunciad*, Thomas Cooper, book IV, 629–632.

93. John Ashton, "Why Environmentalists Need Europe", *Green Futures*, 46, May/June 2004, p 51.

94. St. Paul's Epistle to the Philippians, 4:7.

95. These comments on the text are influenced by Eckhart Tolle (1997), *The Power of Now*, p 183.

96. Johann Friedrich Herbart (1824–1825), *Psychology as Science*, pp 135 and passim.

97. Aldo Leopold, "The Land Ethic", in (1949), *A Sand County Almanac*, p 210 (quotation abridged: the original reads ". . . sold, fed, eaten . . .").

98. *Ibid*, pp 210–211.

99. *Ibid*, p 223. Julianne Lutz Newton (2006), *Aldo Leopold's Odyssey*, Island Press, p 349. For the Prince of Wales, see David Lorimer (2003), *Radical Prince*.

100. Donald Worster (1977), *Nature's Economy*, p 262.

101. Worster (1977), p 262 (Merriam); p 265 (progressive leaders).

102. For Pinchot, see Worster (1977), pp 266–268. For Leopold's 1920 remark, see Worster (1977), p 273. See also Aldo Leopold (1916–1948), *Aldo Leopold's Southwest*, p 11.

103. Raymond L. Lindeman's paper, "The Trophic-Dynamic Aspect of Ecology", *Ecology*, 23, 1942, pp 399–417, is quoted in Worster (1977), p 306.

104. Worster (1977), chapter 14. H.G. Wells, Julian Huxley, and P.G. Wells (1929), *The Science of Life*.

105. Worster (1977), p 270. Also Joseph Wood Krutch, "Conservation Is Not Enough", 1961, in Joseph Wood Krutch, ed. (1969), *The Best Nature Writing of Joseph Wood Krutch*, p 377.

106. Aldo Leopold, "Arizona and New Mexico", in (1949), *A Sand County Almanac*, pp 129–130. "Cunning", "diabolical" and "depraved" are Worster's words to describe the depiction of wolves in the anti-wolf propaganda of the early twentieth century. "Vermin" was in general use, and the colloquial noun "'varmint' has been the very worst epithet in America's moral lexicon". Worster (1977), pp 265, 258–261 and 260.

107. Stephan Harding (2006), *Animate Earth*, p 58. For systems thinking, see Fritjof Capra (1996), *The Web of Life*, especially chapter 3.

108. Worster (1997) p 317. Alfred North Whitehead (1925), *Science and the Modern World*, p 109.

109. This argument on amateur tradition is made by Worster (1977), p 335.

110. Quotation from Joseph Wood Krutch (1954), *The Measure of Man*, p 221. For "reverence and love", see also Joseph Wood Krutch (1956), *The Great Chain of Life*, p 161.

111. William Morton Wheeler quotation from a 1922 talk to the American Association for the Advancement of Science, in Mary Alice Evans and Howard Ensign Evans, eds. (1970), *William Morton Wheeler, Biologist*, p 314.

112. Antonio Damasio (1994), *Descartes' Error*. Lean Logic's summary should be placed in the context of recent discussion and developments in the field.

113. Damasio (1994), pp xxi–xix (summary) and *passim*.

114. Daniel J. Schneck and Dorita S. Berger (2006), *The Music Effect*, p 98.

115. See, for example, Daniel Goleman (1994), *Emotional Intelligence*, pp 102–110.

116. Damasio (1994), summarises research on the smile on pp 139–143, and cites references.

117. Damasio (1994), *Descartes' Error*, pp 3–19 (further reading pp 20–79).

118. *Ibid*.

119. *Ibid*, chapters 3 and 4.

120. Daniel Goleman (1994), *Emotional Intelligence*, pp 234–239.

121. Antonio Damasio (2003), *Looking for Spinoza*, p 151. Lewis Mumford (1961), *The City in History*, pp 267 and 272. See also Steve Biddulph (1994), *Manhood*.

122. Baruch Spinoza (1677), *Ethics*, part 3, cited in Damasio (2003), p 36.

123. Jean Hatton (2005), *Betsy: The Dramatic Biography of Prison Reformer Elizabeth Fry*. The significance of the religious context for Elizabeth Fry's work is noted in Charles Moore, "No Faith in Prisons Means There's No Hope for Prisoners", *The Daily Telegraph*, 8 July 2006. For references to the soul, see Damasio (1994), p xxvii.

124. "Report from the Select Committee of the House of Lords on the Present State of the Gaols and Houses of Correction in England and Wales", UK House of Commons, 28 July 1835, quoted in Hatton (2005), p 272.

125. Dick Taverne, "You Have to Be Green to Swallow the Organic Food Myth", *The Times*, 7 October 2003, p 20.

126. James G. Frazer (1922), *The Golden Bough*, chapter 48.

127. Christopher Tindale (2007), *Fallacies and Argument Appraisal*, pp 19–28; Frans H. van Eemeren and Rob Grootendorst (1992), *Argumentation, Communication and Fallacies*, pp 128–131 and 215; Anthony Weston (1987), *A Rulebook for Arguments*, pp 6–8.

128. See, for example, Walter Wright Arthen, "The Wicker Man: A Ritual of Transformation", 2008, available at www.earthspirit.org/fireheart/fhwkman.html ; and cf. the Green Man, e.g., at www.greenmanenigma.com .

129. Julius Caesar (58–50 BC), *Gallic War*, book VI, chapter 16.

130. Lawrence Kohlberg (1981), *The Philosophy of Moral Development*. See also Lawrence Kohlberg, Charles Levine and Alexandra Hewer, eds. (1983), *Moral Stages: A Current Formulation and a Response to Critics*. Kohlberg's work is also cited in Charles Hampden-Turner (1969), *Radical Man*, p 162. The summary of moral stages is an edited version of Kohlberg's text.

131. For a discussion of moral judgment and failed argument in this context, see Hampden-Turner (1969).

132. For the perils of positive thinking, see Barbara Ehrenreich (2010), *Smile or Die: How Positive Thinking Fooled America and the World*.

133. Mark, 9:24.

134. Mary-Ann Sieghart, *The Today Programme*, BBC Radio 4, 17 May 2004.

135. This bias and other ways in which the evidence can mislead are discussed by Nassim Nicholas Taleb (2001), *Fooled by Randomness*.

136. Karl-Henrik Robèrt (1997), *The Natural Step*.

137. Richard Heinberg (2007), *Peak Everything*, pp 88–95.

138. For further reading, see Jonathon Porritt (2005), *Capitalism as if the World Matters*. Richard Heinberg (2007), *Peak Everything*.

139. Herman E. Daly (1996), Beyond Growth ("biospheric carrying capacity" means "environmental regenerative and absorptive capacities"), p 167.

140. Daly is a little coy here on his own position on this. He writes "*Many believe* that the present scale is beyond long-term carrying capacity" (italics added). But he leaves us in no doubt that he is among the many. Daly (1996), p 167.

141. The World Commission on Environment and Development (1987), "Our Common Future", aka 'The Brundtland report', chapter 2, available at www.un-documents.net/our-common-future.pdf.

142. If a growing population is added in here, even greater improvements in such technology would be needed to stabilise the impact on the biosphere. The interaction between environmental impact, population, the scale of economic activity and technology is summarised in the 'IPAT equation', by Paul and Anne Ehrlich: Impact = Population × Affluence × Technology.

If environmental impact is to be held constant, and population is assumed to be constant, any advance in AFFLUENCE must be offset by a matching improvement in TECHNOLOGY (i.e., technologies which reduce environmental impact). If POPULATION increases—and especially if affluence increases at the same time—technological improvement must achieve extreme reductions in order to hold the IMPACT constant. If the environmental impact is to be made to fall, the task of efficiency-improvements required of the technology must of course be more extreme—and more remote from reality.

See Paul Ekins, "Sustainability First", in Paul Ekins and Manfred Max-Neef, eds. (1992), *Real-Life Economics*, pp 412–422, (specifically pp 418–419). For the famous debate on this, see Paul R. Ehrlich and John P. Holdren, "Impact of Population Growth", *Science*, vol 171, 26 March 1971, pp 1212–1217, and http://tinyurl.com/p5vnt4s . See also M.R. Chertow, "The IPAT Equation and its Variants: Changing Views of Technology and Environmental Impact", *Journal of Industrial Ecology*, 4, 4, 2001, pp 13–19; and R. York, E.A. Rosa and T. Dietz, "STIRPAT, IPAT AND ImPACT: Analytic Tools for Unpacking the Driving Forces of Environmental Impacts", *Ecological Economics*, 46, 3, 2003, pp 351–365.

143. For a discussion of the eco-efficiency of manual skills and advanced technology, relative to that of conventional industrial-scale systems, see Oliviero Bernardini and Riccardo Galli, "Dematerialization: Long Term Trends in the Intensity of Use of Materials and Energy", *Futures*, vol 25, 4, 1993, pp 431–448. Their work is based on Wilfred Malenbaum (1978), *World Demand for Raw Materials in 1985 and 2000*.

144. Decoupling is discussed in the context of degrowth in Tim Jackson (2009), *Prosperity Without Growth*, chapter 5.

145. Jonathon Porritt (2005), *Capitalism as if the World Matters*, chapter 14.

146. For an extended discussion and critique of sustainable development, see Donald Worster (1993), *The Wealth of Nature*, chapter 5, "The Shaky Ground of Sustainable Development".

147. Peter B. Checkland and John Poulter (2006), *Learning for Action*; Brian Wilson (2001), *Soft Systems Methodology*.

148. For hierarchy, see Arthur Koestler (1967), *The Ghost in the Machine*, especially chapter 3. For panarchy, see Lance

H. Gunderson and C.S. Holling, eds. (2002), *Panarchy*, especially chapters 1 and 3. For a summary, see Brian Walker and David Salt (2006), *Resilience Thinking*, pp 88–89.

149. Changes in the form of systems over time are noted by Walker and Salt (2006), p 31.

150. Diagram from Wikimedia Commons, used under the GNU Free Documentation License. Image available at https://tinyurl.com/o7d3zae .

151. Albert-László Barabási (2002), *Linked*, chapters 2, 6 and 7; and Mark Newman, Albert-László Barabási and Duncan J. Watts (2006), *The Structure and Dynamics of Networks*, pp 9–19, pp 229–239 and on pp 349–352 a reprinting of Albert-László Barabási and Réka Albert, "Emergence of Scaling in Random Networks", originally in *Science*, vol 286, 1999, pp 509–512. For a summary, see also Thomas Homer-Dixon (2006), *The Upside of Down*, chapter 5, especially pp 116–120. Diagram from Wikimedia Commons, used under the GNU Free Documentation License. Image available at https://tinyurl.com/o7d3zae .

152. As for barter, the formula is n(n-1)/2, where *n* is the number of towns, so the exact number for direct links between 1,000 towns is 499,500 two-way flights. For hub-based links it is simply 2(n-1)/2, or 999 two-way flights. For a more normal distribution—with, say, each town being linked four ways with the nearest four towns, the number of two-way links rises at the rate of 2n, less the smaller number of links maintained by towns near the edge of the system—and those edges may be expected to be irregular, with some towns having only one link.

153. See Barabási (2002); John Scott (1991), *Social Network Analysis*; Mark Buchanan (2003), *Nexus*; Newman, Barabási and Watts (2006); and Homer-Dixon (2006), chapter 5. For a discussion of the idea of "six degrees of separation" (that you are no more than six handshakes away from any other person on the planet), see Barabási (2002), chapter 3. The two key papers on this "small world" hypothesis are Ithiel de Sola Pool and Manfred Kochen, "Contacts and Influence", *Social Networks*, 1, 1978, pp 5–51 (a mathematical analysis); and Jeffrey Travers and Stanley Milgram, "An Experimental Study in the Small World Problem", *Sociometry*, 43, 1969, pp 425–443. Both of these articles are reprinted in Newman, Barabási and Watts (2006), pp 83–148. For a discussion of redundancy, see Charles Perrow (2007), *The Next Catastrophe*, pp 258, 301 and 327–330.

154. The internet's reliance on a relatively small number of hubs—and the implications of this for its ability to cope with breakdown—was pointed out in 2002, as reported, for instance, in Bobbie Johnson, "Web Providers Must Limit Internet's Carbon Footprint, Say Experts", *The Guardian*, 3 May 2009. It is discussed in more detail in Barabási (2002), chapter 11. For additional references on this fast-moving subject, look for "critical infrastructure", such as Ted G. Lewis (2006), *Critical Infrastructure Protection in Homeland Security: Defending a Networked Nation*, Wiley-Blackwell; and the series *Critical Infrastructure Protection*, US Congressional Sales Office. The source for computers accounting for 2 percent of carbon emissions is Phil McKenna, "Can We Stop the Internet Destroying our Planet?", *New Scientist*, 2637, 3 January 2008 (citing a report from UK charity Global Action Plan). For the energy consumption and carbon emissions of the internet, see, e.g., Professor Jaafar Elmirghani's ongoing projects and research at Leeds University, or Duncan Clark and Mike Berners-Lee, "What's the carbon footprint of . . . the internet", *The Guardian*, 12 August 2010.

155. Benoit B. Mandelbrot and Richard L. Hudson (2004), *The (Mis)behaviour of Markets*.

156. The example of people's heights if distributed according to the power law is from Albert-László Barabási (2002), *Linked*, p 67. For the Great Moderation see, for instance, Gary Duncan, "Fight to Sustain Recovery May Be Ultimate Battle", *The Times*, 16 February 2009, p 37. For examples of the unexpected, see Nassim Nicholas Taleb (2007), *The Black Swan*.

157. The example of the DC-3 is from Peter M. Senge (1990), *The Fifth Discipline*, p 6.

158. The governor was invented by Matthew Boulton and James Watt in 1788.

159. For further reading on feedback, see Brian Walker and David Salt (2006), *Resilience Thinking*; Fritjof Capra (1996), *The Web of Life*, especially chapter 2; Joseph O'Connor and Ian McDermott (1997), *The Art of Systems Thinking*; Henrich R. Greve (2003), *Organisational Learning from Performance Feedback*.

160. For a full description of causal loops—and illustrations of the diagrams that can be used to analyse them—see Dennis Sherwood (2002), *Seeing the Forest for the Trees*.

161. The significance of stability in systems is discussed in Edward Goldsmith (1992), *The Way*, chapter 22.

162. Lovelock here quotes William Shakespeare (c.1595), *A Midsummer Night's Dream*, act II, scene 1, lines 235–238.

163. James Lovelock (1988), *The Ages of Gaia*, pp 49–52.

164. Eugene P. Odum and Howard T. Odum (1953), *Fundamentals of Ecology*, p 13. See also Stephan Harding (2006), *Animate Earth*, pp 214–216; and Edward Goldsmith (1992), *The Way*, pp 136, 143 and 331–335.

165. Lovelock (1988), pp 50–57 (quotation from p 52).

166. For more on emergence, see Dennis Sherwood (2002), *Seeing the Forest for the Trees*; Peter B. Checkland (1981), *Systems Thinking, Systems Practice*, especially chapter 3; Mitchell M. Waldrop (1992), *Complexity*; and John Holland (1998), *Emergence*. For a classic exploration of emergence from a few rules, see Richard Dawkins (1986), *The Blind Watchmaker*.

167. There is an excellent summary and review of key questions arising in Homer-Dixon (2006), chapter 5. See also Malcolm Gladwell (2000), *The Tipping Point: How Little Things Can Make a Big Difference*.

168. Ervin László (2006), *The Chaos Point*, p 11.

169. Marvin Harris (1977), *Cannibals and Kings*, pp 246–247. Complexity economist W. Brian Arthur explores this in his (2009), *The Nature of Technology*.

170. Walker and Salt (2006), pp 59–62 (slow variables); pp 15–27 (the Everglades).

171. Peter M. Senge (1990), *The Fifth Discipline*, chapter 3.

172. Common and Stagl (2005), p 29.

173. Here again a recommended starting point for further reading is Homer-Dixon (2006), chapter 5.

174. Francis Darwin, ed. (1898), *The Life and Letters of Charles Darwin*, John Murray, p 345, quoted in Goldsmith (1992), p 137.

175. See John Gribbin (2004), *Deep Simplicity*. The definition of resonance is on p 61.

176. Buckminster Fuller, in February 1972 *Playboy* interview, quoted in *Bulletin of the Buckminster Fuller Institute*, available at https://bfi.org/sites/default/files/attachments/pages/CandidConversation-Playboy.pdf .

177. Richard H. Thaler and Cass R. Sunstein (2008), *Nudge*, p 253.

178. For discussions of leverage, see Senge (1990), chapter 7; Donella Meadows, "Leverage Points: Places to Intervene in a System", The Sustainability Institute, 1999, available at www.tellusmater.org.uk/pdf/Leverage_Points_%20Places_to_Intervene_in_a_System.pdf .

179. Eve Balfour (1943), *The Living Soil*.

180. Nicholas Carr (2010), *The Shallows*. For suggested reading on systems, see Fritjof Capra (1996), *The Web of Life* (the science of systems and ecology); Peter B. Checkland (1981), *Systems Thinking, Systems Practice* (a core text, including a rich literature review up to 1999); Anthony M.H. Clayton and Nicholas J. Radcliffe (1996), *Sustainability: A Systems Approach* (a comprehensive text on systems and the ecosystem). Edward Goldsmith (1992), *The Way* (a profound application of systems thinking to ecology); Joseph O'Connor and Ian McDermott (1997), *The Art of Systems Thinking* (an engaging beginners' guide); Peter M. Senge (1990), *The Fifth Discipline* (a brilliantly readable guide to systems thinking in management); Dennis Sherwood (2002), *Seeing the Forest for the Trees: A Manager's Guide to Applying Systems Thinking* (develops Senge's work on causal loops); Brian Walker and David Salt (2006), *Resilience Thinking* (an excellent summary, with many examples, seeing systems from the perspective of resilience).

Foundation texts include Norbert Wiener (1948), *Cybernetics, or Control and Communication in the Animal and the Machine* (ambitious, historical reading); Ludwig von Bertalanffy (1968), *General System Theory*; and Paul A. Weiss (1971), *Hierarchically Organised Systems in Theory and Practice*. Jay Wright Forrester (1961), *Industrial Dynamics* developed a systems thinking approach which he applied in (1970), *Urban Dynamics*, and which provided the basis for Meadows et al. (1972), *The Limits to Growth*. A survey of the present state and possible future developments in systems thinking is in Jamshid Gharajedaghi (1999), *Systems Thinking: Managing Chaos and Complexity*.

T

1. See Ashley Montague (1986), *Touching: The Human Significance of the Skin*, especially pp 224–228. For further reading on touch, see Linda Holler (2002), *Erotic Morality*; Ben E. Benjamin and Cherie Sohnen-Moe (2005), *The Ethics of Touch*; Tiffany Field (2001), *Touch*; and Frank Forencich (2006), *Exuberant Animal*. For an outline of the harrowing Harlow experiments with juvenile primates deprived of contact with their mother, see Herbert L. Petri (1986), *Motivation*, chapter 8.

2. On the links between touch and conversation, see Robin Dunbar (1996), *Grooming, Gossip and the Evolution of Language*.

3. This idea of 'the way a thing will develop if unobstructed' also underpins the meaning of "good" suggested by Aristotle and Thomas Aquinas, with its idea of individuation—the evolution by people and places of their uniqueness, character and distinctiveness. See Thomas Aquinas (1264), *On the Truth of the Catholic Faith*.

4. Edward Goldsmith (1992), *The Way*, pp 401–407.

5. From Lenin's 1920 speech to the Third Congress of the Komsomol, quoted in Françoise Thom (1987), *Newspeak*, p 85.

6. Thom (1987), p 85.

7. The key references on TEQs are David Fleming (2005), *Energy and the Common Purpose: Descending the Energy Staircase with Tradable Energy Quotas*, available at www.theleaneconomyconnection.net/downloads.html#TEQs ;

and David Fleming and Shaun Chamberlin (2011), *TEQs (Tradable Energy Quotas): A Policy Framework for Peak Oil and Climate Change,* available at www.teqs.net/download/.

For a regularly updated list of links to the key discussions of TEQs taking place in policy circles, academia and popular media, see www.teqs.net/links.html.

The model of Tradable Energy Quotas, formerly "tradable quotas" and "domestic tradable quotas", was first described in David Fleming, "Stopping the Traffic", *Country Life,* vol 140, 19, 9 May 1996, pp 62–65;

—"Tradable Quotas: Setting Limits to Carbon Emissions", Discussion Paper 11, The Lean Economy Connection ,1996 and 1997;

—"Tradable Quotas: Using Information Technology to Cap National Carbon Emissions", *European Environment,* 7, 5, Sept-Oct 1997, pp 139–148;

—"Your Climate Needs You", *Town & Country Planning,* 67, 9, October 1998, pp 302–304;

—ed., "Domestic Tradable Quotas as an Instrument to Reduce Carbon Dioxide Emissions", European Commission, *Proceedings,* Workshop 1–2 July 1998, EUR 18451;

—"Building a Lean Economy for a Fuel-Poor Future", in Richard Douthwaite, ed. (2003), *Before the Wells Run Dry: Ireland's Transition to Renewable Energy;*

—"The Credit System that Can Really Cut Global Warming", *Radical Economics,* 27, 2005, p 4.

For summaries of TEQs (formerly known as DTQs), see, e.g., David Boyle (2002), *The Money Changers;* James Bruges (2004), *The Little Earth Book;* George Monbiot (2007), *Heat: How We Can Stop the Planet Burning,* Penguin.

For formal reviews of TEQs and related schemes see, e.g., Simon Roberts and Joshua Thumim, "A Rough Guide to Individual Carbon Trading", Report to the UK Department for Environment, Food and Rural Affairs, November 2006, available at http://tinyurl.com /nequdmy ; UK House of Commons Environmental Audit Committee, "Personal Carbon Trading", Fifth Report of Session 2007–08, May 2008, available at https:// tinyurl.com/ost75a2 .

For more information on TEQs, including FAQs, or to subscribe to a newsletter for updates, see www.teqs.net .

Editor's note: For a more recent, peer-reviewed treatment of TEQs, including a summary of the system's impact up to 2015, see Shaun Chamberlin, Larch Maxey and Victoria Hurth, "Reconciling Scientific Reality with Realpolitik: Moving Beyond Carbon Pricing to TEQs— An Integrated, Economy-Wide Emissions Cap", *Carbon Management,* 5, 4, 16 Apr 2015, pp 411–427. Available at https://tinyurl.com/nq76xet.

8. Both diagrams created by author.

9. Andy Kerr and William Battye (2008), *Personal Carbon Trading: Economic Efficiency and Interaction with Other Policies,* report for the RSA, pp 5 and 46–47.

10. Numerous suggested frameworks exist for international agreement on national budgets; see, e.g., Aubrey Meyer (2000), *Contraction and Convergence,* and www.gci.org.uk /contconv/cc.html . TEQs is designed to implement those national budgets, once agreed. It could, of course, also be used for unilateral or multilateral reduction in energy-dependence.

11. For example, the DEFRA report commissioned from Accenture (2008), *An Analysis of the Technical Feasibility and Potential Costs of a Personal Carbon Trading Scheme,* produced estimated running costs of between £1 and £2 billion per annum, p 6. For a commentary on this report, see David Fleming and Shaun Chamberlin (2008), DEFRA's *Pre-Feasibility Study into Personal Carbon Trading—A Missed Opportunity,* available at www.teqs .net/DEFRAPFSresponse.pdf.

12. For lessons learnt from historical rationing and applied to tradable carbon rationing, see Mark Roodhouse (2007), "Rationing Returns: A Solution to Global Warming?", *History and Policy,* available at http://tinyurl.com/nwjojtf.

13. *Editor's note*: Much of this entry was reproduced (in a slightly different format) in David Fleming and Shaun Chamberlin (2011), *TEQs (Tradable Energy Quotas): A Policy Framework for Peak Oil and Climate Change,* available at www.teqs.net/download/ . For more on the political history and progress of TEQs to that date, see chapter 6 of that report, "Policy Update, including A Brief History of TEQs".

Or for a more recent, peer-reviewed treatment of TEQs, including a summary of the system's impact up to 2015, see Shaun Chamberlin, Larch Maxey and Victoria Hurth, "Reconciling Scientific Reality with Realpolitik: Moving Beyond Carbon Pricing to TEQs—An Integrated, Economy-Wide Emissions Cap", *Carbon Management,* 5, 4, 16 Apr 2015, pp 411–427. Available at https://tinyurl.com/nq76xet.

Note that TEQs is not only suited as a *catalyst* to adequate global agreement on emissions reductions; it is equally suited as an *alternative* to such negotiations. As discussed in the 2015 paper above, any unilateral or multilateral implementation of TEQs would make import tariffs necessary, to ensure that manufacturers in the countries concerned were not disadvantaged relative to international competitors (*Protection; see also www .teqs.net/faqs/#Tariffs). These tariffs will generate revenue for the TEQs countries when they import goods. And importantly, this will in turn provide a strong incentive for the exporting countries to themselves implement TEQs or a similar policy, so that they can collect this revenue, instead of letting it flow overseas. In this way, effective climate policy spreads around the world.

14. David Hackett Fischer (1970), *Historians' Fallacies* discusses errors in historians' treatment of time.

15. Dr. Anthony Seldon, "Enough of this Educational Apartheid", *The Independent*, 15 January 2008.

16. Mary Warnock, "We Need Have No Fear of Interference with Nature", *The Guardian*, 15 May 2001.

17. For Thomas Jefferson reference, see, e.g., Jim Cullen (2001), *Restless in the Promised Land: Catholics and the American Dream*, Sheed & Ward, p 8.

18. John Milton (1667), *Paradise Lost*, book II, line 274.

19. See Walt Whitman Rostow (1952), *The Process of Economic Growth*, chapters 11–13 and *passim*.

20. T.S. Eliot, "Tradition and the Individual Talent", in (1932), *Selected Essays, 1917–1932*.

21. David L. Miller (1967), *Individualism: Personal Achievement and the Open Society*, chapter 5.

22. Edmund Burke, Letter to James Barry, 1769, in Fintan Cullen (2000), *Sources in Irish Art*, p 181.

23. "The Rain", in W.H. Davies (1908), *Nature Poems and Others*, A.C. Fifield.

24. For number (and location) of Transition communities, see www.transitionnetwork.org/initiatives. Note that there are also hundreds of 'mullers': communities that have expressed interest in joining the movement, and in some cases are getting on with it all, but have not yet registered themselves.

For introductions to Transition, see Rob Hopkins (2008), *The Transition Handbook*; Shaun Chamberlin (2009), *The Transition Timeline*; and Jacqi Hodgson and Rob Hopkins (2010), *Transition in Action*. For an early take on the subject, see Rob Hopkins, "The Food Producing Neighbourhood", 2000, in Hugh Barton, ed. (1999), *Sustainable Communities: The Potential for Eco-Neighbourhoods*, or for an academic study see Rob Hopkins, "Localisation and resilience at the local level: the case of Transition Town Totnes (Devon, UK)", PhD dissertation, University of Plymouth, 2010. See also the entry on *Energy Descent Action Plans, and the Transition Culture website at http://transitionculture.org . For the latest developments, see www.transitionnetwork.org.

Editor's note: As of 2015, there are now thousands of Transition initiatives, spread over more than 50 countries.

25. *Editor's note*: "The Big Society" was a flagship policy of the UK Conservative Party in their manifesto for the 2010 general election, aiming "to create a climate that empowers local people and communities, building a big society that will take power away from politicians and give it to people . . . encouraging people to take an active role in their communities." After the election, Conservative Prime Minister David Cameron stated that he wanted his vision of such a 'Big Society' to be one of the great legacies of his Government. See, e.g., www.gov.uk/government /news/government-launches-big-society-programme--2.

26. Charles Perrow (2007), *The Next Catastrophe*, pp 3, 325. See also Denis Smith, ed. (2006), *Key Readings in Crisis Management*.

27. Atul Gawande (2009), *The Checklist Manifesto*, pp 107–110.

28. *Editor's note*: In a 2015 interview, Transition movement founder Rob Hopkins stated that: "The one social/ political/cultural policy change that would most assist my work/hopes/dreams would be David Fleming's rather brilliant idea of Tradable Energy Quotas. It would unlock so much." From "Scaling This Stuff Up: Resilience Reflections with Rob Hopkins", *Resilience.org*, 30 September 2015, available at: https://tinyurl.com /pf3upu9 . See also this Dictionary's entry on *TEQs (Tradable Energy Quotas).

29. Francis Fukuyama (1992), *Trust: The Social Virtues and the Creation of Prosperity*, p 25. Trust and its central role in business is also discussed by Peter Taylor-Gooby in, "Markets and Motives: Trust and Egoism in Welfare Markets", *Journal of Social Policy*, 28, 1999, pp 97–114.

30. See, for example, the UK's Independent Safeguarding Authority. For a comment on its implications for trust, and on contact between adults and children, see Camilla Cavendish, "We Are All Suspects in the New Inquisition's Eyes", *The Times*, 1 May 2009, p 31.

31. Onora O'Neill, "A Question of Trust: the 2002 Reith Lectures", BBC Radio 4, available at www.bbc.co.uk /radio4/reith2002/.

32. For an extended discussion of the difference between trust and expectation, see Adam B. Seligman (1997), *The Problem of Trust*, especially chapter 4.

33. Onora O'Neill, "A Question of Trust: the 2002 Reith Lectures", BBC Radio 4, lecture 4, "Trust and Transparency".

34. See Mark K. Smith, "Carl Rogers, Core Conditions and Education", *The Encyclopaedia of Informal Education*, 1997, available at www.infed.org/thinkers/et-rogers.htm.

35. Carl Rogers, "A Tentative Formulation of a General Law of Interpersonal Relationships", chapter 18 of (1961), *On Becoming a Person*, pp 338–346 (quotation from p 344). The formulation of congruence continues with a contrast with incongruence.

36. Carl Rogers, "A Client-Centered/Person-Centered Approach to Therapy", in Irwin L. Kutash and Alexander Wolf, eds. (1986), *Psychotherapist's Casebook*, Jossey-Bass, pp 197–208, republished in Rogers (1942–1987), *The Carl Rogers Reader*, pp 135–152 (quotation from pp 136-137).

37. *Editor's note*: "The Big Society" was a flagship policy of the UK Conservative Party in their manifesto for the 2010 general election, aiming "to create a climate that empowers local people and communities, building a big society that will take power away from politicians and give it to people . . . encouraging people to take an active role in their communities." After the election, Conservative Prime Minister David Cameron stated that he wanted his vision of such a 'Big Society' to be one of the great legacies of his Government. See, e.g., www.gov.uk/government /news/government-launches-big-society-programme--2 .

38. For the notion of metaphor as a means of communicating material truth see, for instance, Catherine Elgin, "Metaphor and Reference", in Zdravko Radman, ed. (1995), *From a Metaphorical Point of View*.

39. A key text in the field of narrative truth is Erich Auerbach (1946), *Mimesis*.

40. Quotation from marginal gloss in Samuel Taylor Coleridge, "The Rime of the Ancient Mariner", part 4, in (1817), *Sibylline Leaves*.

41. John L. Austin (1962), *How To Do Things With Words*, p 62.

42. See, e.g., Luca Castagnoli (2010), *Ancient Self-Refutation: The Logic and History of the Self-Refutation Argument from Democritus to Augustine*, Cambridge University Press.

43. Tim Smit quoted at http://startups.co.uk/tim-smit-the -eden-project/ .

44. See Douglas N. Walton (1999), *One-Sided Arguments*, p 107.

U

1. Karl Popper (1945), *The Open Society and Its Enemies*, vol II, p 260.

2. For further reading, see Steve Fuller (2003), *Kuhn vs. Popper: The Struggle for the Soul of Science* (reviewed by Vincent Deary, "Great White Males Still At Large", *Times Literary Supplement*, 7 November 2003); Karl Popper (1959), *The Logic of Scientific Discovery*; Thomas S. Kuhn (1962), *The Structure of Scientific Revolutions*.

3. For Ptolemy's epicycles, see, e.g., Arthur Koestler (1959), *The Sleepwalkers*, pp 66–75.

4. Jonathan Swift (1726), *Gulliver's Travels*, book 3, chapter 5.

5. Karl Popper (1945), *The Open Society and Its Enemies*, vol II, chapter 25; and, for a more extended discussion of falsifiability and testability, see Karl Popper (1962),

Conjectures and Refutations. For giant water projects, see Fred Pearce (2005), *When the Rivers Run Dry*.

6. Main sources for this entry: Marvin Harris (1977), *Cannibals and Kings*; and Karl A. Wittfogel (1957), *Oriental Despotism*.

Wittfogel's work has had its critics, notably among historians, who have suspected a political motive, and also objected that a society's character is shaped by its inherited culture as much as by its physical environment. But it was quickly recognised by anthropologists such as Julian Steward, and later by Marvin Harris and Robert Netting, who argued simply that there are basic environmental and technological forces that shape a society, and that we will get nowhere in understanding how cultures work if we blithely assume that a people's ideas simply come from other ideas. The debate surrounding Wittfogel's work, and Steward's and Netting's contribution to it, is described by Donald Worster (1993), *The Wealth of Nature*, pp 32–41. Note that, even if a society's culture were substantially shaped by its inheritance of ideas rather than by its environment, it would not follow that it had much choice in the matter, as there is "path dependence": its inheritance of ideas shapes its mindset and there is little that it can do about that inheritance. If it does succeed in doing something, it is a slow process (*Systems Thinking ❭ Feedback ❭ Path Dependence).

7. For "two hours a day" see Marshall Sahlins (1972), *Stone Age Economics*, p 27.

8. Population levels in China, northern India, Mesopotamia and Egypt can be found in Harris (1977), pp 234–235.

9. Wittfogel (1957), pp 23–27. Harris (1977), pp 244–245.

10. Sources report that, of the million labourers conscripted to build the Great Wall, over half died. See Raymond Dawson (1972), *Imperial China*, p 62. Regarding "men with spades", a system in which there is a very high death rate would quickly collapse if women were included in it to any significant extent.

Editor's note: David Fleming's former colleague Judith Thornton highly recommends Steven Mithen (2012), *Thirst: Water and Power in the Ancient World*, Weidenfeld & Nicolson, as a valuable supplementary resource on this topic, published after Fleming's death.

11. *The Laws of Manu*, a Hindu sacred text from the first millennium BC, translated by George Bühler (1886), quotation abridged from chapter 7, verses 14, 17, 18, 20, 22, 23 and 25.

12. All cited in Wittfogel (1957), pp 139–145.

13. Ira Maurice Price, ed. (1899), *The Great Cylinder Inscriptions A & B of Gudea*. Extracts from Cylinder B 17:17–21;

A 13:6 and 9; A 12:24–25; A 13:1. "Even" is inserted, indicating the extraordinary nature of the circumstance.

14. Wittfogel (1957), p 150 (good life); pp 150–151 (Confucius' good society). For small people and mutualism, see Raymond Dawson (1972), *Imperial China*, p 41.

15. Wittfogel (1957), pp 152–153 (kotow); pp 152–154 (Pharaoh); p 159 (Sima Qian, aka Ssŭma Ch'ien).

16. *Ibid*, p 134.

17. *Ibid*, p 50.

18. Harris (1977), pp 264–265.

19. Wittfogel (1957), p 329.

20. There ought to be a "probably" in here. The troubadours were singers and poets who travelled around Europe in the 12th—14th centuries. The source of the fragment is unknown, but many anthologies cite and discuss it. See a brief discussion in R.T. Davies, ed. (1963), *Medieval English Lyrics*, p 367.

21. For instance, John King Fairbank and Merle Goldman (1992) write, "An estimated population of 60 million as of AD 2 in mid-Han had been matched by roughly the same figure in mid-Tang, suggesting a thousand years of ups and downs with only a modest overall increase." *China: A New History*, p 167. For the usual sense of "steady state economy", see, e.g., Herman E. Daly (1992), *Steady-State Economics*.

22. Wittfogel (1957), pp 174 and 191–193. This is a plausible hypothesis. Wittfogel had an anti-Marxist interest, but it remains true that successful and stable political formulae do travel.

23. Deuteronomy 23:19–20.

24. Richard Henry Tawney (1926), *Religion and the Rise of Capitalism*, pp 49, 58 and 49.

25. For Shakespeare, see John Bossy (1985), *Christianity in the West: 1400–1700* , p 77. For radical environmental movement, see Michael Rowbotham (1998), *The Grip of Death: A Study of Modern Money, Debt Slavery and Destructive Economics*; Norman Cohn (1975), *Europe's Inner Demons*.

26. Tawney (1926), p 132.

27. *Ibid*, p 42.

28. Matthew 25, 14–30.

29. Machiavelli (1513), *The Prince*, chapter 15.

30. Machiavelli (1517), *The Discourses on the First Ten Books of Titus Livy*, I. 9.

31. Quoted in John R. Hale (1961), *Machiavelli and Renaissance Italy*, p 9. Original:

> Io spero, e lo sperar cresce il tormento,
> Io piango, e il pianger ciba il lasso core;
> Io rido, e il rider mio non passa drento;
> Io ardo, e l'arsion non par di fuore; . . .

Undated poem by Niccolò Machiavelli, "Strambotti", I, available at www.classicitaliani.it/machiav/mac63 _poes.htm .

32. William H. Koetke, "The Final Empire: The Collapse of Civilization and the Seed of the Future", 1993, in John Zerzan, ed. (1999), *Against Civilization*, pp 155–161.

33. William Morris (1891), *News from Nowhere*, pp 64–65.

34. *Ibid*.

35. Edmund Spenser (1596), *The Faerie Queene*, book III, canto VI.

36. Hesiod, Ovid, Pindar, Cockaigne are cited in Gregory Claeys and Lyman Tower Sargent, eds. (1999), *The Utopia Reader*.

37. The following citations are drawn from John Carey, ed. (1999), *The Faber Book of Utopias*: for population control see, e.g., H.G. Wells (1891), *Anticipations*; for baby factories: Marge Piercy (1979), *Woman on the Edge of Time*; for abolition of heterosexual sex: Naomi Mitchison (1975), *Solution Three*; for depopulated landscape: Richard Jefferies (1885), *After London*; for abolition of money: W.H. Hudson (1887), *A Crystal Age*; Edward Bellamy (1888), *Looking Backward*; William Morris (1891), *News from Nowhere*; for surrender to the passions: Charles Fourier, see Jonathan Beecher and Richard Bienvenu, eds. (1972), *The Utopian Vision of Charles Fourier*; for industrial army: Edward Bellamy (1888), *Looking Backward*; for universal language: Newman Watts (1939), *The Man Who Did Not Sin*; for literary education, the greening of Europe, subsistence farming and the simple life: Adolf Hitler (1939), *Mein Kampf* and *Hitler's Table Talk*, 1941–44; for manual skills: William Morris (1891), *News from Nowhere*; and for noble savage: Jean-Jacques Rousseau (1762), *The Social Contract*.

38. John MacNie, quoted in Northrop Frye, "Varieties of Literary Utopias", 1965, in Frank E. Manuel, ed. (1967), *Utopias and Utopian Thought*, p 30.

39. This was originally outlined in J.D. Bernal (1929), *The World, the Flesh and the Devil: An Inquiry into the Future of the Three Enemies of the Rational Soul*, K. Paul, Trench, Trübner & Co., and elaborated by Freeman J. Dyson in, "The World, the Flesh and the Devil", the third J.D. Bernal lecture, delivered at Birkbeck College, London, 1972.

40. Astolphe de Custine (1843), *Journey for Our Time: The Russian Journals of the Marquis De Custine*, p 176.

41. For a helpful account of Desiderius Erasmus and his life, see A.H.T. Levi's (1971) introduction to the Penguin edition of Erasmus' (1511), *In Praise of Folly*. For Julius II's army, see Erasmus (1511), p 179; for the spin doctors see p 181. For Erasmus' visit to More, see Cornelis Augustijn (1991), *Erasmus: His Life, Works and Influence*, p 57.

42. Erasmus (1511), p 135; see also Levi (1971), p 13 (a social evil).

43. Norman Cohn (1957), *The Pursuit of the Millennium*, pp 281, 282 and 286.

44. Thomas More (1516), *Utopia*.

45. The source for the Renaissance Utopias is Miriam Eliav-Feldon (1982), *Realistic Utopias*: for Anton Doni, see pp 20–21; for Francesco Patrizi, see p 45. For defenestration, see, for instance, Geoffrey Parker (1979), *Europe in Crisis 1598–1648*.

46. Eliav-Feldon (1982), p 38 (Tommaso Campanella), p 38 (Ludovico Zuccolo), p 39 (Robert Burton).

47. Eliav-Feldon (1982), pp 41 and 43 (Johan Andreae), p 50 (I.D.M.), p 69 (Francis Bacon).

48. William Shakespeare (c.1611), *The Tempest*, act II, scene 1, lines 144–165.

49. Northrop Frye, "Varieties of Literary Utopias", 1965, in Frank E. Manuel, ed. (1967), *Utopias and Utopian Thought*.

V

1. James P. Womack and Daniel T. Jones (1996), *Lean Thinking*, pp 16–19; quotation from p 353.

2. Womack and Jones (1996), p 353.

3. Edward Goldsmith discusses the concept of the vernacular (but not the actual word) in "The Last Word", in Edward Goldsmith and Gerry Mander, eds. (1996), *The Case Against the Global Economy*. For an extended discussion (using the word), see Goldsmith (1992), The Way, chapter 59.

4. St. Paul:1 Corinthians 13:13. These are seen as gifts of faith (itself a gift), in that they cannot be achieved by human effort. Arguably, *charity can come with trying, but "love" — which is less obviously capable of forming on demand — is used in its place in most English translations of the Bible.

5. Plato usually writes of four virtues: courage, godliness, righteousness and temperance, but both he and Aristotle recognised that righteousness is actually the same thing as areté — the whole principle of political and moral virtue. *Lean Logic*'s summary of the Greek virtues is open to criticism on the grounds that (a) it has "fortitude" instead of the more usual "courage"; and (b) it changes the order. In the *Republic*, Plato has "philosophical wisdom" instead of godliness. For a discussion of these matters, see Werner Jaeger (1935), *Paideia: The Ideals of Greek Culture*, pp 103–105.

6. The cardinal virtues are usually quoted as prudence, justice, temperance, fortitude. They were derived directly from the Greek virtues. Jaeger (1935) writes that it is "irrelevant" that Plato used "philosophical wisdom" instead of "godliness" in the *Republic* (see previous note), so there may therefore be some justification in seeing "justice and temperance" in the cardinal virtues as closely related in meaning to Plato's godliness.

7. John Henry Newman (1873), *The Idea of a University*, pp xxxxviii, 185, 186 and xxxi (i.e., the introduction and part 1, discourse xiii, chapter 10).

W

1. The following are not necessarily the latest books, but provide an excellent introduction to water. For the state of the water-world, see Fred Pearce (2005), *When the Rivers Run Dry*. For water and permaculture, see Patrick Whitefield (2004), *The Earth Care Manual*. For the treatment of sewage, see Peter Harper and Louise Halestrap (1999), *Lifting the Lid: An Ecological Approach to Toilet Systems*; Nick Grant, Mark Moodie and Chris Weedon (1996), *Sewage Solutions: Answering the Call of Nature*. For community and water, see Ton Schouten and Patrick Moriarty (2003), *Community Water, Community Management*. For examples of community action, and links, see Paul Hawken (2007), *Blessed Unrest*.

    Editor's note: Since David Fleming's death his former colleague Judith Thornton has herself published a definitive guide to the practicalities of water supply: Judith Thornton (2012), *Choosing Ecological Water Supply and Treatment*, Centre for Alternative Technology Publications. For a historical perspective on water, she highly recommends Steven Mithen (2012), *Thirst: Water and Power in the Ancient World*, Weidenfeld & Nicolson.

2. For an extended study of well-being and a discussion of "accomplishment" as a defining property, see James Griffin (1986), *Well-Being*. For a discussion of what well-being means, and of ways of measuring it, see David Boyle and Andrew Simms (2009), *The New Economics*.

3. Simon Kuznets, "A Report on National Income, 1929–32", in response to Senate Resolution no. 220, United States Government Printing Office, 1934, pp 6–7, available at http://tinyurl.com/nrgwqs9 .

4. William H. Branson (1979), *Macroeconomic Theory and Policy*, chapter 2; David Begg et al. (1984), *Economics*, chapters 19, 29; Boyle and Simms (2009), pp 37–39.

5. *Ibid*.

6. E.J. Mishan (1977), *The Economic Growth Debate*, chapter 3. Clothes (such as overalls for workshops and formal clothing for offices) are in Mishan's list but are omitted from this summary. For a more recent discussion, see Boyle and Simms (2009), chapter 3.

7. See Richard Easterlin, "Does Economic Growth Improve the Human Lot?", in Paul A. David and Melvin Warren Reder, eds. (1974), *Nations and Households in Economic Growth*, pp 89–125; see also the entry on the *Composition Fallacy.

8. Frederick Herzberg (1962), *Work and the Nature of Man*, especially chapter 6.

9. Oliver James (1997), *Britain on the Couch*, pp 29–31, For more detail, see chapters 1 and 9, and *passim*.

10. For a useful account of methods of adjusting conventional accounts for environmental costs, see Paul Ekins (2000), *Economic Growth and Environmental Sustainability*, chapter 5, "Accounting for Production and the Environment".

11. Property income is the income earned from overseas assets. For example, the income earned by a French company operating in the UK would count as part of the UK's GDP, and part of France's GNP.

12. Net Economic Welfare, described in David Begg, Stanley Fischer and Rüdiger Dornbusch (1984), *Economics*. See also William D. Nordhaus and James Tobin's Measure of Economic Welfare (MEW) in "Is Growth Obsolete?" National Bureau of Economic Research, Fiftieth Anniversary Colloquium, 1973, available at www.nber.org/chapters/c3621.pdf .

13. GPI is derived from the Index of Sustainable Economic Welfare (ISEW), and based on consumption, rather than incomes. It was designed by Herman E. Daly and John B. Cobb and is described in detail in the appendix of their (1989), *For the Common Good*.

14. The Happy Planet Index was designed by the New Economics Foundation, 2006. See www.happyplanetindex.org

15. Politics' most conspicuous failure to make sense of GDP consists in not realising that it is *per capita* GDP that is at stake here: aggregate GDP has no direct relevance whatsoever. This error was pointed out by the UK House of Lords Select Committee on Economic Affairs, "The Economic Impact of Immigration", First Report of Session 2007–8, published 1 April 2008, Her Majesty's Stationery Office, volume 1, chapter 1, paragraph 69. Also see *Growth, *Instrumentalism, *Population.

16. See Lance H. Gunderson and C.S. Holling, eds. (2002), *Panarchy*, especially chapter 2, "Resilience and Adaptive Cycles". Diagram from p 34.

17. The "r" label came originally from R. Pearl, "The Growth of Populations", *Quarterly Review of Biology*, 2, 1927, pp 532–548, cited in Gunderson and Holling, eds. (2002), p 33. The notation became widely established with the publication of Robert H. MacArthur and Edward O. Wilson (1967), The Theory of Island Biogeography.

18. The "K" label comes from the same sources as "r" (see previous note). MacArthur and Wilson's (1967) definition is "the carrying capacity of the environment", p ix.

19. Gunderson and Holling, eds. (2002), p 34.

20. *Ibid*, p 35.

21. *Ibid*, p 35.

22. Quotation from Gunderson and Holling, eds. (2002), p 34. The authors also note that "in a sustainable ecosystem, the accumulated resources that determine ecological potential might be eroded, might partially leak away, but are only partially reduced. If they were completely or largely eliminated, recovery would be impossible, and the system would slip into a different, degraded state. Such a condition would occur, for example, if species critical in maintaining structure and function became extinct" (p 38).

For further exploration of *resilience* in the cycle, Gunderson and Holling add it as a third axis—in addition to potential and connectedness—to create a three-dimensional diagram (ibid, p 41). See also Brian Walker, C. S. Holling, Stephen R. Carpenter, and Ann P. Kinzig, "Resilience, adaptability and transformability in social–ecological systems", *Ecology and Society*, 9, 2, 2004, available at www.ecologyandsociety.org/vol9/iss2/art5/ .

23. Diagram created by author.

24. Brian Walker and David Salt (2006), *Resilience Thinking*, pp 85–87.

25. The short time taken by the back loop, relative to the fore loop, is noted by Brian Walker and David Salt (2006), *Resilience Thinking*, p 29.

26. Stewart Brand (1999), The Clock of the Long Now. See note 29 for the extensive analysis of timings by Holling, Gunderson and colleagues.

27. Nadia Johanisova, personal communication. But see Daniel M. Brooks, Richard E. Bodmer and Sharon Matola, eds. (1997), *Tapirs: Status Survey and Conservation Action Plan*, International Union for Conservation of Nature and Natural Resources.

28. Diagram created by author.

29. On the relationship between size and timing, see Brand (1999). For the adaptive cycle of panarchical relationships across scales, see Lance H. Gunderson, C.S. Holling and Stephen S. Light, "Breaking Barriers and Building Bridges: A Synthesis", in Gunderson, Holling and Light, eds. (1995), *Barriers and Bridges to the Renewal of Ecosystems and Institutions*; and F. Günther and C. Folke, "Characteristics of Nested Living Systems", *Journal of*

Biological Systems, 1, 1993, pp 257–274; both cited and summarised in C.S. Holling, Fikret Berkes and Carl Folke, "Science, Sustainability and Resource Management", in Fikret Berkes and Carl Folke, eds. (1998), *Linking Social and Ecological Systems: Management Practices and Social Mechanisms for Building Resilience.*

30. Regarding the idea that enabling or encouraging subsystems within a larger system to go through their adaptive cycles on a small scale can be a means of delaying (perhaps preventing) the crash of the whole system, Walker and Salt (2006) comment that "generating disturbances at lower scales can keep a system at a higher scale from progressing to a late *K* phase" (p 88)—that is, to the release phase.

The relationship between small-scale (fast-moving) and large-scale (slow-moving) cycles is discussed in Fikret Berkes, Johan Colding and Carl Folke, "Introduction"; in Berkes, Colding and Folke, eds. (2003), *Navigating Social-Ecological Systems*, pp 1–29; and in C.S. Holling, Lance H. Gunderson and Garry D. Peterson, "Sustainability and Panarchies", in Gunderson and Holling, eds. (2002), *Panarchy*, pp 63–102.

31. Horst Rittel and Melvin Webber, "Dilemmas in a General Theory of Planning", *Policy Sciences*, 4, 1973, pp 155–169. Wicked problems are discussed in Roy Madron and John Jopling (2003), *Gaian Democracies.*

32. Warnings of oil depletion have come from: Esso/Exxon, by W.P. Ryman, deputy exploration manager of Standard Oil, 1967, cited in Edward Goldsmith and Robert Prescott-Allen (1972), *A Blueprint for Survival*, p 18; UK Department of Energy, "Energy Research and Development in the United Kingdom", *Energy Paper No. 11*, 1976; M. King Hubbert, "World Oil and Natural Gas Reserves and Resources", in Congressional Research Services (1977), *Project Independence: U.S. and World Energy Outlook Through 1990*, US Government Printing Office; United States Council on Environmental Quality and Department of State, "The Global 2000 Report to the President", 1980; World Bank, "Global Energy Prospects", Staff Working Paper No 489, 1981; Colin J. Campbell and Jean Laherrère, "The World's Supply of Oil 1930–2050", Petroconsultants, 1995; L.F. Ivanhoe, "Updated Hubbert Curves Analyze World Oil Supply", *World Oil*, 217, 11, November 1996, pp 91–93; Colin J. Campbell (1997), *The Coming Oil Crisis*; Kenneth S. Deffeyes (2001), *Hubbert's Peak: The Impending World Oil Shortage*; and Roger W. Bentley, "Global Oil & Gas Depletion: An Overview", *Energy Policy*, 30, 2002, pp 189–205.

33. The sceptical statement comes from Peter Davis (Chief Economist, BP) in oral evidence to the UK House of Lords Committee on the European Union, considering the EU Green Paper, "Towards a European Strategy for the Security of Energy Supply", November 2000. House of Lords Committee on the European Union, "Energy Supply: How Secure Are We?", session 2001–02, 14th report, HL paper 82, published 12 February 2002, page 79.

Y

1. "Yonder" is used in this sense in Gerard Manley Hopkins' poem "The Leaden Echo and the Golden Echo", 1884.

BIBLIOGRAPHY

The first date given for each book is the date of original authorship/publication. If a later edition is cited in the endnotes, details for this are given in parentheses.

Abramovitz, Moses (1989), *Thinking About Growth and Other Essays on Economic Growth and Welfare*, Cambridge University Press.

Adams, Douglas (1992), *Mostly Harmless: Volume Five in the Hitchhiker's Guide to the Galaxy*, Heinemann (Pan Books edition, 2009).

Adán, José Pérez (1992), *Reformist Anarchism 1800–1936: A Study of the Feasibility of Anarchism*, Merlin Books.

Ainsworth, William Harrison (1854), *The Flitch of Bacon: The Custom of Dunmow: a Tale of English Home*, Routledge.

Alexander, Christopher (1967), *Notes on the Synthesis of Form*, Harvard University Press.

Alexander, Christopher, Sara Ishikawa, Murray Silverstein, et al. (1977), *A Pattern Language: Towns, Buildings, Construction*, Oxford University Press.

Alexander, David E. and Rhodes W. Fairbridge, eds. (1999), *Encyclopaedia of Environmental Science*, Kluwer.

Alt, James E., Margaret Levi and Elinor Ostrom, eds. (1999), *Competition and Cooperation: Conversations with Nobelists about Economics and Political Sciences*, Russell Sage Foundation.

Altieri, Miguel (1987), *Agroecology: The Science of Sustainable Agriculture*, Westview Press (second edition, 1995).

Altman, Irwin and Setha Low (1992), *Place Attachment*, Plenum.

Amsler, Charles D., ed. (2008), *Algal Chemical Ecology*, Springer (second edition, 2009).

Andersen, Heine and Lars Bo Kaspersen, eds. (1996), *Klassisk Og Moderne Samfundsteori*, Hans Reitzels Forlag. English: *Classical and Modern Social Theory* (Wiley-Blackwell edition, 2000).

Aquinas, Thomas (1264), *Summa contra Gentiles*. English: *On the Truth of the Catholic Faith*.

Arblaster, Anthony (1987), *Democracy*, Open University Press (third edition, 2002).

Arendt, Hannah (1961), *Between Past and Future: Eight Exercises in Political Thought*, Viking (Penguin edition, 2006).

Arendt, Hannah (1963), *On Revolution*, Viking (Penguin edition, 1990).

Arendt, Hannah (1971), *The Life of the Mind*, Secker & Warburg (second edition, 1978).

Argyle, Michael (1987), *The Psychology of Happiness*, Routledge.

Argyle, Michael (1991), *Cooperation: The Basis of Sociability*, Routledge.

Aristotle (c.350 BC), *On Sophistical Refutations* (Loeb Classical Library/Heinemann edition, 1955).

Aristotle (c.350 BC), *Politics* (Penguin edition, 1962).

Armstrong, Karen (1993), *A History of God*, Heinemann.

Armstrong, Karen (2006) *The Great Transformation: The Beginning of Our Religious Traditions*, Alfred A. Knopf.

Arnold, Matthew (1865), *Essays in Criticism*, Macmillan & Co. (BiblioBazaar edition, 2009).

Arnold, Matthew (1869), *Culture and Anarchy*, Macmillan & Co. (Jane Garnett, ed., Oxford World's Classics edition, 2009).

Aronson, Elliott (1973), *Readings About the Social Animal*, W.H. Freeman (seventh edition, 1995).

Arthur, W. Brian (2009), *The Nature of Technology: What It Is, and How It Evolves*, Free Press.

Asad, Talal (1993), *Genealogies of Religion: Discipline and Reasons of Power in Christianity and Islam*, Johns Hopkins University Press.

Ashton, T.S. and Joseph Sykes (1929), *The Coal Industry of the Eighteenth Century*, Manchester University Press (second edition, 1964).

Ashwell, Margaret, ed. (1993), *McCance and Widdowson: A Scientific Partnership of 60 Years*, British Nutrition Foundation.

Ashworth, William (1986), *The History of the British Coal Industry, Volume 5, 1946–1982: The Nationalized Industry*, Clarendon Press.

Atiyah, P.S. (1979), *The Rise and Fall of Freedom of Contract*, Clarendon Press.

Auden, W.H. (1965), Auden's introduction to Sylvan Barnet ed., *The Sonnets*, Signet Classic Shakespeare.

Auerbach, Erich (1946), *Mimesis*, Verlag (Princeton edition, 1953).

Augustijn, Cornelis (1991), *Erasmus: His Life, Works and Influence*, Toronto University Press.

Austen, Jane (1813), *Pride and Prejudice*, T.Egerton.

Austin, John L. (1962), *How To Do Things With Words*, Oxford University Press.

Axelrod, Robert (1984), *The Evolution of Cooperation* (Penguin edition, 1990).

Bachelard, Gaston (1969), *The Poetics of Space*, Beacon Press.

Backhouse, Roger (2002), *The Penguin History of Economics*, Penguin.

Bacon, Francis (1625), *Essayes or Counsels, Civill and Morall,* John Haviland.

Baden, John A. and Douglas S. Noonan, eds. (1998), *Managing the Commons,* Indiana University Press.

Baker, John Alec (1967), *The Peregrine,* Harper & Row.

Bakhtin, Mikhail (1930), *Tvorchestvo Fransua Rable,* Khudozhest-vennia Literatura. English: *Rabelais and His World* (MIT edition, translation by Hélène Iswolsky, 1968).

Balfour, Eve (1943), *The Living Soil,* Faber & Faber (revised edition, 1949).

Banton, Michael, ed. (1965), *The Relevance of Models for Social Anthropology,* Tavistock.

Barabási, Albert-László (2002), *Linked: How Everything is Connected to Everything Else,* Perseus Books (Plume edition, 2003).

Barber, Benjamin (1984), *Strong Democracy: Participatory Politics for a New Age,* University of California Press.

Barell, John (2007), *Problem-Based Learning: An Inquiry Approach,* Corwin Press.

Barker, Paul (1984), *Founders of the Welfare State,* Heinemann.

Barnett, Anthony and Roger Scruton, eds. (1998), *Town and Country,* Jonathan Cape.

Bartholomew, James (2004), *The Welfare State We're In,* Politicos.

Barton, Hugh, Geoff Davis and Richard Guise (1995), *Sustainable Settlements: A Guide for Planners, Designers and Developers,* University of the West of England/The Local Government Management Board.

Barton, Hugh, ed. (1999), *Sustainable Communities: The Potential for Eco-Neighbourhoods,* Routledge (Earthscan edition, 2002).

Bar-Yam, Yaneer (1997), *Dynamics of Complex Systems,* Perseus Books.

Bar-Yam, Yaneer (2004), *Making Things Work: Solving Complex Problems in a Complex World,* NECSI Knowledge Press.

Bataille, Georges (1967), *La Part Maudite,* Les Editions de Minuit. English: *The Accursed Share* (Zone Books edition, translation by Robert Hurley, 1988).

Bateson, Gregory (1972), *Steps to an Ecology of Mind: Collected Essays in Anthropology, Psychiatry, Evolution, and Epistemology,* The University of Chicago Press.

Becker, Gary S. (1976), *The Economic Approach to Human Behaviour,* The University of Chicago Press.

Becker, Marvin B. (1994), *The Emergence of Civil Society in the Eighteenth Century: A Privileged Moment in the History of England, Scotland, and France,* Indiana University Press.

Beckerman, Wilfred (1968), *An Introduction to National Income Analysis,* Weidenfeld & Nicolson.

Beckett, J.V. (1989), *A History of Laxton: England's Last Open-field Village,* Blackwell.

Beecher, Jonathan (1986), *Charles Fourier: The Visionary and His World,* University of California Press.

Beeton, Isabella Mary (1861), *The Book of Household Management,* S.O. Beeton Publishing.

Begg, David, Stanley Fischer and Rüdiger Dornbusch (1984), *Economics,* McGraw-Hill (second edition, 1987).

Benjamin, Ben E. and Cherie Sohnen-Moe (2003), *The Ethics of Touch: The Hands-on Practitioner's Guide to Creating a Professional, Safe and Enduring Practice,* Sohnen-Moe Associates, Inc.

Bennett, Deborah J. (2004), *Logic Made Easy: How to Know When Language Deceives You,* W.W. Norton & Co (Penguin edition, 2005).

Bentham, Jeremy (1824), The *Book of Fallacies: from unfinished papers of Jeremy Bentham,* University of California Libraries.

Benyus, Janine (1997), *Biomimicry: Innovation Inspired by Nature,* William Morrow (HarperCollins paperback edition, 1998).

Berkes, Fikret and Carl Folke, eds. (1998), *Linking Social and Ecological Systems: Management Practices and Social Mechanisms for Building Resilience,* Cambridge University Press.

Berkes, Fikret, Johan Colding and Carl Folke, eds. (2003), *Navigating Social-Ecological Systems: Building Resilience for Complexity and Change,* Cambridge University Press.

Berlin, Isaiah (1953), *The Hedgehog and the Fox: An Essay on Tolstoy's View of History* (Phoenix edition, 1999).

Berlin, Isaiah (1969), *Four Essays on Liberty* (Oxford University Press edition, 2002).

Bernick, Michael and Robert Cervero (1997), *Transit Villages in the 21st Century,* McGraw-Hill.

Berry, Wendell (1977), *The Unsettling of America: Culture & Agriculture,* Sierra Club Books.

Bertalanffy, Ludwig von (1968), *General System Theory: Foundations, Development, Applications,* George Braziller (Penguin edition, 1973).

Biddulph, Steve (1994), *Manhood,* Vermillion.

Bird, Alexander (2000), *Thomas Kuhn,* Acumen Publishing Limited.

Birnbaum, Pierre, Jack Lively and Geraint Parry, eds. (1978), *Democracy, Consensus and Social Contract,* Sage Publications.

Blake, William (1804–1808), *Milton,* William Blake.

Bloch, Maurice (1989), *Ritual, History and Power: Selected Papers in Anthropology,* Athlone Press.

Blowers, Andrew, ed. (1992), *Planning for a Sustainable Environment,* Routledge.

Bly, Robert (1990), *Iron John: A Book About Men,* Addison-Wesley.

Blyth, Catherine (2009), *The Art of Conversation: How Talking Improves Lives,* John Murray.

Blythe, Ronald (1969), *Akenfield: Portrait of an English Village,* Allen Lane.

Boccaccio, Giovanni (1349–1351), *Il Decameron.* English: *The Decameron of Giovanni Boccaccio* (first translated 1886, by John Payne), The Villon Society (Gutenberg ebook edition, 2007).

Bohm, David (1985), *Unfolding Meaning: A Weekend of Dialogue with David Bohm*, Routledge-Ark Paperbacks.

Bookchin, Murray (1980), *Toward an Ecological Society*, Black Rose Books.

Booker, Christopher (2004), *The Seven Basic Plots: Why We Tell Stories*, Continuum.

Booker, Christopher and Richard North (2007), *Scared to Death: From BSE to Global Warming: Why Scares are Costing Us the Earth*, Bloomsbury.

Booker, Richard and Earl Boysen (2005), *Nanotechnology for Dummies*, John Wiley & Sons.

Borsodi, Ralph (1933), *Flight from the City: An Experiment in Creative Living on the Land* (Harper Colophon edition, 1972).

Boserup, Ester (1965), *The Conditions of Agricultural Growth: The Economics of Agrarian Change under Population Pressure* (Earthscan edition, 1993).

Bossel, Hartmut (2007), *Systems and Models: Complexity, Dynamics, Evolution, Sustainability*, Books on Demand GmbH.

Bossy, John (1985), *Christianity in the West: 1400–1700*, Oxford University Press.

Boulding, Kenneth E. (1970), *Economics as a Science*, McGraw-Hill.

Bourne, George (1912), *Change in the Village*, Duckworth & Co.

Boyle, David (1999), *Funny Money: In Search of Alternative Cash*, HarperCollins.

Boyle, David (2002), *The Money Changers: Currency Reform from Aristotle to E-cash*, Earthscan.

Boyle, David and Andrew Simms (2009), *The New Economics: A Bigger Picture*, Earthscan.

Boyle, Godfrey, ed. (2004), *Renewable Energy: Power for a Sustainable Future*, Oxford University Press.

Brand, Stewart (1999), *The Clock of the Long Now: Time And Responsibility*, Basic Books.

Branson, William H. (1979), *Macroeconomic Theory and Policy*, Harper & Row.

Brody, Hugh (1973), *Inishkillane: Change and Decline in the West of Ireland*, Allen Lane.

Brody, Hugh (2000), *The Other Side of Eden: Hunter-Gatherers, Farmers and the Shaping of the World*, Faber & Faber.

Bronner, Stephen Eric and Douglas MacKay Kellner, eds. (1989), *Critical Theory and Society: A Reader*, Routledge.

Brontë, Charlotte (1849), *Shirley*, Smith, Elder and Co. (Penguin edition, 2006).

Broome, Jon and Brian Richardson (1995), *The Self-Build Book: How to Enjoy Designing and Building Your Own Home*, Green Earth Books.

Brown, Keith C., ed. (1965), *Hobbes Studies*, Blackwell.

Brown, Stuart L. (2009), *Play: How it Shapes the Brain, Opens the Imagination, and Invigorates the Soul*, Avery.

Bruges, James (2004), *The Little Earth Book*, Alastair Sawday Publishing.

Bruner, Jerome S., Alison Jolly and Kathy Sylva, eds. (1976), *Play: Its Role in Development and Evolution*, Basic Books.

Bryson, Bill (1996), *Notes from a Small Island*, Black Swan.

Buchanan, Mark (2000), *Nexus: Small Worlds and the Groundbreaking Theory of Networks*, W.W. Norton & Co. (reissue edition, 2003).

Buchheim, Hans (1968), *Totalitarian Rule: Its Nature and Characteristics*, Wesleyan University Press.

Bunyan, John (1678–1684), *The Pilgrim's Progress* (Clarendon Press, second edition, 1960).

Bunyard, Peter (1999), *The Breakdown of Climate: Human Choices or Global Disaster?*, Floris Books.

Burger, Joanna, Elinor Ostrom, Richard B. Norgaard, David Policansky and Bernard D. Goldstein, eds. (2001), *Protecting the Commons: A Framework for Resource Management in the Americas*, Island Press.

Burke, Edmund (1748–1797), *Burke's Politics: Selected Writings and Speeches of Edmund Burke on Reform, Revolution and War*, Hoffman, Ross J.S. and Paul Levack, eds., Alfred A. Knopf (fourth edition, 1970).

Burke, Edmund (1774–1780), *The Writings and Speeches of Edmund Burke, Volume 3: Party, Parliament, and the American War: 1774–1780*, Paul Langford, ed. (1996), Clarendon Press.

Burke, Edmund (1789–1794), *The Writings and Speeches of Edmund Burke, Volume 7: India: The Hastings Trial: 1789–1794*, Paul Langford, ed. (2000), Clarendon Press.

Burke, Edmund (1790), *Reflections on the Revolution in France* (Leslie G. Mitchell, ed., Oxford World's Classics edition, 2009).

Burke, Edmund (1794–1797), *The Writings and Speeches of Edmund Burke, Volume 9: I: The Revolutionary War, 1794–1797; II: Ireland*, Paul Langford, ed. (1991), Clarendon Press.

Burton, Robert (1621), *The Anatomy of Melancholy* (Thomas C. Faulkner, Nicolas K Kiessling, Rhonda L Blair eds., Clarendon Press edition, 1990).

Busby, Rebecca L. (2005), *Hydrogen and Fuel Cells: A Comprehensive Guide*, PennWell Books.

Buttimer, Anne and David Seamon, eds. (1980), *The Human Experience of Space and Place*, Croom Helm.

Byrne, Richard W. and Andrew Whiten (1988), *Machiavellian Intelligence: Social Expertise and the Evolution of Intellect in Monkeys, Apes, and Humans*, Clarendon Press.

Byrne, Richard W. and Andrew Whiten (1997), *Machiavellian Intelligence II: Extensions and Evaluations*, Cambridge University Press.

Cahn, Edgar S. (2000), *No More Throw-Away People: The Co-Production Imperative*, Essential Books.

Caillois, Roger (1958), *Les jeux et les hommes*, Gallimard. English: *Man, Play and Games* (translation by Meyer Barash, 1961. University of Illinois Press edition).

Calhoun, Craig, ed. (1992), *Habermas and the Public Sphere*, MIT.

Calhoun, Craig (1995), *Critical Social Theory: Culture, History and the Challenge of Difference*, Blackwell.

Cameron, Deborah (2000), *Good to Talk: Living and Working in a Communication Culture*, Sage.

Campbell, Colin (1987), *The Romantic Ethic and the Spirit of Modern Consumerism*, Blackwell.

Campbell, Colin J. (1991), *The Golden Century of Oil 1950–2050: The Depletion of a Resource*, Kluwer.

Campbell, Colin J. (1997), *The Coming Oil Crisis*, Multi-Science.

Capra, Fritjof (1982), *The Turning Point: Science, Society and the Rising Culture*, Simon & Schuster (Picador edition, 1983).

Capra, Fritjof (1996), *The Web of Life: A New Synthesis of Mind and Matter*, HarperCollins.

Carew-Reid, Jeremy, Robert Prescott-Allen, Stephen Bass and Barry Dalal-Clayton (1994), *Strategies for National Sustainable Development: A Handbook for Their Planning and Implementation*, Earthscan.

Carey, John (1980), *John Donne: Life, Mind and Art*, Faber & Faber.

Carey, John, ed. (1999), *The Faber Book of Utopias*, Faber & Faber.

Carlyle, Thomas (1837), *The French Revolution: A History* (G. Bell and Sons edition, 1902).

Carr, Nicholas (2010), *The Shallows: How the Internet is Changing the Way We Think, Read and Remember*, Atlantic.

Carrasco, Davíd (1999), *City of Sacrifice: The Aztec Empire and the Role of Violence in Civilization*, Beacon Press.

Carrithers, Michael, Steven Collins and Steven Lukes, eds. (1985), *The Category of the Person*, Cambridge University Press.

Carroll, Lewis (1896), *Symbolic Logic*, Macmillan and Co. (Dover Publications edition, *Symbolic Logic and the Game of Logic*, 1958).

Catton, William R. (1980), *Overshoot: The Ecological Basis of Revolutionary Change* (University of Illinois Press edition, 1982).

Cawley, Arthur C., ed. (1961), *Everyman and Medieval Miracle Plays*, Manchester University Press (content first published c.1509).

Chamberlin, Shaun (2009), *The Transition Timeline: For a Local, Resilient Future*, Green Books.

Chartres, Richard (2004), *Tree of Knowledge, Tree of Life*, Continuum.

Chaucer, Geoffrey (c.1400), *The Canterbury Tales*, William Caxton (Modern English translation by Neville Coghill, 1958. Penguin edition).

Checkland, Peter B. (1981), *Systems Thinking, Systems Practice*, John Wiley & Sons (30 year retrospective edition, 1999).

Checkland, Peter B. and John Poulter (2006), *Learning for Action: A Short Definitive Account of Soft Systems Methodology and its Use for Practitioners, Teachers and Students*, John Wiley & Sons.

Christian, Diana Leafe (2003), *Creating a Life Together*, New Society Publishers.

Claeys, Gregory and Lyman Tower Sargent, eds. (1999), *The Utopia Reader*, New York University Press.

Clanchy, Michael T. (1997), *Abelard: A Medieval Life*, Blackwell.

Clark, Duncan (2009), *The Rough Guide to Green Living*, Rough Guides.

Clark, Kenneth E. and Miriam B. Clark, eds. (1990), *Measures of Leadership*, Leadership Library of America.

Clark, Michael (2002), *Paradoxes from A to Z*, Routledge.

Clayton, Anthony M.H. and Nicholas J. Radcliffe (1996), *Sustainability: A Systems Approach*, Earthscan.

Clayton, Paul (2001), *Health Defence*, Accelerated Learning Systems.

Cleave, T.L. (1974), *The Saccharine Disease: Conditions Caused by the Taking of Refined Carbohydrates, such as Sugar and White Flour*, John Wright.

Clover, Charles (2006), *The End of the Line: How Overfishing is Changing the World and What We Eat*, Ebury Press.

Cobbett, William (1821), *Cottage Economy*, C. Clement (Oxford University Press paperback edition, 1979).

Cohen, Robert S., Paul K. Feyerabend and Marx W. Wartofsky, eds. (1976), *Essays in Memory of Imre Lakatos*, Springer.

Cohn, Norman (1957), *The Pursuit of the Millennium*, Secker & Warburg (Oxford University Press revised and expanded edition, 1970).

Cohn, Norman (1975), *Europe's Inner Demons: An Enquiry Inspired by the Great Witch-Hunt*, Sussex University Press and Heinemann Educational Books (Paladin edition, 1976).

Colborn, Theo, Dianne Dumanoski and John Peterson Myers (1996), *Our Stolen Future: Are We Threatening our Fertility, Intelligence and Survival? A Scientific Detective Story*, Little Brown (Abacus edition, 1997).

Coleridge, Samuel Taylor (1817) *Sibylline Leaves*, Rest Fenner.

Collard, David, David W. Pearce and David Ulph, eds. (1988), *Economics, Growth and Sustainable Environments*, Macmillan.

Collis, John Stewart (1973), *The Worm Forgives the Plough*, Charles Knight (Penguin edition, 1975).

Common, Michael and Sigrid Stagl (2005), *Ecological Economics: An Introduction*, Cambridge University Press.

Commoner, Barry (1971), *The Closing Circle: Nature, Man and Technology*, Jonathan Cape.

Confucius (c.300 BC), *Analects*.

Conrad, Joseph (1900), *Lord Jim*, William Blackwood.

Conservative Party (2010), *Conservative Manifesto 2010: An Invitation to Join the Government of Britain*, Conservative Party.

Cook, Guy (2004), *Genetically Modified Language: The Discourse of Arguments for GM Crops and Food*, Routledge.

Cooper, Tim (1990), *Green Christianity*, Hodder and Stoughton.

Coote, Anna, Jane Franklin and Andrew Simms (2010), *21 Hours: Why a Shorter Working Week Can Help Us All to Flourish in the 21st Century*, New Economics Foundation.

Copi, Irving (1953), *Introduction to Logic*, Macmillan (second edition, 1961).

Corrigan, John, ed. (2008), *The Oxford Handbook of Religion and Emotion*, Oxford University Press.

Coulton, George Gordon (1925), *Medieval Village, Manor and Monastery* (Kessinger edition, 2010).

Coupe, Laurence, ed. (2000), *The Green Studies Reader: From Romanticism to Ecocriticism*, Routledge.

Coverdale, Myles (1537), *Remains of Myles Coverdale* (George Pearson, ed., Cambridge University Press edition, 1846).

Cox, John D. (2005), *Climate Crash: Abrupt Climate Change and What It Means for Our Future*, Joseph Henry Press.

Crawford, Martin (2010), *Creating a Forest Garden: Working with Nature to Grow Edible Crops*, Green Books.

Crawford, Matthew (2010), *The Case for Working with Your Hands: Or Why Office Work is Bad for Us and Fixing Things Feels Good*, Viking.

Crick, Bernard (1962), *In Defence of Politics*, Continuum (fifth edition, 2005).

Crick, Bernard (2002), *Democracy: A Very Short Introduction*, Oxford University Press.

Csikszentmihalyi, Mihaly (1975), *Beyond Boredom and Anxiety: The Flow Experience in Work and Play*, Jossey Bass (25th anniversary edition, 2000).

Csikszentmihalyi, Mihaly (1996), *Creativity: Flow and the Psychology of Discovery and Invention*, Harper.

Csikszentmihalyi, Mihaly (2002), *Flow: The Psychology of Happiness: The Classic Work on How to Achieve Happiness*, Rider.

Cullen, Fintan (2000), *Sources in Irish Art*, Cork University Press.

Cumming, John (1844), *Fox's Book of Martyrs: The Acts and Monuments of the Church*, G. Virtue.

Cyert, Richard M. and James G. March (1963), *A Behavioural Theory of the Firm*, Prentice Hall.

Dalby, Andrew (2005), *The Story of Bacchus*, British Museum Press.

Dalrymple, Theodore (2005), *Our Culture, What's Left of It: The Mandarins and The Masses*, Ivan R. Dee.

Daly, Herman E., ed. (1980), *Economics, Ecology, Ethics: Essays Toward a Steady State Economy*, W.H. Freeman.

Daly, Herman E. and John B. Cobb (1989), *For the Common Good: Redirecting the Economy toward Community, the Environment, and a Sustainable Future*, Green Print.

Daly, Herman E. (1992), *Steady-State Economics*, Earthscan.

Daly, Herman E. and Kenneth Neal Townsend, eds. (1993), *Valuing the Earth: Economics, Ecology, Ethics*, MIT.

Daly, Herman E. (1996), *Beyond Growth: The Economics of Sustainable Development*, Beacon.

Damasio, Antonio (1994), *Descartes' Error: Emotion, Reason and the Human Brain* (Vintage edition, 2006).

Damasio, Antonio (2000), *The Feeling of What Happens: Body, Emotion and the Making of Consciousness*, Vintage.

Damasio, Antonio (2003), *Looking for Spinoza: Joy, Sorrow and the Feeling Brain*, Vintage (New Ed edition, 2004).

Dante (1320), *La Divina Commedia*. English: *The Divine Comedy*.

David, Paul A. and Melvin Warren Reder, eds. (1974), *Nations and Households in Economic Growth: Essays in Honour of Moses Abramovitz*, Academic Press.

Davies, Glyn (1994), *History of Money: From Ancient Times to the Present Day*, University of Wales Press.

Davies, J.C. (1995), Davies' introduction to André Gide's (1925) *Les Faux-Monnayeurs*, Methuen.

Davies, R.T., ed. (1963), *Medieval English Lyrics: A Critical Anthology*, Faber & Faber.

Dawkins, Richard (1986), *The Blind Watchmaker*, Longman (Penguin edition, 1988).

Dawson, Jonathan (2006), *Ecovillages: New Frontiers for Sustainability*, Green Books.

Dawson, Raymond (1972), *Imperial China*, Hutchinson (Pelican edition, 1976).

de Bono, Edward (1967), *The Use of Lateral Thinking* (Penguin edition, 1990).

de Bono, Edward (1977), *Lateral Thinking: A Textbook of Creativity* (Penguin edition, 1990).

de Botton, Alain (2000), *The Consolations of Philosophy*, Hamish Hamilton (Penguin edition, 2001).

de Custine, Astolphe (1843), *La Russie en 1839*. English: *Journey for Our Time: The Journals of the Marquis de Custine*, George Prior (translation by Phyllis Penn Kohler, 1980).

De George, Richard T. (1985), *The Nature and Limits of Authority*, University Press of Kansas.

de Montaigne, Michel Eyquem (1580–1591), *Essais*. English: *Essays* (translation by E.J. Trechmann, 1927. Oxford University Press edition, 1942).

de Saint-Exupéry, Antoine (1943), *Lettre à un otage*. English: *Letter to a Hostage* (translation by Jacqueline Gerst, 1950. Pushkin Press edition, 1999).

de Schweinitz, Karl (1943), *England's Road to Social Security: from the Statute of Laborers in 1349 to the Beveridge Report of 1942*, University of Pennsylvania Press.

de Selincourt, Kate (1997), *Local Harvest: Delicious Ways to Save the Planet*, Lawrence & Wishart.

de Tocqueville, Alexis (1835), *De la Démocratie en Amérique*. English: *Democracy in America*, Penguin (translation by Gerard E. Bevan, 2003).

de Vries, Jan (2008), *The Industrious Revolution: Consumer Behaviour and the Household Economy, 1650 to the Present*, Cambridge University Press.

de Waal, Frans (1982), *Chimpanzee Politics: Power and Sex Among Apes* (Johns Hopkins University Press edition, 2007).

Deane, Phyllis (2001), *The Life and Times of J. Neville Keynes: A Beacon in the Tempest*, Edward Elgar.

Deffeyes, Kenneth S. (2001), *Hubbert's Peak: The Impending World Oil Shortage*, Princeton University Press.

Deffeyes, Kenneth S. (2006), *Beyond Oil: The View from Hubbert's Peak*, Hill & Wang.

Dennett, Daniel C. (1991), *Consciousness Explained*, Penguin.

Dennett, Daniel C. (1995), *Darwin's Dangerous Idea: Evolution and the Meanings of Life*, Simon & Schuster.

Descartes, René (1618–1650), *The Philosophical Writings of Descartes*, Cambridge University Press (translation by John Cottingham, Robert Stoothof, Dugald Murdoch and Anthony Kenny, 1991).

Devall, Bill and George Sessions (1985), *Deep Ecology: Living as if Nature Mattered*, Gibbs M. Smith.

Dewey, John (1899–1924), *The Middle Works of John Dewey, Volume 1, 1899–1924*, Jo Ann Boydston and Joe R. Burnett, eds. (2008), Southern Illinois University Press.

Diamond, Jared (1991), *The Rise and Fall of the Third Chimpanzee: The Evolution and Future of the Human Animal*, Harper.

Diamond, Jared (1997), *Guns, Germs and Steel*, W.W. Norton & Co.

Diamond, Jared (2005), *Collapse: How Societies Choose to Fail or Survive*, Allen Lane.

Dickens, Charles (1843), *A Christmas Carol*, Chapman & Hall.

Dickens, Charles (1854), *Hard Times*, Household Words.

Diener, Ed, ed. (2009), The *Science of Well-Being: The Collected Works of Ed Diener – General Reviews and Theories of Subjective Well-Being*, Springer.

Dixon, Norman F. (1976), *On the Psychology of Military Incompetence*, Jonathan Cape (Futura edition, 1979).

Dobson, Andrew, ed. (1991), *The Green Reader: Essays Toward a Sustainable Society*, Mercury House.

Dolšak, Nives and Elinor Ostrom, eds. (2003), *The Commons in the New Millennium: Challenges and Adaptation*, MIT.

Donne, John (1609–1620), *The Divine Poems of John Donne*, Helen Gardner, ed. (1952), Clarendon Press (second edition, 1978).

Doob, Leonard W. (1988), *Inevitability: Determinism, Fatalism and Destiny*, Greenwood Press.

Dooley, Peter C. (2005), *The Labour Theory of Value: Economics or Ethics*, Routledge.

Douglas, Mary (1970), *Natural Symbols: Explorations in Cosmology*, Cambridge University Press.

Douglas, Mary and Baron Isherwood (1979), *The World of Goods: Towards an Anthropology of Consumption* (Penguin edition, 1980).

Douglas, Mary (1982), *In the Active Voice*, Routledge.

Douthwaite, Richard (1992), *The Growth Illusion: How Economic Growth has Enriched the Few, Impoverished the Many and Endangered the Planet*, Green Books.

Douthwaite, Richard (1996), *Short Circuit: Strengthening Local Economies for Security in an Unstable World*, Green Books.

Douthwaite, Richard (1999), *The Ecology of Money*, Green Books.

Douthwaite, Richard, ed. (2003), *Before the Wells Run Dry: Ireland's Transition to Renewable Energy*, Feasta.

Dowding, Charles (2007), *Organic Gardening: The Natural No-Dig Way*, Green Books.

Drexler, K. Eric (1986), *Engines of Creation*, Fourth Estate (Oxford Paperbacks edition, 1992).

Duesenberry, James Stemble (1949), *Income, Saving and the Theory of Consumer Behaviour*, Harvard University Press.

Duffy, Eamon (1992), *The Stripping of the Altars: Traditional Religion in England 1400–1580*, Yale University Press.

Dunbar, Robin (1996), *Grooming, Gossip and the Evolution of Language*, Faber & Faber.

Dundes, Alan and Alessandro Falassi (1975), *La Terra in Piazza: An Interpretation of the Palio of Siena*, University of California Press.

Durkheim, Émile (1893), *The Division of Labour in Society* (Palgrave Macmillan edition, 1984).

Dweck, Carol S. (2000), *Self-Theories: Their Role in Motivation, Personality and Development*, Psychology Press.

Earl, Peter E. (1983), *The Economic Imagination: Towards a Behavioural Analysis of Choice*, Wheatsheaf Books.

Ehrenreich, Barbara (2007), *Dancing in the Streets: A History of Collective Joy*, Granta Books.

Ehrenreich, Barbara (2010), *Smile or Die: How Positive Thinking Fooled America and the World*, Granta Books.

Eisenberg, Nancy, ed. (1995), *Social Development*, Sage.

Ekins, Paul, ed. (1986), *The Living Economy: A New Economics in the Making*, Routledge.

Ekins, Paul (1992), *A New World Order: Grassroots Movements for Global Change*, Routledge.

Ekins, Paul and Manfred Max-Neef, eds. (1992), *Real-Life Economics: Understanding Wealth Creation*, Routledge.

Ekins, Paul (2000), *Economic Growth and Environmental Sustainability: The Prospects for Green Growth*, Routledge.

Elgin, Duane (1981), *Voluntary Simplicity: Toward a Way of Life That Is Outwardly Simple, Inwardly Rich*, William Morrow.

Eliav-Feldon, Miriam (1982), *Realistic Utopias: Ideal Imaginary Societies of the Renaissance, 1516–1630*, Clarendon Press.

Eliot, George (1860), *The Mill on the Floss*, William Blackwood.

Eliot, T.S. (1932), *Selected Essays, 1917–1932*, Harcourt, Brace & Co.

Elkington, John, Peter Knight and Julia Hailes (1991), *The Green Business Guide*, Gollancz.

Elkington, John (1997), *Cannibals with Forks: The Triple Bottom Line of 21st Century Business*, Capstone.

Elkington, John and Pamela Hartigan (2008), *The Power of Unreasonable People: How Social Entrepreneurs Create Markets That Change the World*, Harvard Business School Press.

Ellul, Jacques (1965), *Propaganda: The Formation of Men's Attitudes*, Random House (Vintage edition, 1973).

Elster, Jon (1989), *The Cement of Society: A Study of Social Order*, Cambridge University Press.

Elster, Jon (2007), *Explaining Social Behaviour: More Nuts and Bolts for the Social Sciences*, Cambridge University Press.

Emerson, Ralph Waldo, represented in Mark van Doren, ed. (1946), *The Portable Emerson*, Viking (Penguin edition, 1977).

Empson, William (1930), *Seven Types of Ambiguity*, Chatto (Penguin edition, 1995).

Empson, William (1955), *Collected Poems*, Chatto and Windus.

Epstein, Seymour (1998), *Constructive Thinking: The Key to Emotional Intelligence*, Praeger.

Erasmus, Desiderius (1511), *Stultitiae Laus*. English: *In Praise of Folly* (first translated 1549, by Thomas Chaloner), Early English Text Society (translation by Betty Radice. Penguin edition, *The Praise of Folly and Letter to Martin Dorp 1515*, 1971).

Erickson, Glenn W. and John A. Fossa (1988), *Dictionary of Paradox*, University Press of America.

Estés, Clarissa Pinkola (1992), *Women Who Run with the Wolves: Contacting the Power of the Wild Woman*, Rider.

Etzioni, Amitai (1993), *The Spirit of Community: Rights, Responsibilities, and the Communitarian Agenda*, Crown.

Etzioni, Amitai, ed. (1995), *New Communitarian Thinking: Persons, Virtues, Institutions and Communities*, University of Virginia Press.

Evans, George Ewart (1966), *The Pattern under the Plough* (Faber & Faber edition, 1971).

Evans, Mary Alice and Howard Ensign Evans (1970), *William Morton Wheeler, Biologist*, Harvard University Press.

Eyton, Audrey (1982), *The F-Plan Diet*, Penguin.

Fairbank, John King and Merle Goldman (1992), *China: A New History*, Harvard University Press (second enlarged edition, 2006).

Fairlie, Simon (1996), *Low Impact Development: Planning and People in a Sustainable Countryside*, Jon Carpenter.

Fairtlough, Gerard (1994), *Creative Compartments: A Design for Future Organisation*, Adamantine Press.

Farnham, Willard (1936), *The Medieval Heritage of Elizabethan Tragedy*, University of California Press (Blackwell edition, 1956).

Feinberg, Joel (1980), *Rights, Justice and the Bounds of Liberty: Essays in Social Philosophy*, Princeton University Press.

Ferguson, Niall (2005), *1914: Why the World Went to War*, Penguin.

Fern, Ken (1997), *Plants for a Future: Edible and Useful Plants for a Healthy World*, Permanent Publications (second edition, 2000).

Festinger, Leon (1957), *A Theory of Cognitive Dissonance*, Stanford University Press (second edition, 1962).

Feyerabend, Paul (1999), *Knowledge Science and Relativism: Philosophical Papers*, Cambridge University Press.

Field, John (2003), *Social Capital*, Routledge.

Field, Tiffany (2001), *Touch,* MIT (second edition, 2003).

Finaldi, Gabriele (2000), *The Image of Christ: Catalogue of the Exhibition "Seeing Salvation"*, The National Gallery.

Finer, Herman (1933), *English Local Government*, Methuen (fourth edition, 1950).

Finnegan, William (1998), *Cold New World: Growing Up in a Harder Country*, Picador (paperback edition, 1999).

Fischer, David Hackett (1970), *Historians' Fallacies: Toward a Logic of Historical Thought*, Harper Torchbooks (Routledge & Kegan Paul edition, 1971).

Fischer, Frank (2000), *Citizens, Experts and the Environment: The Politics of Local Knowledge*, Duke University Press.

Flathman, Richard Earl (1987), *The Philosophy and Politics of Freedom*, University of Chicago Press.

Fleming, David (1988), *After Affluence: A Study of the Market for Positional Goods*, unpublished PhD dissertation, University of London.

Fleming, David, ed. (1997), *The Countryside in 2097*, Country Life.

Fleming, David (2005), *Energy and the Common Purpose: Descending the Energy Staircase with Tradable Energy Quotas*, The Lean Economy Connection (third edition, 2007).

Fleming, David (2007), *The Lean Guide to Nuclear Energy: A Life-Cycle in Trouble*, The Lean Economy Connection.

Fleming, David and Shaun Chamberlin (2011), *TEQs (Tradable Energy Quotas): A Policy Framework for Peak Oil and Climate Change*, All Party Parliamentary Group on Peak Oil and The Lean Economy Connection.

Fleming, William (1856), *Vocabulary of Philosophy, Mental, Moral, and Metaphysical*, Charles Griffin (fourth edition, 1887).

Fletcher, Colin and Neil Thompson (1980), *Issues in Community Education*, Falmer Press.

Flew, Antony (1984), *God: A Critical Enquiry*, Open Court.

Flew, Antony (1998), *How to Think Straight: An Introduction to Critical Reasoning*, Prometheus.

Flintoff, John-Paul (2010), *Sew Your Own: Man Finds Happiness and Meaning of Life Making Clothes*, Profile Books.

Forencich, Frank (2006), *Exuberant Animal: The Power of Health, Play and Joyful Movement*, AuthorHouse.

Forrester, Jay Wright (1961), *Industrial Dynamics* (Pegasus edition, 1999).

Forrester, Jay Wright (1969), *Urban Dynamics*, MIT.

Forsyth, Neil (1987), *The Old Enemy: Satan and the Combat Myth*, Princeton University Press.

Foster, Richard, Pierre Van Beneden and Sarah Kaplan (2001), *Creative Destruction: Turning Built-to-Last into Built-to-Perform*, Prentice Hall.

Fox, Matthew (1988), *The Coming of the Cosmic Christ: The Healing of Mother Earth and the Birth of a Global Renaissance*, Harper & Row.

France, Robert L. (2007), *Handbook of Regenerative Landscape Design*, CRC Press.

Frankfurt, Harry G. (2005), *On Bullshit*, Princeton University Press.

Frazer, James G. (1922), *The Golden Bough* (Macmillan abridged paperback edition, 1957).

Freestone, David and Ellen Hey, eds. (1995), *The Precautionary Principle and International Law*, Kluwer Law International.

Friedman, Benjamin M. (2005), *The Moral Consequences of Economic Growth*, Vintage.

Fucini, Joseph J. and Suzy Fucini (1990), *Working for the Japanese: Inside Mazda's American Auto Plant*, Free Press.

Fukuyama, Francis (1992), *Trust: The Social Virtues and the Creation of Prosperity*, The Free Press (paperback edition, 1996).

Fuller, Steve (2003), *Kuhn vs. Popper: The Struggle for the Soul of Science*, Icon.

Galbraith, John Kenneth (1958), *The Affluent Society*, Hamish Hamilton.

Gallie, Duncan, Catherine Marsh and Carolyn M. Vogler, eds. (1994), *Social Change and the Experience of Unemployment*, Oxford University Press.

Gammon, Max (1976), *Health and Security: Report on Public Provision for Medical Care in Great Britain*, St. Michael's Organization.

Gardner, Howard (2004), *Five Minds for the Future*, Paidos (Harvard Business School Press edition, 2006).

Gardner, Howard (2006), *Multiple Intelligences: New Horizons*, Basic Books.

Garnett, Tara (1996), *Growing Food in Cities: A Report to Highlight and Promote the Benefits of Urban Agriculture in the UK*, National Food Alliance and SAFE Alliance.

Garnett, Tara (1999), *City Harvest: The Feasibility of Growing More Food in London*, Sustain.

Gawande, Atul (2009), *The Checklist Manifesto: How To Get Things Right*, Metropolitan Books (Profile Books edition, 2010).

Geddes, Patrick and John Arthur Thomson (1889), *The Evolution of Sex*, Walter Scott.

Geddes, Patrick (1915), *Cities in Evolution: An Introduction to the Town Planning Movement and to the Study of Civics* (Bryan S. Turner, ed., Routledge edition, 1997).

Geiser, Kenneth (2001), *Materials Matter: Towards a Sustainable Materials Policy*, MIT.

Geltner, Guy (2008), *The Medieval Prison: A Social History*, Princeton University Press.

George, Henry (1879), *Progress and Poverty: An Inquiry into the Cause of Industrial Depressions and of Increase of Want with Increase of Wealth: The Remedy*, The Country Life Press.

Georgescu-Roegen, Nicholas (1971), *The Entropy Law and the Economic Process*, Harvard University Press.Harvrd.

Gershon, David and Gail Straub (1989), *Empowerment: The Art of Creating Your Life as You Want It*, High Point Press.

Gharajedaghi, Jamshid (1999), *Systems Thinking: Managing Chaos and Complexity*, Butterworth-Heinemann.

Ghazi, Polly and Rachel Lewis (2007), *The Low Carbon Diet: Wise Up, Chill Out and Save the World*, Short Books.

Gibbon, Edward (1788), *The Decline and Fall of the Roman Empire* (Penguin abridged edition, 2000).

Gibson, Clark C., Margaret A. McKean and Elinor Ostrom, eds. (2000), *People and Forests: Communities, Institutions and Governance*, MIT.

Gibson, Tony (1984), *Counterweight: The Neighbourhood Option*, Town and Country Planning Association and Education for Neighbourhood Change.

Giddens, Anthony (1991), *Modernity and Self-Identity*, Polity Press.

Gilbert, Richard and Anthony Perl (2007), *Transport Revolutions: Moving People and Freight Without Oil*, Earthscan.

Gill, Eric (1983), *A Holy Tradition of Working: An Anthology of Writings*, Golgonooza Press.

Giono, Jean (1953), *The Man Who Planted Trees*, Harvill Press.

Girardet, Herbert (1992), *The Gaia Atlas of Cities: New Directions For Sustainable Urban Living*, Gaia Books.

Girardet, Herbert (1999), *Creating Sustainable Cities*, Green Books.

Gladwell, Malcolm (2000), *The Tipping Point: How Little Things Can Make a Big Difference*, Little Brown (Abacus edition, 2002).

Gleick, James (1987), *Chaos: Making a New Science*, Viking (Cardinal edition, 1988).

Gleick, James (1992), *Genius: Richard Feynman and Modern Physics*, Little Brown.

Gluck, Andrew L. (2007), *Damasio's Error and Descartes' Truth: An Inquiry into Consciousness, Metaphysics and Epistemology*, University of Scranton Press.

Gobat, Jean-Michel, Michel Aragno and Willy Matthey (2004), *The Living Soil: Fundamentals of Soil Science and Soil Biology*, Science Publishers.

Godwin, William (1793), *An Enquiry Concerning Political Justice and its Influence on Morals and Happiness*, G.G. and J. Robinson.

Godwin, William (1794), *Things as They Are; or The Adventures of Caleb Williams*, B. Crosby.

Goldsmith, Edward and Robert Prescott-Allen (1972), *A Blueprint for Survival*, The Ecologist.

Goldsmith, Edward (1992), *The Way: An Ecological Worldview*, Rider (Themis Books edition, 1996).

Goldsmith, Edward and Jerry Mander, eds. (1996), *The Case Against the Global Economy: And for a Turn toward Localization*, Sierra Club (Earthscan edition, 2001).

Goldsmith, Oliver (1756–1774), *The Complete Poetical Works of Oliver Goldsmith*, N. Douglas (edited by Austin Dobson, 1906; Oxford University Press edition, 1927).

Goldsmith, Oliver (1774), *A History of the Earth, and Animated Nature*, J. Nourse.

Goldsmith, Zac (2009), *The Constant Economy: How to Create A Stable Society*, Atlantic Books.

Goleman, Daniel (1994), *Emotional Intelligence: Why It Can Matter More Than IQ*, Bantam (Bloomsbury edition, 1996).

Gombrich, Ernst H. (1960), *Art and Illusion*, Phaidon Press (third edition, 1968).

Goodall, Chris (2007), *How to Live a Low-Carbon Life: The Individual's Guide to Stopping Climate Change*, Earthscan.

Goodman, Percival and Paul Goodman (1947), *Communitas: Means of Livelihood and Ways of Life*, Vintage (Columbia University Press edition, 1990).

Gorski, Philip S. (2003), *The Disciplinary Revolution: Calvinism and the Rise of the State in Early Modern Europe*, University of Chicago Press.

Gosse, Edmund (1899), *The Life and Letters of John Donne*, Heinemann.

Gottfried, Paul Edward (1999), *After Liberalism: Mass Democracy in the Managerial State*, Princeton University Press.

Gould, Stephen Jay (2002), *The Structure of Evolutionary Theory*, Harvard University Press.

Gowers, Ernest (1902), *The Complete Plain Words*, Her Majesty's Stationery Office (revised edition, 1973).

Grahame, Kenneth (1908), *The Wind in the Willows*, Methuen.

Gramsci, Antonio (1935), *Selections from the Prison Notebooks of Antonio Gramsci*, Quintin Hoare and Geoffrey Nowell-Smith, eds. (1971), Lawrence & Wishart.

Grant, Nick, Mark Moodie and Chris Weedon (1996), *Sewage Solutions: Answering the Call of Nature*, Centre for Alternative Technology (second edition, 2000).

Grant, Robert (1990), *Oakeshott*, The Claridge Press.

Gray, John (1998), *False Dawn: The Delusions of Global Capitalism*, Granta (revised edition, 2002).

Gray, Lez (2003), *A Survivor's Guide to Building Your Own Home*, Self Build & Design.

Green, Don W. and G. Paul Willhite (1998), *Enhanced Oil Recovery*, Society of Petroleum Engineers.

Green, Martin (1993), *Curious Customs and Festivals: A Guide to Local Customs and Festivals Throughout the British Isles*, Impact Books.

Green New Deal Group (2008), *A Green New Deal*, New Economics Foundation.

Greene, Thomas M. (1970), *Rabelais: A Study in Comic Courage*, Prentice Hall.

Greenleaf, Robert K. (1977), *Servant Leadership: A Journey into the Nature of Legitimate Power and Greatness*, Paulist Press.

Greer, John Michael (2008), *The Long Descent: A User's Guide to the End of the Industrial Age*, New Society Publishers.

Greve, Henrich R. (2003), *Organisational Learning from Performance Feedback*, Cambridge University Press.

Gribbin, John (2004), *Deep Simplicity: Chaos, Complexity and the Emergence of Life*, Allen Lane (Penguin edition, 2005).

Grice, Paul (1989), *Studies in the Way of Words*, Harvard University Press.

Griffin, James (1986), *Well-Being: Its Meaning, Measurement and Moral Importance*, Clarendon Press.

Grint, Keith (1991), *The Sociology of Work*, Polity Press (third edition, 2005).

Gunderson, Lance H., C.S. Holling and Stephen S. Light, eds. (1995), *Barriers and Bridges to the Renewal of Ecosystems and Institutions*, Columbia University Press.

Gunderson, Lance H. and C.S. Holling, eds. (2002), *Panarchy: Understanding Transformations in Human and Natural Systems*, Island Press.

Haakonssen, Knud (1981), *The Science of a Legislator: The Natural Jurisprudence of David Hume and Adam Smith*, Cambridge University Press.

Habermas, Jürgen (1962), *Strukturwandel der Öffentlichkeit*, Hermann Luchterhand Verlag. English: *The Structural Transformation of the Public Sphere: An Inquiry into a Category of Bourgeois Society*, (translation by Thomas Burger, 1989. MIT Press edition, 1992).

Hahn, Frank H. and Frank P.R. Brechling, eds. (1965), *The Theory of Interest Rates*, Macmillan.

Hahn, Frank H. (1984), *Equilibrium and Macroeconomics*, Blackwell.

Haldane, J.B.S. (1927), *On Being the Right Size and Other Essays* (John Maynard Smith, ed., Oxford University Press edition, 1985).

Hale, John R. (1961), *Machiavelli and Renaissance Italy*, English University Press (Penguin edition, 1971).

Hale, William J. (1934), *The Farm Chemurgic: Farmward the Star of Destiny Lights our Way*, The Stratford Company.

Hall, Peter (1975), *Urban and Regional Planning*, Routledge (third edition, 1992).

Hall, Peter (1988), *Cities of Tomorrow: A Intellectual History of Urban Planning and Design in the Twentieth Century*, Blackwell (second edition, 1996).

Hall, Peter and Colin Ward (1998), *Sociable Cities: The Legacy of Ebenezer Howard*, John Wiley & Sons.

Halpern, David (2009), *The Hidden Wealth of Nations*, Polity Press.

Halweil, Brian (2004), *Eat Here: Reclaiming Homegrown Pleasures in a Global Supermarket*, W.W. Norton & Co.

Hama, Noriko (1996), *Disintegrating Europe: The Twilight of the European Construction*, Adamantine Press.

Hamblin, Charles Leonard (1970), *Fallacies*, Methuen.

Hamilton, William G. (1808), *Parliamentary Logic*, W. Heffer & Sons.

Hammond, Nicholas, ed. (2003), *The Cambridge Companion to Pascal*, Cambridge University Press.

Hampden-Turner, Charles (1969), *Radical Man: The Process of Psycho-Social Development*, Schenkman (Duckworth edition, 1971).

Hansen, Anne Larkin (2010), *The Organic Farming Manual: A Comprehensive Guide to Starting and Running, or Transitioning to, a Certified Organic Farm*, Storey Publishing.

Hansson, Mats G. (2008), *The Private Sphere*, Springer.

Hardin, Garrett (1993), *Living Within Limits: Ecology, Economics and Population Taboos*, Oxford University Press.

Harding, Stephan (2006), *Animate Earth: Science, Intuition and Gaia*, Green Books.

Hardy, Dennis and Colin Ward (1984), *Arcadia for All: The Legacy of a Makeshift Landscape*, Mansell.

Hardy, Dennis (1991), *From Garden Cities to New Towns: Campaigning for Town and Country Planning 1899–1946*, Routledge.

Hardy, Dennis (2006), *Poundbury: The Town that Charles Built*, Town and Country Planning Association.

Hardy, Thomas (1868–1928), *The Collected Poems of Thomas Hardy* (Wordsworth Poetry Library edition, 1994).

Harford, Tim (2007), *The Undercover Economist*, Abacus.

Harford, Tim (2008), *The Logic of Life: Uncovering the New Economics of Everything*, Abacus.

Harling, Robert (1976), *The Letter Forms and Type Designs of Eric Gill*, Eva Svensson (The Typophiles edition, 1978).

Harper, Peter and Louise Halestrap (1999), *Lifting the Lid: An Ecological Approach to Toilet Systems*, Centre for Alternative Technology.

Harremoës, Poul, David Gee, Malcolm MacGarvin, et al., eds. (2002), *The Precautionary Principle in the 20th Century: Late Lessons from Early Warnings*, Earthscan.

Harris, Cindy and Pat Borer (2001), *The Whole House Book: Ecological Building Design and Materials*, Centre for Alternative Technology (second edition, 2005).

Harris, Marvin (1977), *Cannibals and Kings: Origins of Cultures* (Vintage edition, 1991).

Hart, Herbert L.A. (1961), *The Concept of Law*, Oxford University Press (second edition, 1997).

Hart, Robert A. de J. (1991), *Forest Gardening*, Green Books.

Hart, Robert A. de J. (1996), *Beyond the Forest Garden*, Gaia Books.

Hatcher, John (1993), *The History of British Coal: Volume 1, Before 1700: Towards the Age of Coal*, Clarendon Press.

Hatton, Jean (2005), *Betsy: The Dramatic Biography of Prison Reformer Elizabeth Fry*, Monarch Books.

Hawken, Paul, Amory B. Lovins and L. Hunter Lovins (1999), *Natural Capitalism: The Next Industrial Revolution*, Earthscan.

Hawken, Paul (2007), *Blessed Unrest: How the Largest Social Movement in the World Is Restoring Grace, Justice and Beauty to the World*, Penguin.

Hay, Donald Andrew and Derek J. Morris (1979), *Industrial Economics: Theory and Evidence*, Oxford University Press.

Hayek, Friedrich A. (1944), *The Road to Serfdom*, Routledge & Kegan Paul.

Hayek, Friedrich A. (1952), *The Sensory Order: An Inquiry into the Foundations of Theoretical Psychology*, University of Chicago Press.

Hayek, Friedrich A. (1976), *Law, Legislation and Liberty: A New Statement of the Liberal Principles of Justice and Political Economy*, Routledge.

Hazlitt, William (1778–1830), *Selected Essays of William Hazlitt 1778–1830*, Geoffrey Keynes, ed. (1930), Nonesuch Press.

Hefling, Charles and Cynthia Shattuck (2006), *The Oxford Guide to The Book of Common Prayer*, Oxford University Press.

Heinberg, Richard (2003), *The Party's Over: Oil, War and the Fate of Industrial Societies*, New Society Publishers.

Heinberg, Richard (2004), *Powerdown: Options and Actions for a Post-Carbon World*, New Society Publishers.

Heinberg, Richard (2006), *The Oil Depletion Protocol: A Plan to Avert Oil Wars, Terrorism and Economic Collapse*, Clairview Books.

Heinberg, Richard (2007), *Peak Everything: Waking Up to the Century of Declines*, Clairview Books.

Heinberg, Richard (2009), *Blackout: Coal, Climate and the Last Energy Crisis*, New Society Publishers.

Heinrichs, Jay (2007), *Thank You for Arguing: What Aristotle, Lincoln, and Homer Simpson Can Teach Us About the Art of Persuasion*, Three Rivers Press.

Hennessy, Peter (2002), *The Secret State: Whitehall and the Cold War*, Allen Lane.

Herbart, Johann Friedrich (1824–1825), *Psychologie als Wissenschaft: neu gegründet auf Erfahrung, Metaphysik und Mathematik*. English: *Psychology as Science: an attempt to found the science of psychology on experience, metaphysics and mathematics* (University of Michigan Press edition, 2008).

Herman, Arthur (2003), *The Scottish Enlightenment: The Scots' Invention of the Modern World*, Fourth Estate.

Herzberg, Frederick (1962), *Work and the Nature of Man*, Crowell (Staples Press edition, 1968).

Herzen, Alexander (1847–1851), *From the Other Shore*, Oxford University Press (translation by Moura Budberg and Richard Wollheim, with an introduction by Isaiah Berlin, 1979).

Heywood, William (1904), *Palio and Ponte: An Account of the Sports of Central Italy from the Age of Dante to the XXth Century*, Methuen (Hacker Art Books edition, 1969).

Hibbert, Christopher (1987), *The English: A Social History, 1066 – 1945* (HarperCollins paperback edition, 1988).

Hill, Bridget (1996), *Servants: English Domestics in the Eighteenth Century*, Clarendon Press.

Hines, Colin (2000), *Localization: A Global Manifesto*, Earthscan.

Hintikka, Jaakko and Fernand Vandamme, eds. (1985), *Logic of Discovery and Logic of Discourse*, Plenum Press.

Hirsch, Fred (1976), *Social Limits to Growth*, Routledge.

Hirschman, Albert O. (1970), *Exit, Voice and Loyalty: Responses to Decline in Firms, Organisations, and States*, Harvard University Press.

Hirschman, Albert O. (1977), *The Passions and the Interests: Political Arguments for Capitalism Before Its Triumph*, Princeton University Press.

Hobbes, Thomas (1651), *Leviathan* (Michael Oakeshott, ed., Blackwell edition, 1960).

Hodgkinson, Tom (2005), *How To Be Idle*, HarperCollins.

Hodgson, Jacqi and Rob Hopkins (2010), *Transition in Action: Totnes and District 2030, an Energy Descent Action Plan*, Transition Town Totnes.

Hoggart, Richard (1995), *The Way We Live Now*, Chatto & Windus.

Holland, John (1998), *Emergence: From Chaos to Order*, Oxford University Press.

Holler, Linda (2002), *Erotic Morality: The Role of Touch in Moral Agency*, Rutgers University Press.

Holmgren, David (2002), *Permaculture: Principles & Pathways Beyond Sustainability*, Holmgren Design Services.

Homans, George C. (1951), *The Human Group* (Routledge edition, 1968).

Homer (c.700 BC), *The Odyssey* (translation by E.V. Rieu, 1946. Penguin edition, 1991).

Homer-Dixon, Thomas (2000), *The Ingenuity Gap*, Alfred A. Knopf.

Homer-Dixon, Thomas (2006), *The Upside of Down: Catastrophe, Creativity and the Renewal of Civilisation*, Souvenir Press.

Hook, Judith (1976), *The Baroque Age in England*, Thames and Hudson.

Hopkins, Rob (2008), *The Transition Handbook: From Oil Dependency to Local Resilience*, Green Books.

Horace (23 BC), *Odes*.

Horace (c.19 BC), *Ars Poetica*.

Hosking, Geoffrey (2001), *Russia and the Russians: A History*, Penguin.

Hostetler, John A. (1963), *Amish Society*, Johns Hopkins University Press (fourth edition, 1993).

Howard, Albert (1940), *An Agricultural Testament*, Oxford University Press (Other India Press edition, 1996).

Howard, Ebenezer (1898), *To-Morrow: A Peaceful Path to Real Reform*, Swan Sonnenschein (Attic Books edition, *Garden Cities of To-Morrow*, 1985).

Howarth, Robert W., J.W.B. Stewart and Mikhail V. Ivanov (1992), *Sulphur Cycling on the Continents: Wetlands, Terrestrial Ecosystems and Associated Water Bodies*, John Wiley & Sons.

Howatson Margaret C. and Ian Chilvers, eds. (1993), *The Concise Oxford Companion to Classical Literature*, Oxford University Press.

Huizinga, Johan (1936), *In the Shadow of Tomorrow: A Diagnosis of the Spiritual Ills of Our Time*, Heinemann.

Huizinga, Johan (1949), *Homo Ludens: A Study of the Play Element in Culture*, Routledge (Paladin edition, 1970).

Hume, David (1739), *A Treatise of Human Nature: Being an Attempt to Introduce the Experimental Method of Reasoning into Moral Subjects* (Oxford University Press edition, 1978).

Hume, David (1740–1776), *Essays Moral, Political and Literary* (Eugene F. Miller, ed. , 1777. Liberty Fund edition, 1987).

Hume, David (1748), *An Enquiry Concerning Human Understanding* (Oxford World's Classics edition, 2008).

Hunter Blair, Peter (1970), *The World of Bede*, Cambridge University Press (reprint edition, 1990).

Huppert, George (1986), *After the Black Death: A Social History of Early Modern Europe*, Indiana University Press.

Hurley, Patrick J. (1972), *A Concise Introduction to Logic*, Wadsworth (fourth edition, 1991).

Hussen, Ahmed M. (2000), *Principles of Environmental Economics: Economics, Ecology and Public Policy*, Routledge.

Huxley, Aldous (1932), *Brave New World* (Zodiac edition 1948).

Hyde, Lewis (1983), *The Gift: Imagination and the Erotic Life of Property*, Vintage Books.

Hyne, Norman J. (1995), *Nontechnical Guide to Petroleum Geology, Exploration, Drilling and Production*, Penn Well Corporation (second edition, 2001).

Illich, Ivan (1974), *Energy and Equity*, Calder and Boyars.

IPCC (Intergovernmental Panel on Climate Change): Solomon, S., D. Qin, M. Manning, et al., eds. (2007), *Climate Change 2007: The Physical Science Basis. Contribution of Working Group I to the Fourth Assessment Report of the Intergovernmental Panel on Climate Change*, Cambridge University Press.

Jackson, Tim (1996), *Material Concerns: Pollution, Profit and the Quality of Life*, Routledge.

Jackson, Tim (2009), *Prosperity Without Growth: Economics for a Finite Plane*, Earthscan.

Jacobs, Jane (1961), *The Death and Life of Great American Cities*, Random House (Jonathan Cape edition, 1962).

Jacobs, Jane (1984), *Cities and the Wealth of Nations: Principles of Economic Life*, Random House (Vintage edition, 1985).

Jaeger, Werner (1935), *Paideia: The Ideals of Greek Culture*, Blackwell (translation by Gilbert Highet, 1939).

James, Oliver (1997), *Britain on the Couch: Treating a Low-Serotonin Society*, Century.

James, Oliver (2007), *Affluenza*, Vermilion.

James, Peter (1982), *The Future of Coal*, Macmillan (second edition, 1984).

James, Sarah and Torbjörn Lahti (2004), *The Natural Step for Communities: How Cities and Towns Can Change to Sustainable Practices*, New Society Publishers.

Jamieson, Dale, ed. (2001), *A Companion to Environmental Philosophy*, Blackwell.

Jamison, Christopher (2006), *Finding Sanctuary: Monastic steps for Everyday Life*, Weidenfeld & Nicolson.

Jeavons, John (1995), *How to Grow More Vegetables Than You Ever Thought Possible on Less Land Than You Could Possibly Imagine*, Ten Speed Press.

Jenks, Mike, Elizabeth Burton and Katie Williams, eds. (1999), *The Compact City: A Sustainable Urban Form?*, Chapman and Hall.

Jensen, Derrick (2006), *Endgame: Volume I: The Problem of Civilization*, Seven Stories Press.

Johanisova, Nadia (2005), *Living in the Cracks: A Look at Rural Social Enterprises in Britain and the Czech Republic*, Feasta.

Johnson, Bond (2000), *The Mode of Parody: An Essay at Definition and Six Studies*, Peter Lang.

Johnson, David W. and Frank P. Johnson (1975), *Joining Together: Group Theory and Group Skills*, Prentice Hall (Allyn & Bacon edition, 1995).

Johnson, Neil (2007), *Simply Complexity, A Clear Guide to Complexity Theory*, Oneworld (paperback edition, 2009).

Johnson, Paul (1988), *Intellectuals*, Weidenfeld & Nicolson.

Johnson, Steven (2001), *Emergence: The Connected Lives of Ants, Brains, Cities and Software*, Penguin.

Jones, Howard (2008), *The Tao of Holism: A Blueprint for 21st Century Living*, O Books.

Jones, Martin (2007), *Feast: Why Humans Share Food*, Oxford University Press.

Jonsen, Albert and Stephen Toulmin (1988), *The Abuse of Casuistry: A History of Moral Reasoning*, University of California Press.

Jordan, William Chester (2002), *Europe in the High Middle Ages*, Penguin.

Jorgensen, Sven E. and Yuri M. Svirezhev, eds. (2004), *Towards a Thermodynamic Theory for Ecological Systems*, Pergamon Elsevier.

Julian of Norwich (1373), from *A Book of Showings to the Anchoress Julian of Norwich*, Edmund Colledge and James Walsh, eds. (1978), Pontifical Institute of Mediaeval Studies.

Jung, Carl G. (1947, revised 1954), *On the Nature of the Psyche* (Routledge Classics edition, 2001).

Kabata-Pendias, Alina and Henryk Pendias (1984), *Trace Elements in Soils and Plants*, CRC Press (third edition, 2001).

Kafka, Franz (1915), *Metamorphosis and Other Stories* (Penguin edition, 2007).

Kafka, Franz (1922), *The Castle* (Penguin edition, 2000).

Kahneman, Daniel, Paul Slovic and Amos Tversky, eds. (1982), *Judgment Under Uncertainty: Heuristics and Biases*, Cambridge University Press.

Kanter, Rosabeth Moss (1972), *Commitment and Community: Communes and Utopias in Sociological Perspective*, Harvard University Press.

Kay, John (2004), *Everlasting Light Bulbs: How Economics Illuminates the World*, The Erasmus Press.

Keats, John (1795–1821), *Selected Letters of John Keats*, Grant F. Scott, ed. (2002), Harvard University Press.

Keen, David (1994), *The Benefits of Famine: A Political Economy of Famine and Relief in Southwestern Sudan 1983–1989*, Princeton University Press.

Keen, Maurice , ed. (1999), *Medieval Warfare: A History*, Oxford University Press.

Keller, David R., ed. (2010), *Environmental Ethics: The Big Questions*, Blackwell.

Keynes, John Maynard (1931), *Essays in Persuasion* (Macmillan edition, 1972).

Keynes, John Maynard (1936), *The General Theory of Employment, Interest and Money* (Macmillan edition, 1978).

Keys, Ancel and Margaret Keys (1959), *Eat Well and Stay Well*, Doubleday (Hodder & Stoughton edition, 1960).

Klein, Carol (2007), *Grow Your Own Veg*, Mitchell Beazley.

Knight, Amy (1993), *Beria: Stalin's First Lieutenant*, Princeton University Press.

Koestler, Arthur (1941), *Scum of the Earth*, Macmillan (Eland edition, 1991).

Koestler, Arthur (1959), *The Sleepwalkers* (Hutchinson edition, 1968).

Koestler, Arthur (1967), *The Ghost in the Machine*, Hutchinson (Danube edition, 1976).

Kohlberg, Lawrence (1981), *The Philosophy of Moral Development: Moral Stages and the Idea of Justice*, Harper & Row.

Kohlberg, Lawrence, Charles Levine and Alexandra Hewer, eds. (1983), *Moral Stages: A Current Formulation and a Response to Critics*, S. Karger.

Kohn, Alfie (1993), *Punished by Rewards: The Trouble with Gold Stars, Incentive Plans, A's, Praise, and Other Bribes*, Houghton Mifflin (second edition, 1999).

Kohr, Leopold (1957), *The Breakdown of Nations*, Routledge & Kegan Paul (Green Books edition, 2001).

Kohr, Leopold (1989), *The Inner City: From Mud to Marble*, Y Lolfa Cyf.

Korovicz, David (2010), *Tipping Point: Near-Term Systemic Implications of a Peak in Global Oil Production*, Feasta.

Korten, David C. (1995), *When Corporations Rule the World*, Earthscan.

Kosko, Bart (1993), *Fuzzy Thinking: The New Science of Fuzzy Logic*, Hyperion (Flamingo edition, 1994).

Koutsoyiannis, Anna (1975), *Modern Microeconomics*, Macmillan (second edition, 1979).

Krabbe, Judith K. (1989), *The Metamorphoses of Apuleius*, Peter Lang.

Kropotkin, Peter (1890–1896), *Mutual Aid: A Factor of Evolution*, Heinemann.

Kropotkin, Peter (1892), *La Conquête du Pain*. English: *The Conquest of Bread* (first translated 1906), Chapman and Hall (Cornell University Press edition, 2009).

Kropotkin, Peter (1899), *Fields, Factories and Workshops Tomorrow* (Colin Ward, ed., George Allen & Unwin edition, 1974).

Krutch, Joseph Wood (1954), *The Measure of Man*, Bobbs-Merrill (Alvin Redman edition, 1956).

Krutch, Joseph Wood (1956), *The Great Chain of Life*, Houghton Mifflin (paperback edition, 1977).

Krutch, Joseph Wood, ed. (1969), *The Best Nature Writing of Joseph Wood Krutch*, William Morrow.

Kuhn, Thomas S. (1962), *The Structure of Scientific Revolutions*, University of Chicago Press (third edition, 1996).

Kumar, Satish (2002), *You Are, Therefore I Am: A Declaration of Dependence*, Green Books.

Kumar, Satish (2007), *Spiritual Compass: The Three Qualities of Life*, Green Books.

Lakatos, Imre and Alan Musgrave, eds. (1970), *Criticism and the Growth of Knowledge*, Cambridge University Press.

Lakatos, Imre (1973), *Lectures on Scientific Method*, in Matteo Motterlini (1999), *For and Against Method*, University of Chicago Press.

Lampkin, Nicolas (1990), *Organic Farming*, Farming Press (second edition, 1994).

Landsburg, Steven E. (1993), *The Armchair Economist: Economics and Everyday Life*, Free Press (Simon & Schuster paperback edition, 1995).

Lang, Tim and Colin Hines (1993), *The New Protectionism: Protecting the Future Against Free Trade*, Earthscan.

Lang, Tim, David Barling and Martin Caraher (2009), *Food Policy: Integrating Health, Environment and Society*, Oxford University Press.

Lange, Roderyk (1970), *The Nature of Dance: An Anthropological Perspective*, Laban Art of Movement Guild (Macdonald and Evans edition, 1975).

Laqueur, Walter (2007), *The Last Days of Europe: Epitaph for an Old Continent*, St. Martin's Press.

Larvor, Brendan (1998), *Lakatos: An Introduction*, Routledge.

Lasch, Christopher (1979), *The Culture of Narcissism: American Life in an Age of Diminishing Expectations*, W.W. Norton & Co.

Laslett, Peter (1965), *The World We Have Lost*, Methuen (second edition, 1971).

László, Ervin (2006), *The Chaos Point: The World at the Crossroads*, Piatkus.

Laughland, John (1997), *The Tainted Source: The Undemocratic Origin of the European Idea*, Little Brown (Warner Books edition, 1998).

Lawrence, D.H. (1913–1930), *Selected Critical Writings*, Michael Herbert, ed. (1998), Oxford University Press.

Leakey, Richard and Roger Lewin (1995), *The Sixth Extinction*, Doubleday.

Le Bon, Gustave (1896), *Psychologie des Foules*, Ernest Benn. English: *The Crowd: A Study of the Popular Mind*.

Lee-Gosselin Associates Ltd (1985), *Approaches and Attitudes to Fuel Conservation, Final Report to Energy, Mines and Resources, Ottawa, Canada*.

Leibenstein, Harvey (1976), *Beyond Economic Man: A New Foundation for Microeconomics*, Harvard University Press.

Leiber, Justin (1993), *Paradoxes*, Duckworth.

Leighton, Albert C. (1972), *Transport and Communication in Early Medieval Europe AD 500–1100*, David & Charles.

Leiss, William (1976), *The Limits to Satisfaction: An Essay on the Problem of Needs and Commodities*, University of Toronto Press.

Leopold, Aldo (1916–1948), *Aldo Leopold's Southwest*, Brown, David E. and Neil B. Carmony, eds. (1995), New Mexico Press.

Leopold, Aldo (1949), *A Sand County Almanac*, Oxford University Press.

Leroi, Armand Marie (2003), *Mutants: On the Form, Varieties and Errors of the Human Body*, HarperCollins.

Lester, David and Bijou Yang (1997), *The Economy and Suicide: Economic Perspectives on Suicide*, Nova Science.

Levi, A.H.T. (1971), Levi's introduction to the Penguin edition of Erasmus' (1511) *In Praise of Folly*.

Levin, Simon A., ed. (2009), *The Princeton Guide to Ecology*, Princeton University Press.

Levitt, Steven D. and Stephen J. Dubner (2005), *Freakonomics: A Rogue Economist Explores the Hidden Side of Everything*, Allen Lane.

Light, Andrew and Holmes Rolston III, eds. (2002), *Environmental Ethics: An Anthology*, Blackwell (second edition, 2003).

Lindbeck, Assar and Dennis Snower (1988), *The Insider-Outsider Theory of Employment and Unemployment*, MIT.

Lindbeck, George A. (1984), *The Nature of Doctrine: Religion and Theology in a Postliberal Age*, SPCK.

Linder, Staffan B. (1970), *The Harried Leisure Class*, Columbia University Press.

Livy (c.32 BC), *History of Rome, Volume VI, Books 23–25* (Harvard University Press edition, translation by Frank Gardner Moore, 1940).

Locke, John (1689), *Two Treatises of Government*, Awnsham Churchill.

Locke, John (1690), *An Essay Concerning Human Understanding* (Pauline Phemister, ed., Oxford World Classics edition, 2008).

Lohmann, Larry, ed. (2006), *Carbon Trading: A Critical Conversation on Climate Change, Privatisation and Power*, The Corner House.

Lomborg, Bjørn (2001), *The Skeptical Environmentalist*, Cambridge University Press.

Long, Martyn (2000), *The Psychology of Education*, Routledge.

Lorimer, David (2003), *Radical Prince: The Practical Vision of the Prince of Wales*, Floris.

Lovejoy, Arthur O. (1936), *The Great Chain of Being: A Study in the History of an Idea*, Harvard University Press (Harper & Row edition, 1960).

Lovelock, James (1979), *Gaia: A New Look at Life on Earth*, Oxford University Press.

Lovelock, James (1988), *The Ages of Gaia: A Biography of Our Living Earth*, Oxford University Press (paperback edition, 1989).

Lovelock, James (2006), *The Revenge of Gaia: Why the Earth is Fighting Back and How We Can Still Save Humanity*, Allen Lane.

Loveridge, Denis (2007), *Foresight: the Art and Science of Anticipating the Future*, Routledge.

Lovins, Amory B., E. Kyle Datta, Odd-Even Bustnes, et al. (2005), *Winning the Oil Endgame: Innovation for Profits, Jobs and Security*, Earthscan.

Lucas, Caroline (2001), *Stopping the Great Food Swap*, The Greens/European Free Alliance, European Parliament.

Lundin, Roger (1993), *The Culture of Interpretation: Christian Faith and the Postmodern World*, William B. Eerdmans Publishing Company.

Luo, Yiqi and Harold A. Mooney, eds. (1999), *Carbon Dioxide and Environmental Stress*, Academic Press.

Lutz, Mark A. and Kenneth Lux (1988), *Humanistic Economics: The New Challenge*, Bootstrap.

Lutz, Wolfgang, Warren C. Sanderson and Sergei Scherbov, eds. (2004), *The End of World Population Growth in the 21st Century: New Challenges for Human Capital Formation and Sustainable Development*, Earthscan.

Lynas, Mark (2007), *Six Degrees: Our Future on a Hotter Planet*, Fourth Estate.

Lyons, Glenn and Kiron Chatterjee, eds. (2001), *Transport Lessons from the Fuel Tax Protests of 2000*, Ashgate.

Mabey, Richard (1972), *Food for Free*, Collins.

Mabey, Richard (2005), *Nature Cure*, Chatto & Windus (Vintage edition, 2008).

MacArthur, Robert H. and Edward O. Wilson (1967), *The Theory of Island Biogeography*, Princeton University Press.

Macaulay, Thomas Babington (1849), *The History of England*, Phillips, Sampson and Company.

MacCarthy, Fiona (1994), *William Morris: A Life for Our Time*, Faber & Faber.

Machiavelli, Niccolò (1513), *The Prince* (Penguin edition, 2004).

Machiavelli, Niccolò (1517), *The Discourses on the First Ten Books of Titus Livy* (Penguin edition, 1983).

MacIntyre, Alasdair (1981), *After Virtue: A Study in Moral Theory*, Duckworth (second edition, 1985).

MacIntyre, Alasdair (1990), *Three Rival Versions of Moral Enquiry*, Duckworth.

MacKay, David J.C. (2008), *Sustainable Energy – Without the Hot Air*, UIT Cambridge.

Madron, Roy and John Jopling (2003), *Gaian Democracies: Redefining Globalisation and People-Power*, Green Books.

Magee, Bryan (1973), *Popper*, Fontana Modern Masters.

Makhijani, Arjun and Kevin Gurney (1995), *Mending the Ozone Hole*, MIT.

Malenbaum, Wilfred (1978), *World Demand for Raw Materials in 1985 and 2000*, McGraw-Hill.

Malpas, Jeff (1999), *Place and Experience: A Philosophical Topography*, Cambridge University Press.

Malthus, Thomas (1798–1826), *An Essay on the Principle of Population* (Anthony Flew, ed., Penguin edition, 1970).

Mandelbrot, Benoit B. and Richard L. Hudson (2004), *The (Mis)behaviour of Markets: A Fractal View of Financial Turbulence*, Profile Books (paperback edition, 2008).

Mandeville, Bernard (1714), *The Fable of the Bees*, James Roberts.

Mansbridge, Albert (1920), *An Adventure in Working-Class Education: Being the Story of the Worker's Educational Association 1903–1915*, Longmans, Green and Co.

Manuel, Frank E., ed. (1967), *Utopias and Utopian Thought: A Timely Appraisal*, Beacon Press (Souvenir Press edition, 1973).

Marcuse, Herbert (1964), *One Dimensional Man: Studies in the Ideology of Advanced Industrial Society*, Routledge.

Marshack, Alexander (1972), *The Roots of Civilization: Cognitive Beginnings of Man's First Art, Symbol and Notation*, McGraw-Hill.

Marshall, Peter (1992), *Demanding the Impossible: A History of Anarchism*, HarperCollins (PM Press edition, 2010).

Marshall, Sybil (1963), *An Experiment in Education*, Cambridge University Press.

Martin, Geoffrey H. (2003), Martin's introduction to *Domesday Book: A Complete Translation*, Penguin.

Massingham, H.J. (1882–1952), *A Mirror of England: An Anthology of the Writings of H.J. Massingham*, Edward Abelson, ed. (1988), Green Books.

Mauss, Marcel (1950), *Essai sur le don*, Presses Universitaires de France. English: *The Gift: The Form and Reason for Exchange in Archaic Societies* (first translated 1954), Cohen & West (Routledge edition, 1990).

Mawson, Andrew (2008), *The Social Entrepreneur: Making Communities Work*, Atlantic Books.

Mazower, Mark (1998), *Dark Continent: Europe's Twentieth Century*, Penguin.

McCarrison, Robert and Hugh M. Sinclair (1953), *Nutrition and Health*, Faber & Faber.

McCarthy, Patrick and Richard Hawkes (1999), *Northside of the Mizen: Tales, Customs and History from the South-West of County Cork in Ireland*, Mizen Productions.

McCraw, Thomas K. (2007), *Prophet of Innovation: Joseph Schumpeter and Creative Destruction*, Harvard University Press.

McCue, Jim (1997), *Edmund Burke and Our Present Discontents*, Claridge Press.

McDonough, William and Michael Braungart (2002), *Cradle to Cradle: Remaking the Way We Make Things*, North Point Press.

McGregor, Douglas (1960), *The Human Side of Enterprise*, McGraw-Hill.

McKee, Alan (2004), *The Public Sphere: An Introduction*, Cambridge University Press.

McKibben, Bill (2007), *Deep Economy: Economics as if the World Mattered*, Oneworld.

McKisack, May (1959), *The Oxford History of England, Volume V: The Fourteenth Century, 1307–1399*, Oxford University Press.

Meadows, Andrew and Kirsty Shipton, eds. (2001), *Money and its Uses in the Ancient Greek World*, Oxford University Press.

Meadows, Donella H., Dennis L. Meadows, Jørgen Randers and William W. Behrens III (1972), *The Limits to Growth*, Earth Island.

Meadows, Donella H., Dennis L. Meadows and Jørgen Randers (1992), *Beyond the Limits: Global Collapse or a Sustainable Future*, Earthscan.

Meehan, Patricia (1992), *The Unnecessary War: Whitehall and the German Resistance to Hitler*, Sinclair-Stevenson.

Mehta, Lyla and Synne Movik (2010), *Shit Matters: The Potential of Community-Led Total Sanitation*, Practical Action Publishing.

Meller, Helen (1990), *Patrick Geddes: Social Evolutionist and City Planner*, Routledge.

Metcalf, Peter and Richard Huntington (1981), *Celebrations of Death: The Anthropology of Mortuary Ritual*, Cambridge University Press (second edition, 1991)

Meyer, Aubrey (2000), *Contraction and Convergence: The Global Solution to Climate Change*, Green Books.

Michelli, Joseph (1998), *Humor, Play and Laughter: Stress-Proofing Life with your Kids*, Love and Logic Press.

Mill, John Stuart (1848), *Principles of Political Economy*, Longmans, Green and Co.

Mill, John Stuart (1859), *On Liberty* (Everyman edition, 1962).

Mill, John Stuart (1861), *Considerations on Representative Government*, Parker, Son and Bourn.

Miller, Arthur (1943), *The Man Who Had All the Luck* (Methuen edition, 2008).

Miller, David (2000), *Citizenship and National Identity*, Polity Press.

Miller, David L. (1967), *Individualism: Personal Achievement and the Open Society*, University of Texas Press.

Miller, G. Tyler (1975), *Living in the Environment: Principles, Connections, and Solutions*, Brooks Cole (fifteenth edition, 2006).

Miller, James (1987), *Democracy is in the Streets: From Port Huron to the Siege of Chicago*, Simon and Schuster.

Miller, John H. and Scott E. Page (2007), *Complex Adaptive Systems: An Introduction to Computational Models of Social Life*, Princeton University Press.

Miller, Stephen (2006), *Conversation: A History of a Declining Art*, Yale University Press.

Milton, John (1667), *Paradise Lost*, Peter Parker.

Minkler, Meredith (1997), *Community Organizing and Community Building for Health*, Rutgers University Press (second edition, 2005).

Minogue, Kenneth R. (1997), *The Silencing of Society: True Cost of the Lust for News*, Social Affairs Unit.

Mises, Ludwig von (1949), *Human Action: A Treatise on Economics*, William Hodge.

Mishan, E.J. (1977), *The Economic Growth Debate: An Assessment*, George Allen and Unwin.

Mitchell, Melanie (2009), *Complexity: A Guided Tour*, Oxford University Press.

Mitchell, Wesley Clair (1912), *The Backward Art of Spending Money and Other Essays* (Kelley edition, 1950).

Mithen, Steven (2003), *After the Ice: A Global Human History, 20,000 - 5000 BC*, Weidenfeld & Nicolson.

Mollison, Bill and David Holmgren (1978), *Permaculture One: A Perennial Agriculture for Human Settlements*, Tagari Publications (second edition, 1982).

Mollison, Bill (1988), *Permaculture: A Designers' Manual*, Tagari Publications.

Montagu, Ashley (1986), *Touching: The Human Significance of the Skin*, Harper & Row.

Moore, Mike (2003), *A World Without Walls: Freedom, Development, Free Trade and Global Governance*, Cambridge University Press.

More, Thomas (1516), *Utopia* (Richard Marius, ed., J.M. Dent edition, 1985).

Morford, Mark P.O. and Robert J. Lenardon (1971), *Classical Mythology*, McKay (Oxford University Press sixth edition, 1999).

Morrill, John, Paul Slack and Daniel Woolf, eds. (1993), *Public Duty and Private Conscience in Seventeenth Century England*, Clarendon Press.

Morris, Colin (1972), *The Discovery of the Individual 1050–1200*, SPCK.

Morris, John E. (1901), *The Welsh Wars of Edward I*, Clarendon Press.

Morris, William (1891), *News from Nowhere* (Oxford University Press edition, 2003).

Mounier, Emmanuel (1950), *Personalism*, Routledge & Kegan Paul (translation by Philip Mairet, 1952).

Muir, John (1838–1914), *Journeys in the Wilderness: A John Muir Reader*, Graham White, ed. (2009), Birlinn.

Mullen, Peter (2000), *The Real Common Worship*, Edgeways Books.

Mumford, Lewis (1961), *The City in History: Its Origins, Its Transformations, and Its Prospects*, Harcourt, Brace & World (Pelican edition, 1966).

Næss, Arne (1989), *Ecology, Community and Lifestyle: Outline of an Ecosophy*, Cambridge University Press (translation and editing by David Rothenberg, working with Næss, and based on his 1976 work of the same title, *Økologi, samfunn og livsstil*).

Nash, Manning (1966), *Primitive and Peasant Economic Systems*, Chandler.

Netting, Robert McCorkle, Richard R. Wilk and Eric J. Arnould, eds. (1984), *Households: Comparative and Historical Studies of the Domestic Group*, University of California Press.

Newman, John Henry (1873), *The Idea of a University* (Charles Frederick Harrold, ed., Longman edition, 1957).

Newman, Mark, Albert László Barabási and Duncan J. Watts (2006), *The Structure and Dynamics of Networks*, Princeton University Press.

Nicholson-Lord, David (1987), *The Greening of Cities*, Routledge & Kegan Paul.

Nietzsche, Friedrich (1883–1885), *Thus Spake Zarathustra* (in *The Portable Nietzsche*, Viking edition, 1954).

Nietzsche, Friedrich (1887), *On the Genealogy of Morality* (in *The Portable Nietzsche*, Viking edition, 1954).

Nolan, Richard L. and David C. Croson (1995), *Creative Destruction: A Six-Stage Process for Transforming the Organization*, Harvard Business School Press.

Norberg-Hodge, Helena (1991), *Ancient Futures: Learning from Ladakh* (Rider & Co edition, 1992).

Nordhoff, Charles (1875), *American Utopias* (originally *The Communistic Societies of the United States*), Harper & Brothers.

Norman, Jesse, ed. (1993), *The Achievement of Michael Oakeshott*, Duckworth.

North, F.K. (1985), *Petroleum Geology*, Allen & Unwin.

North, Peter (2010), *Local Money: How to Make it Happen in Your Community*, Green Books.

Northbourne, Walter James: Lord (1940), *Look to the Land*, Dent.

Nussbaum, Martha C. (1994), *The Therapy of Desire: Theory and Practice in Hellenistic Ethics*, Princeton University Press.

Oakeshott, Michael (1946), Oakeshott's introduction to Thomas Hobbes' (1651) *Leviathan* (Michael Oakeshott, ed., Blackwell edition, 1960).

Oakeshott, Michael (1962), *Rationalism in Politics and Other Essays* (Timothy Fuller, ed., Liberty Fund edition, 1991).

Oakeshott, Michael (1975), *On Human Conduct*, Oxford University Press.

Oborne, Peter (2007), *The Triumph of the Political Class*, Simon & Schuster.

O'Connor, Joseph and Ian McDermott (1997), *The Art of Systems Thinking: Essential Skills for Creativity and Problem Solving*, Thorsons.

O'Day, Rosemary (1994), *The Family and Family Relationships 1500–1900*, Palgrave Macmillan.

Odum, Eugene P. and Howard T. Odum (1953), *Fundamentals of Ecology*, W.B. Saunders (third edition, 1971).

Odum, Howard T. and Elizabeth C. Odum (2001), *A Prosperous Way Down: Principles and Policies*, University Press of Colorado.

Ohno, Taiichi (1978), *Toyota Production System: Beyond Large-Scale Production*, Daiyamondosha (Productivity Press edition, 1988).

Olson, Mancur (1965), *The Logic of Collective Action: Public Goods and the Theory of Groups*, Harvard University Press.

Open University Course Team (2007), *Energy for a Sustainable Future: Energy Systems and Sustainability*, Open University Worldwide.

Orwell, George (1945–1950), *The Collected Essays, Journalism and Letters of George Orwell, Volume 4: In Front of Your Nose, 1945–1950*, Sonia Orwell and Ian Angus, eds. (1968), Secker & Warburg.

Orwell, George (1949), *Nineteen Eighty-Four*, Secker & Warburg.

Ostrom, Elinor (1971), *Community Organization and the Provision of Police Services*, Indiana University Press (Sage edition, 1973).

Ostrom, Elinor (1990), *Governing the Commons: The Evolution of Institutions for Collective Action*, Cambridge University Press.

Ostrom, Elinor and James A. Walker, eds. (2002), *Trust and Reciprocity: Interdisciplinary Lessons for Experimental Research*, Russell Sage.

Ostrom, Elinor (2005), *Understanding Institutional Diversity*, Princeton University Press.

Ostrom, Vincent (1997), *The Meaning of Democracy and the Vulnerabilities of Democracies: A Response to Tocqueville's Challenge*, University of Michigan Press.

Owens, Susan (1986), *Energy, Planning and Urban Form,* Pion.

Ozouf, Mona (1976), *La Fête Révolutionnaire 1789–1799*, Gallimard. English: *Festivals and the French Revolution* (Harvard University Press edition, translation by Alan Sheridan, 1988).

Papanek, Victor (1995), *The Green Imperative: Ecology and Ethics in Design and Architecture*, Thames and Hudson.

Parker, Geoffrey (1979), *Europe in Crisis 1598–1648*, Cornell University Press (Fontana Press edition, 1987).

Pascal, Blaise (1670), *Pensées*, Guillaume Desprez and Jean Desessartz. English: *Thoughts* (first translated 1688, by John Walker).

Pearce, David W. and R. Kerry Turner (1989), *Economics of Natural Resources and the Environment*, Johns Hopkins University Press.

Pearce, Fred (2005), *When The Rivers Run Dry: What Happens When Our Water Runs Out?*, Beacon Press (Eden Project Books edition, 2007).

Pearce, Fred (2006), *The Last Generation: How Nature Will Take Her Revenge for Climate Change*, Eden Project Books.

Pearce, Fred (2010), *Peoplequake: Mass Migration, Ageing Nations and the Coming Population Crash,* Eden Project Books.

Pellegrini, Anthony D. and Peter K. Smith, eds. (2005), *The Nature of Play: Great Apes and Humans*, Guilford Press.

Penn, Dustin J. and Iver Mysterud, eds. (2007), *Evolutionary Perspectives on Environmental Problems*, Aldine Transaction.

Pereira, Winin and Jeremy Seabrook (1990), *Asking the Earth: Farms, Forestry and Survival in India*, Earthscan.

Perrow, Charles (2007), *The Next Catastrophe: Reducing Our Vulnerabilities to Natural, Industrial and Terrorist Disasters*, Princeton University Press.

Petri, Herbert L. (1986), *Motivation: Theory, Research and Applications*, Wadsworth (third edition, 1991).

Petrie, W.M. Flinders (1911), *The Revolutions of Civilisation*, Harper & Brothers.

Piaget, Jean (1923–1979), *The Essential Piaget*, Howard E. Gruber and J. Jacques Vonèche, eds. (1977), Basic Books.

Pickstock, Catherine (1997), *After Writing: On The Liturgical Consummation of Philosophy*, Blackwell.

Pink, Daniel H. (2009), *Drive: The Surprising Truth About What Motivates Us*, Riverhead (Canongate Books edition, 2010).

Pinker, Steven (2002), *The Blank Slate: The Modern Denial of Human Nature*, Allen Lane (Penguin edition, 2003).

Pinkerton, Tamzin and Rob Hopkins (2009), *Local Food: How to Make It Happen in Your Community*, Transition Books.

Pirie, Madsen (2006), *How to Win Every Argument: The Use and Abuse of Logic,* Continuum.

Pittenger, William Norman (1969), *Alfred North Whitehead*, Lutterworth Press.

Playfair, Guy Lyon (1990), *The Evil Eye: The Unacceptable Face of Television*, Jonathan Cape.

Plutarch (c.100 AD), *Moralia* (Heinemann edition, translation by Frank Cole Babbitt et al., 2004).

Polanyi, Karl (1944), *The Great Transformation* (Beacon paperback edition, 1957).

Ponting, Clive (1991), *A Green History of the World: The Environment and the Collapse of Great Civilisations*, Sinclair-Stevenson (Penguin edition, 1992).

Popper, Karl (1934), *Logik der Forschung*, Springer Verlag. English: *The Logic of Scientific Discovery*, Hutchinson & Co.

Popper, Karl (1945), *The Open Society and Its Enemies*, Routledge (paperback fourth edition, 1962).

Popper, Karl (1962), *Conjectures and Refutations: The Growth of Scientific Knowledge*, Basic Books (Routledge & Kegan Paul edition, 1963).

Porritt, Jonathon (2000), *Playing Safe: Science and the Environment*, Thames & Hudson.

Porritt, Jonathon (2005), *Capitalism as if the World Matters*, Earthscan.

Porter, Roy (2000), *Enlightenment: Britain and the Creation of the Modern World*, Allen Lane.

Portwood, Madeleine (2000), *Understanding Developmental Dyspraxia*, David Fulton.

Powicke, Maurice (1953), *The Thirteenth Century 1216–1307*, Clarendon Press.

Pretty, Jules (1998), *The Living Land: Agriculture, Food and Community Regeneration in Rural Europe*, Earthscan.

Pretty, Jules (2002), *Agri-Culture: Reconnecting People, Land and Nature*, Earthscan.

Price, Ira Maurice, translator and editor (1899), *The Great Cylinder Inscriptions A & B of Gudea*, J.C. Hinrichs'sche Buchandlung.

Price, Weston A.V. (1939), *Nutrition and Physical Degeneration*, Price-Pottenger Nutrition Foundation.

Proctor, Robert (1996), *Cancer Wars: How Politics Shapes What We Know And Don't Know About Cancer*, Basic Books.

Putnam, Robert D. (2000), *Bowling Alone: The Collapse and Revival of American Community*, Simon and Schuster.

Putnam, Robert D., Lewis M. Feldstein and Donald Cohen (2003), *Better Together: Restoring the American Community*, Simon & Schuster.

Quigley, Joan (2007), *The Day the Earth Caved In: An American Mining Tragedy*, Random House.

Rabelais, François (c.1532–1564), *Gargantua and Pantagruel* (Penguin edition, translation by John Michael Cohen, 1955).

Radman, Zdravko, ed. (1995), *From a Metaphorical Point of View: A Multidisciplinary Approach to the Cognitive Content of Metaphor*, de Gruyter.

Ralls, Karen (2003), *The Templars and the Grail: The Knights of the Quest*, Quest Books.

Ramsbotham, Oliver, Tom Woodhouse and Hugh Miall (1999), *Contemporary Conflict Resolution: The Prevention, Management and Transformation of Deadly Conflicts*, Polity Press (second edition, 2005).

Ratner, Mark and Daniel Ratner (2002), *Nanotechnology: A Gentle Introduction to the Next Big Idea*, Prentice Hall.

Raz, Joseph (1986), *The Morality of Freedom*, Oxford University Press.

Rees, Martin (2003), *Our Final Century: Will the Human Race Survive the Twenty-first Century?*, Heinemann.

Renfrew, Colin and Kenneth L. Cooke, eds. (1979), *Transformations: Mathematical Approaches to Culture Change*, Academic Press.

Rescher, Nicholas (2001), *Paradoxes: Their Roots, Range and Resolution*, Open Court.

Revel, Jean-François (2003), *L'obsession anti-américaine: Son fonctionnement, ses causes, ses inconséquences*, Plon.

Rhie, Marilyn M. and Robert A.F. Thurman (1991), *Wisdom and Compassion: The Sacred Art of Tibet*, Thames and Hudson.

Ricardo, David (1817), *On the Principles of Political Economy and Taxation*, John Murray.

Robbins, Lionel (1932), *An Essay on the Nature and Significance of Economic Science*, Macmillan.

Robèrt, Karl-Henrik (1997), *The Natural Step: A Framework for Achieving Sustainability in our Organizations*, Pegasus Communications.

Roberts, Paul (2005), *The End of Oil*, Bloomsbury.

Roberts, Paul (2008), *The End of Food*, Houghton Mifflin.

Robertson, James (1998), *Transforming Economic Life: A Millennial Challenge*, Green Books.

Rogers, Carl (1942–1987), *The Carl Rogers Reader*, Howard Kirschenbaum and Valerie Land Henderson, eds. (1989), Houghton Mifflin (Constable edition, 1990).

Rogers, Carl (1961), *On Becoming a Person: A Therapist's View of Psychotherapy*, Houghton Mifflin.

Rogers, H.C.B. (1961), *Turnpike to Iron Road*, Seeley, Service & Co.

Röhl, John C.G. (1987), *Kaiser, Hof und Staat: Wilhelm II und die deutsche Politik*. English: *The Kaiser and His Court: Wilhelm II and the Government of Germany* (Cambridge University Press edition, 1996).

Röhl, John C.G. (1993), *Wilhelm II. Die Jugend des Kaisers 1859–1888*. English: *Young Wilhelm: The Kaiser's Early Life 1859–1888* (Cambridge University Press edition, 1998).

Rolston, Holmes, III (1986), *Philosophy Gone Wild: Environmental Ethics*, Prometheus.

Roose-Evans, James (1994), *Passages of the Soul: Ritual Today*, Element Books.

Rosillo-Calle, Frank and Francis X. Johnson (2010), *Food versus Fuel: An Informed Introduction to Biofuels*, Zed Books.

Rostow, Walt Whitman (1952), *The Process of Economic Growth*, W.W. Norton & Co.

Rowbotham, Michael (1998), *The Grip of Death: A Study of Modern Money, Debt Slavery and Destructive Economics*, Jon Carpenter.

Rowell, Alexis (2010), *Communities, Councils and a Low Carbon Future: What We Can Do if Governments Won't*, Green Books.

Royal College of General Practitioners (1993), *Better Living, Better Life*, Knowledge House.

Ruggles, Clive L.N. (2005), *Ancient Astronomy: An Encyclopedia of Cosmologies and Myth*, ABC-CLIO.

Ruskin, John (1843–1889), *John Ruskin: Selected Writings*, Dinah Birch, ed. (2004), Oxford University Press.

Ruskin, John (1866), *The Crown of Wild Olive* (George Allen edition, 1902).

Sabine, George H. (1937), *A History of Political Theory*, Harrap (second edition, 1948).

Sacks, Jonathan (2000), *Radical Then, Radical Now: The Legacy of the World's Oldest Religion*, The Free Press (HarperCollins edition, 2001).

Sacks, Jonathan (2002), *The Dignity of Difference: How to Avoid the Clash of Civilizations*, Continuum (revised edition, 2003).

Sacks, Jonathan (2007), *The Home We Build Together: Recreating Society*, Continuum.

Sahlins, Marshall (1972), *Stone Age Economics*, Aldine-Atherton (Routledge edition, 2004).

Sainsbury, R.M. (1987), *Paradoxes*, Cambridge University Press.

Sale, Kirkpatrick (1980), *Human Scale*, Secker & Warburg.

Sale, Kirkpatrick (1985), *Dwellers in the Land: The Bioregional Vision*, Sierra Club Books.

Sale, Kirkpatrick (1995), *Rebels Against the Future: The Luddites and their War on the Industrial Revolution*, Addison-Wesley.

Sampson, Geoffrey (2005), *The 'Language Instinct' Debate*, Continuum.

Samuelson, Paul A. (1964), *Economics*, McGraw-Hill.

Sandel, Michael J. (1982), *Liberalism and the Limits of Justice*, Cambridge University Press.

Saunders, Peter (2010), *Social Mobility Myths*, Civitas.

Scarre, Geoffrey (1996), *Utilitarianism*, Routledge.

Schaffer, Robert H. (1988), *The Breakthrough Strategy: Using Short-term Successes to Build the High Performance Organization*, HarperCollins.

Schelling, Thomas C. (1984), *Choice and Consequence: Perspectives of an Errant Economist*, Harvard University Press.

Schlosser, Eric (2001), *Fast Food Nation: What the All-American Meal is Doing to the World*, Allen Lane (Penguin edition, 2002).

Schmidt, Jeff (2000), *Disciplined Minds: A Critical Look at Salaried Professionals and the Soul-Battering System That Shapes Their Lives*, Rowman and Littlefield.

Schneck, Daniel J. and Dorita S. Berger (2006), *The Music Effect: Music Physiology and Clinical Applications*, Jessica Kingsley.

Schon, Donald A. (1971), *Beyond the Stable State*, W.W. Norton & Co.

Schor, Juliet B. (1992), *The Overworked American: The Unexpected Decline of Leisure*, Perseus Books.

Schor, Juliet B. and Betsy Taylor (2002), *Sustainable Planet: Solutions for the Twenty-first Century*, Beacon Press.

Schouten, Ton and Patrick Moriarty (2003), *Community Water, Community Management: From System to Service in Rural Areas*, Intermediate Technology Development Group.

Schumacher, E.F. (1973), *Small is Beautiful: A Study of Economics as if People Mattered*, Blond & Briggs (Abacus edition, 1974).

Schumacher, E.F. (1997), *This I Believe, and Other Essays*, Green Books.

Schumpeter, Joseph (1942), *Capitalism, Socialism and Democracy* (Allen and Unwin edition, 1976).

Scitovsky, Tibor (1976), *The Joyless Economy: The Psychology of Human Satisfaction*, Oxford University Press.

Scott, John (1991), *Social Network Analysis: A Handbook*, Sage (second edition, 2000).

Scott Cato, Molly (2009), *Green Economics: An Introduction to Theory, Policy and Practice*, Earthscan.

Scruton Roger (1994), *Modern Philosophy: An Introduction and Survey*, Sinclair-Stevenson (Mandarin edition, 1996).

Scruton, Roger (1998a), *An Intelligent Person's Guide to Modern Culture*, Duckworth.

Scruton, Roger (1998b), *On Hunting*, Yellow Jersey Press.

Scruton, Roger (2000), *England: An Elegy*, Chatto & Windus (Continuum edition, 2006).

Scruton, Roger (2005), *Gentle Regrets: Thoughts from a Life*, Continuum.

Scruton, Roger (2006a), *A Political Philosophy: Arguments for Conservatism*, Continuum.

Scruton, Roger (2006b), *England and the Need for Nations*, Civitas.

Scruton, Roger (2007), *Culture Counts: Faith and Feeling in a World Besieged*, Encounter Books.

Seaford, Richard (1994), *Reciprocity and Ritual: Homer and Tragedy in the Developing City-State*, Clarendon Press.

Seaford, Richard (2004), *Money and the Early Greek Mind: Homer, Philosophy, Tragedy*, Cambridge University Press.

Seaford, Richard (2006), *Dionysos: Gods and Heroes of the Ancient World*, Routledge.

Seddon, John (2003), *Freedom from Command and Control: A Better Way to Make the Work Work*, Vanguard Education.

Selden, John (1689), *Table Talk* (Selden Society edition, Frederick Pollock, ed., 1927).

Seligman, Adam B. (1997), *The Problem of Trust*, Princeton University Press.

Sen, Amartya (2006), *Identity and Violence: The Illusion of Destiny*, W.W. Norton & Co.

Senge, Peter M. (1990), *The Fifth Discipline: The Art & Practice of The Learning Organization*, Century Business.

Senge, Peter M., Joseph Jaworski, C. Otto Scharmer and Betty Sue Flowers (2004), *Presence: Exploring Profound Change in People, Organizations and Society*, Crown Business (Nicholas Brealey edition, 2005).

Sennett, Richard (1970), *The Uses of Disorder: Personal Identity and City Life*, Alfred A. Knopf (Penguin edition, 1971).

Sennett, Richard (1974), *The Fall of Public Man*, Random House (Faber & Faber edition, 1986).

Shakespeare, William (c.1592), *Richard III* (Signet Classic Shakespeare edition).

Shakespeare, William (c.1597), *Henry IV, Part 1* (Signet Classic Shakespeare edition).

Shakespeare, William (c.1599), *Much Ado About Nothing* (Signet Classic Shakespeare edition).

Shakespeare, William (c.1604), *Measure for Measure* (Signet Classic Shakespeare edition).

Shakespeare, William (c.1606), *Coriolanus* (Signet Classic Shakespeare edition).

Shakespeare, William (1609), *The Sonnets*. Auden, W.H. (Signet Classic Shakespeare edition, 1965).

Shakespeare, William (c.1611), *The Tempest* (Signet Classic Shakespeare edition).

Shapiro, Howard-Yana and John Harrisson (2000), *Gardening for the Future of the Earth*, Bantam.

Shawcross, William (2003), *The Allies: The US, Britain, Europe and the War in Iraq*, PublicAffairs (Atlantic edition, 2004).

Sheldrake, Rupert (1988), *The Presence of the Past*, William Collins (Fontana edition, 1989).

Sherwood, Dennis (2002), *Seeing the Forest for the Trees: A Manager's Guide to Applying Systems Thinking*, Nicholas Brealey.

Shiva, Vandana (1991), *The Violence of the Green Revolution: Third World Agriculture, Ecology and Politics*, Zed Books.

Shiva, Vandana (2000), *Tomorrow's Biodiversity*, Thames & Hudson.

Shiva, Vandana (2008), *Soil Not Oil: Environmental Justice in an Age of Climate Crisis*, South End Press.

Shlaes, Amity (2007), *The Forgotten Man: A New History of the Great Depression*, Jonathan Cape.

Siedentop, Larry (2000), *Democracy in Europe*, Allen Lane.

Sigman, Aric (2005), *Remotely Controlled: How Television is Damaging Our Lives*, Vermilion.

Simms, Andrew and Joe Smith, eds. (2008), *Do Good Lives Have to Cost the Earth?*, Constable.

Sinclair, John (1831), *The Correspondence of the Right Honourable Sir John Sinclair*, Henry Colburn and Richard Bentley.

Slanina, Sjaak, ed. (1997), *Biosphere-Atmosphere Exchange of Pollutants and Trace Substances*, Springer.

Smil, Vaclav (2010), *Energy Myths and Realities: Bringing Science to the Energy Policy Debate*, AEI Press.

Smith, Adam (1759), *The Theory of Moral Sentiments* (Otto Zeller edition, 1963).

Smith, Adam (1776), *The Wealth of Nations* (Oxford World Classics edition, 2008).

Smith, Anthony D. (2000), *The Nation in History: Historiographical Debates about Ethnicity and Nationalism*, University Press of New England.

Smith, Denis, ed. (2006), *Key Readings in Crisis Management Systems and Structures for Prevention and Recovery*, Routledge.

Smith, Peter K. (2009), *Children and Play: Understanding Children's Worlds*, Wiley-Blackwell.

Smolin, Lee (2006), *The Trouble with Physics: The Rise of String Theory, the Fall of a Science, and What Comes Next*, Houghton Mifflin.

Solo, Robert A., ed. (1955), *Economics and the Public Interest*, Rutgers.

Sorensen, Roy (2001), *Vagueness and Contradiction*, Oxford University Press.

Sorensen, Roy (2003), *A Brief History of the Paradox: Philosophy and the Labyrinths of the Mind*, Oxford University Press (paperback edition, 2005).

Spencer, Paul, ed. (1985), *Society and the Dance: The Social Anthropology of Process and Performance*, Cambridge University Press.

Spenser, Edmund (1596), *The Faerie Queene*, William Ponsonby.

Spratt, David and Philip Sutton (2008), *Climate Code Red: The Case for Emergency Action*, Scribe Publications.

Sprott, W.J.H. (1958), *Human Groups*, Penguin.

Spufford, Francis (2003), *The Backroom Boys: The Secret Return of the British Boffin*, Faber & Faber.

Stanton, William (2003), *The Rapid Growth of Human Populations 1750–2000: Histories, Consequences, Issues – Nation by Nation*, Multi-Science Publishing Company.

Stanway, Andrew (1976), *Fibre in The Diet: Taking the Rough with the Smooth*, Souvenir Press.

Stenton, Frank (1943), *Anglo-Saxon England*, Oxford University Press (third edition, 1971).

Sterelny, Kim (2001), *Dawkins vs. Gould: Survival of the Fittest*, Icon (second edition, 2007).

Sternberg, Robert J., ed. (1982), *Handbook of Human Intelligence*, Cambridge University Press (expanded edition, *Handbook of Intelligence*, 2000).

Stewart, Michael (1967), *Keynes and After*, Penguin.

Steyn, Mark (2006), *America Alone: The End of the World as We Know It*, Regnery.

Stickland, Sue (1998), *Heritage Vegetables: The Gardener's Guide to Cultivating Diversity*, Gaia.

Strahan, David (2007), *The Last Oil Shock: A Survival Guide to the Imminent Extinction of Petroleum Man*, John Murray.

Strogatz, Steven (2003), *Sync: The Emerging Science of Spontaneous Order*, Hyperion (Penguin edition, 2004).

Sturt, George (1923), *The Wheelwright's Shop*, Cambridge University Press (paperback edition, 1963).

Sutherland, Stuart (1992), *Irrationality*, Pinter & Martin.

Swift, Jonathan (1726), *Gulliver's Travels*, Benjamin Motte (Everyman's Library edition, 1954).

Sylvan, Richard and David Bennett (1994), *The Greening of Ethics*, White Horse Press.

Tainter, Joseph A. (1988), *The Collapse of Complex Societies* (Cambridge University Press paperback edition, 1990).

Taleb, Nassim Nicholas (2001), *Fooled by Randomness: The Hidden Role of Chance in Life and in the Markets*, Texere (Penguin edition, 2007).

Taleb, Nassim Nicholas (2007), *The Black Swan: The Impact of the Highly Improbable*, Penguin.

Tawney, Richard Henry (1926), *Religion and the Rise of Capitalism*, John Murray (Penguin edition, 1990).

Taylor, Alan J.P. (1965), *English History 1914–1945*, Oxford University Press.

Taylor, Arthur (2009), *Played at the Pub: The Pub Games of Britain*, English Heritage.

Taylor, Charles (1991), *The Ethics of Authenticity*, Harvard University Press.

Tenner, Edward (1996), *Why Things Bite Back: New Technology and the Revenge Effect*, Fourth Estate.

Tennyson, Alfred (1829–1864), *The Works of Alfred Lord Tennyson*, Rosemary Gray, ed. (1994), Wordsworth.

Thaler, Richard H. and Cass R. Sunstein (2008), *Nudge: Improving Decisions about Health, Wealth and Happiness*, Yale University Press (Penguin edition, 2009).

The Land Is Ours (1999), *Defining Rural Sustainability: Fifteen Criteria for Sustainable Developments in the Countryside*, The Land Is Ours.

Thirsk, Joan (1984), *The Rural Economy of England: Collected Essays*, The Hambledon Press.

Thirsk, Joan (1997), *Alternative Agriculture: A History, from the Black Death to the Present Day*, Oxford University Press.

Thom, Françoise (1987), *La langue de bois*, Julliard. English: *Newspeak: The Language of Soviet Communism* (Claridge Press edition, translation by Ken Connelly, 1989).

Thomas, David St John (1963), *The Rural Transport Problem*, Routledge.

Thomas, Keith (1983), *Man and the Natural World: Changing attitudes in England 1500–1800*, Allen Lane.

Thompson, Edward Palmer (1991), *Customs in Common*, Merlin.

Thompson, Flora (1945), *Lark Rise to Candleford* (Penguin edition, 1973).

Thompson, Kenneth and Jeremy Tunstall, eds. (1971), *Sociological Perspectives: Selected Readings*, Penguin.

Thompson, Michael, Richard Ellis and Aaron Wildavsky (1990), *Cultural Theory*, Westview Press.

Thomson, Hugh (2009), *Tequila Oil: Getting Lost in Mexico*, Weidenfeld & Nicolson.

Thoreau, Henry David (1837–1861), *Journals* (John C. Broderick, ed., Princeton University Press edition, 1981).

Thoreau, Henry David (1854a), *Walden* (Oxford University Press edition, 2008).

Thoreau, Henry David (1854b), *Walden and Civil Disobedience* (Penguin edition, 1986).

Thorpe, David (2010), *Sustainable Home Refurbishment: The Earthscan Expert Guide to Retrofitting Homes for Efficiency*, Routledge.

Thouless, Robert H. (1930), *Straight and Crooked Thinking* (English Universities Press edition, 1952).

Tian-Shanskaia, Olga Semyonova (1993), *Village Life in Late Tsarist Russia*, David L. Ransel, ed., Indiana University Press.

Tindale, Christopher (2007), *Fallacies and Argument Appraisal*, Cambridge University Press.

Toffler, Alvin (1980), *The Third Wave*, Collins (Pan paperback edition, 1981).

Tolle, Eckhart (1997), *The Power of Now*, Namaste Publishing (New World Library edition, 1999).

Tönnies, Ferdinand (1887), *Gemeinschaft und Gesellschaft*, Fues's Verlag. English: *Community and Civil Society*, Jose Harris, ed. (Cambridge University Press edition, translation by Margaret Hollis, 2001).

Toulmin, Stephen, Richard D. Rieke and Allan Janik (1979), *An Introduction to Reasoning*, Macmillan.

Toulmin, Stephen (2001), *Return to Reason*, Harvard University Press.

Toynbee, Arnold (1933), *A Study of History* (Oxford University Press abridged edition, 1946).

Traherne, Thomas (c.1670), *Centuries of Meditations* (first edition edited and published by Bertram Dobell, 1908).

Trainer, Ted (1995), *The Conserver Society: Alternatives for Sustainability*, Zed Books.

Trainer, Ted (2007), *Renewable Energy Cannot Sustain a Consumer Society*, Springer.

Trilling, Lionel (1971), *Sincerity and Authenticity*, Harvard University Press (Oxford University Press edition, 1972).

Trisoglio, Alex (1997), *Managing Complexity*, London School of Economics Working Paper.

Trowell, H.C., Denis P. Burkitt and K.W. Heaton, eds. (1985), *Dietary Fibre, Fibre-Depleted foods and Disease*, Academic Press.

Tuan, Yi-Fu (1972), *Topophilia: A Study of Environmental Perception, Attitudes and Values*, University of Minnesota Press (Prentice Hall edition, 1974).

Tuchman, Barbara (1984), *The March of Folly: From Troy to Vietnam*, Ballantine.

Tudge, Colin (2003), *So Shall We Reap: the Concept of Enlightened Agriculture*, Penguin.

Tulip, Kathryn and Lucy Michaels (2004), *A Rough Guide to the UK Farming Crisis*, Corporate Watch.

Uglow, Jenny (2002), *The Lunar Men: The Friends Who Made the Future*, Faber & Faber.

Unger, Aryeh (1974), *The Totalitarian Party: Party and People in Nazi Germany and Soviet Russia*, Cambridge University Press.

United States Council on Environmental Quality and Department of State (1980), *The Global 2000 Report to the President*, US Government Printing Office.

Urdan, Timothy C. (2001), *Statistics in Plain English*, Routledge (third edition, 2010).

van Eemeren, Frans H. and Rob Grootendorst (1992), *Argumentation, Communication and Fallacies: A Pragma-Dialectical Perspective*, Lawrence Erlbaum.

Van Rooy, Alison, ed. (1998), *Civil Society and the Aid Industry*, Earthscan.

Veblen, Thorstein (1899), *The Theory of the Leisure Class: An Economic Study of Institutions*, Macmillan (Unwin Books edition, 1970).

Vellvé, Renée (1992), *Saving the Seed: Genetic Diversity and European Agriculture*, Earthscan.

Vickery, Margaret (1998), *The Gentleman's Daughter: Women's Lives in Georgian England*, Yale University Press.

Victor, Peter A. (2008), *Managing Without Growth: Slower by Design, Not Disaster*, Edward Elgar.

Viljoen, André, ed. (2005), *CPULs: Continuous Productive Urban Landscapes*, Architectural Press.

Vita-Finzi, Claudio (2008), *The Sun: A User's Manual*, Kluwer.

Wackernagel, Mathis and William Rees (1996), *Our Ecological Footprint: Reducing Human Impact on the Earth*, New Society Publishers.

Waldrop, M. Mitchell (1992), *Complexity: The Emerging Science at the Edge of Order and Chaos*, Simon & Schuster (Penguin paperback edition).

Walker, Brian and David Salt (2006), *Resilience Thinking: Sustaining Ecosystems and People in a Changing World*, Island Press.

Walker, David (1979), *Energy, Plants and Man*, Packard Publishing (Oxygraphics edition, 1992).

Walker, Greg (2000), *Medieval Drama: An Anthology*, Blackwell.

Walton, Douglas N. (1986), *Courage: A Philosophical Investigation*, University of California Press.

Walton, Douglas N. (1989), *Informal Logic: A Handbook for Critical Argument*, Cambridge University Press.

Walton, Douglas N. (1995), *A Pragmatic Theory of Fallacy*, University of Alabama Press.

Walton, Douglas N. (1999), *One-Sided Arguments: A Dialectical Analysis of Bias*, State University of New York Press.

Walton, Izaak (1653), *The Compleat Angler* (Oxford World's Classics edition, 2000).

Walzer, Michael (1983), *Spheres of Justice: A Defence of Pluralism and Equity*, Basic Books.

Wanless, Derek (2002), *Securing Our Future Health: Taking a Long-Term View*, Her Majesty's Treasury.

Ward, Calvin Herbert, John A. Cherry and Marion R. Scalf, eds. (1997), *Subsurface Restoration*, CRC Press.

Ward, Colin (1973), *Anarchy in Action*, George Allen & Unwin (Freedom Press edition, 1985).

Ward, Colin (1991), *Influences: Voices of Creative Dissent*, Green Books.

Ward, Colin (1993), *New Town, Home Town: The Lessons of Experience*, Calouste Gulbenkian Foundation.

Ward, Colin (1997), *Reflected in Water: A Crisis of Social Responsibility*, Cassell.

Ward, Peter and Donald Brownlee (2002), *The Life and Death of Planet Earth: How the New Science of Astrobiology Charts the Ultimate Fate of Our World*, Henry Holt and Company (Piatkus edition, 2003).

Ward, Peter (2009), *The Medea Hypothesis: Is Life on Earth Ultimately Self-Destructive?*, Princeton University Press.

Ward-Perkins, Bryan (2005), *The Fall of Rome and the End of Civilization*, Oxford University Press.

Watson, Gary, ed. (1982), *Free Will*, Oxford University Press.

Watson, John Steven (1960), *The Reign of George III, 1760–1815*, Oxford University Press.

Webber, Christopher L., ed. (2004), *Give Us Grace: An Anthology of Anglican Prayers*, Morehouse Publishing.

Weber, Karl (2009), *Food Inc.: How Industrial Food is Making Us Sicker, Fatter and Poorer – And What You Can Do About It*, PublicAffairs.

Weber, Max (1904), *The Protestant Ethic and the Spirit of Capitalism* (Unwin edition, 1971).

Weber, Max (1921), *Economy and Society* (University of California Press edition, 1992).

Weeks, Dudley (1994), *The Eight Essential Steps to Conflict Resolution: Preserving Relationships at Work, at Home and in the Community*, Tarcher.

Weeks, John R. (1978), *Population: An Introduction to Concepts and Issues*, Wadsworth (tenth edition, 2008).

Weil, Simone (1943), *L'Enracinement, prélude à une déclaration des devoirs envers l'être humain*, Gallimard. English: *The Need for Roots: Prelude to a Declaration of Duties Towards Mankind* (Routledge edition, 2001).

Weiss, Paul A. (1971), *Hierarchically Organized Systems in Theory and Practice*, Hafner.

Weizsäcker, Ernst, Amory B. Lovins and L. Hunter Lovins (1997), *Factor Four: Doubling Wealth, Halving Resource Use*, Earthscan.

Wells, H.G. (1910), *The History of Mr. Polly*, Nelson (Everyman edition, 1993).

Wells, H.G., Julian Huxley, and P.G. Wells (1929), *The Science of Life*, Amalgamated Press.

West, Edwin George (1965), *Education and the State: A Study in Political Economy*, Institute of Economic Affairs (Liberty Fund revised and expanded edition, 1994).

West, Patrick (2004), *Conspicuous Compassion: Why Sometimes it Really Is Cruel to Be Kind*, Civitas.

Weston, Anthony (1987), *A Rulebook for Arguments*, Avatar.

White, Gilbert (1788), *The Natural History and Antiquities of Selborne*, White, Cochrane and Co.

White, Robert E. (1979), *Principles and Practice of Soil Science: The Soil as a Natural Resource*, Wiley-Blackwell (fourth edition, 2006).

Whitefield, Patrick (1996), *How to Make a Forest Garden*, Permanent Publications.

Whitefield, Patrick (2004), *The Earth Care Manual: A Permaculture Handbook for Britain and other Temperate Climates*, Permanent Publications.

Whitehead, Alfred North (1925), *Science and the Modern World*, Macmillan (Free Press paperback edition, 1967).

Whitehead, Alfred North (1929), *Process and Reality*, Harper.

Whitman, Walt (1855), *Leaves of Grass*, Brooklyn.

Whyte, Jamie (2003), *Bad Thoughts: A Guide to Clear Thinking*, Corvo Books.

Wicksteed, Philip H. (1910), *The Common Sense of Political Economy, Volume II* (Routledge and Kegan Paul edition, 1933).

Wiener, Norbert (1948), *Cybernetics, or Control and Communication in the Animal and the Machine*, MIT.

Wilkinson, Paul F., ed. (1980), *In Celebration of Play*, St. Martin's Press.

Wilkinson, Richard G. (1973), *Poverty and Progress: Ecological Model of Economic Development*, Methuen.

Wilkinson, Richard G. and Kate Pickett (2009), *The Spirit Level: Why More Equal Societies Almost Always Do Better*, (Penguin edition, 2010).

Williams, James (1971), *Give Me Yesterday*, J.D. Lewis & Sons.

Williams-Ellis, Clough (1928), *England and the Octopus*, Geoffrey Bles.

Williamson, Oliver E. (1985), *The Economic Institutions of Capitalism*, Collier Macmillan.

Willoughby, Kelvin W. (1990), *Technology Choice: A Critique of the Appropriate Technology Movement*, Intermediate Technology Development Group.

Wilson, Brian (2001), *Soft Systems Methodology: Conceptual Model Building and Its Contribution*, Wiley.

Witte, Erich H. and James H. Davis, eds. (1996), *Understanding Group Behaviour*, Lawrence Erlbaum.

Wittfogel, Karl A. (1957), *Oriental Despotism: A Comparative Study of Total Power*, Yale University Press.

Wolpert, Stanley (1977), *A New History of India*, Oxford University Press (seventh edition, 2003).

Womack, James P., Daniel T. Jones and Daniel Roos (1990), *The Machine that Changed the World*, Simon & Schuster.

Womack, James P. and Daniel T. Jones (1996), *Lean Thinking: Banish Waste and Create Wealth in Your Corporation*, Simon & Schuster (Free Press Business edition, 2003).

Womack, James P. and Daniel T. Jones (2005), *Lean Solutions: How Companies and Customers Can Create Value and Wealth Together*, Simon & Schuster.

Woodcock, Alexander and Monte Davis (1978), *Catastrophe Theory*, Penguin.

Woodham-Smith, Cecil (1962), *The Great Hunger: Ireland: 1845–1849*, Hamish Hamilton.

Wood, Michael (1986), *The Domesday Quest: A Search for the Roots of England*, BBC Books (reprint edition, *The Domesday Quest: In Search of the Roots of England*, 2005).

Woods, Frederick, ed. (1983), *The Oxford Book of English Traditional Verse*, Oxford University Press.

Worster, Donald (1977), *Nature's Economy: A History of Ecological Ideas*, Sierra Club Books (Cambridge University Press edition, 1985).

Worster, Donald, ed. (1988), *The Ends of the Earth: Perspectives on Modern Environmental History*, Cambridge University Press.

Worster, Donald (1993), *The Wealth of Nature: Environmental History and the Ecological Imagination*, Oxford University Press.

Wrangham, Richard (2009), *Catching Fire: How Cooking Made Us Human*, Profile Books.

Wratislaw, A.H. (1890), *Sixty Folk Tales from Exclusively Slavic Sources* (Forgotten Books edition, 2008).

Wrench, Guy Theodore (1938), *The Wheel of Health*, C.W. Daniel.

Wright, Ronald (2004), *A Short History of Progress*, Canongate.

Yeats, W.B. (1921), *Michael Robartes and the Dancer*, Cuala Press.

Yeats, W.B. (1939), *Last Poems and Two Plays*, Cuala Press.

Young, Gavin (1977), *Return to the Marshes: Life with the Marsh Arabs of Iraq*, Faber & Faber.

Yudkin, John (1972), *Pure, White and Deadly: the problem of sugar*, Davis-Poynter.

Yunus, Muhammad and Alan Jolis (1998), *Banker to the Poor: The Story of the Grameen Bank*, Aurum Press (paperback edition, 2003).

Zerzan, John, ed. (1999), *Against Civilization: Readings and Reflections*, Uncivilized Books (Feral House expanded edition, 2005).

Zimbardo, Philip (2007), *The Lucifer Effect: How Good People Turn Evil*, Rider.

Zimmerman, Michael, J. Baird Callicott, John Clark, et al., eds. (2001), *Environmental Philosophy: From Animal Rights to Radical Ecology*, Prentice Hall.

Zweig, Stefan (1942), *Die Welt von Gestern*, Bermann-Fischer Verlag AB. English: *The World of Yesterday* (Pushkin Press edition, translation by Anthea Bell, 2009).

ILLUSTRATION CREDITS

Front cover	Conrad Gesner (1551), see "Hippopotamus" illustration credit and entry.
Dedication	Howard Phipps. Figure in a Landscape.
Ad Hominem	François Maréchal. Voyeur. From Brett.
Begging the Question	Cyril Bouda. Autumn.
Big Stick, The	Chris Daunt. The Big Stick.
Butterfly Effect	Sarah van Niekerk. Lioness.
Butterfly Effect	Anne Hayward. Butterfly.
Cant	Anne Hayward. Wolf Granny.
Cant	Harry Brockway. Wolf Granny. Drawing.
Causes	Julia Mavrogordato. Autumn Morning.
Climate Change	Norman Janes (1935). Coke Ovens. From James Hamilton (1994), *Wood Engravings and the Woodcut in Britain 1890–1990*, p 130.
Climate Change	Maria Bushra Elvorith. Leaf (specimen). Gift to author.
Commons, The	Vivien Gribble. Tail-Piece.
Courtesy	Howard Phipps. The River Alde.
Disconnection	Pam Pebworth. Boat Coming To Shore.
Division	George Tute. Marsh Mouse.
Ecology	Thomas Bewick. The Scarecrow.
Empowerment	Hilary Paynter. A Seed Growing Secretly. From Gwasg Gregynog's *The Texture of the Universe*. Used with their kind permission.
Energy Prospects	John Watson. Robin's Castle.
Eroticism	Eric Gill. Ibi Dabo Tibi.
Expertise	Gwen Raverat. Ploughing. From Rosemary Davidson, ed. (2003), *Gwen Raverat: Wood Engravings of Cambridge and Surroundings*, p 75.
False Analogy	John Lawrence. Mouse. From Brett.
False Consistency	Christopher Cunliffe. Skylark. From Brett.
Food Prospects	Christopher White. Cultivating Biofuels. Cartoon.
Gaia	Christopher White. Daisyworld. Drawing.
Hippopotamus	Conrad Gesner (1551), in C. Froschauer, *Animalium*, Zürich. Reproduced in Gaston Duchet Sucheux and Michel Pastoureau (2002), *Le Bestiaire Medieval: Dictionnaire historique and bibliographique*, Paris: Le Léopard d'Or.
Home	Howard Phipps. Cottage Interior.
Humility	Andy English. Ratty and Mole.
Identity	Howard Phipps. Figure in a Landscape.
Ideology	Cross of the Knights Templar. Graphic.
Incrementalism	Patrick Geddes (1889). An Opossum Carrying its Young on its Back. Drawing. From Patrick Geddes and John Arthur Thomson (1889), *The Evolution of Sex*.
Innocence	Kathleen Lindsley. March Hare.
Instrumentalism	Frank Martin. Kantharos. From Brett.
Internal Evidence	Reynolds Stone (c.1930). Calf. From James Hamilton (1994), *Wood Engravings and the Woodcut in Britain 1890–1990*, p 154.

Ironic Space	Simon Brett. Noli Me Tangere.
Land	Rosalind Atkins. Cypress, Mt Noorat. From Brett.
Lean Education	Shirley Smith. Wheel and Sledgehammer.
Lean Food	Edward Stamp. Winter Landscape.
Lean Food	Vivien Gribble. Whitfield.
Lean Food	Christopher Wormell. Cock. From Brett.
Lean Food	John Morley. Moving the Bell Jars. From Brett.
Lean Health	Anne Hayward. Five a Day.
Lean Law and Order	Harry Brockway. Hue and Cry.
Lean Materials	Anne Hayward. Mending.
Metamorphosis	Albrecht Dürer (1515). Rhinoceros.
Modularity	Sarah van Niekerk. Herd of Antelope.
Multiculturalism	Chris Daunt. Candles.
Needs and Wants	Edward Stamp. Jackdaw.
New Domestication	Sarah van Niekerk. Boar.
Paradigm	Herringbone pattern as described in Arthur Koestler (1967), *The Ghost in the Machine*, chapter 12.
Peasant	Sue Scullard. Candleford Green. From the Folio Society's edition of *Lark Rise to Candleford*. Used with their kind permission.
Pharisee, The	Chris Daunt. Mandolin.
Place	Sue Scullard. English Village.
Play	Sue Scullard. Country Playtime. From the Folio Society's edition of *Lark Rise to Candleford*. Used with their kind permission.
Rationalism	John Lawrence. Devil. From Brett.
Reflection	Christopher White. Reflection. Drawing.
Relevance	Simon Brett. Balinese water temples.
Religion	Henno Arrak. Old Wooden Church on Ruhnu. From Brett.
Responsibility	Sarah van Niekerk. Lion.
Shifting Ground	Harry Brockway. Shifting Ground.
Slippery Slope	Harry Brockway. The Slippery Slope.
Social City	Ebenezer Howard (1898). Detail of Garden City. Drawing.
Social City	Ebenezer Howard (1898). Cluster of Garden Cities. Drawing.
Social City	Ebenezer Howard (1898). Garden City in Local Setting. Drawing.
Straw Man	Chris Daunt. Straw Man.
Straw Man	Gregory Lago. Straw Man. From Brett.
Tao	Tao. Graphic.
Tradition	Anne Hayward. Leaves.
Unfalsifiability	Chris Daunt. Scientist with Cucumbers.

Editor's note: All illustrations were commissioned or selected by David Fleming, and are wood engravings except where noted.

Engravings labelled "From Brett" are reproduced from Simon Brett's *An Engraver's Globe: Wood Engraving in the Twenty-first Century* (Primrose Hill Press, 2002), with his permission. I owe Simon great thanks for the invaluable assistance provided in tracing the artists and works in this book.

Fleming's notes record his communication with the artists, and extensive efforts have been made to inform the artists or their estates, and confirm their permission for this publication.

INDEX

Words/numbers in **bold** denote entries in the dictionary; page numbers
followed by *t* refer to tables; page numbers followed by *s* refer to sidebars.